TORT LAW

TORT LAW

Responsibilities and Redress

John C. P. Goldberg
Professor of Law
Vanderbilt University

Anthony J. Sebok
Professor of Law
Brooklyn Law School

Benjamin C. Zipursky
Professor of Law
Fordham University

PUBLISHERS

1185 Avenue of the Americas, New York, NY 10036
www.aspenpublishers.com

Permissions
Aspen Publishers
1185 Avenue of the Americas
New York, NY 10036

Printed in the United States of America.

1 2 3 4 5 6 7 8 9 0

ISBN 0-7355-2620-6

Library of Congress Cataloging-in-Publication Data

Goldberg, John C., 1961-
     Tort law: responsibilities and redress/John C.
Goldberg, Anthony J. Sebok, Benjamin C. Zipursky
          p.   cm.
     Includes bibliographical references and index.
     ISBN 0-7355-2620-6 (alk paper)
     1. Torts—United States.   2. Torts—United States—
Cases.   I. Sebok, Anthony James, 1963-   .
II. Zipursky, Bejamin Charles, 1960-   .   III. Title.

KF1250.G65 2004
346.7303—dc22

                                              2004046153

About Aspen Publishers

Aspen Publishers, headquartered in New York City, is a leading information provider for attorneys, business professionals, and law students. Written by preeminent authorities, our products consist of analytical and practical information covering both U.S. and international topics. We publish in the full range of formats, including updated manuals, books, periodicals, CDs, and online products.

Our proprietary content is complemented by 2,500 legal databases, containing over 11 million documents, available through our Loislaw division. Aspen Publishers also offers a wide range of topical legal and business databases linked to Loislaw's primary material. Our mission is to provide accurate, timely, and authoritative content in easily accessible formats, supported by unmatched customer care.

To order any Aspen Publishers title, go to *www.aspenpublishers.com* or call 1-800-638-8437.

To reinstate your manual update service, call 1-800-638-8437.

For more information on Loislaw products, go to *www.loislaw.com* or call 1-800-364-2512.

For Customer Care issues, e-mail *CustomerCare@aspenpublishers.com*; call 1-800-234-1660; or fax 1-800-901-9075.

Aspen Publishers
A Wolters Kluwer Company

SUMMARY OF CONTENTS

PART FOUR
LIABILITY WITHOUT FAULT AND PRODUCTS LIABILITY 737

PART FIVE
TORTS AT THE SUPREME COURT   957

TABLE OF CONTENTS

CHAPTER 3
THE BREACH ELEMENT
135

CHAPTER 4
THE CAUSATION ELEMENT
209

CHAPTER 5
ALIGNING THE ELEMENTS:
PROXIMATE CAUSE AND *PALSGRAF*   265

CHAPTER 6
STATUTORY SUPPLEMENTS: NEGLIGENCE
PER SE, WRONGFUL DEATH ACTS, AND
IMPLIED RIGHTS OF ACTION   325

PART THREE
DIGNITARY TORTS AND NEGLIGENT INFLICTION
OF EMOTIONAL DISTRESS   **535**

CHAPTER 9
BATTERY, ASSAULT, AND FALSE
IMPRISONMENT   **537**

CHAPTER 10
INFLICTION OF EMOTIONAL DISTRESS   **627**

PART FOUR
LIABILITY WITHOUT FAULT AND PRODUCTS LIABILITY   737

CHAPTER 11
PROPERTY TORTS AND ULTRAHAZARDOUS ACTIVITIES   739

PREFACE

This book has been written to help a new generation of law students learn an area of law — Torts — that is at once ancient and contemporary, rule-governed and flexible, well-established and controversial.

American tort law traces back to the law of medieval England, a time and place in which government efforts to secure citizens' security from injury were relatively modest. Today, tort law — itself a complex institution — exists within a vastly more complex regulatory state that devotes substantial effort to promoting safety and to providing for citizens' welfare. We hope to give students a sense of where tort law has come from, and of the roles it plays, and might play, in our modern system of government.

As an evolving body of doctrine shaped in courtrooms around the country, tort law simultaneously empowers and limits individuals in their ability to invoke the legal system, and likewise empowers and limits legal decision-makers such as judges and juries faced with the task of deciding whether to hold one person liable for another's injuries. We aim to help students appreciate both the constraining and the power-conferring aspects of tort law.

Tort has been a part of American law since the nation's founding. Today, however, it is at a crossroads: Lawyers, politicians, and academics disagree sharply about its continued utility and viability. We seek to enable students to see why tort law is basic to our legal system, but also why it has become a source of controversy.

In pursuing these pedagogic goals, we have been guided by five themes:

1. As its title suggests, this book is organized around the general theme of responsibilities and redress. Tort law, in our view, has two fundamental features. First, it articulates and imposes on members of society a set of legal obligations — i.e., *responsibilities* — to avoid injuring others. Second, it empowers persons to bring suit to establish that they have been injured by another's failure to heed this sort of obligation — i.e., to pursue and obtain *redress*. Tort is a core part of the first-year curriculum for these reasons: It examines the law's imposition of basic obligations not to injure others, as well as the law's recognition of the right of aggrieved persons to seek redress through the courts for violations of those obligations.

2. We have edited the cases in this book lightly, in a conscious effort to allow readers to experience the "thick" contexts out of which tort law emerges. Put simply, we aim to allow students to read the facts of each

case for themselves. We also try to let the judges speak for themselves through their opinions. Our hope is that this approach will help beginning law students appreciate the degree to which judgments about legal responsibilities are sensitive to facts, and to see that common-law principles are not extracted from some "heaven of legal concepts," but instead derive from ordinary experience. Further, we hope that, by presenting cases edited in this way, we will aid them in developing the capacity to read carefully, an essential tool for good lawyering.

3. The cases and the notes in this book aim to demonstrate to students how the substance of a body of law like torts is heavily influenced by rules of procedure, by the institutions that have been created to handle tort litigation, and by other bodies of law that address some of the same conduct and issues addressed by tort law. Thus, throughout the book, we point out ways in which the demands of trial and appellate processes shape tort doctrine. In various places, we also explore the role played by legislatures in developing, or responding to developments in, tort doctrine. Another of the book's aspirations is to ensure that students appreciate that tort is but one part of the law, and that it can only be adequately understood in relation to other areas of law, including civil procedure, contracts, property, employment law, anti-discrimination law, and constitutional law.

4. Apart from retaining "classic" tort opinions that all law students are expected to know, we have sought as much as possible to use contemporary cases presenting situations that students will be able to recognize. We hope that, by employing these sorts of cases to illuminate the basic concepts of tort law, we will make the subject less archaic and mysterious to novice lawyers, while also helping them to begin to think for themselves about the various choices that courts and lawmakers must make as they carry tort law forward into the future. We also believe that the use of relatively recent cases will help students perceive the relevance of the subject and the significance of the issues that are currently in play in the law of tort.

5. This book adopts a perspective on law that we hope is refreshing. It is, of course, vital that first-year law students come to appreciate that "the law" is not a rule book — that there is play in its joints and deep tensions in its soul. Yet it is equally important that students not be left with the skeptical lesson that law is nothing more than what a particular judge or jury says it is. Thus, in these materials, we strive to help students grasp how the key concepts of tort — concepts such as "reasonable care," "causation," and "intent" — structure and organize legal analysis even as they point it in new directions. A good lawyer, we hope to demonstrate, is one who appreciates both the limits and the flexibility of tort doctrine; one who has a sense of how to make innovative and progressive arguments from *within the law*. For these reasons, our book has a number of distinctive features. Particularly in its early chapters, it contains a good deal of expository text, in part to help students overcome the steep learning curve encountered in the first weeks of law school. It also contains a number of opinions from intermediate appellate courts, in part because these courts

tend to approach cases as presenting problems in the application of law, rather than occasions to rework it. The book also includes some "easy" cases. These opinions can help students avoid basic confusions by providing clear examples of certain torts, or certain concepts. Lastly, the notes following the principal cases strive to be explanatory rather than Delphic. If our own engagement with this subject has taught us anything, it is that tort law, even when presented in a relatively straightforward way, is more than rich enough to captivate students and professors alike.

John C. P. Goldberg
Anthony J. Sebok
Benjamin C. Zipursky

Nashville, Brooklyn, Manhattan
April 2004

ACKNOWLEDGMENTS

We owe more debts than we can acknowledge. Thanks to the numerous faculty members of Brooklyn, Fordham, NYU, Vanderbilt, and many other law schools who gave of their time to respond to our queries and to correct our mistakes. Equal thanks to our students for bearing with us as we field-tested the manuscript, and for helping us to improve it. The final product was also aided immeasurably by the careful and insightful comments provided by several anonymous reviewers.

For excellent research assistance, thanks to Vijay Baliga, Lia Brooks, Will Edmonson, Kristina Hill, James Killelea, Erin McMurray, John Rue, Michael Samalin, Lillith Shilton, Elizabeth TeSelle, and Allen Woods. Renee Cote and Curt Berkowitz provided expert editorial assistance in preparing the manuscript for publication. Jessica Barmack, Melody Davies, Elizabeth Kenny, Carol McGeehan, and Richard Mixter of Aspen were instrumental in launching this project, helping it take shape, and seeing it through to completion. Renee Hawkins generously served double-duty as word processor and editorial advisor. Enid Zafran prepared the Table of Cases and the Index.

Finally, thanks to Brooklyn Law School, Fordham University School of Law, and Vanderbilt University Law School for supporting our research and writing.

The following have granted us permission to reproduce their copyrighted works:

American Law Institute: Sections from the First, Second, and Third Restatements of Torts, and the First Restatement of Agency.

American Lawyer Media, Inc.: Catherine Aman & Gary Young, "Wal-Mart Shifting Litigation Strategy . . . ," *National Law Journal*, September 30, 2002.

New York State Unified Court System: Excerpts from Pattern Jury Instruction — Civil 2:278 (2004).

NOTES ON THE TEXT

Omissions from the judicial opinions reproduced herein are marked with ellipses, except for omitted internal citations, which are not marked (unless only part of a citation has been removed). In some opinions, we have added paragraph breaks to improve their comprehensibility. For the same reason, we have also at times deleted headings and subheadings. Numbered footnotes appear as in the original texts. Our own additions to the text of opinions are marked with square brackets and/or asterisked footnotes.

References to scholarly books and articles mentioned in our notes can be found in the *References/Further Reading* section at the end of each chapter.

Appendices B and C, as well as Modules I and II, which are referenced in the text, can be found on the CD that accompanies this hardbound volume.

TORT LAW

PART ONE

OVERVIEW

CHAPTER 1

An Introduction to Torts

I. WHAT IS A TORT?

Among the courses listed on your schedule, Torts might seem one of the more mysterious. Most entering law students have a rough idea of what a contract or a crime is. The term *tort*, by contrast, tends not to conjure up a clear mental picture or definition.

A brief turn to history may shed some light. Lawyerly usage of the word *tort* dates back to medieval England. There it served primarily as a synonym for "wrong" or "trespass."* Each of these nouns described a category or generic type of misconduct. But what kind? Proceeding still further back in time, we learn that tort derives from the Latin word *torquere*: to twist. This derivation proves quite illuminating. When a person commits a tort, he acts in a manner that is figuratively "twisted": His acts lack rectitude; they are *wrongful*. Beyond this, a tort is a special sort of wrongful act, one that literally involves a twisting—an *injuring*—of another. And a tort is a special sort of wrong in a second, related sense. When the law identifies misconduct as a tort, it determines that it is the sort of misconduct that entitles the victim to invoke the legal system to respond to the twisting: it empowers the victim to *set things straight* as between her and the person who has wronged her.

In sum, to commit a *tort* is to act in a manner that is wrongful toward and injurious to another. *Torts* in turn refers to the collection of recognized legal claims that enable a person (or entity) to obtain redress from another on the ground that he (or it) has suffered injury by virtue of having been wronged by that other. Today, these include actions for assault, battery, conversion, defamation, defective products (products liability), false imprisonment, fraud, intentional infliction of emotional distress, intentional interference with contract or economic advantage, invasion of privacy, negligence, nuisance, and trespass to land or chattel. *Tort law* consists of the rules and principles that define right conduct, as well as the circumstances under which a victim can obtain redress, and the form that such redress may take. As this book's title suggests, tort law articulates legal responsibilities or duties that persons owe to one another, and provides victims of conduct breaching those duties with redress against those who have wronged them.

* Here we mean trespass in its older, broader sense—the sense one finds, for example, in the biblical counsel that we "forgive the trespasses of others."

3

Torts is a first-year course for a number of reasons. Tort suits tend to present legal disputes that are manageable for students untrained in the law. Tort has also become a visible and politically contested part of the American legal landscape. As such it provides a platform for discussion of current policy issues surrounding law. Finally, tort introduces law students to basic legal categories (e.g., civil liability, private rights of action) and basic concepts (e.g., duty, unreasonableness, causation) that will continue to figure prominently in upper-level courses ranging from employment law to securities law to constitutional law. To begin to understand the distinctive domain and concerns of tort law, these materials commence with a judicial opinion concerning a suit that raises a claim for the particular tort of *negligence*.

II.   AN EXAMPLE OF A TORT SUIT

The judicial decision you are about to read — Walter v. Wal-Mart Stores, Inc. — arises out of an appeal from a $550,000 judgment against Wal-Mart. That judgment was entered by a trial judge at the conclusion of a two-day jury trial held in Knox County, Maine, in 1999. The trial in turn arose out a suit brought by the plaintiff, Ms. Antoinette Walter. Walter sued Wal-Mart because a pharmacist named Henry Lovin, who worked in the pharmacy department at a Wal-Mart store, misread her prescription for cancer medication and gave her the wrong drug, causing her to suffer serious illness.

As you will see, Wal-Mart had relatively little to say in its own defense. In this respect, the case was unusually one-sided. Indeed, the trial judge took the unusual step of announcing that, based on the evidence presented at trial, any reasonable jury would have to conclude that Walter had proven she was the victim of Wal-Mart's negligence. In other words, the judge found that the plaintiff had so clearly proven her case that he was entitled to conclude, without the aid of the jury, that Wal-Mart had acted carelessly toward her so as to injure her. However, the judge's determination that Wal-Mart had committed negligence against Walter still left one open issue for the jury: the amount of compensation she was entitled to receive from Wal-Mart in light of the injury it had wrongly inflicted upon her. On that issue, the jury decided on the figure of $550,000.

The text that follows is an edited version of an opinion issued by the Maine Supreme Court in response to Wal-Mart's appeal of the trial court's entry of judgment against it. As you will see, in appealing, Wal-Mart argued to the supreme court that the trial judge erred in concluding that the jury should not even have had a chance to decide for Wal-Mart. It also argued that the amount of the jury's verdict was excessive, and that the trial was defective in various other ways. In light of these alleged problems in the trial, Wal-Mart's appeal sought an order from the supreme court setting aside the trial court's judgment. Further, Wal-Mart asked the court either to dismiss Walter's tort suit altogether, or to order a new trial so that Wal-Mart could raise its defenses without being handicapped by the erroneous rulings allegedly committed by the trial judge.

The seven members of the Maine Supreme Court unanimously concluded that the trial judge did not commit any of the errors alleged by Wal-Mart. In particular, they ruled that the judge was correct in determining that this was an open-and-shut case for Walter. Notice that, in upholding this determination, the court first defines the tort of negligence in terms of constituent parts or "elements." It then explains why the plaintiff's evidence clearly established that these elements were satisfied in this case. Along the way, the Court's opinion also explains why Wal-Mart's main defense was so weak that the trial judge was entitled to reject it without sending that issue to the jury, and why the jury's decision to award Walter $550,000 was not excessive.

As you read the opinion, pay attention to what Walter had to prove to make out a claim of negligence, and to why the members of the court concluded that she provided ample proof. Also, consider whether the $550,000 award was appropriate, and if so, what it is meant to represent or accomplish. Finally, think about the role that the parties' lawyers played and should have played in resolving this dispute.

Walter v. Wal-Mart Stores, Inc.
748 A.2d 961 (Me. 2000)

Calkins, J.

[¶ 1] Wal-Mart Stores, Inc. appeals from a judgment entered in the Superior Court (Knox County, *Marsano, J.*) following a jury trial awarding damages to Antoinette Walter in the amount of $550,000 for her claim of pharmacist malpractice. . . .

I.   FACTS

[¶ 2] Walter, an eighty-year-old resident of Rockland, was diagnosed with a type of cancer which attacks the lymphatic system. Dr. Stephen Ross, Walter's treating physician and a board-certified oncologist, termed her condition treatable with the proper medication. Dr. Ross prescribed Chlorambucil, a chemotherapy drug, for Walter. On the prescription slip, he explicitly called for Chlorambucil, the generic name, because he feared that the drug's brand name, Leukeran, could be confused with other drugs with similar trade names.

[¶ 3] Walter took the prescription for Chlorambucil to the pharmacy in the Wal-Mart store in Rockland on May 7, 1997. Henry Lovin, a Maine licensed pharmacist and an employee of Wal-Mart, was on duty at the pharmacy. Instead of giving Walter Chlorambucil, as called for in the prescription, Lovin gave her a different drug with the brand name of Melphalen. The generic name for Melphalen is Alkeran. Lovin did not speak with Walter at the time he filled the prescription, but he provided her with an information sheet which described the effects of Melphalen. Melphalen is also a chemotherapy drug, but it is a substantially more powerful medication than Chlorambucil. Melphalen is typically given in smaller doses over shorter periods of time than is Chlorambucil, and doctors monitor it more closely. Melphalen has a very toxic effect on the body, and it substantially suppresses bone marrow. It has a longer life in the body than Chlorambucil, which means that any side effects from it last longer.

[¶ 4] To the extent that Walter noticed that the information sheet and bottle label read Melphalen, it did not make an impression on her. She assumed that the drug she had been given was the same as Dr. Ross had prescribed, and she began taking the prescribed dosage. Within seven to ten days of starting the drug treatment, Walter began to suffer from nausea and lack of appetite. When she referred to the information sheet, Walter saw that such side effects are common for chemotherapy drugs. She continued to take the Melphalen. During the third week after starting the medication Walter noticed bruises on her arms and legs, and during the fourth week she developed a skin rash on her arms and legs. Although the information sheet warned that bruises and rashes should prompt a call to the doctor, Walter waited a few days before attempting to contact Dr. Ross.

[¶ 5] Dr. Ross testified at trial that his notes indicated that Walter should have had blood tests two weeks after starting medication and that she was to have scheduled an appointment with him within four weeks of beginning the medication. He also testified that because Chlorambucil is slow-acting, he does not insist that his patients have blood tests done in fourteen days but only that they have blood work periodically. Walter testified that she understood she was to have a follow-up appointment with Dr. Ross in four weeks and blood tests sometime before that appointment.

[¶ 6] On the twenty-third day after starting the medication, Walter had blood tests done. She attempted to reach Dr. Ross by phone to tell him about the side effects, but she was unsuccessful until June 3, 1997. On that day Dr. Ross told her that her blood levels were low and to stop taking the medication immediately. He scheduled an appointment for June 5. Walter, however, was rushed to the hospital later in the day on June 3 when she suffered gastrointestinal bleeding. Following her emergency admission, Walter remained in the hospital five weeks and received numerous blood transfusions. She suffered several infections, and a catheter was placed in her chest. The bruising and skin rash continued. For a period of time she was unable to eat because of bleeding gums and an infection in her mouth. Because of her weakened immune system, Walter's visitors could not come within ten feet of her.

[¶ 7] Prior to receiving the Melphalen, Walter lived independently and was active. Following her hospital discharge on July 7, 1997, she was physically weak. She initially had to make daily trips to the hospital and later went less frequently. She had to have additional transfusions after she left the hospital. Melphalen did have the effect of causing her cancer to go into remission. Walter's total medical bills for her treatment came to $71,042.63.

[¶ 8] The two-day jury trial was held in February 1999. Wal-Mart moved for judgment as a matter of law at the close of Walter's case on the grounds that she had failed to present expert testimony on the standard of care by pharmacists, and the motion was denied. At the close of the evidence Walter moved for a judgment as a matter of law, and the court granted Walter's motion concluding that she was entitled to judgment on liability. During Walter's closing argument, Wal-Mart moved for a mistrial arguing that certain comments by Walter's counsel were improper, and the motion was denied. The jury awarded Walter $550,000 in damages. Wal-Mart's post-trial motion for judgment as a matter of law or a new trial was denied.

II. WALTER'S MOTION FOR JUDGMENT ON LIABILITY

. . .

[¶ 10] The effect of the [trial] court's grant of Walter's motion was a determination, as a matter of law, that[:] Wal-Mart had a duty to Walter which it breached; that breach caused Walter harm; and Walter was not negligent — or if she was negligent, her negligence [could not entirely exculpate Wal-Mart]. The only issue left for the jury was the amount of damages caused by Wal-Mart's negligence and whether those damages should be reduced because of any action or inaction by Walter. . . . [Wal-Mart now seeks reversal of the Court's ruling. Walter insists that is was proper.]

A. WAL-MART'S REPRESENTATIONS TO THE JURY

[¶ 11] . . . Walter contends that Wal-Mart . . . admitted liability in its [attorney's] opening statement to the jury. . . .[1]

1. Wal-Mart's counsel began his opening statement by explaining the process of a lawsuit and why Wal-Mart denied liability in [filing its formal answer to the complaint by which Walter commenced this lawsuit]. He then stated:

> What I'm here to tell you right now is since the filing of the complaint and filing of the answer, Wal-Mart has never denied responsibility for this incident. Never.
>
> Going back to what happened. [Walter's attorney] and I are in substantial agreement in terms of what happened on May 7, 1997, and what has to [sic] occurred since. . . . [We] have a difference of opinion as to what constitutes fair, reasonable and just compensation for Mrs. Walter. That's why we are here. We can't agree. It's as simple as that. We just can't agree on that issue. We need your help. . . .
>
> It's not because we are blaming Mrs. Walter. It's not because we are trying to deflect blame. And it's not because we are trying to sort of make the issues obscure or distracting. We are going to put all the cards on the table. There are no secrets. There are no major disputes as to what occurred. . . .
>
> The hardest issue and the one that is going to be in your laps at the end of tomorrow is what monetary amount represents fair and just compensation for Mrs. Walter? You will be asked to consider medical bills and what she went through during the hospitalization and what she has done [sic] through since then. Wal-Mart is here, and I'm here to ask you as the conscience of the community what that figure is. That's really why we are here. . . .
>
> The evidence in this case will show that . . . on May 7, 1997 . . . Mr. Lovin was given a prescription for Chlorambucil. What came to his mind was Alkeran. And from there the mistake was made. And it was sort of on a path of not being able being [sic] corrected in his mind. He was confident that Chlorambucil was Alkeran. It was a mistake. And it's a mistake for which he's deeply sorry. But that's irrelevant.
>
> The fact is that a mistake was made. That he didn't realize it at the time and wasn't told of the mistake until June 3rd when he received a call from Dr. Ross. . . .

[¶ 13] Wal-Mart's [attorney's] opening statement admitted the error made by its pharmacist in filling the prescription but . . . there was no . . . admission of negligence. Furthermore, the statement taken in its entire context, does not contain an unequivocal admission that the mistake in filling the prescription caused Walter's harm. . . . For these reasons, we cannot conclude that there was [an] . . . admission that Wal-Mart was liable for Walter's damages. . . .

B.   WAL-MART'S NEGLIGENCE

[¶ 14] Walter had the burden to prove that Wal-Mart, through its pharmacist employee, owed a duty to Walter that it breached, thereby causing her harm. In Tremblay v. Kimball, 107 Me. 53, 77 A. 405 (1910), we held that pharmacists owe their customers a duty of ordinary care, but that "ordinary care" for a pharmacist means that "the highest practicable degree of prudence, thoughtfulness, and vigilance and the most exact and reliable safeguards" must be taken. *Id.* at 53, 77 A. at 408.

[¶ 15] Lovin, the Wal-Mart pharmacist, readily admitted that he made an error in filling Walter's prescription. He testified that he thought that the brand name for Chlorambucil was Alkeran, and he filled the prescription with Alkeran, which is Melphalen. Lovin said that he made a "serious error" that did not "satisfy the proper standard of care for a pharmacist." He admitted that he would have discovered the error if he had followed the standard four-step process utilized to check for errors. He acknowledged that to comply with the standard of pharmacy care he should have checked the stock bottle against the prescription. He further admitted that the standard of practice required that he counsel Walter when she picked up the prescription, at which time he would have showed her the drug and discussed it with her. He testified that he did not counsel her, but if he had done so, he would have discovered the error. He also said that Walter would have no reason to suspect that she was given the wrong drug.

[¶ 16] Pursuant to the standard of "the highest practicable degree of prudence, thoughtfulness, and vigilance and the most exact and reliable safeguards" . . ., Lovin's testimony established that the standard was breached. Even if we were to determine that the standard of practice for pharmacists is the skill and diligence exercised by similar professionals, Lovin's testimony established that standard and the breach of it. None of this evidence was disputed. A jury, acting reasonably, could not have found that Wal-Mart was not negligent.

C.   CAUSATION

[¶ 17] In order to establish liability a plaintiff in any negligence action must show that the defendant's negligence was the . . . cause of the plaintiff's harm. Wal-Mart argues that Walter's motion should have been denied because she failed to prove that Wal-Mart's negligence in filling the prescription was the cause of her injury. Causation means "that there be some reasonable connection between the act or omission of the defendant and the damage which the plaintiff has suffered." Wheeler v. White, 1998 ME 137, ¶ 7, 714 A.2d 125. . . .

[¶ 18] There was uncontroverted medical evidence that Melphalen, which Wal-Mart provided Walter erroneously, caused damage to her body. . . . Dr. Ross testified that the Melphalen made Walter seriously ill, to the point that he was not sure she would survive, and that her lack of energy after her release from the hospital was the result of the illness caused by the wrong medication. Wal-Mart's expert oncologist also testified that the side effects of Melphalen caused the lengthy hospitalization, and the hospitalization itself likely caused Walter's malaise and depression after her discharge.

[¶ 19] Wal-Mart['s] . . . expert speculated that if a blood test had been done fourteen days after starting the medication it might have shown lowered blood levels and, depending on how low those levels were, Walter's physician might have stopped the medication, and if the medication had been stopped sooner, the harmful effect may have been less. Wal-Mart's expert did not testify that there would have been no damage if a blood test had been done on the fourteenth day. In fact, in his description of Melphalen, he noted it has a long life in the body and that its side effects last longer.[3] . . . No reasonable factfinder could have found that Wal-Mart's negligent act in misfilling the prescription was not a substantial cause in bringing about Walter's suffering. "[W]hen the totality of the evidence adduced in *any particular case* is so overwhelming that it leaves open to a fact-finder, acting rationally, only one conclusion on the issue, the issue is then determined as a matter of law." Laferriere v. Paradis, 293 A.2d 526, 528 (Me. 1972). The trial court did not err in granting judgment as a matter of law to Walter on the issue of causation.

D.   COMPARATIVE NEGLIGENCE AND MITIGATION OF DAMAGES

[¶ 20] Wal-Mart argues that Walter's motion for judgment on liability should have been denied because Wal-Mart raised the defense of comparative negligence and it was entitled to have the jury decide whether Walter was negligent. Wal-Mart claims that Walter should have realized that the drug name on the medicine container did not match the medication that she had discussed with Dr. Ross. Wal-Mart also argues that Walter was negligent when she did not contact Dr. Ross immediately upon noticing the rash and bruising.

[¶ 21] Under Maine's comparative negligence statute, the damages owing to a plaintiff may be reduced when the plaintiff's harm is partly the result of the plaintiff's own fault, and fault is defined as the negligence that would give rise to the defense of contributory negligence. *See* 14 M.R.S.A. § 156 (1980). If the plaintiff's fault is equal to or greater than that of the defendant, the plaintiff cannot recover damages.

3. The blood tests alone did not reveal that the wrong medication had been given. Dr. Ross did not discover that she was taking the wrong medication until after she was admitted to the hospital.

1.   Walter's Failure to Discover Wal-Mart's Error

[¶ 22] Turning first to Wal-Mart's contention that Walter was contributorily negligent in failing to discover that she had been given the wrong medication, we conclude that a jury, acting rationally, on this evidence could not find that she was negligent. Lovin testified that Walter "would have no way of knowing" that she had been given the wrong medication, and there was no evidence that Walter should have been expected to discover Wal-Mart's negligence.[5] Thus, it was not error to refuse to instruct the jury on comparative negligence concerning Walter's failure to discover Wal-Mart's error.

2.   Walter's Failure to Notify Her Doctor Immediately of Side Effects

[¶ 23] Wal-Mart claims that Walter's delay in calling her doctor to report the skin rash and bruising was negligence on her part that contributed to her suffering. . . .

[Wal-Mart had requested the trial judge to instruct the jury to consider assigning some or all of the responsibility for Walter's injuries to Walter herself based on her failure to promptly contact Dr. Ross. The trial judge declined to give this comparative fault instruction, but did instruct the jury that it could consider Walter's inaction as a "failure to mitigate" her injuries, and hence as a reason to reduce her damage award. The Maine Supreme Court concluded that, although there are conceptual differences between the doctrines of comparative fault and failure to mitigate, as applied to the facts of this case, the two doctrines are indistinguishable. It therefore concluded that the judge's instruction adequately permitted the jury to adjust its award in light of any fault on the part of Walter in failing to report her symptoms. — EDS.]

III.   WAL-MART'S MOTION FOR JUDGMENT AS A MATTER OF LAW

[¶ 31] Wal-Mart moved for judgment as a matter of law on the ground that Walter failed to present any expert evidence on the pharmacist's standard of care. It points out that Lovin was not designated as an expert. In

---

5. We are aware of two cases from other jurisdictions in which a comparative negligence instruction was given when a pharmacist gave the plaintiff the wrong medication. The facts in one case, however, make it distinguishable from Walter's situation. In Forbes v. Walgreen Co., 566 N.E.2d 90, 91 (Ind. App. 1991), the plaintiff had been taking medication for headaches. When she had the prescription refilled, she noticed that the medication she was given was different in size, shape, and color from what she had been taking, but she took it anyway for several months. The wrong medication did not cause her to be sick, but it was ineffective on her headaches. See id. Walter had never taken her medication previously and had no reason to be suspicious of its size, shape, or color. In the other case, the ten percent reduction of plaintiff's damages for comparative negligence was not appealed or discussed. . . .

this case the testimony of an expert was not necessary. We have said that where professional negligence and its harmful results "are sufficiently obvious as to lie within common knowledge" no expert testimony is necessary. . . . The negligence of the pharmacist and the harmful results were sufficiently obvious to be within the common knowledge of a lay person. It does not take an expert to know that filling a prescription with the wrong drug and failing to take the steps in place in that pharmacy to check for the wrong drug is negligence.

IV.   WAL-MART'S MOTION FOR MISTRIAL

[¶ 32] Wal-Mart moved for a mistrial because of three comments made by Walter's counsel during closing argument. First, Walter's attorney stated that the pharmacist attempted to accept responsibility but his employer, Wal-Mart, refused to accept responsibility for Walter's injury. Wal-Mart objected, and the objection was sustained. The court admonished counsel that the only issue was damages and told the jury that they were not to be swayed by any bias or predisposition towards one party or the other. [Wal-Mart's second objection is omitted. — EDS.] Third, while referring to the amount of damages the jury could award, during rebuttal, Walter's counsel told the jury it should consider how much money professional basketball players are paid. Wal-Mart objected and the objection was sustained. Wal-Mart argues that the effect of the three comments was to prejudice the jury against Wal-Mart so that it would punish Wal-Mart by the amount of damages.

[¶ 33] We review a refusal to grant a motion for a mistrial for abuse of discretion. *See* Sheltra v. Rochefort, 667 A.2d 868, 871 (Me. 1995). The judge sustained the objections to the comments, told the jurors to ignore the comments, and gave curative instructions. The trial judge did not abuse his discretion. . . .

V.   WAL-MART'S MOTION FOR NEW TRIAL

[¶ 34] After the verdict Wal-Mart moved for a new trial. . . . Wal-Mart . . . contends that the damages were excessive and the size of the verdict demonstrates that the judge and jury were biased against Wal-Mart.

[¶ 35] "When a court refuses to grant a new trial on the ground of an excessive damage award, the ruling will not be reversed except for clear and manifest abuse of discretion." Gilmore v. Central Maine Power Co., 665 A.2d 666, 670 (Me. 1995). . . .

[¶ 36] Walter's total medical bills and expenses equalled $71,042.63. The jury awarded Walter $550,000 in damages. Presumably, the additional $479,000 of Walter's recovery is in compensation for her pain and suffering. The jury heard several witnesses, including Walter herself, testify about the painful treatment she received in the hospital, the long recovery process, and the continuing difficulties she faces. In light of this evidence, which must be considered favorably to Walter, the jury's award of damages is rational. "Although the verdict may seem large, it reflects the considered opinion of the jury within the range of evidence of sufficient probative character. . . ." *Michaud*, 390 A.2d at 537 (quoting Fotter v. Butler, 145 Me. 266, 273, 75 A.2d 160, 164 (1950)). . . .

Judgment affirmed.

[Concurring opinion omitted. — EDS.]

A.   Common Law and Statute

1. *Appellate Courts*. The Maine Supreme Court is comprised of seven justices, one of whom, Justice Calkins, wrote the majority or main opinion in this case. As is evident from *Walter*, the court is an appellate court — it decides appeals brought to it by litigants who believe there are legal grounds for challenging adverse lower-court decisions. Because it filed the appeal, Wal-Mart is dubbed the *appellant*. (For the appellate phase of the litigation, Ms. Walter, the plaintiff at the trial level, is deemed the *respondent*.) As indicated by its name, the Maine Supreme Court is the court of last resort for issues governed by Maine law. Thus, the decision in *Walter* — issued in April of 2000 — conclusively resolved a lawsuit that had been commenced two years earlier, and that concerned an act of carelessness that took place another year before that.[*]

2. *Negligence and Judge-Made Law*. We stated above that torts are wrongs that generate injuries for which victims are entitled to seek redress. In *Walter*, the tort alleged is negligence. Much of this book aims to provide insight into that particular tort. For now, we can define it as a failure to heed a duty of reasonable care that causes an injury to a person to whom that duty is owed. Thus, to establish that she was a victim of negligence, Walter had to prove (1) that Wal-Mart owed her a *duty* of reasonable care, (2) that it *breached* that duty, (3) that the breach of duty *caused* her to suffer adverse effects, and (4) that these effects are recognized by the law as an *injury*.

In most U.S. jurisdictions, torts such as negligence are *common law causes of action*. This means that the plaintiff's ability to sue in the first place, and the terms on which she can obtain redress, are established by judicial decisions, rather than by a statute passed by a legislature and authorized by the chief executive. In *Walter*, for example, the Maine Supreme Court states in ¶ 14 that, "Walter had the burden to prove that Wal-Mart, through its pharmacist employee, owed a duty to Walter that it breached, thereby causing her harm." This description of the tort of *negligence* — which is consistent with the one we provided a moment ago — derives from prior Maine judicial decisions that have defined negligence in

---

[*] State and federal courts now maintain websites from which recently issued opinions may be downloaded. (For Maine Supreme Court decisions from 1997, see www.courts.state.me.us/opinions/supreme/index.html.) Publishing companies also reproduce these opinions in hardbound volumes found in libraries, as well as in databases accessible to subscribers. The citation that follows the case-caption at the beginning of Walter v. Wal-Mart — 748 A.2d 961 — informs you that the decision can be found starting at page 961 of volume 748 of the Atlantic Reporter, Second Series, published by West Publishing Co.

terms of the four elements of duty, breach, causation, and harm (injury). The court did not provide a citation to those earlier decisions, perhaps because this basic description of negligence is so well established as to not warrant the effort. By contrast, the court does cite earlier decisions to help define the elements of breach and causation. *See* ¶¶ 14, 17. Likewise, it cites earlier decisions for procedural rules, such as the rule that the trial court's decision not to grant a new trial can only be overturned if it constitutes a clear abuse of discretion. *See* ¶ 35.

3. *The Principle of* Stare Decisis. The court's reliance on earlier decisions to guide its legal analysis was not simply a matter of choice. Rather, the court was obligated to rely on them. This obligation stems from a core principle of the common law called *stare decisis*. *Stare decisis* — which translates as "let the decision stand" — is a complex notion. Here is a rough description of its content:

> A court that is presently required to resolve an issue of law ("the present court") must accept the resolution of that issue contained in a prior judicial decision involving other litigants if:
> a.   the prior decision was rendered by a court with the *authority* to issue decisions that are *binding* on the present court;
> b.   the issue was *actually resolved* in the prior decision, rather than assumed away;
> c.   the resolution of the issue was *necessary* to the prior decision; and
> d.   the issue arose in the prior decision in *comparable circumstances* to those of the present decision.

By obliging subsequent courts to follow prior courts' decisions, the principle of *stare decisis* functions to promote a reasonable degree of consistency across decisions within a jurisdiction, and thereby to advance basic values associated with the rule of law, such as predictability and comparable treatment of similarly situated litigants.

The application of *stare decisis* can sometimes be straightforward and sometimes subtle. For example, the citation of the *Walter* court to the 1910 *Tremblay* decision in ¶ 14 for the proposition that pharmacists owe their patients "ordinary care" was routine. Contrast the treatment in footnote 5 of two prior decisions that indicated a willingness to assign some degree of responsibility to patients who failed to prevent or mitigate injuries caused by an erroneous prescription. The first thing to observe is that the Maine court was not obligated to follow these precedents for a very basic reason: They were issued by judges within other states' court systems. Each state's tort law forms a distinct body of law. Thus, the courts of one state do not have *authority* to issue decisions about substantive tort law that are binding on the courts of another state. Rather, out-of-state precedents such as these are at best *persuasive* authorities — helpful or informative, but not *controlling*.

Second, even if we were to imagine that these earlier decisions had been issued by the Maine Supreme Court itself, the *Walter* court would

2

still have had reasons not to follow them. Thus, footnote 5 asserts that the first precedent is *distinguishable* — it was decided on facts sufficiently different from those in *Walter* that one can say without contradiction that the plaintiff in the earlier case failed to mitigate her damages, while Ms. Walter did not. As for the second out-of-state precedent, the court avoided it on the ground that it resolved the issue of plaintiff's failure to mitigate without analysis, and therefore was not entitled to deference. In other instances, a court might decline to follow a prior decision's resolution of an issue on the ground that the resolution was not *necessary* to the decision — that the earlier court could have resolved the dispute in front of it without ever addressing the issue in question. This idea is sometimes conveyed by saying that the prior resolution was not part of the *holding* of the case, but instead constituted *dictum.*

Finally, note that, even though the principle of *stare decisis* is central to the operation of the common law system, it is not understood by courts — particularly courts of last resort, as is the Maine Supreme Court on issues of Maine law — to state an absolute or inexorable rule that controlling precedents must be followed no matter what. Indeed, courts sometimes conclude that precedents ought to be overruled or abandoned because social or economic circumstances have changed since the time of the original decision, or because the precedent runs counter to important policies or principles, or because they conclude that the initial decision was erroneous at the time it was rendered. As we will see, the question of when departure from otherwise binding precedent is warranted is one of the most difficult issues in common law analysis.

4. *The Varying Role of Statutes.* Tort law need not be judicial in origin. Many European countries have statutes that create and define the general parameters of tort liability. For example, Section 823(1) of the German Civil Code translates in part as follows:

> Anyone who intentionally or negligently injures life, body, health, freedom ownership or any other right of another in a manner contrary to the law shall be obliged to compensate the other for the loss arising.

A handful of states, including California and Louisiana, whose legal systems reflect the influence of European civil law (as opposed to English common law) have similar provisions. However, because these statutes are written so broadly, they require extensive judicial interpretation as they are applied to concrete cases. As a result, the tort law of those states is in many respects indistinguishable from that of a common law jurisdiction such as Maine.

In European and Anglo-American jurisdictions, statutes can also create what amount to new tort causes of action for specific situations. For example, Massachusetts General Laws, Chapter 93A, is a statute that protects consumers against unfair business practices. In aid of that goal, it states:

> Any person who . . . suffers any loss of money or property . . . as a result of the use . . . by another person . . . of . . . an unfair or deceptive act or prac-

tice . . . [may sue for damages and may also recover reasonable attorneys' fees and litigation costs if sucessful].

Chapter 93A and its counterparts sometimes permit suits for injuries caused by questionable business practices even though, for one reason or another, the practices do not amount to fraud or some other common law tort.

In addition to creating new tort causes of action, statutes interact with the common law of tort in other ways. For example, statutes can limit tort remedies that would otherwise be available by setting dollar caps on damage awards. Alternatively, as discussed in Chapter 6, statutes that specify certain standards of conduct — for example, laws that require cars to be driven with their headlights on after dusk and before sunrise — are sometimes treated by the courts as setting the standard of care that will govern the resolution of a tort suit by someone who is injured by a failure to comply with these standards. As noted in *Walter*, the legislature and governor of Maine enacted a statute — 14 M.R.S.A. § 156 — with very important ramifications for tort law. Under that statute, which was originally passed in 1965, if there is some evidence presented at trial that the plaintiff's fault helped bring about her own injuries, the jury will be asked to consider that evidence and to assign a percentage fault to both the plaintiff and the negligent defendant, which assignment will have the effect of reducing or barring any recovery by the plaintiff. The place of statutes in tort law will be a recurring issue in these materials.

5. *The Torts Restatements*. Courts dealing with tort cases often consult a set of documents known as the Restatement of Torts. The Restatement is written and published by the American Law Institute (ALI), a private organization founded in the 1920s that is comprised of judges, lawyers, and scholars, and whose stated mission is to promote clarity and consistency in the application of the law. Specifically, the Restatement aims to gather together and interpret decisional law coming out of all U.S. jurisdictions in an effort to identify "black letter" law: rules and standards on which there is a wide degree of consensus among judges. Unlike statutes, regulations, and prior judicial decisions within a jurisdiction, a Restatement does not itself have the force of law. However, Restatements have been enormously influential, and particular provisions often are incorporated into common law by judicial decision. (In an omitted portion of *Walter*, the court cites a comment to Section 918 of the Second Restatement of Torts to help define the relationship between the defenses of comparative fault and failure to mitigate damages.)

Each Restatement is shepherded through the ALI by a "Reporter" or set of Reporters. The Reporters, eminent scholars in the field, serve as the primary authors of the Restatements; thus the Restatements tend to reflect a particularly scholarly "take" on the law. The Restatement of Torts has already gone through two editions, and its third iteration is presently underway. The First Restatement was published in the mid-1930s. The Second was published in the mid-1960s and early 1970s. The Third Restatement is being developed, in stages, by several Reporters responsible for different subject areas.

B.   Responsibilities in Tort

Negligence suits like Ms. Walter's aim to establish that another person or entity was legally at fault, and hence legally responsible, for the plaintiff having suffered an injury. Yet, even in an apparently simple case such as this one — which involves a single victim allegedly injured as the result of an in-person interaction with a single careless actor — allegations and attributions of responsibility are not as straightforward as they might first seem. Consider, for example, a seemingly simple question. Why is the caption of this case *Walter v. Wal-Mart Stores, Inc.?* More specifically, why isn't it *Walter v. Lovin?*

1. *Respondeat Superior*. A negligence suit such as Ms. Walter's alleges that a specific individual engaged in conduct that was careless as to her well-being. Yet, in many instances, a negligence plaintiff will often seek to establish not (or not only) that *the careless individual* owes her compensation, but instead (or also) that *the entity* for which that individual worked owes her compensation. Ms. Walter, for example, did not seek any compensation from the pharmacist, Henry Lovin, which is why he is not named in court documents as a party to the suit. Instead, she sought compensation from the corporate bank accounts of Wal-Mart, Lovin's employer.

Plaintiffs who sue entities such as corporations often are able to recover from them because of a longstanding substantive rule of tort law called *respondeat superior* (literally, "let the master answer [for the wrongs of the servant]"). Under that rule, an employer is held *vicariously liable* for wrongful acts of its employees committed within the scope of their employment. This responsibility attaches even if the employer (i.e., the firm's managers) were careful in supervising the employee's job performance.

In *Walter* itself the evidence produced at trial revealed that Wal-Mart policy requires all of its pharmacists to follow certain procedures to protect against errors. Thus, each is supposed to check the bottle from which he dispenses medication against the original prescription to ensure that they match. In addition, the pharmacist is always supposed to discuss with the patient the drug he is dispensing to her, which provides another opportunity to catch mistakes. Lovin, however, did neither of these things. Given this policy, and depending on whether Wal-Mart and its store manager took reasonable measures to implement it, one can argue that Wal-Mart *management* was *not* careless in terms of how it set up and operated the pharmacy from which the medication was dispensed to Ms. Walter. Even so, Wal-Mart would still be subject to liability. This is because, under *respondeat superior*, liability attaches to Wal-Mart vicariously, that is, simply because Lovin acted carelessly in performing his job as a Wal-Mart pharmacist, notwithstanding that his actions were perhaps in violation of company policies.

The doctrine of *respondeat superior* is not the only basis for holding corporations, organizations, and government entities liable in tort law, but it is perhaps the primary basis for doing so. (We consider the content and justifications for the doctrine more fully in Chapter 8.) To the extent it does function to impose liability on employers, it does *not* thereby immunize careless employees from liability. In other words, the doctrine functions to *add* another entity to the roster of potentially responsible parties, not to substitute one for another. Given this fact, it is worth asking one more question about the caption of the *Walter* case: Why doesn't it read *Walter v. Wal-Mart Stores, Inc. & Lovin?* The immediate answer is that Ms. Walter did not bring suit against Lovin. But, given that she could have, that answer simply provokes another question: Why didn't Ms. Walter sue Lovin in addition to suing Wal-Mart? Can you think of any strategic reasons why her lawyer might advise against it?

2. *Multiple Tortfeasors*. *Respondeat superior* adds an important layer to tort attributions of responsibility. Another source of complexity is that tort cases often allege or identify wrongdoing on the part of multiple actors. Reexamine the facts laid out in ¶¶ 2-8 of the majority opinion. Do they identify anyone else (other than Wal-Mart or Lovin) who might be found to have carelessly contributed to Ms. Walter's injury?

What about Walter's physician, Dr. Ross? Did he act with ordinary care in failing to arrange a blood test within two weeks of the commencement of her treatment? Alternatively, or in addition, was it careless of him to respond to her description of her symptoms by arranging for her to come into the office two days later, by which time she had been hospitalized? Suppose this was carelessness, and that it did have some role in producing Walter's injuries. How would these suppositions affect your assessment of Wal-Mart's responsibility? Should one or the other be held responsible, or both? Interestingly, although it was probably open to each of them, neither Walter's attorney nor Wal-Mart's attorney sought to add Dr. Ross as an additional party to the lawsuit, which perhaps would have enabled the jury, at its discretion, to assign some responsibility to him.

It is increasingly common for modern negligence suits to involve claims against and among multiple parties, each of whom is alleged by the others to have been partly or wholly responsible for a given victim's injury. In this respect, at least, *Walter* is helpfully old-fashioned in its simplicity. Much of the discussion of "duty," "cause," and "apportionment" in Chapters 2, 4, 5, and 7 concern the complexities introduced into negligence law by the presence of multiple potentially responsible parties.

3. *Comparative Responsibility*. There is another group of actors whose conduct must be considered in gauging tort law as a system for articulating and enforcing responsibilities. This group consists of the victims who are bringing the tort suits. To what extent does their own conduct bear on the question of responsibility for their injuries? As noted above, under the Maine comparative fault statute, a party who can be deemed to have been at fault for her own injuries may find that her recovery is reduced or barred because of that fact. Most U.S. jurisdictions apply similar rules. Principles of comparative responsibility are discussed further in Chapter 7.

4. *Insurance*. Although it did not figure in *Walter*, there is often one other key player that figures in modern tort suits alleging negligence, namely, an insurance company that has provided *liability insurance* to the

defendant. A liability insurance policy is a special kind of contract. In exchange for regular payments (premiums), the insurer agrees to pay for (indemnify) certain liabilities incurred by persons insured under the policy. So, for example, a physician or attorney will typically maintain malpractice insurance to cover liability if she is successfully sued by a patient or client. Retailers likewise often carry liability insurance for injuries caused to customers and others in the course of their operations. Wal-Mart is so large and wealthy that it "self-insures." Rather than paying premiums to an insurance company, it sets aside a portion of its assets to cover anticipated liabilities. Liability insurance is discussed further in Chapter 8.

Insurance can also relate to tort litigation in another way. Sometimes victims have insurance — so-called first-party insurance — that covers certain costs they might incur, such as health insurance to cover the costs of one's medical care. Walter was in fact covered by Medicare, which is a federal insurance program by which the government pays for certain health care services provided to persons over the age of 65. However, under the substantive tort law of Maine, Wal-Mart was barred from arguing that *it* should benefit, by way of a reduced damages award, from the fact that Walter's medical expenses were mostly or entirely covered by Medicare. As we note in Chapter 8, whether juries in tort cases should be given information as to first- and third-party insurance coverage is currently a hotly debated topic.

C.   The Role of Lawyers

The legal rules and economic realities that help determine the ability of clients to secure representation and proceed with or fend off tort suits are of central importance to the operation of tort law. Indeed, a practicing tort lawyer would likely tell you that, for purposes of practicing law, a working knowledge of the "nuts and bolts" of getting a case to and through court is of primary importance. The point of such an observation is not that knowledge of tort law is irrelevant to practice. Rather, it is a way of emphasizing that an understanding of tort doctrine can only get the aspiring torts practitioner so far.

Unfortunately, given space constraints, and the complexity of substantive tort doctrine alone, we can here only touch upon basic procedural aspects of tort litigation. Other courses, such as civil procedure and evidence, will provide you with greater knowledge of these topics. *In the discussion that follows, we simplify matters by limiting the discussion to a two-party tort lawsuit in which a plaintiff such as Ms. Walter brings a single tort claim against a defendant such as Wal-Mart.* As cases in later chapters demonstrate, tort cases can involve many parties, as well as various different claims raised by different parties.

1. *Attorneys and Contingent Fees.* Tort actions are lawsuits that are conducted by lawyers who are paid to represent their clients. Lawyers arrange for payment by means of either a contingent fee contract or an hourly-rate contract. Under an hourly-rate contract, the attorney and client

agree to a per-hour rate, the lawyer keeps track of the hours worked on the case, then sends regular bills to the client during the pendency of the litigation. The hourly-rate contract is the prevalent form of contract between corporate clients and their counsel.

Contingent fee contracts free the client from any obligation to provide the lawyer with up-front or interim compensation for his labor. In exchange, the lawyer is given the right to obtain a specified percentage of any recovery, usually about 33 percent. Under this type of contract, if the tort suit results in no recovery, the client pays nothing by way of fees. However, the client is obligated to pay certain costs—for example, copying costs and court filing fees—regardless of outcome. In the United States, most personal injury plaintiffs secure legal representation through a contingent fee contract.

2. *The Contingent Fee Contract: History.* The shape of modern American tort law has been driven at least in part by significant changes in the regulation of contracts between attorneys and their clients. Early American law, like the English law from which it derived, treated attorneys not so much as private-sector service providers but as public officials. Accordingly, the amount a lawyer could charge his client was determined based on schedules developed and implemented by courts and legislatures. More strikingly, at least to the modern eye, contingent fee contracts, regardless of the percentage charged, were deemed not only void but *criminal*. Any person who financed or otherwise assisted the progress of another's lawsuit in return for a portion of the proceeds of that suit could be prosecuted for the crime of *champerty* and, if found guilty, fined or imprisoned.* Finally, early American law adopted the *loser-pays* rule. Under this rule, the party who loses the suit must pay the legal costs incurred by the prevailing party. As indicated, these sums were set by the courts, but they still threatened to impose a significant burden on the unsuccessful plaintiff (as well as the unsuccessful defendant). Each of these features of Revolutionary era law served in some degree to hinder tort litigation.

Early in the 1800s, this regulatory scheme began to break down. In part, this happened because the idea that legislatures and courts should heavily regulate lawyers' fees ran counter to the professional interest of the emerging bar, as well as two core tenets of American political culture: anti-elitism and faith in free markets. The notion that a person should be denied the ability to assert his legal rights simply because he lacked disposable income struck many as fundamentally unjust. Likewise, the notion that the attorney and client should not be free to set the terms of their business relationship increasingly seemed an unwarranted piece of paternalism.

Between 1800 and 1850, state and federal courts began to enforce attorney-client contracts in which clients voluntarily agreed to pay higher-than-statutory fees to their attorneys. Likewise, courts started to rule that contingent fee contracts between lawyers and their clients fell outside the

---

* Champerty was closely related to two other crimes: *maintenance* and *barratry*. Maintenance was defined as officious intermeddling in the lawsuit of another. Barratry was broadly defined to include any effort to stir up litigation.

definition of champerty and were therefore enforceable. Eventually, the blanket ban on contingent fee contracts gave way to much more selective bans; contingent fees were decriminalized, except with respect to certain representations. That pattern holds true today: Most states still do not permit lawyers to represent criminal defendants or persons in divorce proceedings on the basis of a contingent fee contract, but do permit them to do so for other representations, including representation in tort suits.

By the early twentieth century, American courts had also shifted away from the loser-pays rule, which meant that the prevailing party was no longer *allowed* to recover its litigation costs from the other party. For plaintiffs, the rejection of the loser-pays rule arguably reduced the down-side risks of litigation and thus may have encouraged the commencement of tort litigation. Because this rule stood in contrast to the English approach, it soon came to be dubbed the "American rule."

3. *Modern Practice.* With some important exceptions, U.S. law today tends not to set caps or otherwise limit the rates charged in contingent fee contracts. In this regard, lawyers are treated no differently than other service providers such as building contractors or repairmen: We rely on the "market" to set fair rates. The market for lawyers has a number of imperfections, however. For example, only in the last 50 years have lawyers been able to advertise widely for clients instead of relying on referrals. There is some evidence that, as the supply of lawyers has increased, and as bans on advertising have been lifted, contingent fees have gone down in response to competition. Today, the rate is likely to be in the vicinity of 33 percent. Beyond this, the degree to which personal injury lawyers compete on price is unclear.

Also, important aspects of the older conception of the lawyer as public official have endured, and provide the basis for judicial regulation of lawyer-client contracts. Every state court system has adopted binding rules of professional conduct that, among other things, prohibit lawyers from collecting clearly excessive fees. Violations of these rules do not constitute a crime, nor even the tort of legal malpractice. They do, however, subject attorneys to disciplinary actions, including disbarment. The standard for "clearly excessive" fees is obviously vague, and its application depends on factors such as the complexity of the case, the likelihood of success on the merits, etc.*

---

* English law still bans contingent fees. However, it also provides some legal aid to assist the poor in asserting their rights. In the 1990s, Parliament began permitting lawyers in personal injury cases to charge "conditional fees." A conditional fee arrangement, like a contingent fee contract, frees the client of the obligation to pay for the attorney's labor up front. It also conditions reimbursement for that labor upon the plaintiff's suit prevailing. But, unlike contingent fees, conditional fees are not tied to the size of the settlement or award obtained on behalf of the client. Instead, the lawyer is to receive a fee set by a schedule indexed to the type of lawsuit, but in addition stands to receive an "uplift" — a 100 percent increase — over that scheduled amount if the suit prevails. In Germany, plaintiffs' attorneys receive compensation equal to a fixed percentage of the sum demanded in the lawsuit. These payments are not contingent on how much is actually recovered, and the percentages are set by statute in the form of a schedule. British (and European) countries also continue to adhere to the loser-pays rule.

In common law tort actions in the United States, the American rule against fee shifting continues to predominate. However, federal and state statutes have carved out important exceptions to the rule. You may have noticed, for example, that the Massachusetts Consumer Protection Act, quoted above, provides that a plaintiff who prevails is entitled to attorneys' fees from the defendant. Likewise, federal statutes authorizing persons to sue for certain acts of race, gender, and disability discrimination entitle successful plaintiffs to recover fees from the opposing party. Fee-shifting provisions encourage individuals with meritorious claims to bring suit. Consider, as we proceed through these materials, why legislatures might use them selectively to encourage some types of suits but not others.

Even though the legal validity of contingent fee contracts in tort suits is thus now well established, courts and commentators in the last 30 years have expressed many concerns over their use. These modern critics argue that the pendulum has swung too far in the direction of plaintiffs, and that contingent fees foment litigation by eliminating most of the up-front cost of suing. These criticisms call to mind the picture of "ambulance-chasing" lawyers aggressively promoting litigation regardless of the client's interests.* Other critics suggest that contingent fee contracts are bad even for clients with meritorious claims because they encourage lawyers to push for quick settlements that generate very high returns relative to the effort put into the case, rather than to pursue their clients' best interests. Many, however, continue to defend contingent fees both on freedom of contract grounds, and as necessary to ensure widespread access to justice, particularly in a country reluctant to fund legal services for the poor. Empirical studies seem to indicate that the rate of return on contingent fee contracts is not significantly higher than on hourly contracts.

D.   Proceeding Through Court

1. *Complaints and Private Rights of Action.* In tort suits, the sequence of legal events begins at the behest of the injured person, who, if represented by an attorney, will have his lawyer draft a document called a *complaint*. Roughly speaking, we can say that a tort suit is commenced when the complaint is *served on* (i.e., delivered to) the defendant, and filed with the court that will preside over the lawsuit. A typical tort complaint is a modest document. It briefly identifies the most basic allegations contained in the plaintiff's suit, demands a jury trial, and requests that the court order the award of appropriate relief in the event that the defendant is held liable. A copy of the complaint in the *Walter* case is provided in Appendix A.

The role of the plaintiff's complaint in commencing a tort suit attests that tort is in an important sense *private* law rather than public law. Of

---

* In fairness, we should note that the defense bar is just as frequently accused of manipulating hourly fee arrangements by overstaffing cases and otherwise "padding" their bills.

course, the public might have an interest in a given tort suit. Indeed, the outcome of Ms. Walter's suit might conceivably affect how Wal-Mart, a national retailer, goes about dispensing prescription medications. Still, the matter is private in that tort law operates in the particular manner of empowering a private citizen, rather than a government official, to commence a legal proceeding, at her option. Likewise, the point of the suit, at least in the first instance, is for that citizen to obtain redress from the person who has allegedly wronged her.

2. *Answers and Motions to Dismiss.* Typically, a tort defendant will respond to a complaint by having his attorney file an *answer* — a document that will probably admit certain basic facts alleged in the complaint, while also denying others, as well as liability. (Wal-Mart's answer to Walter's complaint is reproduced in Appendix A.) In lieu of an answer, a defendant might instead file a *motion to dismiss* the plaintiff's complaint. (A *motion* is a formal request for a ruling from the court, usually made by a party to the lawsuit.) As its name suggests, a motion to dismiss requests that the trial judge enter judgment for the defendant at the very outset of the suit, on the basis of nothing more than the paper pleadings. Because there has been no opportunity for the plaintiff to build her case, a heavy burden is placed on the movant/defendant. Essentially, the defendant has to demonstrate that, no matter what evidence the plaintiff may be able to present in support of her tort claim as the suit goes forward, the claim contains some fatal defect that prevents the court from affording any manner of relief to the plaintiff.

By their nature, motions to dismiss will only be granted on issues that can be resolved with minimal or no factfinding. As a result, they are usually — though not exclusively — granted on procedural issues. Thus, motions to dismiss often assert that the plaintiff has commenced her tort suit in a court that has no jurisdiction (no authority) to resolve the dispute. Alternatively, they might assert that the plaintiff has waited too long to commence her action and has thus lost the right to sue. For example, suppose a plaintiff files a complaint alleging that she broke her leg after slipping on a carelessly maintained floor in defendant's restaurant. Suppose further that the complaint demonstrates on its face that the plaintiff served and filed her complaint three years after the slip-and-fall, thereby failing to comply with a statutory rule specifying that such a suit must be commenced within two years of the accident. In such a situation, a court would grant a motion to dismiss the suit on the ground that the suit is time-barred, which renders it impossible for the plaintiff to prevail no matter what evidence she might discover and present at trial. *Cf.* Meiselmann v. McDonald's Restaurants, 759 N.Y.S.2d 506 (App. Div. 2003).

3. *Discovery.* If the suit is not resolved on a motion to dismiss, the lawyers commence the process called *discovery*, whereby they attempt to secure information relevant to the tort suit. Discovery often takes the form of *document requests*, which seek copies of relevant documents in the possession of adversaries or third parties. It also may consist of *interrogatories* — written questions — addressed to the parties to the lawsuit. As indicated in Appendix A, the attorney for Ms. Walter invoked these mechanisms

to obtain documents describing Wal-Mart's internal policies for the dispensation of prescription medicines, to identify the particular pharmacist who mishandled her prescription, and to identify persons whom Wal-Mart intended to call as witnesses at trial. Likewise, Wal-Mart's attorney sought to obtain records as to Walter's medical condition before and after her treatment, and records of the expenses she incurred in obtaining medical treatment, including records as to which of those expenses were covered by health insurance.

Another important discovery tool is the *deposition*. A deposition is an interview that is conducted by an attorney for one of the parties in the presence of counsel for the other party. Often a deposition will take place in a conference room at a law firm or at the office of the person being interviewed (the *deponent*). During a deposition, the deponent is under oath, and the questions put to her, as well as her answers, are recorded by a stenographer. Deponents in a tort suit may include anyone who possesses information about the dispute, especially those who may end up serving as testifying witnesses should the case proceed to trial. In *Walter*, for example, Wal-Mart's attorney deposed the plaintiff to get further information about her account of how events unfolded. Among other things, depositions allow counsel to learn more about the strengths and weaknesses of the opponent's case and the likely impact that a given witness will have at trial.

4. *The Jury Trial.* The Seventh Amendment to the United States Constitution grants to each party involved in the litigation of certain suits, including tort suits, the right to demand a jury trial. That right, however, only applies to suits tried in federal courts. Still, most state constitutions provide the same guarantee for suits in state court. (The relevant provision of the Maine Constitution is Article I, Section 20.) Thus, unless the parties agree to forgo that right, if their case goes to trial, they will litigate it to a jury. If they do agree to waive that right and present evidence to the trial judge without a jury, the proceeding is known as a *bench trial*.

At a jury trial, the attorneys for the parties, overseen by the judge, select a jury of six to twelve men and women drawn from a pool made up of those who have received a notice to report for jury duty. (Individuals receive such notices based on random selections from lists such as lists of registered voters in the relevant locality.) The process of jury selection is beyond the scope of this discussion. Still, it is worth noting that many lawyers regard it as one of the most critical phases of the trial, because it will help determine the jurors' receptivity to the parties' evidence and arguments. Probably most civil juries today are comprised of six jurors. As specified by Maine law, *Walter* was heard by a jury of nine, although one juror was excused because of illness.

After a jury has been selected, the attorneys for the plaintiff and defendant take turns making opening statements that describe in general terms what the dispute is about and the kind of decisions the jurors will be asked to make. Although opening statements often are dramatic, they rarely garner legal analysis of the sort given by the justices of the Maine Supreme Court to the opening statement of Wal-Mart's attorney, Mr. Franco.

Next, the plaintiff's attorney, and then the defendant's attorney, present evidence by calling witnesses to testify and by introducing documents and other forms of physical evidence. In complex cases, the presentation of evidence can take weeks or even months. In a simple case, this process may take only a day or two. In *Walter*, for example, Walter's attorney called four witnesses. The first two were Dr. Morse — a longtime friend of the plaintiff — and Walter herself. Both testified primarily to how the episode affected Walter's health and quality of life. The third witness, Dr. Ross, testified to the medical effects of the misfilled prescription. Finally, Henry Lovin, the Wal-Mart pharmacist, testified as to the circumstances and character of his mistake. The defense offered the testimony only of Dr. Pickus, an oncologist who testified that the drug mistakenly given to Walter had the desired effect of causing her cancer to go into remission. He further opined that the depression experienced by Ms. Walter after being released from the hospital was unlikely to be linked *biologically* to the medication. (As the majority opinion notes in ¶ 18, however, Dr. Pickus also stated that Ms. Walter's depression likely was linked to her hospitalization, which he admitted was caused at least in part by her ingesting the wrong medicine.)

After the evidence is submitted, the attorneys give their closing arguments. Then it is the trial judge's job to instruct the jury on the applicable law. This entails informing the jury of the elements that must be proven before the plaintiff can prevail. The judge will also instruct the jury on any defenses potentially available to the defendant that would prevent or limit the assignment of responsibility to the defendant. For example, in *Walter*, the trial judge instructed the jury on the legal definition of the partial defense of mitigation of damages.

Once the relevant legal rules are framed by the judge, the jury retires to the jury room to determine on the basis of the evidence presented at trial whether the plaintiff has proved her tort claim, and whether the defendant has proved its defenses. The *Walter* jury, for example, was required to determine the extent of the injuries that Ms. Walter suffered as a result of ingesting the wrong medication, and the amount of compensation that Wal-Mart was obligated to pay her for those injuries. Different jurisdictions have different rules, but most do not require unanimity among jurors for the resolution of civil cases such as tort suits. (The rules are different for criminal prosecutions.) Under Maine law, a verdict agreed to by three-quarters of the jurors will be deemed the verdict of the jury. *See* Me. R. Civ. Proc. 48(a). As indicated by the verdict form reproduced in Appendix A, the eight jurors who deliberated over the issues in *Walter* agreed unanimously on the verdict.

The civil jury is an institution unique to U.S. tort law. (England, by contrast, abolished use of the jury for most civil actions in 1933.) As we will see, the proper role of judge and jury is a central and contested issue in U.S. tort law. Defenders of the institution maintain that the jury helps ensure that the parties' conduct is evaluated by their peers, keeps law in contact with ordinary citizens' notions of right and wrong, and promotes public participation in the law. Critics maintain that juries make decisions that are arbitrary, or systematically biased in favor of "sympathetic" plaintiffs against "unsympathetic" defendants, including corporations. In the remainder of this book, we will have many occasions to consider what is and is not asked of juries by our tort system, and whether they are well suited to live up to those responsibilities.

5. *Questions of Law and Fact.* Courts and commentators sometimes divide the questions raised by lawsuits into two categories: questions of *law* and questions of *fact*. By drawing this distinction, they mean to emphasize that, even when a case is conducted before a jury, some issues—issues of law—are reserved for the judge. For example, the first "element" or component of negligence, which poses the issue of whether the defendant owed a duty of reasonable care to the plaintiff, is said to pose a question of law for the judge rather than a question of fact for the jury. Thus, the trial judge in *Walter* never asked the jury to make a finding as to whether Wal-Mart owed a duty of reasonable care in dispensing prescription medication to Walter. Rather, he relied on Maine precedents to conclude that such a duty was owed.

Dividing questions for the court and questions for the jury by reference to the distinction between law and fact is very common, but in some ways confusing. This is because many of the questions that are reserved for the jury call on jurors to do more than make factual findings. For example, in his "mitigation" instruction, the trial judge told the jurors to consider whether Walter should have figured out more promptly that she had been given the wrong medicine. The judge further instructed them that, if they concluded that she had unreasonably delayed in making this discovery, they should factor that failure into their damages award. Neither the initial task of assessing what Ms. Walter should have done, nor the subsequent task of adjusting damages so that they would fairly reflect her failure to mitigate, involved a purely factual inquiry. Instead, they required the jury to make factual determinations (e.g., as to the symptoms actually experienced by Ms. Walter) but also to *evaluate* her conduct in light of those determinations. In this sense, many questions of "fact" submitted to juries are actually questions that require both factual findings and normative judgments. These questions are thus sometimes referred to as mixed questions of law and fact.

6. *Judgment as a Matter of Law.* Consistent with the importance attached to the jury by the federal Constitution and its state counterparts, juries are ordinarily given wide berth to determine those issues that are within their province. Moreover, once they have rendered a decision, their determinations are not lightly disturbed. However, a trial judge is sometimes empowered to preempt or second-guess a jury even on issues that are normally reserved for it. One device by which a judge may do so was the device most centrally at issue in the *Walter* appeal—the entry of *judgment as a matter of law*. Precisely because the entry of such a judgment amounts to a circumvention of the jury, a party who makes a motion for judgment as a matter of law bears an onerous burden: The judge may grant such a motion only if she concludes that, in light of the presumed or

proven facts, *no reasonable jury faithfully applying governing law could find in favor of the party opposing the motion*. By contrast, such a motion cannot be granted merely because the judge thinks that the evidence more strongly favors the moving party. Thus, Wal-Mart appealed the trial court's judgment in part because it believed that the judge erred in concluding that, based on the evidence presented by Walter at trial, a reasonable jury would be *required* to find for the plaintiff on issues such as breach and causation.

7. *Timing: Entry of Judgment as a Matter of Law Before, During, and After Trial.* All motions for judgment as a matter of law ask the trial judge finally to resolve one or more of the issues in the case. Thus, all require that the moving party meet the onerous standard just described in order for the motion to be granted. These constant features notwithstanding, motions for judgment as a matter of law come in three different varieties, depending on the point in the litigation at which they are brought.

a. *Before Trial.* After some discovery has taken place, but before a jury has been empaneled, either party may seek entry of judgment as a matter of law on any or all of the legal issues raised by the plaintiff's lawsuit. Such a motion is usually fashioned as a motion for *summary judgment*.* Motions for summary judgment are typically brought by a defendant seeking to have some or all of the issues in the case determined in its favor prior to trial, although they can be brought by the plaintiff.

A judge may grant a summary judgment motion only if she makes two findings:

First, she must conclude that, as to one (or more) of the dispositive legal issues in the case, there are no genuine disputes between the parties as to "material" facts — that is, facts relevant to the resolution of that issue (or those issues).

Second, she must conclude that, in light of these undisputed facts and the applicable law, a reasonable jury could not find for the party opposing the motion.

For example, if a negligence defendant convinces a trial judge that the undisputed facts obtained through discovery that bear on the "breach" element establish that no reasonable juror could deem the conduct of the defendant to have been careless (i.e., a breach of duty), the judge will enter summary judgment for the defendant and the plaintiff's negligence claim will be resolved at that point in the defendant's favor. However,

* For ease of presentation we are here treating motions for summary judgment as if they are one kind of motion for judgment as a matter of law. Strictly speaking, this is inaccurate. A motion for summary judgment is a distinct type of motion that is authorized by separate rules from those governing motions for judgment as a matter of law. For example, in federal courts, motions for summary judgment are provided for by Federal Rule of Civil Procedure 56, whereas motions for judgment as a matter of law are provided for by Rule 50. Still, the substantive *standard* for granting motions for summary judgment is the same standard that governs judgments as a matter of law. Anderson v. Liberty Lobby, Inc., 477 U.S. 242, 250 (1986).

precisely because the question of breach or carelessness is ordinarily for the jury, courts generally express reluctance to grant such a motion.*

b. *During Trial.* The next opportunity for one or both of the parties to make a motion for judgment as a matter of law occurs after the attorneys have presented evidence to the jury, but before the jury receives its instructions and retires to deliberate. Such motions are made after the plaintiff has finished presenting all of her evidence, and/or at the close of all evidence. Like motions for summary judgment, motions for judgment as a matter of law made at the close of plaintiff's evidence or the close of all evidence can seek complete resolution or partial resolution of the case (i.e., resolution of only certain issues). Also like motions for summary judgment, they are not supposed to be granted lightly.**

Motions for judgments as a matter of law filed at the close of evidence were once commonly described as *directed verdict* motions. Today, however, courts tend to designate them simply as motions of judgment as matter of law. Thus, under the older usage, which is still invoked today by some states' courts, the motions that were filed by Wal-Mart and Walter and discussed by the Maine Supreme Court would have been deemed directed verdict motions because they were made, respectively, at the close of plaintiff's evidence and the close of all evidence. Employing currently predominant usage, however, the Maine Supreme Court in ¶ 8 of its opinion simply refers to them as motions for judgment as a matter of law.

c. *After Trial.* After the jury has rendered its verdict, a party who is disappointed by it can again seek judgment as a matter of law. In essence, such a motion asks the trial judge to "overrule" the jury on the ground that a reasonable jury could not have ruled as the jury actually did. In federal courts, a post-verdict motion of this sort is treated as simply renewing the motion for judgment as a matter of law that was filed prior to the submission of the case to the jury. (Thus, in federal court, the filing of a motion for judgment as a matter of law at the close of all evidence is a prerequisite to filing a motion for judgment after the verdict has been rendered — if the earlier motion was not filed, there is nothing to renew.) Under older usage, still employed in some jurisdictions, a post-verdict motion for judgment as a matter of law is deemed a motion for *judgment notwithstanding the verdict* (J.N.O.V.).

8. *New Trial Orders.* Trial judges enjoy another supervisory power that resembles, yet is distinct from, the power to order judgment as a

---

* For a recent case that produced a division among the justices of the South Dakota Supreme Court over whether to grant summary judgment on the issue of breach, see Schuck v. Perkins County, 577 N.W.2d 584 (S.D. 1998). The plaintiff in that case was the widow of a driver who had crashed his car while trying to avoid colliding with cattle on a rural road. The majority upheld the trial judge's determination that no reasonable jury could find that the defendant cattle-rancher acted unreasonably by failing to take steps to prevent the cows from crossing the road at certain points.

** Because such motions are made after the presentation of some or all of the evidence to the jury, even a trial judge who is inclined to grant such a motion may decide to let the process run its course by having the jury render a verdict. As explained below, the judge can feel comfortable doing this because she will have an opportunity *after* the verdict has been rendered to enter judgment as a matter of law if she believes such a judgment is warranted.

matter of law. This is the power to set aside the jury's verdict and *order a new trial*. New trial motions, like post-verdict motions for judgment as a matter of law, are made by a party disappointed with the jury's verdict. Moreover, like the power to enter judgment as a matter of law, the new trial power is meant to be exercised sparingly by trial judges. However, the formal threshold for the exercise of this power is somewhat lower. This is because the entry of a new trial order does not resolve any issues in the litigation, whereas entry of judgment as a matter of law is dispositive of some or all of those issues. Instead, when a court grants a motion for a new trial, it is essentially ordering a "do-over."

The grounds on which new trials are sought are numerous and varied. Most commonly, tort defendants who are faced with a jury finding of liability move for a new trial on the ground that the jury's determination in favor of the plaintiff, even viewing the proof presented at trial most favorably to the plaintiff, runs *substantially against the weight of the evidence*. In the alternative, they argue, as did Wal-Mart, that the damages award set by the jury was so large as to evidence "passion and prejudice" against the defendant on the part of the jury, thus warranting a new trial on the issue of damages. Do you find the sum awarded by the jury to Walter reasonable? Unreasonably high? Unreasonably low? Is your assessment influenced by the fact that almost 90 percent of her recovery seems to have been meant to compensate her for intangible harms such as pain, suffering, and depression? Damages are a major topic for consideration in Chapter 8.

The *Walter* opinion informs you that Wal-Mart also unsuccessfully moved for a new trial on other grounds, including alleged misconduct by opposing counsel. What was the alleged misconduct? Does any of it relate to the size of the jury's damage award? Does the supreme court's majority opinion deny that this misconduct occurred? If not, why does it decline to award Wal-Mart a new trial?

9. *Reconsidering* Walter. In light of what you have just read about the procedural devices available to trial judges, re-examine ¶ 8 of the supreme court's opinion in *Walter*. Is it more comprehensible than the first time you read it? Among other things, it tells you that, after the presentation of evidence at trial, *both* Walter and Wal-Mart made motions for judgment as a matter of law. In other words, Walter thought that the evidence produced at trial clearly established liability, while Wal-Mart, looking at the same evidence, thought it clearly established that there could be no liability. Here it may be worthwhile briefly to consider each of these positions, starting with the latter.

At the close of plaintiff's evidence, Wal-Mart's attorney argued that his client was entitled to judgment as a matter of law. How could he do that with a straight face? What, according to Wal-Mart, was so obviously defective about the plaintiff's presentation of evidence? As we see in Chapter 3, courts commonly require a plaintiff who is suing for carelessness committed by a member of a profession — that is, malpractice — to present expert testimony as to the standards of care of the profession, and as to whether the defendant failed to meet those standards. Why then did the Maine Supreme Court conclude that no such witness was required in this case?

Now consider Walter's motion. We said in the introductory remarks to this section that *Walter* was written to resolve an appeal of a very unusual trial court ruling. In saying that, we were referring to the trial court's decision to *grant* the plaintiff's motion for judgment as a matter of law on the issues of breach, causation, and comparative fault. In fact, this decision is not at all representative of litigation practice as you are likely to encounter it. Perhaps this helps explain why, after the jury returned its verdict, the trial judge *apologized* to the jurors, explaining that it was the first time in his six years on the bench that he had taken the issue of negligence into his own hands. Indeed, the judge was no doubt aware that his ruling was not just rare, but doubly rare.

First, it was rare because, as indicated in the earlier discussion of summary judgment, trial judges tend not to enter judgment as a matter of law on fact-intensive issues such as breach and causation. (Recall what the judge needed to conclude in order to grant the plaintiff's motion. As to breach, for example, he had to conclude not merely that a reasonable jury *could* find that Henry Lovin failed to act with reasonable care, but that such a jury *would have to* make that finding.) Second, even when trial courts do enter judgments as a matter of law, nine out of ten, if not 99 out of 100, are entered on behalf of *defendants* rather than plaintiffs. This strongly asymmetric pattern is not coincidental. Rather, it reflects two important procedural features of tort cases that we discuss in subsequent chapters: (1) the plaintiff ordinarily bears the *burden of proving* that a tort has occurred, and (2) jurors are ordinarily free to discredit or second-guess witness testimony and other forms of evidence offered by either party. In sum, because there are almost always some grounds for a reasonable juror to doubt the plaintiff's evidence, and because it is the plaintiff who bears the onus of convincing the jury that her account of what the defendant did is probably the correct account, a reasonable jury should almost always be able to conclude that the plaintiff has not done enough to prove her case.

Given this asymmetry, what was it about *Walter* that enabled both the trial court and the Supreme Court to treat it as one of the extraordinary cases in which judgment on several key issues was properly entered for the plaintiff prior to verdict? Are you satisfied with the high court's explanation? Was there anything else about the trial proceedings that might have warranted its conclusion?

10. *A Final Thought: Litigating Responsibility.* Materials provided in Appendix A pose additional questions about the procedural, substantive, and tactical issues raised by *Walter*. For now, we conclude the present analysis by considering *Walter* in light of the organizing themes of this book. As we suggested at the outset, tort law is concerned to identify situations in which one person (or entity) can be held responsible for injuring another. It is no surprise, then, that Mr. Silin, Walter's attorney, emphasized notions of responsibility in his opening and closing arguments to the jury. Here is an excerpt from his closing argument:

> . . . This is a case in which all of the parties have tried in many ways to move forward as expeditiously as possible; and to some extent we've been successful, and in other ways we haven't.

I told you [yesterday] . . . the only real issue in this case is the issue of damages. What are the damages to which Antoinette Walter is entitled to [sic]? What is fair compensation for what she suffered as a result of the negligence of the Wal-Mart Pharmacy store going back to May 7, 1997? I told you that would be the issue.

I also told you that although this should be the only issue, that Wal-Mart Stores, Incorporated nevertheless continued to refuse to accept responsibility and continued to deny the liability. It was okay to substitute these drugs or it doesn't matter, or it was all her fault or all Dr. Ross's fault. We've heard much of that. What we now heard [sic] is that despite all that stuff, His Honor ruled the obvious, which is that there is no question of fact as to whether Wal-Mart was negligent. There is no question of fact as to whether Ms. Walter contributed to her negligence [sic]. She didn't. There is no question she was damaged. . . .

Mr. Franco, the defense lawyer, attempted throughout the litigation to deal with Silin's emphasis on Wal-Mart's failure to accept responsibility for Lovin's mistake. What follows is an excerpt from his opening statement (the last part of which is quoted in the *Walter* opinion):

. . . Attorney Silin represented to you why he thought we were here, and it's my chance now to tell you why we are here.

First of all, going back to how lawsuits begin and how cases end up in courts such as this, usually a plaintiff, such as Ms. Walter, has a claim against a defendant, in this case Wal-Mart. And there is a filing, a formal complaint. From the time that the complaint is filed the defendant has 30 days in which to answer the complaint. And depending on what information the defendant has in its possession, they either admit or deny the allegations in the complaint.

It's important I think at the outset for you to understand that the complaint made some pretty strong accusations in this case against Wal-Mart, and used some strange words such as negligent[,] careless, reckless conduct. . . . Within the 30-day time period it was my role to deny or admit these allegations. And given the time frame involved, there was a general denial made. It's common practice to do that until the investigation continues.

There was [sic] also allegations of severe pain, physical permanent injuries. There is no way that a defendant, Wal-Mart or anybody in this situation, would be able to know or admit those types of allegation without further investigation and further inquiry in terms of what is alleged.

So I'm not making any apologies on behalf of Wal-Mart or myself for making denials of those allegations. What I'm here to tell you right now is since the filing of the complaint and filing of the answer, Wal-Mart has never denied responsibility for this incident. Never.

The obvious suggestion contained in the excerpted portion of Silin's closing argument is that the jury should take a dim view of "Wal-Mart Stores, Incorporated," not only because its employee's carelessness injured Walter, but also because Wal-Mart persisted in contesting responsibility even though its responsibility was "obvious." In what way was Wal-Mart's decision to litigate liability a culpable failure to "accept responsibility"? Would an offer from Wal-Mart to settle the case prior to trial have constituted an acceptance of responsibility?* Is Franco correct to point out that, in a system of adversarial litigation, we should expect individuals and entities who have been sued to mount a vigorous defense at trial? Or is Silin right to link the ideas of responsibility and acceptance of responsibility? Based on this admittedly limited introduction, do you think that there might be ways in which the institutions and procedures that have been developed for making determinations of responsibility might distort those determinations? If so, are such problems necessary costs of a system of litigation, or can we devise better ways to proceed?

III.   TORT LAW IN CONTEXT

A.   Tort Contrasted with Other Areas of Law

The preceding discussion offers an in-depth examination of how the tort system permits and requires individuals to respond to situations that gave rise to cases like Walter v. Wal-Mart in a particular way. Tort, however, is but one area of the law, and many other areas also have relevance to the type of situation that gave rise to *Walter*. Contrasting these other areas of law will help further define the distinctive features of tort law. For purposes of introduction, these contrasts are intentionally overdrawn. At times, the boundary lines between these different areas are fuzzy, and the ideas and methods of one frequently crop up in others.

1. *Criminal Law*. Criminal law is closely related to tort law both historically and conceptually, in that it, too, is primarily concerned with identifying and sanctioning wrongful conduct. For this reason, "assault" and "battery" are names of both crimes and torts. Also like tort law, criminal law leaves an important role for the jury in applying the law: The jury typically determines whether the evidence presented by the prosecution is sufficient to establish that the defendant's conduct constituted a given crime.

However, there are also important differences between tort and crime. For one thing, negligence, which is perhaps the most prominent cause of action in modern torts, is less commonly the basis for criminal liability. For example, Lovin's inadvertent error probably would not provide the basis for a criminal conviction. (So far as we know, he was not criminally prosecuted.) Likewise, a driver who runs over and kills a pedestrian simply because he looked down to adjust his car's CD player probably cannot be found guilty of the crime of negligent homicide. To be sure,

---

* Settlement agreements almost always contain language by which the defendant explicitly disavows responsibility, but nonetheless agrees to pay compensation in order to resolve the lawsuit. Obviously, the parties' attorneys were unable to reach a pre-trial settlement in this case. Attorney Silin proposed to settle at a figure about half the size of the jury's eventual award. Franco countered with a substantially lower offer. For more on the dynamics of the *Walter* litigation, see Appendix A.

criminal law contains provisions that criminalize certain instances of "negligence." Still, the term negligence in the criminal context usually refers to more substantial misconduct than a simple slip or a momentary lapse. Thus, lawyers sometimes distinguish between "gross" or "criminal" negligence, on the one hand, and "simple" negligence on the other.*

Suppose, however, Lovin had not simply been careless, but had acted for the very purpose of poisoning Ms. Walter. If that were the case, he would be subject to criminal prosecution, perhaps for the crime of battery. Had such a prosecution been filed, the caption on the court documents would have read *State v. Lovin* or *People v. Lovin*.** This caption would indicate that the action was being commenced not by the victim, but by a government official, such as a district attorney, who represents all the citizens of the jurisdiction. As a result, Walter would have very little formal control over whether such a proceeding were brought, or whether the criminal case were disposed of by a plea agreement or a jury verdict. This in turn indicates that the primary purpose of a criminal prosecution would be for the government, on behalf of the people, to punish the individual wrongdoer, Lovin, and to deter future actors from behaving in a like manner.

Given the potentially harsher nature of criminal punishment — in particular, the prospect of imprisonment — the prosecution would also face a higher set of hurdles in proving its case than did Walter in suing Wal-Mart for negligence. For example, it would have to prove that Lovin's conduct satisfied the elements of the crime of battery *beyond a reasonable doubt*. A tort plaintiff, by contrast, need only prove the elements of her claim by a *preponderance of the evidence*, that is, she must show that it is more likely than not that each element of her claim is satisfied.

Tort differs from crime in another important way: The issue of the victim's responsibility, mentioned in Section II.B above, is usually irrelevant to criminal prosecutions. Put simply, there is no doctrine of comparative fault in criminal law. For example, suppose, contrary to the facts of the actual case, Walter could have taken reasonable steps to prevent herself from being poisoned in the first place. Her failure to do so would, at least as a matter of formal legal rules, be irrelevant to Lovin's criminal culpability.

---

* It may be tempting to extrapolate from this brief discussion that criminal conduct is simply a subset of tortious conduct (i.e., that crimes are just particularly serious torts). This temptation should be resisted, because certain forms of misconduct can be criminal without being tortious. For example, it is a crime to possess various controlled substances, or to attempt to shoot someone, even if the attempt fails. Tort, however, does not recognize liability for mere possession, and does not impose liability for attempts unless they generate certain consequences for the victim (e.g., causing him to fear for his physical well-being).

** Modern criminal law, particularly federal criminal law, sometimes permits the imposition of criminal fines payable by corporations and other entities for criminal acts committed by their employees while acting within the scope of employment *and* for the benefit of the entity. It is highly unlikely that Wal-Mart would be at risk of criminal punishment in our imagined case in which Lovin, for his own purposes, deliberately poisons Walter.

Another critical difference between tort and the imagined criminal prosecution is that its resolution would not likely include an order from the court specifying redress for Ms. Walter. Although criminal penalties can include payment of restitution to the victims of the crime, such penalties are relatively rarely enforced as compared to jail terms and fines payable to the government. Finally, although criminal law was once part of the common law, today the criminal laws that the district attorney would accuse Lovin of breaking would not be of judicial creation, but rather would be found in statutes enacted by the legislative branches of the jurisdiction and endorsed by its governor. In all of these respects, criminal law may be described as primarily public, rather than a law of private redress.

Just to avoid confusion, it is worth pointing out that the same acts and events often can give rise to both criminal prosecution and a tort suit. A famous example of this phenomenon involved former football star O.J. Simpson. Simpson was criminally prosecuted for the murder of his ex-wife Nicole Brown Simpson and her acquaintance Ronald Goldman, and acquitted. Notwithstanding the acquittal, the victims' parents brought a tort suit against Simpson, essentially for the tort of battery. The jury in the tort suit found him liable for millions of dollars in damages. Although the "double jeopardy" clause of the Fifth Amendment to the U.S. Constitution forbids a second prosecution for the same crime following an acquittal, it does not preclude a subsequent action in tort. How is it that one person can, on the same facts, be found innocent of murder yet liable for the tort of battery? (Keep in mind the different standards of proof in criminal and civil cases, mentioned above.)

2. *Administrative Regulation.* Throughout the twentieth century, federal and state governments came increasingly to rely on administrative agencies to study and remedy problems that, in prior centuries, were regulated, if at all, exclusively by the common law of tort. For example, at the national level, the Consumer Protection Agency (CPA) now monitors product safety, the Environmental Protection Agency (EPA) addresses issues of harms posed by toxins in air, soil, and water, and the Occupational Safety and Health Administration (OSHA) regulates workplace hazards.

Another agency whose work is particularly relevant to modern tort law is the National Highway and Transportation Safety Administration (NHTSA), which sets standards for automobile and road safety. *See generally* www.nhtsa.dot.gov. NHTSA, a branch of the U.S. Department of Transportation, was created by a statute passed by the United States Congress and signed into law by President Lyndon Johnson in 1966. The statute authorizes NHTSA, among other things, to prescribe automobile design standards to ensure safety. Relying on this delegation of authority, NHTSA has, for example, required automobile manufacturers to phase in air bags into all new car models, and has required anti-lock brakes on certain vehicles. NHTSA is also empowered to request data from manufacturers, and to test automobiles and component parts for compliance with its standards. If the agency determines that automobiles and other products fail to meet its standards, it can order the manufacturer(s) to recall the model(s) and correct the defect(s). Manufacturers that fail to abide by these regulations are subject to penalties, including fines payable to the government.

State governments also include numerous regulatory agencies. Indeed, the State of Maine maintains an agency called the Office of Licensing and Registration (OLR). The OLR in turn includes an entity called the Board of Commissioners of the Profession of Pharmacy. *See* www.state.me.us/pfr/olr. The pharmacy board is empowered to issue licenses, without which it is unlawful to operate as a pharmacist in Maine. It also sets the terms of those licenses through, among other things, regulations concerning procedures that pharmacists must follow. The board in addition employs inspectors who monitor pharmacists to check for compliance with board regulations. Finally, it is empowered to issue certain penalties for violations, including monetary fines, as well as license suspensions and revocations. (By means of the OLR's website, one can search to determine if a particular licensee in any of a number of professions has been subject to disciplinary action.)

As it turns out, the Maine pharmacy board received a report from one of its inspectors concerning Henry Lovin's erroneous filling of Ms. Walter's prescription in February of 1998, several months before the complaint in *Walter* was filed. (It is unclear how Lovin's mistake came to the attention of the inspector. It is possible that Wal-Mart notified her, or that she discovered it in the course of reviewing the pharmacy's files.) The filing of the inspector's report led the board to take action against Lovin, which in turn led to their entry into a "consent agreement," reproduced in Appendix A. Under the terms of this agreement, Lovin admitted his mistake, and accepted penalties that included a $500 fine, a 14-day suspension, and 15 hours of professional education. In this way, the administrative apparatus of the State of Maine responded to Lovin's mistake independently of the litigation by Walter against Wal-Mart.

Administrative law is a vast and complex subject in its own right, so generalizations are hazardous. For present purposes, however, we may here note two broad features of that body of law. First, like criminal and tort law, administrative law seeks to set substantive standards of conduct, for example, standards of how certain chemicals may be discharged into the environment, or whether passenger vehicles must be equipped with certain safety devices. Also like criminal law, but unlike tort law, its primary mechanism for executing or enforcing these standards is via directives and suits initiated by government officials seeking to set standards and impose penalties on violators. As such, administrative regulations typically provide no redress to victims of unlawful conduct. (Lovin's $500 fine was paid to Maine's treasury.) Finally, as with criminal law, even where regulations are in place governing specific conduct, aggrieved private citizens generally have little, if any, control over agency actions. For example, they are usually *not* entitled to demand investigation of, or the issuance of sanctions against, those who have allegedly violated agency regulations. To be sure, concerned citizens and groups may petition agencies to take action, and may participate in the development of administrative standards of conduct, but they have no legal right to force agencies to initiate regulatory action, and instead must rely on the use of political pressure.

Second, in contrast to both tort and criminal law, administrative standards of conduct are set not by judges or lay-juries but by officials within the agency, who have expertise concerning the conduct in question. Moreover, regulatory law is often created through the process of notice-and-comment rulemaking. Here, the agency, concerned with a particular problem — say, for example, the problem of trains colliding with cars at railroad grade crossings — announces an intention to regulate the activity and solicits input from any actors who might be affected by the issuance of regulations, as well as the public generally. Based on this input, the agency then issues regulations addressing the conduct in question. In contrast to tort suits, this sort of rulemaking proceeds on an aggregate, forward-looking basis. The agency treats a problem such as grade-crossing accidents as an ongoing social problem, rather than a discrete occasion calling for an inquiry into whether a particular actor was responsible for a particular injury. Thus, it seeks to adopt rules that will, in the aggregate, best achieve a balance between objectives such as safety and efficiency.*

Each of these distinctive features of administrative rulemaking — its reliance on experts, its solicitation of information from many sources rather than the parties to a particular dispute, its forward-looking and aggregate orientation — distinguish it to some degree from tort law. Whether these features further suggest that administrative regulation is generally superior to tort law as a response to undesirable conduct is a complex and contested normative question.

3. *Social Welfare Programs and Public Compensation Funds*. Underlying each tort suit is the idea that someone has suffered an injury. Tort law responds to that fact in a particular way: by empowering the alleged victim to bring a claim for redress against the person responsible for the alleged wrongdoing and the resulting injury. Other forms of law might respond to the victim's loss in a way that does not focus on responsibility and redress, but only on the individual victim's need for compensation.

For example, the federal government operates a program popularly known as Medicare. *See* 42 U.S.C. §§ 1395 et seq. In a nutshell, Medicare collects revenues from taxes on worker's wages and uses them to help cover certain healthcare expenses incurred by designated groups of persons, including persons older than 65. Thus, as indicated earlier, Walter's medical expenses were paid partly or wholly by the federal government under the auspices of the Medicare program. In addition to broadly applicable compensation schemes such as Medicare, Congress has adopted a number of programs designed to assist the victims of particular types of

---

* Agency decisions frequently can take a form similar to judicial proceedings. In such agency *adjudications*, the relevant agency files a complaint against a person or entity alleged to have violated a given regulation, such as the Federal Trade Commission's regulation barring "unfair trade practices." The complaint, however, is not filed with a conventional court, but instead with an administrative law judge, who (without the aid of a jury) hears evidence and issues a ruling as to whether the conduct in question violated the regulation. The extent to which agencies should rely on adjudications to make and enforce policy, rather than notice-and-comment rulemaking, is one of the central debates of modern administrative law.

injuries or diseases, including children made ill by vaccines, as well as coal miners who suffer from black lung disease. Most recently it enacted legislation designed in part to compensate victims of the September 11 terrorist attack on the World Trade Center and the Pentagon.

In these and other ways, government can in principle provide injury victims relatively easy access to compensation with a minimum of procedure. Certainly nothing approaching the time, effort, and money expended on litigating a tort suit is required in order for a recovery to be secured by an eligible claimant. In part this stems from the fact that, unlike tort law, compensation schemes of this sort make no attempt to identify or deter wrongful conduct, to impose responsibility on a wrongdoer who has injured another, or to provide the victim with individualized redress. Programs such as Medicare and compensation funds are supported by taxes, not by payments from persons deemed responsible for the victims' injuries. In this regard, compensation funds might apply equally to those injured by natural disasters such as earthquakes or hurricanes as to those injured by wrongdoing. The point of such a fund is not to identify a person or entity responsible for a bad outcome, but to tend to the needs of the victim.

4. *Contract Law.* Consider next how the law might enable the parties themselves to anticipate and respond to problems of the sort that gave rise to *Walter*. The sale of the prescription medicine by Wal-Mart to Ms. Walter was accomplished by means of a contract. It specified, among other things, the price and quantity of the medicine sold to her. In principle, the sales contract might also have addressed the issue of what would happen if Walter were injured because of some problem in the filling of the prescription. For example, Wal-Mart might have included in the fine print on the package containing Walter's medicine the following language: "By purchasing this prescription medicine, purchaser agrees that Wal-Mart shall not be liable for any harm caused as a result of the use of this prescription medicine." Should a court enforce this sort of contractual allocation of the risk of harm? If not, why not? As we see in Chapter 7, courts are often reluctant to enforce contractual provisions that relieve actors from liability for injuries, particularly physical injuries, caused by their misconduct.

Like tort law, contract law is private law. It requires an aggrieved party to commence a lawsuit seeking redress against another whose conduct has caused an injury. Likewise, the application of the law to that suit will be the job of judges and juries. However, unlike tort law, a contract suit seeks redress for the failure of the other party to do what he or she has *promised* to do. Thus, were the facts of *Walter* to have given rise to a contract action, the issue would be to determine what was promised to whom and on what terms. Did Wal-Mart in its contract with Walter promise to take due care to ensure that her prescription was filled correctly? Did it disavow any such promise? If the latter, and if the Maine Supreme Court were to conclude that this contractual disavowal operates to void any tort duties owed by Wal-Mart, Walter would have no claim. (Given these assumptions, Wal-Mart did not break any promise to her because it made no promise whatsoever as to the correctness of the prescription.)

As briefly noted earlier in this chapter, there is a different way in which contract law might figure in this scenario that would involve not a contract between Walter and Wal-Mart, but one between Walter and an insurance company (or between Wal-Mart and an insurance company). To the extent Walter was concerned about the risk of accidental injury, she might have been able to make provision for such injuries by purchasing insurance that would entitle her to reimbursement for any expenses or losses she incurred in the event such an injury came about. First-party insurance of this sort is common today. Examples include health insurance, under which the insurer pays the insured's medical bills, or fire insurance, providing reimbursement for fire damage to the insured's home. First-party insurance, which covers injuries or damage to the insured, her family, or her property, is distinguished from third-party insurance, which protects against losses in the form of liabilities incurred by the insured to others. For example, a homeowner or business might have third-party insurance to cover liabilities incurred when guests or customers suffer injuries on the premises as a result of dangerous conditions on their premises, such as slippery or poorly lit steps.

If Ms. Walter had been insured by a private insurer for injuries caused by others, she could have filed a claim to receive reimbursements for the health care expenses she incurred by virtue of having been poisoned by the wrong medicine. If a dispute arose as to whether she was entitled to such reimbursements, she would eventually have to commence a suit — essentially for breach of contract — to obtain what she believes she was owed under the policy. The critical questions in that suit would be whether or to what extent her injuries were covered under her contract for health insurance.

As the preceding examples emphasize, contract law empowers parties to mold for themselves the terms of their interactions. This flexibility is both a virtue and vice. In principle, and often in practice, contract permits individuals to get exactly what they want out of interactions with others. However, it is sometimes the case in the real world that parties lack the information, judgment, or resources to enter into beneficial contracts. For example, many Americans have not contracted for health insurance, some because it is unavailable to them, others because they lack the resources to pay for it, others because they choose (wisely or unwisely) to forgo insurance for other goods and services. Likewise, in the case of a liability limitation provision of the sort imagined above, one would suspect that an ordinary consumer would not be in a position to make a knowing and voluntary decision to waive her right to sue in tort on the basis of fine print on a package. Tort law, in contrast to contract, is not optional in this way. It specifies a set of responsibilities that, absent some legally recognized excuse or justification, actors are not permitted to avoid. When contract ought to prevail — when parties ought to be able to set for themselves the terms of their interaction — is a regularly recurring question in tort and contract law.

B.   The Politics of Tort Law

In light of the foregoing discussion, one can begin to get a better sense of the distinctive domain of tort. Tort law is private law that provides injured parties with redress from those who have wronged and injured them. Moreover, it specifies those wrongs at least partly independently of how the parties have structured their relationship. In this way, it is a law of responsibility and redress. Because tort law sets out mandatory responsibilities, it is sometimes in conflict with contract law, although contractual arrangements can also give rise to, and help define, tort liability. Criminal law and administrative regulation often work in conjunction with tort law, although these forms of law, too, can sometimes clash with tort. For example, when administrative standards of conduct demand less care of a certain class of actors than tort law might, those actors often will assert that judges and juries should not be allowed to identify and impose standards that ask more of them than those set by agencies. Finally, tort bears the same sort of complex relationship to compensation funds and private insurance. Liability insurance, for example, often enables victims to recover in tort where they otherwise would not. On the other hand, liability insurance can also reduce incentives for care, and lessen the impact on wrongdoers of tort judgments against them.

Although tort has in one form or another been a part of Anglo-American law for hundreds of years, it was not until the late 1970s that it became a subject of intense political and ideological battles, at least in the United States. To be sure, particular tort rules had from time to time generated criticism and reform. At the turn of the twentieth century, for example, legislatures began modifying or supplanting the tort system as it applied to the industrial workplace because certain tort doctrines made it very difficult for workers to recover from their employers for injuries caused by unsafe working conditions. Still, it is only in the last 30 years that the two major political parties, as well as pundits, have come to adopt general — and polarized — stances toward the tort system.

The explanation for the emergence of tort as a hot-button issue is complex. As we will see, certain changes in mid-twentieth-century law — both procedural and substantive — have expanded the potential reach of tort liability. In addition, with the economic downturns of the 1970s came the recognition that U.S. businesses, even giants such as General Motors, were vulnerable to recessions and global competition, and thus could be hurt by a system that had the potential to saddle them with large liabilities. The 1970s also witnessed the first liability "crisis." Doctors, for example, claimed that they could no longer afford to practice in certain high-risk areas, such as obstetrics, because malpractice insurance premiums had risen dramatically. Likewise, some municipalities shut down recreational facilities and essential services, claiming that tort liability had rendered insurance too expensive. Whether the tort system was the prime culprit, or whether other factors, such as poor returns on insurance companies' investments, played a more important role than tort liability, has been, and still is, hotly contested.

Regrettably, debates about the tort system today tend to degenerate into the overheated, polarized discourse of talk radio and television commentary. Critics of the tort system, such as the American Tort Reform Association (ATRA), which was founded in 1986 on behalf of industry to limit tort liability, claim that tort law is crippling the U.S. economy, clogging the courts, and undeservedly enriching the plaintiff's bar. Relying heavily on colorful examples of frivolous lawsuits, ATRA and other political organizations have lobbied vigorously and successfully for the enactment of damage caps, limitations on joint and several liability, and other means of reducing tort awards and deterring the filing of tort suits. *See* www.atra.org; www.overlawyered.com.

In response, or perhaps retort, consumer advocates such as Public Citizen, founded by Ralph Nader, as well as the American Trial Lawyers' Association (ATLA) have argued that the tort reform movement is a barely disguised effort to shield corporations and other actors from scrutiny and responsibility for harms caused by their irresponsible conduct. In their view, the claims of organizations such as ATRA as to the harmful effects of the tort system are exaggerated, and have been fueled by a misinformation campaign that relies on dubious anecdotes seized upon by a sensation-hungry media, and gladly digested by a public desirous of being outraged rather than informed. Just as ATRA has lobbied aggressively for legislation cutting back on tort liability, ATLA has funded candidates and reforms friendly to the maintenance or expansion of the existing tort regime. *See* www.publiccitizen.org; www.atla.org.

Apart from political debates over tort law, there has been a longstanding sense among many members of the legal academy that tort law's time has passed. Indeed, with the rise of administrative regulation and public assistance programs, along with the increasing availability of both private insurance and publicly available information about the dangers associated with different activities, many scholars have questioned whether tort law still has an important role to play in the twenty-first century.

It is not our purpose, nor within our abilities, to settle these disputes. Rather, we hope in this book to give the student a better sense of how tort law hangs together as a law of responsibilities and redress. In doing this, of course, we are inevitably taking a certain position with respect to these debates. In our view, tort law should not be dismissed simply as a device by which plaintiffs' lawyers are empowered to manipulate the law and jurors' emotions to feast off business earnings. Yet we also reject a depiction of tort law as mainly a means by which unelected and unaccountable litigants empower themselves to police corporate behavior on behalf of the public good. Finally, while we believe that there is a vital place for expert regulation, as well as a social safety net, we do not share the prevailing academic sense that we as a nation have somehow grown out of the need for a body of law that assigns responsibilities to individuals and entities and provides redress for victims of their misconduct.

In fact, the United States continues to give greater prominence to tort law than any other industrialized nation. Its relative prominence in U.S. law is fueled by several features of our political system. The contingent fee system likely lowers the barriers to lawsuits as compared with a pay-as-you-go model of the sort employed in other countries. Moreover, in contrast to many European countries, the lack of nationalized health care and other features of a strong social safety net encourages a greater percentage of injured U.S. citizens and residents to seek relief via tort suits. Finally, and perhaps most basically, tort law reflects our political culture. In some nations, the obligations that one owes to be careful toward another, or to otherwise refrain from injuring another, tend to be viewed as created by, and owed exclusively to, the state. Americans, however, tend to view this class of obligations as part of "civil society," as obligations owed to one another. Tort law, as we have said, is all about the articulation of the responsibilities that persons (and entities) owe to others, whether it is the obligation of care that a pharmacy owes to its customers, or the responsibility of a driver to drive safely so as to avoid injuring those around him.

C.   Some Statistics Concerning the Tort System

It may be helpful to put certain features of the tort system in empirical perspective. Tort suits constitute about 10 percent of all civil actions filed in state and federal courts. (The category of civil actions include claims brought under contract, property, and family law.) Evidence gleaned from state courts indicates that the number of tort suits filed rose 75 percent between 1975 and 1986, but declined by about 10 percent between 1990 and 2001. Changes in filing rates during these periods varied enormously from state to state, although only eight states have experienced increases in filings since 1992. All told, tort filings in state courts were about 40 percent higher in 2001 as compared to 1975, although this number must be adjusted for changes in population and other variables. In contrast to the general trend for tort filings, medical malpractice filings in state courts have risen slightly since 1992.

A 1992 survey studied the resolution of tort cases in the courts of the 75 largest counties in the United States. Sixty percent of these arose out of injuries stemming from automobile accidents. (4.2 million people were injured in the United States in 1998 as a result of car accidents.) The next biggest category — about 17 percent — consisted of actions against property owners by persons injured on the property, such as store customers suing for injuries incurred while in stores. Medical malpractice claims form the third biggest category, at about 5 percent.

Of all tort suits filed, about three-quarters settle prior to trial. After allowing for the percentage of suits dismissed prior to trial, the percentage of cases resolved by a trial in front of a jury or judge is quite small — in the neighborhood of 3 percent. (Medical malpractice claims are slightly more likely to be resolved by a jury trial than other claims.) Of those few claims that do go to trial, half are automobile accident cases. With respect to tort claims tried to a jury, plaintiffs and defendants each win about half of the time. Again, the medical malpractice figures are different: Medical providers win at trial almost three-quarters of the time. Perhaps counterintuitively, plaintiffs are slightly more likely to win at trial if the parties agree to waive their right to a jury trial and conduct a bench trial.

For those plaintiffs who prevail at trial, the median compensatory award in 1996 was about $30,000. The median award for the most common tort claim — for injuries arising out of an automobile accident —

was about $18,000. By contrast, in those medical malpractice and product liability actions in which the plaintiff prevailed, the plaintiff stood to receive an award of several hundred thousand dollars. Juries award punitive damages in a very small percentage of tort trials (3 to 4 percent).

IV. USING THIS BOOK

In thinking about torts it is important to remember that there are many forms of wrongful conduct—hence the many distinct torts denominated at the outset of this chapter. Moreover, conduct can be wrongful in different ways. Certain conduct might be egregiously wrongful and blameworthy: for example, intentional and unjustified infliction of physical harm on another person. Other conduct may be less egregious, as was the case with the careless conduct in *Walter*.

Because negligence has come to dominate the torts landscape in the last 150 years, most introductory torts courses focus primarily on the ins and outs of liability for carelessly caused injuries. This book shares that focus. The various chapters of Part Two thus provide detailed analysis of core issues in negligence, introducing along the way concepts that will be integral to other topics in tort, such as causation.

Part Three examines tort suits alleging a different kind of wrongdoing—namely interferences with others' "dignitary" interests. In addition, it revisits negligence law as it applies to a special kind of injury, namely harm to one's emotional well-being. Part Four introduces students to actions for interferences with property interests. It also discusses no-fault (or "strict") liability for abnormally dangerous activities and under statutory workers' compensation schemes as a segue into an analysis of products liability.

In Part Five, the book concludes by presenting five recent decisions issued by the U.S. Supreme Court that have had, and will in the foreseeable future continue to have, a significant impact on the operation of modern tort law. Finally, Appendix A provides supplemental materials, including litigation documents, concerning the *Walter* case.

REFERENCES/FURTHER READING

Attorneys and Tort Law

Randolph E. Bergstrom, *Courting Danger: Injury and the Law in New York City, 1870-1910* (1992).

Peter Karsten, *Enabling the Poor to Have Their Day in Court: The Sanctioning of Contingency Fee Contracts, A History to 1940*, 47 DePaul L. Rev. 231, 241 (1998).

John Leubsdorf, *Toward a History of the American Rule on Attorney Fee Recovery*, 47 Law & Contemp. Probs. 9 (1984).

H. Laurence Ross, *Settled Out of Court: The Social Process of Insurance Claims Adjustment* (1980).

Douglas E. Rosenthal, *Lawyer and Client: Who's in Charge?* (1974).

The Jury

Sheri S. Diamond & Jonathan D. Casper, *Understanding Juries* (2000).

Phoebe Ellsworth, *Jury Reform at the End of the Century: Real Agreement, Real Changes*, 32 U. Mich. J.L. Reform 213 (1999).

Neil Feigensen, *Legal Blame: How Jurors Think and Talk About Accidents* (2000).

Edith Greene et al., *Jurors' Attitudes About Civil Litigation and the Size of Damage Awards*, 40 Am. U. L. Rev. 805 (1995).

Valerie P. Hans, *Business on Trial: The Civil Jury and Corporate Responsibility* (2000).

Valerie P. Hans & Neil Vidmar, *Judging the Jury* (1986).

Robert E. Litan (ed.), *Verdict: Assessing the Civil Jury System* (1993).

Lars Noah, *Civil Jury Nullification*, 86 Iowa L. Rev. (2001).

Neil Vidmar, *The Performance of the American Civil Jury: An Empirical Perspective*, 40 Ariz. L. Rev. 849 (1998).

Developments in the Law — The Civil Jury, 110 Harv. L. Rev. 1408 (1997).

Symposium on the American Civil Jury, 48 DePaul L. Rev. 197 et seq. (1998).

Statistics and Modern Debates About Tort Law

Richard L. Abel, *Questioning the Counter-Majoritarian Thesis: The Case of Torts*, 49 DePaul L. Rev. 533 (1999).

Peter A. Bell & Jeffrey O'Connell, *Accidental Justice: The Dilemmas of Tort Law* (1997).

Robert G. Bone, *The Economics of Civil Procedure* (2003) (providing, among other things, statistics on civil litigation).

Thomas Eaton & Susette M. Talarico, *A Profile of Tort Litigation in Georgia and Reflections on Tort Reform*, 30 Ga. L. Rev. 627 (1996).

Marc Galanter, *Real World Torts: An Antidote to Anecdote*, 55 Md. L. Rev. 1093 (1996).

John C. P. Goldberg, *Unloved: Tort in the Modern Legal Academy*, 55 Vand. L. Rev. 1501 (2002).

Mark M. Hager, *Civil Compensation and Its Discontents: A Response to Huber*, 42 Stan. L. Rev. 539 (1990).

Valerie Hans & William Lofquist, *Jurors' Judgments of Business Liability in Tort Cases: Implications for the Litigation Explosion Debate*, 26 L. & Soc'y Rev. 85 (1992).

Deborah R. Hensler et al., *Trends in Tort Litigation: The Story Behind the Statistics* (1987).

Peter Huber, *Liability: The Legal Revolution and Its Consequences* (1988).

Thomas Koenig & Michael Rustad, *In Defense of Tort Law* (2001).

Deborah Jones Merritt & Kathryn Ann Barry, *Is the Tort System in Crisis? New Empirical Evidence*, 60 Ohio St. L.J. 315 (1999).

Walter K. Olson, *The Rule of Lawyers: How the New Litigation Elite Threatens America's Rule of Law* (2002).

Michael J. Saks, *Do We Really Know Anything About the Behavior of the Tort Litigation System—And Why Not?*, 140 U. Pa. L. Rev. 1147 (1992).

Peter Schuck (ed.), *Tort Law and the Public Interest* (2001).

Charles Silver, *Does Civil Justice Cost Too Much?*, 80 Tex. L. Rev. 2073 (2002).

Symposium: What We Know and Do Not Know About the Impact of Civil Justice on the American Economy and Polity, 80 Tex. L. Rev. 1537 et seq. (2002).

www.ncsconline.org/D_Research/csp/CSP_Main_Page.html (data from state courts).

www.ircweb.org/IRCProducts/ProductsIndex.html (insurance research council data).

PART TWO

NEGLIGENCE: LIABILITY FOR PHYSICAL HARMS

CHAPTER 2

The Duty Element

I. NEGLIGENCE: A BRIEF OVERVIEW

A. Elements of the Prima Facie Case

As we saw in Walter v. Wal-Mart, the tort of negligence is cast in broad terms, rendering potentially actionable any failure to heed a duty of reasonable care owed to another that causes injury to that other. Because of its breadth, negligence is today the tort most commonly relied upon by accident victims to obtain redress from an alleged wrongdoer. Suits for injuries caused by careless driving, incompetently rendered professional services, and unsafe premises are usually suits for negligence.

Negligence has not always played the prominent role it plays in modern tort law. Before 1800, it was relatively rare for an English or American court faced with a tort case explicitly to analyze an accident victim's claim as a negligence claim. See Appendix B. This is *not* to say that common law prior to 1800 failed to recognize tort liability for accidentally caused injuries. Instead, it is only to say that complaints seeking to establish such liability invoked different labels to describe the plaintiff's cause of action. So, for example, if a pedestrian in 1750 were run over by a carelessly driven wagon, he would sue the driver for "trespass" — a category that included any claim for an injury arising out of a "direct" and "forcible" wrong inflicted upon another, whether intentional or careless. Meanwhile, a patient who claimed to have been injured by the malpractice of her physician would bring an action for "trespass on the case." Whether these differences of labeling reflect substantive differences in doctrine is debated among historians, as discussed in Appendix B.

Historians also disagree about when one finds the earliest instances in which lawyers and judges invoke the term *negligence* in its modern sense (i.e., as the name for a distinct tort). For our purposes, it is enough to note that such usage became increasingly common in the period from 1825 to 1875. By the end of that period, moreover, courts had begun to define negligence in terms quite similar to those used in contemporary cases such as Walter v. Wal-Mart. These formulations typically identify four "elements" that a plaintiff must prove to make out a prima facie negligence claim:*

---

* This formulation sets out the elements that, *at a minimum*, a negligence plaintiff must prove to be eligible for a remedy. Even if the plaintiff can make these out, the defendant may be able to avoid liability on the basis of an affirmative defense. This is the import of the phrase "prima facie case."

Negligence: Prima Facie Case

Actor *A* is subject to liability to other person *P* for negligence if:
1. *P* has suffered an *injury*;
2. *A* owed a *duty* to a class of persons including *P* to take care not to cause an injury of the kind suffered by *P*;
3. *A breached* that duty of care;
4. *A*'s breach was an *actual* and *proximate cause* of *P*'s injury.

One can perhaps get a better sense of this formulation by plugging into it the facts alleged and proven in *Walter*:

1. Walter suffered a serious illness (*injury*);
2. Defendant Wal-Mart was obligated to customers of its pharmacy to exercise reasonable care for their physical well-being (*duty*);
3. Wal-Mart, through its employee, failed to exercise reasonable care for Walter's physical well-being when, without appropriate checks, he dispensed the wrong medication to her (*breach of duty*);
4. Wal-Mart's breach functioned as a cause of Walter's illness, which illness was the sort of injury one could expect to be caused by such a breach (*actual* and *proximate cause*).

Our analysis in the next several chapters tracks this account of negligence. After a brief discussion of injury, this chapter concentrates on the duty element. Chapters 3 and 4 turn, respectively, to breach and actual cause. Chapter 5 discusses doctrines such as proximate cause, which concern how the elements of the prima facie case must align with one another before liability will attach.

B.   The Injury Element

Many standard formulations of negligence place "injury" as the last of the tort's four elements. If one thinks of a tort unfolding chronologically, this ordering makes sense: The victim's injury always follows temporally from the injurer's breach of duty. Nonetheless, we have instead identified injury as the first element of the prima facie case. We do this because it helps better capture the role that injury plays in negligence, and throughout tort law. An injury is the first and most basic condition for a viable tort claim. It is only if the plaintiff can demonstrate that she has suffered the right kind of *adverse effect* that she is entitled to pursue her action for redress from another. By contrast, if another person commits a wrong that has no such effect on her, she will have no tort claim.

1.   What Can Count as an Injury in Negligence Law?

Suppose *A* drives carelessly past *B*, narrowly missing her. Suppose also that *A*'s driving is witnessed by a police officer, but that *B* was and is

oblivious to the threat to her well-being. *A* can be cited for a traffic violation, but *B* will have no tort claim against *A*. Because *B* has suffered no
adverse consequence in connection with *A*'s careless driving, *B* cannot
point to anything that would count as an injury, and thus has no grounds
for demanding of *A* that *A* provide her with redress.

Even where a person can point to some adverse effect on her, the
effect still may not count as an injury in the eyes of negligence law. Imagine
that *A* and *B* are standing in a slow-moving supermarket checkout line. *B* is
chattering mindlessly on his cell phone, much to *A*'s annoyance. Even
though it is intelligible to say that *B*'s conduct has caused *A* to suffer some
sort of adverse effect (i.e., annoyance), this will not of itself suffice to establish that *A* has suffered an injury.

So what does count as an injury? Perhaps the most obvious category
is *physical harms*. By physical harms we refer to two sub-categories of
adverse effects. First, we have in mind bodily harms, including fatal and
non-fatal lacerations, broken bones, damaged internal organs, diseases,
and physical illnesses. Second, we refer to damage to, or destruction of,
tangible property including land, structures, and personal possessions.
Returning to the case of *A* and *B* mentioned above, if, when *A* drove carelessly past *B*, *A* struck *B*, causing *B* to suffer contusions and internal bleeding, or damage to a vase of hers that she was carrying, *B* will be deemed to
have suffered an injury. (Whether *B* can hold *A* responsible for those
injuries is a separate question. For now we are concerned only to isolate
the kind of adverse effect that can trigger an inquiry into the issue of
responsibility.)

Loss of wealth can also count as an injury in the law of negligence.
Suppose, for example, beloved nephew *P* were to lose an inheritance that
had been bequeathed to him by his recently departed aunt because his
aunt's lawyer, *L*, incorrectly drew up her will. *P* has suffered an injury, and,
depending on how the other elements of the negligence tort play out, may
be able to establish a negligence claim against *L* for the lost wealth.
Although, as we will see in Chapter 10, negligence law at one time
declined to treat serious *emotional distress* as an injury in its own right,
today it is recognized as an injury. Thus, if in the careless driving example,
B was seriously upset because she was aware that *A* almost ran her over, *B*
might be deemed to have suffered an injury and may be able to recover
compensation from *B* for it (although this is unlikely).

Whether other sorts of effects beyond these will suffice to count as
injuries is a sometimes contested matter, as we will see. For now it is
enough to note that physical harms, economic loss, and emotional distress
are all examples of adverse effects recognized as injuries by the law of
negligence.*

* Torts other than negligence recognize distinct categories of adverse effects as
injuries. For example, as explained in Chapter 9, assault and battery treat interferences
with one's dignity as injuries, even if those interferences do not generate bodily harm or
emotional distress. The torts of defamation and invasion of privacy treat loss of reputation
and loss of privacy, respectively, as injuries on which tort actions can be founded.

C.   *Focusing on Physical Harms*

Chapters 2 through 8 of this book focus primarily on claims of negligence arising out of one kind of injury, namely *physical harms*. This is not because physical harms are as a group more basic, or more serious, than other injuries. (Most of us probably would prefer to suffer a broken arm than to suffer emotional or economic devastation.) Rather, that focus is driven by several pedagogic considerations.

First, as an empirical matter, negligence claims tend to arise out of physical harms. Suits resulting from car accidents, medical errors, and unsafe premises — which together make up the vast bulk of modern negligence suits — typically allege bodily harm or property damage as the relevant injury. Thus, a focus on physical harms helps provide a realistic sense of the world of negligence outside the classroom.

Second, an emphasis on physical harms is probably the most effective way to put to one side any questions concerning the injury element. When a complaint alleges a broken limb or an illness, there is simply no controversy whether the plaintiff is alleging the sort of effect that counts as an injury — she is. Again, this is not to suggest that claims alleging other sorts of injuries are necessarily less valid than claims for physical harms. Rather, it is to say that that physical harms often provide particularly compelling examples of injuries.

Third, as explained below, claims in which the injury alleged is emotional distress, intangible economic loss, or some other adverse effect not involving physical harm often raise complex questions of "duty" that are best analyzed in contrast to the issues raised by physical harm cases.

Finally, we note that our organization of negligence law is consistent with that of the draft Restatement (Third) of Torts, which also isolates negligence claims alleging physical harms for separate treatment from claims alleging other sorts of harms. Restatement (Third) of Torts: Liability for Physical Harm (Basic Principles) § 4 at 75 (Tentative Draft No. 1, Mar. 28, 2001). Thus, our presentation tracks, and perhaps will help make sense of, what is likely to be a presentation of tort doctrine that will have significant influence on judicial decisions in future tort cases.

II.   THE DUTY ELEMENT AND THE GENERAL DUTY OF REASONABLE CARE

On the assumption that the plaintiff alleges and will be able to prove that she has suffered a bodily harm or damage to her property, we now turn our attention to the second element of the prima facie case of negligence: duty. The duty element will occupy us for the rest of this chapter.

Speaking generally and somewhat loosely, one can say that the duty element requires a negligence plaintiff to establish that the defendant owed her, or a class of persons including her, an obligation to take care not to cause the type of injury that she has suffered.* To put the same point negatively: If an actor was *not* under an obligation to take precautions against causing the sort of injury suffered by the victim to persons in the position of the victim, then he cannot be held liable for failing to take those precautions. Understood on these terms, the duty question is distinct from the subsequent breach question. The latter assumes the existence of a duty of care, and asks whether the defendant did enough to satisfy the duty. Unfortunately, this neat analytic separation of duty from breach can become blurry in particular cases, as we will see.

A.   Easy Cases: The Unqualified Duty to Conduct Oneself with Reasonable Care for the Person and Property of Others

Just as a plaintiff who comes into court with evidence of having suffered broken bones or a diagnosed disease will have little trouble satisfying the injury element, so, too, many plaintiffs will have little or no trouble establishing that the defendant owed it to them to take care for their physical well-being. The latter may be termed *easy* duty cases — cases in which neither the litigants nor the court will spend much time on the issue because all are satisfied that the person being sued owed it to the complainant to take reasonable care. Many easy duty cases are ones in which the plaintiff's allegation is that the defendant *carelessly pursued an affirmative course of conduct that caused the plaintiff physical harm*. As indicated above, that is part of the reason why we limit our focus to physical harms in the opening chapters of the book. More difficult duty cases, by contrast, tend to arise out of allegations that the defendant's carelessness consisted of a *failure to act for the benefit of the plaintiff*, or that the defendant caused *some other kind of injury* besides physical harm. We consider some of these cases in Section III of this chapter, and others in Chapter 10. As we also note in Section II.B, however, even cases alleging careless affirmative conduct causing physical harm will sometimes give rise to more difficult duty cases.

Easy duty cases are easy in the sense that the existence of a duty owed by the defendant to the plaintiff tends to be taken for granted. Yet these cases bear a second and related feature that distinguishes them from more difficult cases. In the category of easy duty cases, courts are quite comfortable articulating the duty owed by the injurer to the victim in *unqualified* or *general* terms. So, for example, courts are content to say, as did the court in *Walter*, that a physician or pharmacist owes reasonable care to his patients, without further specifying what reasonable care entails, or when exactly that duty is triggered. Likewise, courts will routinely assert or assume that a driver owes it to others around him to drive reasonably, without saying anything more about the circumstances in which that duty attaches, or its contours or limitations. By contrast, in the harder-case categories, as we will

---

* This description technically fits only "negative" duties to take care to avoid causing harms. As discussed below in Section III.C, persons are sometimes under "positive" or "affirmative" duties to make reasonable efforts to protect or rescue another.

see, even when courts recognize a duty owed to the plaintiff, they will tend to take pains to *qualify* that duty with various limitations. In these cases — which we explore in Section III — the courts are not content to speak in terms of a general duty of reasonable care, but instead identify relatively specific duties to which the defendant must attend.

B. A Sampling of Easy Duty Cases Drawn from English Law

The American Revolution notwithstanding, the common law of tort in this country derives from English law. Indeed, after the Revolution, the new states enacted "reception statutes" that explicitly incorporated English law into their law. Not surprisingly, then, many cases falling into the easy duty case category reflect obligations that have been part of the fabric of the common law for centuries. For example, as noted in Appendix B, the duty owed by Wal-Mart to Antoinette Walter traces back hundreds of years to the recognition of duties owed by medieval surgeons to take care not to commit malpractice on their patients. Likewise, members of various others trades and callings — veterinarians, innkeepers, ferry operators, and others — have for centuries been held to an unqualified or general obligation to take reasonable care for the physical well-being of their customers and/or their customers' property. In each of these scenarios, the provider of services was treated as having *undertaken* to be careful for the benefit of certain other persons.

Although duties of care often were recognized in old English common law on the basis of well-defined roles and relationships, they also attached to certain activities irrespective of any such connection between wrongdoer and victim, as evidenced by two seventeenth-century decisions issued by the English King's Bench court.* In the famous decision of Weaver v. Ward, 80 Eng. Rep. 284 (1616), the court presumed that the victim of an accidental shooting could sue the shooter under the writ of "trespass" notwithstanding the absence of any preexisting relationship between them. Likewise, in Mitchil v. Alestree, 86 Eng. Rep. 190 (1676), the court held the owner of a horse could be sued under the writ of trespass on the case for carelessly arranging to have his horse trained in a public park, during which training it ran down the plaintiff, a stranger.

The operation of horse-drawn carriages and sailboats provides another example of the sort of activity to which an unqualified duty of care to be vigilant of others' physical well-being attached regardless of whether any such duty was assumed by the driver or owner for the benefit of the victim. In Cotterill v. Starkey, 173 Eng. Rep. 676 (N.P. 1839), the plaintiff,

---

* At the time of *Weaver* and *Mitchil*, the King's Bench — or Queen's Bench, if a woman was sitting on the English throne — was one of the three royal courts that sat in Westminster Hall in London and resolved the legal issues raised by private disputes governed by the common law. The other two were the Exchequer Court and the Court of Common Pleas. Each of these courts was ultimately answerable to Parliament's House of Lords, which sat as the high court in England. See Appendix B.

a pedestrian, had been run down by the defendant as he drove his horse-drawn wagon.* The judge presiding over the trial of the case explained the law to the jury as follows:

> [I]t is quite clear that a foot passenger has a right to cross [a public road] and that persons driving carriages along the road are liable if they do not take care so as to avoid driving against the foot passengers who are crossing the road. . . .

Two years earlier, the justices of the English Court of Common Pleas in the case of Vaughan v. Menlove, 132 Eng. Rep. 490 (1837), upheld a claim for liability arising out of a carelessly started fire that spread from defendant's to plaintiff's property. In doing so, they rejected the defendant's argument that he was at liberty to do as he pleased with his own property, regardless of the risks of physical harm it posed to others around him. Said one justice:

> The principle on which . . . [the plaintiff's] action proceeds, is by no means new. It has been urged that the Defendant in such a case takes no duty on himself; but I do not agree in that position: every one takes upon himself the duty of so dealing with his own property as not to injure the property of others.

As the foregoing paragraphs suggest, even before the tort of negligence emerged as a widely recognized cause of action, English tort law had recognized an array of situations and activities giving rise to a presumptive and unqualified duty to take reasonable care against causing physical harms to others. By the end of the nineteenth century, jurists and lawyers sought to "induce" from these instances a general rule as to when a person can be said to owe such a duty to others. In the famous case of Heaven v. Pender, 11 Q.B.D. 503 (Eng. C.A. 1883), Justice Brett, a member of England's Court of Appeal,** offered the following observations:

> If a person contracts with another to use ordinary care or skill towards him or his property the obligation need not be considered in the light of a duty; it is an obligation of contract. It is undoubted, however, that there may be

* As explained in the preceding footnote, common law tort cases usually were filed in, and resolved by, one of three multi-member courts that sat in Westminster Hall in London. However, at certain times during the year, the justices of these courts traveled throughout England to preside individually over local jury trials. The judges would then reconvene in London to discuss and resolve legal issues that had arisen while they were out "riding circuit." The local proceedings before individual justices were called *nisi prius* proceedings; hence the N.P. notation in the caption of *Cotterill*.

** By 1883, Parliament had reorganized the English judiciary. The courts of Common Pleas, Exchequer, and King's Bench were replaced by a single set of courts still known today as the Queen's Bench Division (or King's Bench Division, should a male heir ascend to the throne). The Queen's Bench Division hears tort and contract claims, among others. It forms one branch of the "High Court of Justice," which is the name for the civil side of the English court system.

Appeals from the Queen's Bench Division are heard by a single Court of Appeal, which is the Court that decided *Heaven*. Court of Appeal justices are dubbed "Lord Justices of Appeal." The chief judge responsible for the civil side of the Court of Appeal's docket is titled Master of the Rolls. (That title refers to a now obsolete responsibility for keeping the obligation of such a duty from one person to another although there is no contract between them with regard to such duty. Two drivers meeting have no contract with each other, but under certain circumstances they have a reciprocal duty towards each other. So two ships navigating the sea. So a railway company which has contracted with one person to carry another has no contract with the person carried but has a duty towards that person. So the owner or occupier of house or land who permits a person or persons to come to his house or land has no contract with such person or persons, but has a duty towards him or them. . . . The question[ ] which we have to solve in this case [is] — what is the proper definition of the relation between two persons . . . which imposes on the one of them a duty towards the other to observe, with regard to the person or property of such other, such ordinary care or skill as may be necessary to prevent injury to his person or property. . . . When two drivers or two ships are approaching each other, such a relation arises between them when they are approaching each other in such a manner that, unless they use ordinary care and skill to avoid it, there will be danger of an injurious collision between them. This relation is established in such circumstances between them, not only if it be proved that they actually know and think of this danger, but whether such proof be made or not. It is established, as it seems to me, because any one of ordinary sense who did think would at once recognise that if he did not use ordinary care and skill under such circumstances there would be such danger. And every one ought by the universally recognised rules of right and wrong, to think so much with regard to the safety of others who may be jeopardised by his conduct; and if, being in such circumstances, he does not think, and in consequence neglects, or if he neglects to use ordinary care or skill, and injury ensue, the law, which takes cognisance of and enforces the rules of right and wrong, will force him to give an indemnity for the injury. In the case of a railway company carrying a passenger with whom it has not entered into the contract of carriage the law implies the duty, because it must be obvious that unless ordinary care and skill be used the personal safety of the passenger must be endangered. . . . It follows . . . that there must be some larger proposition which involves and covers both sets of circumstances. The logic of inductive reasoning requires that where two major propositions lead to exactly similar minor premises there must be a more remote and larger premiss which embraces both of the major propositions. . . . The proposition which these recognised cases suggest, and which is, therefore, to be deduced from them, is that whenever one person is by circumstances placed in such a position with regard to another that every one of ordinary sense who did think would at once recognise that if he did not use ordinary care and skill in his own conduct with regard to those circumstances he would cause danger of injury to the person or property of the other, a duty arises to use ordinary care and skill to avoid such danger. . . .

---

court records on rolls of parchment paper.) Justice Brett was Master of the Rolls at the time *Heaven* was decided.

With permission, Court of Appeal decisions can be appealed to the House of Lords, which still operates as the court of last resort in England for most cases. (Certain of its decisions can be appealed to the European Court of Human Rights.) By convention, the House of Lords does not deliberate over or decide cases as a body. Rather, it adopts the decisions of an Appellate Committee. That Committee is comprised mainly of senior jurists appointed at the direction of the Prime Minister and his or her cabinet for the purpose of deciding appellate cases. These jurists are known as the "Law Lords."

Justice Brett's central claim — that an unqualified duty to take reasonable care not to cause physical harms is owed to another whenever a person "of ordinary sense" would recognize that careless conduct on his part would cause "danger of injury to the person or property of the other" — has today been recast by lawyers and judges in the language of *reasonable foreseeability*. Thus, in modern legal parlance, one says that drivers owe a duty to take care not to cause physical harm to those around them simply because it is a reasonably foreseeable consequence of careless driving that such persons might suffer physical harms.

C. The Evolution of Duty Rules

By identifying "easy" duty cases, the previous section emphasized pockets of duty law that have been relatively stable for centuries. Insofar as this emphasis creates the impression that the duty element is always or even typically governed by a static set of rules, it is misleading, even as applied to claims for physical harms arising out of careless conduct. One of the hallmarks of the common law is that it steadily evolves as judges apply existing rules to new disputes arising in new circumstances. Indeed, as the remainder of the materials in this chapter will attest, doctrine pertaining to the issue of duty has evolved on several fronts throughout the twentieth century, and in some instances has changed quite dramatically within a relatively brief period of time. As you read the two main cases in this section, consider what might have prompted the judges who decided them to expand or otherwise alter the rules contained in precedents. Also, consider carefully the content of the new rules that they put in place of the old ones. Do they comport with the notion, emerging from twentieth-century interpretations of Heaven v. Pender, that so long as physical harm to a person such as the plaintiff is a reasonably foreseeable consequence of an actor's careless conduct, the actor owes a duty to take care not to cause such harm to the plaintiff?

1. *Winterbottom v. Wright: The Privity Rule*. Historically, the most infamous instance of a rule declining to recognize a duty to regulate one's conduct with care not to cause physical harms to another was the "privity" rule first announced by the English Court of Exchequer in Winterbottom v. Wright, 152 Eng. Rep. 402 (1842) (decided 41 years prior to Heaven v. Pender). Wright built and maintained carriages. He entered into a contract with the English Postmaster General to provide coaches fit for delivering mail. The Postmaster General in turn obtained drivers by contracting with another company, of which the plaintiff, Winterbottom, was an employee. (Thus, Winterbottom had no contractual relationship with the Postmaster or with Wright, only to the company that employed him.)

Winterbottom was lamed when a wheel on the coach he was driving collapsed. He sued Wright, essentially arguing that Wright had breached a duty of care owed to drivers such as him to take reasonable care to ensure the soundness of the coaches being supplied to the Postmaster General. The justices of the Exchequer Court (titled "Barons") rejected this argument.

According to the Chief Baron, Lord Abinger, it was necessary to reject emphatically the duty posited by Winterbottom's claim lest the court invite "an infinity of actions."

> Here the action is brought simply because the defendant was a contractor with a third person; and it is contended that thereupon he became liable to every body who might use the carriage.
>
>   . . . Unless we confine the operation of such contracts as this to the parties who entered into them, the most absurd and outrageous consequences, to which I can see no limit, would ensue. . . . The plaintiff in this case could not have brought an action on the contract; if he could have done so, what would have been his situation, supposing the Postmaster-General had released the defendant? that would, at all events, have defeated his claim altogether. By permitting this action, we should be working this injustice, that after the defendant had done every thing to the satisfaction of his employer, and after all matters between them had been adjusted, and all accounts settled on the footing of their contract, we should subject them to be ripped open by this action of tort being brought against him.

Likewise, Baron Rolfe opined:

> The breach of the defendant's duty stated in this declaration is his omission to keep the carriage in safe condition. . . . The duty [arose] . . . solely from the contract; and the fallacy consists in the use of that word "duty." If a duty to the Postmaster-General be meant, that is true; but if a duty to the plaintiff be intended, (and in that sense the word is evidently used,) there was none. This is one of those unfortunate cases in which there certainly has been damnum, but is *damnum absque injuria*; it is, no doubt, a hardship upon the plaintiff to be without a remedy, but, by that consideration we ought not to be influenced.* Hard cases, it has been frequently observed, are apt to introduce bad law.

Does *Winterbottom*'s ruling contradict the principle induced from other English cases by Justice Brett in Heaven v. Pender? Recall that Brett's principle states, roughly, that a duty of reasonable care attaches whenever it is reasonably foreseeable that careless conduct on one's part may risk physical harm to persons such as the plaintiff. Wasn't it reasonably foreseeable to Wright that if he provided an unsound coach to the Postmaster General, a driver hired by the Postmaster could be physically injured? If so, on what ground can *Winterbottom* be distinguished from cases such as Cotterill v. Starkey and Vaughan v. Menlove?**

* *Damnum absque injuria* ("harm without wrong") — the maxim invoked by Baron Rolfe — describes a loss or harm that, even though a burden on the injured victim, does not support a legal claim against another person.

** Justice Brett was aware of the obstacle that *Winterbottom* posed to his effort to "induce" a general account of the conditions under which a duty to take reasonable care not to cause physical harm attaches. Thus, in *Heaven*, he sought to distinguish *Winterbottom* on various grounds. For example, he suggested that *Winterbottom* was not really a decision about duty at all, but instead denied liability on the ground that the harm suffered by Winterbottom was too "remote" in time and space from the careless acts committed by Wright. Remoteness mattered, according to Brett, in part because it indicated that various other actors were in a position to identify and address the problem in the coach between the time it left Wright's possession and the time it collapsed. Consider the significance of these observations in light of *MacPherson* and *Mussivand, infra*.

Whether consistent with other English case law or not, *Winterbottom*'s rule that a plaintiff who is injured by carelessness on the part of a product manufacturer may not recover in tort absent contractual privity between plaintiff and the manufacturer served to set an important limitation on U.S. and British manufacturers' responsibilities for the next 75 years.

2. *Thomas v. Winchester: Imminently Dangerous Products.* Even as *Winterbottom* was being imported into American law, it was also being limited. For example, in Thomas v. Winchester, 6 N.Y. 397 (1852), the New York Court of Appeals — the state's highest court — permitted the plaintiff, Mrs. Thomas, to proceed against a company that had carelessly mislabeled a bottle of poison as if it were medicine, thereby causing her to be accidentally poisoned. The company argued, under *Winterbottom*, that it owed Mrs. Thomas no duty of care because it sold the mislabeled bottle to a distributor named Aspinwall, who sold it to a pharmacist, who sold it to the plaintiff's husband. The court rejected this argument:

> If, in labeling a poisonous drug with the name of a harmless medicine, for public market, no duty was violated by the defendant, excepting that which he owed to Aspinwall, his immediate vendee, in virtue of his contract of sale, this action cannot be maintained. If A. build a wagon and sell it to B., who sells it to C., and C. hires it to D., who in consequence of the gross negligence of A. in building the wagon is overturned and injured, D. cannot recover damages against A., the builder. A.'s obligation to build the wagon faithfully, arises solely out of his contract with B. The public have nothing to do with it. Misfortune to third persons, not parties to the contract, would not be a natural and necessary consequence of the builder's negligence; and such negligence is not an act imminently dangerous to human life. . . .
>
> This was the ground on which . . . *Winterbottom* . . . was decided. . . . The reason of [that] decision is best stated by Baron Rolfe. A.'s duty to keep the coach in good condition, was a duty to the postmaster general, with whom he made his contract, and not a duty to the driver employed by the owners of the horses.
>
> But the case in hand stands on a different ground. The defendant was a dealer in poisonous drugs. . . . The death or great bodily harm of some person was the natural and almost inevitable consequence of the sale of [poison] by means of the false label. . . .
>
> No such imminent danger existed in [*Winterbottom*]. . . . [Winchester's] negligence put human life in imminent danger. Can it be said that there was no duty on the part of the defendant, to avoid the creation of that danger by the exercise of greater caution? or that the exercise of that caution was a duty only to his immediate vendee, whose life was not endangered? The defendant's duty arose out of the nature of his business and the danger to others incident to its mismanagement. Nothing but mischief like that which actually happened could have been expected from sending the poison falsely labeled into the market; and the defendant is justly responsible for the probable consequences of the act. The duty of exercising caution in this respect did not arise out of the defendant's contract of sale to Aspinwall. The wrong done by the defendant was in putting the poison, mislabeled, into the hands of Aspinwall as an article of merchandise to be sold and afterwards used as [medicine], by some person then unknown. The owner of a horse and cart who leaves them unattended in the street is liable for any

damage which may result from his negligence. . . . The owner of a loaded gun who puts it into the hands of a child by whose indiscretion it is discharged, is liable for the damage occasioned by the discharge. . . .

Which of the following reasons stated by the Court of Appeals provides the best ground for distinguishing *Thomas* from *Winterbottom*: (a) "The death or great bodily harm of some person was the natural and almost inevitable consequence of the sale of [poison] by means of [a] false label"; (b) because drug manufacturers typically sell their products through intermediaries, rather than directly to consumers, whatever injury was likely to result from the mislabeled poison will not befall those in privity with the manufacturer, but will instead affect only third parties; (c) the defendant's negligence put human life in "imminent" danger? Is there a common thread among these grounds? Can you think of others?

3. *New York Case Law: 1870-1910.* The New York Court of Appeals decided several other "privity" cases in the period between 1870 and 1910. The five most prominent of these can be briefly summarized as follows. The first two align themselves with *Winterbottom*, whereas the last three follow *Thomas*.

In Loop v. Litchfield, 42 N.Y. 351 (1870), the defendant manufactured a piece of machinery that included a cast-iron wheel that spun when in use. As originally manufactured, the wheel was missing a portion of its rim, so the defendant had patched it by riveting some lead to the wheel. The defendant then sold the machinery to Collister. Several years later, Collister leased the frame to Loop, who was fatally injured when the wheel burst at the point of the patch. Loop's estate sued and obtained a jury verdict against the manufacturer. That verdict was overturned by the Court of Appeals for lack of duty under *Winterbottom*'s privity rule.

In Losee v. Clute, 51 N.Y. 494 (1873), the defendant manufactured a steam boiler for use in a paper mill that the defendant knew to be located adjacent to other businesses. The mill owner tested and accepted the boiler, which operated without incident for three months, then exploded, causing damage to Losee's property adjacent to the mill. Citing *Winterbottom*, and stressing that the boiler manufacturer exercised no control over the operation and maintenance of the boiler upon its installation, the Court of Appeals concluded that the manufacturer owed no duty of care to avoid causing property damage to the plaintiff.

In Devlin v. Smith, 89 N.Y. 470 (1882), the plaintiff, a painter, was killed because of the defendant's carelessness in erecting scaffolding on which the painter was standing. In contrast to *Loop* and *Losee*, the Court of Appeals reversed lower-court judgments for the *defendant* by invoking *Thomas*. A poorly constructed scaffold was imminently dangerous to human life, the court reasoned. Therefore, the defendant owed a duty of care to third parties who might use the scaffolding.

In Torgesen v. Schultz, 192 N.Y. 156 (1908), the plaintiff, a domestic servant, lost an eye after a bottle of carbonated water bottled by the defendant and sold to her employer exploded as she was placing it on ice. As in *Devlin*, the Court of Appeals reversed the trial court's dismissal of the claim on the ground that a bottle of aerated water is an inherently dangerous instrument. In Statler v. George A. Ray Mfg. Co., 195 N.Y. 478 (1909), the court reached the same conclusion with respect to the negligent manufacture of a steam-driven coffee urn that exploded and injured the plaintiff.

4. *The* MacPherson *Decision.* The New York Court of Appeals' struggle with the privity rule in negligence law was largely resolved in 1916, in the now famous decision of MacPherson v. Buick. Consider as you read Judge Cardozo's opinion his treatment of precedent. Consider also the new rule of duty that his opinion articulates. Is it fair to say that *MacPherson* embraces Justice Brett's notion, suggested in Heaven v. Pender, that reasonable foreseeability of physical harm flowing from one's activities is sufficient to generate an unqualified duty to take reasonable care against causing such harms? If not, why isn't Cardozo willing to go that far?

MacPherson v. Buick Motor Co.
217 N.Y. 382 (N.Y. 1916)

Cardozo, J.   The defendant is a manufacturer of automobiles. It sold an automobile to a retail dealer. The retail dealer resold to the plaintiff. While the plaintiff was in the car, it suddenly collapsed. He was thrown out and injured. One of the wheels was made of defective wood, and its spokes crumbled into fragments. The wheel was not made by the defendant; it was bought from another manufacturer. There is evidence, however, that its defects could have been discovered by reasonable inspection, and that inspection was omitted. There is no claim that the defendant knew of the defect and willfully concealed it. . . . The charge is one, not of fraud, but of negligence. The question to be determined is whether the defendant owed a duty of care and vigilance to any one but the immediate purchaser.

The foundations of this branch of the law, at least in this state, were laid in Thomas v. Winchester (6 N.Y. 397). A poison was falsely labeled. The sale was made to a druggist, who in turn sold to a customer. The customer recovered damages from the seller who affixed the label. "The defendant's negligence," it was said, "put human life in imminent danger." A poison falsely labeled is likely to injure any one who gets it. Because the danger is to be foreseen, there is a duty to avoid the injury. Cases were cited by way of illustration in which manufacturers were not subject to any duty irrespective of contract. The distinction was said to be that their conduct, though negligent, was not likely to result in injury to any one except the purchaser. We are not required to say whether the chance of injury was always as remote as the distinction assumes. Some of the illustrations might be rejected to-day. The *principle* of the distinction is for present purposes the important thing.

Thomas v. Winchester became quickly a landmark of the law. In the application of its principle there may at times have been uncertainty or even error. There has never in this state been doubt or disavowal of the principle itself. The chief cases are well known, yet to recall some of them will be helpful. Loop v. Litchfield (42 N.Y. 351) is the earliest. . . . The risk [there] can hardly have been an imminent one, for the wheel lasted five years before it broke. In the meanwhile the buyer had made a lease of the machinery. It was held that the manufacturer was not answerable to the lessee. Loop v. Litchfield was followed in Losee v. Clute (51 N.Y. 494), the case of the explosion of a steam boiler. That decision has been criticised but it must be confined to its special facts. . . . The buyer in that case had not only accepted the boiler, but had tested it. The manufacturer knew that his own test was not the final one. The finality of the test has a bearing on the measure of diligence owing to persons other than the purchaser.

These early cases suggest a narrow construction of the rule. Later cases, however, evince a more liberal spirit. First in importance is Devlin v. Smith (89 N.Y. 470). The defendant, a contractor, built a scaffold for a painter. The painter's servants were injured. The contractor was held liable. He knew that the scaffold, if improperly constructed, was a most dangerous trap. He knew that it was to be used by the workmen. He was building it for that very purpose. Building it for their use, he owed them a duty, irrespective of his contract with their master, to build it with care.

From Devlin v. Smith we pass over intermediate cases and turn to . . . Statler v. Ray Mfg. Co. (195 N.Y. 478, 480). . . . We held that the [coffee urn] manufacturer was liable. We said that the urn "was of such a character inherently that, when applied to the purposes for which it was designed, it was liable to become a source of great danger to many people if not carefully and properly constructed."

It may be that Devlin v. Smith and Statler v. Ray Mfg. Co. have extended the rule of Thomas v. Winchester. If so, this court is committed to the extension. The defendant argues that things imminently dangerous to life are poisons, explosives, deadly weapons — things whose normal function it is to injure or destroy. But whatever the rule in Thomas v. Winchester may once have been, it has no longer that restricted meaning. A scaffold is not inherently a destructive instrument. It becomes destructive only if imperfectly constructed. A large coffee urn may have within itself, if negligently made, the potency of danger, yet no one thinks of it as an implement whose normal function is destruction. What is true of the coffee urn is equally true of bottles of aerated water (Torgeson v. Schultz, 192 N.Y. 156). We have mentioned only cases in this court. But the rule has received a like extension in our courts of intermediate appeal. . . . We are not required at this time either to approve or to disapprove the application of the rule that was made in these cases. It is enough that they help to characterize the trend of judicial thought.

Devlin v. Smith was decided in 1882. A year later a very similar case came before the Court of Appeal in England (Heaven v. Pender, L.R. [11 Q.B.D.] 503). We find in the opinion of Brett, M.R., afterwards Lord Esher the same conception of a duty, irrespective of contract, imposed upon the manufacturer by the law itself: "Whenever one person supplies goods, or machinery, or the like, for the purpose of their being used by another person under such circumstances that every one of ordinary sense would, if he thought, recognize at once that unless he used ordinary care and skill with regard to the condition of the thing supplied or the mode of supplying it, there will be danger of injury to the person or property of him for whose use the thing is supplied, and who is to use it, a duty arises to use ordinary care and skill as to the condition or manner of supplying such thing." He then points out that for a neglect of such ordinary care or skill whereby injury happens, the appropriate remedy is an action for negligence. The right to enforce this liability is not to be confined to the immediate buyer. The right, he says, extends to the persons or class of persons for whose use the thing is supplied. It is enough that the goods "would in all probability be used at once . . . before a reasonable opportunity for discovering any defect which might exist," and that the thing supplied is of such a nature "that a neglect of ordinary care or skill as to its condition or the manner of supplying it would probably cause danger to the person or property of the person for whose use it was supplied, and who was about to use it." On the other hand, he would exclude a case "in which the goods are supplied under circumstances in which it would be a chance by whom they would be used or whether they would be used or not, or whether they would be used before there would probably be means of observing any defect," or where the goods are of such a nature that "a want of care or skill as to their condition or the manner of supplying them would not probably produce danger of injury to person or property." What was said by Lord Esher in that case did not command the full assent of his associates. . . . Perhaps it may need some qualification even in our own state. Like most attempts at comprehensive definition, it may involve errors of inclusion and of exclusion. But its tests and standards, at least in their underlying principles, with whatever qualification may be called for as they are applied to varying conditions, are the tests and standards of our law.

   We hold, then, that the principle of Thomas v. Winchester is not limited to poisons, explosives, and things of like nature, to things which in their normal operation are implements of destruction. If the nature of a thing is such that it is reasonably certain to place life and limb in peril when negligently made, it is then a thing of danger. Its nature gives warning of the consequences to be expected. If to the element of danger there is added knowledge that the thing will be used by persons other than the purchaser, and used without new tests, then, irrespective of contract, the manufacturer of this thing of danger is under a duty to make it carefully. That is as far as we are required to go for the decision of this case. There must be knowledge of a danger, not merely possible, but probable. It is *possible* to use almost anything in a way that will make it dangerous if defective. That is not enough to charge the manufacturer with a duty independent of his contract. Whether a given thing is dangerous may be sometimes a question for the court and sometimes a question for the jury. There must also be knowledge that in the usual course of events the danger will be shared by others than the buyer. Such knowledge may often be inferred from the nature of the transaction. But it is possible that even knowledge of the danger and of the use will not always be enough. The proximity or remoteness of the relation is a factor to be considered. We are dealing now with the liability of the manufacturer of the finished product, who puts it on the market to be used without inspection by his customers. If he is negligent, where danger is to be foreseen, a liability will follow. We are not required at this time to say that it is legitimate to go back of the manufacturer of the finished product and hold the manufacturers of the component parts. To make their negligence a cause of imminent danger, an independent cause must often intervene; the manufacturer of the finished product must also fail in *his* duty of inspection. It may be that in those circumstances the negligence of the earlier members of the series is too remote to constitute, as to the ultimate user, an actionable wrong. We leave that question open. . . . There is here no break in the chain of cause and effect. In such circumstances, the presence of a known danger, attendant upon a known use, makes vigilance a duty. We have put aside the notion that the duty to safeguard life and limb, when the consequences of negligence may be foreseen, grows out of contract and nothing else. We have put the source of the obligation where it ought to be. We have put its source in the law.

From this survey of the decisions, there thus emerges a definition of the duty of a manufacturer which enables us to measure this defendant's liability. Beyond all question, the nature of an automobile gives warning of probable danger if its construction is defective. This automobile was designed to go fifty miles an hour. Unless its wheels were sound and strong, injury was almost certain. It was as much a thing of danger as a defective engine for a railroad. The defendant knew the danger. It knew also that the car would be used by persons other than the buyer. This was apparent from its size; there were seats for three persons. It was apparent also from the fact that the buyer was a dealer in cars, who bought to resell. The maker of this car supplied it for the use of purchasers from the dealer just as plainly as the contractor in Devlin v. Smith supplied the scaffold for use by the servants of the owner. The dealer was indeed the one person of whom it might be said with some approach to certainty that by him the car would not be used. Yet the defendant would have us say that he was the one person whom it was under a legal duty to protect. The law does not lead us to so inconsequent a conclusion. Precedents drawn from the days of travel by stage coach do not fit the conditions of travel to-day. The principle that the danger must be imminent does not change, but the things subject to the principle do change. They are whatever the needs of life in a developing civilization require them to be. . . .

In England the limits of the rule are still unsettled. Winterbottom v. Wright (10 M. & W. 109) is often cited. . . . [However,] in Heaven v. Pender (*supra*) the defendant, a dock owner, who put up a staging outside a ship, was held liable to the servants of the shipowner. [Judge Cardozo then reviewed other English decisions.] From these cases a consistent principle is with difficulty extracted. The English courts, however, agree with ours in holding that one who invites another to make use of an appliance is bound to the exercise of reasonable care. That at bottom is the underlying principle of Devlin v. Smith. The contractor who builds the scaffold invites the owner's workmen to use it. The manufacturer who sells the automobile to the retail dealer invites the dealer's customers to use it. The invitation is addressed in the one case to determinate persons and in the other to an indeterminate class, but in each case it is equally plain, and in each its consequences must be the same.

There is nothing anomalous in a rule which imposes upon A, who has contracted with B, a duty to C and D and others according as he knows or does not know that the subject-matter of the contract is intended for their use. We may find an analogy in the law which measures the liability of landlords. If A leases to B a tumbledown house he is not liable, in the absence of fraud, to B's guests who enter it and are injured. This is because B is then under the duty to repair it, the lessor has the right to suppose that he will fulfill that duty, and, if he omits to do so, his guests must look to him. But if A leases a building to be used by the lessee at once as a place of public entertainment, the rule is different. There injury to persons other than the lessee is to be foreseen, and foresight of the consequences involves the creation of a duty (Junkermann v. Tilyou R. Co., 213 N.Y. 404, and cases there cited).

. . . Subtle distinctions are drawn by the defendant between things inherently dangerous and things imminently dangerous, but the case does not turn upon these verbal niceties. If danger was to be expected as reasonably certain, there was a duty of vigilance, and this whether you call the danger inherent or imminent. In varying forms that thought was put before the jury. We do not say that the court would not have been justified in ruling as a matter of law that the car was a dangerous thing. If there was any error, it was none of which the defendant can complain.

We think the defendant was not absolved from a duty of inspection because it bought the wheels from a reputable manufacturer. It was not merely a dealer in automobiles. It was a manufacturer of automobiles. It was responsible for the finished product. It was not at liberty to put the finished product on the market without subjecting the component parts to ordinary and simple tests. . . . The obligation to inspect must vary with the nature of the thing to be inspected. The more probable the danger, the greater the need of caution. . . .

. . . The judgment should be affirmed with costs.

Bartlett, Ch. J. (dissenting) . . .

It has heretofore been held in this state that the liability of the vendor of a manufactured article for negligence arising out of the existence of defects therein does not extend to strangers injured in consequence of such defects but is confined to the immediate vendee. The exceptions to this general rule which have thus far been recognized in New York are cases in which the article sold was of such a character that danger to life or limb was involved in the ordinary use thereof; in other words, where the article sold was inherently dangerous. . . . [T]he learned trial judge instructed the jury that an automobile is not an inherently dangerous vehicle. . . .

The doctrine of [*Winterbottom*] was recognized as the law of this state by the leading New York case of Thomas v. Winchester (6 N.Y. 397, 408), which, however, involved an exception to the general rule. . . . Chief Judge Ruggles, who delivered the opinion of the court, distinguished between an act of negligence imminently dangerous to the lives of others and one that is not so, saying: "If A. build a wagon and sell it to B., who sells it to C. and C. hires it to D., who in consequence of the gross negligence of A. in building the wagon is overturned and injured, D. cannot recover damages against A., the builder. A.'s obligation to build the wagon faithfully, arises solely out of his contract with B. The public have nothing to do with it. . . ."

I do not see how we can uphold the judgment in the present case without overruling what has been so often said by this court and other courts of like authority in reference to the absence of any liability for negligence on the part of the original vendor of an ordinary carriage to any one except his immediate vendee. The absence of such liability was the very point actually decided in the English case of Winterbottom v. Wright, and the illustration quoted from the opinion of Chief Judge Ruggles in Thomas v. Winchester assumes that the law on the subject was so plain that the statement would be accepted almost as a matter of course. In the case at bar the defective wheel on an automobile moving only eight miles an hour was not any more dangerous to the occupants of the car than a similarly defective wheel would be to the occupants of a carriage drawn by a horse at the same speed; and yet unless the courts have been all wrong on this question up to the present time there would be no liability to strangers to the original sale in the case of the horse-drawn carriage.

NOTES AND QUESTIONS

1. *Benjamin Cardozo.* Although foreshadowed by other decisions, including *Heaven* and Huset v. J. I. Threshing Machine Co., 120 F. 865 (8th Cir. 1903), *MacPherson* proved to be a landmark. Its rejection of *Winterbottom* helped bring about the rejection of the privity rule in the vast majority of state courts, and also helped pave the way toward the development of the modern doctrine of strict products liability, discussed in Part Four of this book. *MacPherson* also secured a national reputation for its author, Judge Benjamin Cardozo, who would go on to write many of the leading tort opinions of his time. Cardozo served on the New York Court of Appeals until 1931, and then on the U.S. Supreme Court until his death in 1937.

2. *The Importance of Facts.* In a recent book chapter, Professor Henderson has argued that Buick's account of the accident in *MacPherson* — that Mr. MacPherson lost control of his car on some loose gravel, which caused him to skid into a telephone pole, which in turn caused his injuries and caused the wheel to break — was probably the right account of what happened. What, then, explains how the plaintiff's version arose and came to be the basis for the Court of Appeals' decision? According to Henderson, the explanation lies in the interaction of many forces, including:

- Mr. MacPherson's psychological need to attribute his misfortune to some other responsible party;
- the existence of some circumstantial evidence (wheel fragments) that, on first glance, seemed to point toward the broken wheel as a cause rather than a consequence of the accident;
- the availability and willingness of a local lawyer, as well as experts, who were prepared to maintain that the wheel caused the accident;

- the jury's acceptance of these experts' accounts over those of the defendant (which itself may have turned on considerations such as the experts' demeanor in the courtroom, as well as possible jury sympathy for the plaintiff, or hostility toward the out-of-state, corporate defendant); and
- a tactical decision by Buick not to focus its appeals on the questionable nature of the jury's factual findings, and instead to focus on the privity argument.

As against Professor Henderson's analysis, however, it should be noted that the five-member intermediate appellate court that heard the case prior to the Court of Appeals concluded unanimously that a reasonable jury could accept Mr. MacPherson's account of the accident given the evidence presented at trial.

3. *Appellate Opinions: Facts and the Importance of Narrative.* Appellate courts, particularly high courts like the New York Court of Appeals, being far removed from the actual trial and presentation of evidence, rarely second-guess juries' factual findings. Indeed, they ordinarily will not overturn findings of fact made by trial judges or juries unless they conclude such findings are "clearly erroneous" — a very difficult standard to satisfy. Thus, the Court of Appeals probably believed that they were compelled to decide the legal issues that Buick raised on appeal on the assumption that the accident had been caused by a defect in the wheel that Buick should have detected. (Even Chief Judge Bartlett, who dissented, did not question these aspects of the case.)

Granted the court's limited power to revisit factual questions, reconsider how Cardozo's opinion describes those facts. Notice that he omits most of the details of the accident, as well as that the defendant contested this depiction of the facts at trial. Notice also his use of the terms *suddenly* and *thrown out*. What sort of mental image of the accident does he create? Suppose Cardozo had mentioned the fact, apparently uncontested at trial, that Mr. MacPherson had owned the car for a year prior to the accident, and had frequently driven it, sometimes carrying heavy loads, without incident during that time? Would that have made it harder for him to distinguish certain precedents?

Judge Richard Posner, a prominent present-day federal judge and legal scholar, has argued that the most effective judicial writing is literary and rhetorical rather than merely analytical, and that Cardozo's writing exemplifies this sort of writing. Are there ways in which the *MacPherson* opinion is particularly literary? If so, does that attribute of his analysis affect your own analysis of the legal issues in the suit?

4. *Manufacturer versus Dealer.* What account of the dealer's role in the sale of the car to the consumer does Cardozo seem to have in mind? Why might the role played by the dealer matter to the proper resolution of the case? It was not clear at the time that Mr. MacPherson could have successfully sued the dealer for his personal injuries on a breach of contract theory. In any event, local dealers may not have had the financial wherewithal to pay damages.

5. *Users versus Bystanders.* Suppose that, when the wheel on Mr. MacPherson's Buick crumbled, it did not cause physical injury to him, but caused the automobile to veer into and injure a nearby pedestrian walking lawfully along the side of the road. In *Winterbottom*, Lord Abinger maintained that permitting a bystander to sue the manufacturer in negligence would be "absurd and outrageous." Does Cardozo's opinion indicate whether the pedestrian is entitled to recover? Subsequent decisions by other courts clearly permitted bystander recovery. *See, e.g.,* Flies v. Fox Bros. Buick Motor Co., 218 N.W. 855 (Wis. 1929).

6. *Things of Danger?* Does Cardozo launch a frontal assault on the rule of *Winterbottom?* To what degree does the holding of the case turn on the relative dangerousness of an automobile? Would Cardozo apply the same analysis to an injury resulting from the collapse of an ordinary desk chair?

7. *Contract, Tort, and Duty.* By the early part of the twentieth century, many commentators had come to view *Winterbottom* and its privity rule as a leading example of a harshly individualistic conception of law that privileged the right of business owners to use contracts to limit their potential obligations to those they might injure, particularly consumers and employees. By elevating freedom of contract to a paramount virtue, the critics maintained, courts like the Exchequer Court enabled businesses to avoid responsibility for the mounting toll of injuries associated with the industrial revolution. By the same token, Cardozo's *MacPherson* opinion was hailed by these critics as an enlightened decision that recognized changing economic and political realities, including the fact that manufacturers and users of products increasingly interacted with one another through intermediaries.

Because *Winterbottom*'s privity rule was cast by the Exchequer Barons as a "limited duty" rule, it was perhaps inevitable that some progressive critics of mid- to late-nineteenth-century tort law, including most prominently the British legal historian Percy Winfield, concluded that the duty element itself is an inherently regressive component of the negligence tort, one that was inserted by judges who were anxious to limit liability through matter-of-law rulings on the duty issue. Reconsider Cardozo's opinion in light of Winfield's "guilt by association" criticism of the role the duty element plays in the negligence tort. Does Cardozo's opinion suggest that he believed that the duty element is inexorably linked to "regressive" tort rules?

8. *What Is the Holding?* What rule of duty is articulated by *MacPherson?* Does Cardozo's opinion embrace Justice Brett's unqualified duty of care to those who might foreseeably be injured by one's carelessness? If not, what qualifications or limits are built into the duty? Why? What is distinctive about manufacturing and selling products as compared to driving or providing medical services? Consider, in this regard, a modern case that arguably raises some of the same concerns as *MacPherson*.

Mussivand v. David
544 N.E.2d 265 (Ohio 1989)

[Tofigh Mussivand sued Dr. George David for injuries allegedly stemming from a sexual liaison between David and Dr. Dixie West, who at the time was Mussivand's wife. Mussivand's complaint alleged that David infected his wife with a sexually transmitted disease, and that she in turn infected him. In his first cause of action, Mussivand alleged that David was negligent toward him by engaging in sex with West without disclosing his infection to her or taking precautions against infecting her. In response, David filed a motion to dismiss the complaint, arguing, among other things, that he owed no duty of care to Mussivand. The trial court granted the motion. The intermediate appellate court reversed, concluding that certain facts, if proven, would establish that David owed a duty to Mussivand. — EDS.]

Syllabus by the Court

1. A person who knows, or should know, that he or she is infected with a venereal disease has the duty to abstain from sexual conduct or, at a minimum, to warn those persons with whom he or she expects to have sexual relations of his or her condition.
2. A spouse is a foreseeable sexual partner and a person who has a venereal disease who fails to inform a married person with whom he or she is engaging in sexual contact of his or her condition is liable to the third-party spouse until the initially infected spouse knows or should have known he or she is infected with a venereal disease.

Resnick, J.   This case comes to us on a dismissal of a complaint for failure to state a cause of action. The complaint basically states that appellee contracted a venereal disease due to the acts of the appellant. Therefore we do not know whether the venereal disease was gonorrhea, syphilis, genital herpes, venereal warts or some other sexually transmitted disease. [An unpublished opinion from the lower court reports that the disease complained of was venereal warts. — EDS.]. . .

It long has been held that one who has a contagious disease must take the necessary steps to prevent the spread of the disease. This standard of care has been imposed by the courts in cases concerning the spread of communicable diseases such as tuberculosis. . . .

A similar standard of care exists for preventing the spread of a venereal disease. In Duke v. Housen (Wyo. 1979), 589 P.2d 334, the plaintiff alleged that her former paramour was grossly negligent when he infected her with gonorrhea. Although her action was barred by the statute of limitations, the court held that "[o]ne who negligently exposes another to an infectious or contagious disease, which such other person thereby contracts, can be held liable in damages for his actions. . . ." (Citations omitted.) *Id.* at 340. . . .

Recently several jurisdictions have allowed tort actions for negligent . . . transmission of genital herpes where the person infected with genital herpes fails to disclose to his or her sexual partner that he or she is infected with such a disease. . . . In other words, people with a venereal disease have a duty to use reasonable care to avoid infecting others with whom they engage in sexual conduct. . . .

. . . [T]he above-cited cases differ from the cause before us in one very important aspect: that is, appellee herein alleges that appellant owed him a duty even though appellee was not appellant's sexual partner and had no direct sexual contact with appellant.

The issue which we must decide in this case, therefore, is what duty, if any, does a person infected with a venereal disease owe to the spouse of his paramour. Determining whether a duty exists is crucial since "[a] person's failure to exercise ordinary care in doing or failing to do something will not amount to actionable negligence unless such person owed to someone injured by such failure a duty to exercise such ordinary care." United States Fire Ins. Co. v. Paramount Fur Service, Inc. (1959), 168 Ohio St. 431, 7 O.O. 2d 267, 156 N.E.2d 121, paragraph three of the syllabus.

. . . The existence of a duty in a negligence action is a question of law for the court to determine. There is no formula for ascertaining whether a duty exists. Duty ". . . is the court's 'expression of the sum total of those considerations of policy which lead the law to say that the particular plaintiff is entitled to protection.' (Prosser, Law of Torts (4th ed. 1971) pp. 325-326.) Any number of considerations may justify the imposition of duty in particular circumstances, including the guidance of history, our continually refined concepts of morals and justice, the convenience of the rule, and social judgment as to where the loss should fall.

The common-law duty of due care is that degree of care which an ordinarily reasonable and prudent person exercises, or is accustomed to exercising, under the same or similar circumstances. A person is to exercise that care necessary to avoid injury to others. (Prosser, *Palsgraf Revisited* (1953), 52 Mich. L. Rev. 1, 15)."

A person who has a venereal disease does not have the duty to disclose his condition to everyone. As has been stated, "[i]t should be made clear that this court is not stating here that herpes victims have a specific duty to warn any person of their condition; however, they, like all citizens, are to be guided by those considerations which ordinarily regulate the conduct of human affairs, and they may be sued in this state for negligence in the omission to do something which a reasonable person would do. . . ." Long v. Adams, [175 Ga. App. 538, 540 [(1985)], 333 S.E.2d at 855].

We find the reasoning of these other jurisdictions persuasive and accordingly hold that a person who knows, or should know, that he or she is infected with a venereal disease has the duty to abstain from sexual conduct or, at the minimum, to warn those persons with whom he or she expects to have sexual relations of his or her condition.

There is a strong public policy behind imposition of this duty. In general, we are reminded that ". . . [t]he health of the people is an economic asset. The law recognizes its preservation as a matter of importance to the state. To the individual nothing is more valuable than health. The laws of this state have been framed to protect the people, collectively and individually, from the spread of communicable diseases. . . ." [Skillings v. Allen, 143

Minn. 323,] 325-326 [(1919)], 173 N.W. at 664. More specifically, we recognize that venereal diseases are often serious, and, in some instances, there is no known cure for them. Transmission of a venereal disease is generally through sexual contact. The likelihood that one will contract a venereal disease from someone infected with such a disease is often high.

Furthermore, there is statutory support for this duty. R.C. 3701.81 (A) states: "No person, knowingly or having reasonable cause to believe that he is suffering from a dangerous, contagious disease, shall knowingly fail to take reasonable measures to prevent exposing himself to other persons, except when seeking medical aid." . . .

Appellant argues, however, that while he may have had a duty to appellee's wife to disclose his condition, this duty does not extend to appellee. The existence of a duty will depend on the foreseeability of the injury to appellee. *See* Menifee v. Ohio Welding Products, Inc. (1984), 15 Ohio St. 3d 75, 77, 15 OBR 179, 180, 472 N.E.2d 707, 710. "The test for foreseeability is whether a reasonably prudent person would have anticipated that an injury was likely to result from the performance or nonperformance of an act. . . ." *Menifee, supra* [internal citations omitted]. Thus whether appellant owed appellee a duty turns on whether a reasonably prudent person would have anticipated that appellee would be injured by way of appellant's alleged negligence. In this case appellant, allegedly infected with a venereal disease, engaged in sexual relations with a married woman. A reasonably prudent person would anticipate that a wife and husband will engage in sexual relations. In addition, Dr. David is a medical doctor who, more than most people, should be aware of the method of transmitting a venereal disease, its likelihood of spreading through sexual contact, and its potentially devastating effect. If one negligently exposes a married person to a sexually transmissible disease without informing that person of his exposure, it is reasonable to anticipate that the disease may be transmitted to the married person's spouse. Hence liability to a third party for failure to disclose to the original sexual partner turns on whether, under all the circumstances, injury to the third-party spouse was foreseeable. . . .

We do not, however, mean to say that appellant, subsequent to his affair with appellee's wife, will be liable to any and all persons with whom she may have sexual contact. A spouse, however, is a foreseeable sexual partner. Furthermore, the liability of a person with a sexually transmissible disease to a third person, such as a spouse, would be extinguished as soon as the paramour spouse knew or should have known that he or she was exposed to or had contracted a venereal disease. She or he then would become a "conscious and responsible agency which could or should have eliminated the hazard." [Citation omitted.] . . . Whether appellee's wife knew, or should have known, of her exposure to a venereal disease is a question of fact to be decided by the trier of fact. . . .

Appellant also contends that appellee's complaint is barred by R.C. 2305.29, the so-called "anti-heart balm" statute. Appellee's claim, however, clearly is not based on any amatory cause of action, such as . . . alienation of affections, criminal conversation, or seduction. On the contrary, appellee alleges that he has been seriously injured and suffers from an incurable disease as a result of appellant's conduct. The fact that appellee is married to appellant's former paramour does not turn this into an amatory action. Accordingly, appellee's complaint is not barred by R.C. 2305.29.[11] . . .

[The court affirmed the intermediate appellate courts' reinstatement of Mussivand's negligence claim against David. — EDS.]

NOTES AND QUESTIONS

1. *Ohio Syllabi.* Under rules promulgated by the Ohio Supreme Court, the judge who is assigned to write the opinion for the majority of the court must prepare a separate syllabus for the approval of the majority. The syllabus is then treated as specifying the holding that courts must apply in subsequent cases.

2. *Duty: Law and Fact.* The court indicates the question of duty is a question of law for the court to decide, rather than a question for the jury. By this it means that the court must decide, without deference to the jury, whether the defendant was required to act with vigilance for the well-being of a person such as the plaintiff. As we will see, the duty element stands in contrast to the breach and cause elements, both of which are treated as questions primarily for the jury, with the court limited to a supervisory role.

To say that duty is a question of law for the court is *not* to say that the application of duty rules can always or even typically be made without reference to factual determinations. Indeed, sometimes findings of fact are necessary to determine whether a given rule of duty applies in a particular case. Here, for example, a factual determination must be made, presumably by the jury, as to whether David *knew or should have known* he was infected at the time of his affair with West. Only if a jury so finds would the duty identified by the court apply.

A question to be revisited throughout our analysis of negligence is why negligence law assigns primary responsibility for the resolution of disputes over the different elements to different actors within the legal system. What is it about the duty issue that renders it appropriate for resolution by judges rather than jurors?

3. *Negligence versus Battery.* Suppose it turns out that David despised Mussivand, and that his entire reason for taking up with West was to pass along his communicable illness to Mussivand. Such a purposeful transmission of a disease to another can constitute the distinct tort of battery. See Chapter 9. David could also be found to have committed a battery if a jury determined that he was *nearly certain* that Mussivand would be infected. Thus, assuming that the STD in question was highly

---

11. R.C. 2305.29 states in pertinent part:

No person shall be liable in civil damages for . . . alienation of affections, or criminal conversation, and no person shall be liable in civil damages for seduction of any person eighteen years of age or older, who is not incompetent. . . .

infectious, it is possible that, had David actually known of his condition, he could be found by a jury to have committed a battery on Mussivand.

4. *Knowledge versus Reason to Know.* Assume for purposes of analysis that David did *not* actually know he was infected, but should have known (say, because he was experiencing symptoms that would reveal to an ordinarily attentive person that he was suffering from an infection). Is it plausible to conclude under these circumstances that David owed a duty to monitor his own health for the benefit of persons such as Mussivand?

5. *Foreseeability and Duty.* Courts faced with duty questions often focus, as did this court, on the issue of whether injury of the type suffered by the plaintiff was foreseeable to a reasonable person in the position of the defendant. As noted above, the foreseeability inquiry is similar to the one described by Justice Brett in Heaven v. Pender: Would a person of ordinary sense recognize that, if she pursued the conduct at issue without vigilance for the physical well-being of others, her conduct would pose a meaningful risk of physical injury to persons in the position of the plaintiff? Framed this way, the foreseeability test for duty seems easily to cover Mussivand. Surely David could recognize that inattentiveness to his infectiousness while he carried on sexual relations with a woman whom he knew to be married (and not separated from her husband) posed a nontrivial risk of injury to her husband.

Does the realm of foreseeability extend further than this? What if, unbeknownst to David, West had another lover, who, without West's knowledge, also became infected. Would foreseeability analysis entail a duty owed by David to *L*? What if West unknowingly transmitted an STD to her friend *F* by donating blood to be transfused into *F* during an operation? Would the court find a duty owed by David to *F*? Suppose David and West were both single and in a noncommitted relationship, such that each was dating and sexually active with several partners. Could David foresee that, if he failed to protect West against infection, he would put her other partners at risk? Is the *Mussivand* court prepared to recognize such a duty? If not, what has happened to the role of "foreseeability" in determining duty?

6. *Multiple and Superseding Causes: A Preview.* Notice the "until" clause that concludes paragraph two of the court's syllabus. It limits the scope of David's liability by specifying that his responsibilities were at an end once West knew or had reason to know that she was infected. Why does that conclusion follow? Suppose they were both careless as to the spread of infection. Why would that fact relieve David of his responsibilities to Mussivand? The issue of how a third party's misconduct affects the attribution of responsibility to a careless defendant is discussed in Chapters 4 and 5. Suppose West should have known of her infection. Would it follow that Mussivand can proceed with a negligence claim against his wife? (In fact, Mussivand did file a separate claim of negligence against West. The Ohio Supreme Court did not address that claim.) The doctrine of interspousal immunity from tort liability is discussed in Chapter 7.

7. *The "Amatory" Torts.* At the end of its opinion, the court distinguishes Mussivand's negligence claim against David — which seeks compensation for physical harms — from claims for "criminal conversation" and "alienation of affections." In most states, these torts were abolished by legislatures in the mid-twentieth century by means of "heart balm" statutes of the sort quoted in footnote 11 of the court's opinion.

Criminal conversation was a euphemism for adultery. The tort of that name originally permitted a husband to sue another man for "seducing" his wife. The theory of the case was that the seducer had "damaged" the husband's property, besmirched his honor, and possibly confused the line of succession to his property (since the paternity of male children was now thrown into doubt). As such, the action was available only to husbands: Wives were "owned," not owners, and husbands' affairs were not regarded as besmirching wifely honor. Alienation of affections likewise permitted a husband to sue another — stereotypically, his in-laws — for officiously intermeddling in his marriage so as to cause his wife to abandon him. In the 1700s and early 1800s, numerous high profile and high stakes criminal conversation actions were filed in English courts and dutifully reported in scandalous detail by the forerunners of modern tabloid newspapers.

When in the second half of the nineteenth century legislatures began according married women the status of full legal persons, the question arose as to whether women could now take advantage of the amatory actions. Most courts concluded that it was only fair to let them do so. By so ruling, however, the courts were forced to reconceptualize the claim underlying these torts. No longer was a husband complaining of destruction of his property, honor, or patrimony. Instead, one spouse was complaining that a third party had shattered his or her domestic bliss — albeit with the apparently active participation of the other spouse. Skepticism as to the existence of causation and injury in many of these cases, doubt as to whether the law is well positioned to provide redress for broken hearts, and evidence that the criminal conversation tort was being used collusively by spouses to generate false proofs of infidelity as a basis for securing illegitimate divorces, led Parliament and most American legislatures to enact statutes abolishing these torts. Where legislatures have not done so, courts often have. *See, e.g.,* Helsel v. Noellsch, 107 S.W.3d 231 (Mo. 2003) (abolishing alienation of affections). In recent years, courts in states that continue to recognize these actions have seen them enjoy a modest revival.

III. QUALIFIED DUTIES OF CARE

As noted in Section II.A, modern courts dealing with negligence cases tend to approach the duty element quite differently depending on the type of negligence claim before them. As we have seen, when the plaintiff alleges that the defendant's *own negligent misfeasance caused another to suffer physical harm*, courts tend to be comfortable positing an unqualified duty of reasonable care owed by the defendant to the plaintiff. However, even in this category, as we learn from *MacPherson* and *Mussivand*, courts will sometimes qualify or limit the duty. Moreover, outside of it, courts often resist the embrace of a general or unqualified duty of reasonable care. This section explores four broad categories of "qualified" or "limited" duty cases.

The first three of these categories involve, respectively, cases in which the defendant is alleged to have:

1. carelessly permitted or maintained hazardous conditions on property in his or her possession (*premises liability* cases);
2. acted without reasonable care for the plaintiff's economic prospects (*"pure" economic loss* cases); and
3. unreasonably failed to act for the benefit or protection of the plaintiff (*affirmative duty* or *duty-to-rescue* cases).

In the fourth category, the defendant is alleged to have

4. engaged in affirmative misconduct so as to risk physical harm to others, yet, even though these allegations bring the case within the "easy" or "unqualified" duty category, courts nonetheless impose limits on the duty owed because pressing reasons of policy warrant the imposition of ad hoc limitations on the unqualified duty (*exemption* cases).

As was noted earlier, a fifth category of "qualified duty" cases — cases in which the plaintiff alleges failure on the part of the defendant to be vigilant of her emotional well-being — is reserved for discussion in Chapter 10.

It is important to emphasize that, in drawing a line between easy and harder duty cases, we are not drawing a distinction between "duty" and "no duty" cases. After all, courts often recognize duties of care in premises liability, pure economic loss, and affirmative duty cases. Instead, it is to note, first, that the duty issue will likely be "in play": The court will be looking to the plaintiff for a showing as to why the defendant was obligated to take care with respect to the plaintiff's interests. (Often, but not always, the showing will consist of an assertion that the parties stood in some relationship, other than strangers to one another, at the time of the alleged tortious conduct. Thus, claims, such as those for pure economic loss, that might be non-actionable absent some sort of preexisting relationship between the parties — such as the infliction of pure economic loss — can become actionable given the existence of such a relationship.) Second, it is to alert you to the fact that, when such duties are recognized, they are likely to be *qualified* by the court rather than treated as creating a broad or unqualified duty of reasonable care. This aspect of more difficult duty cases can be made clearer by consideration of the next case.

A.   *Premises Liability*

Owning or possessing land can be described as a form of conduct. Indeed, the terms *owning* and *possessing* are active verbs: They connote that a person is doing something to or with land or chattel. Yet, as contrasted to the acts of providing medical care to a patient, or driving a car, the conduct involved in possessing land seems quite distinct. Much of the time, possession is passive. Moreover, the conditions on one's property, depending on its size and other characteristics, often exist without any immediate participation of the possessor/owner. In part because land ownership is distinctive in these ways, courts have long recognized special duty rules in cases alleging carelessness in the maintenance of real property. However, as noted below, some courts have questioned whether these rules are still warranted in the modern world.

Salaman v. City of Waterbury
717 A.2d 161 (Conn. 1998)

McDonald, J.   [T]he city of Waterbury (city), appeals from the Appellate Court's decision reversing the trial court's judgment granting the city's motion for judgment notwithstanding the verdict. . . . The jury reasonably could have found the following facts. The plaintiff's decedent drowned while attempting to swim across the East Mountain Reservoir (reservoir) in Waterbury on September 2, 1991. Approximately halfway across the reservoir, he experienced difficulty swimming and called for help. Two people tried to rescue the decedent, but were unsuccessful.

At the time of his death, the decedent was part of a group of people from the defendant New Opportunities for Waterbury, Inc. (NOW), a residential counseling program. Following a picnic and a basketball game, the group, supervised by the defendant Michael Trotman, a residential supervisor employed by NOW, had traveled by van to the reservoir to swim. The reservoir, which was owned by the city, was not surrounded by a fence. There was an area to the side of the access road that was used for parking, and a trail that led to the water. The reservoir had not been used as a public water supply for more than thirty years, and the city allowed fishing with a permit. On occasion, some people may have used the reservoir for swimming. The city, however, did not permit swimming in the reservoir. There were no lifeguards or lifesaving equipment at the reservoir. There were several old signs posted on the reservoir property which read: "City of Waterbury, No Trespassing, Public Water Supply." There were no such signs in the parking area, on any of the trails or at the beach area. The decedent, a twenty-two year old former high school athlete, was an excellent swimmer who had been swimming since childhood.

After the conclusion of the plaintiff's case, the city moved for a directed verdict on all counts. The court . . . denied the motion as to the negligence count that was based on premises liability. The basis for the city's motion for a directed verdict on that count was that the decedent was a trespasser as a matter of law.

In its charge to the jury, the trial court, after explaining the status of a trespasser on a landowner's property, stated: "Therefore, if you find that the plaintiff's decedent, Jaime Salaman, was a trespasser upon the reservoir property, then you must further find the defendant city of

Waterbury owed no duty to [him]. If you find no duty, then you must return a verdict in favor of the defendant city. . . ." The trial court also instructed as to the duty owed a licensee as follows: "But if you find that the group had express or implied authority to be on the premises, then they are licensees. And in order to establish liability as to a licensee, three essential elements must be present. One, that the [city] knew of the presence of the [decedent]; two, that it thereafter failed to . . . warn him of a dangerous condition of which it knew and of which it could not reasonably assume the licensee knew of or which by reasonable use of his faculties would observe; and three, that such failure constituted the proximate cause of the [decedent's] injuries. . . . In order for the plaintiff to prevail, evidence must show that the circumstances were such that the knowledge of [the decedent's] presence could be imputed to the [city]. Such circumstances are sufficient to impute knowledge of presence to the [city] only where they are the equivalent of actual knowledge. This equivalent arises where the [city] could have and should have reasonably anticipated the [decedent's] presence on the premises because of the regular pattern of such presence at the approximate time of day and the place of injury."

The jury returned a verdict in favor of the plaintiff. . . . [T]he city's allocation amounted to $343,354.08. . . . Thereafter, the trial court granted the city's motions to set aside the verdict and for judgment notwithstanding the verdict, concluding that the evidence was insufficient to impose liability on the city. The trial court concluded that trespasser liability could not be imposed as there was no evidence that the city's intentional or reckless conduct caused the drowning. The trial court also concluded that licensee liability could not be imposed because there was insufficient evidence to demonstrate that: (1) the city had actual or constructive knowledge of the presence of the decedent; (2) the city failed to exercise reasonable care by failing to warn him of any dangerous conditions that it reasonably could not have assumed the licensee knew of or by reasonable use of his faculties could observe; and (3) the city's failure to exercise reasonable care caused the decedent's drowning.

The Appellate Court reversed the trial court's judgment, concluding that the jury could have found that the decedent was a licensee because the jury reasonably could have inferred that the city had constructive knowledge of the general public's use of the reservoir for swimming. The Appellate Court concluded that this constructive knowledge gave rise to the duty "to exercise reasonable care to warn . . . of conditions posing an unreasonable risk of harm." On the basis of that conclusion, the Appellate Court further concluded that the verdict should not have been set aside. This appeal followed.

I

. . . The status of an entrant on another's land, be it trespasser, licensee or invitee, determines the duty that is owed to the entrant while he or she is on a landowner's property. . . . In this case, the jury was properly instructed as to the city's duty to the decedent if he was either a trespasser or a licensee. If the decedent was a trespasser, the city's only duty was to refrain from causing him injury "intentionally, or by willful, wanton or reckless conduct." [Citation for quotation marks omitted.] It is undisputed that the city did not intentionally or recklessly injure the decedent and the trial court was correct in its instructions. Therefore, as the Appellate Court observed, the jury must have concluded that the decedent was a licensee or it could not have imposed liability on the city.

"A licensee is a person who is privileged to enter or remain upon land by virtue of the possessor's consent, whether given by invitation or permission." (Internal quotation marks omitted.) Laube v. Stevenson, 137 Conn. 469, 473, 78 A.2d 693 (1951). The duty that a landowner "owes to a licensee . . . does not ordinarily encompass the responsibility to keep the property in a reasonably safe condition, because the licensee must take the premises as he [or she] finds them. . . . If the licensor actually or constructively knows of the licensee's presence on the premises, however, the licensor must use reasonable care both to refrain from actively subjecting him [or her] to danger and to warn him [or her] of dangerous conditions which the possessor knows of but which he [or she] cannot reasonably assume that the licensee knows of or by reasonable use of his [or her] faculties would observe." (Citations omitted; internal quotation marks omitted.) The trial court's instruction to the jury on licensee liability was consistent with these principles and therefore correct.

In order to prove that the decedent was a licensee, the plaintiff was required to prove that the decedent was on the city's land with its permission or by its express or implied invitation. In this case, we need not examine the record to determine if there was some evidence from which the jury reasonably might have concluded that the decedent was a licensee. Even if it is assumed that he was a licensee, we conclude that the evidence does not support a finding that the city breached any duty to the decedent as a licensee.

The plaintiff was required to establish that the city breached the duty owed a licensee. After reviewing the evidence, we conclude that the jury reasonably could not have found that the city breached that duty. There was no claim or evidence to support a finding that the city actively subjected the decedent to danger. The city's duty, therefore, concerned warnings as to the hidden hazards upon its property. The city's duty to a licensee was to warn of "dangerous conditions which the owner knows of but which [the owner] cannot reasonably assume that the licensee knows of or by a reasonable use of [the licensee's] faculties would observe." Laube v. Stevenson, supra, 137 Conn. 474; Deacy v. McDonnell, 131 Conn. 101, 104, 38 A.2d 181 (1944).

The plaintiff argues that, because the reservoir was a dangerous condition, the city was required to post signs advising "Danger: Swimming is absolutely prohibited. No lifeguards on duty. No lifesaving equipment." We cannot conclude, however, that the body of water constituting the reservoir itself should be considered a hidden, dangerous condition and the plaintiff did not offer any evidence indicative of hidden hazards in the reservoir. The city's expert witness inspected the reservoir and testified that it contained no "hidden hazards." He concluded that "there were no drop-offs, there were no currents, there was no underwater debris, there were no waves." There was no contrary evidence.

The plaintiff argues that the decedent should have been warned that there were no lifeguards or lifesaving equipment at the reservoir. Under the circumstances of this case, the dangers of swimming in an unguarded body of water were such that the decedent should have, by the reasonable use of his faculties, been aware of such dangers and no such warning was necessary. Here, there was no evidence that the city encouraged or permitted swimming at the reservoir or that NOW, Trotman, the decedent or anyone else had a permit, invitation or permission to swim there. The city was entitled to assume that any reasonable person would appreciate the risk of drowning while swimming in the reservoir. We conclude that the city was not required to remind adult swimmers of the obvious and commonly known danger of drowning inherent in swimming.

A rule requiring a property owner to post warning signs about the dangers inherent in swimming is unreasonable. In Connecticut, a small state, hundreds of miles of shoreline would be exposed to this unreasonable requirement. Property owners who have water on their land are entitled to assume that a reasonable adult would be aware of the risk of drowning in a body of water.

We conclude that the evidence does not support a finding that the city breached any duty to warn the decedent, an adult swimmer, of hidden dangers. We, therefore, reverse the judgment of the Appellate Court.

NOTES AND QUESTIONS

1. *The Plaintiff-Status Categories.* As the Connecticut Supreme Court notes, even with respect to physical harms, the common law of negligence has created special duty rules for injuries suffered because of dangerous conditions existing on property possessed by another. These rules depend on the status of the plaintiff. In addition to the categories of *trespasser* and *licensee*, discussed by the court, the traditional common law of landowner liability recognizes a third category, that of *invitee*. Like a licensee, an invitee is a person who enters property with the consent of the possessor. Invitees are distinguished as a class because they are invited onto the property for the material benefit of the possessor, or in furtherance of the institutional purpose of the possessor. A paradigmatic example of an invitee is a customer who enters a store to shop there. In contrast to trespassers and licensees, invitees *are* owed reasonable care for their safety.

2. *Ownership, Possession, and Occupation.* A person need not own the property to be treated as a possessor. A tenant who rents an apartment is a possessor of that property for purposes of tort liability. Indeed, even one who unlawfully occupies land can be a possessor for purposes of liability. Also, one who is entitled to occupy land can be held liable as a possessor even if he or she does not exercise that entitlement. *See* Restatement (Second) of Torts § 328E (1965).

3. *Hazardous Conditions versus Hazardous Activities.* It is important to stress that, to the extent special duty rules apply in premises liability

cases, they are designed to address dangerous *conditions* on property — traps, holes, uneven surfaces, etc. — rather than dangerous activities that take place on property. For example, suppose Farmer *F* is driving a large tractor on a path on one edge of his farm. Suppose further that he is driving at an unsafe rate of speed while playing a hand-held electronic game that distracts him from keeping an eye on where he is going. As a result, *F* runs over *P*, who intentionally walks onto the path from a public road. *P* is a trespasser (see Note 4), but a court would likely not apply the special duty rules applicable to trespassers bringing premises liability actions, because in this instance the injury arose not from a dangerous condition on the land, but rather a dangerous activity that happened to take place on the land.

4. *Trespassers.* The trespasser category is not limited to those entering another's land intending to do wrong, such as a burglar or vandal. A trespasser is anyone who intentionally enters property without the possessor's actual or implied permission. Suppose adult hiker *H* unwittingly loses the path of a public trail, proceeds a quarter-mile into woods owned by *O*, and is injured by an unmarked animal trap lawfully placed by *O* on his property. Under the traditional rule, absent special circumstances described in the next note, *H* cannot sue *O* for carelessness in his placement of the traps or for failure to warn of their presence. What might be the justification for such a rule?

5. *Exceptions to the Rule for Trespassers.* The general rule of no duty of care applies only to adult trespassers. By contrast, possessors of property must take reasonable care to avoid causing injuries to child trespassers who are not old enough to appreciate a danger presented by the property. In the early years of the twentieth century, the courts tended to speak in terms of an obligation not to maintain an "attractive nuisance" on one's land — that is, a condition that would pique a child's natural curiosity but that contained a danger that would not be apparent to such a child, such as an artificial pond or swimming pool.

Modern courts tend to regard the attractive nuisance formulation as too restrictive, in that it seems to limit liability to those cases in which the plaintiff can prove that it was the dangerous condition that first drew the child onto the property, as opposed to cases in which the child stumbled onto the danger. The typical modern formulation requires only that the land-possessor have reason to foresee that children might enter the property and be endangered by the condition. *See* Restatement (Second) of Torts § 339 (1965). In addition, many localities have enacted ordinances that protect children against particular dangers. Owners of private swimming pools, for example, are often required by ordinance to erect fences with self-latching gates around swimming pools to prevent young children from accidentally drowning. Plaintiffs can sometimes invoke such ordinances to establish duty (and, in cases of noncompliance, breach). *Compare* Johnson v. Harris, 530 P.2d 1136 (Ariz. Ct. App. 1975) (fencing ordinance and violation thereof establish duty and breach) *with* Osterman v. Peters, 272 A.2d 21 (Md. 1971) (fencing ordinance does not create duty of care to trespassers).

The no-duty-to-trespassers rule also does not apply to adults when the possessor knows, or, based on facts known to her, has reason to know, of the presence of trespassers on the property. For example, when a landowner is aware that individuals often use a portion of her property as a shortcut, she is obligated to warn of dangers along the path, at least if the dangers are not open and obvious.

6. *Licensees versus Invitees.* The classic example of a licensee is a guest who visits the residence of another to attend a social function. As the main opinion indicates, possessors owe licensees a duty only under the special conditions specified by the court. Thus, the disposition of landowner cases not involving trespassers often will hinge on whether the court defines the plaintiff as a licensee or invitee. Although there are relatively clear examples of each category, the line between them is sometimes blurry. Is a person who goes into a store merely to use a restroom on the premises an invitee or a licensee? *See* Martin v. B.P. Exploration & Oil, 769 So. 2d 261 (Miss. Ct. App. 2000) (plaintiff who stops to use gas station restroom is an invitee if the jury determines that a reasonable person would perceive that the station invited the public to use its restrooms irrespective of purchase).

7. *Rejecting the Invitee-Licensee Distinction.* Even assuming that one can coherently place different plaintiffs into the two categories of licensee and invitee, is their distinctive treatment justified? Church *C* fails to notice, when it should have, that its front steps are deceptively and dangerously uneven. If churchgoer *A* is injured on her way to services because of the condition of the steps, she may — absent a special immunity, described in Chapter 7 — sue the church for negligence as an invitee. Now suppose that homeowner *H* fails to notice that the steps to the front door of her home are uneven. Suppose further that *H* invites *B* to come to *H*'s house for Bible study. If *B* trips and injures herself as she enters the house, *B*, as a mere licensee, may not recover. Is this disparate treatment of *A* and *B* warranted? *See* Carter v. Kinney, 896 S.W.2d 926 (Mo. 1995) (person invited to defendant's home for Bible study is a licensee, not an invitee). Dissatisfaction with the licensee-invitee distinction has caused approximately half the states to abolish it, so as to create a duty of reasonable care to all those who enter property by permission, while retaining the traditional common law rules for trespassers. *See, e.g.,* Tantimonico v. Allendale Mut. Ins. Co., 637 A.2d 1056, 1062 (R.I. 1994).

8. *Rowland v. Christian and the Elimination of the Categories.* A smaller group of states has gone further and abolished all three categories in favor of a general duty of reasonable care owed to all persons, regardless of their status. The leading opinion advocating this approach is Rowland v. Christian, 443 P.2d 561 (Cal. 1968).

Rowland stopped by an apartment being rented by Christian. He asked to use the bathroom, and suffered a deep laceration when he grabbed a faucet handle that contained a concealed, jagged crack. Christian apparently knew of the existence of the crack. However, California law prior to *Rowland* was unusual in stating that a possessor of land was under no duty even to *licensees* to take reasonable care to protect them against *known* but hidden dangerous conditions. On the basis of that rule, the lower courts dismissed Rowland's negligence action.

Rather than taking the occasion to bring California law in line with that of most other states by imposing a duty to protect licensees against known but hidden dangers, a majority of the California justices instead voted to abolish altogether the common law categories. It thereby created an unqualified duty rule that would permit all premises liability cases to go to the jury on the question of whether the possessor failed to act with reasonable care for the well-being of any person who is injured by dangerous conditions on the premises. In support of its ruling, the majority emphasized the difficulty of applying the traditional categories and their exceptions, suggesting that they no longer functioned well in modern society. Furthermore, it reasoned:

> A man's life or limb does not become less worthy of protection by the law nor a loss less worthy of compensation under the law because he has come upon the land of another without permission or with permission but without a business purpose. Reasonable people do not ordinarily vary their conduct depending on such matters, and to focus upon the status of the injured party . . . to determine the question whether the landowner has a duty of care, is contrary to our modern social mores and humanitarian values.

Rowland, 443 P.2d at 568.

According to *Rowland*, although the plaintiff's status would henceforth be irrelevant to *duty* analysis in premises liability cases, the jury was entitled to consider that status in deciding the *breach* question of whether the land-possessor failed to take reasonable care. (This raises the question of whether *Rowland* changed the legal inquiry, or simply changed the decision-maker from judge to jury.) Note that, under the *Rowland* formulation, even criminal trespassers would be entitled to bring negligence claims against the owners of premises on which they are injured.

Rowland was a significant decision in several respects. First, it aspired to lead a charge for law reform in this corner of tort law. In that endeavor, it enjoyed partial success. As many as ten states have followed its lead by abolishing the categories outright. More ambitiously, the California court in *Rowland* and other negligence cases decided in the 1960s sought to undermine a range of traditional limits on negligence liability, particularly limited duty rules. As discussed above in connection with *Winterbottom* and *MacPherson*, the court was convinced that abolition of traditional limited duty rules was necessary to rid negligence law of the ghost of its hyper-individualistic and plaintiff-unfriendly past.

9. *Legislative Responses.* Subsequent to *Rowland*, the California legislature enacted statutes that limited the decision in two important respects. First, it immunized possessors from liability to trespassers injured on the premises in the course of committing certain felonies. Thus, for example, courts were once again authorized to dismiss claims brought by would-be robbers against a homeowner for injuries caused to them by dangerous conditions on the property they were attempting to rob.

Second, it created specific exceptions to the duty of reasonable care for plaintiffs who are injured when on another's property for "sport or recreational" uses, such as ice skating on a private pond or driving an all-terrain vehicle in an open field. *See* Cal. Civ. Code §§ 846-847. Like California, most other states have enacted statutes granting "recreational use" immunities to owners of property. Some courts have interpreted these statutes so broadly as to cut back sharply on possessors' common law duties to persons entering the land. For a general discussion, see Dan B. Dobbs, *The Law of Torts* § 238, 620-624 (2000).

10. *Liability to Non-entrants.* What about injuries caused by conditions on land to persons not on the land? Suppose *C*, cycling down a public street, is knocked off his bike by a difficult-to-see, low-hanging branch from a tree on *D*'s property. Was a duty owed by *D* to *C*? The general rule is that *D* is not liable to take care to protect against harms caused by "natural" conditions, such as trees on the land. The Restatement, however, states that *D* may be obligated to take care to ensure that trees on his property do not injure travelers on public roads "where traffic is relatively frequent, land is less heavily wooded, and acreage is small." Restatement (Second) of Torts § 363, comment e (1965). The no-duty rule also does not apply when the danger is posed by "artificial" conditions (man-made structures) created by, or known to, the possessor, as well as to activities undertaken on the property, such as the burning of leaves. *Id*. at §§ 364-370.

11. *Municipal Liability.* As the owners of thousands of miles of sidewalks, cities are commonly sued for unsafe conditions on property. According to New York City authorities, that city has in recent years faced about 14,000 claims per year for sidewalk-related injuries, and has annually paid out about $60 million in damages. (Under city law, an injured plaintiff cannot prevail on a claim alleging failure to correct a sidewalk defect unless the city has received *written* notice of the hazard at least 15 days prior to the incident causing the injury. Although one might have expected this limitation to minimize the city's liability, an association of New York lawyers created the Big Apple Pothole and Sidewalk Corporation, which hires surveyors to walk the city's streets and to mark sidewalk defects, as well as potholes, on a map that is regularly sent to city officials.) In response to the high volume of sidewalk claims, the city enacted in 2003 City Code §§ 7-210 to 7-212, which transfer liability for hazardous conditions on a given stretch of sidewalk to the owner(s) of the property fronted by the stretch of sidewalk. Special provision is made for those who are injured but unable to collect a judgment because of the insolvency of the owner.

12. *Acts of Third Parties on the Premises.* A burgeoning class of negligence claims involves suits against property owners alleging that they failed to take adequate steps to protect tenants or other users of the property from criminal activity on the premises. For example, an office worker who is robbed in an underground parking garage might sue the owner of the office complex for failing to adequately light or patrol the garage, thus

facilitating the robbery. Claims such as these are discussed below in the context of duties to protect and rescue. See Section III.C, *infra*.

B.   *Pure Economic Loss*

As noted at the outset of this chapter, negligence law recognizes loss of wealth as a form of injury. Thus, persons who lose existing wealth, or even expected income, may stand to recover from another who has carelessly caused such a loss. Of course, proof of injury is not enough. The plaintiff must further establish that the injury came about as the result of a breach of a duty to take care not to cause such a loss. As it turns out, negligence law is generally reluctant to recognize duties to look out for another person's wealth. Indeed, whereas actors are generally obligated to take reasonable care not to cause foreseeable *tangible property damage*, they have no such general obligation to avoid depriving persons of intangible property, although they do incur the latter sort of duty in special situations.

The following decision is emblematic of the widespread judicial rejection of a general, unqualified duty to conduct oneself with care not to cause "pure" economic loss to others. The notes that follow the decision further explore those rationales and give illustrations of special situations in which such a duty is recognized. As you read these materials, ask yourself what might justify the sharp line drawn by negligence law between harm to property and loss of wealth.

State of Louisiana v. M/V Testbank
752 F.2d 1019 (5th Cir. 1985) (en banc)

Higginbotham, J.   We are asked to abandon physical damage to a proprietary interest as a prerequisite to recovery for economic loss in cases of unintentional maritime tort. We decline the invitation.

I

In the early evening of July 22, 1980, the M/V SEA DANIEL, an inbound bulk carrier, and the M/V TESTBANK, an outbound container ship, collided at approximately mile forty-one of the Mississippi River Gulf outlet. At impact, a white haze enveloped the ships until carried away by prevailing winds, and containers aboard TESTBANK were damaged and lost overboard. The white haze proved to be hydrobromic acid and the contents of the containers which went overboard proved to be approximately twelve tons of pentachlorophenol, PCP, assertedly the largest such spill in United States history. The United States Coast Guard closed the outlet to navigation until August 10, 1980 and all fishing, shrimping, and related activity was temporarily suspended in the outlet and four hundred square miles of surrounding marsh and waterways.

Forty-one lawsuits were filed and consolidated before the same judge in the Eastern District of Louisiana. These suits presented claims of shipping interests, marina and boat rental operators, wholesale and retail seafood enterprises not actually engaged in fishing, seafood restaurants, tackle and bait shops, and recreational fishermen. They proffered an assortment of liability theories, including [negligence]. . . .

Defendants moved for summary judgment as to all claims for economic loss unaccompanied by physical damage to property. The district court granted the requested summary judgment as to all such claims except those asserted by commercial oystermen, shrimpers, crabbers and fishermen who had been making a commercial use of the embargoed waters. The district court found these commercial fishing interests deserving of a special protection akin to that enjoyed by seamen. . . .

On appeal a panel of this court affirmed, concluding that claims for economic loss unaccompanied by physical damage to a proprietary interest were not recoverable in maritime tort. . . . Judge Wisdom specially concurred, agreeing that the denial of these claims was required by precedent, but urging reexamination en banc. We then took the case en banc for that purpose. After extensive additional briefs and oral argument, we are unpersuaded that we ought to drop physical damage to a proprietary interest as a prerequisite to recovery for economic loss. . . . Ultimately we conclude that without this limitation foreseeability loses much of its ability to function as a rule of law. . . .

III

The meaning of Robins Dry Dock v. Flint, 275 U.S. 303, 48 S. Ct. 134, 72 L. Ed. 290 (1927) (Holmes, J.) is the flag all litigants here seek to capture. We turn first to that case and to its historical setting.

Robins . . . applied a principle, then settled both in the United States and England, which . . . denied a plaintiff recovery for economic loss if that loss resulted from physical damage to property in which he had no proprietary interest. . . .

1

In *Robins*, the time charterer of a steamship sued for profits lost when the defendant dry dock negligently damaged the vessel's propeller. The propeller had to be replaced, thus extending by two weeks the time the vessel was laid up in dry dock, and it was for the loss of use of the vessel for that period that the charterer sued. The Supreme Court denied recovery to the charterer, noting:

> . . . no authority need be cited to show that, as a general rule, at least, a tort to the person or property of one man does not make the tort-feasor liable to another merely because the injured person was under a contract with that other unknown to the doer of the wrong (citation omitted). The law does not spread its protection so far.

275 U.S. at 309, 48 S. Ct. at 135. . . .

2

The principle that there could be no recovery for economic loss absent physical injury to a proprietary interest was not only well established when *Robins Dry Dock* was decided, but was remarkably resilient as well. Its strength is demonstrated by the circumstance that *Robins Dry Dock* came ten years after Judge Cardozo's shattering of privity in MacPherson v. Buick Motor Co., 217 N.Y. 382, 111 N.E. 1050 (1916). . . . Indeed this limit on liability stood against a sea of change in the tort law. Retention of this conspicuous bright-line rule in the face of the reforms brought by the increased influence of the school of legal realism is strong testament both to the rule's utility and to the absence of a more "conceptually pure" substitute. The push to delete the restrictions on recovery for economic loss lost its support and by the early 1940's had failed. *See* W. Prosser, *Law of Torts* § 129, at 938-940 (4th ed. 1971). In sum, it is an old sword that plaintiffs have here picked up. . . .

IV

Plaintiffs urge that the requirement of physical injury to a proprietary interest is arbitrary, unfair, and illogical, as it denies recovery for foreseeable injury caused by negligent acts. At its bottom the argument is that questions of remoteness ought to be left to the trier of fact. Ultimately the question becomes who ought to decide — judge or jury — and whether there will be a rule beyond the jacket of a given case. . . .

Those who would delete the requirement of physical damage have no rule or principle to substitute. Their approach fails to recognize limits upon the adjudicating ability of courts. We do not mean just the ability to supply a judgment; prerequisite to this adjudicatory function are preexisting rules, whether the creature of courts or legislatures. Courts can decide cases without preexisting normative guidance but the result becomes less judicial and more the product of a managerial, legislative or negotiated function.

Review of the foreseeable consequences of the collision of the SEA DANIEL and TESTBANK demonstrates the wave upon wave of successive economic consequences and the managerial role plaintiffs would have us assume. The vessel delayed in St. Louis may be unable to fulfill its obligation to haul from Memphis, to the injury of the shipper, to the injury of the buyers, to the injury of their customers. Plaintiffs concede, as do all who attack the requirement of physical damage, that a line would need to be drawn — somewhere on the other side, each plaintiff would say in turn, of its recovery. Plaintiffs advocate not only that the lines be drawn elsewhere but also that they be drawn on an ad hoc and discrete basis. The result would be that no determinable measure of the limit of foreseeability would precede the decision on liability. We are told that when the claim is too remote, or too tenuous, recovery will be denied. Presumably then, as among all plaintiffs suffering foreseeable economic loss, recovery will turn on a judge or jury's decision. There will be no rationale for the differing results save the "judgment" of the trier of fact. Concededly, it can "decide" all the claims presented, and with comparative if not absolute ease. The point is not that such a process cannot be administered but rather that its judgments would be much less the products of a determinable rule of law. In this important sense, the resulting decisions would be judicial products only in their draw upon judicial resources.

The bright line rule of damage to a proprietary interest, as most, has the virtue of predictability with the vice of creating results in cases at its edge that are said to be "unjust" or "unfair." Plaintiffs point to seemingly perverse results, where claims the rule allows and those it disallows are juxtaposed — such as vessels striking a dock, causing minor but recoverable damage, then lurching athwart a channel causing great but unrecoverable economic loss. The answer is that when lines are drawn sufficiently sharp in their definitional edges to be reasonable and predictable, such differing results are the inevitable result — indeed, decisions are the desired product. But there is more. The line drawing sought by plaintiffs is no less arbitrary because the line drawing appears only in the outcome — as one claimant is found too remote and another is allowed to recover. The true difference is that plaintiffs' approach would mask the results. The present rule would be more candid, and in addition, by making results more predictable, serves a normative function. It operates as a rule of law and allows a court to adjudicate rather than manage. . . .

VII

. . . Denying recovery for pure economic losses is a pragmatic limitation on the doctrine of foreseeability, a limitation we find to be both workable and useful. . . .

Accordingly, the decision of the district court granting summary judgment to defendants on all claims for economic losses unaccompanied by physical damage to property is AFFIRMED.

Gee, J. (concurring) (joined by Clark, C.J.) . . .

. . . [T]he dispute-resolution systems of courts are poorly equipped to manage disasters of [this] magnitude and that we should be wary of adopting rules of decision which, as would that contended for by the dissent, encourage the drawing of their broader aspects before us.

An exhaustive study of the deficiencies of applying a mechanism originally developed to decide who owns title to Blackacre, or whether it was Smith or Jones who ran the stop sign in his wagon, to the management of general disasters is beyond either the demands of this writing or the competence and available time of its writer. . . .

. . . Such a system as ours works tolerably well in the traditional case for which it was developed, where the stakes are limited to who owns the farm or to some other finite benefit. Its deficiencies become immediately and painfully apparent, however, when the consideration of factors inherently extraneous to the dispute becomes necessary or desirable to resolving it. Of these factors, perhaps the most often encountered is that of financial reality. . . . The . . . problem arises whenever individual courts contemporaneously grant sweeping awards against the same entity, perhaps a governmental one, in unconnected causes. However just each particular award may be, the cumulative effect — produced by individual proceedings to which questions of fiscal limitations and necessary trade-offs are foreign and irrelevant — may be irrational. It follows that we should decline to adopt rules of decision which set ourselves such tasks, tasks that are of their nature beyond our competence to deal with justly. Because I believe that the well-intentioned rule advanced for adoption by the dissent is such a one, and that the rule of the majority roughly and approximately restrains us to matters within the competence of our procedures, I join in the majority opinion. . . .

Wisdom, J. (dissenting) (joined by Rubin, Politz, Tate and Johnson, JJ.) . . .

With deference to the majority, I suggest, notwithstanding their well reasoned opinion, that the utility derived from having a "bright line" boundary does not outweigh the disutility caused by the limitation on recovery imposed by the physical-damage requirement. *Robins* and its progeny represent a wide departure from the usual tort doctrines of foreseeability and proximate cause. . . .

Foreseeability provides a mechanism for limiting claims . . . related to the accident. The requirement of foreseeability precludes recovery for damages resulting from gains that are allegedly lost because the accident altered the course of events upon which the expected gain was predicated. For example, the law should not compensate a shipper for purely speculative profits. Such predictions of the future are limitless in variety and incalculable in scope. Foreseeability requires that we confine the scope of claims to those arising from activities in process at the time of the accident or to claims that can be proven with certainty.

. . . [A] plaintiff must [also] assert a "particular" damage that distinguishes him from the general population. . . . In a maritime accident, a business suffers "particular" damages to the extent that the accident prevents the business from engaging in primary maritime activities, such as fishing or use of the waterways, or supplying commodities or services vital to primary maritime activities, such as those of bait and tackle shops, drydocks, marinas, and seafood wholesalers or processors. All other losses . . . not peculiar to maritime activities are part of the general economic dislocation caused by the accident and are . . . not "particular." . . .

Shrimpers, crabbers, oystermen, and other commercial fishermen who routinely operated in those parts of the Mississippi River Gulf Outlet and the surrounding areas that were temporarily closed by the Coast Guard should recover. It is foreseeable that a ship carrying PCP might be in a collision and that some of the PCP containers might be lost overboard. . . . It is also foreseeable that a PCP spill would result in the closure of fishing areas. Commercial fishermen have suffered damages that are proximately caused by this closure. Finally, they have suffered "particular" damages because, unlike members of the general public, the tort has denied them their livelihood in the maritime industry. . . .

The land-based businesses that have claimed damages include drydocks, marinas, bait and tackle shops, seafood processors, seafood wholesalers, and restaurants. It is here that drawing the line becomes difficult, for these businesses have been affected by the PCP spill, but all would agree that a seafood restaurant in New Orleans should not recover for a loss of business from consumers' concern over contaminated products.

The general test of recovery for these claimants is whether their business of supplying a vital commodity or service to those engaged in the maritime industry has been interrupted by the collision, the closure, or the embargo. Marinas, for example, in the afflicted area should be allowed to recover. If all shipping and boating is suspended, then a marina or drydock in the area affected is unable to supply docking or repair services to users of the waterway. . . . Bait and tackle shops present a similar situation: The condemnation of a large fishing area damages or destroys the livelihood of those shops whose business is exclusively predicated upon supplying direct inputs (bait, fuel) to those whose commercial undertakings have been foreclosed by the quarantine and embargo. . . . Finally, seafood processors and seafood wholesalers that provide services for the condemned area should recover.

There is a point beyond which we cannot allow recovery. Seafood restaurants, for example, are not providers of a vital service to the afflicted area. . . . The bar would [also] arise . . . if a bait and tackle shop were only partially connected with a foreclosed area. Basically, a claim for damages that is indistinguishable from a general grievance furnishes no basis for recovery. . . .

The advantages of this alternate rule of recovery are that it compensates damaged plaintiffs, imposes the cost of damages upon those who have caused the harm, is consistent with economic principles of modern tort law, and frees courts from the necessity of creating a piecemeal quilt of exceptions to avoid the harsh effects of the *Robins* rule. . . .

It is true that application of foreseeability and proximate causation would necessitate case-by-case adjudication. But I have a more optimistic assessment of courts' ability to undertake such adjudication than the majority.[38] Certainly such an inquiry would be no different from our daily task of weighing such claims in other tort cases.

I would apply a rule of recovery based on conventional tort principles of proximate cause and foreseeability and limit eligibility only by the requirement that a claimant prove "particular" damages.

Rubin, J. (dissenting) (joined by Wisdom, Politz and Tate, JJ.) . . .
I agree with Judge Gee and Chief Judge Clark that the subject calls for legislative consideration and that the necessary application of principle accompanied by suitable line drawing can be better accomplished by

---

38. The majority opinion favors a bright line rule, as opposed to a case-by-case determination of liability, because it enables courts to "adjudicate" rather than to "manage." A bright line rule such as the one the majority proposes, however, requires no adjudication whatsoever. Judges need merely to preside over a self-executing system of limited liability where recovery is predicated upon an easily determined physical injury. The application of such a rule, rather than a case-by-case determination, seems more "management" than adjudication.

statute. However, I would not await such action. . . . The constitutional grant of jurisdiction to federal courts over cases and controversies . . . empowers and requires us to decide . . . cases within our jurisdiction . . . even when we think Congress should have acted and has not done so.

Robins should not be extended beyond its actual holding and should not be applied in cases like this, for the result is a denial of recompense to innocent persons who have suffered a real injury as a result of someone else's fault. We should not flinch from redressing injury because Congress has been indifferent to the problem.

NOTES AND QUESTIONS

1. *Federal Courts and Federal versus State Law.* The typical negligence action is brought in state court. In turn, resolution of the substantive issues posed by that suit—such as the existence or nonexistence of a duty owed by the defendant to the plaintiff—are determined by the application of state tort law. (Whether to apply the law of the state in which the court sits, or some other state's law, is an issue addressed by rules governing "conflicts of law.") Sometimes, however, tort suits fall within the jurisdiction of the federal courts, and may be brought there. *Testbank* provides an example of such a suit. It was decided by a federal court—the Court of Appeals for the Fifth Circuit—rather than a state court. When a tort claim is brought in federal court, a special set of procedural issues arise. You will likely cover these issues in detail in Civil Procedure. Here we aim to give you only the most basic information about them.

The most common basis by which plaintiffs with ordinary tort claims can get into federal court is when the plaintiff and defendant reside in different states. If, for example, *D* injures *P*, and *P* is a resident of New York and *D* a resident of New Jersey, then, subject to certain qualifications, *P* may bring a tort suit against *D* in federal court. By contrast, if both *P* and *D* are New Yorkers, a suit purely based on common law tort claims could not be brought in federal court. The authority of federal courts to hear conventional tort and contract claims between citizens of different states is known as the federal courts' *diversity jurisdiction*.

When such suits are brought, the question arises: Whose tort law should govern? Prior to 1938, the answer was that the federal courts were free to shape their own substantive common law of tort, without regard to state law. In that year, however, the U.S. Supreme Court decided Erie R.R. v. Tompkins, 304 U.S. 64. *Erie* is complex, but its basic message is that federal courts entertaining cases on the basis of diversity jurisdiction have no authority to set substantive rules in areas such as tort and contract. (The same rule sometimes applies when federal jurisdiction rests on grounds other than diversity, but we can leave those cases aside.) Thus, a federal court adjudicating the P v. D suit described above would today have to apply *state* tort law to resolve questions of duty, breach, etc. Most likely, the court would apply the tort law of New York or New Jersey.

The *Erie* rule that federal courts presiding over diversity cases must apply state law does *not* apply to "procedural" rules such as the rule that sets the legal standard as to when a court may grant summary judgment. Also, it does not apply to suits brought in federal court on other jurisdictional bases. For example, Congress long ago passed the Federal Employers' Liability Act (FELA), 45 U.S.C. §§ 51 *et seq.*, which by its terms empowers railroad workers to sue for injuries caused to them by the carelessness of their employers. Railroad workers can bring suit in federal court under FELA regardless of diversity, and their suits are governed by the substantive rules set in the statute, not state tort law. (As we will see, a federal court faced with a question of statutory construction of FELA is not barred from consulting state tort law for guidance on how to interpret FELA. Still, it is not bound to do so.)

As state tort law would not control the disposition of a suit brought under the provisions of the FELA statute, so too it did not control in *Testbank* for a related reason. Federal courts enjoy a separate grant of jurisdiction to hear maritime tort claims, that is, claims arising out of accidents occurring on the navigable waters of the United States. Thus, because the plaintiffs in *Testbank* were invoking a separate body of federal admiralty law, the Fifth Circuit Court of Appeals was left to fashion a federal-law rule of duty. The federal rule adopted by the majority is more or less in line with the rule contained in the tort law of most states, not because the federal courts are obligated to apply state law (as they are in diversity cases), but because they look for guidance from state law in fashioning federal maritime law.

2. *En Banc.* Federal appellate court decisions are ordinarily made by panels consisting of three judges. The "en banc" designation in the caption of *Testbank* indicates that this decision was rendered with the participation of all the judges then sitting on the Fifth Circuit Court of Appeals. En banc decisions are rendered after a decision has been issued by a three-judge panel, usually after one or more members of that panel has identified an issue that he or she suggests is worthy of consideration by all members of the Circuit. Different circuits follow different rules, but usually a case cannot be heard en banc unless an absolute majority of the circuit's judges vote in favor of so proceeding. Some state high courts that allow appeals to be decided by less than the full membership of the court also sit en banc.

3. *Quasi-Property?* The next four notes consider possible rationales for the absence of an unqualified duty to take care to avoid causing economic loss to another. We can begin this exploration by considering on what grounds one might distinguish the claims of the commercial fishermen, which the *Testbank* court permits to go forward, from those of the businesses who are denied the right to recover. Is the suggestion that damage to tangible property is sufficient to support an award for pure economic loss even when the person who suffers loss does not "own" the property, but rather has a right to use it? Why is that an intelligible line to draw? Consider in this regard J'Aire Corp. v. Gregory, 598 P.2d 60 (Cal. 1979). There, a restaurant operated in space leased from an airport. The airport authority hired a contractor to undertake repairs on the airport. As a result of the contractor's negligence, the restaurant was

closed for a period of time and lost business. The California Supreme Court held that the contractor owed a duty to the lessee/restaurant. Is the reasoning of *J'Aire* consistent with the holding in *Robins*?

4. *Floodgates.* Some have argued that policy considerations of excessive litigation and liability are foremost in justifying the general no-duty rule. Consider, for example, then-Judge, now Justice, Breyer's opinion in a case very similar to *Testbank*.

> . . . The number of persons suffering foreseeable financial harm in a typical accident is likely to be far greater than those who suffer . . . physical harm. . . . That possibility—a large number of different plaintiffs each with somewhat different claims—in turn threatens to raise significantly the cost of even relatively simple tort actions. Yet the tort action is already a very expensive administrative device for compensating victims of accidents. . . .
>
> [Another] set of considerations focuses on the "disproportionality" between liability and fault. . . . [L]iability for pure financial harm, insofar as it proved vast, cumulative and inherently unknowable in amount, could create incentives that are perverse. . . . Might not unbounded liability for foreseeable financial damage, for example, make auto insurance premiums too expensive for the average driver?

Barber Lines A/S v. M/V Donau Maru, 764 F.2d 50, 54-55 (1st Cir. 1985). Are judges in a good position to make the various claims on which Breyer relies? Suppose it were the case that one could confidently predict non-ruinous levels of liability—should recovery then be permitted? In any event, why should an actor be excused from liability simply because his conduct threatens to generate many lawsuits, or a great deal of harm? Today, if a manufacturer physically injures a large number of people by selling a defective product, tort law ordinarily will require it to compensate all of its victims, if it can do so. Why is economic loss different?

5. *Proportionality.* Some commentators have fastened on the vast potential scope of liability for negligently inflicted economic loss as supporting a fairness argument against the imposition of such liability. Professor Rabin, for example, suggests that judicial concern that liability not be disproportionate to the nature of the defendant's wrongdoing explains the absence of a general duty to take care not to cause economic loss. Suppose the owner of the M/V TESTBANK is made to pay a total of $25 million to all of the fishermen, dock owners, and others who suffered injuries that are compensable under the majority's rule. Suppose further that the carelessness proved at trial amounted to an error on the part of the TESTBANK's captain in plotting the course of the ship, combined with a failure to maintain an adequate lookout as she proceeded out into the Gulf of Mexico. Would the liability be proportionate to the wrong?

6. *A Hierarchy of Interests and Duties.* Others have argued that enforcement of a general duty to take care to avoid causing economic losses would run against basic principles of liberalism (and capitalism). Professor Perry, for example, has noted that a person's interest in maintaining his wealth is already more vulnerable to interferences through

perfectly lawful means such as market competition, boycotts, and true but unfavorable publicity. Negligence law, he suggests, is rendered consistent with the law's assignment of second-class status to this interest by not according it general protection, but instead protecting it only in certain specified situations.

7. *The* People Express *decision.*   A prominent state case purporting to reject the majority rule is People Express Airlines, Inc. v. Consolidated Rail Corp., 495 A.2d 107 (N.J. 1985). Defendant Conrail negligently operated trains in its yard so as to cause a chemical fire that required the evacuation and temporary closure of plaintiff's nearby airport terminal, which in turn resulted in lost bookings and flight cancellations, but no tangible property damage. Relying in part on *Testbank*'s willingness to permit recovery by the commercial fishermen in that case, the New Jersey Supreme Court held that actors owe a general duty to take care not to cause economic injury to "particular plaintiffs or plaintiffs comprising an identifiable class with respect to whom defendant knows or has reason to know are likely to suffer such damages from its conduct." *Id.* at 116. Distinguishing drivers who happened to be delayed while passing in the vicinity of the fire, or salespersons who happened to be delayed in traveling because of the fire, the court held that economic injury to People Express, as the owner of a nearby airport terminal, was "particularly foreseeable" to Conrail. Is this reasoning really inconsistent with the general rule? How broad a scope of responsibility does it entail?

8. *Accountants' Liability.*   The rule against recovery in negligence for pure economic loss admits of important exceptions. Perhaps the most important of these is a recognized duty on the part of accountants to take reasonable care in conducting audits of their clients' finances so as not to mislead certain creditors of the client. The scope of this duty, however, varies significantly by jurisdiction.

An early and relatively narrow recognition of accountants' malpractice liability is Ultramares Corp. v. Touche, 174 N.E. 441, 447 (N.Y. 1931). Touche, an accounting firm, was hired by Fred Stern & Co. to review Stern's records and prepare a balance sheet that Touche was to certify as providing an accurate reflection of the company's assets and debts. Touche knew that it was hired to perform this function so that Stern could present copies of the certified balance sheet to creditors whenever it might need to convince them that the company was in sound financial health and thus in a position to pay back creditors' loans. Touche failed to realize that certain listings of assets in Stern's books were false, a fact that could have been readily discovered if proper accounting procedures were followed. As a result, Touche certified Stern to be in sound financial health when in fact it was insolvent.

Plaintiff, a company that had loaned money to Stern in reliance on Touche's audit, sued Touche for negligently causing it to lose the value of the loan when Stern defaulted. The court, in an opinion by Judge Cardozo, rejected the idea that accountants owe a broad duty of reasonable care to all those who might foreseeably rely on the results of its audits. However, the opinion also reaffirmed earlier decisions recognizing that such a duty is owed to a third-party creditor if the accountant knew or should have known that the audit was being undertaken specifically in order to facilitate a particular transaction between the audited company and that creditor.

Subsequent courts have expanded the scope of this duty, holding that it is owed to any identifiable third party who might be expected to rely on the accuracy of the audit. *See* Bethlehem Steel Corp. v. Ernst & Whinney, 822 S.W.2d 592 (Tenn. 1991) (surveying different rules for accountants' liability to third-party creditors and adopting the majority rule of Restatement (Second) of Torts § 552).

9. *Other Situations Supporting a Duty to Take Care Not to Cause Economic Loss.* Tort duties to take care not to cause pure economic loss are owed by other actors besides accountants, including attorneys. Suppose *A* hires lawyer *L* to draft a will under which all of *A*'s assets will pass upon her death to her favorite nephew *N. L* negligently drafts the will, so that it is invalid, as a result of which the assets go to *A*'s son *S* and not to *N.* May *N* sue *L* for negligently causing *N* to lose claim to the assets? The majority of the courts to consider the question have answered yes. *See, e.g.,* Lucas v. Hamm, 364 P.2d 685 (Cal. 1961). In part, the majority rule has been supported by the notion that only disappointed beneficiaries will have an incentive to sue negligent estate lawyers, since the estate itself usually suffers no economic harm as a result of the lawyer's error.

The majority rule was rejected by the Texas Supreme Court in Barcelo v. Elliot, 923 S.W.2d 575 (Tex. 1996). The *Barcelo* court was concerned that recognition of a duty of care owed to beneficiaries would interfere with the attorney's primary obligation to his client. It also expressed concern over disruption of the disposition of wills, offering the following example: "Suppose . . . that a properly drafted will is simply not executed at the time of the testator's death. The document may express the testator's true intentions, lacking signatures solely because of the attorney's negligent delay. On the other hand, the testator may have postponed execution because of second thoughts regarding the distribution scheme." *Id.* at 578. One of two dissenting judges in *Barcelo* countered that "these are matters subject to proof, as in all other cases. . . . The Court fails to consider that the beneficiaries will in each case bear the burden of establishing that the attorney breached a duty to the testator, which resulted in damages to the beneficiaries. Lawyers, wishing to protect themselves from liability, may document the testator's intentions." *Id.* at 581 (Cornyn, J.).

The Texas Supreme Court revisited attorney liability to nonclients in McCamish, Martin, Brown & Loeffler v. F.E. Appling Interests, 991 S.W.2d 787 (Tex. 1999). There, plaintiff, a real estate developer, was locked in a dispute with a bank that had promised to finance certain construction. The dispute was resolved by a settlement agreement under which all debts owed by the developer to the bank were forgiven. To be effective, the debt forgiveness provision had to be formally approved by the bank's board. Defendants, lawyers for the bank, told the developer that the settlement had been approved, when in fact it had not. As a result, the settlement was later deemed ineffective.

Plaintiff sued for negligent misrepresentation. The attorneys, however, argued that *Barcelo* foreclosed attorney liability to nonclients.

The court rejected this argument, drawing a sharp distinction between lawyer *malpractice* and negligent *misrepresentation*. Liability for misrepresentations, according to the court, would not pose a danger of unlimited liability, in part because lawyers can control to whom they make such representations.

C. Affirmative Duties to Rescue and Protect

An important category of negligence cases raising duty issues concerns suits in which the plaintiff cannot allege affirmative misconduct by the defendant, but rather claims that the defendant failed to act in a situation where action on his part would have prevented plaintiff's injury. In the language of the common law, these cases allege negligence in the form of careless *nonfeasance* rather than careless *misfeasance*.

Like the categories of licensee and invitee, the categories of nonfeasance and misfeasance admit both of clear examples and close calls. A straightforward example of negligent nonfeasance would be the following case. Defendant *D*, taking a stroll in a public park with a swimming hole, happens to come upon stranger *S*, who is flailing in the water. Although he could do so at no risk to himself, *D* declines to throw a nearby life preserver to *S*, who drowns. As *D* played no role in bringing about *S*'s peril, and merely stood by as an inert observer, *D*'s conduct is described as nonfeasance. At the opposite extreme, suppose *D* is a boat owner who invites *S* onto his boat. *D* drives carelessly, executing a series of turns at excessive speed. As a result, the boat capsizes, pinning *S* underwater and drowning him. Clearly, this is an instance of misfeasance — negligent operation of the boat.

Although the distinction between misfeasance and nonfeasance is sometimes equated with a distinction between acting and omitting to act, that equation has to be handled with care. Suppose *C*, operating his car on a city street at a reasonable speed, sees pedestrian *P* lawfully in a crosswalk in front of him but does nothing to turn or stop the car, thus hitting *P* when he could have avoided doing so. If we consider only the temporal sequence immediately prior to the accident, one can intelligibly say *C* did not undertake an affirmative act — he did not turn the wheel of the car toward *P*, did not press his foot down on the accelerator, etc. Rather, he merely "omitted" to apply his brakes. Still, few would describe this as an instance of nonfeasance, or as *C* failing to rescue or protect *P*. Rather, we would assess *C*'s failure to change course or apply his brakes in light of the fact that he had earlier in the time sequence commenced driving. In other words, *C*'s omissions were part of *a bundle of acts and omissions* that is appropriately described as *misfeasance* in the form of careless driving. As this example indicates, drawing the line between misfeasance and nonfeasance will often require judgments about which among the various features of a defendant's conduct ought to be taken into account.

However drawn in particular cases, the nonfeasance-misfeasance distinction has important implications for duty analysis. The general duty to take care not to cause foreseeable physical injury or property damage applies to *mis*feasance. Thus, duty in these cases is ordinarily presumed.

More or less the opposite presumption — the absence of a duty of care — attaches to true instances of nonfeasance, such as that of the indifferent passerby who fails to rescue the drowning man. To say the same thing, a plaintiff must establish special circumstances in order to prevail on a claim of negligent nonfeasance. Again, the presence or absence of a preexisting relationship between plaintiff and defendant is one such special circumstance that will affect duty analysis.

Osterlind v. Hill
160 N.E. 301 (Mass. 1928)

Braley, J.   This is an action of tort, brought by the plaintiff as administrator of the estate of Albert T. Osterlind to recover damages for the conscious suffering and death of his intestate. There are four counts in the original declaration and five counts in the amended declaration, to each of which the defendant demurred. The first count of the original declaration alleges that, on or about July 4, 1925, the defendant was engaged in the business of letting for hire pleasure boats and canoes to be used on Lake Quannapowitt in the town of Wakefield; that it was the duty of the defendant to have a reasonable regard for the safety of the persons to whom he let boats and canoes; that the defendant, in the early morning of July 4, 1925, in willful, wanton, or reckless disregard of the natural and probable consequences, let for hire, to the intestate and one Ryan, a frail and dangerous canoe, well knowing that the intestate and Ryan were then intoxicated, and were then manifestly unfit to go upon the lake in the canoe; that, in consequence of the defendant's willful, wanton, or reckless disregard of his duties, the intestate and Ryan went out in the canoe, which shortly afterwards was overturned and the intestate, after hanging to it for approximately one-half hour, and making loud calls for assistance, which calls the defendant heard and utterly ignored, was obliged to release his hold, and was drowned; that in consequence of the defendant's willful, wanton, or reckless conduct the intestate endured great conscious mental anguish and great conscious physical suffering from suffocation and drowning. Count 2 differs materially from count 1 only in so far as negligent conduct is alleged as distinguished from willful, wanton, or reckless conduct. . . . The amended declaration adds allegations to the effect that the plaintiff's intestate and Ryan were intoxicated and incapacitated to enter into any valid contract or to exercise any care for their own safety and that the condition of the intestate was involuntary and induced through no fault of his own.

The trial court sustained demurrers to both the original and amended declarations and reported the case for the determination of this court.

. . . The declaration must set forth facts which, if proved, establish the breach of a legal duty owed by the defendant to the intestate. . . .

In the case at bar . . . it is alleged in every count of the original and amended declaration that after the canoe was overturned the intestate hung to the canoe for approximately one-half hour and made loud calls for assistance. On the facts stated in the declaration the intestate was not in a helpless condition. He was able to take steps to protect himself.

The defendant [thus] violated no legal duty in renting a canoe to a man in the condition of the intestate. . . .

In view of the absence of any duty to refrain from renting a canoe to a person in the condition of the intestate, the allegations of involuntary intoxication relating as they do to the issues of contributory negligence become immaterial. The allegations of willful, wanton or reckless conduct also add nothing to the plaintiff's case. The failure of the defendant to respond to the intestate's outcries is immaterial. No legal right of the intestate was infringed. The allegation common to both declarations that the canoe was "frail and dangerous" appears to be a general characterization of canoes. It is not alleged that the canoe was out of repair and unsafe.

It follows that the order sustaining each demurrer is affirmed.

Theobald v. Dolcimascola
690 A.2d 1100 (N.J. App. Div. 1997)

Dreier, J.   Plaintiffs, Colleen Theobald as Administrator . . . for the heirs of Sean Theobald and as administrator of his estate, and Colleen Theobald and Harold Theobald (the parents of the late Sean Theobald), individually, appeal from summary judgments dismissing their complaint against the three remaining defendants, Michael Dolcimascola, Robert Bruck, and Amy Flanagan. . . .

On January 20, 1991, plaintiffs' decedent, Sean Theobald, was in the second floor bedroom of his house with five of his friends. His father was downstairs watching television. The friends had gathered at 6:00 P.M. for a birthday party for one of the friends, Robert Bruck. The other teenagers present were Charles Henn, Michael Dolcimascola, Amy Flanagan and Katherine Gresser. At some time during the evening, the decedent produced an unloaded revolver and ammunition, both of which were examined by all of the teenagers. The discussion turned toward another friend of theirs who had died playing Russian Roulette, and the decedent indicated that he also would try the "game." According to the predominant version of the varying testimony, Sean put a bullet into the gun, pointed it at his head and pulled the trigger several times. He then put the gun down, checked the cylinder, and tried again three or four more times. The gun then went off, killing him. Other versions had the gun going off on the first occasion he tried, or the gun firing by accident without his putting the barrel to his head. There was, however, ample testimony that there were several attempts made while the five other teenagers merely sat around and watched. The trial judge determined that if none of the teenagers actively participated, they had no duty to stop the decedent, and therefore summary judgment was entered.

I

The first question before us is whether any of the defendants, if they were mere observers to this tragic event, can be held civilly liable to plaintiffs. We are at a loss for a viable theory. Had this been a joint endeavor in which all were participating in the "game" of Russian Roulette, there is some authority that each of the participants in the enterprise might be held responsible, although the only cases we have been able to retrieve involve the criminal responsibility of participants. There is no reason to suppose that if the participants could be found criminally responsible, they could not also be held civilly liable. A line, however, has been drawn by the courts between being an active participant and merely being one who had instructed a decedent how to "play" Russian Roulette. In the latter case, a defendant was determined to be free of any potential criminal liability. Lewis v. State, 474 So. 2d 766, 771 (Ala. Crim. App. 1985). Another court, in dictum, stated that inducing an individual to engage in Russian Roulette creates a sufficiently foreseeable harm to engender potential civil liability.

The most comprehensive New Jersey statement of the existence of a duty to another was expressed in Wytupeck v. City of Camden, 25 N.J. 450, 136 A.2d 887 (1957). Although the case involved the question of liability for the use of a dangerous instrumentality on defendant's land, the case explored when a duty to act arises in inter-personal relationships:

> "Duty" is not an abstract conception; and the standard of conduct is not an absolute. Duty arises out of a relation between the particular parties that in right[,] reason and essential justice enjoins the protection of the one by the other against what the law by common consent deems an unreasonable risk of harm, such as is reasonably foreseeable. In the field of negligence, duty signifies conformance "to the legal standard of reasonable conduct in the light of the apparent risk"; the essential question is whether "the plaintiff's interests are entitled to legal protection against the defendant's conduct." Prosser on Torts, (2d ed., section 36). Duty is largely grounded in the natural responsibilities of social living and human relations, such as have the recognition of reasonable men; and fulfillment is had by a correlative standard of conduct. [25 N.J. at 461-62 (some citations omitted).]

If defendants had either been participants or had induced decedent to play Russian Roulette, or even if there had been some other factor by which we could find a common enterprise, then defendants may have had a duty to act to protect Sean from the consequences of his foolhardy actions. Such a duty would nevertheless invoke the usual principles of comparative negligence. Cf. Yount v. Johnson, 121 N.M. 585, 915 P.2d 341, 342-43 (N.M. Ct. App. 1996) (addressing the term "duty"). The problem with such potential liability, however, is the significant factor of a decedent's own negligence which, when measured against any participant's breach of a duty of care, would probably preclude recovery in most cases.

What we are left with in the case before us, positing that there was no proof of encouragement or participation, is a claim which is grounded in a common law duty to rescue. As has been explained in texts and reiterated in case law, there is no such duty, except if the law imposes it based upon some special relationship between the parties. See W. Page Keeton, et al., Prosser and Keaton on Torts, § 56, at 375 (5th ed. 1984) ("The law has persistently refused to impose on a stranger the moral obligation of common humanity to go to the aid of another human being who is in danger, even if the other is in danger of losing his life."); J.D. Lee and Barry

A. Lindahl, Modern Tort Law, § 3.07, at 36 (1994 and Supp. 1996) ("With regard to rescues, it has been stated that the general rule is that there is no liability for one who stands idly by and fails to rescue a stranger. . . ."); Restatement (Second) of Torts, § 314 (1965) ("The fact that the actor realizes or should realize that action on his part is necessary for another's aid or protection does not of itself impose upon him a duty to take such action."). The Restatement's Illustration 1 is instructive. It posits the actor, A, viewing a blind man, B, stepping into the street in the path of an approaching automobile, where a word or touch by A would prevent the anticipated harm. The Restatement concludes that "A is under no duty to prevent B from stepping into the street, and is not liable to B."

Recent New Jersey decisions have focused upon the exceptions to this general rule and involve situations where a duty to act exists as a result of the relationship between the parties, namely, police-arrestee (Del Tufo v. Township of Old Bridge, 147 N.J. 90, 685 A.2d 1267 (1996); Hake v. Manchester Township, 98 N.J. 302, 486 A.2d 836 (1985)) and physician-patient (Olah v. Slobodian, 119 N.J. 119, 574 A.2d 411 (1990)). These cases also address the liability of a ship's captain for failing to attempt to rescue a drowning seaman.

All of these cases are distinguishable from the situation before us, assuming the five observers were mere bystanders upon whom the law places no duty to have protected the decedent. While we may deplore their inaction, we, as did the trial judge, find no legal authority to impose liability. We note the ease with which defendants could have reached out and taken away the revolver when Sean put it down between his two series of attempted firings, or the simple act of one of the five walking to the door and summoning Sean's father, or even remonstrating with Sean concerning his actions. But such acts would have been no more or less than the simple preventatives given in the Restatement Illustration of a word or touch necessary to save a blind pedestrian. Where there is no duty, there is no liability. We recognize that the Supreme Court in Wytupeck v. City of Camden, *supra,* has defined duty as a flexible concept:

> "Duty" is not a rigid formalism according to the standards of a simpler society, immune to the equally compelling needs of the present order; duty must of necessity adjust to the changing social relations and exigencies and man's relation to his fellows; and accordingly the standard of conduct is care commensurate with the reasonably foreseeable danger, such as would be reasonable in the light of the recognizable risk, for negligence is essentially "a matter of risk . . . that is to say of recognizable danger of injury."

[Wytupeck v. City of Camden, *supra*, 25 N.J. at 462 (citation omitted).] But, if a legally actionable duty is to be found in a situation such as the one before us, it must be declared by the Supreme Court.

II

[The Appellate Division then remanded the case for a re-determination by the trial judge as to whether to admit into evidence certain testimony excluded at the first trial, which tended to show that some of the defendants had a more active role in Sean's death. — EDS.]

In sum, we determine that there was no common law duty owed by defendants to the decedent if defendants were mere observers of his shooting. If, however, there is admissible evidence against one or more of the defendants that they participated in deceiving the decedent into assuming the weapon was not loaded when in fact one of them had placed a bullet in the cylinder, then liability may be imposed against such defendant or defendants for such conduct.

NOTES AND QUESTIONS

1. *Ames on Primitive versus Modern Law.* The absence of a general duty to take reasonable steps to rescue has long been a source of academic commentary. Writing in 1908, Professor Ames opined that the no-duty rule is a vestige of "primitive" law which, in its overriding need for clarity and simplicity, adopted formal, across-the-board rules — such as the blanket rule of no duty to rescue — that rode roughshod over basic principles of ordinary morality. Ames proposed that modern tort law could afford to align itself more closely with morality by recognizing a limited duty to rescue others from imminent physical danger where performing the rescue would cause little or no inconvenience to the rescuer.

2. *Epstein and Liberalism.* Contrary to Ames, others have argued that, even if there is a moral duty to rescue strangers, such a duty should not be recognized in the law. Professor Epstein argues, among other things, that the law would violate basic principles of liberalism if it required more of individuals than simply refraining from injuring others. Epstein also argues that it is impossible to draw a principled line between a duty to rescue someone in imminent peril and a more general duty of beneficence, which, for example, would impose liability on individuals for failing to donate a portion of their earnings to prevent persons from starving to death.

Epstein has drawn responses from various quarters. Professor Heyman has argued that classical liberalism recognized a duty on each citizen to assist government officials in maintaining order and protecting the rights of all citizens. He further claims that this theory found expression in common law, which imposed criminal liability on individuals who failed to take steps to prevent serious crimes. Finally, he suggests that it would be consistent with this tradition to recognize tort liability running parallel to this criminal liability. Against Epstein, Professor Weinrib has argued that a limited duty to rescue can be distinguished from a more general duty of beneficence.

3. *Statutory Recognition of a General Duty.* A few states have enacted generally applicable statutes requiring all persons, on pain of fine or even a short stint in prison, to render aid to others in peril. Vermont's Duty to Aid the Endangered Act, VT. Stat. Ann. Tit. 12, 519(a),

which imposes a limited duty to rescue another in imminent peril, is the broadest in the United States. *See also* Wis. Stat. Ann. § 940.34 (a person who knows that a crime is being committed that exposes its victim(s) to bodily harm has a duty to summon police or intervene when he can do so without danger to himself and without ignoring duties owed to others). Confusingly, these provisions sometimes appear within "good Samaritan statutes" which, as discussed in Note 6, below, immunize voluntary rescuers from tort liability for negligence. *See, e.g.,* Wis. Stat. Ann. § 940.34(3) (incorporating Wisconsin rescuer-immunity provision).

General duty-to-rescue statutes are more frequently found outside the United States, particularly in civil law countries such as France, although there is little evidence of enforcement on either side of the Atlantic. This nominal contrast between American and French law was much discussed in 1997, when Princess Diana died in a Paris car crash, and it was thought that paparazzi trailing her car took photographs of the wreck instead of rendering assistance. (The photographers were eventually cleared.) Is any purpose served in enacting under-enforced or unenforced statutes of this sort?

4. *Common Law Exception: Imminent Peril to Plaintiff Caused by Defendant.* The rule of no duty to make a reasonable attempt at rescue is subject to a number of important exceptions. In examining these exceptions, it is important to stress that, for each, the duty in question is not a duty actually to accomplish a rescue, but rather a duty to *make reasonable efforts* to rescue.

A widely, although not universally, recognized exception to the rule arises when the actor knows or should know that he has by his own conduct caused the victim to be physically injured and at risk of further injury, or physically imperiled. Under such circumstances, the actor has a duty to make reasonable efforts to prevent the victim from suffering further harm, or to prevent the risk of harm from being realized. *See* Restatement (Second) of Torts §§ 321-322 (1965). This exception applies in cases in which the defendant injures or imperils the plaintiff through a wrongful act. *See* Heffern v. Perry, 2000 Conn. Super. LEXIS 2708 (2000) (person who buys narcotics for consumption by another has duty to assist that other when he overdoses). According to the Restatement provisions cited above, it also applies in some instances in which the defendant innocently injures or imperils the plaintiff. So, for example, if through no fault of its own, a railroad company's train collides with the victim's truck, causing injuries to the victim that leave him unable to seek medical attention, the railroad's employees thereby incur a duty to make reasonable efforts to secure medical care for the plaintiff. *See* Maldonado v. S. Pac. Transp. Co., 629 P.2d 1001 (Ariz. Ct. App. 1981).

Osterlind appears to have involved an instance of innocent imperilment: The defendant's decision to rent a canoe to the intoxicated decedent was deemed by the court not wrongful, but it seems to have played a role in the decedent coming to face an imminent risk of drowning. Thus, if Section 321 of the Second Restatement — or, for that matter, Section 321 of the First Restatement, which stated roughly the same rule in 1934 — were applied to the case, the decedent's estate presumably would have stood to recover. However, the Massachusetts Supreme Judicial Court has never adopted Section 321 or 322 (and has never purported to overrule *Osterlind*). *See* Panagakos v. Walsh, 749 N.E.2d 670 (Mass. 2001) (noting that the court has yet to adopt Section 321 or 322 and refusing to invoke them as a basis for imposing a duty on friends of the 18-year-old decedent to take steps to prevent him from being run over as he walked home in an intoxicated state after they helped him gain entry to a bar by using fake I.D.s). Why should a causal connection to a plaintiff's peril create a duty to make reasonable rescue efforts? Some scholars, including Professor Honoré, have argued that once a person is causally connected to an outcome affecting others, even if only fortuitously, she is morally not at liberty to disavow them entirely.

5. *Common Law Exception: Voluntary Undertakings.* A second exception to the no-duty-to-rescue rule concerns situations in which the defendant has volunteered to protect another from physical injury or property damage, or to rescue another from physical peril. Such a voluntarily assumed duty may arise from a contractual promise or a less formal undertaking. *See* Wicker v. Harmony Corp., 784 So. 2d 660 (La. Ct. App. 2001) (contractor who agrees in contract to ensure safety of workers owes duty to take safeguards against plaintiff-employee from being injured on the job); Wilmington Gen. Hospital v. Manlove, 174 A.2d 135 (Del. 1961) (hospital that customarily accepted emergency patients effectively undertook to provide care to all such patients). Under this exception, does a trade association that voluntarily circulates safety information about above-ground pools owe a duty to update that information when aware of new risks against which it has not warned? *See* Meneely v. S.R. Smith, Inc., 5 P.3d 49 (Wash. Ct. App. 2000) (such a duty exists).

A related exception to the general rule of no duty holds that, once a rescue is voluntarily undertaken, the rescuer owes a duty to the victim to perform the rescue with reasonable care. *Compare* Hurd v. United States, 134 F. Supp. 2d 745 (D.S.C. 2001) (although under no duty to commence a rescue, the Coast Guard owes a duty under South Carolina law to exercise reasonable care once rescue is commenced) *with* Adams v. City of Fremont, 80 Cal. Rptr. 2d 196 (Ct. App. 1998) (police owe no duty to suicidal man to exercise care in their attempts to prevent his suicide). Suppose *V* volunteers to aid motorist *M*, whose car is stalled on a public road. *V* fails to suggest moving the car to the shoulder or turning on its hazard lights. *P*, another driver, crashes into *M*'s car and suffers injury. May *P* sue *V* for failing to go about his rescue of *M* with due care for *P*'s safety? *See* Redman v. Stone, 667 N.E.2d 526 (Ill. App. 1996) (holding that *V* owed a duty of care to *M* but not to *P*).

6. *Good Samaritan Immunities.* Recognition of a duty to take reasonable care in voluntarily performing a rescue has the potential to deter such rescues. In part because of this concern, every state has enacted "good Samaritan" statutes, which immunize certain persons who undertake rescues from liability for negligence — and in some cases, even gross

negligence — in rescuing. These statutes usually are limited in application to "off-duty" professionals, for example, doctors who undertake rescues outside of their ordinary duties. Some also cover volunteer firefighters and even "lay" rescuers. *See* Hirpa v. IHC Hospitals, Inc., 948 P.2d 785 (Utah 1997) (applying Utah good Samaritan statute and upholding it against constitutional challenge). If the statute in question is not explicit as to the persons it covers, should it be interpreted to protect "official" rescuers performing their official duties, such as police officers while on duty? *See* Praet v. Sayreville, 527 A.2d 486 (N.J. App. Div.), *rev. denied*, 532 A.2d 253 (N.J. 1987) (because the purpose of the good Samaritan statute is to encourage rescue, it should not apply to police and fire personnel, who are already under a duty to perform such rescues). In general, these immunities are not understood as designed to shield emergency medical technicians or emergency room doctors and nurses from ordinary malpractice liability.

7. *Common Law Exception: Special Relationships.* A third exception to the rule attaches when a "special relationship" exists between the victim and would-be rescuer. Some well-recognized categories of relationships supporting a duty to rescue include carrier-passenger (e.g., a railroad or airline owes a duty to take reasonable steps to protect and rescue passengers in transit) and landowner-guest. *See* Foster v. Wal-Mart Stores, Inc., 2000 U.S. Dist. LEXIS 6266 (D. Kan. 2000) (store owes duty to customer injured on premises to summon medical personnel). Other relationships that can, at least under certain circumstances, generate an affirmative duty to protect or rescue include: school-student, employer-employee, hospital-patient, and prison-prisoner. *See* Restatement (Third) of Torts: Liability for Physical Harm (Basic Principles) §§ 41-42 (Council Draft No. 4, Nov. 13, 2003) (discussing affirmative duties arising out of special relationships). Does a store owe a duty to "rescue" customers from an armed robber who threatens to injure them unless a cashier hands over cash from the register? *See* Kentucky Fried Chicken v. Superior Court, 927 P.2d 1260 (Cal. 1997) (no duty to rescue by complying with robber's demands).

Finally, courts will sometimes recognize the existence of a special relationship based on the facts of particular cases. A famous example is *Farwell v. Keaton*, 240 N.W.2d 217 (Mich. 1976). Farwell, age 18, and Siegrist, age 16, consumed some beer. After attempting to make conversation with two young women, they were attacked by the women's friends. Siegrist escaped harm, but Farwell was badly beaten. Siegrist gave Farwell some ice to apply to his head, then the two drove around for about two hours, at which time Farwell lay down in the back of the car. At about midnight, Siegrist drove the car to the driveway of Farwell's grandparents' house, unsuccessfully attempted to rouse Farwell, then left him there. Farwell's grandparents discovered him the next morning and took him to the hospital, but he died from the beating. The court held that, as "companions on a social venture," Siegrist owed Farwell a duty to make reasonable efforts to obtain medical care for him, and, alternatively, that the voluntary-undertaking exception applied, and also warranted the recognition of a duty.

Does *Theobald* reject *Farwell?* Can the *Panagakos* decision, mentioned in Note 4, *supra*, be reconciled with *Farwell?*

8. *Reporting Obligations.* Some states have enacted statutes placing a duty on certain individuals who know that a child has suffered injuries, and who have reason to believe those injuries were caused by abuse or neglect, to report their suspicions to authorities. *See, e.g.,* Ham v. Hospital of Morristown, 917 F. Supp. 531 (E.D. Tenn. 1995) (discussing Tennessee's statute, which imposes a duty to report suspected abuse on physicians, teachers, neighbors, and friends of the child(ren) in question). Those who fall within the statute and negligently fail to report suspicions of abuse are subject to a modest fine. What if the report turns out to be erroneous: May the falsely accused parents sue the person who reported the alleged abuse for defamation? The Tennessee statute protects reporting parties against this risk by requiring a parent complaining of a false report to prove that the reporting party was not merely careless, but acted in "bad faith," that is, out of hostility or malice toward the parent. *See* Bryant-Bruce v. Vanderbilt Univ., 974 F. Supp. 1127 (M.D. Tenn. 1997).

Tarasoff v. The Regents of the University of California
551 P.2d 334 (Cal. 1976)

Tobriner, J.   On October 27, 1969, Prosenjit Poddar killed Tatiana Tarasoff. Plaintiffs, Tatiana's parents, allege that two months earlier Poddar confided his intention to kill Tatiana to Dr. Lawrence Moore, a psychologist employed by the Cowell Memorial Hospital at the University of California at Berkeley. They allege that on Moore's request, the campus police briefly detained Poddar, but released him when he appeared rational. They further claim that Dr. Harvey Powelson, Moore's superior, then directed that no further action be taken to detain Poddar. No one warned plaintiffs of Tatiana's peril.

Concluding that these facts set forth causes of action against neither therapists and policemen involved, nor against the Regents of the University of California as their employer, the superior court sustained defendants' demurrers to plaintiffs' second amended complaints without leave to amend.[2] This appeal ensued.

Plaintiffs' complaints predicate liability on two grounds: defendants' failure to warn plaintiffs of the impending danger and their failure to bring about Poddar's confinement pursuant to [California statutory provisions

---

2. The therapist defendants include Dr. Moore, the psychologist who examined Poddar and decided that Poddar should be committed; Dr. Gold and Dr. Yandell, psychiatrists at Cowell Memorial Hospital who concurred in Moore's decision; and Dr. Powelson, chief of the department of psychiatry, who countermanded Moore's decision and directed that the staff take no action to confine Poddar. The police defendants include Officers Atkinson, Brownrigg and Halleran, who detained Poddar briefly but released him; Chief Beall, who received Moore's letter recommending that Poddar be confined; and Officer Teel, who, along with Officer Atkinson, received Moore's oral communication requesting detention of Poddar.

specifying the conditions under which persons can be involuntarily committed for psychological treatment]. Defendants, in turn, assert that they owed no duty of reasonable care to Tatiana and that they are immune from suit under the California Tort Claims Act of 1963.

We shall explain that defendant therapists cannot escape liability merely because Tatiana herself was not their patient. When a therapist determines, or pursuant to the standards of his profession should determine, that his patient presents a serious danger of violence to another, he incurs an obligation to use reasonable care to protect the intended victim against such danger. The discharge of this duty may require the therapist to take one or more of various steps, depending upon the nature of the case. Thus it may call for him to warn the intended victim or others likely to apprise the victim of the danger, to notify the police, or to take whatever other steps are reasonably necessary under the circumstances.

In the case at bar, plaintiffs admit that defendant therapists notified the police, but argue on appeal that the therapists failed to exercise reasonable care to protect Tatiana in that they did not confine Poddar and did not warn Tatiana or others likely to apprise her of the danger. Defendant therapists, however, are public employees. Consequently, [they enjoy statutory immunity for certain "discretionary" acts, including their failure to confine Poddar]. No . . . statutory provision, however, shields them from liability based upon failure to warn Tatiana or others likely to apprise her of the danger. . . .

Plaintiffs therefore can amend their complaints to allege that, regardless of the therapists' unsuccessful attempt to confine Poddar, since they knew that Poddar was at large and dangerous, their failure to warn Tatiana or others likely to apprise her of the danger constituted a breach of the therapists' duty to exercise reasonable care to protect Tatiana.

Plaintiffs, however, plead no relationship between Poddar and the police defendants which would impose upon them any duty to Tatiana, and plaintiffs suggest no other basis for such a duty. Plaintiffs have, therefore, failed to show that the trial court erred in sustaining the demurrer of the police defendants without leave to amend.

1.   Plaintiffs' Complaints . . .

Plaintiffs' first cause of action, entitled "Failure to Detain a Dangerous Patient," alleges that on August 20, 1969, Poddar was a voluntary outpatient receiving therapy at Cowell Memorial Hospital. Poddar informed Moore, his therapist, that he was going to kill an unnamed girl, readily identifiable as Tatiana, when she returned home from spending the summer in Brazil. Moore, with the concurrence of Dr. Gold, who had initially examined Poddar, and Dr. Yandell, assistant to the director of the department of psychiatry, decided that Poddar should be committed for observation in a mental hospital. Moore orally notified Officers Atkinson and Teel of the campus police that he would request commitment. He then sent a letter to Police Chief William Beall requesting the assistance of the police department in securing Poddar's confinement.

Officers Atkinson, Brownrigg, and Halleran took Poddar into custody, but, satisfied that Poddar was rational, released him on his promise to stay away from Tatiana. Powelson, director of the department of psychiatry at Cowell Memorial Hospital, then asked the police to return Moore's letter, directed that all copies of the letter and notes that Moore had taken as therapist be destroyed, and "ordered no action to place Prosenjit Poddar in 72-hour treatment and evaluation facility."

Plaintiffs' second cause of action, entitled "Failure to Warn on a Dangerous Patient," incorporates the allegations of the first cause of action, but adds the assertion that defendants negligently permitted Poddar to be released from police custody without "notifying the parents of Tatiana Tarasoff that their daughter was in grave danger from Prosenjit Poddar." Poddar persuaded Tatiana's brother to share an apartment with him near Tatiana's residence; shortly after her return from Brazil, Poddar went to her residence and killed her. . . .

2. *Plaintiffs Can State a Cause of Action Against Defendant Therapists for Negligent Failure to Protect Tatiana*

The second cause of action can be amended to allege that Tatiana's death proximately resulted from defendants' negligent failure to warn Tatiana or others likely to apprise her of her danger. . . . Defendants, however, contend that in the circumstances of the present case they owed no duty of care to Tatiana or her parents and that, in the absence of such duty, they were free to act in careless disregard of Tatiana's life and safety.

In analyzing this issue, we bear in mind that legal duties are not discoverable facts of nature, but merely conclusory expressions that, in cases of a particular type, liability should be imposed for damage done. As stated in Dillon v. Legg (1968) 68 Cal. 2d 728, 734, 69 Cal. Rptr. 72, 76, 441 P.2d 912, 916: "The assertion that liability must . . . be denied because defendant bears no 'duty' to plaintiff 'begs the essential question — whether the plaintiff's interests are entitled to legal protection against the defendant's conduct. . . . (Duty) is not sacrosanct in itself, but only an expression of the sum total of those considerations of policy which lead the law to say that the particular plaintiff is entitled to protection.' (Prosser, Law of Torts (3d ed. 1964) at pp. 332-333.)"

In the landmark case of Rowland v. Christian (1968) 69 Cal. 2d 108, 70 Cal. Rptr. 97, 443 P.2d 561, Justice Peters recognized that liability should be imposed "for an injury occasioned to another by his want of ordinary care or skill" as expressed in section 1714 of the Civil Code. Thus, Justice Peters, quoting from Heaven v. Pender (1883) 11 Q.B.D. 503, 509 stated: "whenever one person is by circumstances placed in such a position with regard to another . . . that if he did not use ordinary care and skill in his own conduct . . . he would cause danger of injury to the person or property of the other, a duty arises to use ordinary care and skill to avoid such danger."

We depart from "this fundamental principle" only upon the "balancing of a number of considerations"; major ones "are the foreseeability of harm to the plaintiff, the degree of certainty that the plaintiff suffered injury, the closeness of the connection between the defendant's conduct and the injury suffered, the moral blame attached to the defendant's conduct, the policy of preventing future harm, the extent of the burden to the defendant and consequences to the community of imposing a duty to exercise care with resulting liability for breach, and the availability, cost and prevalence of insurance for the risk involved."

The most important of these considerations in establishing duty is foreseeability. As a general principle, a "defendant owes a duty of care to all persons who are foreseeably endangered by his conduct, with respect to all risks which make the conduct unreasonably dangerous." [Quoted authority omitted. — EDS.] As we shall explain, however, when the avoidance of foreseeable harm requires a defendant to control the conduct of another person, or to warn of such conduct, the common law has traditionally imposed liability only if the defendant bears some special relationship to the dangerous person or to the potential victim. Since the relationship between a therapist and his patient satisfies this requirement, we need not here decide whether foreseeability alone is sufficient to create a duty to exercise reasonably [sic] care to protect a potential victim of another's conduct.

Although, as we have stated above, under the common law, as a general rule, one person owed no duty to control the conduct of another,[5] nor to warn those endangered by such conduct, the courts have carved out an exception to this rule in cases in which the defendant stands in some special relationship to either the person whose conduct needs to be controlled or in a relationship to the foreseeable victim of that conduct. Applying this exception to the present case, we note that a relationship of defendant therapists to either Tatiana or Poddar will suffice to establish a duty of care; as explained in section 315 of the Restatement Second of Torts, a duty of care may arise from either "(a) a special relation . . . between the actor and the third person which imposes a duty upon the actor to control the third person's conduct, or (b) a special relation . . . between the actor and the other which gives to the other a right of protection."

Although plaintiffs' pleadings assert no special relation between Tatiana and defendant therapists, they establish as between Poddar and defendant therapists the special relation that arises between a patient and his doctor or psychotherapist. Such a relationship may support affirmative duties for the benefit of third persons. Thus, for example, a hospital must exercise reasonable care to control the behavior of a patient which may endanger other persons.[7] A doctor must also warn a patient if the patient's

5. This rule derives from the common law's distinction between misfeasance and nonfeasance, and its reluctance to impose liability for the latter. Morally questionable, the rule owes its survival to "the difficulties of setting any standards of unselfish service to fellow men, and of making any workable rule to cover possible situations where fifty people might fail to rescue . . ." (Prosser, Torts (4th ed. 1971) s 56, p. 341). Because of these practical difficulties, the courts have increased the number of instances in which affirmative duties are imposed not by direct rejection of the common law rule, but by expanding the list of special relationships which will justify departure from that rule.

7. When a "hospital has notice or knowledge of facts from which it might reasonably be concluded that a patient would be likely to harm himself *or others* unless preclusive measures were taken, then the hospital must use reasonable care in the circumstances to

condition or medication renders certain conduct, such as driving a car, dangerous to others.[8]

Although the California decisions that recognize this duty have involved cases in which the defendant stood in a special relationship both to the victim and to the person whose conduct created the danger,[9] we do not think that the duty should logically be constricted to such situations. Decisions of other jurisdictions hold that the single relationship of a doctor to his patient is sufficient to support the duty to exercise reasonable care to protect others against dangers emanating from the patient's illness. The courts hold that a doctor is liable to persons infected by his patient if he negligently fails to diagnose a contagious disease, or, having diagnosed the illness, fails to warn members of the patient's family.

Since it involved a dangerous mental patient, the decision in Merchants Nat. Bank & Trust Co. of Fargo v. United States (D.N.D. 1967) 272 F. Supp. 409 comes closer to the issue. The Veterans Administration arranged for the patient to work on a local farm, but did not inform the farmer of the man's background. The farmer consequently permitted the patient to come and go freely during nonworking hours; the patient borrowed a car, drove to his wife's residence and killed her. Notwithstanding the lack of any "special relationship" between the Veterans Administration and the wife, the court found the Veterans Administration liable for the wrongful death of the wife. . . .

Defendants contend, however, that imposition of a duty to exercise reasonable care to protect third persons is unworkable because therapists cannot accurately predict whether or not a patient will resort to violence. In support of this argument amicus representing the American Psychiatric Association and other professional societies cites numerous articles which indicate that therapists, in the present state of the art, are unable reliably to predict violent acts; their forecasts, amicus claims, tend consistently to overpredict violence, and indeed are more often wrong than right. Since predictions of violence are often erroneous, amicus concludes, the courts should not render rulings that predicate the liability of therapists upon the validity of such predictions. . . .

_____

prevent such harm." (Vistica v. Presbyterian Hospital (1967) 67 Cal. 2d 465, 469, 62 Cal. Rptr. 577, 580, 432 P.2d 193, 196.) (Emphasis added.) A mental hospital may be liable if it negligently permits the escape or release of a dangerous patient (Semler v. Psychiatric Institute of Washington, D.C. (4th Cir. 1976) 44 U.S.L.Week 2439; Underwood v. United States (5th Cir. 1966) 356 F.2d 92; Fair v. United States (5th Cir. 1956) 234 F.2d 288). Greenberg v. Barbour (E.D. Pa. 1971) 322 F. Supp. 745, upheld a cause of action against a hospital staff doctor whose negligent failure to admit a mental patient resulted in that patient assaulting the plaintiff.

8. Kaiser v. Suburban Transp. System (1965) 65 Wash. 2d 461, 398 P.2d 14; see Freese v. Lemmon (Iowa 1973) 210 N.W.2d 576 (concurring opn. of Uhlenhopp, J.).

9. Ellis v. D'Angelo (1953) 116 Cal. App. 2d 310, 253 P.2d 675, upheld a cause of action against parents who failed to warn a babysitter of the violent proclivities of their child; Johnson v. State of California (1968) 69 Cal. 2d 782, 73 Cal. Rptr. 240, 447 P.2d 352, upheld a suit against the state for failure to warn foster parents of the dangerous tendencies of their ward; Morgan v. City of Yuba (1964) 230 Cal. App. 2d 938, 41 Cal. Rptr. 508, sustained a cause of action against a sheriff who had promised to warn decedent before releasing a dangerous prisoner, but failed to do so.

We recognize the difficulty that a therapist encounters in attempting to forecast whether a patient presents a serious danger of violence. Obviously we do not require that the therapist, in making that determination, render a perfect performance; the therapist need only exercise "that reasonable degree of skill, knowledge, and care ordinarily possessed and exercised by members of (that professional specialty) under similar circumstances." Within the broad range of reasonable practice and treatment in which professional opinion and judgment may differ, the therapist is free to exercise his or her own best judgment without liability; proof, aided by hindsight, that he or she judged wrongly is insufficient to establish negligence.

In the instant case, however, the pleadings do not raise any question as to failure of defendant therapists to predict that Poddar presented a serious danger of violence. On the contrary, the present complaints allege that defendant therapists did in fact predict that Poddar would kill, but were negligent in failing to warn.

Amicus contends, however, that even when a therapist does in fact predict that a patient poses a serious danger of violence to others, the therapist should be absolved of any responsibility for failing to act to protect the potential victim. In our view, however, once a therapist does in fact determine, or under applicable professional standards reasonably should have determined, that a patient poses a serious danger of violence to others, he bears a duty to exercise reasonable care to protect the foreseeable victim of that danger. While the discharge of this duty of due care will necessarily vary with the facts of each case,[11] in each instance the adequacy of the therapist's conduct must be measured against the traditional negligence standard of the rendition of reasonable care under the circumstances. . . .

The risk that unnecessary warnings may be given is a reasonable price to pay for the lives of possible victims that may be saved. We would hesitate to hold that the therapist who is aware that his patient expects to attempt to assassinate the President of the United States would not be obligated to warn the authorities because the therapist cannot predict with accuracy that his patient will commit the crime.

Defendants further argue that free and open communication is essential to psychotherapy; that "Unless a patient . . . is assured that . . . information (revealed by him) can and will be held in utmost confidence, he will be reluctant to make the full disclosure upon which diagnosis and treatment . . . depends." (Sen. Com. on Judiciary, comment on Evid. Code, § 1014.) The giving of a warning, defendants contend, constitutes a breach of trust which entails the revelation of confidential communications.

We recognize the public interest in supporting effective treatment of mental illness and in protecting the rights of patients to privacy, and the consequent public importance of safeguarding the confidential character of psychotherapeutic communication. Against this interest, however, we

---

11. Defendant therapists and amicus also argue that warnings must be given only in those cases in which the therapist knows the identity of the victim. We recognize that in some cases it would be unreasonable to require the therapist to interrogate his patient to discover the victim's identity, or to conduct an independent investigation. But there may also be cases in which a moment's reflection will reveal the victim's identity. The matter thus is one which depends upon the circumstances of each case. . . .

must weigh the public interest in safety from violent assault. The Legislature has undertaken the difficult task of balancing the countervailing concerns. In Evidence Code section 1014, it established a broad rule of privilege to protect confidential communications between patient and psychotherapist. In . . . section 1024, the Legislature created a specific and limited exception to the psychotherapist-patient privilege: "There is no privilege . . . if the psychotherapist has reasonable cause to believe that the patient is in such mental or emotional condition as to be dangerous to himself or to the person or property of another and that disclosure of the communication is necessary to prevent the threatened danger."

We realize that the open and confidential character of psychotherapeutic dialogue encourages patients to express threats of violence, few of which are ever executed. Certainly a therapist should not be encouraged routinely to reveal such threats; such disclosures could seriously disrupt the patient's relationship with his therapist and with the persons threatened. To the contrary, the therapist's obligations to his patient require that he not disclose a confidence unless such disclosure is necessary to avert danger to others, and even then that he do so discreetly, and in a fashion that would preserve the privacy of his patient to the fullest extent compatible with the prevention of the threatened danger.

The revelation of a communication under the above circumstances is not a breach of trust or a violation of professional ethics; as stated in the Principles of Medical Ethics of the American Medical Association (1957), section 9: "A physician may not reveal the confidence entrusted to him in the course of medical attendance . . . [u]nless he is required to do so by law or unless it becomes necessary in order to protect the welfare of the individual or of the community." We conclude that the public policy favoring protection of the confidential character of patient-psychotherapist communications must yield to the extent to which disclosure is essential to avert danger to others. The protective privilege ends where the public peril begins.

Our current crowded and computerized society compels the interdependence of its members. In this risk-infested society we can hardly tolerate the further exposure to danger that would result from a concealed knowledge of the therapist that his patient was lethal. If the exercise of reasonable care to protect the threatened victim requires the therapist to warn the endangered party or those who can reasonably be expected to notify him, we see no sufficient societal interest that would protect and justify concealment. The containment of such risks lies in the public interest. For the foregoing reasons, we find that plaintiffs' complaints can be amended to state a cause of action against defendants Moore, Powelson, Gold, and Yandell and against the Regents as their employer, for breach of a duty to exercise reasonable care to protect Tatiana. . . .

Turning now to the police defendants, we conclude that they do not have any such special relationship to either Tatiana or to Poddar sufficient to impose upon such defendants a duty to warn respecting Poddar's violent intentions. Plaintiffs suggest no theory, and plead no facts that give rise to any duty to warn on the part of the police defendants absent such a special relationship. They have thus failed to demonstrate that the trial court erred in denying leave to amend as to the police defendants.

3.   Defendant Therapists Are Not Immune from Liability for Failure to Warn

[The court next concluded that a state statutory provision granting immunity from tort liability to public employees for their discretionary acts did not bar plaintiffs' claims against the therapist defendants for failure to warn. For a discussion of immunities for the performance of discretionary functions, see Chapter 7. The Court also concluded that other statutes did grant the therapist and police defendants immunity from liability for failure to confine Poddar. — Eds.]. . . .

Mosk, J. (concurring and dissenting).   I concur in the result in this instance only because the complaints allege that defendant therapists did in fact predict that Poddar would kill and were therefore negligent in failing to warn of that danger. Thus the issue here is very narrow: we are not concerned with whether the therapists, pursuant to the standards of their profession, "should have" predicted potential violence; they allegedly did so in actuality. Under these limited circumstances I agree that a cause of action can be stated. . . .

Clark, J. (dissenting).   [Justice Clark first asserted that the duty recognized by the majority was inconsistent with California statutory law protecting the confidentiality of patient-therapist communications. He next turned to the majority's common law analysis. — Eds.]

Generally, a person owes no duty to control the conduct of another. Exceptions are recognized only in limited situations where (1) a special relationship exists between the defendant and injured party, or (2) a special relationship exists between defendant and the active wrongdoer, imposing a duty on defendant to control the wrongdoer's conduct. The majority does not contend the first exception is appropriate to this case.

Policy generally determines duty. Principal policy considerations include foreseeability of harm, certainty of the plaintiff's injury, proximity of the defendant's conduct to the plaintiff's injury, moral blame attributable to defendant's conduct, prevention of future harm, burden on the defendant, and consequences to the community.

Overwhelming policy considerations weigh against imposing a duty on psychotherapists to warn a potential victim against harm. While offering virtually no benefit to society, such a duty will frustrate psychiatric treatment, invade fundamental patient rights and increase violence.

The importance of psychiatric treatment and its need for confidentiality have been recognized by this court. . . .

Assurance of confidentiality is important for three reasons.

DETERRENCE FROM TREATMENT

First, without substantial assurance of confidentiality, those requiring treatment will be deterred from seeking assistance. It remains an unfortunate fact in our society that people seeking psychiatric guidance tend to become stigmatized. Apprehension of such stigma — apparently increased by the propensity of people considering treatment to see themselves in the worst possible light—creates a well-recognized reluctance to seek aid. This reluctance is alleviated by the psychiatrist's assurance of confidentiality.

FULL DISCLOSURE

Second, the guarantee of confidentiality is essential in eliciting the full disclosure necessary for effective treatment. The psychiatric patient approaches treatment with conscious and unconscious inhibitions against revealing his innermost thoughts. "Every person, however well-motivated, has to overcome resistances to therapeutic exploration. These resistances seek support from every possible source and the possibility of disclosure would easily be employed in the service of resistance." [Quoted authority omitted. — EDS.] Until a patient can trust his psychiatrist not to violate their confidential relationship, "the unconscious psychological control mechanism of repression will prevent the recall of past experiences." (Butler, Psychotherapy and *Griswold*: Is Confidentiality a Privilege or a Right? (1971) 3 Conn. L. Rev. 599, 604.)

SUCCESSFUL TREATMENT

Third, even if the patient fully discloses his thoughts, assurance that the confidential relationship will not be breached is necessary to maintain his trust in his psychiatrist—the very means by which treatment is effected. . . . Patients will be helped only if they can form a trusting relationship with the psychiatrist. All authorities appear to agree that if the trust relationship cannot be developed because of collusive communication between the psychiatrist and others, treatment will be frustrated.

Given the importance of confidentiality to the practice of psychiatry, it becomes clear the duty to warn imposed by the majority will cripple the use and effectiveness of psychiatry. Many people, potentially violent—yet susceptible to treatment—will be deterred from seeking it; those seeking it will be inhibited from making revelations necessary to effective treatment; and, forcing the psychiatrist to violate the patient's trust will destroy the interpersonal relationship by which treatment is effected.

VIOLENCE AND CIVIL COMMITMENT

By imposing a duty to warn, the majority contributes to the danger to society of violence by the mentally ill and greatly increases the risk of civil commitment—the total deprivation of liberty—of those who should not be confined. The impairment of treatment and risk of improper commitment resulting from the new duty to warn will not be limited to a few patients but will extend to a large number of the mentally ill. Although under existing psychiatric procedures only a relatively few receiving treatment will ever present a risk of violence, the number making threats is huge, and it is the latter group—not just the former—whose treatment will be impaired and whose risk of commitment will be increased.

Both the legal and psychiatric communities recognize that the process of determining potential violence in a patient is far from exact, being fraught with complexity and uncertainty. . . .[5] In fact precision has not even been attained in predicting who of those having already committed violent acts will again become violent, a task recognized to be of much simpler proportions.

This predictive uncertainty means that the number of disclosures will necessarily be large. As noted above, psychiatric patients are encouraged to discuss all thoughts of violence, and they often express such thoughts. However, unlike this court, the psychiatrist does not enjoy the benefit of overwhelming hindsight in seeing which few, if any, of his patients will ultimately become violent. Now, confronted by the majority's new duty, the psychiatrist must instantaneously calculate potential violence from each patient on each visit. The difficulties researchers have encountered in accurately predicting violence will be heightened for the practicing psychiatrist dealing for brief periods in his office with heretofore nonviolent patients. And, given the decision not to warn or commit must always be made at the psychiatrist's civil peril, one can expect most doubts will be resolved in favor of the psychiatrist protecting himself.

Neither alternative open to the psychiatrist seeking to protect himself is in the public interest. The warning itself is an impairment of the psychiatrist's ability to treat, depriving many patients of adequate treatment. It is to be expected that after disclosing their threats, a significant number of patients, who would not become violent if treated according to existing practices, will engage in violent conduct as a result of unsuccessful treatment. In short, the majority's duty to warn will not only impair treatment of many who would never become violent but worse, will result in a net increase in violence.

The second alternative open to the psychiatrist is to commit his patient rather than to warn. Even in the absence of threat of civil liability, the doubts of psychiatrists as to the seriousness of patient threats have led psychiatrists to overcommit to mental institutions. This overcommitment has been authoritatively documented in both legal and psychiatric studies. This practice is so prevalent that it has been estimated that "as many as twenty harmless persons are incarcerated for every one who will commit a violent act." (Steadman & Cocozza, Stimulus/Response: We Can't Predict Who Is Dangerous (Jan. 1975) 8 Psych. Today 32, 35.)

5. A shocking illustration of psychotherapists' inability to predict dangerousness, cited by this court in People v. Burnick, . . . 14 Cal. 3d 306, 326-327, fn.17, 121 Cal. Rptr. 488, 535 P.2d 352, is cited and discussed in Ennis, Prisoners of Psychiatry: Mental Patients, Psychiatrists, and the Law (1972): "In a well-known study, psychiatrists predicted that 989 persons were so dangerous that they . . . would have to be kept in maximum security hospitals. . . . Then, because of a United States Supreme Court decision, those persons were transferred to civil hospitals. After a year, the Department of Mental Hygiene reported that one-fifth of them had been discharged to the community, and over half had agreed to remain as voluntary patients. During the year, only 7 of the 989 committed or threatened any act that was sufficiently dangerous to require retransfer to the maximum security hospital. Seven correct predictions out of almost a thousand is not a very impressive record. . . . Other studies, and there are many, have reached the same conclusion: psychiatrists simply cannot predict dangerous behavior." (Id. at p. 227.) . . .

Given the incentive to commit created by the majority's duty, this already serious situation will be worsened. . . .

NOTES AND QUESTIONS

1. *The Special Obligations of Physicians?* How much of the *Tarasoff* court's holding rests on the superior ability of professional psychiatrists and psychologists to assess accurately the intentions of their patients? Suppose Poddar had confessed his intentions to his lawyer, or his best friend. Under the majority's analysis, would either of them be under the same duty to warn Tatiana? Some victims of shootings by students at schools have attempted to sue the shooters' friends, parents, guidance counselors, and teachers for failing to take steps to prevent the shootings. *See, e.g.,* James v. Wilson, 95 S.W.3d 875 (Ky. App. 2002) (rejecting, on various grounds, claims of negligence brought on behalf of victims of a school shooting against parents, fellow students, and teachers of the shooters).

2. *Contagious Diseases.* Most states have statutes that require physicians who are aware of a patient having a contagious disease to report that fact to public health officials. As indicated in the majority opinion in *Tarasoff*, some courts have also recognized a common law duty on the part of a physician to protect immediate family members, as well as significant others, from contracting infectious diseases diagnosed in the patient. *See* DiMarco v. Lynch Homes-Chester County, 583 A.2d 422 (Pa. 1990) (physicians aware that nurse may have contracted hepatitis from accidental needle-stick owed duty to nurse's boyfriend, who contracted hepatitis from nurse, to convey accurate information about duration of latency period for hepatitis). This duty to warn has sometimes been extended to cases in which the diagnosis suggests a heightened risk not from infection by the patient, but from the source that caused the patient's illness. *See* Bradshaw v. Daniel, 854 S.W.2d 865 (Tenn. 1993) (physician who diagnoses patient with Rocky Mountain Spotted Fever has duty to warn patient's family members that they may have been exposed to ticks carrying the disease).

3. *Duty and Causation.* Our concern in this chapter is the duty issue, but it is worth noting that many cases involving failure to warn raise difficult issues of causation. Consider, for example, a suit brought by *P*, who contracts an infectious disease from *Q*, a patient of physician *D*. Because *D* may be under legal requirements of confidentiality — and because *D* may be unaware of *P*'s existence — *P* would stand to benefit from the omitted warning only if (1) *D* transmitted a warning to *Q*; (2) *Q* in turn informed *P* of the risk of infection; and (3) *Q* and *P* then altered their behavior to avoid infection. On what basis can a trier of fact determine whether *Q* would have actually transmitted a warning to *P*, or whether *Q* and *P* would have acted on that information? Such questions are usually left to the jury's discretion, often on the basis of testimony from friends and family as to the patient's or plaintiff's character as a generally responsible person. *Cf.* Reisner v. Regents of the University of California, 31 Cal. App. 4th 1195 (1995) (physician who learns that patient is infected

with HIV owes duty to patient's subsequent boyfriend to warn him, via a warning to the patient, of risk of infection; burden of proof is on boyfriend to establish that patient would have warned him, and that he and patient would have taken effective steps to avoid infection).

4. *Scope of* Tarasoff *Duties.* *Tarasoff* holds that a treating physician need not be *actually aware* that the patient is contemplating an attack on someone, so long as the physician reasonably should have known of the risk. Other states recognizing similar duties have split on what is required for a duty to attach. *Compare* Schuster v. Altenberg, 424 N.W.2d 159 (Wis. 1988) (duty applies when psychologist should have known of danger) *with* Van Horn v. Chambers, 970 S.W.2d 542 (Tex. 1998) (no duty unless physician actually knows that patient poses danger to another). To whom does the duty to warn recognized in *Tarasoff* extend? Must the particular victim be known to the treating psychiatrist by name or description? The California Supreme Court in a subsequent decision answered this question with a "yes." *See* Thompson v. County of Alameda, 614 P.2d 728 (Cal. 1980) (county that released a juvenile offender with a known propensity to commit violent assaults to the custody of his mother not liable to parents of minor killed by offender; minor was not "identifiable" as required by *Tarasoff*, and the county had no duty to issue general warnings to mother's neighbors). Statutes such as "Megan's Law" make it a criminal offense for certain violent sex offenders to fail to provide information to authorities, including their current whereabouts. The attempt to extend *Tarasoff*-type duties to other professions has largely failed. In 1988, for example, the California Supreme Court refused to impose a comparable duty to warn on clergy. *See* Nally v. Grace Comm. Church of the Valley, 763 P.2d 948 (Cal. 1988).

5. *Duties to Protect Third Parties from Physical Lapses.* The *Tarasoff* majority supposes that physicians are under a duty to third parties to warn patients with disorders such as epilepsy that they may suddenly become incapacitated while driving, risking injuries to others. However, some prominent courts have rejected such a duty. *See* Praesel v. Johnson, 967 S.W.2d 391 (Tex. 1998) (given that a physician has no authority to take away a patient's driver's license, and that the patient is likely aware of risks associated with epilepsy, no duty is owed by the physician to protect a third-party driver killed when the patient suffered a seizure while driving and crashed into plaintiff). Should courts be more willing to impose liability if the accident stems from the physician's failure to advise of the risks associated with an active course of treatment — for example, the prescription of a particular drug that causes drowsiness? In *Praesel*, the Texas Supreme Court noted an earlier intermediate appellate court decision upholding liability on such facts. For a contrary analysis, see Kirk v. Michael Reese Hosp., 513 N.E.2d 387 (Ill. 1987) (finding no duty).

6. *Forgotten Keys.* An important type of negligence claim in which the duty question is often hotly contested alleges that defendant *D*'s conduct was careless because it provided the occasion for wrongful conduct by third-party *T*, thereby resulting in injury to plaintiff *P*. One of

the earliest and most frequently encountered examples of this sort of claim involved the following fact pattern: Driver *D* carelessly leaves her keys in her car's ignition, enabling thief *T* to steal the car; *T* proceeds to drive the car carelessly or recklessly, causing injury to plaintiff *P*. Allegations of this form initially tended to fail because *T*'s intervening wrongful acts were regarded by judges as "breaking" the causal chain between *D*'s carelessness and *P*'s injury. However, some courts adopt the view that *T*'s misconduct does not necessarily cancel out *D*'s carelessness, and hence that *each* may be held partly responsible for *P*'s injury. *See generally* Southern Heritage Ins. Co. v. C. E. Frazier Constr. Co., 809 So. 2d 668 (Miss. 2002) (noting the split among the states on the disposition of these cases and declining to impose liability). Consider how the following decision addresses a different form of risk creation.

McGuiggan v. New England Tel. & Tel. Co.
496 N.E.2d 141 (Mass. 1986)

Wilkins, J.   We consider, on direct appellate review, whether a social host who furnished alcoholic beverages to an adult guest may be liable for a death caused shortly thereafter by that guest's negligent operation of a motor vehicle while under the influence of alcohol. We conclude that, although in certain circumstances liability properly could be imposed on such a social host, on the facts presented on the social hosts' motion for summary judgment, they are not liable. . . .

The McGuiggans held a high school graduation party for their eighteen year old son Daniel on June 11, 1978. Perhaps thirty people were present, most of whom were relatives considerably older than Daniel. Four of his contemporaries, including eighteen year old James Magee, were also present. Several people acted as bartender serving alcoholic beverages provided by the McGuiggans at a bar in the cellar playroom, and guests also served themselves. Mr. McGuiggan testified on deposition that he may have given Magee one drink when he arrived, but thereafter did not see him drinking and did not know how many drinks Magee had. He claimed that Magee seemed perfectly normal just before he left their home. Mrs. McGuiggan testified on deposition that she had spoken to Magee before he left with her son and three other young guests to drive David Doherty home. She knew Magee was driving and would have said something to him if she had believed him incapable of driving. Other passengers in the vehicle confirmed that Magee seemed sober. Magee, however, admitted that he had had four or five rum-cokes that evening. . . . [H]e later pleaded guilty to a charge of operating under the influence.

While traveling with his friends in the vehicle driven by Magee on Lowell Street in Peabody, shortly after leaving the party, Daniel McGuiggan became sick to his stomach and leaned his head and upper body out of a window of the vehicle. Daniel's head apparently struck a cement post which the defendant telephone company maintained inside the curb to mark the location of an underground conduit. Daniel died at a local hospital about four hours later. . . .

Approximately three hours after Magee left the party, a breathalyzer test administered to Magee recorded a value of .140. According to an affidavit of a physician submitted on the summary judgment motion, in the circumstances, a person who registered a .140 value on a breathalyzer test three hours after his last drink would have had a blood alcohol content of between .185 and .215 three hours earlier. Unless tolerant to alcohol, a person with a blood alcohol content over .10 would be recognizably intoxicated, and one with a blood alcohol content of between .185 and .215 would be unmistakably intoxicated. No evidence indicated when Magee ate his dinner or when he took his last drink or how strong it was.

The claim against the McGuiggans is based on common law principles and does not rely in any respect on a statutory violation. Under traditional common law tort analysis, our inquiry is whether a social host violated a duty to an injured third person by serving an alcoholic beverage to a guest whose negligent operation of a motor vehicle, while adversely affected by the alcohol, caused injury to a third person. Such an inquiry would require us to consider whether the social host unreasonably created a risk of injury to a person who the social host should reasonably have foreseen might be injured as a result of the guest's intoxication. If a social host acted negligently in serving an alcoholic beverage to a guest when there was such a foreseeable risk of injury to another and injury resulted from the guest's negligence caused by his intoxication, the law would ordinarily impose liability in tort on the social host, barring some statutory restriction or consideration of public policy weighing against the imposition of a duty in the circumstances.

Although this court has never announced a common law rule on the issue, the traditional view supported by the weight of authority has been that the drinker's voluntary consumption alone is the "proximate" cause of the third party's injury and that a person who sold or gave liquor to an intoxicated adult drinker is not liable for subsequent injuries caused by his intoxication. . . .

In the case of licensed vendors, [however] the "proximate cause theory" . . . has [not] attracted this court's favor. This court has held that a licensed commercial vendor of alcoholic beverages owes a duty to a third person who is injured in a motor vehicle accident caused by the negligence of a customer to whom the vendor sold a drink when he knew or reasonably should have known the customer was intoxicated. Cimino v. Milford Keg, Inc., 385 Mass. 323, 327 (1982). In Adamian v. Three Sons, Inc., 353 Mass. 498, 500 (1968), the court rejected arguments that liability could be imposed only by statute and that the drinker alone would be responsible for the consequences of his intoxication. Grounding liability on common law negligence, we held that injury to another on the highways was within "the foreseeable risk created by the sale of liquor to an already intoxicated individual." Adamian v. Three Sons, Inc., *supra* at 501. Although the plaintiff must show that the vendor defendant was on notice that the consumer was intoxicated (Cimino v. Milford Keg, Inc., *supra* at 328), we do not require specific proof that the vendor knew or reasonably should have known that the intoxicated customer would drive a motor vehicle. *Id.* at 330-331. . . . The question for the trier of fact is whether the vendor failed "to exercise that degree of care for the safety of travelers that ought to be exercised by a tavern keeper of ordinary prudence in the same or similar circumstances." *Id.* at 331.

There are, of course, differences between the operation of a commercial establishment selling alcoholic beverages for consumption on the premises and the furnishing of alcoholic beverages to guests in one's home. Balancing these differences, courts have found it easier to impose a duty of care on the licensed operator than on the social host. The threat of tort liability may serve the public purpose of offsetting the commercial operator's financial incentive to encourage drinking. The means of serving beverages in a bar, tavern, or restaurant normally permits closer control and monitoring of customers and their consumption than is typically possible in private gatherings. The commercial vendor may generally (but certainly not always) have more experience in identifying intoxicated drinkers than would social hosts and would be better able to "shut off" consumption without the embarrassment that a social host would suffer. It has also been suggested that licensed operators can be expected to have insurance against loss whereas a private individual would not. Some courts have regarded these various differences sufficient to justify imposing a duty on licensed vendors but not on social hosts. Others have considered the distinctions insignificant in assessing whether a duty should be imposed, although the differences might have a bearing on whether particular conduct was negligent.

A line of cases, most of which rely on statutory violations, imposes social host liability for the adverse consequences of serving alcoholic beverages to a minor. . . .[7]

There are a few cases which have imposed social host liability when, as here, the intoxicated guest who operated a motor vehicle was an adult. In Coulter v. Superior Court, 21 Cal. 3d 144, 149-150 (1978), the Supreme Court of California concluded, on both statutory and common law grounds, that "a social host or other noncommercial provider of alcoholic beverages owes to the general public a duty to refuse to furnish such beverages to an obviously intoxicated person if, under the circumstances, such person thereby constitutes a reasonably foreseeable danger or risk of injury to third persons."[8] The "social hosts" in the *Coulter* case were the owner-operator and the manager of an apartment complex alleged to have served a guest (apparently an adult) large quantities of alcoholic beverages when they knew or should have known that she was becoming "excessively intoxicated," that she customarily drank to excess, and that she would be driving a motor vehicle. *Id.* at 148.

On purely common law grounds, the Supreme Court of New Jersey held that a social host who serves liquor to an adult guest, "knowing both that the guest is intoxicated and will thereafter be operating a motor

7. The legal drinking age at the relevant time in this case was eighteen. The legal drinking age is now twenty-one. In deciding whether a guest was a minor or an adult, for purposes of determining the tort liability of a social host, the legal drinking age under the law at the time the alcoholic beverages are served is the appropriate consideration.

8. The California Legislature rather promptly adopted statutory provisions rejecting the concept of social host liability expressed in the *Coulter* opinion.

vehicle, is liable for injuries inflicted on a third party as a result of the negligent operation of a motor vehicle by the adult guest when such negligence is caused by the intoxication." Kelly v. Gwinnell, 96 N.J. 538, 548 (1984). The court emphasized that it was passing on the duty of a social host who "directly serves the guest and continues to do so even after the guest is visibly intoxicated." *Id.* at 556. . . .*

The paucity of cases in this country imposing social host liability cannot be explained solely on the ground that a social host does not, as a matter of law, create a reasonably foreseeable risk of harm to highway travelers in serving an alcoholic drink to a drunken guest. The risk created by serving liquor to an intoxicated person who is about to operate a motor vehicle is far too apparent to permit the conclusion that the social host's act could not have been the "proximate" cause of a third person's injury. The reluctance of courts to impose liability in these circumstances has been founded, rightly or wrongly, on policy considerations, particularly consideration of the effect that a rule of social host liability would have on a multitude of personal relationships in a variety of social settings.

Virtually every case we have discussed in which social host liability was acknowledged as a possibility or as a fact has been decided in the past decade. This trend toward imposing liability is no doubt a response to the greater concern of society in recent years regarding the problems of drunken driving. It is understandable that the law of torts, which in many aspects measures one's duty by what is reasonable conduct in the circumstances, should begin to respond to society's increasing concern. But the problems and implications of imposing liability are extensive, prompting some courts to abandon the field entirely to their Legislatures. These concerns also explain why more cases impose liability for serving a minor than for serving an adult. It is easier to find a violation of a standard of reasonableness when the intoxicated guest is underage, a person to whom, generally in this country, it is thought to be wrong to furnish an alcoholic drink. Similarly, those cases which have recognized the liability of social hosts for serving adult guests have involved the most flagrant circumstances calling for liability, a defendant furnishing an alcoholic drink directly to a person who was obviously intoxicated.

Cases of this character must be decided one by one, applying common law principles. The facts here do not present a case for social host liability. There is no evidence that either of the McGuiggans knew that Magee was intoxicated at any time while he was at their home. Nor does the evidence show that Magee was obviously intoxicated at any relevant time. There is evidence, admittedly from the McGuiggans and from Magee's sister and friends, which tends to show that Magee was not obviously intoxicated that evening. We pass by the question whether a social host may avoid liability by letting his guests serve drinks to themselves and each other. The crucial consideration has been the condition of the guest (or customer) at the time the social host (or licensee) served him or her an alcoholic drink. Where, on this record, there is no showing that the

* [In 1987, the New Jersey Legislature abrogated social host liability for injuries caused by their intoxicated adult guests. N.J. Stat. Ann. 2A: 15-5.7. — Eds.]

McGuiggans knew Magee was intoxicated and there is a showing that he was not obviously intoxicated at any time that night (thus including the time when he served himself or was served his last drink), there is no case for liability.

We would recognize a social host's liability to a person injured by an intoxicated guest's negligent operation of a motor vehicle where a social host who knew or should have known that his guest was drunk, nevertheless gave him or permitted him to take an alcoholic drink and thereafter, because of his intoxication, the guest negligently operated a motor vehicle causing the third person's injury. In deciding whether the social host exercised ordinary prudence in such circumstances, a relevant consideration will be whether the social host knew or reasonably should have known that the intoxicated guest might presently operate a motor vehicle.

Inherent in what we have said is a rejection of the claim that evidence of Magee's blood alcohol content raises a dispute on a material factual issue. The doctor's affidavit might be thought to raise a factual dispute as to what Magee's apparent condition was just before he left the McGuiggans' home. That evidence, however, has no bearing on what Magee's apparent condition was at the time he took his last drink.[10] We need only say that the record does not raise a dispute on any material fact concerning what the McGuiggans knew or reasonably should have known about Magee's sobriety at any relevant time.

Judgment Affirmed.

Lynch, J. (concurring). I concur in the result. . . .

I would follow the traditional view, alluded to by the majority that the drinker's consumption of alcohol alone is the proximate cause of injuries to third parties. I accept this view out of concern for judicial restraint and not because of any lack of concern with the problem of drunken driving. Sorting out the conflicting social policies involved in imposing liability in such circumstances cries out for a legislative rather than a judicial solution. There are several reasons not to modify the traditional common law rule but to await a legislative solution.

First, in determining when a host should have known his guest was intoxicated and unable to drive safely a jury are, after all, acting as the paradigm of the "Monday morning quarterback." Not only does the jury decide what facts were "known" to the host but they have the ability to analyze the host's conduct in the light of the subsequent, sometimes tragic, events. . . .

Second, . . . [a] social host is by definition not in a commercial setting where furnishers of goods or services can protect themselves from the catastrophic effects of liability by obtaining adequate insurance. The homeowners of the Commonwealth are already sorely burdened and their

10. For the purposes of our discussion we assume that the affidavit, which is generalized, presents an opinion that would be admissible at trial and thus should be considered in deciding whether summary judgment should be entered for the McGuiggans. The doctor's opinion does not deal, however, with specific circumstances such as when Magee consumed his drinks or when Magee ate his dinner.

ability to protect themselves from catastrophic loss may be limited to restricting the activities that are permitted on their property. The Supreme Court of the United States recently held that certain kinds of private, aberrant sexual acts are beyond the bounds of constitutional protection. Bowers v. Hardwick, 478 U.S. 186 (1986).* I suggest that the views of the court expressed here will have a far more pervasive effect on the private activities of consenting adults than that highly criticized decision.

Third, the majority is responding to a serious problem in modern society, but is doing so without the consideration of aspects of the problem that would be appropriate for the Legislature to examine. For example, is it necessary, or desirable, to expose to liability the equity in the home or perhaps the entire life savings of citizens of the Commonwealth who do nothing more than make available alcoholic beverages to social guests whom a jury later determines that the host should have known were intoxicated and would drive? Is the social guest a statistically significant contributor to highway accidents in which alcohol is a factor? After all, social activities themselves usually impose constraints on extreme behavior. Moreover, can a homeowner (who is not in the business of serving alcohol) be expected to recognize when a guest is approaching his individual "limit," and, in what circumstances should a host be charged with knowledge that his guest would drive? What action, if any, might protect the host from liability when he learns that his guest, now perceived to be under the influence, intends to drive? To what extent, if any, should the reasonable availability of insurance affect the policy decision to impose liability?

One other matter requires some comment. A subtle message attaches to the rule of liability proposed by the court. Imposing liability on the host partially excuses the drunken driver from the consequences of his own acts. Instead of placing all of society's opprobrium on the individual who makes the free choice of both drinking too much and then driving, the rule advanced by the court divides that opprobrium and thus defuses it. I suggest that this is not the message that we wish to send to those who make the decision to drink to excess and then drive.

NOTES AND QUESTIONS

1. *More on* McGuiggan. The suit in *McGuiggan* was initially brought by the estate representing the interests of the decedent, Daniel. The estate brought suit only against New England Telephone (NET), alleging negligence in placing the cement post too close to the side of the road. However, NET brought the elder McGuiggans into the suit by means of a procedural device called a third-party complaint. By means of this complaint, NET sought to establish that the McGuiggans were responsible for Daniel's death, and were obligated to pay all or part of any damages awarded to Daniel. See Chapter 8 (discussing apportionment). Thus, the social host theory being presented to the court was not being pressed by

* [Overruled, Lawrence v. Texas, __ U.S. __ , 123 S. Ct. 2472 (2003). — Eds.]

Daniel's representative. Rather, defendant NET offered the theory in an effort to shift responsibility away from the company to Daniel's parents. Do you think the fact that the social host theory was presented by NET for this reason may have affected the court's analysis?

2. *Liability of Commercial Establishments.* As *McGuiggan* notes, in most states, commercial establishments that sell alcohol to "obviously intoxicated" adult patrons, or to minor patrons, are subject to either statutory or common law liability to certain third parties injured by those patrons as a result of their being intoxicated. The typical suit involves a suit by *P* for injuries sustained in a crash caused by intoxicated driver *D* against establishment *E* that had served alcohol to *D* even though he was obviously intoxicated. A recent empirical study conducted by Professor Sloan and others suggests that such liability has encouraged commercial establishments to monitor patrons' consumption of alcohol.

3. *Premises Liability Revisited.* In most jurisdictions, businesses open to the public are under an obligation to maintain or monitor their premises with due care for the possibility of criminal attack on one of their patrons. Likewise, landlords are responsible to take reasonable steps to prevent attacks on tenants. *See* Kline v. 1500 Massachusetts Ave. Apt. Corp., 439 F.2d 477 (D.C. Cir. 1970). Thus, a victim who is assaulted on the property can often point to the failure to provide adequate lighting, or a security patrol, as the basis for a claim in negligence. Courts usually analyze these claims in terms of an affirmative duty to protect or rescue. The prerequisites to, and scope of, these obligations vary by jurisdiction. Some, for example, impose a duty of care when there is some particular reason to foresee criminal activity, such as publicly available information as to a relatively high rate of similar crimes in the immediate vicinity of the property. *See* Timberwalk Apts. v. Cain, 972 S.W.2d 749 (Tex. 1998). Others have adopted a more open-ended approach. *See* McClung v. Delta Square Partnership, 937 S.W.2d 891 (Tenn. 1996) (surveying alternative duty rules and adopting one that permits courts to impose a duty of reasonable care based on a balancing of various considerations). As the relationship between defendant and victim becomes more attenuated, courts are less inclined to find a duty. *See* Doe v. Linder Constr. Co., 845 S.W.2d 173 (Tenn. 1992) (no duty owed by seller of real estate to eventual purchaser to take care to ensure that keys to units are safeguarded so as to prevent criminal from using keys to enter units).

4. *Gun Litigation.* Some of the most complex and contentious recent suits alleging negligence that enables the wrongful acts of others have been brought by gunshot victims against manufacturers of handguns on the ground that the manufacturers' careless marketing and distribution practices have enabled the victims' shooters to more easily obtain guns than they could otherwise. Thus far, these claims have received a mostly skeptical reception in the courts. *See, e.g.,* Merrill v. Navegar, Inc., 28 P.3d 116 (Cal. 2001) (dismissing shooting victims' negligence claims against manufacturer of assailant's semi-automatic weapon on common law and statutory grounds); Hamilton v. Beretta U.S.A. Corp., 750 N.E.2d 1055

(N.Y. 2001) (holding that, on the evidence presented by the plaintiffs, defendant gun manufacturers owed no duty to shooting victims to reduce the risk of their guns being sold via retailers to criminal users); McCarthy v. Olin Corp., 119 F.3d 148 (2d Cir. 1997) (denying a cause of action under New York negligence law against hollow-point bullet manufacturer on the ground that manufacturer owed no duty to gunshot victims to minimize the risk that the bullets would be used unlawfully). *But see* Ileto v. Glock, Inc., 349 F.3d 1191 (9th Cir. 2003) (applying California law and reversing the dismissal of negligent marketing claims by survivors of shooting victims against certain gun manufacturers). Some cities and organizations have also brought suits against gun manufacturers on the theory that their products amount to a public nuisance. See Chapter 11.

D.   Policy-Based Duty Exemptions

The preceding cases and notes have canvassed areas recognized by courts as falling outside the general duty to take care not to cause reasonably foreseeable physical harm or tangible property damage. In each of these areas — premises liability, pure economic loss, and affirmative duties — special qualified duty rules apply instead, and it is often on the plaintiff to explain why the court ought to recognize a duty of care running from the defendant to persons such as the plaintiff. As the following case indicates, even in cases that seem to fall under the ambit of the general duty of care, courts will occasionally invoke special duty rules on grounds of "policy."

Strauss v. Belle Realty Co.
482 N.E.2d 34 (N.Y. 1985)

Kaye, J.   On July 13, 1977, a failure of defendant Consolidated Edison's power system left most of New York City in darkness. In this action for damages allegedly resulting from the power failure, we are asked to determine whether Con Edison owed a duty of care to a tenant who suffered personal injuries in a common area of an apartment building, where his landlord — but not he — had a contractual relationship with the utility. We conclude that in the case of a blackout of a metropolis of several million residents and visitors, each in some manner necessarily affected by a 25-hour power failure, liability for injuries in a building's common areas should, as a matter of public policy, be limited by the contractual relationship. . . .

Plaintiff, Julius Strauss, then 77 years old, resided in an apartment building in Queens. Con Edison provided electricity to his apartment pursuant to agreement with him, and to the common areas of the building under a separate agreement with his landlord, defendant Belle Realty Company. As water to the apartment was supplied by electric pump, plaintiff had no running water for the duration of the blackout. Consequently, on the second day of the power failure, he set out for the basement to obtain water, but fell on the darkened, defective basement stairs, sustaining injuries. In this action against Belle Realty and Con Edison, plaintiff alleged negligence against the landlord, in failing to maintain the stairs or warn of their dangerous condition, and negligence against the utility in the performance of its duty to provide electricity.

Plaintiff moved for partial summary judgment against Con Edison . . . to establish that Con Edison owed a duty of care to plaintiff. . . . Con Edison cross-moved for summary judgment dismissing the complaint, maintaining it had no duty to a noncustomer.

The court . . . denied Con Edison's cross motion to dismiss the complaint, finding a question of fact as to whether it owed plaintiff a duty of care. The Appellate Division reversed and dismissed the complaint against Con Edison. Citing Moch Co. v. Rensselaer Water Co. (247 N.Y. 160), the plurality concluded that "Con Ed did not owe a duty to plaintiff in any compensable legal sense" (98 A.D.2d 424, 428). . . . On public policy grounds, we now affirm the Appellate Division order dismissing the complaint against Con Edison.

A defendant may be held liable for negligence only when it breaches a duty owed to the plaintiff (Pulka v. Edelman, 40 N.Y.2d 781, 782). The essential question here is whether Con Edison owed a duty to plaintiff, whose injuries from a fall on a darkened staircase may have conceivably been foreseeable, but with whom there was no contractual relationship for lighting in the building's common areas.

Duty in negligence cases is defined neither by foreseeability of injury (Pulka v. Edelman, *supra*, at p. 785) nor by privity of contract. As this court has long recognized, an obligation rooted in contract may engender a duty owed to those not in privity, for "[there] is nothing anomalous in a rule which imposes upon A, who has contracted with B, a duty to C and D and others according as he knows or does not know that the subject-matter of the contract is intended for their use" (MacPherson v. Buick Motor Co., 217 N.Y. 382, 393). In Fish v. Waverly Elec. Light & Power Co. (189 N.Y. 336), for example, an electric company which had contracted with the plaintiff's employer to install ceiling lights had a duty to the plaintiff to exercise reasonable care. And in Glanzer v. Shepard (233 N.Y. 236), a public weigher, hired by a seller of beans to certify the weight of a particular shipment, was found liable in negligence to the buyer.

But while the absence of privity does not foreclose recognition of a duty, it is still the responsibility of courts, in fixing the orbit of duty, "to limit the legal consequences of wrongs to a controllable degree" (Tobin v. Grossman, 24 N.Y.2d 609, 619; *see also*, Howard v. Lecher, 42 N.Y.2d 109), and to protect against crushing exposure to liability (*see*, Pulka v. Edelman, 40 N.Y.2d 781, *supra*; Ultramares Corp. v. Touche, 255 N.Y. 170). "In fixing the bounds of that duty, not only logic and science, but policy play an important role" (De Angelis v. Lutheran Med. Center, 58 N.Y.2d 1053, 1055; *see also*, Becker v. Schwartz, 46 N.Y.2d 401, 408). The courts' definition of an orbit of duty based on public policy may at times result in the exclusion of some who might otherwise have recovered for losses or injuries if traditional tort principles had been applied.

Considerations of privity are not entirely irrelevant in implementing policy. Indeed, in determining the liability of utilities for consequential damages for failure to provide service — a liability which could obviously be "enormous," and has been described as "*sui generis*," rather than strictly governed by tort or contract law principles (*see*, Prosser and Keeton, Torts § 92, at 663 [5th ed.]) — courts have declined to extend the duty of care to noncustomers. For example, in Moch Co. v. Rensselaer Water Co. (247 N.Y. 160, *supra*), a water works company contracted with the City of Rensselaer to satisfy its water requirements. Plaintiff's warehouse burned and plaintiff brought an action against the water company in part based on its alleged negligence in failing to supply sufficient water pressure to the city's hydrants. The court denied recovery, concluding that the proposed enlargement of the zone of duty would unduly extend liability. . . .

In the view of the Appellate Division dissenter, *Moch* does not control because the injuries here were foreseeable and plaintiff was a member of a specific, limited, circumscribed class with a close relationship with Con Edison. . . .

. . . Here, insofar as revealed by the record, the arrangement between Con Edison and Belle Realty was no different from those existing between Con Edison and the millions of other customers it serves. Thus, Con Edison's duty to provide electricity to Belle Realty should not be treated separately from its broader statutory obligation to furnish power to all other applicants for such service in New York City and Westchester County. When plaintiff's relationship with Con Edison is viewed from this perspective, it is no answer to say that a duty is owed because, as a tenant in an apartment building, plaintiff belongs to a narrowly defined class.[2]

. . . If liability could be found here, then in logic and fairness the same result must follow in many similar situations. For example, a tenant's guests and invitees, as well as persons making deliveries or repairing equipment in the building, are equally persons who must use the common areas, and for whom they are maintained. Customers of a store and occupants of an office building stand in much the same position with respect to Con Edison as tenants of an apartment building. . . . While limiting recovery to customers in this instance can hardly be said to confer immunity from negligence on Con Edison, permitting recovery to those in plaintiff's circumstances would, in our view, violate the court's responsibility to define an orbit of duty that places controllable limits on liability.

Finally, we reject the suggestion of the dissent that there should be a fact-finding hearing to establish the alleged catastrophic probabilities

2. In deciding that public policy precludes liability to a noncustomer injured in the common areas of an apartment building, we need not decide whether recovery would necessarily also be precluded where a person injured in the home is not the family bill payer but the spouse. In another context, where this court has defined the duty of a public accounting firm for negligent financial statements, we have recognized that the duty runs both to those in contractual privity with the accountant and to those whose bond is so close as to be, in practical effect, indistinguishable from privity, and we have on public policy grounds precluded wider liability to persons damaged by the accountant's negligence. (*See*, Credit Alliance Corp. v. Andersen & Co., 65 N.Y.2d 536 [decided herewith].)

flowing from the 1977 blackout and prospective blackouts, before any limitation is placed on Con Edison's duty to respond to the public for personal injuries. In exercising the court's traditional responsibility to fix the scope of duty, for application beyond a single incident, we need not blind ourselves to the obvious impact of a city-wide deprivation of electric power, or to the impossibility of fixing a rational boundary once beyond the contractual relationship, or to the societal consequences of rampant liability.

In sum, Con Edison is not answerable to the tenant of an apartment building injured in a common area as a result of Con Edison's negligent failure to provide electric service as required by its agreement with the building owner. Accordingly, the order of the Appellate Division should be affirmed, with costs.

Meyer, J. (dissenting).   My disagreement with the majority results not from its consideration of public policy as a factor in determining the scope of Con Ed's duty, but from the fact that in reaching its public policy conclusion it has considered only one side of the equation and based its conclusion on nothing more than assumption. I, therefore, respectfully dissent.

As Professors Prosser and Keeton have emphasized (Prosser and Keeton, Torts, at 357-358 [5th ed.]), "The statement that there is or is not a duty begs the essential question — whether the plaintiff's interests are entitled to legal protection against the defendant's conduct. . . . It is a shorthand statement of a conclusion, rather than an aid to analysis in itself. . . . But it should be recognized that 'duty' is not sacrosanct in itself, but is only an expression of the sum total of those considerations of policy which lead the law to say that the plaintiff is entitled to protection." . . .

There is, of course, legislative intervention in the regulation of gas and electric companies. But the only "legislative" limitation upon the liability of such companies consists of Public Service Commission acceptance and approval of Con Ed's rate schedule, which incorporates the rule, previously enunciated by this court, that liability "be limited to damages arising from the utility's willful misconduct or gross negligence" (Food Pageant v. Consolidated Edison Co., 54 N.Y.2d 167, 172). But, as *Food Pageant* establish[es], what caused the injuries for which compensation is sought in this action was Con Ed's gross negligence. . . .

Criteria more extensive than the unsupported prediction of disaster for determining liability are not wanting. . . . Thus, in Tarasoff v. Regents of Univ. (17 Cal. 3d 425, 434, 551 P.2d 334, 342), the Supreme Court of California listed the major factors to be balanced in determining duty as "the foreseeability of harm to the plaintiff, the degree of certainty that the plaintiff suffered injury, the closeness of the connection between the defendant's conduct and the injury suffered, the moral blame attached to the defendant's conduct, the policy of preventing future harm, the extent of the burden to the defendant and consequences to the community of imposing a duty to exercise care with resulting liability for breach, and the availability, cost and prevalence of insurance for the risk involved." Prosser and Keeton (*op. cit., supra*, at 359), on the basis of the *Tarasoff* case and [another case], list similar factors, which are discussed at greater length in section 4 of their treatise. As to the loss distribution factor, they note (*op. cit.*, at 24-25) that, "The defendants in tort cases are to a large extent public utilities, industrial corporations, commercial enterprises, automobile owners, and others who by means of rates, prices, taxes or insurance are best able to distribute to the public at large the risks and losses which are inevitable in a complex civilization. Rather than leave the loss on the shoulders of the individual plaintiff, who may be ruined by it, the courts have tended to find reasons to shift it to the defendants," except where there are "limitations upon the power of a defendant to shift the loss to the public . . . [as] where the liability may extend to an unlimited number of unknown persons, and is incapable of being estimated or insured against in advance."

The majority's blind acceptance of the notion that Consolidated Edison will be crushed if held liable to the present plaintiff and others like him ignores the possibility that through application to the Public Service Commission Con Ed can seek such reduction of the return on stockholders' equity or [an] increase in its rates, or both, as may be necessary to pay the judgments obtained against it. It ignores as well the burden imposed upon the persons physically injured by Con Ed's gross negligence or, as to those forced to seek welfare assistance because their savings have been wiped out by the injury, the State. Doing so in the name of public policy seems particularly perverse, for what it says, in essence, is the more persons injured through a tort-feasor's gross negligence, the less the responsibility for injuries incurred.

I agree that there are situations encompassed by our tort system that require such a result, perverse though it may be, but before granting public utilities absolution beyond that which they already enjoy through the limitation of their liability to acts of gross negligence, I would put the burden upon the utility to establish the necessity for doing so. I am not suggesting that the issue is to be determined by a jury for, as already noted, I do not question that "duty" is a question of law to be determined by the courts. But the law is not without illustrations of preliminary issues involving facts to be determined by a Judge. . . . All that I am suggesting is that it is Con Ed which claims that its duty does not encompass plaintiff, not because Con Ed was not grossly negligent, but because the effect of that negligence if Con Ed is held liable for it would be to cripple Con Ed as well as the victims of the negligence. There simply is no basis other than the majority's say so for its assumptions that the impact of a city-wide deprivation of electric power upon the utility is entitled to greater consideration than the impact upon those injured; that a rational boundary cannot be fixed that will include some (apartment tenants injured in common areas, for example), if not all of the injured; that the consequence of imposing some bystander liability will be more adverse to societal interests than will follow from blindly limiting liability for tort to those with whom the tort-feasor has a contractual relationship. Before we grant Con Ed's motion to dismiss, therefore, we should require that a rational basis for such assumptions be established.

Con Ed may well be able to do so, but before its motion is granted at the expense of an unknown number of victims who have suffered injuries the extent and effects of which are also unknown, it should be required to establish that the catastrophic probabilities are great enough to warrant the limitation of duty it seeks.

I would, therefore, deny the summary judgment motions of both sides and remit to Supreme Court for determination of the preliminary fact issues involved.

NOTES AND QUESTIONS

1. *MacPherson to Moch: Back to Privity?* In *Strauss*, the New York Court of Appeals relies on Cardozo's 1928 opinion for the same court in Moch Co. v. Rensselaer Water Co. There, the defendant water company contracted with the City of Rensselaer to provide sufficient water for the needs of its residents. Because of carelessness, the company failed to pump an adequate supply of water to the city's fire hydrants, as a result of which firefighters were unable to stop a fire that eventually burned down Moch's warehouse.

Cardozo, writing for the court, first concluded that individual citizens such as Moch were not parties to, or intended beneficiaries of, the contract between the city and the water company, and hence Moch had no right to sue for breach of contract. He then reasoned that, given the absence of any binding promise to Moch to supply water, the company's carelessness toward Moch's property amounted to mere *nonfeasance*, rather than misfeasance. Finally, given that the company's carelessness consisted of nonfeasance, and that none of the standard exceptions to the no-duty-to-rescue rule applied, he concluded that Moch could not sue the company for negligence.

The combined effect of *Moch*'s contract and tort rulings was startling. Cardozo, the author of *MacPherson*, had 12 years later issued an opinion that looked a lot like Winterbottom v. Wright. Essentially, it concluded that, absent privity, a party such as Moch could *not* sue for physical harm proximately caused by the carelessness of a utility such as the water company. How could Cardozo (or anyone else) reconcile the dismantling of privity in *MacPherson* with the resurrection of privity in *Moch*?

As indicated, Cardozo thought that the critical distinction between the two cases was that the former involved actionable misfeasance, whereas the latter involved nonfeasance — the mere failure to confer a gratuitous benefit. Essentially, he likened the position of the water company to that of a private citizen who happened to drive his giant tanker truck filled with water past the scene of the fire. Just as the truck owner would not have been obligated to Moch to stop and lend his truck to aid the firefighters, so too the company owed Moch no duty.

Most commentators are unconvinced by this distinction, in part because they have found it difficult to see what renders the water company's "failure to act" so dramatically different from the carelessness of Buick in *MacPherson*. (The latter, after all, consisted of a *failure* to inspect and detect a defective wheel.) Indeed, it is probably fair to say that *Moch* is widely regarded as Cardozo's least convincing effort at legal reasoning. This is not to say that commentators uniformly criticize the *result* he reached by means of that reasoning. Like the court in *Strauss*, many have embraced his conclusion that the liability of utilities for carelessness has to be limited by a special duty rule.

2. *Utilities*. Traditionally, because water and power companies provide necessary goods and have been thought naturally to form into local monopolies, they have been subject to substantially greater degrees of government regulation than other businesses, such as product manufacturers. For example, federal and state agencies charged with regulating these businesses often mandate that they provide service to all members of the general public, and that they do so at particular rates. Rate setting is accomplished through an elaborate administrative process that involves hearings that often include consideration of whether rates paid by utility customers should be calculated to include payment of liabilities incurred as a result of utility carelessness. For various reasons, regulators often conclude that it is desirable to limit utilities' liabilities, particularly for economic losses, flowing from an interruption of services. A question lurking beneath the surface of *Strauss* is whether the existence of this alternative scheme of regulation should affect tort analysis. If heavily regulated industries are entitled to a break in terms of tort liability, what should happen if and when they are deregulated?

3. *What Is the Worry?* Some more information about the events of 1977 might be helpful in analyzing *Strauss*. A strong July storm caused several lightning strikes that hit power-generating or transmission facilities located north of New York City. These strikes, combined with Con Edison's negligence in responding to them, triggered circuit breakers and other devices that had been installed after an earlier blackout as a means of preventing electrical overloads and equipment damage. Unfortunately, resetting the system was a time-consuming affair, as most of the equipment in question was underground and had to be reset manually.

The result was a citywide blackout that started at about 9:30 P.M. and was not fully rectified for 25 hours. As the court's opinion indicates, the loss of power cut off lights and water to city residents. It also shut down air conditioners in the midst of a summer heat wave. Thousands were trapped in elevators and subways. Thousands more had to climb and descend innumerable flights of stairs in the dark and heat. Traffic signals were rendered nonoperational. Planes lost sight of runways at the city's airports and had to be diverted. During the first night of the blackout, parts of the city were in chaos, with looters causing damage to thousands of businesses and police arresting more than 3,500 suspects. Both the state and federal governments subsequently launched investigations into the causes and consequences of the blackout. *See* http://blackout.gmu.edu/archive/a_1977.html.

As we have seen in this chapter, and will see again in Chapter 4, the Court of Appeals had at its disposal doctrines by which to cut off Con Edison's liability for a great deal of the economic loss suffered as a result of the blackout, as well as physical harms caused by the intervening criminal acts of looters. Why then, did it feel the need to deny Strauss's claim? What parade of horribles did the majority have in mind?

4. *Should the Breadth of the Tort Matter?* As noted by the dissent, there is something counterintuitive about a judicial ruling that says, in effect, "because this tortfeasor has caused substantial and widespread damage by means of its carelessness, we must find a way to limit its liability." One might have thought that exactly the opposite conclusion ought to be drawn: Because of the huge amount of harm generated, the tortfeasor does not deserve the benefit of any special, limited duty rules. Is *Strauss* simply a bow to expedience, in which the court concludes that, for the public good, Con Edison is entitled to a one-time exemption from the normal rules of tort law? If so, is the dissent right to insist that such an exemption should be granted only upon a showing by Con Edison as to the dire consequences of being held responsible to all foreseeable plaintiffs, as opposed to those with whom it had contracted?

5. *Duty as Element versus No-Duty as Liability Exemption.* The majority casts its holding as a "no duty" ruling. If we recall Heaven v. Pender's conception of duty, the implication seems to be that, as Con Edison goes about the business of providing electricity, it is not obligated (except to those in privity) to take care to prevent unnecessary blackouts and the physical injuries one might expect to attend a blackout. As "foreseeability" provides the default test for duty in cases of misfeasance involving physical harm, the implication would seem to be that Con Edison could not have foreseen that its carelessness might cause harm to persons such as Strauss. Given that New York City had experienced a blackout just 12 years earlier, in 1965, which in turn led Con Edison to adopt measures to prevent future blackouts, is that a plausible conclusion? Does the majority opinion so conclude? Or is the dissenting judge right to suggest that the substance of the court's "duty" ruling is not that Strauss failed to establish that Con Edison was obligated to be vigilant of his physical well-being, but instead a ruling that the utility might be entitled to a special affirmative defense that excuses it from liability *notwithstanding* that Strauss can make out all the traditional elements of a negligence cause of action?

6. *From* Strauss *to* Hamilton. Should *Strauss* be read as standing for anything other than an ad hoc limitation of duty arising from a catastrophic one-off event? In fact, *Strauss* is often cited by courts applying New York law for the proposition that, in addition to foreseeability, they must take into account the risk of exposing the defendant to "crushing liability" when determining whether or to what extent a duty was owed by the defendant to the plaintiff. *See, e.g.*, Kazanoff v. United States, 945 F.2d 32, 37 (2d Cir. 1991). Not surprisingly, tort defendants frequently invoke the threat of crushing liability as a reason to grant them judgment as a matter of law.

In Hamilton v. Beretta U.S.A. Corp., 750 N.E.2d 1055 (N.Y. 2001), a group of plaintiffs who had been shot by third parties with illegally obtained handguns sued various gun manufacturers on the theory that the handguns were negligently marketed so as to make it easier for the shooters to obtain guns unlawfully. Specifically, the defendant manufacturers were said to owe a duty to the plaintiffs because it was foreseeable that, as a result of specific marketing choices, handguns sold legally in other states would find their way into New York illegally. The Court of Appeals rejected the plaintiffs' duty argument, relying to a significant degree on *Strauss* and its progeny. Thus, it emphasized that the duty proposed by the plaintiffs would have extended to thousands of victims of gun violence. (It also noted the lack of any evidence suggesting that the defendants were in a position to prevent the illegal migration of guns.)

Thus described, does *Hamilton* strike you as a fair application of *Strauss?* Should *Strauss* apply whenever there is a potentially large class of negligence claimants? In what ways are gun manufacturers (which are not, for the most part, based in New York State) similar to Con Edison? In what ways are they dissimilar?

7. *Calabresi and the Cheapest Cost Avoider.* Legal economists are concerned to study and predict the effects that different legal rules will have on behavior. In particular, they want to know how different legal rules promote the efficient allocation of the resources at society's disposal. To oversimplify, in torts, the economic issue is whether dollars spent on preventing accidents are spent efficiently, that is, achieve the efficient mix of precaution-taking and injury. See Appendix C.

While it may seem odd to posit an efficient mix of precautions and injuries, the notion can be quite intuitive. For example, every once in a while, people who go for walks in urban parks, such as New York's Central Park, collide with one another, causing injuries. To avoid such collisions and injuries, pedestrians could carry with them a small boom box that broadcasts a tape-recording of a beeping sound akin to the sound made by trucks backing up. Taking such a precaution likely would reduce the risk of injury to others (as well as oneself) through collisions. Still, doing so would probably be inefficient: The precaution is too costly (in dollars, time, and inconvenience) given the low probability of injury. With respect to this precaution, at least, it is more efficient to tolerate a few injuries from collisions. Economists analyzing tort law want to know whether its rules — like the boom box idea — lead actors to take too many (or too few) precautions as measured from the standpoint of efficiency. We encounter this facet of economic analysis again in Chapter 3.

In addition to inquiring about *what* sort of precautions ought or ought not to be taken, economists are also concerned with the question of *who* is in the best position to take precautions. In Judge Guido Calabresi's famous phrase, tort law should, from this perspective, aspire to assign liability to the *cheapest cost avoider*: the person or entity who can identify and adopt the most efficient precaution more readily than anyone else.

Does the idea of the cheapest cost avoider help make sense of *Strauss?* As between Con Edison, Belle Realty, and Strauss, who was in the better position to minimize the risk of Strauss falling on darkened and defective stairs? If cheapest-cost-avoider analysis suggests that Strauss or Belle Realty were better able to minimize the risk of Strauss falling in the dark, would the same conclusion follow for a person who suffers a heart attack because he was forced during the blackout to ascend numerous flights of stairs in his high-rise apartment building? Who else might have prevented that sort of injury?

Does cheapest-cost-avoider analysis help make sense of other duty decisions we've seen to this point? For an interesting application of the concept in connection with a no-duty ruling, see Edwards v. Honeywell, Inc., 50 F.3d 484 (7th Cir. 1995). There, the widow of a firefighter who was killed when he fell through the floor of a burning house sued the company that provided fire alarm service to the owner of the house. The theory of liability was that the alarm company had received an automatic signal that the home was on fire, but carelessly failed to contact the firefighter's unit in a timely manner, as a result of which the floor was substantially weaker than it would have been had the firefighters responded to a timely notification from the alarm company. The Court of Appeals ruled that the alarm company owed no duty of care to the firefighter. Although acknowledging that its ruling allowed a careless actor to escape liability, it maintained that such a conclusion was justified in part for the following reasons:

> . . . [T]he defendant may not be in the best position to prevent a particular class of accidents, and placing liability on it may merely dilute the incentives of other potential defendants. In most cases the best way to avert fire damage is to prevent the fire from starting rather than to douse it with water after it has started. The water company represents a second line of defense, and it has no control over the first. It cannot insist that people not leave oil-soaked rags lying about or that they equip their houses and offices with smoke detectors and fire extinguishers.
>
> How [much weight these arguments should carry] is a matter of fair debate; but they are especially powerful in *this* case. . . . The provider of an alarm service not only has no knowledge of the risk of a fire in its subscribers' premises, and no practical ability to reduce that risk (though we suppose an alarm service like a fire insurer could offer a discount to people who installed smoke detectors in their premises); it also lacks knowledge of the risk of a fire to firemen summoned to extinguish it. That risk depends not only on the characteristics of the particular premises but also on the particular techniques used by each fire department, the training and qualifications of the firemen, and the quality of the department's leadership. The alarm company knows nothing about these things and has no power to influence them.

Id. at 490-491. Notably, *Edwards* was authored by Judge Richard Posner, who, along with Judge Calabresi, is one of the leaders of the "Law and Economics" movement.

8. *Prosser and the Sacrosanctity of Duty.* We have repeatedly seen courts invoking Prosser's claim that "'duty' is not sacrosanct in itself, but only an expression of the sum total of those considerations of policy that lead the law to say that the particular plaintiff is entitled to protection." William L. Prosser, *Handbook of the Law of Torts* § 31, at 180 (1941). It is therefore appropriate to conclude this chapter by briefly reflecting on the meaning of this oft-quoted statement. Arguably, it can be read as containing two propositions: one negative and modest, the other positive and more controversial.

In its negative cast, Prosser's quip serves as a warning against decisions such as *Osterlind*, which seem to treat concepts of duties and rights as if they are self-defining. Essentially, the claim is that courts cannot resolve disputes simply by invoking the word *duty*. That duty is not "sacrosanct in itself" means that judges need to articulate reasons in support of their duty rulings.

Understood in these terms, Prosser's quip is helpful, but also quite modest in its implications. It cautions against a certain kind of "mechanical" decisionmaking, but says nothing about the sorts of reasons a court engaged in *non*mechanical decisionmaking might invoke. Suppose, for example, the *Osterlind* court did not simply rely on a conclusory invocation of duty to resolve that case in favor of the defendant, but instead cited precedents espousing the general rule of no duty to rescue. Had it done so, the court would have provided a reason for its ruling: namely, that it was following a rule that it was obligated to follow under the principle of *stare decisis*.*

At least in the hands of some courts, such as the California Supreme Court, Prosser has been interpreted to assert a second claim about the duty element, one with more robust implications for how courts go about (and should go about) deciding duty issues. On this reading, the claim is that the duty element only *seems* to pose a question about *the existence and scope of the defendant's obligation to be vigilant of some aspect of the plaintiff's well-being*. Contrary to these appearances, the duty issue in fact turns on the very different question of *whether, on balance, it would be good for society to impose liability on the defendant*, that is, whether the "sum total" of policy considerations warrant the attachment of liability to the defendant's conduct. Analyses of duty, in this view, always boil down to considerations of aggregate social welfare. Thus, cases such as *Strauss* — which essentially ignore the issue of obligation and instead "forthrightly" inquire as to the policy ramifications of the decision to impose liability — stand as a model of honest, self-conscious judicial decisionmaking on the issue of duty. By contrast, decisions such as *MacPherson* and *McGuiggan*, although perhaps correct in result, are not ideal, because they are not entirely forthcoming in explaining how their holdings advance overall welfare or utility.

In this "positive" rendition, Prosser's claim carries substantially more bite. Precisely because of that, it is also substantially more controversial than the negative claim described above. To be sure, it is *possible* to recast each of the duty decisions we have seen in this chapter as resting on (unstated) judicial conclusions or assumptions about how different rules will contribute to overall social welfare. (It is also possible to recast each of them as turning on various other unstated factors, such as the political affiliations of the justices who made up the majority in each case, or their

---

* In a related vein, one might interpret Prosser as insisting that negligence law's duty rules became embedded in the law not by happenstance, but by the conscious decisions of judges who were swayed by certain considerations of principle and policy. This claim is also unobjectionably modest. To observe that the legal rules courts employ for the disposition of negligence claims were and are grounded in a variety of considerations is not to deny that the rules exist, nor to deny that the rules themselves provide judges with reasons to rule for or against a particular plaintiff, nor to establish that each judge confronted with a negligence case must or ought to ignore those rules and re-think whether, all things considered, they are the right rules.

religious affiliations, or their formative childhood experiences.) Still, the question remains whether a concern for policy *best* explains these decisions. It is evident from the text of the majority opinion that *Strauss* was driven to a large extent by the policy implications of imposing liability. Were those implications equally integral to the decision in *MacPherson? Salaman? Tarasoff? McGuiggan?*

REFERENCES/FURTHER READING

Injury

Stephen Perry, *Harm, History and Counterfactuals,* 40 San Diego L. Rev. 1283 (2003).

The Duty Element

John C. P. Goldberg & Benjamin C. Zipursky, *The Moral of* MacPherson, 146 U. Pa. L. Rev. 1733 (1998).

John C. P. Goldberg & Benjamin C. Zipursky, *The Restatement (Third) and the Place of Duty in Negligence Law,* 54 Vand. L. Rev. 657 (2001).

Peter F. Lake, *Common Law Duty in Negligence Law: The Recent Consolidation of a Consensus on the Expansion of the Analysis of Duty and the New Conservative Liability Limiting Use of Policy Considerations,* 34 San Diego L. Rev. 1503 (1997).

Michael L. Richmond, *The Development of Duty:* Landgridge *to* Palsgraf, 31 St. Louis U. L.J. 903 (1989).

Winterbottom *and* MacPherson

Frances Bohlen, *Studies in The Law of Torts* 76-81 (1926).

Robert M. Davis, *A Re-examination of the Doctrine of* MacPherson v. Buick *and Its Application and Extension in the State of New York,* 24 Fordham L. Rev. 204 (1955).

Martin P. Golding, *Legal Reasoning* 112-143 (1984).

James A. Henderson, Jr., MacPherson v. Buick Motor Co.: *Simplifying the Facts While Reshaping the Law,* in Robert L. Rabin & Stephen D. Sugarman (eds.), *Tort Stories* 41-71 (2003).

Edward H. Levi, *An Introduction to Legal Reasoning* 8-27 (1949).

Vernon Palmer, *When Privity Entered Tort — An Historical Reexamination of* Winterbottom v. Wright, 27 J. Am. Leg. Hist. 85 (1983).

David W. Peck, *Decision at Law* 38-69 (1961).

William L. Prosser, *The Assault upon the Citadel (Strict Liability to the Consumer),* 69 Yale L.J. 1099, 1099-1102 (1960).

Michael A. Stein, Priestley v. Fowler (1837) *and the Emerging Tort of Negligence,* 64 B.C. L. Rev. 689 (2003).

Benjamin Cardozo

John C. P. Goldberg, *Book Review: The Life of the Law*, 51 Stan. L. Rev. 1419 (1999).
Andrew L. Kaufman, *Cardozo* (1998).
Richard Polenberg, *The World of Benjamin Cardozo* (1998).
Richard A. Posner, *Cardozo: A Study in Reputation* (1990).

Amatory Torts

Lawrence Stone, *Road to Divorce: England 1530-1987*, Ch. 9 (1990).

Premises Liability

Jane Larson, *Women Understand So Little, They Call My Good Nature "Deceit": A Feminist Rethinking of Seduction*, 93 Colum. L. Rev. 374 (1993).
Robert L. Rabin, Rowland v. Christian: *Hallmark of an Expansionary Era*, in Robert L. Rabin & Stephen D. Sugarman (eds.), *Tort Stories* (2003).

Pure Economic Loss

Peter Benson, *The Basis for Excluding Liability for Economic Loss in Tort Law*, in David G. Owen (ed.), *Philosophical Foundations of Tort Law* 427 (1995).
Victor P. Goldberg, *Accountable Accountants: Is Third-Party Liability Necessary?*, 17 J. Leg. Stud. 295 (1988).
Stephen R. Perry, *Protected Interests in Undertakings in the Law of Negligence*, 17 U. Toronto L.J. 247 (1992).
Robert L. Rabin, *Tort Recovery for Negligently Inflicted Economic Loss: A Reassessment*, 37 Stan. L. Rev. 1513 (1985).
John C. Siliciano, *Negligent Accounting and the Limits of Instrumental Tort Reform*, 86 Mich. L. Rev. 1929 (1988).
Howard Weiner, *Common Law Liability of the Certified Public Accountant for Negligent Misrepresentation*, 20 San Diego L. Rev. 233 (1983).

Oliver Wendell Holmes, Jr.

Thomas C. Grey, *Accidental Torts*, 54 Vand. L. Rev. 1225 (2001).
Sheldon Novick, *Honorable Justice: The Life of Oliver Wendell Holmes* (1989).
Richard A. Posner (ed.), *The Essential Holmes* (1990).
G. Edward White, *Justice Oliver Wendell Holmes: Law and the Inner Self* (1993).

Duties to Rescue and Protect

James Barr Ames, *Law and Morals*, 22 Harv. L. Rev. 97 (1908).
Richard A. Epstein, *A Theory of Strict Liability*, 2 J. Leg. Stud. 151 (1973).
Steven J. Heyman, *Foundations of the Duty to Rescue*, 47 Vand. L. Rev. 673 (1994).
Tony Honoré, *Responsibility and Luck*, 104 Law Q. Rev. 530 (1988).
Peter F. Lake, *Boys, Bad Men, and Bad Case-Law: Re-Examining the Historical Foundations of No-Duty-To-Rescue Rules*, 43 N.Y.L. Sch. L. Rev. 385 (1999).
Timothy D. Lytton, *Tort Claims Against Gun Manufacturers for Crime-Related Injuries: Defining a Suitable Role for the Tort System in Regulating the Firearms Industry*, 65 Mo. L. Rev. 1 (2000).
John T. Pardun, *Comment: Good Samaritan Laws: A Global Perspective*, 20 Loy. L.A. Int'l & Comp. L.J. 591 (1998).
Robert L. Rabin, *Enabling Torts*, 49 DePaul L. Rev. 435 (1999).
Anthony J. Sebok, *What's Law Got to Do With It? Duty, Tort Doctrine and the 9/11 Victims Compensation Fund*, 53 DePaul L. Rev. 901 (2003).
Frank A. Sloan, et al., *Drinkers, Drivers, and Bartenders: Balancing Private Choices and Public Accountability* (2000).
Ernest J. Weinrib, *The Case for a Duty to Rescue*, 90 Yale L.J. 247 (1980).

Liability of Public Utilities

Richard J. Pierce, Jr., *Regional Transmission Organizations: Federal Limitations Needed for Tort Liability*, 23 Energy L.J. 63 (2002).

Cheapest Cost Avoider

Guido Calabresi, *The Cost of Accidents* (1971).

CHAPTER 3

The Breach Element

I. Duty, Breach, and the Two Meanings of Negligence

Analytically, duty precedes breach: A judge must first determine if a duty of care was owed by the defendant to persons such as the plaintiff before the question of whether that duty was fulfilled can be put to the jury. So far, we have paid relatively little attention to the latter question of what exactly a defendant is duty-bound to do. For example, once *MacPherson* was decided, auto manufacturers subject to New York law clearly owed a duty to users of cars to take reasonable care to protect them against defective wheels. Granted this duty, what course of conduct on the part of auto manufacturers would be sufficient to discharge it? Were they now required to inspect every wheel, or would it be sufficient to check random samples? How would they have to inspect them: visually, or under stress tests? What failure of precaution, in other words, would constitute breach of this duty?

Before proceeding, it is important to note a common terminological confusion that often inhibits clear analysis. We refer to the third element of our formulation of the negligence tort as the "breach" element. This element poses the question of whether the defendant acted with the degree of care that she was duty-bound to exercise. Courts and commentators, however, frequently refer to the breach element by using the terms *negligence* and *negligent*. When they do so, they are *not* referring to the tort of negligence, but to the act of being careless. So, for example, a lawyer or judge might say that the failure of a defendant to take appropriate precautions while driving (e.g., by speeding or being inattentive) constitutes "negligent driving." In doing so, the lawyer or court is not addressing whether the driver was under a duty of care to the plaintiff, nor whether the "negligent driving" proximately caused an injury to the plaintiff.

It is critical to keep in mind that negligence in the sense of careless conduct is *not* sufficient to establish that the defendant can be held liable for having committed the tort of negligence. The latter conclusion, as we have seen, also requires a determination as to injury, duty, and actual and proximate cause. Unfortunately, it is easy even for trained lawyers to become confused between these two different senses of negligence. To help avoid confusion, some lawyers and commentators distinguish between *big "N" Negligence*, which refers to the tort, and *small "n" negligence*, which refers to carelessness. In this book, we use the term *negligence* to refer to the prima facie case. By contrast, we use the terms *breach*, *carelessness*, and *fault* to refer to its third element, concerning the degree of care that the defendant was supposed to have exercised.

Rogers v. Retrum
825 P.2d 20 (Ariz. App. 1991)

Fidel, J.   Plaintiff Kevin C. Rogers appeals from summary judgment entered for defendants Randolph Retrum and Prescott Unified School District on plaintiff's negligence claim. We affirm summary judgment because plaintiff's injury did not result from an unreasonable risk that may be charged to the conduct of these defendants. . . .

On the morning of February 5, 1989, Kevin C. Rogers, a sixteen-year-old junior at Prescott High School, completed an advanced electronics test. Although Rogers anticipated a good grade, the teacher, Randolph Retrum, publicly gave him a failing grade. When Rogers asked why, Retrum threw the test in his direction and answered, "Because I don't like you."

Although class was not over, Retrum permitted students to leave class as they pleased, and Prescott High School permitted students to enter and leave the campus freely. Humiliated and upset, Rogers left class with a friend named Natalo Russo, punching a wall and kicking some trash cans on his way to Russo's car. As Russo tried to calm him, the friends left campus in Russo's car by a meandering route that eventually led them eastward on Iron Springs Road. There Russo, the driver, accelerated and lost control, passing in a curve at a speed exceeding 90 miles per hour. When the car struck an embankment, landed on its nose, and slid several hundred feet, Rogers was ejected and sustained the injuries for which he sues.

After the accident, Retrum admitted that Rogers had actually passed the test. Retrum had falsely given Rogers a failing grade because Rogers had always done well in the class and Retrum "wanted [Rogers] to know what it felt like to fail."

Rogers settled negligence claims against Natalo Russo and his parents, and the trial court granted summary judgment rejecting Rogers's negligence claims against Retrum and the district. From this judgment, Rogers appeals.

We first point out that Retrum's alleged conduct, however egregious, is not the causal focus of plaintiff's claim. If, in the flush of first reaction, plaintiff had blindly run into harm's way, we would examine the range of foreseeable, unreasonable risks that might be attributed to a teacher's false and deliberate humiliation of an impressionable teenager entrusted to his class.

Plaintiff, however, stepped into his friend Natalo Russo's car. And plaintiff's counsel has conceded at oral argument that there is no evidence that Retrum's words to Rogers affected Russo's operation of his car.

Counsel instead targets Retrum's "open class" and the district's "open campus" policies as the causal negligence in this case. By these policies, according to counsel, defendants breached their supervisory duty to plaintiff and exposed him to the risk of highway injury when he should have been in class. We confine our analysis to this claim.

DUTY

The first question in a negligence case is whether the defendants owed a duty to the plaintiff. We find that defendants had a relationship with plaintiff that entailed a duty of reasonable care.

Our supreme court has distilled, as the essence of duty, the obligation to act reasonably in the light of foreseeable and unreasonable risks. *See* Coburn v. City of Tucson, 143 Ariz. 50, 52, 691 P.2d 1078, 1080 (1984). . . .

Clearly, school teachers and administrators are "under [an] obligation for the benefit of" the students within their charge. *See id.* This obligation includes the duty not to subject those students, through acts, omissions, or school policy, to a foreseeable and unreasonable risk of harm. . . .

[Under the separate heading of "Legal Cause," the court next turned to consideration of the defendant's argument that Russo's reckless driving was so unforeseeable that, even granted a duty owed by the school to be vigilant of Rogers' physical well-being, this was not the sort of injury-producing event against which they were duty-bound to guard. The doctrines of legal (or "proximate") cause and superseding cause are discussed more fully in Chapter 5. — EDS.] . . .

We decline to affirm the trial court's judgment on this ground.

First, "we must take a broad view of the class of risks and victims that are foreseeable, and the particular manner in which the injury is brought about need not be foreseeable." Schnyder v. Empire Metals, Inc., 136 Ariz. 428, 431, 666 P.2d 528, 531 (App. 1983) (citing McFarlin v. Hall, 127 Ariz. 220, 222, 619 P.2d 729, 731 (1980)). It is not unforeseeable that mobile high school students, permitted to leave campus during classroom hours, will be exposed to the risk of roadway accidents.

Second, the reckless or criminal nature of an intervenor's conduct does not place it beyond the scope of a duty of reasonable care if that duty entails foresight and prevention of precisely such a risk. *See* Rossell v. Volkswagen of America, 147 Ariz. 160, 169, 709 P.2d 517, 526 (1985), *cert. denied*, 476 U.S. 1108, 106 S. Ct. 1957, 90 L. Ed. 2d 365 (1986) ("[T]he scope of the risk created by the negligence of the original actor may include the foreseeable negligent or criminal conduct of others.") . . .

. . . The condition created by defendants' negligent conduct, according to plaintiff, was exposure to a preventable risk of vehicular injury off school grounds. Inherent in the risk of vehicular injury is the prospect of an intervenor's negligent or reckless driving of a car; to foresee the injurious end is to foresee that a careless intervenor, one way or another, may be the means. For this reason, it does not advance analysis in this case to focus on the details of the intervenor's conduct. The essential question is not whether the district might have foreseen the risk of vehicular injury but whether the district, given its supervisory responsibilities, was obliged to take precautionary measures. This question, we conclude, is [not] one of duty . . . it is one of breach.

UNREASONABLE RISK

Not every foreseeable risk is an unreasonable risk. It does not suffice to establish liability to prove (a) that defendant owed plaintiff a duty of reasonable care; (b) that an act or omission of defendant was a contributing cause of injury to plaintiff; and (c) that the risk of injury should have been foreseeable to defendant. The question whether the risk was unreasonable remains. This last question merges with foreseeability to set the scope of the duty of reasonable care. *Cf.* 3 F. Harper, F. James & O. Gray, *The Law of Torts* § 18.2, at 656-57 (2d ed. 1986). . . .

To decide whether a risk was unreasonable requires an evaluative judgment ordinarily left to the jury. "Summary judgment is generally not appropriate in negligence actions." Tribe v. Shell Oil Co., Inc., 133 Ariz. 517, 518, 652 P.2d 1040, 1041 (1982). However, in approaching the question of negligence or unreasonable risk,

> the courts set outer limits. A jury will not be permitted to require a party to take a precaution that is clearly unreasonable. . . . Thus, for example, the jury may not require a train to stop before passing over each grade crossing in the country. 3 F. Harper, F. James & O. Gray, *supra* § 15.3, at 355-57.[4]

Coburn v. City of Tucson is a recent example of the court's preemption of the question of unreasonable risk. There, a child eastbound on a bicycle was struck and killed by a southbound driver in an intersection collision. 143 Ariz. at 51, 691 P.2d at 1079. The child had ignored a stop sign and entered the intersection in the lane of westbound (oncoming) traffic. The child could not see the driver approaching because a bush at the northwest corner obscured his view. The child's parents sued the city for failure to remove the bush; the city both controlled the street and owned the lot where the bush grew. The evidence established, however, that the bush would not have obstructed the view of south- or northbound traffic for any eastbound cyclist or driver who had stayed in the eastbound lane and stopped at the stop sign. The supreme court affirmed summary judgment for the city, finding that the city had not breached its duty to provide intersections that are reasonably safe.

> The lack of liability may be framed in terms of duty, but we prefer that duty be recognized as a distinct element involving the obligation of the actor to

---

4. In describing the question whether a risk was unreasonable as requiring evaluative judgment, we acknowledge that the question does not fall neatly into the category of question of fact or the category of question of law. These categories serve less as guides to analysis than as labels that attach after the court has decided whether to leave evaluation to the jury or preempt it for the court. *See* James, *Functions of Judge and Jury in Negligence Cases*, 58 Yale L.J. 667, 667-68 (1949) . . . ; *see also* Farrell v. Waterbury Horse R.R., 60 Conn. 239, 247, 21 A. 675, 676 (1891) ("[T]he result of comparing the conduct with the standard is generally spoken of as 'negligence' or the 'finding of negligence.' Negligence, in this last sense, is always a conclusion or inference, and never a fact in the ordinary sense of that word.") . . .

protect the other from harm. Here, there was a duty, but no negligence; therefore, there is no liability.

Id. (citations omitted).

We make the same determination in this case. Members of our mobile society face the risk of collision whenever they are in cars. This risk is arguably higher for teenage passengers of teenage drivers. The school in this case, however, did nothing to increase this general risk. It did not, for example, leave students inadequately supervised or instructed in a driver's education class. It did not tolerate drinking at a school affair. It simply chose not to restrict students to campus during the school day and thereby shield them from the ordinary risk of vehicular harm that they would face when out of school. We conclude that "the standard of reasonable conduct [did] not require the defendant[s] to . . . take precautions against" that risk. [Quoted authority omitted. — EDS.] More simply stated, the defendants' omission did not create an unreasonable risk of harm.

Although, in taking this issue from the jury, we find that reasonable persons could not differ, we do not mask the element of policy in our choice. First, the question of the legal consequence of an open campus high school policy is not a random judgment best left to case-by-case assessment, but a question likely to recur and one on which school boards need some guidance. Second, policy considerations appropriate to local school boards — local transportation options, inter-school transfer arrangements, and extracurricular activity locations, for example — are pertinent to the decision whether restrictions should be placed on high school students coming and going from the campus during ordinary hours. Finally, and most significantly, we decline to make high school districts that adopt an open campus policy insurers against the ordinary risks of vehicular injury that students face in driving off school grounds.

This is not to suggest that a school's supervisory omissions can never give rise to liability for an accident off campus. We do not pretend that the range of foreseeable and unreasonable risks from supervisory omissions is automatically circumscribed by the school fence.

Nor do we suggest that a calculus of unreasonable risk will yield equivalent results at every level of the schools. We leave for resolution in other unsupervised egress cases such questions as whether parents' supervisory expectations may reasonably differ at differing levels of the schools and whether the risks that may be deemed unreasonable may likewise differ with the age of the student involved. Our limited holding in this case is that the defendant high school and its teacher did not subject the plaintiff high school student to an unreasonable risk of vehicular injury by permitting unsupervised egress from class and campus during the school day.

CONCLUSION

Because plaintiff's injury was not a result within an unreasonable risk created by defendants, we hold that defendants were not negligent. The trial court's summary judgment in favor of defendants is affirmed.

Caliri v. New Hampshire Dept. of Transportation
620 A.2d 1028 (N.H. 1993)

Brock, J.   This negligence action arises out of a one-car accident that caused the death of Dale Hobart. The plaintiff, Claire Caliri, is the administratrix of Mr. Hobart's estate. . . . [T]he jury returned a verdict for the defendant, the State of New Hampshire, Department of Transportation (DOT). The plaintiff appeals, arguing that the trial court erred in its jury charge. We affirm.

The accident occurred on April 1, 1987, after the driver of the automobile, in which Mr. Hobart was a passenger, lost control upon hitting a patch of ice on Hampstead Road in Derry.

The plaintiff argued below that the DOT had a duty to maintain Hampstead Road for the safety of its travelers and that in furtherance of that duty, it was required to conduct ditching on private property abutting Hampstead Road; that the purpose of ditching was to prevent hazardous conditions by diverting water from flowing on the road; and that the performance of ditching on the private property was not a discretionary function under RSA 541-B:19, I(c) (Supp. 1991), which would immunize the State from suit for breach of its duty. The plaintiff asserted that because the DOT breached its duty to properly ditch the abutting property, water flowed from the ditch onto the road, forming ice that caused the accident resulting in Mr. Hobart's death.

At trial, the State conceded that the DOT was responsible for the maintenance of Hampstead Road, a Class II Highway, *see* RSA 230:3, and the State did not deny that certain of its employees owed a duty of due care to Mr. Hobart. . . .

On appeal, the plaintiff first argues that the trial court erred when it refused to give her requested instructions involving the State's duty owed to travelers on its roadways, thereby leaving the jury with no guidance upon which to judge the defendant's conduct. We disagree.

. . . [T]he plaintiff requested that the trial court give the following instructions on the State's duty:

> In New Hampshire the highway traveller [*sic*] may act upon the assumption that public authorities have performed their duty to maintain the highway and that the public way is in a reasonably safe condition. [citation omitted] The State of New Hampshire, Department of Transportation is "bound to constant vigilance and circumspection in regard to [its] highways, and [is] liable for damages happening in consequence of existing defects therein, which [it] had reasonable opportunity to remedy, or which may have arisen from [its] own negligence in [its] original construction, or [its] want of fidelity in properly looking after and repairing them." [citations omitted]

The court was under no obligation to give these instructions, because they would impose a standard of care on the State that is not supported by either common or statutory law.

The general purpose of the court's charge is to state and explain to the jury the rules of law that are to be applied to the facts material to the resolution of the case. . . . "A jury charge is sufficient as a matter of law if, taken as a whole, it fairly presents the case to the jury in such a manner that no injustice is done to the legal rights of the litigants." Broderick v. Watts, 136 N.H. 153, 163, 614 A.2d 600, 607 (1992) (quotations and brackets omitted). It is well settled that the court need not use the identical language requested by a party as long as the court adequately states the law as applied to the case. *Id.*

. . . Although no duty of care towards individuals using the highways was statutorily imposed on the DOT at the time of the accident, we accept the State's concession that a duty of due care was owed to Mr. Hobart. *Cf.* Laws 1992, ch. 188 (codified at RSA 230:78 to :82 (Supp. 1992)) (legislation effective January 1, 1993, limiting the DOT's liability in the exercise of its statutory duty to maintain certain highways and highway bridges by determining that it should not be held to the standard of ordinary negligence for tort claims under certain circumstances).

. . . [T]he trial judge gave the standard negligence instruction, *see* N.H. Civil Jury Instructions, 6.1 (rev. ed. 1992). He instructed the jury that

> [n]egligence is simply the want of due care by some act or some omission. It is a deviation from that degree of care that would be exercised by the reasonable person of ordinary prudence. That individual is a fictional individual in the eyes of the law from whose conduct the rest of our conduct is measured. . . . To the extent that a defendant's conduct deviates from what a reasonable man would have done or what a reasonable man or reasonable person wouldn't have done, we say that that deviation is negligence. So negligence is doing what a reasonable person of ordinary prudence wouldn't do, or it is not doing what a reasonable person of ordinary prudence would do under the same or similar circumstances. . . .

These instructions adequately presented the law of negligence. Under the general dictates of tort law, "liability is ordinarily imposed upon persons for injuries caused by their failure to exercise reasonable care under all the circumstances." Ouellette v. Blanchard, 116 N.H. at 553, 364 A.2d at 632. . . . ["T]he test of due care is what reasonable prudence would require under similar circumstances." Weldy v. Town of Kingston, 128 N.H. 325, 330-31, 514 A.2d 1257, 1260 (1986) (citation omitted). Accordingly, we find that the court adequately instructed the jury on the issue of negligence and did not err by refusing to give the requested instructions.

Pingaro v. Rossi
731 A.2d 523 (N.J. Super. App. Div. 1999)

Havey, P.J.   A jury awarded $300,000 in damages to plaintiff Ellen Pingaro, a meter reader for . . . New Jersey Natural Gas Company (NJNG), for injuries she sustained as a result of a dog bite she suffered from a German Shepherd owned by defendant Joseph Rossi. . . .

. . . [O]n June 27, 1996, [Pingaro was] performing her meter reading duties for NJNG [on] a route in Beachwood, Ocean County. When she arrived at Rossi's house, her data cap, a hand-held computer, "beeped" a message: "[b]ad dog, knock." The data cap provides the meter reader with the name of the street and location of the meter and at times displays specialized messages pertaining to the customer, such as whether a "bad dog" may be present.

According to plaintiff, she had never been to Rossi's home before. She knocked on Rossi's door but received no answer. She proceeded to the fenced-in backyard, rattled the gate and her keys and yelled "gas company." There was no response. She looked around the backyard for dogs or other animals. After satisfying herself that the yard was clear, she unhooked the gate and walked towards the meter. Immediately upon entering the back yard two dogs approached her. One dog, a large German Shepard, jumped up, knocked her down and bit her on both arms, legs and head. She subdued the dog by hitting it with her flashlight, exited the yard and called for help. A nearby construction worker summoned an ambulance which took her to Community Medical Center where she received numerous stitches and was released later that afternoon.

[Plaintiff received physical therapy and was unable to work or engage in normal activities for more than a month. She also suffered scars on her arms and on one leg, as well as anxiety, fear, and depression related to the incident. — EDS.] . . .

Rossi testified that the dog which attacked plaintiff was kept fenced in his backyard. The only gate to the backyard was the gate utilized by plaintiff in entering the yard. He stated that a large "Beware of Dog" sign was posted on the gate.

According to Rossi, over the course of ten years he had spoken with several meter readers about his dog and told them they should not enter his yard if no one was home. The meter readers responded that they would comply with his request. Rossi noted that this arrangement had worked for over ten years, and when he was not at home the meter readers would estimate his bill, leave a card for him to mail in or come back at a later date. . . .

The so-called "dog bite" statute, N.J.S.A. 4:19-16, reads in pertinent part:

> The owner of any dog which shall bite a person while such person is on or in a public place, or lawfully on or in a private place, including the property of the owner of the dog, shall be liable for such damages as may be suffered by the person bitten, regardless of the former viciousness of such dog or the owner's knowledge of such viciousness.

There is no question that plaintiff fulfilled the three elements necessary to establish Rossi's liability under the statute. Rossi was the owner of the dog, the dog bit plaintiff and the bite occurred while plaintiff was lawfully on Rossi's property. Satisfaction of the elements of the statute imposes strict liability upon Rossi for damages sustained by plaintiff. . . .

In order for plaintiff to prevail under the "dog-bite" statute, she need not prove scienter; that is, that Rossi knew of the dog's dangerous propensities.

[The Court proceeded to rule on various other issues raised on appeal. — EDS.]

Jones v. Port Authority of Allegheny County
583 A.2d 512 (Pa. Comm. 1990)

Barry, J. Oscar and Mary Jones, husband and wife . . . appeal an order of the Court of Common Pleas . . . which entered judgment for the defendant, the Port Authority of Allegheny County (PAT), following a jury verdict in favor of PAT and the denial of the Jones' post-trial motions.

Oscar Jones testified that he was injured on a PAT bus. He testified that he had entered the bus and was climbing the stairs to the platform on which the seats were located. Before reaching the platform, the bus pulled out and stopped suddenly. According to Mr. Jones' testimony the doors to the bus had not closed at the time of the accident. He testified that he injured his arm in the incident. PAT posited at trial that the accident never occurred. It took the further position that, if the incident actually happened, there was no negligence on the part of PAT's driver. The jury brought a verdict in favor of PAT. Appellants filed post-trial motions which were denied. This appeal followed.

Appellants make three allegations of error, all of which deal with the trial court's charge to the jury. . . .

Appellants first argue that the trial court erred in refusing to charge the jury that PAT, as a common carrier, owes the highest duty of care to its fare paying passengers. The trial court charged the jury as follows on this question:

> Now, the Port Authority or the Defendant . . . owes a duty to passengers to operate the vehicles in which the passengers are boarding and which they are situated, to use that degree of care which they hold itself out to possess.
>
> Now, this degree of care is different than would be for an ordinary person. An ordinary person doesn't say ["]look [w]e're specialists in transporting you from point A to point B in a safe manner,["] but the Port Authority holds itself out to be an instrumentality that is transporting people and that they possess the skill and the knowledge and the training to do this in safety; and this is a duty they owed to Mr. Jones on this particular day in 1986 when he was allegedly injured or as he contends he was injured.
>
> Now, if they breach this duty, if they didn't exercise the degree of care that a reasonably prudent person would who's in the position of the Port Authority, then they would be negligent; . . .

Section 3.05 of the Pennsylvania Suggested Standard Civil Jury Instructions contains the following instruction regarding common carriers.

> The defendant in this case is a common carrier who is required by law to use a higher degree of care for the safety of its passengers than that ordinarily imposed on others and must be judged by a much stricter standard. Although this legal duty does not make the carrier absolutely responsible for the plaintiff's safety in all cases, it does obligate this carrier to exercise the highest degree of diligence and care in the (operation of its vehicle) and the (maintenance of its equipment and facilities). Any failure of the defendant to use such care under all of the circumstances of the particular situation in this case is negligence.

In Burch v. Sears, Roebuck and Co., 320 Pa. Superior Ct. 444, 467 A.2d 615 (1983), the court held that a trial court is to be given broad latitude in the choice of language used in charging a jury. Nevertheless, if the trial court's charge does not adequately explain the principle involved, a new trial must be granted. . . .

The law has long been well settled that a common carrier owes a heightened duty of care to its fare paying passengers. Over a century ago, the Supreme Court held that such a common carrier owed the duty of "extraordinary care." Philadelphia and Reading R.R. Co. v. Boger, 97 Pa. 91, 101 (1881). Cases of a more recent vintage have used the language "highest degree of care" as suggested by the Standard Civil Jury Instructions. . . .

All of the appellate courts of this Commonwealth have made clear that a common carrier owes the "highest duty of care" to its passengers. While the trial court attempted to explain the heightened level of care, we do not believe that attempt was sufficient, when we review the charge in its entirety as we must. . . . Accordingly, a new trial must be granted. . . .

NOTES AND QUESTIONS

1. *Foreseeability versus Reasonableness (I)*. *Rogers* lays out the distinction between duty and breach in terms of a contrast between foresight and reasonableness. The *foreseeability* of the risk of physical harm to students driving to and from campus is necessary to establish that the school owed a duty to take care to prevent such harm to them. (It also establishes, at least in this case, that reckless student driving was among the risks that the school was duty-bound to take care to prevent from being realized.) That such harms and events were foreseeable, however, does not of itself establish that the school was careless with respect to these risks by deciding to maintain its open door policy. Rather, a separate inquiry is required into whether it was *reasonable* for the school, in light of the foreseeable risks, to leave the building open. In effect, then, the court concludes that the school had a duty to take care to protect its students from being injured in car accidents, but that it fulfilled that duty in this instance. How did the school do so? In what other school-related scenarios might the court be willing to let a jury find a breach of this duty?

2. *Foreseeability versus Reasonableness (II)*. While foreseeability plays a special role in duty analysis — if harm to persons such as the plaintiff was truly unforeseeable, then likely there was no duty of care to be vigilant of such harm — courts sometimes invoke that concept of foreseeability in analyzing the breach issue of whether an actor used reasonable care. In other words, as *Rogers* informs us, the test for breach is reasonableness, not foreseeability, yet the foreseeability of a particular harm may bear on the issue of what sort of precautions, if any, a reasonable person would take. So, for example, a court might say that, because the occurrence of a particular kind of harm was completely unforeseeable, it follows

that the defendant's conduct was reasonable as a matter of law. Alternatively, a court might take notice of the degree to which a harm was foreseeable as a factor in assessing what sort of precautions a reasonable person would take in a given situation.

3. *Shifting Sands*. As *Rogers* notes, the decision to frame the issue in the case as one of breach rather than duty is contestable. A different court *could* have framed the dispositive issue in terms of duty: cases do not present themselves with pre-drawn partitions between issues or elements. If it was open to the *Rogers* court to justify its decision on the ground that the school owed no duty of care to its students with respect to the risks posed to them by their driving to or from school, why did it decline to rest its decision on that basis?

Other courts sometimes parse breach and duty differently. For example, in Washington v. City of Chicago, 720 N.E.2d 1030 (Ill. 1999), the plaintiff sued the city after a fire engine winding its way through traffic drove onto a raised median, hit a planter box, went out of control, and struck plaintiff's car. Plaintiff alleged that the city was negligent in designing medians that increased the risk of traffic accidents. The Illinois Supreme Court rejected the claim, reasoning that the city owed no duty of care to the plaintiffs, because "the accident that gave rise to plaintiff's injuries was not a reasonably foreseeable consequence of the condition of the median." Is it really plausible to say that the installation of planter boxes creates no foreseeable risk of harm to drivers, and that a city owes no duty to users of its streets to design those streets with reasonable care for the physical safety of users? Would it be more accurate to say, with *Rogers*, that the city bears such a duty, but that the mere installation of planters into street medians cannot, as a matter of law, be a breach of that duty, since their inclusion likely does not significantly increase the risk of injurious traffic accidents? In other words, wouldn't it be more plausible to assert, in the language of *Rogers*, that the planter boxes posed a fore-seeable-but-not-unreasonable risk of physical harm to drivers?

Decisions such as *Washington* may reflect judicial discomfort, acknowledged by the *Rogers* court, with the issuance of as-a-matter-of-law rulings on the breach question. Indeed, as *Rogers* emphasizes, its decision is unusual in that the breach issue, in contrast to the duty issue, is ordinarily a question for the jury. Recall from Chapter 1 that a judge may only take the breach issue from the jury if the evidence in a given case points so strongly in one direction — usually against a finding of breach — that the judge is entitled to conclude that no reasonable jury could find that a breach did (or did not) occur. By framing what might appear to be a breach question as if it were a duty question, a court such as the *Washington* court may, for better or worse, be helping itself to overcome qualms about substituting its judgment for the jury's.

4. *Judge and Jury*. Because of this allocation of decisionmaking authority between duty and breach, any discussion of breach is necessarily bound up with a discussion of the institution of the jury. As you proceed through the materials, consider again why the courts have employed this division of labor between duty and breach. Is the distinction rooted in a

conception of relative institutional competence: that judges will do a better job of reasoning through duty questions, whereas jurors are better at assessing breach? What other considerations might support or undercut this arrangement?

5. *The Breach Instruction.* Juries resolve the breach issue by reference to the reasonable person standard, which is explained to them by trial judges in instructions provided after closing arguments and before they deliberate. The jury instruction approved by *Caliri* is representative of modern jury instructions on the breach element in most states. What was wrong, exactly, with plaintiff's proposed instruction? How does it misstate the legal standard to be applied by the jury? Does *Pingaro* shed any light on the problem with the proposed instruction?

6. *Strict Liability.* Is the ruling in *Pingaro* that Rossi, the dog owner, failed to behave reasonably even though he erected fencing, posted a clear warning sign at the only entrance to the premises, and arranged with previous meter readers not to have them enter the premises when there was no one at home to control the dogs? Suppose Rossi had also penned the dogs into an area away from the meter using fencing that he had bought from a reputable store, and that had been represented by the store to be adequate to restrain German Shepherds. Suppose further that, against all odds, the dogs still managed to break loose and attack Pingaro. Would liability still attach under the statute? If so, what can Rossi do to avoid liability for dog bites?

Notice how the dog-bite statute, as applied to attacks on the premises, departs from the rules we encountered in Chapter 2 concerning dangerous conditions located on real property. Even absent such a statute, the common law has long held owners of dogs and other animals strictly liable for injuries caused by them, whether on or off the owner's property. However, in contrast to the standard set by the statute, the common law rule of strict liability applies only to owners who know or have reason to know that the animal in question is prone to be vicious or otherwise abnormally dangerous. Thus, under the common law, so long as the plaintiff can establish that a dog owner knew or should have known his dog was prone to viciousness, the owner cannot escape liability even if he employed all reasonable means to control the animal.* Strict liability for injuries caused by domestic animals and livestock will be discussed in greater detail in Chapter 11.

7. *Reasonable Care versus Extraordinary Care.* As noted by the appellate court in *Jones,* "common carriers" — commercial and governmental operators of boats, buses, planes, and trains — have long been held to owe their passengers greater-than-ordinary care. Implicit in the court's

* To say that the dog bite statute and common law impose strict liability (albeit in different forms) is not to say that dog owners have no defenses available to them. For example, owners might be able to eliminate or mitigate liability by establishing that the victim goaded the dog (assumption of risk) or failed to take reasonable care for her own safety (comparative fault). Defenses are discussed in Chapter 7.

ruling is its sense that, with the proper instruction, the jury might have rendered a verdict for the plaintiffs instead of the defendant. Do you think the bus driver's conduct satisfies the standard of ordinary care, but fails the test of extraordinary care?

Many modern courts and commentators have urged that the conduct of common carriers toward their passengers be judged under the ordinary reasonable person standard. *See, e.g.,* Bethel v. New York City Transit Auth., 703 N.E.2d 1214 (N.Y. 1998). *Bethel* reasoned that common carriers are not sufficiently distinct from other actors as to warrant the imposition of a higher standard of care, and that a heightened standard is unnecessary because the reasonable person standard takes into account all relevant factors, including the character of the relationship between defendant and plaintiff. Do you find these rationales convincing? Are there downsides to "flattening" all standards of care into a single standard of reasonableness?

Compare the effort of the California Supreme Court in *Rowland v. Christian* (discussed in the notes following *Salaman, supra,* Chapter 2). There, the California Court aimed to achieve a similar flattening by getting rid of the plaintiff-status categories for claims arising out of hazardous conditions on land. Eliminating the clutter and seeming arbitrariness of multiple standards of care, or multiple status categories, can achieve a certain kind of intellectual tidiness. In doing so, however, might it also be avoiding, rather than addressing, questions that are highly pertinent to the assignment of responsibility?

8. *Unreasonable versus Reckless Behavior.* We saw in Chapter 2 that, in some jurisdictions, owners and occupiers of land owe lesser duties of care to certain persons, such as trespassers. Consider the following instruction, provided in a case in which a train passenger was killed when, after disembarking from a local train at a station, she attempted to cross a set of tracks on foot, at which point she was run down by a different train, owned by Amtrak. Under Massachusetts law, the passenger was deemed a trespasser because she did not cross the tracks at an established crossing. Thus, Amtrak owed her only the lesser duty of not causing her injury through willful or reckless conduct. The trial court instructed the jury as follows on the recklessness standard:

> To prove that Amtrak was reckless in this case, plaintiff must prove that Amtrak intentionally or unreasonably disregarded a risk that presented a high degree of probability that substantial harm would result to another. The risk of death or grave bodily injury must have been known or reasonably apparent to Amtrak, and the harm must have been a probable consequence of Amtrak's election to run that risk or its failure to reasonably recognize it.
>
> To intentionally disregard a risk means to ignore or neglect it deliberately, rather than by accident or mistake.
>
> To unreasonably disregard a risk means to ignore or neglect a risk that a person of ordinary prudence would act to reduce or eliminate.
>
> In this case, plaintiff must also prove that any risk that was intentionally or unreasonably disregarded involved a high probability of substantial harm. This means that plaintiff must prove that substantial harm was more than a foreseeable possibility or likely to occur. Rather, plaintiff must prove

that a reasonable person in Amtrak's position would recognize that substantial harm was highly likely to occur. Plaintiff does not, however, have to prove that substantial harm was certain to occur. . . .

So, to prove recklessness, plaintiff must prove that there was a high probability that a person would be seriously injured or killed crossing the tracks at the Attleboro station and that Amtrak intentionally or unreasonably disregarded that risk.

The mere fact that an accident occurred does not mean that Amtrak was reckless. Moreover, in this case, it would be insufficient for the plaintiff to prove only what is called negligence, which is a failure to use reasonable care. . . . To prevail, the plaintiff must meet a higher standard and prove recklessness, as I defined that term for you today. . . .

Beausoleil v. National R.R. Passenger Corp., 145 F. Supp. 2d 119, 125-126 (D. Mass. 2001). Earlier, Amtrak had moved for summary judgment on the ground that there was insufficient evidence to support a jury finding of recklessness. In rejecting this argument, the court noted that, even though Amtrak had posted warning signs and provided partial fencing, it knew that passengers continued to cross the tracks despite these precautions, and that another passenger had previously been killed under similar circumstances. It had also been warned by a state legislator of the grave dangers posed at this location. Finally, the driver of the train acknowledged in deposition testimony that he knew that passengers who disembarked from other trains routinely crossed the tracks at this station, and that he failed to radio ahead to determine if any trains had just left the station. Beausoleil v. National R.R. Passenger Corp., 138 F. Supp. 2d 189, 205 (D. Mass. 2001).

Does the recklessness instruction, in conjunction with the extraordinary care instruction in *Jones*, help refine the idea of reasonable care? If you were serving as a juror, how might these different formulations affect your deliberations?

9. *Emergencies.* Courts are divided over whether to give specific instructions to juries on certain special instances of breach, for example, breaches that allegedly occur in emergency contexts. Suppose *D* is driving down the highway at a safe distance behind a truck. Several crates suddenly fall off the back of the truck directly in front of *D*. *D* swerves to avoid them and collides with *P*, who is injured and sues *D* for carelessly swerving her car into his. All courts agree that a jury is entitled to take into account that *D* swerved in response to an unforeseen emergency in determining whether *D* behaved like a reasonable person under the circumstances. They differ, however, over whether the jury should receive a general reasonable person instruction as seen in *Caliri*, or whether that instruction should be supplemented with an instruction specifically informing the jury that it may take into account the emergency in assessing the allegedly negligent party's conduct. *See* Dan B. Dobbs, *The Law of Torts* § 131, at 307 (2000) (discussing the debate).

10. *No Breach as a Matter of Law.* Grant that, in most cases, the breach question ought to be committed to the jury's discretion. In what instances will judges take the question away from the jury? Cardozo famously confronted this question in Adams v. Bullock, 125 N.E. 93 (N.Y. 1919). The plaintiff, a 12-year-old boy, was walking across a railroad bridge

that ran over a street, swinging an eight-foot-long piece of wire. The wire, dangling over the side wall of the bridge, came into contact with uninsulated electrical lines located about four and a half feet below the top of the bridge wall. The wires were used by defendant to operate its trolley cars. As a result, the plaintiff suffered an electrical shock and burns. The Court of Appeals reversed a jury verdict for plaintiff, finding no breach as a matter of law. Cardozo wrote as follows:

> There was, of course, a duty to adopt all reasonable precautions to minimize the resulting perils. We think there is no evidence that this duty was ignored. The trolley wire was so placed that no one standing on the bridge or even bending over the parapet could reach it. Only some extraordinary casualty, not fairly within the area of ordinary prevision, could make it a thing of danger. Reasonable care in the use of a destructive agency imports a high degree of vigilance. But no vigilance, however alert, unless fortified by the gift of prophecy, could have predicted the point upon the route where such an accident would occur. It might with equal reason have been expected anywhere else. At any point upon the route, a mischievous or thoughtless boy might touch the wire with a metal pole, or fling another wire across it. If unable to reach it from the walk, he might stand upon a wagon or climb upon a tree. No special danger at this bridge warned the defendant that there was need of special measures of precaution. No like accident had occurred before. No custom had been disregarded. We think that ordinary caution did not involve forethought of this extraordinary peril. It has been so ruled in like circumstances by courts in other jurisdictions. . . . There is, we may add, a distinction, not to be ignored, between electric light and trolley wires. The distinction is that the former may be insulated. Chance of harm, though remote, may betoken negligence, if needless. Facility of protection may impose a duty to protect. With trolley wires, the case is different. Insulation is impossible. Guards here and there are of little value. To avert the possibility of this accident and others like it at one point or another on the route, the defendant must have abandoned the overhead system, and put the wires underground. Neither its power nor its duty to make the change is shown. To hold it liable upon the facts exhibited in this record would be to charge it as an insurer.

11. *Holmes versus Cardozo.* Some have urged that judges should more frequently issue as-a-matter-of-law rulings on breach. For example, in *The Common Law*, Holmes argued as follows:

> [A]ny legal standard must, in theory, be capable of being known. When a man has to pay damages, he is supposed to have broken the law, and he is further supposed to have known what the law was.
>
> [Accordingly], it is . . . clear that the featureless generality that the defendant was bound to use such care as a prudent man would do under the circumstances, ought to be continually giving place to the specific one, that he was bound to use this or that precaution under these or those circumstances. . . . If . . . courts . . . left every case, without rudder or compass, to the jury, they would simply confess their inability to state a very large part of the law which they required the defendant to know, and would assert, by implication, that nothing could be learned by experience.

Oliver W. Holmes, Jr., *The Common Law* 111-112 (1881).

Later, as a Supreme Court Justice, Holmes had occasion to practice what he preached. In Baltimore & O. R. Co. v. Goodman, 275 U.S. 66 (1927), the Court was confronted with a case involving a grade-crossing collision between plaintiff's car and defendant's train. The issue was whether the plaintiff was contributorily negligent — and hence, under the law of the time, barred from recovering any damages — because he failed to come to a complete stop and check for oncoming trains before proceeding across the tracks. Overturning lower court rulings that the issue of contributory fault was for the jury to decide under the reasonable person standard, Holmes, for the Court, declared a rule for grade cross-ing cases specifying that all drivers must, at a minimum, stop at the tracks and look for oncoming trains to avoid being found at fault. Moreover, the Court held, if a driver's view is obstructed at the stopping point, he is further obliged to get out of his car and reconnoiter. While granting that "the question of due care is very generally left to the jury," Holmes reasoned that "we are dealing with a standard of conduct, and where the standard is clear it should be laid down once and for all by the courts." 275 U.S., at 70.

Seven years later, Cardozo, the author of *Adams*, now sitting in the Supreme Court seat vacated by Holmes, substantially undid the work of his predecessor. While reaffirming "stop, look, and listen" as a per se rule of reasonable conduct for drivers approaching grade crossings, Cardozo's opinion abandoned *Goodman*'s "get out and reconnoiter" rule. Noting that the latter was not in keeping with normal driving practices and that it creates dangers of its own, Cardozo emphasized "the need for caution in framing standards of behavior that amount to rules of law," particularly where "there is no background of experience out of which the standards have emerged." The courts, he said, should not impose rules that they have "artificially developed." Rather, in the absence of "the guide of customary conduct, what is suitable for the traveler caught in a mesh where the ordinary safeguards fail him is a judgment for the jury." Pokora v. Wabash Ry. Co., 292 U.S. 98, 106 (1934).

II.   DEFINING THE REASONABLE PERSON

We noted in Chapter 2 that English courts long ago recognized duties owed by owners and possessors of property to take care in undertaking activities on their property so as not to injure others nearby. As it turns out, the decision cited for that proposition — Vaughan v. Menlove — is more famous for its discussion of breach than of duty.

Vaughan v. Menlove
132 Eng. Rep. 490 (C. P. 1837)

[What follows is a syllabus or summary of the case prepared by a professional case reporter. It begins with the reporter's recitation of the facts and procedural history of the case, and then is followed by his transcription of the judges' opinions, which were issued orally. — EDS.]

The declaration stated, that before and at the time of the grievance and injury, hereinafter mentioned, certain premises, to wit, two cottages . . . in the county of Salop, were . . . in the respective possessions and occupations of certain persons as tenants thereof to the Plaintiff . . . : that the Defendant was then possessed of a certain close near to the said cottages, and of certain buildings of wood and thatch, also near to the said cottages; and that the Defendant was then also possessed of a certain rick or stack of hay before then heaped, stacked, or put together, and then standing, and being in and upon the said close of the Defendant. That on the 1st of August 1835, while the said cottages so were in the occupation of the said tenants, . . . the said rick or stack of hay of the Defendant was liable and likely to . . . break out into a flame . . . ; and by reason of . . . the state and condition of the said rick or stack of hay, the same then was and continued dangerous to the said cottages; of which said several premises the Defendant then had notice; yet the Defendant well knowing the premises, but not regarding his duty in that behalf, . . . wrongfully negligently, and improperly, kept and continued the said rick or stack of hay, so likely and liable to . . . take fire, and in a state and condition dangerous to the said cottages, although he could, and might, and ought to have removed and altered the same, so as to prevent the same from being and continuing so dangerous as aforesaid; and by reason thereof the said cottages for a long time, . . . were in great danger of being consumed by fire. That by reason of the . . . carelessness, negligence, and improper conduct of the Defendant, . . . the said rick or stack of hay of the Defendant, . . . did . . . break out into flame, and by fire and flame thence issuing and arising, the said buildings of the Defendant . . . were set on fire; and thereby . . . fire and flame so occasioned as aforesaid by the igniting and breaking out into flame, . . . was thereupon . . . communicated unto the said cottages in which the Plaintiff was interested . . . , which were thereby then respectively set on fire, and then . . . were consumed, damaged and wholly destroyed, the cottages being of great value, to wit, the value of 500 [pounds].* . . .

At the trial it appeared that the rick in question had been made by the Defendant near the boundary of his own premises; that the hay was in such a state when put together, as to give rise to discussions on the probability of fire; that though there were conflicting opinions on the subject, yet during a period of five weeks, the Defendant was repeatedly warned of his peril; that his stock was insured; and that upon one occasion, being advised to take the rick down to avoid all danger, he said "he would chance it." He made an aperture or chimney through the rick; but in spite, or perhaps in consequence of this precaution, the rick at length burst into

---

* [Combustion caused by the release of chemicals from stacked hay that is rotting because of exposure to excessive moisture apparently remains a problem today. *See* www.montana.edu/wwwpb/ag/hayfire.html. — EDS.]

flames from the spontaneous heating of its materials; the flames communicated to the Defendant's barn and stables, and thence to the Plaintiff's cottages, which were entirely destroyed.

Patteson J. before whom the cause was tried, told the jury that the question for them to consider, was, whether the fire had been occasioned by gross negligence on the part of the Defendant; adding, that he was bound to proceed with such reasonable caution as a prudent man would have exercised under such circumstances.

A verdict having been found for the Plaintiff, a rule nisi for a new trial was obtained, on the ground that the jury should have been directed to consider, not, whether the Defendant had been guilty of gross negligence with reference to the standard of ordinary prudence, a standard too uncertain to afford any criterion; but whether he had acted bona fide to the best of his judgment; if he had, he ought not to be responsible for the misfortune of not possessing the highest order of intelligence. . . .

Tindal, C.J. . . .

It is contended . . . that the learned Judge was wrong in leaving this to the jury as a case of gross negligence, and that the question of negligence was so mixed up with reference to what would be the conduct of a man of ordinary prudence that the jury might have thought the latter the rule by which they were to decide; that such a rule would be too uncertain to act upon; and that the question ought to have been whether the Defendant had acted honestly and bona fide to the best of his own judgment. That, however, would leave so vague a line as to afford no rule at all, the degree of judgment belonging to each individual being infinitely various: and though it has been urged that the care which a prudent man would take, is not an intelligible proposition as a rule of law, yet such has always been the rule adopted in cases of bailment, as laid down in Coggs v. Bernard (2 Ld. Raym. 909). Though in some cases a greater degree of care is exacted than in others, yet in "the second sort of bailment, viz. commodatum or lending gratis, the borrower is bound to the strictest care and diligence to keep the goods so as to restore them back again to the lender; because the bailee has a benefit by the use of them, so as if the bailee be guilty of the least neglect he will be answerable; as if a man should lend another a horse to go westward, or for a month; if the bailee put this horse in his stable, and he were stolen from thence, the bailee shall not be answerable for him: but if he or his servant leave the house or stable doors open and the thieves take the opportunity of that, and steal the horse, he will be chargeable, because the neglect gave the thieves the occasion to steal the horse." The care taken by a prudent man has always been the rule laid down; and as to the supposed difficulty of applying it, a jury has always been able to say, whether, taking that rule as their guide, there has been negligence on the occasion in question.

Instead, therefore, of saying that the liability for negligence should be co-extensive with the judgment of each individual, which would be as variable as the length of the foot of each individual, we ought rather to adhere to the rule which requires in all cases a regard to caution such as a man of ordinary prudence would observe. That was in substance the criterion presented to the jury in this case, and therefore the present rule must be discharged. . . .

Vaughan, J. . . . It was, if anything, too favourable to the Defendant to leave it to the jury whether he had been guilty of gross negligence; for when the Defendant upon being warned as to the consequences likely to ensue from the condition of the rick, said, "he would chance it," it was manifest he adverted to his interest in the insurance office. The conduct of a prudent man has always been the criterion for the jury in such cases: but it is by no means confined to them. In insurance cases, where a captain has sold his vessel after damage too extensive for repairs, the question has always been, whether he had pursued the course which a prudent man would have pursued under the same circumstance. Here, there was not a single witness whose testimony did not go to establish gross negligence in the Defendant. He had repeated warnings of what was likely to occur, and the whole calamity was occasioned by his procrastination.

Rule discharged.

Appelhans v. McFall

757 N.E.2d 987 (Ill. App. 2001)

Byrne, J. . . .

On October 4, 1999, plaintiff, who was 66 years old at the time, was walking north along the eastern edge of McCabe Road in the Township of Nunda when William [McFall], who was five years old, rode his bicycle and struck plaintiff from behind. Plaintiff fell and suffered a fractured hip. At the time of the accident, it was daylight outside, the pavement was clear and dry, and no other pedestrians, automobiles, or bicyclists were present. The roadway in the area was straight and flat.

In count I, plaintiff alleged that William's parents negligently failed to (1) instruct their son on the proper use of his bicycle, or (2) supervise him while he rode his bicycle on a public roadway because they knew or should have known that his youth would prevent him from considering the safety of pedestrians such as plaintiff. Plaintiff alleged that her injuries were proximately caused by the parents' failure to supervise their son or teach him how to use his bicycle properly. In count II, plaintiff generally asserted that William negligently caused the collision.

Defendants filed a motion to dismiss. . . . The trial court granted the motion, concluding that William's youth rendered him incapable of negligence and that plaintiff failed to allege specific facts that would have put William's parents on notice that he might ride his bicycle negligently. This timely appeal followed.

THE TENDER YEARS DOCTRINE

Defendants' motion to dismiss . . . admits all well-pleaded facts in the complaint and all reasonable inferences drawn therefrom. . . . The fact that disposes of this issue is undisputed: William was five years old when he collided with plaintiff.

On appeal, plaintiff contends that we should abandon the well-settled rule that a child is incapable of negligence if he is less than seven years old. She argues that we should adopt the "Massachusetts Rule," under which any child will be found capable of negligence if the fact finder decides that the child failed to exercise a degree of care that is reasonable for similarly situated children.

Section 283A of the Restatement (Second) of Torts (Restatement) mirrors the Massachusetts Rule and provides that "[if] the actor is a child, the standard of conduct to which he must conform to avoid being negligent is that of a reasonable person of like age, intelligence, and experience under like circumstances." Restatement (Second) of Torts § 283A (1965). Comment b to section 283A further provides in relevant part:

> "Some courts have endeavored to lay down fixed rules as to a minimum age below which the child is incapable of being negligent, and a maximum age above which he is to be treated like an adult. Usually these rules have been derived from the old rules of the criminal law, by which a child under the age of seven was considered incapable of crime, and one over fourteen was considered to be as capable as an adult. The prevailing view is that in tort cases no such arbitrary limits can be fixed. Undoubtedly there is a minimum age, probably somewhere in the vicinity of four years, below which negligence can never be found; but with the great variation in the capacities of children and the situations which may arise, it cannot be fixed definitely for all cases." Restatement (Second) of Torts § 283A, Comment b (1965).

In 1886, our supreme court held that an injured child who was seven years and three months old at the time of the accident "was too young, at the time she was injured, to observe any care for her personal safety." Chicago, St. Louis & Pittsburgh R.R. Co. v. Welsh, 118 Ill. 572, 574, 9 N.E. 197 (1886). The court later expressly adopted the tender years doctrine, which states that a child is incapable of . . . negligence if he is less than seven years old. Chicago City Ry. Co. v. Tuohy, 196 Ill. 410, 422, 63 N.E. 997 (1902). . . . The rationale for the tender years doctrine is the belief that a child under the age of seven is incapable of recognizing and appreciating risk and is therefore deemed incapable of negligence as a matter of law. Chu [v. Bowers], 275 Ill. App. 3d 861, 864 [(1995)]. The child's immaturity limits his liability regardless of whether, as a litigant, he is the plaintiff or the defendant.

. . . Plaintiff [argues] that profound societal changes since the adoption of the rule undermine . . . stare decisis. Specifically, plaintiff asserts that the judiciary that crafted the rule did not envision "cable television, video games, the internet, pre-teen gangs, and violent crime." She argues that, in response to these modern-day challenges, children are instructed at an early age that they must exercise good judgment for themselves and others and therefore we may hold them to a reasonable standard of care based upon their age.

In reaffirming its preference for the Massachusetts Rule, the Supreme Court of Minnesota quoted an opinion it drafted in 1936:

"'Under present-day circumstances a child of [tender years] is permitted to assume many responsibilities. There is much opportunity for him to observe and thus become cognizant of the necessity for exercising some degree of care. Compulsory school attendance, the radio, the movies, and traffic conditions all tend to have this effect. . . . The Illinois rule has no basis in sound reason or logic. It is based upon an outworn historical rule of criminal law which refused to acknowledge any capacity on the part of any child under seven years of age to distinguish between right and wrong.'" (Emphasis omitted.) Toetschinger [v. Ihnot], 312 Minn. 59, 65-66 [(1977)], 250 N.W.2d at 208, quoting Eckhardt v. Hanson, 196 Minn. 270, 272, 264 N.W. 776, 777 (1936).

The Minnesota high court recognized that children were sufficiently sophisticated in 1936 to be held to a reasonable standard of care. As society has changed dramatically since the *Eckhardt* court made its observations, children have become even more sophisticated. Because the tender years doctrine is based on the assumption that young children cannot recognize or appreciate risk, the rule is increasingly undermined as society more thoroughly educates them on safety issues. We find *Eckhardt* to be persuasive, and it lends great weight to plaintiff's argument that Illinois children under the age of seven may be negligent.

Plaintiff further contends that the tender years doctrine . . . leads to "ridiculous" results because a child does not "magically" know to exercise due care after his seventh birthday. In *Chu*, the Third District acknowledged that several jurisdictions have accepted this argument and rejected the tender years doctrine accordingly. *Chu*, 275 Ill. App. 3d at 864-65. . . . We agree with plaintiff that the arbitrariness of the rule supports its abandonment. However, we reluctantly conclude that the principle of stare decisis requires this court to reassert the tender years doctrine.

It is well settled that where it is clear that a court has made a mistake in adopting a rule, it should not decline to correct it, even though the rule may have been reasserted and acquiesced in for many years. No person has a vested right in any rule of law entitling him to insist that it shall remain for his benefit. However, when a rule of law has been settled, it should be followed unless a party can show that serious detriment prejudicial to the public interest is likely to arise. The rule of stare decisis is founded upon sound principles in the administration of justice, and a court should not depart from rules long recognized as the law merely because the court believes that it might decide the issue differently if the question were novel.

. . . The modification in the law that plaintiff advocates is . . . far-reaching . . . , and we decline to announce such a sweeping change here. Instead, we invite our supreme court or the legislature to revisit the viability of the tender years doctrine.

When a child is between 7 and 14 years old, the trier of fact must consider the "age, capacity, intelligence, and experience of the child" in light of the rebuttable presumption that a child between the ages of 7 and 14 is incapable of negligence. Savage v. Martin, 256 Ill. App. 3d 272, 281, 195 Ill. Dec. 142, 628 N.E.2d 606 (1993). However, it is well settled in

Illinois that a child who is 14 years old or who engages in an adult activity is held to an adult standard of care. Because bicycle riding on a public street is not an adult activity, a bicyclist between the ages of 7 and 14 is held to a reasonable standard of care based upon his age and experience. *Chu*, 275 Ill. App. 3d at 865. Therefore, one could argue that, when a child under the age of 7 engages in an activity that children between the ages of 7 and 14 normally pursue, such as riding a bicycle, the child should be held to the standard of care of a reasonable 7-year-old. However, we do not answer this question here.

. . . We conclude that the trial court correctly dismissed count II of plaintiff's complaint because William was incapable of negligence at the time of the accident.

NEGLIGENT PARENTAL SUPERVISION

Plaintiff next asserts that William's parents were negligent for failing to supervise William or instruct him on the proper use of his bicycle. . . . [T]he parent-child relationship does not automatically render parents liable for the torts of their minor children. [Lott v. Strang, 312 Ill. App. 3d 521, 524 (2000).] Parents may be liable, however, if they do not adequately control or supervise their child. To prove a claim of negligent supervision, a plaintiff must show that (1) the parents were aware of specific instances of prior conduct sufficient to put them on notice that the act complained of was likely to occur and (2) the parents had the opportunity to control the child. *Lott*, 312 Ill. App. 3d at 523-24 . . . ; Restatement (Second) of Torts §316 (1965).

Here, plaintiff alleged that the parents' mere knowledge of William's age sufficiently informed them that ongoing supervision was necessary. Plaintiff did not assert that the parents knew of a specific prior incident where William negligently struck a pedestrian while he rode his bicycle. Plaintiff essentially contends that parents should be liable for all negligent acts of their children. However, we conclude that holding parents strictly liable for failing to prevent their child's negligence is unreasonable and unsupported by the law. *Cf. Chu*, 275 Ill. App. 3d at 865 ("it is in the nature of children to be careless and thoughtless on occasion, and society must be ever aware of the need to exercise extraordinary caution when children are present").

In *Lott*, the plaintiffs sued the parents of an unemancipated minor who caused a traffic collision while he was allegedly intoxicated. In support of their negligent parental supervision claim, the plaintiffs alleged that the parents knew that their son was likely to drive negligently because he had been at fault in an earlier traffic accident. The . . . Appellate Court affirmed the dismissal, concluding that section 316 of the Restatement does not require parents to "prevent their children from ever entering into a situation where they might commit a negligent act." *Lott*, 312 Ill. App. 3d at 525. . . . The court further noted that the parents had no duty to discipline their child and regulate his conduct on a long-term ongoing basis. Parents are not liable for such broadly defined omissions. *Lott*, 312 Ill. App. 3d at 525. . . .

In this case, plaintiff defines the omission in parenting even more broadly than the alleged parental negligence addressed in *Lott*. Furthermore, plaintiff does not allege that the parents had an opportunity to follow William to ensure that he rode his bicycle safely. We conclude that plaintiff did not allege the two elements of negligent parental supervision. . . .

NOTES AND QUESTIONS

1. *The Objective Standard. Vaughan* is perhaps the leading early decision for the proposition that the issue of whether a defendant has lived up to the standard of reasonable care is to be determined by the application of an *objective* standard of care, not a *subjective* one. The objective/subjective distinction with regard to the issue of reasonable care has at least two different ideas packed into it.

The first is a distinction between whether the *conduct of the defendant was reasonably careful* (objective) versus whether *the defendant's attitude was one of trying to be reasonably careful* (subjective). Here, the term "objective" means conduct-based, whereas "subjective" means state-of-mind based. As to this version of the objective/subjective distinction, the standard of reasonable care in negligence law is clearly objective — the primary question is whether the "external" conduct of the defendant was reasonably careful, not whether he maintained an "internal" attitude of concern or care as he went about his business.

A second iteration of the objective/subjective distinction concerns the criteria against which to assess the (external) reasonableness of the defendant's conduct. On the one hand, one could compare the defendant's conduct to how an *ordinary person*, acting reasonably, would have behaved under the circumstances (objective). On the other hand, one could assess the defendant's conduct by considering *how a person with defendant's attributes*, acting reasonably, would have behaved, under the circumstances (subjective). Here "objective" is generalized, using a non-individualized norm to set the standard, while "subjective" particularizes or individualizes the standard of care to fit the individual defendant's personal attributes. Again, the black-letter law of negligence is that reasonable care is to be determined in the objective, generalized manner, not in a subjective manner that particularizes. However, as we will see, there are some pockets of case law where courts are willing to raise or lower the standard of care depending on defendant's attributes.

Vaughan holds that the standard of care employed by negligence law is and should be objective in both of the foregoing respects. For what reason(s)? Oliver Wendell Holmes, later Justice Holmes, justified this decision as follows:

> If . . . a man is born hasty and awkward, is always having accidents and hurting himself or his neighbors, no doubt his congenital defects will be allowed for in the courts of Heaven, but his slips are no less troublesome to his neighbors than if they sprang from guilty neglect. His neighbors, accordingly require him, at his proper peril, to come up to their standard. . . .

Oliver W. Holmes, Jr., *The Common Law* 108 (1881). Others, including Professor Ripstein, have argued that, once Menlove undertook an activity posing risk of physical harm to others, those others were entitled to rely on his competence, and hence Menlove is precluded (estopped) from claiming an incapacity to foresee and protect against those harms. Ripstein also suggests that employment of a subjective standard would violate an entitlement of each person to enjoy an equal degree of protection from others' risky conduct. Are there additional (or alternative) arguments, more pragmatic in nature, for the use of the objective standard? What incentives might a subjective standard create for future actors? How compelling are the administrative concerns identified by Chief Judge Tindal?

2. *Inadvertence and Breach*. Menlove's case was not aided by the evidence indicating that he was aware of the risk that the hay rick would ignite, but decided to "chance it." This evidence suggests that Menlove might not even have benefitted from the subjective standard for which his lawyers argued. It also raises an important point about the nature of faulty or careless conduct. It is natural to equate negligence with inadvertence. Usually when one is being careless, it is because one is not paying attention to certain risks. However, there are instances of "advertent" negligence (*Vaughan* itself appears to have been one).

Suppose *D* is driving 40 m.p.h. on a seemingly deserted street with a posted speed limit of 25 m.p.h. Suppose further that he is fully aware that he is speeding. *P*, exercising due care, backs his car out of his driveway onto the street. Because *D* is speeding, *D* cannot stop in time to avoid colliding with *P*. The fact that *D* was aware of his speeding does not of itself establish that he has committed anything graver than the tort of negligence. For example, it is highly doubtful he can be found to have committed an intentional wrong (likely his *purpose* in speeding was not to injure *P*; equally likely he did not *know* that he would injure *P*). Nor is it obvious that *D* was reckless — so far as he knew, the risks attending his speeding were quite small. Rather, it may be that this is an instance of carelessness in which the defendant was aware that he was acting unreasonably.

3. *Physical Disabilities*. The "objective" standard entails that a given defendant's conduct is to be measured by reference to the abilities ordinarily found in other persons. *Which* other persons are to provide the basis for that comparison varies, depending on the type of incapacity alleged by the defendant, and perhaps the type of conduct in question. A court likely would never hold that a completely blind person who, while walking down a sidewalk, bumps into someone else, has failed to exercise reasonable care *because she did not look where she was going*, even though the ordinary person surely does take such care. In this instance, the basis for comparison is not the ordinary person (who is sighted), but the ordinary blind person. This change in reference point does *not* mean that the blind pedestrian is insulated from all claims of negligence. Rather it means that, to prevail in such a case, the plaintiff must show that the pedestrian failed to take precautions that a prudent blind person would

take (e.g., failed to use a cane to sense the presence of others and to alert others to her blindness). *Cf.* Poyner v. Loftus, 694 A.2d 69 (D.C. Ct. App. 1997) (visually impaired pedestrian at fault for not using cane or guide dog that would have prevented his fall); Stephens v. Dulaney, 428 P.2d 27 (N.M. 1967) (plaintiff with no sense of smell must exercise reasonable care in light of that incapacity), *overruled in part on other grounds*, 491 P.2d 1147 (N.M. 1971). Note, however, if a blind person were to attempt to drive a car, he would presumably be found to have acted unreasonably as a matter of law. Is this because he would have failed to act like a sighted person of ordinary prudence? (It is surely unreasonable for a sighted person to drive with her eyes closed.) Or is it consistent with the application of a "reasonable blind person" standard, in that no reasonable blind person would get into a car and drive it?

4. *Awkward versus Young. Vaughan* establishes that Holmes's "hasty and awkward" adult is held to an objective standard of reasonable care. *Appelhans* indicates that very young children are not held to that standard. Indeed, in jurisdictions that adopt the tender years doctrine, they are deemed incapable of being careless as a matter of law. In both instances, the actor in question lacks the capacity to comport with the standard of reasonable care, yet the law treats those incapacities in opposite ways. Is this disparate treatment intelligible?

5. *Older Children and Adult Activities.* With regard to children who are over seven and who are engaged in activities typical of childhood, such as bicycle riding, the courts ask the jury to gauge the child's behavior in comparison to that of "other children of the same age, experience, and intelligence." Although this standard is in some ways objective, by factoring in the particular child's experience and intelligence, it points toward a more subjective standard. This rule, however, has exceptions. Most importantly, as the *Appelhans* court notes, minors who engage in "adult" activities, such as driving cars or snowmobiles, are held to the reasonable care standard for competent adults.

6. *Parental Liability: Direct versus Vicarious.* It is rare for a child to be the defendant in a negligence action. In part this is because children tend not to be in a position to provide adequate redress to their victims, except with respect to certain activities covered by an insurance policy taken out by their parents. Moreover, parents are not held *vicariously liable* for their child's faulty conduct in the way that employers can often be held vicariously liable for their employees' careless acts. Thus, a person injured by a child's carelessness who wishes to recover from the child's parents must establish some form of *direct* negligence, that is, carelessness on the part of the parent.

One such form consists of *negligent supervision.* As *Appelhans* explains, the negligent supervision theory is available only in a narrow range of circumstances. For an example of a statute codifying this form of liability, see Tenn. Code. Ann. § 37-10-101-103 (where a minor willfully or maliciously causes personal injury or property damage to another, his parents can be held liable up to the amount of $10,000 if they knew or should have known of the minor's tendency to commit wrongful acts, and also failed to exercise reasonable means to restrain him, thereby enabling his tortious conduct); Lavin v. Jordan, 16 S.W.3d 362 (Tenn. 2000) (interpreting and applying these provisions).

Another ground for direct parental liability consists of *negligent entrustment*, whereby a parent carelessly gives a child access to a dangerous instrumentality, such as a gun or a car, that the child is not equipped to handle safely. *See, e.g.*, Rios v. Smith, 744 N.E.2d 1156 (N.Y. 2001) (owner of all-terrain vehicle can be found by a jury to have carelessly entrusted it to his teenage son).

7. *The Reasonable Child and Comparative Fault.* The issue of the standard of care applicable to children is of considerably more practical importance on the question of comparative fault. For example, a careless driver who strikes a child pedestrian or cyclist may try to establish that the child acted unreasonably and so contributed to her own injury by darting out into the street. Likewise, parental carelessness is more often "in play" when evidence of such carelessness is being offered not by the plaintiff to establish parental liability, but instead by a defendant seeking to assign a percentage of responsibility and liability to the parents for an injury to their child. Thus, if the tables were turned and the McFalls were bringing an action on behalf of William against Appelhans for carelessly riding *her* bicycle into William as he crossed a street, a court might in that context be more willing to permit the attribution of fault to the senior McFalls for not keeping a close enough eye on William. See Chapter 8 (discussing apportionment).

8. *Mental Incompetence, Battery, and Negligence.* Menlove may have been prone to ignore risks, but there is no suggestion in the opinion that he lacked basic mental competence. How should tort law apply to actors who suffer from a mental disorder that leaves them unable to comprehend the significance of their actions, or to control them? Mental incompetence ("insanity") can sometimes serve as a defense to criminal prosecution. However, there is no equivalent to the insanity defense in tort law. Indeed, the black letter rule states that a defendant's insanity does not even defeat the attribution of intent to her in a suit for torts such as battery. (Battery, for present purposes, can be defined as intentionally or knowingly causing harmful contact with another person.) For example, suppose adult *A* is under the delusion that *P*, standing next to her, is a Martian bent on conquering earth. *A* therefore attacks *P*. In principle, *P* can sue *A* for battery. *See* Anicet v. Gant, 580 So. 2d 273 (Fla. Ct. App. 1991) (stating the rule, but refusing to apply it).

Some courts have suggested that insanity should sometimes defeat liability for torts such as battery precisely because those torts, unlike the tort of negligence, require the defendant to have acted with a certain subjective mental state — with a *purpose* to cause harmful contact to another person, or *knowing* that such contact would result. On this view, if the jury finds that the defendant in a battery suit was so incapacitated as to be incapable of forming the relevant purpose, or possessing the relevant knowledge, he should not be held liable for battery. Even these courts, however, are prepared to hold a mentally incompetent person liable under *Vaughan*'s objective reasonable person standard. *See* White v. Muniz, 999 P.2d 814 (Col. 2000) (en banc) (if the jury finds that defendant's Alzheimer's disease rendered her incapable of forming an intent to cause harmful contact, she cannot be held liable for battery, although she can be held liable in negligence); Burch v. American Family Mut. Ins. Co., 543 N.W.2d 277 (Wis. 1996) (severely retarded girl held to reasonable person standard in gauging whether she was careless in causing parked truck to slip into gear). As it turns out, those plaintiffs facing the prospect of suing a mentally incompetent defendant might often prefer to sue for negligence rather than battery, for, as explained in Chapter 8, liability insurance tends not to cover intentional wrongful acts.

What is the justification for holding a person who is incapable of controlling her conduct to the *Vaughan* standard? Does it suggest that legal fault really is quite a different concept than fault as we ordinarily use that term? Or are there special considerations that attend the actions of insane persons that warrant the imposition of what is, in effect, a form of strict liability? If the latter, on what basis can the cases that excuse carelessness by young children be distinguished? *See* Creasy v. Rusk, 730 N.E.2d 659 (Ind. 2000) (identifying policy factors thought by courts to warrant the imposition of the objective standard on insane persons, including (1) the desirability of allocating losses between two innocent parties to the one who caused or occasioned the loss; (2) providing an incentive to family members and other guardians of persons with mutual disabilities to control the behavior of those persons; (3) removing inducements for alleged tortfeasors to fake a mental disability in order to escape liability; (4) avoiding administrative problems that are created by requiring courts and juries to identify and assess the significance of an actor's disability; and (5) forcing persons with disabilities to pay for the damage they do if they are to live active lives).

9. *Fault versus Comparative Fault.* As with negligence litigation involving the conduct of children, the issue of the standard of care to apply to mentally incompetent persons usually arises in assessing a victim's *comparative responsibility* for her injuries. Should there be any difference between the standard of care to which injurers ought to adhere for the protection of potential victims, and the standard of care that victims "owe" to themselves? Commentators frequently deny that there is or ought to be any difference. *See, e.g.*, Dan Dobbs, *The Law of Torts* § 125, at 294 (2000). Consider the rationales for the application of the objective standard to incompetent persons listed above. Do any of them offer a basis for distinguishing the breach inquiry as it pertains to *comparative fault* from the inquiry as it applies to *fault*?

10. *"Temporary" Insanity.* A leading decision holding the mentally disabled to the objective standard is Breunig v. American Family Ins. Co., 173 N.W.2d 619 (Wis. 1970). In that case, the plaintiff was injured when another driver, Veith, operating under the delusion that she could make her car fly, rammed into plaintiff's truck. Veith's insurer defended on the ground that Veith was schizophrenic, and hence utterly incapable of

driving as would a reasonably prudent person. The Wisconsin Supreme Court declined to recognize this broad defense. Still, although it rejected a general insanity defense to negligence claims, *Breunig* distinguished instances of "temporary" insanity that occur without forewarning to the afflicted defendant.

Suppose one can make sound medical distinctions between permanent and temporary forms of insanity. Does *Breunig*'s distinction make sense in light of the reasons justifying the rule of liability for general incapacity specified by *Creasy*, *supra* Note 8? The differing treatment of "sudden" incapacities is consistent with judicial treatment of sudden physical incapacities. For example, a driver who, without any forewarning, suffers a heart attack that causes him to drive carelessly and injure another, will be held to have not acted unreasonably — at least in this regard — as a matter of law. *See, e.g.*, Goodrich v. Blair, 646 P.2d 890 (Ariz. Ct. App. 1982) (affirming jury instruction on sudden physical incapacity). Sudden incapacity will not defeat a finding of breach, however, when its onset was foreseeable to the actor. *See* Storjohn v. Fay, 519 N.W.2d 521 (Neb. 1994) (epileptic who blacked out while driving, causing injury to plaintiff, cannot claim benefit of sudden incapacity: he knew or should have known that he was subject to losing consciousness without notice and thus was careless as a matter of law for driving at all).

11. *The Elderly*. If youth is sometimes taken account of in the application of the standard of care, should old age likewise be taken into account? Can an elderly defendant, for example, argue that slower reflexes or lack of attentiveness, which often accompany aging, should be considered? A few courts have recognized such arguments — again, however, primarily in connection with determinations of comparative fault.

12. *Gender*. Today's "reasonable person" standard historically was stated as the "reasonable man" standard. Professor Schlanger has discussed nineteenth-century cases in which courts differed over whether to apply a distinct standard of reasonableness to women. In one 1873 case, for example, the trial judge instructed the jury to take into account the plaintiff's gender in determining whether she was comparatively at fault in riding her horse. The presumption, apparently, was that this would permit the jury to apply a less-demanding standard that would benefit the plaintiff. What if studies show that, on average, women have better reflexes than men? Should the jury take that higher standard into account in determining the reasonableness of a particular woman's driving? Is the use of gender-specific standards appropriate or discriminatory? Professor Minow has argued that feminist theory faces a dilemma on this issue: Women's interests can, in different ways, be served both by recognition of a different standard of care and insistence upon application of a uniform reasonable person standard. Case law interpreting federal statutes barring gender discrimination has sometimes employed a "reasonable woman" standard in connection with determining, for example, whether an employer is responsible for maintaining a harassing or otherwise hostile work environment. *See, e.g.*, Hurley v. Atlantic City Police Dept., 174 F.3d 95 (3d Cir. 1999). Again, theorists have divided over the value of this approach.

13. *Cultural Reasonableness*. Should negligence law ever recognize a culturally relative standard of care? An analogous issue has arisen in criminal law. For example, in Ha v. Alaska, 892 P.2d 184 (Alaska Ct. App. 1995), Ha, a Vietnamese man, shot and killed another Vietnamese man named Buu, who had attacked and threatened him the night before. When Ha was prosecuted for murder, he sought to establish the justification of self-defense, which, under Alaska law, permits the use of deadly force against another if one *reasonably* believes that its use is necessary to avoid *imminent* death or serious bodily harm. Ha's attorney argued that, in assessing the reasonableness of Ha's perception of imminent harm at the hands of Buu, the jury should consider that death threats are taken very literally in Vietnamese culture. The trial court refused to so instruct the jury, insisting that the perception of imminent harm was to be judged by an objective standard and that Ha had no reasonable basis for perceiving an imminent threat from Buu. The Court of Appeals upheld the trial court on a slightly different rationale, concluding that, even taking into account knowledge of Vietnamese culture, Ha had no basis for perceiving an imminent threat from Buu at the time Ha shot him.

14. *Time Frame for Assessing Conduct*. Following *Vaughan*, American negligence law focuses on a defendant's conduct, not his or her ostensibly good intentions. But the directive to look at his conduct still leaves many questions open, including the question of the time frame for evaluating it. Should a defendant's conformity to the standard of reasonable care be determined by his or her conduct over a lifetime, a year, a day, or a moment? Negligence law generally permits a plaintiff to prevail (on the breach issue) if she can identify any time-slice in which the conduct fell below reasonable care. It therefore encourages plaintiffs to divide up courses of conduct into discrete episodes or snapshots, rather than connecting them to an individual defendant's record of careful or careless behavior over time. For example, suppose two surgeons, *A* and *B*, are sued for malpractice, each for carelessly leaving an object (e.g., a sponge) inside one of her patients during surgery. For purposes of determining whether one or the other should be held liable, it makes no difference that *A* has a long and sordid history of botching operations, whereas *B*'s record is spotless. The question is whether, *in this instance*, *A* or *B* adhered to the relevant standard of care.* Professor Grady has argued that this snapshot approach to breach introduces a pocket of strict liability into negligence law, simply because even the most careful person can be expected to err once in a while. Grady regards this liability as strict, because it seems to entail that, no matter how careful one is, one cannot avoid sooner or later being careless.

---

* Evidence of *A*'s or *B*'s record might be admitted as relevant to a factual dispute as to how *A* or *B* actually conducted him- or herself on the occasion in question. However, *B* could not introduce the evidence of his past performance as a reason for the jury to excuse his breach on that occasion.

III. INDUSTRY AND PROFESSIONAL CUSTOM

The T.J. Hooper
60 F.2d 737 (2d Cir. 1932)

L. Hand, J.   The barges No. 17 and No. 30, belonging to the Northern Barge Company, had lifted cargoes of coal at Norfolk, Virginia, for New York in March, 1928. They were towed by two tugs of the petitioner, the "Montrose" and the "Hooper," and were lost off the Jersey Coast on March tenth, in an easterly gale. The cargo owners sued the barges under the contracts of carriage; the owner of the barges sued the tugs under the towing contract, both for its own loss and as bailee of the cargoes; the owner of the tug filed a petition to limit its liability. All the suits were joined and heard together, and the judge found that all the vessels were unseaworthy; the tugs, because they did not carry radio receiving sets by which they could have seasonably got warnings of a change in the weather which should have caused them to seek shelter in the Delaware Breakwater en route. He therefore entered an interlocutory decree holding each tug and barge jointly liable to each cargo owner, and each tug for half damages for the loss of its barge. The petitioner appealed, and the barge owner appealed and filed assignments of error.

Each tug had three ocean going coal barges in tow, the lost barge being at the end. The "Montrose," which had the No. 17, took an outside course; the "Hooper" with the No. 30, inside. The weather was fair without ominous symptoms, as the tows passed the Delaware Breakwater about midnight of March eighth, and the barges did not get into serious trouble until they were about opposite Atlantic City some sixty or seventy miles to the north. The wind began to freshen in the morning of the ninth and rose to a gale before noon; by afternoon the second barge of the Hooper's tow was out of hand and signalled the tug, which found that not only this barge needed help, but that the No. 30 was aleak. Both barges anchored and the crew of the No. 30 rode out the storm until the afternoon of the tenth, when she sank, her crew having been meanwhile taken off. The No. 17 sprang a leak about the same time; she too anchored at the Montrose's command and sank on the next morning after her crew also had been rescued. The cargoes and the tugs maintain that the barges were not fit for their service; the cargoes and the barges that the tugs should have gone into the Delaware Breakwater, and besides, did not handle their tows properly.

The evidence of the condition of the barges was very extensive, the greater part being taken out of court. As to each, the fact remains that she foundered in weather that she was bound to withstand. . . . As to the cargoes, the charters excused the barges if "reasonable means" were taken to make them seaworthy; and the barge owners amended their answers during the trial to allege that they had used due diligence in that regard. As will appear, the barges were certainly not seaworthy in fact, and we do not think that the record shows affirmatively the exercise of due diligence to examine them. The examinations at least of the pumps were perfunctory; had they been sufficient the loss would not have occurred. . . .

A more difficult issue is as to the tugs. [The critical issue here is whether the tug captains acted carelessly in not turning into the Delaware Breakwater given the information that was available up to the time at which they passed it. — EDS.]

The weather bureau at Arlington broadcasts two predictions daily, at ten in the morning and ten in the evening. Apparently there are other reports floating about, which come at uncertain hours but which can also be picked up. The Arlington report of the morning read as follows: "Moderate north, shifting to east and southeast winds, increasing Friday, fair weather to-night." The substance of this [forecast] . . . reached a tow bound north to New York about noon, and, coupled with a falling [barometer], [convinced] the master [of that tow] to put in to the Delaware Breakwater in the afternoon. The [barometer] had not indeed fallen much and perhaps the tug was over cautious; nevertheless, although the appearances were all fair, he thought discretion the better part of valor. Three other tows followed him, the masters of two of which testified. . . . Courts have not often such evidence of the opinion of impartial experts, formed in the very circumstances and confirmed by their own conduct at the time.

Moreover, the "Montrose" and the "Hooper" would have had the benefit of the evening report from Arlington had they had proper receiving sets. This predicted worse weather. . . . The bare "increase[ing]" of the morning had become "fresh to strong." To be sure this scarcely foretold a gale of from forty to fifty miles for five hours or more, rising at one time to fifty-six; but if the four tows thought the first report enough, the second ought to have laid any doubts. The master of the "Montrose" himself, when asked what he would have done had he received a substantially similar report, said that he would certainly have put in. The master of the "Hooper" was also asked for his opinion, and said that he would have turned back also, but this admission is somewhat vitiated by the incorporation in the question of the statement that it was a "storm warning," which the witness seized upon in his answer. All this seems to us to support the conclusion of the judge that prudent masters, who had received the second warning, would have found the risk more than the exigency warranted; they would have been amply vindicated by what followed. . . . Taking the situation as a whole, it seems to us that these masters would have taken undue chances, had they got the broadcasts.

They did not, because their private radio receiving sets, which were on board, were not in working order. These belonged to them personally, and were partly a toy, partly a part of the equipment, but neither furnished by the owner, nor supervised by it. It is not fair to say that there was a general custom among coastwise carriers so to equip their tugs. One line alone did it; as for the rest, they relied upon their crews, so far as they can be said to have relied at all. An adequate receiving set suitable for a coatwise tug can now be got at small cost and is reasonably reliable if kept up; obviously it is a source of great protection to their tows. Twice every day they can receive these predictions, based upon the widest possible information, available to every vessel within two or three hundred miles and more. Such a set is the ears of the tug to catch the spoken word, just as the master's binoculars are her eyes to see a storm signal ashore. Whatever may be said as to other vessels, tugs towing heavy coal laden barges, strung out for half a mile, have little power to maneuvre, and do not, as this case proves, expose themselves to weather which would not turn back stauncher craft. They can have at hand protection against dangers of which they can learn in no other way.

Is it then a final answer that the business had not yet generally adopted receiving sets? There are, no doubt, cases where courts seem to make the general practice of the calling the standard of proper diligence; we have indeed given some currency to the notion ourselves. Indeed in most cases reasonable prudence is in fact common prudence; but strictly it is never its measure; a whole calling may have unduly lagged in the adoption of new and available devices. It never may set its own tests, however persuasive be its usages. Courts must in the end say what is required; there are precautions so imperative that even their universal disregard will not excuse their omission. Wabash R. Co. v. McDaniels, 107 U.S. 454, 459-461, 2 S. Ct. 932, 27 L. Ed. 605; Texas & P. R. Co. v. Behymer, 189 U.S. 468, 470, 23 S. Ct. 622, 47 L. Ed. 905; Shandrew v. Chicago, etc., R. Co., 142 F. 320, 324, 325 (C.C.A. 8); Maynard v. Buck, 100 Mass. 40. But here there was no custom at all as to receiving sets; some had them, some did not; the most that can be urged is that they had not yet become general. Certainly in such a case we need not pause; when some have thought a device necessary, at least we may say that they were right, and the others too slack. . . . We hold the tugs therefore because had they been properly equipped, they would have got the Arlington reports. The injury was a direct consequence of this unseaworthiness.

Johnson v. Riverdale Anesthesia Assocs., P.C.
563 S.E.2d 431 (Ga. 2002)

Sears, J.   Certiorari was granted in this medical malpractice action in order to consider the Court of Appeals' ruling forbidding the plaintiff from cross-examining the defendants' expert witness as to how he personally would have treated the plaintiffs' decedent. We conclude that because the standard of care in medical malpractice cases is that which is employed by the medical profession generally, and not what one individual physician would do under the same or similar circumstances, how a testifying medical expert personally would have treated a plaintiff or a plaintiff's decedent is not relevant to the issue of whether a defendant physician committed malpractice. Moreover, we conclude that how a testifying medical expert personally would have treated a plaintiff or a plaintiff's decedent cannot be used to impeach the . . . expert's credibility. Therefore, we affirm.

The decedent, Clair Johnson, suffered a severe adverse reaction to anesthesia she received during surgery. The reaction caused Mrs. Johnson's oxygen supply to be interrupted, resulting in massive brain trauma and death. Her husband, Donald Johnson, along with the administratrix of her estate (collectively "Johnson"), sued the anesthesiologist, Dr. Lawhead, and his employer, Riverdale Anesthesia Associates, Inc. (collectively "Anesthesia Associates"), alleging malpractice.

At trial, Johnson alleged that Anesthesia Associates had committed malpractice by failing to "preoxygenate" Mrs. Johnson. Preoxygenation is a procedure where, before surgery, a patient is given a measure of pure oxygen, providing her with a reserve to draw from, should her oxygen supply be interrupted during surgery. The trial court granted Anesthesia Associates' motion in limine to prevent Johnson from cross-examining the defendants' medical expert, Dr. Caplan, about whether he, personally, would have preoxygenated Mrs. Johnson.

After the jury found in favor of Anesthesia Associates, Johnson appealed, claiming the trial court erred by preventing Johnson from cross-examining Dr. Caplan as to whether he would have elected to preoxygenate Mrs. Johnson. The Court of Appeals affirmed, and this Court granted certiorari.

1. The crux of Johnson's complaint against Anesthesia Associates was the contention that the latter violated the applicable standard of care by failing to preoxygenate Mrs. Johnson. Johnson attempted to establish this breach of care through the testimony of an expert witness.[3] Johnson claimed that if preoxygenation had been administered, Mrs. Johnson would have been protected against the low oxygen levels that occurred during surgery and that led to her death. For its part, Anesthesia Associates claimed that because its decision not to preoxygenate Mrs. Johnson was consistent with the applicable standard of care, no malpractice occurred. In support of this argument, Anesthesia Associates presented the testimony of its own medical expert, Dr. Caplan.

It is axiomatic that in order to establish medical malpractice,

> "the evidence presented by the patient must show a violation of the degree of care and skill required of a physician. Such standard of care is that which, under similar conditions and like circumstances, is ordinarily employed by the medical profession generally." Thus, in medical malpractice actions, "the applicable standard of care is that employed by the medical profession generally and not what one individual doctor thought was advisable and would have done under the circumstances."

[McNabb v. Landis, 223 Ga. App. 894, 896 (1996).]

Accordingly, in cases where expert medical testimony has been presented either to support or to rebut a claim that the applicable standard of care was breached, Georgia case law holds that questions aimed at

---

3. See Slack v. Moorhead, 152 Ga. App. 68 (1979) (except in rare instances, the question of compliance with the required medical standard of care must be presented through expert testimony).

determining how the expert would have personally elected to treat the patient are irrelevant. The questioning of a medical expert witness should be disallowed as irrelevant when it "pertains to [the expert's] personal views and opinion as to the care and treatment he himself would have rendered." [*Id.*, at 896.] Contrary to Johnson's argument, this is true regardless of whether the expert's personal views are sought through direct testimony or cross-examination; as held by the trial court in this case, a defendant's expert witness is not required to answer questions on cross-examination "as to what course of treatment he personally would have followed."

It follows that the trial court did not abuse its discretion in granting Anesthesia Associates' motion in limine to prohibit Johnson from cross-examining the defendant's expert witness as to whether he personally would have preoxygenated the decedent, because such questioning was irrelevant to the issue of whether Anesthesia Associates breached the applicable standard of care.[8]

2. Questions aimed at determining how a defendant's medical expert personally would have treated a plaintiff or a plaintiff's decedent also are irrelevant for purposes of impeaching the expert. As explained above, a medical expert's personal practices are irrelevant to the issues in controversy in a malpractice case. It is axiomatic that a witness may not be impeached with irrelevant facts or evidence, and cross-examination should be confined to matters that are relevant to the case.

Moreover, when confronted with the same or similar situation, different physicians will, quite naturally, often elect to administer differing treatments, and will exercise their judgments regarding a patient's care differently. However, merely because these procedures and treatments differ, it does not automatically follow that one of them fails to comply with the applicable standard of care.

Georgia precedent holds that "'testimony showing a mere difference in views between surgeons as to operating techniques, or as to medical judgment exercised,'" is irrelevant in a medical malpractice action when the differing views or techniques are both acceptable and customary within the applicable standard of care. Accordingly, questions asked on cross-examination as to how a defendant's medical expert "personally would have treated [a patient are] . . . not proper for impeachment." [Cited authority omitted. — EDS.]

Therefore, the trial court did not improperly curtail Johnson's ability to impeach the testimony of Anesthesia Associates' medical expert, Dr. Caplan, by granting the defendants' motion in limine.

3. . . . For the reasons explained above, the trial court did not abuse its discretion in this case by prohibiting the cross-examination of the

---

8. The portion of *Prevost v. Taylor*, 196 Ga. App. 368 (4) (1990), that holds otherwise is hereby overruled.

defendants' medical expert as to his personal medical practices, because such information was irrelevant to any issue of fact in controversy.

Judgment affirmed. . . .

Carley, J. (dissenting) (joined by Benham and Hunstein, JJ). In a one-sentence footnote, the majority overrules *Prevost v. Taylor*, 196 Ga. App. 368, 369 (4) (396 S.E.2d 17) (1990), which was not even cited by the Court of Appeals. In my opinion, *Prevost* was simply overlooked by the Court of Appeals and should not be overruled by this Court because the rationale of that decision is so persuasive:

> It is true, as defendant argues, that the issue in a medical professional negligence action is whether the treatment met the standard of care of the profession generally and not what any one individual doctor believes is advisable. However, those cases cited by defendant involved instances where the only testimony presented to support plaintiff's claim is the individual view of one doctor and no testimony was presented as to the standard of care generally practiced by the profession. [Cits.] Here, plaintiff did not present the individual opinion of defendant's expert for the purpose of establishing the acceptable standard of care but offered it to impeach the expert's opinion that the surgery performed by defendant met the standard of care of the profession generally. "Evidence tendered for impeachment purposes need not be of the kind or quality required for proving the facts." [Cits.]

Prevost v. Taylor, supra at 369-370 (4).

"The right of a thorough and sifting cross-examination shall belong to every party as to the witnesses called against him." O.C.G.A. § 24-9-64.

> Over one hundred years ago, this Court held that it is the [trial] court's duty to allow a searching and skillful test of the witness' "intelligence, memory, accuracy and veracity(,)" [cit.], and that it is better for cross-examination to be "too free than too much restricted." . . . [Cit.]

Eason v. State, 260 Ga. 445, 446 (1990), *overruled on other grounds*, State v. Lucious, 271 Ga. 361, 365 (1999). " '(W)here the purpose is to impeach or discredit the witness, great latitude should be allowed by the [trial] court in cross-examination. . .[.]' [Cit.]" *Corley v. Harris*, 171 Ga. App. 688, 689 (1984).

> As a general rule, the liability test to be employed by the court and the jury is the "standard of care" that a reasonably prudent physician would exercise under the same or similar circumstances as the defendant. Therefore, the ultimate test is not whether the expert would perform a medical act and/or teach a medical act in the same way or a different way as a particular defendant. *However*, such a line of inquiry *usually is admissible* on the issue of credibility. If, for example, the plaintiff's expert testifies that a defendant deviated from a certain standard of care, said expert's credibility certainly would be severely shaken if, in fact, it can be shown that this expert has performed a medical act in the same or similar manner as the defendant. *If a defense expert has testified that a defendant's medical act conformed with*

a certain acceptable standard of care, the credibility of said testimony
certainly would be severely shaken, if said expert conceded on cross-exam-
ination that he personally does not perform and/or teach the medical act
in the same manner. (Emphasis supplied.)

2 Pegalis & Wachsman, American Law of Medical Malpractice 2d § 14:7 (e),
p.492 (1993). The identical circumstances are present in this case. As demonstrated by an offer of proof, the defendants' medical expert would have testified on cross-examination that he would have preoxygenated Mrs. Johnson if
she had been his patient. Plaintiffs' counsel also sought to ask Dr. Caplan
how he teaches his medical students to treat patients in similar situations.
Such testimony is particularly relevant to credibility here, because Dr. Caplan
testified on direct examination that there was nothing that could have been
done to make it safer for Mrs. Johnson to have the anesthesia.

"'A material abridgement or denial of the substantial right of cross-
examination of opposing witnesses is material error and requires the
grant of a new trial. (Cits.)'" Hyles v. Cockrill, 169 Ga. App. 132, 140
(1983) (on motion for rehearing), *overruled on other grounds*, Ketchup
v. Howard, 247 Ga. App. 54, 61 (2000). Because the trial court did not
allow plaintiffs to conduct "a thorough and sifting cross-examination" of
the defendant's medical expert, I dissent to the affirmance of the Court of
Appeals' judgment.

Largey v. Rothman
540 A.2d 504 (N.J. 1988)

Per Curiam.   This medical malpractice case raises an issue of a
patient's informed consent to treatment. The jury found that plaintiff
Janice Largey had consented to an operative procedure performed by the
defendant physician. The single question presented goes to the correctness of the standard by which the jury was instructed to determine
whether the defendant, Dr. Rothman, had adequately informed his patient
of the risks of that operation.

The trial court told the jury that when informing the plaintiff Janice
Largey of the risks of undergoing a certain biopsy procedure, described
below, defendant was required to tell her "what reasonable medical practi-
tioners in the same or similar circumstances would have told their patients
undertaking the same type of operation." By answer to a specific interrogatory on this point, the jurors responded that defendant had not "fail[ed] to
provide Janice Largey with sufficient information so that she could give
informed consent" for the operative procedure. On plaintiffs' appeal the
Appellate Division affirmed in an unreported opinion, noting that the trial
court's charge on informed consent followed the holding in Kaplan v. Haines,
96 N.J. Super. 242, 257 (App. Div. 1967), which this Court affirmed. . . .

Plaintiffs argued below, and repeat the contention here, that the
proper standard is one that focuses not on what information a reasonable
doctor should impart to the patient (the "professional" standard) but rather
on what the physician should disclose to a reasonable patient in order that

the patient might make an informed decision (the "prudent patient" or "materiality of risk" standard). The latter is the standard announced in Canterbury v. Spence, 464 F.2d 772 (D.C. Cir.), *cert. den.*, 409 U.S. 1064, 93 S. Ct. 560, 34 L. Ed. 2d 518 (1972). The Appellate Division rejected the *Canterbury* standard, not because it disagreed with that standard but because the court felt itself bound, correctly, by the different standard of *Kaplan*, which represents "the latest word" from this Court.

. . . We now discard *Kaplan*'s "reasonable physician" standard and adopt instead the *Canterbury* "reasonable patient" rule. Hence, we reverse and remand for a new trial.

I

[The New Jersey Supreme Court quotes and adopts the Appellate Division's recitation of the fact. — EDS.]

In the course of a routine physical examination plaintiff's gynecologist, Dr. Glassman, detected a "vague mass" in her right breast. The doctor arranged for mammograms to be taken. The radiologist reported two anomalies to the doctor: an "ill-defined density" in the subareola region and an enlarged lymph node or nodes, measuring four-by-two centimeters, in the right axilla (armpit). The doctor referred plaintiff to defendant, a surgeon. Defendant expressed concern that the anomalies on the mammograms might be cancer and recommended a biopsy. There was a sharp dispute at trial over whether he stated that the biopsy would include the lymph nodes as well as the breast tissue. Plaintiff claims that defendant never mentioned the nodes.

Plaintiff submitted to the biopsy procedure after receiving a confirmatory second opinion from a Dr. Slattery. During the procedure defendant removed a piece of the suspect mass from plaintiff's breast and excised the nodes. The biopsies showed that both specimens were benign. About six weeks after the operation, plaintiff developed a right arm and hand lymphedema, a swelling caused by inadequate drainage in the lymphatic system. The condition resulted from the excision of the lymph nodes. Defendant did not advise plaintiff of this risk. Plaintiff's experts testified that defendant should have informed plaintiff that lymphedema was a risk of the operation. Defendant's experts testified that it was too rare to be discussed with a patient.

Plaintiff and her husband . . . advanced two theories of liability. . . . They claimed that they were never told that the operation would include removal of the nodes and therefore that procedure constituted an unauthorized battery. Alternatively, they claimed that even if they had authorized the node excision, defendant was negligent in failing to warn them of the risk of lymphedema and therefore their consent was uninformed. The jury specifically rejected both claims.

II

The origins of the requirement that a physician obtain the patient's consent before surgery may be traced back at least two centuries. The doctrine is now well-embedded in our law. In Schloendorff v. The Soc'y of the N.Y. Hosp., 211 N.Y. 125, 105 N.E. 92 (1914), Justice Cardozo announced a patient's right to be free of uninvited, unknown surgery, which constitutes a trespass on the patient: "Every human being of adult years and sound mind has a right to determine what shall be done with his own body; and a surgeon who performs an operation without his patient's consent commits an assault, for which he is liable in damages." 211 N.Y. at 129-30, 105 N.E. at 93. Earlier case law recognized that theories of fraud and misrepresentation would sustain a patient's action in battery for an unauthorized intervention. *See* State v. Housekeeper, 70 Md. 162, 16 A. 382 (1889); W. Keeton, D. Dobbs, R. Keeton, D. Owen, *Prosser and Keeton on The Law of Torts* §§ 18, 32 (5th ed. 1984). . . . Although that cause of action continues to be recognized in New Jersey, *see* Perna v. Pirozzi, 92 N.J. 446, 459-63 (1983) (operation on a patient by a surgeon to whom the patient has not given any consent constitutes a battery), there is no "battery" claim implicated in this appeal because the jury determined as a matter of fact that plaintiff had given consent to the node excision performed by Dr. Rothman.

Although the requirement that a patient give consent before the physician can operate is of long standing, the doctrine of *informed* consent is one of relatively recent development in our jurisprudence. It is essentially a negligence concept, predicated on the duty of a physician to disclose to a patient such information as will enable the patient to make an evaluation of the nature of the treatment and of any attendant substantial risks, as well as of available options in the form of alternative therapies.

An early statement of the "informed consent" rule is found in Salgo v. Leland Stanford, Jr. Univ. Bd. of Trustees, 154 Cal. App. 2d 560, 317 P.2d 170 (Dist. Ct. App. 1957), in which the court declared that "[a] physician violates his duty to his patient and subjects himself to liability if he withholds any facts which are necessary to form the basis of an intelligent consent by the patient to the proposed treatment." *Id.* at 578, 317 P.2d at 181. *Salgo* recognized that because each patient presents a "special problem," the physician has a certain amount of discretion in dismissing the element of risk, "consistent, of course, with the full disclosure of facts necessary to an informed consent." *Id.* at 578, 317 P.2d at 181.

Further development of the doctrine came shortly thereafter, in Natanson v. Kline, 186 Kan. 393, 350 P.2d 1093, *modified on other grounds*, 187 Kan. 186, 354 P.2d 670 (1960), which represented one of the leading cases on informed consent at that time. In *Natanson* a patient sustained injuries from excessive doses of radioactive cobalt during radiation therapy. Even though the patient had consented to the radiation treatment, she alleged that the physician had not informed her of the nature and consequences of the risks posed by the therapy. Thus, the case sounded in negligence rather than battery. 186 Kan. at 400-404, 350 P.2d at 1100-01. The court concluded that when a physician either affirmatively misrepresents the nature of an operation or fails to disclose the probable consequences of the treatment, he may be subjected to a claim of unauthorized treatment. *Id.* at 406, 350 P.2d at 1102. The *Natanson* court established the standard of care to be exercised by a physician in an informed consent case as "limited to those disclosures which a reasonable medical practitioner would make under the same or similar circumstances." *Id.* at 409, 350 P.2d at 1106. At bottom the decision turned on the principle of a patient's right of self-determination:

> Anglo-American law starts with the premise of thorough self-determination. It follows that each man is considered to be master of his own body, and he may, if he be of sound mind, expressly prohibit the performance of life-saving surgery, or other medical treatment. A doctor might well believe that an operation or form of treatment is desirable or necessary but the law does not permit him to substitute his own judgment for that of the patient by any form of artifice or deception. [*Id.* at 406-07, 350 P.2d at 1104.]

After *Salgo* and *Natanson* the doctrine of informed consent came to be adopted and developed in other jurisdictions, which, until 1972, followed the "traditional" or "professional" standard formulation of the rule. Under that standard, as applied by the majority of the jurisdictions that adopted it, a physician is required to make such disclosure as comports with the prevailing medical standard in the community — that is, the disclosure of those risks that a reasonable physician in the community, of like training, would customarily make in similar circumstances. 2 D. Louisell and H. Williams, *Medical Malpractice* § 22.08 at 22-23 (1987) (hereinafter Louisell and Williams). A minority of the jurisdictions that adhere to the "professional" standard do not relate the test to any kind of community standard but require only such disclosures as would be made by a reasonable medical practitioner under similar circumstances. *Id.* at 22-34. In order to prevail in a case applying the "traditional" or "professional" standard a plaintiff would have to present expert testimony of the community's medical standard for disclosure in respect of the procedure in question and of the defendant physician's failure to have met that standard. *Id.* § 22.09 at 22-35 to -37.

In both the majority and minority formulations the "professional" standard rests on the belief that a physician, and *only* a physician, can effectively estimate both the psychological and physical consequences that a risk inherent in a medical procedure might produce in a patient. The burden imposed on the physician under this standard is to "consider the state of the patient's health, and whether the risks involved are mere remote possibilities or real hazards which occur with appreciable regularity. . . ." Louisell and Williams, *supra*, § 22.08 at 22-34. A second basic justification offered in support of the "professional" standard is that "a general standard of care, as required under the prudent patient rule, would require a physician to waste unnecessary time in reviewing with the patient *every* possible risk, thereby interfering with the flexibility a physician needs in deciding what form of treatment is best for the patient." *Ibid.* (footnotes omitted).

It was the "professional" standard that this Court accepted when, twenty years ago, it made the doctrine of informed consent a component part of our medical malpractice jurisprudence. *See* Kaplan v. Haines, *supra*, 51 N.J. 404, *aff'g* 96 N.J. Super. 242. In falling into step with those other jurisdictions that by then had adopted informed consent, the Court approved the following from the Appellate Division's opinion in *Kaplan*:

> The authorities . . . are in general agreement that the nature and extent of the disclosure, essential to an informed consent, depends upon the medical problem as well as the patient. Plaintiff has the burden to prove what a reasonable medical practitioner of the same school and same or similar community, under the same or similar circumstances, would have disclosed to his patient and the issue is one for the jury where, as in the case *sub judice*, a fact issue is raised upon conflicting testimony as to whether the physician made an adequate disclosure. [96 N.J. Super. at 257.]

In 1972 a new standard of disclosure for "informed consent" was established in Canterbury v. Spence, *supra*, 464 F.2d 772. The case raised a question of the defendant physician's duty to warn the patient beforehand of the risk involved in a laminectomy, a surgical procedure the purpose of which was to relieve pain in plaintiff's lower back, and particularly the risk attendant on a myelogram, the diagnostic procedure preceding the surgery. After several surgical interventions and hospitalizations, plaintiff was still, at the time of trial, using crutches to walk, suffering from urinary incontinence and paralysis of the bowels, and wearing a penile clamp. *Id.* at 778.

The *Canterbury* court announced a duty on the part of a physician to "warn of the dangers lurking in the proposed treatment" and to "impart information [that] the patient has every right to expect," as well as a duty of "reasonable disclosure of the choices with respect to proposed therapy and the dangers inherently and potentially involved." *Id.* at 782. The court held that the scope of the duty to disclose

> must be measured by the patient's need, and that need is the information material to the decision. Thus the test for determining whether a particular peril must be divulged is its materiality to the patient's decision: all risks potentially affecting the decision must be unmasked. And to safeguard the patient's interest in achieving his own determination on treatment, the law must itself set the standard for adequate disclosure. [*Id.* at 786-87 (footnotes omitted).]

The breadth of the disclosure of the risks legally to be required is measured, under *Canterbury*, by a standard whose scope is "not subjective as to either the physician or the patient," *id.* at 787; rather, "it remains *objective* with due regard for the patient's informational needs and with suitable leeway for the physician's situation." *Ibid.* (emphasis added). A risk would be deemed "material" when a reasonable patient, in what the physician knows or should know to be the patient's position, would be "likely to attach significance to the risk or cluster of risks" in deciding whether to forego the proposed therapy or to submit to it. *Ibid.*

The foregoing standard for adequate disclosure, known as the "prudent patient" or "materiality of risk" standard, has been adopted in a number of jurisdictions.

The jurisdictions that have rejected the "professional" standard in favor of the "prudent patient" rule have given a number of reasons in support of their preference. Those include:

(1) The existence of a discernible custom reflecting a medical consensus is open to serious doubt. The desirable scope of disclosure depends on the given fact situation, which varies from patient to patient, and should not be subject to the whim of the medical community in setting the standard.

(2) Since a physician in obtaining a patient's informed consent to proposed treatment is often obligated to consider non-medical factors, such as a patient's emotional condition, professional custom should not furnish the legal criterion for measuring the physician's obligation to disclose. Whether a physician has conformed to a professional standard should . . . be important [only] where a pure medical judgment is involved, e.g. in ordinary malpractice actions, where the issue generally concerns the quality of treatment provided to the patient.

(3) Closely related to both (1) and (2) is the notion that a professional standard is *totally* subject to the whim of the physicians in the particular community. Under this view a physician is vested with virtually unlimited discretion in establishing the proper scope of disclosure; this is inconsistent with the patient's right of self-determination. As observed by the court in Canterbury v. Spence: "Respect for the patient's right of self-determination . . . demands a standard set by law for physicians rather than one which physicians may or may not impose upon themselves."

(4) The requirement that the patient present expert testimony to establish the professional standard has created problems for patients trying to find physicians willing to breach the "community of silence" by testifying against fellow colleagues. [Louisell and Williams, *supra*, § 22.12 at 22-45 to -47 (footnotes omitted).]

Taken together, the reasons supporting adoption of the "prudent patient" standard persuade us that the time has come for us to abandon so much of the decision by which this Court embraced the doctrine of informed consent as accepts the "professional" standard. To that extent Kaplan v. Haines, 51 N.J. 404, *aff'g* 96 N.J. Super. 242, is overruled.

As indicated by the foregoing passages from Louisell and Williams, the policy considerations are clear-cut. At the outset we are entirely unimpressed with the argument, made by those favoring the "professional" standard, that the "prudent patient" rule would compel disclosure of *every* risk (not just *material* risks) to *any* patient (rather than the *reasonable* patient). As *Canterbury* makes clear,

[t]he topics importantly demanding a communication of information are the inherent and potential hazards of the proposed treatment, the alternatives to that treatment, if any, and the results likely if the patient remains untreated. The factors contributing significance to the dangerousness of a medical technique are, of course, the incidence of injury and the degree of harm threatened. [464 F.2d at 787-88.]

The court in *Canterbury* did not presume to draw a "bright line separating the significant [risks] from the insignificant"; rather, it resorted to a "rule of reason," *id.* at 788, concluding that "[w]henever non-disclosure of particular risk information is open to debate by reasonable-minded men, the issue is one for the finder of facts." *Ibid.* The point assumes significance in this case because defendant argues that the risk of lymphedema from an axillary node biopsy is remote, not material. Plaintiff's experts disagree, contending that she should have been informed of that risk. Thus there will be presented on the retrial a factual issue for the jury's resolution: would the risk of lymphedema influence a prudent patient in reaching a decision on whether to submit to the surgery?

Perhaps the strongest consideration that influences our decision in favor of the "prudent patient" standard lies in the notion that the physician's duty of disclosure "arises from phenomena apart from medical custom and practice": the patient's right of self-determination. *Canterbury*, *supra*, 464 F.2d at 786-87. The foundation for the physician's duty to disclose in the first place is found in the idea that "it is the prerogative of the patient, not the physician, to determine for himself the direction in which his interests seem to lie." *Id.* at 781. In contrast the arguments for the "professional" standard smack of an anachronistic paternalism that is at odds with any strong conception of a patient's right of self-determination. *Id.* at 781, 784, 789. . . .

III

Finally, we address the issue of [causation]. As with other medical malpractice actions, informed-consent cases require that plaintiff prove not only that the physician failed to comply with the applicable standard for disclosure but also that such failure was the proximate cause of plaintiff's injuries.

Under the "prudent patient" standard "causation must also be shown: *i.e.*, that the prudent person in the patient's position would have decided differently if adequately informed." Perna v. Pirozzi, *supra*, 92 N.J. at 460 n.2 (citing *Canterbury, supra*, 464 F.2d at 791; Louisell and Williams, *supra*, § 2208 at 22-32 to -35). As *Canterbury* observes,

> [t]he patient obviously has no complaint if he would have submitted to the therapy notwithstanding awareness that the risk was one of its perils. On the other hand, the very purpose of the disclosure rule is to protect the patient against consequences which, if known, he would have avoided by foregoing the treatment. The more difficult question is whether the factual issue on causality calls for an objective or a subjective determination. [464 F.2d at 790.]

Canterbury decided its own question in favor of an objective determination. The subjective approach, which the court rejected, inquires whether, if the patient had been informed of the risks that in fact materialized, he or she would have consented to the treatment. The shortcoming of this approach, according to *Canterbury*, is that "it places the physician in jeopardy of the patient's hindsight and bitterness. It places the factfinder in the position of deciding whether a speculative answer to a hypothetical question is to be credited. It calls for a subjective determination solely on testimony of a patient-witness shadowed by the occurrence of the undisclosed risk." [*Id*. at 790-91.]

The court therefore elected to adopt an objective test, as do we. Because we would not presume to attempt an improvement in its articulation of the reasons, we quote once again the *Canterbury* court:

> Better it is, we believe, to resolve the causality issue on an objective basis: in terms of what a prudent person in the patient's position would have decided if suitably informed of all perils bearing significance. If adequate disclosure could reasonably be expected to have caused that person to decline the treatment because of the revelation of the kind of risk or danger that resulted in harm, causation is shown, but otherwise not. The patient's testimony is relevant on that score of course but it would not threaten to dominate the findings. And since that testimony would probably be appraised congruently with the factfinder's belief in its reasonableness, the case for a wholly objective standard for passing on causation is strengthened. Such a standard would in any event ease the fact-finding process and better assure the truth as its product. [*Id*. at 791.] . . .

IV

The judgment of the Appellate Division is reversed. The cause is remanded for a new trial consistent with this opinion.

NOTES AND QUESTIONS

1. *Per Se versus Evidentiary Approaches.* *T.J. Hooper*, along with the *Behymer* decision it cites, are the leading authorities for the widely accepted rule that, outside of professional negligence, adherence to customary business practices does not of itself establish that the defendant acted with reasonable care. Some nineteenth-century and early-twentieth-century decisions had endorsed the now-rejected *per se* approach. *See* Titus v. Bradford, B. & K. R.R. Co., 20 A. 517 (Pa. 1890) ("the unbending test of negligence in methods, machinery and appliances is the ordinary usage of business. No man is held to a higher degree of skill than the fair average of his profession or trade. . . ."). There is some suggestion in these decisions that judges believed that the *per se* rule helped to constrain pro-plaintiff juries.

2. *Is Custom Probative of Reasonableness?* To conclude that customary precaution is not of itself reasonable precaution is not to conclude that evidence of customary precaution is *irrelevant* to the issue of reasonableness. As Holmes, the author of *Behymer*, explained: "What usually is done may be evidence of what ought to be done, but what ought to be done is fixed by a standard of reasonable prudence, whether it was usually complied with or not." 189 U.S. at 470. If, as Hand suggests, entire industries might lag behind evolving standards of due care, why should one presume that evidence of customary care tells us anything

about the standard of reasonable care? *See* Mayhew v. Sullivan Mining Co., 76 Me. 100 (1884) (excluding evidence of custom as irrelevant to the question of reasonable care). In a related vein, Professor Morris once argued that evidence of custom does not so much tell us what reasonable care is, but instead serves to focus the deliberation of jurors on the practical difficulties defendants may have faced in taking precautions against harming persons such as the plaintiff.

3. *Custom as Sword or Shield.* Should the weight given by courts to custom vary depending on whether it is the plaintiff who seeks to introduce nonconformity with custom as a sword for establishing fault, or the defendant who seeks to introduce compliance with custom as a shield against a finding of fault? Alternatively, should it vary depending on whether the plaintiff and defendant were strangers or maintained some sort of preexisting relationship? Judge Richard Posner has argued that a *per se* equation of customary and reasonable care ought to apply when the parties were in a relationship, but not when they were strangers, because parties in a relationship can in principle bargain to adopt practices that provide the appropriate level of care. Does *T.J. Hooper* endorse this rationale?

4. *Types of Custom.* Should the rules bearing on custom depend on the type of custom at stake? Professor Hetcher argues that customs develop out of several different circumstances and warrant different legal treatment depending on their type. For example, observance of certain customs enables individuals to "coordinate" their behavior — such as the custom, now enshrined in American law, that drivers should drive on the right side of the road. Other customs serve an informational role. For example, if a person unfamiliar with carpentry observes a carpenter wearing protective goggles, she may infer that there is a risk of eye injury present, and that goggles will help protect against it. Still other customs may have an expressive function, or may be mere vestiges of outdated patterns of conduct. Hetcher argues that the legal treatment of compliance with custom ought to vary according to the type of custom at issue. Which of the foregoing custom-types was in play in *T.J. Hooper?*

5. *Proof of Custom.* How does one prove the existence of a custom? Must adherence be uniform across the entire practice or industry? If not uniform, then what degree of adherence will suffice? Courts typically maintain that a practice must be "widespread" or "common" to count as a custom. *See, e.g.,* Trimarco v. Klein, 436 N.E.2d 502 (N.Y. 1982) (discussing whether usage of shatterproof glass for shower doors had become customary).

6. *Professionals versus Nonprofessionals.* As *Johnson* attests, prevailing practices play a special role in suits alleging professional malpractice. For example, the standard of care for doctors incorporates the notion of customary care into the very definition of reasonableness: A doctor is required to exercise the same level of care as is considered standard by members of the profession. Thus, in medical cases, proof of compliance with professional custom often *does* establish reasonable care.

7. *Local versus National Custom*. At one time, courts tended to require medical malpractice plaintiffs to show that the defendant's conduct departed from the custom of other doctors in the same locality. Now courts and statutes tend to speak, as does Georgia law, in terms of "general" custom, or the custom of "similar" localities. In part, this change of rules has been motivated by concern that plaintiffs residing in relatively sparsely populated localities would have a hard time finding a second physician or other expert willing to testify against a treating physician. In addition, the change was spurred by the judicial sense that modern medical training is more standardized, and medical information more readily available today than it once was. Can you see how this change as to which custom ought to be considered by the jury might affect the application of the *per se* rule in particular cases? By permitting comparisons and contrasts with practices in other jurisdictions, does the rule of custom promise at least some plaintiffs a basis for challenging prevailing local customs?

8. *Expert Testimony and Standard of Care*. As *Johnson* notes, unless the professional conduct at issue is so unrelated to professional expertise that lay jurors can assess it based on their experience, the plaintiff in a malpractice action must introduce expert testimony to establish that the defendant failed to heed standard of care. (Recall from *Walter*, discussed in Chapter 1, the high court's conclusion that Ms. Walter did not need to produce an expert to testify as to Wal-Mart's carelessness because its pharmacist's error was so basic that the jury could assess the issue of breach without the aid of expert analysis.) The expert must, moreover, testify in a way that identifies a standard of conduct that the defendant failed to observe. *See, e.g.*, Locke v. Pachtman, 521 N.W.2d 786 (Mich. 1994) (plaintiff's expert failed to identify a standard of care for injections by testifying that hypodermic needles usually break off in a patient only because of the caregiver's improper technique; the expert offered no description of how the defendant should have acted). The identification of an expert who is not only competent to testify, but also will make an effective witness, is among the most significant challenges facing a plaintiff's attorney contemplating the commencement of a malpractice action.

The *Johnson* court bars the plaintiff from asking defendant's expert, Dr. Caplan, whether he would have pre-oxygenated plaintiff's decedent. Is this because such testimony sheds *no* light for the jury on the applicable standard of care? How can that be? Mr. Johnson's lawyer argued that, even if it would not help define customary care, the question would help the jury assess whether Dr. Caplan was being sincere in asserting that Dr. Lawhead's conduct conformed to professional standards. Why did the court not permit the question for this more limited purpose of impeaching Dr. Caplan's credibility?

9. *Administrative versus Professional Judgments*. The professional standard of care applies to treatment and other care-related decisions. By contrast, administrative decisions do not fall under the rubric of professional malpractice. *See, e.g.*, Rice v. St. Lukes Roosevelt Hosp. Cent., 739 N.Y.S.2d 384 (App. Div. 2002) (claim for injuries allegedly arising from

inadequate hospital security are claims for ordinary negligence, rather than professional malpractice); Doe v. Vanderbilt, 958 S.W.2d 117 (Tenn. Ct. App. 1997) (hospital's decision not to notify patients who received blood transfusions that they may have been exposed to HIV was administrative rather than medical; motion for summary judgment on the ground of compliance with custom denied), *rev'd on other grounds*, 62 S.W.3d 133 (Tenn. 2001).

10. *Helling v. Carey*. A few decisions have assaulted the *per se* rule head on. A well-known example is Helling v. Carey, 519 P.2d 981 (Wash. 1974). Plaintiff, who was nearly blinded by glaucoma, sued her ophthalmologist for failing to administer a "pressure" test, a simple, painless procedure for detecting the disease. The accepted practice among ophthalmologists at the time was to administer this test only to certain high-risk patients (of which class plaintiff was not a member). Hence plaintiff stood to lose her suit under an application of the *per se* rule. The Washington Supreme Court, however, ruled that the ordinary, reasonable person standard ought to control, in part because the decision not to apply the test seemed on its face unreasonable. (Can you think of any reason justifying a failure not to provide a cheap, safe, and efficacious test such as this one?) Even more controversially, the court was so sure of its analysis that it held, as a matter of law, that the ophthalmologist had acted carelessly because the benefits of administering the test so clearly outweighed its costs.

11. *Informed Consent. Largey* indicates another limitation recognized by some courts on the *per se* rule for professional malpractice: It does not apply to claims of malpractice that assert a tortious failure to inform the patient of risks attending medical procedures. About half the states now recognize this exception. What is the strongest basis for *Largey*'s rule that informed consent cases are different?

12. *Exceptions to the Rule of Informed Consent*. The rule of informed consent admits of exceptions. For example, no informed consent need be obtained to operate on an unconscious patient in need of immediate surgery (although if a guardian or close relative is present or immediately available, it may be necessary to obtain her consent). *See, e.g.*, Miller v. Rhode Island Hosp., 625 A.2d 778 (R.I. 1993) (discussing the scope of the emergency exception and holding that the issue of whether a severely intoxicated emergency-room patient lacked the capacity to consent, such that a surgeon could proceed to operate over his objection, is a question for the jury). Harder cases concern whether a doctor is entitled to refrain from disclosing risks for paternalistic reasons, such as a fear that a particular patient will severely overestimate the risks disclosed and thus make an irrational decision not to opt for the procedure. Courts have suggested that such reasoning runs against the autonomy principle undergirding informed consent analysis. As a matter of informed consent law, must a surgeon disclose that he is HIV positive? *See* Faya v. Almaraz, 620 A.2d 327 (Md. 1993) (disclosure required). Must a physician disclose that she is under a contract with an HMO that provides financial incentives to

the physician to avoid, if possible, performing certain tests or procedures? *See* Neade v. Portes, 739 N.E.2d 496 (Ill. 2000) (failure to disclose incentives does not support an independent cause of action, but, if physician testifies as to the propriety of patient's course of treatment at trial, evidence of the nondisclosure of incentives can be admitted to impeach physician's credibility).

13. *Medical Malpractice Statutes.* In the last 25 years, medical malpractice actions have become increasingly governed by statutory rules designed in large part to limit physicians' liability. These statutes were enacted in response to a perceived crisis in medical malpractice insurance markets that threatened to vastly escalate the cost, or reduce the availability of, medical services. The provisions of these statutory regimes vary widely and may include rejection of the national standard of care in favor of a similar localities standard; adoption of shorter statutes of limitations, as well as statutes of repose (see Chapter 7); abolition of the collateral source rule (see Chapter 8); damage caps (see Chapter 8); and caps on attorneys' fees. *See* Newton v. Cox, 878 S.W.2d 105 (Tenn. 1994) (discussing Tennessee's medical malpractice statute and upholding its cap on contingent fees). Some statutes also set up administrative schemes, such as medical review boards, through which malpractice claimants must proceed before being eligible to sue in tort. In 2003, the U.S. House of Representatives took the unprecedented step of passing a bill that would have created national medical malpractice law by setting damage caps for medical malpractice actions, but the bill died in the Senate. Do these developments shed any light on the *Johnson* decision?

14. *MCOs and ERISA.* Medical care increasingly is provided through managed care organizations (MCOs). MCOs differ in their particulars, but their basic goal is to impose cost-benefit analysis on health care decisions so as to promote efficient expenditures on medical procedures. As more and more health care services are delivered through MCOs, administrators — as opposed to physicians — have gained a larger say over whether patients will be reimbursed for particular procedures. This in turn has raised the issue of whether they can be held liable for negligently determining that a particular medical procedure is not necessary or otherwise not covered by the relevant health plan, thus preventing the procedure from taking place and the patient from receiving the benefit of it. Judicial treatment of this issue has been enormously complicated by the presence of a federal statute, the Employee Retirement Income Security Act (ERISA), 29 U.S.C. §§ 1001 *et seq.* ERISA was enacted by Congress to bring order and fairness to employee pension plans. However, it also governs health insurance plans provided to employees through their employer, which plans provide a significant percentage of the health insurance in the country. ERISA includes a "preemption" provision stating that its provisions supersede conflicting state law, including state tort law. (Preemption is discussed further in Chapter 13 in connection with the *Geier* decision.) For patients seeking to sue MCOs for negligence, the problem is that ERISA seemingly confines the patient's remedy to a recovery of "benefits

denied," — for example, the cost of the procedure — rather than the damages suffered by the plaintiff from having been wrongfully denied the procedure. The scope of ERISA preemption and MCO liability are very much in play in the state and federal courts today. For an interesting recent analysis, see Cicio v. Does, 321 F.3d 83 (2d Cir. 2003).

15. *Other Professions.* The same *per se* rule extends to other professions, including the legal and accounting professions. The textbook example of legal malpractice consists of failing to file suit within the time period set by the relevant statute of limitations, thus causing the client to forfeit her claim. *See, e.g.,* Carpenter v. Cullen, 581 N.W.2d 72 (Neb. 1998) (affirming a $270,000 jury verdict against an attorney who failed to file suit prior to the expiration of the statute of limitations period). However, lawyers can also commit malpractice in other ways, for example, by breaching the duty of confidentiality owed to their clients, by failing to keep them apprised of the progress of their cases, by failing to conduct a diligent examination of documents related to a transaction, or by failing to consult their clients before making critical decisions, such as those pertaining to settlement. Legal malpractice claims, like their medical counterparts, require expert testimony to establish breach of the relevant standard of care, except in cases where the attorney's alleged carelessness is straightforward enough for a lay person to assess. *Cf.* Boyle v. Welsh, 589 N.W.2d 118 (Neb. 1999) (just as the general requirement of expert testimony in medical malpractice suits can be relaxed in certain cases, such as those in which a sponge is left inside a surgical patient, so certain legal malpractice cases will not require expert testimony on the issue of breach).

16. *Breach and Cause-in-Fact.* As with informed consent cases, legal malpractice claims can present thorny issues of causation and damages. If, for example, the allegation is that Lawyer *L* was negligent in handling the litigation of client *C*'s breach of contract claim, *C* is damaged only insofar as the contract suit was likely to succeed, either in the form of a favorable verdict or a settlement. In other words, as malpractice plaintiff, *C* is required to establish that, but-for *L*'s malpractice, she would have prevailed on her underlying contract claim. Thus, in suing *L*, she must prove "a case within a case," that is, the validity of the contract claim, as well as the tort claim against *L* for mishandling the contract claim. This can be a formidable burden.

IV. REASONABLENESS, BALANCING, AND COST-BENEFIT ANALYSIS

We mentioned in the notes to Part I of this chapter that Justice Holmes thought it would be desirable for judges to replace the "featureless generality" of the reasonable person standard with more specific rules as to what constitutes carelessness. We also noted that Holmes's vision has not been realized. Are there other ways to refine and systematize the breach inquiry? Or is reasonableness necessarily bound up with the particular context and type of behavior at issue?

United States v. Carroll Towing Co.
159 F.2d 169 (2d Cir. 1947)

[This suit arose out of events taking place at three piers extending out in a westerly direction into the Hudson River (which runs north-south) from the Manhattan side of the river. The three piers, in order from north to south, were the Public Pier, Pier 52, and Pier 51. On January 4, 1944, four barges were attached to the Public Pier in a "tier" formation, in which the first (easternmost) barge is tied to the end of the pier, the second barge, further out in the river, is tied to the first barge, the third is tied to the second, and so forth. Six barges were attached in the same formation to Pier 52, directly south of the Public Pier. For reasons unknown, someone had attached a line from the fourth (outermost) barge of the tier attached to the Public Pier to the sixth (outermost) barge of the tier attached to Pier 52.

The inner barge in the Pier 52 tier — the one attached to the pier — was named the "Anna C." The Anna C. was owned by Conners Marine Co., was being chartered (leased) by the Pennsylvania Railroad Company, and had on its decks flour owned by the United States Government. Under the terms of the lease between Conners and Pennsylvania Railroad, Conners was obligated to provide a bargee between the hours of 8 A.M. and 4 P.M. (A bargee is charged with looking after the vessel, often living on it.) However, the Anna C.'s bargee was not on board at the relevant times.

At about noon, the harbormaster ordered a tugboat named the Carroll, which was owned by Carroll Towing Co., and was being leased at the time by Grace Line, Inc., to tow away one of the barges in the Public Pier tier. In order to get to that barge, it had to first release the line attaching the outermost barges of the two tiers. Before undertaking that task, the Carroll pulled alongside, and attached itself with a line to the outermost barge of the Pier 52 tier. Two men from the Carroll, one of whom was the harbormaster, proceeded to board each of the barges in the Pier 52 tier and to inspect and adjust the lines holding the tier together, including the two lines holding the Anna C. to Pier 52. With that effort completed, the crew of the Carroll released the line attaching it to the outermost barge of the Pier 52 tier, as well as the line connecting the two outermost barges of the respective tiers, then backed away.

Soon thereafter, the entire Pier 52 tier broke away from Pier 52 and floated southward toward Pier 51. The Anna C., the innermost barge, struck a tanker docked at Pier 51. The propeller of the tanker punched a hole in the Anna C.'s hull. Because the hole was below the water line, its presence was not immediately obvious to the crew of the Carroll and others in the area. The Anna C. was pushed to a spot in between Piers 52 and 51, where it soon sunk. Evidence presented to the lower court indicated that, had they been made aware of the hole, both the Carroll and

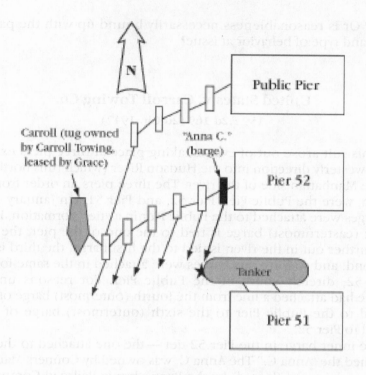

Carroll (tug owned
by Carroll Towing,
leased by Grace)

"Anna C."
(barge)

Public Pier

Pier 52

Tanker

Pier 51

United States v. Carroll Towing Co.
159 F.2d 169 (2d Cir. 1947)

another tug had the opportunity and ability to push the Anna C. to shore after it hit the tanker so as to prevent it from sinking.

Various claims and counter-claims were filed. The lower court held that Carroll Towing and Grace were both equally negligent in inspecting and/or adjusting the lines holding the Anna C. and the rest of the Pier 52 tier to that pier. Essentially, the court held each of these two defendants liable to Conners for half of the value of the damage to the Anna C.

On appeal to the Second Circuit, Carroll and Grace argued that Conners should also have been found at fault for the sinking of the Anna C. for failing to have a bargee on board at the time of the mishap. Unlike most states' negligence law, which at this time applied the all-or-nothing rule of contributory negligence, admiralty law apportioned liability for property damage on a *pro rata* basis among all persons deemed legally responsible for an injury. Thus, to oversimplify, if Conners could not be charged with the negligence of its bargee, the lower court's assignment of 50/50 responsibility would stand and Conners could recover all of its damages from Carroll Towing and Grace. By contrast, if Conners were charged with fault, it would be assigned responsibility for 1/3 of its own losses as one of three at-fault parties. Then it would stand to recover only 2/3 of its damages: 1/3 each from Carroll Towing and Grace. — EDS.]

L. Hand, J.   [After laying out the facts and the lower court's rulings, Judge Hand turned to the question of Conners' comparative responsibility. — EDS.] [E]ven though we assume that the [Anna C.'s] bargee was responsible for [inspecting and maintaining the lines holding the Anna C. to Pier 52] after the other barges were added outside, there is not the slightest ground for saying that [the Carroll crewmen] would have paid any attention to any protest which he might have made, had he been there. We do not therefore attribute it as in any degree a fault of the "Anna C." that the flotilla broke adrift. Hence she may recover in full against the Carroll Company and the Grace Line for any injury she suffered from the contact with the tanker's propeller, which we shall speak of as the "collision damages." On the other hand, if the bargee had been on board, and had done his duty to his employer, he would have gone below at once, examined the injury, and called for help from the "Carroll" and the Grace Line tug. Moreover, it is clear that these tugs could have kept the barge afloat, until they had safely beached her, and saved her cargo. This would have avoided what we shall call the "sinking damages." Thus, if it was a failure in the Conner Company's proper care of its own barge, for the bargee to be absent, the company can recover only one third of the "sinking" damages from the Carroll Company and one third from the Grace Line. For this reason the question arises whether a barge owner is slack in the care of his barge if the bargee is absent.

As to the consequences of a bargee's absence from his barge there have been a number of decisions; and we cannot agree that it is never ground for liability even to other vessels who may be injured. As early as 1843, Judge Sprague in Clapp v. Young, held a schooner liable which broke adrift from her moorings in a gale in Provincetown Harbor, and ran down another ship. The ground was that the owners of the offending ship had left no one on board, even though it was the custom in that harbor not to do so. Judge Tenney in Fenno v. The Mary E. Cuff, treated it as one of several faults against another vessel which was run down, to leave the offending vessel unattended in a storm in Port Jefferson Harbor. Judge Thomas in *The On-the-Level*, held liable for damage to a stake-boat, a barge moored to the stake-boat "south of Liberty Light, off the Jersey shore," because she had been left without a bargee; indeed he declared that the bargee's absence was "gross negligence." In *The Kathryn B. Guinan*, Ward, J., did indeed say that, when a barge was made fast to a pier in the harbor, as distinct from being in open waters, the bargee's absence would not be the basis for the owner's negligence. However, the facts in that case made no such holding necessary; the offending barge in fact had a bargee aboard though he was asleep. In the *Beeko*, Judge Campbell exonerated a power boat which had no watchman on board, which boys had maliciously cast loose from her moorings at the Marine Basin in Brooklyn and which collided with another vessel. Obviously that decision has no bearing on the facts at bar. In United States Trucking Corporation v. City of New York, the same judge refused to reduce the recovery of a coal hoister, injured at a foul berth, because the engineer was not on board; he had gone home for the night as was apparently his custom. We reversed the decree, but for another reason. In *The Sadie*, we affirmed Judge Coleman's holding that it was actionable negligence to leave without a bargee on board a barge made fast outside another barge, in the face of storm warnings. The damage was done to the inside barge. In *The P. R. R. No. 216*, we charged with liability a lighter which broke loose from, or was cast off, by a tanker to which she was moored, on the ground that her bargee should not have left her over Sunday. He could not know when the tanker might have to cast her off. We carried this so far in *The East Indian*, as to hold a lighter whose bargee went ashore for breakfast, during which the stevedores cast off some of the lighter's lines. True, the bargee came back after she was free and was then ineffectual in taking control of her before she damaged another vessel; but we held his absence itself a fault, knowing as he must have, that the stevedores were apt to cast off the lighter. *The Conway No. 23* went on the theory that the absence of the bargee had no connection with the damage done to the vessel itself; it assumed liability, if the contrary had been proved. In *The Trenton*, we refused to hold a moored vessel because another outside of her had overcharged her fasts. The bargee had gone away for the night when a storm arose; and our exoneration of the offending vessel did depend upon the theory that it was not negligent for the bargee to be away for the night; but no danger was apparently then to be apprehended. In Bouker Contracting Co. v. Williamsburgh Power Plant Corporation, we charged a scow with half damages because her bargee left her without adequate precautions. In O'Donnell Transportation Co. v. M. & J. Tracy, we refused to charge a barge whose bargee had been absent from 9 A.M. to 1:30 P.M., having "left the vessel to go ashore for a time on his own business."

It appears from the foregoing review that there is no general rule to determine when the absence of a bargee or other attendant will make the owner of the barge liable for injuries to other vessels if she breaks away from her moorings. However, in any cases where he would be so liable for injuries to others obviously he must reduce his damages proportionately, if the injury is to his own barge. It becomes apparent why there can be no such general rule, when we consider the grounds for such a liability. Since there are occasions when every vessel will break from her moorings, and since, if she does, she becomes a menace to those about her; the owner's duty, as in other similar situations, to provide against resulting injuries is a function of three variables: (1) The probability that she will break away; (2) the gravity of the resulting injury, if she does; (3) the burden of adequate precautions. Possibly it serves to bring this notion into relief to state it in algebraic terms: if the probability be called P; the injury, L; and the burden, B; liability depends upon whether B is less than L multiplied by P: i.e., whether B [is] less than PL. Applied to the situation at bar, the likelihood that a barge will break from her fasts and the damage she will do, vary with the place and time; for example, if a storm threatens, the danger is greater; so it is, if she is in a crowded harbor where moored barges are constantly being shifted about. On the other hand, the barge must not be the bargee's prison, even though he lives aboard; he must go ashore at times. We need not say whether, even in such crowded waters as New York Harbor a bargee must be aboard at night at all; it may be that the custom is otherwise, as Ward, J., supposed in *The Kathryn B. Guinan, supra*; and that, if so, the situation is one where custom should control. We leave that question open; but we hold that it is not in all cases a sufficient answer to a bargee's absence without excuse, during working hours, that he has properly made fast his barge to a pier, when he leaves her. In the case at bar the bargee left at five o'clock in the afternoon of January 3rd, and the flotilla broke away at about two o'clock in the afternoon of the following day, twenty-one hours afterwards. The bargee had been away all the time, and we hold that his fabricated story was affirmative evidence that he had no excuse for his absence. At the locus in quo — especially during the short January days and in the full tide of war activity — barges were being constantly "drilled" in and out. Certainly it was not beyond reasonable expectation that, with the inevitable haste and bustle, the work might not be done with adequate care. In such circumstances we hold — and it is all that we do hold — that it was a fair requirement that the Conners Company should have a bargee aboard (unless he had some excuse for his absence), during the working hours of daylight.

[Judge Hand's opinion proceeds to apportion liability among the various parties in light of the ruling on Conners' comparative fault and various other procedural facts about the case, then remands the entire matter for further proceedings in accordance with its dictates. — EDS.]

Rhode Island Hosp. Trust Nat'l Bank v. Zapata Corp.
848 F.2d 291 (1st Cir. 1988)

Breyer, J.   The issue that this appeal presents is whether Zapata Corporation has shown that the system used by Rhode Island Hospital Trust National Bank for detecting forged checks — a system used by a majority of American banks — lacks the "ordinary care" that a bank must exercise under the Uniform Commercial Code § 4-406(3) (1977), embodied here in Rhode Island General Laws, § 6A-4-406(3) (1985). The question arises out of the following district court determinations. . . .

1. In early 1985, a Zapata employee stole some blank checks from Zapata. She wrote a large number of forged checks, almost all in amounts of $150 to $800 each, on Zapata's accounts at Rhode Island Hospital Trust National Bank. The Bank, from March through July 1985, received and paid them.

2. Bank statements that the Bank regularly sent Zapata first began to reflect the forged checks in early April 1985. Zapata failed to examine its statements closely until July 1985, when it found the forgeries. It immediately notified the Bank, which then stopped clearing the checks. The Bank had already processed and paid forged checks totaling $109,247.16.

3. The Bank will (and legally must) reimburse Zapata in respect to all checks it cleared before April 25, 1985 (or for at least two weeks after Zapata received the statement that reflected the forgeries). *See* U.C.C. §§ 3-401(1), 4-406(2) (1977).

4. In respect to checks cleared on and after April 25, the Bank need not reimburse Zapata because Zapata failed to "exercise reasonable care and promptness to examine the [bank] statement." U.C.C. § 4-406(1) (1977).

The question before us is whether this last-mentioned conclusion is correct or whether Zapata can recover for the post-April 24 checks on the theory that, even if it was negligent, so was the Bank.

To understand the question, one must examine U.C.C. § 4-406, R.I. Gen. Laws § 6A-4-406. Ordinarily a bank must reimburse an innocent customer for forgeries that it honors, § 6A-3-401(1) (1985), but § 6A-4-406 makes an important exception to the liability rule. The exception operates in respect to a series of forged checks, and it applies once a customer has had a chance to catch the forgeries by examining his bank statements and notifying the bank but has failed to do so.

The statute, in relevant part, reads as follows:

> (1) *When a bank sends to its customer a statement of account* accompanied by items paid in good faith in support of the debit entries or holds the statement and items pursuant to a request or instructions of its customer or otherwise in a reasonable manner makes the statement and items available to the customer, *the customer must exercise reasonable care and promptness to examine the statement* and items *to discover his unauthorized signature* or any alteration on an item *and must notify the bank promptly* after discovery thereof.
>
> (2) *If the bank establishes that the customer failed* with respect to an item *to comply with* the duties imposed on the customer by *subsection (1) the customer is precluded from asserting against the bank.*
>
>> (a) *His unauthorized signature* or any alteration on the item if the bank also establishes that it suffered a loss by reason of such failure; *and*
>>
>> (b) *An unauthorized signature or alteration by the same wrongdoer on any other item paid in good faith by the bank after the* first item and *statement was available to the customer for a reasonable period not exceeding fourteen (14) calendar days* and before the bank receives notification from the customer of any such unauthorized signature or alteration.

§ 6A-4-406(1)-(2) (emphasis added).

The statute goes on to specify an important exception to the exception. It says:

> (3) The preclusion under subsection (2) does not apply if the customer establishes lack of ordinary care on the part of the bank in paying the item(s).

§ 6A-4-406(3). Zapata's specific claim, on this appeal, is that it falls within this "exception to the exception" — that the bank's treatment of the post-April 24 checks lacked "ordinary care." . . .

. . . The statute . . . says that strict bank liability terminates fourteen days after the customer receives the bank's statement unless "*the customer establishes* lack of ordinary care." § 6A-4-406(3) (emphasis added). . . . And, the U.C.C. commentary makes clear that the statute [places the burden on the customer to prove lack of ordinary care]. . . .

The record convinces us that Zapata failed to carry its burden of establishing "lack of ordinary care" on the part of the Bank. First, the Bank described its ordinary practices as follows: The Bank examines all signatures on checks for more than $1,000. It examines signatures on checks between $100 and $1,000 (those at issue here) if it has reason to suspect a problem, *e.g.*, if a customer has warned it of a possible forgery or if the check was drawn on an account with insufficient funds. It examines the signatures of a randomly chosen one percent of all other checks between $100 and $1,000. But, it does not examine the signatures on other checks between $100 and $1,000. Through expert testimony, the Bank also established that most other banks in the nation follow this practice and that banking industry experts recommend it. Indeed, Trust National Bank's practices are conservative in this regard, as most banks set $2,500 or more, not $1,000, as the limit beneath which they will not examine each signature.

This testimony made out a *prima facie* case of "ordinary care." U.C.C. § 4-103(3) (1977); R.I. Gen. Laws § 6A-4-103(3) (1985) ("action or nonaction . . . consistent with . . . a general banking usage not disapproved by this [Article or] chapter, prima facie constitutes the exercise of ordinary care"). . . . Of course, Zapata might still try to show that the entire industry's practice is unreasonable, that it reflects lack of "ordinary care." *The T.J. Hooper*, 60 F.2d 737, 740 (2d Cir.), *cert. denied*, 287 U.S. 662, 53 S. Ct. 220, 77 L. Ed. 571 (1932). In doing so, however, "the *prima facie* rule does . . . impose on the party contesting the standards to establish that they are *unreasonable, arbitrary*, or *unfair*." U.C.C. § 4-103 comment 4 (emphasis added).

Second, both bank officials and industry experts pointed out that this industry practice, in general and in the particular case of the Trust National Bank, saved considerable expense, compared with the Bank's pre-1981 practice of examining each check by hand. To be specific, the change saved the Bank about $125,000 annually. Zapata accepts this testimony as accurate.

Third, both a Bank official and an industry expert testified that changing from an "individual signature examination" system to the new "bulk-filing" system led to *no* significant increase in the number of forgeries that went undetected. Philip Schlernitzauer, a Bank vice-president . . . testified that under the prior "individual signature examination" system, some forgeries still slipped through. The Bank's loss was about $10,000 to $15,000 per year. He also determined through a feasibility study that by implementing a "bulk-filing" system in which 99 percent of checks under $1,000 were not individually screened, the loss would remain between $10,000 and $15,000. Dr. Lipis, an executive vice-president of a large consulting firm to the financial industry, testified that among its purposes was the following:

Well, it improves the ability to return checks back to customers more correctly, simply that the checks do not get misplaced when they are handled; generally [it] can improve the morale within th[e] bank because . . . the signature verification is very tedious, very difficult, and not a function that is liked by anybody who does it. In addition, *it does not impact the amount of forgeries that are produced at the bank.*

Rec. App. 179 (emphasis added).

Zapata points to *no* testimony or other evidence tending to contradict these assertions. An industry-wide practice that saves money without significantly increasing the number of forged checks that the banks erroneously pay is a practice that reflects at least "ordinary care." *Cf.* Vending Chattanooga [, Inc. v. American Nat'l Bank & Trust Co., 730 S.W.2d 624, 628-29 (Tenn. 1987)] (weighing economic feasibility and business practice into definition of "ordinary care" or "reasonable commercial standards").

Fourth, even if one assumes . . . that the new system meant *some* increase in the number of undetected forged checks, Zapata still could not prevail, for it presented *no* evidence tending to show any such increased loss unreasonable in light of the costs that the new practice would save. Instead, it relied simply upon the assertion that costs saved the bank are irrelevant. But, that is not so, for what is reasonable or unreasonable insofar as "ordinary care" or "due care" or "negligence" (and the like) are concerned is often a matter of costs of prevention compared with correlative risks of loss. *See Vending Chattanooga*, 730 S.W.2d at 628-29; United States v. Carroll Towing Co., 159 F.2d 169, 173 (2d Cir. 1947) (Hand, J.) ("duty" defined by calculating probability of injury times gravity of harm to determine "burden of precaution" that is warranted). One does not, for example, coat the base of the Grand Canyon with soft plastic nets to catch those who might fall in, or build cars like armored tanks to reduce injuries in accidents even though the technology exists. . . . In arguing that the Bank provided "no care" in respect to the checks it did not examine, Zapata simply assumed the very conclusion (namely, the unreasonableness of a selective examination *system*) that it sought to prove. Aside from this assumption, its evidentiary cupboard is bare. . . .

We have found a few, more modern cases that arguably support Zapata's view, but they involve practices more obviously unreasonable than those presented here. *See, e.g.*, Hanover Insurance Cos. v. Brotherhood State Bank, 482 F. Supp. 501 (D. Kan. 1979) (no ordinary care where *no* examination of *any size* checks, conspicuous forgeries); Perley v. Glastonbury Bank and Trust Co., 170 Conn. 691, 702-03 (1976) (no ordinary care where *no* authentication of endorsements of *any size* checks). . . . And, in any event, we believe Rhode Island would follow the more significant body of modern case law suggesting analysis along the lines we have undertaken.

For these reasons, the judgment of the district court is *Affirmed*.

NOTES AND QUESTIONS

1. *Learned Hand*. Judge Hand, whom we encountered earlier as the author of *T.J. Hooper*, was, along with Holmes and Cardozo, one of the most influential American judges of the first half of the twentieth century. He spent most of his career on the federal Court of Appeals for the Second Circuit, where he sat with his cousin Augustus, another distinguished

jurist. Hand is regarded by many to have been the most able judge of his time not to have served on the Supreme Court. Although sophisticated in matters of private and corporate law, he also earned his reputation by authoring an influential decision broadly protecting the free speech rights of political dissenters, and by academic writings that (ironically) urged courts to maintain a modest role in American government.

2. *Where Was the Bargee?* At trial, the bargee insisted that he was actually on the Anna C. at the relevant time, but failed to notice that it was taking on water after its collision. The master who presided over the trial found the bargee's testimony utterly incredible. Based on other witnesses' testimony, he concluded that the bargee had not been on the barge on the day in question, and that the bargee had lied to avoid revealing the apparently unimpressive explanation as to why he was not on board. Does the reason for the bargee's absence matter to the analysis of comparative fault? Suppose the bargee had just left the Anna C. one hour prior to the incident in response to an emergency summons from his spouse, who needed medical assistance. Would that change the result? Why?

3. *What Is a General Rule?* Why does Hand recite the various precedents on liability for accidents caused in part by the absence of bargees? What lesson or principle do they establish, in his view? In what way do they lead him to consider that the element of carelessness or fault might usefully be described abstractly, as inquiring whether the burden on the company of taking "precautions" (B) is less than the harm that probably will result from not having taken the precautions (P × L)?

4. T.J. Hooper *versus* Carroll Towing. Hand's opinion states that "the barge must not be the bargee's prison, even though he lives aboard; he must go ashore at times." How does this consideration figure into his formula for addressing the fault issue? Hand acknowledges that it may be the custom not to have bargees on board during nighttime hours. How does that observation affect his analysis? Is his treatment of custom in *Carroll Towing* consistent with that of *T.J. Hooper?* What is the relationship of ordinary or customary care to the level of care demanded by Hand's algebraic formulation?

5. *Reasonableness and Balancing.* That the determination of whether a person has behaved reasonably requires consideration of the burdens and expected benefits of taking precautions was not especially novel or controversial when Hand expressed it in 1947. For example, Section 291 of the First Restatement of Torts, published in 1934, following the earlier analysis of Professor Henry Terry, fleshed out the notion of acting as a reasonable person in the following terms:

> Where an act is one which a reasonable man would recognize as involving a risk of harm to another, the risk is unreasonable and the act is negligent if the risk is of such magnitude as to outweigh what the law regards as the utility of the act or of the particular manner in which it is done.

About 75 years prior to the publication of the First Restatement, the Exchequer Barons had ruled that a waterworks company could not be found to have acted carelessly in failing to take precautions against their pipes cracking during an unprecedented winter freeze. Blythe v. Birmingham Water Works Co., 156 Eng. Rep. 1047 (Exch. 1856). Implicit in the Barons' analysis was the notion that not every precaution is worth taking, and hence not every failure to take a precaution constitutes carelessness.

If judges and lawyers were already alert to the idea that the breach inquiry calls for an assessment of both the burdens and the benefits of taking certain precautions, how much does Hand's algebraic rendition add?

6. *Risk/Utility Balancing.* The First Restatement's formulation speaks in terms of balancing the risk of harm against the "utility" of the actor's conduct. In so doing, it evokes the doctrine of utilitarianism, formulated most influentially by the English philosopher Jeremy Bentham. Although it comes in many variations, utilitarianism's central claim is that the goal of social arrangements should be to maximize the *aggregate level* of utility or happiness in the world. If many car drivers experience great pleasure from careening down local streets for the fun of it, might their happiness outweigh the displeasure of the few unlucky persons who are injured or killed because the happy drivers were not proceeding more cautiously? The First Restatement's formulation is careful to note that courts should consider "*what the law regards* as the utility of the act." What does that qualification mean? Why did the ALI put it in there?

7. *Hand on the Hand "Formula."* In other opinions, Hand made quite clear that he himself did not regard his algebraic rendering of reasonable care to be the sort of formula into which a judge could simply place well-defined inputs so as to generate a determinate result. For example, a 1950 decision raised the issue whether a car driver had acted with gross negligence. After noting that the formal legal standard for gross negligence was clear enough, Hand emphasized the difficulties in applying the standard to particular cases, noting that

> the same difficulties inhere in the concept of "ordinary" negligence. It is indeed possible to state an equation for negligence in the form, C equals P times D, in which the C is the care required to avoid risk, D, the possible injuries, and P, the probability that the injuries will occur, if the requisite care is not taken. But of these factors care is the only one ever susceptible of quantitative estimate, and often that is not. The injuries are always a variable within limits, which do not admit of even approximate ascertainment; and, although probability might theoretically be estimated, if any statistics were available, they never are; and, besides, probability varies with the severity of the injuries. It follows that all such attempts are illusory, and, if serviceable at all, are so only to center attention upon which one of the factors may be determinative in any given situation. It assists us here to center on the factor of probability, because the difference between "gross" and "ordinary" negligence consists in the higher risks which the putatively wrongful conduct has imposed upon the injured person. The requisite care to avoid the injuries and the possible injuries themselves are the same.

Moisan v. Loftus, 178 F.2d 148, 149 (2d Cir. 1950). Is Hand being appropriately skeptical or too skeptical? Consider *Zapata*, which involves a contract dispute that, because of the wording of the Uniform Commercial Code, raises the issue of whether the bank exercised ordinary care in honoring stolen checks. In the hands of then-Judge Breyer, *Zapata* seems to provide a particularly promising context for application of a fairly rigorous rendition of Hand's algebra. Is this because the case involves "only" money? Or because the parties were in a contractual relationship? Because of other features unusual to the case? Do any of the negligence cases we have seen thus far lend themselves to such analysis in the same way?

8. *Posner on the Hand Formula.* Judge Posner's 1972 article, *A Theory of Negligence*, is primarily responsible for elevating Hand's invocation of algebra into a negligence "formula" that purports to advance the ability of lawyers and academics to analyze questions of breach. It also provided a launching pad for the influential "Law and Economics" movement in the legal academy.

In his article, Posner argued that Hand's formula, whether intended to or not, provided the basis for a more rigorous conception of balancing that asks the factfinder to measure the *dollar cost* of precautions against the *dollar value* of expected harm. Whenever the former is greater than the latter, Posner argued, the precaution ought not to be taken, simply because it is wasteful of society's resources to take a precaution that is more expensive than the harm it is meant to prevent. According to Posner, Hand's use of the $B < P \times L$ formula is a key piece of evidence establishing that the law of negligence is primarily concerned to maximize aggregate social wealth by encouraging actors to take only cost-efficient precautions. Posner further argues that the law has been wise to pursue this goal, because the minimization of waste is a cause that persons with otherwise diverse interests can endorse.

As a judge on the Seventh Circuit Court of Appeals, Posner has had occasion to apply his rendition of the Hand formula in concrete settings. For example, in McCarty v. Pheasant Run, Inc., 826 F.2d 1554 (7th Cir. 1987), the plaintiff was attacked while in her second-floor hotel room. Police later determined that the attacker gained access to the room through a sliding glass door that opened onto a walkway that in turn connected to a stairway that was accessible to the public at ground level. The sliding door had a handle-lock that had not been used. It also featured a chain lock that was in place, but was broken by the intruder.

Plaintiff sued, alleging that the hotel carelessly failed to equip the door with a better lock; ensure that the door was locked when she was first shown to her room; warn her to keep the sliding glass door locked; employ more security guards; and/or bar public access to the stairway leading to the second-floor walkway. The jury returned a defense verdict. On appeal, the court, per Judge Posner, affirmed:

> . . . Unreasonable conduct is merely the failure to take precautions that would generate greater benefits in avoiding accidents than the precautions would cost.
>   . . . Conceptual as well as practical difficulties in monetizing personal injuries may continue to frustrate efforts to measure expected accident costs

with the precision that is possible, in principle at least, in measuring the other side of the equation — the cost or burden of precaution. For many years to come juries may be forced to make rough judgments of reasonableness, intuiting rather than measuring the factors in the Hand Formula; and so long as their judgment is reasonable, the trial judge has no right to set it aside, let alone substitute his own judgment.

Having failed to make much effort to show that the mishap could have been prevented by precautions of reasonable cost and efficacy, Mrs. McCarty is in a weak position to complain about the jury verdict. No effort was made to inform the jury what it would have cost to equip every room in the Pheasant Run Lodge with a new lock, and whether the lock would have been jimmy-proof. . . . No effort was made, either, to specify an optimal security force for a resort the size of Pheasant Run. No one considered the fire or other hazards that a second-floor walkway not accessible from ground level would create. A notice in every room telling guests to lock all doors would be cheap, but since most people know better than to leave the door to a hotel room unlocked when they leave the room — and the sliding glass door [opened onto] a walkway, not a balcony — the jury might have thought that the incremental benefits from the notice would be slight. Mrs. McCarty testified that she didn't know there was a door behind the closed drapes, but the jury wasn't required to believe this. Most people on checking into a hotel room, especially at a resort, are curious about the view; and it was still light when Mrs. McCarty checked in at 6:00 P.M. on an October evening.

It is a bedrock principle of negligence law that due care is that care which is optimal given that the potential victim is himself reasonably careful; a careless person cannot by his carelessness raise the standard of care of those he encounters. The jury may have thought it was the hotel's responsibility to provide a working lock but the guest's responsibility to use it. We do not want to press too hard on this point. A possible explanation for the condition of the door as revealed by the police investigation is that Mrs. McCarty on leaving the room for the evening left the door unlocked but with the safety chain fastened, and she might have been reasonable in thinking this a sufficient precaution. But it would not follow that the hotel was negligent, unless it is negligence to have sliding doors accessible to the public, a suggestion the jury was not required to buy. We doubt whether a boilerplate notice about the dangers of unlocked doors would have altered the behavior of the average guest; in any event this too was an issue for the jury.

Now it is true that in Illinois an innkeeper . . . is required to use a high (not merely the ordinary) standard of care to protect its guests from assaults on the innkeeper's premises. . . .

. . . Ordinarily the innkeeper knows much more about the hazards of his trade than the guest, and can take reasonable (= cost-justified) steps to reduce them, while ordinarily the guest can do little to protect himself against them. Pheasant Run, Inc. knows more about the danger of break-ins to guest rooms at its lodge than the guests do, and more about the alternative methods for preventing such break-ins, as well. Maybe this asymmetry in the parties' position should make the defendant's standard of care higher than it would be in, say, an ordinary collision case. But it does not make the defendant's liability strict. In this case there was evidence of negligence but not so much as to establish liability as a matter of law or . . . to require a new trial. And the rule, based as it seems to be on an asymmetry in the parties' abilities to prevent mishaps, has a certain hollowness in a case such as this, where the victim may have failed to take an elementary precaution—locking the sliding door before leaving the room.

Id. at 1557-1558.

9. *Criticisms of Posner's Rendition of the Hand Formula.* Suppose Posner's interpretation of Hand's formula is adopted. Does it entail that the level of precaution one takes ought to vary according to what sort of person or property might be injured by one's conduct? For example, should D spend less effort on care when driving his car in a generally less affluent neighborhood, on the theory that the expected future income of the persons D might hurt, as well as the value of property D is likely to harm ($P \times L$), will be lower as contrasted to the incomes and properties of persons in more affluent neighborhoods? If so, does this disqualify Posner's interpretation of the Hand formula as fundamentally unjust? What might Posner offer by way of response?

In a related vein, Professor Keating poses the following hypothetical as a counterexample to the economic interpretation of *Carroll Towing*. D drives on a quiet local road at a speed well above the speed limit solely to secure a good tanning spot on the local beach. D's speeding results in a collision with cyclist P that causes P a broken leg. Is D permitted to argue that the statistical probability of hitting someone was so low that the loss of welfare he stood to experience by not getting his desired spot on the beach outweighs the expected loss to others, such that his speeding was not negligent? Keating suggests that the moral significance that society attaches to particular activities and purposes matters in the fault determination, and cannot adequately be captured by an economic account.

Recall that much conduct that is careless consists of momentary lapses and other forms of inadvertent behavior, as contrasted to calculated decisions, such as Menlove's decision to build his hayrick a certain way. Do balancing notions such as the Hand formula capture the concept of fault at work in cases of *inadvertence?* In what way has one failed to properly balance burdens and benefits by failing to check one's mirrors, or signal before changing lanes? By unknowingly driving above the speed limit? By slipping up during the course of surgery, or while performing an audit?

10. *Lord Reid's "Disproportionate Cost" Test*. Some commentators have pointed to the opinion of Lord Reid in the House of Lords decision in Bolton v. Stone, [1951] A.C. 850, as providing a more satisfactory account of the balancing that ought to take place in analyzing the breach issue.

In that case, a batsman hit a cricket ball over the fence encircling the cricket pitch. The ball struck Mrs. Stone in the head as she stood in her yard, about 50 feet beyond the wall, causing her serious injury. The residences that included Mrs. Stone's had been constructed 30 years earlier, and, although there was evidence that a ball had left the pitch about once every five years, there was no record of a cricket ball ever having caused physical harm to anyone during that time. Nonetheless, Mrs. Stone argued that the club that owned the pitch had been careless for not erecting a higher wall to prevent balls from escaping.

The trial judge ruled that the club had not been negligent. The Court of Appeal reversed by a 2 to 1 decision. On appeal, the House of Lords reinstated the trial court's ruling. In stating his judgment, Lord Reid justified the Lords' decision by invoking a three-tiered mode of analysis, which can be summarized as follows:

1. If, at the time of acting, the risk that the actor's conduct would cause harm of the sort suffered by the plaintiff was exceedingly small, there was no obligation to take precautions against it;
2. If the risk of harm was not far-fetched — "real" — but still very small, the actor was obligated to take precautions against the harm unless the taking of those precautions would have imposed a burden on the actor entirely *disproportionate* to the harm risked;
3. If the risk of harm was "material" or "substantial," the actor was obligated to do everything *possible* to prevent the harm, even if that would entail adopting very expensive precautions to avoid a modest expected loss.

Lord Reid concluded that Mrs. Stone's suit fell under prong (2). Given that balls had occasionally left the pitch, and that there were residences nearby, the risk of someone getting hit was not preposterous, but was still very low. Because the only precautions apparently available to the club were expensive — erecting a higher fence or ceasing to play cricket — the club was under no obligation to take these precautions.

On the assumption that Lord Reid intended prongs (1) and (2) to be reserved for unusual cases, and hence that (3) was meant to cover the vast bulk of suits alleging careless wrongdoing, scholars including Professors Weinrib and Wright argue that it provides a better account of reasonable care than Posner's Hand formula because it requires an actor whose conduct poses substantial risk of injury to take precautions even when they are not cost-efficient. This, they argue, better captures the intuitive idea that safety (physical well-being) is a more important interest than money or modest restrictions on liberty. Do you agree? Professor Gilles has suggested that Lord Reid's opinion was an outlier, and that English judges, like their American counterparts, attend to costs of precaution more than prong (3) of Reid's test would permit.

11. *The Third Restatement.* Section 3 of the new Torts Restatement construes the reasonable person standard to embrace a version of balancing. It reads:

§3. NEGLIGENCE

A person acts with negligence if the person does not exercise reasonable care under all the circumstances. Primary factors to consider in ascertaining whether the person's conduct lacks reasonable care are the foreseeable likelihood that it will result in harm, the foreseeable severity of the harm that may ensue, and the burden that would be borne by the person and others if the person takes precautions that eliminate or reduce the probability of harm. Restatement (Third) of Torts: Physical Harm (Basic Principles) § 3, at 38 (Discussion Draft, Mar. 28, 2001).

It is unclear whether the authors of the Third Restatement anticipate that juries will be instructed to balance "costs" and "benefits" instead of, or in addition to, being instructed on the reasonable person standard. Given that the jury usually has broad discretion to make the breach determination, if jurors will not be instructed on balancing, what is the use of framing "breach" in these terms?

12. *The Utility of Formulae*. Review the instances of faulty conduct provided in the cases in this chapter and earlier chapters. In what ways do the formulae offered by the Restatements, Judge Hand, Judge Posner, and/or Lord Reid enhance your ability to grasp what it means for a person to act carelessly?

V. PROVING BREACH: *RES IPSA LOQUITUR*

To say that breach is one of the elements of the plaintiff's prima facie negligence case is to say that the onus of establishing that the defendant acted carelessly is on the plaintiff. Often this onus is described as the plaintiff's "burden of proof." This phrase is somewhat misleading, in that it refers to two different burdens: the burden of *production* and the burden of *persuasion*.

The burden of production is the requirement of providing to the court some evidence in support of an alleged fact or set of facts that the party bearing the burden seeks to establish. So, for example, a negligence plaintiff seeking to establish that a defendant drove carelessly might seek to introduce into evidence a copy of a police report in which the police officer reports having observed the defendant speeding. Evidence offered in satisfaction of the burden of production will often be "circumstantial" rather than in the form of an eyewitness or videotaped account. For example, our imagined plaintiff might have to rely on skid marks at the accident scene, or the extent of damage to the cars involved in the collision, to support an inference that the defendant was driving carelessly. Often a plaintiff in this situation will seek to enlist the testimony of experts who can help establish such an inference based on circumstantial evidence.

The burden of persuasion comes into play only after there is evidence before a judge or jury upon which it must make a decision. As noted in Chapter 1, in criminal prosecutions, the prosecutor bears a high burden of persuasion. With respect to those elements for which she bears the burden, she must establish them *beyond a reasonable doubt*. However, in most civil lawsuits, including most tort suits, the burden of persuasion is phrased in terms of a lower standard, namely, the *preponderance of the evidence* standard. To say that a negligence plaintiff bears the burden of persuasion on an element such as breach therefore entails that the plaintiff must persuade the judge or jury that *it is more likely than not* that the defendant acted as the plaintiff alleges. To say the same thing in reverse, if the plaintiff's evidence establishes that it is equally likely (or less likely than not) that the defendant did or did not engage in the conduct alleged by the plaintiff, then the judge or jury must find for the defendant.*

In sum, the rule that a negligence plaintiff usually bears the burden of proving the breach element requires her to produce enough evidence concerning the defendant's conduct such that a judge or jury can conclude that it is more likely than not that the alleged careless conduct actually occurred. Yet, as we see below, in some situations, a negligence plaintiff will have only two pieces of circumstantial evidence available to her: (1) that the defendant acted *in some undetermined manner* toward the plaintiff, and (2) that, during or subsequent to the interaction, the plaintiff suffered an injury. The question arises: Is this minimal showing ever sufficient to satisfy the plaintiff's burden of proof on breach?

Byrne v. Boadle
159 Eng. Rep. 299 (Exch. 1863)

. . . At the trial before the learned Assessor of the Court of Passage at Liverpool, the evidence adduced on the part of the plaintiff was as follows: — A witness named Critchley said: "On the 18th July, I was in Scotland Road, on the right side going north, defendant's shop is on that side. When I was opposite to his shop, a barrel of flour fell from a window above in defendant's house and shop, and knocked the plaintiff down. He was carried into an adjoining shop. A horse and cart came opposite the defendant's door. Barrels of flour were in the cart. I do not think the barrel was being lowered by a rope. I cannot say: I did not see the barrel until it struck the plaintiff. It was not swinging when it struck the plaintiff. It struck him on the shoulder and knocked him towards the shop. No one called out until after the accident." The plaintiff said: "On approaching Scotland Place and defendant's shop, I lost all recollection. I felt no blow. I saw nothing to warn me of danger. I was taken home in a cab. I was helpless for a fortnight." (He then described his sufferings.) "I saw the path clear. I did not see any cart opposite defendant's shop." Another witness said: "I saw a barrel falling. I don't know how, but from defendant's." The only other witness was a surgeon, who described the injury which the plaintiff had received. It was admitted that the defendant was a dealer in flour.

It was submitted, on the part of the defendant, that there was no evidence of negligence for the jury. The learned Assessor was of that opinion, and nonsuited the plaintiff, reserving leave for him to move the Court of Exchequer to enter the verdict for him with 50l. damages, the amount assessed by the jury. . . .

* Some find it helpful to think of the preponderance standard mathematically. It requires the plaintiff to establish at least a 50.00001 percent probability that her allegations describe what actually happened. By contrast, a "tie" — that is, a 50/50 likelihood — goes to the defendant.

[On appeal, defense counsel argued that the facts established at trial] do not disclose any evidence for the jury of negligence. The plaintiff was bound to give affirmative proof of negligence. But there was not a scintilla of evidence, unless the occurrence is of itself evidence of negligence. There was not even evidence that the barrel was being lowered by a jigger-hoist as alleged in the declaration. [Pollock, C.B. There are certain cases of which it may be said res ipsa loquitur, and this seems one of them. In some cases the Courts have held that the mere fact of the accident having occurred is evidence of negligence, as, for instance, in the case of railway collisions.] On examination of the authorities, that doctrine would seem to be confined to the case of a collision between two trains upon the same line, and both being the property and under the management of the same Company. . . . The law will not presume that a man is guilty of a wrong. It is consistent with the facts proved that the defendant's servants were using the utmost care and the best appliances to lower the barrel with safety. Then why should the fact that accidents of this nature are sometimes caused by negligence raise any presumption against the defendant? There are many accidents from which no presumption of negligence can arise. . . . In a case of this nature, in which the sympathies of a jury are with the plaintiff, it would be dangerous to allow presumption to be substituted for affirmative proof of negligence. . . .

Pollock, C.B.   We are all of opinion . . . to enter the verdict for the plaintiff. The learned counsel was quite right in saying that there are many accidents from which no presumption of negligence can arise, but I think it would be wrong to lay down as a rule that in no case can presumption of negligence arise from the fact of an accident. Suppose in this case the barrel had rolled out of the warehouse and fallen on the plaintiff, how could he possibly ascertain from what cause it occurred? It is the duty of persons who keep barrels in a warehouse to take care that they do not roll out, and I think that such a case would, beyond all doubt, afford prima facie evidence of negligence. A barrel could not roll out of a warehouse without some negligence, and to say that a plaintiff who is injured by it must call witnesses from the warehouse to prove negligence seems to me preposterous. So in building or repairing a house, or putting pots on the chimneys, if a person passing along the road is injured by something falling upon him, I think the accident alone would be prima facie evidence of negligence. . . . The present case upon the evidence comes to this, a man is passing in front of the premises of a dealer in flour, and there falls down upon him a barrel of flour. I think it apparent that the barrel was in the custody of the defendant who occupied the premises, and who is responsible for the acts of his servants who had the control of it; and in my opinion the fact of its falling is prima facie evidence of negligence, and the plaintiff who was injured by it is not bound to show that it could not fall without negligence, but if there are any facts inconsistent with negligence it is for the defendant to prove them. . . .

Kambat v. St. Francis Hosp.
678 N.E.2d 456 (N.Y. 1997)

Kaye, C.J.   In this medical malpractice action, an 18-by-18-inch laparotomy pad was discovered in the abdomen of plaintiffs' decedent following a hysterectomy performed by defendant physician at defendant hospital. The question before us is whether plaintiffs were entitled to submit the case to the jury on the theory of res ipsa loquitur. Contrary to the trial court and Appellate Division, we conclude that the jury could have inferred negligence under the doctrine of res ipsa loquitur, and that defendants' evidence of due care and alternative causes of the injury did not remove the doctrine from the case. The trial court's refusal to instruct the jury regarding res ipsa loquitur thus mandates reversal and a new trial.

I

In August 1986, defendant physician Ralph Sperrazza performed an abdominal hysterectomy on decedent, Florence Fenzel, at defendant St. Francis Hospital. Ten laparotomy pads were marked and available for the operation, and Dr. Sperrazza placed several of these pads in decedent's peritoneal cavity, next to the bowel, during the surgery. The patient was unconscious throughout the procedure.

In the months following the operation decedent's condition was at first unremarkable. Eventually, however, she began to complain of stomach pain, and on November 30, 1986 X-rays taken at another hospital revealed a foreign object in her abdomen. On December 5, a laparotomy pad measuring 18-by-18 inches — similar to those used during the hysterectomy — was discovered fully or partially inside decedent's bowel, and it was removed by Dr. Robert Barone. This finding was so unanticipated that a photographer was called to document it. Decedent's condition continued to deteriorate, and she died on December 29, 1986, from infection-related illnesses.

Plaintiffs, decedent's husband and children, commenced this medical malpractice action against Dr. Sperrazza and St. Francis Hospital, alleging that defendants were negligent in leaving the laparotomy pad inside decedent's abdomen. At trial, plaintiffs presented evidence that the pad removed from decedent was the same type and size as those supplied to St. Francis Hospital in 1986 and commonly used during hysterectomies. Plaintiffs also adduced testimony that the pads were provided only to hospitals with operating rooms, where patients would not have access to them.

Plaintiffs called three expert witnesses, who disagreed as to the precise abdominal area where the pad was discovered. Two experts testified that the pad was both partially inside and partially outside decedent's bowel. A third testified that the pad had originally been left outside the bowel, in the peritoneal cavity, where it caused an abscess to develop outside the bowel, which in turn created an artificial opening through which the pad had migrated into the bowel. According to this expert witness, the pad was completely within the decedent's bowel when removed.

In response, defendants introduced evidence that standard procedures were followed during the operation, and that the number of sponges, medical instruments and laparotomy pads used and removed were counted several times, carefully and accurately. Defendants' experts, moreover, opined that the pad had not been left inside decedent but, rather, that she had swallowed it. According to defendants' witnesses, laparotomy pads were frequently left in places accessible to patients in hospitals; decedent suffered from chronic depression; overuse of sleeping pills could suppress the gag reflex and permit her to swallow the pad; and the human gastrointestinal tract would allow the pad to pass to the small bowel. Plaintiffs' expert witnesses, by contrast, agreed that it would be anatomically impossible to swallow the laparotomy pad or for a swallowed pad to reach the bowel.

The trial court denied plaintiffs' request to charge res ipsa loquitur, and the jury returned a defendants' verdict. Plaintiffs moved to set aside the verdict and either enter judgment in their favor or grant a new trial, arguing that the trial court erred in refusing to deliver the requested charge. The court denied the motion, concluding that the lengthy and inconsistent expert testimony demonstrated that resolution of the case was not within a lay jury's experience and, thus, res ipsa loquitur was not applicable. The Appellate Division affirmed Supreme Court's dismissal of the complaint, two Justices dissenting, and we now reverse.

II

Where the actual or specific cause of an accident is unknown, under the doctrine of res ipsa loquitur a jury may in certain circumstances infer negligence merely from the happening of an event and the defendant's relation to it (*see*, Abbott v. Page Airways, 23 N.Y.2d 502, 510; Restatement [Second] of Torts § 328 D, comments *a, b*). Res ipsa loquitur "simply recognizes what we know from our everyday experience: that some accidents by their very nature would ordinarily not happen without negligence" (Dermatossian v. New York City Tr. Auth., 67 N.Y.2d 219, 226).

Once a plaintiff's proof establishes the following three conditions, a prima facie case of negligence exists and plaintiff is entitled to have res ipsa loquitur charged to the jury. First, the event must be of a kind that ordinarily does not occur in the absence of someone's negligence; second, it must be caused by an agency or instrumentality within the exclusive control of the defendant; and third, it must not have been due to any voluntary action or contribution on the part of the plaintiff.

To rely on res ipsa loquitur a plaintiff need not conclusively eliminate the possibility of all other causes of the injury. It is enough that the evidence supporting the three conditions afford a rational basis for concluding that "it is more likely than not" that the injury was caused by defendant's negligence (Restatement [Second] of Torts § 328 D, comment *e*). Stated otherwise, all that is required is that the likelihood of other possible causes of the injury "be so reduced that the greater probability lies at defendant's door" (2 Harper and James, Torts § 19.7, at 1086). Res ipsa loquitur thus involves little more than application of the ordinary rules of circumstantial evidence to certain unusual events (see, Prosser and Keeton, Torts § 40, at 257 [5th ed.]), and it is appropriately charged when, "upon 'a commonsense appraisal of the probative value' of the circumstantial evidence, . . . [the] inference of negligence is justified" (George Foltis, Inc. v. City of New York, 287 N.Y. 108, 115).

Submission of res ipsa loquitur, moreover, merely permits the jury to infer negligence from the circumstances of the occurrence. The jury is thus allowed — but not compelled — to draw the permissible inference. In those cases where "conflicting inferences may be drawn, choice of inference must be made by the jury" (George Foltis, Inc. v. City of New York, 287 N.Y. at 118, *supra*).

Here, the Appellate Division majority concluded that plaintiffs' proof at trial failed to satisfy any of the three conditions. With regard to the first requirement in particular, the appellate court agreed with the trial court that a lay jury could not determine whether the occurrence was of a kind that ordinarily does not occur in the absence of negligence without evaluating the parties' expert testimony and, therefore, res ipsa loquitur did not apply.

In the typical res ipsa loquitur case, the jury can reasonably draw upon past experience common to the community for the conclusion that the adverse event generally would not occur absent negligent conduct. In medical malpractice cases, however, the common knowledge and everyday experience of lay jurors may be inadequate to support this inference. Courts and commentators across the country have come to varying conclusions as to whether expert testimony can be used to educate the jury as to the likelihood that the occurrence would take place without negligence where a basis of common knowledge is lacking. Courts in this State, as well, have differed as to whether expert testimony can supply the necessary foundation for consideration of res ipsa loquitur by a jury.

Widespread consensus exists, however, that a narrow category of factually simple medical malpractice cases requires no expert to enable the jury reasonably to conclude that the accident would not happen without negligence. Not surprisingly, the oft-cited example is where a surgeon leaves a sponge or foreign object inside the plaintiff's body. As explained by Prosser and Keeton in their classic treatise:

> "There are, however, some medical and surgical errors on which any layman is competent to pass judgment and conclude from common experience that such things do not happen if there has been proper skill and care. *When an operation leaves a sponge or implement in the patient's interior*, . . . the thing speaks for itself without the aid of any expert's advice." (Prosser and Keeton, Torts § 40, at 256-257 [5th ed.] [emphasis added].)

Manifestly, the lay jury here did not require expert testimony to conclude that an 18-by-18-inch laparotomy pad is not ordinarily discovered inside a patient's abdomen following a hysterectomy in the absence of negligence. Thus, plaintiffs' undisputed proof that this occurred satisfied the first requirement of res ipsa loquitur. We therefore need not resolve today the question whether res ipsa loquitur is applicable in medical malpractice cases in which the jury is incapable of determining whether the first res ipsa loquitur condition has been met without the aid of expert testimony.

Plaintiffs' expert testimony regarding how the presence of the pad led to decedent's ultimate injury and contradicting defendants' alternative theory that decedent swallowed the pad did not render res ipsa loquitur inapplicable. This evidence was probative of the questions of exclusive control and absence of contributory conduct on the part of decedent — the second and third foundational elements of res ipsa loquitur. The debate over the use of expert testimony in res ipsa loquitur cases, however, centers primarily on the first element, since it is with regard to the likelihood that the accident would not happen without negligence that the jury is generally expected to draw upon its common knowledge.

Turning to these remaining res ipsa loquitur conditions, plaintiffs' evidence that similar pads were used during decedent's surgery, that decedent was unconscious throughout the operation, that laparotomy pads are not accessible to patients and that it would be anatomically impossible to swallow such pads sufficed to allow the jury to conclude that defendants had exclusive control of the laparotomy pad "at the time of the alleged act of negligence" (Dermatossian v. New York City Tr. Auth., 67 N.Y.2d at 227, *supra*) and that it did not result from any voluntary action by the patient.

We agree with the Appellate Division dissenters, moreover, that defendants' evidence tending to rebut the three conditions did not disqualify this case from consideration under res ipsa loquitur. Plaintiffs were not obligated to eliminate every alternative explanation for the event. Defendants' evidence that they used due care and expert testimony supporting their competing theory that decedent might have had access to laparotomy pads and inflicted the injury upon herself by swallowing the pad merely raised alternative inferences to be evaluated by the jury in determining liability. The undisputed fact remained in evidence that a laparotomy pad measuring 18 inches square was discovered in decedent's abdomen: "[f]rom this the jury may still be permitted to infer that the defendant's witnesses are not to be believed, that something went wrong with the precautions described, that the full truth has not been told" (Restatement [Second] of Torts § 328 D, comment *n*). Thus, the inference of negligence could reasonably have been drawn "upon 'a commonsense appraisal of the probative value' of the circumstantial evidence," and it was error to refuse plaintiffs' request to charge res ipsa loquitur.

In light of this determination, we need not address plaintiffs' remaining contentions.

Accordingly, the orders of the Appellate Division should be reversed, with costs, and a new trial granted as to the first and second causes of action of the complaint.

NOTES AND QUESTIONS

1. *Mode of Proof versus Cause of Action. Res ipsa loquitur* — Latin for "the thing speaks for itself" — is sometimes described by courts as a distinct cause of action; for example, the plaintiff is said to sue on a

res ipsa theory. Strictly speaking, this usage is inaccurate. *Res ipsa loquitur* is an evidentiary doctrine applicable to certain tort causes of action, including negligence. When applicable in negligence actions, it permits a jury to infer that the plaintiff's injury was caused by defendant's careless-ness even when the plaintiff presents no evidence of particular acts or omissions on the part of the defendant that might constitute carelessness. The question for the court, then, is the preliminary question of whether the case before it is the *type of case* in which the jury will be permitted to draw such an inference. As indicated by *Kambat*, this type of case has tradi-tionally been defined by three features: (1) the injury must be of a kind that ordinarily does not result from absent carelessness on someone's part; (2) the instrumentality causing the injury must have been in the defendant's exclusive control; and (3) the injury must not have arisen from acts or carelessness on the part of the plaintiff.

2. *Effect of* Res Ipsa. Notice the effect of *res ipsa*, once successfully invoked. It relieves the plaintiff of the burden of producing evidence as to what exactly the defendant did wrong. As *Byrne* notes, it is still open to the defendant to introduce evidence to rebut the inference of careless-ness that *res ipsa* permits. In this way, *res ipsa* can be understood in part as an information-forcing rule. It asks the party in the better position to identify what happened to come forth with evidence as to what really did happen.

3. *The Inapplicability of* Res Ipsa Loquitur *in Standard Cases.* The first element of *res ipsa* precludes its application in the vast majority of negligence cases, even if it turns out that plaintiff has no means of deter-mining or proving whether defendant acted negligently. For example, even though many surgical patients cannot testify to what went wrong in a surgical procedure (because they were anesthetized), the general rule is that they still must provide expert testimony as to the defendant-physi-cian's failure to meet the standards of his profession. This is because surgery, even when properly performed, often fails or produces complica-tions. Therefore, these complications cannot be presumed to be the sort of outcome that only comes about from carelessness. If a malpractice complaint avers that a surgeon failed to remove a tumor in its entirety, or failed properly to insert an artificial joint, *res ipsa* will likely be unavailable — these are complex procedures that often go badly without carelessness on anyone's part. Accordingly, plaintiff will have to employ the pre-trial discovery process to obtain documents and testimony that will permit plaintiff's expert witnesses to reconstruct what, if anything, went wrong during the procedure.

4. *Medical Events That Tend Not to Happen Without Carelessness.* When *res ipsa* can be invoked in medical malpractice, it is because the plaintiff, like Ms. Fenzel's survivors, can establish that, in the particular case at hand, the injuries suffered are so unlikely to occur without care-lessness on the physician's or hospital's part that no proof of specific care-less acts need be proffered. As the Court of Appeals indicates, the post-operative presence of medical instruments or materials in a surgical

patient's body is the paradigmatic example of such a case. *See also* Umeugo v. Milford Hospital, 2000 Conn. Super. LEXIS 1943 (2000) (*res ipsa* applicable to claim of malpractice against surgeon who performed circumcision; presence of substantial portion of foreskin after procedure indicates the likelihood of carelessness in performing the procedure). By way of contrast, consider Locke v. Pachtman, 521 N.W.2d 786 (Mich. 1994), discussed above in the notes on professional custom. There the plaintiff attempted to invoke *res ipsa* by asserting that a broken hypodermic needle is not ordinarily left in a patient's body without carelessness. The Michigan Supreme Court rejected this argument.

Kambat ducked the question of whether *res ipsa* is available even if expert testimony is required to establish that the events leading to the plaintiff's injury would not likely happen without carelessness. Subsequently, however, in States v. Lourdes Hospital, 792 N.E.2d 151 (N.Y. 2003), the Court held that *res ipsa* can be invoked in such circumstances. Plaintiff, a surgical patient, complained that the attending anesthesiologist had injured her arm during surgery. In support of this contention, she submitted expert medical opinions stating that her injuries could not have occurred except by careless manipulation of her arm to administer anesthetic. The court held that expert testimony could be used to "educate" the jury as to what sort of injuries tend to come about only through medical error.

5. *Other Accidents*. Since *Byrne*, *res ipsa* has been successfully invoked in many other cases involving injuries caused by objects falling, moving, or exploding. For example, the modern trend is to permit passengers killed in airline crashes for which there is no evidence as to the cause to invoke *res ipsa* as a means of establishing pilot fault. *See* Dan B. Dobbs, *The Law of Torts* § 155, at 374 (2000) (providing examples).

Compare, in this regard, two car accident cases, Broadnax v. ABF Freight Systems, Inc., 1998 U.S. Dist. LEXIS 4662 (N.D. Ill. 1998), and Martinez v. CO2 Services, Inc., 2001 U.S. App. LEXIS 6195 (10th Cir. 2001). In *Broadnax*, the plaintiff's decedent was killed when his car was struck by defendant's truck. Apparently, no evidence existed as to what caused the defendant's driver to strike plaintiff's car. The court permitted plaintiff to invoke *res ipsa*. In *Martinez*, plaintiff's decedent was killed when defendant's tractor-trailer veered across two lanes and struck him. The driver of the truck was later found to have died of cardiac arrest. Given this finding, the court held that *res ipsa* was unavailable, as the accident could have just as easily been caused by the driver suffering an unforeseen heart attack as by any carelessness on his part.

6. *Exclusive Control*. Read literally, the "exclusivity" prong would require plaintiff to establish that the defendant exercised such a degree of physical control over the instrumentality or events that led to plaintiff's injury that it is impossible to suppose any other actor contributed to it. Modern courts, however, have not read the requirement so strictly. In most jurisdictions, it is enough to show that the defendant is likely to be the only one to have undertaken or omitted the relevant acts. When numerous others have access to the place of, or instrumentality causing, the

harm, courts are likely not to permit a *res ipsa* argument. *See* Flowers v. Delta Air Lines, Inc., 2001 U.S. Dist. LEXIS 19878 (E.D.N.Y. 2001) (extensive review of New York case law on exclusivity; plaintiff who suffered injury as a result of alleged failure to repair broken chairs at airport terminal cannot invoke *res ipsa*; widespread public access to the chairs indicates that many other persons could have been responsible for their being broken).

Imagine a suit in which the plaintiff alleges that her elderly decedent inexplicably fell out of a train car in the middle of the night. The car is equipped with doors located in the middle of the car that are latched, but can be opened by a passenger. Granted a weak version of the exclusivity requirement, can *res ipsa* be invoked? *See* Harris v. Amtrak, 79 F. Supp. 2d 673 (E.D. Tex. 1999) (denying plaintiff use of *res ipsa* on the ground that defendant lacked exclusive control over the doors).

7. *Multiple Defendants.* Are there situations in which, notwithstanding the exclusive control requirement, a plaintiff can use *res ipsa* to establish carelessness on the part of several defendants? In the famous case of Ybarra v. Spangard, 154 P.2d 687 (Cal. 1945), the otherwise healthy plaintiff underwent an appendectomy under general anesthetic. He woke up suffering partial paralysis in his shoulder. The theory of the complaint was that he had been positioned on the operating table in such a way as to damage nerves in his neck and shoulder. His position on the table, however, could have been affected by the acts of several nurses and doctors. Citing the inequity of forcing the plaintiff to prove what happened while he was unconscious, as well as a concern that the defendants in this instance each stood to benefit by remaining silent, the California Supreme Court permitted the plaintiff to invoke *res ipsa* to establish the carelessness of each. Contrast Samson v. Riesing, 215 N.W.2d 662 (Wis. 1974), in which a plaintiff who was caused a prolonged illness from ingesting contaminated turkey salad was prevented by the court from invoking *res ipsa* to impose liability on each of eleven mothers who prepared the dish for a band fundraiser.

8. *Plaintiff's Participation.* The third *res ipsa* requirement — that plaintiff establish that she did not voluntarily participate in causing her injury — is arguably just a particular application of the "exclusive control" requirement. If plaintiff played a significant role in bringing about her injury, the likelihood of the defendant's negligence having been the major contributing cause of plaintiff's injury significantly decreases, barring the jury from presuming that defendant's carelessness must have been what brought about plaintiff's injury. Thus, some courts will rebuff a car accident victim's attempt to invoke *res ipsa* if there is evidence of plaintiff having driven carelessly. Needless to say, unconscious surgical patients who suffer injuries during surgery ordinarily will not be found to be contributors to their injuries. In light of the existing requirement of "exclusivity," as well as the fact that modern negligence law takes plaintiff's fault into account in determining liability or damages, some courts have explicitly dropped this requirement. Peplinksi v. Forbes Roofing, Inc., 531 N.W.2d 597 (Wis. 1995).

9. *Spoliation of Evidence.* If, after an accident, the defendant intentionally (or in some states) negligently destroys evidence tending to establish its carelessness as the cause of plaintiff's injury, the plaintiff may have a separate cause of action against the defendant for spoliation of evidence.

REFERENCES/FURTHER READING

The Reasonable Person

Patrick J. Kelley & Laurel A. Wendt, *What Judges Tell Juries About Negligence: A Review of Pattern Jury Instructions*, 77 Chi.-Kent L. Rev. 587 (2002).

The Objective Standard

Leslie Bender, *A Lawyer's Primer on Feminist Theory and Torts*, 38 J. Leg. Educ. 3 (1988).

Anita Bernstein, *Treating Sexual Harassment with Respect*, 111 Harv. L. Rev. 446 (1997).

Mark Grady, *Res Ipsa Loquitur and Compliance Error*, 142 U. Pa. L. Rev. 887 (1994).

Martha Minow, *Making All the Difference: Inclusion, Exclusion, and American Law* (1990).

Arthur Ripstein, *Equality, Responsibility and the Law* 85-86 (1999).

Carol Sanger, *The Reasonable Woman and the Ordinary Man*, 65 S. Cal. L. Rev. 1411 (1992).

Margo Schlanger, *Gender Matters: Teaching a Reasonable Woman Standard in Personal Injury Law*, 45 St. Louis U. L.J. 759 (2001).

Reasonableness and Custom

Steven Hetcher, *Creating Safe Social Norms in a Dangerous World*, 73 S. Cal. L. Rev. 1 (1999).

Clarence Morris, *Custom and Negligence*, 42 Colum. L. Rev. 1147 (1942).

Richard A. Posner, *Economic Analysis of Law* 168 (4th ed. 1992).

Medical Malpractice

Patricia M. Danzon, *Medical Malpractice: Theory Evidence and Public Policy* (1990).

Neal C. Hogan, *Unhealed Wounds, Medical Malpractice in the Twentieth Century* (2003).

David W. Louisell & Harold Williams (eds.), *Medical Malpractice* (1987).

Frank A. Sloan, et al., *Suing for Medical Malpractice* (1993).

Paul C. Weiler, et al., *A Measure of Malpractice: Medical Injury, Malpractice Litigation, and Patient Compensation* (1993).

Learned Hand

Gerald Gunther, *Learned Hand: The Man and the Judge* (1994).

Reasonableness, Balancing, and Cost-Benefit Analysis

Mark Geistfeld, *Reconciling Cost-Benefit Analysis with the Principle that Safety Matters More than Money*, 76 N.Y.U. L. Rev. 114 (2001).
Stephen G. Gilles, *On Determining Negligence: Hand Formula Balancing, the Reasonable Person Standard, and the Jury*, 54 Vand. L. Rev. 813 (2001).
Stephen G. Gilles, United States v. Carroll Towing Co.: *The Hand Formula's Home Port*, in Robert L. Rabin & Stephen D. Sugarman (eds.), *Tort Stories* 11-39 (2003).
Michael Green, *Negligence = Economic Efficiency: Doubts >*, 75 Tex. L. Rev. 1605 (1997).
Gregory C. Keating, *Pressing Precaution Beyond the Point of Cost-Justification*, 56 Vand. L. Rev. 653 (2003).
Gregory C. Keating, *Reasonableness and Rationality in Negligence Theory*, 48 Stan. L. Rev. 311 (1996).
Geoffrey R. Marczyk & Ellen Wertheimer, *The Bitter Pill Of Empiricism: Health Maintenance Organizations, Informed Consent and the Reasonable Psychotherapist Standard Of Care*, 46 Vill. L. Rev. 33 (2001).
Richard A. Posner, *A Theory of Negligence*, 1 J. Leg. Stud. 29 (1972).
Henry T. Terry, *Negligence*, 29 Harv. L. Rev. 40 (1915).
Ernest J. Weinrib, *The Idea of Private Law* 147-152 (1995).
Richard W. Wright, *Hand, Posner and the Myth of the "Hand Formula,"* 4 Theoretical Inquiries in Law 145 (2003).
Symposium on the Third Restatement of Torts, 54 Vand. L. Rev. 813-940 (2001) (commentary by Professors Gilles, Hetcher, Perry, and Simons).

Res Ipsa Loquitur

Mark F. Grady, *Res Ipsa Loquitur and Compliance Error*, 142 U. Pa. L. Rev. 887 (1994).
Saul Levmore, *Gomorrah to* Ybarra and Mac: *Overextraction and the Puzzle of Immoderate Group Liability*, 81 Va. L. Rev. 1561 (1995).
Allan H. McCoid, *Negligence Actions Against Multiple Defendants*, 7 Stan. L. Rev. 480 (1955).

CHAPTER 4

The Causation Element

I. KEY TERMS AND CONCEPTS

A. Actual and Proximate Cause

Negligence law imposes liability only when careless acts have injurious consequences. Imagine two drivers, A and B, both of whom carelessly throw half-filled, jumbo-sized paper cups of coffee out of their car windows as they drive on a moderately busy public street. The cup thrown by A splatters on the car windshield of nearby driver Z, startling Z, which causes him to crash his car into a tree. B, by contrast, is luckier. His cup neither hits nor endangers anyone, but falls harmlessly to the ground. Both A and B were careless in the same way, and both A and B can be cited for littering, but A alone is subject to liability in negligence, because only A's carelessness *actually caused* injury to another.

Even when a careless act causes injury, liability often will not attach if the injury comes about in an entirely haphazard or otherwise attenuated manner. Imagine another driver, C, who acts in the same manner as A and B. Like B, driver C is lucky and does not hit or endanger anyone with his coffee cup. But C happens to do his littering in the sight of P, a pedestrian walking on a sidewalk parallel to the road. C's act poses no physical danger to P, and P does not perceive himself to be in danger. However, P does have strong feelings about people who potentially endanger others by throwing coffee cups. Thus, upon seeing C toss the cup, P instinctively expresses his outrage by stopping in his tracks and lifting his arms over his head. Unfortunately, in doing so, P brushes his hand against a hidden bee's nest in an overhanging tree limb. P is stung repeatedly. The stings cause him painful welts that require medical treatment.

C's careless act was almost certainly a breach of a duty of care owed to persons such as P.* That breach in turn was an actual cause of P's bodily injury—so far as we know, if C had not acted carelessly in the presence of P, P would not have stopped walking, would not have raised his arms, and would never have been stung. Nonetheless, C would have a strong argument that he should not be held liable to P because the connection between his carelessness and P's injury is too fortuitous. In negligence law, such argument is typically phrased in terms of the concept of *proximate cause*. Thus, C will argue that *even though* his carelessness was an

---

* Consider a variation on the example of A and Z, above. A tosses his cup and it splatters on Z's windshield, distracting Z. However, instead of hitting a tree, Z runs over pedestrian P. It seems very plausible that such a result was a foreseeable consequence of tossing a half-filled coffee cup out of a moving car in a populated area.

actual cause of *P*'s injury, it was not a proximate cause, and he should therefore not be held responsible for that injury.

The distinction just drawn between the actual cause question — Did actor *A*'s carelessness play some role in bringing about victim *V*'s injury? — and the proximate cause question — Did *A*'s carelessness bring about *V*'s injury in such a fortuitous manner that it is inappropriate to hold *A* responsible for an injury that his carelessness helped to cause? — may seem reasonably clear in the context of artificial hypothetical situations. In practice, however, lawyers, judges, and academic commentators routinely confuse the two. This confusion results in part from an unhealthy tendency to use the phrase "proximate cause" (or "legal cause") as a shorthand reference for *both* the actual and proximate cause issues. For example, it is not uncommon for a court to assert in its opinion, or a jury instruction, that the defendant cannot be held liable to the plaintiff unless the defendant's negligence was a "proximate cause" of plaintiff's injury. See Skinner v. Square D Co., *infra*. By this, the court conveys in potentially confusing shorthand that the plaintiff must prove that defendant's carelessness *actually caused* plaintiff's injury, *and* that it did so *proximately* (i.e., nonfortuitously).

To avoid confusion as much as possible, we will endeavor to keep the concepts of actual cause and proximate cause as distinct as possible. Thus, the present chapter is almost entirely concerned with the issue of actual cause, which is also sometimes labeled as the issue of "cause-in-fact" or "factual cause." Chapter 5 takes up the subject of proximate cause.

B.   *Actual Cause, the Jury, and the But-For Test*

The actual cause inquiry lies at the core of the causation element of the plaintiff's prima facie case. Given the preponderance of the evidence standard of proof (discussed in Chapter 3 in connection with *res ipsa loquitur*), this means that the typical negligence plaintiff must prove that the defendant's breach of duty more likely than not functioned as a cause of the plaintiff's injury. Like the breach determination, the decision as to whether a plaintiff has met this burden is generally left to the jury, subject to the judge's power to rule on the issue as a matter of law. Moreover, just as the jury's breach inquiry is usually guided by the legal standard of the reasonable person, its actual causation inquiry is usually guided by a particular legal standard. This standard is known as the *but-for* test of causation, also called the "sine qua non"* or "counterfactual" test. In U.S. jurisdictions, the but-for test is the predominant test for actual causation. In certain situations, however, courts employ an alternative test known as the *substantial factor* test.**

---

* [Without which not. — EDS.]

** Some courts have introduced still more terminological confusion by purporting to *replace* (rather than supplement) the but-for test with the substantial factor test. Thus, one sometimes encounters opinions in which the court states (or instructs a jury) that the

The basic content of the but-for test is easy enough to grasp. It calls on the factfinder to answer the following question: *Would the plaintiff have been injured if the defendant had acted with reasonable care?* If the answer to this question is no, the but-for test is satisfied and actual causation is established. If the answer is yes, plaintiff's claim fails the but-for test and, except in certain special cases discussed below, actual causation is not established.

An example will demonstrate the but-for standard in action. Suppose that *D* gets into her car, parked in her driveway, at noon on a Saturday, intending to run an errand. *D* backs her car out of the driveway, running over and injuring *P*, her neighbor's four-year-old child. Assume that *P*'s lawyers can establish that *D* owed persons such as *P* a duty of care, and that *D* breached that duty by not looking behind the car before entering it, and by not checking her rearview mirror once in it. The next question is actual causation—whether *P* would have been injured if *D* had been careful. Suppose *D*'s lawyers locate an authentic videotape of the incident. It shows that *P* stealthily approached *D*'s car on his hands and knees from a point directly behind the car just *after D* had entered the car, then sat down directly under the car's rear bumper. Given the facts revealed by the video, *P*'s case fails on the causation element. *D*'s having been careful *would have made no difference* because *D* would not have seen *P* even if she had taken reasonable care. Thus, *D*'s unreasonable conduct cannot be deemed a but-for cause of *P*'s injuries.

C.   Two Meanings of "Caused"

At the outset of Chapter 3, we warned against confusing the breach element (small "n" negligence) with the entire prima facie case (big "N" Negligence). Because of the imprecision of ordinary English language, it is easy to make a similar mistake in analyzing causation. Consider, for example, a collision of two cars at an intersection that are driven, respectively, by *X*, who is driving with all due care, and *Y*, who is driving carelessly. If you were talking to a friend about the accident, it would be perfectly normal for you to assert that it was *Y* who "caused" the accident. However, if one were to use the word "caused" in a different sense, one could say that *both Y* and *X* caused the accident. To adopt this latter usage is not to deny that *Y*'s careless driving contributed to the accident's occurring. Rather, it is to insist that the accident resulted from *both Y*'s careless driving and *X*'s careful driving. After all, had *X* not been driving carefully when and where she was driving, *Y* would never have had occasion to hit *X*'s car.

This latter usage of "caused" may strike you as odd, yet its apparent oddity results from failure to attend to a distinction between two senses in which the term is commonly used. Speaking as a friend, family member, or interested observer trying to figure out how someone ended up getting hurt, one tends to use a notion of "cause" that imports ideas of responsibility.

---

test for actual causation is whether the relevant actor's carelessness was a "substantial factor" in bringing about the victim's injury. As explained below, use of substantial factor as a generally applicable test for cause-in-fact is misleading.

Thus, when we imagined you saying to your friend that Y 'caused' the accident that injured X, the word "caused" was being used to convey a complex judgment that mixes notions of causation and responsibility. In other words, "caused" functions there as shorthand for a longer statement along the following lines: "Because Y was the one driving carelessly, he is the one who is *responsible for causing* the accident that injured X."

By contrast, we can imagine a somewhat different inquiry into causation that is largely divorced from any assessment of moral or legal responsibility. For example, consider how a physicist or highway engineer might go about analyzing the roles played by X and Y in their car accident. Their analyses might be largely indifferent to issues of blame and responsibility and instead concerned with assessing how the actions of these two actors happened to interact to produce a certain result. From this perspective, it makes perfect sense to assert that the actions of both X and Y contributed to causing their collision.

When factfinders in negligence cases are asked to focus on the particular question of whether actor A's careless conduct has functioned as an actual cause of an injury to victim V, they are principally being asked to assess causation in the nonblaming sense just described. That is, they have already determined or are assuming that V has suffered an injury, and that A has acted carelessly, and are now trying to figure out whether that carelessness helped to bring about that injury. Of course, this relatively neutral inquiry into causation is one step in a broader inquiry that aims to determine fault and to assign responsibility. But the limited inquiry conducted within this step itself is focused on determining which of the parties' actions, if any, brought about the injury.

Appreciation of the limited nature of the actual causation inquiry may help ward off certain confusions often associated with causation. One common misconception is that actual causation analysis involves a search for *the* (sole) cause of a victim's injury. This conception of the inquiry must be avoided. To attribute a causal relation between a victim's injury and a particular actor's carelessness is *not* to deny that the injury was caused by the conduct of many other actors. Rather, it serves to isolate a particular actor as having played a special role in bringing about a victim's injury by virtue of having caused it through a breach of a duty owed to the victim.

Reconsider the car accident in which Y's careless driving functioned as a cause of the collision with X. To notice this feature of the incident is *not* to deny that the conduct of innumerable other actors helped to bring about the accident. For example, one can go so far as to say that Y's parents played a role in causing the accident by giving birth to Y years earlier. (Much the same could be said of X's parents, and X's and Y's parents' parents, etc.) Needless to say, even if the accident between X and Y gives rise to litigation, there will be no inquiry into whether Y's parents should be held *responsible* for contributing to the accident *simply by virtue of giving birth to Y*. But this is not because the parents' conduct played no causal role in bringing about the accident — it did. Rather, it is because there is no remotely plausible basis for holding Y's parents responsible for having participated in causing the accident. (It is preposterous to suppose that they owed any duties to X and Y in this regard, or breached any such duties simply by giving birth to a child.) The causation question is not even raised because the threshold condition of duty has not been met.

For similar reasons, it is important to recognize that a finding of an actual causal link between actor A's carelessness and victim V's injury does *not necessarily entail* the conclusion that A is the *only* person whose *carelessness* (or otherwise wrongful conduct) played a role in bringing about V's injury. Suppose that X and Y would not have collided if another careless driver, T, had not entered the intersection at the same time they did. In that scenario, T's carelessness *and* Y's carelessness both played a role in bringing about the collision. Likewise, by virtue of the doctrines of contributory negligence and comparative fault — which we have encountered in previous chapters and discuss more thoroughly in Chapter 7 — the careless conduct of a victim herself may sometimes function as one among two or more careless acts that bring about the victim's injuries.

II. PROVING BUT-FOR CAUSATION UNDER THE PREPONDERANCE STANDARD

In a garden-variety negligence suit, if there is a "live" issue as to the actual causation component of the causation element, it is usually one of evidence and proof. In these sorts of cases, because the preponderance-of-the-evidence standard applies to causation, the issue is whether the plaintiff has offered evidence sufficient to permit the fact-finder to conclude that defendant's carelessness was *probably* a but-for cause of plaintiff's injury. We avoided that inquiry in our driveway hypothetical by assuming — quite fancifully — the availability of a videotape.

As we noted in Chapter 3, proof of the breach element sometimes will come in the form of circumstantial evidence. Thus, for example, the victim of a car collision might call an expert to the witness stand to testify that skid marks at the scene indicate that the defendant was driving at an unreasonable speed just prior to the collision. As the next cases demonstrate, the same holds true with respect to the issue of actual causation. Absent an eyewitness account or authentic videotape of the events in question, a plaintiff's lawyer typically will have to present circumstantial evidence that is sufficient to permit a reasonable factfinder to infer a probable causal connection between the defendant's carelessness and the plaintiff's injury. Yet, as we will also see, just as courts invoke doctrines such as *res ipsa loquitur* to relieve certain plaintiffs of the burden of producing evidence as to breach, courts will sometimes permit findings of causation notwithstanding an apparent lack of evidence sufficient to meet the preponderance standard.

Skinner v. Square D Co.
516 N.W.2d 475 (Mich. 1994)

Cavanagh, C.J. Plaintiffs, representatives for the decedent Chester W. Skinner, appeal from the Court of Appeals decision affirming the trial court's grant of the defendant's motion for summary disposition. . . .

We find that the plaintiffs failed to offer evidence from which reasonable minds could infer that the alleged defect [in defendant's product] caused the decedent's death. . . .

I

We borrow from the Court of Appeals' accurate summary of the relevant facts in this case:

> Plaintiffs brought this products liability action against defendant, Square D Company, following the death of plaintiffs' decedent, Chester W. Skinner. Mr. Skinner was electrocuted by his own homemade tumbling machine on which he had installed a switch manufactured by defendant.
>
> [Mr. Skinner] was in the business of cleaning and finishing metal parts. To this end, [he] routinely used a homemade tumbling machine that he had designed and built himself. Essentially, the machine consisted of a large metal drum mounted on a frame. Rough metal parts were placed inside the drum along with a quantity of abrasive detergent. An electric motor then rotated the drum in one direction to wash the parts. After allowing the drum to rotate for a period of time, the operator would reverse the direction of the tumbler and the finished parts would be ejected from the drum.
>
> Because of the way Mr. Skinner had designed the machine, reversing the direction of the drum's rotation was a dangerous task. The motor that turned the drum was controlled by a switch manufactured by defendant. Mr. Skinner had connected the Square D switch to the motor by using three wires with insulated "alligator clips" on the ends. In order to reverse the direction of the machine, the operator was required to disconnect two of the alligator clips from the motor by hand and reverse them. For obvious reasons, it was important for the operator to make sure that the Square D switch was in the "off" position before disconnecting the wires from the motor.
>
> On February 21, 1986, Mr. Skinner was in his shop, working in the room with the tumbling machines. Mrs. Skinner and two other women, Beulah McBride and Violet Whiting, were in another room, racking parts. Suddenly, the women heard Mr. Skinner cry out. They ran into the room where Mr. Skinner was, and found him standing with his hands above his head, each hand grasping an alligator clip. Electric current was passing through Mr. Skinner's body. Aware of what was hap-pening, Mr. Skinner cried out to the women, "don't touch me!" He then freed his left hand from the alligator clip and reached for the Square D switch. Mr. Skinner threw the switch into the "off" position, twisted, and fell over dead. [195 Mich. App. 665-666.]

Plaintiffs claim that the Square D switch was defectively designed because it had a large "phantom zone" that sometimes made the switch appear to be "off" when it was actually "on." Plaintiffs assert that this defect proximately caused Mr. Skinner's death.

The defendant responds that, even assuming the switch is defective, the plaintiffs' evidence does not show that Mr. Skinner was misled by the switch when he was fatally electrocuted. [Following extensive discovery,] the defendant filed a motion for summary disposition . . . , effectively claiming that because plaintiffs are unable to establish a genuine issue of causation, it is entitled to judgment as a matter of law.

The trial court granted the defendant's motion, ruling that the "Plaintiff has produced no evidence to show a specific fact issue to support his theory that the switch somehow caused Plaintiff's decedent's death." The Court of Appeals affirmed, over the dissent of Judge Michael J. Kelly. The majority found that "at no time did plaintiffs advance a plausible theory regarding how the defective switch caused the accident." 195 Mich. App. 668. . . .

II

. . . [A] prima facie case for products liability requires proof of a causal connection between an established defect and injury. Mulholland v. DEC Int'l, 432 Mich. 395, 415; 443 N.W.2d 340 (1989). While the plaintiff bears the burden of proof, the plaintiff is not required to produce evidence that positively eliminates every other potential cause. Rather, the plaintiff's evidence is sufficient if it "establishes a logical sequence of cause and effect, notwithstanding the existence of other plausible theories, although other plausible theories may also have evidentiary support." *Id.* . . .

IV

. . . Under Michigan . . . law . . . a plaintiff must show that the manu-facturer's negligence was the proximate cause of the plaintiff's injuries. . . . We have previously explained that proving proximate cause actually entails proof of two separate elements: (1) cause in fact, and (2) legal cause, also known as "proximate cause." Moning v. Alfono, 400 Mich. 425, 437; 254 N.W.2d 759 (1977).

The cause in fact element generally requires showing that "but for" the defendant's actions, the plaintiff's injury would not have occurred. . . . A plaintiff must adequately establish cause in fact in order for legal cause or "proximate cause" to become a relevant issue. We find that the plaintiffs here were unsuccessful in showing a genuine issue of factual causation. Accordingly, we need not and do not address legal cause or "proximate cause" in this case.

Because no one was present in the shop with the decedent immedi-ately before the accident, the plaintiffs had to rely on circumstantial evidence to establish that the alleged defective switch was the cause in fact of the decedent's death. This Court has repeatedly recognized that plain-tiffs may utilize circumstantial proof to show the requisite causal link between a defect and an injury in products liability cases. . . .

While plaintiffs may show causation circumstantially, the mere happening of an unwitnessed mishap neither eliminates nor reduces a plaintiff's duty to effectively demonstrate causation:

> That there was no eyewitness to the accident does not always prevent the making of a possible issue of fact for the jury. But the burden of establishing proximate cause . . . always rests with the complaining party, and no presumption of it is created by the mere fact of an accident. [Howe v. Michigan C. R. Co., 236 Mich. 577, 583-584; 211 N.W. 111 (1926), *cert. denied*, 274 U.S. 738, 71 L. Ed. 1317, 47 S. Ct. 576 (1927).]

To be adequate, a plaintiff's circumstantial proof must facilitate reasonable inferences of causation, not mere speculation. In Kaminski v. Grand Trunk W. R. Co., 347 Mich. 417, 422; 79 N.W.2d 899 (1956), [we] highlighted the . . . distinction between a reasonable inference and impermissible conjecture with regard to causal proof:

> As a theory of causation, a conjecture is simply an explanation consistent with known facts or conditions, but not deducible from them as a reasonable inference. There may be 2 or more plausible explanations as to how an event happened or what produced it; yet, if the evidence is without selective application to any 1 of them, they remain conjectures only. On the other hand, if there is evidence which points to any 1 theory of causation, indicating a logical sequence of cause and effect, then there is a juridical basis for such a determination, notwithstanding the existence of other plausible theories with or without support in the evidence.

We want to make clear what it means to provide circumstantial evidence that permits a reasonable inference of causation. As *Kaminski* explains, at a minimum, a causation theory must have some basis in established fact. However, a basis in only slight evidence is not enough. Nor is it sufficient to submit a causation theory that, while factually supported, is, at best, just as possible as another theory. Rather, the plaintiff must present substantial evidence from which a jury may conclude that more likely than not, but for the defendant's conduct, the plaintiff's injuries would not have occurred. . . .

In light of the above pronouncements, we concur with the observation made in 57A Am. Jur. 2d, Negligence, § 461, p.442:

> All that is necessary is that the proof amount to a reasonable likelihood of probability rather than a possibility. The evidence need not negate all other possible causes, but such evidence must exclude other reasonable hypotheses with a fair amount of certainty. Absolute certainty cannot be achieved in proving negligence circumstantially; but such proof may satisfy where the chain of circumstances leads to a conclusion which is more probable than any other hypothesis reflected by the evidence. However, if such evidence lends equal support to inconsistent conclusions or is equally consistent with contradictory hypotheses, negligence is not established.

Our case law effectively illustrates the degree of circumstantial proof required to enable jurors to reasonably infer the existence of a causal relationship between a defendant's actions and a plaintiff's injuries. For example, in [Schedlbauer v. Chris-Craft Corp., 381 Mich. 217, 223; 160 N.W.2d 889 (1968)], a plaintiff boat owner suffered injuries when his pleasure boat exploded. The plaintiff filed suit against the boat manufacturer, claiming that a defectively porous fuel pump caused gasoline to leak into the boat's bilge area, ultimately resulting in the explosion. The controlling question was whether the plaintiff could offer enough evidence to establish that the gasoline entered the bilge area via the allegedly defective fuel pump, thereby producing the blast.

The plaintiff relied upon circumstantial proof to verify his causation theory. The proofs included: the plaintiff's testimony that, while the boat had operated without incident in the past, immediately before the explosion, the engine started to "run 'rough'"; the plaintiff's expert testimony that if there had been a leak in the fuel pump, the engine would not turn off, but it would "'run roughly'"; the expert's opinion that the gasoline entered the bilge area through the fuel pump and caused the explosion; the expert's view that if gasoline had entered the bilge area in any other way, the engine would have necessarily shut off automatically during the explosion; and the plaintiff's testimony that during the explosion the motor continued to run until he manually turned it off.

In particular, this Court emphasized that the expert's testimony "fairly indicated 'a logical sequence of cause and effect'" between the alleged defect and resulting injury. The Court also acknowledged the defendant's alternative causation theories, but found them to be less than probable. On the basis of the plaintiff's circumstantial evidence, the Court concluded that a jury would have sufficient ground to infer that the defendant's defective fuel pump caused the explosion and, in turn, the plaintiff's injuries.

Kaminski also highlights the level of circumstantial evidence needed to adequately establish causation. A plaintiff factory worker incurred injuries when he was hit by a trailer that was parked near a railroad track. The plaintiff filed suit against the defendant railroad company, claiming that the conductor's negligent failure to see the trailer caused the train to push the trailer into the plaintiff, injuring him. The collision occurred at night, and there were no eyewitnesses to the accident.

The plaintiff's circumstantial proof showed that moments before the accident the plaintiff had stopped within six feet of the train track, the dark green trailer was parked near the track on the same side that the plaintiff had stopped, and the train was approaching the area where both the plaintiff and trailer were located. Nearer to the time of the collision, the evidence indicated that the train conductor heard a screeching noise coming from the side of the train where both the plaintiff and trailer were situated. At the time of the collision, the plaintiff, also having heard the same screeching noise, was suddenly struck by something he could not see. Immediately after the collision, the plaintiff found himself lying on top of the trailer. The evidence also indicated that, other than the moving train, there were no other objects in the area that could have pushed the trailer into the plaintiff.

The Court found that these circumstantial proofs could facilitate a jury in inferring a logical causal relationship between the defendant's negligence and the plaintiff's injuries. The Court mentioned the defendant's contrary causation theories, but in the end dismissed them, explaining that while they were "possible," they were "not probable." . . .

In *Howe*, [by contrast,] the circumstantial causal proof was . . . deficient. A brakeman for a railroad company . . . fell to his death from the bridge on which the car [he was in] had stopped. The brakeman's representative brought suit against the railroad company, claiming that the railroad's negligent failure to provide more space between the track and the edge of the bridge resulted in the decedent's death. The misadventure occurred on a dark and rainy night, and no one observed the actual fall.

The circumstantial evidence established that the train had stopped on the bridge, and, pursuant to his duties, the decedent prepared to get off the train to set up flagman signals. The decedent was last seen buttoning his coat by the rear door of the car with two lanterns at his feet. The decedent's representative argued that it was reasonable to infer that the decedent thereafter alighted from the train, and that the insufficient landing space caused the decedent to fall off the bridge. The Court regarded this causation theory as unlikely without additional facts and circumstances for support, reasoning:

> This is one possible explanation of the manner decedent came to his death. It is by no means the only one. No eye saw him after he left the car. No one even knows from which side of the car he left. Is it not just as possible that he stumbled or slipped from the platform or steps of the car and fell into the river? If he did, the space afforded him for walking between the car and the edge of the bridge had nothing to do with it. One theory is as reasonable as the other. Additional ones might be and have been advanced, but the jury should not be permitted to conjecture that he fell from one cause and not from another. [*Id.* at 583-584.]

V

Unlike the circumstantial proofs submitted in *Schedlbauer* and *Kaminski*, and more like those offered in . . . *Howe*, the plaintiffs' circumstantial evidence here did not afford a reliable basis from which reasonable minds could infer that more probably than not, but for the defect in the Square D switch, Mr. Skinner would not have been electrocuted.

Plaintiffs' causation theory is that the faulty switch caused the decedent to be confused about whether the machine was on or off; that this confusion induced him to touch the live wires; and that this contact resulted in his electrocution. To support this theory, the plaintiffs offered testimony from co-workers who stated that, in the past, the decedent was always a careful worker, and always turned the power off before he manually reversed the alligator clips. On the basis of this testimony, the plaintiffs urge that the switch must have confused the decedent regarding whether the machine was on or off on the day that he touched the wires and that this confusion led to his electrocution. The lower courts explicitly exposed the critical problem with this theory.

If the machine had been operating, the decedent could not have been confused by the switch in the way that the plaintiffs contend. The plaintiffs do not dispute that when the tumbler is running, it makes a considerable amount of noise, and that the drum moves in a circular motion. The decedent could not have been confused regarding the power's status because either the noise or the visual appearance of movement would have affirmatively cued him regarding whether the power was on or off—regardless of what the switch may have indicated.

In view of this factually established phenomenon, the plaintiffs had to offer an alternative sequence of cause and effect, whereby the decedent was confused by the switch, but the machine was not in operation.

The plaintiffs proposed an hypothesis under which Mr. Skinner thought that the machine was off because of a faulty indication from the switch, the power was actually on, but the machine was not running *because the wires were not attached to the alligator clips*. . . . This scenario is fatally flawed in two respects.

First, the plaintiffs failed to produce any evidence from which a jury could reasonably conclude that the wires were unhooked when Mr. Skinner began using the machine just before the accident. In fact, the only record evidence pertaining to how the wires and clips were maintained indicated that they would probably have been connected. Second, the plaintiffs did not offer any proof from which it rationally could be inferred how the machine would have been turned back on after the wires had been unhooked.

Of course, the plaintiffs' offered scenario is a *possibility*. However, so are countless others. As explained above, causation theories that are mere possibilities or, at most, equally as probable as other theories do not justify a grant of summary judgment.

Plaintiffs further argue that the testimony of their experts proved factual causation. [E]xpert opinion based upon only hypothetical situations is not enough to demonstrate a legitimate causal connection between a defect and injury. Moreover, in *Mulholland* at 411, we stated that "there must be facts in evidence to support the opinion testimony of an expert."

Plaintiffs' expert testimony did not sufficiently establish causation. Plaintiffs' experts maintained that the switch was defective, and that the defect was the proximate cause of the decedent's death. The experts' causation theories were deficient, however, because each lacked a basis in established fact. Specifically, each expert either assumed, or was asked to assume, that (somehow) the wires were unhooked, and that the power was on when Mr. Skinner began working on the machine. Because the experts' conclusions regarding causation are premised on mere suppositions, they did not establish an authentic issue of causation.

Taking the record evidence in the light most favorable to the plaintiff, we conclude that the record facts do not manifest a genuine issue of factual causation. The offered evidence only established that an accident took place. Michigan law does not permit us to infer causation simply because a tragedy occurred in the vicinity of a defective product. The plaintiffs were required to set forth specific facts that would support a reasonable inference of a logical sequence of cause and effect. Instead, the plaintiffs posited a causation theory premised on mere conjecture and possibilities.

We recognize that . . . the jury's role [is] to decide questions of material fact. [However,] litigants do not have any right to submit an evidentiary record to the jury that would allow the jury to do nothing more than guess. . . .

   Levin, J. (dissenting). . . .
   . . . I would hold that the estate produced sufficient evidence to require jury submission of the question whether Skinner's death was caused by the defect in design and failure to insulate so in effect conceded. . . .

The estate's theory of causation is that the defective on/off switch caused Chester Skinner's death in the following manner. Skinner entered, or had been working in, the room containing the tumbling machine. The tumbling machine was not being operated immediately before Skinner touched or picked up the electrical wires. Before touching the wires, in accordance with his habit, he looked at the on/off switch.

The . . . defective on/off switch falsely indicated that it was in the off position, and thus that there was no electricity flowing through the wires. Relying on his reading of the on/off switch, Skinner touched the wires and suffered the excruciating electrical shock. . . .

The majority asserts that there are two "fatal flaws" in the plaintiff's theory. First, "the plaintiffs failed to produce any evidence from which a jury could reasonably conclude that the wires were unhooked when Mr. Skinner began using the machine just before the accident."

The majority ignores that there is substantial evidence that the tumbling machine was *not* operating when Skinner touched the wires. If the wires had been connected to the tumbler and had power been running through them, the tumbler would have been operating. Since there is substantial evidence that it was not operating, a trier of fact could reasonably conclude, without resorting to conjecture, that the electrified wires were not connected to the tumbler when Skinner touched them. . . .

This brings us to the second "fatal flaw" highlighted by the majority when it states that the plaintiff failed to "offer any proof from which it rationally could be inferred how the machine would have been turned back on after the wires had been unhooked."[11]

[The dissent proceeded to consider various theories of how the power might have been turned on with the wires unattached to the tumbling machine, rejecting them as unsupported by the evidence. — EDS.]

That leaves only the possibilities that either Skinner[16] or some other person restored power to the wires. Under both of these remaining explanations of how power was restored to the wires — either by Skinner accidentally before he touched or picked up the wires or by another person — Skinner would have had an opportunity to rely on the faulty on/off switch before touching the wires.

Beswick v. City of Philadelphia
185 F. Supp. 2d 418 (E.D. Pa. 2001)

Giles, C.J.

I.   INTRODUCTION

Ralph Raymond Beswick, Jr. and Rose Wiegand, Co-Administrators of the Estate of Ralph Richard Beswick, Sr., bring . . . state law negligence

---

11. Again, the majority misspeaks. The question is not whether it can be inferred "how the *machine* would have been turned back on after the wires had been unhooked" (emphasis added), but rather how the *power* would have been turned back on after the wires had been unhooked.

16. To be sure, if Skinner had turned on the power and then had forgotten that he had done so, that would have been a lot of comparative negligence. But the issue on which summary disposition was granted was the absence of the requisite causal relationship.

claims against Julie Rodriguez, and Father and Son Transport Leasing Inc., d/b/a CareStat Ambulance and Invalid Coach Transportation, Inc. ("CareStat"), a private ambulance service, its record owner, Slawomir Cieloszcyk, a purported owner and manager, Gregory Sverdlev, and two CareStat employees, Ruslan Ilehuk and Ivan Tkach (collectively "CareStat defendants").

Before the court [are motions] for Summary Judgment filed by . . . the CareStat defendants, for alleged failure to establish proximate cause. . . . For the reasons that follow, . . . the motions are denied. . . .

II.   FACTUAL BACKGROUND

. . . Consistent with the review standards applicable to motions for summary judgment, Fed. R. Civ. P. 56(c), the alleged facts, viewed in the light most favorable to the plaintiffs, follow.

On the evening of February 11, 2000, Ralph Richard Beswick, Sr. collapsed on the dining room floor of the South Kensington home that he and Wiegand had shared for 23 years. From the living room where she had been watching television, Wiegand heard the "thump" of Beswick falling and went to him. Upon entering the kitchen and finding Beswick lying prone on the floor, Wiegand immediately dialed the City's medical emergency response number, 911, and told the answering call-taker, Julie Rodriguez, that Beswick had fallen and needed urgent assistance, and requested an ambulance. Rodriguez asked if Beswick was breathing. Wiegand responded that he was. Without obtaining any further information, Rodriguez told Wiegand that "somebody" was "on the way."

Fire Department regulations require 911 operators to refer all emergency medical calls to the Fire Department, which then dispatches Fire Rescue Units appropriately equipped and staffed to respond to medical emergencies. The mechanical protocol of the job of 911 call-taker requires that the call be transferred immediately to the dispatcher upon termination of the emergency call. The last step of the mechanical protocol of the call-taker job is to punch a sequential button on a console to connect the dispatcher and transmit the acquired information from the caller. The dispatcher forwards the call to the Rescue Unit closest to the response site.

Instead of following established procedure, which would have continued the process to trigger the Rescue Unit's response, Rodriguez abandoned protocol and used a telephone located next to her console to call a private ambulance company, CareStat, to see if it could respond to the Wiegand call. Rodriguez, without the knowledge of the City, had recently begun working for CareStat as a dispatcher in her off hours, and had a secret deal with CareStat to refer to it all calls received in her City 911 capacity that she believed CareStat could handle. Under the City's protocol, Rodriguez was required to treat all 911 calls as emergencies requiring the City's Rescue Unit response. She had no discretion to act otherwise.

Immediately after speaking with Wiegand, Rodriguez telephoned Slawomir Cieloszcyk (also known as "Slavik"), the owner and dispatcher of CareStat. Upon telling Cieloszcyk that Ralph Beswick, Sr. was age 65 and unconscious from a fall, Rodriguez asked how long it would take CareStat to get to the Beswick home. Neither Rodriguez nor Cieloszcyk knew that the 911 call was, in fact, a situation other than an emergency, such as a heart attack or other serious medical event. Cieloszcyk estimated a response time of fifteen minutes. He ended the conversation by saying, "We're on the way."

Arguably, corruptly, in violation of Pennsylvania's statutory requirements applicable to private ambulances, Cieloszcyk undertook a response to a medical situation to which CareStat was not authorized to respond. All 911 calls are assumed to be medical emergencies unless and until actual response and evaluation by the City Fire Department might determine otherwise. CareStat had no permission from the City to use 911 call-taker Rodriguez to refer calls to it and knew that the 911 call was being diverted from the City's established response system. Under these circumstances, Cieloszcyk nevertheless gave the Beswick response assignment to employees Ilehuk and Tkach, neither of whom had completed the requisite training to become a licensed EMT or paramedic. Ilehuk and Tkach, having the same knowledge as Cieloszcyk, including the deal with Rodriguez to compromise her City 911 job responsibilities, accepted the call and set out for the Beswick residence.

Ten minutes after the first 911 call had been made, because there was yet no emergency vehicle at the Beswick home, Wiegand's sister placed another 911 call at 8:02 P.M. to make sure that the City's rescue services had already been dispatched. This call also happened to have been received and handled by Rodriguez. Despite this second urgent call, Rodriguez did not punch it over to the City's emergency dispatch system. She called CareStat again, seeking assurance that its ambulance dispatched would arrive soon. Cieloszcyk assured Rodriguez that the CareStat ambulance was on the way as he had promised her.

Because an emergency equipped unit still had not arrived, Wiegand called 911 a third time. The third call came to a call-taker other than Rodriguez. He followed all Fire Department procedures and within a very short time period a City Fire Department Rescue Unit arrived at the Beswick home. Rodriguez became aware of the third Wiegand call. She promptly called Cieloszcyk at CareStat and told him that a City paramedic unit was responding to the Beswick home, and requested that he hide her involvement in the misdirecting of the 911 calls. By the time that the CareStat ambulance arrived, the Fire Rescue Unit had already removed Beswick from the home. It was then that the Beswick family realized that the 911 call-taker had caused a private ambulance to attempt to respond to their emergency call, and that it was ill-equipped to have dealt with the Beswick medical emergency had it arrived earlier.

The first emergency telephone call concerning Beswick was received by Rodriguez at the Fire Command Center ("FCC") at 19:53:41. The second call, placed by Wiegand's sister, was received by Rodriguez at 20:02:54. The third Wiegand call was received at the FCC by dispatcher Jose Zayes at 20:04:57, and the City Fire Department response was immediately dispatched.

Fire Battalion Chief William C. Schweizer confirmed that at the time Rodriguez received the first call at 19:53:41, Medic Unit No. 2 would have been available to respond from its base . . . which was within several minutes of the Beswick home. Medic Unit No. 2 . . . was staffed with paramedics, who have more training than EMTs. However, at 20:04:57, when Zayes received the third call, Medic Unit No. 2 was no longer available. Nor was the next closest Medic Unit, No. 8, based at Boudinot and Hart Streets. In response to the 20:04:47 call, Medic Unit 31, the third closest of the City's Medic Units, was dispatched from Second Street, and Fire Department Engine No. 7 was dispatched from [Unit 2's base]. However, Engine No. 7 is staffed only with EMTs, and EMTs are not permitted to administer epinephrine or atropine to patients. Medic Unit 31 took 8 minutes and 34 seconds to arrive at 959 East Schiller Street. Engine No. 7 took 3 minutes and 34 seconds to arrive. Engine No. 7 and Medic Unit No. 2 — which was available for the first call but was never contacted by Rodriguez — . . . would have had to travel the same distance to get to the Beswick residence. Based upon this information, the total delay in getting a Medic Unit to respond to Beswick has been estimated by Battalion Chief Schweizer to be 16 minutes and 16 seconds.

Plaintiffs have introduced evidence that this 16 minute, 16 second delay caused or contributed to the cause of Beswick's death, through the deposition testimony of Kale Etchberger and Joanne Przeworski, the two Fire Department paramedics who arrived on the scene as part of Medic Unit 31. Both testified that when they arrived, Engine No. 7's EMTs were already tending to Beswick. However, those EMTs, unlike paramedics, cannot administer medications. As indicated in these paramedics' depositions, Engine No. 7's Lifepack 500 defibrillator machine received a "shock advised" message at 20:07:48, which suggests that at the time, Beswick was either in a state of v-fib or v-tack; in other words, his heartbeat was not totally flat. Additionally, upon the administration of medications by Etchberger and Przeworski, Beswick's heart rate was temporarily restored. Both paramedics testified that they believed he had a chance to be saved when they first came to the scene. Plaintiffs' expert, Dr. Norman Makous, a cardiologist, would opine to a reasonable degree of medical certainty that based on established medical literature regarding observed cardiac arrests due to ventricular fibrillation, and assuming that Beswick was still breathing at the time of the first 911 call, that had Medic Unit No. 2 arrived after the first call, Beswick's chance of survival would have equaled, if not exceeded, thirty-four (34) percent. . . .

III.   DISCUSSION

. . . CareStat defendants argue that on its face, a statistical survival rate of 34 percent, which plaintiffs' medical expert concludes is the chance for survival Beswick would have had if a City ambulance had been appropriately dispatched, is insufficient as a matter of law to establish proximate cause. In the alternative, CareStat defendants argue that additional factors unique to Beswick, such as preexisting heart and stroke conditions, as well as chronic obstructive pulmonary disease, necessarily served to reduce his chances of survival well below 34 percent; further, they contend that Wiegand's deposition testimony indicates that she waited "five or ten minutes" before responding to Beswick's collapse, therefore Dr. Makous' conclusions, which are based on *observed* cardiac arrests, are inadmissible. . . .

Addressing defendants' alternative argument first, for summary judgment purposes, this court must accept plaintiffs' allegation that Wiegand heard Beswick collapse and responded immediately, as she stated in the police report taken eleven days after Beswick's death. Further, Dr. Makous' conclusions are predicated upon an article from the New England Journal of Medicine, which states that "the rate of survival to hospital discharge for patients with a witnessed collapse who are found to be in ventricular fibrillation is 34 percent." Mickey S. Eisenberg, M.D., Ph.D., & Terry J. Mengert, M.D., "Cardiac Resuscitation," N. Eng. J. Med., vol. 344, no. 17, at 1304 (April 26, 2001). The article further states that "when cardiopulmonary resuscitation is started within four minutes after collapse, the likelihood of survival to hospital discharge doubles." *Id.* at 1305. Viewing all facts of record in the light most favorable to plaintiffs, this court must assume that Wiegand called 911 immediately after Beswick's collapse, and that at that time, Medic Unit No. 2, with licensed paramedics, was available for dispatch and 3 minutes and 34 seconds from the Beswick residence. Thus, a jury could conclude that Beswick's chances for survival were at least 34 percent, if not more, had the 911 call not been diverted to CareStat. Moreover, the 34 percent survival rate noted in the article and in Dr. Makous' conclusions does not assume only patients who are experiencing their first cardiac arrest, or patients without other pre-existing conditions. Thus, for the purposes of summary judgment, the court must assume that the factors surrounding the cardiac arrest of an individual with Beswick's medical history were taken into account by both the article and Dr. Makous. . . .

The court finds Dr. Makous, a licensed physician who has spent more than fifty years practicing cardiology, is basing his opinions upon established modern medicine, stated, inter loci, in the New England Journal of Medicine, and thus is scientifically reliable. . . . The 34 percent probability that Dr. Makous cites should not be confused with the degree of his medical certainty as to the accuracy of that opinion. . . .

Pennsylvania tort law follows the Restatement Second of Torts, § 323, which provides:

> § 323. Negligent Performance of Undertaking to Render Services. One who undertakes, gratuitously or for consideration, to render services to another which he should recognize as necessary for the protection of the other's person or things, is subject to liability to the other for physical harm resulting from his failure to exercise reasonable care to perform his undertaking, if (a) *his failure to exercise such care increases the risk of such harm,* or (b) the harm is suffered because of the other's reliance upon the undertaking (emphasis added).

See Hamil v. Bashline, 481 Pa. 256, 392 A.2d 1280, 1286 (1978). In *Hamil*, plaintiff's husband, who was suffering from severe chest pains, was brought to the defendant hospital. Due to a faulty electrical outlet, the EKG machine failed to function. A second EKG machine could not be found and, upon receiving no further aid or treatment, Hamil transported her husband to a private doctor's office, where he died of cardiac arrest while an EKG was being taken. Plaintiff's expert witness estimated that the decedent would have had a 75 percent chance of surviving the attack had he been appropriately treated upon his arrival at the hospital. Following the introduction of all evidence, the trial court determined that plaintiff's medical expert had failed to establish, with the required degree of medical certainty, that the alleged negligence of the defendant was the proximate cause of plaintiff's harm, and directed a verdict for the defendant. The Supreme Court reversed, finding that cases such as this "by their very nature elude the degree of certainty one would prefer and upon which the law normally insists before a person may be held liable." *Id.* at 1287. The court interpreted the effect of § 323(a) of the Restatement as to address these situations, and relaxed the degree of evidentiary proof normally required for plaintiff to make a case for the jury as to whether a defendant may be held liable for the plaintiff's injuries. Accordingly, the court adopted the following standard:

> Once a plaintiff has introduced evidence that a defendant's negligent act or omission increased the risk of harm to a person in plaintiff's position, and that the harm was in fact sustained, it becomes a question for the jury as to whether or not that increased risk was a substantial factor in producing the harm. Such a conclusion follows from an analysis of the function of Section 323(a).

Id.

In determining the burden of proof required ultimately to warrant a jury verdict for the plaintiff, the *Hamil* court again relied on the Restatement Second of Torts, which reflected the state of the law at the time of its adoption in 1965; namely that the quantum of proof, or "substantial factor," necessary is a preponderance of the evidence. 392 A.2d at 1288 n.9 (citing Restatement (Second) of Torts § 433B, comment (a)).[9] Accordingly, this court will permit Dr. Makous' testimony regarding the increased risk of harm to Beswick of 34 percent, and will allow the jury to determine, by a preponderance of the evidence, whether this increased risk brought about Beswick's death. . . .

NOTES AND QUESTIONS

1. *Products Liability.* The plaintiffs in *Skinner* sought to establish liability based on injuries caused by a defective product. As we saw in

---

9. Comment (a) of Section 433B states:

a. Subsection (1) states the general rule as to the burden of proof on the issue of causation. As on other issues in civil cases, the plaintiff is required to produce evidence that the conduct of the defendant has been a substantial factor in *bringing about the harm* he has suffered, and to sustain his burden of proof by a *preponderance of the evidence*. This means that he must make it appear that it is more likely than not that the conduct of the defendant was a substantial factor in bringing about the harm. A mere possibility of such causation is not enough; and when the matter remains one of pure speculation and conjecture, or the probabilities are at best evenly balanced, it becomes the duty of the court to direct a verdict for the defendant. [Emphasis added.—EDS.]

MacPherson, one way to assign liability for injuries caused by a product is through negligence law, under which the plaintiff must make out the usual elements of the prima facie case. Since the mid-1960s, however, claims for injuries caused by products have increasingly been brought under a separate branch of tort law known as products liability. Products liability law is explored in Chapter 12. For purposes of analyzing the cause-in-fact issue in *Skinner*, its differences from negligence law are not important.

2. *Judge versus Jury.*   Skinner's co-worker, Carl Jacobs, testified in his deposition that he (Jacobs) sometimes operated the machine, although he apparently did not testify as to whether he was the last person to use the machine before Skinner was electrocuted. Is the *Skinner* majority saying that there is *no* chance that Skinner, Jacobs, or some other person turned the power to the machine on after it had last been used and before Skinner picked up the wires? Did the justices conclude that this set of operations would have been physically impossible (like claiming a gunshot wound was caused by a gun that was not loaded), or are they saying that the likelihood of the plaintiff's theory is so low as to be virtually zero? If the latter, on what basis does their assessment rest? Why not allow a jury to decide the issue?

3. *Framing the Sequence of Events.*   Both the majority and dissent assume that it was the plaintiff's burden to establish that someone — whether Skinner, Jacobs, or another person — caused the switch to *revert back* to being on *after* the switch had been successfully turned to the off position. Can you think of an alternative narrative by which the plaintiffs could have more readily established that Skinner was fooled by the phantom zone problem?

Suppose that Skinner or Jacobs first used the machine, *then* disconnected the wires *before* turning the power off, *and only then* flicked the switch into what he erroneously took to be the off position. (One might imagine him taking this last step to avoid wasting electricity, or to avoid accidental electrocution of other persons who might come into contact with the wires.) Given this scenario, the user who detached the wires and flicked the switch would not have known that he had failed to turn the power off. (Because the wires would have already been unhooked, the flicking of the switch would not have been expected to have any effect on the movement of the machine.) Likewise, in this scenario, when Skinner at a later time picked up the wires, he would have had no warning that the power was on because the wires would have been unhooked from the machine, and because the switch would have been in the phantom zone.

So far as one can tell from both opinions, plaintiffs' attorneys appear not to have offered this scenario. Assuming it was available — that is, not contradicted by the evidence — is there any explanation as to why they did not?

4. *Statistics versus Individual Cases.*   As explained in connection with the doctrine of *res ipsa loquitur*, the preponderance-of-the-evidence standard means that a jury may only deem a fact proven if the jurors reasonably and actually conclude that it is more likely than not to have

occurred. This suggests that a judge ought not to allow a jury to find a fact if the plaintiff admits that the odds of its hypothesis on cause-in-fact are 50 percent or less.

In theory, then, a judge should direct a verdict for the defendant in cases in which there were no eyewitnesses and the circumstantial evidence is simply too scant to allow an educated guess as to what happened. Consider this example. A sailor is swept overboard during a storm at sea while other crew members are on deck. Assume that it is the duty of the owner of a ship to have life preservers on hand so that other crew members can throw one to a sailor before he drowns. Assume also that it is well known that, in stormy conditions, the chances of a promptly thrown life preserver saving the life of a sailor in the water is less than 50 percent — say 33 percent. (The wind may blow the preserver astray, or a wave may carry it away, and even if the sailor catches it, he may succumb to the storm before he can be pulled up from the sea.) Now suppose the sailor's estate brings a negligence action against the ship owner, and can prove only that the sailor fell overboard during a typical storm, that other sailors were on hand to throw him a life preserver, and that the ship was not equipped with life preservers. Must the judge direct a verdict for the defendant? Given that, statistically, the life preserver was not likely to have saved the sailor, is the jury entitled to find that the defendant's breach was a cause-in-fact of the sailor's death?

If the answer to the last question is no, note the following problem. In a random distribution of sailors who go overboard during storms, one of three will be saved by means of a life preserver. However, no individual plaintiff can show that it was *his decedent* who would likely have survived, since it is 67 percent likely for each individual sailor that he would not have survived. Thus, even though statistically one in three would survive but for the boat owner's carelessness, no single plaintiff alleging negligent failure to maintain rescue equipment will ever recover under the preponderance standard. Is this a tolerable result?

5. *Giving the Jury Room for Inference.* What exactly is the holding of *Beswick* with respect to proof of cause-in-fact? Does the court rule that the evidence established that Mr. Beswick had no more than a 34 percent chance at survival had the 911 call been correctly routed? If so, why does the court deny the defendants' motion for summary judgment? Or is it saying that the jury was entitled to make its own judgment as to the probabilities of Mr. Beswick's survival and thus can conclude on the basis of Dr. Makous's testimony that the probability was in fact over 50 percent? *Compare* Kallenberg v. Beth Israel Hosp., 357 N.Y.S.2d 508 (N.Y. App. Div. 1974) (jury can find that plaintiff proved causation by a preponderance of the evidence where plaintiff's expert testifies that if patient had been properly treated, he would have had "a 20, say 30, maybe 40% chance of survival"). If the latter is the right description of the *Beswick* court's holding, is *Beswick* consistent with *Skinner?*

6. Hamil. *Beswick* was decided by a federal court applying Pennsylvania negligence law to the causation issue. Accordingly, it looked to the Pennsylvania Supreme Court's decision in the *Hamil* case for

authoritative guidance. *Hamil* is an unusual decision in two respects. First, as *Beswick* notes, the plaintiff's expert in *Hamil* testified that the plaintiff had a 75 percent chance of surviving had the defendant not been careless. Given this testimony, the *Hamil* jury was presumably entitled to conclude that defendant's carelessness more likely than not was a cause of plaintiff's injury, and there was simply no need in *Hamil* to consider whether it might sometimes be appropriate to lower the burden of proof on causation. (Perhaps the expert testified that the defendant's negligence reduced the plaintiff's chance of survival from 75 percent to some smaller percentage, say 50 percent. This sort of testimony would have directly posed the issue of whether to lower the burden of proof.)

As noted towards the end of *Beswick*, *Hamil* apparently found in the conjunction of Sections 323 and 433B of the Second Restatement a separate legal test for proof of actual causation known as the "substantial factor" test. Implicit in *Hamil*'s articulation of this test is the notion that it may enable a victim of negligence to prove that the defendant's careless act caused her harm even though the proof offered would not suffice to establish that the act probably was a but-for cause of that harm. Numerous commentators, including the drafters of the Third Restatement, have criticized as unwarranted *Hamil*'s claim that Sections 323 and 433B support the employment of "substantial factor" as an alternative and more plaintiff-friendly test for actual causation. See Section III of this chapter; see also Dan B. Dobbs, *The Law of Torts* § 178, at 435 (2000). Does *Beswick* invoke "substantial factor" as an alternative to the but-for test, or for some other purpose?

7. *Causation and Nonfeasance.* Might there be another justification for a relaxation of the burden of proof in *Beswick?* In *Beswick*, as in the overboard sailor cases discussed in Note 4, the plaintiff is attempting to prove the causal significance of the defendant's failure to fulfill an affirmative duty to aid an already imperiled victim. By contrast, in a suit such as *Skinner*, the assertion is that the defendant's affirmative misconduct (misfeasance) created the peril that resulted in the victim's injury. One sometimes finds courts being similarly disposed toward lenience on the issue of causation when dealing with other claims grounded in affirmative duties. For example, we observed in a note following the *Tarasoff* case that courts sometimes permit juries wide leeway to determine that a given victim would have heeded the warning omitted by the defendant, had it been given. As we see in Chapter 12, when plaintiffs complain that they have been injured because a product manufacturer has failed to warn them of a hidden danger in the product, courts will often adopt a "presumption" that the plaintiff would have heeded the warning had there been one. Likewise, the U.S. Supreme Court has held that when the defendant breaches an affirmative duty to disclose material information, a court may presume that the person(s) to whom the duty was owed would have changed their conduct had the information been provided. Affiliated Ute Citizens v. United States, 406 U.S. 128, 153-154 (1972). Does attending to the nature of the defendant's duty help to explain why the courts are sometimes willing to adopt more plaintiff-friendly approaches to cause-in-fact

than one seems to observe in *Skinner?* If so, what is special about these sorts of duties that might warrant this judicial disposition toward lenience?

Falcon v. Memorial Hospital
462 N.W.2d 44 (Mich. 1990)

Levin, J.   The deposition testimony of plaintiff Ruby Falcon's expert witness tended to show that had the defendant physician, S.N. Kelso, Jr., followed the procedures the expert witness claims should have been followed, the patient, Nena J. Falcon, [plaintiff's granddaughter] would have had a 37.5 percent opportunity of surviving the medical accident that was a cause of her death.

The trial court dismissed the complaint because Falcon's evidence did not show that Nena Falcon probably — defined as more than fifty percent — would have survived if the procedure had not been omitted. The Court of Appeals reversed, stating that Falcon need only "establish that the omitted treatment or procedure had the potential for improving the patient's recovery or preventing the patient's death." Falcon v. Memorial Hosp., 178 Mich. App. 17, 26-27; 443 N.W.2d 431 (1989). The Court added that "while a plaintiff must show some probability that the treatment would be successful, that probability need not be greater than fifty percent." We affirm.

I

. . . The defendants contend that because the proofs at a trial of Falcon's claim would not show that it was probable, measured as more than fifty percent, that Nena Falcon would have avoided physical harm had the procedure not been omitted, Falcon cannot show that the asserted negligence of defendants caused her physical harm. They also contend that Falcon cannot maintain an action for wrongful death because such an action can only be maintained where the plaintiff can establish that the act or omission caused death, and, again, Falcon's proofs will fall short because they will show only that there would have been a 37.5 percent opportunity of avoiding death and not a more than fifty percent opportunity had the procedure not been omitted.

II

Some courts disallow recovery for lost opportunity unless the plaintiff can establish that the patient would not have suffered the physical harm but for the defendant's negligence, or, at least, that it is more probable, measured as more than fifty percent, that, but for such negligence, the patient would not have suffered the physical harm.

Under the more probable, measured as more than fifty percent, approach to causation, a plaintiff who establishes that the patient would have had more than a fifty percent opportunity of not suffering physical harm had the defendant not acted negligently, recovers one hundred percent of the damages. The better than even opportunity is compensated as if it were a certainty, although the patient's chances of a better result are significantly less than one hundred percent.[7]

To say that a patient would have had a ninety-nine percent opportunity of survival if given proper treatment, does not mean that the physician's negligence was the cause in fact if the patient would have been among the unfortunate one percent who would have died. A physician's carelessness may, similarly, be the actual cause of physical harm although the patient had only a one percent opportunity of surviving even with flawless medical attention. . . .

III

Other courts have permitted recovery for physical harm on a showing that the lost opportunity was a substantial, albeit fifty percent or less, factor in producing the harm:

> An evolving trend has developed to relax the standard for sufficiency of proof of causation ordinarily required of a plaintiff to provide a basis upon which the jury may consider causation in the "lost chance of survival" cases. McKellips v. St. Francis Hosp., Inc., 741 P.2d 467, 471 (Okla. 1987).

Some courts have held that the plaintiff need only show that the defendant's conduct was a substantial factor in producing the physical harm.[11] Other courts allow recovery for loss of a fifty percent or less opportunity of achieving a better result without clearly articulating a standard of causation.[12] A number of courts have so held on the basis of language in [Section 323 of] the Restatement Torts, 2d. [excerpted above, in *Beswick*].

IV

Nena Falcon, a nineteen-year-old woman, gave birth to a healthy baby, Justice Eugene Falcon, in the early morning hours of March 21, 1973. Moments after delivery, Nena Falcon coughed, gagged, convulsed, became cyanotic, and suffered a complete respiratory and cardiac collapse. Attempts to revive her were unsuccessful. She was pronounced dead soon thereafter.

The autopsy report indicated that amniotic fluid embolism, an unpreventable complication that occurs in approximately one out of ten or

---

7. The more probable than not approach thus tends to over compensate particular plaintiffs. Professor McCormick stated:

> Should the courts insist, in claims for loss of a single specific advantage, upon a showing that the chances were substantially better than even and upon giving all or nothing? To adopt this attitude seems to result in oscillation between overlavishness and niggardliness. McCormick, Damages, § 31, p.119.

11. Hamil v. Bashline, 481 Pa. 256; 392 A.2d 1280 (1978). . . .
12. Kallenberg v. Beth Israel Hosp., 357 N.Y.S.2d 508 (1974), . . . *aff'd* 337 N.E.2d 128 (1975). . . .

twenty thousand births, was the cause of death. The survival rate of amniotic fluid embolism is, according to Falcon's expert witness, 37.5 percent if an intravenous line is connected to the patient before the onset of the embolism. In this case, an intravenous line had not been established.

Falcon's theory is that had a physician or nurse anesthetist inserted an intravenous line before administering the spinal anesthetic to assist the physician in dealing with any of several complications, the intravenous line could have been used to infuse life-saving fluids into Nena Falcon's circulatory system, providing her a 37.5 percent opportunity of surviving. By not inserting the intravenous line, the physician deprived her of a 37.5 percent opportunity of surviving the embolism.

V

The question whether a defendant caused an event is not readily answered, and is especially perplexing in circumstances such as those present in the instant case where the defendant's failure to act is largely responsible for the uncertainty regarding causation.

Had the defendants in the instant case inserted an intravenous line, one of two things would have happened, Nena Falcon would have lived, or she would have died. There would be no uncertainty whether the omissions of the defendants caused her death. Falcon's destiny would have been decided by fate and not possibly by her health care providers. The United States Court of Appeals for the Fourth Circuit, observed:

> When a defendant's negligent action or inaction has effectively terminated a person's chance of survival, it does not lie in the defendant's mouth to raise conjectures as to the measure of the chances that he has put beyond the possibility of realization. If there was any substantial possibility of survival and the defendant has destroyed it, he is answerable. Rarely is it possible to demonstrate to an absolute certainty what would have happened in circumstances that the wrongdoer did not allow to come to pass. The law does not in the existing circumstances require the plaintiff to show to a *certainty* that the patient would have lived had she been hospitalized and operated on promptly. Hicks v. United States, 368 F.2d 626, 632 (4th Cir. 1966) [internal citation and footnote omitted — EDS.].

VI

In an ordinary tort action seeking recovery for physical harm, the defendant is a stranger to the plaintiff and the duty imposed by operation of law is imposed independently of any undertaking by the defendant. In an action claiming medical malpractice, however, the patient generally is not a stranger to the defendant. Generally, the patient engaged the services of the defendant physician. The physician undertook to perform services for the patient, and the patient undertook to pay or provide payment for the services.

The scope of the undertakings by a physician or hospital to the patient and by the patient to the physician or hospital is not generally a matter of express agreement. There is, however, an understanding that the law enforces in the absence of express agreement. The patient expects a physician to do that which is expected of physicians of like training in the community, and the physician expects the patient to pay or provide payment for the services, whether the likelihood of there in fact being any benefit to the patient is only one through fifty percent or is greater than fifty percent.

The defendants assert, in effect, that the scope of their undertaking did not include acts or omissions likely to benefit the patient only to the extent of one through fifty percent — or at least they should not be subject to liability for acts or omissions likely to have caused harm to the extent only of one through fifty percent. They contend that they should be subject to liability only for acts or omissions likely, to the extent of more than fifty percent, to have caused physical harm to the patient. . . .

Patients engage the services of doctors, not only to prevent disease or death, but also to delay death and to defer or ameliorate the suffering associated with disease or death. If the trier of fact were to decide, on the basis of expert testimony, that the undertaking of the defendant physician included the implementation of tasks and procedures that, in the case of Nena Falcon, would have enabled the physician and other medically trained persons, who were present at the time of delivery, to provide her, in the event of the medical accident that occurred, an opportunity to survive the accident, a failure to do so was a breach of the understanding or undertaking.

Nena Falcon, if the testimony of Falcon's expert witness is credited, would have had a 37.5 percent opportunity of surviving had the defendants implemented the procedures Falcon's expert asserts should have been implemented. In reducing Nena Falcon's opportunity of living by failing to insert an intravenous line, her physician caused her harm, although it cannot be said, more probably than not, that he caused her death. A 37.5 percent opportunity of living is hardly the kind of opportunity that any of us would willingly allow our health care providers to ignore. If, as Falcon's expert asserts, the implementation of such procedures was part of the understanding or undertaking, the failure to have implemented the procedures was a breach of the understanding or undertaking. The physician is, and should be, subject to liability for such breach, although Nena Falcon was likely, measured as more than fifty percent, to die as soon as the medical accident occurred and the negligence of the physician eliminated a less than fifty percent opportunity of surviving.

We thus see the injury resulting from medical malpractice as not only, or necessarily, physical harm, but also as including the loss of opportunity of avoiding physical harm. A patient goes to a physician precisely to improve his opportunities of avoiding, ameliorating, or reducing physical harm and pain and suffering.

Women gave birth to children long before there were physicians or hospitals or even midwives. A woman who engages the services of a physician and enters a hospital to have a child does so to reduce pain and suffering and to increase the likelihood of her surviving and the child surviving childbirth in a good state of health even though the likelihood of the woman and child not surviving in good health without such services is far less than fifty percent. That is why women go to physicians. That is what physicians undertake to do. That is what they are paid for. They are, and should be, subject to liability if they fail to measure up to the standard of care.

VII

A number of courts have recognized, as we would, loss of an opportunity for a more favorable result, as distinguished from the unfavorable result, as compensable in medical malpractice actions. Under this approach, damages are recoverable for the loss of opportunity although the opportunity lost was less than even, and thus it is not more probable than not that the unfavorable result would or could have been avoided.

Under this approach, the plaintiff must establish more-probable-than-not causation. He must prove, more probably than not, that the defendant reduced the opportunity of avoiding harm. . . .

The trier of fact should determine whether defendant's negligence was a substantial factor in reducing plaintiff's chances of obtaining a better result.

In DeBurkarte v. Louvar, 393 N.W.2d 131, 135 (Iowa 1986), the Supreme Court of Iowa explained the difference between viewing the injury as a loss of life and viewing it as a loss of opportunity to survive an illness:

> We recognize that the plaintiff's injury may be viewed as a shortening of her life, in which case we would agree with the defendant that the plaintiffs did not produce substantial evidence on causation: there was no evidence the plaintiff's cancer probably spread after September, 1981, preventing her from being cured. [Citation omitted.] On the other hand, as the Restatement [§ 323(a)] indicates, her injury may also be viewed as a lost chance to survive the cancer. The jury could then find from the evidence that the defendant's failure to diagnose and treat the cancer probably caused a substantial reduction in the plaintiff's chance to survive it.

The court concluded: "We believe the better approach is to allow recovery, but *only* for the lost chance of survival." *Id.*, p.136. (Emphasis in original.) . . .

VIII

. . . The harm resulting from defendants' asserted malpractice occurred immediately before Nena Falcon's death when the medical accident occurred and, by reason of the failure to have inserted an intravenous line, it became certain that she would die. At that moment, immediately before her death, Nena Falcon had a cause of action for the harm, the denial of any opportunity of living, that had been caused her. Her claim therefor survived her death because "[a]ll actions and claims survive death." RJA § 2921.

We are persuaded that loss of a 37.5 percent opportunity of living constitutes a loss of a substantial opportunity of avoiding physical harm. We need not now decide what lesser percentage would constitute a substantial loss of opportunity.

IX

In the instant case, while Nena Falcon's cause of action accrued before her death, she did not suffer conscious pain and suffering from the failure to implement the omitted procedures between the moment that the medical accident occurred and the time of her death a few minutes later—she was sedated throughout the entire time period. In this case, 37.5 percent times the damages recoverable for wrongful death would be an appropriate measure of damages. . . .

We would affirm the Court of Appeals reversal of the entry of summary judgment for the defendants, and remand the case for trial.

Boyle, J. (concurring).   I concur in the recognition of "lost opportunity to survive" as injury for which tort law should allow recovery in proportion to the extent of the lost chance of survival, *ante*, p.466, provided that the negligence of the defendant more probably than not caused the loss of opportunity. However, I would emphasize that the Court today is called upon to decide the viability of a claim for "lost opportunity" only where the ultimate harm to the victim is death. Thus, any language in the lead opinion suggesting that a similar cause of action might lie for a lost opportunity of avoiding lesser physical harm is dicta. Whether the social and policy factors which justify compensation for a lost chance of survival would justify recovery for the loss of a chance to avoid some lesser harm is a question for another day.

Riley, C.J. (dissenting).   I would hold that a wrongful death action may not survive a motion for summary disposition where it is uncontested that the plaintiff cannot show that defendant's negligence caused the decedent's death, and will produce evidence only that the decedent would have had an increased chance of survival if the defendant, as in this case, had not negligently failed to insert an intravenous line before or immediately after administering saddle block anaesthesia. Where plaintiff cannot show that defendants' omission was probably a cause of the death of Nena Falcon, the degree of certitude which would justify the imposition of liability on defendants is lacking. The recognition of mere chance as a recoverable item of loss fundamentally contradicts the essential notion of causation. By definition, the lost chance theory would compensate plaintiff for a mere possibility that defendants' omission caused the death of Nena Falcon. . . .

IV

Even where there is causation in fact, a weighing of social interests requires a limit on how far the consequences of negligence will extend.

> As a practical matter, legal responsibility must be limited to those causes which are so closely connected with the result and of such significance that the law is justified in imposing liability. Some boundaries must be set to liability for the consequences of any act, upon the basis of some social idea of justice or policy. Prosser & Keeton, *Torts*, 5th ed., § 41, p.264.

Thus, "[b]y adjusting the causation requirement, the court is able to strike a balance between deterring harmful behavior and encouraging useful activity." Abel v. Eli Lilly & Co., 418 Mich. 311, 324, n.8; 343 N.W.2d 164 (1984), *cert. denied*, 469 U.S. 833 (1984). If liability is to be imposed in proportion to any chance at survival, then the medical profession will be subjected to a burden which is not imposed on any other group of defendants. I submit that nothing is to be gained by extracting payment from a defendant who cannot be shown to have caused the adverse result. Such a rule will not serve the deterrence function of tort law. It more likely will encourage the practice of costly defensive medicine in an attempt to avoid practically certain liability in the event of an unfavorable outcome.

The utility of the physician's conduct militates against a relaxation of the causation requirement in medical malpractice cases. "The physician serves a vital function in our society, a function which requires the assumption of a duty to the patient. Yet, his profession affords him only an inexact and often experimental science by which to discharge his duty." [Herskovits v. Group Health Co-op., 664 P.2d 474, 488 (Wash. 1983)] (Brachtenbach, J., dissenting). *See also* Malone, *Ruminations on Cause-in-Fact*, 9 Stan. L. R. 60, 86-87 (1956).

. . . In this case, the question is not who caused Nena Falcon's death; the question, for which we have no answer, is whether any human act or omission caused her death. I do not mean to minimize the tragedy of such events, but only to question the assumption that a human cause may be located.

V

. . . Where the plaintiff can show no more than a possibility that the defendants' conduct was a cause of the harm, I would conclude that the plaintiff has not produced adequate evidence to create a factual issue regarding causation. Inherent in the concept of causation is a degree of certitude which is absolutely lacking in this case. Our case law wisely requires evidence from which it may be inferred that the defendant *probably* caused the ultimate harm before the jury may be allowed to infer that the defendant did cause such harm and should compensate the plaintiff in damages. . . .

NOTES AND QUESTIONS

1. *Duty, Cause, and Injury: Loss of a Chance.* One way of understanding loss-of-a-chance doctrine is as attempting to solve the proof-of-causation problem faced by certain plaintiffs by redefining the injury suffered. Take, for example, Mr. Beswick. As presented to the *Beswick* court, the claim was that the defendants breached a duty to take care to protect Mr. Beswick from physical injury (including death), thereby allowing him to suffer that injury. Now suppose one alternatively framed his claim as follows: "Defendants owed Mr. Beswick a duty to take care *not to reduce his chances for survival*, yet by acting carelessly they robbed him

of those chances." Notice that, on this rendering of the claim, the injury complained of is not Beswick's death, but the reduction in his chances for surviving. In effect, the assertion is that plaintiff asked of the defendants that they not carelessly deny him whatever opportunity for survival his circumstances permitted, even if that opportunity was a less-than-50 percent likelihood. Once the injury is recharacterized, are any new obstacles posed to the plaintiffs in proving their prima facie case?

2. *Measuring Damages.* If the injury complained of is identified as the loss of a chance to survive, a question arises as to the appropriate measure of damages. A wrongful death plaintiff such as Ruby Falcon — usually a surviving family member of the victim — is entitled to compensation for loss of economic support from the decedent, including compensation for loss of the decedent's companionship. See Chapter 6. Under *Falcon*, the wrongful death plaintiff who prevails on a loss-of-a-chance theory will only get a percentage of this compensation corresponding to the percentage chance of which the decedent was deprived. Is that measure of damages obviously correct? Some judges have suggested that, in loss-of-a-chance cases, the jury should be left, as it ordinarily is in tort cases, to come up with an appropriate damage award unconstrained by the sort of ceiling set in *Falcon.*

3. Falcon*'s Fate. Falcon*'s holding proved short-lived in Michigan. M.C.L. § 600.2912a(2), enacted by the Michigan legislature in 1993 in response to *Falcon*, provides:

> In an action alleging medical malpractice, the plaintiff has the burden of proving that he or she suffered an injury that more probably than not was proximately caused by the negligence of the defendant or defendants. In an action alleging medical malpractice, the plaintiff cannot recover for loss of an opportunity to survive or an opportunity to achieve a better result unless the opportunity was greater than 50%.

Notwithstanding the enactment of this statute, the loss-of-a-chance issue returned to the Michigan Supreme Court in *Weymers v. Khera*, 563 N.W.2d 647 (Mich. 1997). There, the Court was faced with the question of whether a malpractice plaintiff who alleged a nonfatal injury should be permitted to use *Falcon*'s loss-of-a-chance doctrine. The alleged malpractice had occurred in the brief window of time after *Falcon* had been decided, but before the effective date of the statute, hence the statute did not determine the resolution of the issue. Nonetheless, the Court declined to extend *Falcon* to medical malpractice suits alleging injuries other than death.

4. *For Doctors Only*? Loss-of-a-chance doctrine has been formally adopted by only a handful of state courts in the context of suits for medical malpractice. Dan B. Dobbs, *The Law of Torts* § 178, at 436 (2000). The *Falcon* court seems to have thought that there was something special about claims against physicians that favored the application of loss-of-a-chance doctrine to at least some claims of medical malpractice. What is special about them? That they are brought against professionals? If so,

should loss of a chance apply to solve the problem of proof faced by many legal malpractice claimants — namely, the claimant's inability to establish by a preponderance of the evidence that she would have prevailed in the "case within the case"? Or are there special considerations at work that apply to physicians but not attorneys or other professionals? If there is nothing special about professionals, should loss of a chance be available to any tort plaintiff who may otherwise fail to prove causation?

III.   MULTIPLE NECESSARY AND MULTIPLE SUFFICIENT CAUSES

As noted at the outset of this chapter, it is sometimes the case that the search for the careless conduct that produced the victim's injury will turn up more than one actor whose carelessness may have contributed to the occurrence of the injury. In this section we consider how the presence of multiple tortfeasors affects application of the but-for test for actual causation.

McDonald v. Robinson
224 N.W. 820 (Iowa 1929)

Stevens, J.   The injuries of which appellee complains were received by her near the northwest corner of the intersection of Fourth Street and Avenue G in the city of Cedar Rapids, and occurred in the following manner: Avenue G lies east and west, and Fourth Street north and south. Appellant Robinson was driving his car westerly along the north side of Avenue G, and Max Padzensky, the son of Dave, who owned the car, was driving his car northerly along the center line of Fourth Street. When near the center of the intersection, the automobiles collided, and as a result, became interlocked. They were thrown out of their course toward the northwest of the intersection. The Padzensky car struck appellee near the corner of the curbing, knocked her down, and she was dragged under the car until it was stopped, 56 feet farther north. After proceeding north-ward from the corner of the curbing, the cars became separated, and the Robinson car was stopped on the opposite side of the street. [Plaintiff's] injuries were serious, and, she claims, permanent. The petition alleged that each car was being negligently driven, and that the injury resulted from the concurrent negligence of the two drivers.

The chief ground of error alleged by appellant, to wit, that there is a misjoinder of causes of action and of parties, was raised at every step of the proceeding and in every way known to the profession. All, of course, concede that joint tort-feasors, properly so defined, may be sued jointly, and a joint judgment recovered against them. The point of divergence has its origin in other propositions, on which the courts are somewhat divided. . . .

. . . The real point of controversy between counsel, when carefully analyzed, is as to what wrongful or tortious acts are necessary, to render two or more persons joint tort-feasors. A common intent, purpose, and design on the part of the wrongdoers to do a particular wrong or injury, — as, for example, where a conspiracy is charged, — is not always essential. There is a large class of cases in which joint liability may exist, from which the element of intent and unity of design and purpose is wholly absent. If the acts of two or more persons concur in contributing to and causing an accident, and but for such concurrence the accident would not have happened, the injured person may sue the actors jointly or severally, and recover against one or all, according to the proven or admitted facts of the case.

This rule has the support of the great weight of authority [from other jurisdictions]. . . .

The question here to be decided is, Was there such concurrence of negligent acts on the part of appellant and Max Padzensky which united and concurred to produce the injury complained of, as to render them jointly or severally liable? We think there was. The jury may well have found that both defendants were negligent, and it must have found that, but for the concurrence of such negligence, the injury to appellee could not possibly have happened.

It was said by the New York Court of Appeals in Sweet v. Perkins, 196 N.Y. 482 (90 N.E. 50), that, "Where concurrence in causes is charged, the test is, simply, could the accident have happened without their co-operation?" The injury in this case was indivisible. There was no possible way by which it could be said that the negligence of one or of the other of the defendants was the sole or proximate cause thereof. . . .

The conclusion reached in the court below, that the accident was caused solely by reason of the combined and concurrent negligence of the appellants Robinson and Max Padzensky, and that, but for such combined and concurrent negligent acts, the injury would not have happened, cannot be avoided. . . .

NOTES AND QUESTIONS

1. *"The" Cause versus "A" Cause.* The opinion in *McDonald* reminds us that a defendant's carelessness need not be *the* only careless conduct functioning as a but-for cause of an accident for him to be subject to liability in negligence. Rather, it is enough if his carelessness was *a* but-for cause. In a case such as *McDonald*, the carelessness of each defendant must occur for the accident to occur: But for *each* actor's carelessness there would have been no accident and no injury to the plaintiff.

2. *Illustrations of Multiple Necessary Causes.* Careless acts by different actors can function as multiple but-for causes of a plaintiff's injury even without the literal interlock among the negligent parties in *McDonald*. (Reconsider some of the opinions that appear in the duty and breach chapters. Can you identify some that involve multiple tortfeasors?) For example, suppose driver *D* carelessly stops his vehicle in the middle of

the road on the far side of a curve to watch the sunset. Taxi driver *T*, who is driving unreasonably fast, comes around the curve, and because he is speeding, cannot avoid colliding with *D*'s car. As a result, *P*, a passenger in *T*'s taxi, suffers injury. If *P* were to sue *D* and/or *T*, and the foregoing facts were established at trial, neither *D* nor *T* could deny that its carelessness was a cause of *P*'s injury: the carelessness of each was required in order for *P* to have been injured. *See* Stemler v. Burke, 344 F.2d 393 (6th Cir. 1965). Likewise, if, after the accident, *P* is rushed to a hospital and then suffers an additional injury via the malpractice of emergency room doctor *E*, then, with respect to that injury, the respective carelessness of *D*, *T* and *E* each is a but-for cause of the injury.

3. *Actual versus Proximate Cause Again.* To say that the carelessness of each of two or more actors helped to bring about plaintiff's injury is *not necessarily* to say that each should be held responsible or liable for that injury. Some actual causes of a plaintiff's harm, as we will see, will not be deemed *proximate* causes of that harm, in which case no liability attaches to those causes. For example, whether, in the foregoing example, *D* and *T* will be liable for the injury *P* suffered most immediately through *E*'s subsequent malpractice will turn on whether *D*'s and *T*'s respective acts can be deemed to have been proximate causes of that injury. See Chapter 5.

4. *Multiple Necessary Causes versus Apportionment of Liability.* Even if multiple negligent actors such as *D*, *T*, and *E* are all deemed responsible as actual and proximate causes of a plaintiff's injury, there still remains the question of how to apportion their responsibility, that is, who among them has to pay what percentage of plaintiff's damages. In *McDonald*, the court concluded that "a joint judgment could be recovered against [both defendants]." By saying this, it applied a particular rule of apportionment known as joint and several liability. Joint and several liability is a complex idea. For now, we can say that it entitles a not-at-fault plaintiff such as Mrs. McDonald to recover up to 100 percent of her damages from any one of two or more defendants who is found liable for her injuries. As a result, McDonald was in this case free to recover all her damages from Robinson, all from Padzensky, or some from each. (However, she was not allowed to recover more than 100 percent in total.) Apportionment is governed by a separate body of rules discussed in Chapter 8.

5. *Omissions.* A negligent omission to take a precaution, where there is a duty to act, can be deemed one of two or more but-for causes of a victim's injury. *See, e.g.*, LeJeune v. Allstate Ins. Co., 365 So. 2d 471 (La. 1978) (jury could find that a deputy sheriff's failure to clear an intersection for a funeral procession was, along with the careless driving of defendant driver, a but-for cause of plaintiff hearse-driver's injuries). Assume that utility company *U* owes pedestrians and drivers a duty to build telephone poles capable of withstanding a modest (say, 10 mph) impact from an ordinary passenger vehicle without toppling over. Assume further that *U* breached that duty by failing to inspect or test its poles, which turn out

not to be capable of meeting the 10 mph standard. Negligent driver *R* crashes into one of *U*'s poles, causing it to fall on *P*, who sues *R* and *U* for negligence. Can *U* be held liable? Under what circumstances? *See* Bernier v. Boston Edison Co., 403 N.E.2d 391 (Mass. 1980) (utility held liable as one cause of plaintiff's injury given evidence that the driver was not going so fast as to render the utility's negligence causally irrelevant).

6. *Plaintiff's Fault as One Among Multiple Necessary Causes.* In any case in which the factfinder determines that the plaintiff's recovery must be reduced because her own fault contributed, along with the defendant's fault, to her injury, the factfinder is treating the plaintiff's faulty conduct as one of (at least) two careless but-for causes of her injury. See Chapter 7 (discussing principles of comparative responsibility).

Aldridge v. Goodyear Tire & Rubber Co.
34 F. Supp. 2d 1010 (D. Md. 1999)*

Harvey, J.   In this consolidated case, this Court has once again been called upon to address the viability of claims asserted against the Goodyear Tire & Rubber Company ("Goodyear") by former employees or survivors of employees of Kelly-Springfield Tire Company ("Kelly-Springfield").[1] Like other plaintiffs in earlier suits filed against Goodyear in this Court, the plaintiffs in these sixty-six consolidated cases have alleged that they are entitled to compensation from Goodyear under various tort theories for occupational diseases contracted by them during the course of their employment with Kelly-Springfield.

In his Memorandum Opinion filed in this case on March 5, 1997, Judge Smalkin granted summary judgment in favor of the defendant against all plaintiffs in all cases. . . . The plaintiffs appealed Judge Smalkin's summary judgment Order, and in Aldridge v. Goodyear Tire & Rubber Co., 145 F.3d 1323 (Table), 1998 WL 230986 (4th Cir. May 11, 1998), the Fourth Circuit vacated the judgment entered and remanded the case to this Court for further proceedings. . . .

The Court has now had an opportunity to consider the lengthy memoranda and voluminous exhibits submitted by the parties in support of and in opposition to defendant's pending motion for summary

---

* [On appeal to the Fourth Circuit Court of Appeals, the opinion reproduced here was vacated and remanded for consideration as to whether plaintiffs were entitled to additional discovery on the issue of causation. 223 F.3d 263 (4th Cir. 2000). After further proceedings, Judge Harvey concluded that further discovery was unwarranted, and again granted summary judgment for the defendants. In the process, he "reaffirm[ed]" the conclusions reached in the excerpted opinion. 198 F.R.D. 72, 81 (D. Md. 2000). When Judge Harvey's second grant of summary judgment was challenged on appeal, the Fourth Circuit affirmed it in an unpublished opinion. 2002 WL 340629. Excerpts from Judge Harvey's vacated opinion are included here on the premise that its analysis was incorporated by reference into Judge Harvey's second ruling when he reaffirmed his initial ruling. —Eds.]

1. Although Kelly-Springfield is a wholly owned subsidiary of Goodyear, the two corporations are separate and distinct entities.

judgment. A massive record has been presented to the Court, and lengthy oral argument has been heard. For the reasons to be stated herein, the Court has concluded that the motion for summary judgment of defendant Goodyear must be granted. . . .

I BACKGROUND FACTS

Kelly-Springfield formerly operated a tire manufacturing plant in Cumberland, Maryland. Goodyear supplied some of the chemicals used by Kelly-Springfield in its manufacturing operations. Plaintiffs or their decedents are former employees of Kelly-Springfield who worked at the Cumberland plant at various times between 1940 and 1987. The plant closed in 1987. Plaintiffs allege that they or their decedents developed various diseases as a result of their contact with toxic chemicals to which they were exposed during the manufacturing process at Kelly-Springfield.

The plaintiffs here are the fourth group of [Kelly] employees who have sought damages from Goodyear based on similar tort claims. The first group . . . filed an action against Goodyear in this Court in 1980. Heinrich v. Goodyear Tire & Rubber Company, 532 F. Supp. 1348 (D. Md. 1982). A second group sued . . . in 1987, McClelland v. Goodyear Tire and Rubber Company, 735 F. Supp. 172 (D. Md. 1990), and a third group sued in 1989. Jewell v. Goodyear Tire & Rubber Co., Civil No. S-89-3235. Finally, commencing in 1990, plaintiffs comprising this fourth group filed the first of these sixty-six pending cases, alleging claims similar to those asserted in the earlier cases. Although there were settlements in the first group . . . , summary judgment in favor of Goodyear has previously been entered in all of the cases comprising the second and third group.

II PRIOR RELATED PROCEEDINGS

In Heinrich v. Goodyear Tire & Rubber Company, 532 F. Supp. 1348 (D. Md. 1982), an employee of Kelly-Springfield and his spouse sought damages in connection with the occupational disease contracted by him while working at Kelly-Springfield's Cumberland plant. Ruling on Goodyear's motion to dismiss, Judge Miller of this Court held that plaintiffs had properly stated claims against Goodyear sounding in negligence and fraud. After the parties engaged in extensive discovery, settlement was reached as to all claims in this first group of cases.

The next group of cases were consolidated and were addressed by Judge Smalkin in McClelland v. Goodyear Tire & Rubber Co., 735 F. Supp. 172 (D. Md. 1990) (McClelland I). Defendant Goodyear moved for summary judgment in those consolidated cases on the ground that plaintiffs could not prove causation. . . . Judge Smalkin concluded that Goodyear's motion for summary judgment should be granted. . . .

. . . After reviewing the record *de novo*, [Judge Smalkin] said the following:

> Plaintiffs' attempts to hold Goodyear responsible . . . for the total "toxic soup" they claim existed in their workplace, without the ability to adduce compe-

tent evidence that a reasonable fact-finder could view as showing a greater than 50% chance of a causal connection between any such product and the specific injuries they allegedly suffered, must fail. . . . 735 F. Supp. at 174.

The Court is of the opinion that plaintiffs have not adduced evidence that would allow a reasonable fact-finder to conclude that it was more likely than not that any particular, identifiable negligent or intentional conduct by Goodyear (and not by K-S) was the cause of any of the plaintiffs' particular illnesses. Because, even taking the inferences to be drawn from the plaintiffs' experts testimony in the light most favorable to plaintiffs, as the Court must do on summary judgment, it would be impossible for them to show by a preponderance that any particularly, identifiable conduct by Goodyear was in any sense the proximate cause of their particular illnesses, defendant is entitled to summary judgment on the negligence and fraud claims. To hold otherwise would be . . . [to] impose liability on too slender a reed to be tolerated under Maryland law, one not rising above the level of *post hoc, ergo propter hoc.** Blame, in the legal sense, cannot be so easily assigned, even where unfortunate consequences ensue. *Id.* at 174-75. . . .

Twelve consolidated cases were involved in *McClelland I.* Thereafter, defendant Goodyear moved for summary judgment in five similar cases. In his Memorandum of May 9, 1990 entered in Jewell v. Goodyear Tire & Rubber Co., Civil No. S-89-3235, Judge Smalkin granted summary judgment in favor of defendant Goodyear in those five cases as well, relying on the reasons set forth in his *McClelland I* ruling.

Plaintiffs in both *McClelland I* and *Jewell* appealed to the Fourth Circuit. In its unpublished *per curiam* opinion of March 25, 1991, the Fourth Circuit affirmed the entry of summary judgment in favor of defendant Goodyear in all of the *McClelland* and *Jewell* cases. McClelland v. Goodyear Tire & Rubber Co., Nos. 90-3087, 90-3090, 90-3091, 90-3092, 90-3093 and 90-3094, 929 F.2d 693 (Table), 1991 WL 38700 (4th Cir. March 25, 1991) (*McClelland II*). . . .

III   SUMMARY JUDGMENT PRINCIPLES

One of the purposes of Rule 56 of the Federal Rules of Civil Procedure is to require a plaintiff, in advance of trial and after a motion for summary judgment has been filed and properly supported, to come forward with some minimal facts to show that a defendant may be liable under the claims alleged. *See* Rule 56(e). If the nonmoving party "fail[s] to make a sufficient showing on an essential element of her case with respect to which she has the burden of proof," then "the plain language of Rule 56(c) mandates the entry of summary judgment." [Citation omitted.]

While the facts and all reasonable inferences drawn therefrom must be viewed in the light most favorable to the party opposing the motion, "when the moving party has carried its burden under Rule 56(c), its opponent must do more than simply show that there is some metaphysical doubt as to the material facts." Matsushita Elec. Indus. Co. v. Zenith Radio

---

* ["After this, therefore because of this." — EDS.]

Corp., 475 U.S. 574, 586, 106 S. Ct. 1348, 89 L. Ed. 2d 538 (1986). "A mere scintilla of evidence is not enough to create a fact issue; there must be evidence on which a jury might rely.'" Barwick v. Celotex Corp., 736 F.2d 946, 958-59 (4th Cir. 1984) (quoting Seago v. North Carolina Theatres, Inc., 42 F.R.D. 627, 640 (E.D.N.C. 1966), *aff'd*, 388 F.2d 987 (4th Cir. 1967), *cert. denied*, 390 U.S. 959 (1968)). . . .

IV   THE CLAIMS AND DEFENSES

. . . Plaintiffs contend that Goodyear manufactured and sold to Kelly-Springfield specific toxic chemicals, that each worker plaintiff was exposed to these toxic substances and that such exposure caused or contributed to a certain disease contracted by the worker.[6] Plaintiffs further assert that Goodyear undertook an obligation to ensure general plant safety at Kelly-Springfield and claim that Goodyear is also responsible in tort for the harm caused by toxic substances which Goodyear did not supply.

The principal contention advanced by Goodyear in support of its motion for summary judgment is that, as in prior similar cases brought by other Kelly-Springfield workers, the plaintiffs here have failed to produce evidence upon which a reasonable juror could rely to conclude that Goodyear-supplied chemicals or those supplied by another entity in fact caused their various ailments. Relying on the rulings made by Judge Smalkin in *McClelland I* and by the Fourth Circuit in *McClelland II*, defendant argues that the principles of law applied by this Court and by the Fourth Circuit to similar facts bar any recovery by plaintiffs [here].

. . . Mindful of the determinations in *McClelland I* and *McClelland II* that the plaintiffs in that litigation had failed to provide any evidence linking a particular, identifiable chemical to their diseases, the plaintiffs have here submitted voluminous affidavits, exhibits and other evidentiary materials which were not a part of the record in *McClelland* or *Jewell*. They present this additional evidence largely in the form of supplemental affidavits which attempt to link the plaintiffs' diseases to specific chemicals supplied by Goodyear to Kelly-Springfield. Plaintiffs argue at length that sufficient evidence has now been produced by them to create a dispute of material fact in each case as to the causation issue. . . .

V   GOODYEAR-SUPPLIED CHEMICALS

Proof of . . . causation has always been a significant hurdle faced by a plaintiff seeking a recovery in tort for an occupational disease. Plaintiffs' decision to seek tort recoveries from Goodyear, which was not their employer, must face "the availability to Goodyear . . . of defenses, primarily absence of causality. . . ." *McClelland II*, 1991 WL 38700 at *1. Because of problems faced by a claimant in overcoming a defense based on lack of

---

6. In the *McClelland* and *Jewell* cases and in this case, the plaintiffs have alleged that they contracted the same types of diseases. More than fifty different illnesses are claimed to have been caused by Goodyear's wrongful conduct. Cancer, cardiovascular disease and lung disease are the predominate illnesses alleged.

causation, workers' compensation laws, which do not require proof of causation, have in Maryland and other states been extended to cover occupational diseases. Indeed, the plaintiffs in this case have filed workers' compensation claims against Kelly-Springfield, and these claims have been stayed pending the outcome of this litigation. But, in here seeking under various tort theories much larger recoveries for their occupational diseases from an entity which was not their employer, plaintiffs face what the Court in *McClelland II* characterized as one of the "landmines" presented by Goodyear's causation defense "which would have to be overcome to make out a viable claim in tort." 1991 WL 38700 at *2.

As disclosed by the record here, workers at the Kelly-Springfield plant were exposed to a great many chemicals. However, Goodyear supplied only ten percent of the plaintiffs' list of approximately two hundred potentially hazardous chemicals to which they were exposed. Affidavits of plaintiffs' own experts reveal the extreme difficulties faced by plaintiffs in their effort to defeat summary judgment in this case.

For example, according to Dr. Michael M. Lipsky, Jr., plaintiffs' principal expert witness, as many as twenty-eight different chemicals at the Kelly-Springfield plant have the capacity to be a substantial contributing cause of cancer if sufficient exposure to each of the chemicals has occurred. However, only three of these are Goodyear-supplied chemicals, namely N-Nitrosodimethylamine ("NDMA"), Nitrosomorpholine ("NMOR") and 4-amino-biphenyl ("4AB"). But even these three cannot be attributed exclusively to Goodyear. According to Dr. Donohue, another one of plaintiffs' experts, many of the Goodyear-supplied chemicals are not toxic until they decompose in the various hot processes of the tire plant. The toxic elements of the chemicals are often the byproduct of the interaction between many different chemicals, the vast majority of which were not supplied by Goodyear.

In his deposition in the *Heinrich* case, Dr. Lipsky was asked to explain his testimony that at any level of exposure the chemicals listed in his affidavits substantially increased the risk of causing cancer. When asked what he meant by the phrase "substantially," he stated that he could not give a quantitative assessment for the term, namely a number or percent. He explained that he was merely saying that the risk was greater with the exposure than it would have been without the exposure. This testimony hardly constitutes competent evidence which "a reasonable fact-finder could view as showing a greater than 50% chance of a causal connection" between a Goodyear product and the specific illnesses alleged by plaintiffs.

Defendant notes that the deposition testimony of Dr. Lipsky in *Heinrich* is inconsistent with statements contained in his affidavits filed in this case. In contrast to the opinions proffered here, Dr. Lipsky testified in the *Heinrich* case that he could not say that any of the particular chemicals listed in his affidavits contributed to the cancer of any specific plaintiff. He also stated that he was not qualified to testify as to the concentration of any individual chemical necessary to cause harm and that he was not expressing any opinion as to whether the exposure of any plaintiff to any particular chemical was sufficient to be a substantial contributing factor to the individual's disease. It appears that Dr. Lipsky has now re-fashioned his opinions to meet the deficiencies in plaintiffs' proof described in *McClelland I* and *McClelland II*. This Court would note that the Fourth Circuit has held that a district court is justified in disregarding the affidavit of an expert when it conflicts with that expert's earlier deposition testimony.

In any event, it is apparent from the Court's review of all of the affidavits submitted by plaintiffs that their experts have not been able to isolate the toxic effects of the Goodyear-supplied chemicals from the effects of the host of other chemicals not supplied by Goodyear. Many chemicals at the Kelly-Springfield plant which are toxic in and of themselves were not supplied by Goodyear. In one of his affidavits, Dr. Lipsky confirmed that many chemicals, most of which were not supplied by Goodyear, are potential contributing causes of one or more of the diseases claimed by plaintiffs. Dr. Donohue's affidavits acknowledge that, while the carcinogens NDMA, NMOR and 4AB can in theory be derived exclusively from Goodyear-supplied chemicals, the NDMA, NMOR and 4AB present at the Kelly-Springfield plant were necessarily derived from a few chemicals supplied by Goodyear, from many chemicals not supplied by Goodyear, and from the countless interactions between all these chemicals which occurred during the hot processing of rubber at the plant. Plaintiffs' own evidence thus indicates that Goodyear at most supplied only a small fraction of the total chemicals at Kelly-Springfield which may have caused or contributed to their various illnesses.

As indicated by the *McClelland* litigation, plaintiffs in this case must produce evidence that a "particular, identifiable chemical supplied by Goodyear" was a legal cause of their injuries. This they have failed to do. It is not possible to determine from facts of record whether any Goodyear-supplied chemical in fact caused plaintiffs' illnesses. That the presence of a particular chemical may have increased the risk of harm hardly constitutes causation in fact. In view of the presence at the Kelly-Springfield plant of a host of different chemicals interacting with each other, some supplied by Goodyear and some not, and in view of the complicating effects of other potential contributing factors to plaintiffs' cancer and heart disease such as genetics, overall health considerations, diet and smoking habits, a reasonable fact-finder would not be able to conclude that any one of the identifiable chemicals supplied by Goodyear caused plaintiffs' illnesses. Cancer and cardiovascular disease are common illnesses suffered by a significant proportion of the general population. As the Fourth Circuit stated in *McClelland II*, the plaintiffs have "failed to produce adequate evidence that the injuries to them resulted from Goodyear's activities *rather than other causes*." 1991 WL 38700 at *2. (Emphasis added). . . .

In their attempt to avoid the decisive application of the *McClelland* rulings, plaintiffs argue that there has been a change or clarification of Maryland law since the Fourth Circuit decided *McClelland II*. Relying on Eagle-Picher Industries, Inc. v. Balbos, 326 Md. 179, 604 A.2d 445 (1992) . . . plaintiffs argue that Maryland has now replaced in a case of this sort the "but-for" causation standard with a "substantial factor" test. . . .

As plaintiffs have correctly stated, the substantial factor test for causation rather than a "but-for" test should under Maryland law be applied in a case involving multiple causes of a particular harm. However, plaintiffs miscomprehend the underlying requirements for the application of the substantial factor test in a case like this one. The critical question here is whether Goodyear's chemicals or conduct were independently *sufficient* causes of harm to the plaintiffs. A cause must be sufficient before it can be substantial. *See* Restatement (Second) of Torts, § 432(2) ("if . . . each [force] of itself is sufficient to bring about harm to another, the actor's negligence may be found to be a substantial contributing factor"). The *Balbos* case itself recognizes that this sufficiency requirement must first be met in a case involving multiple causes of a particular harm. As the Court of Appeals of Maryland there observed, "'[i]f two causes concur to bring about an event, *and either one of them, operating alone, would have been sufficient to cause the identical result*,' some test of proximate causation, other than 'but-for' is needed." 326 Md. at 208, 604 A.2d 445 (quoting W. Keeton, *Prosser & Keeton on the Law of Torts* § 41 at 266 (5th ed. 1984) (emphasis added).)

Balbos and the other cases relied upon by plaintiffs were asbestos cases. Asbestos is known to cause asbestosis and mesothelioma, and that this product is a sufficient cause of harm is rarely a contested issue in asbestos litigation. Thus, since asbestos in itself is sufficient to cause harm, the substantial factor test has been properly applied in *Balbos* and other Maryland asbestos cases to determine whether there has been adequate proof of causation. Here, each chemical supplied by Goodyear must be an independently sufficient cause of harm before it can be a substantial contributing factor.[14] As discussed hereinabove, the proof relied upon by plaintiffs does not show by a preponderance of the evidence that any particular, identifiable Goodyear-supplied chemical was of itself sufficient to cause harm to the plaintiffs. . . .

For all these reasons, this Court concludes that defendant Goodyear is entitled to the entry of summary judgment as to all of plaintiffs' claims based on their exposure to chemicals supplied by Goodyear to Kelly-Springfield. . . .

VII   ADMISSIBILITY OF EXPERT OPINIONS

As an alternative argument in support of its motion for summary judgment, Goodyear contends that the conclusory affidavits submitted by plaintiffs are not admissible because the opinions rendered by plaintiffs' experts do not satisfy the requirements of Rule 702, [of the Federal Rules of Evidence] and Daubert v. Merrell-Dow Pharmaceuticals, Inc., 509 U.S. 579, 113 S. Ct. 2786, 125 L. Ed. 2d 469 (1993). According to Goodyear, the expert opinions relied upon by plaintiffs are too vague and conclusory to be received as admissible evidence in this case.

---

14. Professor David W. Robertson has cogently noted in *The Common Sense of Cause-in-Fact*, 75 Tex. L. Rev. 1765, 1778-80 (1997) that courts often err in applying the substantial factor test in a case involving multiple causes of a particular harm. As he observed:

> The only "combined active conduct" cases in which the substantial factor test is needed are those in which the defendant's conduct was by itself sufficient to accomplish the harm but did not seem to be a but-for cause of the harm because it was fortuitously joined by the causal conduct of another that was also by itself sufficient to accomplish the harm. . . .

Only Dr. Lipsky and Dr. Caplan have opined that chemicals supplied by Goodyear were a substantial contributing factor to the illnesses contracted by the plaintiffs. Their affidavits contain essentially the same boilerplate language:

> It is my opinion with a reasonable degree of medical probability that each of the chemicals identified above was a substantial contributing cause of Mr. _____'s (*disease*). I base this opinion on my training and experience, my own scientific research, and my knowledge of the scientific literature, as well as Mr. _____'s occupational history as provided to me by counsel for Mr. _____.

Daubert requires that when considering the admissibility of an expert opinion under Rule 702, a federal judge must exercise a "gatekeeping responsibility" to insure that admitted scientific testimony is both relevant and reliable. 509 U.S. at 589, n.7, 600, 113 S. Ct. 2786, 125 L. Ed. 2d 469. Before the Court can consider expert opinions of the sort relied upon here by plaintiffs, threshold standards for the admissibility of such evidence must be met. As Judge Young noted in Marder v. G.D. Searle & Co., 630 F. Supp. 1087, 1089 (D. Md. 1986), *aff'd*, 814 F.2d 655 (4th Cir. 1987) (Table), the Fourth Circuit has cautioned that special care should be taken when assessing the sufficiency of causation evidence in a case where such evidence is wholly circumstantial. In performing its "gatekeeping" task, a district judge must engage in a two-part analysis. The Court must first make essentially a reliability inquiry and determine whether the proffered expert testimony consists of "scientific knowledge." Particularly in establishing causation in product liability and toxic tort actions, expert opinion testimony must be grounded on reliable data. Second, the Court must inquire further to ascertain whether the proposed testimony is relevant, that is, whether under Rule 702 it will "assist the trier of fact." [Citation omitted.] In determining whether challenged expert evidence properly satisfies the reliability component of the test, the Supreme Court in *Daubert* held that a trial court may consider several factors: (1) whether the theory or technique used by the expert can be, and has been, tested; (2) whether the theory or technique has been subjected to peer review and publication; (3) the known or potential rate of error of the method used; and (4) the degree of the method's or conclusion's acceptance within the relevant scientific community.

Applying in this case the principles of *Daubert* and subsequent decisions interpreting it, this Court concludes that the affidavits of Dr. Lipsky and Dr. Caplan submitted by plaintiffs must be excluded. Vague and conclusory terms like "substantial contributing cause" and "knowledge of the scientific literature" standing alone do little to satisfy the reliability requirement. As the Supreme Court recently stated, "[n]othing in either *Daubert* or the Federal Rules of Evidence requires a district court to admit opinion evidence which is connected to existing data only by the *ipse dixit* of the expert." General Electric Co. v. Joiner, 522 U.S. 136, 118 S. Ct. 512, 519, 139 L. Ed. 2d 508 (1997).

To be properly admissible under Rule 702, expert testimony "requires some objective, independent validation of the expert's methodology. The expert's assurances that he has utilized generally accepted scientific methodology is insufficient." Moore v. Ashland Chem. Co., 151 F.3d 269, 276 (5th Cir. 1998); *see also* Cavallo v. Star Enterprise, 892 F. Supp. 756, 760-61 (E.D. Va. 1995), *aff'd in part*, 100 F.3d 1150, 1159 (4th Cir. 1996). In a comment directly relevant to the circumstances of this case, the Court in *Cavallo* referred to evidence indicating that "all chemicals can cause health problems at some level" and noted that it is therefore critical that an expert testifying as to the effects of exposure to chemicals identify the threshold level required to cause a particular effect. 892 F. Supp. at 764. In a toxic tort case, "the extrapolation or leap from one chemical to another must be reasonable and scientifically valid." *Moore*, 151 F.3d at 279 (citing *Daubert*, 43 F.3d at 1319-20 and *Cavallo*, 892 F. Supp. at 769).

In their affidavits, neither Dr. Lipsky nor Dr. Caplan state (1) what training or experience they have relied upon in reaching conclusions that particular chemicals cause specific illnesses, (2) what scientific research they have conducted and what experience they have that renders them qualified to give their opinions, (3) what "scientific literature" supports their conclusions, and (4) what threshold level of exposure to a particular chemical is necessary to cause a particular disease. Most significantly, all of plaintiffs' experts have failed to adequately address possible alternative causes of plaintiffs' illnesses. Many of these illnesses, including cancer and cardiovascular disease, are commonly known to be influenced by a complex, and as yet poorly understood, interplay of genetic and environmental factors. Plaintiffs' experts have not explained how a particular chemical in fact caused a particular disease when each worker was exposed not only to a number of other chemicals at the Kelly-Springfield plant but also to various environmental factors with similar effects. As the Court noted in *Cavallo*: "*Daubert* commands that in court, science must do the speaking, not merely the scientist." 892 F. Supp. at 761. The failure of an expert to address alternative causes has been held to constitute an adequate ground for excluding the testimony of that expert.

In the performance of its gatekeeping responsibility, this Court concludes that, insofar as the causation issue in this case is concerned, the affidavits of Dr. Lipsky and Dr. Caplan do not satisfy the reliability component of the *Daubert* test. The evidence in question must therefore be excluded. As a result of such exclusion, there is insufficient evidence of causation in the record here to create a triable issue of fact for the jury. Plaintiffs' failure to satisfy the *Daubert* test provides an alternative ground for the Court's conclusion that defendant's motion for summary judgment must be granted.

NOTES AND QUESTIONS

1. *Tort Law and Workers' Compensation.* Part V of the *Aldridge* opinion mentions that the workers who are suing Goodyear were employed not by Goodyear, but by Kelly-Springfield, a distinct corporate entity. It further notes that any claim to compensation the workers might have against Kelly-Springfield would have to be made through workers' compensation

rather than tort law. This is because, in the early decades of the twentieth century, state governments enacted schemes designed to compensate workers for such injuries outside of the tort system. These workers' compensation schemes apply to a wide array of private-sector employees, as well as to persons employed by state and local governments. (The federal government has since adopted a workers' compensation scheme for federal employees; it does not apply to private-sector workers. *See* 5 U.S.C. §§ 8101 *et seq.* (Federal Employees' Compensation Act (FECA)).

The displacement of negligence law as it applied to suits against employers for workplace injuries was fueled in part by the sense that negligence doctrine had developed in ways extremely unfavorable to injured workers and their dependents. For one thing, workers could not take advantage of *respondeat superior*: If an employee's injury was caused by the carelessness of another employee — a "fellow servant" — the injured employee could only sue his co-worker, not the company. Moreover, some courts presiding over suits arising from workplace injuries gave broad reign to defense doctrines such as assumption of risk and contributory negligence. See Chapter 7. Thus, a worker might be found to have assumed the risk of being injured by workplace dangers simply by virtue of showing up to work. Finally, given the norm of high-risk work and the absence of modern safety equipment, it was not always easy to establish that the employer had failed to maintain a reasonably safe workplace.

Railroad workers — a group particularly vulnerable to workplace injury — received relief from some of these burdens at the turn of the twentieth century when Congress passed the Federal Safety Appliance Acts, as well as the Federal Employers' Liability Act (FELA), 45 U.S.C. §§ 51 *et seq.* FELA, in particular, created national statutory tort law by enabling railroad workers to sue their employers for injuries on the job caused by the employer's negligence. The big advantage of FELA was that it eliminated the defenses of contributory negligence and assumption of risk.

By contrast to FELA, workers' compensation statutes were predominantly enacted by state legislatures and are designed to cover workers in a wide variety of industries and businesses. Also in contrast to FELA, these statutes departed more radically from the negligence framework. The defenses of contributory negligence and assumption of risk were again eliminated. In addition, however, employers were now held *strictly liable* for workplace injuries. This means that the injured worker is no longer required to prove fault on the part of anyone, only that he incurred an injury in the course of his employment. Moreover, as we learn from *Aldridge*, employees can recover workers' compensation benefits for occupational diseases without having to run the gauntlet of proving exactly what caused their illnesses.

For their part, employers secured an important benefit. Employees injured as a result of a workplace accident are barred from suing in negligence.* Thus, they can no longer obtain compensatory damage

* Under most workers' compensation laws, employees who are the victims of intentional torts such as battery and false imprisonment at the hands of fellow workers are permitted to invoke the tort system against those workers. However, as explained in

awards set by a jury. Instead, they receive payments in accordance with certain formulae. For example, an employee who loses a digit or limb on the job receives a payment according to a schedule or chart that attaches a fixed monetary value to that sort of injury. Likewise, an employee who is injured and totally disabled typically receives a percentage of lost wages for a set period of time (usually a certain number of months or years) plus medical expenses.

The advantage of workers' compensation systems is that they deliver relatively prompt and predictable payments to employees injured in workplace accidents, and therefore promise predictable costs to employers, while diverting fewer resources to lawyers and litigation. However, these systems have come under criticism from both labor and management. Scheduled payments under workers' compensation schemes have not kept pace with increases in jury awards. Survivors of workers killed on the job, in particular, receive small sums of money as compared to successful wrongful death plaintiffs. The administrative costs of workers' compensation systems are lower than those of the tort system, but lawyers still are often needed to hash out disputes. Employers, meanwhile, complain that employees are increasingly able to circumvent the workers' compensation system by alleging a "knowing or intentional" wrong on the part of the employer. See Chapter 9.

As *Aldridge* attests, workers' compensation laws bar only negligence actions for workplace injuries by employees *against their employers* — that bar does not extend to other actors whose tortious conduct played a role in causing injurious accidents in the workplace. Thus, for example, if a worker is injured while using a machine installed on a shop floor, the workers' compensation system bars him from suing his employer for negligence, but does not bar him from pursuing a products liability claim against the machine's manufacturer. Of course, as *Aldridge* also attests, injured workers may face other hurdles in trying to recover in tort from persons other than their employer.

2. *Problems of Proof Revisited: Toxic Torts. Aldridge* is an example of a "toxic tort" claim. These claims are characterized by allegations that victims have contracted an illness or disease after having been exposed to a carelessly or defectively manufactured product such as a pharmaceutical product or a pesticide. Given limitations in scientific and medical knowledge about how certain diseases and illnesses develop, it is often difficult for individual toxic tort plaintiffs to establish actual causation. This problem can be alleviated if the substance in question causes a "signature" illness that appears only in connection with exposure to it. (For example, as the court explains, certain lung diseases are known to be caused only by asbestos exposure.) If not, however, medical studies often only suggest

---

Chapter 8, the doctrine of *respondeat superior* often does not extend to individual employees' intentional torts, in which case the injured employee will likely have no recourse against her employer. As explained in Chapter 9, courts have occasionally (and contentiously) invoked an expanded notion of intent to permit employees to bring claims of battery against employers whose managers have "knowingly" exposed employees to a risk of bodily harm.

— rather than establish as more likely than not — a general causal relation-ship between exposure to a particular substance and a generic disease (say, cancer of the liver).

Moreover, even if a plaintiff can establish the likelihood of a "general" causal linkage between a substance produced by the defendant and her illness, she faces another problem: She must further convince the jury that *her* individual illness is an instance of that general causal linkage. Defense counsel will look to establish, by contrast, that factors personal to the plaintiff, such as genetic predispositions, exposure to other environmental factors, and personal health habits (e.g., smoking), acted as the relevant causal agents.

3. Daubert, *Experts, and Proof of Causation.* A toxic tort plaintiff will usually have to rely on expert witnesses to make the case that defen-dant's carelessness operated as a but-for cause of plaintiff's illness. As the last part of the *Aldridge* excerpt explains, the U.S. Supreme Court in the *Daubert* case directed federal courts to screen such experts to ensure, as much as possible, that the experts present jurors with scientifically valid theories of causation. Thus, federal trial court judges are now expected to review the studies on which an expert's testimony will be based to deter-mine if they provide a reliable basis for the expert's assessment of the causal relation between one party's carelessness and another's injury. If, as in *Aldridge*, the court determines that there is no reliable basis, the expert is not permitted to testify and the plaintiff's case will likely collapse.

As a result of *Daubert*, it is often the case in federal courts that the issue of proof of causation is aired out in the first instance not at trial, but instead at a pre-trial hearing on whether the testimony of the plaintiff's expert is sufficiently well supported to be admitted into evidence at trial. The draft Third Restatement has gone to great lengths to attempt to assist judges in thinking through what ought to count as reliable expert testi-mony on issues of causation. Restatement (Third) of Torts: Liability for Physical Harm (General Principles) § 28, comment c (Tentative Draft No. 3, Apr. 7, 2003).

The *Daubert* requirement derived from the Supreme Court's inter-pretation of Rule 702 of the Federal Rules of Evidence, which governs the admissibility of expert testimony in federal courts. Whether state courts ought to follow *Daubert*'s lead is currently a very contentious issue. In 2000, Rule 702 — the initial source of *Daubert* — was revised to reflect that decision's interpretation of the rule. It now provides as follows:

> If scientific, technical, or other specialized knowledge will assist the trier of fact to understand the evidence or to determine a fact in issue, a witness qualified as an expert by knowledge, skill, experience, training, or educa-tion, may testify thereto in the form of an opinion or otherwise, if (1) the testimony is based upon sufficient facts or data, (2) the testimony is the product of reliable principles and methods, and (3) the witness has applied the principles and methods reliably to the facts of the case.

According to the revised rule's drafters, its current language "affirms the trial court's role as gatekeeper and provides some general standards that the trial court must use to assess the reliability and helpfulness of proffered expert testimony."

In an important subsequent ruling, the Supreme Court extended the rule of *Daubert* to a wide range of experts, not simply experts opining on medical-scientific evidence. Kumho Tire Co., Ltd. v. Carmichael, 526 U.S. 137 (1999) (applying *Daubert* to an expert testifying on the causes of a tire explosion). Again, the 2000 amendments to Rule 702 track the Court's analysis by incorporating its broad holding into the text of the rule. Chapter 13 reproduces in part, and further discusses, *Daubert*.

4. *Substantial Factor and Restatement (Second) §§ 431 and 432.* The plaintiffs in *Aldridge* (unsuccessfully) attempted to invoke the "substantial factor" test as an alternative to the but-for test for actual causation. The phrase "substantial factor" has long been a source of controversy and confusion in this area of negligence law, and tort law more generally. It first appeared in the First Restatement of Torts, and then reappeared in two of the main provisions on causation in the Second Restatement, Sections 431 and 432. They read in part as follows:

§ 431.   Legal Cause; What Constitutes

[An] actor's negligent conduct is a legal cause of harm to another if
　　(a) his conduct is a substantial factor in bringing about the harm. . . .

§ 432.   Negligent Conduct as Necessary Antecedent of Harm

　　(1) Except as stated in Subsection (2), the actor's negligent conduct is not a substantial factor in bringing about harm to another if the harm would have been sustained even if the actor had not been negligent.
　　(2) If two forces are actively operating, one because of the actor's negligence, the other not because of any misconduct on his part, and each of itself is sufficient to bring about harm to another, the actor's negligence may be found to be a substantial factor in bringing it about.

Plaintiffs have often argued, sometimes successfully, that by employing the language of substantial factor, these provisions aimed to supplant the but-for test with an *alternative* test that sets a lower threshold for proof of causation. On this reading, the substantial factor test permits a plaintiff to prevail even if she cannot prove by a preponderance of the evidence that her injury would not have happened without defendant's carelessness, so long as she can show that that carelessness played some ill-defined (albeit "substantial") role in relation to the plaintiff's injury. *See, e.g.*, Mitchell v. Gonzales, 819 P.2d 872 (Cal. 1991) (eliminating the then-standard California jury instruction incorporating the but-for test and holding that the jury in every negligence case ought to be given an instruction incorporating a substantial factor test).

A careful reading of these admittedly confusing provisions reveals that they were not intended to have this effect. Instead, they were intended to serve two very different goals. The first, discussed in the next note, was to explain the result in an unusual set of cases involving what are known as *multiple sufficient causes*. These cases raise a genuine puzzle as to *actual causation* because they present instances in which it is quite intuitive to say that the defendant's carelessness caused plaintiff's injury, yet the but-for test cannot be satisfied. However, because this puzzle only emerges in one particular circumstance, the solution achieved by the application of the substantial factor test to these cases does not entail scrapping the but-for test for actual causation in most other cases.

The second goal of these provisions bore only indirectly on the issue of actual causation. Here the aim was to graft onto the standard but-for test for actual causation a *proximate cause restriction* that would bar the assignment of responsibility to a defendant whose carelessness functions as a trivial (i.e., non-"substantial") but-for cause of the plaintiff's injury. The nature of this restriction is discussed in Note 6 below.

5. *Substantial Factor (I): § 432(2) and Multiple Sufficient Causes.* Sections 431 and 432 can be reconstructed along the following lines:

> An actor's carelessness must be a *substantial factor* in bringing about an injury in order to be deemed a legal cause of that injury. Carelessness will be deemed a substantial factor in bringing about an injury if it constitutes:
> (i) a *non-trivial necessary condition* for the occurrence of the plaintiff's injury; or
> (ii) one of two or more forces that is *each sufficient* to bring about harm to another.

This reconstruction makes clear that Section 431 does not invoke the language of substantial factor to *supplant* the but-for test. After all, a version of the but-for test is incorporated into the substantial factor test by branch (i) Rather, it is invoked primarily so that the alternative test for actual causation stated in branch (ii) can be seen to fall within the umbrella of Section 431's general statement of the requirement of proof of actual causation.

Branch (ii) — which simply restates § 432(2) — reflects a doctrine most commonly attributed to the Minnesota Supreme Court's decision in Anderson v. Minneapolis St. P & S.S.M. Ry. Co., 179 N.W. 45 (Minn. 1920). In *Anderson*, the defendant negligently generated a fire that merged with another fire of unknown origin. The merged fires then caused damage to plaintiff's property. The court first upheld as reasonable the jury's finding that *each fire was itself of sufficient magnitude* to have reached the plaintiff's property and caused the damage. It then concluded that each fire should be treated as a cause of that injury, even though, given the jury's finding, *neither fire could be deemed a but-for cause of the damage*.

Cases such as *Anderson* are commonly referred to today as cases involving *multiple sufficient causes*. They are also described as cases of *overdetermined* or *concurrent* causation. Make sure that you understand why, given the *Anderson* jury's finding, neither of the two fires constituted a but-for cause of the property damage. Contrast, in this regard, *McDonald* and other multiple *necessary* cause cases. Does that contrast help you to grasp why the *Aldridge* court refused to permit the plaintiffs to invoke an *Anderson*-type analysis to establish that Goodyear's provision of toxic chemicals to Kelly-Springfield constituted a cause of each plaintiff's injuries?

The *Anderson* court's treatment of the defendant's conduct as a cause of the plaintiff's injury has struck courts and commentators ever since as intuitive. Do you share that intuition? If the property was going to be damaged anyway by the other fire, in what sense did the defendant's care-lessness cause that damage? Is it because the defendant should not benefit from being lucky enough to have carelessly set a fire in the vicinity of another fire? Does it matter to your thinking whether the other fire was of tortious or innocent origin? (The *Anderson* court held that it should not matter.)

6. *Substantial Factor (II): Section 431 and Trivial Necessary Conditions.* We can grasp the other aspiration underlying the Restatement's employment of the language of substantial factor by considering another aspect of the holding in *Aldridge*. At various points in its analysis, the district court seems to suppose that Goodyear should be excused from liability because its careless provision of toxic chemicals to the Kelly-Springfield plant, even if perhaps a but-for cause of plaintiffs' injuries, constituted a *de minimis* or trivial but-for cause. As conveyed by his expressions of concern over the plaintiff's "toxic soup" theory, the trial judge seems to have concluded that Goodyear's chemicals were, in all likelihood, but a drop in the bucket.

If that was the *Aldridge* court's thinking, its decision perfectly captures the second aim behind the Restatement's adoption of substantial factor language. This alternative aspiration is made clear in comment a to Section 431:

> *a. Distinction between substantial cause and cause in the philosophic sense.* In order to be a legal cause of another's harm, it is not enough that the harm would not have occurred had the actor not been negligent. . . . The negligence must also be a substantial factor as well as an actual factor in bringing about the plaintiff's harm. The word "substantial" is used to denote the fact that the defendant's conduct has such an effect in producing the harm as to lead reasonable men to regard it as a cause, using that word in the popular sense in which there always lurks the idea of responsibility, rather than in the so-called "philosophic sense," which includes every one of the great number of events without which any happening would not have occurred. Each of these events is a cause in the so-called "philosophic sense," yet the effect of many of them is so insignificant that no ordinary mind would think of them as causes.

Thus, as used in § 431(a), the phrase "substantial factor" was not meant to supplant the but-for test, but to *narrow* the class of but-for causes that ought to be recognized as a basis for liability by excluding insubstantial or trivial but-for causes. Notice that, strictly speaking, this use of substantial factor has nothing to do with actual causation. Instead it concerns the distinct issue of proximate cause. (Recall the discussion of the bee-sting hypothetical at the beginning of this chapter.) Its point is to enable an actor whose carelessness has functioned as an actual cause of a victim's injury to escape responsibility *notwithstanding actual causation* on the ground that the causal role played by his carelessness was so miniscule as to make it unfair to assign any responsibility to him.*

7. *Criticisms of Substantial Factor Language.* Precisely because the Second Restatement used "substantial factor" to try to kill two very different birds with one stone, a number of commentators, and now the Reporters for the draft Third Restatement, have criticized this language as needlessly confusing. In addition, although they do not question the desire of the Restatement to carve out an exception to the but-for test for multiple sufficient cause cases such as *Anderson*, many object to § 431(a)'s use of "substantial factor" as a proximate cause doctrine. These critics argue that it is neither necessary nor appropriate to carve out a *per se* rule of proximate cause that grants an automatic exemption from liability for carelessness that functions as a trivial but-for cause of an injury. As the Reporters for the Third Restatement put it, in at least some circumstances, "the actor who tortiously provides the straw that breaks the camel's back is subject to liability for the broken back." *See* Restatement (Third) of Torts: Liability for Physical Harm (Basic Principles) § 29, cmt. q (Tentative Draft No. 3, Apr. 7, 2003).**

---

* Notice in turn that most of the perceived "unfairness" that is driving § 431(a)'s use of "substantial factor" as a proximate cause limitation derives from the assumption that an actor whose trivial contribution to a plaintiff's injury runs the risk of being held liable for more than a trivial percentage of the plaintiff's damages. (In *Aldridge*, the concern would be that Goodyear would end up paying most of the many millions of dollars in damages sought by the plaintiffs, even though its carelessness played only a modest role, if any, in causing those injuries.) That assumption in turn derives from the fact that many defendants will be subject to "joint and several liability," as were the defendants in *McDonald*. An alternative rule of apportionment that imposed liability only in proportion to a given defendant's contribution to a plaintiff's injury would thus obviate the main concern underlying § 431(a)'s invocation of the language of substantial factor.

** The Reporters do, however, allow an exception for trivial causes in a special kind of case in which the actor's conduct is deemed a trivial yet sufficient cause of the plaintiff's injury. *See* Restatement (Third) of Torts: Liability for Physical Harm (Basic Principles) § 29, cmt. q & illus. 12 (Tentative Draft No. 3, Apr. 7, 2003). There, the Reporters describe a case involving eight persons leaning against a car so as to cause it to tip over, seven of whom exert considerable force against it, while the eighth exerts only a modest force against it. On the assumption that the efforts of any four of the seven would have been sufficient, the Reporters deem the efforts of the eighth person to be a sufficient but trivial cause of the tipping, to whose conduct liability should not attach.

Further analysis of proximate cause will have to await the next chapter. Here we can only note that the Third Restatement's rejection of a per se exception for trivial but-for causes does not necessarily entail that a defendant whose carelessness constitutes an insignificant contribution to a plaintiff's injury will be held liable for any or all of the damages associated with that injury. For example, it is possible that some defendants whose carelessness played a relatively minor role in bringing about a plaintiff's injury will be deemed not to have proximately caused that injury under one of the general tests for proximate cause. See Chapter 5. Alternatively, the defendant may be responsible for only a small percentage of the plaintiff's damages, depending on the rules for apportioning liability among multiple tortfeasors. See Chapter 8. The limited point of comment q to Section 29 is that there should be no separate doctrinal limitation that automatically blocks the imputation of liability just because an actor's carelessness operates as a trivial but-for cause of another's injury.

In light of these and other problems, the Reporters of the Draft Third Restatement are strongly committed to purging "substantial factor" language from the analysis of actual causation in tort law. Instead, the relevant provisions on actual causation quite explicitly render the but-for test as the appropriate legal standard against which to determine actual causation, *except* for those rare cases involving multiple sufficient causes:

§ 26. FACTUAL CAUSE

An actor's tortious conduct must be a factual cause of another's physical harm for liability to be imposed. Conduct is a factual cause of harm when the harm would not have occurred absent the conduct. Tortious conduct may also be a factual cause of harm under § 27.

§ 27. MULTIPLE SUFFICIENT CAUSAL SETS

When an actor's tortious conduct is not a factual cause of physical harm under the standard in § 26 only because another causal set exists that is also sufficient to cause the physical harm at the same time, the actor's tortious conduct is a factual cause of the harm.

Restatement (Third) of Torts: Liability for Physical Harm (Basic Principles) §§ 26-27 (Tentative Draft No. 2, Mar. 25, 2002).

8. *Preempted Causes and "Doomed" Plaintiffs.* Closely related to cases of multiple sufficient causation are instances of so-called preempted causation. Suppose *D1* negligently strikes pedestrian *P* with his car, killing him, and that *P*'s body remains on the road. A few minutes later, *D2* negligently runs over *P*. *D2* cannot be said to have caused bodily injury or death to *P*, since *P* was already dead. This sort of scenario is sometimes referred to as a case of "preempted" causation.

A related fact pattern that poses an interesting but perhaps distinct issue consists of a situation in which victim *V* is tortiously injured by actor *A*, yet it turns out that, because of the operation of some independent human or natural force, *V* was about to suffer, or did suffer, that same injury (or death) shortly thereafter. For example, in the English case of Baker v. Willoughby, 2 W.L.R. 50 (H.L. 1970), the plaintiff's leg was injured by the defendant in an automobile accident. However, at some point before trial, the plaintiff's leg was injured again by the negligent act of a third party, which injury resulted in the leg's amputation. The House of Lords concluded that the defendant ought to be held liable for damages flowing from the initial injury to the leg measured for the expected duration of the plaintiff's life, without regard to the subsequent injury and amputation. This approach has been followed by some U.S. courts. *See* Spose v. Ragu Foods, Inc., 537 N.Y.S.2d 739, 740 (Sup. Ct. 1989) (in awarding the plaintiff damages for a partial disability caused by the defendant's tortious conduct, the jury should not take into account the fact that the plaintiff subsequently was rendered totally disabled by a third party).

Compare the famous case of Dillon v. Twin State Gas & Electric Co., 163 A. 111 (N.H. 1932). There a young boy playing on the superstructure of a bridge lost his balance and was electrocuted when he grabbed a nearby high voltage wire maintained by the defendant. The court first held that the defendant could be found to have acted carelessly in arranging its exposed wires so as to leave them in reach of persons such as the boy. However, it also held that if the factfinder were to conclude that the boy would have probably died anyway in falling from the bridge, the defendant would not be liable for any damages except those that would compensate for the increment of suffering he experienced as a result of being electrocuted to death (as compared to falling to his death). Likewise, if the factfinder were to determine that the boy would likely have been crippled by the fall, it was instructed to award only those damages reflecting the difference between the boy's being killed and being crippled.

Finally, consider a variation on these scenarios involving nonfeasance rather than misfeasance. Suppose patient X is dying of an untreatable, incurable disease that physician Y negligently fails to diagnose. Has Y's negligence caused X's death? *See* Candia v. Estepan, 734 N.Y.S.2d 37 (App. Div. 2001) (no cause of action on these facts).

The issue posited by examples of "doomed" plaintiffs is often thought to present a conundrum as to actual causation. Do you find that characterization satisfactory? Might they be better understood as raising an issue of damages — that is, the amount of compensation that, in fairness, ought to be paid to the victim (or his estate) by the tortfeasor? See Chapter 8 (discussing damage measures).

IV.   CAUSATION AND BURDEN-SHIFTING

As we saw in Chapter 3 in connection with *res ipsa loquitur*, courts confronted with a class of plaintiffs whose members face systematic challenges in proving breach will sometimes permit them to proceed without evidence identifying what exactly the defendant did that can be considered careless. We consider in this section an example of a comparable doctrinal adjustment on the issue of actual causation in the face of an unusual problem of proof.

Summers v. Tice
199 P.2d 1 (Cal. 1948)

Carter, J.   Each of the two defendants appeals from a judgment against them in an action for personal injuries. . . .

Plaintiff's action was against both defendants for an injury to his right eye and face as the result of being struck by bird shot discharged from a shotgun. The case was tried by the court without a jury and the court found that on November 20, 1945, plaintiff and the two defendants were hunting quail on the open range. Each of the defendants was armed with a 12 gauge shotgun loaded with shells containing 7½ size shot. Prior to going hunting plaintiff discussed the hunting procedure with defendants, indicating that they were to exercise care when shooting and to "keep in line." In the course of hunting plaintiff proceeded up a hill, thus placing the hunters at the points of a triangle. The view of defendants with reference to plaintiff was unobstructed and they knew his location. Defendant Tice flushed a quail which rose in flight to a 10-foot elevation and flew between plaintiff and defendants. Both defendants shot at the quail, shooting in plaintiff's direction. At that time defendants were 75 yards from plaintiff. One shot struck plaintiff in his eye and another in his upper lip. Finally it was found by the court that as the direct result of the shooting by defendants the shots struck plaintiff as above mentioned and that defendants were negligent in so shooting and plaintiff was not contributorily negligent.

. . . There is evidence that both defendants, at about the same time or one immediately after the other, shot at a quail and in so doing shot toward plaintiff who was uphill from them, and that they knew his location. That is sufficient from which the trial court could conclude that they acted with respect to plaintiff other than as persons of ordinary prudence. . . .

The problem presented in this case is whether the judgment against both defendants may stand. It is argued by defendants that they are not joint tort feasors, and thus jointly and severally liable, as they were not acting in concert, and that there is not sufficient evidence to show which defendant was guilty of the negligence which caused the injuries — the shooting by Tice or that by Simonson. Tice argues that there is evidence to show that the shot which struck plaintiff came from Simonson's gun because of admissions allegedly made by him to third persons and no evidence that they came from his gun. Further in connection with the latter contention, the court failed to find on plaintiff's allegation in his complaint that he did not know which one was at fault — did not find which defendant was guilty of the negligence which caused the injuries to plaintiff.

Considering the last argument first, we believe it is clear that the court sufficiently found on the issue that defendants were jointly liable and that thus the negligence of both was the cause of the injury or to that legal effect. It found that both defendants were negligent and "[t]hat as a direct and proximate result of the shots fired by *defendants, and each of them*, a birdshot pellet was caused to and did lodge in plaintiff's right eye and that another birdshot pellet was caused to and did lodge in plaintiff's upper lip." In so doing the court evidently did not give credence to the admissions of Simonson to third persons that he fired the shots, which it was justified in doing. It thus determined that the negligence of both defendants was the legal cause of the injury — or that both were responsible. Implicit in such finding is the assumption that the court was unable to ascertain whether the shots were from the gun of one defendant or the other or one shot from each of them. The one shot that entered plaintiff's eye was the major factor in assessing damages and that shot could not have come from the gun of both defendants. It was from one or the other only.

It has been held that where a group of persons are on a hunting party, or otherwise engaged in the use of firearms, and two of them are negligent in firing in the direction of a third person who is injured thereby, both of those so firing are liable for the injury suffered by the third person, although the negligence of only one of them could have caused the injury.

(Moore v. Foster, 182 Miss. 15, 180 So. 73 (1938); Oliver v. Miles, 144 Miss. 852, 110 So. 666 (1926); Reyher v. Mayne, 90 Colo. 586 [10 P.2d 1109]; Benson v. Ross, 143 Mich. 452 [106 N.W. 1120, 114 Am. St. Rep. 675].) The same rule has been applied in criminal cases . . . , and both drivers have been held liable for the negligence of one where they engaged in a racing contest causing an injury to a third person. Saisa v. Lilja, 76 F.2d 380. These cases speak of the action of defendants as being in concert as the ground of decision, yet it would seem they are straining that concept and the more reasonable basis appears in Oliver v. Miles, *supra*. There two persons were hunting together. Both shot at some partridges and in so doing shot across the highway injuring plaintiff who was travelling on it. The court stated they were acting in concert and thus both were liable. The court then stated: "We think that . . . each is liable for the resulting injury to the boy, although no one can say definitely who actually shot him. *To hold otherwise would be to exonerate both from liability, although each was negligent, and the injury resulted from such negligence.*" [Emphasis added.] . . . Dean Wigmore has this to say:

"When two or more persons by their acts are possibly the sole cause of a harm, or when two or more acts of the same person are possibly the sole cause, and the plaintiff has introduced evidence that the one of the two persons, or the one of the same person's two acts, is culpable, then the defendant has the burden of proving that the other person, or his other act, was the sole cause of the harm. (b) . . . The real reason for the rule that each joint tortfeasor is responsible for the whole damage is the practical unfairness of denying the injured person redress simply because he cannot prove how much damage each did, when it is certain that between them they did all; let them be the ones to apportion it among themselves. Since, then, the difficulty of proof is the reason, the rule should apply whenever the harm has plural causes, and not merely when they acted in conscious concert. . . ." (Wigmore, Select Cases on the Law of Torts, § 153.) . . .

When we consider the relative position of the parties and the results that would flow if plaintiff was required to pin the injury on one of the defendants only, a requirement that the burden of proof on that subject be shifted to defendants becomes manifest. They are both wrongdoers — both negligent toward plaintiff. They brought about a situation where the negligence of one of them injured the plaintiff, hence it should rest with them each to absolve himself if he can. The injured party has been placed by defendants in the unfair position of pointing to which defendant caused the harm. If one can escape the other may also and plaintiff is remediless. Ordinarily defendants are in a far better position to offer evidence to determine which one caused the injury. This reasoning has recently found favor in this court. In a quite analogous situation this court held that a patient injured while unconscious on an operating table in a hospital could hold all or any of the persons who had any connection with the operation even though he could not select the particular acts by the particular person which led to his disability. (Ybarra v. Spangard, 25 Cal. 2d 486, 154 P.2d 687.) . . . Similarly in the instant case plaintiff is not able to establish which of defendants caused his injury. . . .

In addition to that, however, it should be pointed out that the same reasons of policy and justice shift the burden to each of defendants to absolve himself if he can — relieving the wronged person of the duty of apportioning the injury to a particular defendant, apply here where we are concerned with whether plaintiff is required to supply evidence for the apportionment of damages. If defendants are independent tort feasors and thus each liable for the damage caused by him alone, and, at least, where the matter of apportionment is incapable of proof, the innocent wronged party should not be deprived of his right to redress. The wrongdoers should be left to work out between themselves any apportionment. . . .

It is urged that plaintiff now has changed the theory of his case in claiming a concert of action; that he did not plead or prove such concert. From what has been said it is clear that there has been no change in theory. The joint liability, as well as the lack of knowledge as to which defendant was liable, was pleaded and the proof developed the case under either theory. We have seen that for the reasons of policy discussed herein, the case is based upon the legal proposition that, under the circumstances here presented, each defendant is liable for the whole damage whether they are deemed to be acting in concert or independently.

The judgment is affirmed.

NOTES AND QUESTIONS

1. *Implications.* The *Summers* rule has the immediate effect of taking the onus with respect to proving actual causation off the plaintiff and placing it onto each defendant to *disprove* that his carelessness was a cause of plaintiff's injury. In some jurisdictions, including California at the time *Summers* was decided, a plaintiff who can avail herself of this rule also obtains the benefit of joint and several liability, discussed in Note 4 following the *McDonald* case. Under this rule, as the court explains, each defendant is subject to liability for the full amount of plaintiff's damages. (Plaintiff is not entitled to recover 200 percent of her actual, proven damages. Rather, she is given the option of seeking the entire amount from either defendant. This can be critically important when, for example, one of the defendants lacks assets or is otherwise unavailable to pay a judgment.)

2. *Burden Shfiting or Element Elimination?* How likely is it that a person in the position of the *Summers* defendants will be able to *disprove* that he caused plaintiff's injury? If the answer is "not at all likely," does this mean that *Summers* is not so much a burden-shifting rule as a rule that simply dispenses with the actual causation component of the causation element? If so, would courts be justified in dispensing with actual causation in other situations in which plaintiffs face seemingly insurmountable problems of proof? Are there special reasons for burden shifting in *Summers*?

3. *Alternative Causation versus Multiple Necessary Causes.* *Summers* applies in situations in which *one* of two (or perhaps more than two) negligent actors acts independently of the other to cause injury to the plaintiff. As

such it must be distinguished from three related tort doctrines, discussed in this note and Note 4.

The first is that of *multiple necessary cause* cases. As discussed above in connection with *McDonald*, multiple necessary causation analysis applies when the independent careless conduct of two (or more) actors each functions as a cause of plaintiff's injury. Unlike the rule of *Summers*, this doctrine applies only when each of two or more careless acts functions as a but-for cause of the injury to the plaintiff. In *Summers*, by contrast, only one actor's careless shooting functioned as a but-for cause of the plaintiff's injury. The other's is presumed to have had no effect whatsoever on the plaintiff.

Are there any theories of negligence that would apply to the facts of *Summers* and that would permit a jury to identify careless acts by Simonson and Tice that each operated as but-for causes of Summers' injury? What about the decision of the shooters to form a "triangle" rather than a straight-line hunting formation?

4. *Aiding and Abetting and Concert of Action.* The other doctrines to be distinguished from alternative causation are *conspiracy* and *concert of action*. Suppose Summers found evidence indicating that Simonson and Tice actually set up the hunting expedition as part of a plan to shoot Summers. If that were the case, Summers would not need the benefit of a burden-shifting rule, because no matter who actually shot Summers, the other would be responsible for "aiding and abetting" the shooting. On these imagined facts, the two shooters would not be acting independently, but rather as part of a planned effort to injure Summers.

Concert of action, like aiding and abetting, treats two tortfeasors as acting jointly, rather than independently. However, it does not require the existence of a plan or undertaking to injure the plaintiff. As *Summers* notes, the classic application of concert-of-action doctrine involves a plaintiff who is struck by one of two speeding cars involved in an illegal drag race. Regardless of which racer's car hits the plaintiff, the two racers are held jointly to have caused plaintiff's injury: their separate acts of careless driving are, in effect, fused into a single coordinated course of conduct. *See, e.g.*, Bierczynski v. Rogers, 239 A.2d 218 (Del. 1968).

5. *Extending* Summers. Is the *Summers* rule applicable only when there are two defendants? *See* Huston v. Konieczny, 556 N.E.2d 505 (Ohio 1990) (plaintiff injured by minor who could have received alcohol from any one of a number of defendants can sue those defendants on alternative causation theory). The draft Third Restatement would extend *Summers* to cases involving "two or more" defendants. Restatement (Third) of Torts: Liability for Physical Harm (Basic Principles) § 28(b) (Tentative Draft No. 2, Mar. 25, 2002). Can you think of any reasons to draw the line at two?

6. *From Alternative to Market Share Liability:* Sindell. For a plaintiff to avail herself of alternative causation, each of the possible causers of her injury must be joined as a party to her lawsuit; otherwise, the person who actually caused the harm might escape liability. However, in an important

subsequent decision, the California Supreme Court expanded *Summers* to impose liability even in the absence of all possible tortfeasors. *See* Sindell v. Abbott Labs., 607 P.2d 924 (Cal. 1980). The defendants in these cases were manufacturers of DES, a generic, defective drug that injured a large number of women while they were in utero. Because the drug was generic, the victim usually could not prove which of the more than 150 manufacturers of the drug produced the pills that injured her. Extending *Summers*, the Court held — with some important qualifications — that even if the plaintiff did not join all the manufacturers in one suit, the burden of proof was on each defendant to disprove that its drug caused the plaintiff's injury. As to any defendant who could not disprove causation, the plaintiff could recover a percentage of her proven damages equal to the defendant's percentage share of the relevant market for DES. As a result, this scheme has been dubbed "market share liability." For the most part, courts have restricted its application to the unusual facts of DES cases. For a discussion of market share liability, see Chapter 12.

7. *Other Instances of Burden Shifting.* The *Summers* rule is confined to an unusual situation. Another, more prominent area of tort law in which some courts permit burden shifting on the issue of causation is in products liability suits alleging that the manufacturer of a product failed adequately to warn users of the product of dangers it poses. Here, the causation issue hinges in part on whether the plaintiff would have heeded the warning that the manufacturer f ailed to provide. Some courts adopt a presumption that the plaintiff would have heeded the warning, and leave it to the manufacturer to try to prove that the warning would not have been heeded. See Chapter 12. Recall Chapter 2's discussion of negligence cases such as *Tarasoff*, in which the allegation is that the defendant acted carelessly by failing to alert the plaintiff of a danger posed by another person. Should these plaintiffs also benefit from a presumption that they would have heeded the warning?

REFERENCES/FURTHER READING

Actual Causation

Arno C. Becht & Frank W. Miller, *The Test of Factual Causation in Negligence and Strict Liability Cases* (1961).

Guido Calabresi, *Concerning Cause and the Law of Torts: An Essay for Harry Kalven, Jr.*, 43 U. Chi. L. Rev. 69 (1975).

H. L. A. Hart & Tony Honoré, *Causation in the Law* (2d ed. 1985).

J. L. Mackie, *The Cement of the Universe: A Study of Causation* (1974).

David Robertson, *The Common Sense of Cause in Fact*, 75 Tex. L. Rev. 1765 (1997).

David Rosenberg, *The Causal Connection In Mass Exposure Cases: A "Public Law" Vision of the Tort System*, 97 Harv. L. Rev. 851 (1984).

John D. Rue, *Note: Returning to the Roots of the Bramble Bush: The "But For" Test Regains Primacy in Causal Analysis in the American Law Institute's Proposed Restatement (Third) of Torts*, 71 Fordham L. Rev. 2679 (2003).

Richard W. Wright, *Causation in Tort Law*, 73 Cal. L. Rev. 1735 (1985).

Richard W. Wright, *Causation, Responsibility, Risk, Probability, Naked Statistics, and Proof: Pruning the Bramble Bush by Clarifying the Concepts*, 73 Iowa L. Rev. 1001 (1988).

Symposium: *Causation in the Law of Torts*, 63 Chi.-Kent L. Rev. 397 *et seq.* (1987).

Symposium on the Third Restatement of Torts, 54 Vand. L. Rev. 941 *et seq.* (2001) (article and commentaries by Profs. Stapleton, Geistfeld, Kelley, and Wright).

Causation in Rescue Cases

Wex S. Malone, *Ruminations on Cause-in-Fact*, 9 Stan. L. Rev. 60 (1956).

Loss of a Chance

David Fischer, *Tort Recovery for Loss of a Chance*, 36 Wake Forest L. Rev. 605 (2001).

Joseph H. King, Jr., *Causation, Valuation and Chance in Personal Injury Torts*, 90 Yale L.J. 1353 (1981).

John C. P. Goldberg, *What Clients Are Owed: Some Preliminary Cautions on Loss-of-a-Chance in Legal Malpractice*, 52 Emory L.J. 1201 (2003).

John C. P. Goldberg & Benjamin C. Zipursky, *Concern for Cause: A Comment on the Twerski-Sebok Plan for Administering Negligent Marketing Claims Against Gun Manufacturers*, 32 Conn. L. Rev. 1411 (2000).

Andrew R. Klein, *A Model for Enhanced Risk Recovery in Tort*, 56 Wash. & Lee L. Rev. 1173 (1999).

Stephen R. Perry, *Risk, Harm and Responsibility*, in *Philosophical Foundations of Tort Law* 321, 330-339 (David G. Owen ed., 1995).

Aaron Twerski & Anthony J. Sebok, *Liability Without Cause? Further Ruminations on Cause-in-Fact as Applied to Handgun Liability*, 32 Conn. L. Rev. 1379 (2000).

Burden Shifting/Summers

Arthur Ripstein & Benjamin C. Zipursky, *Corrective Justice in an Age of Mass Torts*, in Gerald J. Postema (ed.), *Philosophy and the Law of Torts* 214 (2001).

CHAPTER 5

Aligning the Elements: Proximate Cause and *Palsgraf*

You have now been introduced to the elements of the prima facie case of negligence. One element — injury — received only brief mention. The others — duty, breach, and cause — received more extensive treatment. This chapter completes the inquiry into the prima facie case by introducing you to two additional (and elusive) components of negligence law: (1) *proximate cause* and (2) the *relational aspect of duty*.

To emphasize the distinctive nature of the inquiry under each element, we have up to now treated each largely in isolation from the others. However, as the cases in this chapter help to demonstrate, the prima facie case of negligence cannot be captured without considering how its parts relate to one another. Indeed, each of two elements in particular — duty and causation — contains a concept or set of concepts that filters out claims by plaintiffs who can make out each element, yet cannot establish that they *line up with one another in the right way*.

We briefly encountered the first of these "alignment" concepts — the concept of proximate cause — at the outset of Chapter 4. As noted there, the proximate cause inquiry proceeds on the assumption that the plaintiff has proven or can prove that a breach of a duty owed to the plaintiff by the defendant was a cause-in-fact of the plaintiff's injury. (Again, in this sense, the presumption is that each of the elements of the plaintiff's prima facie case is met.) Yet proximate cause — an alignment concept built into the causation element — specifies that liability will not attach unless the judge and jury are satisfied that the breach has caused the injury *in a non-fortuitous manner.** The second "alignment" concept built into the tort of negligence is housed not in the causation element, but in the element of duty. We refer to it as "the relational aspect" of duty. As we will see, it demands of the plaintiff that she demonstrate that the breach of duty about which she is complaining is a breach of a duty *owed to her*, rather than a duty owed only to persons differently situated from her.

Both the proximate cause component of the causation element and the relational aspect of the duty element can be difficult to apply. In fact, each has proved confusing, if not maddening, to lawyers, judges, and scholars. In part, the difficulty is inherent in the concepts — they are complex and subtle. Adding to the problem is the tendency among many

---

* The draft Third Restatement favors eliminating any reference to "proximate cause" and adding a fifth element requiring that the plaintiff's injury be "within the scope of the risk" posed by defendant's carelessness. Restatement (Third) of Torts: Liability for Physical Harm (Basic Principles) § 29 (Tentative Draft No. 3, Apr. 7, 2003).

to muddy the waters further by using these concepts, particularly the concept of proximate cause, to refer not only to the alignment issue mentioned above, but also to various other considerations that might affect attributions of responsibility to those whose tortious conduct has caused injury to another. Thus, a central aim of Section I of this chapter is to untangle different senses of "proximate cause," in part so that its primary sense becomes more intelligible. Similarly, we hope to articulate and clarify what it means to locate within the duty element a "relational aspect."

Section II elaborates the distinct component of negligence law that we refer to as the relational aspect of duty. Whereas proximate cause primarily concerns the alignment of the breach and injury elements, the relationality requirement addresses the alignment of duty and breach. In short, relationality demands that a plaintiff complaining of a breach of a duty of reasonable care must establish that the breach consisted of *carelessness toward her*, rather than carelessness toward other persons situated differently than her. In analyzing this relational aspect of duty, we have occasion to consider what is arguably the most famous (and misunderstood) torts case of the modern era: Palsgraf v. Long Island Railroad.

Finally, just as we saw in the concluding section of Chapter 2 that courts sometimes invoke the duty element to set "policy-based" limits on liability in situations in which a careless actor appears to be threatened with the prospect of crushing liability, so in Section III of this chapter we discuss how courts sometimes invoke proximate cause and *Palsgraf* in a similar manner.

I. PROXIMATE CAUSE

As noted at the outset of Chapter 4, the issue of proximate cause must be distinguished clearly from the issue of actual cause (or cause in fact). Proximate cause only arises in cases in which actual cause is proven or presumed: In the absence of actual causation the issue of proximate cause need not be entertained. In other words, the primary issue posed by proximate cause doctrine is whether there is something about the causal connection between defendant's carelessness and plaintiff's injury that warrants freeing the defendant from responsibility for that injury *notwithstanding* that connection.

A. History

Lawyers and commentators have employed various concepts that function to bar the attribution of responsibility for harms linked to carelessness by an attenuated causal connection. However, there has been little agreement as to which among these concepts are most appropriate. Indeed, the search for a general description of the idea of proximate cause has frustrated legions of scholars since the negligence tort first emerged in the mid-nineteenth century.

1. *Proximity versus Remoteness.* To some degree, this frustration owes to the very language employed in the phrase "proximate cause." That language derives from a principle of law traceable back at least to Francis Bacon, the great seventeenth-century English politician and scientist, who offered this maxim: *In jure non remota causa, sed proxima, spectatur* ("In law, not the remote cause, but the proximate, is looked to").

On a superficial reading, the language of "proximate" suggests that liability should attach for carelessness causing injury only if that carelessness is sufficiently near to the injury in time or space. However, notions of spatial or temporal distance do not accurately convey the substance of the proximate cause requirement, at least as it is invoked by modern courts. Consider the imagined case of the bee-sting plaintiff provided at the beginning of Chapter 4. There, the driver's negligence was not far removed from the pedestrian's injury either in time or space. Yet we have supposed that it would not be deemed a proximate cause of that damage. Moreover, many injuries complained of in negligence result from careless acts that took place hundreds or even thousands of miles from the locus of the plaintiff's injury (think of *MacPherson*), or that took place years before the plaintiff's injury emerged (think of *Aldridge*). Thus, although in some instances time and distance may matter in determining whether carelessness can count as a proximate cause of an injury, it is clear that proximate cause is not determined simply by reference to temporal or spatial proximity.

2. *Causes versus Conditions.* Others have attempted to "cash out" the difference between proximate and remote causes by reference to a distinction between careless acts that count as causes of injuries and careless acts that merely provide the (pre-)conditions for injuries. Reconstructing our bee-sting hypothetical in this language, one might say that the nest of bees functioned as the immediate cause of the pedestrian's injury, whereas the defendant's careless act was merely a background condition. To be sure, the careless tossing of the coffee cup functioned as a but-for cause of the pedestrian being hurt. But it was necessary to that result in such a minimal sense that it no more makes sense to deem it a cause of the pedestrian's injury than it does to say that the tree's owner was a cause of the injury by planting the tree.

The condition-cause distinction may bring us a bit closer to the mark, but it still does not seem to capture the limitations on responsibility generally recognized in existing case law. To see why, recall the facts of the *McGuiggan* case, discussed in Chapter 2, in which the court endorsed a limited conception of social host liability. Suppose, contrary to the facts of that case, there was evidence that the hosts actually knew that the driver was drunk before leaving their party. Given these facts, according to the court, a jury could impose liability for negligence. If liability were imposed, note that it would attach notwithstanding the remarkable array of unfortunate circumstances that had to coalesce before the social host's breach of duty led to the plaintiff's death. (The plaintiff had to enter the car of the drunk driver, the driver had to drive too close to the side of the road, the plaintiff had to become nauseated and stick his head out the car window just at the moment that the car was driving too close to the side, and the telephone company's pole had to be close enough to the street to permit impact between the plaintiff's body and the pole.) Assuming, as we are, the existence of a duty, most courts would likely say that the breach of this duty was a proximate cause of plaintiff's death notwithstanding the complexity of the causal chain connecting the social host's breach to the plaintiff's death. Nor is this an isolated example: One sees similar analyses in many duty-to-protect cases, and even in some plain-vanilla negligence cases. In short, there is ample case authority to suggest that, while the greater complexity of a causal chain might be relevant to the issue of proximate cause, it does not of itself establish lack of proximate causation.

3. *The Rise and Fall of the "Directness" Test in Commonwealth Law.* In the mid-twentieth century, English and Australian courts struggled to come to terms with proximate cause in a famous sequence of opinions. We describe them briefly here, starting, oddly enough, with a 1921 King's Bench decision that resolved a *contractual* dispute over who should bear the cost associated with the destruction of a leased ship: In re Arbitration Between Polemis and Furness, Withy & Co. Ltd., 3 K.B. 560 (1921).

a. Polemis *and Directness.* Furness leased a steamship from Polemis. Clause 5 of the lease specified that Furness was obligated to return the boat "in same good order and condition as when delivered to [it], fair wear and tear excepted." However, Clause 21 exempted Furness from liability for damage to the ship caused by, among other things, *"fire on board. . . ."*

The ship carried in one of its cargo holds containers of flammable benzene. Some of these were leaking, which allowed benzene vapor to accumulate in the hold. While the ship was docked, workers employed by Furness were in the process of hoisting the containers up to the ship's deck by means of a rope that passed through a winch. In the process, they knocked a wooden plank off the deck into the hold. The fall of the plank "was instantaneously followed by a rush of flames from the . . . hold, and this resulted eventually in the total destruction of the ship."

Polemis initiated an arbitration seeking compensation from Furness equal to the value of the lost ship. The main question raised in the arbitration was whether the fire could fairly be attributed to the negligence of Furness's employees. This was the main question because the arbitrators concluded that the "fire on board" provision of Clause 21 did not immunize Furness from liability (under Clause 5) for failing to return the boat intact if that failure was attributable to the fault of Furness or its employees.

The arbitrators found as follows: (1) Furness's workers had been careless in how they used the rope apparatus; (2) the fire arose from a spark that ignited flammable vapors in the hold emitted by the leaky containers; and (3) the spark *could not reasonably have been anticipated* from the falling of the plank. Notwithstanding this last finding, the arbitrators concluded that the fire was attributable to the workers' carelessness simply because their carelessness functioned as a cause of it. Thus, they concluded that Furness could not take advantage of the "fire on board" exception to its duty to return the ship in good order. Accordingly, they awarded Polemis nearly £200,000 — a huge sum.

On appeal, Furness's lawyers argued that, even if the arbitrators were correct to read Clause 21 as not immunizing Furness from liability for failure to return an intact ship because of fire damage attributable to Furness's carelessness, they erred in attributing *this* fire to Furness's carelessness. True, the employees' carelessness functioned as a but-for cause of the fire. Nonetheless, the unforeseeability of a falling plank causing an explosion — its freakishness — entailed that Furness could not be held responsible for it.

The three Kings Bench justices who heard the appeal rejected this argument and upheld the award. In different opinions, each maintained that, because Furness's employees' careless acts *directly caused* the explosion, Furness could not benefit from the "fire on board" exemption of Clause 21. That the workers could not have foreseen that their carelessness in causing the plank to fall would cause an explosion was deemed by the justices to be "irrelevant."

b. Wagon Mound (No. 1) *and Foreseeability.* Even though the *Polemis* judges were faced with the question of whether arbitrators had properly interpreted a clause in a particular lease, their decision apparently came to stand for the proposition that the test in negligence for proximate cause is whether the defendant's carelessness *directly* caused plaintiff's injuries. Unfortunately, the courts soon became bogged down in confusion over what counted as a directly inflicted injury. Although not formally overruled, *Polemis* was effectively put to rest in the early 1960s by a pair of decisions again concerning fire damage in a marine setting, commonly referred to as *The Wagon Mound (No. 1)* and *The Wagon Mound (No. 2)*.

The ship *Wagon Mound* was moored at a wharf in Sydney Harbor. Its crew carelessly released a large slick of furnace oil into the harbor. Workers at a nearby dock, known as Morts Dock, were repairing another ship named the *Corrimal.* Their repairs involved the use of acetylene torches for welding. Upon becoming aware of the oil spill, the supervisor who worked for Morts Dock ordered his workers to suspend their activities. He then inquired of the owner of the wharf at which the *Wagon Mound* was moored whether the oil in the harbor water might ignite. Based on that discussion, he concluded that there was no risk of ignition and ordered his men back to work. The next day, sparks from the welding operations ignited some debris floating in the water, which in turn ignited the oil, resulting in a fire that destroyed Morts Dock and the *Corrimal.*

The first *Wagon Mound* decision primarily concerned an action for negligence brought by the owners of Morts Dock against the owners of the *Wagon Mound.* The trial court in that action, relying in part on the testimony of a "distinguished scientist," concluded that the crew of the *Wagon Mound* could *not* have foreseen that, by spilling large quantities of furnace oil into the harbor, they might cause a fire. Said the trial court: "The raison d'etre of furnace oil is, of course, that it shall burn, but I find the [crew] did not know and could not reasonably be expected to have known that it was capable of being set afire when spread on water." Nonetheless, the trial court went on to conclude that, because the spilled oil made *direct contact* with the dock, thereby mucking it up, the owners of the *Wagon Mound* were liable for the destruction of Morts Dock under *Polemis*'s directness test.

On appeal, the Australian Privy Council (akin to the English Law Lords) reversed. *See* Overseas Tankship (U.K.), Ltd. v. Morts Dock & Eng'g Co., 1 All E.R. 404 (Privy Council Austl. 1961). In a lengthy and arduous opinion, Viscount Simonds reviewed precedents before and after *Polemis*, then concluded that *Polemis* "should no longer be regarded as good law." Instead, the test for proximate cause should be whether the type of harm suffered by the plaintiff was reasonably foreseeable to the defendants at the time they acted carelessly. In support of this conclusion, Simonds reasoned in part as follows:

> . . . it does not seem consonant with current ideas of justice of morality that, for an act of negligence, however slight or venial, which results in some trivial foreseeable damage, the actor should be liable for all consequences, however unforeseeable and however grave, so long as they can be said to be "direct."
>
> It is a principle of civil liability, subject only to qualifications which have no present relevance, that a man must be considered to be responsible for the probable consequences of his act. To demand more of him is too harsh a rule, to demand less is to ignore that civilised order requires the observance of a minimum standard of behaviour.

Elsewhere, Simonds wrote:

> the Polemis rule works in a very strange way. After the event even a fool is wise. Yet it is not the hindsight of a fool, but it is the foresight of the reasonable man which alone can determine responsibility. The Polemis rule, by substituting "direct" for "reasonably foreseeable" consequence, leads to a conclusion equally illogical and unjust.

In short, given the trial court's conclusion that no reasonable person could have foreseen that the careless spilling of oil posed a risk of fire damage, the defendant could not be held liable for having caused it. Viscount Simonds' opinion further rejected the idea that liability for the fire damage ought to attach because the defendant clearly could have foreseen that the oil spill risked *some* adverse effect on the dock — that is, mucking it up with oil. That the defendant could foresee one form of property damage was not, in the court's view, sufficient to hold it responsible for causing an entirely different sort of damage.

c. Wagon Mound (No. 2). Five years later, the Privy Council considered the claim of the *Corrimal*'s owner against the owners of the *Wagon Mound*. Overseas Tankship (U.K.) Ltd. v. The Miller Steamship Co., 2 All E.R. 709 (Austl. Privy Council 1966) (*Wagon Mound (No. 2)*). In contrast to its first *Wagon Mound* decision, the Privy Council here concluded that the very same fire that destroyed Morts Dock *was* a foreseeable consequence of the furnace-oil spill, and hence the spill should be deemed a proximate cause of damage to the *Corrimal*. The Council justified this about-face on the ground that "the evidence [in *Wagon Mound (No. 2)*] . . . was substantially different from the evidence . . . in *Wagon Mound (No. 1)*." This difference, they continued, owed not to differences in the quality of the lawyering in the two cases, but because the plaintiffs in the first case were "embarrassed by a difficulty" that did not affect the owner of the *Corrimal*. Can you identify this difficulty? What would have been the legal consequence if the owners of Morts Dock had set out to prove in *Wagon Mound (No. 1)* that the ignition of the oil was foreseeable?

B. Foreseeable Risks and the Risk Rule

With the foregoing in mind, particularly the suggestion of Viscount Simonds that the proximate cause inquiry should turn on a notion of foreseeability, consider the efforts of the judges in the following cases to grasp more clearly the proximate cause requirement. Ask yourself if "proximate cause" is a unitary concept, or instead shorthand for several different concepts pertaining to the attribution of responsibility for injuries caused by careless acts.

Union Pump Co. v. Allbritton
898 S.W.2d 773 (Tex. 1995)

Owen, J. The issue in this case is whether the condition, act, or omission of which a personal injury plaintiff complains was, as a matter of law, too remote to constitute legal causation. Plaintiff brought suit alleging negligence . . . and the trial court granted summary judgment for the defendant. The court of appeals reversed and remanded, holding that the plaintiff raised issues of fact concerning proximate and producing cause. Because we conclude that there was no legal causation as a matter of law, we reverse the judgment of the court of appeals and render judgment that plaintiff take nothing.

On the night of September 4, 1989, a fire occurred at Texaco Chemical Company's facility in Port Arthur, Texas. A pump manufactured by Union Pump Company caught fire and ignited the surrounding area. This particular pump had caught on fire twice before. Sue Allbritton, a trainee employee of Texaco Chemical, had just finished her shift and was about to leave the plant when the fire erupted. She and her supervisor Felipe Subia, Jr., were directed to and did assist in abating the fire.

Approximately two hours later, the fire was extinguished. However, there appeared to be a problem with a nitrogen purge valve, and Subia was instructed to block [off] the valve. Viewing the facts in a light most favorable to Allbritton, there was some evidence that an emergency situation existed at that point in time. Allbritton asked if she could accompany Subia and was allowed to do so. To get to the nitrogen purge valve, Allbritton followed Subia over an aboveground pipe rack, which was approximately two and one-half feet high, rather than going around it. It is undisputed that this was not the safer route, but it was the shorter one. Upon reaching the valve, Subia and Allbritton were notified that it was not necessary to block it off. Instead of returning by the route around the pipe rack, Subia chose to walk across it, and Allbritton followed. Allbritton was injured when she hopped or slipped off the pipe rack. There is evidence that the pipe rack was wet because of the fire and that Allbritton and Subia were still wearing fireman's hip boots and other firefighting gear when the injury occurred. Subia admitted that he chose to walk over the pipe rack rather than taking a safer alternative route because he had a "bad habit" of doing so.

Allbritton sued Union Pump. . . . But for the pump fire, she asserts, she would never have walked over the pipe rack, which was wet with water or firefighting foam.

. . . The question before this Court is whether Union Pump established as a matter of law that neither its conduct nor its product was a legal cause of Allbritton's injuries. Stated another way, was Union Pump correct in contending that there was no causative link between the defective pump and Allbritton's injuries as a matter of law?

Negligence requires a showing of proximate cause. . . . Proximate cause consists of both cause in fact and foreseeability. Cause in fact means that the defendant's act or omission was a substantial factor in bringing about the injury which would not otherwise have occurred. . . .

At some point in the causal chain, the defendant's conduct or product may be too remotely connected with the plaintiff's injury to constitute legal causation. As this Court noted in City of Gladewater v. Pike, 727 S.W.2d 514, 518 (Tex. 1987), defining the limits of legal causation "eventually mandates weighing of policy considerations." *See also* Springall v. Fredericksburg Hospital and Clinic, 225 S.W.2d 232, 235 (Tex. Civ. App. — San Antonio 1949, no writ), in which the court of appeals observed:

> [T]he law does not hold one legally responsible for the remote results of his wrongful acts and therefore a line must be drawn between immediate and remote causes. The doctrine of "proximate cause" is employed to determine and fix this line and "is the result of an effort by the courts to avoid, as far as possible the metaphysical and philosophical niceties in the age-old discussion of causation, and to lay down a rule of general application which will, as nearly as may be done by a general rule, apply a practical test, the test of common experience, to human conduct when determining legal rights and legal liability."

Id. at 235 (quoting City of Dallas v. Maxwell, 248 S.W. 667, 670 (Tex. Comm'n App. 1923, holding approved)).

Drawing the line between where legal causation may exist and where, as a matter of law, it cannot, has generated a considerable body of law. Our Court has considered where the limits of legal causation should lie in the factually analogous case of Lear Siegler, Inc. v. Perez, [819 S.W.2d 470 (Tex. 1991)]. The threshold issue was whether causation was negated as a matter of law in an action where negligence and product liability theories were asserted. Perez, an employee of the Texas Highway Department, was driving a truck pulling a flashing arrow sign behind a highway sweeping operation to warn traffic of the highway maintenance. The sign malfunctioned when wires connecting it to the generator became loose, as they had the previous day. Perez got out of the truck to push the wire connections back together, and an oncoming vehicle, whose driver was asleep, struck the sign, which in turn struck Perez. Perez's survivors brought suit against the manufacturer of the sign. In holding that any defect in the sign was not the legal cause of Perez's injuries, we found a comment to the Restatement (Second) of Torts, section 431, instructive on the issue of legal causation:

> In order to be a legal cause of another's harm, it is not enough that the harm would not have occurred had the actor not been negligent. . . . The negligence must also be a substantial factor in bringing about the plaintiff's harm. The word "substantial" is used to denote the fact that the defendant's conduct has such an effect in producing the harm as to lead reasonable men to regard it as a cause, using that word in the popular sense, in which there always lurks the idea of responsibility, rather than in the so-called "philosophic sense," which includes every one of the great number of events without which any happening would not have occurred.

Lear Siegler, 819 S.W.2d at 472 (quoting Restatement (Second) of Torts § 431 cmt. a (1965)).

As this Court explained in *Lear Siegler*, the connection between the defendant and the plaintiff's injuries simply may be too attenuated to constitute legal cause. Legal cause is not established if the defendant's conduct or product does no more than furnish the condition that makes the plaintiff's injury possible. *Id.* . . .

This Court similarly considered the parameters of legal causation in Bell v. Campbell, 434 S.W.2d 117, 122 (Tex. 1968). In *Bell*, two cars collided, and a trailer attached to one of them disengaged and overturned into the opposite lane. A number of people gathered, and three of them were attempting to move the trailer when they were struck by another vehicle. *Id.* at 119. This Court held that the parties to the first accident were not a proximate cause of the plaintiffs' injuries, reasoning:

> All acts and omissions charged against respondents had run their course and were complete. Their negligence did not actively contribute in any way to the injuries involved in this suit. It simply created a condition which attracted [the plaintiffs] to the scene, where they were injured by a third party.

Id. at 122. . . .

Even if the pump fire were in some sense a "philosophic" or "but for" cause of Allbritton's injuries, the forces generated by the fire had come to rest when she fell off the pipe rack. The fire had been extinguished, and Allbritton was walking away from the scene. Viewing the evidence in the light most favorable to Allbritton, the pump fire did no more than create the condition that made Allbritton's injuries possible. We conclude that the circumstances surrounding her injuries are too remotely connected with Union Pump's conduct or pump to constitute a legal cause of her injuries.

Cornyn, J. (concurring). I concur in the Court's judgment, but for different reasons than those given in its opinion. I would hold that although the defective pump was a cause-in-fact of Sue Allbritton's injury, neither Union Pump's negligence nor the defective pump was a legal cause of her injury. Because the Court's opinion conflates foreseeability and other policy issues with its cause-in-fact analysis, I do not join its opinion. . . .

[Justice Cornyn proceeded to undertake an exhaustive review of how cause-in-fact and proximate cause have been analyzed by academics and the Texas courts.] . . .

This case does not present a question of cause-in-fact. The pump defect clearly was a "but for" cause of Allbritton's injuries: assuming the truth of Allbritton's allegations, as we must in this summary judgment case, if the pump had not been defective, there would have been no fire, and Allbritton would have gone home uninjured at the end of her shift. . . .

But determining that the defect was the cause-in-fact of Allbritton's injuries does not end the inquiry. We must decide whether the pump defect meets the second prong of . . . proximate cause. . . . In proximate cause, this other element is foreseeability, but it also incorporates policy driven decisions such as when subsequent events will be treated as intervening causes. In this case, the injury to Allbritton was not foreseeable. Allbritton's injuries were the result of a needlessly dangerous shortcut taken after the crisis had subsided.[4] Holding Union Pump liable for Allbritton's failure to use proper care in exiting the area of the fire after the crisis has ended is akin to holding it liable for an auto accident she suffered on the way home, even though the accident probably would not have occurred had she left after her normal shift. Foreseeability allows us to cut off Union Pump's liability at some point; I would do so at the point the crisis had abated or at the point that Allbritton and Subia departed from their usual, safe path. . . .

Spector, J. (dissenting). . . .
The record reflects that at the time Sue Allbritton's injury occurred, the forces generated by the fire in question had *not* come to rest. Rather, the emergency situation was continuing. The whole area of the fire was covered in water and foam; in at least some places, the water was almost knee-deep. Allbritton was still wearing hip boots and other gear, as required to fight the fire. Viewing all the evidence in the light most favorable to Allbritton, I agree with Justice Cornyn that the pump defect was . . . a cause in fact [of Allbritton's injury].

This case is markedly different from the two main cases on which the majority relies: Lear Siegler, Inc. v. Perez, 819 S.W.2d 470 (Tex. 1991), and

---

4. My conclusion might be different had Allbritton taken the shortcut under emergency conditions because it is foreseeable that workers might take extraordinary risks in trying to extinguish a dangerous fire.

Bell v. Campbell, 434 S.W.2d 117 (Tex. 1968). In each of those cases, a defendant's negligence simply created a condition that attracted an individual to the scene, where a negligent third party inflicted an injury. Here, in contrast, there was no negligent third party. To whatever extent Allbritton's own negligence may have contributed to her injury, a jury should be allowed to allocate comparative responsibility. . . .

Metts v. Griglak
264 A.2d 684 (Pa. 1970)

Pomeroy, J. This action arose out of a rear-end collision in which a bus owned by Albert and Cyril Griglak and John Stolarik, doing business as the Perry Bus Lines, struck from behind an automobile driven by Mrs. Helen R. Harshman. The accident occurred on the afternoon of February 6, 1966 on Route 51 in Westmoreland County. At the place of the accident Route 51 is a divided four-lane highway, and at the time the vehicles collided the stretch of highway in question was slippery and covered with snow and ice.

Joseph H. Metts was a passenger on the Perry bus when the accident occurred. Thereafter, he brought suit for personal injuries against the Griglaks and Stolarik (hereinafter collectively referred to as Perry); Mikael R. Torkysh, the driver of the bus; and Mrs. Harshman. By a third party complaint . . . Mrs. Harshman joined the Greyhound Corporation (hereinafter Greyhound) as an additional defendant. In Mrs. Harshman's third party complaint, she averred that immediately before the accident she was traveling south on Route 51 when a bus owned and operated by Greyhound overtook and passed her car in the left-hand lane; that in doing so the Greyhound bus had crowded her automobile into a snowbank on the right side of the highway causing her to lose control of its operation; that immediately thereafter her automobile was struck by the Perry bus; that this collision was the direct result of the negligent operation of the Greyhound bus; and that any injuries sustained by plaintiff Metts were proximately caused by the concurrent negligence of Perry, Torkysh, and Greyhound.

After trial the jury returned a verdict in favor of the plaintiff and against all the defendants, including the additional defendant Greyhound. Greyhound filed motions for judgment n.o.v. and for new trial; the court En banc granted the n.o.v. and ordered the entry of judgment in favor of Greyhound and against all original defendants. From the judgment, the original defendants have taken this appeal.

. . . Viewed in [the light most favorable to the plaintiffs], the facts of this case are as follows: Shortly before the accident Mrs. Harshman and the Perry bus were proceeding south on Route 51 several car lengths apart from each other at speeds of approximately 30 to 35 miles per hour. Both vehicles were in the right-hand lane, and the Perry bus was traveling behind the Harshman automobile. They were overtaken and passed by a Greyhound bus traveling in the left southbound lane at approximately 60 miles per hour or some 10 miles per hour over the posted speed limit.

The Greyhound bus, in so passing the other vehicles, splashed slush and raised a cloud of snow which obscured the vision of the other drivers. Although he was unable to see, Torkysh, the Perry driver, continued ahead without reducing the speed of his bus. When the road ahead again became visible, Torkysh saw the Harshman automobile immediately ahead of him, apparently in a slight skid but fully in the right-hand lane. Torkysh was unable to avoid colliding with it, and Metts, a passenger on the bus, sustained an injury to his back in the collision. Neither the bus nor the Harshman automobile were using chains at the time, nor was Torkysh using the sander with which his bus was equipped. At the point of the accident there was an uninterrupted view of the highway for one-half mile, and all parties agreed that the Greyhound bus was out of sight when the accident took place. The point of collision was 1,500 to 2,000 feet from the point the Greyhound bus passed the other vehicles. While the exact position of Mrs. Harshman's automobile at the point of collision was a matter of some conjecture, no evidence was produced to support the theory of the third party complaint that the Greyhound bus, in passing the Harshman vehicle had forced it from the highway into a snowbank and caused Mrs. Harshman to lose control.

As to Greyhound, the case was submitted to the jury on the theory that Greyhound had been negligent in operating the bus at an excessive speed. Clearly Greyhound did owe other travelers on the highway a duty to exercise reasonable caution and in operating its bus at an excessive speed it may have been negligent; certainly it was in violation of the speed limit. But Greyhound could be properly liable only with respect to those harms which proceeded from a risk or hazard the foreseeability of which rendered its conduct negligent. Brusis v. Henkels, 376 Pa. 226, 102 A.2d 146 (1954) and Dahlstrom v. Shrum, 368 Pa. 423, 84 A.2d 289 (1951). Thus, Greyhound's operation of a bus at excessive speeds under these conditions created a risk that the driver might lose control of his vehicle or be unable to stop within his assured clear distance and avoid any collision. In the present case, as it happened, these risks did not mature into harm. Similarly, Greyhound's negligent operation of its vehicle might have jeopardized another driver's control of his own vehicle. As noted above, the third party complaint averred such a chain of actions, but there was no evidence to support this factual allegation. Other reasonably foreseeable risks might easily be imagined.[2] But in the case at hand, we cannot say that a collision occurring when the Greyhound bus was over one-half mile from the scene, and alleged to have resulted from the creation of a snow swirl

2. "Thus the duty to exercise reasonable care in driving an automobile down the highway is established for the protection of the persons or property of others against all of the unreasonable possibilities of harm which may be expected to result from collisions with other vehicles, or with pedestrians, or from the driver's own automobile leaving the highway, or from narrowly averted collisions or other accidents. When harm of a kind normally to be expected as a consequence of the negligent driving results from the realization of any one of these hazards, it is within the scope of the defendant's duty of protection." Restatement (Second) of Torts, § 281, comment E (1965). *Cf.* Marshall v. Nugent, 222 F.2d 604 (1st Cir. 1955).

(or the throwing of slush) was a harm within the risk foreseeably created by Greyhound's operation of its bus at an excessive speed. . . .

In granting Greyhound's motion for judgment n.o.v., the court below stated that a snow swirl caused by one vehicle's passing another was a normal hazard of winter driving which for all practical purposes was unavoidable.[3] Appellants have cited no case, nor has our research uncovered any, in which defendant's alleged negligence as to plaintiffs has consisted in the creation of a snow swirl. The situation at hand is perhaps analogous to one in which a driver blinded by the headlights of an approaching vehicle nonetheless proceeds without diminution of speed and collides with a car in front of it. Such accidents, and such cases, are numerous, but so far as we can determine it has not been argued that the approaching vehicle was negligent by virtue of the blinding effect of its headlights. Such an effect has always been considered a natural hazard of road travel, and the blinding effect of the instant snow swirl is in the same category.

In conclusion, we find that if Greyhound was negligent, its negligence lay only in exceeding the speed limit. The harm suffered by Metts, however, was not the result of a risk the foreseeability of which rendered Greyhound's excessive speed negligent. Rather that harm was attributable to Greyhound's non-negligent raising of a snow swirl and the subsequent and unforeseeable negligence of Perry and Mrs. Harshman. On the facts of this case, we find no error in the grant of judgment n.o.v. in favor of Greyhound.

   Roberts, J. (dissenting). . . .
   I believe that it was for the jury to determine whether Greyhound's conduct was negligent and the risk of accident foreseeable. There was testimony to the effect that the Greyhound Bus passed the Perry Bus going "at least" 60 m.p.h., ten miles in excess of the posted limit; that it had been snowing during the day; that the road conditions were "deplorable," the road being coated with a combination of freezing rain and snow; and that there was more snow in the passing lane than in the right hand lane. People at all familiar with high-speed driving know the danger involved in passing under such conditions, and know that the visibility of other drivers may be temporarily impaired by slush thrown onto their windshields by high-speed passing vehicles, especially by large buses. It is certainly foreseeable that when a driver's visibility is impaired by such conduct, even temporarily, a collision may occur. These are conclusions which reasonable men can draw from the present record and their common experience.

   In my view the majority is incorrect in holding that reasonable men could not find this accident foreseeable, that this was not a question for the jury to decide. The majority forgets what Mr. Justice Holmes said over fifty years ago: "It was not necessary that the defendant should have had

---

3. There is no suggestion in the record before us that the snow flurry in the wake of the Greyhound bus was a result of its excessive speed, nor is there evidence that the snow cloud raised by a bus proceeding within the 50 m.p.h. speed limit would not have similarly interfered with the vision of other drivers using the highway.

notice of the particular method in which an accident would occur, if the possibility of an accident was clear to the ordinarily prudent eye." Munsey v. Webb, 231 U.S. 150, 156, 34 S. Ct. 44, 45, 58 L. Ed. 162 (1913). I think the possibility of an accident was clear in the instant case. The jury so found. I would not disturb its conclusion, and I must therefore dissent.

NOTES AND QUESTIONS

1. *Actual Cause versus Proximate Cause.* In *Allbritton*, concurring Justice Cornyn agrees with the majority's conclusion but criticizes its reasoning for conflating actual and proximate cause. Is that criticism valid? To what use is the majority putting the concept of "substantial factor" causation? Does it mean what it meant in the multiple sufficient cause cases discussed in Chapter 4? If not, why would the majority seize on it to help explain its denial of liability here? Can one argue, particularly in light of Justice Spector's dissent, that Justice Cornyn's opinion is guilty of a different sort of confusion?

2. *Judge and Jury.* Proximate cause is generally held to be a question for the jury, subject to the judge's power to decide issues as a matter of law. The question is whether a jury might reasonably find that the relevant harm or harm-producing event was "foreseeable," or the sort of harm that the prohibition violated by defendant was meant to prevent. Our (impressionistic) sense — borne out, perhaps, by cases such as *Allbritton* and *Metts* — is that judges are, on the whole, less prone to defer to juries on this issue than they are on the issues of breach and cause-in-fact. If so, what might explain such a difference in attitude?

3. *Proximate Cause and Foreseeability.* Like Viscount Simonds in *Wagon Mound (No. 1)* and the majority in *Allbritton*, courts and commentators often invoke the concept of foreseeability to help give content to the concept of proximate cause. If the type of harm that resulted to the plaintiff was not reasonably foreseeable to a person in the position of the defendant, they reason, the defendant should not be held liable. Consider in this regard Ventricelli v. Kinney Sys. Rent A Car, Inc., 383 N.E.2d 1149 (N.Y. 1978). Plaintiff rented an automobile from Kinney. The car had a defective trunk lid that repeatedly flew open so as to obstruct the operator's rear view while the vehicle was moving, despite several returns to the lessor for repair. On the day of the accident, plaintiff had parked the car alongside the curb on a New York City street. While plaintiff and a passenger were attempting to slam the trunk lid shut, the defendant Maldonado's automobile, parked several lengths behind them, unexpectedly jerked forward and severely injured the plaintiff. The jury apportioned fault 80 percent to Kinney and 20 percent to Maldonado. However, the intermediate appellate court concluded that no act of defendant Kinney proximately caused plaintiff's injuries. The Court of Appeals affirmed.

> That Kinney's negligence in providing an automobile with a defective trunk lid would result in plaintiff's repeated attempts to close the lid was reasonably

foreseeable. Not "foreseeable," however, was the collision between vehicles both parked a brief interval before the accident. Plaintiff was standing in a relatively "safe" place, a parking space, not in an actively traveled lane. He might well have been there independent of any negligence of Kinney, as, for example, if he were loading or unloading the trunk. Under these circumstances, to hold the accident a foreseeable consequence of Kinney's negligence is to stretch the concept of foreseeability beyond acceptable limits.

Id. at 1149. Is the *Ventricelli* majority asserting that the defendant could not reasonably foresee that a user of the rental car might be injured by another driver after getting out of the car to fix the defective trunk lid?

4. *Examples*. Consider the following hypotheticals. Do they shed light on the reasoning in the main cases?

a.   Driver *D* drives unreasonably fast—say, 20 miles over the posted speed limit—on a highway for a period of ten minutes without incident. He then exits the highway and proceeds down a local street exercising all due care. Despite his exercise of due care, *D* collides with another car on the local street, driven by *P*, thereby injuring *P*. Suppose *P* learns of *D*'s highway speeding and sues on the theory that *D*'s carelessness on the highway caused the accident. Should the court rule that *D*'s speeding was a but-for cause of *P*'s injuries? If so, was it a proximate cause? If not, is it because *D* could not foresee that his speeding might lead him to collide with another car?

b.   Father *F* returns from target practice and carelessly hands his five-year-old son *S* a small loaded pistol. The gun is no more heavy, sharp, or cumbersome than many toys designed for five-year-olds. *S* accidentally drops the pistol on playmate *P*'s toe, breaking it. Was *F*'s carelessness a but-for cause of *P*'s injury? A proximate cause? If not the latter, why not?

c.   Restaurant owner *O* places an unlabeled can of what he knows to be rat poison on a shelf directly above a stove used for preparing food. The rat poison is flammable (which *O* had no reason to know). It explodes, injuring chef *C*. Was *O*'s negligence the proximate cause of *C*'s injury?

d.   Driver *D*, proceeding carelessly down a residential street, loses control of his car and crashes into the picket fence of *P*'s yard. Minutes later, *P*, who was inside his house at the time, discovers the damage and proceeds down the steps to his basement to obtain some tools to repair the fence. In doing so, *P* slips and breaks his arm. Was *D*'s careless driving a but-for cause of *P*'s injury? A proximate cause? If not the latter, why not?

5. *Tortious-Aspect Causation*. Professor Wright has argued that many proximate cause cases can be resolved with a refined understanding of actual cause.

Recall from the beginning of Chapter 4 the example of driver *D*, who fails to check behind her car, and fails to look in her rear view mirror, before backing out of her driveway, which results in child *P* being run over. Because the evidence clearly demonstrated that *D* would *not* have seen *P* even if she had been careful, we concluded that *P* could not establish actual causation. Yet, in that example, *D* clearly *acted carelessly* toward *P* by not checking behind her before or as she drove. Moreover, it is clear from the facts that *D*'s *conduct* — her backing up the car — *was* a cause-in-fact of *P*'s injury. (After all, had *D* not backed up, *P* would not have been injured.) Still, we concluded that *P* could not establish actual causation.

According to Professor Wright, examples such as this one indicate that a negligence plaintiff has to establish something more than that (1) *D*'s conduct was negligent, and that (2) *D*'s conduct caused *P*'s injury. In addition, *P* has to show that (3) the *careless aspect* of *D*'s conduct played a part in bringing about *P*'s injury. In this view, the precise issue posed by the actual causation inquiry concerns whether the *careless features of the actor's conduct* — the acts or omissions that rendered the conduct unreasonable — operated as a but-for cause of the other's injury. By attending to the tortious aspect of the defendant's conduct, Wright maintains, courts would exclude liability in many of the cases in which they purport to rely on proximate cause grounds.

Do you find this analysis helpful in resolving some of the hypotheticals in Note 4? Is there a "tortious aspect" problem in *Metts*, or is it fair to say that the bus's speeding mattered in terms of making it possible for the Greyhound bus to momentarily blind the driver of the Perry bus with a snow swirl?

6. *The Risk Rule Formulation.* Professor Keeton offered variants on many of the foregoing examples in aid of illustrating what he dubbed the "risk rule." In one formulation, that rule states: "A negligent actor is legally responsible for the harm . . . that . . . (1) is caused in fact by his conduct but also (2) is a result within the scope of the risks by reason of which the actor is found to be negligent." Under that rule, there would arguably be no liability in any of the examples in Note 4 because none of the risks there realized were of the sort that prompts one to label the defendant's conduct as careless.

In an earlier formulation of a similar idea, Professor Bingham articulated the primary question posed by proximate cause doctrine as follows: "Were the . . . consequences which constituted plaintiff's harm within any of the dangers that provoked legal condemnation of defendant's conduct?" Writing in 1927, Dean Green also framed the proximate cause inquiry in similar terms: "[W]as this the sort of hazard protected against by the rule which the [actor] violated?" According to Green, this question cannot be answered simply by employing a test of foreseeability but instead requires a sensitive inquiry into the underlying purposes and policies of the rule in question.

The draft Third Restatement adopts a variant of these formulations by framing the proximate cause inquiry in terms of whether the injury suffered by the victim is one of the harms whose risks rendered the actor's conduct careless. *See* Restatement (Third) Torts: Liability for Physical Harm (Basic Principles) § 29, at 2 (Tentative Draft No. 3, Apr. 7, 2003).

7. *Expiration of the Risk.* Do *Allbritton* and *Metts* "flunk" Keeton's risk rule for the same reasons or different reasons? What was problematic about the way in which the defective valve functioned as a cause of Allbritton's injury? Compare another famous proximate cause case, Marshall v. Nugent, 222 F.2d 604 (1st Cir. 1955). There, a truck driver (call him *T*) negligently crossed over the center line of a road while taking a sharp curve, thereby forcing off the road a car in which plaintiff *M* was a passenger. Luckily, *M* and the other occupants of the car were unhurt. *T* pulled his truck up alongside the car as part of an effort to get it back on to the road. *M*, perhaps at *T*'s suggestion, walked to one end of the curve to warn oncoming traffic of the obstruction formed by the stopped truck. As *M* was getting into position, driver *N* approached the accident scene and, in an effort to avoid colliding with the stopped truck, skidded into a guardrail and struck *M*, severely injuring him. The court held that the question of whether *T*'s initial negligence in driving the truck was a proximate cause of *M* being injured by *N* was for the jury:

> Regarding motor vehicle accidents . . . one should contemplate a variety of risks which are created by negligent driving. . . . In a traffic mix-up due to negligence, before the disturbed waters have become placid and normal again, the unfolding of events between the culpable act and the plaintiff's eventual injury may be bizarre indeed; yet the defendant may be liable for such a result. . . .
>
> Though this particular act of negligence was over and done with when the truck pulled up alongside the stalled [car] without having actually collided with it, still the consequences of such past negligence were in the bosom of time, as yet unrevealed.

The court contrasted a case in which the car in which *M* was riding was successfully restored to the road, but then was involved in a collision with some other car five miles away from the original accident scene. If *M* were injured in that situation, the court reasoned, *T* would be entitled to a judgment as a matter of law that *T*'s negligence was not a proximate cause of *M*'s injuries.

C. Superseding Cause

We have seen in this chapter and elsewhere that an injury often can occur as the result of the wrongful acts of multiple tortfeasors. We have also seen that, in such cases, tort law is at least sometimes prepared to hold two or more tortfeasors responsible for the injury. One aspect of proximate cause doctrine that deserves separate attention concerns the question of whether the subsequent acts of a second tortfeasor can sometimes function to block an attribution of responsibility to an earlier tortfeasor. The issue, in legal terminology, is whether a second wrongdoing can function as a *superseding* cause that relieves the perpetrator of a prior wrongdoing of responsibility, even though the prior wrongdoing was a but-for cause of the victim's injury.

Britton v. Wooten
817 S.W.2d 443 (Ky. 1991)

Leibson, J.   On May 8, 1983, Wooten's Pic Pac Grocery in Louisa, Kentucky, was destroyed by fire. A portion of the grocery store premises consisted of a building owned by the movant, Genoa Britton (the lessor), and leased to L. Wayne Wooten d/b/a Wooten's Pic Pac and Wooten's Grocery Company, Inc. (collectively, the lessee). The movant filed suit against her lessee alleging negligence in the operation of the grocery store. Allegedly, the store employees stacked trash that was flammable, combustible material next to the building all the way up to the eaves, in violation of the fire marshal's regulations and the fire code of the State of Kentucky. Consequently, a fire originating in the trash progressed up the exterior wall to the combustible roof, causing the building to burn to the ground.

The only evidence of record specifically identifying how the fire started was the testimony of Andrew Reed, an arson investigator from the Kentucky State Police, who had investigated the cause of the fire at length. He stated that in his opinion "someone set fire to the paper boxes in or near the dempsey dumpsters." There was testimony from other witnesses that these dumpsters, located next to the building, were overflowing with trash which had been accumulating for days. The arson investigator also opined that the "first part of the building that became involved" was the overhanging exposed wooden eaves "as the fire went up the wall." Thus there was substantial evidence that the fire started in the trash and that the manner in which the trash was accumulated and stored violated portions of the Kentucky Fire Safety Standard Regulations 815 KAR 10:020, relating to accumulating combustible waste and refuse, and to disposal of rubbish, from which a jury could reasonably conclude fire safety code violations were a substantial factor in the spread of the fire and the burning of the building. Nevertheless, the trial court rendered Summary Judgment in favor of the respondent. The primary reason stated for granting the Summary Judgment was that the lease, as a matter of law, contracted away the lessor's right to sue the lessee for the destruction of the premises by fire. . . .

In seeking Summary Judgment, the lessee had also relied upon "several general principles of law pertaining to proximate causation" and, more specifically, "that the act of the arsonist in setting the fire was a superseding cause as a matter of law, thereby breaking the chain of causation."

[The Court of Appeals affirmed the trial court's grant of summary judgment.]

We . . . decide for the lessor . . . : in this case neither the terms of the lease nor tort law principles relating to proximate cause . . . insulate the lessee from liability for negligent conduct contributing to the destruction of the leased premises.

I. THE LEASE

[The Court concluded that lease provisions excusing nonpayment of rent because of fire damage to the property were not intended to shield the lessee from liability for damage caused by fire resulting in part from its own negligence. *Compare Polemis,* discussed *supra.* — EDS.]

II. CAUSATION

. . . [S]tacking rubbish and boxes close to a building and too high in the dumpsters, to such extent that if a fire started it would climb the masonry wall to the inflammable material in the roof of the building constitutes acts which might well be viewed as actionable negligence.

At oral argument the respondent conceded there would be no basis for the summary judgment if the proof showed that the fire started accidentally. The real basis of the respondent's argument is, as stated in his Brief, that "the cause of the fire was an act of arson," "this is and can be the only substantial factor," and the negligent acts of his employees, if any, must be viewed as "an act that only furnishes the occasion of an injury [and] cannot be a proximate cause." . . .

To begin with, at this point the evidence that this fire constituted the crime of arson is far short of overwhelming. As we stated earlier in this Opinion, the only evidence on this subject was from the arson investigator who concluded, "my opinion is that someone set fire to the paper boxes in or near the dempsey dumpsters." Movant argues that this statement hardly even suffices to prove the fire was set intentionally, let alone sufficient to establish the elements of arson as related in the Penal Code, KRS Chapter 513. Respondent counters that at the time of Summary Judgment both parties and the trial court were operating on the assumption the arson investigator's deposition established that at least the fire in the trash, if not also the destruction or damage to the building, was started as an intentional act. Respondent insists that therefore this appeal should be decided on this same premise. We need not decide this subissue because we reject any all-inclusive general rule that, as respondent contends, "criminal acts of third parties . . . relieve the original negligent party from liability."

This archaic doctrine has been rejected everywhere. The only Kentucky case movant cites in support of it [is] Watson v. Kentucky & Indiana Bridge and R. Co., 137 Ky. 619, 126 S.W. 146 (1910), a case over 80 years old. In it the court draws a distinction in the railroad company's liability for a fire ignited following a train derailment and gas spillage on the basis of a fact question presented as to whether the man who ignited the gasoline did so maliciously or inadvertently. That case indeed holds that the railroad company is "not bound to anticipate the criminal act of others by which damage is inflicted and hence is not liable therefor." *Id.* at 151. . . . The question is whether that case is still viable.

Respondent cites Restatement (Second) of Torts, § 448, in support of the continued viability of criminal acts, per se, as sufficient to cut the chain of causation. That section postulates that "an intentional tort or crime is a superseding cause" where the defendant's "negligent conduct" only creates "a situation which afforded an opportunity" for another to commit an intentional tort or crime, but it adds an all important caveat: ". . . unless the actor [the defendant] at the time of his negligent conduct realized or should have realized the likelihood that such a situation might be created, and that a third person might avail himself of the opportunity to commit such a tort or crime."

Restatement (Second) of Torts, § 449, expands on the meaning of § 448. Section 449 postulates:

> If the likelihood that a third person may act in a particular manner is the hazard or one of the hazards which makes the actor [the defendant] negligent, such an act [by another person] whether innocent, negligent, intentionally tortious, or criminal, does not prevent the actor [the defendant] from being liable for harm caused thereby.

And these two sections, 448 and 449, also must be read in conjunction with Restatement (Second) of Torts, § 302B, "Risk of Intentional or Criminal Conduct," which states:

> An act or an omission may be negligent if the actor realizes or should realize that it involves an unreasonable risk of harm to another through the conduct of the other or a third person which is intended to cause harm, even though such conduct is criminal.

The fact is that the appendices to the Restatement (Second) of Torts, §§ 448 and 449, are replete with numerous cases, perhaps one hundred in number, from throughout these United States, acknowledging the Restatement (Second) of Torts §§ 448 and 449 as authority and deciding the negligence of a defendant is actionable as a contributing cause, wherein the immediate cause is a subsequent criminal act. We will not burden this Opinion by trying to cover the field, but we will review four cases because they represent factual situations strikingly similar to the present case:

1) Arneil v. Schnitzer, 173 Or. 179, 144 P.2d 707 (1944), affirmed the liability of the property owners where litter in a junk yard created a fire hazard, and a trespasser then started a fire on the premises which spread to adjoining premises. The court states:

> "The intervention of a criminal act, however, does not necessarily interrupt the relation of cause and effect between negligence and an injury. If at the time of the negligence, the criminal act might reasonably have been foreseen, the causal chain is not broken by the intervention of such act." [Citations omitted.]
>   . . . "We know of no decision which holds that one who maintains his property so negligently that it menaces his neighbors, is liable for the destruction of their premises by a fire which started upon his, only in the event that he himself applied the match. To the contrary, we are satisfied that

the owner's negligence is the proximate cause of the damage to the neighbor, even if a stranger communicated the spark. . . ."

"One who suspends a sword of Damocles over the head of his neighbor must respond in damages for the consequences if another, allured by the temptation, cuts the tender cord. . . ."

. . . We are satisfied that when the defendants littered their property with piles of combustible material it was their duty to anticipate trespasses by such persons as Ellis Miller, and also to anticipate that the intruders might cast about lighted tobacco."

2) d'Hedouville v. Pioneer Hotel Co., 552 F.2d 886 (9th Cir. 1977), a wrongful death action. It involved a claim against the manufacturer of acrylic fiber used in carpeting in a hotel, charging the product was highly inflammable and unreasonably dangerous, and as such a contributing cause in the rapid spread of a fire started by an arsonist. The Court states:

"Monsanto [the defendant carpet manufacturer] argues that under Arizona decisions the criminal act of a third person constitutes a superseding cause as a matter of law. While this appears to have been the rule stated in early Arizona cases, more recent decisions apply the general principle of foreseeability to intervening criminal acts." Id. at 894.

3) Mozer v. Semenza, 177 So. 2d 880 (Fla. 1965), another negligence action by guests against a hotel owner for injuries from a fire started by an arsonist. The Court states:

"In the instant case the act of the arsonist was not an 'independent intervening cause.' The scope of defendant's duty to maintain reasonably safe premises does not include a duty to foresee a particular fire but it does include a duty to reasonably guard against the risk of fire. Viewed from this standpoint it is not important to the liability of the appellant whether the fire started in one way or another. . . . We therefore conclude that the record reveals a reasonable basis upon which the jury could find that the injuries to the appellees were proximately caused by the negligent maintenance of appellant's Hotel." Id. at 883.

4) Hodge v. Nor-Cen, Inc., 527 N.E.2d 1157 (Ind. App. 2 Dist. 1988), holding that the act of an arsonist in setting the fire was not an intervening event which broke the causal connection between the landlord's negligence in failing to provide a second means of egress and the injury occasioned to tenants by inability to escape during the fire. This recent Indiana case is strikingly similar in facts to the Kentucky case, Higgins Investments, Inc. v. Sturgill, Ky., 509 S.W.2d 266 (1974) (discussed earlier in this Opinion), with the added factor that, whereas in the Higgins Investments case the cause of the fire is unknown (or if known was not set out in the opinion), in Hodge v. Nor-Cen, arson was positively identified as the factor starting the fire. The Indiana court holds:

"While Nor-Cen correctly states the rule of [Restatement (Second) of Torts], § 448], its application of the rule to these facts is faulty. . . .

. . . Fire, whether by accident or design, is not an intervening event which breaks the causal connection between the act of failing to provide a second means of egress and the injury occasioned by the inability to escape; it is merely an event in the chain of causation.

. . . Because the undisputed facts do not negate the elements of a claim of negligence, appellants' claim should have survived summary judgment. . . ." *Id.* at 1161.

The lengthy and authoritative treatise by Harper, James and Gray, *The Law of Torts*, 2d ed. (1986), addresses the point at issue as follows:

"It is often said that an actor may assume that others will act lawfully and carefully. Rightly understood this is sound enough, and no more than a corollary of the general [negligence] principle. . . . But in this connection two things must be noted. The first is that such an assumption does not always correspond to the facts. It does not in situations where a law is generally disobeyed. . . . And it does not wherever the actor's [defendant's] conduct exposes some interest to risk from a large and indeterminate group of people that will probably include some who will be negligent or commit crime, so that the likelihood of some negligence or some crime is considerable, though the number of those who will be responsible for it is relatively small. . . . Perhaps the most significant trend that has taken place in this particular field, in recent years, has been the increasing liberalization in allowing the wrongs of other people to be regarded as foreseeable where the facts warrant that conclusion if they are looked at naturally and not through the lens of some artificial archaic notion." *Id.* § 16.12 at 495-96.

And from the same treatise, § 20.5, "Legal Cause," pp.154-56:

So far as scope of duty (or, as some courts put it, the relation of proximate cause) is concerned, it should make no difference whether the intervening actor is negligent or intentional or criminal. Even criminal conduct by others is often reasonably to be anticipated.

Parenthetically, Harper, James and Gray back up the above quotations from the treatise with a vast number of cases in point, cases which only serve to supplement the numerous cases found in the appendices to the Restatement (Second) of Torts alluded to earlier. . . .

. . . We return for further instruction as to what constitutes a superseding cause to the definitive case of House v. Kellerman, Ky., 519 S.W.2d 380 (1975), being mindful that in that case the intervening act argued as a superseding cause was that of the passenger in the automobile, who awakened when the car began to slide and grabbed the steering wheel in a "sudden reflex action . . . that caused [the defendant/host driver] to lose control of the automobile." This act was rejected as a superseding cause. The reasoning in House v. Kellerman is that to be a superseding cause the intervening act must be so "highly extraordinary" that antecedent negligence should be ruled out as a matter of law as a substantial factor in causing the accident. Peterson v. Bailey, Ky. App., 571 S.W.2d 630 (1978), uses the same reasoning. It is a fire case with a role reversal: the defendant whose negligence started the fire sought to shift sole responsibility to the building owner and the fire department claiming it was their negligent acts after the fire started that actually caused the building to burn down. The Court of Appeals, rejecting the superseding cause argument, held that the failure to take appropriate actions to stop the spread of the fire was not of such "utterly foolhardy or extraordinary" nature as to insulate the liability of the defendant who caused the fire.

In the present case whether the spark ignited in the trash accumulated next to the building was ignited negligently, intentionally, or even criminally, or if it was truly accidental, is not the critical issue. The issue is whether the movant can prove that the respondent caused or permitted trash to accumulate next to its building in a negligent manner which caused or contributed to the spread of the fire and the destruction of the lessor's building. If so, the source of the spark that ignited the fire is not a superseding cause under any reasonable application of modern tort law.

The Summary Judgment in the trial court is vacated, and the decision in the Court of Appeals affirming it is reversed.

NOTES AND QUESTIONS

1. *What Is Left of the* Per Se *Rule?* Under the *per se* rule of earlier decisions such as the *Watson* case (discussed in *Britton*), an intervening criminal act would automatically bar the attribution of responsibility to a defendant whose carelessness also played a role in bringing about plaintiff's injury. After rejecting *Watson*'s *per se* rule as "archaic," what does *Britton* put in its place? Does it adopt the position that an intervening criminal act can never function as a superseding cause?

2. *Affirmative Duties and Superseding Cause. Britton* holds that a tenant can be responsible for destruction of the leased property caused both by the tenant's carelessness and by a third party's criminal act. To the extent that attribution of responsibility is plausible, does it gain its plausibility from the court's (unstated) premise that, absent a specific term in the lease to the contrary, tenants owe their landlords an affirmative duty to protect the leased property from vandalism and other such risks?* Suppose the driver of a delivery truck, after completing his delivery to the same store, piled up some empty boxes against the back of the store, which were later set fire by an arsonist, causing the building to burn down. Would *Britton*'s holding apply to the driver?

The interrelation of duty and superseding cause can be appreciated by flipping the role of landlord and tenant. As we saw in Chapter 2, a property owner often is under affirmative duties to protect persons on the

---

* Whether such a duty in fact exists as a matter of property law is questionable. Under the doctrine of "waste," a tenant has some obligations to avoid causing damage or devaluation to the rental property. However, this obligation consists mainly of a negative duty to refrain from damaging the property through one's own conduct. To the extent waste doctrine imposes affirmative duties, they usually consist of circumscribed duties, such as a duty to place a tarp over a leaky roof to prevent interior damage.

property by permission from the wrongful acts by third parties. For example, a court might well conclude that the owner of an apartment building owes its tenants a duty to protect them against crime by providing reasonably secure locks on room doors. If a guest is attacked in his room by an assailant who was able to gain access only because of the absence of adequate locks, the court presumably would not treat the assailant's intentional wrongdoing as a superseding cause of the plaintiff's injury. Restatement (Third) of Torts: Liability for Physical Harm (Basic Principles) § 34, illus. 1, at 104-05 (Tentative Draft No. 3, Apr. 7, 2003); *see also* Nixon v. Mr. Prop. Mgmt. Co., 690 S.W.2d 546 (Tex. 1985) (the owner of a tenement without secure doors and windows can be held liable to the resident of neighboring building who was dragged to the tenement and assaulted there, especially given evidence of prior criminal activity at the tenement).

If the characterization of the lessees' duty in *Britton* as an affirmative duty to protect the premises against third-party misconduct generated the court's conclusion as to superseding cause, does it follow that the *per se* rule might still have a role to play in the absence of an affirmative duty to protect?

3. *Fire.* Is there something special about conduct that is careless because it poses the risk of fire damage, such that a person who creates such a risk should be held responsible regardless of whether a resulting fire was generated by intervening criminal conduct?

4. *Superseding Cause: Effect.* In situations in which a judge or jury concludes, contrary to *Britton*, that intervening criminal conduct *does* constitute a superseding cause, the defendant being sued for negligence is relieved of all liability. Conversely, when intervening criminal misconduct is held not to constitute a superseding cause, *both* actors — the negligent defendant and the criminal actor — are in principle subject to liability to the plaintiff. It will often be the case, as was the situation in *Britton* itself, that the identity of the criminal actor will never be determined, and hence no claim will be brought against him or her. This raises the question of whether a careless actor such as Wooten can be held liable for the entire amount of damages suffered by the plaintiff, even though the damages would not have come about without the participation of the other, perhaps more culpable, wrongdoer. *See* Chapter 8 (discussing apportionment when not all tortfeasors are parties to plaintiff's suit).

5. *Judge and Jury.* Recall that, in contrast to the duty issue, proximate cause is supposed to be assessed by the jury. Thus, the issue for judges in addressing a superseding cause argument is whether a reasonable juror could find that a third party's intervening wrongful act constitutes a superseding cause. Consider the following hypotheticals. Should a jury be permitted to enter a verdict for any of these negligence defendants on superseding cause grounds?

    a.   Defendant *D* manufactures large metal pipes, prepares them for delivery by bundling them together with metal bands, and loads them onto trucks owned by another company, *T*. Plaintiff's decedent is killed when a load of pipes that had been carelessly bundled by *D* falls off the back of one of *T*'s trucks. It turns out that, shortly before the accident, the driver of the truck, an employee of *T*'s, had stopped at a gas station and observed that several of the bands holding the pipes together had broken. Thus, he knew that there was a very high risk of the pipes coming loose. He continued driving nonetheless. *Cf.* Georgia Pipe Co. v. Lawler, 584 S.E. 2d 634 (Ga. Ct. App. 2003) (on similar facts, the issue of whether the driver's misconduct constitutes superseding cause is for the jury).

  b.   Dockowner *D* carelessly permits a tanker ship captained by *C* to break loose from its moorings. *C* and his crew are on board. Although *C* has ample opportunity to steer the ship to safety, *C* unjustifiably ignores standard procedures, instead executing a series of maneuvers that ultimately cause the ship to crash into a reef and sink. *Cf.* Exxon Co., U.S.A. v. Sofec, Inc., 517 U.S. 830, 833-837 (1996) (noting lower courts' determination that captain's gross negligence constituted a superseding cause).

  c.   Plaintiff *P* purchases a new car manufactured by *D*. Because of a mechanical problem resulting from negligence on *D*'s part, the car "dies" without warning as plaintiff crosses a busy intersection. Another driver, *R*, could easily avoid colliding with *P*'s stalled car, but decides instead that it would be "interesting" to see whether his colossal SUV can collide with *P*'s car without sustaining damage. *R* collides with *P*, injuring her.

  d.   Production company *C* produces a daytime TV show that is known for staging confrontations among guests that often lead to fist fights in the television studio. Indeed, fights are so common that *C* employs security personnel to break them up when they occur. *C* invites *A* to come on the show to meet his "secret admirer"—*P*—for the first time. *C* knows, but does not tell *A*, that *P* is another man. When *P*'s identity is revealed on the air, *A*, who is homophobic, is mortified. Two weeks later *A* shoots and kills *P*. *Cf.* Graves v. Warner Bros., 656 N.W.2d 195 (Mich. Ct. App. 2002) (holding that defendant owed "'no duty'" to protect guest against such violence).

  e.   Manufacturer *M* produces fertilizer. *M* is aware, or reasonably should be aware, that the fertilizer can be used in conjunction with other materials to make powerful explosives, and has thus far declined to render the fertilizer less volatile by changing its chemical composition. Terrorists use the fertilizer to bomb a building, killing and injuring numerous victims. Superseding cause? *See* Port Authority of NY & NJ v. Arcadian Corp., 189 F.3d 305 (3d Cir. 1999) (applying New York and New Jersey law) (1993 terrorist bombing of World Trade Center constitutes a superseding cause of victims' injuries).

  6. *Can Negligence Count as a Superseding Cause?* We saw in Chapter 4 in connection with the *McDonald* case that two negligent acts

frequently can count as independent but-for causes of a victim's injury. At times, however, courts will treat intervening negligence as sufficiently unforeseeable to amount to a superseding cause. In Roberts v. Benoit, 605 So. 2d 1032 (La. 1991), the plaintiff was accidentally shot by *C*, who was employed as a cook by defendant sheriff's office (*S*). *C* had been deputized by *S* solely to render *C* eligible for supplementary pay. However, in order to be deputized, *C* had to undergo training in the use of firearms, which apparently included "encouragement" that all deputies ought to carry a firearm. While drunk and playing with his gun one evening, *C* shot *P*. Granting that *S* breached a duty owed to the plaintiff by its careless training and encouragement of *C*, the court nonetheless held that *S* was relieved of responsibility because of the "foolhardy" nature of *C*'s conduct.

Consider also Martinez v. Lazaroff, 411 N.Y.S.2d 955 (App. Div. 1978). There, defendant landlord *L* carelessly failed to provide hot water to tenant *T*'s apartment. To provide hot water for bathing, *T* heated water in a pot on the stove, then carried the pot to the bathroom. Along the way, however, he collided with his infant child *C*, causing *C* to suffer burns. The court ruled that *C*'s suit against *L* was barred because *T*'s carelessness constituted a superseding cause. Might this result be explicable (although not necessarily defensible) as an indirect means of ruling that *T*'s fault was substantial and in some sense chargeable to *C* (given that *C* would be left to collect damages from his parents)?

7. *Intervening Malpractice.* Suppose that drunk driver *D* crashes into the car of *P*, and that *P* suffers a broken leg. As emergency medical technicians transport *P* to the hospital, however, they carelessly mistreat the injury. Because of this carelessness, *P*'s leg must be amputated. Does the EMTs' carelessness count as a superseding cause that relieves *D* of responsibility for the amputation? Uniformly, the courts have held that ordinary medical malpractice committed in the course of treating injuries created by the negligence of a defendant is a foreseeable consequence of causing bodily injury to someone, and hence cannot be deemed a superseding cause. Restatement (Third) of Torts: Liability for Physical Harm (General Principles) § 35, at 127 (Tentative Draft No. 3, Apr. 7, 2003). Suppose *P* is taken by the EMTs to the hospital without incident, and treated and released with instructions to return two weeks later for a follow-up examination. When *P* returns for that examination, the examining physician commits malpractice by using unsterilized instruments, causing *P* to suffer a serious infection. Should *D* be on the hook for having been a but-for cause of these harms as well?

Returning to the original hypothetical above, suppose that the EMTs are not careless in treating *P*, but that a second drunk driver, *S*, carelessly crashes into the ambulance, which again necessitates amputation of *P*'s leg. May a jury conclude that *S*'s carelessness constitutes a superseding cause of the damages associated with amputation, such that *D* cannot be held liable for those damages? *Cf.* Coates v. Contl. Vinyl Window Co., 2003 WL 21540440 (Mich. App. 2003) (per curiam) (accident caused by a second drunk driver is a superseding cause). If *S*'s carelessness does constitute a superseding cause, is that because it was unforeseeable? Less foreseeable than medical malpractice?

Finally, suppose a third variation on this scenario, in which one of the EMTs, without warning, has a psychotic episode that causes him to strangle *P* en route to the hospital. Superseding cause as a matter of law?

8. *"Acts of God."* Can a natural event ever operate as a superseding cause? Imagine the following variation on hypothetical c in Note 5, *supra*. *P*'s car breaks down in the middle of a busy intersection because of *D*'s carelessness. Just then, a bolt of lightning strikes a telephone pole that falls onto *P*'s car, injuring *P*. Superseding cause?

9. *An Outmoded Doctrine?* Some commentators maintain that the practical justification for the doctrine of superseding cause has disappeared. Under older negligence law, if the wrongful acts of two or more tortfeasors functioned as but-for causes of a single, indivisible injury, the plaintiff could, under the rule of joint and several liability, recover *all* of his damages from any one of them, even one who was much less culpable and responsible than the other(s).* Given this framework, superseding cause doctrine permitted a kind of rough justice by sparing the minimally culpable party from bearing the entirety of the liability. Now, however, with the advent of comparative fault and the move toward apportioned (rather than joint) liability, a jury is permitted to allocate responsibility among multiple wrongdoers on a percentage basis. See Chapter 8. Thus — the argument concludes — the need for the crude rule of superseding cause has largely been obviated.

In a recent admiralty case, the U.S. Supreme Court pointedly rejected this argument. *See* Exxon Co., U.S.A. v. Sofec, Inc., 517 U.S. 830, 837 (1996). Apart from the rough justice idea just described, what other justifications might there be for the doctrine? Reconsider the following passage from the concurring opinion in *McGuiggan, supra,* Chapter 2, which expressed concern over the adoption of even a limited form of social host liability. Although it is addressed to a different aspect of negligence law, does the opinion help capture a concern underlying superseding cause doctrine?

> A subtle message attaches to the rule of [limited social host] liability [adopted by the majority]. Imposing liability on the host partially excuses the drunken driver from the consequences of his own acts. Instead of placing all of society's opprobrium on the individual who makes the free choice of both drinking too much and then driving, the rule advanced by the court divides that opprobrium and thus defuses it. I suggest that this is not the message that we wish to send to those who make the decision to drink to excess and then drive.

Does this "anti-diffusion" idea likewise provide an argument for sometimes treating intervening wrongful conduct as constituting a superseding cause?

---

* As explained in Chapter 8, in principle, if one to two or more tortfeasors responsible for a plaintiff's injuries is made to pay the entire cost of those injuries because of the rule of joint and several liability, it is open to that tortfeasor to seek "contribution" — partial reimbursement — from the other(s). If, however, the other tortfeasors are judgment-proof or otherwise unavailable, the tortfeasor made to pay the plaintiff's damages will be left to bear that cost alone.

II.   THE PERSISTENT PUZZLE OF *PALSGRAF*

The next opinion is probably the most famous of twentieth-century tort law. As you read it, consider why it might have achieved that status. Consider also how the analyses of Judge Cardozo for the majority, and Judge Andrews in dissent, relate to the preceding materials on proximate cause.

Palsgraf v. Long Island Railroad Co.
162 N.E. 99 (N.Y. 1928)

Cardozo, C.J.   Plaintiff was standing on a platform of defendant's railroad after buying a ticket to go to Rockaway Beach. A train stopped at the station, bound for another place. Two men ran forward to catch it. One of the men reached the platform of the car without mishap, though the train was already moving. The other man, carrying a package, jumped aboard the car, but seemed unsteady as if about to fall. A guard on the car, who had held the door open, reached forward to help him in, and another guard on the platform pushed him from behind. In this act, the package was dislodged, and fell upon the rails. It was a package of small size, about fifteen inches long, and was covered by a newspaper. In fact it contained fireworks, but there was nothing in its appearance to give notice of its contents. The fireworks when they fell exploded. The shock of the explosion threw down some scales at the other end of the platform, many feet away. The scales struck the plaintiff, causing injuries for which she sues.

The conduct of the defendant's guard, if a wrong in its relation to the holder of the package, was not a wrong in its relation to the plaintiff, standing far away. Relatively to her it was not negligence at all. Nothing in the situation gave notice that the falling package had in it the potency of peril to persons thus removed. Negligence is not actionable unless it involves the invasion of a legally protected interest, the violation of a right. "Proof of negligence in the air, so to speak, will not do." Pollock, Torts (11th Ed.), p.455; Martin v. Herzog, 228 N.Y. 164, 170; *cf.* Salmond, Torts (6th Ed.), p.24. "Negligence is the absence of care, according to the circumstances." Willes, J., in Vaughan v. Taff Vale Ry. Co., 5 H. & N. 679, 688; 1 Beven, Negligence (4th Ed.), 7; Paul v. Consol. Fireworks Co., 212 N.Y. 117; Adams v. Bullock, 227 N.Y. 208, 211; Parrott v. Wells-Fargo Co., 15 Wall. [U.S.] 524. The plaintiff as she stood upon the platform of the station might claim to be protected against intentional invasion of her bodily security. Such invasion is not charged. She might claim to be protected against unintentional invasion by conduct involving in the thought of reasonable men an unreasonable hazard that such invasion would ensue. These, from the point of view of the law, were the bounds of her immunity, with perhaps some rare exceptions, survivals for the most part of ancient forms of liability, where conduct is held to be at the peril of the actor. If no hazard was apparent to the eye of ordinary vigilance, an act innocent and harmless, at least to outward seeming, with reference to her, did not take to itself the quality of a tort because it happened to be a wrong, though apparently not one involving the risk of bodily insecurity, with reference to some one else. "In every instance, before negligence can be predicated of a given act, back of the act must be sought and found a duty to the individual complaining, the observance of which would have averted or avoided the injury." McSherry, C.J., in [W. Va.] Central & P. R. Co. v. State, 96 Md. 652, 666. . . . "The ideas of negligence and duty are strictly correlative." (Bowen, L.J., in Thomas v. Quartermaine, 18 Q.B.D. 685, 694. The plaintiff sues in her own right for a wrong personal to her, and not as the vicarious beneficiary of a breach of duty to another.

A different conclusion will involve us, and swiftly too, in a maze of contradictions. A guard stumbles over a package which has been left upon a platform. It seems to be a bundle of newspapers. It turns out to be a can of dynamite. To the eye of ordinary vigilance, the bundle is abandoned waste, which may be kicked or trod on with impunity. Is a passenger at the other end of the platform protected by the law against the unsuspected hazard concealed beneath the waste? If not, is the result to be any different, so far as the distant passenger is concerned, when the guard stumbles over a valise which a truckman or a porter has left upon the walk? The passenger far away, if the victim of a wrong at all, has a cause of action, not derivative, but original and primary. His claim to be protected against invasion of his bodily security is neither greater nor less because the act resulting in the invasion is a wrong to another far removed. In this case, the rights that are said to have been violated, the interests said to have been invaded, are not even of the same order. The man was not injured in his person nor even put in danger. The purpose of the act, as well as its effect, was to make his person safe. If there was a wrong to him at all, which may very well be doubted, it was a wrong to a property interest only, the safety of his package. Out of this wrong to property, which threatened injury to nothing else, there has passed, we are told, to the plaintiff by derivation or succession a right of action for the invasion of an interest of another order, the right to bodily security. The diversity of interests emphasizes the futility of the effort to build the plaintiff's right upon the basis of a wrong to some one else. The gain is one of emphasis, for a like result would follow if the interests were the same. Even then, the orbit of the danger as disclosed to the eye of reasonable vigilance would be the orbit of the duty. One who jostles one's neighbor in a crowd does not invade the rights of others standing at the outer fringe when the unintended contact casts a bomb upon the ground. The wrongdoer as to them is the man who carries the bomb, not the one who explodes it without suspicion of the danger. Life will have to be made over, and human nature transformed, before prevision so extravagant can be accepted as the norm of conduct, the customary standard to which behavior must conform.

The argument for the plaintiff is built upon the shifting meanings of such words as "wrong" and "wrongful," and shares their instability. What the plaintiff must show is "a wrong" to herself, i.e., a violation of her own right, and not merely a wrong to some one else, nor conduct "wrongful" because unsocial, but not "a wrong" to any one. We are told that one who drives at reckless speed through a crowded city street is guilty of a negligent act and therefore of a wrongful one irrespective of the consequences. Negligent the act is, and wrongful in the sense that it is unsocial, but wrongful and unsocial in relation to other travelers, only because the eye of vigilance perceives the risk of damage. If the same act were to be committed on a speedway or a race course, it would lose its wrongful quality. The risk reasonably to be perceived defines the duty to be obeyed, and risk imports relation; it is risk to another or to others within the range of apprehension. This does not mean, of course, that one who launches a destructive force is always relieved of liability if the force, though known to be destructive, pursues an unexpected path. "It was not necessary that the defendant should have had notice of the particular method in which an accident would occur, if the possibility of an accident was clear to the ordinarily prudent eye." Munsey v. Webb, 231 U.S. 150, 156; Condran v. Park & Tilford, 213 N.Y. 341, 345; Robert v. U. S. E. F. [U.S.S.B.E.F.] Corp., 240 N.Y. 474, 477. Some acts, such as shooting are so imminently dangerous to any one who may come within reach of the missile, however unexpectedly, as to impose a duty of prevision not far from that of an insurer. Even today, and much oftener in earlier stages of the law, one acts sometimes at one's peril. Jeremiah Smith, Tort and Absolute Liability, 30 H. L. Rv. 328; Street, Foundations of Legal Liability, vol. 1, pp.77, 78. Under this head, it may be, fall certain cases of what is known as transferred intent, an act willfully dangerous to A resulting by misadventure in injury to B. Talmage v. Smith, 101 Mich. 370, 374. These cases aside, wrong is defined in terms of the natural or probable, at least when unintentional. Parrot v. Wells-Fargo Co. (The Nitro-Glycerine Case), 15 Wall. [U.S.] 524. The range of reasonable apprehension is at times a question for the court, and at times, if varying inferences are possible, a question for the jury. Here, by concession, there was nothing in the situation to suggest to the most cautious mind that the parcel wrapped in newspaper would spread wreckage through the station. If the guard had thrown it down knowingly and willfully, he would not have threatened the plaintiff's safety, so far as appearances could warn him. His conduct would not have involved, even then, an unreasonable probability of invasion of her bodily security. Liability can be no greater where the act is inadvertent.

Negligence, like risk, is thus a term of relation. Negligence in the abstract, apart from things related, is surely not a tort, if indeed it is understandable at all. Bowen, L.J., in Thomas v. Quartermaine, 18 Q.B.D. 685, 694. Negligence is not a tort unless it results in the commission of a wrong, and the commission of a wrong imports the violation of a right, in this case, we are told, the right to be protected against interference with one's bodily security. But bodily security is protected, not against all forms of interference or aggression, but only against some. One who seeks redress at law does not make out a cause of action by showing without more that there has been damage to his person. If the harm was not willful, he must show that the act as to him had possibilities of danger so many and apparent as to entitle him to be protected against the doing of it though the harm was unintended. Affront to personality is still the keynote of the wrong. Confirmation of this view will be found in the history and development of the action on the case. Negligence as a basis of civil liability was unknown to mediaeval law. 8 Holdsworth, History of English Law, p.449; Street, Foundations of Legal Liability, vol. 1, pp.189, 190. For damage to the person, the sole remedy was trespass, and trespass did not lie in the absence of aggression, and that direct and personal. Holdsworth, op. cit. p.453; Street, op. cit. vol. 3, pp.258, 260, vol. 1, pp.71, 74. Liability for other damage, as where a servant without orders from the master does or omits something to the damage of another, is a plant of later growth. Holdsworth, op. cit. 450, 457; Wigmore, Responsibility for Tortious Acts, vol. 3, Essays in Anglo-American Legal History, 520, 523, 526, 533. When it emerged out of the legal soil, it was thought of as a variant of trespass, an offshoot of the parent stock. This appears in the form of action, which was known as trespass on the case. Holdsworth, op. cit. p.449; *cf.* Scott v. Shepard, 2 Wm. Black. 892; Green, Rationale of Proximate Cause, p.19. The victim does not sue derivatively, or by right of subrogation, to vindicate an interest invaded in the person of another. Thus to view his cause of action is to ignore the fundamental difference between tort and crime. Holland, Jurisprudence (12th Ed.), p.328. He sues for breach of a duty owing to himself.

The law of causation, remote or proximate, is thus foreign to the case before us. The question of liability is always anterior to the question of the measure of the consequences that go with liability. If there is no tort to be redressed, there is no occasion to consider what damage might be recovered if there were a finding of a tort. We may assume, without deciding, that negligence, not at large or in the abstract, but in relation to the plaintiff, would entail liability for any and all consequences, however novel or extraordinary. Bird v. St. Paul [F. & M.] Ins. Co., 224 N.Y. 47, 54; Ehrgott v. Mayor, etc., of [N.Y.], 96 N.Y. 264; Smith v. London & S. W. Ry. Co., L. R. 6 C.P. 14; 1 Beven, Negligence, 106; Street, op. cit. vol. 1, p.90; Green, Rationale of Proximate Cause, pp.88, 118; *cf.* Matter of Polemis, L. R. 1921, 3 K. B. 560; 44 Law Quarterly Review, 142. There is room for argument that a distinction is to be drawn according to the diversity of interests invaded by the act, as where conduct negligent in that it threatens an insignificant invasion of an interest in property results in an unforseeable invasion of an interest of another order, as, e.g., one of bodily security. Perhaps other distinctions may be necessary. We do not go into the question now. The consequences to be followed must first be rooted in a wrong.

The judgment of the Appellate Division and that of the Trial Term should be reversed, and the complaint dismissed, with costs in all courts.

Andrews, J. (dissenting). Assisting a passenger to board a train, the defendant's servant negligently knocked a package from his arms. It fell between the platform and the cars. Of its contents the servant knew and could know nothing. A violent explosion followed. The concussion broke some scales standing a considerable distance away. In falling they injured the plaintiff, an intending passenger.

Upon these facts may she recover the damages she has suffered in an action brought against the master? The result we shall reach depends upon our theory as to the nature of negligence. Is it a relative concept — the breach of some duty owing to a particular person or to particular persons? Or where there is an act which unreasonably threatens the safety of others, is the doer liable for all its proximate consequences, even where they result in injury to one who would generally be thought to be outside the radius of danger? This is not a mere dispute as to words. We might not believe that to the average mind the dropping of the bundle would seem to involve the probability of harm to the plaintiff standing many feet away whatever might be the case as to the owner or to one so near as to be likely to be struck by its fall. If, however, we adopt the second hypothesis we have to inquire only as to the relation between cause and effect. We deal in terms of proximate cause, not of negligence.

Negligence may be defined roughly as an act or omission which unreasonably does or may affect the rights of others, or which unreasonably fails to protect oneself from the dangers resulting from such acts. Here I confine myself to the first branch of the definition. Nor do I comment on the word "unreasonable." For present purposes it sufficiently describes that average of conduct that society requires of its members. . . .

But we are told that "there is no negligence unless there is in the particular case a legal duty to take care, and this duty must be one which is owed to the plaintiff himself and not merely to others." Salmond Torts (6th Ed.), 24. This, I think too narrow a conception. Where there is the unreasonable act, and some right that may be affected there is negligence whether damage does or does not result. That is immaterial. Should we drive down Broadway at a reckless speed, we are negligent whether we strike an approaching car or miss it by an inch. The act itself is wrongful. It is a wrong not only to those who happen to be within the radius of danger but to all who might have been there — a wrong to the public at large. Such is the language of the street. Such the language of the courts when speaking of contributory negligence. Such again and again their language in speaking of the duty of some defendant and discussing proximate cause in cases where such a discussion is wholly irrelevant on any other theory. Perry v. Rochester Line Co., 219 N.Y. 60. As was said by Mr. Justice Holmes many years ago, "the measure of the defendant's duty in determining whether a wrong has been committed is one thing, the measure of liability when a wrong has been committed is another." Spade v. Lynn & B. R. Co., 172 Mass. 488. . . . Due care is a duty imposed on each one of us to protect society from unnecessary danger, not to protect A, B or C alone.

It may well be that there is no such thing as negligence in the abstract. "Proof of negligence in the air, so to speak, will not do." In an empty world negligence would not exist. It does involve a relationship between man and his fellows, but not merely a relationship between man and those whom he might reasonably expect his act would injure; rather, a relationship between him and those whom he does in fact injure. If his act has a tendency to harm some one, it harms him a mile away as surely as it does those on the scene. We now permit children to recover for the negligent killing of the father. It was never prevented on the theory that no duty was owing to them. A husband may be compensated for the loss of his wife's services. To say that the wrongdoer was negligent as to the husband as well as to the wife is merely an attempt to fit facts to theory. An insurance company paying a fire loss recovers its payment of the negligent incendiary. We speak of subrogation — of suing in the right of the insured. Behind the cloud of words is the fact they hide, that the act, wrongful as to the insured, has also injured the company. Even if it be true that the fault of father, wife or insured will prevent recovery, it is because we consider the original negligence not the proximate cause of the injury. Pollock, Torts (12th Ed.), 463.

In the well-known *Polemis Case* [1921] 3 K.B. 560, Scrutton, L.J., said that the dropping of a plank was negligent for it might injure "workman or cargo or ship." Because of either possibility the owner of the vessel was to be made good for his loss. The act being wrongful the doer was liable for its proximate results. Criticized and explained as this statement may have been, I think it states the law as it should be and as it is. Smith v. London & S. W. R. Co. R. R. (1870-71) L. R. 6 C.P. 14; Anthony v. Staid, 52 Mass. 290; Wood v. Pa. R. Co., 177 Pa. St. 306; Trashansky v. Hershkovitz, 239 N.Y. 452.

The proposition is this. Every one owes to the world at large the duty of refraining from those acts that may unreasonably threaten the safety of others. Such an act occurs. Not only is he wronged to whom harm might reasonably be expected to result, but he also who is in fact injured, even if he be outside what would generally be thought the danger zone. There needs be duty due the one complaining but this is not a duty to a particular individual because as to him harm might be expected. Harm to some one being the natural result of the act, not only that one alone, but all those in fact injured may complain. We have never, I think, held otherwise. Indeed in the *Di Caprio* case we said that a breach of a general ordinance defining the degree of care to be exercised in one's calling is evidence of negligence as to every one. We did not limit this statement to those who might be expected to be exposed to danger. Unreasonable risk being taken, its consequences are not confined to those who might probably be hurt.

If this be so, we do not have a plaintiff suing by "derivation or succession." Her action is original and primary. Her claim is for a breach of duty to herself — not that she is subrogated to any right of action of the owner of the parcel or of a passenger standing at the scene of the explosion.

The right to recover damages rests on additional considerations. The plaintiff's rights must be injured, and this injury must be caused by the negligence. We build a dam, but are negligent as to its foundations. Breaking, it injures property down stream. We are not liable if all this happened because of some reason other than the insecure foundation. But when injuries do result from our unlawful act we are liable for the consequences. It does not matter that they are unusual, unexpected, unforeseen and unforeseeable. But there is one limitation. The damages must be so connected with the negligence that the latter may be said to be the proximate cause of the former.

These two words have never been given an inclusive definition. What is a cause in a legal sense, still more what is a proximate cause, depend in each case upon many considerations, as does the existence of negligence itself. Any philosophical doctrine of causation does not help us. A boy throws a stone into a pond. The ripples spread. The water level rises. The history of that pond is altered to all eternity. It will be altered by other causes also. Yet it will be forever the resultant of all causes combined. Each one will have an influence. How great only omniscience can say. You may speak of a chain, or if you please, a net. An analogy is of little aid. Each cause brings about future events. Without each the future would not be the same. Each is proximate in the sense it is essential. But that is not what we mean by the word. Nor on the other hand do we mean sole cause. There is no such thing.

Should analogy be thought helpful, however, I prefer that of a stream. The spring, starting on its journey, is joined by tributary after tributary. The river, reaching the ocean, comes from a hundred sources. No man may say whence any drop of water is derived. Yet for a time distinction may be possible. Into the clear creek, brown swamp water flows from the left. Later, from the right comes water stained by its clay bed. The three may remain for a space, sharply divided. But at last, inevitably no trace of separation remains. They are so commingled that all distinction is lost.

As we have said, we cannot trace the effect of an act to the end, if end there is. Again, however, we may trace it part of the way. A murder at Serajevo may be the necessary antecedent to an assassination in London twenty years hence. An overturned lantern may burn all Chicago. We may follow the fire from the shed to the last building. We rightly say the fire started by the lantern caused its destruction.

A cause, but not the proximate cause. What we do mean by the word "proximate" is that, because of convenience, of public policy, of a rough sense of justice, the law arbitrarily declines to trace a series of events beyond a certain point. This is not logic. It is practical politics. Take our rule as to fires. Sparks from my burning haystack set on fire my house and my neighbor's. I may recover from a negligent railroad. He may not. Yet the wrongful act as directly harmed the one as the other. We may regret that the line was drawn just where it was, but drawn somewhere it had to be. We said the act of the railroad was not the proximate cause of our neighbor's fire. Cause it surely was. The words we used were simply indicative of our notions of public policy. Other courts think differently. But somewhere they reach the point where they cannot say the stream comes from any one source.

Take the illustration given in an unpublished manuscript by a distinguished and helpful writer on the law of torts. A chauffeur negligently collides with another car which is filled with dynamite, although he could not know it. An explosion follows. A, walking on the sidewalk nearby, is killed. B, sitting in a window of a building opposite, is cut by flying glass. C, likewise sitting in a window a block away, is similarly injured. And a further illustration. A nursemaid, ten blocks away, startled by the noise, involuntarily drops a baby from her arms to the walk. We are told that C may not recover while A may. As to B it is a question for court or jury. We will all agree that the baby might not. Because, we are again told, the chauffeur had no reason to believe his conduct involved any risk of injuring either C or the baby. As to them he was not negligent.

But the chauffeur, being negligent in risking the collision, his belief that the scope of the harm he might do would be limited is immaterial. His act unreasonably jeopardized the safety of any one who might be affected by it. C's injury and that of the baby were directly traceable to the collision. Without that, the injury would not have happened. C had the right to sit in his office, secure from such dangers. The baby was entitled to use the sidewalk with reasonable safety.

The true theory is, it seems to me, that the injury to C, if in truth he is to be denied recovery, and the injury to the baby is that their several injuries were not the proximate result of the negligence. And here not what the chauffeur had reason to believe would be the result of his conduct, but what the prudent would foresee, may have a bearing — May have some bearing, for the problem of proximate cause is not to be solved by any one consideration. It is all a question of expediency. There are no fixed rules to govern our judgment. There are simply matters of which we may take account. We have in a somewhat different connection spoken of "the stream of events." We have asked whether that stream was deflected — whether it was forced into new and unexpected channels. This is rather rhetoric than law. There is in truth little to guide us other than common sense.

There are some hints that may help us. The proximate cause, involved as it may be with many other causes, must be, at the least, something without which the event would not happen. The court must ask itself whether there was a natural and continuous sequence between cause and effect. Was the one a substantial factor in producing the other? Was there a direct connection between them, without too many intervening causes? Is the effect of cause on result not too attentuated? Is the cause likely, in the usual judgment of mankind, to produce the result? Or by the exercise of prudent foresight could the result be foreseen? Is the result too remote from the cause, and here we consider remoteness in time and space. Bird v. St. Paul & M. Ins. Co., 224 N.Y. 47, where we passed upon the construction of a contract — but something was also said on this subject. . . . Clearly we must so consider, for the greater the distance either in time or space, the more surely do other causes intervene to affect the result. When a lantern is overturned the firing of a shed is a fairly direct consequence. Many things contribute to the spread of the conflagration — the force of the wind, the direction and width of streets, the character of intervening structures, other factors. We draw an uncertain and wavering line, but draw it we must as best we can.

Once again, it is all a question of fair judgment, always keeping in mind the fact that we endeavor to make a rule in each case that will be practical and in keeping with the general understanding of mankind.

Here another question must be answered. In the case supposed it is said, and said correctly, that the chauffeur is liable for the direct effect of the explosion although he had no reason to suppose it would follow a collision. "The fact that the injury occurred in a different manner than that which might have been expected does not prevent the chauffeur's negligence from being in law the cause of the injury." But the natural results of a negligent act — the results which a prudent man would or should foresee — do have a bearing upon the decision as to proximate cause. We have said so repeatedly. What should be foreseen? No human foresight would suggest that a collision itself might injure one a block away. On the contrary, given an explosion, such a possibility might be reasonably expected. I think the direct connection, the foresight of which the courts speak, assumes prevision of the explosion, for the immediate results of which, at least, the chauffeur is responsible.

It may be said this is unjust. Why? In fairness he should make good every injury flowing from his negligence. Not because of tenderness toward him we say he need not answer for all that follows his wrong. We look back to the catastrophe, the fire kindled by the spark, or the explosion. We trace the consequences — not indefinitely, but to a certain point. And to aid us in fixing that point we ask what might ordinarily be expected to follow the fire or the explosion.

This last suggestion is the factor which must determine the case before us. The act upon which defendant's liability rests is knocking an apparently harmless package onto the platform. The act was negligent. For its proximate consequences the defendant is liable. If its contents were broken, to the owner; if it fell upon and crushed a passenger's foot, then to him. If it exploded and injured one in the immediate vicinity, to him also as to A in the illustration. Mrs. Palsgraf was standing some distance away. How far cannot be told from the record — apparently 25 or 30 feet. Perhaps less. Except for the explosion, she would not have been injured. We are told by the appellant in his brief, "It cannot be denied that the explosion was the direct cause of the plaintiff's injuries." So it was a substantial factor in producing the result — there was here a natural and continuous sequence — direct connection. The only intervening cause was that instead of blowing her to the ground the concussion smashed the weighing machine which in turn fell upon her. There was no remoteness in time, little in space. And surely, given such an explosion as here it needed no great foresight to predict that the natural result would be to injure one on the platform at no greater distance from its scene than was the plaintiff. Just how no one might be able to predict. Whether by flying fragments, by broken glass, by wreckage of machines or structures no one could say. But injury in some form was most probable.

Under these circumstances I cannot say as a matter of law that the plaintiff's injuries were not the proximate result of the negligence. That is all we have before us. The court refused to so charge. No request was made to submit the matter to the jury as a question of fact, even would that have been proper upon the record before us.

NOTES AND QUESTIONS

1. *What's the Big Deal?* It seems unlikely that *Palsgraf* significantly affected the liability of railroads for injuries caused to their passengers. Indeed, as compared to a decision such as *MacPherson*, *Palsgraf* seems of little practical import precisely because it deals with an odd sequence of events. What, then, explains its continued notoriety? Can a torts

decision be significant even if it does not immediately change the liability landscape? How?

2. *Cardozo and the ALI.* As a judge, Cardozo bore the reputation of being moralistic to a fault. Perhaps this is why Dean Prosser found it irresistible to report the claim of another scholar that Cardozo had engaged in a minor impropriety in rendering the *Palsgraf* decision. Cardozo was a founding member of the American Law Institute (ALI), the organization of judges, lawyers, and scholars that issues the Restatements. The ALI met to discuss the draft First Restatement of Torts in December of 1927, at which time the intermediate appellate court had just handed down its decision in *Palsgraf.* According to the story circulated by Prosser, even though Cardozo knew he would be asked to rule on the case when it arrived at his court, he attended the ALI meeting and listened intently as members were presented with the facts and debated intensively its proper resolution. Professor Kaufman has since discovered that this story is almost certainly false: Cardozo appears not to have been at the meeting in question.

3. *Cardozo and the Facts of* Palsgraf. Others have criticized Cardozo for being inattentive to, if not creative with, the facts of the case. For example, some have maintained that Mrs. Palsgraf was quite a bit closer to the explosion than Cardozo suggests when he described her as standing "at the other end of the platform, many feet away." Judge Andrews mentions that the record was unclear, but placed her at about 25 to 30 feet from the point where the package was dropped. Suppose Andrews had the distance right and that Cardozo wrongly implied a greater distance. Would that change the outcome under Cardozo's analysis? *See* Palsgraf v. Long Island R.R. Co., 164 N.E. 564 (N.Y. 1928) (denying motion for reargument) ("If we assume that the plaintiff was nearer the scene of the explosion than the prevailing opinion would suggest, she was not so near that injury from a falling package, not known to contain explosives, would be within the range of reasonable prevision.").

In a related vein, Judge Noonan has suggested that Cardozo was insensitive to the plight of a working-class woman such as Mrs. Palsgraf, as evidenced by the court's decision to impose the cost of the appeal on her notwithstanding her poverty and the railroad's wealth. In response, Judge Posner has noted that imposition of costs on the losing party, although discretionary with the court, was the norm, and that Mrs. Palsgraf's attorney made no request to deviate from that norm.

4. Palsgraf *versus* MacPherson. Is there an inconsistency between *MacPherson*'s elimination of the privity rule and *Palsgraf*'s holding? How could Cardozo maintain in the former that a duty was owed irrespective of privity, yet then turn around and say that the railroad did not breach a duty to a customer with whom it had a contract in the form of a train ticket? *MacPherson* was decided 12 years before *Palsgraf.* Do the different outcomes suggest that Cardozo had grown more conservative, or had become more concerned about the floodgates he had opened earlier in his career? Professor White has suggested as much. Professors Goldberg and Zipursky have argued that the opinions are quite consistent.

5. *Empty Rhetoric?* By far the most common criticism of Cardozo's opinion is that it is empty or circular. For example, although Judge Posner is favorably disposed to the result, he describes Cardozo's opinion as "subtle bluff." By this he means that it is rhetorically effective, but does not actually convey any reason for denying Mrs. Palsgraf's claim. In this, Posner follows Prosser, who famously argued that the main lesson of *Palsgraf* is that efforts to employ legal concepts such as duty to resolve difficult questions are hopeless. Proof of this, he claimed, resides in the evident vacuity of Cardozo's duty analysis (as well as Andrews' proximate cause analysis). More recently, Professors Schwartz and Powers, two of the Reporters for the Third Restatement of Torts, have taken up the mantle of Prosser and Posner by contending that Cardozo's opinion consists of smoke and mirrors. No doubt their attitude helps explains why, as Professor Weinrib has observed, one of the primary goals of the Third Restatement's provisions on duty and proximate cause has been to excise *Palsgraf* entirely from the modern law of negligence.

Is Cardozo's opinion mere blather or does it contain an argument from legal principle? Critics of the opinion have made much of the fact that Cardozo's opinion seems to suggest — absurdly — that the railroad owed no duty of care to a paying customer such as Mrs. Palsgraf. Does Cardozo deny that a duty was owed by the railroad to Mrs. Palsgraf? Assuming that he does not, what element did she fail to make out, such that the railroad was entitled to a judgment as a matter of law?

6. *Relational versus Nonrelational Conceptions of Negligence.* English grammar distinguishes between transitive and intransitive verbs. To use transitive verbs correctly, one must specify or imply a direct object that is *being acted upon*. Intransitive verbs, by contrast, do not take a direct object because they do not describe actions that involve acting upon someone or something. The verb "injures" is an example of a transitive verb. Thus, to write the phrase "*X* injured" without stating or implying *whom or what X* has injured is to write a sentence fragment rather than a complete sentence. An example of an intransitive verb is "littered," as used in the sentence "*X* littered."

Obviously, Cardozo and Andrews are not fighting over rules of grammar. Nonetheless, does the distinction between these two types of verbs help capture the meaning of Cardozo's claim that "negligence . . . is a term that imports relation"? Or Andrews' claim that "[d]ue care is a duty imposed on each one of us to protect society from unnecessary danger, not to protect A, B, or C alone"?

7. *Foreseeability, Duty, and Breach.* Recall Rogers v. Retrum, excerpted in Chapter 3. There, the court distinguished the duty inquiry — which in cases of physical harm caused by affirmative acts turns mostly on foreseeability — from the breach inquiry, which turns on the reasonableness of the defendant's conduct. Recall also that duty is ordinarily a question for the judge, whereas breach is for the jury. Cardozo opines that "no hazard [to Mrs. Palsgraf] was apparent to the eye of ordinary vigilance." Later, he states that an injury to Mrs. Palsgraf was, so far as the conductors were concerned, out of the "range of reasonable apprehension." At

another point, he proclaims that "[l]ife will have to be made over, and human nature transformed, before prevision so extravagant can be accepted as the norm of conduct." Are these observations addressed to the issue of duty or breach? If breach, what happened to the idea of deferring to the jury (which, in this case, must have found a breach since it imposed liability on the railroad)?

8. *Rights, Wrongs, and Torts.* Cardozo's opinion reasons that, because "[n]othing in the situation gave notice that the falling package had in it the potency of peril to persons [far] removed," the defendant's conduct was "not a wrong in its relation to" Mrs. Palsgraf. Even if one assumes that Cardozo is correct in saying this, why does it follow that Mrs. Palsgraf should lose? His answer seems at first blush to rely on a principle that restates the problem, rather than solving it: "What the plaintiff must show is 'a wrong' to herself, i.e., a violation of her own right, and not merely a wrong to some one else, nor conduct 'wrongful' because unsocial, but not 'a wrong' to anyone." *Why, then, must a negligence plaintiff show a wrong to herself?* Consider the following passage from the opinion:

> Affront to personality is the keynote of the wrong. . . . The victim does not sue derivatively, or by right of subrogation, to vindicate an interest invaded in the person of another. Thus to view his cause of action is to ignore the fundamental difference between tort and crime. . . . [The plaintiff] sues for breach of a duty owing to himself.

What is Cardozo getting at here? Why does Judge Andrews reject this argument?

Professor Zipursky argues that the "relational" aspect of negligence law identified by Cardozo in *Palsgraf* also features prominently in other torts. For example, he notes that under the common law of fraud, even if *P* suffers a loss because of *D*'s knowing misrepresentation, *P* cannot prevail unless she can show that *she herself actually relied* on the content of misrepresentation. If the misrepresentation was not one on which *P* relied, *D*'s utterance of it is not actionable by *P* because its utterance does not constitute a *defrauding of P*, in the same way that the railroad's carelessness was not *carelessness toward Mrs. Palsgraf*. Likewise, even if *P* foreseeably suffers damage to his reputation by virtue of a defamatory statement made by *D*, *P* cannot recover unless the statement was "of and concerning" *P*—that is, a *libeling or slandering of P*. According to Zipursky, each of these doctrines reflects a basic and distinctive feature of tort law, namely, that it empowers a person or entity (*P*) to complain about another's conduct only if that conduct constitutes a wrong to *P* (or persons similarly situated to *P*), as opposed to a wrong to someone else that happens to injure *P*. He labels this general requirement the rule of "substantive standing."

9. *Andrews' Dissent. Palsgraf* has become part of the torts canon as much for Judge Andrews' dissent as Cardozo's majority opinion. Why does Andrews claim that *Palsgraf* is a case whose outcome turns on proximate cause rather than duty? Does Andrews conceive of proximate cause in a manner consistent with the opinions that we studied in Section I of this

chapter? Is the dispute between him and Cardozo about whether to analyze the case under duty or proximate cause purely verbal, or is it substantive? Andrews and Cardozo locked horns in other important decisions. *See, e.g.,* People v. Westchester County Natl. Bank, 132 N.E. 241 (N.Y. 1921).

10. *Duty versus Proximate Cause.* Cardozo says that the law of proximate cause has no bearing on the resolution of the case. However, he goes on to assume that, if the problem he identifies in Mrs. Palsgraf's claim were somehow overcome, liability would attach for "any and all consequences" flowing from the railroad's negligence, "however novel or extraordinary." Does this mean that Cardozo rejected the foreseeable risk/risk rule conception of proximate cause? Does he offer any authority for doing so? In his biography of Cardozo, Professor Kaufman has produced the record of a fascinating pre-*Palsgraf* interchange among Bohlen, Cardozo, Learned Hand, and others, in which Cardozo appears to reject a scope-of-the-risk conception of proximate cause. According to Professor Powers, New York proximate cause doctrine at the time of *Palsgraf* rejected "scope of the risk" as a limitation on liability. Indeed, Powers concludes that Cardozo invoked the rhetoric of duty as a way of getting to a sound result in *Palsgraf* without overruling existing New York proximate cause doctrine.

Suppose one adopts the modern foreseeable risk/risk rule approach. Would the jury be entitled to conclude that the railroad's breach was a proximate cause of Mrs. Palsgraf's injuries? If not, what additional requirement does *Palsgraf* set beyond the requirement of proximate cause?

11. *Androzo (I).* Although indisputably a canonical case, *Palsgraf* has sometimes been transformed by subsequent courts into a bizarre hybrid that melds certain aspects of the majority opinion — namely, that Mrs. Palsgraf ought not to prevail because harm to her was an unforeseeable consequence of pushing the package-carrying passenger — with certain aspects of the dissent — namely, that the case ought to be resolved by application of proximate cause doctrine. On this view, which has essentially been adopted by the Reporters for the Third Restatement, Cardozo's opinion reaches the right result for the right reason, but misstates the doctrinal "hook" for applying those reasons. Meanwhile, Judge Andrews is understood to have properly framed the question of the case as one of proximate cause, but then reached the wrong result by misunderstanding proximate cause to turn on a blunderbuss inquiry concerning expedience (instead of the narrower scope-of-the-risk question). As Professor Zipursky has noted, "[T]his is an odd way to read any case, especially a central case of our torts canon. . . . [N]either of the famous opinions in the case agrees with — or even presents — the argument most commonly attributed to it."

12. *Androzo (II).* Influential courts — including the California Supreme Court and later iterations of the New York Court of Appeals — have proceeded to meld Cardozo's and Andrew's *Palsgraf* opinions in a different way. According to them, Andrews was correct to conclude that the question of liability in odd cases such as *Palsgraf* cannot be resolved by employing a subtle understanding of how the elements of negligence

align with one another. Instead, they require an "all things considered" assessment as to whether "expedience" or "policy" suggests that the defendant ought to be let off the hook notwithstanding that its carelessness helped to cause plaintiff's injury. Yet, while these courts agree with Andrews as to the nature of the question being asked, they also "agree" with Cardozo to the following (limited) extent: The question of expedience ought to be asked under the heading of duty rather than proximate cause. Thus, prominent decisions such as Rowland v. Christian and Strauss v. Belle Realty each ask roughly the same question that Judge Andrews asked in *Palsgraf*. Yet each does so under the heading of duty rather than proximate cause. While the choice of label for this policy inquiry may seem trivial, notice the important procedural effect of this shift. What Andrews conceived as primarily a mixed question of law and fact for the jury has been converted by these courts into a question of law for the courts.

13. Palsgraf *versus* Wagner. Seven years prior to *Palsgraf*, Cardozo authored the court's opinion in Wagner v. International Railway Co., 133 N.E. 437 (N.Y. 1921). Defendant operated an electric tram. In order to proceed over the tracks of another railway, the tram proceeded up a graded ramp that rose to a height of 25 feet, then took a sharp left turn as the ramp segued into a bridge that spanned the other railway's tracks. The bridge itself had a railing, but the ramp leading to the bridge did not. At the point of the sharp left turn, one side of the tram cars extended out over the edge of the ramp.

Plaintiff Arthur Wagner and his cousin Herbert were standing in the doorway of a crowded tram car. The car had doors, but the tram's conductor did not close them. As the tram was navigating the left turn at about 7 mph, "there was a violent lurch," and Herbert was thrown out near the point where the ramp joined the bridge. The tram went on across the bridge, then stopped. By this time, the sun had set. Several other passengers went to look beneath the bridge to see if Herbert was in need of assistance. Arthur, however, walked back along the track, a distance of 400 feet, until he arrived at the bridge. "Reaching the bridge, he had found upon a beam his cousin's hat, but nothing else. About him, there was darkness. He missed his footing, and fell."

The trial court held that Arthur could not recover for injuries from his fall *unless* the jury found that the conductor had *invited* him to go upon the bridge, thus actively endangering him. The jury found in favor of the defendant. The Court of Appeals held this instruction in error, and ordered a new trial. According to Cardozo, the defendant could be held liable even if its conductor had not explicitly invited the plaintiff to participate in a dangerous rescue attempt:

> Danger invites rescue. The cry of distress is the summons to relief. The law does not ignore these reactions of the mind in tracing conduct to its consequences. It recognizes them as normal. It places their effects within the range of the natural and probable. The wrong that imperils life is a wrong to the imperilled victim; it is a wrong also to his rescuer. . . . The state that leaves an opening in a bridge is liable to the child that falls into the stream, but liable

also to the parent who plunges to its aid. The railroad company whose train approaches without signal is a wrongdoer toward the traveler surprised between the rails, but a wrongdoer also to the bystander who drags him from the path. . . . The risk of rescue, if only it be not wanton, is born of the occasion. The emergency begets the man. The wrongdoer may not have foreseen the coming of a deliverer. He is accountable as if he had. . . .

Cardozo assumed for purposes of decision that the doctrine of danger-invites-rescue applies to any rescue effort that, like Arthur's, is carried out both reasonably and contemporaneously with the carelessly created peril. He left it to the jury on remand to determine whether Arthur was barred from suing under the doctrine of contributory negligence.

If Arthur was entitled to sue for the railroad's wrong to Herbert, why did Cardozo later hold that Mrs. Palsgraf was not entitled to sue for a railroad's wrong to another? What distinguishes the two cases? (Might it help here to recall the special duty principles discussed in Chapter 2, such as attractive nuisance doctrine, as well as the rule that one is obligated to make efforts to rescue persons whom one has imperiled?) In keeping with its hostility to *Palsgraf* and duty analysis generally, the draft Third Restatement has recast *Wagner*'s rescuer doctrine as a special rule of proximate cause. *See* Restatement (Third) of Torts: Liability for Physical Harm (General Principles) § 32, at 81 (Tentative Draft No. 3, Apr. 7, 2003).

III.   PROXIMATE CAUSE AND *PALSGRAF* REVISITED

Ryan v. New York Cent. R. R. Co.
35 N.Y. 210 (1866)

On the 15th day of July, 1854, in the city of Syracuse, the defendant, by the careless management, or through the insufficient condition, of one of its engines, set fire to its wood-shed, and a large quantity of wood therein. The plaintiff's house, situated at a distance of one hundred and thirty feet from the shed, soon took fire from the heat and sparks, and was entirely consumed, notwithstanding diligent efforts were made to save it. A number of other houses were also burned by the spreading of the fire. [The plaintiff sued the railroad company to recover the value of his building thus destroyed. The trial judge entered judgment for the defendant and the intermediate appellate court affirmed. — EDS.]

Hunt, J.   The question may be thus stated: A house in a populous city takes fire, through the negligence of the owner or his servant; the flames extend to and destroy an adjacent building: Is the owner of the first building liable to the second owner for the damage sustained by such burning?

It is a general principle that every person is liable for the consequences of his own acts. He is thus liable in damages for the proximate results of his own acts, but not for remote damages. It is not easy at all times to determine what are proximate and what are remote damages.

In Thomas v. Winchester 6 N.Y. [397], Judge Ruggles defines the damages for which a party is liable, as those which are the natural or necessary consequences of his acts. Thus, the owner of a loaded gun, who puts it in the hands of a child, by whose indiscretion it is discharged, is liable for the injury sustained by a third person from such discharge. The injury is a natural and ordinary result of the folly of placing a loaded gun in the hands of one ignorant of the manner of using it, and incapable of appreciating its effects. The owner of a horse and cart, who leaves them unattended in the street, is liable for an injury done to a person or his property, by the running away of the horse, for the same reason. The injury is the natural result of the negligence. . . . So if an engineer upon a steamboat or locomotive, in passing the house of A., so carelessly manages its machinery that the coals and sparks from its fires fall upon and consume the house of A., the railroad company or the steamboat proprietors are liable to pay the value of the property thus destroyed.

Thus far the law is settled and the principle is apparent. If, however, the fire communicates from the house of A. to that of B., and that is destroyed, is the negligent party liable for his loss? And if it spreads thence to the house of C., and thence to the house of D., and thence consecutively through the other houses, until it reaches and consumes the house of Z., is the party liable to pay the damages sustained by these twenty-four sufferers? The counsel for the plaintiff does not distinctly claim this, and I think it would not be seriously insisted that the sufferers could recover in such case. Where, then, is the principle upon which A. recovers and Z. fails?

It has been suggested that an important element exists in the difference between an intentional firing and a negligent firing merely; that when a party designedly fires his own house or his own fallow land, not intending, however, to do any injury to his neighbor, but a damage actually results, that he may be liable for more extended damages than where the fire originated in accident or negligence. It is true that the most of the cases where the liability was held to exist, were cases of an intentional firing. The case, however, of Vaughan v. Menlove (3 Bing. N.C. 468) was that of a spontaneous combustion of a hay-rick. The rick was burned, the owner's buildings were destroyed, and thence the fire spread to the plaintiff's cottage, which was also consumed; the defendant was held liable.

Without deciding upon the importance of this distinction, I prefer to place my opinion upon the ground that, in the one case, to wit, the destruction of the building upon which the sparks were thrown by the negligent act of the party sought to be charged, the result was to have been anticipated the moment the fire was communicated to the building; that its destruction was the ordinary and natural result of its being fired. In the second, third or twenty-fourth case, as supposed, the destruction of the building was not a natural and expected result of the first firing. That a building upon which sparks and cinders fall should be destroyed or seriously injured must be expected, but that the fire should spread and other buildings be consumed, is not a necessary or an usual result. That it is possible, and that it is not unfrequent, cannot be denied. The result, however, depends, not upon any necessity of a further communication of the fire, but upon a concurrence of accidental circumstances, such as the degree of the heat, the state of the atmosphere, the condition and materials of the adjoining structures and the direction of the wind. These are accidental and varying circumstances. The party has no control over them, and is not responsible for their effects.

My opinion, therefore, is, that this action cannot be sustained, for the reason that the damages incurred are not the immediate but the remote result of the negligence of the defendants. The immediate result was the destruction of their own wood and sheds; beyond that, it was remote. . . .

That the defendant is not liable in this action may also be strongly argued, from the circumstance that no such action as the present has ever been sustained in any of the courts of this country, although the occasion for it has been frequent and pressing. Particular instances are familiar to all, where such claims might have been made with propriety. The instance of the Harpers, occurring a few years since, is a striking one. Their large printing establishment, in the city of New York, was destroyed by the gross carelessness of a workman, in throwing a lighted match into a vat of camphene. The fire extended, and other buildings and much other property was destroyed. The Harpers were gentlemen of wealth, and able to respond in damages to the extent of their liability. Yet we have no report in the books, and no tradition, of any action brought against them to recover such damages. The novelty of the claim, as was said by Judge Beardsley, in Costigan v. M. & H. R. R. Co., where the occasion for its being made had been so common, is a strong argument against its validity. . . .

To sustain such a claim as the present, and to follow the same to its legitimate consequences, would subject to a liability against which no prudence could guard, and to meet which no private fortune would be adequate. Nearly all fires are caused by negligence, in its extended sense. In a country where wood, coal, gas and oils are universally used, where men are crowded into cities and villages, where servants are employed, and where children find their home in all houses, it is impossible that the most vigilant prudence should guard against the occurrence of accidental or negligent fires. A man may insure his own house or his own furniture, but he cannot insure his neighbor's building or furniture, for the reason that he has no interest in them. To hold that the owner must not only meet his own loss by fire, but that he must guarantee the security of his neighbors on both sides, and to an unlimited extent, would be to create a liability which would be the destruction of all civilized society. No community could long exist, under the operation of such a principle. In a commercial country, each man, to some extent, runs the hazard of his neighbor's conduct, and each, by insurance against such hazards, is enabled to obtain a reasonable security against loss. To neglect such precaution, and to call upon his neighbor, on whose premises a fire originated, to indemnify him instead, would be to award a punishment quite beyond the offense committed. It is to be considered, also, that if the negligent party is liable to the owner of a remote building thus consumed, he would also be liable to the insurance companies who should pay losses to such remote owners. The principle of subrogation would entitle the companies to the benefit of every claim held by the party to whom a loss should be paid. . . .

The remoteness of the damage, in my judgment, forms the true rule on which the question should be decided, and which prohibits a recovery by the plaintiff in this case.

NOTES AND QUESTIONS

1. *Unnatural and Improbable?* Under *Ryan*'s analysis, the defendant's carelessness was a proximate cause only of the fire damage to its own shed because the shed was the only structure that was contacted by flames or heat emanating from the burning engine itself. By contrast, because the fire had to make a second leap to get to the plaintiff's house, the carelessly caused fire was deemed a "remote" cause of the damage to that structure. What might justify this 'first leap' account of proximity? The court insists that the causal relation between carelessness and injury must be "natural and probable" for liability to attach, and that the firing of the plaintiff's house was not a natural and probable consequence of the carelessly started fire. Do you suppose the court really means what it says? How can it, given its acknowledgment that the spread of fire in the manner of this case is "not infrequent." Recall Vaughan v. Menlove from Chapter 3. Is *Ryan*'s implicit suggestion that Vaughan should not have been able to recover from Menlove unless he could show that sparks jumped directly from Menlove's carelessly constructed hayrick to Vaughan's cottages?

2. *Fairness?* Assume that the spread of the fire to Ryan's property was not so improbable as to be unnatural. Is there anything else to support the court's apparent sense that it would be unfair to hold the defendant liable? The court notes that the spread of fire is to a considerable extent determined by factors outside the defendant's control. Isn't that also true with regard to whether the sparks from the engine will ignite the shed in the first place? Have other decisions that we have read limited liability to those injuries caused by carelessness that arose in circumstances of which the defendant was largely in control?

3. *Criticism of* Ryan. *Ryan*'s reasoning was almost immediately criticized by the Massachusetts Supreme Court. Perley v. Eastern R. Co., 98 Mass. 414 (1868). A number of other states rejected it. In 1872, the New York Court of Appeals itself revisited the issue of liability for "remote" fire damage. Webb v. Rome, W. & O. R.R. Co., 49 N.Y. 420 (1872). In *Webb*, the causal sequence ran as follows. The defendant railroad carelessly permitted fired coals to fall onto its track. Once there, the coals ignited a railroad tie. The fire then was communicated to an old tie lying perpendicular to the track, then to accumulated cut grass and weeds at the far end of the old tie, then to a fence owned by the defendant, and finally to the plaintiff's property. *Webb* affirmed recovery for the property owner and purported to distinguish *Ryan* on its facts. Specifically, it held that, under the dry and windy circumstances of the particular day, the transmission of fire to the plaintiff's property was an "an ordinary, a usual, a necessary

result." In the process, the court pointedly rejected defendant's attempt to invoke *Ryan*'s 'first leap' rule:

> The defendant asks in effect that this court hold that it is not liable for the damage to the plaintiff, unless it appears that the coals which escaped from the engine were cast from the engine directly upon the property of the plaintiff which was injured. If the air had been the medium through which was conveyed the same fire which left the engine, it seems to be conceded that the damage was the immediate and natural result of the negligence. I am unable to perceive a reasonable distinction between the air as the medium of conveying the fire, and the denser matter which had accumulated upon the ground there. Nor am I able to confine the act of negligence to the dropping of the coal from the engine, and thus separating it from all the other concurring acts and omissions of the defendant, make that the solitary prime cause of a series of causes. If this were so, it might as well be said that of a hundred growing trees burned by a fire kindled among them by a cinder thrown from a locomotive, the sufferer could recover for only the one upon which the cinder fell, and that as the others took fire from the flame of that, it was not the negligent act which caused their destruction.

4. *From* Ryan *to* Hoffman *and* Homac. That *Webb* amounted to a de facto overruling of *Ryan*'s first-leap rule was recognized in a dissenting opinion in Hoffman v. King, 55 N.E. 401, 404-405 (N.Y. 1899) (Vann, J., dissenting), and acknowledged by the full Court in 1932. *See* Homac Corp. v. Sun Oil Co., 180 N.E. 172, 173 (N.Y. 1932). This is not to say, however, that the court's subsequent decisions permitted *Ryan*'s imagined homeowner "Z" to recover for negligently caused fire damage. Instead, under *Hoffman* and *Homac*, a defendant is liable in negligence for transmitting fire to a plaintiff's property by sparks, or by the ignition of materials in its ownership or control, but *not* for damage caused when the fire spreads to the plaintiff's property by first igniting an intervening property owned by a third party. Here is the court's argument for the new rule just described:

> It is contended that liability ought not to be thus limited; that a fire once set may run across the lines of an abutting owner and upon lands of other proprietors, causing damage. It must be conceded that such a result often happens. It did in the case we have under consideration. But where is the line to be drawn? Shall it be 1 mile, 2 miles, or 10 miles distant from the place of the original starting of the fire? Who is to specify the distance? . . . While we appreciate the force of the argument in favor of extending the rule of liability, and recognize the fact that a limitation of the rule will deprive many persons of a right of action for damages, we are convinced that the old rule is wiser and more just, and that we ought not to depart from it. The limitation may be somewhat arbitrary, but it recognizes the principle that we should live and let live. Fires often occur from the trivial acts of most prudent persons. Great conflagrations are daily reported. Not long since one of our largest cities substantially disappeared within a single day. No person, however cautious, is exempt. Misfortune may overtake him in a forgetful moment, or through fault in the members of his family or servants. No man is able to answer for all the remote consequences of his acts and those for whom he is responsible. Hence, the wisdom of the rule of proximate cause. . . . The fire set by the defendant did not immediately precede

the fire upon the plaintiff's land. Other lands intervened, covered with inflammable material, over which the defendant had no control, and without which the fire could not have extended upon plaintiff's premises. The drought, atmosphere, and wind were the principal agents assisting the fire in its work of destruction, and were the intervening causes of the damage.

Hoffman, 55 N.E., at 403.

Hoffman and *Homac* appear still to state the rule in New York law. Probably the majority of courts, however, permit liability to attach for any carelessly caused fire damage that a reasonable jury might deem to have been foreseeable under the circumstances in which the defendant was acting. *See, e.g.*, Silver Falls Timber Co. v. Eastern & W. Lumber Co., 40 P.2d 703, 730 (Or. 1935); Hardy v. Hines Bros. Lumber Co., 75 S.E. 855 (N.C. 1912).

5. *A Bow to Expedience?* Suppose that the New York rule ceased at some point to rest on *Ryan*'s conceptual confusions and instead became a matter of conscious choice. What is the basis for it? Is fire damage to properties not adjacent to a defendant's property unforeseeable? Is it not the sort of harm that warrants the taking of precautions against its spread in the first place? Is there a *Palsgraf* problem in a case like *Homac?* If not, then what is the justification? *See* Arnhold v. United States, 284 F.2d 326, 329 (9th Cir. 1960) (describing New York decisions on liability for fire damage as employing "the doctrine of 'proximate cause' somewhat arbitrarily to cut off a liability that would otherwise rest upon a negligent actor").

Petitions of the Kinsman Transit Co.
338 F.2d 708 (2d Cir. 1964)

Friendly, J. We have here six appeals from an interlocutory decree in admiralty adjudicating liability. The litigation, in the District Court for the Western District of New York, arose out of a series of misadventures on a navigable portion of the Buffalo River during the night of January 21, 1959. The owners of two vessels petitioned for exoneration from or limitation of liability; numerous claimants appeared in these proceedings and also filed libels against the Continental Grain Company and the City of Buffalo, which filed cross-claims. The proceedings were consolidated for trial before Judge Burke. We shall summarize the facts as found by him:

The Buffalo River flows through Buffalo from east to west, with many turns and bends, until it empties into Lake Erie. Its navigable western portion is lined with docks, grain elevators, and industrial installations; during the winter, lake vessels tie up there pending resumption of navigation on the Great Lakes, without power and with only a shipkeeper aboard. About a mile from the mouth, the City of Buffalo maintains a lift bridge at Michigan Avenue. Thaws and rain frequently cause freshets to develop in the upper part of the river and its tributary, Cazenovia Creek;

currents then range up to fifteen miles an hour and propel broken ice down the river, which sometimes overflows its banks.

On January 21, 1959, rain and thaw followed a period of freezing weather. The United States Weather Bureau issued appropriate warnings which were published and broadcast. Around 6 P.M. an ice jam that had formed in Cazenovia Creek disintegrated. Another ice jam formed just west of the junction of the creek and the river; it broke loose around 9 P.M.

The *MacGilvray Shiras*, owned by The Kinsman Transit Company, was moored at the dock of the Concrete Elevator, operated by Continental Grain Company, on the south side of the river about three miles upstream of the Michigan Avenue Bridge. She was loaded with grain owned by Continental. The berth, east of the main portion of the dock, was exposed in the sense that about 150' of the *Shiras*' forward end, pointing upstream, and 70' of her stern — a total of over half her length — projected beyond the dock. This left between her stem and the bank a space of water seventy-five feet wide where the ice and other debris could float in and accumulate. The position was the more hazardous in that the berth was just below a bend in the river, and the *Shiras* was on the inner bank. None of her anchors had been put out. From about 10 P.M. large chunks of ice and debris began to pile up between the *Shiras*' starboard bow and the bank; the pressure exerted by this mass on her starboard bow was augmented by the force of the current and of floating ice against her port quarter. The mooring lines began to part, and a 'deadman,' to which the No. 1 mooring cable had been attached, pulled out of the ground — the judge finding that it had not been properly constructed or inspected. About 10:40 P.M. the stern lines parted, and the *Shiras* drifted into the current. During the previous forty minutes, the shipkeeper took no action to ready the anchors by releasing the devil's claws; when he sought to drop them after the *Shiras* broke loose, he released the compressors with the claws still hooked in the chain so that the anchors jammed and could no longer be dropped. The trial judge reasonably found that if the anchors had dropped at that time, the *Shiras* would probably have fetched up at the hairpin bend just below the Concrete Elevator, and that in any case they would considerably have slowed her progress, the significance of which will shortly appear.

Careening stern first down the S-shaped river, the *Shiras*, at about 11 P.M., struck the bow of the *Michael K. Tewksbury*, owned by Midland Steamship Line, Inc. The *Tewksbury* was moored in a relatively protected area flush against the face of a dock on the outer bank just below a hairpin bend so that no opportunity was afforded for ice to build up between her port bow and the dock. Her shipkeeper had left around 5 P.M. and spent the evening watching television with a girl friend and her family. The collision caused the *Tewksbury*'s mooring lines to part; she too drifted stern first down the river, followed by the *Shiras*. The collision caused damage to the Steamer *Druckenmiller* which was moored opposite the *Tewksbury*.

Thus far there was no substantial conflict in the testimony; as to what followed there was. Judge Burke found, and we accept his findings as soundly based, that at about 10:43 P.M., Goetz, the superintendent of the Concrete Elevator, telephoned Kruptavich, another employee of

Continental, that the *Shiras* was adrift; Kruptavich called the Coast Guard, which called the city fire station on the river, which in turn warned the crew on the Michigan Avenue Bridge, this last call being made about 10:48 P.M. Not quite twenty minutes later the watchman at the elevator where the *Tewksbury* had been moored phoned the bridge crew to raise the bridge. Although not more than two minutes and ten seconds were needed to elevate the bridge to full height after traffic was stopped, assuming that the motor started promptly, the bridge was just being raised when, at 11:17 P.M., the *Tewksbury* crashed into its center. The bridge crew consisted of an operator and two tenders; a change of shift was scheduled for 11 P.M. The inference is rather strong, despite contrary testimony, that the operator on the earlier shift had not yet returned from a tavern when the telephone call from the fire station was received; that the operator on the second shift did not arrive until shortly before the call from the elevator where the *Tewksbury* had been moored; and that in consequence the bridge was not raised until too late.

The first crash was followed by a second, when the south tower of the bridge fell. The *Tewksbury* grounded and stopped in the wreckage with her forward end resting against the stern of the Steamer Farr, which was moored on the south side of the river just above the bridge. The *Shiras* ended her journey with her stern against the *Tewksbury* and her bow against the north side of the river. So wedged, the two vessels substantially dammed the flow, causing water and ice to back up and flood installations on the banks with consequent damage as far as the Concrete Elevator, nearly three miles upstream. Two of the bridge crew suffered injuries. Later the north tower of the bridge collapsed, damaging adjacent property.

Judge Burke concluded that Continental and the *Shiras* had committed various faults discussed below; . . . that the *Tewksbury* and her owner were entitled to exoneration; and that the City of Buffalo was at fault for failing to raise the Michigan Avenue Bridge. The City was not faulted for the manner in which it had constructed and maintained flood improvements on the river and on Cazenovia Creek, or for failing to dynamite the ice jams. For the damages sustained by the *Tewksbury* and the *Druckenmiller* in the collisions at the Standard Elevator dock, Judge Burke allowed those vessels to recover equally from Continental and from Kinsman. . . . He held the City, Continental and Kinsman equally liable jointly and severally . . . for damages to persons and property sustained by all others as a result of the disaster at the bridge. . . .

The mooring of the *Shiras*, as to which more will be said under the next heading, was the joint work of Kinsman, acting through Captain Davies, her former master, and of Continental. The judge was justified in holding that, with her bow protruding into the river just below a bend and with the eroded bank incapable of taking a long lead line or an anchor chain, the *Shiras* ought to have put out an anchor from her port bow. He was also warranted in finding that Continental was at fault for the inadequately secured "deadman" and the *Shiras* for the shipkeeper's failure to ready the anchors in the interval between 10 P.M. and 10:40 P.M. on January 21. The current and ice conditions on the fateful evening were not so unexpectable as to go beyond the range of foreseeability and hence to come within the principle of inevitable accident; the conditions were of the very sort that had been occurring for years, although not in quite the same degree. . . .

I.   THE CITY'S FAILURE TO RAISE THE BRIDGE

If this were a run of the mine negligence case, the City's argument against liability for not promptly raising the Michigan Avenue Bridge would be impressive: All the vessels moored in the harbor were known to be without power and incapable of controlled movement save with the aid of tugs. The tugs had quit at 4 P.M.; they were not docked in the river, and would not undertake after quitting time to tow a vessel into or out of the inner harbor. Since the breaking loose of a ship was not to be anticipated, it would have been consistent with prudence for the City to relieve the bridge crews of their duties. Neglect by the crews ought not subject the City to liability merely because, out of abundance of caution, it had ordered them to be present when prudence did not so require. . . . [Judge Friendly nonetheless concluded that the conduct of the bridge crew violated applicable federal statutory and regulatory law, and therefore was negligent per se. — EDS.]

II.   THE TIME RELATION OF THE CITY'S FAILURE TO THE PRIOR FAULTS OF THE *SHIRAS* AND CONTINENTAL

. . . Kinsman and Continental contend that the City's failure insulates them from liability for damages to others resulting from the collision at the bridge. . . .

We speedily [reject this contention]. Save for exceptions which are not here pertinent, an actor whose negligence has set a dangerous force in motion is not saved from liability for harm it has caused to innocent persons solely because another has negligently failed to take action that would have avoided this. . . . The contrary argument grows out of the discredited notion that only the last wrongful act can be a cause — a notion as faulty in logic as it is wanting in fairness. The established principle is especially appealing in admiralty which will divide the damages among the negligent actors or non-actors. . . .

III.   THE ALLEGEDLY UNEXPECTABLE CHARACTER OF THE EVENTS LEADING TO MUCH OF THE DAMAGE

The very statement of the case suggests the need for considering Palsgraf v. Long Island R.R., 248 N.Y. 339, 162 N.E. 99, 59 A.L.R. 1253 (1928), and the closely related problem of liability for unforeseeable consequences.

In Sinram v. Pennsylvania R.R., 61 F.2d 767, 770 (2d Cir. 1932), which received *Palsgraf* into the admiralty, Judge Learned Hand characterized the issue in that case as "whether, if A. omitted to perform a positive duty to B., C., who had been damaged in consequence, might invoke the breach, though otherwise A. owed him no duty; in short, whether A. was chargeable for the results to others of his breach of duty to B." Thus stated, the query rather answers itself; Hohfeld's analysis tells us that once it is concluded that A. had no duty to C., it is simply a correlative that C. has no right against A. The important question is what was the basis for Chief Judge Cardozo's conclusion that the Long Island Railroad owed no "duty" to Mrs. Palsgraf under the circumstances.

Certainly there is no general principle that a railroad owes no duty to persons on station platforms not in immediate proximity to the tracks, as would have been quickly demonstrated if Mrs. Palsgraf had been injured by the fall of improperly loaded objects from a passing train. Neither is there any principle that railroad guards who jostle a package-carrying passenger owe a duty only to him; if the package had contained bottles, the Long Island would surely have been liable for injury caused to close bystanders by flying glass or spurting liquid. The reason why the Long Island was thought to owe no duty to Mrs. Palsgraf was the lack of any notice that the package contained a substance demanding the exercise of any care toward anyone so far away; Mrs. Palsgraf was not considered to be within the area of apparent hazard created by whatever lack of care the guard had displayed to the anonymous carrier of the unknown fireworks.[5] The key sentences in Chief Judge Cardozo's opinion are these:

> "Here, by concession, there was nothing in the situation to suggest to the most cautious mind that the parcel wrapped in newspaper would spread wreckage through the station. If the guard had thrown it down knowingly and willfully, he would not have threatened the plaintiff's safety, so far as appearances could warn him. Liability can be no greater where the act is inadvertent." 248 N.Y. at 345, 162 N.E. at 101.

We see little similarity between the *Palsgraf* case and the situation before us. The point of *Palsgraf* was that the appearance of the newspaper-wrapped package gave no notice that its dislodgement could do any harm save to itself and those nearby, and this by impact, perhaps with consequent breakage, and not by explosion. In contrast, a ship insecurely moored in a fast flowing river is a known danger not only to herself but to the owners of all other ships and structures down-river, and to persons upon them. No one would dream of saying that a shipowner who "knowingly and willfully" failed to secure his ship at a pier on such a river "would not have threatened" persons and owners of property downstream in some manner.[6] The shipowner and the wharfinger in this case having thus

---

5. There was exceedingly little evidence of negligence of any sort. The only lack of care suggested by the majority in the Appellate Division was that instead of endeavoring to assist the passenger, the guards "might better have discouraged and warned him not to board the moving train." 222 App. Div. 166, 167, 225 N.Y.S. 412, 413 (2d Dept. 1927). . . .

How much ink would have been saved over the years if the Court of Appeals had reversed Mrs. Palsgraf's judgment on the basis that there was no evidence of negligence at all.

6. The facts here do not oblige us to decide whether the *Shiras* and Continental could successfully invoke *Palsgraf* against claims of owners of shore-side property upstream from the Concrete Elevator or of non-riparian property other than the real and personal property which was sufficiently close to the bridge to have been damaged by the fall of the towers.

owed a duty of care to all within the reach of the ship's known destructive power, the impossibility of advance identification of the particular person who would be hurt is without legal consequence. Similarly the foreseeable consequences of the City's failure to raise the bridge were not limited to the *Shiras* and the *Tewksbury*. Collision plainly created a danger that the bridge towers might fall onto adjoining property, and the crash of two uncontrolled lake vessels, one 425 feet and the other 525 feet long, into a bridge over a swift ice-ridden stream, with a channel only 177 feet wide, could well result in a partial damming that would flood property upstream. As to the City also, it is useful to consider, by way of contrast, Chief Judge Cardozo's statement that the Long Island would not have been liable to Mrs. Palsgraf had the guard wilfully thrown the package down. If the City had deliberately kept the bridge closed in the face of the onrushing vessels, taking the risk that they might not come so far, no one would give house-room to a claim that it "owed no duty" to those who later suffered from the flooding. Unlike Mrs. Palsgraf, they were within the area of hazard. . . .

Since all the claimants here met the *Palsgraf* requirement of being persons to whom the actors owed a "duty of care," we are not obliged to reconsider whether that case furnishes as useful a standard for determining the boundaries of liability in admiralty for negligent conduct as was thought in *Sinram*, when *Palsgraf* was still in its infancy. But this does not dispose of the alternative argument that the manner in which several of the claimants were harmed, particularly by flood damage, was unforeseeable and that recovery for this may not be had — whether the argument is put in the forthright form that unforeseeable damages are not recoverable or is concealed under a formula of lack of "proximate cause."[8]

So far as concerns the City, the argument lacks factual support. Although the obvious risks from not raising the bridge were damage to itself and to the vessels, the danger of a fall of the bridge and of flooding would not have been unforeseeable under the circumstances to anyone who gave them thought. And the same can be said as to the failure of Kinsman's shipkeeper to ready the anchors after the danger had become apparent. The exhibits indicate that the width of the channel between the Concrete Elevator and the bridge is at most points less than two hundred fifty feet. If the *Shiras* caught up on a dock or vessel moored along the shore, the current might well swing her bow across the channel so as to block the ice floes, as indeed could easily have occurred at the Standard Elevator dock where the stern of the *Shiras* struck the *Tewksbury*'s bow. At this point the channel scarcely exceeds two hundred feet, and this was further narrowed by the presence of the *Druckenmiller* moored on the opposite bank. Had the *Tewksbury*'s mooring held, it is thus by no means unlikely that these three ships would have dammed the river. Nor was it

---

8. It is worth underscoring that the ratio decidendi in *Palsgraf* was that the Long Island was not required to use any care with respect to the package vis-a-vis Mrs. Palsgraf; Chief Judge Cardozo did not reach the issue of "proximate cause" for which the case is often cited.

unforeseeable that the drawbridge would not be raised since, apart from any other reason, there was no assurance of timely warning. What may have been less foreseeable was that the *Shiras* would get that far down the twisting river, but this is somewhat negated both by the known speed of the current when freshets developed and by the evidence that, on learning of the *Shiras*' departure, Continental's employees and those they informed foresaw precisely that.

Continental's position on the facts is stronger. It was indeed foreseeable that the improper construction and lack of inspection of the "deadman" might cause a ship to break loose and damage persons and property on or near the river — that was what made Continental's conduct negligent. With the aid of hindsight one can also say that a prudent man, carefully pondering the problem, would have realized that the danger of this would be greatest under such water conditions as developed during the night of January 21, 1959, and that if a vessel should break loose under those circumstances, events might transpire as they did. But such post hoc step by step analysis would render "foreseeable" almost anything that has in fact occurred; if the argument relied upon has legal validity, it ought not be circumvented by characterizing as foreseeable what almost no one would in fact have foreseen at the time.

The effect of unforeseeability of damage upon liability for negligence has recently been considered by the Judicial Committee of the Privy Council, Overseas Tankship (U.K.) Ltd. v. Morts Dock & Engineering Co. (*The Wagon Mound*), (1961) 1 All E.R. 404. The Committee there disapproved the proposition, thought to be supported by Re Polemis and Furness, Withy & Co. Ltd., (1921) 3 K.B. 560 (C.A.), "that unforeseeability is irrelevant if damage is 'direct.'" We have no difficulty with the result of *The Wagon Mound*, in view of the finding, 1 All E.R. at 407, that the appellant had no reason to believe that the floating furnace oil would burn, see also the extended discussion in Miller S.S. Co. v. Overseas Tankship (U.K.) Ltd., *The Wagon Mound No. 2*, (1963) 1 Lloyd's Law List Rep. 402 (Sup. Ct. N.S.W.). On that view the decision simply applies the principle which excludes liability where the injury sprang from a hazard different from that which was improperly risked, see fn.9. Although some language in the judgment goes beyond this, we would find it difficult to understand why one who had failed to use the care required to protect others in the light of expectable forces should be exonerated when the very risks that rendered his conduct negligent produced other and more serious consequences to such persons than were fairly foreseeable when he fell short of what the law demanded. Foreseeability of danger is necessary to render conduct negligent; where as here the damage was caused by just those forces whose existence required the exercise of greater care than was taken — the current, the ice, and the physical mass of the *Shiras*, the incurring of consequences other and greater than foreseen does not make the conduct less culpable or provide a reasoned basis for insulation.[9] The oft

9. The contrasting situation is illustrated by the familiar instances of the running down of a pedestrian by a safely driven but carelessly loaded car, or of the explosion of unlabeled rat poison, inflammable but not known to be, placed near a coffee burner.

encountered argument that failure to limit liability to foreseeable consequences may subject the defendant to a loss wholly out of proportion to
his fault seems scarcely consistent with the universally accepted rule that
the defendant takes the plaintiff as he finds him and will be responsible
for the full extent of the injury even though a latent susceptibility of the
plaintiff renders this far more serious than could reasonably have been
anticipated.

The weight of authority in this country rejects the limitation of
damages to consequences foreseeable at the time of the negligent conduct
when the consequences are "direct," and the damage, although other and
greater than expectable, is of the same general sort that was risked. . . .
Other American courts, purporting to apply a test of foreseeability to
damages, extend that concept to such unforeseen lengths as to raise
serious doubt whether the concept is meaningful,[10] . . .

We see no reason why an actor engaging in conduct which entails a
large risk of small damage and a small risk of other and greater damage, of
the same general sort, from the same forces, and to the same class of
persons, should be relieved of responsibility for the latter simply because
the chance of its occurrence, if viewed alone, may not have been large
enough to require the exercise of care. By hypothesis, the risk of the lesser
harm was sufficient to render his disregard of it actionable; the existence
of a less likely additional risk that the very forces against whose action he
was required to guard would produce other and greater damage than

---

Larrimore v. American Nat. Ins. Co., 184 Okl. 614, 89 P.2d 340 (1939). Exoneration of the
defendant in such cases rests on the basis that a negligent actor is responsible only for
harm the risk of which was increased by the negligent aspect of his conduct. *See* Keeton,
Legal Cause in the Law of Torts, 1-10 (1963); Hart & Honore, *Causation in the Law*,
157-58 (1959). *Compare* Berry v. Borough of Sugar Notch, 191 Pa. 345, 43 A. 240 (1899).

This principle supports the judgment for the defendant in the recent case of Doughty
v. Turner Mfg. Co., (1964) 2 W.L.R. 240 (C.A.). The company maintained a bath of molten
cyanide protected by an asbestos cover, reasonably believed to be incapable of causing an
explosion if immersed. An employee inadvertently knocked the cover into the bath, but
there was no damage from splashing. A minute or two later an explosion occurred as a
result of chemical changes in the cover and the plaintiff, who was standing near the bath,
was injured by the molten drops. The risk against which defendant was required to use
care — splashing of the molten liquid from dropping the supposedly explosion proof cover
— did not materialize, and the defendant was found not to have lacked proper care against
the risk that did. As said by Lord Justice Diplock, (1964) 2 W.L.R. at 247, "The former risk
was well known (that was foreseeable) at the time of the accident; but it did not happen. It
was the second risk which happened and caused the plaintiff damage by burning."
Moreover, if, as indicated in Lord Pearce's judgment, (1964) 2 W.L.R. at 244, the plaintiff
was not within the area of potential splashing, the case parallels *Palsgraf*. . . .

10. An instance is In re Guardian Casualty Co., 253 App. Div. 360, 2 N.Y.S.2d 232 (1st
Dept.), *aff'd*, 278 N.Y. 674, 16 N.E.2d 397 (1938), where the majority gravely asserted that
a foreseeable consequence of driving a taxicab too fast was that a collision with another car
would project the cab against a building with such force as to cause a portion of the building to collapse twenty minutes later, when the cab was being removed, and injure a spectator twenty feet away. Surely this is "straining the idea of foreseeability past the breaking
point," Bohlen, Book Review, 47 Harv. L. Rev. 556, 557 (1934), at least if the matter be
viewed as of the time of the negligent act, as the supposedly symmetrical test of *The Wagon
Mound* demands, (1961) 1 All Eng. R. at 415. . . .

could have been reasonably anticipated should inculpate him further rather than limit his liability. This does not mean that the careless actor will always be held for all damages for which the forces that he risked were a cause in fact. Somewhere a point will be reached when courts will agree that the link has become too tenuous — that what is claimed to be conse- quence is only fortuity. Thus, if the destruction of the Michigan Avenue Bridge had delayed the arrival of a doctor, with consequent loss of a patient's life, few judges would impose liability on any of the parties here, although the agreement in result might not be paralleled by similar unanimity in reasoning; perhaps in the long run one returns to Judge Andrews' statement in *Palsgraf*, 248 N.Y. at 354-355, 162 N.E. at 104 (dissenting opinion). "It is all a question of expediency, . . . of fair judg- ment, always keeping in mind the fact that we endeavor to make a rule in each case that will be practical and in keeping with the general under- standing of mankind." It would be pleasant if greater certainty were possi- ble, see Prosser, Torts, 262, but the many efforts that have been made at defining the locus of the "uncertain and wavering line," 248 N.Y. at 354, 162 N.E. 99, are not very promising; what courts do in such cases makes better sense than what they, or others, say. Where the line will be drawn will vary from age to age; as society has come to rely increasingly on insur- ance and other methods of loss-sharing, the point may lie further off than a century ago. Here it is surely more equitable that the losses from the operators' negligent failure to raise the Michigan Avenue Bridge should be ratably borne by Buffalo's taxpayers than left with the innocent victims of the flooding; yet the mind is also repelled by a solution that would impose liability solely on the City and exonerate the persons whose negligent acts of commission and omission were the precipitating force of the collision with the bridge and its sequelae. We go only so far as to hold that where, as here, the damages resulted from the same physical forces whose exis- tence required the exercise of greater care than was displayed and were of the same general sort that was expectable, unforeseeability of the exact developments and of the extent of the loss will not limit liability. Other fact situations can be dealt with when they arise. . . .

The decree is modified so that [Continental, Kinsman and the City of Buffalo could be held jointly liable for, among other things, property damage caused by the flooding resulting from the damming of the river. — EDS.] . . .

Moore, J. (concurring and dissenting): I do not hesitate to concur with Judge Friendly's well-reasoned and well-expressed opinion as to . . . the extent of the liability of the City of Buffalo, Continental and Kinsman for the damages suffered by the City, the *Shiras*, the *Tewksbury*, the *Druckenmiller* and . . . the division of damages.

I cannot agree, however, merely because "society has come to rely increasingly on insurance and other methods of loss-sharing" that the courts should, or have the power to, create a vast judicial insurance company which will adequately compensate all who have suffered damages. Equally disturbing is the suggestion that "Here it is surely more equitable that the losses from the operators' negligent failure to raise the

Michigan Avenue Bridge should be ratably borne by Buffalo's taxpayers than left with the innocent victims of the flooding." Under any such principle, negligence suits would become further simplified by requiring a claimant to establish only his own innocence and then offer, in addition to his financial statement, proof of the financial condition of the respective defendants. Judgment would be entered against the defendant which court or jury decided was best able to pay. Nor am I convinced that it should be the responsibility of the Buffalo taxpayers to reimburse the "innocent victims" in their community for damages sustained. In my opinion, before financial liability is imposed, there should be some showing of legal liability.

. . . [N]o bridge builder or bridge operator would envision a bridge as a dam or as a dam potential.

By an extraordinary concatenation of even more extraordinary events, not unlike the humorous and almost-beyond-all-imagination sequences depicted by the famous cartoonist, Rube Goldberg, the *Shiras* with its companions which it picked up en route did combine with the bridge demolition to create a very effective dam across the Buffalo River. Without specification of the nature of the damages, claims in favor of some twenty persons and companies were allowed resulting from the various collisions and from "the damming of the river at the bridge, the backing up of the water and ice upstream, and the overflowing of the banks of the river and flooding of industrial installations along the river banks." (Sup. Finding of Fact #26a.)

My dissent is limited to that portion of the opinion which approves the awarding of damages suffered as a result of the flooding of various properties upstream. I am not satisfied with reliance on hindsight or on the assumption that since flooding occurred, therefore, it must have been foreseeable. In fact, the majority hold that the danger "of flooding would not have been unforeseeable under the circumstances to anyone who gave them thought." But believing that "anyone" might be too broad, they resort to that most famous of all legal mythological characters, the reasonably "prudent man." Even he, however, "carefully pondering the problem," is not to be relied upon because they permit him to become prudent "[W]ith the aid of hindsight." . . .

In final analysis the answers to the questions when the link is "too tenuous" and when "consequence is only fortuity" are dependent solely on the particular point of view of the particular judge under the particular circumstances. . . . [T]o me the fortuitous circumstance of the vessels so arranging themselves as to create a dam is much "too tenuous." . . .

NOTES AND QUESTIONS

1. *Within the Scope of the Risk?* Does Judge Friendly conclude that property damage through flooding was one of the risks that rendered the conduct of Kinsman, Continental, and the city careless? If so, does he mean to say that the risk, properly described, was to property damaged by

any means, or property damaged through a specific means, such as flooding or physical impact? Or does he abandon the "scope of the risk" test in favor of some other conception of proximate cause? Does *Kinsman* mark a return to *Polemis* and the directness test?

2. *The Increment of Unforeseeable Harm.* Judge Friendly's opinion maintains that, at least in some circumstances, there is nothing unfair about assigning liability for unforeseeable harms to a defendant found to have acted carelessly. Specifically, he suggests that, since the defendants were already subject to liability for lesser harms foreseeably caused by their negligence, such as damage to the *Tewksbury*, it is perfectly appropriate to add on liability for additional, highly improbable but potentially vast harms, such as property damage caused by flooding. The argument seems to be that if an actor is duty-bound to take precautions for the benefit of the plaintiff against certain types of harm, and his breach happens to cause some other kind of harm, there is no reason *not* to hold the defendant liable for this other kind of harm as well. Wasn't this argument rejected by Viscount Simonds in *Wagon Mound (No. 1)*?

3. *The Relevance of Cost-Spreading.* Judge Friendly, invoking Judge Andrews' *Palsgraf* dissent, further suggests that the determination of proximate cause should be driven at least in part by "policy" considerations, such as the ability of different actors to defray the cost of the harms at issue. Is he right in assuming that the city, as opposed to the property owners, was in the best position to defray those costs through, say, a modest tax increase? What if the property owners could buy flood insurance that would reimburse them for property damage caused by flooding? Wouldn't that be a more efficient way to handle this problem?

4. *Type of Harm versus Manner of Harm.* *Kinsman* raises some difficult questions for the scope-of-the-risk approach to proximate cause. In particular, the question arises as to whether the *manner* of harm — as opposed to the type of harm — should ever be relevant to the inquiry. Consider the *Guardian Casualty* case mentioned in footnote 10 of the *Kinsman* opinion. How should that case be analyzed under the scope-of-the-risk approach? Does a correct description of the risks posed by driving too fast include the risk of all physical harms caused by impacts flowing from the car's movement? Was the court in *Guardian* correct to conclude that the cab driver ought to be subject to liability to the spectator injured by the debris that fell as the cab was being removed from the building? Should this sort of hard case simply be left to the jury?

Suppose, alternatively, that S is a spectator at a stock car race. O, the owner of the racetrack, acts carelessly by not providing adequate fencing to protect spectators from debris that can be expected to fly off cars when they collide or break down. It so happens that this race is being televised, in part by means of a huge camera mounted on a blimp hovering over the stadium. Unexpectedly, and without fault on the part of the television production company, the camera falls, shattering on the track. S is struck and injured by camera shrapnel that would have been blocked by an adequate fence. Was *S*'s injury within the scope of the risk posed by *O*'s carelessness?

5. Kinsman (II). In a subsequent case, the Second Circuit determined that the same defendants who were held liable for the losses discussed in *Kinsman* were not liable for economic losses caused to carriers who could not unload wheat from their ships because of the negligent damming of the Buffalo River. According to the court, the connection between the defendants' negligence and these claimants' damages was "too tenuous and remote" to permit recovery. In re Kinsman Transit Co. (*Kinsman (II)*), 388 F.2d 821 (2d Cir. 1968). Is this conclusion defensible in light of the holding of *Kinsman (I)*?

REFERENCES/FURTHER READING

Proximate Cause

Joseph W. Bingham, *Some Suggestions Concerning "Legal Cause" at Common Law (Part II)*, 9 Colum. L. Rev. 136, 154 (1909).

John C. P. Goldberg, *Comment: Rethinking Injury and Proximate Cause*, 40 S.D. L. Rev. 1315 (2003).

Leon Green, *Rationale of Proximate Cause* 195-196 (1927).

Nicholas St. John Green, *Proximate and Remote Cause*, 4 Am. L. Rev. 201 (1870).

Heidi M. Hurd & Michael S. Moore, *Negligence in the Air*, 3 Theoretical Inq. in Law 333 (2002).

Robert E. Keeton, *Legal Cause in the Law of Torts* (1963).

Patrick Kelley, *Proximate Cause in Negligence Law: History, Theory and the Present Darkness*, 69 Wash. U. L.Q. 49 (1991).

Saul Levmore, *The* Wagon Mound *Cases: Foreseeability, Causation and Mrs. Palsgraf*, in Robert L. Rabin & Stephen D. Sugarman (eds.), *Torts Stories* 129 (2003).

Jane Stapleton, *Legal Cause: Cause-in-Fact and the Scope of Liability for Consequences*, 54 Vand. L. Rev. 941 (2001).

Michael L. Wells, *Proximate Cause and the American Law Institute: The False Choice Between the "Direct-Consequences" Test and the "Risk Standard,"* 37 U. Rich. L. Rev. 389 (2003).

Glanville Williams, *The Risk Principle*, 77 L. Quar. Rev. 179 (1961).

Palsgraf

Andrew L. Kaufman, *Cardozo* 287-295 (1998).

John C. P. Goldberg & Benjamin C. Zipursky, *The Moral of* MacPherson, 146 U. Pa. L. Rev. 1733, 1812-1824 (1998).

John T. Noonan, Jr., *Perons and Masks of the Law: Cardozo, Holmes, Jefferson, and Wythe as Makers of the Masks* 144 (1976).

William E. Nelson, *The Legalist Reformation: Law, Politics and Ideology in New York* 1920-1980 (2001).

David Owen, *Duty Rules*, 54 Vand. L. Rev. 767 (2001).

Richard A. Posner, *Cardozo: A Study in Reputation* 16-17 (1990).

William Powers, *Thaumotrope*, 77 Tex. L. Rev. 1319 (1999).

William L. Prosser, Palsgraf *Revisited*, 52 Mich. L. Rev. 1 (1953).

Gary T. Schwartz, *Cardozo as Tort Lawmaker*, 49 DePaul L. Rev. 305 (1999).

G. Edward White, *Tort Law in America: An Intellectual History* (2d ed. 2002).

Ernest J. Weinrib, *The Passing of* Palsgraf?, 54 Vand. L. Rev. 803 (2001).

Benjamin C. Zipursky, *Rights, Wrongs and Recourse in the Law of Torts*, 51 Vand. L. Rev. 1 (1998).

CHAPTER 6

Statutory Supplements: Negligence Per Se, Wrongful Death Acts, and Implied Rights of Action

Statutes and negligence law interact in numerous ways. Some statutes supplant negligence law. For example, as we saw in connection with the *Aldridge* case in Chapter 4, workers' compensation laws enacted at the beginning of the twentieth century removed most workplace injuries from the ambit of tort law and placed them in an alternative scheme that combines strict liability with scheduled damages. Other statutes eliminate, partially block, or otherwise limit the operation of tort law without providing an alternative scheme of redress. Thus, the *Mussivand* decision in Chapter 2 referred to the outright abolition of "amatory" torts.* Finally, statutes can expressly create tort-like causes of action by empowering a class of plaintiffs to seek redress for injuries caused by conduct that was not actionable at common law. We provide examples of this sort of statute in Chapter 10, which briefly addresses statutory causes of action for housing and employment discrimination.

In this chapter, we deal with three additional ways in which statutes interact with tort law. First, negligence law can sometimes incorporate standards of behavior contained in criminal or regulatory statutes that, on their face, do not say anything about tort liability. This is accomplished primarily through the doctrine of *negligence per se.* Second, statutes can confer on plaintiffs precisely the power that *Palsgraf* denies them as a matter of common law, namely, the power to sue as "vicarious beneficiaries" of rights possessed by others. The most important examples of this sort of statute are the *wrongful death acts* enacted by American legislatures in the nineteenth and early-twentieth centuries. Finally, statutes can effectively combine these two functions. That is, in the course of setting standards of conduct, certain statutes implicitly create a "protected class" — a group whose members are deemed by courts to be the beneficiaries of those standards — thereby conferring on those class members the power to seek redress for violations that cause injury to them. Statutes that have this particular effect are said to contain *implied rights of action*.

---

* In Chapter 13, we consider how laws regulating the use of safety devices in automobiles can "preempt" certain products liability claims. In Chapter 8 and Module III, we discuss caps on damages and other measures used to limit compensation to successful tort claimants.

I.   Negligence Per Se

Dalal v. City of New York
692 N.Y.S.2d 468 (App. Div. 1999)

Per Curiam. . . . [P]laintiff appeals from a judgment . . . which, upon a jury verdict finding, *inter alia*, that the defendant Alicia Ramdhani-Mack was not negligent, is . . . against him. . . .

ORDERED that the judgment is reversed . . . and a new trial is granted, with costs to abide the event.

The instant action arises out of an automobile accident that occurred at the intersection of Booth Street and 66th Avenue in Queens. The action against the defendant City of New York was discontinued prior to trial. At trial, the plaintiff testified that he stopped at the stop sign controlling traffic on 66th Avenue, and looked both ways for a distance of about one block, without seeing anything, before he proceeded into the intersection. When he was about halfway through the intersection, his vehicle was struck on the driver's side by a vehicle operated by Alicia Ramdhani-Mack (hereinafter the defendant). The plaintiff further testified that he never saw the defendant's car until impact. The defendant testified that she was about 10 to 15 feet away from the intersection when she noticed the plaintiff's vehicle, which was about 14 feet behind the stop sign but moving, and that about 5 to 7 seconds elapsed from the time that she observed the plaintiff's vehicle until the collision. She stated that she attempted to swerve out of the way, but could not avoid the collision. The defendant further testified that although she was nearsighted and required prescription glasses, she was not wearing her glasses at the time of the accident. She claimed she was still able to see while driving. There was no evidence that either driver was speeding. The jury returned a verdict finding that only the plaintiff was negligent, and that his negligence was the sole proximate cause of the accident.

The plaintiff contends that the trial court erred in refusing to charge that the defendant's violation of Vehicle and Traffic Law § 509(3) was negligence per se, and erred in refusing to allow him to cross-examine the defendant on that issue. Vehicle and Traffic Law § 509(3) provides that "no person shall operate any motor vehicle in violation of any restriction contained on his license." The defendant testified at her examination before trial that her New York State driver's license contained a restriction requiring her to wear corrective lenses while driving.

It is well established that an unexcused violation of a statutory standard of care, if unexplained, constitutes negligence per se (*see*, Martin v. Herzog, 228 N.Y. 164, 126 N.E. 814 . . .). The defendant's reliance upon the principle that operating a motor vehicle without a license is not negligence per se is misplaced. The absence or possession of a driver's license relates only to the authority for operating the vehicle and not to the manner thereof. However, a restriction placed upon the license requiring the wearing of glasses when driving relates directly to the actual operation of the vehicle. Vehicle and Traffic Law § 509(3) provides that no one shall operate a vehicle in violation of any restriction contained on his or her license, and also relates to the manner in which the vehicle is being operated. Thus, the statute sets up a standard of care, the unexcused violation of which is negligence per se. The trial court erred, therefore, in refusing the plaintiff's request to charge. . . .

In view of the verdict, we cannot conclude that [this and another error] were harmless. The plaintiff is therefore entitled to a new trial.

Bayne v. Todd Shipyards Corp.
568 P.2d 771 (Wash. 1977)

Brachtenbach, J.   Plaintiff sued for personal injuries sustained while unloading goods being delivered to defendant's premises. Plaintiff was not an employee of the defendant, but rather of the trucking company engaged in the delivery. While unloading those goods, plaintiff fell from a loading platform. Plaintiff contended that the defendant's loading platform lacked a guardrail required by a safety standard regulation promulgated by the Department of Labor and Industries, pursuant to statute. The trial court refused to instruct that violation of that administrative regulation was negligence per se, but did instruct that it was evidence of negligence. . . . [T]he Court of Appeals affirmed a judgment for the defendant. . . . We granted review limited to the sole issue whether violation of an administrative safety regulation is negligence per se or only evidence of negligence. We reverse.

The statute in effect at the time of the injury imposed a duty upon the Director of Labor and Industries to promulgate safety regulations to furnish workers a place of work which is as safe as is reasonable and practicable under the circumstances, surroundings and conditions. RCW 49.16.030, .050. . . .

Pursuant to this authority, the Director of Labor and Industries adopted WAC 296-25-515:

> (1) All elevated walks, runways or platforms, except on loading or unloading sides of platforms, if four feet or more from the floor level, shall be provided with a standard railing on platforms. If height exceeds six feet, a toe-board shall be provided, to prevent material from rolling or falling off. . . .

We have long been committed to the principle that violation of an applicable statute or ordinance is negligence per se. Engelker v. Seattle Elec. Co., 50 Wash. 196, 96 P. 1039 (1908); Portland-Seattle Auto Freight, Inc. v. Jones, 15 Wn. 2d 603, 607, 131 P.2d 736 (1942). This is the majority rule. W. Prosser, *Handbook of the Law of Torts* § 36, at 200 (4th ed. 1971).

However, the courts are divided on the question whether violation of an administrative regulation is evidence of negligence or negligence per se. Prosser, *supra* at 201 n.30. . . .

By our decision in Kness v. Truck Trailer Equip. Co., 81 Wn. 2d 251, 501 P.2d 285 (1972), we already have aligned ourselves with those jurisdictions which hold that under appropriate circumstances violation of an administrative order is negligence per se. In *Kness* a regulation had been adopted limiting the hours of work for a minor. The regulation was based on a rather broad statute authorizing the administrative establishment of standards of wages and conditions of labor for women and minors. In holding violation of the regulation was negligence per se we said:

> In deciding whether violation of a public law or *regulation* shall be considered in determining liability, the Restatement (Second) of Torts § 286 (1965) properly states the rules:
>
> > The court may adopt as the standard of conduct of a reasonable man the requirements of a legislative enactment *or an administrative regulation* whose purpose is found to be exclusively or in part
> >
> > (a) to protect a class of persons which includes the one whose interest is invaded, and
> > (b) to protect the particular interest which is invaded, and
> > (c) to protect that interest against the kind of harm which has resulted, and
> > (d) to protect that interest against the particular hazard from which the harm results.
>
> This court has substantially adhered to these principles in a number of cases: . . .

(Citations omitted. Italics ours.) Kness v. Truck Trailer Equip. Co., *supra* at 257. . . .

In this case we had a somewhat more specific statutory directive to adopt standards of safety to make safe the place of work of workmen. RCW 49.16.030 and .050.

This is not an instance of violation of some obscure bureaucratic edict. Under the statute in effect when this regulation was adopted, the Director of Labor and Industries was required to hold a public hearing to consider new standards, or changes or modifications of existing standards. Employers and workmen or their representatives could attend such hearing and present testimony. RCW 49.16.080. Written notice of the hearing had to be mailed to *each* employer whose class or establishment was affected. RCW 49.16.090.

We perceive no reason why such a regulation should be of any less force, effect or significance than a municipal ordinance. We are not alone in this result. *See* Porter v. Montgomery Ward & Co., 48 Cal. 2d 846, 313 P.2d 854 (1957); Pierson v. Holly Sugar Corp., 107 Cal. App. 2d 298, 237 P.2d 28 (1951). . . .

Defendant contends that plaintiff was not within the protected class because he was not an employee of the defendant. The statute requires a safe place of work for workmen. It does not limit it to employees of the defendant employer. A worker who is lawfully on the premises in pursuit of his own employment and at the invitation of the third party, defendant here, is entitled to the benefit of the statute and the regulation. *See* Pierson v. Holly Sugar Corp., *supra,* which so holds, stating that the regulation was a safeguard for the public generally which necessarily included a workman making a delivery who was not an employee of the defendant. Extension of the protection of the regulation to the public generally is not before us.

Finally it is necessary to deal with the defendant's argument that we have a contrary line of cases which were not dealt with in the *Kness* case. Admittedly there has been at least some confusion in our cases concerning the main question. Defendant relies on six cases for its argument that violation of an administrative regulation is only evidence of negligence. Four of those cases are distinguishable and two are in error.

In Engen v. Arnold, 61 Wn. 2d 641, 379 P.2d 990 (1963), the trial court held that violation of safety rules promulgated by the Department of Labor and Industries was contributory negligence as a matter of law. The plaintiff had not elected to be covered by the workmen's compensation act. We held at page 646 that

> [W]hile violation of such rules and regulations may, in a case such as this, afford some evidence of negligence, a violation thereof by one not covered by the Workmen's Compensation Act, even though engaged in an extrahazardous occupation, does not constitute negligence as a matter of law.

We did not hold that in an appropriate case violation would not be negligence per se.

In Vogel v. Alaska S.S. Co., 69 Wn. 2d 497, 419 P.2d 141 (1966), and Cresap v. Pacific Inland Navigation Co., 78 Wn. 2d 563, 478 P.2d 223 (1970), we were concerned with alleged violations of federal safety regulations governing stevedore employers. The defendant there was not such an employer but was the owner of the ship on which the stevedoring work was being done and who had a legal duty to furnish a seaworthy vessel. We held the regulations to be admissible against the shipowner and a violation of them to be evidence of negligence because "they give expression to the minimum standards which must be met in order to render conditions aboard the vessel safe, and hence seaworthy." Vogel v. Alaska S.S. Co., *supra* at 503. . . . That is, the regulations were objective criteria of seaworthiness and though not binding on that defendant were evidence of negligence. Here, the defendant is covered by the workmen's compensation act and is an employer intended to be governed by the regulation.

Next, defendant cites Nordstrom v. White Metal Rolling & Stamping Corp., 75 Wn. 2d 629, 453 P.2d 619 (1969). That case dealt with standards adopted by a trade association. We held that such voluntary standards are relevant on the standard of care, but not determinative. Such standards simply do not have the force of a statute, ordinance or statutorily authorized administrative regulation.

Thorpe v. Boeing Co., 5 Wn. App. 706, 490 P.2d 448 (1971), and Loyland v. Stone & Webster Eng'r Corp., 9 Wn. App. 682, 514 P.2d 184 (1973), held that Department of Labor and Industries safety standards are only evidence of negligence. *Thorpe* erroneously relied upon *Nordstrom* and *Vogel*, failing to draw the distinctions we note here. *Loyland* then relied entirely on *Thorpe*. We do not agree with those cases as they relate to the violation of statutorily authorized administrative regulations.

The judgment is reversed and a new trial ordered.

Hicks, J. (dissenting) (joined by Utter, J.). I dissent. Administrative agencies have a penchant for spawning regulations without end. As a Member of Congress, I served on a subcommittee that had occasion to evaluate regulations promulgated under the Occupational Safety and Health Act (OSHA). While these regulations were generally most appropriate, they were unnecessary, impractical or picayunish (Mickey Mouse) often enough to give me concern as to making violation of any one of them negligence per se in every instance in a damage action.

The court is setting policy in this case and I have no quarrel with that. However, I am more comfortable with the rule that violation of administrative regulations be submitted to the trier of fact as evidence of negligence, as the trial court did in this case, rather than to be submitted as negligence as a matter of law. In my view, when violations of regulations are submitted as evidence of negligence, the trier of fact has a better opportunity to use common sense and reach a more nearly just result between the parties.

Until this case, the state of the law in this jurisdiction did not compel the result the majority reaches. Based on past decisions of this court, I believe the Court of Appeals was correct in both Thorpe v. Boeing Co., 5 Wn. App. 706, 490 P.2d 448 (1971), and Loyland v. Stone & Webster Eng'r Corp., 9 Wn. App. 682, 514 P.2d 184 (1973). . . .

In the instant case, WAC 296-25-515 and its supplement No. 13, 7-1-74 do no more than provide an administratively approved standard of safety. By the fiat of this court, the violation of such administratively promulgated standard now becomes negligence as a matter of law in every instance in a damage action. I believe the better course to be to . . . submit the regulation to the trier of fact only as evidence of an approved standard, as the trial court did in this case. . . .

Victor v. Hedges
91 Cal. Rptr. 2d 466 (Ct. App. 1999)

Dau, J.   Plaintiff Stephani Victor appeals from the judgment entered in favor of defendants Michael Hedges and Thermtech, Inc. (collectively, "Hedges"), following the grant of defendants' motion for summary judgment, and from the denial of her motion for new trial. Michael Hedges parked his auto on the sidewalk in front of his apartment building. Plaintiff and Hedges were standing on the sidewalk behind the car, when an inattentive motorist drove over the curb and into plaintiff, seriously injuring her. We are required to decide whether a statute prohibiting the parking of a vehicle on a sidewalk may be employed to fix upon Hedges the presumption of negligence in the circumstances of this case and whether reasonable people could conclude that he subjected plaintiff to an unreasonable risk of harm. We hold the statute in question was not designed to prevent the type of occurrence that resulted in plaintiff's injury, and plaintiff has failed to raise a triable issue of fact that an ordinarily prudent person in Hedges's place would have foreseen an unreasonable risk of harm to plaintiff. Accordingly, we affirm.

FACTUAL AND PROCEDURAL BACKGROUND

Plaintiff brought an action for damages alleging that . . . defendant Thermtech owned a certain Ford Explorer and defendant Hedges was driving that vehicle with the owner's consent, that defendant Mark Williams was driving a Ford Aerostar van, and that defendants negligently operated and controlled these vehicles so as to cause a collision with plaintiff, who was lawfully upon the sidewalk in the City of Hermosa Beach.

The undisputed facts showed that at approximately 10:00 P.M. Hedges had parked his Ford Explorer on the sidewalk in front of his apartment building, parallel to, and with the driver's side tires three to four feet from, the curb line of Hermosa Avenue in Hermosa Beach. Hedges did this to show plaintiff his new compact disk player, which was located in the rear of the Explorer. Due to construction, northbound traffic along Hermosa Avenue was routed into a single lane along the east curb. There was some gravel on the road, and the surface was rough with bumps and potholes. Immediately before the accident Williams was northbound on Hermosa Avenue, approaching the intersection with First Street, in his Aerostar van. He looked down at the tape deck and, with his right hand, fast forwarded a cassette for approximately two seconds. The steering wheel jostled about an inch each way, Williams's van drifted to the right, and the front and rear passenger side tires hit the First Street curb, causing them to blow out; the van continued in its path. Hedges and plaintiff were standing at the rear of the Explorer, with plaintiff nearer the curb and Hedges to her right, when Williams's van ran into plaintiff and the Explorer about 30 feet from the First Street curb. . . .

DISCUSSION

Plaintiff's claim against Hedges and Thermtech is based on theories of negligence per se and common law negligence. Defendants argued in the court below that a necessary element of plaintiff's case under either theory—proximate cause—could not be established. . . . [W]e will address the negligence per se issue before coming to that of ordinary negligence. We do this, even though the proximate cause argument . . . made by the parties is common to both, for the following reason: If Hedges is not to be presumed negligent, and we will conclude that he is not, the ordinary negligence analysis may proceed uncontaminated by the infraction charge. . . .

B.   NEGLIGENCE PER SE

Plaintiff argues that Hedges must be presumed negligent because he violated Vehicle Code section 22500, subdivision (f), which prohibits parking on a sidewalk.

Section 669, subdivision (a) of the Evidence Code provides: "The failure of a person to exercise due care is presumed if: [¶] (1) He violated a statute . . . [¶] (2) The violation proximately caused death or injury to person or property; [¶] (3) The death or injury resulted from an occurrence of the nature which the statute . . . was designed to prevent; and [¶] (4) The person suffering the death or the injury to his person or property was one of the class of persons for whose protection the statute . . . was adopted." With respect to paragraphs (3) and (4), the Law Revision Commission Comments state: "Whether the death or injury involved in an action resulted from an occurrence of the nature which the statute . . . was designed to prevent . . . and whether the plaintiff was one of the class of persons for whose protection the statute . . . was adopted are questions of law. Nunneley v. Edgar Hotel, 36 Cal. 2d 493, 225 P.2d 497 (1950) (statute requiring parapet of particular height at roofline of vent shaft designed to protect against walking into shaft, not against falling into shaft while sitting on parapet). . . ."

At the time of the accident, section 22500 provided: "No person shall stop, park, or leave standing any vehicle whether attended or unattended, except when necessary to avoid conflict with other traffic or in compliance with the directions of a peace officer or official traffic control device, in any of the following places: . . . [¶] (f) On a sidewalk, except electric carts when authorized by local ordinance, as specified in Section 21114.5."

We are required to determine the nature of the occurrence that section 22500, subdivision (f) was designed to prevent. . . .

Section 22500 designates twelve categories of locations where stopping, standing or parking a vehicle is prohibited. The Legislature specified certain of these with pedestrians obviously in mind. "On a sidewalk" (id., subd. (f)), which the Code defines as "that portion of a highway, other than the roadway, set apart by curbs, barriers, markings or other delineation for pedestrian travel" (§ 555), is one of these. Others are: "[o]n a crosswalk" (§ 22500, subd. (b)); "[b]etween a safety zone and the adjacent right-hand curb" (id., subd. (c)); "[a]longside curb space authorized for the loading and unloading of passengers of a bus engaged as a common carrier in local transportation" (id., subd. (i)); and "[i]n front of that portion of a curb that has been cut down, lowered, or constructed to provide wheelchair accessibility to the sidewalk. . . ." (Id., subd. (l).) With the exception of "on a sidewalk" (id., subd. (f)), vehicles normally operate within each of these designated categories, and, for these, the section's prohibition appears designed both to prevent vehicular obstruction of pedestrian traffic and to lessen the danger of vehicle-pedestrian collision. Thus pedestrians finding it necessary to walk around a vehicle that is illegally parked, stopped or left standing may be put at increased risk of injury from unsure footing, from another vehicle in the roadway, or from the sudden movement of the vehicle that had been at rest. Hedges's parked automobile did not obstruct plaintiff's way and increase her risk of injury in this fashion.

Injury to a pedestrian on a sidewalk, resulting from contact with a vehicle that has been parked, stopped or left standing there, can also occur when the vehicle is at rest or when it is again put in motion. The Legislature's 1998 amendment to subdivision (f) appears to reflect an awareness that a vehicle at rest, even if partially on the sidewalk, can cause injury to a passing pedestrian.[10] In this situation, the pedestrian,

_____

10. Plaintiff argues that the amendment, which was not in effect at the time of the accident in this case, clarifies the Legislature's original intent. The amendment makes more explicit what is meant by "*[o]n* a sidewalk [italics added]." Subdivision (f), as amended, is

insufficiently aware of the presence of the vehicle, walks into it, or a portion of it, and is injured. That is not what occurred in the case at bar. Here, plaintiff was inspecting the Explorer's compact disk player when she was struck by another vehicle, which ran into her and the Explorer.

We conclude that subdivision (f) of section 22500 was designed to prevent (1) vehicular obstruction of pedestrian traffic on sidewalks, and (2) injury to pedestrians that might occur when a pedestrian (a) walks around the obstructing vehicle and is injured by another hazard, (b) walks into the obstructing vehicle, or (c) is struck when the vehicle, previously at rest on the sidewalk, is put in motion. The section was not designed to prevent the type of occurrence that resulted in plaintiff's injury in this case—being struck on the sidewalk by a vehicle other than the illegally parked vehicle. Accordingly, the court correctly denied to plaintiff the presumption, available under Evidence Code section 669, that defendants failed to exercise due care.

C.   ORDINARY NEGLIGENCE

We turn now to the issue of ordinary negligence....

... "[N]egligence is conduct which falls below the standard established by law for the protection of others against unreasonable risk of harm." ([Rest. 2d Torts,] § 282.) Only those circumstances which the actor perceives or should perceive at the time of his or her action are to be considered in determining whether the actor should recognize the risks that are involved in his or her conduct. (*Id.*, § 282, com. h.) The actor is required to give his surroundings the attention which the average person in the community would give under like circumstances and such superior attention as the actor himself or herself has. (*Id.*, § 289.) ...

Plaintiff contends the following undisputed facts are sufficient to defeat defendants' summary judgment motion: Hedges took plaintiff to the sidewalk in front of his apartment at about 10:00 P.M., to see the compact disk player in his car, and stood with plaintiff on the sidewalk within three to four feet of the curb, knowing that the street was undergoing construction, such that traffic was reduced to one lane and the surface of the road had some gravel upon it and was bumpy. In the half-block south of his apartment building Hedges had observed between five and ten dirt mounds; the mounds were six to eight feet in height and four to five feet on the other side of the traffic lane. Hedges acknowledged that due to bumps and potholes in the street, sometimes his car would act a little "squirrelly," causing "momentary [loss of] control of the vehicle for a split second."[12] ...

reproduced here with the language added in italics. "(f) On *any portion of a sidewalk, or with the body of the vehicle extending over any portion of* a sidewalk, except electric carts when authorized by local ordinance, as specified in section 21114.5. *Lights, mirrors, or devices that are required to be mounted upon a vehicle under this code may extend from the body of the vehicle over the sidewalk to a distance of not more than 10 inches.*" (Stats. 1998, ch. 877, § 66.)

12. We acknowledge that plaintiff points to some additional claimed defects in the road, but the record contains no evidence to show that they were either observed by Hedges or would have been observed by the average person in the community....

The cases relied upon by the parties are focused upon determining whether the defendant's conduct was the cause of the injury. . . . [W]e believe that in the case at bar the proper focus lies elsewhere. "There is a clear distinction . . . between the problem of foreseeability . . . in determining whether the defendant's conduct was the proximate cause of an injury, and the problem of foreseeability in determining whether the defendant was negligent at all. In the latter case the problem is whether or not the defendant's conduct was wrongful toward the plaintiff, while in the former it is whether he should be relieved of responsibility for an admitted wrong because another's wrongful conduct also contributed to the injury." (Richards v. Stanley (1954) 43 Cal. 2d 60, 68-69, 271 P.2d 23.) Where it is contended that the element of foreseeability is determinative of proximate cause, the court "should . . . approach the problem as one of determining the nature of the duty and the scope of the risk of the negligent conduct." (Schwartz v. Helms Bakery Limited (1967) 67 Cal. 2d 232, 240-241, 60 Cal. Rptr. 510, 430 P.2d 68, fn. omitted.)

For Hedges to be liable for negligence, his conduct must have fallen below the standard established by law for the protection of those in plaintiff's situation against "unreasonable risk of harm." (Rest. 2d Torts, § 282.) Plaintiff argues that Hedges should have foreseen the likelihood that another vehicle would lose control and come onto the public sidewalk where he and plaintiff were standing, a few feet from the curb. This, says the plaintiff, was negligence because it was near a road made hazardous by construction activity, which Hedges knew about, and it was foreseeable that these conditions could cause a car to lose control and run onto the curb.

In the circumstances of this case these facts do not raise a triable issue that Hedges's conduct was wrongful toward the plaintiff. Reasonable people would not conclude, from these facts, that Hedges's act of taking plaintiff to the sidewalk subjected her to an unreasonable risk of harm. Plaintiff relies solely upon Hedges's knowledge of the following road conditions to establish his negligence: the street was undergoing construction; traffic was reduced to one lane; the road surface was bumpy and had some gravel upon it; and there were dirt mounds four to five feet to the left of the traffic lane. Plaintiff's *expert* declared that these *and other factors*—deficient size of lane of travel, according to applicable manuals and specifications, inadequate delineation of the left side of the roadway, and the asphalt overhang at the gutter—"bias[ed]" the Williams van to the right side of the road, and that the van's drift to the right could be predicted by traffic engineering human factors. But Hedges is not shown to have had the special knowledge of an expert, and his conduct is not judged by that standard. (*See* Rest. 2d Torts, § 289.) Thus, knowledge of the "bias" condition of the roadway, or of what could have been predicted by using traffic engineering human factors, is superior knowledge that Hedges is not chargeable with. There is no evidence in the record that Hedges was aware of any prior accident in this area, and there is no evidence raising a triable issue of fact that an ordinarily prudent person would have understood that he or she was subjecting plaintiff to an unreasonable risk of harm by standing on the public sidewalk at this location. . . .

We conclude that under the undisputed facts here there can be no reasonable difference of opinion as to whether Hedges subjected plaintiff to an unreasonable risk of harm or as to the foreseeability that a driver would become distracted and, due to road conditions that only qualified experts would be able to detect, run up on the sidewalk in the stretch of road in front of Hedges's apartment. We conclude that defendants were entitled to summary judgment. . . .

NOTES AND QUESTIONS

1. *Negligence Per Se: Fault versus Evidence of Fault.* As employed by a majority of jurisdictions, the doctrine of negligence per se permits a negligence plaintiff to satisfy the breach element of her cause of action by proving that the defendant violated a statutory rule of conduct (or as we see in *Bayne*, a regulation issued by an administrative agency). By doing so, it relieves the plaintiff of her burden of proving that the defendant violated the common law's reasonable person standard. Thus, on remand, Dalal will be able to prove that defendant Ramdhani-Mack acted carelessly simply by introducing evidence of her admission that, at the time of the accident, she was driving without contact lenses in violation of the condition on her driver's license, which in turn constituted a violation of New York's motor vehicle laws. Such conduct is *per se* unreasonable in that the state legislature has pronounced it unreasonable. Given this pronouncement, there is no need, indeed no room, for further inquiry into whether the defendant acted reasonably under the circumstances.

In Martin v. Herzog, 126 N.E. 814 (1920), which is cited by the *Dalal* court, Judge Cardozo provided a typically forceful description of the effect of negligence per se. *Martin* involved the crash of two vehicles. The issue was the plaintiff's alleged contributory negligence in failing to use lights while driving after sunset in violation of a statute requiring their use. The trial court instructed the jury that it could consider the plaintiff's violation of the statute as *evidence* of negligence. Cardozo, for the Court of Appeals, disapproved of the instruction:

> We think the unexcused omission of the statutory signals is more than some evidence of negligence. It *is* negligence in itself. Lights are intended for the guidance and protection of other travelers on the highway. By the very terms of the hypothesis, to omit, willfully or heedlessly, the safeguards prescribed by law for the benefit of another that he may be preserved in life or limb, is to fall short of the standard of diligence to which those who live in organized society are under a duty to conform. . . . In the case at hand, we have an instance of the admitted violation of a statute intended for the protection of travelers on the highway, of whom the defendant at the time was one. Yet the jurors were instructed in effect that they were at liberty in their discretion to treat the omission of lights either as innocent or as culpable. They were allowed to "consider the default as lightly or gravely" as they would (Thomas, J., in the court below). . . . Jurors have no dispensing power by which they may relax the duty that one traveler on the highway owes under the statute to another. It is error to tell them that they have. The omission of

these lights was a wrong, and being wholly unexcused was also a negligent wrong. No license should have been conceded to the triers of the facts to find it anything else.

126 N.E., at 815.

Professor Dobbs reports that a few jurisdictions decline to follow this approach and instead treat the doctrine of negligence *per se* as stating a rule that statutory violations may be introduced as evidence of negligence. Dan B. Dobbs, *The Law of Torts* § 134, at 316-317 (2000).

2. *Breach versus Actual Cause.* In another portion of *Martin*, Cardozo warned against the conflation of the issue of breach with that of cause-in-fact:

> We must be on our guard . . . against confusing the question of negligence with that of the causal connection between the negligence and the injury. A defendant who travels without lights is not to pay damages for his fault unless the absence of lights is the cause of the disaster. A plaintiff who travels without them is not to forfeit the right to damages unless the absence of lights is at least a contributing cause of the disaster.

Id. at 816. Consider this admonition in connection with the remand order in *Dalal*. Might a jury still be able to conclude that Dalal should not recover in negligence?

3. *Safety versus Licensing and Other Statutes.* Notice in *Dalal* the defendant's (failed) argument that Dalal should not benefit from the doctrine of negligence *per se* because the statute that Ramdhani-Mack violated was a mere "licensing" statute. This argument attempts to invoke the rule that negligence per se only applies to violations of statutes that are intended to set standards of conduct, rather than serve record-keeping or other administrative functions. For example, most courts hold that the victim of a car accident cannot conclusively establish fault on the part of the defendant driver simply by proving that she was operating her vehicle without a valid driver's license. This is because (apart from the perfunctory quiz on basic rules of the road), the licensing requirement functions as a means of record-keeping, not as a scheme setting standards as to how one should drive. Likewise, courts have held that medical malpractice plaintiffs cannot establish fault simply by proving that their treating physician was unlicensed. *See, e.g.*, Brown v. Shyne, 151 N.E. 197 (N.Y. 1926). To observe that courts tend to refuse to give dispositive effect to violations of licensing and reporting statutes is not to say that such violations are always *irrelevant* to the breach issue. Indeed, plaintiffs typically can introduce evidence of the defendant's failure to possess a required license as evidence in support of a finding that the defendant failed to adhere to the common law's reasonable person standard.

4. *Conditions for the Application of Negligence Per Se.* Establishing a violation of a conduct-oriented statutory command is *necessary* to make out a claim for negligence per se. However, as *Bayne* and *Victor* emphasize, it is not *sufficient*. In addition, the party seeking to invoke the

doctrine must also establish that the law was meant to protect a class of persons including the plaintiff and to protect against the sort of injury suffered by the plaintiff. Restatement (Second) of Torts § 286 (1965). Conversely, if a plaintiff fails to establish either that she was in the protected class, or that she suffered the right sort of injury, she cannot rely on the statutory violation to establish breach as a matter of law, leaving her to proceed under the ordinary reasonable person standard.

5. *The Protected Class.* Todd, the defendant in *Bayne*, argued that the regulatory requirement of railings was not enacted for the benefit of Bayne. Why not? How is one to gauge who was meant to benefit from such a regulation?

Several courts have confronted the parallel question of whether workplace safety regulations issued by the federal Occupational Safety and Health Agency (OSHA) were meant for the benefit only of employees, or also independent contractors and other invitees of a business. For example, in Walton v. Potlach Corp., 781 P.2d 229 (Idaho 1989), the plaintiff was an employee of a company that was hired by the defendant to repair the bleaching tower of defendant's paper mill. While doing so, he was exposed to chlorine dioxide gas that was released because of a leak in the tower. The exposure caused permanent damage to his lungs. Walton sued, claiming that Potlach's release of the gas violated an OSHA regulation stating that owners and operators of paper mills "shall not" release such gas into the atmosphere without first treating and neutralizing it. The majority held that Walton could invoke the regulation, even though he was not an employee, in part because Walton's work was closely monitored and controlled by Potlach. A dissenter, noting a split among courts on this issue, reasoned that Walton should not have been permitted to invoke the regulation because the enabling statutes that created OSHA indicate that their aim was to ensure that employers provide safe workplaces for their employees. The dissent further suggested that, in close cases, courts ought not to apply negligence per se doctrine:

> . . . the effect of a negligence per se instruction is to deprive a litigant of his right to a jury trial on the question of the reasonableness of his conduct. . . . Given the equivocal nature of whether or not OSHA has any authority [over], much less intended its regulations to apply to[,] third parties . . . the strong policy . . . favoring jury trials on issues of fact should not be usurped by an overbroad application of the doctrine. . . .

Id. at 238 (Bakes, C.J., dissenting).

Suppose Bayne was on the loading platform not for a business purpose, but because he was meeting a friend for lunch. Would he still be considered a member of the protected class? In Thoma v. Kettler Bros., Inc., 632 A.2d 725 (D.C. 1993), the plaintiff, a prospective purchaser of townhouse, was on the premises by permission and was injured because of a dangerous condition that amounted to a violation of OSHA regulations. The court held that the plaintiff was not an intended beneficiary of the regulations, and thus could not invoke them to establish *per se* carelessness on the part of the developer and builder. The court did, however, permit her to introduce the statutory violations as evidence of carelessness.

What if Bayne were technically trespassing because he failed to obtain permission to proceed to the loading dock to meet his friend? Would negligence per se apply? Might the categories of landowner liability discussed in Chapter 2 have any bearing here? If so, does that connection shed any light on the type of inquiry to be made under the "protected class" aspect of negligence per se doctrine?

6. *The Right Sort of Injury.* Why did the *Victor* court conclude that Victor could not invoke negligence per se? Because the law in question did not set a standard of safe conduct? Because the plaintiff, as a pedestrian, was not within the protected class? Do you find its interpretation of the statute compelling? Does the negligence per se requirement of the "right sort of injury" resemble a mode of analysis you have encountered in connection with ordinary negligence actions?

7. *Other Cases.* Compare the analysis and result in *Victor* to those of the following four decisions. In Chevron U.S.A., Inc. v. Forbes, 783 So. 2d 1215 (Fla. App. 2001), the plaintiff, a patron of the defendant gas station, slipped in a puddle of gas. The plaintiff attempted to invoke negligence per se on the basis of a statute requiring that self-service gas stations be staffed during business hours by an attendant, and that attendants promptly clean up spills of gasoline. The court held that the staffing and clean-up requirement were fire-safety measures, not measures designed to prevent slips and falls.

In Wawanesa Mut. Ins. Co. v. Matlock, 60 Cal. App. 4th 583 (Cal. App. 1997), *rev. denied*, 1998 Cal. LEXIS 2048, a lumber company (*L*) lost a good deal of lumber because of a fire caused by a minor (*M*) who dropped a lit cigarette onto it. After *L*'s property insurer (*PI*) paid for the loss, it sought to recoup the value of its payment from the defendant (*D*), who had provided cigarettes to *M* in violation of a statute barring the provision of cigarettes to minors. The court rejected *PI*'s argument that *D*'s statutory violation constituted *per se* carelessness. The statute, it reasoned, was enacted to prevent young persons from becoming addicted to cigarettes, not to reduce the risk of fire caused by dropping them while lit.

In the famous English case of Gorris v. Scott, 1874 L.R. 9 Ex. 125, the ship's owner failed to keep sheep in separate pens in violation of a statute. Because the sheep were not penned, several were lost overboard. The owner sued and attempted to argue negligence per se. The Exchequer Court ruled, however, that the statute was enacted for the purpose of preventing the spread of infectious diseases among animals, not to prevent them from washing overboard.

Finally, consider the last tort-law decision that Cardozo wrote for the New York Court of Appeals before ascending to a seat on the U.S. Supreme Court, De Haen v. Rockwood Sprinkler Co., 179 N.E.2d 764 (N.Y. 1932). There, the plaintiff's decedent was killed when another worker bumped into a radiator that had been placed near the edge of a "hoistway" being used to construct a building, whereupon it fell onto the decedent. The plaintiff successfully invoked negligence per se against the building company on the ground that the company failed to comply with a statute requiring that hoistway openings be fully enclosed on two sides, and that the two remaining (open) sides be guarded by a bar at a height of 3 to 4 feet off the floor. Writing for the court, Cardozo affirmed the verdict:

> The chief object of this statute is to protect workmen from the hazard of falling into a shaft. We cannot say, however, that no other hazard was within the zone of apprehension. On two sides of the shaft there must be a solid or comparatively solid fence. Only on the other sides where material is taken on or off may there be a single bar. If there was no thought to give protection against falling missiles or debris, the lawmakers might well have stopped with a requirement that there be a single bar on every side. The fact that they did not stop there is evidence of a broader purpose. True, indeed, it is that on two of the four sides the security is only partial and imperfect. A barrier set in place at a height of four feet will often be of little avail in holding back material or rubbish collected on the floor. Even so, security against the hazard of falling objects will not be lacking altogether. One of the requirements of the statute is that the guard shall be placed at least two feet from the edge. In a barrier so fixed there is warning, if no more. Workmen, who may otherwise be tempted to store material in dangerous proximity to the edge of an open shaft, will be reminded of the danger and will tend to stand afar. The thoughtless will be checked, though the recklessly indifferent will be free to go their way.
>
> The potencies of protection that reside in such a barrier have illustration in the case before us. If the hoistway had been guarded, it is unlikely that the radiators thirty-eight inches high would have been placed as they were within falling distance of the edge. It is still less likely that a worker would heedlessly have brushed against them and so brought about the fall. We do not mean to say that these considerations are decisive. Liability is not established by a showing that as chance would have it a statutory safeguard might have avoided the particular hazard out of which an accident ensued. The hazard out of which the accident ensued must have been the particular hazard or class of hazards that the statutory safeguard in the thought and purpose of the Legislature was intended to correct. None the less, the sequence of events may help to fix the limits of a purpose that would be obscure if viewed alone. A safeguard has been commanded, but without distinct enumeration of the hazards to be avoided. In the revealing light of experience the hazards to be avoided are disclosed to us as the hazards that ensued.

Id. at 765-766.

8. *Excused Violations.* Courts recognize certain grounds on which actors who have violated statutes are nonetheless excused from being held *per se* at fault. For example, young children are often excused from violations on the ground that they cannot be expected to conform to statutory and regulatory commands. (Again, the point is not that children can never be held liable, only that they cannot be found to have acted unreasonably *per se*. Thus, the plaintiff is presumably left to pursue his case under common law standards of reasonableness as they apply to children. See Chapter 3.)

Some courts will also excuse violations where there is evidence that violation of the statute was the more prudent course of conduct for the defendant to follow. For example, in Tedla v. Ellman, 19 N.E.2d 987 (1939), the plaintiff was walking along the side of a busy road with her back to oncoming traffic in violation of a statute requiring pedestrians to walk so as to face oncoming vehicles. On this basis, the defendant argued that the plaintiff's conduct constituted *per se* contributory fault. The court rejected this argument, concluding that traffic and road conditions on that particular stretch of road were such that the plaintiff had chosen the safer course by violating the statute. Courts may also deem statutory violations not to be instances of *per se* carelessness if the defendant can show that it was unable, despite reasonable diligence, to comply. *See* Busby v. Quail Creek Golf & Country Club, 885 P.2d 1326 (Okla. 1994) (country club can be held negligent per se for serving alcohol to the minor plaintiff in violation of statute; however, the club will be excused from its violation if it establishes that it had no means of knowing that the plaintiff was a minor because she produced a realistic false I.D. and appeared to be over 21).

According to comment j to Section 288A of the Second Restatement, it is for the court to determine if the excuse proffered by the statutory violator is of a type recognized by the law of negligence, and for the jury to decide any relevant factual disputes as to whether the conditions necessary to establish the excuse have been made out. Professor Dobbs suggests that decisions such as *Busby* and *Tedla* effectively convert the doctrine of negligence per se into a form of burden shifting. When invoked by a plaintiff, a violation of a statutory standard of conduct relieves her of the burden of proving fault, and places the burden on the defendant to prove an excuse. Likewise, a defendant in a case such as *Tedla* who seeks to establish comparative fault is relieved of his burden by establishing plaintiff's violation, and the plaintiff is then left to establish a valid excuse. Dobbs, *supra*, § 140, at 330-331. Presumably, once a valid excuse is established, the conduct of the statutory violator—at least as it pertains to the conduct that amounted to the violation—has been determined to be reasonable.

9. *Interrelation of Negligence Per Se and "Ordinary" Negligence.* As demonstrated in *Victor*, if a court concludes that a party seeking to invoke *negligence per se* is unable to satisfy the requirements of that doctrine, the court does *not* thereby conclude that the party has no negligence action whatsoever. Rather, it determines that the party has not relieved itself of the burden of persuading the judge or jury that a breach occurred under the reasonable person standard. In other words, the court must still undertake ordinary common law negligence analysis to see whether the party can make out a claim. On what ground did the court subsequently conclude that Victor could not establish liability for ordinary negligence?

II.   WRONGFUL DEATH ACTS

The root idea expressed in *Palsgraf* is that only those who have been wronged by the defendant's misconduct are entitled to sue for injuries caused by that wrong. Thus, *P* is not empowered to sue *D* for conduct that is a wrong only to *T*, even if *D*'s wronging of *T* happens to injure *P*. By focusing on this idea of relationality (or "standing"), one can begin to comprehend the common law's seemingly strange prohibition of tort claims on behalf of persons killed by the careless acts of others, as well as against tortfeasors who die prior to judgment. That understanding can in turn give us perspective on the statutory regime that has developed as a supplement to the common law.

A. *Historical Background*

Instances of careless conduct proximately causing death would seem to count as among the most obvious and egregious forms of actionable negligence. Yet, until about 1850, English law almost never authorized causes of action for negligence resulting in death. This surprising gap emerged from a confluence of several common law rules.

1. Actio Personalis. Common law observed the maxim *actio personalis moritur cum persona* ("a 'personal' cause of action dies with the person.") The reasoning seems to have been as follows. Suppose plaintiff *P* was the only one wronged, in Cardozo's sense, by *D*'s negligence. It follows that, if *P* were to die prior to completion of his tort suit against *D*, there would no longer be anyone alive with "standing" to sue *D* for *P*'s injuries. By parallel reasoning, the common law operated on the rule that the death of the alleged tortfeasor prior to judgment barred tort claims against him simply because the actual perpetrator of the alleged wrong was no longer around to provide redress. In the words of the famous English jurist William Blackstone, the tort action died with the plaintiff or defendant because "neither the [representatives of the deceased] plaintiff have received, nor those of the defendant have committed, in their own personal capacity, any manner of wrong or injury." 3 William Blackstone, *Commentaries on the Law of England* *302 (1765-1769).* It might help to grasp the idea underlying the *actio personalis* maxim to pose the following questions: Why should someone other than the defendant (e.g., his heirs) pay for his wrong? Why should someone other than the wronged plaintiff obtain compensation for that wrong?

2. *Husbands and Loss of Consortium.* One rule of the common law seemed to point toward an exception to the *actio personalis* maxim. This is the rule that permitted suits by husbands for injuries caused to their wives by the wrongful act of another. To these unfortunate husbands, the law made available the action for trespass on the case *per quod consortium amisit* (literally, "a trespass whereby [plaintiff] lost the company of his wife"). 3 Blackstone, *supra*, at *140. In modern terminology, the husband whose wife was tortiously injured had an action for "loss of

---

* These rules did not apply to actions for breach of contract, which were conceived of as actions concerning property rather than the person. One imagines that this variance in treatment encouraged lawyerly manipulation of the categories. For example, claims of medical malpractice causing death were perhaps pleaded as arising in contract (breach of a promise to treat competently) rather than tort.

consortium," by which he could seek compensation from the tortfeasor for the deprivation of the companionship of his wife. In principle, the loss of consortium action applied regardless of whether the deprivation was temporary (i.e., the wife was injured) or permanent (i.e., the wife was killed).

On what basis did the common law recognize an exception to the *actio personalis* maxim for loss of consortium actions seeking compensation for the wrongful killing of plaintiff's wife? Here one has to appreciate that, by modern Anglo-American standards, English common law was patriarchal and sexist. For these purposes, at least, a husband was treated as owning the "services" of his wife.* The action for loss of consortium thus did not seek compensation for the wife's death, nor for the emotional distress of the husband, but for his loss of the value of her services. Given these premises, it followed that wives could not take advantage of the loss of consortium action. Simply put, they were not regarded in this respect as full-fledged, rights-bearing persons. 3 Blackstone, *supra*, at *142-143.**

3. *Husbands and the Felony Merger Rule.*

The consortium action, grounded in this patriarchal conception of ownership, thus empowered one set of persons — husbands — to seek compensation for wrongfully caused death. However, this right was a matter more of theory than practice, because husbands faced a significant practical barrier to bringing such claims, one that arose from a third facet of English common law: the interaction between criminal and tort law.

Under the criminal law of the seventeenth and early eighteenth centuries, all crimes that constituted "felonies" were punishable by forfeiture to the Crown of all the felon's assets. Most felonies also earned the criminal the death penalty. Premeditated killings constituted one class of felonies subject to these penalties. So, too, did killings arising from

---

* Under the common law doctrine of "coverture," a married woman was not recognized as a separate, rights-bearing person for purposes of civil law. (This treatment did not extend to other areas of law. For example, the intentional killing of a married woman was still treated as a murder.) This subsumption of the wife into the husband meant not only that the husband "owned" her services, but also that she lacked the authority to sue in her own name for injuries done to her. Thus, if we imagine an early nineteenth-century suit complaining that one Jones had tortiously injured a Mrs. Smith, the case caption for the suit would usually read *Smith et ux. v. Jones*. By use of the phrase "et ux." — an abbreviation of a Latin phrase meaning "and wife" — this formulation indicated that *Mr.* Smith was suing in his own right for loss of consortium (*his* loss of companionship and support, etc.), while also suing to recover for harm suffered by Mrs. Smith (*her* bodily injury, pain and suffering, etc.). Starting in the mid-nineteenth century, U.S. legislatures began enacting statutes granting married women independent legal status.

** Prior to 1600, wives could institute a proceeding called an "appeal," a hybrid criminal-tort action that, contrary to the suggestion of its name, consisted of a suit in its own right, as opposed to a request for higher-court review of a lower-court ruling. By "appealing" a defendant for allegedly killing her spouse, a widow initiated a private criminal prosecution for the felony of homicide. If the prosecution resulted in conviction, the killer would be executed. Although the wife was not formally entitled to compensation, the parties to these appeals often "settled" these actions, with the blessing of government prosecutors, by means of a monetary payment to the victim's family. By the 1700s, however, the appeal had fallen into disuse as the Crown increasingly claimed the exclusive power to indict and prosecute criminal offenses.

recklessness and perhaps even negligence on the part of the killer. (Blackstone gives as an example of a felony a worker on a platform throwing down a heavy stone onto a busy city street and killing a pedestrian.)

The death penalty and the total forfeiture rule eliminated the practical point of a loss of consortium suit by a husband who might otherwise seek compensation via a tort suit against a person who killed his wife. The execution of the felonious tortfeasor would itself abate any civil action not concluded prior to the criminal punishment. Moreover, given the forfeiture punishment, the defendant's estate would be devoid of assets with which to satisfy a tort judgment. Over time, these *de facto* bars to tort suits complaining of conduct that also constituted a felony became codified into a legal rule called the "felony merger doctrine." That doctrine held that all private rights of action based on felonious conduct were "swallowed up" by the Crown's criminal prosecution and thereby rendered moot. 4 Blackstone, *supra*, at *6.

4. *Baker v. Bolton.* By 1800, then, the state of English law was roughly as follows: (1) the death of the victim precluded any tort action on behalf of the victim for his injuries, and (2) although husbands in theory could sue for the wrongful killing of their wives, the felony merger rule barred suits for intentional, reckless, and perhaps negligent killings. It is possible that this scheme of rules left open room to sue for certain negligent killings not deemed felonies. (In addition, if the standard in the old trespass actions really was a strict liability standard, certain husbands might also be able to sue for the innocent killings of their wives.) However, even if these sorts of killings in theory provided a small window for loss of consortium suits by husbands, that window was closed by the 1808 decision of Baker v. Bolton. Confronted there with a tort claim by a husband for the negligent killing of his wife, Lord Ellenborough declared summarily that, "[i]n a civil court, the death of a human being [cannot] be complained of as an injury." 1 Campb. 493. *Baker* thus established the hard-and-fast rule that a husband whose wife was accidentally killed could not recover by means of a loss of consortium action. (This even though, if she had been accidentally *injured*, he would be entitled to recover both for her injuries and his loss of consortium.)

B. *Lord Campbell's Act and American Statutes*

Dissatisfaction in England with the common law bar on tort actions for negligently caused deaths soon mounted. Many bemoaned a system in which a negligence defendant was better off in terms of liability if his careless conduct killed rather than merely wounded the victim.* (Of course,

---

* Legend has it that, prior to the passage of wrongful death acts, railroad companies designed their cars to ensure that, if there was an accident, the passengers would be killed (nonactionable) rather than merely injured (actionable). This legend transformed into the urban myth that railroad company managers instructed train personnel that, in the event of an accident, they should surreptitiously "finish off" any injured passengers because that would permit the companies to avoid liability.

the killer was better off only with respect to tort liability. If the killing was deemed a felony, as most were, he was subject to execution!) They likewise thought it unjust that widows and their children could be driven into destitution by the negligent killing of the husband/father without any recourse against the wrongdoer.

In 1846, Parliament responded by enacting Lord Campbell's Act. The majority of American states soon followed the English lead by enacting their own statutes. These statutes are now generally referred to as *wrongful death statutes*, even though, as we will see, this is a slight misnomer. The statutes were (and still are) diverse in their particulars, but they typically ushered in two broad changes in tort law. First, they allowed tort litigation to proceed after the death of the plaintiff or defendant, with representatives of the deceased party(ies) now taking over the litigation.* Second, they empowered certain family members to sue, in Cardozo's words, as "vicarious beneficiaries" of breaches of duties owed only to others.

1. *Survival Actions.* The wrongful death statutes substantially modified both aspects of the *actio personalis* maxim. Thus, tort suits may now proceed after the death of a defendant as claims against the defendant's estate. Moreover, certain tort actions — including negligence actions — that the deceased would have been able to bring against the tortfeasor had he not died can now proceed with an administrator serving as the plaintiff. These latter actions are known as *survival* actions.

Damages recoverable in survival actions have a fairly narrow aim: to provide the decedent's estate with compensation for any harm that the decedent suffered *up to the moment of her death*. By contrast, other harms, including loss of future income, are not compensable in survival actions. The theory is that a dead person *herself* does not suffer from being deprived of future gains: After all, she is not around to enjoy them. As such, compensation flowing from these actions is often quite modest, typically being limited to medical expenses incurred prior to death (which may be nonexistent, if death was instantaneous), funeral expenses, and lost earnings between the time of injury and the time of death. However, most states also permit recovery in survival actions for pain and suffering experienced by the decedent prior to death, an element of damages that, where recognized, will often support more substantial damage awards (again, assuming death was not instantaneous).

2. *Wrongful Death Actions.* The same statutes that create survival actions have also authorized *wrongful death* claims by certain family members for at least some of the harms they have suffered by virtue of the

---

* This is why the caption of *McGuiggan*, the social host liability case, *supra*, Chapter 2, reads: *Daniel E. McGuiggan, administrator v. New England Tel. & Tel. Co.* Daniel E. McGuiggan was the father of Daniel Jr., the young man killed when he leaned out of a car at just the wrong moment. Daniel Sr. brought the action against the telephone company as administrator of his son's estate. This fact made the defendant phone company's attempt to invoke the social host theory of liability all the more ironic. Had it prevailed, Daniel Sr. (in his capacity as administrator) would have had a claim against himself (i.e., in his capacity as social host).

wrongful killing of the decedent. "Wrongful" in these statutes is taken to be equivalent of "tortious." Thus, if conduct would have amounted to a tort had the victim been injured, it constitutes "wrongful" death when death rather than injury results. Obviously, by such inclusive wording, the wrongful death statutes laid to rest the felony merger doctrine: An intentional and unjustified killing is "wrongful" and therefore actionable. (Although many states still adhere to the death penalty for especially heinous felonies, modern American criminal law has abandoned the rule that anyone who commits a felony automatically forfeits his assets to the government.)

In contrast to survival actions, wrongful death actions do not seek to impose liability for the *decedent's* losses prior to death. Instead, they compensate immediate family members for the losses that *they have suffered* because of the decedent's death. This is why wrongful death claims are "vicarious" or "derivative" in nature. The idea is that R, close relation of V, is given a means to complain of a wrong to V that has also caused harm to R.

The question then arises: Actionable by whom and for what? Lord Campbell's Act specified the eligible beneficiaries to be the "wife, husband, parent and[/or] child" of the decedent who was wrongfully killed. Thus, it empowered not only husbands to sue for the loss of their wives' (or children's) support and services, but also wives (and children) to sue for loss of support caused by the wrongful killing of their husbands (and fathers). Evidently, the concern was to compensate two classes of victims: widowers who had lost valuable services, and widows and orphans who had lost their breadwinner. As Professor Witt has shown, a slight majority of mid-nineteenth-century American statutes declined to empower husbands to sue for wrongful death. Apparently, these American legislatures rejected the patriarchal notion that a husband owned his wife's services, and were primarily concerned to identify a possible source of economic support for economic dependents who had lost their source of income because of the wrongful act of another. Later, toward the turn of the twentieth century, courts and legislatures added husbands to the list of beneficiaries.

Lord Campbell's Act left it to the jury to specify a wrongful death claimant's damages. In theory, then, the jury was empowered to award surviving family members compensation not only for economic loss but also for their bereavement. However, in keeping with their tendency to exclude claims by husbands, American statutes until recently tended to limit damages exclusively to the *pecuniary losses* suffered by surviving family members, typically measured as the percentage of the decedent's expected future income that would have been devoted to the support of the surviving spouse and/or minor child(ren). This limited conception of damages not only excluded compensation for anguish and loss of companionship caused by the death of a loved one, it also meant that even after husbands were formally empowered to bring wrongful death claims, such claims promised them little compensation, simply because courts tended to assign little or no *economic* value to "wifely" services such as housework.

Consider the following decision on the issue of the type of damages recoverable in survival and wrongful death actions. Does its different treatment of the two make sense?

Nelson v. Dolan
434 N.W.2d 25 (Neb. 1989)

Caporale, J.   In this suit joining an action for the wrongful death of Robert James Nelson with . . . [a survival] action on behalf of his estate, the defendant-appellee, Paul J. Dolan, admitted that his negligence proximately caused decedent Nelson's death. The jury thus returned a verdict in favor of the plaintiff-appellant, Phyllis F. Nelson, personal representative of the estate of the aforenamed decedent, and judgment was rendered accordingly in the total sum of $37,968.26. The personal representative nonetheless appeals, asserting as error the district court's sustainment of Dolan's motion in limine preventing her from adducing evidence concerning (1) the mental anguish suffered by the next of kin of the decedent and (2) the mental anguish suffered by the decedent Nelson himself. . . .

I.   OFFER OF PROOF

. . . [A] collision occurred in the early morning hours of June 22, 1984, between an automobile operated by Dolan and a motorcycle driven by the 17-year-old decedent Nelson, and on which the latter's friend, Kevin Coffin, was riding as a passenger. Decedent Nelson and Coffin had just left the scene of a fight in Grand Island, Nebraska, and were traveling on a Grand Island street when they noticed behind them an automobile driven by Dolan. In an effort to lose the Dolan automobile, decedent Nelson entered a highway and later turned onto an asphalt road, traveling at 85 miles per hour. Dolan nonetheless continued to follow the motorcycle at a distance of about 50 to 75 feet. In his deposition, Coffin said that "[a]t one point, they got really close. And I got scared, so I turned around and hit the hood of the car with my hand." The automobile was at that time about 1 or 2 feet behind the motorcycle.

After Coffin hit the hood of the Dolan automobile, Dolan backed off, sped up, and hit the motorcycle. Upon impact at a point just outside Grand Island, the two vehicles locked together and, according to an accident reconstructionist, traveled thus locked, with decedent Nelson trying to maintain control, for about 268 feet over a period of approximately 5 seconds until the motorcycle struck a light post, fell, and went under the Dolan automobile. Decedent Nelson's body was found underneath the Dolan automobile, and the personal representative acknowledges that decedent Nelson was crushed by Dolan's automobile and that death was instantaneous.

A psychiatrist offered to testify, in effect, that in his opinion decedent Nelson understood he was going to be run down from the moment the Dolan automobile made contact with the motorcycle and that he "must have been absolutely terrified," knowing or thinking that he was going to die for whatever period of time intervened between the two vehicles' coming together and death.

The personal representative's treating physician offered to testify that he thought she suffered from endogenous depression and acute anxiety caused in part by the loss of the decedent Nelson, who was her son. He treated the condition with medication over a 2-year period and is of the opinion that the condition would continue and should be treated by a psychiatrist.

The personal representative offered to testify that she felt a great loss as the result of her son's death, has found it difficult to sleep since his death, has lost 30 to 40 pounds, is mentally unstable, and has lost her job because of her inability to work.

II. ANALYSIS

The personal representative's contentions require an examination of the types of damages which flow from an actionable death and to whose benefit such damages inure.

A. WRONGFUL DEATH ACTION

While adjudication of the first assignment of error requires only an analysis of the nature of a wrongful death action, the second assignment of error requires an analysis of both the nature of such an action and the nature of an action brought on behalf of a decedent's estate. We concern ourselves first with the wrongful death action.

1. Next of Kin's Damages

The first assignment of error asserts that the district court erred by rejecting the offer of proof concerning the mental anguish suffered by decedent Nelson's next of kin. . . .

The Nebraska wrongful death action is found in Neb. Rev. Stat. §§ 30-809 and 30-810 (Reissue 1985). The first of these statutes provides in relevant part:

> Whenever the death of a person shall be caused by the wrongful act, neglect or default, of any person . . . and the act, neglect or default is such as would, if death had not ensued, have entitled the party injured to maintain an action and recover damages in respect thereof, then . . . the person who . . . would have been liable if death had not ensued, shall be liable to an action for damages, notwithstanding the death of the person injured, and although the death shall have been caused under such circumstances as amount in law to felony.

The second statute reads in relevant part:

> Every such action, as described in section 30-809, shall be . . . brought by and in the name of [the decedent's] personal representatives, for the exclusive benefit of the . . . next of kin. The verdict or judgment should be for the amount of damages which the persons in whose behalf the action is brought have sustained. The avails thereof shall be paid to and distributed among the

. . . next of kin in the proportion that the pecuniary loss suffered by each bears to the total pecuniary loss suffered by all such persons.

Thus, the damages recoverable, the disposition of the avails obtained, and the measure of recovery in a wrongful death action are all fixed by statute.

Johnson County v. Carmen, 71 Neb. 682, 99 N.W. 502 (1904), determined that a [predecessor] statute permitting jurors to award such damages, not to exceed $5,000, "as they shall deem a fair and just compensation with reference to the pecuniary injuries, resulting from such death," Gen. Stat. ch. 15, § 2 (1873), did not permit the next of kin to recover for bereavement, mental suffering, or solace. The *Carmen* court ruled that a jury is "limited to giving pecuniary compensation resulting to the next of kin on account of the death of the deceased." *Carmen* at 685, 99 N.W. at 503.

A 1919 amendment to the damages language found in the *Carmen* statute produced the damages language now found in § 30-810. In considering that amendment, this court, in Ensor v. Compton, 110 Neb. 522, 524, 194 N.W. 458, 459 (1923), said:

> This amendment was made by the legislature after this court had, by a long line of decisions, held that damages in this class of cases were limited under the statute to money loss or its equivalent. This change, while significant, does not provide a wide open door to all sorts of claims for damages. The loss under the statute is still a pecuniary loss. *Nothing can be allowed on account of mental suffering or bereavement or as a solace on account of such death.* Only such damages can be recovered as are shown by the evidence to have a monetary value. In states having a statute similar to our own, it has generally been construed as permitting recovery of damages for loss of service and companionship under special circumstances where the evidence shows they have a money value. [Citations omitted.] However, recovery for loss of services and companionship by a surviving husband or wife can only be sustained where the evidence shows a reasonable probability that such services and companionship afforded the survivor was of such a character that it would be of advantage to such survivor, and that a disallowance thereof would cause a pecuniary loss to him or her. [Citation omitted.]

(Emphasis supplied.)

In allowing recovery for the economic value of the society, comfort, and companionship lost by the next of kin, the opinion of this court in Selders v. Armentrout, 190 Neb. 275, 207 N.W.2d 686 (1973), noted that the wrongful death damages statute had been interpreted as limiting recovery to pecuniary loss. The *Selders* opinion then went on to explain that damages for loss of society, comfort, and companionship were recoverable because they constituted services which have a financial value to the next of kin.

This court recently reaffirmed . . . that damages on account of mental suffering or bereavement or as a solace to the next of kin on account of the death are not recoverable. . . .

The personal representative concedes the current status of the law but invites us to abandon our prior interpretation and permit the next of kin to recover for her or his mental anguish in an action for wrongful death on the ground that a number of other states so permit. *See, e.g.*, Tommy's Elbow Room, Inc. v. Kavorkian, 727 P.2d 1038 (Alaska 1986); Moore v. Lillebo, 722 S.W.2d 683 (Tex. 1986). . . .

We decline the invitation without undertaking any comparison of the various statutes of other states with our own, for the invitation overlooks the general and dispositive rule that where a statute has been judicially construed and that construction has not evoked an amendment, it will be presumed that the Legislature has acquiesced in the court's determination of its intent. That being so, it cannot now be judicially declared that the Legislature meant something else; thus, the personal representative's first assignment of error fails.

2.   Decedent Nelson's Damages

In connection with the second assignment of error, the personal representative first argues that she is entitled to recover in the wrongful death action for the mental anguish decedent Nelson himself experienced prior to his death. In doing so, she ignores the plain language of § 30-810 and thus is once again in error. The statutory language plainly limits a wrongful death recovery to the loss suffered by a decedent's next of kin; it provides no basis upon which to recover a decedent's own damages. . . .

The issue is not unlike that presented in Kroeger v. Safranek, 161 Neb. 182, 72 N.W.2d 831 (1955), a wrongful death action in which . . . the jury . . . [heard evidence that] the person killed suffered " 'an excruciating death by electrocution.' " *Id.* at 192, 72 N.W.2d at 840. In reversing a verdict . . . in favor of the plaintiff . . . , this court, quoting from Hindmarsh v. Sulpho Saline Bath Co., 108 Neb. 168, 187 N.W. 806 (1922), said at 192, 72 N.W.2d at 840:

> [I]n the action brought by the personal representative, in behalf of the statutory beneficiaries, to recover damages for the death caused by the wrongful act of the defendant, *the recovery must be measured by the pecuniary loss suffered by those beneficiaries.* . . .
> *Thus any pain or suffering endured by the decedent is not an element upon which appellee can herein base any recovery* and it was error for the court to include the allegations in its instructions.

(Emphasis supplied.)

However, the determination that damages for a decedent's preimpact mental anguish cannot be recovered in a wrongful death action does not resolve the second assignment of error; the petition here joins with the wrongful death action a separate action on behalf of the decedent's estate, a procedure which our law permits.

B.   ESTATE ACTION

Thus, the question becomes whether a decedent's estate may recover for the mental anguish a decedent consciously suffers by the apprehension and fear of impending death prior to sustaining fatal injury.

While we have not heretofore considered this question, we have long permitted a decedent's estate to recover for the conscious physical pain and suffering the decedent endured after a negligently inflicted injury resulting in death. We have also long recognized postinjury mental anguish as an element of damages recoverable in personal injury actions.

Some courts have allowed recovery for conscious preimpact mental anguish suffered by decedents aware of impending death. Most of these cases are federal diversity actions and arise out of airplane crashes.

In one such action, Shu-Tao Lin v. McDonnell Douglas Corp., 742 F.2d 45 (2d Cir. 1984), the decedent was killed when a jet crashed shortly after takeoff. The reviewing court referred with approval to the language of the trial court, 574 F. Supp. 1407, 1416 (S.D.N.Y. 1983), which observed:

> New York provides a cause of action for the pain and suffering of a decedent before his death. In several cases it has been held that a decedent's estate may recover for the decedent's pain and suffering endured *after* the injury that led to his death. [Citations omitted.] From this proposition, it is only a short step to the allowing of damages for a decedent's pain and suffering *before* the mortal blow and resulting from the apprehension of impending death.

(Emphasis in original.) The reviewing court then itself reasoned:

> A decedent's representative unquestionably may recover for pain and suffering experienced in a brief interval between injury and death. . . . We see no intrinsic or logical barrier to recovery for the fear experienced during a period in which the decedent is uninjured but aware of an impending death.

742 F.2d at 53.

In Haley v. Pan American World Airways, 746 F.2d 311 (5th Cir. 1984), *reh'g denied* 751 F.2d 1258, the court interpreting state law concluded that Louisiana would recognize a surviving cause of action for preimpact fear and apprehension of impending death experienced by an airline passenger killed in an airplane crash. In *Haley*, as in our present case, the decedent was killed immediately upon impact. The court based its decision on Louisiana law which permitted recovery for fear suffered during a negligently produced ordeal. . . . [It also] quoted with approval the analysis from its earlier decision in Solomon v. Warren, 540 F.2d 777 (5th Cir. 1976), *cert. denied* 434 U.S. 801, 98 S. Ct. 28, 54 L. Ed. 2d 59 (1977) (interpreting Florida law):

> While in the garden variety of claims under survival statutes, including the Florida Statute — fatal injuries sustained in automobile accidents and the like — the usual sequence is impact followed by pain and suffering, we are unable to discern any reason based on either law or logic for rejecting a claim because in this case as to at least part of the suffering, this sequence was reversed. We will not disallow the claims for this item of damages on that ground.

Haley at 314-15. . . .

Similarly, in Missouri Pacific R. Co. v. Lane, 720 S.W.2d 830 (Tex. App. 1986), the court affirmed an award for mental anguish suffered by the decedent before a train hit his stalled truck. As to the claim that such damages were not recoverable because decedent died instantly, the court reasoned: "Such an argument fails to consider the terror and consequent mental anguish Lane suffered for the six to eight seconds while he faced imminent death." *Id.* at 833.

Similar results were obtained in [several other decisions]. [Citations omitted. — EDS.]

Some courts, however, have denied recovery for preimpact mental anguish. E.g., Nye v. Com., Dept. of Transp., 331 Pa. Super. 209, 480 A.2d 318 (1984) (no damages available under Pennsylvania statute for conscious preimpact fright); In re Air Crash Disaster Near Chicago, Ill. etc., 507 F. Supp. 21 (N.D. Ill. 1980) (no recovery under Illinois law for fright and terror decedent may have suffered in anticipation of physical injury prior to death in an airplane crash); Fogarty v. Campbell 66 Exp., Inc., 640 F. Supp. 953 (D. Kan. 1986) (no recovery is permitted under Kansas law for negligently induced preimpact mental anguish, not itself resulting in physical injury, notwithstanding that the collision caused physical injury).

Nonetheless, we are persuaded that there exists no sound legal or logical distinction between permitting a decedent's estate to recover as an element of damages for a decedent's conscious postinjury pain and suffering and mental anguish and permitting such an estate to recover for the conscious prefatal-injury mental anguish resulting from the apprehension and fear of impending death.

Neb. Rev. Stat. § 25-1401 (Reissue 1985) provides that, among other things, a cause of action for an injury to a personal estate survives the death of the person entitled to the same. Thus, we hold that as an element of a decedent's personal injury action, conscious prefatal-injury fear and apprehension of impending death survives a decedent's death and inures to the benefit of such decedent's estate.

Dolan argues that the personal representative's offer of proof fails in any event to establish that the decedent Nelson knew how closely his motorcycle was being followed or otherwise establishes that the decedent Nelson was consciously aware of and feared his impending death. It is true that courts have denied recovery for preimpact mental anguish for lack of evidence that the decedent was aware of his impending death. E.g., Anderson v. Rowe, 73 A.D.2d 1030, 425 N.Y.S.2d 180 (1980); Shatkin v. McDonnell Douglas Corp., 727 F.2d 202 (2d Cir. 1984). . . .

In *Shatkin*, the reviewing court reversed a jury award for preimpact pain and suffering, finding no evidence that the decedent passenger was awake or was aware that anything was wrong; that the pilot or anyone alerted the passengers as to the danger; nor that the airplane tilted and rolled in an unusual manner. However, in Shu-Tao Lin v. McDonnell Douglas Corp., 742 F.2d 45 (2d Cir. 1984), which arose out of the same accident, the same reviewing court distinguished *Shatkin* and concluded that the jury could reasonably find that a passenger seated over the left wing of the airplane (Shatkin's assigned seat was over the right wing) could have seen the left engine and a portion of the wing break off at the beginning of the flight and suffered preimpact mental anguish during the 30 seconds before the crash. . . .

It is fundamental that the nature and amount of damages cannot be sustained by evidence which is speculative and conjectural. The record must provide some basis for the jury to make a reasonable inference that the decedent suffered conscious mental anguish. While it is true that in the present case there is no evidence that decedent Nelson said anything prior to his death revealing an awareness of his impending death, the personal representative's offers of proof nonetheless provide a basis upon which the jury certainly need not, but could, if it wished, find that decedent Nelson apprehended and feared his impending death during the 5 seconds his motorcycle traveled 268 feet locked with Dolan's automobile before he was crushed and thus killed.

We must therefore conclude that the record sustains the personal representative's second assignment of error.

III.   DECISION

Accordingly, the judgment of the district court is hereby affirmed as to the wrongful death action, and the cause is reversed and remanded for a new trial as to the action on behalf of the decedent's estate.

NOTES AND QUESTIONS

1. *The Action for Loss of Consortium in Modern Law.* As indicated in the notes preceding *Nelson*, the common law long ago recognized a loss of consortium action for a husband who was temporarily deprived of his wife's services because of injuries caused to his wife by the careless acts of another. Needless to say, the conception of spousal relations underwriting this cause of action, by which the wife was treated as akin to a servant of the husband, has been abandoned. One might have predicted that, with this change in social and legal norms, the action for loss of consortium would disappear, much like the amatory actions such as "criminal conversation" (discussed in the notes following the *Mussivand* opinion, *supra*, Chapter 2). Instead, courts have generally gone the other route by *extending* the loss of consortium action to wives. In doing so, they have placed the consortium action on a new conceptual footing. It is no longer an action complaining of interference with a quasi-property interest, but instead an action for tortiously caused injury (other than death) that adversely affects the relationship of a husband and wife.

In principle, a loss of consortium action is available for any tortious conduct that generates the requisite injury to the spouse, and hence to the relationship. Most commonly, however, consortium actions are brought in connection with claims for battery and negligence, as opposed to, say, defamation or fraud. In terms of procedure, actions for loss of consortium are almost always appended to the victim's underlying tort claim, and they are litigated together by the same lawyer who represents the victim.* Some states permit consortium actions to be brought by parents whose minor

---

* Thus, if the complaint in the imagined early nineteenth-century case of *Smith et ux. v. Jones* were brought today, the caption would read *Smith and Smith v. Jones*.

children have been tortiously injured, as well as by children whose parents have been tortiously injured. For a decision in which the judges debate the merits of extending loss of consortium actions to children whose parents are tortiously injured, *see* Berger v. Weber, 303 N.W.2d 424 (Mich. 1981).

  2. *Loss of Consortium Damages*. Loss of consortium *actions* are freestanding causes of action that can be brought by appropriate family members to recover from a defendant for losses they have suffered because the defendant has tortiously *injured* their spouse, child, or parent. By contrast, as indicated in *Nelson*, when a family member is tortiously *killed*, survivors seeking compensation for *their* losses do not bring a loss of consortium action. Instead, they bring a wrongful death action. Still, as *Nelson* attests, wrongful death actions raise the related issue of whether the survivors can recover for loss of consortium *damages* as one component of their wrongful death award.

  Nelson stresses that a jury award of lost consortium damages in a wrongful death action is meant to reflect the expected *economic* benefits that surviving family members would have received by virtue of continuing to have the decedent's companionship and support. As explained by the Tennessee Supreme Court, the pecuniary loss associated with the death of a spouse or parent encompasses

> not only tangible services provided by a family member, but also intangible benefits each family member receives from the continued existence of other family members. Such benefits include attention, guidance, care, protection, training, companionship, cooperation, affection, love, and in the case of a spouse, sexual relations.

Jordan v. Baptist Three Rivers Hospital, 984 S.W.2d 593, 600-601 (Tenn. 1999). Focusing particularly on the issue of the child's loss of a parent, the court further explained:

> A basis for placing an economic value on parental consortium is that the education and training which a child may reasonably expect to receive from a parent are of actual and commercial value to the child. Accordingly, a child sustains a pecuniary injury for the loss of parental education and training when a defendant tortiously causes the death of the child's parent.

Id.

  Conceived as such, consortium damages in wrongful death actions are *not* designed to compensate for a survivor's emotional distress or grief over the death of a loved one, but rather for the reduced quality of life experienced by the surviving family member. *See, e.g.*, Krouse v. Graham, 562 P.2d 1022 (Cal. 1977). As the Texas Supreme Court has explained:

> Mental anguish represents an emotional response to the wrongful death itself. Loss of society, on the other hand, constitutes a loss of positive

---

Obviously, this is not because Mrs. Smith remains dependent on her husband to sue for her injuries. Rather, it is because her underlying negligence claim and Mr. Smith's derivative claim for loss of consortium present mostly the same allegations and facts and hence are more efficiently litigated in one proceeding.

benefits which flowed to the family from the decedent's having been a part of it. Mental anguish is concerned "not with the benefits [the beneficiaries] have lost, but with the issue of compensating them for their harrowing experience resulting from the death of a loved one." 1 S. Speiser, *Recovery for Wrongful Death 2d* § 3:52 at 327 (1975). Loss of society asks, "what positive benefits have been taken away from the beneficiaries by reason of the wrongful death?" Mental anguish damages ask about the negative side: "what deleterious effect has the death, as such, had upon the claimants?" *Id.*

Moore v. Lillebo, 722 S.W.2d 683, 687-688 (Tex. 1986).

3. *Wrongful Death and Emotional Distress Damages*. The Nebraska Supreme Court essentially refuses to entertain the question of whether emotional distress damages ought to be compensable in wrongful death actions. As it notes, however, other courts have permitted them. In Sanchez v. Schindler, 651 S.W.2d 249 (Tex. 1983), the Texas Supreme Court overturned its longstanding adherence to the rule of awarding only pecuniary-loss damages in wrongful death actions:

> Sanchez argues the pecuniary loss rule is based on an antiquated concept of the child as an economic asset, and should be rejected. We agree. It is time for this court to revise its interpretation of the Texas Wrongful Death statutes in light of present social realities and expand recovery beyond the antiquated and inequitable pecuniary loss rule. If the rule is literally followed, the average child would have a negative worth. Strict adherence to the pecuniary loss rule could lead to the negligent tortfeasor being rewarded for having saved the parents the cost and expense of rearing a child. The real loss sustained by a parent is not the loss of any financial benefit to be gained from the child, but is the loss of love, advice, comfort, companionship and society.

Id. at 251. The court noted that, at the time, three other jurisdictions permitted recovery for emotional distress damages under statutes similar to Texas's wrongful death act. It also noted that eight other states' legislatures had enacted statutes that had been construed to permit recovery for emotional distress damages. *Id.* at 254.

Is it so obviously inequitable to exclude recovery for survivors' grief over the loss of loved ones? Does that conclusion depend on how one understands the purposes of wrongful death acts?

4. *Derivative Causes of Action*. Wrongful death and loss of consortium actions each claim that the plaintiff herself — usually a relative of the victim of the underlying tort — suffered an injury as a result of an act that was wrongful to someone else. As such, they remain *derivative* of the victim's underlying claim. The derivative nature of these claims was most clearly apparent when survival and wrongful death actions were brought under the old rule of contributory negligence. Thus, if a judge or jury determined that the decedent's underlying claim would have been barred because his own fault was a cause of his injury, this finding not only defeated a survival action on behalf of the victim, but also any claim for wrongful death, *even if the surviving family members were in no way at*

fault for the death. Likewise, an innocent spouse of an injury victim who sued for loss of consortium would lose that claim if the judge or jury determined that the victim (not the plaintiff) was contributorily negligent. For example, if *D* carelessly ran over and injured *V*, but it turned out that *V* was also careless in stepping out into the street in front of *D*'s carriage, not only would *V* lose his negligence claim because of the complete defense of contributory negligence, *V*'s spouse would also lose her action for loss of consortium.

Arguably, if wrongful death and loss of consortium claims were truly freestanding actions, they should not have been barred by the *victim's* fault. Rather, at most, the victim's fault ought to have been treated as one of two necessary causes (along with the defendant's fault) of the surviving family member's loss of support and companionship. In this important respect, then, the wrongful death or loss of consortium plaintiff sued not in her own right, but derivatively.

Wrongful death and loss of consortium actions remain derivative. Thus, the rule attributing the victim's fault to survivors still applies, notwithstanding the shift to comparative responsibility. See Chapter 7. If the factfinder assigns a percentage responsibility to the decedent greater than zero, the surviving family members' recovery from the defendant is reduced accordingly. (States vary as to the effect they assign to a *beneficiary's* fault in causing the victim's death.) Wrongful death and loss of consortium plaintiffs also "inherit" other defenses that would bar a claim by the dead or injured spouse, such as the failure to meet an applicable statute of limitations.

5. *Nontraditional Relationships.* Not surprisingly, given the period in which they were enacted, wrongful death statutes tend to restrict membership in the class of persons who can bring actions under them to traditional family members. With the increasing prominence of same-sex couples and nontraditional family arrangements, the question has arisen as to whether these classes ought to be redefined by courts or legislatures. Some states have amended their wrongful death statutes to expand the beneficiary class. *See, e.g.*, Cal. Code Civ. Proc. § 377.60 (2002) (authorizing decedent's "domestic partner" to bring action for wrongful death). Vermont recently enacted a law giving full legal effect to same-sex marriages. This has raised an issue for courts in other states as to whether they should give effect to Vermont's law, thereby rendering a party to a same-sex marriage a "spouse" within the meaning of that state's wrongful death statute.

6. *Situation-Specific Statutes.* In addition to wrongful death statutes, the state and federal governments have enacted legislation that generates tort claims for victims of particular kinds of accidents and their survivors. For example, in 1920, Congress enacted the Death on the High Seas Act (DOHSA). DOHSA is essentially a wrongful death statute for admiralty law, which, like the rest of the common law, refused to recognize actions for wrongful death. Whether tort actions will be available to the administrator and/or survivors of an employee killed during the course of employment will depend on the interaction of a given jurisdiction's

wrongful death and workers' compensation statutes. *See* Stuart M. Speiser, et al., *Recovery for Wrongful Death and Injury* § 1:14-24 (3d ed. 1992).

7. *Actions that Do Not Survive.* State statutes vary as to which tort claims may be asserted in survival and wrongful death actions. Some, for example, do not permit claims for defamation of invasion of privacy to continue after the death of the plaintiff. On what basis can one explain this differential treatment? Might the reasons vary depending on whether the claim is a survival action or a wrongful death action? *Compare* Innes v. Howell Corp., 76 F.3d 702 (6th Cir. 1996) (invoking Kentucky's statutory rule that defamation actions do not survive the death of the defamed victim, and upholding it against constitutional challenge) *with* Canino v. New York News, Inc., 475 A.2d 528 (N.J. 1984) (noting that defamation actions survive under New Jersey law).

8. *Committing Torts against the Dead.* Wrongful death statutes permit suits by representatives of a person who was the victim of a tort but died after the commission of the tort. They do not purport to create actions based on torts committed against persons who are already deceased. Can it ever be tortious to mistreat a dead person?

The short answer is: not exactly. A coroner or mortician who mishandles a corpse — say, by losing the body, or cremating it when he had been instructed to bury it — may be subject to liability to persons other than the deceased. In particular, he may be sued for causing emotional distress to surviving family members. See Chapter 10. It may also be tortious to interfere with certain rights that "descend" from the deceased to his or her heirs. For example, if one were to appropriate for commercial use an image of Elvis Presley without the consent of his estate, such conduct might infringe on the estate's ownership of Presley's image or persona.

Suppose that, without obtaining surviving family members' permission, a mortician permits a television crew filming a documentary to film decedent's body, and that the image of his corpse is later broadcast on television. Has the decedent suffered an invasion of privacy by having his dead body shown to the public? Should that invasion be redressable through a tort action brought by his representative? A longstanding rule of defamation law holds that the dead have no legally protected interest in their reputations. Thus, one is free to slander or libel dead persons without fear of liability, at least so long as a living person isn't implicitly defamed in the process. Does this rule make any sense? Could one argue that a person's interest in maintaining her good name continues after death, and that the law ought to be particularly solicitous of a person's reputation when she is no longer around to defend herself against scurrilous attack? Might similar reasoning apply to privacy actions?

III.   IMPLIED RIGHTS OF ACTION

Wrongful death statutes explicitly empower persons to sue in tort who would otherwise lack the right to sue under common law rules. Other sorts of statutes explicitly create what amounts to tort liability for conduct that, prior to their enactment, was not tortious. For example, as we see in Chapter 10, federal laws have expressly made certain forms of workplace discrimination actionable, even when such conduct would not be actionable as a common law tort. This section considers a related question about the intersection of statutes and torts: Can a statute create a cause of action even when it says nothing about whether individuals are entitled to sue for violations of it?

In framing this inquiry it is helpful to recall the doctrine of negligence per se. The issue in applying that doctrine is whether a plaintiff suing for the tort of common law negligence can take advantage of a legislative standard of conduct to prove the element of breach. Implicit in such a claim is the idea that the common law, by recognizing the negligence action, has already provided the plaintiff with the vehicle for bringing suit. Suppose, however, a statute regulates a species of conduct to which no common law tort liability attaches, yet also says nothing explicit about whether it is intended to provide causes of actions to those who are injured by violations of the statute. Can a person aggrieved by a violation of the statute assert that it implicitly has conveyed to them a right to sue?

Tex. & Pac. Ry. Co. v. Rigsby
241 U.S. 33 (1916)

Pitney, J.   . . . [Rigsby was employed by the railway as a switchman in its yard at Marshall, Texas. There, he] was engaged . . . in taking some "bad order" cars to the shops . . . to be repaired. . . . Rigsby, in the course of his duties, rode upon the top of one of the cars (a box car) in order to set the brakes and stop them and hold them upon the main line. He did this, and while descending from the car . . . he fell, owing to a defect in one of the handholds or grab-irons that formed the rungs of the ladder, and sustained personal injuries. This car had been out of service and waiting on the track spur for some days, perhaps a month. The occurrence took place September 4, 1912. In an action for damages, based upon the Federal Safety Appliance Acts [of 1893 and 1910], the above facts appeared without dispute. . . . The trial court instructed the jury, as matter of law, that they should return a verdict in favor of plaintiff, the only question submitted to them being the amount of the damages. . . . The resulting judgment was affirmed by the Circuit Court of Appeals.

. . . This action was . . . [based] upon § 2 of the . . . 1910 [act], which declares: "All cars must be equipped with secure sill steps and efficient hand brakes; all cars requiring secure ladders and secure running boards shall be equipped with such ladders and running boards, and all cars having ladders shall also be equipped with secure handholds or grab irons on their roofs at the tops of such ladders." There can be no question that a box car having a handbrake operated from the roof requires also a secure ladder to enable the employee to safely ascend and descend, and that the provision quoted was intended for the especial protection of employees engaged in duties such as that which plaintiff was performing. . . .

. . . A disregard of the command of [a] statute is a wrongful act, and where it results in damage to one of the class for whose especial benefit the statute was enacted, the right to recover the damages from the party in default is implied, according to a doctrine of the common law expressed in 1 Com. Dig., *tit*. Action upon Statute (F), in these words: "So, in every case, where a statute enacts, or prohibits a thing for the benefit of a person, he shall have a remedy upon the same statute for the thing enacted for his advantage, or for the recompense of a wrong done to him contrary to the said law." (*Per* Holt, C.J., Anon., 6 Mod. 26, 27.) This is but an application of the maxim, *Ubi jus ibi remedium. See* 3 Black. Com. 51, 123; Couch v. Steel, 3 El. & Bl. 402, 411; 23 L.J.Q.B. 121, 125. The inference of a private right of action in the present instance is rendered irresistible by the provision of § 8 of the Act of 1893 that an employee injured by any car, etc., in use contrary to the act shall not be deemed to have assumed the risk, and by the language . . . [, discussed below, of] the proviso in § 4 of the 1910 act. . . .

[The court proceeded to consider defendant's argument against the imposition of liability based on § 4 of the 1910 act. Section 4 provided statutorily set fines for each violation of the substantive requirements of the 1910 act. However, it waived those fines if (a) the railroad car in question was at one time properly equipped with the required safety devices; (b) those devices, through no fault of the railroad, had become defective or inoperative in transit; (c) repairs to them could not be effected on the spot; and (d) the car was being taken to the nearest point at which repairs could be effected. Citing its decision in an earlier case, the court's opinion then continued as follows. — EDS.]

. . . [A]lthough § 4 . . . relieves the carrier from the statutory penalties while a car is being hauled to the nearest available point for repairs, it [contains a proviso] that it shall not be construed to relieve a carrier from liability in a remedial action for the death or injury of an employee caused by or in connection with the movement of a car with defective equipment.* The question whether the defective condition of the ladder was due to defendant's negligence is immaterial, since the statute imposes an absolute and unqualified duty to maintain the appliance in secure condition.

. . . [T]he employee's knowledge of the defect does not bar his suit, for by § 8 of the Act of 1893 an employee injured by any car in use contrary to the provisions of the act is not to be deemed to have assumed the risk, although continuing in the employment of the carrier after the unlawful use of the car has been brought to his knowledge. . . .

---

* [The Section 4 proviso referenced in this paragraph and in the preceding one stated that the movement of railcars with nonconforming equipment, even for the purpose of effecting necessary repairs, "shall be at the sole risk of the carrier, and nothing in this section shall be construed to relieve such carrier from liability in any remedial action for the death or injury of any railroad employee caused to such employee by reason of or in connection with the movement or hauling of such car with equipment which is defective or insecure or which is not maintained in accordance with the requirements of this chapter. . . ." — EDS.]

J. I. Case Co. v. Borak
377 U.S 426 (1964)

Clark, J.   [Borak owned shares of stock in J. I. Case Co. Case's managers sought to merge Case with another company named ATC. The merger could not go through unless a certain percentage of Case's shareholders approved it. Given the difficulty of assembling thousands of shareholders to cast their votes, corporate managers are permitted to *solicit proxies* from shareholders, that is, to ask each shareholder to transfer to managers the authority to vote on the shareholder's behalf. Managers who solicit proxies must provide shareholders with certain specified information about the transaction at issue. Accordingly, Case's managers sent a proxy solicitation to shareholders that included information about the proposed merger that aimed to explain why it was in the shareholders' interest to authorize management to approve the merger.

Borak unsuccessfully sued to block the merger. When that effort failed, he sued for damages. His complaint alleged that: (1) the proxy solicitation sent out by Case's management included false statements; (2) but for these falsehoods, shareholders would not have given management their proxies to approve the merger; and (3) the merger negatively affected the value of Case's stock, including his own shares.

The complaint further alleged that management's issuance of false statements in its proxy solicitation violated Section 14(a) of the federal Securities Exchange Act of 1934. Section 14(a) renders unlawful the solicitation of proxies by means that violate any rules duly promulgated by the Securities and Exchange Commission (SEC), a federal agency that oversees the issuance and sale of stocks and bonds. One such rule — SEC Rule 14a-9 — forbids the use in a proxy solicitation of any statement that is false or misleading with respect to a material fact. The question before the court was whether Section 14(a) creates a private right of action on behalf of those who suffer losses by virtue of conduct that violates it. — EDS.] . . .

The purpose of § 14(a) is to prevent management or others from obtaining authorization for corporate action by means of deceptive or inadequate disclosure [to shareholders]. The section stemmed from the congressional belief that "(f)air corporate suffrage is an important right that should attach to every equity security bought on a public exchange." H.R. Rep. No. 1383, 73d Cong., 2d Sess., 13. It was intended to "control the conditions under which [votes] may be solicited with a view to preventing the recurrence of abuses which . . . (had) frustrated the free exercise of the voting rights of stockholders." *Id.*, at 14. "Too often proxies are solicited without explanation to the stockholder of the real nature of the questions for which authority to cast his vote is sought." S. Rep. No. 792, 73d Cong., 2d Sess., 12. These broad remedial purposes are evidenced in the language of the section which makes it "unlawful for any person . . . to solicit or to permit the use of his name to solicit any proxy or consent or authorization in respect of any security . . . in contravention of such rules and regulations as the Commission may prescribe as necessary or appropriate in the public interest *or for the protection of investors*."

(Italics supplied.) While this language makes no specific reference to a private right of action, among its chief purposes is "the protection of investors," which certainly implies the availability of judicial relief where necessary to achieve that result.

The injury which a stockholder suffers from corporate action pursuant to a deceptive . . . solicitation ordinarily flows from the damage done the corporation, rather than from the damage inflicted directly upon the stockholder. The damage suffered results not from the deceit practiced on him alone but rather from the deceit practiced on the stockholders as a group. To hold that [individual shareholder] actions are not within the sweep of the section would therefore be tantamount to a denial of private relief. Private enforcement of the proxy rules provides a necessary supplement to Commission action. As in anti-trust treble damage litigation, the possibility of civil damages or injunctive relief serves as a most effective weapon in the enforcement of the proxy requirements. The Commission advises that it examines over 2,000 proxy statements annually and each of them must necessarily be expedited. Time does not permit an independent examination of the facts set out in the proxy material and this results in the Commission's acceptance of the representations contained therein at their face value, unless contrary to other material on file with it. Indeed, on the allegations of respondent's complaint, the proxy material failed to disclose alleged unlawful market manipulation of the stock of ATC, and this unlawful manipulation would not have been apparent to the Commission until after the merger.

We, therefore, believe that under the circumstances here it is the duty of the courts to be alert to provide such remedies as are necessary to make effective the congressional purpose. As was said in Sola Electric Co. v. Jefferson Electric Co., 317 U.S. 173, 176, 63 S. Ct. 172, 174, 87 L. Ed. 165 (1942):

"When a federal statute condemns an act as unlawful, the extent and nature of the legal consequences of the condemnation, though left by the statute to judicial determination, are nevertheless federal questions, the answers to which are to be derived from the statute and the federal policy which it has adopted."

It is for the federal courts "to adjust their remedies so as to grant the necessary relief" where federally secured rights are invaded. "And it is also well settled that where legal rights have been invaded, and a federal statute provides for a general right to sue for such invasion, federal courts may use any available remedy to make good the wrong done." Bell v. Hood, 327 U.S. 678, 684 . . . (1946). Section 27 [of the 1934 Act] grants the District Courts jurisdiction "of all suits in equity and actions at law brought to enforce any liability or duty created by this title. . .". In passing on almost identical language found in the Securities Act of 1933, the Court found the words entirely sufficient to fashion a remedy to rescind a fraudulent sale, secure restitution and even to enforce the right to restitution against a third party holding assets of the vendor. Deckert v. Independence Shares Corp., 311 U.S. 282 . . . (1940). This significant language was used:

"The power to *enforce* implies the power to make effective the right of recovery afforded by the Act. And the power to make the right of recovery effective implies the power to utilize any of the procedures or actions normally available to the litigant according to the exigencies of the particular case." [*Deckert*, at 288]. . . .

NOTES AND QUESTIONS

1. *Ubi jus ibi remedium.* This maxim, cited by the *Rigsby* court, translates as "where there is a right, there is a remedy." *Rigsby* seems to presume that whenever a statute sets a standard of conduct a court should permit an individual who is injured by a person's violation of that standard to sue the violator for damages. Is that a plausible presumption? Might a legislature sometimes want to enact rules and regulations that do not give rise to private rights of action? Notice that the *ubi jus* maxim speaks in terms of *rights* demanding remedies, as opposed to harms.

Suppose you live in a state with a law that imposes criminal fines on those who operate industrial plants that emit excessive quantities of airborne pollutants. The law is silent as to whether it empowers individuals to sue for violations. Should a court infer that the law accords a cause of action against the owner of any plant that is in violation of the statute to all those who suffer asthma traceable to excessive levels of the relevant pollutants? All those whose taxes are increased because of additional burdens on the public health system due to a higher rate of respiratory illness resulting from the pollution?

Might certain kinds of legislation aim to accomplish something other than setting standards of right conduct? Each state requires drivers to have valid licenses before driving. Suppose *X* is injured by driver *Y*, who was driving carefully at the time, but never obtained a license. Does *Rigsby* suggest that the licensing law creates a private right of action on *X*'s behalf based solely on the statutory violation? (Recall that most states do not permit a plaintiff to invoke a violation of a licensing statute to establish negligence per se.)

2. *Implied Rights of Action versus Negligence Per Se.* *Rigsby* does not appear to invoke the doctrine of negligence per se — it does not suggest that the federal Safety Appliance Acts provide a standard of care that will govern Rigsby's common law tort action.* Rather, it seems to treat the acts as giving rise to a statutory cause of action. Indeed, the action identified by

---

* At the time *Rigsby* was decided, federal courts were understood to have the power to interpret and apply "general common law." Thus, the *Rigsby* court could have invoked a notion of negligence per se if it had wanted to. The Supreme Court's 1938 *Erie* decision (discussed in the notes following *Testbank, supra,* Chapter 2) held that the substantive common law of tort is almost exclusively the province of the state courts. Therefore, because a federal court today faced with a common law negligence claim would almost always be applying the common law of a given state, the court could not permit the plaintiff to invoke a *federal* statute as specifying a legislative standard of care under the doctrine of negligence per se unless it determined that the relevant state's law has incorporated the federal standard by judicial decision or legislation. *See* Crane v. Cedar Rapids & Iowa City Ry., 395 U.S. 164 (1969).

the court apparently imposes strict liability rather than fault-based liaibility — the court deems "irrelevant" the issue of whether the railroad took reasonable steps to maintain its train car in a safe condition. *Rigsby* was decided in the same year as *MacPherson*. Does the knowledge that railways were sometimes subject to strict liability for injuries caused by defective equipment render more reasonable Cardozo's recognition of a duty on car manufacturers to make reasonable inspections of car wheels?

3. *Jurisdiction and Remedy*. Even more clearly than *Rigsby*, *Borak* locates the source of the plaintiff's cause of action in a statute, here the federal Securities Exchange Act of 1934. Looming large in the court's analysis is Section 27 of the Act, which grants jurisdiction to federal courts to hear and resolve disputes arising under the Act. The court infers from this grant of jurisdiction that courts may supplement explicit statutory provisions with additional remedies, including private rights of action, whenever they deem it necessary to promote the objectives of the statute. Can you imagine situations in which it would not promote justice, or would interfere with the objectives of a statute, to recognize an implied right of action? Or does it follow from *Borak* that courts should always infer the existence of a cause of action when a statute setting standards of conduct is silent on the question?

4. *The Protected Class*. *Rigsby*'s identification of the class of persons eligible to assert a claim under the Safety Appliance Acts seems to incorporate a traditional notion of common law duty. The acts were clearly intended for the benefit of railroad workers, thus the court identifies them as persons empowered to sue. Does *Borak* invoke a similar notion of duty? How does it define the protected class? Do any of *Borak*'s stated rationales support the idea that a right of action ought to be available not just to a disappointed investor, but to anyone? Wouldn't the broadest possible class provide an even more "effective weapon" for enforcing securities laws?

5. *Federalism*. Any full discussion of the issue of implied rights of action must take into account the complex relationship between federal and state courts, a matter that cannot be pursued here. One way to highlight some of these issues is to pose the following question: Why was Borak so anxious to assert a claim under the 1934 Act? Assuming that he could prove his allegations, would his suit have been dismissed on the merits by a state court applying state law? As it turns out, probably not. State law then and now treats managers as "fiduciaries" of their shareholders, that is, as requiring them to make every effort to ensure that transactions undertaken by the company are in shareholders' best interests. Thus, a shareholder such as Borak who believed that the proposed merger benefited management at the expense of shareholders likely could have brought a state law claim for breach of fiduciary duty.

Thus, in contrast to *Rigsby*, *Borak* probably did not help the plaintiff by supplying through federal law a cause of action that state law did not. Instead, the main benefit to Borak was that he avoided a *procedural* requirement imposed by state law. It would have required him to post a bond — that is, pledge a substantial sum of money — in order to pursue his claim. The bond requirement had been set to deter frivolous shareholder suits — if a suit turned out to be groundless, the plaintiff would forfeit the amount specified in the bond.

Should the federal courts be in the business of identifying federal statutory causes of action at the behest of plaintiffs whose primary motivation is to avoid this sort of procedural hurdle? Is the idea that the federal courts provide a better brand of justice than state courts? One can certainly identify types of suits for which this was and is likely the case. Consider, for example, the probable receptivity of federal courts, as compared to Southern state courts, to actions brought by African-Americans for civil rights violations in the mid-1960s. Does litigation over false proxy statements warrant a similar opening up of the federal courts?

6. *Applying the Brakes.* Within ten years of *Borak*, the U.S. Supreme Court began to show greater reticence in identifying implied rights of action in federal statutes. In Cort v. Ash, 422 U.S. 66 (1975), the Court refused to find within a criminal law banning certain campaign contributions by corporations an implied right of action on behalf of shareholders that would empower them to recover for the improper expenditure of corporate funds on campaigns. The Court expressed reluctance to identify a private right of action within general criminal prohibitions. It also identified a four-part test designed to assist courts in determining whether to infer a private right of action from a statute:

> First, is the plaintiff "one of the class for whose especial benefit the statute was enacted," [quoting *Rigsby*] — that is, does the statute create a federal right in favor of the plaintiff? Second, is there any indication of legislative intent, explicit or implicit, either to create such a remedy or to deny one? Third, is it consistent with the underlying purposes of the legislative scheme to imply such a remedy for the plaintiff? And finally, is the cause of action one traditionally relegated to state law, in an area basically the concern of the States, so that it would be inappropriate to infer a cause of action based solely on federal law?

Applying this test, the Court concluded that the ban on corporate contributions to political campaigns was designed primarily to clean up the political process for the benefit of the public, rather than a particular class of persons. It further found no hint of congressional intent to create a private right of action, and reasoned that empowering the shareholders to collect damages for illegal payments that had already been made would not advance the regulatory purposes of the statute. Finally, the Court noted that the plaintiffs might be able to pursue state-law causes of action against management for breach of fiduciary duty.

7. *Making a U-Turn.* Although suggesting that federal courts ought to think twice about recognizing implied rights of action, Cort v. Ash still operated on the assumption of *Rigsby* and *Borak* that the courts had broad discretion to determine whether, *in their judgment*, it would promote justice or the aims of a statute to identify such a right. Four years later, the Court abandoned this posture in favor of an approach much more deferential to Congress.

In Cannon v. University of Chicago, 441 U.S. 677 (1979), the Court identified, by a 6 to 3 vote, an implied cause of action for victims of discrimination within a federal law prohibiting gender discrimination by universities that receive federal funding. Two of the six votes, however, came by means of the following concurrence, written by then-Justice Rehnquist, 441 U.S., at 717-718.

> **Rehnquist, J.** (concurring) (with Stewart, J.).   Having joined the Court's opinion in this case, my only purpose in writing separately is to make explicit what seems to me already implicit in that opinion. I think the approach of the Court, reflected in its analysis of the problem in this case and [other] cases . . . is quite different from the analysis in earlier cases such as [*Borak*]. The question of the existence of a private right of action is basically one of statutory construction. And while state courts of general jurisdiction still enforcing the common law as well as statutory law may be less constrained than are federal courts enforcing laws enacted by Congress, the latter must surely look to those laws to determine whether there was an intent to create a private right of action under them.
>
> . . . . [T]he Court's opinion demonstrates that Congress . . . [has] tended to rely to a large extent on the courts to *decide* whether there should be a private right of action, rather than determining this question for itself. Cases such as [*Borak*] and numerous cases from other federal courts, gave Congress good reason to think that the federal judiciary would undertake this task.
>
> I fully agree with the Court's statement that "[w]hen Congress intends private litigants to have a cause of action to support their statutory rights, the far better course is for it to specify as much when it creates those rights." It seems to me that the factors to which I have here briefly adverted apprise the lawmaking branch of the Federal Government that the ball, so to speak, may well now be in its court. Not only is it "far better" for Congress to so specify when it intends private litigants to have a cause of action, but for this very reason this Court in the future should be extremely reluctant to imply a cause of action absent such specificity on the part of the Legislative Branch.

That same term, in *Touche Ross & Co. v. Redington*, 442 U.S. 560 (1979), Justice Rehnquist wrote an opinion for the Court declining to find a private right of action within Section 17(a) of the Securities Exchange Act of 1934, which mandates that brokerage firms file certain financial reports with the SEC. Treating this provision as setting bookkeeping requirements rather defining wrongful conduct, the Court saw no evidence of congressional intent to create a right of action to those injured by filings containing false statements. The Court also distanced itself from *Borak* and *Cort.* 442 U.S., at 575-579.

> Relying on the factors set forth in Cort v. Ash . . . [respondents, who seek to establish the existence of a cause of action] assert that we . . . must consider whether an implied private remedy is necessary to "effectuate the purpose of the section" and whether the cause of action is one traditionally relegated to state law. . . . We need not reach the merits of the arguments concerning the "necessity" of implying a private remedy and the proper forum for enforcement of the rights asserted by [the respondents], for we believe such inquiries have little relevance to the decision of this case. It is true that in Cort v. Ash, the Court set forth four factors that it considered "relevant" in determining whether a private remedy is implicit in a statute not expressly

providing one. But the Court did not decide that each of these factors is entitled to equal weight. The central inquiry remains whether Congress intended to create, either expressly or by implication, a private cause of action. Indeed, the first three factors discussed in *Cort* — the language and focus of the statute, its legislative history, and its purpose — are ones traditionally relied upon in determining legislative intent. Here, the statute by its terms grants no private rights to any identifiable class and proscribes no conduct as unlawful. And the parties . . . agree that the legislative history of the 1934 Act simply does not speak to the issue of private remedies under § 17(a). At least in such a case as this, the inquiry ends there: The question whether Congress, either expressly or by implication, intended to create a private right of action, has been definitely answered in the negative.

. . . In *Borak*, the Court found in § 14(a) of the 1934 Act . . . an implied cause of action for damages in favor of shareholders for losses resulting from deceptive proxy solicitations. . . . [Respondents] emphasize language in *Borak* that discusses the remedial purposes of the 1934 Act and § 27 of the Act, which, *inter alia*, grants to federal district courts the exclusive jurisdiction of violations of the Act and suits to enforce any liability or duty created by the Act or the rules and regulations thereunder. They argue that Touche Ross has breached its duties under § 17(a) and the rules adopted thereunder and that in view of § 27 and of the remedial purposes of the 1934 Act, federal courts should provide a damages remedy for the breach.

The reliance . . . on § 27 is misplaced. Section 27 grants jurisdiction to the federal courts and provides for venue and service of process. It creates no cause of action of its own force and effect; it imposes no liabilities. The source of plaintiffs' rights must be found, if at all, in the substantive provisions of the 1934 Act which they seek to enforce, not in the jurisdictional provision. The Court in *Borak* found a private cause of action implicit in § 14(a). We do not now question the actual holding of that case, but we decline to read the opinion so broadly that virtually every provision of the securities Acts gives rise to an implied private cause of action. The invocation of the "remedial purposes" of the 1934 Act is similarly unavailing. Only last Term, we emphasized that generalized references to the "remedial purposes" of the 1934 Act will not justify reading a provision "more broadly than its language and the statutory scheme reasonably permit." SEC v. Sloan, 436 U.S. 103, 116, 98 S. Ct. 1702, 1711, 56 L. Ed. 2d 148 (1978). . . . Certainly, the mere fact that § 17(a) was designed to provide protection for brokers' customers does not require the implication of a private damages action in their behalf. To the extent our analysis in today's decision differs from that of the Court in *Borak*, it suffices to say that in a series of cases since *Borak* we have adhered to a stricter standard for the implication of private causes of action, and we follow that stricter standard today. The ultimate question is one of congressional intent, not one of whether this Court thinks that it can improve upon the statutory scheme that Congress enacted. . . .

[Respondents] contend that the result we reach sanctions injustice. But even if that were the case, the argument is made in the wrong forum, for we are not at liberty to legislate. If there is to be a federal damages remedy under these circumstances, Congress must provide it. . . . Obviously, nothing we have said prevents Congress from creating a private right of action on behalf of brokerage firm customers for losses arising from misstatements contained in § 17(a) reports. But if Congress intends those customers to have such a federal right of action, it is well aware of how it may effectuate that intent.

8. *Federal Courts and Limited Jurisdiction.* The Court's newfound unwillingness to infer rights of action proceeds in part from a recognition that federal courts are in a different position vis-à-vis Congress than state courts are with respect to state legislatures. Specifically, federal courts are courts of "limited jurisdiction" — they are only empowered to hear claims when authorized by Congress to do so. By contrast, state courts are often courts of general jurisdiction. As a rule, they can hear any manner of suit, whether grounded in state or federal law. Does it follow that state courts interpreting state regulatory statutes ought to be more inclined to infer rights of action when faced with statutory silence? For a debate among the justices of the Oregon Supreme Court on this issue that includes references to other cases raising the same debate, see Bob Godfrey Pontiac, Inc. v. Roloff, 630 P.2d 840 (1981).

9. *Are There Still Federal Implied Rights of Action to Be Found?* Decisions such as *Redington* have largely put the federal courts out of the business of inferring rights of action. Indeed, by placing the ball in Congress's hands, the Court seems to have indicated that it will not recognize a cause of action unless Congress explicitly indicates an intent to create one. Of course, once Congress has done so, there is little room left for "implied" rights of action: either the statute creates an express cause of action or none will be recognized.

Still, neither *Cannon* nor *Redington* overruled the holdings of decisions such as *Borak*. Thus, the causes of actions recognized by those decisions continue to provide federal-law remedies for plaintiffs. Perhaps most important, the Court declined to second-guess the longstanding assumption that Section 10(b) of the Securities Exchange Act of 1934 creates an implied right of action. Section 10(b) — in particular SEC Rule 10b-5, which was enacted by the SEC under the authority of the 1934 Act — has long provided an important device by which shareholders have sought redress for economic losses caused by misrepresentations made by corporate managers.

10. *From Statutes to Constitution.* Thus far we have considered whether rights of action can be inferred from regulatory statutes that are silent as to whether they mean to empower persons injured by statutory violations to sue for those violations. The same issue has arisen in connection with the "supreme" law of the United States.

Bivens v. Six Unknown Named Agents of Federal Bureau of Narcotics
403 U.S. 388 (1971)

Brennan, J.   The Fourth Amendment provides that:

> The right of the people to be secure in their persons, houses, papers, and effects, against unreasonable searches and seizures, shall not be violated. . . .

In Bell v. Hood, 327 U.S. 678, 66 S. Ct. 773, 90 L. Ed. 939 (1946), we reserved the question whether violation of that command by a federal agent acting under color of his authority gives rise to a cause of action for damages consequent upon his unconstitutional conduct. Today we hold that it does.

This case has its origin in an arrest and search carried out on the morning of November 26, 1965. Petitioner's complaint alleged that on that day respondents, agents of the Federal Bureau of Narcotics acting under claim of federal authority, entered his apartment and arrested him for alleged narcotics violations. The agents manacled petitioner in front of his wife and children, and threatened to arrest the entire family. They searched the apartment from stem to stern. Thereafter, petitioner was taken to the federal courthouse in Brooklyn, where he was interrogated, booked, and subjected to a visual strip search.

. . . [The complaint further alleges] that the arrest and search were effected without a warrant, and that unreasonable force was employed in making the arrest; fairly read, it alleges as well that the arrest was made without probable cause. Petitioner claimed to have suffered great humiliation, embarrassment, and mental suffering as a result of the agents' unlawful conduct, and sought $15,000 damages from each of them. The District Court . . . dismissed the complaint on the ground, inter alia, that it failed to state a cause of action. The Court of Appeals . . . affirmed on that basis. . . .

I

Respondents do not argue that petitioner should be entirely without remedy for an unconstitutional invasion of his rights by federal agents. In respondents' view, however, the rights that petitioner asserts — primarily rights of privacy — are creations of state and not of federal law. Accordingly, they argue, petitioner may obtain money damages to redress invasion of these rights only by an action in tort, under state law, in the state courts. In this scheme the Fourth Amendment would serve merely to limit the extent to which the agents could defend the state law tort suit by asserting that their actions were a valid exercise of federal power: if the agents were shown to have violated the Fourth Amendment, such a defense would be lost to them and they would stand before the state law merely as private individuals. . . .

We think that respondents' thesis rests upon an unduly restrictive view of the Fourth Amendment's protection against unreasonable searches and seizures by federal agents. . . . Respondents seek to treat the relationship between a citizen and a federal agent unconstitutionally exercising his authority as no different from the relationship between two private citizens. In so doing, they ignore the fact that power, once granted, does not disappear like a magic gift when it is wrongfully used. An agent acting — albeit unconstitutionally — in the name of the United States possesses a far greater capacity for harm than an individual trespasser exercising no authority other than his own. Accordingly, as our cases make clear, the Fourth Amendment operates as a limitation upon the exercise of federal power regardless of whether the State in whose jurisdiction that power is exercised would prohibit or penalize the identical act if engaged in by a private citizen. It guarantees to citizens of the United States the absolute right to be free from unreasonable searches and seizures carried out by virtue of federal authority. And "where federally protected rights have been invaded, it has been the rule from the beginning that courts will be alert to adjust their remedies so as to grant the necessary relief." Bell v. Hood, 327 U.S., at 684, 66 S. Ct., at 777 (footnote omitted). . . .

First. Our cases have long since rejected the notion that the Fourth Amendment proscribes only such conduct as would, if engaged in by private persons, be condemned by state law. . . .

Second. The interests protected by state laws regulating trespass and the invasion of privacy, and those protected by the Fourth Amendment's guarantee against unreasonable searches and seizures, may be inconsistent or even hostile. Thus, [one is permitted by law to] bar the door against an unwelcome private intruder, or call the police if he persists in seeking entrance. The availability of such alternative means for the protection of privacy may lead the State to restrict imposition of liability for any consequent trespass. A private citizen, asserting no authority other than his own, will not normally be liable in trespass if he demands, and is granted, admission to another's house. But one who demands admission under a claim of federal authority stands in a far different position. The mere invocation of federal power by a federal law enforcement official will normally render futile any attempt to resist an unlawful entry or arrest by resort to the local police; and a claim of authority to enter is likely to unlock the door as well. "In such cases there is no safety for the citizen, except in the protection of the judicial tribunals, for rights which have been invaded by the officers of the government, professing to act in its name. There remains to him but the alternative of resistance, which may amount to crime." Nor is it adequate to answer that state law may take into account the different status of one clothed with the authority of the Federal Government. For just as state law may not authorize federal agents to violate the Fourth Amendment, neither may state law undertake to limit the extent to which federal authority can be exercised. The inevitable consequence of this dual limitation on state power is that the federal question becomes not merely a possible defense to the state law action, but an independent claim both necessary and sufficient to make out the plaintiff's cause of action.

Third. That damages may be obtained for injuries consequent upon a violation of the Fourth Amendment by federal officials should hardly seem a surprising proposition. Historically, damages have been regarded as the ordinary remedy for an invasion of personal interests in liberty. Of course, the Fourth Amendment does not in so many words provide for its enforcement by an award of money damages for the consequences of its violation. But "it is . . . well settled that where legal rights have been invaded, and a federal statute provides for a general right to sue for such invasion, federal courts may use any available remedy to make good the wrong done." Bell v. Hood, 327 U.S., at 684, 66 S. Ct., at 777 (footnote omitted). The present case involves no special factors counseling hesitation in the absence of affirmative action by Congress. We are not dealing with a question of "federal fiscal policy," as in United States v. Standard Oil Co., 332 U.S. 301,

311, 67 S. Ct. 1604, 1609-1610, 91 L. Ed. 2067 (1947). In that case we refused to infer from the Government-soldier relationship that the United States could recover damages from one who negligently injured a soldier and thereby caused the Government to pay his medical expenses and lose his services during the course of his hospitalization. Noting that Congress was normally quite solicitous where the federal purse was involved, we pointed out that "the United States (was) the party plaintiff to the suit. And the United States has power at any time to create the liability." *Id.*, at 316, 67 S. Ct., at 1612; *see* United States v. Gilman, 347 U.S. 507, 74 S. Ct. 695, 98 L. Ed. 898 (1954). Nor are we asked in this case to impose liability upon a congressional employee for actions contrary to no constitutional prohibition, but merely said to be in excess of the authority delegated to him by the Congress. Finally, we cannot accept respondents' formulation of the question as whether the availability of money damages is necessary to enforce the Fourth Amendment. For we have here no explicit congressional declaration that persons injured by a federal officer's violation of the Fourth Amendment may not recover money damages from the agents, but must instead be remitted to another remedy, equally effective in the view of Congress. The question is merely whether petitioner, if he can demonstrate an injury consequent upon the violation by federal agents of his Fourth Amendment rights, is entitled to redress his injury through a particular remedial mechanism normally available in the federal courts. "The very essence of civil liberty certainly consists in the right of every individual to claim the protection of the laws, whenever he receives an injury." Marbury v. Madison, 1 Cranch 137, 163, 2 L. Ed. 60 (1803). Having concluded that petitioner's complaint states a cause of action under the Fourth Amendment, we hold that petitioner is entitled to recover money damages for any injuries he has suffered as a result of the agents' violation of the Amendment. . . .

The judgment of the Court of Appeals is reversed. . . .

Harlan, J. (concurring). . . .

For the reasons set forth below, I am of the opinion that federal courts do have the power to award damages for violation of "constitutionally protected interests" and I agree with the Court that a traditional judicial remedy such as damages is appropriate to the vindication of the personal interests protected by the Fourth Amendment. . . .

. . . [T]he judiciary has a particular responsibility to assure the vindication of constitutional interests such as those embraced by the Fourth Amendment. To be sure, "it must be remembered that legislatures are ultimate guardians of the liberties and welfare of the people in quite as great a degree as the courts." Missouri, Kansas & Texas R. Co. of Texas v. May, 194 U.S. 267, 270, 24 S. Ct. 638, 639, 48 L. Ed. 971 (1904). But it must also be recognized that the Bill of Rights is particularly intended to vindicate the interests of the individual in the face of the popular will as expressed in legislative majorities; at the very least, it strikes me as no more appropriate to await express congressional authorization of traditional judicial relief with regard to these legal interests than with respect to interests protected by federal statutes.

The question then, is, as I see it, whether compensatory relief is "necessary" or "appropriate" to the vindication of the interest asserted. . . . In resolving that question, it seems to me that the range of policy considerations we may take into account is at least as broad as the range of a legislature would consider with respect to an express statutory authorization of a traditional remedy. In this regard I agree with the Court that the appropriateness of according Bivens compensatory relief does not turn simply on the deterrent effect liability will have on federal official conduct. Damages as a traditional form of compensation for invasion of a legally protected interest may be entirely appropriate even if no substantial deterrent effects on future official lawlessness might be thought to result. Bivens, after all, has invoked judicial processes claiming entitlement to compensation for injuries resulting from allegedly lawless official behavior, if those injuries are properly compensable in money damages. I do not think a court of law — vested with the power to accord a remedy — should deny him his relief simply because he cannot show that future lawless conduct will thereby be deterred.

And I think it is clear that Bivens advances a claim of the sort that, if proved, would be properly compensable in damages. The personal interests protected by the Fourth Amendment are those we attempt to capture by the notion of "privacy"; while the Court today properly points out that the type of harm which officials can inflict when they invade protected zones of an individual's life are different from the types of harm private citizens inflict on one another, the experience of judges in dealing with private trespass and false imprisonment claims supports the conclusion that courts of law are capable of making the types of judgment concerning causation and magnitude of injury necessary to accord meaningful compensation for invasion of Fourth Amendment rights. . . .

[I]t is apparent that some form of damages is the only possible remedy for someone in Bivens' alleged position. It will be a rare case indeed in which an individual in Bivens' position will be able to obviate the harm by securing injunctive relief from any court. However desirable a direct remedy against the Government might be as a substitute for individual official liability, the sovereign still remains immune to suit. Finally, assuming Bivens' innocence of the crime charged, the "exclusionary rule" is simply irrelevant.* For people in Bivens' shoes, it is damages or nothing.

The only substantial policy consideration advanced against recognition of a federal cause of action for violation of Fourth Amendment rights by federal officials is the incremental expenditure of judicial resources that will be necessitated by this class of litigation. There is, however, something ultimately self-defeating about this argument. For if, as the Government contends, damages will rarely be realized by plaintiffs in these cases because of jury hostility, the limited resources of the official concerned, etc., then I am not ready to assume that there will be a significant increase in the expenditure of judicial resources on these claims. Few responsible

---

* [The exclusionary rule states that, subject to certain exceptions, evidence obtained unlawfully — for example, by means of an unconstitutional warrantless search — may not be used in a criminal prosecution to help convict the defendant. — Eds.]

lawyers and plaintiffs are likely to choose the course of litigation if the statistical chances of success are truly de minimis. And I simply cannot agree with my Brother Black that the possibility of "frivolous" claims — if defined simply as claims with no legal merit — warrants closing the courthouse doors to people in Bivens' situation. There are other ways, short of that, of coping with frivolous lawsuits. . . .

. . . [T]he countervailing interests in efficient law enforcement of course argue for a protective zone with respect to many types of Fourth Amendment violations. But, . . . at the very least such a remedy would be available for the most flagrant and patently unjustified sorts of police conduct. Although litigants may not often choose to seek relief, it is important, in a civilized society, that the judicial branch of the Nation's government stand ready to afford a remedy in these circumstances. . . .

Burger, C.J. (dissenting).   I dissent from today's holding which judicially creates a damage remedy not provided for by the Constitution and not enacted by Congress. We would more surely preserve the important values of the doctrine of separation of powers — and perhaps get a better result — by recommending a solution to the Congress as the branch of government in which the Constitution has vested the legislative power. Legislation is the business of the Congress, and it has the facilities and competence for that task — as we do not. . . .

[Chief Justice Burger proceeds with a lengthy critique of the exclusionary rule, see *supra* footnote *, arguing that it largely fails to deter official misconduct while permitting some who have committed crimes to escape conviction on technicalities. — Eds.]

The problems of both error and deliberate misconduct by law enforcement officials call for a workable remedy. Private damage actions against individual police officers concededly have not adequately met this requirement, and it would be fallacious to assume today's work of the Court in creating a remedy will really accomplish its stated objective. . . . Jurors may well refuse to penalize a police officer at the behest of a person they believe to be a "criminal" and probably will not punish an officer for honest errors of judgment. In any event an actual recovery depends on finding non-exempt assets of the police officer from which a judgment can be satisfied.

I conclude, therefore, that an entirely different remedy is necessary but it is one that in my view is as much beyond judicial power as the step the Court takes today. Congress should develop an administrative or quasi-judicial remedy against the government itself to afford compensation and restitution for persons whose Fourth Amendment rights have been violated. The venerable doctrine of respondeat superior in our tort law provides an entirely appropriate conceptual basis for this remedy. If, for example, a security guard privately employed by a department store commits an assault or other tort on a customer such as an improper search, the victim has a simple and obvious remedy — an action for money damages against the guard's employer, the department store. W. Prosser, *The Law of Torts* § 68, pp.470-480 (3d ed., 1964). Such a statutory scheme would have the added advantage of providing some remedy to the completely innocent persons who are sometimes the victims of illegal police conduct. . . .

A simple structure would suffice. . . . Congress could enact a statute [effecting]:

(a)   a waiver of sovereign immunity as to the illegal acts of law enforcement officials committed in the performance of assigned duties;

(b)   the creation of a cause of action for damages sustained by any person aggrieved by conduct of governmental agents in violation of the Fourth Amendment or statutes regulating official conduct;

(c)   the creation of a tribunal, quasi-judicial in nature . . . to adjudicate all claims under the statute. . . .

Black, J. (dissenting). . . . There can be no doubt that Congress could create a federal cause of action for damages for an unreasonable search in violation of the Fourth Amendment. Although Congress has created such a federal cause of action against state officials acting under color of state law,[*] it has never created such a cause of action against federal officials. . . . Congress could, of course, create a remedy against federal officials who violate the Fourth Amendment in the performance of their duties. But the point of this case and the fatal weakness in the Court's judgment is that . . . Congress . . . has [not] enacted legislation creating such a right of action. For us to do so is, in my judgment, an exercise of power that the Constitution does not give us.

Even if we had the legislative power to create a remedy, there are many reasons why we should decline to create a cause of action where none has existed since the formation of our Government. The courts of the United States as well as those of the States are choked with lawsuits. The number of cases on the docket of this Court have reached an unprecedented volume in recent years. A majority of these cases are brought by citizens with substantial complaints — persons who are physically or economically injured by torts or frauds or governmental infringement of their rights; persons who have been unjustly deprived of their liberty or their property; and persons who have not yet received the equal opportunity in education, employment, and pursuit of happiness that was the dream of our forefathers. Unfortunately, there have also been a growing number of frivolous lawsuits, particularly actions for damages against law enforcement officers whose conduct has been judicially sanctioned by state trial and appellate courts and in many instances even by this Court. My fellow Justices on this Court and our brethren throughout the federal judiciary know only too well the time-consuming task of conscientiously poring over hundreds of thousands of pages of factual allegations of misconduct by police, judicial, and corrections officials. Of course, there

---

* "Every person who, under color of any statute, ordinance, regulation, custom, or usage, of any State or Territory, subjects, or causes to be subjected, any citizen of the United States or other person within the jurisdiction thereof to the deprivation of any rights, privileges, or immunities secured by the Constitution and laws, shall be liable to the party injured in an action at law, suit in equity, or other proper proceeding for redress." Rev. Stat. § 1979, 42 U.S.C. § 1983.

are instances of legitimate grievances, but legislators might well desire to devote judicial resources to other problems of a more serious nature.

We sit at the top of a judicial system accused by some of nearing the point of collapse. Many criminal defendants do not receive speedy trials and neither society nor the accused are assured of justice when inordinate delays occur. Citizens must wait years to litigate their private civil suits. Substantial changes in correctional and parole systems demand the attention of the lawmakers and the judiciary. If I were a legislator I might well find these and other needs so pressing as to make me believe that the resources of lawyers and judges should be devoted to them rather than to civil damage actions against officers who generally strive to perform within constitutional bounds. There is also a real danger that such suits might deter officials from the proper and honest performance of their duties.

All of these considerations make imperative careful study and weighing of the arguments both for and against the creation of such a remedy under the Fourth Amendment. I would have great difficulty for myself in resolving the competing policies, goals, and priorities in the use of resources, if I thought it were my job to resolve those questions. But that is not my task. . . . Congress has not provided that any federal court can entertain a suit against a federal officer for violations of Fourth Amendment rights occurring in the performance of his duties. A strong inference can be drawn from creation of such actions against state officials that Congress does not desire to permit such suits against federal officials. Should the time come when Congress desires such lawsuits, it has before it a model of valid legislation, 42 U.S.C. § 1983, to create a damage remedy against federal officers. . . .

[Justice **Blackmun** dissented, largely on the grounds articulated by Justice Black.]

NOTES AND QUESTIONS

1. *Rights of Action Against Whom?* *Bivens* renders *individual* federal officers liable for violating a person's Fourth Amendment rights. It does not purport to give rise to a claim against the federal government as employer of those officers. Under the common law doctrine of sovereign immunity, see Chapter 7, federal and state governments were immune from being held liable for "their" torts. As further explained in Chapter 7, Congress has waived much of its common law immunity in 1946 by means of the Federal Tort Claims Act (FTCA). However, at the time of *Bivens*, the FTCA was written so as *not* to waive immunity for injuries caused by *intentional misconduct* of the sort alleged by Bivens. In 1974, in response to *Bivens*, Congress amended the FTCA to waive federal governmental immunity for intentional torts committed by "investigative or law enforcement officers" in the course of their official duties. Thus, today, Bivens would be able to bring an action against the federal government, as employer of the agents.

2. *Bivens and § 1983.* As indicated in Justice Black's dissent, long before 1971, Congress had enacted a statute — 42 U.S.C. § 1983 — that

enables individuals to bring damage actions for violations of constitutional rights committed by *state* or *local government* officials. Thus, if the agents who had carried out the arrest of Bivens had been employed by the State or City of New York, Bivens could have relied on § 1983 to bring claims seeking to impose liability on those agents individually. The Supreme Court has since held that, under certain circumstances, § 1983 can also be invoked to impose liability on municipalities and other local governmental entities for maintaining policies that violate individuals' constitutional rights. However, the statute does not authorize suits for damages against a *state government* (or the federal government) for the enactment and perpetuation of unconstitutional policies. A great deal of civil rights litigation seeking damages has proceeded under § 1983, creating an area of law that (in conjunction with *Bivens* actions) is sometimes referred to as "constitutional torts."

3. *Implied Constitutional Rights of Action after* Bivens. After *Bivens*, the Court recognized implied rights of action against federal officials arising out of other provisions of the Constitution, including the Fifth Amendment's (implicit) Equal Protection principle, as well as the Eighth Amendment's ban on cruel and unusual punishment. Davis v. Passman, 442 U.S. 228 (1979); Carlson v. Green, 446 U.S. 14 (1980). However, as has been the case with statutory causes of action, the Court has subsequently shown greater reticence in recognizing new rights of action. Bush v. Lucas, 462 U.S. 367 (1983) (federal employee does not have a right of action against his supervisor for violating his First Amendment rights); Schweiker v. Chilicky, 487 U.S. 412 (1988) (plaintiff does not have a right of action against officials for denying him disability benefits without procedures guaranteed by the Due Process Clause). One of the prime motivations for the Court's increasing reticence in statutory cases — the desire to place the ball in Congress's hands — presumably does not apply to the Constitution, which can be amended only with great difficulty. Instead, the Court in these later cases has pointed to the availability of other remedies, including administrative procedures, as a reason not to recognize a private right of action.

4. *State Constitutions.* Should state courts follow the lead of *Bivens* and recognize private rights of action arising out of state constitutions? *See* Darwart v. Caraway, 58 P.3d 128 (Mont. 2002) (reviewing state court decisions on this issue and determining that about half have recognized *Bivens*-type claims).

REFERENCES/FURTHER READING

Negligence Per Se

Caroline Forell, *Statutory Torts, Statutory Duty Actions, and Negligence Per Se: What's the Difference?*, 77 Or. L. Rev. 497 (1998).
Paul Sherman, *Use of Federal Statutes in State Negligence Per Se Actions*, 13 Whittier L. Rev. 831 (1992).

Wrongful Death Acts

Jacob Lippman, *The Breakdown of Consortium*, 30 Colum. L. Rev. 651 (1930).

John F. Witt, *From Loss of Services to Loss of Support: The Wrongful Death Statutes, The Origins of Modern Tort Law, and the Making of the Nineteenth-Century Family*, 25 Law & Soc. Inquiry 717 (2000).

Claudia Zaher, *When a Woman's Marital Status Determined Her Legal Status: A Research Guide on the Common Law of Coverture*, 94 L. Lib. J. 459 (2002).

Private Rights of Action

Robert H. Ashford, *Implied Causes of Action under Federal Law: Calling the Court Back to* Borak, 79 Nw. U. L. Rev. 227 (1984).

Henry H. Drummonds, *The Dance of Statutes and the Common Law: Employment, Alcohol, and Other Torts*, 36 Willamette L. Rev. 939 (2000).

Caroline Forell, *The Statutory Duty Action in Tort: A Statutory/Common Law Hybrid*, 23 Ind. L. Rev. 781 (1990).

Tamar Frankel, *Implied Rights of Action*, 67 Va. L. Rev. 553 (1981).

Thomas Hazen, *Implied Private Remedies under Federal Statutes: Neither a Death Knell Nor a Moratorium — Civil Rights, Securities Regulation, and Beyond*, 33 Vand. L. Rev. 133 (1980).

Susan J. Stabile, *The Role of Congressional Intent in Determining the Existence of Implied Private Rights of Action*, 71 Notre Dame L. Rev. 861 (1996).

Donald H. Zeigler, *Rights, Rights of Action, and Remedies: An Integrated Approach*, 76 Wash. L. Rev. 67 (2001).

CHAPTER 7

Defenses

Even if a victim can establish a prima facie case of negligence against another person or entity, there are various grounds on which that other can defeat or mitigate the attribution of responsibility and liability for negligence. Some of these grounds have to do with the victim's role in bringing about her injury. Others have to do with facts relating to the actor's status or circumstances. Some are provided by common law, others by statute.

If a party defending against a negligence claim believes that, notwithstanding the ability of the claimant to make out a prima facie case, there are grounds for defeating or limiting liability, it is usually up to him to identify those grounds early in the proceedings. Doing so is known as raising an *affirmative defense*. Because the onus is on the defending party, a failure to assert a defense in the manner prescribed by the relevant rules of procedure usually constitutes a waiver of the defense. For example, if a defendant wishes to invoke a statute of limitations to establish that the plaintiff waited too long before bringing suit, he normally must raise that argument in his answer to the plaintiff's complaint, or in a motion to dismiss for failure to state a claim. A defendant who fails to do this loses his right to assert this defense, even if the facts support its application to the case.

In addition to having the obligation to plead defenses, the defendant also usually shoulders the burdens of production and persuasion. At times, however, courts will employ the technique of burden shifting that we have seen them employ to assist plaintiffs in overcoming certain obstacles to proving the prima facie case.

I. CONTRIBUTORY NEGLIGENCE AND COMPARATIVE RESPONSIBILITY

A. *Contributory Negligence*

In the introduction to Chapter 2, we provided a brief excerpt from an 1839 English decision, Cotterill v. Starkey. It stated that Starkey, as the driver of a horse-drawn carriage, owed a duty to take reasonable care not to injure pedestrians such as Mrs. Cotterill. After describing this duty for the jury, and instructing it to deliberate on the question of whether Starkey's running down of Mrs. Cotterill resulted from a want of due care on Starkey's part, the trial judge presented one other issue to the jury for resolution. This issue concerned the question of Mrs. Cotterill's fault:

> [D]efendant says that the [accident] arose from the . . . careless and improper conduct of Mrs. Cotterill, which is denied by the plaintiff. You

must say whether it arose from plaintiff's fault or not. . . . [You must find for the defendant if you are] satisfied that the matter arose from the . . . careless . . . conduct of Mrs. Cotterill.

The logic of this instruction might seem obvious, but it deserves some reflection. Why should the plaintiff lose just because her carelessness combined with the defendant's carelessness to cause her injury? Is the defendant getting off the hook merely because he happened carelessly to hurt someone who was not careful, as opposed to a careful victim? Why should the defendant benefit from that sort of luck? Notice that, under the judge's formulation, *any* carelessness on the part of the plaintiff that contributes to her injury results in a careless defendant paying nothing and the plaintiff suffering the full burden of the loss. This principle, known as *contributory negligence*, at one time conferred on negligence defendants a powerful affirmative defense.

1. *Multiple But-For Causes and Superseding Cause Revisited.* A succinct account of the contributory negligence defense is provided in another early nineteenth-century decision, this one issued by the Massachusetts Supreme Judicial Court, Smith v. Smith, 19 Mass. 621 (1824). Plaintiff was driving a wagon containing barrels of cider down a "circuitous" road at night. Defendant had erected a pile of wood near the road. Plaintiff's horse and wagon struck the wood and the horse was injured. Plaintiff sued for negligence, alleging that defendant had failed to place the wood at a safe distance from the road. The jury was instructed that defendant could not be held liable if the jury found that the plaintiff "had not driven skillfully" and that that lack of skill contributed to the accident. The court upheld a defense verdict. It reasoned that, although a person who carelessly obstructs a highway is "amenable to the public in indictment," he is not to be held liable to an individual plaintiff in tort unless the obstruction "caused" an injury to the plaintiff. When the plaintiff himself was at fault, the court continued, the careless defendant, in the eyes of the law, is not a cause of the injury.

In the introduction to Chapter 4, we stressed that the actual causation inquiry in negligence law should *not* be framed as a search for *the* (single) person or entity responsible for causing an injury, because it may be that two or more persons are legally responsible. According to the jury, the plaintiff in *Smith* could have avoided the collision by driving carefully, hence his carelessness was *a* but-for cause of his own injuries. But so too was the defendant's carelessness. Yet the *Smith* court in effect held that, so long as carelessness on the part of the plaintiff is determined to have been *a* but-for cause of his injury, he is totally responsible, notwithstanding that the defendant's carelessness also caused the injury. ·

It may be that nineteenth-century courts took this position as a result of basic confusion over how to think about actual causation. More likely, they consciously constructed this affirmative defense by analogy to certain proximate cause doctrines. Recall that, at this time, courts tended to treat intervening third-party criminal misconduct as a *per se superseding cause*. The defense of contributory negligence gave similar effect to fault on the part of the plaintiff. If plaintiff's carelessness contributed to his injury, then as a matter of law his conduct would be deemed the only *legally relevant* cause of the injury.

Even granted the intelligibility of this analysis, the rule of contributory negligence did not seem to sit comfortably with other facets of proximate cause analysis. Consider a suit by a *careful* plaintiff against two careless defendants, both of whose carelessness combined to cause injury to the plaintiff. For example, suppose the same facts as *Smith*, except that the driver's horse was not damaged, only the cider barrels he was carrying. Suppose *O* — the owner of the cider barrels — sued the defendant (*D*) for the negligent destruction of his cider. Would the court have thrown out *O*'s claim on the ground that Smith's (*S*'s) intervening act of careless driving superseded *D*'s careless stacking of the wood? Perhaps, but certainly by the early years of the twentieth century, courts would more typically impose liability on both *D* and *S*, given that the carelessness of each functioned as a but-for cause of *O*'s injury. Would it make sense to permit *O* to proceed against *D* for negligence yet at the same time bar *S* from proceeding against *D* for the same negligence? Why should *S*'s carelessness have a different legal effect when *S* is the one suing *D*, rather than *O*?

2. *Limits: Intentional Torts and Last Clear Chance.* The rule of contributory negligence did not extend to claims alleging recklessness or intentional wrongdoing on the part of the defendant. *See, e.g.* Restatement (Second) of Torts § 500 (1965). Thus, carelessness by the plaintiff was treated as irrelevant in a case in which the defendant was alleged to have acted with more than mere carelessness, as in suits for battery of false imprisonment. That rule remains true today, even with the abandonment of contributory negligence in favor of comparative responsibility.

Even in negligence cases, the harshness of the contributory negligence regime was ameliorated both by informal practices and explicit legal rules. Informally, jurors were often made aware of the harsh implications of a finding of contributory negligence. For example, they may have been apprised by the trial judge's instructions, as were the jurors in *Cotterill*, that they would be required to find for the defendant if they found that the plaintiff's fault contributed to her injury. Given this awareness, some jurors may have "nullified" the formal law by declining to assign fault to a plaintiff who they thought deserving of compensation.

Apart from this sort of *ad hoc* adjustment, nineteenth-century judges developed special rules to deal with certain cases in which it seemed counterintuitive to permit a defendant to avoid responsibility for an accident that he could have foreseen and avoided, just because the plaintiff's fault also contributed to the injury. Most important among these was the doctrine of *last clear chance*.

A typical last clear chance case would proceed as follows. Imagine that a railroad engineer employed by defendant *D* operates *D*'s train at a carelessly high speed. Plaintiff *P*, a farmer, carelessly drives his truck across a grade crossing so that it gets stuck on the track. Suppose *P* can prove at trial that, notwithstanding the train's excessive speed, the engineer could have prevented a collision with *P*'s truck by applying the train's brakes, yet for no good reason failed to do so. *D* would not be allowed to raise the affirmative defense of contributory negligence because, even though *P* was careless, *D* had the last clear chance to avoid the accident. (Notice that it is the plaintiff seeking to invoke last clear chance who bears the burden of proving the doctrine's applicability.)

In essence, the doctrine of last clear chance held that, if a defendant has the last opportunity to prevent an accident resulting from careless acts of both the defendant and the plaintiff, the defendant will not enjoy the protection of the contributory negligence defense. Does this doctrine rest on an intelligible principle? Why should the temporal order of a defendant's and a plaintiff's respective careless acts make any difference for purposes of assigning responsibility? Is it because the defendant has, in effect, committed a second careless act by not responding appropriately to the plaintiff's negligence?

3. *Doing Away with Contributory Negligence.*   Dissatisfaction with the regime of contributory negligence mounted among twentieth-century lawyers, judges, and scholars. Finally, in the period from about 1970 to 1990, contributory negligence was eliminated and replaced by schemes of comparative responsibility in all but four U.S. jurisdictions. Sometimes its adoption was brought about by judicial decision, and sometimes through legislation. As indicated below, comparative responsibility regimes differ in many respects. But all of them do away with the idea that *any* degree of carelessness on the part of the plaintiff constitutes a *per se* bar to recovery. As the following notes explain, under many comparative responsibility regimes, a plaintiff's fault can sometimes still function to bar her claim, but only in special circumstances. More typically, the contribution of plaintiff's fault to her injury is taken into account in other, less drastic ways.

4. *Comparative Fault versus Comparative Responsibility.*   Conventional usage refers to the various schemes that have replaced contributory negligence as "comparative fault" regimes. This usage can sometimes be misleading. For example, in some jurisdictions, the definition of what the jury can treat as "fault" when comparing the parties' misconduct encompasses not just carelessness, but also intentional misconduct and even careful conduct. For this reason, we prefer the locution "comparative responsibility" to describe the general framework for allocating responsibility between plaintiff(s) and defendant(s). We use "comparative fault" to refer specifically to instances in which the parties' respective *carelessness* is at issue.

B.   Comparative Responsibility in Action

1.   Comparative Responsibility and Apportionment: Alternatives

To move from a scheme of contributory negligence to one of comparative responsibility is, first and foremost, to reject the rule that a negligence claim must be dismissed upon a finding that some carelessness on the part of the claimant contributed to her injury. However, this negative proposition does not of itself answer the remaining question: How *should* plaintiff's carelessness affect her claim? Conceptually, there are several possibilities.

One would be to give plaintiff's fault *no effect*, that is, to treat it as irrelevant to a negligence defendant's liability, which is how it is treated with respect to injuries caused by defendants who commit intentional torts. That option appears never to have earned serious consideration within American tort law.

Another option would be to adopt the following rule: Responsibility shall be split evenly among the number of parties whose fault is found to have contributed to plaintiff's injury. Under this rule, a careless plaintiff such as the driver in Smith v. Smith, *supra*, would be entitled to recover 50 percent of his damages from a careless defendant simply because there are two at-fault parties among whom to divide legal responsibility. By the same rule, a careless plaintiff who has a claim against two careless defendants would recover 66.67 percent of her damages, and so forth.

This approach to apportioning fault may strike you as intuitive. If so, that may be because you already encountered it in *Carroll Towing, supra*, Chapter 3. *Carroll Towing* was an admiralty case, and admiralty law had long observed the scheme of "divided damages" for claims of property damage, even as the common law of tort applied the rules of contributory negligence. Still, the ancient pedigree of the admiralty rule did not stop the U.S. Supreme Court from reconsidering it.

United States v. Reliable Transfer Co.
421 U.S. 397 (1975)

Stewart, J.   [A tanker owned by Reliable Transfer Co. ended up stranded on a sandbar. Reliable Transfer sued the United States for failing to maintain a flashing light that would have helped the ship's captain avoid the sandbar. The district court found that the vessel's grounding was caused 25 percent by the failure of the Coast Guard to maintain the light and 75 percent by the fault of the boat's captain. In so finding, the district court stated:]

> The fault of the vessel was more egregious than the fault of the Coast Guard. . . .
> Equipped with look-out, chart, searchlight, radiotelephone, and radar, he made use of nothing except his own guesswork judgment. After . . . turning in a loop toward the north so as to pass astern of [another vessel], he should have made sure of his position before setting his new . . . course. The fact that a northwest gale blowing at 45 knots with eight to ten foot seas made it difficult to see, emphasizes the need for caution rather than excusing a turn into the unknown. . . .

The court held, however, that the settled admiralty rule of divided damages required each party to bear one-half of the damages to the vessel.[1] . . .

II.

The precise origins of the divided damages rule are shrouded in the mists of history. . . .

. . . [I]n 1855 this Court adopted the rule of equal division of damages in The Schooner Catharine v. Dickinson, 17 How. 170. The rule was adopted because it was then the prevailing rule in England, because it had become the majority rule in the lower federal courts, and because it seemed the "most just and equitable, and . . . best [tended] to induce care and vigilance on both sides, in the navigation." *Id.*, at 177-178. There can be no question that subsequent history and experience have conspicuously eroded the rule's foundations.

. . . England has long since abandoned the rule and now follows the Brussels Collision Liability Convention of 1910 that provides for the apportionment of damages on the basis of "degree" of fault whenever it is possible to do so. Indeed, the United States is now virtually alone among the world's major maritime nations in not adhering to the Convention with its rule of proportional fault — a fact that encourages transoceanic forum shopping. . . .

The divided damages rule has been said to be justified by the difficulty of determining comparative degrees of negligence when both parties are concededly guilty of contributing fault. Although there is some force in this argument, it cannot justify an equal division of damages in every case of collision based on mutual fault. When it is impossible fairly to allocate degrees of fault, the division of damages equally between wrongdoing parties is an equitable solution. But the rule is unnecessarily crude and inequitable in a case like this one where an allocation of disparate proportional fault has been made. Potential problems of proof in some cases hardly require adherence to an archaic and unfair rule in all cases. Every other major maritime nation has evidently been able to apply a rule of comparative negligence without serious problems, see Mole & Wilson, *A Study of Comparative Negligence*, 17 Corn. L.Q. 333, 346 (1932) . . . and in our own admiralty law a rule of comparative negligence has long been applied with no untoward difficulties in personal injury actions. *See, e.g.*, Pope & Talbot, Inc. v. Hawn, 346 U.S. 406, 409. *See also* Merchant Marine (Jones) Act, 38 Stat. 1185, as amended, 41 Stat. 1007, 46 U.S.C. § 688; Death on the High Seas Act, 41 Stat. 537, 46 U.S.C. § 766.

---

1. The operation of the rule was described in *The Sapphire*, 18 Wall. 51, 56:

It is undoubtedly the rule in admiralty that where both vessels are in fault the sums representing the damage sustained by each must be added together and the aggregate divided between the two. This is in effect deducting the lesser from the greater and dividing the remainder. . . . If one in fault has sustained no injury, it is liable for half the damages sustained by the other, though that other was also in fault.

The argument has also been made that the divided damages rule promotes out-of-court settlements, because when it becomes apparent that both vessels are at fault, both parties can readily agree to divide the damages — thus avoiding the expense and delay of prolonged litigation and the concomitant burden on the courts. It would be far more difficult, it is argued, for the parties to agree on who was more at fault and to apportion damages accordingly. But the argument is hardly persuasive. For if the fault of the two parties is markedly disproportionate, it is in the interest of the slightly negligent party to litigate the controversy in the hope that the major-minor fault rule may eventually persuade a court to absolve it of all liability. And if, on the other hand, it appears after a realistic assessment of the situation that the fault of both parties is roughly equal, then there is no reason why a rule that apportions damages would be any less likely to induce a settlement than a rule that always divides damages equally. Experience with comparative negligence in the personal injury area teaches that a rule of fairness in court will produce fair out-of-court settlements. But even if this argument were more persuasive than it is, it could hardly be accepted. For, at bottom, it asks us to continue the operation of an archaic rule because its facile application out of court yields quick, though inequitable, settlements, and relieves the courts of some litigation. Congestion in the courts cannot justify a legal rule that produces unjust results in litigation simply to encourage speedy out-of-court accommodations. . . .

We hold that when two or more parties have contributed by their fault to cause property damage in a maritime collision or stranding, liability for such damage is to be allocated among the parties proportionately to the comparative degree of their fault, and that liability for such damages is to be allocated equally only when the parties are equally at fault or when it is not possible fairly to measure the comparative degree of their fault. . . .

Hunt v. Ohio Dept. of Rehabilitation & Correction
696 N.E.2d 674 (Ohio Ct. Cl. 1997)

Strausbaugh, J.   In her complaint, plaintiff, Lesa Hunt, alleges that defendant, Department of Rehabilitation and Correction ("ODRC"), negligently instructed and trained her to operate a snowblower, and that she was not provided with supervision while she was operating the snowblower. Plaintiff alleges that as a result, she inserted her hand in the chute in an attempt to unclog the snowblower, thereby causing her bodily injury.

On April 14, 1997, this action came before the court for trial on the sole issue of liability. . . .

At the time of the accident, plaintiff was an inmate in the custody and control of defendant. Plaintiff arrived at Northeast Pre-Release Center towards the end of 1993. On January 23, 1995, plaintiff was operating a Gravely snowblower while working with the outside yard crew. Carl Jenkins was the corrections officer in charge of the yard crew. Plaintiff and fellow inmate, Claudia DeJesus, were assigned to clear the sidewalks of two streets with the snowblower. While plaintiff was operating the snowblower, the chute became clogged with snow. Plaintiff put the snow-blower in neutral and turned the "Power Take Off" ("PTO") switch to the "off" position. The PTO switch shut down the blower. After visually inspecting the chute, plaintiff inserted her hand inside the chute and began cleaning out the packed snow. As she was removing the snow, the machine caught plaintiff's gloved hand and started pulling it into the chute. Although her glove remained caught in the chute, and plaintiff was able to pull her hand out, her right index, middle and third fingers were partially severed.

Prior to her assignment on that day, plaintiff and DeJesus had been instructed by Officer Jenkins on how to operate the snowblower. The training session lasted approximately ten minutes. This was the first time that Officer Jenkins had trained anyone to operate the snowblower, in spite of the fact that he had no prior experience operating the snow-blower. Although Officer Jenkins did not read the operator's manual, he had been trained one week prior to the accident by Woody Meyers, head of the maintenance department, who had instructed him that if the chute became clogged, to push the PTO switch in, turn the power switch off with the key, and clean out the snow with water or some device. Meyers cautioned against placing one's hand down the chute.

The court finds that Officer Jenkins, in good faith, believed that he had instructed plaintiff on all of the above. However, even if he did instruct plaintiff in this manner, there was insufficient emphasis placed on the importance of the safety instructions.

The court finds that plaintiff was under the impression that she needed only to push the PTO switch into the "off" position. Plaintiff did not consider the snowblower a dangerous machine and did not realize that there were moving parts that could still be spinning for a period of time after the snowblower was turned off. The court finds that plaintiff was not made aware that the engine should also be shut off prior to clean-ing out packed snow and that she should never place her hand in the chute.

Plaintiff's claim sets forth a single cognizable action, sounding in negligence. . . .

In the special relationship between the state and its prisoners, the state owes prisoners a duty of reasonable care and protection from unrea-sonable risks of harm. Reasonable care is that which would be utilized by an ordinarily prudent person under certain circumstances. An inmate laborer, such as plaintiff in the case at bar, is not an employee of the state. . . .

The court finds that defendant owed plaintiff a duty to warn her of the potential risks associated with the operation of the snowblower. The court further finds that plaintiff received inadequate safety training concerning what actions to take in the event that the snowblower became clogged. The operation of the machine was relatively new to both plaintiff and Officer Jenkins. Therefore, plaintiff should have received more detailed and hands-on safety training with the snowblower. It is not unrea-sonable to expect that a new user of such a machine may believe that the blades would immediately shut off by putting the PTO switch in the "off" position, without being specifically warned also to turn the ignition switch to the "off" position and wait for the blades to stop. The court finds that defendant did not adequately instruct plaintiff on the proper operation of the snowblower, and defendant is therefore negligent, since it breached its duty of reasonable care to protect plaintiff from harm.

Although the court finds that defendant was negligent, Ohio's comparative negligence statute bars a plaintiff from recovery if his or her actions were a greater cause (more than fifty percent) of his injuries than any acts of defendant. In this case, the court finds that although plaintiff's own negligence was not a greater causative factor, it constituted forty percent of the cause of her injuries.

The court finds that plaintiff disregarded a potential hazard and failed to use common sense when she inserted her hand in the chute of the snowblower.

The court concludes that plaintiff has proven that defendant breached its duty of reasonable care; however, the contributory negligence attributable to plaintiff is forty percent. Judgment is hereby rendered for plaintiff. A trial on the issue of damages will be scheduled in the near future.

Judgment accordingly.

Judgment Entry

Filed January 26, 1998

On June 17, 1997, this court rendered judgment in favor of plaintiff on the sole issue of liability. However, the court found plaintiff to be forty percent contributorily negligent. On December 5, 1997, this matter came to trial on the sole issue of damages.

The court finds that the total damages in this case amount to $18,000, which, when reduced by forty percent, the amount of negligence attributable to plaintiff, equals $10,800. Accordingly, judgment is rendered in favor of plaintiff in the amount of $10,800, which includes, but is not limited to, incurred medical expenses, lost earnings, pain and suffering, inability to perform usual activities, and emotional distress due to defendant's negligence. Court costs are assessed against defendant. The clerk shall serve upon all parties notice of this judgment and its date of entry upon the journal.

NOTES AND QUESTIONS

1. *Divided Damages versus Comparative Responsibility.* The court in *Reliable Transfer* notes that the rule of divided damages operates in a mechanical way that can produce unfair results in particular cases. Is it equally candid about the costs associated with a comparative fault regime?

For example, is it too optimistic about the ability of legal institutions to assign proportionate fault among multiple careless parties? Does your answer to this question vary depending on whether that assignment is made by a judge or a jury?

2. *Comparative Fault Today*. As indicated above, in adopting comparative responsibility, states were leaving behind the regime of contributory negligence, as opposed to the old admiralty rule of divided damages for property losses. Nonetheless, in doing so, they adopted rules of percentage apportionment more or less in keeping with the rule stated in *Reliable Transfer*. Thus, as indicated in *Hunt*, in the vast majority of jurisdictions, a finding that plaintiff's fault contributed to his injury will today entail a reduction in recoverable damages that corresponds to the percentage responsibility assigned to him. (This assumes that the percentage assigned is not so high as to constitute a complete bar within a "modified" comparative responsibility regime, discussed below.)

3. *Apportionment and the Jury*. Suits in admiralty law, such as the suit in *Reliable Transfer*, proceed without juries. Likewise, judges usually act as the factfinder for suits against government entities such as the suit in *Hunt*. In this regard, neither decision is representative. For garden-variety negligence suits that go to verdict, it is the jury who usually bears primary responsibility for implementing the system of comparative responsibility. In a simple P v. D negligence case, the jury will be instructed to assign a percentage responsibility to each party, such that the total responsibility adds up to 100 percent. This instruction is issued by the trial judge just before the jury retires to deliberate. In addition, judges often require the jury to complete a special verdict form. This form leads the jury through a series of yes or no questions as to whether the plaintiff has made out each element of her prima facie case, and whether the defendant has established any applicable defenses.

Consider the following instructions and special verdict form, proposed by the Tennessee Supreme Court for use in simple A v. B negligence actions. McIntyre v. Balentine, 833 S.W.2d 52, 59-60 (Tenn. 1992).

SUGGESTED JURY INSTRUCTIONS

[The following instructions should be preceded by instructions on negligence, proximate cause, damages, etc.]

1. If you find that defendant was not negligent or that defendant's negligence was not a proximate cause of plaintiff's injury, you will find for defendant.

2. If you find that defendant was negligent and that defendant's negligence was a proximate cause of plaintiff's injury, you must then determine whether plaintiff was also negligent and whether plaintiff's negligence was a proximate cause of his/her injury.

3. In this state, negligence on the part of a plaintiff has an impact on a plaintiff's right to recover damages. Accordingly, if you find that each party was negligent and that the negligence of each party was a proximate cause of

plaintiff's damages, then you must determine the degree of such negligence, expressed as a percentage, attributable to each party.

4.   If you find from all the evidence that the percentage of negligence attributable to plaintiff was equal to, or greater than, the percentage of negligence attributable to defendant, then you are instructed that plaintiff will not be entitled to recover any damages for his/her injuries. If, on the other hand, you determine from the evidence that the percentage of negligence attributable to plaintiff was less than the percentage of negligence attributable to defendant, then plaintiff will be entitled to recover that portion of his/her damages not caused by plaintiff's own negligence.

5.   The court will provide you with a special verdict form that will assist you in your duties. . . .

SPECIAL VERDICT FORM

We, the jury, make the following answers to the questions submitted by the court:

1.   Was the defendant negligent?

Answer: _____ (Yes or No)

(If your answer is "No," do not answer any further questions. Sign this form and return it to the court.)

2.   Was the defendant's negligence a proximate cause of injury or damage to the plaintiff?

Answer: _____ (Yes or No)

(If your answer is "No," do not answer any further questions. Sign this form and return it to the court.)

3.   Did the plaintiff's own negligence account for 50 percent or more of the total negligence that proximately caused his/her injuries or damages?

Answer: _____ (Yes or No)

(If your answer is "Yes," do not answer any further questions. Sign this form and return it to the court.)

4.   What is the total amount of plaintiff's damages, determined without reference to the amount of plaintiff's negligence?

Amount in dollars: $_____

5.   Using 100 percent as the total combined negligence which proximately caused the injuries or damages to the plaintiff, what are the percentages of such negligence to be allocated to the plaintiff and defendant?

Plaintiff _____%

Defendant _____%

(Total must equal 100%)

_____

Signature of Foreman

Notice that the court's proposed instruction tells jurors that they must determine "the degree of negligence attributable to each party." Likewise, question 5 on the proposed verdict form asks the jurors to assign percentages of "negligence" to the two parties that add up to 100 percent. Imagine a simple car accident involving *P* and *D*, in which *P* suffers a broken leg. If a jury following the court's instructions and its form were to assign 30 percent responsibility to *P* for not being sufficiently attentive to surrounding traffic, and 70 percent to *D* for speeding, what exactly would those numbers represent? Presumably the jury is *not* concluding that 3/10ths of the break in the bone in plaintiff's leg is traceable to plaintiff's inattentive driving. (It is difficult to imagine what that conclusion would mean, or how a jury could make it. Is the idea that *P* would have suffered a 30 percent smaller fracture? If so, would that necessarily entitle *P* to a smaller award of damages?) But if the 30 percent figure is not measuring the *causal contribution* of plaintiff's carelessness, what is it measuring? Is the jury being asked to determine who between *P* and *D* was driving less carefully? Is that judgment susceptible of numeric expression?

4. *Modified Comparative Responsibility.* The vast majority of jurisdictions have ceased to treat plaintiff's fault as a bar to negligence suits. Still, as indicated by *Hunt* and *McIntyre*, many states' comparative responsibility regimes retain a weaker version of that bar. Under their laws, the plaintiff's fault operates to defeat her cause of action (rather than reduce her recovery) if it passes a certain threshold in relation to the fault of the defendant. For example, under Wisconsin's version of comparative responsibility, a plaintiff suing a single defendant will have her suit dismissed as a matter of law if the jury assigns more fault to her than to the defendant — that is, anything more than 50 percent of the responsibility for the accident.* Where such a bar is retained, the system is commonly described as a *modified* comparative responsibility regime. This is in contrast to a *pure* system, in which a plaintiff could in principle be found 99 percent at fault for her injuries and yet still recover 1 percent of her damages from an at-fault defendant.

The possible variations on modified comparative responsibility expand when the plaintiff is suing multiple defendants. Thus, a jurisdiction might adopt the rule that a careless plaintiff is barred from suing if her comparative fault is equal to the total fault of all those whom she is suing. Under this rule, if *P* is suing *D1* and *D2*, and *P* is found to be 40 percent at fault, whereas *D1* is held 50 percent at fault and *D2* 10 percent at fault, *P* would be able to recover from both *D1* and *D2*, and

* Wisconsin was among the leaders in the movement toward comparative fault, adopting it by legislation in 1931. As originally enacted, the statute specified that the plaintiff's claim would be barred if the jury attributed at least 49 percent responsibility to the plaintiff. The legislature moved to the present threshold of greater than 50 percent in 1971, in part because the 49 percent rule was thought to operate harshly given an apparent tendency among Wisconsin juries to divide fault evenly among plaintiffs and defendants. As indicated below, Wisconsin jurors are not informed of the legal consequences of their assignments of responsibility.

to recover a total of 60 percent of her damages. (How much of that 60 percent she can collect from each will depend on the rules for apportionment of liability, as well as the solvency and amenability to suit of each. See *infra* Note 7.)

5. *Shades of Contributory Negligence?* In light of the fact that most states have adopted modified comparative responsibility regimes, one perhaps should take care not to overstate the significance of the transition from contributory negligence to comparative responsibility. A recent Nebraska decision illustrates how current law to some extent carries forward the spirit of the old regime.

In Baldwin v. City of Omaha, 607 N.W.2d 841 (Neb. 2000), the plaintiff was a college football player who had been hospitalized and medicated for severe mental illness, including a form of psychosis. Weeks after his discharge, he had a psychotic episode, endangering himself and others, which led two female police officers to attempt to subdue him to take him into custody. In the ensuing scuffle, one officer shot Baldwin, leaving him permanently paralyzed from the chest down.

At a bench trial, Baldwin established to the trial judge's satisfaction that he was injured in part because the officers acted unreasonably in effecting his arrest. In particular, by "utterly failing" to follow standard police procedures for detaining suspects known to be mentally ill (as they knew Baldwin to be), and by thereby provoking a physical confrontation with a suspect whom they also knew to be unusually powerful, they unnecessarily created the need for use of deadly force. However, the defendants established that Baldwin was also negligent, if not reckless, because of his decision — made while he was still taking anti-psychotic medication and therefore not delusional — to discontinue the medication notwithstanding his awareness that doing so might cause him to act in ways dangerous to himself and others. The judge then assigned 55 percent responsibility to Baldwin and 45 percent to the officers.

In doing so, the judge was aware that the Nebraska legislature had recently adopted a modified comparative fault regime. Like most states, Nebraska had for most of the twentieth century recognized contributory negligence as a complete bar to recovery. However, unlike many states, Nebraska's law lifted this bar if the plaintiff's fault was deemed by a jury to be "slight" in comparison to the defendant's relatively "gross" negligence. (In a case of relatively slight plaintiff's fault, the jury was instructed to reduce the plaintiff's damages by the percentage of fault attributed to the plaintiff.) In 1992, the state legislature replaced this scheme with a modified comparative responsibility regime under which a claimant's fault serves only to diminish his recovery, except that it bars recovery if the claimant's fault contributes to his injury to an equal or greater degree than the fault of all persons against whom he seeks recovery. 607 N.W.2d at 854. Thus, once the trial judge allocated greater fault to Baldwin, it was compelled to enter judgment for the defendants.

A divided Supreme Court affirmed, concluding that there was credible evidence to support the district court's apportionment of fault. *Id.* at 854. In effect, then, the same result was reached under Nebraska's new comparative fault regime as would have been reached under the old regime that barred claims brought by more than slightly at fault claimants. Assume that the trial judge's apportionment of fault was reasonable. Why should Baldwin lose his entire claim given that he was only a bit more at fault than the defendants? Would it make more sense to adopt a rule that only bars claims — as opposed to reducing damages — if the plaintiff is substantially more at fault than the defendant(s)?

In light of *Baldwin*, do you suppose that Nebraska's shift from the "more than slightly at fault" rule to the "at least as much at fault as the defendant(s)" rule will significantly decrease the number of claims that are barred outright on the grounds of plaintiff's comparative fault? Do you suppose this decrease has been much more significant in jurisdictions that, unlike Nebraska, recognized no exception to the contributory negligence bar for "slight" fault before shifting to modified comparative responsibility? Or might it be the case that, even in these jurisdictions, the plaintiffs who ended up being barred from recovery by judges and juries under the old rules of contributory negligence were by and large the same plaintiffs who today would be found "at least as much at fault" as defendants?

6. *Too Much Information?* Tennessee, like Wisconsin and Nebraska, is a modified comparative responsibility jurisdiction. Notice that the Tennessee-proposed instructions reproduced above, as well as question 3 of the special verdict form, inform jurors that if they assign more fault to the plaintiff than the defendant, judgment will be entered for the defendant. Does it make sense to inform the jury of the legal effects that will follow from certain assignations of percentage fault? Most states either require or permit trial judges to inform jurors of these effects in instructions and/or special verdict forms. *See* Russell v. Stricker, 635 N.W.2d 734 (Neb. 2001) (applying Nebraska's comparative fault statute, which requires that the jury be instructed on the legal effects of its apportionment). However, some state courts and legislatures have forbidden trial judges from informing jurors of such effects. The concern appears to be that jurors will adjust their calculation of percentage fault to avoid seemingly harsh legal consequences that would follow from a "true" assignment of percentages. *See, e.g.,* McGowan v. Story, 234 N.W.2d 325, 328-330 (Wis. 1975) (refusing to abrogate the rule against informing juries of the legal effects of apportionment rulings).* Is it undesirable for jurors to adjust apportionments of responsibility in light of the legal consequences that will follow?

---

* Some lower federal courts have interpreted Federal Rule of Civil Procedure 49(a), which empowers federal trial judges to submit special verdict forms to juries, as barring judges from informing jurors of the legal effects of assignments of percentage fault. This in turn has raised the question of whether, under *Erie R.R. v. Tompkins*, a federal court hearing a tort claim based on the law of a jurisdiction that mandates that juries be instructed as to the effects of their assignments of responsibility, should apply the federal rule or the conflicting state law. *See, e.g.,* Affiliated FM Ins. Co. v. Neosho Const. Co., 192 F.R.D. 662 (D. Kan. 2000) (concluding that rules about informing jurors is procedural rather than substantive, and therefore that the federal rule controls in federal court).

In a related vein, notice also that question 4 of *McIntyre*'s proposed verdict form asks the jury to determine damages *without* regard to its assignment of percentage fault. Is it realistic to ask jurors to determine the dollar amount of damages while ignoring that those damages will be reduced by the percentage fault assigned to the plaintiff?

7. *Comparative Responsibility and Other Apportionment Rules.* Other rules concerning apportionment of damages will influence how a plaintiff's fault affects her recovery. For example, recall the doctrine of joint and several liability, which we encountered in connection with Summers v. Tice, the case of the two careless hunters, only one of whom shot the plaintiff. That doctrine holds that any one of two or more at-fault defendants who cause a single "indivisible" injury can be held liable for 100 percent of plaintiff's damages. Now suppose a case involving a plaintiff adjudged by the jury to be 33 percent at fault for his injuries, and two at-fault defendants who are each deemed 33.5 percent at fault, but whose conduct falls within the rule of joint and several liability. Should plaintiff be able to take advantage of joint and several liability, which would entitle him to recover 67 percent of his total damages from a party found to have been only 33.5 percent responsible? Or would that violate the principle of apportioning responsibility in accordance with each party's percentage fault? *See* Ravo v. Rogatnick, *infra,* Chapter 8.

8. *Comparative Fault and Causation.* It is tempting to think of comparative fault as a doctrine that requires the jury to make a finding only as to the unreasonableness of plaintiff's conduct. In fact, the defense requires a finding of fault *and* causation. Two famous New York cases illustrate this point. Both were decided under the old contributory negligence rules, but they can still illuminate analysis under modern comparative fault systems.

The first decision is Martin v. Herzog, 126 N.E. 814 (N.Y. 1920), which we previously encountered in Chapter 6 under the heading of negligence per se. There, the defendant was driving his car at dusk on the wrong side of the center line and slammed into a buggy driven by the plaintiff's decedent. The buggy was operating without lights in contravention of a New York statute. Writing for the majority, Cardozo held that the defendant driver could rely on the statute to establish that the plaintiff's conduct was *per se* unreasonable. Cardozo noted, however, that establishing the unreasonableness of the plaintiff's conduct was not sufficient to make out the defense of contributory negligence. Rather, the plaintiff's statutory violation would defeat her claim only if *it actually played a role in bringing about the injuries suffered by the decedent.* In other words, a defendant, as part of his burden of proving the affirmative defense of comparative fault, normally has to prove that but for plaintiff's fault, the injury would not have happened.*

---

* In *Martin* itself, Cardozo further concluded that the statute not only set the standard of care that plaintiff's decedent had to meet, but also shifted the burden of proof to the plaintiff, requiring her to *disprove* causation by establishing that, *even if the buggy had used lights, the accident still would have occurred.* Ordinarily, however, the burden of proof will rest on the defendant.

The second case is Spier v. Barker, 323 N.E.2d 164 (N.Y. 1974). There, the defendant drove a truck into plaintiff's car. The plaintiff, who was not wearing a seat belt, was ejected from the car, which rolled over onto her, breaking her leg. Defendant's expert witness testified that the plaintiff likely would not have suffered any serious physical injuries if she had worn her seat belt. The New York Court of Appeals reasoned that plaintiff's failure to use a seat belt could not constitute contributory negligence because there was no evidence that plaintiff's omission was a but-for cause of the *accident*. (It did not, for example, cause her to slide on her seat so as to lose control of her car.) However, the court also held that the jury could consider plaintiff's failure to wear a seat belt in determining whether she failed to take reasonable steps to "mitigate" her damages. (On the issue of mitigation, recall Walter v. Wal-Mart from Chapter 1, and see Chapter 8.) Other courts have disagreed with the reasoning of *Spier*, holding that if the factfinder reasonably concludes that the failure to wear a seat belt was a but-for cause of plaintiff's *injuries*, a judge or jury can assign comparative fault to the plaintiff.*

Although in conflict, *Spier* and the decisions that reject it *both* accept that plaintiff's fault must play a causal role in producing the plaintiff's injury before it may be deemed "comparative fault." They disagree over how exactly to specify that role. *Spier* holds that plaintiff's carelessness must contribute to bringing about the accident that injured the plaintiff before it can be deemed comparative fault. Courts that reject *Spier* conclude that, so long as plaintiff's carelessness contributed to bringing about the *injury* that resulted from the accident, it may be treated as comparative fault, even if it did not make its contribution until after the accident.

The fact that *Spier* was decided under the old rule of contributory negligence perhaps influenced that court's analysis. By characterizing the issue as one of "mitigation" rather than contributory negligence, the court circumvented the all-or-nothing rule of contributory negligence, permitting the jury to factor the plaintiff's carelessness into the amount of damages she would recover. Notice that even today, the choice to characterize plaintiff's failure to wear a seat belt as "comparative fault" or "failure to mitigate" is not simply a matter of semantics. For example, in a modified comparative fault regime, the decision to treat such a failure as comparative fault entails that a plaintiff stands to lose her claim outright if the factfinder assigns a high enough percentage fault to that failure, as compared to the defendant's fault.

II.   Assumption of Risk

Today, comparative fault provides the primary focal point for defense arguments for reducing or eliminating liability on the ground of the complainant's

---

* Still other courts have refused to permit the defendant to raise the issue of the plaintiff's failure to wear a seat belt. Often these are courts in jurisdictions that lack mandatory seat belt laws, thus supporting the inference that individuals are under no legal duty to wear seat belts and hence cannot be found at fault for failing to wear them.

conduct. There is, however, another set of doctrines pertaining to the complainant's conduct that can affect the ability of plaintiff to recover even granted his or her ability to make out a prima facie case. These are the doctrines gathered under the heading of *assumption of risk*. The basic notion is simple enough. Sometimes, a negligent actor will argue that the victim is barred from recovering because she *knowingly and voluntarily* took on the risk that she might be injured *by careless conduct on the part of the defendant(s)*. The issue here is threefold: (1) Did the plaintiff in fact take on such a risk?; (2) Did she do so knowingly and voluntarily?; and (3) Are there policy reasons for courts to decline to enforce such assumptions of risk? As should be apparent, assumption of risk will frequently raise issues that rest on the boundary line between tort and contract.

A. *Express Assumption of Risk*

Jones v. Dressel
623 P.2d 370 (Colo. 1981)

Erickson, J. . . . In an action for damages by the plaintiff for personal injuries sustained in an airplane crash, the trial court granted the defendants' motion for partial summary judgment. Summary judgment was based upon the execution of an exculpatory agreement which the court held insulated the defendants from liability for simple negligence involving the crash of an airplane. A claim alleging willful and wanton negligence is at issue in the trial court. The court of appeals affirmed. We affirm the court of appeals.

On November 17, 1973, the plaintiff, William Michael Jones, who was then seventeen years old, signed a contract with the defendant, Free Flight Sport Aviation, Inc. (Free Flight).[1] The contract allowed Jones to use Free Flight's recreational skydiving facilities, which included use of an airplane to ferry skydivers to the parachute jumping site. A covenant not to sue and a clause exempting Free Flight from liability were included in the contract:

> 2A. EXEMPTION FROM LIABILITY.   The [plaintiff] exempts and releases the Corporation, its owners, officers, agents, servants, employees, and lessors from any and all liability, claims, demands or actions or causes of action whatsoever arising out of any damage, loss or injury to the [plaintiff] or the [plaintiff's] property while upon the premises or aircraft of the Corporation or while participating in any of the activities contemplated by this Agreement, whether such loss, damage, or injury results from the negligence of the Corporation, its officers, agents, servants, employees, or lessors or from some other cause.

---

1. Even though Jones' mother had ratified the terms of this contract on November 16, 1973, it should be noted that the approval by a parent does not necessarily validate an infant child's contract. *See generally*, Kaufman v. American Youth Hostels, 13 Misc. 2d 8, 174 N.Y.S.2d 580 (1957); Fedor v. Mauwehu Council, Boy Scouts of America, 21 Conn. Sup. 38, 143 A.2d 466 (1958).

The contract also contained an alternative provision which would have permitted Jones to use Free Flight's facilities at an increased cost, but without releasing Free Flight from liability for negligence.[2]

On December 28, 1973, Jones attained the age of eighteen. Ten months later, on October 19, 1974, he suffered serious personal injuries in an airplane crash which occurred shortly after takeoff from Littleton Airport. Free Flight furnished the airplane as part of its skydiving operation.

On November 21, 1975, nearly two years after attaining his majority, Jones filed suit against Free Flight alleging negligence and willful and wanton misconduct as the cause of the airplane crash. The defendants included the owners and operators of the airplane, the airport, and Free Flight. Based upon the exculpatory agreement, the trial court granted summary judgment in favor of the defendants. The court of appeals affirmed the trial court.

Jones asserts three grounds for reversal of the summary judgment. First, he claims that he disaffirmed the contract with Free Flight within a reasonable time after he attained his majority by filing suit. Second, he asserts that the exculpatory agreement is void as a matter of public policy. Third, he contends that inasmuch as an exculpatory agreement must be strictly construed against the party seeking to avoid liability for negligence, the injuries which he sustained as a result of the airplane crash were beyond the scope of the agreement. . . .

II.   RATIFICATION

As a matter of public policy, the courts have protected minors from improvident and imprudent contractual commitments by declaring that the contract of a minor is voidable at the election of the minor after he attains his majority. . . . A minor may disaffirm a contract made during his minority within a reasonable time after attaining his majority or he may, after becoming of legal age, by acts recognizing the contract, ratify it.

. . . What act constitutes ratification or disaffirmance is ordinarily a question of law to be determined by the trial court. We conclude, however,

---

2. The record indicates that the alternative provision of the contract was crossed out when Jones signed the contract. However, the record does not establish that Free Flight would have prohibited Jones from participating in skydiving activities if the alternative provision had not been crossed out.

2B. ALTERNATE PROVISION.   In consideration of the deletion of the provisions, 2A, 3, 4, and 5 herein regarding ASSUMPTION OF RISK, EXEMPTION FROM LIABILITY, COVENANT NOT TO SUE, INDEMNITY AGAINST THIRD PARTY CLAIMS, and CONTINUATION OF OBLIGATIONS, the Participant has paid the additional sum of $50.00 upon execution of this agreement, receipt of which is hereby acknowledged by the Corporation.

2C. It is understood that acceptance of this ALTERNATIVE PROVISION does not constitute a contract of insurance, but only waives Corporation's contractual defenses which would otherwise be available.

that the trial court properly determined that Jones ratified the contract, as a matter of law, by accepting the benefits of the contract when he used Free Flight's facilities on October 19, 1974. . . .

III. THE CONTRACT

Jones' assertion that his contract with Free Flight is void as a matter of public policy, raises two issues: (A) whether the contract with Free Flight is an adhesion contract; and (B) the validity of the exculpatory provisions of the contract. . . .

A. ADHESION CONTRACT

An adhesion contract is a contract drafted unilaterally by a business enterprise and forced upon an unwilling and often unknowing public for services that cannot readily be obtained elsewhere. *See* Chandler v. Aero Mayflower Transit Company, 374 F.2d 129 (1967); A. Ehrenzweig, *Adhesion Contracts in the Conflict of Laws,* 53 Col. L. Rev. 1072. An adhesion contract is generally not bargained for, but is imposed on the public for a necessary service on a take or leave it basis.

. . . [T]his Court [has] stated that even though a contract is a printed form and offered on a "take-it-or-leave-it" basis, those facts alone do not cause it to be an adhesion contract. There must be a showing "that the parties were greatly disparate in bargaining power, that there was no opportunity for negotiation, or that [the] services could not be obtained elsewhere." [Quoted authority omitted. — EDS.] . . .

We conclude that the record in the instant case supports the trial court's determination that the contract between Jones and Free Flight was not an adhesion contract as a matter of law. . . .

We also agree with the court of appeals' conclusion that nothing in the record establishes a disparity in bargaining power, or that the services provided by Free Flight could not be obtained elsewhere.

B. THE EXCULPATORY PROVISIONS

Jones asserts that the exculpatory agreement is void as a matter of public policy. We disagree. The defendants contend that Barker v. Colorado Region, 35 Colo. App. 73, 532 P.2d 372 (1974), is dispositive of the issue of the validity of the exculpatory agreement. In *Barker,* the court of appeals held that an exculpatory clause in a contract relating to recreational activities will be given effect where the intention of the parties is expressed in sufficiently clear and unequivocal language and does not fall within any of the categories where the public interest is directly involved.

Jones, however, claims that summary judgment should not have been granted for three reasons. First, he argues that because exculpatory agreements must be strictly construed against the party seeking exemption, the agreement here does not insulate the defendants from liability for negligence in connection with a crash that occurred prior to the time that Jones made a parachute jump. Second, he claims that Free Flight was acting as a common carrier when it carried Jones, for compensation, to an altitude from which he could make a parachute jump, and that a common carrier by air cannot compel a passenger to release or limit the carrier's legal liability for its own negligence. Third, he contends that Free Flight, which is engaged in the private air charter business and operates under a Part 135 Certificate, is subject to FAA regulations which impose standards of safety upon the pilot of an airplane, and that Free Flight cannot contract away its liability for negligence in the performance of a duty imposed by law or where the public interest requires performance.

The determination of the sufficiency and validity of an exculpatory agreement is a question of law for the court to determine. . . .

An exculpatory agreement, which attempts to insulate a party from liability from his own negligence, must be closely scrutinized, and in no event will such an agreement provide a shield against a claim for willful and wanton negligence. In determining whether an exculpatory agreement is valid, there are four factors which a court must consider: (1) the existence of a duty to the public; (2) the nature of the service performed; (3) whether the contract was fairly entered into; and (4) whether the intention of the parties is expressed in clear and unambiguous language. *See* Rosen v. LTV Recreational Development, Inc., 569 F.2d 1117 (10th Cir. 1978); . . . Threadgill v. Peabody Coal Co., 34 Colo. App. 203, 526 P.2d 676 (1974). . . .

Measured against the four factors which determine the validity of an exculpatory agreement, we conclude that the trial court correctly held, as a matter of law, that the exculpatory agreement was valid. Therefore, the granting of defendants' motion for summary judgment was not error.

The duty to the public factor is not present in this case. In Tunkl v. Regents of University of California, 60 Cal. 2d 92, 383 P.2d 441, 32 Cal. Rptr. 33 (1963), the California Supreme Court stated:

> In placing particular contracts within or without the category of those affected with a public interest, the courts have revealed a rough outline of that type of transaction in which exculpatory provisions will be held invalid. Thus the attempted but invalid exemption involves a transaction which exhibits some or all of the following characteristics. It concerns a business of a type generally thought suitable for public regulation. The party seeking exculpation is engaged in performing a service of great importance to the public, which is often a matter of practical necessity for some members of the public. The party holds himself out as willing to perform this service for any member of the public who seeks it, or at least for any member coming within certain established standards. As a result of the essential nature of the service, in the economic setting of the transaction, the party invoking exculpation possesses a decisive advantage of bargaining strength against any member of the public who seeks his services. In exercising a superior bargaining power the party confronts the public with a standardized adhesion contract of exculpation, and makes no provision whereby a purchaser may pay additional reasonable fees and obtain protection against negligence. Finally, as a result of the transaction, the person or property of the purchaser

is placed under the control of the seller, subject to the risk of carelessness by the seller or his agents. *Id.* . . . at 444.

In light of the foregoing factors, we conclude that the contract between Jones and Free Flight does not fall within the category of agreements affecting the public interest. . . .

Jones also claims that Free Flight was operating as a common carrier when it accepted funds and provided an aircraft to ferry him to an altitude from which he could make a parachute jump. He is correct in his statement that releases or limitations of liability in airline tickets issued by a common carrier have uniformly been held invalid. Conklin v. Canadian Colonial Airways, Inc., 266 N.Y. 244, 194 N.E. 692 (1935); Curtiss-Wright Flying Service, Inc. v. Glose, 66 F.2d 710 (3d Cir. 1933), *cert. denied*, 290 U.S. 696, 78 L. Ed. 599, 54 S. Ct. 132 (1938). *See* L. Kreindler, I. *Aviation Accident Law* § 3.13 (rev. 1977). He is in error, however, in his contention that Free Flight was operating as a common carrier in the instant case. C.F.R. § 135.1(a)(3). 14 C.F.R. § 1.1 provides:

"Commercial operator" means a person who, for compensation or hire, engages in the carriage by aircraft in air commerce of persons or property, other than as an air carrier or foreign air carrier or under the authority of Part 375 of this Title. Where it is doubtful that an operation is for "compensation or hire," the test applied is whether the carriage by air is merely incidental to the person's other business or is, in itself, a major enterprise for profit. . . .

Here, the facts are clear that Free Flight was not engaged in "commercial operations" or acting as a common carrier in connection with this skydiving flight. In fact, paragraph four of Jones' complaint alleges that Free Flight was "engaged in the business of operating a service for the general aviation public involving parachuting, soaring, and aerobatics. . . ." Carriage by air was incidental to Free Flight's principal business. . . .

While it is not necessary for a contract to embody all of the characteristics set forth in *Tunkl, supra,* to meet the test, we conclude that an insufficient number of these characteristics are present in the instant case to establish that the contract between Jones and Free Flight affected the public interest. The service provided by Free Flight was not a matter of practical necessity for even some members of the public; because the service provided by Free Flight was not an essential service, it did not possess a decisive advantage of bargaining strength over Jones; and the contract was not an adhesion contract.

Finally, in our consideration of the remaining factors that must be reviewed in considering the validity of an exculpatory agreement, we note that there was no disagreement between the parties that the contract was fairly entered into. Likewise, the agreement expressed the parties' intention in clear and unambiguous language; the contract used the word "negligence" and specifically included injuries sustained "while upon the aircraft of the Corporation."

We conclude that the exculpatory agreement was not void as a matter of public policy, and that there was no genuine issue as to any material fact.

Accordingly, the trial court properly granted a partial summary judgment on the simple negligence issue and we, therefore, affirm the decision of the court of appeals.

Dalury v. S-K-I, Ltd.
670 A.2d 795 (Vt. 1995)

Johnson, J.   We reverse the trial court's grant of summary judgment for defendants S-K-I, Ltd. and Killington, Ltd. in a case involving an injury to a skier at a resort operated by defendants. We hold that the exculpatory agreements which defendants require skiers to sign, releasing defendants from all liability resulting from negligence, are void as contrary to public policy.

While skiing at Killington Ski Area, plaintiff Robert Dalury sustained serious injuries when he collided with a metal pole that formed part of the control maze for a ski lift line. Before the season started, Dalury had purchased a midweek season pass and signed a form releasing the ski area from liability. The relevant portion reads:

RELEASE FROM LIABILITY AND CONDITIONS OF USE

1.   I accept and understand that Alpine Skiing is a hazardous sport with many dangers and risks and that injuries are a common and ordinary occurrence of the sport. As a condition of being permitted to use the ski area premises, I freely accept and voluntarily assume the risks of injury or property damage and release Killington Ltd., its employees and agents from any and all liability for personal injury or property damage resulting from negligence, conditions of the premises, operations of the ski area, actions or omissions of employees or agents of the ski area or from my participation in skiing at the area, accepting myself the full responsibility for any and all such damage or injury of any kind which may result.

Plaintiff also signed a photo identification card that contained this same language.

Dalury and his wife filed a complaint against defendants, alleging negligent design, construction, and placement of the maze pole. Defendants moved for summary judgment, arguing that the release of liability barred the negligence action. The trial court, without specifically addressing plaintiffs' contention that the release was contrary to public policy, found that the language of the release clearly absolved defendants of liability for their own negligence.

The trial court based its decision on Douglass v. Skiing Standards, Inc., 142 Vt. 634, 637, 459 A.2d 97, 99 (1983), in which we held that an exculpatory agreement was sufficient to bar a negligence action by a professional freestyle skier who was injured in a skiing competition, and two subsequent decisions of the United States District Court for the District of Vermont. *See* Estate of Geller v. Mount Snow Ltd., No. 89-66, slip op. at 5-6 (D. Vt. May 21, 1991) (summary judgment granted where plaintiff recreational skier signed release on back of ski pass); Barenthein v. Killington Ltd., No. 86-33, slip op. at 7 (D. Vt. June 17, 1987) (summary judgment granted where plaintiff signed equipment rental agreement which contained a release). The trial court did not view the distinction between professional and recreational skiing as significant, and granted summary judgment on the ground that the release was clear and unambiguous.

On appeal, plaintiffs contend that the release was ambiguous as to whose liability was waived and that it is unenforceable as a matter of law because it violates public policy. We agree with defendants that the release was quite clear in its terms. Because we hold the agreement is unenforceable, we proceed to a discussion of the public policy that supports our holding.

I.

This is a case of first impression in Vermont. While we have recognized the existence of a public policy exception to the validity of exculpatory agreements, see Lamoille Grain Co. v. St. Johnsbury & L.C.R.R., 135 Vt. 5, 7, 369 A.2d 1389, 1390 (1976) (public policy forbids a railroad from limiting its duty of care to the public, but this rule does not extend to the railroad's private contractual undertakings), in most of our cases, enforceability has turned on whether the language of the agreement was sufficiently clear to reflect the parties' intent.

Even well-drafted exculpatory agreements, however, may be void because they violate public policy. Restatement (Second) of Torts § 496B comment e (1965). According to the Restatement, an exculpatory agreement should be upheld if it is (1) freely and fairly made, (2) between parties who are in an equal bargaining position, and (3) there is no social interest with which it interferes. § 496B comment b. The critical issue here concerns the social interests that are affected.

Courts and commentators have struggled to develop a useful formula for analyzing the public policy issue. The formula has been the "subject of great debate" during "the whole course of the common law," and it had proven impossible to articulate a precise definition because the "social forces that have led to such characterization are volatile and dynamic." Tunkl v. Regents of Univ. of Cal., 60 Cal. 2d 92, 383 P.2d 441, 444, 32 Cal. Rptr. 33, 36 (1963).

The leading judicial formula for determining whether an exculpatory agreement violates public policy was set forth by Justice Tobriner of the California Supreme Court. *Id*. at 444-46, 32 Cal. Rptr. at 36-38. An agreement is invalid if it exhibits some or all of the following characteristics:

[The court proceeded to quote the same language from *Tunkl* that is quoted above in Jones v. Dressel. — EDS.]

Applying these factors, the court concluded that a release from liability for future negligence imposed as a condition for admission to a charitable research hospital was invalid. *Id.* at 449, 32 Cal. Rptr. at 41. . . .

[The court reviewed decisions from other states.—EDS.]

Having reviewed . . . various formulations of the public policy exception, we accept them as relevant considerations, but not as rigid factors that, if met, preclude further analysis. Instead, we recognize that no single formula will reach the relevant public policy issues in every factual context. Like the court in Wolf v. Ford, 335 Md. 525, 644 A.2d 522, 527 (Md. 1994), we conclude that ultimately the "determination of what constitutes the public interest must be made considering the totality of the circumstances of any given case against the backdrop of current societal expectations."

II.

Defendants urge us to uphold the exculpatory agreement on the ground that ski resorts do not provide an essential public service. They argue that they owe no duty to plaintiff to permit him to use their private lands for skiing, and that the terms and conditions of entry ought to be left entirely within their control. Because skiing, like other recreational sports, is not a necessity of life, defendants contend that the sale of a lift ticket is a purely private matter, implicating no public interest. . . . We disagree.

Whether or not defendants provide an essential public service does not resolve the public policy question in the recreational sports context. The defendants' area is a facility open to the public. They advertise and invite skiers and nonskiers of every level of skiing ability to their premises for the price of a ticket. At oral argument, defendants conceded that thousands of people buy lift tickets every day throughout the season. Thousands of people ride lifts, buy services, and ski the trails. Each ticket sale may be, for some purposes, a purely private transaction. But when a substantial number of such sales take place as a result of the seller's general invitation to the public to utilize the facilities and services in question, a legitimate public interest arises.

The major public policy implications are those underlying the law of premises liability. In Vermont, a business owner has a duty "of active care to make sure that its premises are in safe and suitable condition for its customers." Debus v. Grand Union Stores, 159 Vt. 537, 546, 621 A.2d 1288, 1294 (1993). We have recognized this duty of care where the defendant's routine business practice creates a foreseeable hazard for its customers. The business invitee "has a right to assume that the premises, aside from obvious dangers, [are] reasonably safe for the purpose for which he [is] upon them, and that proper precaution [has] been taken to make them so." Garafano v. Neshobe Beach Club, 126 Vt. 566, 572, 238 A.2d 70, 75 (1967). We have already held that a ski area owes its customers the same duty as any other business—to keep its premises reasonably safe.

The policy rationale is to place responsibility for maintenance of the land on those who own or control it, with the ultimate goal of keeping accidents to the minimum level possible. Defendants, not recreational skiers, have the expertise and opportunity to foresee and control hazards, and to guard against the negligence of their agents and employees. They alone can properly maintain and inspect their premises, and train their employees in risk management. They alone can insure against risks and effectively spread the cost of insurance among their thousands of customers. Skiers, on the other hand, are not in a position to discover and correct risks of harm, and they cannot insure against the ski area's negligence.

If defendants were permitted to obtain broad waivers of their liability, an important incentive for ski areas to manage risk would be removed, with the public bearing the cost of the resulting injuries.

For these reasons, we disagree with the decisions of the United States District Court for the District of Vermont, upholding exculpatory agreements similar to the one at issue here. We do not accept the proposition that because ski resorts do not provide an essential public service, such agreements do not affect the public interest. A recognition of the principles underlying the duty to business invitees makes clear the inadequacy of relying upon the essential public service factor in the analysis of public recreation cases. While interference with an essential public service surely affects the public interest, those services do not represent the universe of activities that implicate public concerns.

Moreover, reliance on the private nature of defendants' property would be inconsistent with societal expectations about privately owned facilities that are open to the general public. Indeed, when a facility becomes a place of public accommodation, it "render[s] a 'service which has become of public interest' in the manner of the innkeepers and common carriers of old." Lombard v. Louisiana, 373 U.S. 267, 279, 10 L. Ed. 2d 338, 83 S. Ct. 1122 (1963) (Douglas, J., concurring) (citation omitted) (quoting German Alliance Ins. v. Kansas, 233 U.S. 389, 408, 58 L. Ed. 1011, 34 S. Ct. 612 (1914)). Defendants are not completely unfettered, as they argue, in their ability to set the terms and conditions of admission. Defendants' facility may be privately owned, but that characteristic no longer overcomes a myriad of legitimate public interests. Public accommodations laws that prohibit discrimination against potential users of the facility are just one example of limitations imposed by law that affect the terms and conditions of entry. . . .

Reversed and remanded.

NOTES AND QUESTIONS

1. *Assuming the Risk of Injury versus Assuming the Risk of Careless Conduct.* The question posed by *express* assumption of risk doctrine is whether the plaintiff has agreed in advance to take on all responsibility for injuries caused by *careless* conduct on the part of the defendant. Thus, in *Jones*, the issue is *not* whether Jones took on responsibility for risks that attend a well-operated skydiving business. By definition, under a negligence regime, *those* risks are always assumed by the plaintiff.

For example, suppose that a skydiving company exercises reasonable care in selecting a location for the jump, operating its plane, providing training and equipment, and so forth. Suppose further that, notwithstanding these efforts, there is still a 1-in-100 chance that a skydiver will break an ankle upon hitting the ground. A customer who suffers such an injury despite the use of all due care by the skydiving operation has no claim in negligence. True, the company's conduct functioned as a cause of an injury to its customer, but since none of that conduct was faulty, there can be no liability, and so there is no need to inquire about any possible assumption of risk by the plaintiff. By contrast, imagine that the customer breaks his ankle because the pilot employed by the defendant made a navigational error that caused the plaintiff to parachute down onto a dangerously uneven surface. Under these circumstances, the assumption of risk issue may be in play. Again: The express assumption of risk inquiry concerns whether the plaintiff agreed in advance to take responsibility for any injury caused by carelessness on the part of the defendant.

2. *The Importance of Options.* How important to the *Jones* court was it that the defendant offered the plaintiff the option to pay $50 more to reserve his right to sue for negligently caused injuries? If that option were not available, would the court have found that Jones had assumed the risk? What exactly does a customer get for $50? A guarantee that the company would pay all damages if it is found to have negligently caused them? An agreement not to contest liability? Would one worry that customers might misunderstand what they are getting for their money? How did the company arrive at $50 as the price for the right to sue?

3. *Skydiving versus Skiing.* Do the different outcomes in *Jones* and *Dalury* turn on the different characteristics of skydiving and skiing? What characteristics? Why are those salient to the question of how to interpret, and whether to enforce, contractual provisions purporting to exculpate one party from liability for negligence?

4. *Bailments and Common Carriers.* A "bailment" occurs when one person hands over personal property to another for safekeeping. The owner of the property is referred to as the "bailor," and the temporary custodian is deemed the "bailee." Bailees often attempt to relieve themselves from liability for all damage caused to the owner's property during the bailment, even if caused by the bailee's carelessness. A common example is provided by parking garages that, through signs or language on the back of ticket stubs, disclaim liability for "any damage" that befalls cars while parked on the premises. Most courts have refused to permit commercial bailees to exculpate themselves in this manner on the grounds that such provisions are against public policy. As *Jones* and *Dalury* note, the same holds true for attempts by common carriers—commercial operators of boats, buses, planes, taxis, and trains—to exculpate themselves for personal injury and property damage liability. If this is the case, why do some professional bailees and common carriers continue to include exculpatory clauses on signage and ticket stubs?

5. *Express Assumption of Risk, Breach, and Comparative Fault.* The basic holding of *Dalury* is that the trial court erred in granting summary

judgment to the ski resort on the basis of the waiver contained in its passes and photo I.Ds. On remand, Dalury would presumably still have to prove that the placement of the pole was careless and that it proximately caused his injury. Does anything in the court's ruling preclude the defendant from arguing that Dalury was comparatively at fault? In concluding that the resort was not permitted to waive its liability through contract, did the court determine that, as a matter of law, Dalury acted reasonably? If not, how much did Dalury really gain from this ruling?

B.   *Implied Assumption of Risk*

Monk v. Virgin Islands Water & Power Auth.
53 F.3d 1381 (3d Cir. 1995)

Scirica, J.   In this appeal, we are required to interpret and apply . . . the Restatement (Second) of Torts to a lawsuit arising from a tragic construction accident in the Virgin Islands. The primary issue is the viability of Restatement section 343A, involving the doctrine of assumption of risk, in light of the Virgin Islands' adoption of a comparative negligence statute. . . . The district court granted summary judgment to the defendant landowner, holding that the Restatement provisions shielded it from tort claims by a worker injured on the property. We will affirm.

I.

In June 1990, a fire destroyed a building on St. Croix owned by Quality Electric Supply Company. The following month Quality Electric contracted with Benak Construction Company to demolish the remains of the original structure and to construct a new building. Ted Monk, Sr., a partner in Benak and head of the project, named his son, Ted Monk, Jr. ("Monk"), as foreman of the site.

At the time of construction, the Virgin Islands Water & Power Authority ("WAPA") maintained 7,200-volt power lines several feet above part of the proposed building. The power lines were clearly visible, and there is no dispute that everyone involved with the project knew about the lines and that any contact with them would be dangerous. On November 8, 1990, a crane was being used to lift steel joists that would connect the columns of the building frame. The first joist was installed with the use of a "tag line," a rope attached to the beam to prevent it from swinging. Monk decided not to use a tag line to install the next joist, however, because he thought he could better control the joist from swinging by holding it directly with his hands. At this point, Monk, Sr., yelled for his son to use a tag line. As Monk prepared to do so, the steel joist touched an overhead power line, sending an electrical current through his body. He suffered severe burns that resulted in the amputation of both his legs and his left arm. . . .

II.

In the Virgin Islands, the various Restatements of law provide the rules of decision in the absence of local laws to the contrary. . . .[2]

A.

At common law, a plaintiff's contributory negligence barred any subsequent recovery for damages, even if the plaintiff was only slightly at fault. W. Page Keeton et al., *Prosser and Keeton on the Law of Torts* §§ § 65, 67, at 451-52, 468-69 (5th ed. 1984); Restatement (Second) of Torts § 467. Similarly, the common law doctrine of assumption of risk prevented recovery when a plaintiff was deemed to have assumed the risk of a known danger. Keeton et al., *supra*, § 68, at 495-96; Restatement § 496A.

While these rules were still in force throughout most of the United States, the American Law Institute incorporated section 343A on "Known or Obvious Dangers" into the [Second] Restatement. . . . Section 343A provides in relevant part:

A possessor of land is not liable to his invitees[3] for physical harm caused to them by any activity or condition on the land whose danger is known or obvious to them, unless the possessor should anticipate the harm despite such knowledge or obviousness.

(footnote added). Section 343A's focus on dangers "known or obvious" to invitees, along with pertinent commentary,[4] indicated it was intended as a variation on the doctrine of assumption of risk. *See, e.g.*, Koutoufaris v. Dick, 604 A.2d 390, 395-96 (Del. 1992) (noting section "343A's apparent espousal of assumption of risk as a bar to recovery").

Soon after adoption of the Second Restatement in 1965 . . . the principle of apportioning damages between negligent plaintiffs and defendants

---

2. V.I. Code Ann. tit. 1, § 4 (1967) provides:

The rules of the common law, as expressed in the restatements of the law approved by the American Law Institute, and to the extent not so expressed, as generally understood and applied in the United States, shall be the rules of decision in the courts of the Virgin Islands in cases to which they apply, in the absence of local laws to the contrary.

3. . . . . There is no dispute that Monk is an "invitee," within the meaning of the Restatement.

4. For example, comment e to section 343A provides:

. . . If [an invitee] knows the actual conditions, and the activities carried on, and the dangers involved in either, he is free to make an intelligent choice as to whether the advantage to be gained is sufficient to justify him in incurring the risk by entering or remaining on the land. The possessor of the land may reasonably assume that he will protect himself by the exercise of ordinary care, or that he will voluntarily assume the risk of harm if he does not succeed in doing so. . . .

under a comparative fault system began "veritably sweeping the land." Keeton et al., *supra*, § 67, at 479. "Although by the mid-1960s only seven states had replaced contributory negligence with comparative fault, several states switched over in 1969, and the 1970s and early 1980s witnessed a surge of legislative and judicial action accomplishing the switch." *Id.* at 471 (footnotes omitted). All but four states now have adopted the doctrine.

The movement toward comparative negligence . . . raised questions concerning the continued viability of the assumption of risk defense,[6] which often resembled contributory negligence. *See, e.g., id.* § 68, at 495 ("The rise of comparative negligence has forced the courts and commentators to consider afresh the proper role for the assumption of risk defense."). Some jurisdictions that abolished contributory negligence also eliminated assumption of risk by statute. Other states left the issue for their courts to decide, which resulted in a range of decisions across the spectrum. Most courts rejected the defense, others continued it, and some supported certain forms of it but rejected others.

Depending upon their position on the viability of assumption of risk, courts also decided whether to continue using section 343A of the Restatement. As with assumption of risk generally, some courts opted to continue using section 343A, others decided against it, and still others decided the applicability of section 343A depended on the type of assumption of risk involved.

B.

In 1973, the Virgin Islands abolished the common law rule that a plaintiff's contributory negligence barred any recovery. In its place, it adopted a comparative negligence statute that apportioned fault between the plaintiff and defendant. *See* V.I. Code Ann. tit. 5, § 1451 (Supp. 1993). . . .[14] Monk contends this statute implicitly abolished assumption of risk as a defense, thereby contradicting Restatement section 343A and nullifying its viability.

In [Keegan v. Anchor Inns, Inc., 606 F.2d 35 (3d Cir. 1979)], we examined the . . . comparative negligence statute and its effect on the doctrine

---

6. Our discussion involves only the implied form of assumption of risk, not a defense based on an express contract. Defenses based on express assumption of risk remain valid in virtually all jurisdictions. . . .

14. V.I. Code Ann. tit. 5, § 1451(a) (Supp. 1993) provides in relevant part:

In any action based upon negligence to recover for injury to person or property, the contributory negligence of the plaintiff shall not bar a recovery, but the damages shall be diminished by the trier of fact in proportion to the amount of negligence attributable to the plaintiff. The burden of proving contributory negligence shall be on the defendant. If such claimant is found by the trier of fact to be more at fault than the defendant, or, in the case of multiple defendants, more at fault than the combined fault of the defendants, the claimant may not recover.

of assumption of risk. We held the statute abrogated one type of the assumption of risk defense, but left the other form intact:

> Assumption of risk is not necessarily grounded on the concept of fault. Sometimes the defense has been invoked when the plaintiff's conduct could be characterized as negligent; sometimes it has been invoked in its "strict" or "primary" sense when the conduct amounted to consent. In those cases where the plaintiff's conduct amounts to negligence, that fact should be accorded weight only within the comparative scheme of the statute. In such a case assumption of risk is not available as a bar to recovery. . . . It follows that when conduct amounts to a voluntary waiver or consent the absolute bar to recovery should remain.

Id. at 40. We employed this distinction between the two types of assumption of risk in Smollett v. Skayting Development Corp., 793 F.2d 547 (3d Cir. 1986). In *Smollett*, a woman injured while ice skating sued the operator of the rink, complaining that the lack of guardrails and the carpeted floor surrounding the ice caused her injuries. The jury found for the plaintiff, and the district court denied the defendant's motion for a judgment notwithstanding the verdict. On appeal, we reversed and directed the district court to enter judgment for the defendant, holding that the evidence showed the plaintiff "fully understood the risk of harm to herself and voluntarily chose to enter the area of risk. She, therefore, implicitly assumed the risk of injury." *Id.* at 548 (citation omitted). In so ruling, we reiterated the comparative negligence statute's effect on assumption of risk:

> Assumption of risk is still available as a complete defense to a negligence claim but it has been limited by enactment of the comparative negligence statute. Assumption of risk, to the extent it incorporates the concept of fault on the part of the actor and, therefore, overlaps with contributory negligence, is no longer available as a defense. However, assumption of risk can still be applied to "non-negligent conduct which constitutes waiver or consent" but which involved no negligence. In such cases the absolute bar to recovery remains.

Id. (quoting *Keegan*, 606 F.2d at 41 n.8). Therefore, the "primary" form of assumption of risk remains a viable defense in the Virgin Islands. Because Restatement section 343A requires a plaintiff's implicit acquiescence to "known or obvious dangers," the essence of the primary form of assumption of risk, this Restatement provision also remains valid. . . .

We recognize our holding on assumption of risk may not represent the view of a majority of jurisdictions. But many of the contrary cases are distinguishable, largely because relevant statutes eliminating contributory negligence often expressly barred the assumption of risk defense. Furthermore, we have interpreted the statute in this manner consistently since its 1973 enactment. We acknowledge the existence of strong policy reasons for completely abandoning the doctrine of assumption of risk as an absolute bar to recovery, just as there are compelling reasons to maintain the defense in its limited form. But unlike other jurisdictions, where the Restatement merely serves as a summary of general legal principles for courts to accept or reject, the Virgin Islands has designated the Restatement as its law, until a contrary statute is approved. Therefore, if the Virgin Islands wishes to abrogate the doctrine of assumption of risk, along with section 343A of the Restatement, its legislature must say so, as it did in 1973 with contributory negligence.

C.

In applying section 343A of the Restatement to this case, the district court granted summary judgment to Quality Electric because "it was Monk's decision not to use a tag line and instead to hold onto the metal beam that precipitated his injuries. Monk cannot now try to shift the liability to Quality Electric simply because they owned the land where the work was performed." *Monk*, No. 91-0077, slip op. at 12.

To the extent the district court based its decision on Monk's negligence (or contributory negligence), we believe it erred. Instead, the court should have focused on evidence demonstrating Monk's awareness of and consent to a "known or obvious" danger. Evidence of Monk's negligence is relevant only to show the type of secondary assumption of risk that "incorporates the concept of fault on the part of the actor and, therefore, overlaps with contributory negligence." *Smollett*, 793 F.2d at 548. As we have held, such evidence is no longer permitted in the Virgin Islands to bar a plaintiff's cause of action, but rather only may be used to apportion fault between plaintiffs and defendants.

Nevertheless, as in *Smollett*, we have little difficulty in concluding as a matter of law that plaintiff "fully understood the risk of harm to himself and voluntarily chose to enter the area of risk." 793 F.2d at 548. Although the issue of whether a danger was "known or obvious" generally is a question of fact for a jury, *cf.* Restatement § 496D cmt. e, there is no dispute in this case that Monk actually knew of the risk posed by the power lines. As the district court noted, "At all relevant times, the Benak Construction crew knew that the power lines were energized and posed a possible danger." *Monk*, No. 91-0077, slip op. at 3. In his deposition, Monk admitted that "I did pay attention to the location of the lines. I looked at them, everybody else on the job had looked at them." He stated he knew that "if somebody came in contact with [the power lines], then they were going to get electrocuted, get hurt." *Id.* at 4 n.2. As foreman, Monk testified he warned others about the danger posed by the power lines: "As I said earlier, I was always trying to stress how dangerous they were and to be careful around them." *Id.* Although Monk contends he did not know the lines were uninsulated and the level of their voltage, these factors do not change the fact that he knew the location of the lines and that they posed a serious danger. Thus, he "assumed the risk of injury." *Smollett*, 793 F.2d at 549. . . .

IV.

Based on the foregoing reasons, we will affirm the judgment of the district court.

NOTES AND QUESTIONS

1. *Duty and Assumption of Risk.* Restatement (Second) of Torts § 343A, at issue in *Monk*, is a duty provision. It specifies the limited duties owed by a landowner to invitees with respect to obvious dangers on the premises. Why, then, is the issue in the case framed in terms of the continued viability of the doctrine of implied assumption of risk? The Court of Appeals reasoned that if that doctrine was no longer valid under Virgin Islands law, Section 343A's rule of "no duty" would no longer be valid. Does that conclusion follow?

2. *Express versus Implied Assumption of Risk.* As the *Monk* court mentions in a footnote, some comparative responsibility legislation has explicitly eliminated *implied* assumption of risk as a distinct defense. It also notes, however, that these courts have not eliminated *express* assumption of risk. Why this difference in treatment? What is so important about a writing? If defendant can muster evidence of behavior or conversations that supports the conclusion that the plaintiff knowingly and freely subjected herself to the risk of defendant's carelessness, why shouldn't that be sufficient?

3. *Implied Assumption of Risk as Comparative Fault.* Statutes and judicial decisions that have eliminated the implied assumption of risk defense have reasoned that the principles and policies underlying that doctrine are better served by folding it into the jury's comparative responsibility determination. Under the law of these jurisdictions, defendants are still free to argue to the jury that the plaintiff was aware of the risk of carelessly caused injury and voluntarily chose to encounter it. However, a defendant who proves such an argument may no longer earn himself the complete defense of implied assumption of risk. Instead, that proof is factored into the jury's percentage allocation of fault among defendant and plaintiff. (Of course, in a modified comparative fault regime, if the jury finds that the plaintiff's knowing and voluntary assumption of the risk renders the plaintiff more than 50 percent at fault, or more at fault than the defendant, it may function as a total defense in that instance.)

4. *Retaining the Distinction: Sports.* The *Monk* court declines to follow the majority rule that collapses implied assumption of risk into comparative fault. What is distinctive about implied assumption of risk, according to the court?

A number of states that have folded implied assumption of risk into comparative fault have excluded certain activities from that merger. Several, for example, have enacted statutes specifying that all skiers assume the risks that are "inherent" in that sport, including risks associated with the use of ski lifts and tows. *See, e.g.,* N.J.S.A. § 5:13-5 (1979). Others have enacted statutes that specify a general assumption of risk defense against negligence claims based on injuries arising out of participation in any sport. *See, e.g.,* 12 Vt. Stat. Ann. § 1037 (1978) (a person who takes part in a sport "accepts as a matter of law the dangers that inhere therein insofar as they are obvious and necessary").

The references in these statutes to "inherent" risks can be unhelpful. If, for example, "inherent" means "inevitable"—that is, ineliminable even by the exercise of due care—they are merely restating the common law requirement that the plaintiff cannot prevail without proving breach. Apparently, however, the statutes were intended to bar actions arising out of certain forms of careless conduct on the part of resort owners that are commonly encountered in skiing. What sort of careless acts are these?

In the context of claims against the owners and operators of the venues in which sporting activities take place, it is hard to see what, if any, careless activity on *their* part should be deemed "inherent." Consider again claims against ski resorts. Suppose skier *S* is injured when the ski-lift gondola in which she is riding collapses because of the resort's failure to service its equipment. It would be bizarre to say that *S* accepted that sort of carelessness as an inherent risk of skiing. Are there *any* risks of owner/operator carelessness that *S* might plausibly be deemed to have accepted? Failure to remove difficult-to-see man-made obstacles on the slopes? Jumps or moguls carelessly built into beginner slopes? Other skiers carelessly colliding with them?* In an omitted portion of the *Dalury* opinion, the court dismissed the defendant's argument that Vermont's inherent risk statute entailed that Dalury had assumed the risk of running into carelessly placed poles as a matter of law. In doing so, it seemed to question whether the statute could ever be invoked by resort owners:

> The statute places responsibility for the "inherent risks" of any sport on the participant, insofar as such risks are obvious and necessary. A ski area's own negligence, however, is neither an inherent risk nor an obvious and necessary one on the sport of skiing.

Inherent risk statutes are more readily applied to claims of negligence brought by one participant in a sport against another. Under the statutes, participants in events such as amateur softball or basketball games are deemed to have implicitly accepted the risk of injury caused by certain commonly encountered forms of careless conduct. Examples of such conduct might include the careless tossing of a ball or bat during a baseball game. However, if the injury results from recklessness or intentional misconduct on the part of another participant, it may still be actionable. *See, e.g.,* Knight v. Jewett, 834 P.2d 696 (Cal. 1992) (developing these rules in conjunction with a claim for an injury incurred during a recreational

---

* Keep in mind that the focus here is on claims against owners and operators. If the claim is for injuries resulting from being struck by a careless skier, the plaintiff would have to show that the owner/operator was at fault for encouraging, or not taking reasonable measures to control, careless skiing. Presumably this showing could not be made simply by establishing that careless skiing sometimes occurred on the grounds. If an inherent risk statute could be invoked to limit liability in this scenario, it would arguably be denying liability not on assumption-of-risk grounds, but instead by setting a *per se* rule of careful conduct, to wit: "As a matter of law it shall not be careless for the owner and operator of a ski resort merely to fail to prevent instances of careless skiing from occurring on the premises."

football game). Should the statutes bar claims even by novices, who might not actually be aware of risks of careless conduct that more experienced players would find obvious?

5. *New York's "Hybrid" Statute.* New York law has retained implied assumption of risk as a distinctive affirmative defense, yet at the same time has converted it into a partial rather than complete defense. This "hybrid" scheme emerged out of judicial interpretations of the somewhat unusual language of New York's comparative fault statute. That statute directs that plaintiff's damages "shall be diminished in the proportion which the culpable conduct attributable to the claimant . . . bears to the culpable conduct which caused the damages." N.Y. C.P.L.R. § 1411. New York's courts have deemed the plaintiff's assumption of risk to count as "culpable conduct." Thus, the statute converts assumption of risk into a partial defense without subsuming it entirely into comparative fault. As a result, a defendant subject to New York law can, if the facts support it, request that the jury be instructed to assign a percentage of responsibility to the plaintiff *either* because the plaintiff carelessly contributed to his own injury, or because the plaintiff assumed the risk of the defendant's negligence. *See, e.g.,* McCabe v. Easter, 516 N.Y.S.2d 515 (App. Div. 1987). The New York Court of Appeals has, however, read into Section 1411 a complete bar to recovery for those who are injured by carelessness while participating in sports or recreational activities. Turcotte v. Fell, 502 N.E.2d 964 (N.Y. 1986).

6. *Implied Assumption of Risk versus Breach.* As suggested above in Note 4, there are instances in which implied assumption of risk analysis seems strongly to resemble breach analysis. Cardozo provided a famous example of this phenomenon in Murphy v. Steeplechase Amusement Co., 166 N.E. 173 (N.Y. 1929).

Plaintiff, "a vigorous young man," boarded a Coney Island amusement ride known as the "Flopper." It consisted of a conveyer belt moving away from the customer at a very high speed, perhaps as quickly as a gym treadmill set at a rate that would require the user to run rapidly. The belt was surrounded on both sides by padding designed to break customers' falls. The challenge was to step and stay on the belt without losing one's balance. After watching others "flop," plaintiff boarded the ride and fell, breaking his kneecap. He later sued in negligence and obtained a jury verdict of $5,000.

Cardozo's opinion held that, insofar as plaintiff's theory was that the defendant acted carelessly in operating a device that caused its riders to tumble, the claim was barred because the plaintiff had assumed the risk of being injured by that sort of negligence:

> Something more was here, as every one understood, than the slowly-moving escalator that is common in shops and public places. A fall was foreseen as one of the risks of the adventure. There would have been no point to the whole thing, no adventure about it, if the risk had not been there. The very name above the gate, the Flopper, was warning to the timid. If the name was not enough, there was warning more distinct in the experience of

others. We are told by the plaintiff's wife that the members of her party stood looking at the sport before joining in it themselves. Some aboard the belt were able, as she viewed them, to sit down with decorum or even to stand and keep their footing; others jumped or fell. The tumbling bodies and the screams and laughter supplied the merriment and fun. "I took a chance," she said when asked whether she thought that a fall might be expected. . . .

   *Volenti non fit injuria.** One who takes part in such a sport accepts the dangers that inhere in it so far as they are obvious and necessary, just as a fencer accepts the risk of a thrust by his antagonist or a spectator at a ball game the chance of contact with the ball. . . . The antics of the clown are not the paces of the cloistered cleric. The rough and boisterous joke, the horse-play of the crowd, evokes its own guffaws, but they are not the pleasures of tranquillity. The plaintiff was not seeking a retreat for meditation. Visitors were tumbling about the belt to the merriment of onlookers when he made his choice to join them. He took the chance of a like fate, with whatever damage to his body might ensue from such a fall. The timorous may stay at home.

The court then remanded for a new trial on an alternative theory, namely that the padding provided by the defendant to break riders' falls was inadequate.

   It seems fair to say, on these facts, that the plaintiff implicitly assumed the risk of falling *by virtue of the normal motion of the conveyer belt.* But isn't this just an obtuse way of saying that, as a matter of law, it is not careless to operate an amusement ride that causes people to fall down onto a padded surface? (Assume for these purposes that the padding was adequate.) Is Cardozo using implied assumption of risk as a stand-in for no breach as a matter of law?

   As Professor Simons has noted, there is another troubling aspect to Cardozo's analysis in *Murphy,* which is that the above-quoted language fails to engage directly the plaintiff's main allegation of fault. This allegation did not assert that the defendant had acted carelessly in designing the machine. Rather, the claim was that the machine contained a defect that caused the belt to *jerk forward,* rather than to run smoothly, as it was designed to do. Cardozo and his brethren were apparently highly skeptical that a jerk of this sort could have occurred or did occur.** Assuming, however, that a reasonable jury could find that the jerk did occur, would there be any basis for concluding that the plaintiff implicitly accepted the risk that he would be injured by a mechanical malfunction in the machine?

   7. *Assumption of Risk and Consent.* In the context of intentional wrongs, such as claims for intentional batteries, the role played by express and implied assumption of risk in negligence law is played by the related

---

   * ["To one who chooses [to encounter a risk] no wrong is done." — EDS.]
   ** Notice the actual causation problem posed by Murphy's claim. Given that falls were a common feature of — indeed the very point of — the ride, how would a jury determine that, but for the unexpectedly jerky motion of the belt, the plaintiff would not have fallen in the way that he did?

defense of express or tacit consent. Thus, a batterer can sometimes avoid liability by establishing that his victim consented to being hit, as is the case, for example, if the blow occurred during a licensed boxing match. See Chapter 9.

III.   STATUTES OF LIMITATIONS AND REPOSE

Plaintiff-conduct defenses are one important category of complete or partial affirmative defenses available to negligence defendants. Other defenses operate as a matter of law for reasons of policy. Perhaps the most mundane yet important of these are the time limits a claimant must observe in order to have his suit heard in court. In general, these limits take two forms. *Statutes of limitations* start the clock running in relation to the occurrence of (a) the alleged tortious conduct and (b) harm to the claimant caused by that conduct. Typically, they specify that a tort claimant must commence his lawsuit within a certain period of time — usually one to three years — of those events. *Statutes of repose*, by contrast, set limits by reference either to the date of the tortious act alone, or to some other date, such as the date on which a particular product is manufactured or purchased. Thus, for example, a statute of repose for products liability actions might say that no tort action may be brought complaining of a product defect more than ten years after the date of the initial sale of the product.

Although statutes of limitations do not always make for interesting law school discussions, they are of the utmost practical importance. If, for example, a given legislature were anxious to restrict certain negligence causes of action, one very effective way to do so would be to adopt a relatively short statute of limitations, as some states have done with respect to medical malpractice actions.

As you read the following case consider the policies at stake. How important is it for defendants to have prompt knowledge as to whether they will be sued? Does it matter whether the defendant is an individual or a corporate entity? What other goals are served by setting these limitations on tort actions? What risks to defendants or the judicial process are posed by long delays in bringing suit?

Ranney v. Parawax Co.
582 N.W.2d 152 (Iowa 1998)

Ternus, J.   This case involves the application of the discovery rule and the principle of inquiry notice to a latent injury case arising under Iowa's workers' compensation law. *See* Iowa Code ch. 85 (1993). The district court affirmed the industrial commissioner's summary judgment ruling that the appellant's claim was barred by the two-year statute of limitations for workers' compensation claims. *See id.* § 85.26(1). We affirm.

I.   SCOPE OF REVIEW

Judicial review of the industrial commissioner's decisions is governed by the administrative procedure act, Iowa Code chapter 17A. *See id.* § 86.26. The court may reverse if the commissioner's decision is affected by an error of law. *See id.* § 17A.19(8)(*e*). Here, the appellant claims the commissioner erred in his application of the law governing summary judgments. . . .

II.   BACKGROUND FACTS AND PROCEEDINGS

The record shows the following facts, when viewed in a light most favorable to the appellant, Joseph W. Ranney III. Ranney worked for the defendant, Parawax Company, Inc., from 1975 through February 1981. During that time he was exposed to toxic materials in the course of his regular duties. In 1985, Ranney became ill and was diagnosed with Hodgkin's disease.

Ranney suspected from the beginning that his condition might be causally connected to his work with toxic chemicals. The physician he first consulted regarding his symptoms made the following statements in a report dated June 26, 1985: "The patient does report working with paint solvents and he associates this work in some manner with these recent episodes. . . . The relationship to the paint solvents is unclear and may suggest an allergic component; however, the unilateral adenopathy and episodic symptoms argue against this." Ranney testified he questioned subsequent treating physicians about a possible connection between his work with chemicals and his disease but none of "the doctors would commit themselves, one way or the other."

Then in 1987, Ranney's wife started law school. Later that year or in 1988, she took a course in which she read cases discussing occupational diseases caused by exposure to chemicals. Ranney and his wife discussed the possibility that his exposure to toxic materials at Parawax caused his condition. Ranney testified he associated his condition to his chemical exposure at that time. It was not until 1991, however, when Ranney asked a new treating physician whether there was a causal link between his work-related exposure and his Hodgkin's disease, that a doctor confirmed Ranney's theory of causation.

This workers' compensation case was filed in 1992 against Ranney's former employer and its workers' compensation carrier, appellee American States Insurance Company. Ranney claimed his Hodgkin's disease was causally connected to his work-related exposure to toxic chemicals. He relied on the discovery rule to extend the two-year statute of limitations applicable to chapter 85 workers' compensation claims.

The industrial commissioner granted a motion for summary judgment filed by American States, ruling that the limitations period had expired before Ranney filed his petition for benefits. The commissioner's ruling was affirmed on judicial review by the district court and this appeal followed. . . .

III.   DISCUSSION

The resolution of this case requires the application of three related principles of law: the statute of limitations, the discovery rule and inquiry notice. Parawax has the burden to prove its limitations defense; Ranney has the burden to establish any exception to the ordinary limitations period, such as the applicability of the discovery rule. *See* Estate of Montag v. T H Agric. & Nutrition Co., 509 N.W.2d 469, 470 (Iowa 1993); Sparks v. Metalcraft, Inc., 408 N.W.2d 347, 350 (Iowa 1987).

A. *The statute of limitations and the discovery rule.* A petition for benefits under chapter 85 must be filed "within two years from the date of the occurrence of the injury for which benefits are claimed." Iowa Code § 85.26(1). We have interpreted this statute to mean that the injury occurs when it is discovered. *See* Dillinger v. City of Sioux City, 368 N.W.2d 176, 181 (Iowa 1985). Thus, the two-year limitation period begins to run when "the employee discovers or in the exercise of reasonable diligence should . . . discover[] the nature, seriousness and probable compensable character" of his injury or disease. Orr v. Lewis Cent. Sch. Dist., 298 N.W.2d 256, 261 (Iowa 1980).

As applied here, these principles require that Ranney have actual or imputed knowledge of the nature, seriousness and probable compensable character of his disease in order to commence the limitations period. There is no dispute that Ranney had actual knowledge of the nature and seriousness of his condition more than two years prior to filing his petition for benefits. The controversy here is whether he had imputed knowledge of the probable compensable nature of his disease, i.e., that his disease was caused by his workplace exposure to toxic chemicals. That brings us to the issue of inquiry notice.

B. *Inquiry notice.* Knowledge is imputed to a claimant when he gains information sufficient to alert a reasonable person of the need to investigate. *See* Estate of Montag, 509 N.W.2d at 470. . . . As of that date he is on inquiry notice of all facts that would have been disclosed by a reasonably diligent investigation. We reject Ranney's assertion that inquiry notice does not apply here because he suffered from a latent injury. When Ranney was diagnosed with Hodgkin's disease in 1985, his condition was no longer latent; it was then known. At that point, Ranney was subject to the same duty to investigate as is any other plaintiff who knows he has sustained an injury. Thus, we now turn to an analysis of the inquiry notice rule as applied to the undisputed facts of this case.

The record shows that Ranney suspected from the beginning that his Hodgkin's disease was caused by his work-related exposure to toxic materials. By 1987 or 1988, he learned that chemical exposure can cause disease and that persons suffering from such diseases had successfully sued for damages. He concedes he knew of the *possible* compensable nature of his condition at that time. Ranney claims, however, he was not on inquiry notice until he had facts alerting him to the *probable* compensable nature of his condition. We think that once a claimant knows or should know that his condition is possibly compensable, he has the duty to investigate. *See* Roth v. G.D. Searle Co., 27 F.3d 1303, 1307 (8th Cir. 1994) (holding that inquiry notice began when the plaintiff "knew or should have known of her injuries and their *possible* connection to her IUD") (emphasis added) (applying Iowa law); Jones v. Maine Cent. R.R., 690 F. Supp. 73, 75-77 (D. Me. 1988) (holding, as a matter of law, that statute of limitations commenced when plaintiffs were diagnosed with hearing loss and "thought," "suspected," or "presumed" it resulted from workplace noise). The purpose of the investigation is to ascertain whether the known condition is probably, as opposed to merely possibly, compensable.

Similarly, Ranney also argues that he was not on inquiry notice until 1991 when a physician informed him that his disease was causally connected to his work with toxic chemicals. He relies on the federal district court's decision in Brazzell v. United States, 633 F. Supp. 62 (N.D. Iowa 1985). In *Brazzell*, the court held the statute of limitations under the Federal Tort Claims Act did not begin to run until the plaintiff's doctor made a medical determination of causation. 633 F. Supp. at 69. This court, however, has never so interpreted Iowa's statute of limitations. *See Roth*, 27 F.3d at 1308 ("Under Iowa law, actual knowledge of a causal relationship is not required to begin the running of the statute of limitations."). We have held that "positive medical information is unnecessary if [the claimant] has information *from any source* which puts him *on notice* of [the injury's] probable compensable nature." Robinson v. Department of Transp., 296 N.W.2d 809, 812 (Iowa 1980) (emphasis added); *accord* 7 Arthur Larson, *Larson's Workers' Compensation Law* § 78.41(f), at 15-286 (1998). Thus, the duty to investigate does not depend "on exact knowledge of the nature of the problem that caused the injury." [Franzen v. Deere & Co.], 377 N.W.2d [660,] 662 [(Iowa 1985)]. "Once a person is aware of a problem, he has a duty to investigate." *Sparks,* 408 N.W.2d at 352; *accord Franzen,* 377 N.W.2d at 662 ("It is sufficient that the person be aware that a problem existed."). The purpose of the investigation is to ascertain the exact nature of the problem that caused the injury. . . . Consequently, the lack of an expert opinion supporting causation does not prevent commencement of the statute of limitations under the principle of inquiry notice.

If we adopted Ranney's interpretation of when inquiry notice is triggered, the beginning of the limitations period would be postponed until the *successful completion* of the plaintiff's investigation. Such an application of the discovery rule would be contrary to our holdings in *Estate of Montag* and *Franzen*. As we stated in *Franzen*, "the period of limitations is the outer time limit for making the investigation and bringing the action. The period *begins* at the time the person is on inquiry notice." *Franzen*, 377 N.W.2d at 662 (emphasis added). . . .

We agree with the industrial commissioner that by 1987 or 1988, at the latest, Ranney had enough information to trigger his duty to investigate. *See* Nasim v. Warden, 64 F.3d 951, 956 (4th Cir. 1995) (affirming summary dismissal of complaint on statute-of-limitations grounds because the plaintiff was on inquiry notice that his condition was caused by asbestos exposure when (1) he knew that he was exposed to asbestos, that asbestos presented a health hazard and that he suffered physical and psychological injuries, and (2) he believed that his injury and exposure were linked). As of that date, Ranney was on notice of what a reasonably diligent investigation would have disclosed.

Ranney argues, however, that he conducted a reasonably diligent investigation into the cause of his condition, but was unable to obtain confirmation that his work-related exposure caused his Hodgkin's disease. The undisputed facts establish that Ranney's "investigation" consisted of asking his treating physicians whether there was a causal connection between his chemical exposure and his disease. The undisputed facts also show that his physicians would not commit one way or the other or they told him the cause of Hodgkin's disease was unknown. We hold these facts are insufficient to create a factual issue on the applicability of the discovery rule.

The fact that Ranney's actual investigation was unsuccessful in confirming his suspicions does not toll the statute of limitations. In United States v. Kubrick, 444 U.S. 111, 100 S. Ct. 352, 62 L. Ed. 2d 259 (1979), the plaintiff knew of his injury and its probable cause in 1969, but did not know of the defendant's negligence, an additional factual element of his claim, until 1971 when a physician told him the defendant's treatment was improper. . . . The plaintiff then filed suit. . . . In affirming judgment for the defendant on statute-of-limitations grounds, the United States Supreme Court stated:

> [The plaintiff] may be incompetently advised or the medical community may be divided on the crucial issue of negligence, as the experts proved to be on the trial of this case. But however [the plaintiff] is advised, the putative malpractice plaintiff must determine within the period of limitations whether to sue or not, which is precisely the judgment that other tort claimants must make. If he fails to bring suit because he is incompetently or mistakenly told that he does not have a case, we discern no sound reason for visiting the consequences of such error on the defendant by delaying the accrual of the claim until the plaintiff is otherwise informed or himself determines to bring suit, even though more than two years have passed from the plaintiff's discovery of the relevant facts about injury. [*Id.* at 124.] . . .

We think the same reasoning applies here to Ranney's investigation of the probable cause of his Hodgkin's disease. *See* Cochran v. GAF Corp., 542 Pa. 210, 666 A.2d 245, 249 (Pa. 1995) (affirming summary judgment for the defendant despite the plaintiff's claim that he had not discovered the cause of his lung cancer until two years before he filed suit: "It is well settled that the statute of limitations is not tolled by mistake or misunderstanding. Also, a diligent investigation may require one to seek further medical examination as well as competent legal representation.") (citations omitted). By 1988 at the latest, Ranney knew of the possible connection between his disease and his employment; he had two years from that date to complete his investigation and file suit. His inability to find expert support for his theory of causation within that time does not prevent the limitations period from running.

We conclude the commissioner did not err in ruling as a matter of law that Ranney's workers' compensation claim was barred by the statute of limitations. Although this conclusion has the effect of barring a possibly meritorious claim, that is the unfortunate result of any statute of limitations. There must come a time when the interest in preventing stale claims takes precedence over the policy of deciding cases on their merits. That time has arrived in this case.

Andreasen, J., (dissenting in part) (joined by Larson, Lavorato, and Snell, JJ.). . . .

The majority opinion suggests that once Ranney knew of his disease and its possible connection with his employment, he had a duty to investigate *and* the two-year statute of limitation period began to run. Apparently, once Ranney was under a duty to investigate (inquiry notice), it made no difference if a reasonable investigation [would have] revealed the cause of his Hodgkin's disease is unknown. This interpretation of the inquiry notice doctrine conflicts with the majority opinion statements that "the purpose of the investigation is to ascertain whether the known condition is probably, as opposed to merely possibly, compensable," and that, when Ranney had enough information to trigger his duty to investigate, "as of that date, Ranney was on notice of what a reasonably diligent investigation would have disclosed."

Ranney is not asking that the statute be tolled until the *successful completion* of his investigation. Inquiry notice did impose a duty on him to investigate. The limitation period should run only if a reasonably diligent investigation would disclose the probable compensable character of his injury. In our previous application of the inquiry notice doctrine, we stated:

> The information they possessed on the date of the accident was plainly sufficient to put them on inquiry notice concerning possible defects in the wagon. They did not investigate at that time. When they later investigated, they found the alleged defects they now rely on. [Franzen v. Deere & Co., 377 N.W.2d 660, 663 (Iowa 1985), quoted in Vachon v. State, 514 N.W.2d 442, 447 (Iowa 1994).]

In United States v. Kubrick, 444 U.S. 111, 100 S. Ct. 352, 62 L. Ed. 2d 259 (1979), the Court in a medical malpractice suit filed in 1992 stated: "It is undisputed in this case that in January 1969 Kubrick was aware of his injury and its *probable* cause. *Kubrick*, 444 U.S. at 119 (emphasis added). The Court was addressing the application of the discovery rule where the plaintiff was ignorant of his legal rights; rather than ignorant of the fact of his injury or its causes. *Id.* at 123. After recognizing reasonably competent doctors would have known the plaintiff should not have been treated with Neomycin, the Court stated:

> Crediting this finding, as we must, Kubrick need only have made inquiry among doctors with average training and experience in such matters to have discovered that he probably had a good cause of action. The difficulty is that it does not appear that Kubrick ever made any inquiry, although meanwhile he had consulted several specialists about his loss of hearing and had been in possession of all the facts about the cause of his injury since January 1969. Furthermore, there is no reason to doubt that Dr. Soma, who in 1971

volunteered his opinion that Kubrick's treatment had been improper, would have had the same opinion had the plaintiff sought his judgment in 1969. [*Id.* at 122-23.]

. . . There is no suggestion in the record that "in the exercise of reasonable diligence" or "in the exercise of a reasonably diligent investigation" Ranney, or a reasonable person, would have acquired actual or implied knowledge of the probable compensable nature of his claim before June 1990, two years prior to the filing of his claim.

Our court's application of the inquiry notice doctrine when a reasonably diligent investigation would not disclose the probable compensable character of the employee's injury, "guts" the basic requirement of the discovery rule that the limitation period begins when the employee discovered or should have discovered the *probable* compensable character of the injury. I would . . . reverse the ruling dismissing the claim under chapter 85. I would then remand to the industrial commissioner for further proceedings under chapter 85. . . .

NOTES AND QUESTIONS

1. *Workers' Compensation.* As indicated in the notes following the *Aldridge* case from Chapter 4, claims by employees against their employers for workplace injuries arising from accidents or hazardous conditions at the workplace are generally handled through workers' compensation systems rather than tort law. As *Ranney* indicates, however, the operation of these systems is governed by legal rules that still give rise to questions over which judges retain jurisdiction. Here the court reviews a ruling initially issued by a commissioner within the workers' compensation system who is charged with rendering decisions as to what constitutes a compensable injury within that system.

2. *Varying Limits.* Statutes of limitations vary from jurisdiction to jurisdiction, and, within a given jurisdiction, can vary among different torts. In Kentucky, a plaintiff complaining of personal injury, whether by means of a claim for battery, false imprisonment, or negligence, must commence the claim within one year of the relevant start date. Ky. Stat. § 413.140(1). However, if the claim is for "intentional infliction of emotional distress," the plaintiff is given five years. Craft v. Rice, 671 S.W.2d 247 (Ky. 1984). In Florida, a plaintiff alleging injury resulting from negligence or battery has four years to bring her claim, unless the action alleges professional malpractice, or consists of a claim for wrongful death, in which case the limitations period is two years. Fla. Stat. § 95.11. In Tennessee, the statute of limitations for all claims of personal injury is one year from the relevant start date, although certain defendants, including doctors, also get the benefit of special statutes of repose. Tenn. Code § 28-3-104.

3. *Accrual Rule versus Discovery Rule.* Courts faced with statutes of limitations in tort cases used to apply the accrual rule to determine the date on which the limitations period commenced. Under the accrual rule,

the clock on a negligence claim started to run as soon as two things happened: (1) the defendant acted carelessly and (2) that act caused some harm to the plaintiff. The fact that the plaintiff did not know, and perhaps could not know, of the harm or its connection to the defendant was deemed irrelevant. The emergence of new forms of tort liability, particularly toxic torts, put a great deal of pressure on courts and legislatures to modify the accrual rule. Toxic torts often involve injuries that occur gradually over time, and whose connection to a particular substance is not discovered until many years later. The discovery rule stalls the commencement of the limitations clock until such time as (1) the plaintiff knows, or has reason to know, that she has suffered an injury; and (2) there is sufficient reason to believe that the defendant's conduct is causally linked to that injury such that an inquiry into the connection is warranted and would reveal evidence of such a connection.

A current controversy among courts concerns the application of the discovery rule to suits brought by adults against priests and others for acts of sexual abuse alleged to have occurred decades earlier, when the plaintiffs were minors. Among other issues presented by these claims is whether and how to apply the discovery rule to repressed memories of abuse, or to a plaintiff who remembers the abuse but has only recently linked it to current physical or mental illnesses. *See* Dan B. Dobbs, *The Law of Torts* § 222, at 567-568 (2000).

4. *Statutes of Repose.* Although they generally provide a longer window in which to sue than statutes of limitations, statutes of repose are in some ways even harsher than the old accrual rule. They run from the date on which a specified act or event occurs regardless of whether that act is tortious or has yet produced any harm to any plaintiff. Thus, if the relevant statute of repose specifies that suits claiming injury caused by medical malpractice must be brought within three years of the date on which medical services were provided, and the plaintiff suffers an injury because of malpractice that does not manifest itself until after that period has run, the plaintiff is out of luck. Various special interest groups, most notably product manufacturers, but also architects, engineers, and doctors, have successfully lobbied for statutes of repose in recent years. Dobbs, *supra,* § 219, at 557-558. The typical act or event triggering a statute of repose will be the sale of the product, the completion of the construction project, or the conclusion of a course of medical treatment.

5. *Continuing Torts.* Certain forms of tortious conduct consist not of isolated acts of wrongdoing, but continuing patterns of behavior. A common example of the latter category is when one landowner uses his land in a manner that pollutes the property of another. Suppose the polluting activity has occurred regularly over the preceding five years, and was known to the plaintiff throughout that time. Suppose further that the statute of limitations for bringing a tort action for trespass is two years. Most courts will not treat a suit brought at the end of the five-year period as time-barred, even though the trespass and the harm *began* occurring more than two years prior to the filing of the suit, and even though the plaintiff knew this to be the case. In essence, they will permit the plaintiff

to proceed on the theory that the defendant committed a single tort that took place over a five-year period. On the other hand, when a court deems a nuisance "permanent" (as opposed to continuous), the statute of limitations for the plaintiff's claim is deemed to begin running when the nuisance first occurred. *See* Bowen v. Kansas City, 646 P.2d 484 (Kan. 1982).

Continuing tort rules do not figure prominently in negligence cases, although they may come into play in medical malpractice cases in which the complaint concerns a long course of treatment. *See* Dobbs, *supra,* § 220, at 561-563. Some courts have concluded that claims of spousal abuse should be subject to the continuing tort rule, such that a battered spouse can complain of injuries stemming from assaults that occurred outside the limitations period. *See, e.g.*, Feltmeier v. Feltmeier, 33 Ill. App. 3d 1167 (2002) (applying continuous tort theory). *But see* Seaton v. Seaton, 971 F. Supp. 1188 (E.D. Tenn. 1997) (applying Tennessee law and refusing to treat a series of assaults as a single, continuing tort; plaintiff may sue only for injuries stemming from the last act of abuse, which fell within the limitations period).

6. *Tolling.* Statutes of limitations themselves, or judicial interpretations of them, sometimes provide for the *tolling* of limitations periods — that is, a pause in the running of the clock. The classic example is the tolling of limitations periods for torts committed against minors. Depending on the statute in question, the clock on such claims might not begin to run until the minor reaches the age of majority.

IV. IMMUNITIES AND EXEMPTIONS FROM LIABILITY

An immunity, in tort law, is a complete defense to liability granted to certain entities, as well as to actors in certain relationships. Historically, the three most important immunities recognized by the common law of tort have been intra-family immunity, charitable immunity, and sovereign immunity.

Intra-family immunity — specifically, spousal and parental immunity — was designed to prevent family members from suing each other in tort. Traditionally, the rules were defended as outgrowths of the authority of the patriarch over the family, as a means of leaving parents free to discipline children without fear of liability, and as a way of preventing collusive litigation between family members. These broad immunities have generally eroded in recent years in favor of applying general principles of tort liability, although some jurisdictions still grant immunity for certain "discretionary" parental decisions concerning the rearing and supervision of their children. *See* Dan B. Dobbs, *The Law of Torts* § 280 (2000).

In a similar fashion, the doctrine of charitable immunity barred tort actions against charitable organizations, albeit only for their negligent (as opposed to intentional or reckless) wrongs. This immunity was of great significance in the early twentieth century, when many if not most hospitals were run as charitable institutions. Most states have now rejected across-the-board charitable immunity through judicial decision or legislation, although many state legislators have provided charities with other protections, such as damage caps, that are not applicable to other actors.

The doctrine of sovereign immunity was technically a jurisdictional doctrine: It held that courts had no authority to order the federal or state governments into court at the behest of a private citizen, and hence that injured plaintiffs were not permitted to include the federal or state governments as parties to a civil lawsuit. In part, the rationale was one of separation of powers. The thought was that courts, via tort actions, should not be influencing policy decisions of the legislative and executive branches. This blanket immunity did not extend to local or municipal governments, which were not regarded as genuine "sovereigns." Nonetheless, these entities, too, enjoyed certain specific immunities under common law. By means of the Federal Tort Claims Act (1946) and state statutory counterparts, both the federal and state governments have partially waived their common law immunities. The present contours of government liability at the federal, state, and local levels is quite complex; we provide only two illustrations below.

In sum, even though modern legislatures and courts have moved away from blanket immunities, specific immunities often remain intact. Moreover, as the last case reproduced in this section suggests, courts will at times confer what we call liability "exemptions" that, while not falling within the scope of traditional immunities, bear a strong resemblance to them in their substance and rationales.

Schultz v. Roman Catholic Archdiocese of Newark
472 A.2d 531 (N.J. 1984)

O'Hern, J.   We granted certification, 93 N.J. 246 (1983), limited to the issue of whether the Charitable Immunity Act, N.J.S.A. 2A:53A-7 to -11, bars a claim by a beneficiary of a charitable institution based on the charity's alleged negligence in hiring. . . .

The facts alleged are that Christopher Schultz, age 11, was a student at a parish school owned, operated, and controlled by the defendant charity, Roman Catholic Archdiocese of Newark. It is further alleged that the Franciscan Brothers of the Poor were engaged by the Archdiocese to supply instructors for the school. It is alleged that the defendant employed one such Franciscan, Robert Coakley, known as Brother Edmund, as an instructor at the school and as a scoutmaster for the Boy Scout group sponsored by the parish.

During the spring and summer of 1978, Coakley operated the Boy Scout camp that Christopher Schultz attended. It is alleged that while at this camp, in July 1978, Coakley forced Christopher to engage in sexually provocative activities and in sexual contact with him. Coakley threatened Christopher not to reveal what had occurred. These deviant actions and threats continued after the school year started. In the late fall of 1978, Christopher told his parents what had happened. They immediately notified the Archdiocese.

Throughout the winter and spring of 1979, Christopher received extensive psychiatric and medical care and was hospitalized. Finally, in May 1979, Christopher committed suicide by taking drugs.

Following Christopher's death, this action was brought, alleging that the defendant was reckless, careless, and negligent in hiring Coakley and permitting him to have young boys under his care, in failing to determine his prior employment history, in failing to supervise him, and that the defendant was otherwise negligent. Christopher's parents seek compensation for his suffering and death and for their own damages. . . .

The trial court granted defendant's motion to dismiss the complaint based on the Charitable Immunity Act. The Appellate Division affirmed on that issue. . . .

The common law doctrine of charitable immunity was abolished in this State in 1958. Benton v. YMCA, 27 N.J. 67 (1958); Collopy v. Newark Eye and Ear Infirmary, 27 N.J. 29 (1958); Dalton v. St. Luke's Catholic Church, 27 N.J. 22 (1958). The Legislature responded to these decisions by adopting N.J.S.A. 2A:53A-7 to -11.

N.J.S.A. 2A:53A-7 provides:

No nonprofit corporation, society or association organized exclusively for religious, charitable, educational or hospital purposes shall, except as is hereinafter set forth, be liable to respond in damages to any person who shall suffer damage from the negligence of any agent or servant of such corporation, society or association, where such person is a beneficiary, to whatever degree, of the works of such nonprofit corporation, society or association; provided, however, that such immunity from liability shall not extend to any person who shall suffer damage from the negligence of such corporation, society, or association or of its agents or servants where such person is one unconcerned in and unrelated to and outside of the benefactions of such corporation, society or association; but nothing herein contained shall be deemed to exempt the said agent or servant individually from their liability for any such negligence.

Judge, later Justice, Pashman described this statute as having "reinstated the common law doctrine as it had been judicially defined by the courts of this State" prior to *Collopy*. Wiklund v. Presbyterian Church of Clifton, 90 N.J. Super. 335, 338 (Cty. Ct. 1966) (citing Anasiewicz v. Sacred Heart Church, 74 N.J. Super. 532 (App. Div.), cert. denied, 38 N.J. 305 (1962)). Under this analysis we are urged to find that the Legislature crystallized the law as of 1958 and that it is our role to carve out of the statute those exceptions that would have been then recognized.

In New Jersey the central common law exception to immunity allowed "strangers" to a charity—those who gained no benefit—to recover damages for negligence. See Collopy, 27 N.J. at 37; Lindroth v. Christ Hosp., 21 N.J. 588, 592-93 (1956). Plaintiffs urge that there existed as well a common law exception from immunity for administrative negligence. The exception finds support in one case, Fields v. Mountainside Hosp.,

22 N.J. Misc. 72 (Cir. Ct. 1944), in which that court allowed an allegation of administrative negligence to survive a motion to dismiss. But a later Supreme Court decision disapproved that exception:

> Further as to the plaintiffs' suggestion that the immunity rule does not extend to acts or omissions constituting administrative negligence, we are asked thereby to modify the established common law rule in this State. There is no merit in this contention. There can be no logical distinction between the tortfeasors when all act under the charitable corporation. The corporation acts, through its servants or agents, whether they be directors, trustees or instructors. [Jones v. St. Mary's Roman Catholic Church, 7 N.J. 533, 538, *cert. denied*, 342 U.S. 886, 72 S. Ct. 175, 96 L. Ed. 664 (1951).]

. . . Thus prior to the enactment of the statute, it simply was not true that administrative negligence, also called negligent hiring, was an exception to charitable immunity. In *Jones*, the Court sustained the dismissal of a complaint that alleged administrative negligence of a parochial school in the hiring and training of a teacher. That Court relied on two other cases that rejected the cause of action, Fair v. Atlantic City Hosp., 25 N.J. Misc. 65 (Cir. Ct. 1946), and Roosen v. Peter Bent Brigham Hosp., 235 Mass. 66, 126 N.E. 392 (1920). Jones, 7 N.J. at 538.

Plaintiffs further argue that because one of the statute's purposes was to relieve a charity from liability based upon principles of *respondeat superior, see Collopy,* 27 N.J. at 39, it is inapplicable to negligent hiring. Under *respondeat superior*, an employer is liable only for those acts of his employee committed within the scope of employment, while negligent hiring reaches further to cover acts outside the scope of employment. *See* DiCosala v. Kay, 91 N.J. 159, 172-73 (1982). Therefore, it is said, immunity is not available.

Our dissenting colleagues advance a related theory. The argument has attraction because our natural sympathies favor the result, but it presents problems of consistency. It suggests that immunity is lost when the tort is intentional, since the statutory immunity refers consistently and exclusively to "negligence." Thus the fact that the ultimate act that did the damage was intentional takes the entire incident out of the statute in the dissent's view. That would make the church, protected in the past by the common law immunity and now by statutory immunity, more vulnerable than private entities protected by neither common law nor statutory immunity.[1] The dissent asks us to assume that the Legislature decided to disregard all other aspects of the tort and simply focus on the final action. Its premise is that the Legislature, having removed liability for

---

1. The dissent emphasizes the distinction between intentional and negligent torts, but in our cases involving ordinary employers we ask instead whether the tort occurred within the scope of employment. If so, there is liability, whether the tort is negligent or intentional. In practice, only rarely do intentional torts fall within the scope of employment. *See* Gibson v. Kennedy, 23 N.J. 150 (1957) (railroad liable for employee who assaulted fellow employee during dispute as to his right to ride on train); W. Prosser, *Handbook of the Law of Torts* § 70, at 464 (4th ed. 1971).

the most likely situations, implicitly would restore liability for the most unlikely situations. Would not the same logic also apply had the sexual crime been committed by an unsupervised fellow student [?] Yet in *Jones*, the negligent failure to avert the commission of an intentional act by a fellow student did not impose liability. 7 N.J. at 538.

At root is the dissent's notion that the church should be liable when its employees are not pursuing the business of charity. . . . It is ironic that in the dissent's view the more remote the agent's act is from the charity's purposes, the more liable the charity will become. This is contrary to common law doctrine.

We understand the desire to find an exception to immunity here. At the time of *Collopy*, courts naturally sought exceptions to the doctrine of charitable immunity. It was in disfavor as a matter of public policy. In Lindroth v. Christ Hosp., 21 N.J. 588, 590-91 (1956), Justice Brennan wrote:

> The protection of charitable organizations from liability in damages for otherwise just claims arising from their negligence is losing support throughout the country. In . . . his handbook on the law of torts Dean Prosser comments that the law conferring this immunity "is undergoing rapid change," largely influenced by the 1942 decision of the late Mr. Justice Rutledge in President and Directors of Georgetown College v. Hughes, 76 U.S. App. D.C. 123, 130 F.2d 810 (App. D.C. 1942), written while the Justice was a judge of the Court of Appeals of the District of Columbia. That "devastating opinion," says Dean Prosser, "reviewed all of the arguments in favor of the immunity and demolished them so completely as to change the course of the law," and was followed by "a flood of recent decisions holding that a charity is liable for its torts to the same extent as any other defendant." The Dean lists 17 jurisdictions in addition to the District of Columbia where the immunity was formerly recognized and has now been repudiated. He concludes, "The immunity of charities is clearly in full retreat." Prosser, *Law of Torts* (2d ed. 1955), pp.787, 789.

This retreat culminated in the *Collopy* trilogy abolishing the doctrine. Yet, even in rejecting the "historical error and the lack of current utility or justification for the immunity," Justice Jacobs recognized that "[t]here is no doubt that within constitutional limits the Legislature may at any time, if it so chooses, explicitly fix the State's policy as to the immunity of charitable institutions from tort responsibilities." *Collopy*, 27 N.J. at 33, 41.

Within a week, the Legislature acted to restore the doctrine by introduction of an act to provide immunity for all nonprofit corporations organized for religious, charitable, educational, or hospital purposes from negligence suits brought by any person who was a beneficiary, to whatever degree, of the organization's works. *L.* 1958, *c.* 131. That law, enacted on July 22, 1958, was scheduled to expire June 30, 1959.

On June 11, 1959, a successor statute, N.J.S.A. 2A:53A-7 to -11, was enacted. The law was identical to the predecessor but had no expiration date. It remains the law today. The Legislature thus quickly reversed the retreat of the doctrine in New Jersey.

N.J.S.A. 2A:53A-10 provides:

This act shall be deemed to be remedial and shall be liberally construed so as to afford immunity to the said corporations, societies and associations from liability as provided herein in furtherance of the public policy for the protection of nonprofit corporations, societies and associations organized for religious, charitable, educational or hospital purposes.

Whatever this Court's views of immunity, *cf.* Foldi v. Jeffries, 93 N.J. 533 (1983) (limits on parental immunity); Merenoff v. Merenoff, 76 N.J. 535 (1978) (no interspousal immunity for personal injury actions); France v. A.P.A. Trans. Corp., 56 N.J. 500 (1970) (no parental immunity for automobile negligence actions); Immer v. Risko, 56 N.J. 482 (1970) (no interspousal immunity for automobile negligence actions), we should apply this statute as the Legislature intended.

The focus of the legislative process was not on the question of what exceptions were consistent with the historical development of the doctrine of common law charitable immunity. The focus was on the economic effect of abolition of the doctrine upon the charities. *Hearings on S. 204 re Exemption of Religious, Charitable and Hospital Organizations from Negligence Liability, Before the Assembly Judiciary Committee,* (July 17, 1958).

We need not, then, theorize about whether liability for negligent hiring or administrative negligence advances the purposes of charitable immunity as it developed at common law, since the Legislature has "explicitly fix[ed] the State's policy." *Collopy,* 27 N.J. at 41. That policy is that the act shall be deemed to be "remedial and shall be liberally construed so as to afford immunity . . . for the protection of nonprofit corporations . . . organized for religious, charitable, educational or hospital purposes." N.J.S.A. 2A:53A-10. Nowhere does the dissent recognize this statutory mandate or seek to give it effect.

Taken in that light, we believe that the Legislature intended to deal with the reality that corporate charities can act only through employees, whether at the management or field level. Finally, we do not discern in the lack of parallelism between clauses of the statute dealing with strangers and beneficiaries an intention that a charitable organization be liable for its negligence in hiring. . . . Nothing in the legislative history points to so subtle a distinction. . . . As noted, the interim immunity statute, *L.* 1958, *c.* 131, was introduced within seven days of the *Collopy* decision, and on June 16, 1958, the Assembly Committee inserted the specific language because the Senate bill did not distinguish between strangers and beneficiaries. The permanent statute follows the interim statute without change to that provision and nothing in its history sustains a legislative determination to distinguish administrative negligence.

We agree that a statute should be construed in light of probable legislative intent in the context of an evolving common law. . . . We see no evolution of common law doctrine that conflicts with the original legislative policy insofar as ordinary negligence of a charity's employees is involved. . . . Whether immunity should cloak those with a reckless or gross disregard for the safety of others is a question that may have to be addressed. *See* Foldi v. Jeffries, 93 N.J. 533 (1983) (parental immunity does not extend to willful or wanton failure to supervise); Brown v. Anderson Cty. Hosp. Ass'n, 268 S.C. 479, 234 S.E.2d 873 (1977) (no charitable immunity for hospital's heedless and reckless acts). Perhaps the time has come for the Legislature to consider again the scope of the law and its intended application to new theories of liability. *See* Bottari, *The Charitable Immunity Act*, 5 Seton Hall Legis. J. 61 (1980).

The arguments of the dissent, then, are not without appeal but are based upon the premise that we can modify the law to our own views of public policy rather than those set forth by the Legislature. . . . . [T]he Legislature has spoken and has directed the court to interpret the immunity liberally. N.J.S.A. 2A:53A-10.

Others must reconcile the issues of moral responsibility. As to legal responsibility, we find that the act charged against the charity here is negligence in hiring. Under New Jersey's Charitable Immunity Act a charity is not liable for negligence.

The judgment below is affirmed. No costs.

Handler, J. (dissenting) (joined by Pollack and Schreiber, JJ.). . . .

II

The pivotal question . . . is whether an entity, otherwise liable for injuries suffered by an innocent third person resulting from the intentional wrongdoing of its employee on grounds of negligence in the hiring, supervision or retention of the employee can, because of its status as a charitable institution, interpose an absolute defense under the charitable immunity statute. . . .

The earliest English decisions that established the charitable immunity doctrine did not stress general notions of prevailing public policy as the underlying reason for the rule. These cases viewed a charitable entity as the manager of a trust that should be immune from liability to third persons because the award of damages would constitute an unwarranted invasion of the trust fund and its diversion to an unintended purpose. . . . However, in 1865, in the case of Mersey Docks & Harbour Bd. v. Gibbs, 11 Eng. Rep. 1500 (H.L.C. 1864-66), [this] rationale . . . was specifically repudiated. The court declared that a public corporation whose funds were held in trust was liable for the negligence of its servants in causing injury to third persons in the same way as any private corporation would be liable. Subsequently this rule of accountability was carried over to charitable organizations in Hillyer v. The Governors of St. Bartholomew's Hosp., 2 K.B. 800 (1909). . . .

As noted by Justice Jacobs in *Collopy*, the early pre-Act New Jersey decisions did not fully subscribe to the trust fund theory, but spoke primarily in terms of public policy. E.g., D'Amato v. Orange Memorial Hospital, *supra*, 101 N.J.L. at 65. . . . *D'Amato* relied in some measure upon the New York cases that had recognized the common law charitable immunity doctrine, citing Schloendorff v. The Society of New York Hospital, 211 N.Y. 125, 105 N.E. 92 (1914), a leading decision. Judge Cardozo, in a later case, Hamburger v. Cornell Univ., 240 N.Y. 328, 148 N.E. 539, 543 (1925), stressed that the appropriate basis for the common law doctrine was public policy, observing that "[i]n this state . . . the trust fund theory has been rejected." 240 N.Y. at 331, 148 N.E. 539. Thus, *D'Amato*, which was the first authoritative pronouncement of the charitable immunity doctrine in this state, adopted the New York conceptualization of the immunity with its rejection of the trust fund theory and its reliance upon public policy. As previously noted, the New Jersey Legislature itself has recognized public policy to be the proper foundation of its statutory grant of immunity. N.J.S.A. 2A:53A-10.

A public policy that suffers an immunity for tortious acts, thereby tolerating an exception to the overriding principle that injuries from wrongful conduct be redressed, must surely be hostile to a legal sanctuary for aggravated wrongs. E.g., Foldi v. Jeffries, 93 N.J. 533 (1983). Even more so must a sound public policy, reflecting the conscience of the community, be loathe to carve out a legal haven for willful and intentional misconduct. E.g., Tevis v. Tevis, 79 N.J. 422 (1979); Small v. Rockfeld, 66 N.J. 231 (1974). . . .

. . . It is evident that in the commission of an intentional tort, the wrongful conduct is so far removed from the beneficent purposes of the charity that it would serve no salutary societal goal to accord immunity from liability. The immunity protects the charity in its normal endeavors, and not in activities that are antithetical to its charitable ends. . . .

. . . Immunity does not attach simply because the entity is a charity. Rather, its availability is determined by whether the entity is acting charitably when the tortious conduct occurs. The critical conduct must be inspired by and directed to a charitable end. This is central to the charitable immunity doctrine. The conduct of the charity, both in terms of the relationship between the charity and the claimant and in terms of its beneficent works, must in all respects be directly and clearly related to the furtherance of the legitimate purposes of the charity.

In this case, the . . . employee's injurious acts served only his own malicious and salacious ends; they were totally disconnected from his lawful employment and the legitimate work of the charity. . . . The sexual exploitation of an innocent child by a perverted employee destroys any vestige of a beneficent nexus between the charity and its victim. In this tragic and evil setting, it is a misnomer to characterize the child as a beneficiary of the institution. Further, the heinous character of the conduct totally negates any possibility of achieving a charitable end. . . .

III

The second reason that persuades me to recognize a cause of action in this case is based upon an exception in the charitable immunity statute where the asserted negligence involves negligent hiring, supervision or retention of a dangerous or incompetent employee by the institution itself. The public policy that supports the conclusion that the immunity statute has no application to the victim of an intentional tort committed by a dangerous employee of a charity supports as well the exception to the immunity based on negligent hiring. . . .

The immunity has always been restricted to a context in which the charity is both engaged in a proper pursuit of its charitable ends and stands in a beneficent relationship to the injured claimant. A charity failing in either forfeits the immunity. And, a charity that fails to exercise due care in the hiring or supervision of its work force generates a probability of injury to innocent third persons. Such negligence clearly undermines the essential capacity of the charity to do charity and to benefit its intended recipients. Managerial negligence of this sort defeats the essential purpose of the legal protection accorded beneficent entities. Such negligence on the part of a charity properly stands as an exception to the immunity conferred by statute. . . .

Accordingly, I would reverse the judgment below.

NOTES AND QUESTIONS

1. *Complete and Partial Immunities.* Mid- and late-twentieth-century legislatures and courts that abolished across-the-board charitable immunity did so mainly with the goal of permitting medical malpractice actions against not-for-profit hospitals. With the lifting of the blanket immunity, however, plaintiffs began to bring claims against other charities, including churches. Some state legislatures have responded by granting selective protection to particular charities. Others have reinstated a de facto immunity by virtue of tight damage caps. Massachusetts, for example, currently caps charitable institutions' liability for injuries caused by actions in furtherance of such an institution's charitable purpose at $20,000 per claim. Mass. G. L. c. 231 § 85K.

2. *Individual Liability.* Where applicable, charitable immunities such as those provided by the New Jersey statute protect the assets of the charity, not the individual tortfeasor. Some states have granted partial or complete immunities to individuals who accidentally injure others in the course of doing charitable works or volunteerism. For example, a volunteer who knocks someone over in the course of a charity bake sale might be immunized from ordinary negligence liability, but still subject to liability for gross negligence, recklessness, or intentional wrongdoing.

In a case such as *Schultz*, the plaintiffs probably possessed valid survival and wrongful death actions against Brother Edmund individually, but would likely have collected little by way of compensation from such a suit. Needless to say, a successful suit against the Archdiocese would also have sent a very different message about who was responsible — and who would in the future be held responsible — for injuries caused by conduct such as Brother Edmund's.

3. *Direct Liability. Schultz* involves a claim of *direct* liability against the Archdiocese rather than a claim that it is *vicariously* liable for the tortious acts of its employee. In other words, the complaint is that management itself did something wrong so as to cause injury to the plaintiffs' decedent, not that management is responsible for the wrongs of an employee. *See* Taber v. Maine, *infra*, Chapter 8.

What did the Archdiocese do wrong, according to the complaint? Some courts have suggested that by holding a church liable on a direct theory of negligence in hiring or supervision, the courts would interfere with religious practices in violation of the First Amendment's guarantee of freedom of religion. Pritzlaff v. Archdiocese of Milwaukee, 194 Wis. 2d 302 (1995). Others have rejected this argument on the ground that application of facially neutral tort principles does not interfere with church organization or doctrine. Malicki v. Doe, 814 So. 2d 347 (Fla. 2001).

4. *Vicarious Liability.* The plaintiffs' reliance on a theory of direct liability was likely driven in part by the rule that intentional wrongful acts of the sort allegedly perpetrated by Brother Edmund occur "outside the scope" of employment, and hence cannot provide the basis for a claim of vicarious liability against the employer. *See* Taber v. Maine, *infra*, Chapter 8. Some courts have held that, even if other employers can be held vicariously liable for the intentional wrongs of their employees, religious institutions are entitled to the benefit of a narrower orbit of vicarious liability. *See, e.g.*, Byrd v. Faber, 565 N.E.2d 584 (Ohio 1991).

Downs v. United States
522 F.2d 990 (6th Cir. 1975)

Celebrezze, J.   This appeal presents two basic questions concerning the United States' liability for actions of FBI agents resulting in the death of innocent victims of a hijacking. These issues are the applicability of the "discretionary function" exception to the Federal Tort Claims Act and the existence of negligence under Florida law on the facts of this case.

This action arose out of the hijacking of a small passenger airplane in Nashville, Tennessee. Inside the aircraft were the hijacker, an associate, the hijacker's estranged wife, a pilot, and a co-pilot. The hijacker ordered the aircraft flown to Freeport, Bahamas, with a refueling stop in Jacksonville, Florida. After the plane landed in Jacksonville, FBI agents refused to allow refueling, despite the pilot's signals that the hijacker was armed and dangerous and that in his opinion the agents' intervention would prove disastrous. The hijacker allowed the co-pilot, and, later, an associate to deplane to bargain for fuel. The FBI agents took them both into custody. Moments later the agents used rifle fire to disable one of the aircraft's engines and attempted, unsuccessfully, to deflate the aircraft's tires. This attack provoked the hijacker to shoot and kill his wife, the pilot, and himself.

The survivors of the hijacker's victims sued the United States under the Federal Tort Claims Act, alleging that the chief FBI agent had been negligent in handling the situation and had thereby caused the two victims' deaths. . . . The Government defended, asserting that the "discretionary function" exception to the Act barred jurisdiction over the complaint and, in any event, that the agent had not been negligent.

The District Court, sitting without a jury, held that the "discretionary function" exception to the Federal Tort Claims Act did not bar the action. It found, however, that under Florida law the FBI agent had not been negligent. . . .

The first issue we face is whether this action is barred by the "discretionary function" exception to the Federal Tort Claims Act. . . .

The . . . Act constitutes a broad waiver of the United States' sovereign immunity from tort liability. The Act gives federal courts jurisdiction to hear actions

> for injury or loss of property, or personal injury or death caused by the negligent or wrongful act or omission of any employee of the Government while acting within the scope of his office or employment, under circumstances where the United States, if a private person, would be liable to the claimant in accordance with the law of the place where the act or omission occurred. [28 U.S.C. § 1346(b).]

Before the Act's passage, victims of torts committed by federal employees had to pursue the cumbersome route of seeking a private relief bill from Congress. The Act's basic purpose was to relieve Congress of the burden of considering these bills and to entrust their consideration to the courts. . . .

Certain exceptions were provided, however, which limited the waiver of immunity. Among these was the "discretionary function" exception, which the Government contends is applicable. It reasons that the FBI agent in charge of handling the hijacking had the "discretion to make an on-the-scene judgment as to the best course of action during the hijacking." Since there was "room for policy judgment," Appellee argues, the agent's actions fall within the discretionary function exception.

We recognize that the agent was called upon to use judgment in dealing with the hijacking. Judgment is exercised in almost every human endeavor. It is not the mere exercise of judgment, however, which immunizes the United States from liability for the torts of its employees. Driving an automobile was frequently cited in the congressional reports leading to the Act as an example of "non-discretionary" activity which would be outside the discretionary function exception. Driving an automobile involves judgment. The failure to signal a turn, for example, may be said to represent an exercise of judgment, albeit a poor one. Yet, the automobile accident caused by a federal employee while on the job is the archetypal claim which Congress sought to place in the courts. If exercise of judgment were the standard for applying the discretionary function exception, a host of cases have been wrongly decided. These cases would include Indian Towing Co., Inc. v. United States, 350 U.S. 61, 76 S. Ct. 122, 100 L. Ed. 48 (1955) (failure to replace a burned-out lamp in a lighthouse); Rayonier, Incorporated v. United States, 352 U.S. 315, 77 S. Ct. 374, 1 L. Ed. 2d 354

(1957) (failure completely to extinguish intermittently smoldering matter following a forest fire); Underwood v. United States, 356 F.2d 92 (5th Cir. 1966) (decision of psychiatrists to release airman from mental hospital and to provide him access to weapons), and Fair v. United States, 234 F.2d 288 (5th Cir. 1956) (decision to release homicidal patient).

A review of the language of the exception, the provision's legislative history, and the application of this section by the courts offers guidance in applying the exception.

The discretionary function provision . . . is embodied in 28 U.S.C. § 2680(a). The text of that section reads as follows:

> The provisions of this chapter and section 1346(b) of this title shall not apply to
>   (a) Any claim based upon . . . the exercise or performance or the failure to exercise or perform a discretionary function or duty on the part of a federal agency or an employee of the Government, whether or not the discretion involved be abused.

In our view . . . [this] provision . . . immunizes Government employees while they are formulating policy.

The limited legislative history of the section supports this reading. A paragraph discussing the provision, excerpted from testimony given in 1942 before the House Committee on the Judiciary by an Assistant Attorney General, states that liability should not arise "out of an authorized activity, such as a flood-control or irrigation project." The exception was "designed to preclude application of the bill to a claim against a regulatory agency, such as the Federal Trade Commission or the Securities and Exchange Commission, based upon an alleged abuse of discretionary authority by an officer or employee." Claims arising out of "an allegedly negligent exercise by the Treasury Department of the blacklisting or freezing powers are also intended to be excepted." Congressional reports indicate that the regulatory functions of the FTC and SEC were the types of activity to be exempted by this exception. The functions which this sparse legislative history indicates were to be excepted are those involving policy formulation, as distinguished from the day-to-day activities of persons not engaged in determining the general nature of the Government's business.

Supreme Court decisions have not extensively analyzed the exception. In Dalehite v. United States, 346 U.S. 15, 73 S. Ct. 956, 97 L. Ed. 1427 (1953), the Supreme Court first discussed the discretionary function provision. The 4-3 majority opinion concluded that immunized discretion "includes determinations made by executives or administrators in establishing plans, specifications or schedules of operations. (Footnote omitted.) Where there is room for policy judgment and decision there is discretion." 346 U.S. at 35-36, 73 S. Ct. at 968. Later opinions have suggested a more restrictive view of the exception, without setting forth clear guideposts for decision.

Numerous Circuit and District Courts have struggled to mold the sparse legislative history and the language of *Dalehite* into a precise standard, often seizing upon the planning level operational level distinction as a ready solution to the problem. Courts taking this approach have regarded discretionary acts of officials at the planning level as within the discretionary function exception and discretionary acts of operational level officials as outside the exception. This distinction is based on the status of the official making a judgment. While offering some general guidance, it is not a sufficient test for determining whether a Government employee's actions are within the exception.

We believe that the basic question concerning the exception is whether the judgments of a Government employee are of "the nature and quality" which Congress intended to put beyond judicial review. Congress intended "discretionary functions" to encompass those activities which entail the formulation of governmental policy, whatever the rank of those so engaged. We agree with a commentator's analysis of the provision:

> It would seem that the justifications for the exception do not necessitate a broader application than to those decisions which are arrived at through an administrator's exercise of a quasi-legislative or quasi-judicial function. [Citation omitted.]

In this case, the FBI agents were not involved in formulating governmental policy. Rather, the chief agent was engaged in directing the actions of other Government agents in the handling of a particular situation. FBI hijacking policy was not being set as an ad hoc or exemplary matter since it had been formulated before this hijacking. Hijacking policy had previously been promulgated in the FBI Handbook and in a memorandum jointly issued by the Departments of Transportation and Justice. While the Government's guidelines for dealing with hijackings are secret and must remain so, we note that Special Agent O'Connor was not making policy in responding to this particular situation.

The Government argues that United States v. Faneca, 332 F.2d 872 (5th Cir. 1964), *cert. denied*, 380 U.S. 971, 85 S. Ct. 1327, 14 L. Ed. 2d 268 (1965), supports its position that a law enforcement officer choosing among various available methods of enforcing the law in a given situation is performing a discretionary function under the Act. [*Faneca* involved a suit by persons injured when federal marshals, who were present at the University of Mississippi to protect James Meredith, a newly enrolled African-American student, fired tear gas into the crowd. The plaintiffs alleged negligence on the part of Deputy Attorney General Katzenbach and James P. McShane, Chief of the Executive Office of the United States Marshals, in formulating the plan by which federal officials would effect desegregation. However, at that time, government] efforts were underway to integrate colleges and universities throughout the nation. The policy formulated by Katzenbach and McShane was meant to influence and did inevitably serve to guide the actions of other government officials faced with similar situations. The *Faneca* Court recognized that in responding to this particular situation, the Government employees were performing a "discretionary function," as they were determining law enforcement policy.

When a response to a particular situation does not have the policy overtones involved in *Faneca*, however, courts have scrutinized the day-to-day activities of law enforcement officers. . . .

The proper approach is to consider the precise function at issue, and to determine whether an officer is likely to be unduly inhibited in the performance of that function by the threat of liability for tortious conduct. . . .[Carter v. Carlson, 447 F.2d 358, 362 (D.C. Cir. 1971)]. . . .

The prospect of governmental liability for the actions of law enforcement officers should not cause those officers less vigorously to enforce the law. The need for compensation to citizens injured by the torts of government employees outweighs whatever slight effect vicarious government liability might have on law enforcement efforts.

We believe that Congress intended that this action be tried in the courts, not in the halls of Congress. To decide otherwise would be to ignore the "sweeping language" of the Act, the "general trend toward increasing the scope of the waiver," and the need to avoid "whittl(ing) it down by refinements." United States v. Yellow Cab Co., 340 U.S. 543, 547, 550, 71 S. Ct. 399, 404, 95 L. Ed. 523 (1951). . . .

The second issue presented is whether the District Court erred in finding that the FBI agent in charge of handling the hijacking was not negligent. . . .

[The court proceeded to review the sequence of events leading up to the death of plaintiff's decedents. Agent O'Connor was a 21-year FBI veteran. He was alerted to the hijacking at about 4:00 A.M., and arrived at the hangar area of the airport at about 4:50. Two other agents, Murphy and Burns, met O'Connor there. Burns proceeded to the control tower to enable communication with the plane. Additional agents later arrived and took positions around the plane.

The plane landed at 5:10 and taxied to the hangar area at 5:15. By this time, O'Connor had been informed that the plane was low on fuel, and that the pilot was requesting re-fueling, as well as equipment needed to restart the plane. He had also been told that there were two armed hijackers on board, and that, prior to the plane's departure from Nashville, one of them had dragged a woman on board, reportedly his wife, with whom he had a history of marital difficulties.

Burns made contact with the aircraft, identifying himself as an FBI agent. The pilot responded that he needed fuel, and he requested that the area be cleared of personnel. O'Connor instructed Burns to respond that no fuel or starter would be provided. When Burns conveyed this message, the pilot informed Burns, and Burns told O'Connor, that the hijacker had plastic explosives aboard. O'Connor expressed concern to other agents that the airplane might take off without refueling.

At 5:20, the left engine of the hijacked airplane was shut down to allow co-pilot Randall Crump to leave the plane to negotiate for fuel. Crump testified that O'Connor elicited very little information from him, and that when he told O'Connor that explosives were aboard, O'Connor discounted the information as a "bunch of malarky."

Three or four minutes after Crump deplaned, Bobby Wallace, the hijacker's accomplice, exited the airplane. O'Connor and Murphy took Wallace into custody. Wallace indicated that the hijacker was upset and that he had been sent out to bargain for fuel. Wallace, who was carrying a loaded pistol, was disarmed and placed under arrest for air piracy and, consistent with FBI regulations, was not questioned further.

At 5:30, O'Connor decided to employ forcible intervention to prevent the plane from departing. O'Connor ordered agents to block the plane from taxiing and to shoot out its right rear tire. He then approached the plane, identified himself, and ordered all the occupants to exit. Two shots were fired from inside the plane. O'Connor then ordered McBride to shoot out the right engine. When the engine was silenced, he heard moaning, looked into the plane, and discovered the two dead hostages and the fatally wounded hijacker. — Eds.]

The District Court concluded that O'Connor's actions throughout the incident did not amount to negligence. Although moved by the tragic outcome of the FBI's response to the hijacking, the District Court made this ultimate finding:

> . . . O'Connor's challenged decisions were not an unreasonable response under all the circumstances. In traditional negligence terms, O'Connor was under a duty to choose a course of action which would maximize the hostages' safety, and to attempt a capture of the hijacker only if possible by means compatible with the greater interest. While the FBI obviously cannot undertake to guarantee the safety of persons in this situation, the means employed to effect any capture should be consonant with that which would provide the maximum assurance possible that hostages would not be harmed as a result. . . . To the court it seems obvious that the proper decision in this situation is a matter on which reasonable minds could differ; but viewed objectively and without the benefit of hindsight, the court is unable to conclude that the alternatives chosen by Agent O'Connor were unreasonable. 382 F. Supp. at 755.

We are convinced that this finding is clearly erroneous. There did exist, from foresight, "a better-suited alternative to protecting the hostages' well-being." That choice was not to intervene forcibly but to continue the "waiting game."

We recognize that law enforcement officers must make split-second, difficult decisions when confronted with emergency situations. As the District Court pointed out, however, the extent to which "an actor will be excused for errors in judgment under (emergency) circumstances is qualified by training and experience he may have, or be expected to have, in coping with the danger or emergency with which he is confronted." 382 F. Supp. at 752.

Agent O'Connor was trained to handle dangerous situations. He must be held to the standard of the reasonable FBI agent with training in handling such affairs. Indeed, although O'Connor himself had not previously been involved in handling a hijacking, he was familiar with the FBI Handbook's guidelines and the Jacksonville intra-office memorandum on hijackings. While these documents must be kept secret, it is significant that they place a far greater emphasis on hostage safety and pilot cooperation than O'Connor did in confronting his problem. . . . [O]ur review of O'Connor's actions convinces us that O'Connor violated FBI policy and disregarded the substance of the Guidelines, thereby directly resulting in the deaths of the pilot and the hijacker's estranged wife.

While we agree with the District Court that the failure to comply with FBI policy is not a basis for a finding of negligence per se, we are less willing than the District Court to diminish the importance of the fact that O'Connor failed to act in accordance with procedures intended to maximize hostage safety, short of complying with unreasonable hijacker demands.

We find, furthermore, that O'Connor was clearly unreasonable in turning what had been a successful "waiting game," during which two persons safely left the plane, into a "shooting match," which left three persons dead.

O'Connor's reasons for choosing force rather than continued delay were confused and contradictory. O'Connor reasoned that when the hijacker released his associate he demonstrated a rational state of mind and might at that point have been expected to respond reasonably to the agents' disabling of the plane. Yet, O'Connor also concluded that the hijacker would react in an irrational and violent manner to continued delay.

Another of O'Connor's stated reasons for disabling the plane's right engine was to facilitate communication. Yet, up to that point O'Connor had experienced no difficulty communicating with his fellow agents or with the control tower.

O'Connor's basic fear was that the airplane would depart, with what he had heard was less than thirty minutes of fuel left. He reasoned that the hostages would have had a better chance of surviving an on-the-ground assault than "continued flight into the unknown," as the District Court described it. 382 F. Supp. at 754. Yet, the plane had made no movement away from its landing berth, and if delay had continued for a while longer, the plane might have run out of fuel while on the ground, thus accomplishing the purpose of the armed assault without provoking an irrational reaction from the hijacker. In addition, the hijacker had said, "Let's get out of here," upon first hearing the no fuel decision, but the pilot had not complied with the request and the hijacker instead let both the co-pilot and an apparent accomplice leave the plane to bargain for fuel. Thus, the hijacker himself had decided to participate in the "waiting game," and there was no reason to suppose that the plane was about to depart when O'Connor ordered the aircraft forcibly disabled.

The District Court framed only two action alternatives as having been available to O'Connor: (1) the forcible termination chosen by O'Connor or (2) acquiescence in the aircraft's departure. We believe that additional delay and an attempt to reason with the hijacker were other options which were open to O'Connor, and these options were particularly proper in view of the pilot's insistence that armed intervention would result in disaster. We believe a reasonable FBI agent would have tried additional delay and would have ordered an attempt to reason with the hijacker. By the timing of his decisions, O'Connor backed the hijacker into a corner. Force or immediate surrender became the hijacker's only options. Special Agent O'Connor grossly miscalculated in assuming the hijacker would respond peacefully to a show of force.

Where one trained in the field of law enforcement is called upon to make a judgment which may result in the death of innocent persons, he is required to exercise the highest degree of care commensurate with all facts within his knowledge. Such care must be exercised in order to ensure that undue loss of life does not occur. We believe that Agent O'Connor failed to exercise such care. . . .

Riss v. City of New York
240 N.E.2d 860 (N.Y. 1968)

Breitel, J.   This appeal presents, in a very sympathetic framework, the issue of the liability of a municipality for failure to provide special protection to a member of the public who was repeatedly threatened with personal harm and eventually suffered dire personal injuries for lack of such protection. The facts are amply described in the dissenting opinion and no useful purpose would be served by repetition. The issue arises upon the affirmance by a divided Appellate Division of a dismissal of the complaint, after both sides had rested but before submission to the jury.

It is necessary immediately to distinguish those liabilities attendant upon governmental activities which have displaced or supplemented traditionally private enterprises, such as are involved in the operation of rapid transit systems, hospitals, and places of public assembly. Once sovereign immunity was abolished by statute the extension of liability on ordinary principles of tort law logically followed. To be equally distinguished are certain activities of government which provide services and facilities for the use of the public, such as highways, public buildings and the like, in the performance of which the municipality or the State may be liable under ordinary principles of tort law. The ground for liability is the provision of the services or facilities for the direct use by members of the public.

In contrast, this case involves the provision of a governmental service to protect the public generally from external hazards and particularly to control the activities of criminal wrongdoers. The amount of protection that may be provided is limited by the resources of the community and by a considered legislative-executive decision as to how those resources may be deployed. For the courts to proclaim a new and general duty of protection in the law of tort, even to those who may be the particular seekers of protection based on specific hazards, could and would inevitably determine how the limited police resources of the community should be allocated and without predictable limits. This is quite different from the predictable allocation of resources and liabilities when public hospitals, rapid transit systems, or even highways are provided.

Before such extension of responsibilities should be dictated by the indirect imposition of tort liabilities, there should be a legislative determination that that should be the scope of public responsibility. . . .

It is notable that the removal of sovereign immunity for tort liability was accomplished after legislative enactment and not by any judicial arrogation of power (Court of Claims Act, § 8). It is equally notable that for many years, since as far back as 1909 in this State, there was by statute municipal liability for losses sustained as a result of riot (General

Municipal Law, § 71). Yet even this class of liability has for some years been suspended by legislative action (New York State Defense Emergency Act [L. 1951, ch. 784, § 113, subd. 3; § 121, as last amd. by L. 1968, ch. 115]), a factor of considerable significance.

When one considers the greatly increased amount of crime committed throughout the cities, but especially in certain portions of them, with a repetitive and predictable pattern, it is easy to see the consequences of fixing municipal liability upon a showing of probable need for and request for protection. To be sure these are grave problems at the present time, exciting high priority activity on the part of the national, State and local governments, to which the answers are neither simple, known, or presently within reasonable controls. To foist a presumed cure for these problems by judicial innovation of a new kind of liability in tort would be foolhardy indeed and an assumption of judicial wisdom and power not possessed by the courts. . . .

For all of these reasons, there is no warrant in judicial tradition or in the proper allocation of the powers of government for the courts, in the absence of legislation, to carve out an area of tort liability for police protection to members of the public. Quite distinguishable, of course, is the situation where the police authorities undertake responsibilities to particular members of the public and expose them, without adequate protection, to the risks which then materialize into actual losses.

Accordingly, the order of the Appellate Division affirming the judgment of dismissal should be affirmed.

Keating, J. (dissenting).   Certainly, the record in this case, sound legal analysis, relevant policy considerations and even precedent cannot account for or sustain the result which the majority have here reached. For the result is premised upon a legal rule which long ago should have been abandoned, having lost any justification it might once have had. Despite almost universal condemnation by legal scholars, the rule survives, finding its continuing strength, not in its power to persuade, but in its ability to arouse unwarranted judicial fears of the consequences of overturning it.

Linda Riss, an attractive young woman, was for more than six months terrorized by a rejected suitor well known to the courts of this State, one Burton Pugach. This miscreant, masquerading as a respectable attorney, repeatedly threatened to have Linda killed or maimed if she did not yield to him: "If I can't have you, no one else will have you, and when I get through with you, no one else will want you." In fear for her life, she went to those charged by law with the duty of preserving and safeguarding the lives of the citizens and residents of this State. Linda's repeated and almost pathetic pleas for aid were received with little more than indifference. Whatever help she was given was not commensurate with the identifiable danger. On June 14, 1959 Linda became engaged to another man. At a party held to celebrate the event, she received a phone call warning her that it was her "last chance." Completely distraught, she called the police, begging for help, but was refused. The next day Pugach carried out his dire threats in the very manner he had foretold by having a hired thug throw lye in Linda's face. Linda was blinded in one eye, lost a good portion of her vision in the other, and her face was permanently scarred. After the assault the authorities concluded that there was some basis for Linda's fears, and for the next three and one-half years, she was given around-the-clock protection.

No one questions the proposition that the first duty of government is to assure its citizens the opportunity to live in personal security. And no one who reads the record of Linda's ordeal can reach a conclusion other than that the City of New York, acting through its agents, completely and negligently failed to fulfill this obligation to Linda.

Linda has turned to the courts of this State for redress, asking that the city be held liable in damages for its negligent failure to protect her from harm. With compelling logic, she can point out that, if a stranger, who had absolutely no obligation to aid her, had offered her assistance, and thereafter Burton Pugach was able to injure her as a result of the negligence of the volunteer, the courts would certainly require him to pay damages. (Restatement, 2d, Torts, § 323.) Why then should the city, whose duties are imposed by law and include the prevention of crime (New York City Charter, § 435) and, consequently, extend far beyond that of the Good Samaritan, not be responsible? If a private detective acts carelessly, no one would deny that a jury could find such conduct unacceptable. Why then is the city not required to live up to at least the same minimal standards of professional competence which would be demanded of a private detective?

Linda's reasoning seems so eminently sensible that surely it must come as a shock to her and to every citizen to hear the city argue and to learn that this court decides that the city has no duty to provide police protection to any given individual. What makes the city's position particularly difficult to understand is that, in conformity to the dictates of the law, Linda did not carry any weapon for self-defense (former Penal Law, § 1897). Thus, by a rather bitter irony she was required to rely for protection on the City of New York which now denies all responsibility to her.

It is not a distortion to summarize the essence of the city's case here in the following language: "Because we owe a duty to everybody, we owe it to nobody." Were it not for the fact that this position has been hallowed by much ancient and revered precedent, we would surely dismiss it as preposterous. To say that there is no duty is, of course, to start with the conclusion. The question is whether or not there should be liability for the negligent failure to provide adequate police protection.

The foremost justification repeatedly urged for the existing rule is the claim that the State and the municipalities will be exposed to limitless liability. . . .

The fear of financial disaster is a myth. The same argument was made a generation ago in opposition to proposals that the State waive its defense of "sovereign immunity." The prophecy proved false then, and it would now. The supposed astronomical financial burden does not and would not exist. No municipality has gone bankrupt because it has had to respond in damages when a policeman causes injury through carelessly driving a police car or in the thousands of other situations where, by judicial fiat or legislative enactment, the State and its subdivisions have been held liable for the tortious conduct of their employees. Thus, in the past four or five years, New York City has been presented with an average of some 10,000 claims each year. The figure would sound ominous except for the fact the city has been paying out less than $8,000,000 on tort claims each year and this amount includes all those sidewalk defect and snow and ice cases about which the courts fret so often. (Reports submitted by the Comptroller of the City of New York to the Comptroller of the State of New York pursuant to General Municipal Law, § 50-f.) Court delay has reduced the figure paid somewhat, but not substantially. Certainly this is a slight burden in a budget of more than six billion dollars (less than two tenths of 1%) and of no importance as compared to the injustice of permitting unredressed wrongs to continue to go unrepaired. That Linda Riss should be asked to bear the loss, which should properly fall on the city if we assume, as we must, in the present posture of the case, that her injuries resulted from the city's failure to provide sufficient police to protect Linda is contrary to the most elementary notions of justice.

The statement in the majority opinion that there are no predictable limits to the potential liability for failure to provide adequate police protection as compared to other areas of municipal liability is, of course, untenable. When immunity in other areas of governmental activity was removed, the same lack of predictable limits existed. Yet, disaster did not ensue.

Another variation of the "crushing burden" argument is the contention that, every time a crime is committed, the city will be sued and the claim will be made that it resulted from inadequate police protection. . . . [H]ere too the underlying assumption of the argument is fallacious because it assumes that a strict liability standard is to be imposed and that the courts would prove completely unable to apply general principles of tort liability in a reasonable fashion in the context of actions arising from the negligent acts of police and fire personnel. The argument is also made as if there were no such legal principles as fault, proximate cause or foreseeability, all of which operate to keep liability within reasonable bounds. No one is contending that the police must be at the scene of every potential crime or must provide a personal bodyguard to every person who walks into a police station and claims to have been threatened. They need only act as a reasonable man would under the circumstances. At first there would be a duty to inquire. If the inquiry indicates nothing to substantiate the alleged threat, the matter may be put aside and other matters attended to. If, however, the claims prove to have some basis, appropriate steps would be necessary.

The instant case provides an excellent illustration of the limits which the courts can draw. No one would claim that, under the facts here, the police were negligent when they did not give Linda protection after her first calls or visits to the police station in February of 1959. The preliminary investigation was sufficient. If Linda had been attacked at this point, clearly there would be no liability here. When, however, as time went on and it was established that Linda was a reputable person, that other verifiable attempts to injure her or intimidate her had taken place, that other witnesses were available to support her claim that her life was being threatened, something more was required — either by way of further investigation or protection — than the statement that was made by one detective to Linda that she would have to be hurt before the police could do anything for her.

In dismissing the complaint, the trial court noted that there are many crimes being committed daily and the police force is inadequate to deal with its "tremendous responsibilities." The point is not addressed to the facts of this case. Even if it were, however, a distinction must be made. It may be quite reasonable to say that the City of New York is not required to hire sufficient police to protect every piece of property threatened during mass riots. The possibility of riots may even be foreseeable, but the occurrence is sufficiently uncommon that the city should not be required to bear the cost of having a redundancy of men for normal operations. But it is going beyond the bounds of required judicial moderation if the city is permitted to escape liability in a situation such as the one at bar. If the police force of the City of New York is so understaffed that it is unable to cope with the everyday problem posed by the relatively few cases where single, known individuals threaten the lives of other persons, then indeed we have reached the danger line and the lives of all of us are in peril. If the police department is in such a deplorable state that the city, because of insufficient manpower, is truly unable to protect persons in Linda Riss' position, then liability not only should, but must be imposed. It will act as an effective inducement for public officials to provide at least a minimally adequate number of police. If local officials are not willing to meet even such a low standard, I see no reason for the courts to abet such irresponsibility.

It is also contended that liability for inadequate police protection will make the courts the arbiters of decisions taken by the Police Commissioner in allocating his manpower and his resources. We are not dealing here with a situation where the injury or loss occurred as a result of a conscious choice of policy made by those exercising high administrative responsibility after a complete and thorough deliberation of various alternatives. There was no major policy decision taken by the Police Commissioner to disregard Linda Riss' appeal for help because there was absolutely no manpower available to deal with Pugach. This "garden variety" negligence case arose in the course of "day-by-day operations of government" (Weiss v. Fote, 7 N.Y.2d 579, 585). Linda Riss' tragedy resulted not from high policy or inadequate manpower, but plain negligence on the part of persons with whom Linda dealt.

More significant, however, is the fundamental flaw in the reasoning behind the argument alleging judicial interference. It is a complete oversimplification of the problem of municipal tort liability. What it ignores is the fact that indirectly courts are reviewing administrative practices in almost every tort case against the State or a municipality, including even decisions of the Police Commissioner. Every time a municipal hospital is held liable for malpractice resulting from inadequate record-keeping, the courts are in effect making a determination that the municipality should have hired or assigned more clerical help or more competent help to medical records or should have done something to improve its record-keeping procedures so that the particular injury would not have occurred.

Every time a municipality is held liable for a defective sidewalk, it is as if the courts are saying that more money and resources should have been allocated to sidewalk repair, instead of to other public services.

The situation is nowise different in the case of police protection. Whatever effects there may be on police administration will be one of degree, not kind. In McCrink v. City of New York (296 N.Y. 99) we held the city liable where a drunken policeman, while off duty, shot and killed a citizen in an unprovoked assault. The policeman had a long history of being a troublemaker, having been brought up before the Police Commissioner on drunkenness charges on three prior occasions. In imposing liability on the city, were we not in effect overruling the Commissioner's judgment in retaining the policeman on the force and saying his decision was so unreasonable that the city should be required to pay damages?

The truth of the matter, however, is that the courts are not making policy decisions for public officials. In all these municipal negligence cases, the courts are doing two things. First, they apply the principles of vicarious liability to the operations of government. Courts would not insulate the city from liability for the ordinary negligence of members of the highway department. There is no basis for treating the members of the police department differently.

Second, and most important, to the extent that the injury results from the failure to allocate sufficient funds and resources to meet a minimum standard of public administration, public officials are presented with two alternatives: either improve public administration or accept the cost of compensating injured persons. Thus, if we were to hold the city liable here for the negligence of the police, courts would no more be interfering with the operations of the police department than they "meddle" in the affairs of the highway department when they hold the municipality liable for personal injuries resulting from defective sidewalks, or a private employer for the negligence of his employees. In other words, all the courts do in these municipal negligence cases is require officials to weigh the consequences of their decisions. If Linda Riss' injury resulted from the failure of the city to pay sufficient salaries to attract qualified and sufficient personnel, the full cost of that choice should become acknowledged in the same way as it has in other areas of municipal tort liability. Perhaps officials will find it less costly to choose the alternative of paying damages than changing their existing practices. That may be well and good, but the price for the refusal to provide for an adequate police force should not be borne by Linda Riss and all the other innocent victims of such decisions.

What has existed until now is that the City of New York and other municipalities have been able to engage in a sort of false bookkeeping in which the real costs of inadequate or incompetent police protection have been hidden by charging the expenditures to the individuals who have sustained often catastrophic losses rather than to the community where it belongs, because the latter had the power to prevent the losses.

Although in modern times the compensatory nature of tort law has generally been the one most emphasized, one of its most important functions has been and is its normative aspect. It sets forth standards of conduct which ought to be followed. The penalty for failing to do so is to pay pecuniary damages. At one time the government was completely immunized from this salutary control. This is much less so now, and the imposition of liability has had healthy side effects. In many areas, it has resulted in the adoption of better and more considered procedures just as workmen's compensation resulted in improved industrial safety practices. To visit liability upon the city here will no doubt have similar constructive effects. No "presumed cure" for the problem of crime is being "foisted" upon the city as the majority opinion charges. The methods of dealing with the problem of crime are left completely to the city's discretion. All that the courts can do is make sure that the costs of the city's and its employees' mistakes are placed where they properly belong. Thus, every reason used to sustain the rule that there is no duty to offer police protection to any individual turns out on close analysis to be of little substance.

. . . [S]tep by step, New York courts are moving to return — albeit with some notable setbacks — toward the day when the government, in carrying out its various functions, will be held equally responsible for the negligent acts of its employees as would a private employer. . . . But although "sovereign immunity," by that name, supposedly died in Bernardine v. City of New York, it has been revived in a new form. It now goes by the name — "public duty." . . .

The rule [of no duty] is Judge made and can be judicially modified. By statute, the judicially created doctrine of "sovereign immunity" was destroyed. It was an unrighteous doctrine, carrying as it did the connotation that the government is above the law. Likewise, the law should be purged of all new evasions, which seek to avoid the full implications of the repeal of sovereign immunity.

No doubt in the future we shall have to draw limitations just as we have done in the area of private litigation, and no doubt some of these limitations will be unique to municipal liability because the problems will not have any counterpart in private tort law. But if the lines are to be drawn, let them be delineated on candid considerations of policy and fairness and not on the fictions or relics of the doctrine of "sovereign immunity." Before reaching such questions, however, we must resolve the fundamental issue raised here and recognize that, having undertaken to provide professional police and fire protection, municipalities cannot escape liability for damages caused by their failure to do even a minimally adequate job of it. . . .

. . . [S]ince this is an appeal from a dismissal of the complaint, we must give the plaintiff the benefit of every favorable inference. . . A few examples of the actions of the police should suffice to show the true state of the record. Linda Riss received a telephone call from a person who warned Linda that Pugach was arranging to have her beaten up. A detective learned the identity of the caller. He offered to arrest the caller, but plaintiff rejected that suggestion for the obvious reason that the informant was trying to help Linda. When Linda requested that Pugach be arrested, the detective said he could not do that because she had not yet been hurt. The statement was not so. It was and is a crime to conspire to injure someone. True there was no basis to arrest Pugach then, but that was only because the necessary leg work had not been done. No one went to speak to the informant, who might have furnished additional leads. Linda claimed to be receiving telephone calls almost every day. These calls could have been monitored for a few days to obtain evidence against Pugach. Any number of reasonable alternatives presented themselves. A case against Pugach could have been developed which would have at least put him away for awhile or altered the situation entirely. But, if necessary, some police protection should have been afforded.

Perhaps, on a fuller record after a true trial on the merits, the city's position will not appear so damaging as it does now. But with actual notice of danger and ample opportunity to confirm and take reasonable remedial steps, a jury could find that the persons involved acted unreasonably and negligently. Linda Riss is entitled to have a jury determine the issue of the city's liability. This right should not be terminated by the adoption of a question-begging conclusion that there is no duty owed to her. The order of the Appellate Division should be reversed and a new trial granted.

NOTES AND QUESTIONS

1. *Respondeat Superior and the FTCA.* The FTCA states as a general rule that the federal government is subject to liability "if a private person would be liable to the claimant in accordance with the law of the place where the act or omission occurred." 28 U.S.C. § 1346(b). Notice that the statute attaches liability to the government, rather than its individual employees. (As explained below, individual employees often enjoy immunity from liability for torts committed in the course of their government employment.) Thus, the primary effect of the FTCA is to treat the federal government, for purposes of tort liability, as if it were a private employer. This in turn has the effect of rendering the United States subject to the doctrine of *respondeat superior*, under which it is held vicariously liable for tortious acts by its employees committed within the scope of their employment. *See* Taber v. Maine, *infra*, Chapter 8 (on *respondeat superior*). However, as Note 3, *infra*, indicates, the rules of vicarious liability that apply to the government are slightly different from the rules that apply to private employers under modern common law.

2. *The Paradox of Treating Government as a "Private Person."* Certain activities undertaken by government officials have obvious counterparts in the sphere of private activity, making application of the FTCA's basic directive unproblematic. If a U.S. employee carelessly drives his government-owned car into a pedestrian while acting within the scope of his employment, the government can readily be analogized to a private employer. However, there are other functions performed by government that have no private counterpart, such as maintaining the armed forces, and issuing mandatory, binding regulations backed by threat of fine or other punishment. If there is no private counterpart to such regulation, it would seem to follow that no "private person" can ever be held liable for negligence in the issuance or enforcement of such regulations. So how can the government be held liable under the FTCA?

Noticing this paradox, Justice Robert Jackson argued that the federal government should never be held liable for wrongdoing in connection with its performance of regulatory and other functions that only it performs, no matter what the nature of the particular conduct in question. *Feres v. United States*, 340 U.S. 135 (1950). However, the Court's 1955 *Indian Towing* decision, cited in *Downs*, abandoned this line of reasoning. In holding that the federal government could be liable for negligently operating a lighthouse, it concluded that the issue posed by the "private person" clause is whether general tort principles contained in the applicable state's law would call for the imposition of liability, even if the activity is one in which only government engages.

3. *Protections Built into the FTCA.* The FTCA marked an historic waiver of the carte blanche immunity previously enjoyed by the federal government for its torts. Still, Congress proceeded with care, as evidenced by the discretionary function exemption and several other provisions of the act. For example, the act does not accord claimants the right to a jury trial; judges determine all issues of fact and law. 28 U.S.C. § 2402. Moreover, the act adopts a conception of vicarious liability that is somewhat narrower than the rule at common law because it categorically excludes certain intentional wrongdoings from generating liability, even when those wrongs would permit the imposition of *respondeat superior* liability against a private actor. 28 U.S.C. § 2680(h); *see* Taber v. Maine, *infra*, Chapter 8. Also, when proceeding under the FTCA, claimants cannot obtain punitive damages against the government, even if such damages could be awarded were the defendant a private entity. 28 U.S.C. § 2674.

4. *Discretionary Functions and Discretion.* As noted in *Downs*, the fact that an activity entails the exercise of some discretion does not necessarily qualify it for the discretionary function exemption. Rather, the exemption seems to be directed at the exercise of a certain kind of discretion having to do with matters of "policy." So, for example, while the activity of surgery often involves discretionary decisions about what instrument to use, or how much anesthesia to administer, the federal government presumably cannot claim that the discretionary function exemption automatically immunizes it from all vicarious liability for malpractice committed by surgeons in its employ. Some courts, however, have concluded that certain medical decisions do qualify under the exemption. *See* C.R.S. v. United States, 11 F.3d 791 (8th Cir. 1993) (failure to screen blood used in transfusions for HIV infection constitutes a "policy" decision subject to the discretionary function exemption).

In the last 20 years, there has been a general tendency, led by the Supreme Court, to interpret the discretionary function exemption more broadly, and thus to immunize the government from liability for a greater range of carelessness on the part of its employees. Perhaps most important, United States v. Gaubert, 499 U.S. 315 (1991), declined to analyze the discretionary function issue in terms of a categorical distinction between "policy" and "day-to-day" decisions, and instead directed courts to determine whether the conduct in question called for employees to exercise discretion while pursuing the government's policy objectives. *Gaubert* also made clear that, at least in some instances, immunity will attach to a policy decision even if the decision in question was made unreflectively, without actual consideration of relevant policy factors. *See also* Aguehounde v. District of Columbia, 666 A.2d 443 (D.C. App. 1995) (decision on timing of traffic signals is a discretionary function even if no judgment was actually exercised in setting their timing). For a lower court decision representative of this tendency that appears to be inconsistent with *Downs*, see Flax v. United States, 847 F. Supp. 1183, 1187-1192 (D.N.J. 1994) (holding that the discretionary function exemption applies to FBI agents' mishandling of a kidnapping that may have contributed to the death of the kidnap victim; the agents' decisions to follow rather than apprehend the kidnappers, and to follow them in a certain way, were discretionary judgments).

5. *Why the Exemption?* Keep in mind that a plaintiff proceeding with a claim of negligence against the federal government must prove to a judge's satisfaction that a government employee acted carelessly before obtaining recovery. Given that reasonable people often legitimately disagree over the proper resolution of judgment-calls, won't it be the case that most allegations of faulty policymaking will fail on the breach element? Why did Congress feel the need to add a special exemption for discretionary functions? Does the second part of the court's opinion in *Downs* help capture its concern?

6. *Immunity from Liability to Military Personnel: The* Feres *Doctrine.* Although, as noted above, its original rationale is no longer endorsed by the Supreme Court, the holding of Feres v. United States, 340 U.S. 135 (1950) remains intact. In a nutshell, it found implicit in the FTCA a broad rule barring any suits by military servicemen against the government for injuries arising out of, or incident to, their service. *Feres* is discussed below in the context of a case dealing primarily with vicarious liability. *See* Taber v. Maine *infra*, Chapter 8.

7. *Personal Immunity of Government Employees.* In contrast to private employees, federal employees have been exempted by a statute known as the Westfall Act from being held individually liable for torts committed in the scope of their employment. 28 U.S.C. § 2679(b). Many states have enacted similar legislation for state employees. Thus, a person injured by the tortious conduct of a government employee acting within the scope of her employment ordinarily *cannot* recover from the employee, but at most may recover only from the government as employer. In this respect, government employees are at least nominally better off than private sector employees, who enjoy no such *de jure* immunity.

The grant of individual immunity contained in the Westfall Act and its state counterparts, when combined with the remaining pockets of sovereign immunity still recognized under the FTCA and its state equivalents, entail that some persons tortiously injured by government employees will be unable to recover any compensation through the tort system for their injuries either from the individual tortfeasor or the government. Victims placed in such a bind have challenged the federal statute granting individual immunity on constitutional grounds, but these challenges have failed. *See, e.g.,* Carr v. United States, 422 F.2d 1007 (4th Cir. 1970).

Recall from Chapter 6 that, under the *Bivens* decision, individuals sometimes are empowered by the U.S. Constitution to sue individual federal officers for violating certain constitutional rights. In keeping with *Bivens*, the Westfall Act contains an exception that permits the imposition of individual liability for violations of constitutional rights, whether cognizable under *Bivens* or by means of a statutory cause of action. 28 U.S.C. § 2679(b)(2)(A).

8. *State and Local Governments.* As indicated in *Riss*, the New York legislature, like Congress, abolished sovereign immunity at the state level. Most states have followed the same course, although the state statutes differ considerably in their particulars. To the extent generalization is possible, one may say that the state schemes tend to resemble the regime applicable to the federal government under the FTCA. Under the common law, city and local governments did not enjoy sovereign immunity simply because they were not deemed sovereign entities. However, courts tended to exempt them from liability for *governmental* activities — such as the provision of a police force or a fire department — as opposed to *proprietary* activities — such as the operation of a local utility. In many states, municipal and local government liability rules have also been modified by statute.

9. *The Public Duty Rule. Riss* provides an application of what has come to be known as the *public duty rule*. Nominally, this rule does not create an immunity defense, but instead provides a rule affecting the ability of the plaintiff to establish the duty element of her prima facie case. Compare the duty-based exemption granted in *Riss* to the exemption granted to Con Edison by the same court in Strauss v. Belle Realty, *supra*, Chapter 2. Is either of these best understood as a genuine "no duty" opinion? Does either deny that the actor in question was obligated to persons such as the plaintiff to be vigilant of the harm that befell the plaintiff?

Typically, the public duty rule comes up in cases in which the allegation is that a local government entity has acted carelessly in failing to perform, or in performing, an affirmative duty. For example, a plaintiff might sue on a claim that a local government failed to enforce its own building codes, resulting in a dangerous condition that injured the plaintiff. Or a plaintiff whose house has burned down might sue the fire department on the theory that its personnel needlessly delayed in responding, or went about fighting the fire in a careless manner. Or a plaintiff who is attacked by a parolee might sue a local parole board on the theory that they mistakenly released the wrong parolee. When they invoke the public duty rule, courts deny liability on the ground that, although government owes certain duties to the public at large, it does not owe those duties to any individual member of the public. Thus, no individual has "standing" to sue for damages caused by the breach of such a duty. What is the best justification for such a rule? Is it convincing?

For an opposite approach to the one adopted in *Riss*, see Torres v. State, 894 P.2d 386 (1995). There, New Mexico police allegedly were careless in not promptly arresting the prime suspect in a triple murder, as a result of which the suspect was able to travel to Los Angeles, where he murdered plaintiffs' decedents. The New Mexico Supreme Court held that "duty" was no obstacle to the plaintiffs' wrongful death claims given that it was foreseeable that, by carelessly permitting the murder suspect to leave town, the police might endanger the lives of others far away. The court remanded the case for a jury to resolve the issues of breach and causation, and, if necessary, to allocate responsibility as between the police and the suspect.

10. *Exceptions to the Public Duty Rule.* Courts have recognized various exceptions to the public duty rule. To a certain extent, these exceptions track the exceptions to the common law rules on special duties to rescue. Thus, some courts will look to see if government actors made a particular undertaking to the plaintiff (i.e., volunteered to assist her), or if they and the plaintiff interacted in a manner that created a "special relationship" between them. Why was the *Riss* majority convinced that, as a matter of law, Linda Riss could not establish the existence of a special relationship between her and New York City police?

The New York court reaffirmed and arguably extended *Riss* in Kircher v. City of Jamestown, 543 N.E.2d 443 (1981). There, plaintiff was abducted in her own car in front of eyewitnesses who gave chase, then came upon a police officer to whom they described the incident as well as the car (including its license plate number). The officer told the witnesses that he would report the incident, but never did. Plaintiff was brutalized by her kidnapper before later being discovered locked in the trunk of the car. In denying plaintiff a cause of action against the city, the court held that such a claimant could only establish the requisite duty if there were a special relationship between her and police, and that a special relationship requires:

(1) an assumption by the municipality, through promises or actions, of an affirmative duty to act on behalf of the party who was injured; (2) knowledge on the part of the municipality's agents that inaction could lead to harm; (3) some form of direct contact between the municipality's agents and the injured party; and (4) that party's justifiable reliance on the municipality's affirmative undertaking.

Id. at 446.

REFERENCES/FURTHER READING

Comparative Fault

Ellen M. Bublick, *Comparative Fault to the Limits,* 56 Vand. L. Rev. 977 (2003).

Gail D. Hollister, *Using Comparative Fault to Replace the All-or-Nothing Lottery Imposed on Intentional Tort Suits in Which Both Plaintiff and Defendant Are at Fault*, 46 Vand. L. Rev. 121 (1993).

Jordan H. Leibman, et al., *The Effect of Lifting the Blindfold from Civil Juries Charged with Apportioning Damages in Modified Comparative Fault Cases: An Empirical Study of the Alternatives*, 35 Am. Bus. L.J. 349 (1998).

Wex S. Malone, *The Formative Era of Contributory Negligence*, 41 Ill. L. Rev. 151 (1946).

William L. Prosser, *Comparative Negligence*, 41 Cal. L. Rev. 1 (1953).

Gary T. Schwartz, *Contributory and Comparative Negligence: A Reappraisal*, 87 Yale L.J. 697 (1978).

Assumption of Risk

John L. Diamond, *Assumption of Risk after Comparative Negligence: Integrating Contract Theory into Tort Doctrine*, 52 Ohio St. L.J. 717 (1991).

Kenneth W. Simons, Murphy v. Steeplechase Amusement Co.: *While the Timorous May Stay at Home, The Adventurous Ride the Flopper*, in Robert L. Rabin & Stephen D. Sugarman (eds.), *Tort Stories* 179 (2003).

Kenneth W. Simons, *Reflections on Assumption of Risk*, 50 U.C.L.A. L. Rev. 481 (2002).

Stephen D. Sugarman, *Assumption of Risk*, 31 Val. U. L. Rev. 833 (1997).

Immunities

Erwin Chemerinsky, *Against Sovereign Immunity*, 53 Stan. L. Rev. 1201 (2001).

Joseph W. Glannon, *Liability for "Public Duties" under the Tort Claims Act: The Legislature Reconsiders the Public Duty Rule*, 79 Mass. L. Rev. 17 (1994).

Carl Tobias, *The Imminent Demise of Interspousal Tort Immunity*, 60 Mont. L. Rev. 101 (1999).

Jennifer Wriggins, *Interspousal Tort Immunity and Insurance "Family Member Exclusions": Shared Assumptions, Relational and Liberal Feminist Challenges*, 17 Wis. Women's L.J. 251 (2002).

Donald N. Zillman, *Protecting Discretion: Judicial Interpretation of the Discretionary Function Exception to the Federal Tort Claims Act*, 47 Me. L. Rev. 365 (1995).

CHAPTER 8

Damages and Apportionment

Negligence law affords redress to a victim who has been injured by careless conduct that constitutes a wrong to him. In this chapter, we analyze the standard form of tort redress: payment of money damages by the tortfeasor to the victim. In Section I, we consider the legal rules that specify the types and amount of damages a tort plaintiff stands to recover. We then examine in Sections II-IV the extent to which actors other than the individual tortfeasor — including his employer, co-defendant(s), and liability insurer — may be required to pay those damages. The chapter concludes with a brief note on problems successful tort plaintiffs may face in enforcing judgments in their favor. Throughout, the focus remains on negligence, although much of the discussion applies to other torts as well.

I. ELEMENTS AND AVAILABILITY OF DAMAGES

A. *Compensatory Damages*

Smith v. Leech Brain & Co. Ltd.
2 Q.B. 405 (1962)

[William Smith was employed by the defendants at their iron works, which produced "galvanized" articles. The galvanizing process involved dipping items into a large tank filled with extremely hot molten metal. Larger articles were lowered into the tank by means of an overhead crane. The tank was circled by a low brick wall that ran around its circumference about two feet outside the tank's rim. The controls for the crane were located about one foot past this wall.

The location of the controls posed a danger to crane operators, because when items were dipped into the tank, drops of molten metal sometimes spattered out of the tank. To protect operators, the defendants provided a 6.5 × 3-foot sheet of corrugated iron, which was bent over at the top to form a partial roof. Because an operator had to use his hands to manipulate the crane controls, he would deploy this makeshift shield by turning his back to the tank and "sandwiching" the sheet of corrugated iron between his back and the outer side of the low brick wall. Once in this position, the operator would then reach up and operate the crane controls. Because, under this arrangement, the operator's back was to the tank, he could not view the dipping process. Instead, he relied on signals from another employee, standing further away from the boiling metal, who had a view of the tank.

On August 15, 1950, at 1 A.M., Smith was operating the overhead crane and dipping a large article when either he turned around to see what he was doing, or leaned out to look at the man who was giving him instructions, and so inadvertently situated his head outside the shield. As a result, he sustained a burn on his lip from a spattering of molten metal. The wound never healed. In fact, Smith developed cancer at the point of the wound, which caused his death.

Smith's widow brought this negligence action, England not having adopted a comprehensive workers' compensation scheme.—EDS.] . . .

Lord Parker C.J.   . . . On the issue of [fault] I am satisfied that there was a clear and known danger of molten metal flying from the tank when articles were being lowered into it. . . . The dangerous process of lowering was done by remote control, and all that the operator had was the make-shift bit of corrugated iron which was put up and held by the operator himself by leaning against it. Of course, it is only right to say that so long as he stayed behind that shield, it was an adequate protection. But any reasonable employer must reasonably foresee that, men being what they are, the most natural thing in the world is that sooner or later the man will look round. Indeed, the evidence before me is that that is just what was done.

Added to that, in 1950 many galvanisers throughout the country . . . were providing what the defendants, when they altered their works in 1955, provided, namely, a proper shelter akin to a signal box with a window in front whereby the operator could watch what he was doing, and where he was really in complete safety and had no reason to put his head out. . . .

[Judge Parker then rejected the contention that Smith was contributorily negligent.]

The next question is whether the cancer which the plaintiff's husband had admittedly got, and the death resulting from it, were caused in whole or in part by the burn. The burn was treated at the time with picric acid and probably gauze was put on it. He did not get to hospital for a long time — he thought nothing of it. . . . But ultimately it did not heal, the place where the burn had been began to ulcerate and get larger, and he went to his general practitioner. The general practitioner without a doubt felt that he had epithelioma, a form of cancer on the lower lip. He was sent at once to hospital. This cancer was at once diagnosed, and thereafter he was in and out of hospital, having, first, treatment with radium needles which enable the lip to heal and destroy the primary growth. But even when he got to hospital it was noticed that his glands were swelling, and while no great significance was attached to that in the first instance, it became perfectly clear later that secondary growths were taking place. Thereafter, he had a series of operations, some six or seven, and finally he died in October, 1953.

[Judge Parker then reviewed the evidence on actual causation provided by experts at trial. He concluded that it supported the conclusion that the burn was probably a but-for cause of the cancer.]

The third question is damages. Here I am confronted with the recent decision of the Privy Council in [*Wagon Mound (No. 1)*]. But for that case, it seems to me perfectly clear that, assuming negligence proved, and assuming that the burn caused in whole or in part the cancer and the death, the plaintiff would be entitled to recover. . . .

For my part, I am quite satisfied that the [Privy Council's] Judicial Committee in the *Wagon Mound* case did not have what I may call, loosely, the thin skull cases in mind. It has always been the law of this country that a tortfeasor takes his victim as he finds him. It is unnecessary to do more than refer to the short passage in the decision of Kennedy J. in Dulieu v. White & Sons, where he said: "If a man is negligently run over or otherwise negligently injured in his body, it is no answer to the sufferer's claim for damages that he would have suffered less injury, or no injury at all, if he had not had an unusually thin skull or an unusually weak heart." [[1901] 2 K.B. 669, 679.]

. . . [A]s is well known, the work of the courts for years and years has gone on on that basis. There is not a day that goes by where some trial judge does not adopt that principle, that the tortfeasor takes his victim as he finds him. If the Judicial Committee had any intention of making an inroad into that doctrine, I am quite satisfied that they would have said so.

. . . [In distinguishing] Smith v. London & South Western Railway Company[,] [(1870) L.R. 6 C.P. 14.][,] Lord Simonds[' *Wagon Mound (No. 1)* opinion] . . . said: ". . . that the point to which the [*Smith*] court directed its mind was not unforeseeable damage of a different kind from that which was foreseen, but more extensive damage of the same kind." [[1961] A.C. 388, 416.] In other words, Lord Simonds is clearly there drawing a distinction between the question whether a man could reasonably anticipate a type of injury, and the question whether a man could reasonably anticipate the extent of injury of the type which could be foreseen.

The Judicial Committee were, I think, disagreeing with the decision in the *Polemis* case that a man is no longer liable for the type of damage which he could not reasonably anticipate. The Judicial Committee were not, I think, saying that a man is only liable for the extent of damage which he could anticipate, always assuming the type of injury could have been anticipated. . . .

In those circumstances, it seems to me that this is plainly a case which comes within the old principle. The test is not whether these employers could reasonably have foreseen that a burn would cause cancer and that he would die. The question is whether these employers could reasonably foresee the type of injury he suffered, namely, the burn. What, in the particular case, is the amount of damage which he suffers as a result of that burn, depends upon the characteristics and constitution of the victim.

[Judge Parker then considered the question of damages and concluded that they ought to reflect that the decedent might have developed cancer even if he had not suffered the burn. He awarded the plaintiff £3,064.]

NOTES AND QUESTIONS

1. *The Eggshell Skull Rule. Smith* provides a clear statement of the so-called eggshell (or thin) skull rule, which is also expressed in the maxim

that "the tortfeasor takes his victim as he finds him." The idea is that, having wronged and injured another, a tortfeasor cannot be heard to complain that the *amount* of damage caused to that other was much greater than anyone could reasonably have expected because of a hidden physical vulnerability in the plaintiff.

2. Wagon Mound *and Proximate Cause Revisited.*   Recall the holding of the Australian Privy Council's decision in *Wagon Mound (No. 1)*, discussed in Chapter 5. It denied recovery to a dock owner whose dock was destroyed by a fire that resulted from defendant shipowner's careless creation of an oil slick. This holding in turn rested on the conclusion that the ignition of the oil slick was not reasonably foreseeable. Yet the shipowner's carelessness apparently did cause *some* foreseeable damage to the dock—it mucked it up with oil. Still, the Privy Council declined to impose liability for the unforeseeable fire-damage harm based on the foreseeability of the mucking harm. On this point, Lord Simonds reasoned as follows:

> It is not the act but the consequences on which tortious liability is founded. Just as (as it has been said) there is no such thing as negligence in the air, so there is no such thing as liability in the air. Suppose an action brought by A for damage caused by the carelessness (a neutral word) of B, for example, a fire caused by the careless spillage of oil. It may, of course, become relevant to know what duty B owed to A, but the only liability that is in question is the liability for damage by fire. It is vain to isolate the liability from its context and to say that B is or is not liable, and then to ask for what damage he is liable. For his liability is in respect of that damage and no other. If, as admittedly it is, B's liability (culpability) depends on the reasonable foreseeability of the consequent damage, how is that to be determined except by the foreseeability of the damage which in fact happened—the damage in suit? And, if that damage is unforeseeable so as to displace liability at large, how can the liability be restored so as to make compensation payable?
>
> But, it is said, a different position arises if B's careless act has been shown to be negligent and has caused some foreseeable damage to A. Their Lordships have already observed that to hold B liable for consequences however unforeseeable of a careless act, if, but only if, he is at the same time liable for some other damage however trivial, appears to be neither logical nor just. This becomes more clear if it is supposed that similar unforeseeable damage is suffered by A and C but other foreseeable damage, for which B is liable, by A only. A system of law which would hold B liable to A but not to C for the similar damage suffered by each of them could not easily be defended. Fortunately, the attempt is not necessary. For the same fallacy is at the root of the proposition. It is irrelevant to the question whether B is liable for unforeseeable damage that he is liable for foreseeable damage, as irrelevant as would the fact that he had trespassed on Whiteacre be to the question whether he has trespassed on Blackacre. Again, suppose a claim by A for damage by fire by the careless act of B. Of what relevance is it to that claim that he has another claim arising out of the same careless act? It would surely not prejudice his claim if that other claim failed: it cannot assist it if it succeeds. Each of them rests on its own bottom, and will fail if it can be established that the damage could not reasonably be foreseen.

Overseas Tankship (U.K.) Ltd. v. The Miller Steamship Co., [1961] A.C. 388, at 425-426.

Given the foregoing analysis, is *Smith* right to conclude that the eggshell skull rule is consistent with the holding of *Wagon Mound No. 1?* Lord Simonds' opinion defends *Wagon Mound No. 1*'s foreseeable-type-of-harm test for proximate cause on the ground that a contrary rule, which would hold a careless actor responsible for an unforeseeable type of harm, would be profoundly unfair. If so, how can it be fair to saddle a defendant with unforeseeably large damages resulting from the realization of a risk of a foreseeable type of harm? Is the eggshell skull rule consistent with a scope-of-the-risk conception of proximate cause? The drafters of the Third Restatement believe so. *See* Restatement (Third) of Torts: Physical Harm (General Principles) §§ 29, 31 (Tentative Draft No. 3, Apr. 7, 2003) (adopting a scope-of-the-risk conception of proximate cause and the eggshell skull rule).

3. *Eggshell Stuff?* Suppose one were to grant the propriety of the eggshell skull rule as applied to personal injuries. Should it also apply to property damage? Suppose *O* owns a detached garage that contains a hidden structural defect. *D*, driving at a very low speed in *O*'s driveway, fails properly to brake his car and bumps into a corner of the garage, an impact that normally could be expected to leave a small scratch or divot in the structure. Because of the defect, the garage collapses. Should *D* be liable for the value of the entire garage?

4. *Other Sources of Unexpectedly Severe Injuries.* As noted, the eggshell skull rule is formulated to impose liability for foreseeable types of harm whose magnitude is unforeseeable *because of a hidden vulnerability in the plaintiff.* Should the same rule apply when the unforeseeability of the magnitude of harm derives from some other source? In some instances, at least, the black-letter answer appears to be yes. Thus, if motorist *M* carelessly runs down and kills pedestrian *P*, and *P* happens to be the CEO of a hugely successful company, *M* stands to pay much more in compensation for lost income to *P*'s survivors than one would expect to pay based on the incomes of ordinary or average pedestrians. Alternatively, suppose *M* carelessly crashes into the back of another car, owned by *C*. In doing so, *C* destroys a painting in the trunk of *C*'s car that *C* had just purchased at a flea market and was taking to an appraiser. Although *C* did not know it at the time of purchase, the painting turns out to be a Van Gogh that was worth tens of millions before being destroyed. Again, as a matter of black-letter law, *M* would appear to be on the hook for this surprisingly expensive car accident. Would it make a difference if *C* knew that he had a Van Gogh in his trunk?

5. *Permissive or Mandatory?* At a minimum, the eggshell skull rule prohibits the defendant from arguing that the jury is barred from awarding compensation for the unforeseeable portion of plaintiff's damages. This prohibition is in keeping with the wide discretion traditionally granted jurors in setting compensatory awards. Does the eggshell skull rule further entail that the jury *must* award compensation for the unforeseeable

damages suffered by the plaintiff, or does it merely *permit* them to do so if they believe the equities warrant such an award? Consider the award granted by the judge in *Smith*. (Recall that the judge is here playing the role of the jury because English law abolished jury trials for this sort of tort claim.) Does it suggest that the judge felt obligated to compensate the plaintiff for the full value of his losses, or did the judge feel that it was within his discretion to adjust the award downward from full compensation? Jury instructions on the rule vary as to whether they employ permissive or mandatory language. *Compare* Schafer v. Hoffman, 831 P.2d 897 (Colo. 1992) (approving instruction that jurors "*may not* . . . reduce the amount of any . . . damages because of any physical frailties of the plaintiff") *with* Aflague v. Luger, 589 N.W.2d 177 (Neb. App. 1999) (defendant "*may*" be liable for all compensatory damages even though the plaintiff's injury is greater than expected due to the plaintiff's vulnerability).

6. *Vosburg v. Putney*. A famous American decision applying the eggshell skull rule involves intentional rather than careless wrongdoing. In Vosburg v. Putney, 50 N.W. 403 (Wis. 1891), a 12-year-old boy purposely kicked a 14-year-old boy in the shin as they sat in class. The recipient of the kick was lamed. At trial, an expert testified that, at the time of the kick, the victim was recovering from an infection in that leg and that the kick worsened his condition, thereby contributing to the lameness. The jury returned a verdict for the plaintiff. Although the Wisconsin Supreme Court remanded the case for a new trial on other grounds, it held that the defendant could be held liable for the full extent of the injury, notwithstanding its unforeseeability. Should the extent of liability vary in accordance with the egregiousness of the wrongdoing? Which is a worse wrong: a purposeful kick in the shin or a careless failure to provide protection against burns by molten metal?

7. *Mitigation of Damages*. Recall Walter v. Wal-Mart from Chapter 1. There, the trial court refused to let the defendant argue that Ms. Walter, the pharmacy patient, was comparatively at fault for failing to detect that she had been given the wrong medicine by Wal-Mart. However, the court also instructed the jury that it could reduce her award on the ground that, by waiting a certain period of time before notifying her treating physician of her symptoms, she permitted the harmful side effects of the medicine to become worse than they would have had she been reasonably attentive to her condition. The notion that a plaintiff may sometimes bear responsibility for the magnitude of her damages — as opposed to the causing of the accident or the injury itself — is sometimes phrased in terms of a plaintiff's "duty" to mitigate damages. Perhaps it would be more accurate to say that a defendant who is liable in negligence may argue that he is not responsible to compensate for certain damages flowing from that negligence on the ground that the plaintiff could have avoided them, but chose not to.

The classic example is that of plaintiff *P* who, for no reason, refuses to obtain post-accident medical treatment, as a result of which his injuries are exacerbated. This rule of avoidable consequences applies only to *unreasonable* failures to mitigate. Were *P* to argue, and were the factfinder to determine, that he failed to pursue medical treatment because he was deeply depressed as a result of the accident, *D* presumably should not benefit from the mitigation rule. The same would hold true if *P* refused treatment out of sincerely held and "reasonable" religious beliefs. *See* Munn v. Algee, 924 F.2d 568 (5th Cir. 1991).

8. *Pre-Accident Mitigation*. Recall the *Spier* case, discussed in Chapter 7 in connection with comparative responsibility and causation. There, the plaintiff's failure to wear her seat belt was deemed not to be contributory negligence, but was deemed a potential failure to mitigate. *Spier* is a somewhat unusual application of the avoidable consequences rule, in that the plaintiff's unreasonable failure, if any, occurred prior to the accident, as contrasted to a post-accident failure to seek treatment. Should that difference matter? What sort of pre-accident failures to take precautions against injury should count? As noted in Chapter 7, some courts have deemed evidence of the plaintiff's failure to wear a seat belt inadmissible with respect to damages. Professor Dobbs notes the same split over whether to admit evidence that an injured bicyclist was not wearing a helmet. Dan B. Dobbs, *The Law of Torts* § 205, at 514-516 (2000).

Kenton v. Hyatt Hotels Corp.
693 S.W.2d 83 (Mo. 1985)

[On July 17, 1981, two skywalks located in the lobby of the Hyatt Regency Hotel in Kansas City, Missouri, collapsed onto the hotel's crowded lobby floor. The skywalks were constructed of concrete, steel, glass, and other materials and weighed, in the aggregate, more than 15 tons. Numerous victims and their family members sued various defendants, including Hyatt. A partial settlement was reached whereby the settling defendants (again including Hyatt) agreed to stipulate to liability at the outset of each settling victim's trial, thereby leaving the jury to decide only the issue of damages. In exchange for this stipulation, the settling victims agreed not to present evidence bearing on how the defendants conducted themselves in constructing and maintaining the skywalks. They also agreed to a cap on the total amount of punitive damages available to them.*

Plaintiff-respondent Kay Kenton was one of the victims of the Hyatt disaster. The trial of her claim resulted in a jury award of $4 million in compensatory damages. Defendant-appellants filed post-verdict motions seeking a new trial on the ground that the jury's award was excessive. The trial judge concluded that the verdict was excessive and entered an order sustaining a motion for a new trial unless the plaintiff filed a remittitur of $250,000.** Plaintiff-respondent accepted the remittitur. Both sides appealed. — EDS.]

---

* The effect of the settlement achieved by Hyatt was thus comparable to the effect of the trial judge's ruling in *Walter v. Wal-Mart* (see Chapter 1) that Walter had made out a prima facie case of negligence as a matter of law.

** Remittitur is a procedural device that can be invoked by trial judges in response to a defendant's motion for a new trial. Specifically, if the judge concludes that the jury's

The Court of Appeals . . . affirmed the judgment in all particulars but declined to restore the remittitur ordered by the trial court and transferred the case to this court. . . . We affirm the judgment of the trial court, in all respects, except remittitur; we reverse that part of the trial court's order . . . , and, under the principles of the companion case decided this date, Firestone v. Crown Center Redevelopment Corporation, 693 S.W.2d 99 (1985), remand the cause with directions to . . . reinstate the verdict and enter judgment for plaintiff for the verdict sum of $4,000,000. . . .

I

Appellants' first point is that the trial court erred in admitting evidence concerning events at the hotel on July 17, 1981. They contend: "Such evidence was not relevant to any issue relating to respondent's damages, because appellants admitted that respondent's injuries were caused by the accident. Because the evidence was inflammatory and prejudicial to appellants the jury's verdict was based upon improper passion and prejudice and was greatly enhanced." . . .*

[Two witnesses, a fire captain who responded to the disaster, and a TV reporter who happened to be at the hotel to videotape an event there, were permitted by the trial court to testify to the chaos and devastation that followed the collapse. In addition, the trial court let into evidence small portions of videotape taken at the scene, although certain gruesome parts were edited out.]

Respondent's sister, Ann Kenton, who was with her on the evening of the disaster, testified as to her observations of that occurrence. . . . Ann described the sounds she heard coming from people in and around the skywalks after the collapse: "A. It was hysterical, hysteria. There were grown men crying for help and there was nothing I could do for them. There were people crushed everywhere, blood, and I looked in the area where she had been and there was rubble and bodies and I couldn't pick her out of the bodies. And the moans and screams." Ann later found respondent slumped in a chair to the west of the skywalks, and respondent was carried outside and placed on a gurney or a stretcher.

Still photographs of the scene were admitted into evidence, some in color and some in black and white. Ann Kenton identified Exhibit 4K as the area where respondent had been and described it thus: "A. There were people sticking halfway out from under the skywalk, from here up there were grown men screaming for help, moaning and I walked through the

---

award was excessive in light of the evidence of damages presented at trial, she is empowered to grant plaintiff the option of accepting a lower award — that is, *remitting* a specified portion of the damages found by the jury — instead of re-trying the entire case. Without remittitur, the court would, upon a finding of excessiveness, order a new trial of the entire case.

* [In all likelihood, the defendants had stipulated to liability to avoid having the jury consider the gruesome evidence on causation, as well as the evidence as to their carelessness. Obviously, the defendants had hoped that this stipulation would change the tenor of the trial in ways favorable to them. — EDS.]

blood, or there was blood everywhere. And the rescue people were pulling out whoever was more alive than others, I suppose." None of the admitted photographs show any dead or injured persons.

. . . Appellants argue that the testimony concerning the events of July 17, 1981, was neither probative nor material to the issue of respondent's compensation; it was an attempt to incite the jury with evidence of how she was injured; and that the "slight probative value the testimony may have had concerning the nature of Ms. Kenton's injuries was outweighed completely by the gruesome and highly inflammatory nature of the evidence."

. . . Respondent says that . . . the evidence was not offered or received as bearing on appellants' conduct which was not an issue, but was offered instead for the purpose of showing how respondent was injured, both physically and mentally, as well as her location at the time her injuries were sustained. Begley v. Adaber Realty & Investment Company, 358 S.W.2d 785, 792 (Mo. 1962), held that photographs of ductwork which fell upon plaintiff, taken after it had fallen and had been removed to a parking lot, was admissible to show the type of construction, the presence or absence of straps, and what type of object struck plaintiff. Respondent was similarly entitled to show the force, violence and traumatic circumstances of this tragic occurrence as bearing upon the nature, extent and duration of her injuries. Compare Berry v. Harmon, 329 S.W.2d 784, 794 (Mo. 1959) [reversed and remanded on other grounds], where a photograph vividly showing the damaged interior of the automobile evidencing a terrific impact and showing blood stains on the car top was offered to show the force of the impact, a basis for plaintiff's injuries, and the place where the heads of the occupants were wedged after the evidence was held properly admitted as not being so inflammatory as to indicate any abuse of the court's discretion. . . . Even though photographs are gruesome and depict serious injuries they need not be excluded if they satisfy the rules as to the admission of demonstrative evidence. Chism v. Cowan, 425 S.W.2d 942, 947 (Mo. 1967). . . .

The evidence of respondent's injuries is that she suffered a cervical fracture which produced an initial paralysis of her body. In addition, Dr. Walter Menninger stated that she was subjected to the most severe psychosocial stressor imaginable, Grade 7, and the traumatic event and the crippling effects it produced caused a dramatic and profound psychic trauma which is continuing in nature. Dr. Francisco Gomez, respondent's treating psychiatrist, and Dr. Menninger classified her psychiatric injury as post-traumatic stress disorder, chronic and severe. Dr. Menninger testified further that she exhibited symptoms characteristic of a post-traumatic stress disorder: re-experiencing the trauma by either recurrent recollections, recurrent dreams, or suddenly acting or feeling as if the event was happening; and a numbing of responsiveness or reduced involvement with the external world sometime afterward. Certainly, the jury was entitled to consider the evidence of the scene of the collapse, the utter chaos that prevailed, and the effect upon respondent of being pinned beneath the debris, amidst blood, dead and injured bodies, and the sheer terror of the voices around her, in evaluating her physical and mental injuries for the purpose of fixing her compensation. The evidence was relevant, material, and appropriate. Its probative value far outweighed any prejudicial effect it might have had on the jury. There was no error in admitting the evidence, and Point I is overruled. . . .

III

[Respondent had completed two years of law school at the time of the accident.] In Point III, appellants contend . . . that the trial court erred in refusing to exclude the testimony of two law school professors that respondent was unable to return to law school or to practice law. . . . Appellants conclude that because of these (claimed) errors the jury considered evidence incompetent in itself and as foundation for economic projections of respondent's future wage loss, and the award was greatly and improperly enhanced by the use of this evidence.

[The professors testified to the rigors of law school, stating, among other things, that law students devote 48 hours per week to preparation for class. One also opined that, in light of respondent's medical records and condition, she could not function as a law student. The second professor testified that respondent perhaps could return as a part-time student. She also stated that, while respondent might be able to practice law part-time after graduation, she was unaware of any part-time positions in the field of law. — EDS.] . . .

[A lawyer who suffered substantial disabilities from polio testified for the appellants. He opined that, with accommodations, respondent could finish law school and practice law. He conceded on cross-examination that respondent's disabilities would narrow her job opportunities. — EDS.]

The trial court properly determined that expert testimony was needed to inform the jury as to the physical and mental rigors of a person attending law school and practicing law. Members of the jury would not ordinarily have knowledge of that subject, and certainly the two professors, being actively engaged in that field would have superior knowledge and expertise thereof by reason of their education and experience. . . .

In addition to stating their knowledge and experience in the practice of law, and in teaching law school courses, both professors reviewed respondent's academic records, medical records, and reports which were in evidence without objection. [One of the professors] had also personally met and interviewed respondent. There was thus a sufficient factual basis for them to give their opinions. They were not . . . giving medical opinions. . . .

This case falls within the category of those allowing the opinion testimony of a non-medical expert witness on the employability of handicapped persons. Such a case is Chrisler v. Holiday Valley, Inc., 580 S.W.2d 309 (Mo. App. 1979), where a diving accident left plaintiff a quadriplegic, with bowel incontinence, sexual disfunction, and a reliance upon assistance to handle almost any activity or function except eating. Medical evidence established the conditions as permanent. The testimony of an employment counsellor, whose job it was to find employment for hard-to-place persons, including those with handicaps, to the effect that plaintiff was permanently unemployable, was held not to have been error. Defendant sought to strike her testimony on the basis that she was not an expert on para- and quadriplegics. The court said, "This misconceives the nature of Mrs. Maly's expertise. She was an expert on employment opportunities, particularly those for hard-to-place people including those with handicaps. It was about those opportunities that she was testifying and she was aware of the requirements for a vast number of jobs. Her slight experience with para- and quadriplegics did not affect her expertise on employment opportunities. . . ." *Chrisler, supra,* at 313. . . .

Appellants also say that the testimony of the two professors permitted respondent's economist, Dr. Ward, to base his opinion as to her projection of economic losses on incompetent evidence. The answer is found in the *Chrisler* case, *supra,* page 313[4], where the court found no error in the economists' expert testimony as based upon the expert testimony of the employment counselor. The jury had the function of evaluating all the evidence of economic loss, both appellants' and respondent's, and the weight to be given thereto. . . .

VI

Appellants' Point VI contends that the trial court erred in refusing to grant a remittitur of $2,000,000. They contend that as a matter of law the jury's verdict greatly exceeded the upper limits of "fair and reasonable compensation," the proper measure of damages, and that the verdict was, as the trial court itself recognized, the erroneous product of a mistaken evaluation of highly incendiary evidence and [was] improperly disproportionate to awards for comparable or more severe injuries.

Taking respondent's evidence in the light most favorable to her, as this court must do, her loss of income and the reasonably anticipated future loss of income because of the injuries sustained was testified to . . . have been between $1,605,846 as a low, to a high of $2,164,642.

The evidence shows that, to the time of trial, respondent's hospital, medical and therapy expenses incurred amounted to at least $80,000; her future physical therapy and cost of an electronic device (T.E.N.S.) was from $189,759 to $250,000; her homemaking assistance and care, $307,228 to $614,457; her future medical and supplemental insurance, $100,679. This evidence places the low of these items at $677,666, and the high at $1,045,136.

The economic loss, present and future medical, and therapy expenses thus shows a range of between $2,283,512 to $3,209,778.

Respondent's age was 28 years at the time of trial. She has a life expectancy of 51.8 years.

The nature and extent of respondent's injuries, is shown by the following evidence, all shown to have been permanent. She suffered a broken neck with permanent spinal cord damage [with miraculous surgical treatment, she avoided becoming a permanent quadriplegic]; she has spasticity and weakness in all four limbs, inability to walk without crutches, and must wear a knee cage to prevent buckling of the left knee; lack of endurance and easy fatigability; reduced vital capacity and impaired breathing muscles; sensory loss of much of her body below her neck, including female parts. She will not enjoy a normal sexual life or have children normally; she has impaired bladder and bowel function with periods of incontinence. Her bladder condition causes her to retain urine which will eventually produce renal or kidney damage; psychic and emotional trauma diagnosed as chronic and severe post-traumatic stress syndrome, which will require continued psychiatric care; destruction of her athletic lifestyle which will prevent her from ever again playing tennis, skiing, running, jogging, playing softball, raquetball, hiking, backpacking and riding horses; and a commitment to 2 to 4 hours a day to maintain her present limited muscle function.

There was some evidence that respondent's cost of therapy and the T.E.N.S. unit would increase over her lifetime, and her income would also increase should she be employed as a lawyer, these being the effects of inflation.

The jury was entitled to consider the intangibles of the evidence of respondent's past and future pain and suffering, the destruction of her previous lifestyle, along with the evidence of economic loss. All of the matters going to the nature and extent of respondent's injuries were primarily for the jury's consideration because it is in a far better position to appraise them for the assessment of damages which would fairly and reasonably compensate her. . . . In Fowler v. Park Corporation, 673 S.W.2d 749, 758 (Mo. banc 1984), the plaintiff suffered the loss of both legs above the knees. He was 19 years old, with a life expectancy of 50 years. He had not successfully used prosthetic devices; he would need constant care and medical attention, and had doubtful employability. He did not introduce evidence of economic damage other than showing that he stood to lose one million dollars in earnings based upon present wage levels, and the court said that he would obviously be incapable of leading a normal social life. The jury awarded $6 million to Fowler for his damages, and this court declined to interfere with the amount of the verdict.

Appellants cite Chrisler v. Holiday Valley, Inc., 580 S.W.2d 309, 312 (Mo. App. 1979), wherein the plaintiff, 17 years old, was rendered a quadriplegic by reason of a diving accident, and the jury returned a verdict of $2.3 million, which was affirmed. That case does not aid appellants. There was apparently no evidence of economic loss by the plaintiff, but importantly, the court said:

> In most litigation, and particularly in personal injury actions, there is a large range between the damage extremes of inadequacy and excessiveness. Within that range a jury has virtually unfettered discretion to determine the damages incurred and is under no obligation to, and is in fact prohibited from, specifying what amounts have been attributed to each of the various elements of damage. Past and future pain and suffering, embarrassment and humiliation, future care and medical treatment, loss of or reduction in employment opportunities and many other factors, do not lend themselves to precise calculation. 580 S.W.2d at 312.

There is no exact formula to determine whether a verdict is excessive; each case is considered on its own facts. The ultimate test is what fairly and reasonably compensates plaintiff for the injuries sustained. In making this determination consideration is given to the nature and extent of the injuries, diminished earning capacity, economic conditions, plaintiff's age, and a comparison of the compensation awarded and permitted in cases of comparable injuries. . . . This case is not out of line with others. . . .

Turning to the merits of this case, we believe that the trial court abused its discretion in ordering a remittitur of $250,000 after a verdict of $4,000,000 under the circumstances of this case. This amount represents a miniscule percentage (6.25%) of the total verdict which demonstrates judicial hairsplitting and shows the extremes to which the remittitur practice has fallen. [Because of outcomes such as these, the court decided to abolish the practice of remittitur in Missouri in the companion case of Firestone v. Crown Center Redevelopment Corporation, 693 S.W.2d 99 (1985). It applied *Firestone*'s holding to this case. — EDS.] . . .

Accordingly, the verdict of the jury is affirmed and the cause is remanded with directions to set aside the order of remittitur and to reinstate the verdict and enter judgment for the plaintiff, Kay Kenton, in the sum of $4,000,000.00.

Welliver, J., dissented.

NOTES AND QUESTIONS

1. *Damage Elements.* As *Kenton* indicates, the specific items for which a negligence plaintiff may claim compensation are numerous. Commentators often divide compensatory damages into two general categories: (1) *economic* or *out-of-pocket* losses (e.g., past and future medical bills, lost earnings, repair costs) and (2) *noneconomic* losses (e.g., pain and suffering experienced as a result of the tort, depression, anxiety, loss of enjoyment of life). As a rule, economic losses are more readily quantifiable than noneconomic losses. This is not always the case, however. For example, when estimating future expenses or lost earnings, the jury is asked to make predictions, based on expert testimony as to how long the plaintiff would have worked and at what rate of compensation. Noneconomic losses, by contrast, are notoriously difficult to quantify, and, as a result, have become a focal point for debates about whether tort law has gone "out of control."

2. *Correcting or Fairly Compensating?* It is common for courts and commentators to describe the aim of a compensatory damage award as that of "making the plaintiff whole" or "restoring the *status quo ante*." The picture evoked by these metaphors is that an award of money will erase the tort by fully compensating the plaintiff for all the harms associated with it. Indeed, an entire school of thought about tort law — corrective justice theory — is built around this metaphor. Following Aristotle's conception, corrective justice scholars argue that tort law is best understood as concerned to take away whatever the tortfeasor has "gained" from committing the tort (in terms of wealth, or the excess liberty he has implicitly claimed for himself) while restoring to the plaintiff whatever she has lost, thereby restoring a preexisting equilibrium.

As applied to payments reimbursing out-of-pocket expenditures, the imagery of correcting or making whole is appropriate enough. But, as to noneconomic losses, it is inapt. To be sure, the payment of money is an appropriate form of redress for these losses, in large part because it is open-ended, permitting the injured victim, as much as is possible, to craft the remedy as he sees fit. Yet few believe that, at least with respect to serious injuries, monetary compensation restores the plaintiff to the life he had prior to the tort. A person who has physical and emotional scars, permanent disabilities, or merely the experience of being the victim of a tort, leads a different life than he would have otherwise.

There is another reason to resist the "make whole" metaphor. Juries are not instructed to award that measure of compensation. Instead, they are typically told to award an amount that they deem *just and reasonable* in light of their findings as to the injuries plaintiff has suffered and will suffer because of the defendant's tortious conduct. While verbal formulations only go so far in channeling discretion, might the decision to frame the jury's assignment as that of awarding just and reasonable damages, rather than make whole damages, affect its calculation?

3. *Lump Sum versus Structured Payments*. Compensatory damages are normally paid out to the successful negligence plaintiff in one lump sum, rather than periodically over time. This practice presents various challenges for the legal system. For example, as demonstrated by *Kenton*, it requires juries to make educated guesses about future lost earnings and future medical expenses without knowing exactly what the plaintiff's job prospects were, how long she will live, or what her actual medical expenses will end up being. If it subsequently turns out that the jury under- or overestimated these items, there is no recourse for plaintiff or defendant.

Another complication stems from the fact that a dollar in hand today is worth more than a dollar obtained one or five years from now, because of the ability to invest and "grow" assets in one's possession. Furthermore, inflation will reduce the value of a dollar over time. At trial juries are often subjected to expert testimony on how the time value of money, as well as inflation, should be taken into account in setting an appropriate award. *See* Dan B. Dobbs, *The Law of Torts* § 1056, at 1057-1058 (2000).

As Professor Pryor has noted, lump sum awards can also present a different sort of problem for plaintiffs. Although large awards such as the one received by Kay Kenton might be entirely appropriate in light of her suffering and the lifetime of difficulties she faces, the fact remains that she and other successful tort plaintiffs receive compensation in the form of a single check worth thousands or millions of dollars. This sudden influx of wealth can complicate relations with family and friends, and present many other practical problems for persons not savvy about managing money.

4. *Workers' Compensation Benefits Compared*. As indicated in earlier chapters, absent intentional wrongdoing on the part of management, workplace injuries are now ordinarily recompensed through workers' compensation systems. These systems vary substantially, but they typically

limit the injured employee's compensation to medical expenses related to treatment of the workplace injury, plus a fixed percentage of lost wages. The amount of compensation is set by legislative or administrative guidelines that are interpreted by officials employed by the system. These officials' decisions are subject to limited judicial review. Intangible elements of damages such as emotional distress are not separately compensable.

A basic distinction drawn by most systems is between temporary disabilities (e.g., a broken leg that completely heals) and permanent disabilities (e.g., loss of a limb). Those who suffer temporary disabilities are usually entitled to reimbursement for medical expenses and a percentage of lost wages for the period of recovery. Permanent disabilities may be treated differently, depending on whether the victim suffers the loss of a discrete body part (e.g., the loss of a finger, or of hearing in one ear) or suffers a permanent injury or condition that affects the worker's general physical abilities (e.g., a back injury that makes all physical movement difficult).

For discrete injuries, most systems award compensation based on a pre-set schedule. These schedules can make for grisly reading. For example, Neb. Rev. Stat. § 48-121(3) specifies in part that workers suffering discrete injuries shall be compensated as follows:

> For the loss of a thumb, sixty-six and two-thirds percent of daily wages during sixty weeks. For the loss of a first finger . . . sixty-six and two-thirds percent of daily wages during thirty-five weeks. . . . For the loss of a hand, sixty-six and two-thirds percent of daily wages during seventy-five weeks. . . . For the loss of the nose, sixty-six and two-thirds percent of daily wages during fifty weeks.

By contrast, when the injury causes the worker to be partially or totally disabled, she can recover a percentage of her lost wages (often two-thirds) for the length of the disability. (Because workers' compensation benefits are paid out sequentially, rather than in a lump sum, there is usually no need to project future lost income, as is the case in the award of tort damages.) However, these recoveries, too, may be subject to certain ceilings. For example, the Nebraska statute specifies a maximum salary for purposes of calculating permanent disabilities: benefits for a worker suffering a permanent disability who was being paid more than the statutory maximum will be calculated at the amount specified by the statute, rather than the worker's actual salary. Nebraska law also limits recovery for permanent partial disabilities to a maximum of 300 weeks' worth of benefits.

If a worker is killed on the job, surviving family members are not automatically qualified for compensation. Rather, they may receive benefits only if they are economic dependents of the deceased (typically a spouse who relied on the worker's income or a minor child). Qualified dependents are usually entitled to regular payments equal to a fixed percentage of the deceased's lost wages until the period of dependency ends (e.g., the death or remarriage of the widowed spouse, or the minor child's reaching the age of majority). Loss of consortium and emotional distress are, again, not compensable. In the absence of any economic dependents, the employer is often liable only for funeral expenses.

5. *Reproducing Inequality?* Experts who testify as to lost future earnings generally rely on statistics as to how much a person with the same education, background, and traits could have expected to earn before and after suffering the injuries in question. This means that two careless drivers, each of whom causes identical injuries to his victim, may end up paying very different damage awards depending on the economic prospects of the victim. For example, if Kay Kenton were not a law student, but a bicycle messenger, her recovery for lost wages would have been substantially smaller. (See the discussion of the compensation issues arising in connection with the 9/11 Fund in Module II.)

To the extent certain groups have been subject to past discrimination in hiring and pay, these statistics reproduce the effects of that discrimination. Thus, for example, if women have historically been paid less for doing equivalent work to men because of discrimination, statistical evidence of what a particular female plaintiff such as Kay Kenton would have earned will reflect that lower rate of pay. Is the use of gender- or race-specific statistics a violation of the Equal Protection Clause of the Fourteenth Amendment? Even if not, should courts attempt to adjust for biases in statistics by, for example, requiring the presentation of data on the future earnings of all workers in a given field, regardless of race, gender, or other characteristics?

6. *Bifurcation.* As *Kenton* demonstrates, witness testimony and other evidence bearing on the nature and severity of the harms suffered by the victim of a tort can be gut-wrenching. For this reason, defendants who, unlike Hyatt, seek to contest liability, often express concern that jurors' judgments as to the issue of liability — that is, whether the defendant committed a tort against the plaintiff — will be inappropriately swayed in favor of the plaintiff because of their visceral responses to such evidence. Federal and state rules of procedure for civil actions typically grant the trial judge broad discretion to bifurcate the trial of a tort action based on her assessment of whether doing so will promote the efficient and fair resolution of the dispute before her. This grant of discretion notwithstanding, many if not most federal and state trial judges probably maintain a presumption against granting bifurcation motions. For an example of a federal district judge granting a defense motion to bifurcate the issues of liability and damages, see Witherbee v. Honeywell, Inc., 151 F.R.D. 27 (N.D.N.Y. 1993) (invoking Fed. R. Civ. Proc. 42(b) to order a sequential trial of liability, then damages, in a suit by the victim of a gas explosion, in part to ward off possible bias resulting from juror sympathy for the badly injured plaintiff). Plaintiffs' attorneys generally resist bifurcation by arguing, among other things, that it introduces inefficiencies (e.g., by requiring particular witnesses to testify on two different occasions) and that jurors need to have a sense of the severity of a given plaintiff's injuries to be able to reason soundly about issues such as duty and breach.

7. *Jury versus Judge.* Longstanding black-letter doctrine holds that a trial judge should not second-guess a jury's compensatory damage award

unless, after viewing the evidence in the light most favorable to the plaintiff, the verdict "shocks the conscience," or is so out of line with the evidence presented that it was likely the product of "passion, prejudice or other improper motive." Aldrich v. Palmer, 24 Cal. 513 (Cal. 1864). These standards are meant to set a high barrier against judicial second-guessing of jury awards. Such deference is grounded in the notion that, apart from readily quantifiable out-of-pocket items such as medical bills and repair bills, the task of assigning a dollar value to a given plaintiff's injuries is quintessentially one of judgment.

8. *Comparison with Other Awards.* Some jurisdictions, perhaps most, permit trial judges to gauge the alleged excessiveness of a jury award in part by comparing it with awards given in other similar cases. They emphasize, however, that care must be taken in determining what constitutes a similar case. *See, e.g.*, Martell v. Boardwalk Enters., Inc., 748 F.2d 740 (2d Cir. 1984) (applying New York law). Consider, however, the comments of one trial judge on the idea of comparative award analysis:

> Essayists often attempt to re-examine some aspect of our society by viewing it from the p[er]spective of someone who arrives on this planet from Mars. . . . From that p[er]spective, the most striking feature of our system . . . is the total lack of meaningful guidance that we provide to the jury of laym[e]n into whose hands we place [the] decision [on damages].
>
> The charge of the Court does no more than to tell the jury that they are to award a plaintiff a sum that would fairly compensate him for his injury, without the slightest hint or any specific guideline that might help the jury arrive at a figure between $10 or $10 million. Nor, at least in this case, did the jury get any meaningful guidance from defense counsel. . . . [T]he one counsel who did suggest an amount did so . . . by simply mentioning a figure and then recoiling from the subject of damages like someone who has just placed his hand on a hot stove.
>
> . . . [I]t seems strange that, having given the jury no meaningful guidance as to how to fix compensatory damages for an injury that none of us would willingly accept for any amount of money, courts nonetheless second guess the judgment it has reached after conscientious deliberation by comparing it to awards that other juries have given in similar, yet factually distinguishable contexts. Yet this is what the applicable precedent requires this Court to do.

Sundbom v. Erik Riebling Co., 1991 U.S. Dist. LEXIS 812 (S.D.N.Y. 1991) (Martin, J.). Some courts in other jursidictions have gone beyond these skeptical musings by deeming evidence of compensatory awards in other cases irrelevant on the ground that, as to damages, each case stands on its own. *See, e.g.*, Barry v. Owens-Corning Fiberglas Corp., 668 N.E.2d 8 (Ill. App. 1996).

9. *Remittitur and Additur.* The Missouri Supreme Court's abolition of remittitur is unusual. The practice is still used in the federal courts and most state courts. What was it about the trial court's use of remittitur in *Kenton* that so bothered the Supreme Court? Notice that the elimination of

remittitur does *not* take away the power of trial judges to order new trials in cases in which the judge concludes that the jury's verdict is shockingly large. Rather, it prevents the judge from giving the plaintiff the *option* of accepting a lower damage award *in lieu* of a new trial. Given that the court did not change the formal legal standard against which trial judges assess verdicts for excessiveness, and did not bar them from ordering new trials on grounds of excessiveness, what exactly did it expect to accomplish by abolishing remittitur?

Some jurisdictions empower the trial court to offer the defendant, in lieu of a new trial, the option of paying a specified larger award (again, only upon a finding by the judge that the jury's verdict is shocking — in these instances, shockingly low). This device is known as *additur.* Likewise, it is open to appellate courts to review awards for insufficiency, as opposed to excessiveness.

10. *Appellate Review.* Appellate court statements as to the standard by which they are to review jury verdicts, as well as the trial judge's initial review of those verdicts, vary. Some indicate that the trial court's ruling upholding or reversing a jury award is entitled to a presumption of correctness, given that the trial judge observed the trial and the jury first hand. Thus, the question is whether the trial court "abused its discretion" in upholding or second-guessing a jury award. *See, e.g.,* Thrailkill v. Patterson, 879 S.W.2d 836 (Tenn. 1994) (applying Tennessee statute); Kelley v. Montesi, 539 A.2d 1020 (Conn. App. 1988). Others conduct the same sort of deferential review of the jury's verdict as was conducted by the trial court, without reference to the trial court's analysis. Kessel v. Leavitt, 511 S.E.2d 720 (W. Va. 1998).

On the issue of appellate review of damage awards, compare *Kenton* with Southern v. Lyons, 696 So. 2d 128 (La. Ct. App. 1997). Plaintiff, a 13-year-old boy, was struck by a boat and seriously injured while swimming in a lake. Defendant Clark was supposed to be supervising plaintiff, but had left him and his friends to play in the water unattended. The jury exonerated the driver of the boat, and found that plaintiff and Clark were each 50 percent responsible for the accident. Given that his injuries were not disabling, and that his mother was responsible for paying his medical expenses, plaintiff's evidence on damages concerned almost entirely the pain and suffering and lost enjoyment of life he had experienced as a result of the accident. It showed that the boat's propeller had torn large gashes in his side, that he remained conscious while being transported to the emergency room, that he underwent two surgeries and a painful skin graft, that he was bed-ridden for a month, and that he suffered permanent scarring that caused him pain, depression, and embarrassment, and limited his activities. In light of this evidence, the jury awarded him about $14,000. (Given the jury's allocation of fault, the trial court entered judgment for plaintiff for $7,000.) On review, the appellate court concluded that the jury's award was shockingly low. It therefore increased that award to about $85,000 — a figure it described as representing the smallest quantum of damages that a reasonable jury could have found in light of the evidence. The court also found that the jury's assignment of equal fault to plaintiff and Clark was erroneous, and instead held that plaintiff could be assigned no more than 20 percent of the responsibility for the accident. Accordingly, it entered judgment for $68,000.

11. *Compensation for Expenses Not Incurred: The Collateral Source Rule.* As noted in Chapter 1, medical and other expenses incurred by injury victims will often be covered at least in part by insurance purchased by the victim or provided to her by her employer or by governmental programs such as Medicare. Thus, when Antoinette Walter sued Wal-Mart for carelessly poisoning her and offered proof of medical costs amounting to about $70,000, that figure did not represent the amount that she actually paid out of her own assets. Indeed, to the extent these charges were paid, they were paid by Medicare. The *Walter* jury heard no evidence as to who paid what percentage of her medical bills because of the operation of a rule of tort law called the *collateral source rule*. It holds that a tortfeasor is not entitled to present evidence at trial indicating that the victim has received, or stands to receive, compensation for her injuries from some other source.

Various rationales are offered in support of this rule. Some argue that the tortfeasor should not benefit from the "good fortune" of having wrongfully injured a person with insurance or other sources of compensation. Others suggest that, to deduct for insurance proceeds would be to deny the plaintiff the benefit she has secured for herself by obtaining insurance. Still others argue that, as a practical matter, the rule helps counteract the American rule denying successful tort plaintiffs attorneys' fees as part of compensatory damages.

In recent years, as many as half the states have modified or abolished the collateral source rule as it applies to all tort cases or to specific areas of tort, such as medical malpractice. The terms of these statutes vary: Some merely permit the defendant to submit for the factfinder's consideration evidence as to other sources of compensation. Other laws mandate that any recovery by the plaintiff be offset by the value of these other sources. In New York, for example, the legislature has eliminated the collateral source rule in medical malpractice cases. *See* N.Y. C.P.L.R. § 4545 (2003):

In any action for medical, dental or podiatric malpractice where the plaintiff seeks to recover for the cost of medical care, . . . rehabilitation services, loss of earnings or other economic loss, evidence shall be admissible for consideration by the court to establish that any such past or future cost or expense was or will, with reasonable certainty, be replaced or indemnified, in whole or in part, from any collateral source such as insurance (except for life insurance), social security . . . , workers' compensation or employee benefit programs (except such collateral sources entitled by law to liens against any recovery of the plaintiff). If the court finds that any such cost or expense was or will, with reasonable certainty, be replaced or indemnified from any collateral source, it shall reduce the amount of the award by such finding, minus an amount equal to the premiums paid by the plaintiff for such benefits for the two-year period immediately preceding the accrual of such action and minus an amount equal to the projected future cost to the plaintiff of maintaining such benefits.

What might justify the legislature's decision to carve out from this new rule the value of the insurance premiums that the plaintiff paid two years prior to her injury, as well as the premiums she will have to pay to maintain her insurance benefits in the future?

12. *Pain and Suffering Damages and Tort Reform.* As noted above, jury awards designed to compensate plaintiffs for pain and suffering and other intangible losses are the subject of intense debate today. Critics of the current system argue that the impossibility of translating pain and suffering into dollar amounts gives jurors carte blanche to award any amount they feel is appropriate in light of their sympathy for the plaintiff and antipathy for the defendant. They also claim that such awards have risen substantially, in real dollar terms, over the last 20 years. Defenders argue that there has been no such increase and that the jury is the appropriate institution to assign values to intangible injuries.

As courts, commentators, interest groups, and legislatures have become increasingly concerned about the size of jury verdicts, legislatures have responded with various measures, including some that directly address compensatory damages. Some legislatures have set flat caps on the compensatory award that a plaintiff can recover in a certain type of tort litigation. A Virginia statute, for example, imposes a $1.5 million limit on total compensatory damages recoverable in medical malpractice actions.* Thus, even if a jury were to determine, based on a reasonable view of the evidence presented, that the plaintiff faces the prospect of $10 million in medical expenses and lost earnings over his lifetime, the trial judge must adjust the award down to $1.5 million. Va. Code. Ann. § 8.01-581.15. Consider who fares worst under Virginia law. Is such a system intolerably regressive? *See* Pulliam v. Coastal Emerg. Servs., Inc., 509 S.E.2d 307 (Va. 1999) (upholding the cap against constitutional challenge).

Other states have enacted legislation placing a cap only on noneconomic losses. *See, e.g.,* Cal. Civ. Code § 3333.2 (imposing a $250,000 cap on noneconomic damages in medical malpractice cases). Still others eschew caps in favor of more robust judicial review. New York law, for example, instructs judges to examine whether a jury award "deviates materially from what would constitute just compensation," a mandate that courts have construed as requiring them to conduct a more searching review of jury awards than under the traditional "shocks the conscience" standard. N.Y. Civ. Prac. L. & Rules § 5501(c) (1986).

13. *Federal Courts and the Seventh Amendment.* The Seventh Amendment to the U.S. Constitution, which governs proceedings in federal but not state courts, guarantees the right to a jury trial, and also mandates that "no fact tried by a jury, shall be otherwise re-examined in any Court of the United States, than according to the rules of the common law." The Supreme Court has held that this "Reexamination Clause" does not prohibit federal *trial* judges from overturning jury verdicts on grounds

* The Virginia law specifies that this cap shall increase by a specified amount each year ($50,000 or $75,000) through 2008, at which point there shall be no further increases.

of excessiveness. Indeed, as we have seen, they have the power to grant new trials upon a finding that the jury's verdict runs counter to the great weight of the evidence, and even to enter post-verdict judgments as a matter of law if no reasonable jury could find as the jury did. These practices, the Court has reasoned, are permissible because they have a long historic pedigree. Thus, although they involve reexamination of jury findings, that reexamination proceeds "according to the rules of the common law."

The Court has taken a different view of the constitutionality of modern state statutes requiring *courts of appeal* to engage in searching review of juries' damage awards. (Recall that when a federal court hears a tort case under its "diversity" jurisdiction, it is obligated to apply substantive state law.) Specifically, it has held that any form of review more robust than deferential "abuse of discretion" review, when undertaken by appellate judges, would violate the Reexamination Clause. Gasperini v. Center for Humanities, Inc., 518 U.S. 415 (1996) (upholding application in federal court of a New York statute mandating appellate review of jury awards, but only on the understanding that the statute called for nothing more rigorous than abuse-of-discretion review).

14. *Other Forms of Redress: Nominal Damages and Injunctions.* A jury is permitted to find that a given defendant has committed the tort of negligence against a plaintiff, and that the plaintiff was not at fault, yet still conclude that the plaintiff is not entitled to any compensation. For example, suppose car driver *P* is struck from behind by careless car driver *D*. Suppose further, however, the jury believes that *P* suffered only a trivial scratch to the bumper of her car. Under these circumstances, the jury may enter a verdict awarding *P nominal damages* — usually specified by law as $1. Such an award serves as an acknowledgment of the tort notwithstanding the absence of any compensable losses flowing from it.

In seeking recourse, tort plaintiffs are not necessarily limited to monetary compensation. Alternatively, or in addition, some plaintiffs will be entitled to *injunctive* relief. See Chapter 11. Typically, injunctive relief consists of an order from the court mandating that the defendant cease engaging in a particular activity (e.g., discharging pollutants into a stream that runs to plaintiff's land). Failure to comply with the order amounts to contempt of court, which is punishable by fine and/or imprisonment.

B. Punitive Damages

Although pain and suffering damages have drawn the attention of judges, legislators, and scholars, perhaps no issue has garnered more widespread notice among contemporary observers of tort law than punitive damages. Punitive damages — also called "exemplary" or "vindictive" damages — form a special category of damages in two related respects. First, an award of punitive damages stands apart from damages that compensate a tort victim for lost wages, medical expenses, pain and suffering, and lost quality of life.* Second, these "extra-compensatory" damages are not available to all tort plaintiffs, only to those who can demonstrate that they have been victims of certain "aggravated" forms of mistreatment involving "malice, insult, oppression, [or] wanton or willful violence." Towle v. Blake, 48 N.H. 92 (1868).

Punitive damages have been a part of American law from the time of the nation's founding. Since then, they have episodically become the subject of controversy. In the period from about 1850 to 1900, some judges and scholars disparaged punitive damages as introducing a form of criminal punishment into tort law. Although these critics occasionally expressed concern that punitive awards worked injustices against particular defendants, the gist of their complaints was conceptual and legalistic: In their eyes, punitive damages flouted the boundaries separating crime from tort, public law from private law, and punishment from compensation. After this wave of criticism failed to persuade most courts and legislatures to change the common law of punitive damages, a period of relative quiet ensued.** However, in the 1980s, the issue of punitive damages' legitimacy erupted again. In contrast to their nineteenth-century predecessors, contemporary critics argue that punitive awards threaten the vitality of the economy and empower undeserving plaintiffs and their lawyers to extract "windfalls" from corporate defendants. Also in contrast to their predecessors, contemporary critics have had a good deal more success in convincing courts and legislatures to introduce significant new restrictions on the ability of plaintiffs to obtain punitive damages.

The reasons for this shift in the terms of the debate are subtle, and will be explored in more detail in Chapter 13. For now, we note that both debates pose three interrelated questions: (1) Should some tort plaintiffs be permitted to recover an additional quantum of damages beyond the amount that, in principle, compensates for the physical and emotional harms that they have suffered?; (2) If so, which plaintiffs and why?; and (3) By what criteria should judges and jurors determine the size of this additional quantum of damages? We devote some attention to each of these questions below, and consider question (3) in more detail in Chapter 13.

National By-Products, Inc. v. Searcy House Moving Co.
731 S.W.2d 194 (Ark. 1987)

Dudley, J.   The sole issue in this tort case is whether an award of punitive damages should be upheld. We hold there was no substantial evidence to support the award of punitive damages, and reverse the judgment.

---

* Many jurisdictions require the plaintiff to establish that she incurred some actual damages before the jury may consider awarding punitive damages. Among these, there is a split as to whether a punitive award will be permitted upon proof of nominal damages.

** By way of illustration, we note that the index to the 1964 edition of Dean Prosser's Torts treatise contains no separate heading for punitive damages, although they

On July 11, 1985, Robert Foley was driving a large tractor trailer for appellant National By-Products, Inc. from Batesville south on Highway 167. At the same time, appellee Searcy House Moving Company was moving a house north on the same highway. Appellee could not get the house through a bridge which was just north of Bald Knob, and, while the house was being adjusted on the house moving trailer, traffic was stopped and flagged around in the one lane of traffic still open. Stacy McGee and Lorene Staggs were slowly starting to go through the open lane when appellant Foley, speeding in an over-weight truck smashed into the rear of their car, knocking it eighty feet forward, causing it to hit the house and trailer, and then to hit two bystanders. Appellant National's truck also struck the house and then crashed into another tractor-trailer rig. Lorene Staggs died instantly and Stacy McGee died seven hours later. The estates of Lorene Staggs and Stacy McGee filed wrongful death actions against Foley and appellant National By-Products, Inc. and appellee moving company. Defendants Foley and National By-Products and defendant moving company filed cross-complaints against each other, each asking compensatory and punitive damages from the other. The cases were tried before a jury which returned compensatory damage awards of $3,000,000 to the estate of Stacy McGee, $1,400,000 to the estate of Lorene Staggs, and $15,000 to appellee moving company. In addition, separate punitive damage awards of $100,000 were given to each estate and to appellee moving company. The judgments in the wrongful death cases were satisfied and appellee moving company agreed to a remittitur of its compensatory damage award from $15,000 to $1,883.14, the stipulated amount of compensatory damages. Therefore, the only damage award involved in this appeal is the $100,000 punitive damage award made in favor of appellee moving company and against appellant National By-Products Company.

Appellant contends that the trial court erred in refusing to grant its motion for a judgment notwithstanding the verdict. The argument is meritorious. An award of punitive damages is justified only where the evidence indicates that the defendant acted wantonly in causing the injury or with such a conscious indifference to the consequences that malice may be inferred. We have previously defined wantonness and conscious indifference to the consequences. In Ellis v. Ferguson, 238 Ark. 776, 385 S.W.2d 154 (1964), we said:

> Wantonness is essentially an attitude of mind and imparts [. . .] such conduct as manifests a "disposition of perversity." Such a disposition or mental state is shown by a person, when, notwithstanding his conscious and timely knowledge of an approach to an unusual danger and of common probability of injury to others, he proceeds into the presence of danger, with indifference to consequences and with absence of all care. . . .

---

are mentioned briefly in the book's opening remarks on the relation of tort to criminal law. Although the treatise characterizes them as an "anomalous . . . invasion" of criminal principles into tort law, it does not associate their anomalousness with illegitimacy or impropriety. William L. Prosser, *Handbook of the Law of Torts* § 2, at 9 (3d ed. 1964).

It is not necessary to prove that the defendant deliberately intended to injure the plaintiff. It is enough if it is shown that, indifferent to consequences, the defendant intentionally acted in such a way that the natural and probable consequence of his act was injury to the plaintiff.

In Freeman v. Anderson, 279 Ark. 282, 651 S.W.2d 450 (1983), we quoted with approval from St. Louis, I. M. & S. Ry. Co. v. Dysart, 89 Ark. 261, 116 S.W. 224 (1919):

The terms "wilfulness, or conscious indifference to consequences from which malice may be inferred," as used in the decisions of this court, means such conduct in the face of discovered peril. In other words, in order to superadd this element of damages by way of punishment, *it must appear that the negligent party knew, or had reason to believe, that his act of negligence was about to inflict injury, and that he continued in his course with a conscious indifference to the consequences*, from which malice may be inferred.

In the case at bar there was proof of gross negligence, but gross negligence is not sufficient to justify punitive damages.

The facts, when viewed most favorably to appellee, reveal that Foley, appellant's driver, was late leaving Batesville and his truck weighed 80,480 pounds, which is 480 pounds over the legal limit. Foley had received six citations in the last year for driving an overweight truck, and appellant had paid all of the citations. One of appellant's employees testified that the company had a disciplinary procedure for drivers who got an excessive number of overweight tickets, and he testified that Foley had an excessive number of such tickets, but admitted that Foley had not been cautioned or disciplined for driving an overweight truck. Appellee's expert witness on accident reconstruction testified that the 480 pounds excess weight on the 80,000 pound rig was a contributing, but insignificant, factor in the accident.

Between Batesville and the place of the accident, Foley exceeded the 55 miles per hour speed limit while going downhill. He got so close to one car that all the driver of the car could see in his rearview mirror was the grill of Foley's tractor. He got extremely close to another car while "tailgating" downhill. Finally, he came around a curve at the crest of a small hill and had 804 feet of clear visibility to the bridge structure where the accident occurred. The house, which was sitting on the trailer, at the bridge, was 17 feet high, 28 feet wide, and 36 feet long, and because of its added height, could be seen from about 900 feet away. Foley either did not apply his brakes, or he applied them but they did not function properly.

Appellee's witnesses said Foley was going 60 to 70 miles per hour and made no effort to stop even though he went past a vehicle with a flashing warning light. They testified his brake lights did not come on, the tires did not skid, there was no smoke from either the brakes or tires, and there were no skid marks. However, appellee's expert brake witness testified that Foley probably did apply his brakes just before the accident, but the brakes were not working properly. While the expert did not testify about standards in the industry, he did testify that the Ryder Truck Company checks truck brakes every 8,000 miles. One of the appellant's employees testified that the company policy was to adjust the trailer brakes once a month, but the brakes on this trailer had not been adjusted for three and one-half months, and the tractor brakes had not been opened for a complete inspection for almost six months, although they were adjusted about 6 weeks before the accident. He further testified that appellant conducted an internal inspection of the brakes every 50,000 miles as recommended by the American Trucking Association and, in addition, the drivers conducted a daily inspection. There was no evidence that appellant had any knowledge that the brakes were faulty.

As Foley sped downhill at 70 miles per hour, he ran into the rear of the decedent's car and then struck appellee's rig and the house.

The foregoing facts do not show that appellant, either by its own policies or through the actions of its agent Foley, intentionally acted in such a way that the natural and probable consequence was to damage appellee's property. Nor do the facts show that appellant knew that some act of negligence was about to cause damage, but still continued to cause that damage. Accordingly, we reverse the judgment for punitive damages. . . .

Reversed.

Hays, J. (dissenting) (joined by Purtle, J.).   The majority's opinion has examined the evidence supporting punitive damages more from the appellant's standpoint than the appellee's. When viewed most favorably to the appellee, and with its fullest probative force, I believe there was substantial evidence to support the trial court's refusal to grant a motion for a directed verdict. Dalrymple v. Fields, 276 Ark. 185, 633 S.W.2d 362 (1982). . . .

We no longer require actual malice as an essential constituent of punitive damages. It is enough if the defendant acted recklessly or wantonly, or with a conscious indifference to the safety and welfare of others using the highways. In Dalrymple v. Fields, *supra*, we said:

> Before punitive damages may be allowed it must be shown that in the absence of proof of malice or willfulness there was a wanton and conscious indifference for the rights and safety of others on the part of the tortfeasor.

While excessive speed may, in many circumstances, be no more than ordinary negligence, actions are not to be viewed in a vacuum, and what may be no more than negligence in one setting can readily be seen as wantonness or conscious indifference in another context. Thus driving 85 m.p.h. on certain stretches of highway may be relatively safe, or it may be negligence, depending on the traffic, weather, etc. But driving only 35 or 40 m.p.h. past a school at dismissal hour or close to a playground crowded with children with an evident indifference to the known tendencies of children could meet even restrictive concepts of wantonness. In Airco, Inc. v. Simmons First National Bank, 276 Ark. 486, 638 S.W.2d 660 (1982), we upheld a monumental award of punitive damages, not on proof that Airco had any intent to injure, but because the injury was the natural and probable consequence of Airco's conduct. It seems a fair analogy to me to say that when one knowingly drives an overloaded 18-wheeler, with defective brakes, on the highway at speeds of 70 m.p.h. by some accounts, oblivious of warning signals and without slowing down and with no apparent effort at stopping, approaching congestion on the highway, a collision is the natural and probable consequence of such conduct. At least, reasonable minds could differ on the issue of conscious indifference and that is enough.

In sum, the proof was that Robert Foley was several hours late leaving Batesville for Little Rock. His truck, an 18-wheeler, was loaded beyond the lawful limit. His truck, by whatever standard one chooses, was equipped with brakes that were not functioning properly. For some miles prior to the point of impact Mr. Foley drove so fast and so close to preceding vehicles that two of those motorists were alarmed by it and described his conduct at trial as speeding and "tailgating." Rounding a curve bearing into a straight, level stretch of highway some 900 feet from the appellee's house-moving rig, Mr. Foley proceeded at a high rate of speed (70 m.p.h. by one account) and with no discernible attempt to reduce his speed (some witnesses testified that his speed actually increased as he neared the impact point), past one vehicle with a warning light flashing, to strike the Staggs-McGee vehicle, knocking it a considerable distance in the air, and resulting in the deaths of the two occupants, before striking another vehicle and the house. Photographs of the scene attest to extraordinary force of the impact.

There was testimony that one of the brake shoes on the truck was not even touching the brake drum, rendering it useless as a braking device. There was testimony that none of the four rear brakes met Department of Transportation specifications. There was other material evidence from which an inference could be drawn that the brakes on the truck were seriously deficient and that fact was known by Foley and was in derogation of the policies of National By-Products, Inc. Lastly, there was proof from which the jury could quite properly have inferred that National By-Products, Inc., in addition to neglecting the safe operation of the truck involved, engaged in practices which promoted the overloading of its trucks beyond the legal limit, by routinely paying weight fines rather than demanding compliance by its drivers.

The proof, I believe, was such that a jury had a right under the law to exemplify the conduct of both defendants by assessing punitive damages. The judgment should be affirmed.

Mathias v. Accor Economy Lodging, Inc.
347 F.3d 672 (7th Cir. 2003)

Posner, J.   The plaintiffs brought this diversity suit governed by Illinois law against affiliated entities (which the parties treat as a single entity, as shall we) that own and operate the "Motel 6" chain of hotels and motels. One of these hotels (now a "Red Roof Inn," though still owned by the defendant) is in downtown Chicago. The plaintiffs, a brother and sister, were guests there and were bitten by bedbugs, which are making a comeback in the U.S. as a consequence of more conservative use of pesticides. The plaintiffs claim that in allowing guests to be attacked by bedbugs in a motel that charges upwards of $100 a day for a room and would not like to be mistaken for a flophouse, the defendant was guilty of "willful and wanton conduct" and thus under Illinois law is liable for punitive as well as compensatory damages. The jury agreed and awarded each plaintiff $186,000 in punitive damages though only $5,000 in compensatory damages. The defendant appeals, complaining primarily about the punitive-damages award. . . .

The defendant argues that at worst it is guilty of simple negligence, and if this is right the plaintiffs were not entitled by Illinois law to any award of punitive damages. It also complains that the award was excessive — indeed that any award in excess of $20,000 to each plaintiff would deprive the defendant of its property without due process of law. The first complaint has no possible merit, as the evidence of gross negligence, indeed of recklessness in the strong sense of an unjustifiable failure to avoid a *known* risk, was amply shown. In 1998, EcoLab, the extermination service that the motel used, discovered bedbugs in several rooms in the motel and recommended that it be hired to spray every room, for which it would charge the motel only $500; the motel refused. The next year, bedbugs were again discovered in a room but EcoLab was asked to spray just that room. The motel tried to negotiate "a building sweep [by EcoLab] free of charge," but, not surprisingly, the negotiation failed. By the spring of 2000, the motel's manager "started noticing that there were refunds being given by my desk clerks and reports coming back from the guests that there were ticks in the rooms and bugs in the rooms that were biting." She looked in some of the rooms and discovered bedbugs. The defendant asks us to disregard her testimony as that of a disgruntled ex-employee, but of course her credibility was for the jury, not the defendant, to determine.

Further incidents of guests being bitten by insects and demanding and receiving refunds led the manager to recommend to her superior in the company that the motel be closed while every room was sprayed, but this was refused. This superior, a district manager, was a management-level employee of the defendant, and his knowledge of the risk and failure to take effective steps either to eliminate it or to warn the motel's guests are imputed to his employer for purposes of determining whether the employer should be liable for punitive damages. . . . Restatement (Second) of Torts § 909 (1979); Restatement (Second) of Agency § 217C (1958). The employer's liability for compensatory damages is of course automatic on the basis of the principle of respondeat superior, since the district manager was acting within the scope of his employment.

The infestation continued and began to reach farcical proportions, as when a guest, after complaining of having been bitten repeatedly by insects while asleep in his room in the hotel was moved to another room only to discover insects there; and within 18 minutes of being moved to a third room he discovered insects in that room as well and had to be moved still again. (Odd that at that point he didn't flee the motel.) By July, the motel's management was acknowledging to EcoLab that there was a "major problem with bed bugs" and that all that was being done about it was "chasing them from room to room." Desk clerks were instructed to call the "bedbugs" "ticks," apparently on the theory that customers would be less alarmed, though in fact ticks are more dangerous than bedbugs because they spread Lyme Disease and Rocky Mountain Spotted Fever. Rooms that the motel had placed on "Do not rent, bugs in room" status nevertheless were rented.

It was in November that the plaintiffs checked into the motel. They were given Room 504, even though the motel had classified the room as "DO NOT RENT UNTIL TREATED," and it had not been treated. Indeed, that night 190 of the hotel's 191 rooms were occupied, even though a number of them had been placed on the same don't-rent status as Room 504. One of the defendant's motions in limine that the judge denied was to exclude evidence concerning all other rooms — a good example of the frivolous character of the motions and of the defendant's pertinacious defense of them on appeal.

Although bedbug bites are not as serious as the bites of some other insects, they are painful and unsightly. Motel 6 could not have rented any rooms at the prices it charged had it informed guests that the risk of being bitten by bedbugs was appreciable. Its failure either to warn guests or to take effective measures to eliminate the bedbugs amounted to fraud and probably to battery as well. . . . There was, in short, sufficient evidence of "willful and wanton conduct" within the meaning that the Illinois courts assign to the term to permit an award of punitive damages in this case.

But in what amount? . . .

[Judge Posner's opinion here discusses federal constitutional limits on the magnitude of punitive damage awards that have been articulated in a series of decisions issued by the U.S. Supreme Court since 1991. Those limits, which take the form of general "guideposts," rather than fixed amounts, are discussed in Chapter 13. Judge Posner concluded that application of the Court's guideposts for determining whether an award of punitive damages is unconstitutionally large requires lower court judges to consider a given award in light of the reasons for which punitive damages are awarded in the first place. His opinion thus turned to consideration of that issue. — EDS.]

. . . The term "punitive damages" implies punishment, and a standard principle of penal theory is that "the punishment should fit the crime" in the sense of being proportional to the wrongfulness of the defendant's action, though the principle is modified when the probability of detection is very low (a familiar example is the heavy fines for littering) or the crime is potentially lucrative (as in the case of trafficking in illegal drugs). Hence, with these qualifications, which in fact will figure in our analysis of this case, punitive damages should be proportional to the wrongfulness of the defendant's actions.

Another penal precept is that a defendant should have reasonable notice of the sanction for unlawful acts, so that he can make a rational determination of how to act; and so there have to be reasonably clear standards for determining the amount of punitive damages for particular wrongs.

And a third precept, the core of the Aristotelian notion of corrective justice, and more broadly of the principle of the rule of law, is that sanctions should be based on the wrong done rather than on the status of the defendant; a person is punished for what he does, not for who he is, even if the who is a huge corporation. . . .

England's common law courts first confirmed their authority to award punitive damages in the eighteenth century, see Dorsey D. Ellis, Jr., *"Fairness and Efficiency in the Law of Punitive Damages,"* 56 S. Cal. L. Rev. 1, 12-20 (1982), at a time when the institutional structure of criminal law enforcement was primitive and it made sense to leave certain minor crimes to be dealt with by the civil law. And still today one function of punitive-damages awards is to relieve the pressures on an overloaded system of criminal justice by providing a civil alternative to criminal prosecution of minor crimes. An example is deliberately spitting in a person's face, a criminal assault but because minor readily deterrable by the levying of what amounts to a civil fine through a suit for damages for the tort of battery. Compensatory damages would not do the trick in such a case, and this for three reasons: because they are difficult to determine in the case of acts that inflict largely dignatory harms; because in the spitting case they would be too slight to give the victim an incentive to sue, and he might decide instead to respond with violence — and an age-old purpose of the law of torts is to provide a substitute for violent retaliation against wrongful injury — and because to limit the plaintiff to compensatory damages would enable the defendant to commit the offensive act with impunity provided that he was willing to pay, and again there would be a danger that his act would incite a breach of the peace by his victim.

When punitive damages are sought for billion-dollar oil spills and other huge economic injuries, the considerations that we have just canvassed fade. . . . Our case is closer to the spitting case. The defendant's behavior was outrageous but the compensable harm done was slight and at the same time difficult to quantify because a large element of it was emotional. And the defendant may well have profited from its misconduct because by concealing the infestation it was able to keep renting rooms. Refunds were frequent but may have cost less than the cost of closing the hotel for a thorough fumigation. The hotel's attempt to pass off the bedbugs as ticks, which some guests might ignorantly have thought less unhealthful, may have postponed the instituting of litigation to rectify the hotel's misconduct. The award of punitive damages in this case thus serves the additional purpose of limiting the defendant's ability to profit from its fraud by escaping detection and (private) prosecution. If a tortfeasor is "caught" only half the time he commits torts, then when he is caught he should be punished twice as heavily in order to make up for the times he gets away.

Finally, if [the defendant's argument is accepted, and] the total stakes in the case were capped at $50,000 (2 × [$5,000 + $20,000]), the plaintiffs might well have had difficulty financing this lawsuit. It is here that the defendant's aggregate net worth of $1.6 billion becomes relevant. A defendant's wealth is not a sufficient basis for awarding punitive damages. That would be discriminatory and would violate the rule of law, as we explained earlier, by making punishment depend on status rather than conduct. Where wealth in the sense of resources enters is in enabling the defendant to mount an extremely aggressive defense against suits such as this and by doing so to make litigating against it very costly, which in turn may make it difficult for the plaintiffs to find a lawyer willing to handle their case, involving as it does only modest stakes, for the usual 33-40 percent contingent fee.

In other words, the defendant is investing in developing a reputation intended to deter plaintiffs. It is difficult otherwise to explain the great stubborness with which it has defended this case, making a host of frivolous evidentiary arguments despite the very modest stakes even when the punitive damages awarded by the jury are included. . . .

All things considered, we cannot say that the award of punitive damages was excessive, albeit the precise number chosen by the jury was arbitrary. It is probably not a coincidence that $5,000 + $186,000 = $191,000/191 = $1,000: i.e., $1,000 per room in the hotel. . . . [In the absence of guidelines attaching specific damage amounts to particular forms of misconduct], it is inevitable that the specific amount of punitive damages awarded whether by a judge or by a jury will be arbitrary. (Which is perhaps why the plaintiffs' lawyer did not suggest a number to the jury.) The judicial function is to police a range, not a point. . . .

NOTES AND QUESTIONS

1. *Placing Punitive Damages in Context.* Jury awards of punitive damages are rare. Studies of recent tort litigation suggest that they are awarded in less than 5 percent of all tort cases that go to verdict. For reasons explained below, awards in cases in which the underlying theory of liability is *negligence* are even rarer, making up a small fraction of this already small percentage. Instead, when awarded, punitive damages tend to be given to plaintiffs asserting claims for intentional wrongs that today would fall under the headings of assault, battery, false imprisonment, fraud, and tortious interference with contract. (To say that punitive damages are rare is not necessarily to say that they are unimportant. Indeed, even a handful of punitive awards — particularly awards of enormous magnitude — can have the potential to affect the trial and settlement of many other cases.)

In the notes that follow we examine the historical and contemporary bases for awarding punitive damages, some of the procedural rules governing the issuance of such awards, and possible theoretical justifications for punitive damages. *It is important to emphasize at the outset that this treatment of the subject is necessarily incomplete.* In the last 15 years, the U.S. Supreme Court has added an important constitutional-law overlay onto the common law and statutory law of punitive damages. Because the Court's intervention arguably has been motivated in part by developments in modern *products liability* law, which we have not yet encountered, we postpone consideration of it until Chapter 13. In practice, the common law, statutory law, and constitutional law of punitive damages must be considered together.

2. *History.* In the eighteenth and early-nineteenth centuries, punitive damages were most commonly awarded to victims of torts that involved abuses of power or insults to honor or dignity. The former category is exemplified by Wilkes v. Wood, 98 Eng. Rep. 489 (K.B. 1763). There, the court upheld a London jury's imposition of a punitive award of £1000 — a large sum for the time — in a false arrest claim brought against a member of Parliament who arranged for the arrest of plaintiff, a newspaper editor, for allegedly defaming King George III. Eighteenth-century "insult" cases included claims for "criminal conversation" brought by husbands against seducers of their wives. (See Chapter 2, note following Mussivand v. David.) In these cases — the trials of which helped give birth to London's tabloid newspaper industry — juries would occasionally deliver ruinously large verdicts on the order of £10,000 or more. Claims for libel and slander would also sometimes give rise to punitive awards in light of the "insult" to the plaintiff's good name.

In the nineteenth and early twentieth centuries, one finds U.S. decisions upholding jury awards for punitive damages in additional settings. Among the small collection of cases in which they were awarded, one sees them most frequently when employees of railroads and other common carriers mistreated passengers by, for example, forcing them to disembark at locations other than designated stations. *See, e.g.,* Spellman v. Richmond & D. R. Co., 14 S.E. 947 (S.C. 1892) (upholding a punitive award to a passenger against a railroad whose conductor forced him off the train without justification); McLelland v. Burns, 5 Colo. 390 (1880) (upholding an award where a stagecoach driver abandoned his passengers during a snowstorm); *see also* Goddard v. Grand Trunk Ry., 57 Me. 202 (1869) (upholding an award where a railroad brakeman abused and threatened the plaintiff). Punitive damages were also permitted for flagrant intrusions onto, or willful destructions of, property, as well as for instances of deceit or fraud. *See, e.g.,* Duncan v. Stalcup, 18 N.C. 440 (1836) (upholding a punitive award against the defendant for his malicious destruction of plaintiff's dogs, cattle, hogs, and stables); Huffman v. Moore, 115 S.E. 634 (S.C. 1923) (punitive damages appropriate in action for fraudulent sale of used car).

3. *Simple Negligence versus Reckless Indifference. Mathias* notes the black-letter rule that a plaintiff is *ineligible* to receive punitive damages if she can establish *only* that the defendant wronged her by acting carelessly toward her. An equally well-established rule holds that there is a certain subset of negligence suits in which juries retain discretion to award punitive damages. (A jury is never required to award punitive damages.) The Wisconsin Supreme Court described this special subset of negligence cases as instances of:

> gross and criminal negligence — such negligence as evinces on the part of the defendant a *wanton disregard* of the safety of others, and which in law is equivalent to malice.

Pickett v. Crook, 20 Wis. 358 (1866) (emphasis added). In the words of the Second Restatement, a claim of negligence can support a punitive award if the plaintiff establishes that the defendant's unreasonable conduct demonstrates "reckless indifference to the rights of others." Restatement (Second) of Torts § 908(2), at 464 (1979).

In this subset of cases, the tort being sued upon is negligence — the defendant's liability for compensatory damages is established on the same terms as any other negligence case. What marks them as special is the plaintiff's ability to prove, in addition, that the defendant's conduct was *so careless* as to constitute a different order of wrongdoing, one that warrants a supplementary form of relief. Thus, there is a conceptual separation between the grounds of liability (unreasonable conduct toward the plaintiff proximately causing injury to her) and the grounds of punitive damages (conduct so unreasonable as to bespeak wanton disregard or deliberate indifference).

The employment of wanton disregard/deliberate indifference as a separate ground for punitive damages dates back at least to the mid-nineteenth century. *See, e.g.*, Brooke v. Clark, 57 Tex. 105 (1882) (upholding, upon rehearing, an award of punitive damages against a doctor for gross malpractice evincing indifference); Whipple v. Walpole, 10 N.H. 130 (1839) (upholding a punitive award upon evidence of defendant's gross negligence in maintaining a bridge, which resulted in the loss of plaintiff's horses). With the advent of the automobile in the early twentieth century, instances of injury resulting from dangerous driving by intoxicated motorists would provide a common instance of the sort of "aggravated" negligence that permits the imposition of punitive damages. *See* Ross v. Clark, 274 P. 639 (Ariz. 1929); see also *infra* Note 6.

What, if anything, links the sort of conduct described in Note 2 — that is, conduct undertaken for the purpose of harming, oppressing, or insulting identifiable victims — with conduct evincing indifference to the well-being of others?

4. *Recklessness, Wanton Disregard, and Deliberate Indifference*. According to Section 500 of the Second Restatement of Torts, all forms of reckless indifference are distinguished from mere carelessness by the fact that the acts in question not only pose an unreasonable risk of physical harm to another, "but also that such risk is substantially greater than that which is necessary to make his conduct [careless]." Restatement (Second) of Torts § 500, at 587 (1965). Granting that the notion of unreasonable conduct posing particularly grave dangers to others forms the core of recklessness, it will nonetheless be helpful to distinguish two different forms of reckless conduct. The first consists of *reckless disregard* for others' physical well-being. The second involves *deliberate indifference* to others' physical well-being. As these labels suggest, the central distinction between the two forms of recklessness is the degree to which the actor is cognizant of the risks posed by his conduct.

5. *Wanton Disregard*. Section 500 of the Second Restatement states in part that a person acts with reckless indifference when his unreasonable conduct poses a grave danger of harm to others and when he has "reason

to know of facts which would lead a reasonable man to realize [that those dangers attend his conduct]." *Id.* It thus permits a factfinder to conclude that an actor has acted recklessly even though he was not actually aware of the dangers posed by his conduct at the time of acting. By doing so, the clause aims to bring under the heading of reckless indifference the conduct of an actor who fails to appreciate the dangers his actions pose because of his "reckless temperament, or [because of] the abnormally favorable results of previous conduct of the same sort." *Id.*, cmt. c, at 589. Our label for this branch of reckless indifference is *wanton disregard*.

Return now to *National By-Products*. The majority opinion denies Searcy an award of punitive damages because it concludes that National By-Products and its driver Foley at most acted with extreme negligence, which it labels "gross."* It reaches this conclusion in part for a supposed lack of evidence establishing that company management or Foley acted *in the knowledge* that its or his unreasonable conduct posed a grave risk of physical harm to others. Even granting the soundness of this reading of the evidence, couldn't a reasonable jury still have concluded that *Foley* acted with wanton disregard for the physical well-being of others? For example, couldn't it have found that he drove the way he did because he was by disposition extraordinarily willing to risk harm to others (as well as himself), or because he was wildly optimistic about his ability to navigate dangerous traffic situations? Is the majority's apparent refusal to apply the concept of wanton disregard explained by the fact that it confronted the issue of punitive damages in conjunction with Searcy's claim for property damage?** Alternatively, might it be explained by the fact that National By-Products, rather than Foley, would likely be paying those damages? (On the latter point, see *infra* Note 16.)

6. *Recklessness and Deliberate Indifference*. Wanton disregard forms one prong of Section 500's concept of reckless indifference. The other prong consists of conduct undertaken by a person who is *aware* both that his conduct creates an unreasonable risk of physical harm to another, and that such risk is substantially greater than that which is necessary to make his conduct careless. We refer to instances of this sort of conscious recklessness as *deliberate indifference*.

Deliberate indifference "requires a *conscious choice of a course of action*, . . . with knowledge of the serious danger to others involved. . . ." *Id.* cmt. g, at 590 (emphasis added). It thus stands in sharp contrast to

---

* As indicated above in Note 3, Wisconsin law equates "gross and criminal negligence" with wanton disregard, the threshold for permitting an award of punitive damages. Arkansas law, by contrast, uses the term *gross negligence* to refer to conduct that, while more careless than the sort of conduct that will support liability for ordinary negligence, is not so careless as to amount to wanton disregard.

** Of course, Foley's conduct killed two people — Staggs and McGee — but National By-Products apparently paid those punitive damage awards and did not appeal them. Was it appropriate for the jury to provide the *same* punitive damage award ($100,000) to the Searcy House Moving Company as to the estates of Staggs and McGee? Should the punitive damage award to a victim who suffers personal injury because of reckless driving be higher than the award to a victim that suffers only property damage because of the same conduct?

those forms of negligence that involve inadvertence — momentary lapses, slip-ups, etc. It also differs from instances of *advertent* (conscious) carelessness in that "the actor to be reckless must recognize that his conduct involves a risk substantially greater in amount than that which is necessary to make his conduct negligent." *Id*.

To grasp this latter distinction it may be helpful to contrast *Mathias* with Vaughan v. Menlove from Chapter 3. Recall that, after being apprised of the risk of fire associated with his method for stacking hay, Menlove indicated that he would "chance it." Assume that the increased likelihood of fire associated with Menlove's chosen method was sufficient to render his conduct unreasonable, but was still relatively small. (Incurring even a relatively small increased risk of harm can be unreasonable if, for example, it is incurred needlessly.) Given this assumption, one might say of Menlove that he was *consciously careless*. By contrast, the motel owners in *Mathias* had every reason to suppose that their decision not to treat the motel's bedbug infestation would result in their guests being bitten. Thus, it seems natural to say of them that they acted with *deliberate indifference* toward the physical well-being of their guests.

7. *Recklessness and Drunk Driving.* As noted above, many jurisdictions allow punitive damages in cases in which the defendant has caused an accident while operating a vehicle with a blood alcohol level above the limit set by criminal statutes. Some defendants have tried to persuade courts to bar the award of punitive damages in these cases on the ground that, unlike the actors in *Mathias*, drunk drivers who are already drunk when they enter their cars do not knowingly choose to engage in highly risky conduct. This argument has been regularly rejected: If the decision to begin drinking is made in the knowledge that driving may soon follow, the whole series of decisions leading up to the erratic driving is deemed reckless. *See* Taylor v. Superior Court, 598 P.2d 854 (Cal. 1979).

Should liability for compensatory or punitive damages attach if an intoxicated driver *who is driving reasonably* collides with and injures the plaintiff? (Keep in mind that many car accidents do not involve erratic or otherwise abnormal driving on anyone's part, and assume that a defendant might with some credibility contend that, even if drunk, he was not driving in an abnormal or erratic manner.) With respect to *compensatory damages*, it is conceivably open to a drunk-yet-competent driver who is involved in an accident to argue that he should not be held liable because his competent driving would suggest that the tortious aspect of his conduct — driving while drunk — played no role in producing the plaintiff's injury. Might a similar argument be invoked to block the imposition of punitive damages? In Ingram v. Pettit, 340 So. 2d 922 (Fla. 1976), the Florida Supreme Court seemingly rejected such an argument, imposing punitive damages on a drunk driver whose drunkenness appears not to have contributed to the accident resulting in plaintiff's injuries. A dissenting justice responded as follows:

Sundberg, J. (dissenting)   [The majority opinion entails that] in cases where an accident involving an intoxicated driver is concerned, the injured party need only prove the accident, provide evidence of intoxication and, thereupon, the driver will be subject to assessment of punitive damages. This is strict liability, not only for compensatory damages, but for exemplary damages. . . .

I suggest that the law of torts as it has been carefully developed over the years permits an award of punitive damages in personal injury cases involving vehicles where reckless *conduct* is involved, not reckless *attitude*.

The public policy arguments of the majority are enticing. There can be no question that drunk drivers endanger the lives of citizens of our state. But the Legislature can and has dealt with this problem through enactment of criminal statutes. The Legislature is the appropriate body to assert the public policy of Florida in this regard. That body having done so, it is unnecessary and improvident to [permit the award of punitive damages in such a case]. . . .

What "public policy" arguments might sanction the imposition of punitive damages on a tortfeasor who engages in potentially reckless conduct that does not in fact generate the risks that render the conduct reckless?

8. *Trial Procedure (I): Burden of Proof.* As has been discussed in the preceding notes, punitive damages may only be awarded if the evidence is sufficient to permit a reasonable jury to conclude that the defendant not only committed a tort, but acted with malice or indifference toward the plaintiff. We have also seen in Chapters 3 and 4 that tort law typically employs the "more probable than not" or *preponderance of the evidence* standard in setting the burden of proof. Jurisdictions have split over whether plaintiffs ought to face a greater burden on the threshold question of malice or indifference. Many take the position that the plaintiff must present *clear and convincing* evidence of malice or indifference, that is, evidence sufficient to permit a reasonable jury to conclude that it is *quite likely* that the defendant acted with the requisite disposition. The adoption of this heightened standard has been achieved by judicial decision and by statute. *See, e.g.*, Travelers Indem. Co. v. Armstrong, 442 N.E.2d 349 (Ind. 1982); Ga. Code Ann. § 51-12-5.1(b).

Although the clear-and-convincing standard is meant to be more onerous than the preponderance standard, it is also meant to be less onerous than the *beyond a reasonable doubt* standard used in criminal law to help protect citizens from being too readily subject to punishment at the behest of government officials. Is the adoption of this intermediate standard defensible? If punitive damages really are part of tort law, why depart from the preponderance standard? If they really are a form of punishment, shouldn't they be adjudicated under the reasonable doubt standard?

9. *Trial Procedure (II): Jury Instructions.* Assuming that the aforementioned threshold showing is made, the issue of punitive damages is, in the first instance, left to the discretion of the jury. The jury is instructed that, upon finding proof of malice, etc., it *may* — but need not — award punitive damages. Jurors are further instructed to consider various factors in determining the amount of any such award. For example, New York's Pattern Jury Instructions provide in part as follows:

In arriving at your decision as to the amount of punitive damages you should consider the following factors:

1. The nature and reprehensibility of what the defendant did. That would include the character of the wrongdoing, . . . whether the defendant's conduct demonstrated an indifference to, or reckless disregard of, the health and safety of others, whether the plaintiff was financiallly vulnerable, how long the conduct went on, the defendant's awareness of what harm the conduct caused or was likely to cause, any concealment or covering up of the wrongdoing, [and] how often the defendant had committed similar acts of this type in the past. In considering the amount of punitive damages to award, you should weigh this factor heavily.

2. The actual and potential harm created by defendant's conduct. The amount of punitive damages that you award must be both reasonable and proportionate to the actual and potential harm suffered by the plaintiff, and to the compensatory damages you awarded to the plaintiff.

3. The defendant's financial condition and the impact your punitive damages award will have on the defendant.

N.Y. Pattern Jury Instr. — Civil 2:278 (2004).

Plaintiffs' attorneys will attempt to present to jurors a wide range of evidence bearing on defendants' culpability, although their discretion to do so has been narrowed to an as-yet undetermined extent by a recent Supreme Court decision. *See* State Farm Mut. Auto Ins. Co. v. Campbell, 538 U.S. 408 (2003), discussed in Chapter 13, (holding that the Due Process Clause of the Fourteenth Amendment prevents a tort plaintiff seeking punitive damages from introducing evidence of misconduct by the defendant that bears at best indirectly on the defendant's mistreatment of the plaintiff). In principle, it is likewise open to the defendant to offer evidence tending to show that its conduct was less egregious than it might otherwise appear to have been. By definition, such evidence cannot have been sufficient to prevent the imposition of liability in the first place. If so, why should it be permitted to factor into the jury's determination of the size of a punitive award? *See* Prentiss v. Shaw, 56 Me. 427 (1869) (defendants who were found liable for falsely imprisoning the plaintiff may introduce evidence that they imprisoned the plaintiff only after hearing him express gratification upon hearing the news of President Lincoln's assassination; while plaintiff's "provocation" did not justify the defendants' wrongful act, the jury was entitled to take it into account in determining whether to award punitive damages against them and in what amount).

10. *Trial Procedure (III): Bifurcation.* Courts have uniformly deemed evidence of a defendant's wealth to be relevant to the jury's determination of the size of any punitive award. As explained in *Mathias*, this is not because wealthy persons or entities deserve greater punishment, but because an actor's wealth may have factored into its decision to behave as it did, and because a larger award may be necessary to send a meaningful "message" to a wealthy individual or entity. To reduce the risk that evidence of the defendant's wealth will shade jurors' judgments on the underlying issue of liability, some states mandate, and other states permit, a trial judge, at the request of a defendant, to bifurcate trial proceedings.

See, e.g., N.J.S.A. 2A:15-5.13. In the first phase, the jury is presented with evidence pertaining to the elements of the prima facie case, any relevant defenses, and compensatory damages.* Only if the jury determines that liability for compensatory damages should attach for the underlying tort does the court then preside over a second phase on punitive damages, at which evidence of wealth is introduced. *See* Hodges v. S.C. Toof & Co., 833 S.W.2d 896 (Tenn. 1992) (holding that trial courts "shall," upon a motion of the defendant, separate the punitive damages phase of tort cases from the phase in which liability and compensatory damages are determined, in part out of concern that jurors will be biased by evidence as to certain defendants' wealth).

11. *Trial Court and Appellate Review of the Magnitude of Punitive Damage Awards*. The degree of scrutiny applied by trial and appellate judges to juries' punitive damage awards is inextricably bound up with an important set of decisions issued by the U.S. Supreme Court in the last 15 years. For present purposes, it is sufficient to state that both trial and appellate courts are expected closely to scrutinize such awards for excessiveness. A more detailed examination of the constitutional dimensions of punitive damages law is provided in Chapter 13.

12. *Punitive Damages and Punishment*. Because they are reserved for instances of "aggravated" misconduct, and because they are awarded apart from ordinary compensatory damages, it is natural (and quite common) to think of punitive damages as inflicting a kind of punishment. Indeed, their very name suggests as much. As noted at the outset of this section, some judges and scholars have criticized punitive damages as an inappropriate importation of criminal law principles of retribution into the civil law of tort. Reconsider the materials in Chapter 1 distinguishing criminal and tort law. Granted the existence of various differences between the two bodies of law, do you think tort law is or should be distinguished from criminal law on the ground that the former is solely concerned to compensate victims, whereas the latter is concerned to punish wrongdoers? What conception of tort law is presupposed by the critique of punitive damages as an anomalous feature of that law?

13. *Recourse for a Special Class of Wrongs? Mathias* canvases various rationales for punitive damages. One rationale — sometimes emphasized in eighteenth- and nineteenth-century cases imposing punitive damages for "insult" torts — is that they are appropriately given in recognition of the (perhaps justifiably) greater urge toward private reprisal that tends be felt by victims of egregious mistreatment. *See, e.g.*, Perkins v. Towle, 43 N.H. 220 (N.H 1861) (linking the award of punitive damages in cases of insult to the suppression of dueling). Other decisions suggest that punitive awards are an appropriate response to conduct

---

* Recall from Section I.A, *supra*, that bifurcation is also sometimes used to separate the presentation of evidence on liability from the presentation of evidence as to the extent of plaintiff's compensatory damages. Some trials are thus *tri*furcated, with separate phases for (1) liability, (2) extent of compensatory damages, and (3) punitive damages.

demonstrating a disposition on the part of a tortfeasor to treat harm to a particular individual as simply a cost of doing business. Cashin v. Northern Pac. Ry. Co., 28 P.2d 862, 870 (Mont. 1934) (approving an award of punitive damages where the defendant's employees used explosives in the knowledge that their use would damage the plaintiffs' house because it was cheaper to pay for the damage than to employ alternative construction methods). The concern here is that some well-to-do persons or entities will happily treat compensatory damages as the price to be paid for securing the "right" to injure others.*

Some early critics argued that, to the extent they are awarded *because of* a defendant's insulting or opportunistic behavior, punitive damages are really a disguised form of compensatory damages that duplicate the portion of the jury's compensatory award designed to compensate the plaintiff for the emotional distress he experienced by virtue of being mistreated. Fay v. Parker, 53 N.H. 342 (N.H. 1872) (tort law should not recognize a separate category of exemplary damages because they are "the same thing as damages for wounded feelings, as distinguished from damages for an injury to person or property"). Might one accept *Fay*'s insight that punitive damages are in some sense "compensatory" of the plaintiff without drawing the conclusion that they are redundant with damages for emotional distress? If tort compensation is conceived as redress that a victim is entitled to exact from a person who has wronged him, might punitive damages be understood as a special form of recourse appropriately granted to victims of torts who have been subjected to insult on top of injury?

14. *Deterrence of Anti-Social Conduct?* Some of the language in *Mathias* is reminiscent of the Supreme Court's *Borak* decision, see Chapter 6, in which the Court based its willingness to identify implied rights of action within federal securities laws in part on the idea that private suits would assist regulators in enforcing those laws. Thus, Judge Posner suggests that punitive damages can assist in deterring and punishing criminal conduct that would otherwise escape sanction, either because it goes undetected, or because the victim (and her attorney) will not have sufficient incentive to bring suit in light of the psychic and economic costs of litigation (particularly if the defendant is wealthy and inclined to engage in "scorched earth" defense tactics). To what extent can punitive damages be justified as inducing certain tort plaintiffs to play the role of private attorneys general — plaintiffs who sue (and recover) on behalf of the public interest in the enforcement of rules of proper conduct? Would this rationale explain why punitive damages are awarded only in some tort cases? Why they are awarded in response to

---

* To illustrate their concern, nineteenth- and early-twentieth century authorities sometimes pointed to an example drawn from ancient Rome, the law of which required tortfeasors to compensate their victims in pre-set amounts. The example was provided by Lucius Veratius, a Roman citizen who apparently "used to amuse himself by striking those whom he met in the street in the face, and then tendering them the legal amends, which a slave carried after him for that purpose." *Vindictive Damages*, 4 Am. L.J. 61, 75 (1852).

the particular forms of "aggravated" misconduct currently recognized by courts as supporting such awards?

15. *Compensating Others?* Suppose a given defendant has committed the sort of egregious wrong that warrants harsh sanction. Why should that sanction take the form of money paid *to the plaintiff?* Consider, in light of the foregoing rationales, whether any explains why a tort victim or his survivors should be the one(s) to whom the sanction is paid. Some states have enacted statutes mandating that a certain percentage of any punitive damage award be taken from the plaintiff and contributed to the state's treasury, presumably to be allocated for the public good. *See, e.g.,* Ga. Code Ann. § 51-12-5.1(e)(2) (requiring 75 percent of punitive awards to be paid to the state). Plaintiffs whose awards have been reduced under these statutes have challenged their validity on constitutional grounds, with mixed results. *See, e.g.,* Kirk v. Denver Publg. Co., 818 P.2d 262 (Colo. 1991) (en banc) (striking down Colorado's punitive damages splitting statute).

16. *Who Pays?: Punitive Damages, Vicarious Liability and Insurance.* Sections II and IV of this chapter respectively examine the doctrine of *respondeat superior*, by which employers are held responsible for certain torts committed by employees, and the role of liability insurance in permitting tortfeasors to defray the costs of judgments entered against them. As a segue to these discussions, consider the role that *respondeat superior* and insurance might have played in *National By-Products* and *Mathias*.

Note first that both decisions are prepared to impose liability for punitive damages not only on the individual employees who perpetrated the torts in question, but also on the companies that employed them. For all practical purposes, this entails that the judgments in these cases will be paid out of company bank accounts rather than out of the employees' pockets.

With respect to *compensatory* damages, the basic rule, explored in the next section, is that a plaintiff can seek compensation out of company assets if her injuries result from a tort committed by a company employee in the course of his employment. Courts have split on whether this same standard should control employer liability for punitive damages. Arkansas appears to take the view that the same rule should apply. Miller v. Blanton, 210 S.W.2d 293 (Ark. 1948). Thus, if the evidence had been deemed sufficient to support an award of punitive damages against Foley, National By-Products would likely have been on the hook, given that his errant driving occurred during the course of his employment.

Other jurisdictions require great *managerial* involvement before permitting employers to be held liable for punitive damages arising out of employees' tortious acts. Typically, these jurisdictions will only permit liability to be imposed on the employer if the tortious conduct in question was either committed by management-level employees (as was the case in *Mathias*) or was committed by lower-level employees whose conduct was then endorsed or "ratified" by management. Dan B. Dobbs, *The Law of Torts* § 381, at 1063 (2000) (noting split among jurisdictions). Might one argue that the *National By-Products* court's refusal to attribute recklessness to Foley was an indirect means of implementing this more restrictive approach to vicarious liability for punitive damages?

As to insurance, courts have similarly split over whether insurers should be permitted to issue liability insurance policies — such as medical malpractice policies — that cover punitive damage awards. Courts that have barred such coverage reason that it is against public policy to let perpetrators of egregious wrongs "escape" punishment by purchasing insurance to cover the cost of a punitive award issued in response to that conduct.

II.   VICARIOUS LIABILITY

We have seen many negligence suits in which claims are brought against a company or organization instead of, or in addition to, the individual tort-feasor. As noted briefly in Chapter 1, the ability of plaintiffs to establish the liability of these defendants usually turns on the doctrine of *vicarious liability*, by which one person or entity is held responsible for the tortious acts of another who is acting, in some sense, on her or its behalf. The following case presents for consideration the scope of the most important form of vicarious liability, namely, *respondeat superior*. Under that doctrine, a "master" (employer) is subject to liability for tortious conduct committed by its "servant" (employee).

Taber v. Maine
67 F.3d 1029 (2d Cir. 1995)

Calabresi, J.   Twenty-six years ago, in Ira S. Bushey & Sons, Inc. v. United States, 398 F.2d 167 (2d Cir. 1968), this court held that the United States Government was vicariously liable for damage to a drydock caused by a drunken sailor who was returning to ship from a night's liberty. In his celebrated opinion, Judge Henry Friendly described the basis of respondeat superior as the "deeply rooted sentiment that a business enterprise cannot justly disclaim responsibility for accidents which may fairly be said to be characteristic of its activities." *Id.* at 171. Even though the sailor had become drunk while on liberty and far off base, we noted that drinking on leave was so common a part of naval life that the sailor's drunken return to ship could fairly be deemed to be characteristic of the military enterprise and, hence, that the government should be held liable for the damage that he caused. *See id.* at 172.

In *Bushey*, we applied admiralty law. Today — in a case that again involves a seaman who had too much to drink — we must apply the law of Guam. This, in turn, points us to California decisions for guidance. As it happens, California had taken the lead in developing the modern law of respondeat superior even before *Bushey*. And, so, rounding out the circle, we now reach the same conclusion as did Judge Friendly, twenty-six years ago. . . .

BACKGROUND

. . . On the morning of April 13, 1985, Robert S. Maine, ("Maine") a Navy serviceman on active duty at the U.S. Naval Ship Repair Facility on the island of Guam, went on liberty after having completed a grueling 24 hour duty shift. While on liberty he was free to leave the base as he pleased and travel up to 50 miles away. He could also be recalled for duty at any time.

Maine decided to have a good time. By noon, he was relaxing at an on-base beach party and drinking beer with Navy friends. Later that afternoon, he purchased two six-packs of beer at the base PX with his Navy comrade, Karin Conville ("Conville"), and returned with her to his barracks to drink several more cans. At dinnertime, Maine accompanied friends to the enlisted men's club, where he consumed two cocktails with his meal. After dinner, he attended a barracks party in the room of a superior officer, with several other superior officers present. There, Maine drank three or four more beers and — when he left to return to his own barracks at about 11:00 P.M. — Conville and another Navy comrade named Jean Buquet noticed that he seemed to be drunk. At around 11:30 P.M., Maine had difficulty sleeping and decided to drive off base to get something to eat. Feeling tired, he aborted his snack mission and tried to return to base. On the way back, he caused the accident that injured Scott A. Taber ("Taber").

Taber was an enlisted Seabee — a construction worker in the United States Navy — and was stationed at Camp Covington, Guam. At 6:00 P.M. on Friday, April 12th, he too went on liberty. Accordingly, he was free to go off base at any time, to travel anywhere within 50 miles of his base and, unless he was recalled for duty, to do as he pleased until his liberty ended at 6:00 A.M. on the following Monday.

Around 2:00 P.M. on Saturday April 13, Taber's civilian friend, Estelita Stills ("Stills"), met Taber at his base in her car. They planned to spend the weekend together at her house, which was located off the base. Before going there, however, the two drove to her cousins' home for dinner at the nearby U.S. Naval Station. There, Taber enjoyed a meal and, as a friendly gesture in return, helped fix the cousins' car. Shortly before midnight, Stills and Taber left for Stills's house and their weekend of rest and recreation. As fate would have it, they never got there. While they were driving on the public roadway toward Stills's house, Maine crashed into them, injuring Taber severely.

Two years later, Taber started this action for damages under the Federal Tort Claims Act ("FTCA"), 28 U.S.C. §§ 1346(b), 2671, in the United States District Court for the Western District of New York, (David G. Larimer, Judge). Naming both Maine and the United States Government as defendants, Taber complained that he was injured as a result of Maine's negligent driving and that, because Maine was acting within the scope of his Naval employment when he caused the accident, the government was liable on a theory of *respondeat superior*. . . .

Judge Larimer granted summary judgment to the government because "Maine's drunk driving incident on April 13, 1985, was not in the line of duty and therefore the United States is not liable under the doctrine of *respondeat superior*." . . .

The action proceeded against Maine, however. After a bench trial in which Maine appeared pro se, the district court found Maine liable for negligence and assessed Taber's damages at $300,000. A final judgment was entered and Taber appealed. . . .

The FTCA allows civil actions against the government based on the negligent acts or omissions of its employees, see 28 U.S.C. § 1346(b), including those of members of the Armed Services who are acting "in the line of duty." 28 U.S.C. § 2671. The courts have uniformly equated the FTCA's "line of duty" language with the phrase "scope of employment," as that concept is defined by the respondeat superior law of the jurisdiction in which the accident occurred. . . . Because the accident in this case happened in Guam, we must follow Guam's law of respondeat superior. . . .

Where the law of Guam is unclear, the Ninth Circuit, serving as Guam's highest appellate court . . . has instructed courts to look to California law for guidance. . . .

It seems clear to us that California law (and by implication the law of Guam) would hold the government vicariously liable for Maine's actions. California was one of the first states in the nation to adopt an expansive reading of the *respondeat superior* doctrine. . . .

This approach to *respondeat superior* is . . . evident in numerous California cases. . . . For example, in Rodgers v. Kemper Construction Co., 50 Cal. App. 3d 608, 124 Cal. Rptr. 143 (4th Dist. 1975), a subcontractor was held vicariously liable for an assault committed by two of its employees who had lounged around drinking for several hours in what was, ironically, called the "dry house" (a rest area/locker room located on the job site). On a Friday night after their work shift had ended, the employees, though free to go home, stayed in the dry house and got drunk. Later they went outside and got in a fight with the plaintiffs. *See id.* at 615, 124 Cal. Rptr. at 146-47.

In finding *respondeat superior* liability, the court stated that "the inquiry should be whether the risk was one 'that may be fairly regarded as typical of or broadly incidental' to the enterprise undertaken by the employer." 50 Cal. App. 3d at 619, 124 Cal. Rptr. at 149 (citations omitted). The court further noted that under California law,

> where social or recreational pursuits on the employer's premises after hours are endorsed by the express or implied permission of the employer and are "conceivably" of some benefit to the employer or, even in the absence of proof of benefit, if such activities have become "a customary incident of the employment relationship," an employee engaged in such pursuits after hours is still acting within the scope of his employment.

50 Cal. App. 3d at 620, 124 Cal. Rptr. at 150.

In *Rodgers*, the subcontractor "customarily permitted employees to remain on the premises in or about the dry house long after their work shift had ended" and it was also "customary, particularly on Friday evenings, for employees to sit around the dry house after their work shift and talk and drink beer, often . . . joined by their supervisors." 50 Cal. App. 3d at 619-20, 124 Cal. Rptr. at 149. Because it "was neither unusual nor unreasonable" for the assailants to be on the job site drinking before the assault, and because such drinking in the dry house "was a customary incident of the employment relationship," the court ruled that their related tortious actions fell within the scope of their employment. *Id.* Not surprisingly, the court in *Rodgers* relied heavily on our decision in *Bushey. See id.* at 618, 124 Cal. Rptr. at 148-49.

Similarly, in Childers v. Shasta Livestock Auction Yard, Inc., 190 Cal. App. 3d 792, 235 Cal. Rptr. 641 (3d Dist. 1987), Shasta's foreman gave Childers and Abbott (both Shasta employees) the keys to his office at the end of the day and told them to go have a beer. The two employees were later joined by a customer, and the three of them drank both beer and hard liquor for several hours, getting quite drunk. *Id.* at 799, 235 Cal. Rptr. at 642-43. At around 10:00 P.M., Abbott suggested to Childers that they drive off to feed Abbott's horses. Abbott drove her truck off the road, killing herself and injuring Childers. *Id.*

In addressing Childers's claim against Shasta, the court made clear that the fact that Childers's injuries occurred away from the work site did not bar the employer's vicarious liability for Abbott's drunk driving. The court said:

> *respondeat superior* liability is properly applied where an employee undertakes activities within his or her scope of employment that cause the employee to become an instrumentality of danger to others even where the danger may manifest itself at times and locations remote from the ordinary workplace.

190 Cal. App. 3d at 804-05, 235 Cal. Rptr. at 647. . . .

The district court below tried to distinguish these authorities on the ground that the drinking in *Rodgers* and *Childers* took place at the work site while Maine's supposedly did not. We disagree. The drinking in both *Rodgers* and *Childers* occurred at work-site rest areas (the "dry house" and the business office, respectively) — not on the assembly line. Similarly, although Maine did not drink while working at the Naval Ship Repair Facility, he drank at an on-base beach party, at the enlisted men's club, and in the barracks — all of which were located on his base. These places were as much on-site rest areas as the ones involved in both *Rodgers* and *Childers.*

The government understandably seeks to rely on an older conception of *respondeat superior.* This view of the doctrine required a close link between the acts of the "agent" and "profit" accruing to the master before vicarious liability attaches to the latter. *See* Restatement (Second) of Agency § 228 (1984). But today this position is in hasty retreat, if not rout. Thus *Rodgers* and *Childers* held that the employer-benefit requirement is met whenever broad potential effects on morale and customer relations exist, or where the employer has implicitly permitted or endorsed the recreational practices that led to the harm. *See Rodgers,*

50 Cal. App. 3d at 618-21, 124 Cal. Rptr. at 149-50; *Childers*, 190 Cal. App. 3d at 805-06, 235 Cal. Rptr. at 647-48. . . .

Of course drinking by servicemembers *can* be viewed as important to military morale, just as drinking was apparently instrumental to good employee morale and customer relations in *Rodgers* and *Childers*. Hence, "employer-benefit" can be adduced in all these cases. But in the end, "employer-benefit" is significant only because it is one way of showing that the harm that drinking causes can properly be considered a cost of the employer's enterprise.

California courts have said that the doctrine of *respondeat superior* is *"concerned with the allocation of the cost of industrial injury." Childers*, 190 Cal. App. 3d at 801, 235 Cal. Rptr. at 644 (emphasis added). The issue is simply whether the employee's "conduct is not so unusual or startling that it would seem unfair to include the loss resulting from it *among other costs* of the employer's business." *Rodgers*, 50 Cal. App. 3d at 619, 124 Cal. Rptr. at 149 (emphasis added). Thus, our focus must be on the relationship between the servicemember's behavior and the costs of the military enterprise.

Here, it is undisputed that drinking on base during off-duty hours was a commonplace, if not an officially condoned activity. It certainly was a customary incident of Maine's employment relationship with the Navy, as that element is described in *Rodgers*. *See* 50 Cal. App. 3d at 620, 124 Cal. Rptr. at 150. And in the context of the military mission, an occasional drunken servicemember who leaves government premises and causes damage is a completely foreseeable event, in the sense that it is a reasonably obvious risk of the general enterprise. As such, we do not think that it would be either "unfair" or the slightest bit unreasonable to impose that cost on the government. To the contrary, given the pervasive control that the military exercises over its personnel while they are on a base, it is totally in keeping with the doctrine of *respondeat superior* to allocate the costs of base operations to the government. *See* William M. Landes & Richard A. Posner, *The Positive Economic Theory of Tort Law*, 15 Ga. L. Rev. 851, 914-15 (1981) (discussing *respondeat superior* as an incentive for employers to exert their control over employees to induce careful conduct). And this is so quite apart from whether or not the military benefits from the boost in morale achieved through fairly lenient on-base drinking policies.[4]

As the leading Torts treatise has put it, "the integrating principle" of *respondeat superior* is "that the employer should be liable for those faults that may be fairly regarded as risks of his business, whether they are committed in furthering it or not." Fowler V. Harper, Fleming James,

---

4. We make no pronouncement on drunkenness in general. Our point here is simply that drinking *on base* during off-duty hours was a customary incident of Maine's employment relationship with the Navy. . . . It is these on-base activities that bring this case within the ambit of *Rodgers* and *Childers*. . . . We find instructive the example offered by Judge Friendly . . . in *Bushey*, indicating that employer liability would not be imposed for an off-base tort resulting from drinking at an *off-base* bar. . . . [W]e would not deem such an activity incident to the employment relationship. *See Bushey*, 398 F.2d at 172.

Jr. & Oscar S. Gray, *The Law of Torts* § 26.8 (2d ed., 1986). Judge Friendly
made the same point most elegantly in *Bushey*. "The proclivity of seamen
to find solicitude by copious resort to the bottle," he wrote, "has been
noted in opinions too numerous to warrant citation. Once all this is
granted, it is immaterial that [the coastguardsman's] precise action was
not to be foreseen." 398 F.2d at 172. After all, the government "cannot
justly disclaim responsibility for accidents which may fairly be said to be
characteristic of its activities." *Id.* at 171.

We believe the law of Guam reaches the same conclusion. Accordingly, we hold that the government is vicariously liable for Maine's
conduct.

[The United States next argued that even if Maine's actions could be
attributed to it via *respondeat superior*, it could not be held liable because
of the exception to FTCA liability recognized by the U.S. Supreme Court in
Feres v. United States, 340 U.S. 135 (1950). *Feres* held that the FTCA does
not waive sovereign immunity with regard to claims by members of the
armed forces for injuries that "arise out of or are [sustained] in the course
of activity incident to service." *Id.* at 146. The Court offered various rationales for this ban, noting, for example, that civil liability to service members
might interfere with military organization and discipline, and that servicemen are usually eligible for government benefits available outside the tort
system in the event they are injured in the line of duty. After an exhaustive
review of *Feres* and subsequent Supreme Court decisions, Judge Calabresi
concluded that Taber's claim was *not* barred by the *Feres* exception to the
FTCA. Taber's conduct in driving home from a weekend furlough, he
reasoned, was so tangentially related to his service that it would not interfere with military operations or government benefits programs.—EDS.] . . .

For the reasons stated above, we reverse the district court's judgment
and remand the case to the district court for further proceedings consistent with this opinion.

NOTES AND QUESTIONS

1. *Employee versus Employer Liability.* It is critical to distinguish
the issue of an employee's personal liability from that of his employer's
liability. Under the common law of negligence, if an employee drives carelessly while on the job so as to run down a pedestrian, the employee can
ordinarily be held liable for the damages caused. (However, the rules of
personal liability are different for government employees, see Note 13
infra.) But establishing the employee's liability does not of itself establish
that the employer—a separate "person" or entity in the eyes of the law—
should also be held liable. Determining the employer's liability instead
requires the application of additional legal principles.

2. *Direct versus Vicarious Liability.* In general, an employer can be
held liable for the tortious acts of its employees on two different theories:
direct liability and *vicarious* liability. A claim of direct liability asserts that
the employer (i.e., managerial personnel) acted wrongfully by failing to

screen or supervise its employees, and that this wrongful conduct helped bring about plaintiff's injuries. For example, suppose the manager of a trucking company hires a driver without performing a simple check that would have revealed that the driver has recently received a string of citations for drunk driving. Now suppose the driver, while intoxicated, crashes into and injures the plaintiff while driving a company truck on company business. Here, the plaintiff could sue the company directly on the theory that its manager's carelessness helped bring about the crash and his injuries. *See* Schultz v. Roman Catholic Archdiocese, *supra*, Chapter 7 (claim of negligent hiring).

By contrast, an allegation of *respondeat superior* liability does not assert that management itself has done anything wrong. Rather, it asserts that management — and ultimately, the company's owners — are on the hook for the wrong of an employee. As *Taber* explains, an employer is liable for the torts of its employees when those torts arise out of employee acts undertaken within the "scope of employment." However, when *respondeat superior* liability attaches, it does so even to an employer who has carefully screened and monitored its employees. Thus, it is common to regard the doctrine as creating a form of "strict" or "no-fault" liability. Can one argue to the contrary that *respondeat superior* provides for genuinely fault-based liability?

As indicated in the notes following Downs v. United States, *supra*, Chapter 7, as well as in *Taber*, the main effect of the passage of the Federal Tort Claims Act in 1946 was to expose the federal government to state law rules of *respondeat superior* liability. As we have seen and will see, however, these rules differ somewhat from the rules that typically attach to private employers.

3. *Direct Liability and Constitutional Torts.* Before examining *respondeat superior* liability in greater detail, it is worth pausing to note an important example of "direct" liability. Under 42 U.S.C. § 1983, city and local governments can be held liable to individuals whose constitutional rights are violated by virtue of conduct pursuant to policies set by those entities. As we saw in Chapter 6, government officials can be held *individually* liable under *Bivens* (federal officials) or Section 1983 (state and local officials) for violating constitutional rights. In addition, however, city and local governments can themselves be held liable for maintaining unconstitutional policies. For example, if a city were to adopt hiring guidelines for municipal employees that resulted in hiring decisions that discriminated against prospective hires on the basis of gender or race, a victim of those policies stands to obtain redress directly from the city's coffers. *See* Monell v. Department of Social Servs., 436 U.S. 658 (1978) (recognizing direct municipal liability under section 1983). The idea here is akin to the idea that employers can be held liable for negligent hiring or supervision. A distinct wrong is being perpetrated by the managers of the entity, rather than by lower-level employees in the course of their employment.

4. *Scope of Employment: Purpose versus Characteristic Activity.* *Respondeat superior* liability attaches only to employee torts committed within the scope of employment. The meaning of that restriction is, of

course, the central issue in *Taber*. Courts in the early twentieth century tended to address the scope issue in terms of the employee's reason for acting. If the careless employee was acting, at least in part, for the purpose of advancing the interests of the employer, the careless act was deemed within the scope of employment. Modern courts, however, have moved away from that test toward the "characteristic activities" analysis employed by Judge Friendly in *Bushey* and by Judge Calabresi in *Taber*.

5. *Scope of Employment: Detours and Frolics.* In an omitted portion of the excerpted opinion, Judge Calabresi opined that, had the situation in *Taber* been reversed, such that Taber was the negligent driver and Maine the plaintiff, the government would not have been subject to vicarious liability:

> There is nothing characteristically military about an employee who, after working-hours are done, goes off to spend a romantic weekend with a companion. Nor is there anything particularly military about having dinner with that companion's family at their home, and helping to fix their car. Finally, there is nothing especially military about returning to the companion's house intending to spend the rest of the weekend engaged in more intimate rest and recreation.

67 F.3d, at 1051. In drawing this distinction, Judge Calabresi invoked language from old cases distinguishing between an employee *detour* and an employee *frolic*. A detour consists of a slight deviation from the expected course or route that an employee would take in the course of doing his job. A frolic consists of an employee who so far deviates from his employment obligations that he is deemed to be on his own business. An example of a detour might be a delivery-truck driver who, while en route to a customer, goes three city blocks out of his way on a personal errand, and who carelessly injures another driver during that diversion. A frolic would be an instance in which the driver played hooky with the truck, using it to take his jet-ski for a day at the beach. *See, e.g.*, Fiocco v. Carver, 137 N.E. 309 (N.Y. 1922) (Cardozo, J.) (employer not liable for injuries caused to children when driver deviated from his route, stopped his truck at a street fair, and let a horde of costumed children climb onto the truck).

6. *Scope of Employment: Intentional Torts and State and Federal Law.* Under the older, "purpose" test, courts tended to categorically exclude intentional wrongful acts of employees as being outside the scope of employment. Under the "characteristic activities" test state courts have held that some — but not all — forms of intentional employee wrongdoing can be attributed to employers.

For example, a bar will typically be held liable if a bouncer it employs to control crowds takes the occasion to beat severely a patron for no particular reason. However, some intentional acts will be deemed to be too far removed from the business of the employer to provide the basis for vicarious liability. Suppose, for example, the driver of a company's delivery van takes an instant dislike to a customer, as a result of which the driver deliberately backs his van over the customer's dog. Even under the modern approach, a court will be reluctant to hold the company liable under *respondeat superior*. Modern courts have divided over whether schools and churches can be held vicariously liable for sexual assaults by teachers and clergy. *See generally* Dan B. Dobbs, *The Law of Torts* § 335, at 915 (2000).

By means of an explicit statutory command, the FTCA adopts a more restrictive approach to vicarious liability for intentional torts committed by federal employees. Essentially, it excludes such liability unless the intentional tort is committed by an "investigative or law enforcement officer." 28 U.S.C. § 2680(h). See Chapter 6. Obviously, this special statutory limitation was not at issue in *Taber*, which involved a claim for careless employee conduct.

7. *Hostile Work Environment.* Federal antidiscrimination statutes provide private rights of actions to employees who are subject to sexual harassment. Harassment comes in two forms: *quid pro quo* and *hostile work environment*. An example of the former is a situation in which a supervisor makes his supervisee's job advancement contingent on compliance with a request for sex. The latter sort of claim asserts that management has tolerated or endorsed an atmosphere that is pervasively sexist. See Chapter 10. Whereas management is usually held vicariously liable for *quid pro quo* harassment, the rule is different for hostile work environment claims. If the employer has in place a reasonable system for preventing and responding to harassment, the plaintiff is not permitted to recover from the employer without demonstrating that she attempted to invoke that system. In effect, then, the employer will only be liable in this class of harassment case on a *direct* theory of liability, that is, if its system for dealing with harassment is found to be unreasonable. *See* Farragher v. City of Boca Raton, 524 U.S. 775 (1998).

8. *Rationales.* The principle of *respondeat superior* is venerable, running back at least to the law of ancient Rome. As originally cast, it may have been based on the idea that an employee — that is, servant or slave — was not a legally recognized person, but was owned by the master. As such, the master was held to be responsible for the damage caused by his "things." Needless to say, such odious notions no longer provide the rationale for the rule. What rationale does the Second Circuit identify as the most compelling basis for the doctrine? Can you think of others?

9. *Friendly versus Calabresi.* Before ascending to the bench from the deanship of Yale Law School, Judge Calabresi established himself as one of the twentieth century's leading torts scholars. His most important contribution to torts scholarship is rooted in the idea that judges and legislatures dealing with the problem of assigning liability for accidents should base their decisions not on "backward-looking" considerations of responsibility, but instead with the "forward-looking" aim of efficiently deterring future accidents. They could best accomplish this, he argued, by assigning liability to the actor whom they believe could most easily (cheaply) take precautions that would prevent the same sort of accident from arising in the future. In his words, courts should assign liability to the "cheapest cost avoider" of similar accidents.

There is a certain irony in Calabresi's effort to invoke Friendly's opinion in the *Bushey* case. *Bushey* involved a drunken sailor who, for unknown reasons, decided to play with wheels that opened valves controlling the level of water in a drydock, thereby causing property damage to the drydock owner. The trial court invoked Calabresi's notion of the cheapest cost avoider in support of its decision to treat the acts of the drunken sailor as within the scope of employment and hence attributable to the government. A broad rule of *respondeat superior*, the judge suggested, would encourage efficient precaution-taking because it would give the employer an incentive to more closely monitor and control its employees. In essence, it reasoned that the United States as the shipowner and employer was in the best position to protect against shenanigans by drunken sailors.

Friendly's opinion for the Court of Appeals affirmed the trial court's ruling but expressed skepticism that it was supported by a Calabresian "cheapest cost avoider" rationale:

> [T]he suggestion that imposition of liability here will lead to more intensive screening of employees rests on highly questionable premises. . . . The unsatisfactory quality of the [efficient deterrence] rationale is especially striking on the facts of this case. It could well be that application of the traditional rule [which would have excluded employer liability on the facts of the case] might induce drydock owners . . . to install locks on their valves to avoid similar incidents in the future, while placing the burden on shipowners is much less likely to lead to accident prevention.

398 F.2d., at 170-171. Friendly further cast a skeptical eye toward another commonly cited rationale for *respondeat superior*, namely the idea that attaching liability to the employer permits the legal system to "spread the cost" of injuries from a single injured victim (e.g., the dockowner) to a large segment of the population (i.e., the customers of a business, who will "pay" for the tort judgment through higher prices, or taxpayers, who fund the federal government and thus pay the tab for its torts). Said Friendly: "[T]he fact that the defendant is better able to afford damages is not alone sufficient to justify legal responsibility. . . ." *Id.* at 171. Having dismissed these rationales, Friendly then invoked the "deeply rooted sentiment" rationale quoted in Judge Calabresi's *Taber* opinion.

10. *Employees, Independent Contractors, and Co-Workers.* As a matter of black-letter doctrine, the rule of *respondeat superior* applies to employees, but not to independent contractors. For example, suppose business *B* contracts with bicycle messenger *M* to have *M* deliver documents to local clients, and that *M* carelessly injures someone in the course of making a delivery for *B*. *B* should not be held liable on a theory of *respondeat superior*. Even though *M*'s acts presumably provide a benefit to *B*, they are not acts undertaken *by B*, but instead by an independent entity that has contracted to provide a service to *B*. *Cf.* Bailly v. Rudolf Steiner School, 741 N.Y.S.2d 197 (App. Div. 2002) (school not vicariously liable for negligence of bus company hired to transport students).

In particular situations, the line between an employee and an independent contractor will be elusive. The ALI's Restatement of Agency law advises that the distinction be drawn by reference to various considerations. (The Restatement uses the term *servant* to refer to what we have been calling *employee*.)

§ 220.   DEFINITION OF SERVANT

(1) A servant is a person employed to perform services in the affairs of another and who with respect to the physical conduct in the performance of the services is subject to the other's control or right to control.

(2) In determining whether one acting for another is a servant or an independent contractor, the following matters of fact, among others, are considered:

(a) the extent of control which, by the agreement, the master may exercise over the details of the work;

(b) whether or not the one employed is engaged in a distinct occupation or business;

(c) the kind of occupation, with reference to whether, in the locality, the work is usually done under the direction of the employer or by a specialist without supervision;

(d) the skill required in the particular occupation;

(e) whether the employer or the workman supplies the instrumentalities, tools, and the place of work for the person doing the work;

(f) the length of time for which the person is employed;

(g) the method of payment, whether by the time or by the job;

(h) whether or not the work is a part of the regular business of the employer;

(i) whether or not the parties believe they are creating the relation of master and servant; and

(j) whether the principal is or is not in business.

Restatement (Second) of Agency § 220, at 485-486 (1958). Needless to say, the distinction between employees (servants) and independent contractors can be critical to the plaintiff's ability to recover. For example, if the putative employer is solvent, whereas the negligent actor is not, the plaintiff will be unable to collect on any judgment if the actor is deemed an independent contractor rather than an employee.

Common law also sets limits on the ability of employers to circumvent vicarious liability through the use of independent contractors. Under the *non-delegable duty* doctrine, for example, courts have sometimes prohibited commercial landowners from disavowing carelessness by independent contractors performing work on the premises. *See, e.g.*, Strayer v. Lindeman, 427 N.E.2d 781 (Ohio 1981) (landlord held vicariously liable to tenants for property damage caused by the carelessness of an independent contractor hired to fulfill the landlord's statutory obligation to maintain the premises in good repair). Likewise, they have held general contractors liable for the negligence of technically independent subcontractors. *See, e.g.*, Brooks v. Hayes, 395 N.W.2d 167 (Wis. 1986).

11. Respondeat Superior *and Medical Malpractice.* Contrary, perhaps, to public perception, treating physicians at hospitals often are

independent contractors rather than hospital employees. For example, some are staff physicians who merely have permission to use a hospital's facilities as they are available. What about a surgical nurse who is formally employed by the hospital, but makes a mistake that causes injury to the patient during a surgical procedure that is controlled by the surgeon? Is the hospital liable as employer even though the surgeon had complete authority over the nurse's actions while in the operating room? Is the surgeon vicariously liable? *See, e.g.*, Parker v. Vanderbilt University, 767 S.W.2d 412 (Tenn. Ct. App. 1998) (surgeon not vicariously liable for malpractice of surgical nurses).

12. *Joint Liability and Indemnification.* Ordinarily, when a private employer is held liable for the tort of its employee under *respondeat superior*, that holding does *not* relieve the employee who tortiously injured the plaintiff of liability. Rather, the employer and employee are held jointly and severally liable to the plaintiff — that is, each is on the hook to the plaintiff, and the plaintiff may decide from whom he wishes to seek compensation. See *infra* Section III (discussing joint and several liability). As a practical matter, however, the plaintiff will almost always seek recovery from the employer, who is more likely to possess the means to pay the judgment. Once the employer pays the judgment, in principle, it has a right to seek either partial or full reimbursement from the employee. Again, however, this right is more notional than real. Employers who have been made to pay judgments for their employees' torts do not typically seek reimbursement for many reasons, including that the employer is itself not likely to be the one footing the bill for the tort claim, but rather the employer's liability insurer. See *infra* Section IV.

13. *Personal Immunity of Government Employee Revisited.* As noted in Chapter 7, federal employees such as Maine have been formally exempted by the Westfall Act from being held individually liable for torts committed in the scope of their employment. 28 U.S.C. § 2679. In other words, a person injured by the tortious conduct of a federal employee acting within the scope of her employment *cannot* recover from the employee, but may only recover from the government as employer. State legislatures have enacted counterparts for state employees.

Recalling this feature of federal law raises an obvious question: Why was Taber permitted to sue Maine individually, along with the federal government? In a portion of the opinion not reproduced, the Court of Appeals informs us that Maine, who represented himself in the litigation, failed to invoke this statutory provision, which would have immunized him from any personal liability to Taber.

14. *Related Doctrines: Automobile Owners' Liability. Respondeat superior* is a particularly important variant of vicarious liability, one which stems from the employer-employee relationships. Other relationships can sometimes support attributions of vicarious liability. The general partners of a partnership, for example, are vicariously liable for each other's torts. As we saw in connection with the *Appelhans* case in Chapter 3, parents generally are *not* vicariously liable for the careless acts of their children,

although they may sometimes be held *directly liable* if their own carelessness helped bring about the child's negligence, as in cases of negligent supervision (e.g., failing to take any steps to control a child known to have violent or dangerous propensities) or negligent entrustment (e.g., handing a young child a dangerous weapon).

An important exception to this rule concerns the case of parents who permit their children to drive their cars for business or pleasure. In the typical case, the parent/owner permits her teenager to use the car, and the child drives carelessly so as to cause injury to another. In such situations, the parent, *as car owner*, is held liable even if the decision to hand over the car keys to the child was not itself unreasonable. *See, e.g.*, Malchose v. Kalfell, 664 N.W.2d 508 (N.D. 2003) (parents vicariously liable for dependent son's careless driving even though son was away at college at the time of the accident).

Some states have by statute extended this rule of car owners' vicarious liability to any accident resulting from carelessness in the use of the car by a driver who was given permission by the owner to use the car. *See, e.g.*, N.Y. Veh. & Traf. L. § 388. In theory, this version of vicarious liability could extend to an automobile dealer or manufacturer that "sells" cars by means of long-term lease arrangements rather than outright sales. Until quite recently, Connecticut imposed such liability by statute. *See* Conn. Stat. Ann. § 14-154a (lessor of an automobile is liable to the same extent as operator of the car). In 2003, the state legislature repealed this provision and enacted a new statute that excludes passenger car dealers and manufacturers from being held vicariously liable for the negligent operation of passenger vehicles held on long-term leases. *See* Conn. Leg. P.A. No. 03-250 (2003).

III. JOINT LIABILITY AND CONTRIBUTION

We have already touched on the issue of apportionment in connection with comparative responsibility. However, the topic is sufficiently important and complex to warrant separate treatment. The basic issue is this: When two or more persons are adjudged legally responsible for an injury to the plaintiff, how should the courts allocate responsibility and liability among them?

Ravo v. Rogatnick
514 N.E.2d 1104 (N.Y. 1987)

Alexander, J.   In this medical malpractice action, defendant, Dr. Irwin L. Harris, appeals from an order of the Appellate Division unanimously affirming an amended judgment of Supreme Court, entered on a jury verdict, finding him jointly and severally liable with Dr. Sol Rogatnick for injuries negligently inflicted upon plaintiff, Josephine Ravo, and resulting in brain damage that has rendered her severely and permanently retarded. The issue presented is whether joint and several liability was properly imposed upon defendant under the circumstances of this case where, notwithstanding that the defendants neither acted in concert nor concurrently, a single indivisible injury—brain damage—was negligently inflicted. For the reasons that follow, we affirm.

I.

Uncontroverted expert medical evidence established that plaintiff, Josephine Ravo, who at the time of trial was 14 years of age, was severely and permanently retarded as a result of brain damage she suffered at birth. The evidence demonstrated that the child was born an unusually large baby whose mother suffered from gestational diabetes which contributed to difficulties during delivery. The evidence further established that Dr. Rogatnick, the obstetrician who had charge of the ante partum care of Josephine's mother and who delivered Josephine, failed to ascertain pertinent medical information about the mother, incorrectly estimated the size of the infant, and employed improper surgical procedures during the delivery. It was shown that Dr. Harris, the pediatrician under whose care Josephine came following birth, misdiagnosed and improperly treated the infant's condition after birth. Based upon this evidence, the jury concluded that Dr. Rogatnick committed eight separate acts of medical malpractice, and Dr. Harris committed three separate acts of medical malpractice.

Although Dr. Rogatnick's negligence contributed to Josephine's brain damage, the medical testimony demonstrated that Dr. Harris' negligence was also a substantial contributing cause of the injury. No testimony was adduced, however, from which the jury could delineate which aspects of the injury were caused by the respective negligence of the individual doctors. Indeed, plaintiff's expert, Dr. Charash, . . . concluded that neither he nor anybody else could say with certainty which of the factors caused the brain damage. Similarly, Dr. Perrotta, testifying on behalf of plaintiff, opined that she could not tell whether [Dr. Harris' carelessness] contributed "10 percent, 20 percent, or anything like that" to the injury. Nor, as the Appellate Division found, did Dr. Harris adduce any evidence that could support a jury finding that he caused an identifiable percentage of the infant plaintiff's brain damage. Indeed, Dr. Harris' entire defense appears to have been that he was not responsible for the plaintiff's injury to any degree.

The trial court instructed the jury [on the principles of comparative fault and joint and several liability.] . . .

. . . [T]he jury returned a verdict for plaintiff in the total amount of $2,750,000 attributing 80% of the "fault" to Dr. Rogatnick and 20% of the "fault" to Dr. Harris.

In a postverdict motion, Dr. Harris sought an order directing entry of judgment limiting the plaintiff's recovery against him to $450,000 (20% of the $2,250,000 base recovery—the court having set off $500,000 received by plaintiff in settlement of claims against other defendants) based upon his contention that his liability was not joint and several, but rather was independent and successive. This motion was denied. The Appellate Division . . . affirmed. . . .

II.

When two or more tort-feasors act concurrently or in concert to produce a single injury, they may be held jointly and severally liable (*see*, Suria v. Shiffman, 67 N.Y.2d 87; Bichler v. Lilly & Co., 55 N.Y.2d 571; Derby v. Prewitt, 12 N.Y.2d 100, 105; Sweet v. Perkins, 196 N.Y. 482, 485). This is so because such concerted wrongdoers are considered "joint tort-feasors" and in legal contemplation, there is a joint enterprise and a mutual agency, such that the act of one is the act of all and liability for all that is done is visited upon each (. . . *see generally*, Prosser and Keeton, *Torts* § 46 [5th ed]). On the other hand, where multiple tort-feasors "neither act in concert nor contribute concurrently to the same wrong, they are not joint tort-feasors; rather, their wrongs are independent and successive" (Suria v. Shiffman, 67 N.Y.2d 87, 98, *supra; see*, Melodee Lane Lingerie Co. v. American Dist. Tel. Co., 18 N.Y.2d 57, 66; Derby v. Prewitt, 12 N.Y.2d 100, 105, *supra;* Matter of Parchefsky v. Kroll Bros., 267 N.Y. 410, 413). Under successive and independent liability, of course, the initial tort-feasor may well be liable to the plaintiff for the entire damage proximately resulting from his own wrongful acts (Milks v. McIver, 264 N.Y. 267, 270), including aggravation of injuries by a successive tort-feasor (Milks v. McIver, 264 N.Y. 267, 270, *supra*; Matter of Parchefsky v. Kroll Bros., 267 N.Y. 410, 414, *supra*; Derby v. Prewitt, 12 N.Y.2d 100, 105, *supra*). The successive tort-feasor, however, is liable only for the separate injury or the aggravation his conduct has caused (*see*, Suria v. Shiffman, 67 N.Y.2d 87, 98, *supra*; Derby v. Prewitt, 12 N.Y.2d 100, 106, *supra*; Dubicki v. Maresco, 64 A.D.2d 645, 646; *see also*, Zillman v. Meadowbrook Hosp. Co., 45 A.D.2d 267).

It is sometimes the case that tort-feasors who neither act in concert nor concurrently may nevertheless be considered jointly and severally liable. This may occur in the instance of certain injuries which, because of their nature, are incapable of any reasonable or practicable division or allocation among multiple tort-feasors (*see, e.g.*, Hawkes v. Goll, 281 N.Y. 808, *affg* 256 App. Div. 940; Slater v. Mersereau, 64 N.Y. 138; Wiseman v. 374 Realty Corp., 54 A.D.2d 119; *see also*, Prosser and Keeton, *Torts* § 52, at 347 [5th ed]).

We had occasion to consider such a circumstance in Slater v. Mersereau (64 N.Y. 138, *supra*), where premises belonging to the plaintiff were damaged by rainwater as a result of the negligent workmanship by a general contractor and a subcontractor. We held that where two parties by their separate and independent acts of negligence, cause a single, insepa-rable injury, each party is responsible for the entire injury: "Although they acted independently of each other, they did act at the same time in causing the damages . . . each contributing towards it, and although the act of each, alone and of itself, might not have caused the entire injury, under the circumstances presented, there is no good reason why each should not be liable for the damages caused by the different acts of all. . . . The water with which each of the parties were instrumental in injuring the plaintiffs was one mass and inseparable, and no distinction can be made between the different sources from whence it flowed, so that it can be claimed that each caused a separate and distinct injury for which each one is separately responsible. . . . [The] contractor and subcontractors were separately negligent, and although such negligence was not concurrent, yet the negligence of both these parties contributed to produce the damages caused at one and the same time" (Slater v. Mersereau, 64 N.Y. 138, 146-147, *supra*).

Our affirmance in Hawkes v. Goll (281 N.Y. 808, *affg* 256 App. Div. 940, *supra*) demonstrates that simultaneous conduct is not necessary to a finding of joint and several liability when there is an indivisible injury. In that case, the decedent was struck by the vehicle driven by the defendant Farrell and was thrown across the roadway, where very shortly thereafter he was again struck, this time by the vehicle driven by the defendant Goll, and dragged some 40 to 50 feet along the highway. He was taken to the hospital where he expired within the hour. The Appellate Division stated (256 App. Div. 940): "As the result of his injuries the plaintiff's intestate died within an hour. There could be no evidence upon which the jury could base a finding of the nature of the injuries inflicted by the first car as distinguished from those inflicted by the second car. The case was submitted to the jury upon the theory that if both defendants were negligent they were jointly and severally liable. While the wrongful acts of the two defendants were not precisely concurrent in point of time, the defendants may nevertheless be joint tort feasors where, as here, their several acts of neglect concurred in producing the injury." . . .

Similarly, here the jury was unable to determine from the evidence adduced at trial the degree to which the defendants' separate acts of negligence contributed to the [brain damage suffered] by Josephine at birth. Certainly, a subsequent tort-feasor is not to be held jointly and severally liable for the acts of the initial tort-feasor with whom he is not acting in concert in every case where it is difficult, because of the nature of the injury, to separate the harm done by each tort-feasor from the others (*see*, Chipman v. Palmer, 77 N.Y. 51; *see generally*, Prosser, *Joint Torts and Several Liability*, 25 Cal. L. Rev. 413). Here, however, the evidence established that plaintiff's brain damage was a single indivisible injury, and defendant failed to submit any evidence upon which the jury could base an apportionment of damage.

Harris argues, however, that since the jury ascribed only 20% of the fault to him, this was in reality an apportionment of damage, demonstrating that the injury was divisible. This argument must fail. Clearly, the court's instruction, and the interrogatory submitted in amplification thereof, called upon the jury to determine the respective responsibility in negligence of the defendants so as to establish a basis for an apportionment between them, by way of contribution, for the total damages awarded to plaintiff (*see*, CPLR 1401; Dole v. Dow Chem. Co., 30 N.Y.2d 143, *supra*). In that respect, the jury's apportionment of fault is unrelated to the nature of defendants' liability (i.e., whether it was joint and several or independent and successive). . . .

Here, the jury determined that the defendants breached duties owed to Josephine Ravo, and that these breaches contributed to her brain injury. The jury's apportionment of fault, however, does not alter the joint and several liability of defendants for the single indivisible injury. Rather, that aspect of the jury's determination of culpability merely defines the amount of contribution defendants may claim from each other, and does not impinge upon plaintiff's right to collect the entire judgment award from either defendant (CPLR 1402). As we stated in Graphic Arts Mut. Ins. Co. v. Bakers Mut. Ins. Co. (45 N.Y.2d 551, 557): "The right . . . to seek equitable apportionment based on relative culpability is not one intended for the benefit of the injured claimant. It is a right affecting the distributive responsibilities of tort-feasors *inter sese*. . . . It is elementary that injured claimants may still choose which joint tort-feasors to include as defendants in an action and, regardless of the concurrent negligence of others, recover the whole of their damages from any of the particular tort-feasors sued (see Kelly v. Long Is. Light. Co., 31 N.Y.2d 25, 30)." This being so, in light of the evidence establishing the indivisibility of the brain injury and the contributing negligence of Dr. Harris, and of the manner in which the case was tried and submitted to the jury, we conclude that joint and several liability was properly imposed.

Accordingly, the order of the Appellate Division should be affirmed.

NOTES AND QUESTIONS

1. *Joint and Several Liability: Indivisible Harms.* As *Ravo* explains, joint and several liability has long been available when two tortfeasors were found to have conspired together, or to have acted in concert. At least since the turn of the twentieth century, it has also been regularly applied in situations such as the one in *Ravo*, in which two negligent actors, acting independently of one another, caused a single *indivisible* harm to the plaintiff, such that there was no way to tell which tortfeasor caused which portion of the harm. See Chapter 4 (notes following McDonald v. Robinson). For example, suppose *D1* and *D2* drive in opposite directions through an intersection and both unreasonably ignore stop signs so as to smash into pedestrian *P*. *P* suffers serious injuries to his internal organs, resulting in damages of $1 million, but there is no way to figure out how much of that harm resulted from *P* being struck by *D1*, and how much from *P* being struck by *D2*. Under the indivisible injury rule, *D1* and *D2* would be held jointly and severally liable — *P* could ask either *D1* or *D2* to pay the full amount.

2. *Contribution.* Suppose in the foregoing hypothetical that *P* sued *D1* and *D2*, won verdicts against *D1* and *D2*, and then chose to collect the entire judgment of $1 million from *D1*. Does this mean that *D2* gets away with paying nothing, simply because *P* decided to collect from *D1*? Not necessarily. This is because a defendant who is made to pay more than his share of a liability that is jointly owed by another can bring a claim *against that other party*. This claim does *not* sound in tort or contract (*D2* did not commit a tort against *D1*, nor did *D2* breach any contract with *D1*). Instead, the claim sounds in a body of law called *restitution*. Essentially, the claim is that because of the operation of the rule of joint and several liability, *D1* has paid too much, and *D2* too little, and therefore in justice

D2 should transfer some of his wealth to *D1*. As noted in *Ravo*, claims for restitution brought in this special circumstance are called actions for *contribution*. Thus, the rule of joint and several liability, combined with the equitable action for contribution, frees the plaintiff from having to collect from each defendant and in turn *leaves it to the defendants to settle their accounts with one another*.*

3. *Actions for Contribution, Cross-Claims, and Impleaders.* In terms of procedure, it once was the case that a tortfeasor such as *D1* had to wait until he was forced to pay the judgment to *P* before filing a separate suit for contribution against a jointly liable co-defendant such as *D2*. Under modern rules of civil procedure, tortfeasors whose torts cause an injury to the same victim can assert claims for contribution against one another as part of the same lawsuit in which plaintiff brings her claims against the defendants. If a plaintiff has commenced her action against the relevant tortfeasors, such that they are all parties to the suit, they can seek contribution from one another by asserting *cross-claims*. Thus, if *P* were to sue *D1* and *D2*, and if *D1* were held liable for *P*'s entire award, *D1* could assert his claim for contribution in the form of cross-claim against *D2*. Even if for some reason *P* initially chose only to sue *D1*, *D1* would today have the option of bringing *D2* into the suit for purposes of determining to what extent *D2* will be liable to *D1* for contribution. When one defendant brings a co-defendant into a suit for the purpose of determining whether the co-defendant might be responsible for a share of any liability incurred by the original defendant to the plaintiff, the original defendant is said to have *impleaded* the co-defendant.**

4. *Comparative Fault With Joint and Several Liability.* Prior to the adoption of comparative fault, the amount that a jointly and severally liable co-defendant would have to contribute to the unlucky defendant

---

* Historically, an *intentional* tortfeasor subject to joint and several liability for a plaintiff's damages has been barred from seeking contribution from another tortfeasor also responsible for those damages on the ground that one who commits this graver sort of wrong has no basis for asserting that he has "overpaid" and hence no basis for seeking restitution from others. There is today movement among some courts to permit intentional tortfeasors held jointly and severally liable to seek contribution from co-tortfeasors — even merely careless co-tortfeasors — on the ground that intentional wrongs differ merely in degree, rather than in kind, from unintentional wrongs.

** Procedural rules authorizing impleaders typically authorize a defendant (*D*) to commence an action against a third party (*TP*) if *D* has a colorable claim that *TP* will be liable to *D* in the event that *D* is held liable to plaintiff (*P*). Once impleaded, *TP* becomes a party to the underlying suit by *P* against *D*. *TP* is referred to as the *third-party defendant*. For purposes of its claim against *TP*, *D* is referred to as the *third-party plaintiff*.

For an example of an impleader action, recall *McGuiggan, supra*, Chapter 2, the social-host liability case. There, the decedent's estate sued the telephone company for the careless placement of its pole, only to see the company *implead* the decedent's parents as additional defendants under the social host theory of liability. The telephone company was permitted to name the decedent's parents as additional parties to the suit because it had a nonfrivolous basis for asserting that they might be held jointly liable for their son's death, and hence might be someone against whom the company could bring a claim for contribution. As it turned out, of course, the court determined that they could not be held liable, hence the claims against them were dismissed.

who had been chosen by the plaintiff to pay the full judgment was determined on a *pro rata* basis. Thus, to continue the example developed above, if *P* collected her $1 million award from *D1*, and *D1* then sued *D2* for contribution, *D2* would be liable to pay *D1* $500,000 — 50 percent of the amount *D1* paid to *P* — because *D1* and *D2* were the only two responsible parties. With the adoption of comparative fault, *D2*'s share is no longer determined on a *pro rata* basis, but instead by the jury's percentage apportionment of fault. Thus, for example, if *D1* was found by the jury to be 30 percent at fault, and *D2* 70 percent at fault, yet *D1* was made to pay the full judgment, then *D1* would be entitled to seek contribution in the amount of $700,000 from *D2*.

5. *Comparative Fault Without Joint and Several Liability.* With the adoption of comparative responsibility, a question has arisen as to whether the idea of joint and several liability for indivisible harms continues to make sense. After all, comparative responsibility regimes require juries faced with cases such as our imagined intersection collision to assign *percentage* fault to the likes of *D1* and *D2*. If juries can and must *divide responsibility* in this manner, how can it make sense to describe *P*'s injury as *indivisible*, and hence as the sort of injury that requires the special rule of joint and several liability?

Obviously, the *Ravo* court concluded that comparative fault and joint and several liability are compatible with one another. Does the court contradict itself by simultaneously asserting that the plaintiff's injury is divisible for purposes of assigning comparative fault, yet indivisible for purposes of applying joint and several liability? A number of courts have concluded, in opposition to *Ravo*, that comparative fault is inconsistent with the doctrine of joint and several liability for indivisible injuries. *See, e.g.*, McIntyre v. Balentine, 833 S.W.2d 52 (Tenn. 1992).

6. *So What?* What is the practical difference between decisions such as *Ravo* and decisions such as *McIntyre*? In either case, *P* is ultimately entitled to recover 100 percent of her damages, and *D1* and *D2* to pay the share of damages apportioned to them by the jury. True, under *Ravo*, the plaintiff can get her $1,000,000 from *D1 or D2*, whereas under *McIntyre* she must collect it from *D1 and D2*. Is this a distinction without a difference? What risk is being allocated by the different approaches?

7. *Splitting the Difference.* *Ravo* and *McIntyre* are "all or nothing" decisions. If it turns out that one defendant is unreachable or insolvent, either the other defendant(s) (under *Ravo*) or the plaintiff (under *McIntyre*) will bear the full cost of a missing defendant's share of the damages. An alternative perhaps more in keeping with the "equitable" nature of the law of contribution might be to instead allocate the missing share among all parties found to have contributed to the plaintiff's injuries (including, where applicable, the at-fault plaintiff).

Suppose, for example, a jury faced with our hypothetical intersection collision were to conclude that *P* was 10 percent at fault for her own injuries, *D1* was 50 percent at fault, and D2 was 40 percent at fault. Now suppose *D2* is judgment-proof or otherwise unreachable. The value of

D2's "missing" share of liability—$400,000—might be split among *P* and *D1* as the two remaining parties deemed by the jury to have been responsible for *P*'s injuries. Under a *pro rata* version of such a scheme, *P* would recover $700,000 from *D1*—$500,000 based on *D1*'s 50 percent responsibility, plus another $200,000 representing half of *D2*'s missing share. (*P* would thus be forced to bear the other half of *D2*'s share.) Alternatively, a court could divide the value of *D2*'s missing share among *P* and *D1* by reference to the ratio of their percentage responsibilities. Under this approach, *P* would recover $833,333 from *D1*—$500,000 based on *D1*'s 50 percent responsibility, plus another $333,333 representing 5/6ths of *D2*'s missing share. *See, e.g.*, Martignetti v. Haigh-Farr, Inc., 680 N.E.2d 1131 (Mass. 1997) (adopting the latter approach in applying a federal environmental statute that imposes liability for the cost of cleaning up toxic waste sites among parties responsible for creating the site).

8. *The Decline of Joint and Several Liability.* In addition to focusing on statutes of limitations, as well as compensatory and punitive damage reforms, modern tort reform movements have taken aim at the rule of joint and several liability for indivisible injuries. The result has been that most states have adopted rules eliminating or restricting joint and several liability, at least in some classes of tort cases (e.g., actions for medical malpractice), or for certain damage items (e.g., noneconomic losses). For example, in 1986, Colorado enacted a statute that essentially abolished joint and several liability for cases of indivisible physical harms (although it remains applicable to cases of conspiracy and concert of action):

COLO. REV. STAT. § 13-21-111.5

Civil Liability Cases-Pro Rata Liability of Defendants.
   (1) In an action brought as a result of a death or an injury to person or property, no defendant shall be liable for an amount greater than that represented by the degree or percentage of negligence or fault attributable to such defendant that produced the claimed injury, death, damage, or loss, except as provided in subsection (4) of this section. . . .
   (4) Joint liability shall be imposed on two or more persons who consciously conspire and deliberately pursue a common plan or design to commit a tortious act. . . .

Obviously, under this scheme, a plaintiff suing for an indivisible physical harm caused independently by two tortfeasors, one of whom is insolvent or unreachable, bears the entire cost of that tortfeasor's share of liability. Is this fair? Suppose a jury were to find that the available tortfeasor was 75 percent at fault and the unreachable tortfeasor 25 percent at fault. Why should the innocent plaintiff bear the entire burden of the missing amount, as opposed to the available tortfeasor who was, after all, deemed by the jury to be mostly responsible for the plaintiff's injuries?

   In partial contrast to Colorado, New Jersey has adopted a "hybrid" scheme that authorizes joint and several liability in indivisible harms cases, but only as against those tortfeasors whose percentage responsibility reaches or surpasses a certain threshold:

N.J. STAT. 2A:15-5-5.3

Recovery of damages based on party's responsibility . . .
    Except [in suits for environmental harms, a successful claimant] may
recover as follows:
        a. The full amount of the damages of any party determined by the
    trier of fact to be 60% or more responsible for the total damages. . . .
        c. Only that percentage of the damages directly attributable to that
    party's negligence or fault from any party determined by the trier of fact
    to be less than 60% responsible for the total damages.

With the decline of joint and several liability, the issue of to whom a jury
may assign a percentage liability has become increasingly important.
Consider the issues raised under the New Jersey statute in the following
case.

Bencivenga v. J.J.A.M.M., Inc.

609 A.2d 1299 (N.J. Super. App. Div. 1992)

Muir, Jr., J.   In this personal injury action, the trial court denied the
request of J.J.A.M.M., Inc., doing business as Club 35 (Club 35), to instruct
the jury to compare the negligence of the club, the negligence of the plaintiff, and the intentional conduct of an unknown defendant, John Doe, for
the purposes of apportioning liability under the Comparative Negligence
Act, N.J.S.A. 2A:15-5.1, *et seq.* (Act). The jury found Club 35 liable for the
failure to protect the plaintiff, a patron of the club, from an assault by the
unknown defendant who was also a patron of the club. It awarded plaintiff $40,000 in compensatory damages. Club 35 appeals asserting, among
other things, the trial court erred in denying its request. . . .

I.

    Club 35 provides music, dancing, and a soda bar for persons 18 to 21
years of age on the second floor of a building that has an adult bar on the
first floor. The dancing area is approximately 40 feet by 30 feet with a stage
on one side. The club has overhead lighting, which includes a rarely used
strobe (flashing) light. The switch to the strobe light is in a room with a
locked door. Only club employees have keys to the door.
    The club employs personnel to maintain order and "provide safety to
the patrons." The personnel are essentially young, muscular men dressed
in matching outfits that include jackets identifying them as Club 35 staff.
The club operator testified these young men (bouncers) are present to
intervene if any problems arise. Two are located on the stage and two on
opposite sides of the dance floor. These four bouncers sit on bar stools
near the dance floor. They are placed, according to the operator, so
"they're visible to watch if anybody's doing anything." The operator testified all the bouncers are specifically responsible for watching the dance
floor to stop "fooling around[,] . . . unordinary type dancing or kicking,
waving arms around or whatever, what might be damage [sic] to the

customer. . . ." All bouncers have the responsibility to walk back and forth across the dance floor to assure crowd control.

On the evening of January 9, 1988, plaintiff, his brother, and three friends went to Club 35. After being approved for admission by the underage facility manager, defendant Melvin Meszaros, plaintiff, and his companions paid their admission and began dancing. The dance floor was very crowded—"packed elbow to elbow."

After dancing for about twenty minutes, plaintiff and his companions went to the soda bar area to cool off. While there, another male patron walked by a female patron and pinched her. The female, who at the time was talking to one of the bouncers, turned and accused plaintiff. Plaintiff denied he had pinched her. Later, the female again made the accusation, and plaintiff responded by saying he was sorry but he had not done it. The same bouncer then "gave [plaintiff] a dirty look" and suggested plaintiff and his friends leave. Plaintiff did not interpret this to mean leave the club but just to leave the vicinity of the female. Plaintiff and his companions returned to their dancing.

A few minutes later, plaintiff sustained the injury that gave rise to the lawsuit. Plaintiff's companions testified that four young men, two coming from the stage and two others from sides of the dance floor, met next to the stage. None of the four wore the dress of the bouncers. The four then began to cross the dance floor. At the same time the strobe light was turned on making it hard to see. The four proceeded across the floor toward plaintiff with the dancers separating as the men pushed their way through. One of plaintiff's companions testified he was pushed aside. The men left an open path in the dance floor crowd. As the four reached the plaintiff, who had his back to them, one said, "Why'd you pinch my girl's ass?" As plaintiff turned, the speaker punched plaintiff in the face. Plaintiff dropped to the floor bleeding profusely from the nose. Although the bouncers on the stage had a clear view of the floor and the four men crossing it, none interceded before or after the assault and none offered any assistance.

With assistance of his companions, plaintiff went to a bathroom on the first floor of the club. The injury made plaintiff almost unrecognizable. Plaintiff's nose was pushed to the right side of his face. Blood covered plaintiff and areas around him.

Shortly after plaintiff arrived in the bathroom, Melvin Meszaros appeared with three bouncers. Plaintiff's companions asked that a rescue squad and the police be called. They also asked for a towel. Instead of offering assistance, Meszaros took plaintiff by the arm and ushered him out of the building. At the same time, two bouncers carried plaintiff's emotionally distraught brother outside.

As plaintiff and his companions stood outside, a bouncer approached. Plaintiff recognized him as the bouncer who was talking to the female when she got pinched. The bouncer said, "I see you guys got your asses kicked." When asked why plaintiff's attacker also had not been removed from the club, the bouncer responded, "[T]he other guy's got juice. . . ."

Plaintiff needed surgery to repair his nose. . . . Plaintiff's nose contains a scar and a permanent deviation to the right as a result of the incident.

Plaintiff's complaint sought damages from Club 35 and the unnamed intentional tortfeasor, as well as from unnamed employees of the club. The complaint alleged, alternatively, negligent or intentional conduct on the part of Club 35 and its one named and other unnamed employees. Club 35's answer raised defenses that negligent conduct of others caused plaintiff's injuries. . . .

II.

In Blazovic v. Andrich, 124 N.J. 90, 107, 590 A.2d 222 (1991), decided after the trial in this case, the Supreme Court held the Act applies to conduct characterized as intentional. It ruled a jury must be instructed to compare the fault of intentional tortfeasors with that of negligent wrongdoers for the purpose of apportioning liability under the Act. See N.J.S.A. 2A:15-5.1. The Court based its ruling on the premise that parties causing an injury should be liable in proportion to their relative fault. Blazovic v. Andrich, *supra*, 124 N.J. at 109-10, 590 A.2d 222.

. . . Blazovic sought compensatory damages for injuries he sustained in a parking lot of the defendant restaurant when he was assaulted by five defendants who had been patrons of the restaurant. The evidence suggested comments made by Blazovic precipitated the assault. *Blazovic* held the fault of all parties, Blazovic, the restaurant, and the five assaultive defendants, who settled with Blazovic prior to trial, should be compared for purposes of the Act.

Blazovic rested his claim against the restaurant proprietor, as plaintiff rests his claim against Club 35, on the holding in Butler v. Acme Markets, Inc., 89 N.J. 270, 275, 445 A.2d 1141 (1982). *Butler* recognized that the "proprietor of premises to which the public is invited for business purposes of the proprietor owes a duty . . . to exercise reasonable care to discover intentionally harmful acts of third parties are being done or are likely to be done, or to give warning adequate to enable patrons to avoid the harm, or otherwise to protect them against the harm." *Id.* [at 280] (quoting Restatement (Second) of Torts § 344, at 223-24 (1965)).

III.

Club 35 asserts the trial court erred when the court rejected its request to instruct the jury to determine the relative percentages of fault of the plaintiff, the fictitiously named and never identified intentional tortfeasor who assaulted plaintiff, and Club 35. It contends *Blazovic* dictates such a result. We disagree. . . .

We turn first to the issue of whether the trial court erred in refusing to instruct the jury to compare the fault of the unnamed intentional tortfeasor in assessing liability. N.J.S.A. 2A:15-5.1 requires comparison of plaintiff's negligence with the negligence, now fault as the result of *Blazovic*, of the person or persons against whom recovery is sought. N.J.S.A. 2A:15-5.2 requires the trier of fact to return a special verdict on "[t]he percentage of negligence of each *party*" with "the total of all percentages of negligence of all the *parties to the suit*" being fixed at 100%. *Id.* (emphasis added).

We conclude the plain and ordinary meaning of the statutory language precludes inclusion of a fictitiously named tortfeasor from the Act's commands for apportioning fault. The plain language of sections 5.1 and 5.2 make the negligence of the person or persons *against whom recovery is sought* and the negligence of each *party* or *parties to the suit* the prerequisites to apportioning fault. A fictitious person is not someone against whom recovery can be sought because the fictitious person rule, R. 4:26-4, and due process prevent entry of judgment against a person designated by a fictitious name.

Also, a fictitious person is not a party to a suit. The person plaintiff identifies as a fictitious defendant only becomes a party to the suit when the defendant's true name is substituted in an amended complaint and service is effected. . . . It is at the point of service on the true defendant that a court gains jurisdiction, consonant with due process, and a person becomes a party to a suit. It is at that point when the Act requires the person's conduct be compared for the purposes of apportioning liability and not before.

This result is supported by our holding in Ramos v. Browning Ferris Ind. of So. Jersey, Inc., 194 N.J. Super. 96, 476 A.2d 304 (App. Div. 1984), *rev'd on other grounds*, 103 N.J. 177, 510 A.2d 1152 (1986). There we stated,

> A truer verdict is more likely to be returned where the fact finder's attention is ultimately fixed on the conduct of the parties who will be affected by the verdict. . . . With [the] necessary exception [of assessing the negligence of a settling tortfeasor with that of a non-settling tortfeasor for contribution purposes] there is no more reason to have a fact finder assign a percentage of negligence to someone who is not affected by the verdict than to assign a percentage of negligence to acts of God (such as the snow in this case) or a myriad of other causative factors that may have contributed to the happening of an accident. [*Id.* 194 N.J. Super. at 106, 476 A.2d 304.] . . .

Blazovic does not dictate otherwise. *Blazovic* required fault be apportioned among joint or concurrent tortfeasors regardless of the nature of the fault. It did not specifically rule on whether the Act required apportioning fault of an unnamed party. The Court did, however, suggest resolution of the issue in its response to a concern of an Appellate Division dissent. That concern suggested the liability formula enacted in N.J.S.A. 2A:15-5.3a [excerpted above—EDS.] could limit a plaintiff's recovery where there are multipl[e] liable tortfeasors if an intentional tortfeasor is deemed to have greater than 40% fault and is unable to pay the judgment. The Court responded, "We reject that [concern] because it ignores the principle that the *parties* causing an injury should be liable in proportion to their relative fault." *Id.* 124 N.J. at 110, 590 A.2d 222 (emphasis added). The unnamed intentional tortfeasor, John Doe, is not a party as required by the statute. To sanction inclusion of that tortfeasor in the fault allocation-liability format of the Act would engender a result beyond its plain language. . . .

Furthermore, there are strong policy reasons that dictate against including the absent or unnamed tortfeasor from the fact finder's negligence apportionment. The amount of plaintiff's judgment and amount of defendant's liability will vary depending upon whether the absent-unnamed person's negligence is considered by the fact finder. Defendant, however, has a greater incentive to join and name additional potential tort-feasors or to see that they are identified. That greater incentive is the percentage-liability formula. That formula proscribes contribution where fault falls below a certain percentage. *See* N.J.S.A. 2A:15-5.3. Thus, defendant has significant incentive in naming and joining multiple tortfeasors so as to create the potential for diminishing defendant's percentage of liability to a level that avoids contribution. Given that incentive, it is appropriate to place upon defendant the burden of finding and naming any additional person since it is to defendant's advantage to spread the risk or defeat the claim. *See* National Farmers Union Prop. and Cas. Co. v. Frackelton, 662 P.2d 1056, 1060 (Colo. 1983).

These policy dictates are particularly poignant here. The evidence recited reflects Club 35 failed to protect plaintiff in the manner the law requires and had the best opportunity to identify the intentional tortfeasor who assaulted plaintiff. Indeed, the evidence suggests the bouncers knew the intentional tortfeasor, yet Club 35 chose to ignore that knowledge and not identify him. Interestingly, Club 35 chose also not to identify its bouncers who were also unnamed defendants, although the bouncers' conduct might have affected the jury's evaluation of Club 35's responsibility. Consequently, and quite apart from our statutory construction, in absence of language demonstrating a contrary legislative purpose, we are satisfied the most equitable result, in light of the circumstances here, is to preclude the unnamed intentional tortfeasor's conduct from the fault comparison for purposes of allocating liability. . . .

IV.

In conclusion we hold the fault of a fictitious person may not be considered when apportioning negligence among parties to the lawsuit. The Act's plain language precludes fault allocation because a fictitious defendant is not a party to the suit and not one against whom recovery is sought. Moreover, we find sound policy reasons applicable to the facts of this case dictate against allocating fault of the unnamed intentional tortfeasor. . . .

The judgment of the trial court is affirmed.

NOTES AND QUESTIONS

1. *Apples and Oranges?* As this decision notes, the New Jersey Supreme Court, interpreting the state's comparative fault statute, had already held in *Blazovic* that juries should be instructed to allocate percentage "fault" between tortfeasors even if one acted negligently and another acted intentionally. Courts have dealt similarly with cases in which one tortfeasor is being held liable under a strict liability standard whereas another is being held liable under a negligence standard. In these latter cases, the jury is thus being asked to assign a percentage "fault" to a strictly

liable tortfeasor(!). As we noted above in Chapter 6, the fact that juries are asked to make percentage assignments of responsibility to intentional and strictly liable tortfeasors suggests that comparative fault — as opposed to comparative responsibility — is something of a misnomer.

2. *"Phantom" Tortfeasors. Bencivenga* refuses to permit the jury to assign fault to the unknown assailant. What is the most compelling justification for its decision? Is it that the unavailability of the assailant is the defendant's fault? If not, why put the onus on the defendant to bear the risk of the assailant's unavailability?

Other state statutes and judicial decisions permit juries to assign fault to non-parties. *See, e.g.*, Joseph v. Broussard Rice Mill, Inc., 772 So. 2d 94 (La. 2000) (noting that Louisiana statutory law requires the jury to consider the fault of non-parties). Some place the burden of proof with respect to a non-party's comparative fault on the defendant, and require that the non-party be identified by name. Ind. Code. §§ 34-51-2-7 & 2-15. *In these jurisdictions, absent a rule of joint and several liability, the plaintiff cannot collect on the portion of liability assigned to such a non-party.* In a modified comparative fault system, should non-parties' fault also be counted in determining, for example, whether plaintiff's fault exceeded that of the defendants?

3. *Immune Tortfeasors.* As we have seen, various persons who would otherwise be liable in negligence are protected from liability by defenses and immunities, including statutes of limitations and sovereign immunity, as well as particular immunities such as the immunity effectively granted by the exclusive remedy provisions of workers' compensation systems. If actors that are immune from liability are named in the underlying tort suit, yet establish their immunity, should the jury be instructed to assign a percentage fault to these parties if the evidence shows that their carelessness was a cause of the plaintiff's injury? Legislation and judicial decisions vary on this issue, even within a given jurisdiction. *Compare* Dotson v. Blake, 29 S.W.3d 26 (Tenn. 2000) (in suit against multiple tortfeasors, jury should assign a percentage responsibility to any fault attributable to state employees, even though they are immune from liability) *with* Ridings v. Ralph M. Parsons Co., 914 S.W.2d 79 (Tenn. 1996) (in a suit by plaintiff-employee against a third party for injuries suffered at the workplace, the jury should *not* assign a percentage responsibility to the plaintiff's employer, which is immunized from tort liability by workers' compensation law).

4. *Settling Tortfeasors.* What happens when one defendant settles with the plaintiff prior to trial, but another chooses to go to trial over the same incident? Should the jury be instructed that it may assign a percentage fault to a settling defendant as an absent party to the suit? Assuming the abolition of joint and several liability, how should a remaining defendant's liability be adjusted in light of the settlement? Suppose, for example, *D1*, the settling defendant, pays plaintiff an amount that turns out to equal 30 percent of the damages awarded by the jury. Suppose further that the jury assigns 60 percent responsibility to *D1*, and 40

percent to *D2*. Should *D2* be required to pay only 40 percent of the award in light of the jury's apportionment of fault? Or should *D2* be made to pay 50 percent as one of two responsible tortfeasors? Or some other amount? Rules on allocation of damages in light of settlement are enormously complicated and vary substantially among jurisdictions. *See* McDermott, Inc. v. AmClyde, 511 U.S. 202 (1994) (discussing alternative rules).

IV.   INDEMNIFICATION AND LIABILITY INSURANCE

When one tortfeasor is held jointly and severally liable to compensate a victim for her injuries, and then seeks reimbursement from a second tortfeasor who also contributed to the victim's injury but was not made to pay anything, the former brings an action for contribution. As indicated, the action for contribution sounds neither in tort nor contract, but in restitution. The second tortfeasor has been deemed partially responsible for the victim's injury, yet has paid nothing, whereas the first tortfeasor has paid too much. Hence it is equitable to permit the first to obtain reimbursement from the second for a portion of the damages paid out to the victim.

Indemnification is similar to contribution, in that it permits a tortfeasor to look to another person or entity to cover some or all of its liability. However, indemnity is almost always accomplished through contract. By virtue of that contract, a person or entity has *promised* to *indemnify* (reimburse) the tortfeasor for certain liabilities. In tort law, the most important example of a promise to indemnify consists of the issuance of a *liability insurance policy*.

Interinsurance Exch. of the
Automobile Club v. Flores
53 Cal. Rptr. 2d 18 (Ct. App. 1996)

Gilbert, J.   An insured drives his van to a location to allow his passenger to shoot someone from the van. The driver has a standard auto insurance policy that provides coverage for injuries caused by an accident. Does the policy provide the driver with coverage for injuries to the victim? No.

Rosemary and David Flores (Flores) appeal from the judgment in favor of respondent, Interinsurance Exchange of the Automobile Club of Southern California (Automobile Club) in this declaratory relief action. We affirm. . . .

FACTS

. . . An unknown pedestrian punched Eric Michael Sanders in the face while Sanders sat in his van waiting for a traffic light to change. . . . Sanders told Roger Perez of the incident. Perez suggested they return to the scene, locate the assailant and seek retribution. Perez told Sanders he was armed with a handgun before he and others got into the van. Sanders knew that someone was likely to get shot. He drove Perez and the others back to the intersection where Sanders had been punched. David Flores stood on the corner of the intersection. While Sanders drove by, Perez intentionally shot and injured Flores from the van. The van itself did not inflict any injury on Flores, nor was it used to block or pin down Flores.

After his arrest for his involvement in the shooting, Sanders admitted that he knew someone was likely to be shot. In the criminal action Sanders pled [guilty] to the felony of aiding and abetting the shooting of Flores (Pen. Code, § 245, subd. (a)(2)). (People v. Sanders (Super. Ct. Santa Barbara County, 1990, No. 182329).)

Rosemary Flores, individually, and as guardian ad litem for David Flores, filed the underlying civil suit against Sanders and others for conspiracy, battery and negligence. The Floreses' suit alleged, inter alia, that Sanders and Perez "agreed to hunt down, shoot, and either kill or maim the perpetrator of the Sanders attack, using Roger Perez's .22 caliber handgun." These allegations were incorporated into each cause of action in the Floreses' suit.

Sanders owns the van involved and his parents insured it for him under an automobile insurance policy issued by the Automobile Club. The Automobile Club reserved its rights to deny coverage and filed the instant declaratory relief action to determine whether or not it had a duty to defend or indemnify Sanders for liability in the underlying Flores action under the policy.

The trial court denied summary judgment to the Automobile Club and the parties proceeded to trial by the court on the stipulated facts. After trial, the trial court found that the shooting was not an accident, that Sanders acted intentionally in aiding and abetting the shooting and that the injuries inflicted on the Flores family were not covered by the instant policy. In its judgment, the trial court ruled that the Automobile Club is not obligated to indemnify Sanders for liability he may have to the Floreses. This appeal ensued. . . .

DISCUSSION

INTERPRETATION

Interpretation of the insurance policy presents a question of law for this court to decide. (Waller v. Truck Ins. Exchange, Inc. (1995) 11 Cal. 4th 1, 18 [44 Cal. Rptr. 2d 370, 900 P.2d 619]; State Farm Mut. Auto. Ins. Co. v. Partridge (1973) 10 Cal. 3d 94, 100 [109 Cal. Rptr. 811, 514 P.2d 123].) We consider the stipulated facts and the allegations of the Floreses' complaint together with the language of the insurance policy. (Montrose Chemical Corp. v. Superior Court (1993) 6 Cal. 4th 287, 295, 300 [24 Cal. Rptr. 2d 467, 861 P.2d 1153].)

The duty of an insurance company to defend a claim of coverage is broad. . . . Courts first consider whether there may be a potential for coverage under the policy. . . . The insured has the burden to bring the claim within the basic scope of coverage; the insurer must establish the absence of such coverage. . . . Courts will not indulge in a forced construction of the policy's insuring clauses to find coverage. . . . And, courts construe policy terms in their " 'ordinary and popular sense.' " (Bank of the West v. Superior Court (1992) 2 Cal. 4th 1254, 1265 [10 Cal. Rptr. 2d 538, 833 P.2d 545]; *Waller, supra,* at p.18. . . .)

Because the Automobile Club reserved its rights, any allegations or judgment of negligence in the underlying civil suit would not preclude the insurance company from asserting there is no coverage here because Sanders expected or intended harm to occur. . . .

COVERAGE

USE OF THE VEHICLE

In an insurance policy, the phrase "arising out of the use" has broad and comprehensive application. (State Farm Mut. Auto. Ins. Co. v. Partridge, *supra,* 10 Cal. 3d at p.100.) It affords coverage for injuries where the insured vehicle bears "almost *any* causal relation" to the accident at issue, however minimal. (*Id.* at p.100; *see also id.,* at fn.7; *id.* at p.101, fn.8.) Here, Sanders drove to the scene for the purpose of seeking retaliation and left the scene of the shooting by use of the van. The insurer admits that the van "was passing through the intersection" when Perez shot Flores. We agree with the trial court that the Sanders van was being used at all pertinent times within the meaning of the instant policy language.

OCCURRENCE

The instant policy promises to "pay damages for which any person insured is legally liable because of bodily injury . . . *caused by an occurrence* arising out of the ownership, maintenance or use" of the insured vehicle. (Italics added.) "Occurrence" is defined to mean "an *accident* . . . , including injurious exposure to conditions, which results in bodily injury. . . ." (Italics added.) Therefore, the instant policy provides coverage to Sanders only if he accidentally caused the injury to Flores. "[T]he insured has the burden of showing that there has been an 'occurrence' within the terms of the policy." (Waller v. Truck Ins. Exchange, Inc., *supra,* 11 Cal. 4th at p.16. . . .)

When an injury is an unexpected or unintended consequence of the insured's conduct, it may be characterized as an accident for which coverage exists. When the injury suffered is *expected* or *intended,* coverage is denied. When one expects or intends an injury to occur, there is no "accident."

Flores argues that Sanders' acts were not intended or expected because he did not shoot Flores himself or direct that he be shot. Therefore, his conduct was, at most, reckless. (Peterson v. Superior Court (1982) 31 Cal. 3d 147, 158-159 [181 Cal. Rptr. 784, 642 P.2d 1305]; State

Farm Mut. Auto. Ins. Co. v. Partridge, *supra,* 10 Cal. 3d at p.101; National American Ins. Co. v. Insurance Co. of North America (1977) 74 Cal. App. 3d 565, 571 [140 Cal. Rptr. 828].) We disagree. The cases cited by appellant are distinguishable.

In *Peterson*, a driver drove with excessive speed after consuming alcohol. In deciding issues not relevant here, our Supreme Court explained that conduct amounting to a conscious disregard for the safety of others does not constitute willful, intentional conduct within the meaning of Insurance Code section 533. (Peterson v. Superior Court, *supra*, 31 Cal. 3d at pp.158-159.) Section 533 states an insurer is not liable for the willful acts of its insured.

In *Partridge*, the insured filed the trigger mechanism of his pistol at home so that the gun would have a "hair trigger action." The insured took the gun into his Bronco truck and placed it either on his lap or on top of the steering wheel. While the insured was driving, he saw a rabbit crossing the road. He drove off the road onto rough terrain to follow the rabbit. When the truck hit a bump, the gun discharged and caused injury to a passenger in the vehicle.

The insurance company filed a declaratory relief action to determine whether its homeowners or its automobile policy provided coverage for the damages caused by the injuries incurred as a result of the accident. The trial court ruled that both policies afforded coverage and our Supreme Court affirmed.

Filing the trigger mechanism and transporting the gun independently concurred to proximately cause the accident. The insured's automobile policy provided coverage because the insured was using the truck at the time the gun accidentally discharged. The homeowners policy also provided coverage, despite an express exclusion for injuries arising out of use of a vehicle, because the insured's negligent filing of the trigger mechanism was an independent, concurrent covered proximate cause of the accidental injury.

Because coverage clauses are broadly construed in favor of the insured and express exclusions are strictly construed against the insurer, an insurer is liable if one of such multiple causes is a covered one. Even though the circumstances in *Partridge* "can only be described as blatant recklessness" ([State Farm Mut. Auto. Ins. Co. v. Partridge, *supra*, 10 Cal. 3d.] at pp.97, 106-107), the concurrent negligent causes of the incident were covered under the policies.

In *National American*, four teenage boys rode in an automobile indiscriminately throwing eggs at other automobiles, homes and people. While the automobile was traveling about 40 miles an hour, one of the boys flipped an egg towards a pedestrian who lost an eye as a result. The most significant factor causing the injury was the speed of the automobile. A jury returned a verdict of liability for negligence against the boy who flipped the egg. The issue in *National American* was not coverage, but causation.

The Court of Appeal stated that substantial evidence supported the findings of the trial court that the injury resulted from negligent conduct which caused an accident involving the use of an automobile. It affirmed the judgment of the trial court and concluded that the judgment comported with policies of law and equity regarding indemnity and defense costs among insurers.

Drunk driving, leaving a loaded hair trigger weapon on one's lap and flipping eggs out of a car at 40 miles an hour all constitute negligent or reckless conduct which may cause injury. As such, they all constitute "accidents" within the meaning of personal injury insurance policies because the injuries are not intended or expected.

Here, however, the underlying complaint and the stipulated facts establish that the instant shooting was no accident. It was planned. Sanders knew Perez was armed with a deadly weapon. He drove Perez to the place where he thought they might find the person who had punched him. Sanders knew that someone was likely to be shot. Sanders therefore intended and expected injury to result from his acts. The Floreses have not borne their burden to show that Sanders' conduct was accidental within the meaning of the instant insurance policy. Accordingly, the Floreses did not establish potential coverage for the shooting incident.

EXCLUSIONS

INSURANCE CODE SECTION 533

Coverage is also excluded because the acts were willful within the meaning of section 533, which provides a statutory exclusion in every insurance policy. (J. C. Penney Casualty Ins. Co. v. M. K., *supra*, 52 Cal. 3d at p.1019.) Section 533 states, "*An insurer is not liable for* a loss caused by the *wilful act of the insured*; but he is *not exonerated by the negligence* of the insured, or of the insured's agents or others." (Italics added.) We determine the Legislature's intent in passing section 533 by considering the words of the statute. Neither the words of section 533 nor its legislative history establishes its meaning.

Because a negligent act may be done "wilfully" — the act is volitional — the term "wilful act" in section 533 means something more than performing a voluntary act which constitutes negligence. (J. C. Penney Casualty Ins. Co. v. M. K., *supra*, 52 Cal. 3d at p.1021.)

Our Supreme Court has explained that ". . . section 533 does not preclude coverage for acts that are negligent or reckless." (J. C. Penney Casualty Ins. Co. v. M. K., *supra*, 52 Cal. 3d at p.1021.) Where application of section 533 becomes an issue, the insurance company must establish that the insured acted with intent to harm or that the insured committed an inherently wrongful act. (52 Cal. 3d at pp.1021-1027.)

But, the general rule of strict construction against the insurer regarding exclusions does not apply to section 533 because it is a statutory exclusion evincing a fundamental public policy. (*See* J. C. Penney Casualty Ins. Co. v. M. K., *supra*, 52 Cal. 3d at pp.1019, 1020, fn.9.) If coverage is excluded under section 533, we may not consider whether there may be coverage under any express exclusions stated in the insurance policy. (52 Cal. 3d pp.1019-1020, fn.8.) Whether there may be coverage due to section 533 depends upon the facts of the case.

There may be coverage under section 533 for an accident caused by drunk driving because drunk driving, per se, is reckless conduct. (*See generally*, Peterson v. Superior Court, *supra*, 31 Cal. 3d at p.159.) There may not be coverage for an act such as child molestation because that act is deemed to be inherently wrongful or harmful in itself. (*See* J. C. Penney Casualty Ins. Co. v. M. K., *supra*, 52 Cal. 3d at pp.1021-1027.)

Although the Supreme Court expressly limited *J. C. Penney* to child molestation, its dictum establishes that under section 533, an insurer bears no liability if the insured acted with intent to harm or committed an inherently wrongful act without legal justification. (*See* J. C. Penney Casualty Ins. Co. v. M. K., *supra*, 52 Cal. 3d at pp.1025, fn.13, 1021-1027; *see also* Fire Ins. Exchange v. Altieri (1991) 235 Cal. App. 3d 1352, 1357-1358. . . .)

Here, Sanders pled nolo contendere to the felony criminal charge of aiding and abetting an assault with a deadly weapon. "The legal effect of such a [nolo] plea, . . . shall be the same as that of a plea of guilty for all purposes." (Pen. Code, § 1016, subd. 3.) Guilty and nolo pleas are admissible in a subsequent civil action, such as the underlying action, as an admission of the crime. Therefore, Sanders admitted committing the crime of aiding and abetting an assault with a deadly weapon.

The admission is not conclusive, per se, and has no collateral estoppel effect. A plea may reflect a compromise or a choice not to undergo prosecution; it does not necessarily establish the underlying factual matters at issue in the civil litigation.

Under section 533, the question here is whether Sanders' admission of the crime of aiding and abetting assault with a deadly weapon, together with the other stipulated or pleaded facts, constitute [sufficient evidence of] acts which are either inherently harmful or which evince an intent to harm.

The stipulated facts establish that Sanders drove Perez back to the intersection where Sanders had been punched in order to retaliate. Sanders knew someone was likely to get shot. When an offense includes the intent to do some act beyond the actus reus of the crime, one who aids and abets the crime *must share the specific intent of its perpetrator*. Although the stipulated facts do not state the crime for which Perez was charged and convicted, they do state that "Roger Perez intentionally shot David Flores with a .22 caliber revolver while Roger Perez was inside the van."

By aiding and abetting the intentional shooting, Sanders is a principal to it and he is equally guilty for that act. . . . Under these facts, we conclude that Sanders harbored intent to harm within the meaning of section 533.

The underlying complaint also supports our conclusion that Sanders evinced an intent to harm another. Each of its causes of action incorporate by reference the allegation that Sanders and Perez "agreed to hunt down, shoot, and either kill or maim the perpetrator of the Sanders' attack, using Roger Perez' .22 caliber handgun."

The Automobile Club has established that it may deny coverage under the implied exclusion set forth in section 533. (Fire Ins. Exchange v. Altieri, *supra*, 235 Cal. App. 3d at pp.1357-1360 [no duty to indemnify for assault even though assailant asserted he did not intend to injure victim];

Reagen's Vacuum Truck Service, Inc. v. Beaver Ins. Co. (1994) 31 Cal. App. 4th 375, 388 [37 Cal. Rptr. 2d 89].) Because coverage is excluded here under section 533, we need not consider whether there may be coverage under the express policy exclusion for bodily injury intentionally caused by or at the direction of an insured.

CONCLUSION

"The concept of 'fortuity' is basic to insurance law. Insurance typically is designed to protect [against] contingent or unknown risks of harm [citations], not to protect against harm which is certain or expected. [Citation.]" (Chu v. Canadian Indemnity Co., *supra*, 224 Cal. App. 3d at pp.94-95; Waller v. Truck Ins. Exchange, Inc., *supra*, 11 Cal. 4th at pp.16-17.) Sanders expected harm to occur here and he acted deliberately to help bring it about. Under the stipulated facts and allegations in the underlying complaint, the Automobile Club need not defend or indemnify the Floreses' claims against Sanders.

The judgment is affirmed. Each party to bear its own costs.

NOTES AND QUESTIONS

1. *Insurer and Insured.* An insurance policy is a contract. One party to the contract is the insurer. In exchange for a fee ("premium"), the insurer promises to pay certain costs incurred by another person or persons. The person or persons who are entitled to reimbursement for these costs are known as "insureds." Note that one can be an insured without being a party to the insurance contract. Here, the relevant insured was not the purchaser of the automobile insurance policy, but rather a child of the purchasers of that policy. Depending on the terms of the actual automobile insurance policy, a guest who happened to be in the car and injured in an accident might also have qualified as an insured.

2. *First-Party versus Third-Party Coverage.* Policies such as automobile policies often contain two different types of insurance coverage. First, they contain coverage for *first-party* costs, that is, a promise to pay costs incurred directly by one or more of the insureds. First-party coverage typically found in an automobile insurance policy includes collision coverage (a promise to pay for repairs to the insured's vehicle if damaged in an accident) and medical coverage (a promise to pay medical bills incurred by the insured as a result of an accident arising out of use of the insured vehicle). Second, such policies often provide coverage of certain *third-party* costs, that is, costs that are incurred by some person other than the insured. Here, for example, Flores maintained that the contract between Mr. and Mrs. Sanders and the Automobile Club included a promise from Automobile Club to cover third-party costs that they or their son became obligated to pay as a result of using the car. This sort of promise/coverage is commonly known as *liability insurance*: The insured is covered against the risk of being held liable to a third party.

3. *Liability Insurance: The Duties to Indemnify and Defend.* In common usage, liability insurance is often equated with the promise to pay for liabilities incurred by the insured to others. In legal terminology, this is known as a promise to *indemnify* the insured. In the automobile policy at issue in this case, the promise to indemnify read roughly as follows: "Insurer promises to pay damages for which any insured is legally liable because of bodily injury or property damage caused by an occurrence arising out of the use of the insured vehicle."

The promise to indemnify is at the core of any liability insurance policy. However, it is only one of two aspects of the third-party coverage provided in most policies containing liability insurance provisions. The second sort of coverage consists of a promise to pay for and manage the defense of the underlying lawsuit by which the injured party attempts to establish the insured's liability. This promise gives rise to a second duty beyond the duty to indemnify, namely the duty to *defend*. Thus, in *Flores*, the issue was not only whether Automobile Club had to pay for any damages awarded to Flores on his claim that Sanders aided Perez's battery (the duty to indemnify), but also whether it was obligated to defend Sanders against the aiding and abetting claim (the duty to defend). The promise to defend is sometimes described as *litigation insurance*. These notes focus first on the promise to indemnify, then later revisit the promise to defend.

4. *Examples of Liability Coverage.* Liability insurance is provided through many other types of insurance policies beyond automobile policies. For example, a homeowner's insurance policy might include provisions under which the insurer agrees to indemnify the owner in the event a guest is accidentally injured on the premises and successfully sues the homeowner in tort for those injuries. Businesses commonly maintain liability insurance for personal injuries or property damage accidentally caused to third parties by their products or their employees' carelessness. Professionals such as doctors and lawyers maintain insurance to pay for malpractice liabilities.

5. *History.* Liability insurance is ubiquitous today. However, relative to the history of tort, its emergence is a recent development. Early examples of liability insurance policies were those issued in the late 1800s to employers to indemnify them for tort liabilities owed to employees injured on the job. By the turn of the twentieth century, insurers were issuing liability policies to many other types of insureds, including manufacturers (for liabilities resulting from injuries caused by their negligently made products), residential and commercial property owners (for injuries on the premises), professionals (for injuries caused by malpractice), and even participants in sports such as golf (for injuries caused to other participants or bystanders).

6. *The Business of Insurance.* To make a profit, insurers must decide, in the context of competing with other insurers, at what level to set premiums and how much coverage to promise in return for those premiums. To make these judgments, insurers rely on actuaries, experts

who study statistics as to the frequency of particular kinds of occurrences, the typical costs associated with those occurrences, etc. For example, an actuary might determine that, for each of the past five years, 1,000 passenger-vehicle drivers in location L were involved in accidents that caused an average of $10,000 worth of damage to others per accident. Based on this information, an insurer can, with a reasonable degree of confidence, predict how much it can expect to pay in covered claims by insureds and hence can set premiums to cover these costs, plus overhead, plus a margin for profit.* Notice, however, that the insurer can only take advantage of these statistics if it can "pool" the relevant risks — that is, enter into insurance contracts with a large number of the relevant class of passenger-vehicle drivers in the relevant location. This is because statistical correlations, if they hold true, only hold true for large numbers. (Think of it in terms of coin flips. If one flips an honestly weighted coin 10,000 times, the ratio of heads to tails will approach 50/50. If, however, one were to flip only 10 times, one might easily come up with heads 8 out of those 10 times.)

Individual insureds, meanwhile, purchase the security of knowing that if they are one of the unlucky drivers who does incur liability to another as a result of driving, they will not have to pay the actual loss out of their own pockets. Of course, if the actuary has done her job well, for most insureds, the risk will never actually come to pass — in hindsight these persons will have "wasted" their money. But it is precisely because hindsight is 20/20, whereas foresight is not, that they made the decision to purchase insurance in the first place.

7. *The Duty to Indemnify: Scope.* The scope of the promise to indemnify within a given liability insurance provision is determined primarily by the terms of the insurance contract that:

a.   specify who counts as an "insured" under the policy;
b.   define "occurrence" and "exclusion" — that is, the sorts of events that do and do not give rise to the duty to indemnify;
c.   indicate the type of liabilities flowing from an occurrence for which there is coverage (e.g., bodily injury, property damage, and/or business interruption); and
d.   set the dollar-amount ceiling ("coverage amount") for liabilities arising out of a given occurrence, as well as deductible amounts that the insured is responsible to pay.

---

* As it turns out, insurers tend to make their profits not by collecting premiums in excess of payouts and overhead, but from obtaining premiums in advance of making payouts, and thus having in their possession money which they can invest until such time as payouts have to be made. It follows that, as a rule, insurance companies tend to perform poorly when they cannot earn large returns by investing the premium dollars that are in their possession. This feature of the insurance business is noteworthy because insurers often maintain that ever-increasing tort liability is what forces them to raise premiums. Before such claims can be accepted, however, one must discount, among other things, the effect of poor returns on investments on insurers' profitability.

In *Flores*, the liability insurance provisions of the automobile policy contained an additional restriction on the duty to indemnify: that duty only applies to liabilities for injuries "arising out of the use of the insured vehicle." According to the court, is this a significant restriction on the scope of the liability insurance provided by the policy? Suppose that the same car was sitting in the Sanders' driveway, and that Eric Sanders and Roger Perez were taking turns jumping off its roof onto the driveway. If one of them accidentally crashed into Flores as Flores happened to walk by, would the automobile policy cover that liability?

8. *The Duty to Indemnify: To Whom Owed?* It is important to keep in mind that even though the indemnity provisions of a liability insurance policy have the effect of reimbursing third parties injured by the insured, the insurer's obligation to cover those costs is usually owed exclusively to the insured, not to the injured third party. Thus, with one or two exceptions, states do not require or even permit a tort victim to sue the tortfeasor's insurer directly to obtain compensation.* Rather, the victim must sue the tortfeasor to establish his liability, and must leave it up to the tortfeasor to make a claim under the policy. (Of course, the tortfeasor will ordinarily have an interest in doing so.)

Similarly, the victim of a tort typically will not have a freestanding tort cause of action against the tortfeasor's liability insurer. For example, suppose swimming pool owner *D* is insured by *L* Corp. for liabilities associated with accidental bodily injuries suffered by users of the pool. Under the terms of the policy, *L* has the right to inspect *D*'s premises and recommend safety precautions, which *D* in turn is free to accept or reject. Now suppose *P*, a guest invited by *D* to swim at the pool, is injured when she slips off the end of the pool's diving board. *P* brings a negligence claim against *D* for carelessly failing to attach traction strips to the board, but also tries to sue *L* for failing to recommend such a precaution. Even if *P* has a valid cause of action in negligence against *D* — one that, because of the terms of the policy, results in an obligation on the part of *L* to pay for the damages caused by *D* — *P* will not likely have an independent tort cause of action against *L*. *L*'s obligations as insurer to indemnify *D* for liabilities do not include a duty to take steps to protect those who may suffer injury of the sort covered by the policy issued to *D*. *See* Goodwin v. Jackson, 484 So. 2d 1041 (Miss. 1986) (parents of child who drowned in insured's pool do not have a tort cause of action against the pool owner's insurer for failing to insist that the pool owner implement proper safety precautions).

9. *Exclusion of "Intentional" Acts: Policy Provisions.* The central legal issue of *Flores* concerns whether the insured's role in bringing about the shooting of the plaintiffs' son was intentional, on the one hand, or reckless or careless, on the other. The court concluded that Eric Sanders intentionally helped bring about the shooting of Flores. Standard language employed by liability insurers almost always defines "occurrence" to be an

---

* Wisconsin law permits a direct action by the tort victim against the tortfeasor's liability insurer.

event *unintended* by the insured, or *unexpected* from the perspective of the insured. This is just another way of saying, with the *Flores* court, that liability insurance is primarily about fortuities: It is designed to protect against risks that may or may not be realized, not harms that the insured intends to bring about. Thus, as a matter of contract law, the plain wording of the typical liability policy will establish that the insurer makes no promise to indemnify for liabilities resulting from intentionally caused injuries. Can you see how the relative paucity of insurance for intentional wrongs, as compared to careless wrongs, might pressure litigants into framing the issues in tort litigation a certain way?

10. *Exclusion of Intentional Acts: Public Policy.* Ordinarily, the public policy exception for intentional wrongs will not need to be litigated, or will be litigated as a secondary rationale for a decision, as it was in *Flores*. This is because, as just indicated, most liability policies are written to exclude coverage of intentional misconduct. Suppose, contrary to the facts of *Flores*, the policy had been written so as to clearly cover intentional wrongful use of the car of the sort engaged in by Sanders. Would there be coverage then?

The answer, according to the Court of Appeals, is no, but now because of statute rather than contract. By enacting Section 533 of the state insurance code, the California legislature forbade parties from buying and providing insurance for liabilities resulting from willful misconduct. Although California is unusual in having such a statute, the vast majority of states recognize an equivalent ban on insuring intentional wrongs as a matter of judge-made law. Thus, courts around the country routinely hold that there is an implied public policy exception that excludes coverage of "wilful" or "intentional" wrongful acts no matter what the actual contract says. (It should be noted, however, that there are important differences among the states as to what counts as the sort of "intentional act" for which insurance coverage is precluded.)

The origins of the public policy exception apparently derive from first-party insurance contracts. Courts, for example, long ago held that it was against public policy for *B*, the beneficiary of a life insurance policy, to murder the insured *I*, then collect on the policy. The rationale for these decisions was driven by the moral principle that one ought not to profit from his wrong, as well as a concern not to give people a monetary incentive to commit intentional wrongful acts. Without much discussion, the public policy bar was then carried over to liability insurance policies, apparently on the theory that this, too, would help discourage, or at least not encourage, intentional wrongful conduct.

In general, mandatory rules barring competent adults from making contractual arrangements as to economic matters are quite rare — our legal system leaves them largely free to structure their economic transactions. Do you find the rationales articulated for the public policy exception convincing? Can you think of better ones?

11. *The Intentional Acts of Agents and Employees.* We said above that intentional acts are usually excluded from standard liability policies. Note, however, that a loss that is intentionally or knowingly caused by one

actor may still be a fortuity from the perspective of someone else. Mega Corp., for example, might expect that, in any given year, one out of the 1,000 supervisors it employs will commit an act of intentional discrimination against a supervisee on the basis of race, age, or gender. For this reason, although insurers are generally anxious to exclude from coverage any liability arising from intentional acts, one sometimes finds liability policies issued to companies covering certain intentional wrongs by its employees, such as intentional acts of discrimination. A key question in such cases will be whether these policies violate the public policy bar against insuring for intentional wrongs. Courts have split on this issue.

12. *The Duty (and Right) to Defend.* Thus far, the focus in these notes has been on the obligation of a liability insurer to *indemnify* an insured for liability arising out of a covered event. As noted above, however, liability insurance also includes a promise to defend the underlying lawsuit by the third party against the insured seeking to establish the insured's liability. Unlike the provisions in the insurance policy specifying the duty to indemnify, the provisions describing the duty to defend usually do not contain a dollar cap on the amount the insurer will be obligated to defend. However, the duty to defend is typically accompanied by a corresponding set of *rights* conferred on the insurer, namely, the right to select defense counsel and to control the underlying litigation. This right includes the authority to decide on how to dispose of the case—whether to settle or proceed to trial, how much to settle for, etc. As you might expect, the insurer and the insured may often have different views on these sorts of decisions. For example, an insurer backed by substantial assets might be more willing than an impoverished insured to forgo settlement and take the chance of a jury returning a huge verdict against the insured at trial.

As a rough-and-ready generalization, it is fair to say that insurers are under an obligation to their insureds to act reasonably in responding to settlement offers. If they fail to do so, they run the risk of being held liable to their insureds for a breach of the duty to defend. A famous example of this risk coming to fruition is found in Crisci v. The Security Insur. Co. of New Haven, 426 P.2d 173 (Cal. 1967). There, the insurer issued a policy to a landlord that indemnified her for liabilities arising from injuries suffered on the premises up to $10,000 per occurrence. Faced with an obviously strong tort claim brought by an injured tenant against the insured, the insurer chose not to accept an offer to settle the case for the policy limits of $10,000. A jury subsequently rendered a $101,000 verdict against the insured, leaving her to pay $91,000 out of her own pocket, which essentially bankrupted her. The insured then successfully brought an action against the insurer for unreasonably refusing the settlement offer. (A similar action was the basis for State Farm Mut. Auto Ins. Co. v. Campbell, discussed in the notes following BMW v. Gore, *infra* Chapter 13.)

13. *Which Goes First: Tort Liability or Coverage under the Insurance Contract?* The duty to defend is often described as "broader" than the duty to indemnify. This is because, under standard policies, that duty applies to any lawsuit against the insured that contains *allegations* of a

covered liability, even if it turns out subsequently that there is no basis for liability at all, or that the particular liability established is not covered under the policy. Suppose, for example, homeowner D is covered by a policy issued by insurer L for liabilities arising from accidental injuries suffered by others on D's property. Suppose also that plaintiff P sues D in tort, alleging a physical injury that occurred on defendant D's premises. At that point, D will notify L of the pending claim, and L's duty to take over the defense of P's claim against D will commence. In such a case, questions as to whether P actually suffered an injury, whether it occurred on the premises, and whether it occurred by accident, often will not be determined until the judge or jury renders a verdict. However, even if the verdict includes a finding that the injury was not covered, L still must pay D's defense costs. (Whether L might in some circumstances be relieved of the obligation to defend prior to the conclusion of the P v. D litigation is a much-debated question.)

Initially, then, the insurer's duty to defend is largely in the hands of the plaintiff's attorney. If the allegations contained in plaintiff's complaint are crafted so as to specify acts or events that may count as an occurrence under the policy, the duty kicks in. However, insurers are not entirely at plaintiffs' attorneys' mercy. For one thing, plaintiffs' attorneys run certain risks if they simply make up allegations that have no grounding in fact. (For example, they can be fined by the court.) In some jurisdictions, moreover, the insurer can ask the court to resolve the issue of coverage *before* proceeding with the underlying tort litigation. This procedure, under which the insurer seeks a *declaratory judgment* as to coverage, was invoked successfully by Automobile Club in *Flores*. In states that permit declaratory judgment actions, the trial court must decide whether to proceed first by resolving the tort suit, then the coverage issue, or by resolving coverage first and tort liability second. Usually, a court will not permit a declaratory judgment action unless the issue of coverage turns on factual and legal issues that can be decided independently of the underlying tort suit.

Can you identify the features of *Flores* that may have encouraged this judge to tackle the declaratory judgment action first, thus enabling Automobile Club to establish in advance of the tort litigation that it owed no obligation to defend or indemnify? Might all the parties, including the plaintiffs, have wanted that question resolved first?

14. *The Chicken-Egg Problem.* The spread of liability insurance has been integral to the growth in size and significance of tort law as part of the U.S. legal and political system. As Dean Syverud has explained, tort law and liability insurance are "symbiotic" institutions. If there were little or no risk of tort liability, fewer people would buy liability insurance. Likewise, if there were no liability insurance, tort recoveries would be fewer in number and more modest in amount. In this sense, tort law and insurance feed off one another.

Syverud elsewhere notes that Americans consume large amounts of liability insurance by comparison to citizens of other nations. This phenomenon, he hypothesizes, might be part of a cycle that works to the benefit of lawyers and insurers, but causes Americans to over-consume insurance. The cycle runs as follows. Individual insureds are risk-averse; they understandably want to avoid a catastrophic liability. Given a choice between buying a cheaper policy that indemnifies him for up to $100,000 for injuries to a guest on the premises, or a slightly more expensive policy providing $1 million in coverage, the risk-averse homeowner will choose the latter. But the very existence of greater coverage might be the thing that encourages a slip-and-fall victim to sue in the first place, or to demand greater compensation upon suing. Thus, the decision to buy more insurance results in greater liability, which fuels the demand for more insurance, and so on.

15. *Discovery and Insurance Policies.* We have just noted that the presence of liability insurance might sometimes invite tort claims where there otherwise might not be any. How does the availability of insurance affect tort litigation once it is underway? Before 1970, courts were split as to whether, after a tort suit is commenced, a plaintiff's attorney could use the discovery process to obtain information from the defendant as to applicable liability insurance. In that year, the Federal Rules of Civil Procedure were amended to permit such discovery, and most states have followed along. Thus, today, the plaintiff often will have a clear idea of how much coverage is available, a figure that can serve as a benchmark for settlement discussions. As part of recent tort reform efforts, some jurisdictions have barred plaintiffs from obtaining information about insurance coverage in certain tort actions. *See, e.g.*, Ala. Code § 6-5-548(d) (barring discovery of the limits of liability coverage in medical malpractice actions).

16. *Jury Deliberations: Evidence of Insurance.* If the underlying tort case does not settle and instead proceeds to a jury trial, the question arises as to whether the jury can and should be informed of the presence either of liability insurance covering the defendant or first-party insurance such as medical insurance covering the plaintiff. For litigation in federal courts, and many state courts, a rule of evidence exists that, subject to certain exceptions, specifically bars the litigants from presenting evidence that the *defendant* carried liability insurance. *See* Fed. R. Evid. 411. Likewise, as noted earlier in this chapter, about half the states adhere to the *collateral source rule*, which bars admission of evidence that *plaintiff* has been (or will be) compensated, in part or in whole, for her injuries by some other source than the tortfeasor, such as employee benefits or first-party medical insurance.

These rules have been defended on various grounds. One such ground is the belief that jurors might be prejudiced in their thinking about the merits of the underlying tort claim if they know that the defendant will not have to pay the judgment out of his own pocket, or that the plaintiff has access to other sources of compensation apart from payment by the defendant. Based on this sort of thinking, many legislatures that have recently set out to "reform" tort law have abolished the collateral source rule for some or all tort claims. A recent study of 40 tort trials by Professors Diamond and Vidmar found that the jurors' deliberations almost always include discussions of insurance even though little or no evidence on the issue had been presented to them. If this is generally the case, might it make sense to introduce evidence of insurance so that the parties have a chance to educate the jury on the coverages in question?

17. *Liability Insurance and Redress.* We have suggested that tort is fundamentally about permitting individuals to seek redress for those deemed responsible by the law for injuring them. Is the ability of many tortfeasors to "contract out" of the obligation to pay for injuries they cause consistent with that claim? If the insured tortfeasor is not the one who ends up footing the bill for the harm done to the plaintiff, in what way is he held responsible by the law of tort? Looking at the issue from the opposite end, can one make an argument that the availability of liability insurance often ensures that the tort system operates fairly in attributing responsibility?

V.   ENFORCING JUDGMENTS: GETTING TO ASSETS

Even after a tort suit results in a jury verdict (or judicial verdict if the parties have waived jury trial), there are a few more procedural steps left before the case is deemed resolved at the trial level. (We leave aside issues of appellate procedure—assume that neither party will seek an appeal.) If the verdict is rendered by a jury in favor of the plaintiff, the defendant(s) will almost certainly have moved to set aside the verdict either as a matter of law or on the grounds that a new trial is required. Assuming that the trial judge denies these motions, her next job is to enter judgment in the case. A judgment records the amount of the jury's verdict, the defendant or defendants against whom the judgment is rendered, and the plaintiff or plaintiffs to whom the judgment is owed. Ideally, the judgment will be issued in a separate document, signed by the judge. However, judges sometimes enter judgments orally from the bench.

Although it is necessary for a plaintiff seeking redress from a defendant to obtain a judgment, it is hardly sufficient. Now the plaintiff must collect on it. There are a number of potential obstacles to collection, including obstacles created by other areas of law, such as corporate, property, and bankruptcy law. In the following notes we identify in a very preliminary way how some of these areas of law intersect with tort law. Other courses will provide you with a much richer understanding of these subjects.

1. *Judgment-Proof Defendants.* Most tort plaintiffs seek redress in the form of payment by the tortfeasor. If the tortfeasor lacks available assets by which to satisfy the judgment, the tort victim may be out of luck. The presence or absence of liability insurance coverage often matters enormously. If, for example, driver *D* tortiously injures pedestrian *P*, and *D* has no savings or property holdings, *P* still stands to recover if *D*'s careless driving is covered under a liability insurance policy. If not—either because *D* lacked insurance or because his act was intentional and therefore excluded from coverage—*P* may be left without compensation. This latter sort of defendant is sometimes deemed a "judgment proof" defendant.

A few options are still open to Ps who are unlucky enough to have valid claims against judgment-proof defendants. For example, if D were gainfully employed, P might be able to obtain a court order under which a certain percentage of D's wages are "garnished" — that is, handed over to P.

2. *Whose Assets?* Anglo-American law recognizes a number of devices that enable individuals and entities to shield certain assets from being paid over to a tort victim. Perhaps the most important of these is the business corporation. One of the primary purposes of the corporate form is to permit individuals to invest in a business run by others in a manner that limits their potential losses to the amount that they invest. Thus, if a business organized as a corporation incurs tort liability, each shareholder is on the hook for no more than the value of his holdings in the company. Other assets owned by the shareholder — for example, a shareholder's personal bank account or her home — cannot be used to satisfy the corporation's tort liabilities.

This limitation on liability holds not only for shareholders who are "natural" persons, but also for business entities that own shares of other businesses. Recall the *Aldridge* case from Chapter 4, which concerned claims made against Goodyear by workers exposed to toxic chemicals at a Kelly-Springfield plant. As indicated in the court's opinion, Kelly-Springfield was owned by Goodyear. Yet, even if the workers could have prevailed on a tort claim against Kelly-Springfield outside of the workers' compensation system (say, because the evidence established that Kelly-Springfield purposely exposed its workers to toxins), they likely could not have obtained access to assets in Goodyear's bank accounts. Kelly-Springfield was set up as a distinct corporate entity; hence the workers' claims would run only against its assets. If for some reason it lacked the resources to compensate the plaintiffs, they could not look to assets held by Goodyear to make up the deficiency.*

Natural persons and entities can limit access to their assets by placing control of some of their assets with others. For example, suppose A is about to start an accounting business. Although he does not anticipate encountering malpractice liability, he also wants to prepare for the worst. One thing he will likely do is buy malpractice insurance. Another might be to transfer certain assets that he currently owns to others. For example, he might have the deed to his home put in his wife's name, thereby rendering it her asset, rather than his. (But see *infra* Note 3.) Certain foreign jurisdictions and some American states have recently begun to offer individuals the opportunity to place certain of their assets in a special kind of trust account. These are complex and highly controversial financial devices. When they work, they do so by requiring the owner to give up some of his ability to control the assets — for example, he may have access to the income generated by the assets held in trust but not the principal — in exchange for putting them beyond the reach of creditors.

---

* Business entities need not be organized as corporations. For example, they can also be organized (as are many law firms) as partnerships. The rules governing the liability of individual partners for torts vary substantially depending on the type of partnership.

3. *Limits.* The methods briefly described above give individuals and entities the ability to structure their holdings so as to reduce the availability of their assets to tort victims. However, these methods are subject to a number of important limits. In principle, businesses are not permitted to set up sham or phony corporations for the purpose of avoiding liability. Likewise, courts will nullify transfers of assets that amount to "fraudulent conveyances." Suppose, for example, our imagined accountant *A* learns that he has been sued, or is about to be sued, for malpractice. If *under those circumstances* he tries to transfer his assets so that they will be unavailable to satisfy a judgment against him, a court will likely void those transactions as fraudulent. Finally, even in the absence of a fraudulent conveyance, particular courts may decline to recognize the validity of particularly aggressive financial devices designed to limit tort victims' access to assets, such as offshore trust accounts. For example, even if a defendant were to assert in court that the bulk of his assets are unavailable because bound up in an offshore trust, the judge might still order the defendant (or the custodian of the trust) to release the assets from the trust. If a defendant were to fail to comply with that order, the judge could hold the tortfeasor in contempt of court, which would in turn authorize his temporary imprisonment.

4. *Corporate Bankruptcy.* For so-called mass torts — torts that involve injuries to hundreds or thousands of persons — there is often a risk that the tortfeasor, even if it is a large and insured corporation, will lack sufficient assets to pay its tort liabilities. For example, because of the toxicity and widespread use of asbestos, Johns Manville and numerous other asbestos manufacturers have incurred or can expect to incur tort liabilities in excess of the company's insurance and assets. In such situations, a corporation may find itself, voluntarily or involuntarily, in bankruptcy proceedings. When that occurs, payment for any debts and liabilities are suspended ("stayed") while the bankruptcy judge attempts to devise an orderly scheme of payment under the rules of federal bankruptcy law. Unfortunately for tort plaintiffs, those laws generally call for the payment of "secured" debts — such as bank loans issued in exchange for a security interest in assets owned by the corporation — before "unsecured" debts, such as tort liabilities. Often by the time secured debts are paid off, there is little or no money left to pay tort liabilities. If so, the debts are permanently "discharged" and the tort claimants are out of luck. Certain liabilities, however, are not dischargeable in bankruptcy, namely those arising out of egregious misconduct. See Chapter 9.

REFERENCES/FURTHER READING

Compensatory Damages

Randall R. Bovbjerg, et al., *Valuing Life and Limb in Tort: Scheduling "Pain and Suffering,"* 83 Nw. U. L. Rev. 908 (1989).

Martha Chamallas, *Questioning the Use of Race-Specific and Gender-Specific Data in Tort Litigation: A Constitutional Argument*, 63 Fordham L. Rev. 73 (1994).

Heidi Li Feldman, *Harm and Money: Against the Insurance Theory of Tort Compensation*, 75 Tex. L. Rev. 1567 (1997).

Mark Geistfeld, *Placing a Price on Pain and Suffering: A Method for Helping Juries Determine Tort Damages for Nonmonetary Injuries*, 83 Cal. L. Rev. 773 (1995).

Stanley Ingber, *Rethinking Intangible Injuries: A Focus on Remedy*, 73 Cal. L. Rev. 772 (1985).

Louis L. Jaffe, *Damages for Personal Injury: The Impact of Insurance*, 18 Law & Contemp. Probs. 219 (1953).

David Leebron, *Final Moments: Damages for Pain and Suffering Prior to Death*, 64 N.Y.U. L. Rev. 256 (1989).

Edward McCaffery, et al., *Framing the Jury: Cognitive Perspectives on Pain and Suffering Awards*, 81 Va. L. Rev. 1341 (1995).

Clarence Morris, *Liability for Pain and Suffering*, 59 Col. L. Rev. 476 (1959).

Colleen P. Murphy, *Judicial Assessment of Legal Remedies*, 94 Nw. U. L. Rev. 153 (1999).

Ellen S. Pryor, *Rehabilitating Tort Compensation*, 91 Geo. L.J. 659 (2003).

Ellen S. Pryor, *The Tort Law Debate, Efficiency and the Kingdom of the Ill: A Critique of the Insurance Theory of Compensation*, 79 Va. L. Rev. 91 (1993).

Margaret J. Radin, *Compensation and Commensurability*, 43 Duke L.J. 56 (1993).

Alan Schwartz, *Proposals for Products Liability Reform: A Theoretical Synthesis*, 97 Yale L.J. 353 (1988).

Victor E. Schwartz & Leah Lorber, *Twisting the Purpose of Pain and Suffering Awards: Turning Compensation into Punishment*, 54 S. C. L. Rev. 47 (2002).

Warren Seavey, *Torts and Atoms*, 46 Cal. L. Rev. 3 (1958).

Suja Thomas, *Re-Examining the Constitutionality of Remittitur Under the Seventh Amendment*, 64 Ohio St. L.J. 731 (2003).

Neil Vidmar, *Empirical Evidence on the Deep Pockets Hypothesis: Jury Awards for Pain and Suffering in Medical Malpractice Cases*, 43 Duke L.J. 217 (1993).

Albert Yoon, *Damage Caps and Civil Litigation: An Empirical Study of Medical Malpractice Litigation in the South*, 3 Am. L. & Econ. Rev. 199 (2001).

Punitive Damages

Bruce Chapman & Michael Trebilcock, *Punitive Damages: Divergence in Search of a Rationale*, 40 Ala. L. Rev. 741 (1989).

Thomas B. Colby, *Beyond the Multiple Punishment Problem: Punitive Damages as Punishment for Individual, Private Wrongs*, 87 Minn. L. Rev. 583 (2003).

Stephen Daniels & Joanne Martin, *Myth and Reality in Punitive Damages*, 75 Minn. L. Rev. 1 (1990).

Neil R. Feigensen, *Book Review: Can Juries Punish Competently*, 78 Chi.-Kent L. Rev. 239 (2003).

Marc Galanter & David Luban, *Poetic Justice: Punitive Damages and Legal Pluralism*, 42 Am. U. L. Rev. 1393 (1993).

Theodore Eisenberg, et al., *Juries, Judges, and Punitive Damages: An Empirical Study*, 87 Cornell L. Rev. 743 (2002).

Dorsey D. Ellis, Jr., *Fairness and Efficiency in the Law of Punitive Damages*, 56 S. Cal. L. Rev. 1 (1982).

David Friedman, *An Economic Explanation of Punitive Damages*, 40 Ala. L. Rev. 1125, (1989).

2 Simon Greenleaf, *A Treatise on the Law of Evidence* § 253 (16th ed. 1899).

David Owen, *Punitive Damages in Product Liability Litigation*, 74 Mich. L. Rev. 1258 (1976).

David Owen, *The Moral Foundations of Punitive Damages*, 40 Ala. L. Rev. 705 (1989).

Michael L. Rustad, *Unraveling Punitive Damages: Current Data and Further Inquiry*, 1998 Wis. L. Rev. 15.

Michael Rustad & Thomas Koenig, *The Historical Continuity of Punitive Damages Awards: Reforming the Tort Reformers*, 42 Am. U. L. Rev. 1269 (1993).

Gary T. Schwartz, *The Myth of the Ford Pinto Case*, 43 Rutgers L. Rev. 1013 (1991).

Anthony J. Sebok, *What Did Punitive Damages Do? Why Misunderstanding the History of Punitive Damages Matters Today*, 78 Chi.-Kent L. Rev. 163 (2003).

Theodore Sedgwick, *A Treatise on the Measure of Damages* 515-540 (5th ed. 1869).

Catherine M. Sharkey, *Punitive Damages as Societal Damages*, 113 Yale L.J. 347 (2003).

A. Mitchell Polinsky & Steven Shavell, *Punitive Damages: An Economic Analysis*, 111 Harv. L. Rev. 869 (1998).

Cass Sunstein, et al., *Punitive Damages: How Juries Decide* (2002).

W. Kip Viscusi, *Why There Is No Defense of Punitive Damages*, 87 Geo. L.J. 381, 384-387 (1998).

Vicarious Liability

William O. Douglas, *Vicarious Liability and Administration of Risk* (Pts. I & II), 38 Yale L.J. 584, 720 (1929).

Young B. Smith, *Frolic and Detour* (Pts. I & II), 23 Colum. L. Rev. 444, 716 (1923).

Michael Wells & Thomas A. Eaton, *Constitutional Remedies* 96-117 (2002).

Joint Liability and Contribution

Restatement (Third) of Torts: *Apportionment of Liability* (1998).

Insurance

Randall R. Bovbjerg, *Liability and Liability Insurance: Chicken and Egg, Destructive Spiral, or Risk and Reaction*, 72 Tex. L. Rev. 1655 (1994).

Clyde J. Crobaugh & Amos E. Redding, *Casualty Insurance* 394-491 (1929).

Shari Seidman Diamond & Neil Vidmar, *Jury Room Ruminations on Forbidden Topics*, 87 Va. L. Rev. 1857 (2001).

Sean W. Gallagher, *Note: The Public Policy Exclusion and Insurance for Intentional Employment Discrimination*, 92 Mich. L. Rev. 1256 (1994).

Mary C. McNeeley, *The Genealogy of Liability Insurance*, 7 U. Pitt. L. Rev. 169 (1941).

Ellen S. Pryor, *The Stories We Tell: Intentional Harm and the Quest for Insurance Funding*, 75 Tex. L. Rev. 1721 (1997).

Adam F. Scales, *Man, God and the Serbonian Bog: The Evolution of Accidental Death Insurance*, 86 Iowa L. Rev. 173 (2000).

Gary T. Schwartz, *The Ethics and Economics of Liability Insurance*, 75 Cornell L. Rev. 313 (1990).

Kent D. Syverud, *The Duty to Settle*, 76 Va. L. Rev. 1113 (1990).

Kent D. Syverud, *On the Demand for Liability Insurance*, 72 Tex. L. Rev. 1629 (1994).

PART THREE

DIGNITARY TORTS AND NEGLIGENT INFLICTION OF EMOTIONAL DISTRESS

CHAPTER 9
Battery, Assault, and False Imprisonment

I. DIGNITARY TORTS

Part Two of this book provided an in-depth treatment of the tort of negligence as it applies to claims for bodily injury and property damage. In Part Three, we shift our attention to torts that enable victims to obtain redress for other forms of wrongdoing and other kinds of injuries. This chapter introduces three torts that have been recognized by name since the Middle Ages: *battery*, *assault*, and *false imprisonment*. The next chapter begins with consideration of an important modern descendant of these ancient torts: *intentional infliction of emotional distress* (IIED). In doing so, it also introduces you to related causes of action created by federal statutes that bar discrimination on the basis of race, gender, and age. Chapter 10 concludes by returning to negligence law to examine a group of claims not covered in Part Two. This group consists of claims seeking recovery for *negligent infliction of emotional distress* (NIED) — emotional distress caused by conduct that is unreasonable because of the risk it poses to the emotional well-being of others.

The organization just described departs from the conventional pattern. Indeed, it is now standard for scholars, judges, and lawyers to place battery, assault, and false imprisonment together with IIED and the "property torts" of trespass and conversion within a single category called *intentional torts*. This standard categorization makes some sense — in many instances, a plaintiff who sues for one of the aforementioned torts is complaining that the defendant acted for the purpose of causing harm to her or to interfere with her property rights. Still, it is in other ways awkward and confusing. The most basic confusion it generates derives from the implicit claim that assault, battery, false imprisonment, IIED, trespass, and conversion employ a single and uniform concept of "intent." In fact, as we see in Chapter 11, trespasses to land and personal property do not always or even typically involve the same sort of purposeful conduct that characterizes batteries, assaults, and false imprisonments. Likewise, the IIED cause of action sometimes permits liability to attach to conduct that is wrongful because it is reckless rather than intentional.

In place of "intentional torts," we employ the category *dignitary torts* and limit its applicability to battery, assault, false imprisonment, and IIED. We prefer use of the latter phrase to categorize these four causes of action because it better captures a quality that they actually share. In contrast to standard claims of negligence, which aim to vindicate a person's interest in being free from certain *harms*, the core interest vindicated by each of these causes of action is the interest in not being subjected to certain kinds of indignities.

To begin to grasp this distinction, consider the follow hypothetical. Suppose *V*, who wears his hair in a ponytail, falls asleep on the lawn of a public park. When he wakes up, *V* discovers that a stranger, *S*, has expertly cut off his ponytail. Even though *V* has not suffered any physical wound, and even if we suppose that *V* in fact likes his new appearance, *V* can still claim to have been mistreated by *S* simply because *S*'s touching of *V*'s body was unauthorized and inappropriate. Absent extenuating circumstances, *V* will be able to seek redress from *S* for subjecting him to this particular indignity by means of a claim for battery. (Of course, this example is highly stylized. In the real world, invasions of one's "bodily space" are usually accompanied by harm in the form of physical harm or emotional distress. The point is that such invasions need not generate harm to be actionable — they constitute actionable injuries in and of themselves.)

As the judicial decisions excerpted in this chapter attest, tort and related bodies of law contain various rules marking dignitary torts as involving a separate species of wrongdoing. State laws sometimes impose shorter statutes of limitation on claims asserting the torts covered in this chapter. Liabilities arising from conduct amounting to one of these three torts is often uninsured, and sometimes uninsurable. Punitive damages are more commonly awarded to victims of these torts than to victims of negligence. Torts such as battery are excluded from workers' compensation coverage, thus permitting employees victimized by these torts to obtain damage awards from fellow employees and their employers. Finally, whereas liabilities arising out of careless and even reckless conduct are dischargeable in bankruptcy, those incurred by virtue of assaults, batteries, and false imprisonments tend not to be.

Battery, assault, and false imprisonment constitute the historical and conceptual core of the dignitary torts, which is why they are presented together in this chapter. Indeed, before the collapse of the writ system in the early nineteenth century, each provided a paradigmatic example of the sort of direct, forcible harming that was cognizable under the old English writ of trespass *vi et armis*. (This is not to say that they provided the *only* sort of claims cognizable under that writ.) It is thus no surprise to find that these torts "hang together" in their conceptual structure and animating principles. Still, they do not exhaust the category of dignitary torts. Other venerable torts, including libel and slander, probably fall within it. Moreover, as tort law has evolved, courts have self-consciously developed new causes of action that build on the core dignitary torts. One of these, IIED, is discussed in Chapter 10. (Others include various actions for invasions of privacy.) Some of the statutory causes of action encountered in Chapter 10 are also perhaps best understood as actions designed to vindicate one's dignitary interest in not being demeaned or disrespected. Finally, although the NIED cause of action does not belong in the category of dignitary torts, its formation and current composition reflect its links to dignitary actions such as assault and IIED.

II. BATTERY, ASSAULT, AND FALSE IMPRISONMENT: ELEMENTS

A. *Battery*

We described the above example of an uninvited haircut as "highly stylized." This is because, although liability for battery can attach without violence or harm to the victim, real-world batteries typically involve both. Intentional physical beatings, in particular, have long served as a paradigm case of battery. Thus, one finds references to thirteenth-century English "trespass" actions that are essentially actions for battery — the allegation is that the defendant set upon, beat, and wounded the plaintiff. Other purposeful touchings that are not physically harmful but nonetheless inappropriate and offensive also have long been recognized as batteries. Here the classic example is that of *A* purposely spitting in *B*'s face. *See* Draper v. Baker, 21 N.W. 527 (Wis. 1884) (upholding a $1,200 jury award for the plaintiff, who sued in battery after defendant spat on her). We consider in more detail the defining characteristics that unite this category of wrongs. Before doing so, however, it is important to note the basic distinction between battery and its close cousin, the tort of assault. That distinction will become clearer as you read the cases in this section.

1. *Assault versus Battery*. Suppose *D* intentionally hits *P* with a metal pipe in order to render him unconscious and rob him of his wallet. In ordinary language, one might describe *D* as having "assaulted" *P*, or as having committed an "assault and battery" against *P*. In the technical parlance of tort law, however, *D*'s act, although clearly a battery, may or may not have amounted to an assault. If *P* apprehended the attack as it was coming, it would give rise to a claim for assault as well as battery. If *P* did not sense the attack, the facts would only support a claim for battery. In other situations, discussed below, an actor can commit an assault without committing a battery. The tendency to lump together assault and battery is certainly understandable. Most attacks that generate assault liability will generate a claim of battery as well, and vice versa. Moreover, as we will see, there is a particular way in which tort law itself links the two causes of action by means of a special doctrine called *transferred intent*. Still, for purposes of clear legal analysis, it is important to keep in mind that assault and battery are distinct causes of action.

2. *Elements of Battery*. A prima facie case of battery may be described as follows:

Battery: Prima Facie Case

Actor *A* is subject to liability to other person *P* for battery if:
1.   *A* acts,
2.   intending to cause

    a.   harmful contact with *P*, or

    b.   contact with *P* that is offensive; and

3.   *A*'s act causes such contact.

The first element of battery — the act requirement — is rarely at issue: It builds a minimal volitional component into the tort. One standard example of a *non-act* in this context would be if *D*, against *C*'s will, were to grab *C*'s hand and use it to slap *P*'s face. *P* would not have a battery claim against *C* even though *C*'s hand made contact with *P*'s body, because *C* did not act, much less act with an intent to slap *P*. Likewise, suppose bus passenger *B* is standing on a crowded city bus and holding firmly onto an overhead rail to keep his balance. If the bus unexpectedly comes to a sudden stop, thereby causing *B* to crash into fellow passenger *F*, *B* has not "acted," at least not within the time frame relevant to a potential claim for battery.*

3. Intent and Proof of Intent. The second element (intent) is also *sometimes* very straightforward. Bringing about a harmful or inappropriate touching on purpose — for example, a deliberate punch in the nose — is a paradigmatic instance of acting with the sort of intent required by the second element of battery. However, as discussed below in this section, as well as in Section II.D, analysis of the intent element can, in other circumstances, be substantially more subtle and complicated.

As should be apparent even from this very preliminary description, the intent element of torts such as assault and battery concerns the mental state of the alleged tortfeasor. Mental states, needless to say, are not directly observable. Thus, even in a straightforward case, a battery plaintiff must rely on circumstantial evidence to establish that the defendant probably acted with the requisite intent. In some cases, plaintiffs will have access to evidence "from the horse's mouth." For example, imagine that *A* crashes into and knocks down *B* as they pass one another on the street, and that *B* sues *A* for battery. At her deposition, *A* initially denies she acted for the purpose of knocking over *B*. However, under withering examination from *B*'s attorney, *A* finally blurts out: "All right, yes, I meant to knock over *B*, and I'm glad I did it." Alternatively, suppose that *B* is fortunate enough to discover that *W*, a witness to the incident, will testify that, moments before the incident, *A* told *W* that she was planning to knock over *B*. In either situation, *B* would seem to have compelling evidence of *A*'s intent from *A* herself.

More typically, a battery plaintiff will have to rely on evidence pertaining to the defendant's behavior to support an inference that the defendant acted with the requisite intent. At times, that inference will be relatively easy to draw. Suppose *D*, a champion darts player, is playing an ordinary game of darts in a pub. In typical fashion, *D* is defeating her opponents with an extraordinary display of throwing accuracy. Suppose further that *D*

---

* Of course *B* acted when he boarded and took his position on the bus, but those actions are not relevant to an inquiry into whether *B* committed battery against *F* (unless *F* is prepared to show that *B* took the position on the bus that he did as part of an elaborate plan to slam into *F*).

spears *P* with a dart, even though *P* was standing 15 feet away from the dartboard at the time. Finally, suppose that the jury is presented with evidence that *D* and *P* had been seen arguing heatedly earlier that day. Even if *D* were to insist that the dart "slipped," a jury would almost certainly be entitled to infer from this evidence that *D* acted for the purpose of spearing *P* with the dart.

Circumstantial evidence can also be used for other purposes besides proving intent. For example, a plaintiff who is subjected to an intentional physical attack can sometimes rely on it to identify the defendant as the perpetrator. *Compare* Lackie v. Fulks, 2002 WL 1308646 (Mich. App. 2002) (plaintiff, attacked in a bar, did not see his assailant, but circumstantial evidence permitted the jury to conclude that it was the defendant), *app. denied*, 655 N.W.2d 562, *with* O'Connell v. Jacobs, 583 N.Y.S.2d 61 (N.Y. App. Div. 1992) (minor plaintiff who was attacked in her bed but unable to identify her assailant could not prove assault and battery claims brought against one of several older children staying in the house at the time; no evidence indicated who among the older children committed the assault), *aff'd*, 611 N.E.2d 289 (N.Y. 1993).

4. *Contact: Direct and Indirect.* The tort of battery is all about indignities in the form of impermissible *touchings* of the body. Indeed, its emphasis on physical contact is the feature that most clearly distinguishes battery from assault. Thus, the third element of the prima facie case of battery requires that the plaintiff prove that the defendant's act caused physical contact with the plaintiff's body. In a prototypical battery, such as the deliberate punch in the nose, the contact aspect of battery is readily apparent. However, as the foregoing darts example suggests, touching need not be flesh-on-flesh, nor directly caused, to satisfy the third element. Shootings and bombings that cause bodily injury to another can count as batteries, assuming the other elements are met. So too would an attack by a dog that is ordered by the dog's owner. Bernadsky v. Erie R. Co., 70 A. 189 (N.J. Err. & App. 1908) (affirming a jury verdict for the minor plaintiff where the defendant's employee "sicked" his dog on the plaintiff).

5. *Battery versus Negligence.* The foregoing examples ought to give you a feel for the sort of conduct that amounts to a battery. A fuller appreciation of the distinctive features of the tort can now be gained by considering its application in more complex settings. The next cases provide two such settings. Each also illuminates the contours of battery by demanding consideration of the differences between battery and the distinct cause of action for negligence. As explained briefly in Chapter 1, and in detail in Chapters 2 through 6, the crux of a claim of negligence is that the defendant has wronged the plaintiff by *failing to take sufficient care* to avoid harming her. One classic example of such a failure is that of a medical professional — such as the pharmacist in Walter v. Wal-Mart — who, in providing services to a patient or customer, fails to take reasonable care to avoid causing bodily harm to the patient or customer. In such cases, the negligence plaintiff, like a battery plaintiff, is often complaining of physical harms. Yet, as the next case demonstrates, there are important conceptual and practical differences between a claim that a physician has battered his

patient and a claim that the physician has committed negligence toward her (i.e., malpractice).

Newland v. Azan
957 S.W.2d 377 (Mo. Ct. App. 1997)

Howard, J.   . . . Brenda Newland sought dental treatment from Dr. Nohaud Azan, a dentist licensed in the State of Missouri, for a root canal and related dental procedures. . . . Newland alleged that on May 8, 1995, while she was in the dental chair, Dr. Azan sexually assaulted her after giving her several painkiller shots. Newland alleged that Dr. Azan touched her pubic area, kissed her, caressed her cheek and hand, rubbed his own genital area, and made sexually suggestive comments. All of these events occurred while Dr. Azan was treating Newland and performing dental services.

Newland filed a petition stating claims for professional negligence, battery, and infliction of emotional distress, and [sought] punitive damages. Dr. Azan filed a motion for partial summary judgment on the claim of professional negligence, claiming there were no material facts in dispute showing that Dr. Azan committed professional negligence in sexually assaulting Newland. The trial court granted the motion for partial summary judgment. Newland then dismissed the remaining counts without prejudice, and this appeal ensued. . . .

We find that Newland has not presented a valid malpractice claim, and the trial court did not err in granting Dr. Azan's motion for summary judgment. . . .

STANDARD OF CARE

First, Newland must show that Dr. Azan's acts fell below the requisite standard of care for a dentist. For a health care worker, the standard of care requires the worker to use the degree of skill and learning ordinarily used under the same or similar circumstances by members of the worker's profession. Expert testimony generally must be introduced to establish the standard of care in a medical negligence case. Edward Mosby, D.D.S., an expert witness retained by Newland, testified in his deposition that the behavior of Dr. Azan fell below the standard of care of a practicing dentist. . . .

This is a case of first impression in Missouri. However, several jurisdictions have decided cases with [similar] facts. . . . In these cases, the issue was whether the dentist's malpractice insurance covered injuries resulting from a sexual assault on a patient that took place while the dentist was performing dental services. The courts considered whether sexual assault constituted "professional services" rendered by the dentist, for the purpose of determining coverage by the insurance policy. All of the courts found that "professional services" did not include sexual assault. While the insurance coverage issue differs from the issue presented here, we find the reasoning of these cases persuasive in determining whether Dr. Azan's sexual conduct could fall below the standard of care for a dentist.

Whether an act results from a professional service is determined by focusing on the act itself, rather than the place where the act occurred. The fact that an act occurred in a professional's office does not automatically transmute the act into a professional service. Likewise, when there is a complaint of malpractice, attention should focus on the act or service performed rather than the fact that the alleged wrongdoer was a dentist because "the scope of professional services does not include all forms of a medical professional's conduct simply because he or she is a . . . dentist." [Cited authority omitted.] Therefore, the fact that Dr. Azan is a dentist and the sexual conduct took place in his office is not determinative of liability in this case.

There must be some causal connection between the act that caused the harm and the nature of the dentist-patient relationship. That is, it must be a dental act or service that caused the harm, not an act or service that requires no professional skill. Newland's allegations of assault and battery do not describe professional services. Rather, the allegations present "factual issues capable of resolution . . . without application of the standard of care prevalent in the . . . medical community." Roe v. Madison Ctr. Hosp., 652 N.E.2d 101, 104 (Ind. Ct. App. 1995).[1]

Newland does not allege that the actual dental services, including the root canal and related tooth and gum care, were not properly done or performed or that Dr. Azan lacked the skill and learning of a dentist to perform a root canal. Therefore, Newland has failed to show that Dr. Azan's conduct fell below the standard of care for a dentist.

Most of the cases Appellant cites in support of her claim of professional negligence involve psychiatrists, therapists, and other mental health professionals. In most cases where malpractice actions based on sexual assault of a patient by a mental health professional have succeeded, the court found that the professional failed to properly handle the "transference phenomenon."[2] We find that the cases involving mental health professionals are distinguishable from the present case. First, a mental health professional's mishandling of a patient's transference is directly related to providing mental health services, while a dentist's sexual assault on a patient is completely unrelated to dental services. Moreover, Newland does not argue that she believed, or that Dr. Azan ever maintained, that sexual contacts were a part of her dental treatment. In addition, unlike the therapist-patient relationship, there is nothing

---

1. . . . [We] note the absurd precedent that would be set by allowing Newland to sue Dr. Azan under the theory of malpractice for sexual assault that did not involve dental care. . . . [U]nder the rule proposed by Newland, if a dentist shot his patient or tied the patient to a chair in the dentist's office, [such conduct] would also fall within the realm of malpractice.

2. Transference occurs when a patient transfers to the psychiatrist the emotions he or she feels toward another person. . . .

inherent in the typical relationship between a patient and a dentist that makes the patient unusually susceptible to accept the sexual advances of the dentist.[3] . . .

We next consider the issue of whether the administration of the anesthetic affects Dr. Azan's liability for professional negligence. Newland was administered novocaine or a similar drug to numb her gums for the dental work. However, Newland does not allege that her ability to resist the alleged advances by Dr. Azan was impaired or that she was vulnerable in any way because of the administration of the drug. Newland testified that the painkiller shots made her "very groggy," but she did not suggest that the drug made her more susceptible to Dr. Azan's advances. In addition, Newland does not allege that the drug was administered negligently or for an improper purpose. Therefore, we find that the administration of the drug has no effect on Dr. Azan's liability for professional negligence. . . .

NOTES AND QUESTIONS

1. *More on Battery versus Negligence.* Why, according to the *Newland* court, is it incorrect to describe Dr. Azan's conduct as constituting negligence? Does a reasonable dentist behave as he is alleged to have behaved? If not, why is it inappropriate to describe the wrong he committed as the wrong of careless dentistry? Alternatively, don't the allegations suggest that Dr. Azan exploited the power and trust accorded to him by the doctor-patient relationship to perpetrate his misdeed? If so, why wouldn't that be enough to render his conduct malpractice?

2. *Intent versus Motive.* As we noted above, in some cases—*Azan* appears to be one of them—a battery plaintiff is able to allege or prove conduct that, given the circumstances, readily demonstrates that the defendant acted with the requisite intent. However, this issue can also be quite subtle, as the next several notes attest. We can begin our exploration of the complexities of intent by exploring the distinction between *intent* and *motive*.

Suppose *U*, an adult, sincerely believes that it is a vital part of each person's maturation to experience some bodily trauma. Accordingly, *U* purposely punches his 18-year-old nephew *N*, leaving *N* with a bloody nose. *N* sues *U* for battery. *U* testifies credibly that he delivered the punch "for *N*'s own good; . . . to prepare him for life's hard knocks." Has *U* acted with intent to cause a harmful touching? Yes. It is true that *U* acted out of benevolent *motives*. He sought to provide a net benefit to *N* by causing *N* to suffer an unwelcome and harmful touching. Still, that this was his ultimate

---

3. "Transference involves more than the trust that could be reposed in any professional to whose procedures a patient submits. . . . Rather, it involves the emotional fragility for which treatment may have been sought, and permits the exploitation of the vulnerability that may be present during the course of treatment. This nexus is what brings the tort within the ambit of professional malpractice." Steven G. v. Herget, 178 Wis. 2d 674, 505 N.W.2d 422, 427 (App. 1993).

purpose does not change the fact that U sought to achieve that purpose by acting for the immediate purpose of causing such a touching. (Evidence of U's "benevolent" motive might be permitted by a judge to figure in the jury's damage calculation, although one could argue that U's paternalistic attitude toward N's welfare is precisely the sort of disposition the law means to check by recognizing claims for interferences with dignitary interests. See Largey v. Rothman, Chapter 3.)

As discussed in Section III of this chapter, batteries can sometimes be *justified* on slightly different grounds from those unsuccessfully invoked by U. For example, rescuer R would be justified in performing the Heimlich maneuver on choking victim C, even though it entails forceful compression of the area above C's abdomen. Here, the justification for R's battery of C does *not* reside in the fact that R acted with good motives — a desire to help C by battering C — but in the fact that R reasonably believed that touching C in this way was necessary to save C from serious injury or death. See Section III.B (discussing defense of self and others).

3. *Intent and Knowledge.* In the famous case of Garratt v. Dailey, 279 P.2d 1091 (Wash. 1955), Brian Dailey, who was just under six years old, pulled a chair out from under his aunt as she began to sit in it. As a result, she fell and broke her hip. At a bench trial of the aunt's battery claim, Brian testified that he had moved the chair before realizing that his aunt was about to sit down on it, then hurriedly tried to move it back under her, but failed. Based on this testimony, the judge found for Brian.

On appeal, the Washington Supreme Court reversed, relying in part on comment d to Section 13 of the First Restatement. That comment read as follows:

> *Character of actor's intention.* In order that an act may be done with the intention of bringing about a harmful or offensive contact . . . to a particular person . . . the act must be done for the purpose of causing the contact . . . or *with knowledge* on the part of the actor that such contact . . . *is substantially certain* to be produced.

Restatement (First) of Torts § 13, cmt. d, at 29 (1934) (emphasis added). According to the court, on the facts found by the trial judge, Brian could have committed a battery under the "knowledge" prong of comment d's test for intent. Upon remand, the trial court found that Brian was "substantially certain" that his aunt would fall as a result of his moving the chair, and therefore imposed liability. That decision was affirmed by the supreme court.* 304 P.2d 681 (Wash. 1956).

---

* Although *Garratt* has come to stand as a leading authority for the existence of a separate "knowledge" standard for battery liability, the facts of the case do not seem to have necessitated or even warranted application of that standard. If, as his aunt contended, Brian moved the chair as a prank, he acted for the purpose of causing his aunt to suffer a harmful touching, and no separate knowledge standard is required to establish that he acted with the requisite intent. If, however, Brian had no idea that his aunt was about to sit down in the chair when he moved it, it would seem that he failed to act with the requisite intent even under the knowledge standard. After all, if he didn't know she was about to sit, how could he be *certain* that, by moving it, he would cause her to fall?

Comment d's rule was incorporated, with certain changes, into Section 8A of the Second Restatement. A version of it also appears in Section 1 of the Draft Third Restatement. Thus, each of the three torts Restatements appears to treat the knowledge prong to constitute a separate substantive liability standard for torts such as battery and assault. In other words, they seem to assert that one can commit a battery by knowingly touching a person even if one does not act for the purpose of causing that touching. Restatement (Second) of Torts § 8A, cmt. b (1965) ("If the actor knows that the consequences are . . . substantially certain . . . to result from his act, and still goes ahead, he is treated by the law *as if* he had in fact desired to produce the result.") (emphasis added). Some courts, however, employ "knowledge" differently. In their view, proof that a defendant knew that his conduct would cause a harmful or offensive touching of the plaintiff is *not* sufficient of itself to establish that the defendant intended to cause such a touching. Rather, it provides *circumstantial evidence* from which a jury can infer that the defendant acted for the purpose of causing a harmful or offensive contact. *See, e.g.*, Travis v. Dreis & Krump Mfg. Co., 551 N.W.2d 132 (Mich. 1996) (proof that plaintiff's employer had actual knowledge that injury to the plaintiff was certain to occur as a result of the employer's conduct creates an inference that the employer acted for the purpose of injuring the plaintiff, thereby permitting him to sue in tort, rather than collect workers' compensation benefits). The difference between these two accounts of the role played by "knowledge" in the law of assault and battery is subtle: In most cases the two will permit the same result. However, as indicated in Note 7, *infra*, there may be an important class of cases for which they generate disparate results.

4. *Knowledge: Sufficient, Not Necessary.* On either account of the knowledge standard, proof that the defendant knew his act would cause a harmful or offensive touching is deemed *sufficient* but *not necessary* to satisfy the intent element. It is not necessary because the plaintiff can prove intent by proving that the defendant acted for the purpose of causing such a touching, even if he did not know that his conduct would have that effect, a point illustrated by the following hypothetical. Suppose that T is an inept darts player. While playing darts in a bar, T spots his enemy E standing near the darts board. T throws the dart at E, very much hoping it will spear E in the leg. T is *not certain* that the dart will hit E. Indeed, given his ineptitude, he has every reason to believe that the dart will *not* hit E. If, nonetheless, the dart miraculously does hit E, T will have committed a battery because he acted for the purpose of causing a harmful (if improbable) contact with T so as to cause such a contact.

5. *Knowledge: Subjective or Objective Standard?* To the extent the knowledge prong is meant to instantiate the idea of a dignitary tort, it probably ought to be read as setting a *subjective* rather than an *objective* standard. Suppose that host H serves store-bought food to guest G. Unbeknownst to G, the food contains nuts, to which G is very allergic. G eats the food and has a severe allergic reaction. If H actually knew that the food contained nuts and that G was allergic to them, he has committed a

battery. Essentially, he has intentionally poisoned *G*. If *H* did not know either of those things, he has not committed a battery — he did not set out to "poison" *G*, nor was he certain that his conduct would do so. Perhaps a reasonable person in *H*'s position should have known that the food contained nuts and that *G* was allergic to them. If so, *H* should be held liable for negligence, not battery.* For a contrary argument that the substantial certainty standard ought to be objective, along with citations to contrary cases defending a subjective standard, see Turner v. PCR, Inc., 754 So. 2d 683 (Fla. 2000).

6. *Knowledge versus Foresight.*   The standard of knowledge is much more exacting than the standard of foreseeability encountered in negligence law. The issue is *not* whether the actor knows that his actions pose a *risk* of harmful or offensive contact, but rather whether he knows that his actions *will cause* such contact. German Mut. Ins. Co. v. Yeager, 554 N.W.2d 116 (Minn. Ct. App. 1996), illustrates this important point. Yeager, a teenager, demonstrated a homemade bomb to his friends by tossing it over his shoulder, away from where they were sitting. Despite this precaution, shrapnel from the bomb severely injured one of them. Yeager's insurer sought to deny coverage for any tort liability Yeager would incur to his friends on the ground that Yeager's act was "intentional" and thus excluded from coverage by the terms of his insurance policy. The court of appeals rejected this argument noting that while Yeager clearly was aware of the risks of harm associated with his conduct, he was not substantially certain that someone would be injured by it — indeed, he acted in the belief that no one would get hurt. Thus, his conduct was an instance of carelessness or recklessness, rather than an intentional wrong.

7. *Knowledge and Ongoing Activities.*   The knowledge prong most obviously applies when the defendant is nearly certain that his conduct will result in the harmful or inappropriate touching of a particular person or particular persons. Should it also be satisfied if the defendant knows to a certainty that, by virtue of its ongoing conduct, *someone* will sooner or later be hurt? For example, suppose delicatessen owner *O* knows that, in each of the last five years, he has sold 10,000 cups of piping hot coffee in styrofoam cups. Suppose *O* also knows that, in each of these years, two customers have suffered severe burns because of leaky cups. Now suppose that, in the current year, customer *C* is scalded and sues *O* for battery. In a statistical and predictive sense, *O* was perhaps substantially certain that his conduct — selling coffee in the manner that he did — would eventually cause a harmful touching to someone. Yet it does not necessarily follow that he has committed battery against *C*. Rather, one could argue that if *O* has wronged *C*, it is because he acted carelessly toward *C*, or perhaps with reckless indifference to *C*'s physical well-being.

---

* We assume that *H* did not serve food to *G* for the purpose of causing some other unwanted touching of *G*; for example, for the purpose of causing him to choke or to burn his tongue. If *H* acted with such a purpose, and then ended up causing the desired injury to *G* by the unexpected means of generating an allergic reaction, he might be held liable for battery. See *infra* Section II.D.

The choice between these alternative descriptions of O's conduct can have great practical significance. Recall, for example, that the bar imposed by workers' compensation laws on lawsuits by employees against employers for workplace injuries typically does not apply to "intentional" wrongs. If an employer's knowledge that its ongoing business will eventually cause injury to some employee suffices to establish intent, a wide range of workplace injuries would seem to fall within the intentional wrongs exception and hence outside of workers' compensation schemes. *See, e.g.*, Turner v. PCR, Inc., 754 So. 2d 683 (Fla. 2000) (if the jury finds that the employer should have known that some workers would almost certainly be injured by workplace activities and conditions, those workers who do suffer injury are not limited to workers' compensation benefits, and may instead sue in tort for battery).

Courts have split over whether "statistical" knowledge is sufficient to establish intent. That split is related to the split, discussed above, over whether to treat knowledge as sufficient in its own right to generate liability for battery, or instead to view it as circumstantial evidence of purpose. The latter view, in particular, can help capture why statistical knowledge strikes some courts and commentators as insufficient to prove intent. Simply put, it is very implausible to infer a *purpose* to cause a harmful touching from mere statistical knowledge. For example, there is little, if any, reason to suppose that deli owner O acted out of any desire to harm his customers. More likely, he regarded these incidents as a necessary evil; a matter for regret. To point this out is not to say that O acted appropriately, nor to assert that O is immune from liability for a tort other than battery, such as negligence. It is only to conclude that his willingness to act in a manner that subjects a small number of customers per year to serious burns does not amount to conduct undertaken *for the purpose* of causing harmful touchings of those persons.

8. *Intent and Mental Incompetence.* Suppose D is suffering from a severe mental illness, as a result of which she believes that P is a Martian who has come to earth to conquer it. If D strikes P in a sincere effort to "stop P's evil plot," should P be able to recover for battery? As noted in Chapter 3, the black-letter rule is that insanity does not defeat the attribution of intent, which suggests that liability should attach, notwithstanding that D sincerely believed that she was causing harmful contact with a Martian rather than a person. Some courts, however, have qualified or rejected this rule. *See* White v. Muniz, 999 P.2d 814 (Colo. 2000) (en banc) (jury may find that Alzheimer's sufferer who punched caregiver committed battery only if it finds that she had the capacity to appreciate that such contact would be harmful or offensive); Edwards v. Stills, 984 S.W.2d 366 (Ark. 1998) (insanity is not generally a defense in tort but can be invoked to defeat liability if the actor's mental incapacity renders him incapable of maintaining the intent necessary to establish liability). As indicated in Chapter 3, even if an actor is deemed incapable of committing a dignitary tort by virtue of mental incapacity, he still can be found to have acted carelessly by failing to adhere to the reasonable person standard.

As also noted in Chapter 3, common law has traditionally regarded children of a certain age (under seven, for example) to be incapable of acting unreasonably as a matter of law. No such blanket rule has attached to conduct amounting to a battery or assault. Instead, the factfinder must determine whether the particular minor being sued was capable of forming the requisite intent and acted with such intent. *See, e.g.*, Weisbart v. Flohr, 67 Cal. Rptr. 114 (Ct. App. 1968) (given trial testimony concerning the seven-year-old defendant's capacities, as well as his state of mind when he shot the plaintiff with an arrow, the trial court should have entered judgment for the plaintiff on the ground that the defendant committed battery as a matter of law).

Herr v. Booten
580 A.2d 1115 (Pa. Super. Ct. 1990)

Montemuro, J.   This appeal is based upon the sad and tragic death of a very young man, Eric B. Herr. At the time of his death, Eric was a college student at the West Chester University. Eric was born on January 17, 1963. On January 17, 1984, Eric's college roommates entered his bedroom and discovered that Eric had died during the night. The cause of his death was acute ethanol poisoning. . . .

This litigation was commenced in March of 1986 by Eric's parents in their own right, and by Eric's father, Benjamin A. Herr, as Administrator of the Estate of Eric B. Herr. The defendants include Eric's college roommates: Paul Booten, John Raymer, and Robb Aspril, Jr. The fourth defendant, Alex Orolyn, did not reside with Eric at college but he was a college acquaintance.

It is undisputed that in the afternoon of January 16, 1984, Eric and his three roommates decided to buy beer to celebrate Eric's impending twenty-first birthday. All four of the young men contributed money toward the purchase of the beer. Defendant Raymer drove Eric to a beer distributorship where several cases of beer were purchased. The roommates began drinking the beer in their apartment in the late afternoon of January 16, 1984. Later in the evening, defendant Orolyn arrived. Eric, along with Orolyn and Raymer, then left the apartment and attended a party at a fellow student's house where they consumed more beer. They later left this party to stop at Orolyn's apartment in order to obtain a nearly full bottle of Jack Daniels whiskey which Orolyn gave to Eric as a birthday present. When the group returned to Eric's apartment, which he shared with Booten, Raymer, and Aspril, other people had arrived to celebrate Eric's birthday. That evening, Eric Herr consumed most of the bottle of whiskey himself, apparently in two sustained gulps. It appears to be undisputed that the first gulp occurred before midnight.

The present action is based in tort. It is claimed that the defendants committed the intentional tort of battery by providing alcohol to Eric. Secondly, it is claimed that the defendants were negligent in providing Eric with alcohol, challenging or encouraging him to drink the alcohol, and then failing to render care when his physical condition became serious. The trial court entered summary judgment in favor of the defendants, concluding that no cause of action for battery or negligence had been set forth as a matter of law. We affirm in part and reverse in part. . . .

We agree with the trial court's conclusion that no cause of action can be established for battery in the present case, even when the evidence is viewed in the light most favorable to the non-moving party. "As traditionally stated, the elements of the tort of battery are 'a harmful or offensive contact with a person, resulting from an act intended to cause the plaintiff or a third person to suffer such a contact, or apprehension that such a contact is imminent.' Prosser & Keeton, *Law of Torts,* at 39 (5th ed. 1984)." Levenson v. Souser, 384 Pa. Super. 132, 146, 557 A.2d 1081, 1088 (1989). There was no "harmful contact" or "offensive touching" with the body of Eric Herr so as to give rise to a cause of action for battery in the present case. We are unwilling to view the supplying of an alcoholic beverage to a person as an act intending to cause "offensive or harmful bodily contact."

"A bodily contact is offensive if it offends a reasonable sense of *personal dignity.*" Restatement (Second) of Torts § 19 (emphasis added). Implicit in the tort of battery is the recognition that an individual has a right to be free from unwanted and offensive or harmful intrusions *upon his own body.* The tort of battery has traditionally been employed to redress this precise grievance. The essence of the tort "consists in the offense to the dignity involved in the unpermitted and intentional invasion of the inviolability of [the plaintiff's] person. . . ." *See* Restatement (Second) of Torts § 18, Comment c. Thus, the Restatement recognizes that an intrusion upon the plaintiff's physical or personal dignity does occur where the defendant "throws a substance, such as water, upon the [plaintiff] or if [the defendant] sets a dog upon him" even though the defendant and the plaintiff have not physically touched each other. *Id.* Additionally, "if the actor daubs with filth a towel which he expects another to use in wiping his face with the expectation that the other will smear his face with it and the other does so, the actor is liable as fully as though he had directly thrown the filth in the other's face or had otherwise smeared his face with it." *Id.* Although the supplying of alcohol to a person may be improper or contrary to the law because the person is a minor or, perhaps, because he is already visibly intoxicated, it is not an act which impinges upon that individual's sense of physical dignity or inviolability. Such an expansion of the traditional notion of battery has never been sanctioned by the courts of this Commonwealth. Consequently, we affirm the entry of summary judgment in favor of the defendants as to the battery cause of action.

In entering summary judgment in favor of the defendants as to the negligence claims, the trial court first determined that Eric B. Herr was twenty-one years of age, and thus an adult, at the time the defendants participated in the distribution of alcohol to him. This is a critical determination [because, in Klein v. Raysinger, 504 Pa. 141, 470 A.2d 507 (1983), the Pennsylvania Supreme Court declined to hold social hosts liable to third parties for injuries caused most immediately by an intoxicated *adult* guest on the ground that any such injuries are the responsibility of the guest, not the host. Thus, if Eric were adjudged to be an adult at the time of the alleged tort, he would be deemed solely responsible for his death.]

The *Klein* decision stands in sharp contrast to a decision rendered by the Pennsylvania Supreme Court on the same day: Congini v. Portersville Valve Company, 504 Pa. 157, 470 A.2d 515 (1983). In *Congini,* an eighteen year old employee of Portersville Valve Company ("Portersville") was injured when, in an intoxicated condition, he drove his vehicle into the rear of another vehicle. Prior to the accident, the employee had attended a Christmas party held by Portersville where he was served alcoholic beverages. The *Congini* Court . . . depart[ed] from the common law rule it had relied upon in *Klein,* recognizing that:

> . . . our legislature has made a legislative judgment that persons under twenty-one years of age are incompetent to handle alcohol. Under Section 6308 of the Crimes Code 18 Pa. C.S. § 6308, a person "less than 21 years of age" commits a summary offense if he "attempts to purchase, purchases, consumes, possesses or transports any alcohol, liquor or malt or brewed beverages." Furthermore, under Section 306 of the Crimes Code, 18 Pa. C.S.A. § 306, an adult who furnishes liquor to a minor would be liable as an accomplice to the same extent as the offending minor.

Congini, supra at 161, 470 A.2d at 517. The Supreme Court thus held that the serving of alcohol to a person less than twenty-one years of age is negligent per se. *Id.* (citing Restatement (Second) of Torts § 286). The affirmative action on the part of the defendant which gives rise to this negligence is the "furnishing of intoxicants to a class of persons legislatively determined to be incompetent to handle its effects." *Id.* at 163, 470 A.2d at 518.

In determining that Eric Herr was twenty-one years of age during the day *preceding* his twenty-first birthday, the trial court relied upon a general rule of common law in this jurisdiction which provides that a person is deemed to attain a given age on the day before his or her birthday. While this general rule of common law remains a viable one, it is not applicable in the instant case. . . . [I]t is common knowledge and common practice that an individual may not legally be served alcohol, or purchase or consume alcohol, until the day of his twenty-first birthday. When an individual is "carded" at a liquor store or tavern, . . . alcohol will not be served to him or sold to him unless he has proof that it is . . . his twenty-first birthday, or after.

. . . In drafting the criminal statutes at issue in the case at bar, we are convinced that the Legislature was cognizant of this commonly understood and practiced rule for determining the legal age for the purchase and consumption of alcohol. . . . [W]e are bound to presume that the General Assembly did not "intend a result that is absurd, impossible of execution or unreasonable." Further, we are permitted to examine the practical consequences of a particular interpretation." Commonwealth v. Stewart, 375 Pa. Super. 585, 544 A.2d 1384 (1984) (citations omitted). Our Legislature did not intend 18 Pa. C.S.A. § 6308 to be interpreted in a manner which ignores, and indeed contravenes, the commonly accepted and practiced method for determining the legal age for the purchase and consumption of alcohol. . . .

Based upon our view of the correct statutory construction of Section 6308 of the Crimes Code, as well as Section 6310.1, we are firmly convinced that an individual born on January 17, 1963, such as Eric B. Herr, could not have legally purchased or consumed alcohol on January 16, 1984; but he could have legally done so on the following day, the day of his birth, January 17. Thus, the furnishing of alcohol to Eric B. Herr on January 16, [1984], amounted to negligence per se. . . .

In vacating the summary judgment which was entered in favor of the defendants in this case, we express no opinion concerning the ultimate finding of liability. A social host may assert, as a defense, the minor's contributory negligence. Questions of accusation as between the appellees and as between the appellees vis-a-vis Eric Herr must be resolved in the trial court by the finder of fact. Consequently, the summary judgment entered in favor of the defendants as to the cause of action in negligence for furnishing alcohol to Eric Herr is vacated and reversed.[2] . . .

Del Sole, J. (dissenting) (joined by Rowley, Johnson, and Hudock, JJ.). I agree with the majority's conclusion that no cause of action can be established for battery in the present case. . . . However, I can not agree that Appellees [were] negligent in providing alcohol to Eric Herr, because he was not a minor when his excessive drinking took place, on the day before his twenty-first birthday. [The dissent argues that statutory law barring provision of alcohol to minors was intended to incorporate the common law's "day-before-one's-birthday" rule. — EDS.]

NOTES AND QUESTIONS

1. *What Must Be Touched?* The interest underlying the tort of battery is the interest in controlling others' access to one's body. In protecting that interest, however, tort law creates a protective zone or space around the body by rendering actionable certain contacts with things closely connected to it. For example, if *D* shoots at *P*, but manages only to make a bullet hole in the sleeve of the shirt that *P* is wearing,

---

2. We reject appellants' claim that a cause of action in negligence is set forth by the allegations that appellees urged or challenged Eric Herr to consume the alcohol which ultimately caused his death. The only authority relied upon for this cause of action is Yania v. Bigan, 397 Pa. 316, 155 A.2d 343 (1959), wherein [the defendant cajoled the plaintiff,] an adult . . . [into] jump[ing] into a water-filled trench at a mining site and [the plaintiff] had died as a result. . . . The Supreme Court held that such alleged conduct would not constitute actionable negligence when directed to an adult in possession of all his mental faculties. The Court also stated that if the decedent "had been a child of tender years or a person mentally deficient then it is conceivable that taunting and enticement could constitute actionable negligence if it resulted in harm." . . . 155 A.2d at 345. We are unwilling, as an intermediate appellate court, to extend . . . *Yania* . . . to find a cause of action for the appellees' alleged "challenging conduct" in the present case. It is clear that Eric Herr was not a child of tender years and was not mentally deficient. . . . Even though Eric Herr was no doubt intoxicated . . . before he consumed the bottle of whiskey, he was in control of himself and made decisions regarding what and how much alcohol he would consume. . . .

D has caused a touching of *P* sufficient to generate a claim for battery. In Fisher v. Carrousel Motor Hotel, Inc., 424 S.W.2d 627 (Tex. 1967), plaintiff, an African-American, was standing in a buffet line at defendant's motel while holding an empty plate in his hands. One of defendant's employees snatched the plate away from him, telling Fisher that the restaurant did not serve African-Americans. The court upheld a jury award of compensatory and punitive damages for battery on the ground that the employee's snatching of the plate amounted to an offensive touching of Fisher. *Fisher* provides an example of what is sometimes referred to as the doctrine of *extended personality*.

The touching of an object with which a person happens to be in contact will not always count as a touching of the person. For example, if *R* were angrily to kick a lamppost against which *S* happened to be leaning, the kick would not likely of itself suffice to establish a touching of *S*.

2. *How Touched?* The notion of contact or touching conveys the idea of physical contact between two objects. However, there are other perhaps less obvious forms of contact. To take a gruesome example, some persons killed by explosions die not because they are crushed by falling objects or hit by shrapnel, but by virtue of an intense shock wave of energy, or by massive increases in air pressure (if, for example, the explosion occurs in a confined space). Such persons are treated for purposes of battery law as having been touched. Likewise, if *M* fills *Q*'s house with odorless, colorless, and deadly carbon monoxide gas, *Q* suffers harmful contact by inhaling the gas. Suppose *B* purposefully blows cigarette smoke in *F*'s face. Is this a harmful or offensive *touching?* What about a forceful current of air? Suppose *L* is listening to headphones that are plugged into a stereo system located on a bookshelf six feet behind where *L* is sitting. As a practical joke, *K* sneaks up behind *L*, then sharply increases the volume on the stereo, causing *L* momentary but extreme discomfort from the loud music. Is this a touching of *L* by *K*? Would the result change if *L* had been listening to a portable MP3 player attached to his belt?

3. *Contact and Causation.* Reconsider in light of what you now know the *Herr* majority's explanation as to why the plaintiffs could not sue for battery. Couldn't a reasonable jury have found that Eric's friends knew that, by supplying him with large quantities of alcohol, he would suffer some form of physical harm — for example, nausea — as the result of ingesting alcohol? If so, shouldn't the plaintiffs have been permitted to go forward with their battery claim? Would the plaintiffs have had a plausible battery claim if Eric's friends had secretly "spiked" what he thought was a soft drink in order to make him dizzy or nauseous, or if they had physically forced him to ingest vast quantities of hard liquor? If so, what's different about this case? The majority reasons that Eric's friends' actions did not constitute "intrusions upon his . . . body." Which element of the prima facie case of battery requires that the defendant's act constitute such an intrusion?

Suppose *P*, whom *D* knows to be careless at times, indicates to *D* that he desires to juggle kitchen knives. Suppose further that *D* provides *P* with knives even though *D* is substantially certain that *P*, an inexperienced juggler, will hurt himself by juggling them. Finally, suppose *P* suffers a serious laceration while juggling. Has *D* committed a battery by providing to *P* a dangerous instrument with which *P* injures himself? Would your analysis change if, instead of cutting himself, *P* broke a toe when one of the knives fell, handle-first, onto it?

4. *Offensive Contact*. The concept of "offensive" contact requires care in application. The issue is not whether the person touched *actually takes offense* at the contact. Usually the plaintiff will feel offended, but such a reaction is not sufficient for a contact to count as offensive. Rather, the issue is whether the contact *offends against prevailing standards of acceptable touchings*. As noted above, to be spat upon by a stranger is a quintessential instance of suffering an offensive contact. By contrast, if two strangers, *X* and *Y*, are standing at a public street corner, and *Y* taps *X* on the shoulder to ask for directions, the touching will not be deemed offensive, even if *X* is in fact offended. The same act of touching might be inoffensive in some contexts, yet offensive in others, depending on who is doing the touching, who is being touched, what the relationship is between them, the setting in which the touching occurs, etc. Thus, the question of offensiveness will often be for the factfinder. *See, e.g.*, Paul v. Holbrook, 696 So. 2d 1311 (Fla. Ct. App. 1997) (the question of whether male co-employee's uninvited rubbing of female employee's shoulders constitutes offensive contact is for the jury); Newsome v. Cooper-Wiss, Inc., 347 S.E.2d 619 (Ga. App. 1986) (a jury may find that an office worker who repeatedly rubbed against his secretary committed an offensive-contact battery). Some courts, following the Restatements, express the idea of offensiveness in terms of whether the contact "offends a reasonable sense of personal dignity." Restatement (Second) of Torts § 19 (1965).

Notice that our description of the elements of a prima facie case of battery describes the intent element for the "offensive contact" version of battery somewhat differently than for the "harmful contact" version of the tort. This difference reflects the fact that a defendant's unawareness of prevailing norms as to what constitutes an unacceptable touching provides no basis for avoiding battery liability. Because actors are in this sense expected to know and observe social norms as to the propriety of different sorts of touchings, they may be held liable for battery even if they "meant no offense" by intentionally touching the victim. *See, e.g.*, Wal-Mart Stores, Inc. v. Odem, 929 S.W.2d 513 (Tex. App. 1996) (contact can amount to battery if the defendant "should reasonably believe" that the contact would be offensive). So long as one has intended the sort of bodily contact that law or social norms deems inappropriate, one has acted with the requisite intent.

5. *Interplay of Intent and Offensiveness*. Certain contacts that might otherwise be deemed inoffensive as a matter of law can be rendered offensive if the defendant knows that the plaintiff is unusually averse to being touched in a particular way. *See, e.g.*, Cohen v. Smith, 648 N.E.2d 329 (Ill. Ct. App. 1995) (when patient's religion enjoins her to avoid having her

skin touched directly by males, and when hospital has notice of, and agrees to abide by, this restriction, the touching of her skin by a male nurse during surgery can constitute offensive contact battery). In this instance, the offensiveness of the contact is generated in part by the particular intent behind it. The plaintiff is entitled to take offense when the defendant fails to heed what he knows to be her disposition about being touched in certain ways.

6. *Compensatory and Punitive Damages*. As explained in detail in Chapter 8, the typical relief accorded to a successful tort plaintiff comes in the form of a damage payment made by the tortfeasor to the plaintiff. As the name suggests, compensatory damages aim to compensate the plaintiff for losses he has suffered as a result of the tort. Punitive damages, by contrast, provide an additional increment of redress to the victim, while also "sending a message" to the tortfeasor that such conduct is unacceptable, as well as a message to others that similar conduct may result in significant penalties. Compensatory damages are available to any tort claimant who can prove that he has suffered loss as a proximate result of the tort. These include economic (out-of-pocket) losses, such as medical bills incurred, losses in the form of property damage, and loss of past and future income. They also include noneconomic losses, such as pain and suffering. Punitive damages, by contrast, are only available to claimants who can establish that the tortfeasor committed a malicious or willful wrong, or a wrong that displays reckless disregard for the victim's well-being. Even then, their award is entirely discretionary with the factfinder.

Because batteries often consist of violent attacks, successful battery plaintiffs typically recover damages reflecting out-of-pocket losses such as medical bills. However, in the case of offensive-contact batteries, out-of-pocket losses may be quite modest. Still, even this sort of battery victim may recover a substantial compensatory award reflecting any pain, embarrassment, or humiliation he experienced. In addition, to the extent a battery plaintiff has been the victim of acts undertaken for the purpose of causing harm or offense to him, he often will be in a position to seek punitive damages. On the other hand, some batteries—for example, an offensive touching caused intentionally by a defendant who was unaware of prevailing social norms—might not display sufficient malice, willfulness, or wantonness to warrant a punitive award.

B. Assault

Recorded instances of English assault pleas date back at least to the fifteenth century. As explained in the case below, the interest vindicated by the action for assault is that of not being put in apprehension of imminent harmful or offensive contact. Assault, like battery, thus derives from a concern to protect individual bodily integrity. However, assault differs from battery because it gives effect to that right by protecting against certain apprehensions of contact, rather than contact itself.

A prima facie case of assault can be defined as follows:

Assault: Prima Facie Case

Actor A is subject to liability to other person P for assault if:
1. A acts,
2. intending to cause in P the apprehension of:
   a.   an imminent harmful contact with P, or
   b.   an imminent contact with P that is offensive; and
3. A's act causes P reasonably to apprehend an imminent harmful or offensive contact with P.

One occasionally sees assault described as an "attempted battery," or as a "failed" or "inchoate" battery. These formulations can be misleading. As the cases below demonstrate, a person can be the victim of an assault that is not a battery. Likewise, as we saw in the preceding subsection, a battery need not include an assault, as is the case with respect to batteries committed on unconscious plaintiffs, or surreptitious batteries, such as poisonings. Moreover, an assault might arise from an attempt at battery, but it need not. For example, the defendant's purpose may have been all along to scare rather than touch the plaintiff.

An assault is also not properly described as an action for an inchoate — that is, unrealized or incomplete — battery. Rather, an assault is a suit for a fully realized wrong, one that is completed when the requisite apprehension is generated in the victim. In this respect, the law of assault differs fundamentally from the criminal law, which sometimes criminalizes failed efforts to commit other crimes. Suppose, for example, S fires a loaded gun equipped with a silencer intending to shoot and kill V, but misses his target. V, for her part, is completely oblivious to the attempt. By happenstance, S's conduct is observed by a witness who reports S's behavior to the police. S can be convicted of attempted murder, but V has no action against S for assault.

Beach v. Hancock
27 N.H. 223 (1853)

TRESPASS, for an assault.

. . . [I]t appeared that the plaintiff and defendant, being engaged in an angry altercation, the defendant stepped into his office, which was at hand, and brought out a gun, which he aimed at the plaintiff in an excited and threatening manner, the plaintiff being three or four rods distant.* The evidence tended to show that the defendant snapped the gun twice at the plaintiff, and that the plaintiff did not know whether the gun was loaded or not, and that, in fact, the gun was not loaded.

* [1 rod ≈ 16.5 feet. — Eds.]

The court ruled that the pointing of a gun, in an angry and threatening manner, at a person three or four rods distant, who was ignorant whether the gun was loaded or not, was an assault, though it should appear that the gun was not loaded, and that it made no difference whether the gun was snapped or not. . . .

The jury, having found a verdict for the plaintiff, the defendant moved for a new trial. . . .

Gilchrist, C.J. . . .

One of the most important objects to be attained by the enactment of laws and the institutions of civilized society is, each of us shall feel secure against unlawful assaults. Without such security society loses most of its value. Peace and order and domestic happiness, inexpressibly more precious than mere forms of government, cannot be enjoyed without the sense of perfect security. We have a right to live in society without being put in fear of personal harm. But it must be a reasonable fear of which we complain. And it surely is not unreasonable for a person to entertain a fear of personal injury, when a pistol is pointed at him in a threatening manner, when, for aught he knows, it may be loaded, and may occasion his immediate death. The business of the world could not be carried on with comfort, if such things could be done with impunity.

We think the defendant guilty of an assault, and we perceive no reason for taking any exception to the remarks of the court. . . .

Brooker v. Silverthorne
99 S.E. 350 (S.C. 1919)

Hydrick, J.   Defendant appeals from judgment for plaintiff for $2,000 damages for mental anguish and nervous shock alleged to have been caused by abusive and threatening language addressed to plaintiff by defendant over the telephone.

Plaintiff alleges: That on October 27, 1916, she was night operator at the telephone exchange at Barnwell. That defendant called the exchange over the telephone and asked for a certain connection, which she promptly tried to get for him, but, upon her failing to do so, he cursed and threatened her in an outrageous manner, saying to her: "You God damned woman! None of you attend to your business." That she tried to reason with him, telling him that she had done all that she could to get the connection he wanted, but he continued to abuse and threaten her, saying to her: "You are a God damned liar. If I were there, I would break your God damned neck." That the language and threat of defendant put her in great fear that he would come to the exchange and further insult her, and that she was so shocked and unnerved that she was made sick and unfit for duty, and had to take medicine to make her sleep. That for weeks afterwards, when defendant's number would call, she would become so nervous that she could not answer the call. And that her nervous system was so shocked and wrecked that she suffered and continues to suffer in health, mind, and body on account of the abusive and threatening language addressed to her by defendant. . . .

Although it cannot affect the decision, because the truth of the facts alleged is concluded by the verdict, it is nevertheless due to the defendant to say that he denied emphatically using the language attributed to him, and his denial was corroborated by the testimony of his wife and a lineman of the telephone company. Defendant testified, also, that, on hearing that plaintiff was offended, he went to her and told her that he did not intend to say anything to offend her, and did not remember having done so, and asked her what he had said that offended her, and she replied that he had spoken a little harshly to her; that he told her he did not remember having done so, but, if she thought so, he was very sorry, and she seemed to be satisfied with this apology. This conversation was not denied by plaintiff.

The question is whether plaintiff stated or proved a cause of action. That question was decided in the negative in Rankin v. Railroad Co., 58 S.C. 532, 36 S.E. 997. In that case, Mrs. Rankin alleged that the railroad company's agents trespassed upon her premises, and were about to cut down some trees of great value and beauty, and, when she approached them and requested them not to do so, the foreman of the gang "cursed her and ordered her to get away from there, or he would put her in the penitentiary, and threatened to strike her, she being an old woman, and otherwise maltreated and abused her to her great damage." A demurrer to this complaint was sustained. The court considered the complaint as having attempted to set forth two causes of action, one for trespass on the plaintiff's property, and the other for the abusive and threatening language. After showing that no cause of action for trespass was stated, the question whether an action would lie for the abusive and threatening language was considered, and it was held that it would not. . . .

The circuit court rested its conclusions in part upon the following quotations from Cooley on Torts:

> "An act or omission may be wrong in morals, or it may be wrong in law. It is scarcely necessary to say that the two things are not interchangeable. No government has undertaken to give redress whenever an act was found to be wrong, judged by the standard of strict morality; nor is it likely that any government ever will." Cooley on Torts, p.3.
>
> "A threat to commit an injury is also sometimes made a criminal offense, but it is not actionable private wrong. Many reasons may be assigned for distinguishing between this case and that of an assault, one of them being that the threat only promises a future injury, and usually gives ample opportunity to provide against it, while an assault must be resisted on the instant. But the principal reason, perhaps, is found in the reluctance of the law to give a cause of action for mere words. Words never constitute an assault, is a time-honored maxim. Words may be thoughtlessly spoken; they may be misunderstood; they may have indicated to the person threatened nothing but momentary spleen or anger, though when afterwards reported by witnesses they seem to express deliberate malice and purpose to injure. . . . And comparing assaults and threats, another important difference is to be noted: In the case of threats, as has been stated, preventive remedies are available; but against an assault there are usually none beyond what the

party assaulted has in his own power of physical resistance." Cooley on Torts, p.29.

The plaintiff in this case relies upon the case of . . . Lipman v. R. Co., 108 S.C. 151, 93 S.E. 714, L.R.A. 1918A, 596 in which it was held that a carrier is liable in damages for abusive language addressed to a passenger by the carrier's servants. It was pointed out in [that case] that the ground of the carrier's liability for abusive language to a passenger is exceptional, on account of the special and peculiar relations, obligations, and duties existing between carrier and passenger, which differ in kind and degree from almost every other legal or contractual relation, since the carrier is in duty bound to protect his passengers from assault or insult by his servants, and to afford them courteous and respectful treatment. When the ground of liability is considered, the want of analogy between [that case] and this becomes apparent, for the defendant in this case was under no legal or contractual obligation or duty to protect the plaintiff from insult, abusive language, or assault. Every decision has tacit reference to the facts and circumstances of the case decided. Therefore, when it was said in the *Rankin* Case that no action would lie for mere threats or abusive words spoken, the court was careful to qualify the statement by confining it to the circumstances stated; for, as we have seen, abusive language addressed to a passenger by a carrier's servants is actionable. And it is not absolutely true that no action will lie for threats. Blackstone says that injury may be committed "by threats and menaces of bodily hurt, through fear of which a man's business is interrupted. A menace alone, without a consequent inconvenience makes not the injury, but to complete the wrong, there must be both of them together. The remedy for this is in pecuniary damages, . . . this being inchoate, though not an absolute violence." 3 Black. Com. 120. But the threat which causes the fear must be such as the law will recognize as adequate to produce the result. There must be just and reasonable ground for the fear; hence a vain or idle threat is not sufficient. It must be of such nature and made under such circumstances as to affect the mind of a person of ordinary reason and firmness, so as to influence his conduct; or it must appear that the person against whom it is made was peculiarly susceptible to fear, and that the person making the threat knew and took advantage of the fact that he could not stand as much as an ordinary person.

If it should be conceded that the language of defendant contained a threat, it was not of such nature or made under such circumstances as to put a person of ordinary reason and firmness in fear of bodily hurt. And it is not alleged that plaintiff was not a person of ordinary reason and firmness and that defendant knew it; and, in the absence of such allegation, it will not be presumed. A person of ordinary reason and firmness should have known that the profane and vulgar language alleged to have been used by defendant was the result of a momentary fit of passion, caused by his failure to get the connection he asked for, and that he had no intention of doing or attempting to do plaintiff any bodily hurt. But the words used did not amount to a threat. Defendant said: "If I were there, I would break your . . . neck." But he was not there, and plaintiff knew it; and there is nothing in what he said expressive of an intention to go there and injure plaintiff. Webster defines a "threat" as "the expression of an intention to inflict evil or injury on another." The law dictionaries give practically the same definition. A threat therefore looks to the future. As Judge Cooley says, in the passage above quoted, "a threat only promises a future injury." Here there was no expression of an intention to injury in the future, and therefore no threat.

The language attributed to defendant — especially when used by a man to a woman — merits severest condemnation and subjects the user to the scorn and contempt of his fellow men. But it is not civilly actionable. . . .

Vetter v. Morgan

913 P.2d 1200 (Kan. App. 1995)

Briscoe, C.J.   Laura Vetter appeals the summary judgment dismissal of her . . . assault . . . and negligence claims against Chad Morgan for injuries sustained in an automobile accident. We . . . reverse and remand for further proceedings on . . . [these] claims. . . .

Vetter was injured when her van ran off the road after an encounter with a car owned by Morgan's father and driven by Dana Gaither. Morgan and Jerrod Faulkner were passengers in the car. Vetter was alone at 1:30 or 1:45 A.M. when she stopped her van in the right-hand westbound lane of an intersection at a stoplight. Morgan and Gaither drove up beside Vetter. Morgan began screaming vile and threatening obscenities at Vetter, shaking his fist, and making obscene gestures in a violent manner. According to Vetter, Gaither revved the engine of the car and moved the car back and forth while Morgan was threatening Vetter. Vetter testified that Morgan threatened to remove her from her van and spat on her van door when the traffic light turned green. Vetter stated she was very frightened and thought Morgan was under the influence of drugs or alcohol. She was able to write down the license tag number of the car. Morgan stated he did not intend to scare, upset, or harm Vetter, but "didn't really care" how she felt. He was trying to amuse his friends, who were laughing at his antics.

When the traffic light changed to green, both vehicles drove forward. According to Vetter, after they had driven approximately 10 feet, the car driven by Gaither veered suddenly into her lane, and she reacted by steering her van sharply to the right. Vetter's van struck the curb, causing her head to hit the steering wheel and snap back against the seat, after which she fell to the floor of the van. Morgan and Gaither denied that the car veered into Vetter's lane, stating they drove straight away from the intersection and did not see Vetter's collision with the curb.

Vetter filed this action against Morgan and Gaither, alleging their negligent or intentional actions had caused her injuries. The trial court granted summary judgment in favor of Morgan, ruling Vetter could not raise a negligence claim against Morgan for unintended results of his intentional acts. The court concluded that Morgan could not be liable for Gaither's actions because Morgan did not participate in driving the car. The court also concluded Morgan's actions did not constitute assault . . . and dismissed all claims against Morgan. Gaither settled with Vetter, and the trial court approved the settlement. . . .

II. ASSAULT

Vetter argues the trial court erred in dismissing her assault claim against Morgan. Assault is defined as "an intentional threat or attempt, coupled with apparent ability, to do bodily harm to another, resulting in immediate apprehension of bodily harm. No bodily contact is necessary." *Taiwo*, 249 Kan. at 596, 822 P.2d 1024 (quoting PIK Civ. 2d 14.01).

The trial court concluded there was no evidence that Morgan threatened or attempted to harm Vetter, that he had no apparent ability to harm her because her van was locked and the windows were rolled up, and there was no claim of immediate apprehension of bodily harm. Vetter contends all of these conclusions involved questions of fact that should have been resolved by a jury.

There was evidence of a threat. Vetter testified in her deposition that Morgan verbally threatened to take her from her van. Ordinarily, words alone cannot be an assault. However, words can constitute assault if "together with other acts or circumstances they put the other in reasonable apprehension of imminent harmful or offensive contact with his person." Restatement (Second) of Torts § 31 (1964).

The record is sufficient to support an inference that Morgan's threat and the acts and circumstances surrounding it could reasonably put someone in Vetter's position in apprehension of imminent or immediate bodily harm. Morgan's behavior was so extreme that Vetter could reasonably have believed he would immediately try to carry out his threat. It is not necessary that the victim be placed in apprehension of instantaneous harm. It is sufficient if it appears there will be no significant delay. *See* Restatement (Second) of Torts § 29(1), comment b (1964).

The record also supports an inference that Morgan had the apparent ability to harm Vetter. Although Vetter's van was locked and the windows rolled up, the windows could be broken. The two vehicles were only six feet apart, and Morgan was accompanied by two other males. It was late at night, so witnesses and potential rescuers were unlikely. Although Vetter may have had the ability to flee by turning right, backing up, or running the red light, her ability to prevent the threatened harm by flight or self-defense does not preclude an assault. It is enough that Vetter believed that Morgan was capable of immediately inflicting the contact unless prevented by self-defense, flight, or intervention by others.

The trial court erred in concluding there was no evidence that Vetter was placed in apprehension of bodily harm. Whether Morgan's actions constituted an assault was a question of fact for the jury.

[In the remainder of its opinion, the court concluded that Morgan could be subject to liability in negligence on the theory that his conduct was unreasonable and that it functioned as an actual and proximate cause

of Vetter's crash. The court further held that Morgan could be liable for
Gaither's misconduct in swerving the van toward Vetter's car on a concert-
of-action theory.]

NOTES AND QUESTIONS

1. *Apprehension versus Fear*. A plaintiff can make out a prima facie
case of assault without having to establish that she was fearful that she was
about to suffer a harmful or offensive contact. It is enough that she was
aware that such contact might occur. Thus, a plaintiff who testifies to her
awareness that the defendant had tried unsuccessfully to dump garbage
over her head, or to caress her in an inappropriate but nonviolent manner,
need not establish that she was afraid for her physical well-being to make
out a prima facie case of assault. Still, these sorts of plaintiffs may sometimes find that their lack of fear will affect the amount of compensatory
damages they can expect to recover.

2. *"Mere" Words: Conditional or Indeterminate Threats*. As indicated in *Brooker*, for a threat to constitute an assault, it must be conveyed
in a way that creates a reasonable belief in the hearer that the threatened
contact is imminent. Absent special circumstances, a statement to the
effect of "One of these days, you're gonna get it" will not constitute an
assault. Some courts have generalized from this sort of example to the
proposition, mentioned in *Brooker* and *Vetter*, that "words alone" can
never constitute an assault. However, this proposition is more confusing
than helpful, given that real-world cases of assault never consist of words
alone. Instead, they are uttered in a context that is created by, among other
things, the speaker's tone of voice, accompanying gestures, the physical
circumstances in which the statement is uttered, the relationship or lack
thereof between defendant and plaintiff, and differentials between the
assailant and the victim such as physical size or gender.

3. *Present Ability and Reasonableness of Apprehension*. Not all
apprehensions caused by the intentional act of another count as assaults.
Rather, as with respect to offensive-contact batteries, social norms play an
important role in determining the circumstances under which an individual is justified in apprehending imminent harmful contact. Thus, some of
the cases thought to exemplify the "words alone" maxim are perhaps
better explained in terms of a judicial insistence that the victim's apprehension have some objective basis. For example, given the apparent lack
of physical proximity between the caller and the operator in *Brooker*, one
might conclude that, as a matter of law, the operator was not reasonable in
apprehending *imminent* harmful contact. What aspects of the situation in
Vetter provided the plaintiff with objective grounds for apprehending
imminent harmful contact?

In the famous case of Western Union Tel. Co. v. Hill, 150 So. 709 (Ala.
Ct. App.), *cert. denied*, 150 So. 711 (Ala. 1933), Mrs. Hill entered a telegraph office looking for one Sapp, a Western Union employee, to request

of Sapp that he repair a broken clock in her husband's store. Sapp, who had been drinking, reached across a countertop that separated them and stated to Mrs. Hill that, if she would "love and pet him," he would "fix her clock." The appellate court held that the jury could find that, given his height, and the height and width of the counter, Sapp was in a position to reach past the counter's far edge and touch Mrs. Hill. Thus, Sapp's propositioning of Mrs. Hill, when combined with evidence of his "present ability" to act on it, permitted the jury to conclude, first, that he acted with intent to create an apprehension of imminent offensive contact, and, second, that the plaintiff was reasonable to apprehend such contact.

4. *Aiding and Abetting.* Could Vetter successfully sue Gaither, the driver of the car in which Morgan was sitting, for playing a role in the assault? That would depend on whether a jury could find that Gaither "aided or abetted" Morgan's assault, that is, encouraged, incited, or helped to carry it out. Aiding and abetting closely resembles the idea of "concert of action" mentioned briefly in the notes following Summers v. Tice in Chapter 4. Indeed, as indicated at the end of the excerpted *Vetter* opinion, the court held that Morgan could be held liable for Gaither's careless driving, which functioned as a cause of Vetter's crash, on the ground that Morgan and Gaither were co-venturers. Presumably a similar rationale would apply to establish that Gaither aided and abetted Morgan's assault. *See* Halberstam v. Welch, 705 F.2d 472 (D.C. Cir. 1983) (discussing the scope of aiding and abetting liability in tort).

For a decision that provides an interesting application of assault law, while also invoking a seemingly narrow conception of aiding and abetting, see Phelps v. Bross, 73 S.W.3d 651 (Mo. App. 2002). Phelps worked as a "Budweiser girl" who accompanied male golfers during organized golf outings. According to the allegations in Phelps' complaint, at the conclusion of one such outing, her supervisor coerced her into accepting a ride back to her hotel from two golfers, Bross and Church. The two men then drove Phelps to Bross's house, where Church provided Phelps with a beer containing a drug that rendered her unconscious. While Phelps was unconscious, Church sexually assaulted her. When Phelps awoke, she found herself naked in a bed with Bross sitting next to her, fully clothed. Phelps ran from the house and contacted the police. She later sued Bross, among others, for assault and for aiding and abetting Church's battery. The appellate court concluded that, notwithstanding his active participation in the transportation of Phelps to his own house, Bross could not be held to have aided and abetted Church's battery because there was no evidence that he incited, encouraged, or participated in the attack itself. However, the court reversed the trial court's entry of summary judgment on Phelps' assault claim against Bross, concluding that a jury could reasonably find that Bross assaulted Phelps by getting into bed next to her and thereby causing her to fear imminent harmful or offensive contact when she awoke.

Two recent high-profile cases have also raised the issue of the breadth of aiding and abetting liability. In Rice v. Paladin Enterprises, Inc., 128 F.3d 233 (4th Cir. 1997), *cert. denied*, 523 U.S. 1074 (1998), the federal Court of Appeals was faced with a lawsuit against the publisher of a manual, entitled

"Hit Man," that instructs would-be assassins on how to commit and get away with murders. The plaintiffs, survivors of a decedent who was killed by a person who used the book's methods, claimed that the publisher had aided and abetted the killing. The court's opinion was devoted to rejecting the defendant's assertion that the First Amendment creates a blanket immunity from liability for book publishers. The case also poses an interesting question of substantive tort law: Does the publication of an instruction manual not directed to or at any particular person amount to the aiding and abetting of a battery committed in accordance with the manual's instructions?

In the second case, presently before the Ninth Circuit Court of Appeals, representatives of Myanmar citizens who allegedly were killed, raped, tortured, dispossessed, and/or conscripted by Myanmar military personnel have brought suit against Unocal Corporation under the Alien Tort Claims Act (ATCA), a federal statute that permits non-U.S. citizens to sue in American courts for redress for certain human rights violations. The suit alleges that Unocal, a participant in a joint venture responsible for building a gas pipeline in Myanmar, supervised and paid Myanmar soldiers to provide security for the project, and in the process knowingly assisted or encouraged the soldiers' human rights abuses. Although a three-judge panel initially ruled that the plaintiffs' complaint stated cognizable claims, that decision was vacated upon the subsequent granting of Unocal's motion to have the full (en banc) court rule on Unocal's motion to dismiss. Doe v. Unocal, 2003 WL 359787 (9th Cir. 2003).

C. False Imprisonment

The right to liberty has long been identified as one of the most important rights that Anglo-American law aspires to protect. Liberty has many dimensions, including freedom of thought and conscience, freedom of speech, and freedom to associate with others. But perhaps the most basic component of liberty is physical freedom — freedom of movement. It is no surprise, then, to find that the common law of tort has long accorded redress to those who have been subjected to the indignity of being confined by another. The primary doctrine by which that relief has been provided is through the tort of false imprisonment. Consider how this venerable cause of action applies in the following modern setting.

Fojtik v. Charter Med. Corp.
985 S.W.2d 625 (Tex. Ct. App. 1999)

Chavez, J.   Felix Fojtik appeals from . . . summary judgment entered against him on his claim against Charter Medical Corporation. Fojtik had brought a false imprisonment cause of action against Charter arising from his stay at a Charter hospital where he was treated for alcoholism. . . . We affirm the judgment of the trial court. . . .

BACKGROUND FACTS

Fojtik's admission to Charter was preceded by an "intervention," where Dorrill Nabours and Valerie Bullock from Charter, along with a group of Fojtik's family and friends, confronted him and told him that he needed to go through an inpatient treatment at Charter for alcohol abuse. Fojtik's medical records indicate that he told Charter staff he had admitted himself to Charter because those conducting the "intervention" had told him that, if he did not voluntarily admit himself, they would have him committed to the hospital and have him brought in wearing handcuffs.[2] When admitted, Fojtik was angry about being at Charter and refused to be photographed or to agree to permit Charter to contact him after he left the treatment program. While at the hospital Fojtik made several requests for a "pass" permitting him to leave the Charter facility. His initial requests were denied on the ground that he was not "eligible" for a pass until he was further into his stay. Fojtik expressed his opinion that he was getting a "raw deal" because he was "locked up and couldn't get away." Later Fojtik was granted passes for a few hours at a time, and always returned to Charter voluntarily and on time. Fojtik explained that he had vowed to follow all of the rules at Charter. Although nothing in the record explains the reason Fojtik made this "vow," he argues on appeal that he had decided to follow all the rules only because he hoped that obedient behavior might speed his release.

Charter produced summary judgment evidence that Fojtik was free to leave at any time. Charter employees explained that, although they used a system of "passes" and preferred to follow certain procedures when patients left the hospital, if a patient insisted on leaving without following Charter procedures, Charter would permit the patient to leave. Charter also refers us to Fojtik's admission documents, which indicate that he consented to inpatient treatment.

LEGAL STANDARDS

. . . . The elements of a false imprisonment cause of action are: (1) willful detention by the defendant, (2) without consent of the detainee, and (3) without authority of law. A detention may be accomplished by violence, by threats, or by any other means that restrain a person from moving from one place to another. Randall's Food Mkts., Inc. v. Johnson, 891 S.W.2d 640, 645 (Tex. 1995).

Where it is alleged that a detention is effected by a threat, the plaintiff must demonstrate that the threat was such as would inspire in the threatened person a just fear of injury to his person, reputation, or property. Id. Threats to call the police are not ordinarily sufficient in themselves to effect an unlawful imprisonment. Morales v. Lee, 668 S.W.2d 867, 869 (Tex.

---

2. Upon a showing that a person is chemically dependent and evidences an imminent, substantial risk of serious harm to himself or to others, a judge or magistrate may order that such person be apprehended and transported to a treatment facility. Tex. Health & Safety Code Ann. §§ 462.042-43 (Vernon 1992 & Supp. 1998).

App. — San Antonio 1984, no writ) (citing W. Prosser, Torts § 11 (4th ed. 1971)). In determining whether such threats are sufficient to overcome the plaintiff's free will, factors such as the relative size, age, experience, sex, and physical demeanor of the participants may be considered. . . .

WHETHER FOJTIK WAS RESTRAINED

Although Fojtik was not physically restrained, he alleges that he was detained against his will by threats that, if he did not submit to his detention, he would be forcibly committed and "brought in in handcuffs." Fojtik also contends that Charter used "other means" in addition to threats of commitment in order to restrain him. We first consider whether the evidence raises a question of fact regarding whether Fojtik was restrained by threats.

A review of false imprisonment case law is instructive. In Black v. Kroger, 527 S.W.2d 794 (Tex. App. — Houston [1st Dist.] 1975, writ dism'd) an eighteen year old woman with a tenth grade education and a two-year-old daughter was accused by her employers of stealing. She was led into a small, windowless room lit by bare light bulbs, where the store manager and another man who worked for "Kroger Security" were waiting. She was told repeatedly that they knew she had been stealing, and that if she did not admit to stealing they would handcuff her and take her to jail. She testified that she made a false confession, explaining "I just had it in my head that they were going to put me in jail no matter what I did, and I wasn't going to see my little girl for a long, long time." The court noted the woman's lack of business experience and the harsh and intimidating nature of her questioning. *Black*, 527 S.W.2d at 800. The court held that under these facts the jury could have reasonably concluded that the threats to the woman intimidated her to the point where she was not free to leave and was unreasonably detained. *Id.* at 801.

Skillern & Sons, Inc. v. Stewart, 379 S.W.2d 687 (Tex. Civ. App. — Fort Worth 1964, writ ref'd n.r.e) presents a similar set of facts. A female employee was accused of stealing. She was led by the arm to a room where two men she had never met beat on a desk while telling her "we have the goods on you . . . we know you've been stealing money." She was threatened with imprisonment, and told that she could not leave until she wrote a confession. She managed to leave, but was ordered back, and again told that she would either sign a confession or she would go to jail, but that she could not leave without confessing. When she tried to stand up she was physically pushed back into a chair by her accusers. These facts were held to support a recovery for false imprisonment.

In Safeway Stores, Inc. v. Amburn, 388 S.W.2d 443 (Tex. App. — Fort Worth 1965, no writ) the evidence was held insufficient to support a finding that the plaintiff was falsely imprisoned. In this case as well, an employee was led to a secluded room where others were waiting to accuse him of theft. The employee's path to the door, if he had desired to leave, was not blocked. The only physical contact between the employee and his accusers was a handshake. When the employee denied stealing anything he was accused of lying and threatened with jail. The employee spent thirty to forty minutes with his accusers. The court held that, where there is nothing else particularly overbearing about this kind of meeting, threats of imprisonment are not enough to establish a claim for false imprisonment, and the court reversed the jury's verdict in the plaintiff's favor.

In Randall's Food Markets, Inc. v. Johnson, 891 S.W.2d 640 (Tex. 1995), the plaintiff was a store employee accused of stealing. She was told to either wait in an office or to work on a volunteer project in a particular area. She waited in the office, but left twice and returned each time. The Texas Supreme Court rejected the plaintiff's contention that the store management had impliedly threatened her person, because no one was guarding her and she had in fact left the office twice. Summary judgment in favor of the store on the employee's false imprisonment claim was upheld.

In evaluating Fojtik's claim of false imprisonment, the issue is essentially this: to what extent must plaintiffs insist on their freedom and have it denied to them before they can recover for false imprisonment? Under some circumstances, a combination of the plaintiff's vulnerability and oppressive circumstances permit recovery, even when the plaintiff does not actually resist their detention. Comparing the facts of this case to previous reported cases, however, indicates that this is not one of those cases. None of the factors that are considered in evaluating whether threats are sufficient to overcome the plaintiff's free will, i.e., the relative size, age, experience, sex, and physical demeanor of the participants, weigh in Fojtik's favor. Fojtik was a forty-five-year-old man who had run several businesses. He was not a young, inexperienced woman, like the plaintiff in *Black*. He was not physically restrained, like the plaintiff in *Skillern*. Although he was threatened with the police, there were no other factors adding to the intimidating effect of those threats, and, as in *Amburn*, such threats, standing alone, are not enough to establish false imprisonment. Fojtik left and voluntarily returned, as the plaintiff did in *Johnson*, where the plaintiff's actions were held to negate her false imprisonment theory.

Fojtik contends that his frequent comments at Charter about being "locked up" and his generally uncooperative attitude are evidence that he did not consider himself free to leave. While it may be true that Fojtik considered himself restrained, the issue is not Fojtik's subjective interpretation of his situation, but rather whether he had a "*just* fear of injury." Randall's v. Johnson, 891 S.W.2d at 645. The facts of this case do not raise a fact issue on whether Fojtik had a "just fear" of injury. The record before us indicates that, while Fojtik certainly complained about being at Charter, he never insisted that he be permitted to leave. As discussed above, there is nothing in this case to suggest that Fojtik was a person whose weakness or susceptibility to intimidation might excuse his failure to insist on leaving. . . .

Aside from threats of legal commitment, the "other means" of restraint identified by Fojtik are: (1) constantly telling him that he was an alcoholic and treating him as though he were, and (2) permitting him to leave on temporary passes. Appellant's argument appears to be that these methods lessened his will to insist on being released. We do not believe that such trifling matters as these constitute restraint. Treating Fojtik as an

alcoholic did not restrain him; if it contributed to his ongoing presence at
the Charter hospital, it did so by persuading Fojtik that he did have a
problem with alcohol that should be addressed, not by any actual restraint.
The fact that Charter permitted Fojtik to leave on passes undermines his
claim for false imprisonment rather than supporting it. . . .

NOTES AND QUESTIONS

1. *Elements.* By including "lack of consent" and "absence of authority" as "elements," the *Fojtik* court's description of the false imprisonment
tort incorporates into the plaintiff's prima facie case what many jurisdictions instead describe and analyze as affirmative defenses. Following
Section 35 of the Second Restatement, one could alternatively define the
prima facie case of false imprisonment as follows:

False Imprisonment: Prima Facie Case

Actor *A* is subject to liability to other person *P* for false imprisonment
if:
1.   *A* acts,
2.   intending to confine *P*;
3.   *A*'s act causes *P* to be confined; and
4.   *P* is aware of her confinement.

2. *Damages versus Release: Habeas Corpus.* Like other torts, false
imprisonment can be perpetrated by a private citizen or by a government
official. False imprisonment, however, is more closely linked with official
misconduct than some other torts because confinements, as opposed to
other injuries, often come in the form of detentions at the behest of
governmental officials or via government processes such as criminal
prosecutions.

The immediate legal remedy sought by most persons who believe that
they have been unjustifiably detained by government officials is to obtain
not damages, but release. English common law long provided means for
individuals being held by executive-branch officials to apply to the courts
for their release. One particularly important device for doing so has been
the writ of *habeas corpus*, whereby a prisoner could ask a judge to order
the relevant officials to "produce the body," that is, appear with the prisoner before the court to justify the detention. If that justification was not
forthcoming, the judge could order that the prisoner to be released.

Prior to the late eighteenth century, the habeas writ was primarily
available only to persons who were being held without judicial proceedings of any kind. By contrast, in modern American law, the habeas writ,
which has been codified in federal statutes, now serves to provide prisoners with the ability to raise *collateral* challenges to a criminal conviction
obtained in a state court. (The challenge is a "collateral" challenge because

it is not raised by appealing a trial-level conviction to a higher court, but instead involves the initiation of a separate lawsuit subsequent to and independent of the original criminal prosecution.) Typically, such a challenge asserts that the prisoner's conviction or confinement violates rights accorded to him by the U.S. Constitution, such as the right to effective assistance of legal counsel or to legal procedures in accordance with due process of law.

3. *Civil Rights Laws and False Imprisonment.* Apart from obtaining release, a person wrongfully subject to official detention can also sue for damages. Here, she can rely not only on the common law tort of false imprisonment, but also on federal civil rights laws. The Fourth and Fifth Amendments to the U.S. Constitution respectively grant individuals the right not to be subjected to unreasonable seizure by government officials and the right to "Due Process of Law." In turn, a federal statute, 42 U.S.C. § 1983, empowers persons who have suffered violations of these (and other) constitutional rights at the hands of state and local officials, as well as certain private citizens, to sue those persons for damages. The Supreme Court in the *Bivens* decision, *supra*, Chapter 6, authorized similar actions against federal officials who deprive individuals of their constitutional rights.

Because these federal remedies tend to provide certain advantages to claimants over common law actions — for example, successful Section 1983 claimants can recover attorneys' fees — suits alleging wrongful detention brought about by state and federal officials such as police officers tend to be framed primarily as federal law civil rights claims, with common law false imprisonment claims tacked on as redundancies. *See, e.g.*, Daley v. Harber, 234 F. Supp. 2d 27 (D. Mass. 2002) (proof that the plaintiff's unjustified arrest was actionable as a civil rights violation under Section 1983 is sufficient to establish as a matter of law that defendant also committed the tort of false imprisonment). When the alleged detention is committed by a private citizen or entity, such as private hospitals and private security personnel, the claim for wrongful detention may still be actionable under Section 1983 if the private actor is deemed to have been acting "under color of law."* Suits complaining of detentions caused by private actors not deemed to be acting under color of law must invoke state-law claims for false imprisonment (and perhaps other torts such as battery).

4. *What Counts as Confinement?* A confinement occurs when the tortfeasor causes the victim to be within a bounded physical space. Confinement can occur in a relatively small space, such as a closet, or in large spaces, such as a home. However, certain boundaries may be so

---

* A private actor may be deemed to have acted under color of law if his conduct toward the plaintiff was undertaken in coordination with government officials or if he enjoyed special authority to detain the plaintiff by virtue of a delegation of authority from the government. *See, e.g.*, Payton v. Rush-Presbyterian-St. Luke's Medical Center, 184 F.3d 623, 628 (7th Cir. 1999) (holding that hospital security guards acted under color of law in detaining the plaintiff because of the authority delegated to them by Illinois law).

broad and permissive of free movement as to not count as confinement as a matter of law. *See* Shen v. Leo A. Daly Co., 222 F.3d 472 (8th Cir. 2000) (applying Arkansas law) (employee who was barred from leaving Taiwan by the Taiwanese government because of his employer's willful and unjustified refusal to file certain papers with the government was not "confined" by the employer's misconduct). Likewise, conduct that bars a person from traveling along a particular route, or to a particular destination, will not, absent special circumstances, count as confinement. Smith v. Comair, Inc., 134 F.3d 254 (4th Cir. 1998) (applying Kentucky law) (airline's refusal to allow a connecting passenger to board any flights other than a flight that would return him to the city from which he initially flew does not constitute confinement); Lloyd v. Jefferson, 53 F. Supp. 2d 643 (D. Del. 1999) (applying Delaware law) (no confinement when daughter, who sought to accompany her father as he was being brought into a private entrance of a police station, was barred by an officer from using that entrance and told instead to use a public entrance). Confinement can occur in a non-stationary space. *See* Wilson v. Houston Funeral Home, 50 Cal. Rptr. 2d 169 (Ct. App. 1996) (confinement occurred when deceased's relatives were, against their wishes, driven by a funeral home employee in a company limousine to a bank rather than to the burial site).

The paradigmatic instance of confinement is being placed within a space, such as a jail cell, that renders exit physically impossible. However, confinement can occur even absent the impossibility of departure. If an exit is available to the victim, but can only be used by the victim in a manner that poses a risk of physical harm to himself or others, the victim is deemed confined. Likewise, if the victim reasonably perceives that the tortfeasor will seek to prevent her from leaving, she is also confined. *See* Ball v. Wal-Mart, Inc., 102 F. Supp. 2d 44 (D. Mass. 2000) (applying Massachusetts law) (shopper who reasonably apprehended that the defendant store owner would take steps physically to prevent her from leaving was confined). Other forms of pressure can constitute confinement even if the plaintiff is literally free to move. For example, a threat to detain plaintiff's children or to seize plaintiff's property if plaintiff were to leave can suffice. *See* National Bond & Inv. Co. v. Whithorn, 123 S.W.2d 263 (Ky. App. 1938) (threat by the defendant to seize the plaintiff's automobile deemed to generate confinement). Lesser constraints on exit, including risk of loss of reputation or embarrassment, may also be sufficient. Jacques v. Childs Dining Hall Co., 138 N.E. 843 (Mass. 1923) (customer who was openly accused by waiter of trying to leave without paying her bill was "confined" for the period it took to establish that the accusation was unfounded; in light of the public accusation, the customer's leaving could have been viewed by other diners as an admission of guilt).

By contrast, if the victim can exit with only minimal inconvenience, or there is no reason to suppose that his effort to exit will be met with resistance, there is no confinement. *See* Caswell v. BJ's Wholesale Co., 5 F. Supp. 2d 312 (E.D. Pa. 1998) (customer who was brought to an office in a store was not confined, even though a store manager stood in the doorway, because there was nothing in the circumstances to suggest that the manager would block her departure). Also, threats of certain consequences not pertaining directly to the confinement, such as subsequent dismissal from employment or prosecution, are often deemed insufficient to establish confinement. *See* Grant v. Stop-and-Go Market, *infra*, Section III (discussing Texas cases); Foley v. Polaroid Corp., 508 N.E.2d 72 (Mass. 1987) (an at-will employee is not confined in an office simply because he was concerned that, if he left, he would be fired).

5. *Awareness of Confinement.* Section 35 of the Second Restatement and several state high court decisions require the plaintiff to prove that she was aware of her confinement as it happened. These authorities treat false imprisonment in one respect like assault, that is, as requiring apprehension of the condition of being confined. So, a victim who is locked in a room but sleeps for the duration of the confinement, or an infant who is too young to appreciate that she is being confined, cannot maintain a claim for false imprisonment. *See* Sager v. Rochester Gen. Hosp., 647 N.Y.S.2d 408 (Super. Ct. 1996) (five-month-old infant has no claim for false imprisonment absent proof that she was conscious of her confinement). Other authorities have questioned the requirement of awareness or apprehension. *See* Scofield v. Critical Air Medicine, Inc., 52 Cal. Rptr. 2d 915 (Cal. App. 1996) (noting and criticizing the contemporaneous awareness requirement in part on the ground that it would bar recovery by persons who only later learn that their confinement was unlawful).

6. *Willful versus Accidental Confinement.* To prevail on a claim of false imprisonment, the victim must prove by a preponderance of the evidence that the tortfeasor acted for the purpose of causing her to be confined, or with knowledge that she would be confined. Green v. Donroe, 440 A.2d 973 (Conn. 1982) (noting these two liability standards, albeit describing the latter as "extreme recklessness"); Stewart v. Williams, 255 S.E.2d 699 (Ga. 1979) (false imprisonment is an "intentional" tort). Accidental confinements, such as confinements arising out of misunderstandings, are ordinarily not actionable as false imprisonments. *But see* Ortiz v. Hampden County, 449 N.E.2d 1227 (Mass. App. 1983) (rejecting government's motion to dismiss a claim for negligence brought by a plaintiff who was arrested and imprisoned allegedly because a county employee carelessly and mistakenly wrote plaintiff's name on an arrest warrant). If the confinement results in harm such as bodily injury, the person who causes the confinement may be liable in negligence. So, for example, if *A* were carelessly to cause *B* to be trapped in a small, unventilated shed that became so hot as to cause *B* to suffer heatstroke before being freed, *B* may have a negligence claim against *A*.

The Wisconsin Supreme Court has permitted an action for negligent confinement resulting in emotional distress unaccompanied by physical injury. *See* La Fleur v. Mosher, 325 N.W.2d 314 (Wis. 1982) (police officer who took custody of a physically ill teenager for the purpose of returning her to her parent's home, but then forgetfully left her in a locked area of the police station overnight without food, water, or blankets can be held liable for negligent infliction of emotional distress). *But cf.* Garrett v. City of New Berlin, 362 N.W.2d 137 (Wis. 1985) (emphasizing that *La Fleur* was a "narrow" decision, grounded in the special situation of a police officer taking custody of an essentially helpless minor). The California Supreme Court has held that a plaintiff may recover in negligence from a bank that failed to honor a check written out by the plaintiff, which in turn caused the plaintiff's arrest at the behest of the merchant to whom the bounced check was paid. Although the complaint alleged that the arrest had resulted in physical harm, the court seems to have treated the causation of confinement as sufficient to support a claim in negligence, at least given the preexisting relationship of bank and customer. Weaver v. Bank of America Natl. Trust & Sav. Assn., 380 P.2d 644 (Cal. 1963). (Harms associated with bank failures to honor checks are today governed by a provision in Article 4 of the Uniform Commercial Code.)

7. *Causing Confinement: Malicious Prosecution and Abuse of Process.* False imprisonment can be achieved indirectly, by arranging for others to confine the victim. For example, if the tortfeasor causes the victim to be detained by officials while knowing that there is no basis for such confinement, he can be sued for false imprisonment.

Malicious prosecution and *abuse of process* are two closely related causes of action. The former sometimes permits a claim by a victim who is subjected to an unfounded criminal prosecution against the person(s) who instigated the prosecution. In contrast to false imprisonment claimants, a person suing for malicious prosecution need not establish that she was confined. To recover, the victim must establish, first, that the instigator acted (a) without probable cause to believe that the victim had engaged in the reported misconduct *and* (b) with malice or ill-will toward the victim. Second, she must prove that, but for the instigator's activities, the prosecution would not have gone forward. Finally, she must establish that the prosecution terminated in a manner that establishes or supports the conclusion that she did not engage in the alleged misconduct. Dan B. Dobbs, *The Law of Torts* § 430, at 1215 (2000) (listing elements of malicious prosecution). Thus, a store owner who, out of personal hostility toward the plaintiff, falsely informs police that the plaintiff has stolen goods from his store and thereby subjects the plaintiff to prosecution for shoplifting can be held liable to the victim for malicious prosecution. Mere carelessness in falsely instigating a prosecution ordinarily is not sufficient. Prosecutors themselves, as opposed to instigators of those prosecutions, are generally granted immunity from any tort liability for prosecutions that turn out to be unfounded.

Although the label "malicious prosecution" tends to be reserved for instigations of criminal proceedings against another, comparable causes of action exist for malicious instigation of civil litigation. Actions such as these are sometimes referred to such as *malicious use of process* or *wrongful litigation*. Dobbs, *supra*, § 436, at 1228. The separate tort of *abuse of process* applies to a particular subset of malicious prosecutions and malicious uses of process in which one person invokes the legal system for the particular purpose of extorting, threatening, or harassing the victim, rather than in a good-faith effort to vindicate some interest or right of hers. For example, a person who knowingly launches an utterly unfounded tort suit against another merely to coerce the other into paying her has committed the tort of abuse of process.

8. *Damages*. As with other dignitary torts, courts sometimes award nominal damages out of recognition of the violation of plaintiff's rights independently of any harm suffered, while harms parasitic on the dignitary violation — bodily injury, lost wages and expenses, loss of reputation, and emotional distress associated with the confinement — are generally compensable. *See* Banks v. Fritsch, 39 S.W.3d 474 (Ky. App. 2001) (perennially absent student who was chained to a tree by a teacher partly in jest is entitled to recover nominal damages for the dignitary harm as well as compensatory damages for subsequent emotional distress). Punitive damages may also be awarded upon the requisite showing of malice or reckless indifference. *See, e.g.*, Edwards v. Stills, 984 S.W.2d 366 (Ark. 1998) (upholding $1.5 million punitive award in suit for false imprisonment and other torts brought by an attorney whose client abducted, bound, and threatened to kill him).

D. Unintended Consequences and Transferred Intent

Many dignitary torts — consider, for example, batteries involving beatings, poisonings, or shootings — present straightforward and relatively simple issues as to the intent element. In these cases, the evidence likely will establish clearly that the assailant acted with the requisite purpose, and that his act led directly and predictably to the intended outcome. In certain cases, however, the analysis of intent is complicated by the fact that the assailant intended one sort of consequence but ended up causing a different consequence than the one he intended.

Cole v. Hibberd
1994 WL 424103 (Ohio App. 1994)

Young, J. Plaintiff-appellant, Debbie L. Cole, appeals the judgment of the Warren County Common Pleas Court granting summary judgment in favor of defendant-appellee, Sheri L. Hibberd.

Cole filed a personal injury complaint against Hibberd on June 11, 1993, based on an incident that occurred on June 15, 1991. She set forth the operative facts of this action in paragraph two of her complaint: "At said time and place, defendant negligently struck said plaintiff in the lower lumbar area, which negligence directly caused injuries and damages hereinafter set forth." Cole described Hibberd's actions more completely in her deposition taken on August 12, 1993. At the deposition, Cole described the incident as follows:

> The Hibberds had been drinking and Sheri was acting a little rambunctious. While I was standing there leaning over, I had ahold of my daughter with one hand and my niece with the other, I was holding them by the hand,

I leaned over to look at her children in her stroller, and she hauled . . . off and kicked me.

Hibberd's attorney asked Cole to describe the incident in more detail, and she responded:

Well, she kicked me. And I stood up and said, damn it, Sheri, that hurt. She started laughing. And Gary, [Hibberd's husband] Gary called me something fowl [*sic*] and started laughing and thought it was funny. And I told my husband, I said, come on. I was, I was extremely hot about it. She hurt me.

When asked whether she believed Hibberd's action was intentional or accidental, Cole stated:

I'd say she didn't, she meant to kick me. I mean, she didn't mean to hurt me, she was just horsing around. I guess she thought it wouldn't hurt me. . . .

No, she meant to kick me playingly, but I don't think she meant to hurt me like she did. She basically thought it was funny. I mean, that's how, how she was, really.

R.C. 2305.111 establishes a one-year statute of limitations for claims involving assault and battery. On the other hand, R.C. 2305.10 requires that an action for bodily injury must be brought within two years after the cause arises. Cole filed her complaint more than one year, but less than two years after June 15, 1991, the date Hibberd kicked her.

Hibberd filed a motion for summary judgment contending that her alleged actions constituted a battery which was no longer actionable under R.C. 2305.111 since the complaint was not filed within one year of the incident. The trial court granted Hibberd's motion for summary judgment by entry filed January 14, 1994.

In a single assignment of error, Cole contends that the court erred in concluding that her claim amounted to an action in assault and battery instead of negligence. Basically, Cole argues that a genuine issue of material fact exists as to whether Hibberd made intentional, offensive contact with Cole. . . .

In Love v. Port Clinton (1988), 37 Ohio St. 3d 98, 99-100, the Ohio Supreme Court stated that "[w]here the essential character of an alleged tort is an intentional, offensive touching, the statute of limitations for assault and battery governs even if the touching is pleaded as an act of negligence. To hold otherwise would defeat the assault and battery statute of limitations."

An individual is liable for battery when he or she acts intending to cause offensive or harmful contact, and such contact results. *Id.* at 99, citing Restatement of the Law 2d, Torts (1965) 25, Section 13. "Offensive contact" is contact that would be offensive to a reasonable sense of personal dignity. *Id.*

Cole insists that Hibberd did not act with an intention to cause harm. However, it is the intentional nature of the contact with the plaintiff that controls the definition, not the intent to cause actual harm or injury. See Restatement of the Law 2d, Torts (1965) 25, Section 13, Comment *c*.

Construing the facts most strongly in favor of Cole, this court concludes that the essential character of her complaint is grounded in the intentional tort of assault and battery. From the evidence presented, reasonable minds can only conclude that Hibberd intended to kick Cole. We also conclude that Hibberd's contact, as testified to by Cole in her deposition, would be considered offensive to a reasonable sense of personal dignity. It is irrelevant to this determination whether or not Hibberd intended to cause injury.

In this case, the statute of limitations for assault and battery applies over the statute of limitations for bodily injury. Accordingly, Cole had only one year from the time of the incident, or until June 15, 1991, to file this lawsuit. The filing of this suit on June 11, 1993, was therefore untimely. . . .

Jones, P.J. (dissenting). Summary judgment was simply inappropriate. A factual question existed with respect to Hibberd's intentions. A jury could, would, and should find that Hibberd's playful "kick in the rear" was not intended to cause offensive or harmful conduct. Hibberd wasn't assaulting her friend Cole any more than one would "assault" a friend by slapping him on the back. Hibberd's "kick" was simply misdirected, striking the coccyx, and a jury could certainly conclude that such was merely negligence. The two-year statute of limitations applies.

NOTES AND QUESTIONS

1. *Collateral Consequences of Characterizing the Tort.* As indicated at various points in this chapter, a number of important legal consequences flow from conduct being deemed a dignitary tort such as battery rather than negligence. *Cole* illustrates one such consequence: The statute of limitations governing the plaintiff's suit depends on whether she is understood by the court to be alleging a battery or negligence. The difference between the two types of tort can be equally important in other contexts. For example, employees who suffer injuries on the job resulting from intentional torts can sue in tort rather than being limited to disability benefits. Most homeowners' insurance policies cover acts of negligence by the insured but not intentional wrongs.

For reasons such as these, litigants — such as Ms. Newland, the patient in Newland v. Azan — will sometimes strive mightily to characterize the event that caused the injury in terms that fit their litigation strategy. For an example of an insurance company attempting a similar stretch to avoid having to pay out under one of its policies, *see* North Star Mut. Ins. Co. v. R.W., 431 N.W.2d 138 (Minn. App. 1988) (policyholder's unknowing transmission of an STD to a sexual partner was not excluded from coverage by a policy provision that denied coverage for liabilities arising out of "intentional" misconduct — that the policyholder intended to have consensual sex does not suffice to establish a battery).

One can perhaps expect litigants' attorneys to press on the distinctions between different types of torts to secure favorable outcomes for their clients. Should judges also be mindful of these sorts of consequences in making their determinations as to the correct conceptualization of the defendant's conduct? Did the majority in *Cole* have in mind the consequences of its determination when it determined that Cole's claim sounded in battery? Consider, on this question, Villa v. Derouen, 614 So. 2d 714 (La. 1993). Derouen and Villa were co-workers. Apparently as a practical joke, Derouen pointed the unlit compressed-air blowtorch that he was using at Villa, intending only to annoy him with the stream of air. The air ignited, however, causing Villa to suffer burns. The Louisiana Supreme Court concluded that because Derouen intended to touch Villa by blowing air on him, his conduct constituted a battery rather than negligence. As such, it fell outside the ambit of workers' compensation, which in turn permitted Villa to recover a jury award of about $175,000.

2. Vosburg, *Battery, and the Eggshell Skull Rule Revisited*. *Cole* presents facts similar to a famous older battery case, Vosburg v. Putney, 50 N.W. 403 (Wis. 1891). George Putney, a 12-year-old, kicked his 14-year-old schoolmate Andrew Vosburg in the shin as they sat in class. According to Vosburg's doctor, the kick aggravated an existing infection, and had the effect of leaving Vosburg lame. Putney's attorney argued that Putney should not be held liable for battery because he did not intend to injure Vosburg's leg by kicking it. He further argued that Putney should not be held liable for the damages associated with Vosburg's lameness, as that result was an unforeseeable consequence of the kick.

The Supreme Court of Wisconsin rejected both arguments. Noting that class had already come to order prior to the kick, the court held that it was sufficient that Putney had intended a kick that was "unlawful," that is, against school rules. In modern legal parlance, one might say that in the context of a class that has been called to order — as opposed to a situation such as roughhousing in a park or on a school playground — the kick constituted an intended and offensive contact. As a result, the *Vosburg* court deemed irrelevant the fact that the injury being complained of (lameness) was not the injury intended (annoyance). As to the damages issue, the court invoked against Putney the eggshell skull rule (see Chapter 8), explaining that, in tort, "the wrongdoer is liable for all injuries resulting directly from the wrongful act, whether they could or could not have been foreseen by him." *See also* Nelson v. Carroll, 735 A.2d 1096 (Md. 1999) (defendant struck plaintiff in the head with his loaded gun and was about to do so again when it accidentally went off, resulting in plaintiff being shot; because the shooting occurred in the course of a purposeful beating, it constitutes battery even though apparently accidental).

3. *Intending Contact versus Intending a Certain Type of Harm*. Most courts endorse the negative proposition that a plaintiff suing for battery or assault need *not* establish that the defendant intended the particular injury, or even the type of injury, that was suffered by the victim. *See, e.g.,* Frey v. Kouf, 484 N.W.2d 864 (S.D. 1992) (reversing a defense verdict in a battery action because of an erroneous instruction to the jury specifying that the jury could find for the plaintiff only if it concluded that the defendant threw a beer mug at plaintiff's head with intent to cause the

injuries that the plaintiff suffered). A notable exception to this rule is *Spivey v. Battaglia*, 258 So. 2d 815 (Fla. 1972). Battaglia playfully put his arm around his co-worker Spivey's neck and pulled her toward him, even though he apparently knew that she was shy and would not welcome the contact. Quite unexpectedly, his action caused her to suffer paralysis in the left side of her face. As in *Cole*, the plaintiff in *Spivey* sued after the statute of limitations for battery had expired, but before the negligence limitations period had run. However, unlike the *Cole* court, the Florida Supreme Court held that Spivey's action sounded in negligence rather than battery, and hence was not time-barred.

The *Spivey* court's stated reason for its conclusion seems problematic — it deemed Battaglia's conduct negligent rather than intentional simply because he did not intend to cause, or know that he would cause, partial paralysis. 258 So. 2d, at 817. This reasoning ignores the fact that Battaglia seems to have intended a contact that was inappropriate because he knew it would be offensive to Spivey. To make the same point, the Florida court seems to have misdescribed Battaglia's "wrong" by treating it as a failure to take reasonable care against causing physical harm to Spivey. To the extent a playful hug of this sort is objectionable, the objection derives not from the fact that it poses an unreasonable risk of physical harm, but rather from its offensiveness.*

Do the facts of *Cole* present a more compelling basis than those of *Spivey* for concluding, with the dissent, that Hibberd was at most liable for negligence? Why, in apparent contrast to the *Spivey* court, might the *Cole* court have been more willing to leave the plaintiff remediless?

4. *Intentional Torts, Actual Cause, and Proximate Cause*. Actual causation is generally analyzed in battery and assault cases just as it is analyzed in negligence. See Chapter 4. Thus, the plaintiff ordinarily has the burden of proving that, but for the defendant's intentional act, she would not have suffered the injury of which she now complains. So, for example, a defendant who acts intending to cause bodily harm to, or apprehension of imminent bodily harm in, the plaintiff, yet fails to produce either, cannot be sued for battery or assault.

What about instances of intentional conduct that function as a cause of injury, but only fortuitously? As explained in Chapter 5, in negligence cases, the issue of fortuitous causation tends to be handled under the doctrine of proximate cause. By contrast, courts rarely mention proximate cause in connection with dignitary torts. Instead, fortuity tends to be analyzed under the rubric of intent. Would invocation of a rule analogous to the "scope of the risk" rule developed by courts for negligence cases

---

* The *Spivey* court's ruling may have been driven more by a desire to ensure plaintiff a remedy than by an adequate account of the intent element of battery. It also seems to have assumed that Florida law would permit Spivey to proceed with her negligence claim against Battaglia even though workplace injuries caused by a co-employee's negligence were at the time (as they are now) covered by Florida workers' compensation law. In fact, Spivey later received workers' compensation benefits from the company, either in addition to, or instead of, recovering on her "negligence" claim against Battaglia. *See* Spivey v. Battaglia Fruit Co., 287 So. 2d 302 (1973).

help set appropriate limits on responsibility for dignitary torts? If the objectionable feature of the defendant's conduct is *not* that it posed risks of certain kinds of harm to others, is it helpful to ask whether a given harm constitutes the realization of one of the risks that rendered the defendant's conduct tortious? If not expressed in terms of risk, how should a principle of proximate cause for dignitary torts be expressed? As we have now seen, it would be incorrect as a matter of black-letter law to say that an actor is subject to liability only for those harms that he intended to cause or knew he would cause. Should the imposition of responsibility for injuries fortuitously caused bother us less when it comes to dignitary torts, as opposed to negligence? *See* Restatement (Third) of Torts: Liability for Physical Harm (Basic Principles) § 33, at 90-91 (Tentative Draft No. 3, Apr. 7, 2003) ("An actor who intentionally or recklessly causes physical harm is subject to liability for a broader range of harms than the harms for which that actor would be liable if acting negligently.").

In re White
18 B.R. 246 (Bankr. E.D. Va. 1982)

Shelley, Bankr. J. . . .

STATEMENT OF THE FACTS

On September 10, 1977 Walter Calvin White, Jr. (White) shot Ralph Edward Davis (Davis) in the stomach with a handgun. White was arrested for the shooting and on November 29, 1978 the Circuit Court of the City of Richmond found him guilty of maiming Davis and sentenced him to serve five years in the state penitentiary. On February 26, 1980 Davis obtained a default judgment against White in the amount of $50,000.00 in the Circuit Court for the City of Richmond on the ground that White willfully and maliciously wounded Davis. White subsequently filed his petition in bankruptcy and Davis now asks this Court to declare White's debt on account of that judgment nondischargeable in bankruptcy.

On the day of the shooting Davis and his brother, Marvin W. Davis, were washing cars in front of their mother's house on Fairmont Avenue in Richmond, Virginia. At the same time White, a neighbor who lives less than one block away on the same street, was having a conversation with William Tipton (Tipton). In that conversation White and Tipton continued an argument which had begun approximately one week earlier. White had obtained a gun in anticipation of seeing Tipton. White was carrying the pistol in a container on his motorcycle and pulled it out of the container during the course of that argument.

When White pulled the gun Tipton mounted his motorcycle and sped away. White shot at Tipton as Tipton passed within twenty-five feet of Davis. He missed Tipton and the bullet hit Davis in the stomach. White fled the scene.

White testified at the trial that he obtained the gun with the intent of scaring Tipton. He said that he drew the gun after Tipton insulted his mother but that he did not intentionally fire the gun. He claimed the gun went off when he tripped over a rock in the street.

Davis and White did not know each other before the shooting incident. White said he pulled the gun intending to scare Tipton and that it accidently fired. This Court believes that White's testimony that the gun accidently fired when he tripped over a rock is unworthy of belief. White testified that he obtained the gun earlier that week with another meeting with Tipton in mind. Although Davis was located almost a full block from White, the bullet hit him as Tipton passed within twenty-five feet of him. White clearly intended to shoot Tipton; however, he missed and the bullet hit Davis instead.

CONCLUSIONS OF LAW

A debt incurred from an action based upon a willful and malicious injury by the debtor to another person may be nondischargeable in bankruptcy. 11 U.S.C. § 523(a)(6). The word "willful" means deliberate or intentional.[2]

It is clear . . . that "reckless disregard" is no longer sufficient to make a debt non-dischargeable. . . . [However,] the [Bankruptcy] Act does not necessarily restrict the penalty of nondischargeability . . . [to] cases in which the debtor injured the person he intended to injure. ". . . The word 'willful' means 'deliberate or intentional,' a deliberate and intentional act which necessarily leads to injury. Therefore, a wrongful act done intentionally, which necessarily produces harm and is without just cause or excuse, may constitute a willful and malicious injury." *Collier on Bankruptcy,* para. 523.16[1] (15th ed. 1981) (footnotes omitted).

White committed the wrongful act when he shot at Tipton. The act was intentional and it produced an injury although not to the person White intended to injure. White's actions cannot be excused solely because he missed his intended victim and instead hit someone else. The injury is not required to be directed against the victim, but includes any entity other than the intended victim.

Under the doctrine of transferred intent one who intends a battery is liable for that battery when he unexpectedly hits a stranger instead of the intended victim. W. Prosser, *The Law of Torts,* 33 (4th ed. 1971). If one intentionally commits an assault or battery at another and by mistake strikes a third person, he is guilty of an assault and battery of the third person if "defendant's intention, in such a case, is to strike an unlawful

---

2. Congress stated in . . . legislative history . . . that "paragraph (6) excepts debts for willful and malicious injury by the debtor to another person or to the property of another person. Under this paragraph, 'willful' means deliberate or intentional. To the extent that Tinker v. Colwell, 193 U.S. 473, 24 S. Ct. 505, 48 L. Ed. 754 (1902), held that a looser standard is intended, and to the extent that other cases have relied on *Tinker* to apply a 'reckless disregard' standard, they are overruled." H.R. Rep. 95-595, 95th Cong., 1st Sess., 365 (1977), U.S. Code Cong. & Admin. News 1978, pp.5787, 6320-21.

blow, to injure some person by his act, and it is not essential that the injury be to the one intended." Morrow v. Flores, 225 S.W.2d 621, 624, Tex. Civ. App. (1949), *rehearing denied* 1950.

Virginia courts have adopted the doctrine of transferred intent reasoning that ". . . every person is liable for the direct, natural and probable consequence of his acts, and that every one doing an unlawful act is responsible for all of the consequential results of that act." Bannister v. Mitchell, 127 Va. 578, 104 S.E. 800, 801 (1920). There need be no actual intent to injure the particular person who is injured. *Id.* . . .

The evidence here clearly shows that the shooting was a wrongful act intentionally done and that Davis's injuries resulted from that act. White deliberately, intentionally and maliciously fired the gun and injured Davis and the debt resulting from that act is nondischargeable in bankruptcy. . . .

An appropriate order will issue.

NOTES AND QUESTIONS

1. *Transferred Intent (I): Same Victim, Different Tort.* The doctrine of transferred intent invoked by the *White* court is in reality a collection of doctrines, some of which may be more intelligible than others. It will therefore be worthwhile to attempt to disaggregate the various rules that fall under that label.

At times when a court invokes transferred intent it is specifying a rule that the intent element of torts such as battery and assault can be satisfied even if the actor intended one of these torts, but ended up committing another. Suppose, for example, White had succeeded in his efforts to shoot Tipton, and had not shot Davis. Suppose further that the bankruptcy judge credited White's testimony that he shot at Tipton only to scare him. The judge should still conclude that White committed a battery against Tipton because an act undertaken with intent to create the apprehension of an imminent harmful contact in a person provides the basis for liability in battery if the act happens to cause actual harmful contact to that person. Weisbart v. Flohr, 67 Cal. Rptr. 114 (Ct. App. 1968). (By the same token, intent can "transfer" from an intended battery to a completed assault.)

In this iteration, the doctrine of transferred intent presumably permits mixing and matching among certain other torts as well. Thus, if *D* slams a door intending to lock *P* in a room, but *P*'s fingers are crushed in the closing door, *D*'s intent to confine *P* will likely suffice to establish the intent element of *P*'s claim for battery even though *D* never intended to touch *P*. What explains the willingness of tort law to mix and match intents and consequences, and with them, different wrongs?

2. *Transferred Intent (II): Across Victims.* As *White* indicates, courts sometimes also use transferred intent to convey a different idea, namely that victims of certain acts that were intended to injure others may sue even if they were not among the persons whom the defendant intended to injure. Talmage v. Smith, 59 N.W. 656 (Mich. 1894) is often held out as a leading instance of a court permitting intent to transfer from an intended

to an unintended victim. In that case, Mr. Smith saw several boys playing on the roof of a shed on his property. He sought to chase them away by hurling a large stick at one of them. The stick instead hit another boy who was on the shed (Talmage) and blinded him in one eye. Smith argued as an affirmative defense that he was entitled to throw the stick at the boys as a reasonable means of defending his property. See *infra* Section III.D. The trial judge instructed the jury that if it found that Smith's action involved excessive rather than reasonable force, it should hold Smith liable regardless of whether he intended to hit Talmage or the other boy. The Michigan Supreme Court upheld this instruction.

Is Talmage properly understood as an instance in which the defendant acts with the intent to cause a harmful contact with *A*, but ends up causing harmful contact with unintended victim *B*? Or is it an example of an act undertaken with intent to cause harm to any one of several possible victims? If the latter, does it support the result reached by the bankruptcy judge in *White?* Of course, White's wrongful conduct obviously caused harm to Davis. But did White subject Davis to the sort of indignity characteristic of batteries? Is there a better way to describe the wrong perpetrated by White against Davis? If so, would that description also bar White from discharging his liability to Davis in bankruptcy under the terms of the Bankruptcy Code?

Assume that the bankruptcy judge correctly deemed White's conduct to constitute a battery against Davis. Would the same analysis apply if, upon hearing the gunshot, Davis instinctively (and reasonably) dove to the ground, breaking his arm? What if Tipton, in his haste to avoid being shot, drove his motorcycle into pedestrian *P*, who was crossing the street 50 yards from where White fired his weapon. Could *P* establish a claim of battery against White? If not, why not?

3. *Transferred Intent (III): Across Torts and Victims.* In principle, it is open to courts to combine the foregoing forms of transferred intent to create a third category, in which the tortfeasor is held liable to actual victim (*AV*) for tort *T1*, even though he acted for the purpose of injuring potential victim (*PV*) in a manner that, had he been successful, would have constituted tort *T2*. Indeed, if the bankruptcy judge credited White's testimony that he shot at Tipton only to scare him, then White v. Davis is such a case: White intended to engage in conduct that amounted to an assault of Tipton but ended up being held liable for committing battery against Davis.

4. *Transferred Intent (IV): From Things to Persons.* As noted at the outset of this chapter, commentators often place property torts such as trespass to land or chattels into the category of intentional torts. As a result, they sometimes go so far as to suggest that intent should transfer from property torts to battery and assault. For example, Dean Prosser once suggested that if *D* were knowingly to shoot at a domestic dog, intending to kill it, but ended up shooting person *P* instead, *D*'s intent to commit trespass to "chattel" (i.e., the owned dog) should suffice to provide the necessary intent for *P* to make out a case of battery, even if *D* had no reason to know that *P* was anywhere nearby.

Prosser seems to have based this conclusion primarily on Corn v. Sheppard, 229 N.W. 869 (Minn. 1930). There, the defendant sought to avoid liability by arguing that at the time he shot the plaintiff, he was unaware of plaintiff's presence and was instead shooting at a domesticated dog. Noting that the shooting of a domestic animal was unlawful under state statute, and that the discharge of a firearm is an inherently dangerous activity, the court concluded that, "[w]here a person intentionally discharges a firearm for a wrongful purpose and another is hit, he is liable for the injuries inflicted, although he did not intend to hit the other nor even know that any person was within range." *Id.* at 871. Is *Corn* an instance of the sort of broad transferred intent that Prosser describes, or does it impose negligence (or strict) liability on the activity of discharging a firearm?

Compare *Corn* to Lynn v. Burnette, 531 S.E.2d 275 (N.C. Ct. App. 2000). Defendant Burnette tailed plaintiff Lynn and his friend Pratt, who was Burnette's ex-boyfriend, as Lynn and Pratt drove to a motel with two other women. Later, as he was leaving the motel, Lynn caught sight of Burnette in her car in a gas station parking lot across from the motel. Lynn drove his car to the parking lot, got out, and confronted Burnette. He then returned to his car. As Lynn drove away, Burnette fired a gun out of the window of her car, striking Lynn in the neck. Lynn sued Burnette after the statute of limitations for battery had run, but prior to the expiration of the limitations period for negligence actions. Burnette admitted in her deposition that she purposely fired in the direction of the car, but claimed that she was aiming for one of its rear tires and simply missed her target. She thus moved for summary judgment on the ground that the action was time-barred because, in effect, it sought redress for a transferred-intent battery — a harmful touching of a person resulting from an intended trespass to chattel (i.e., the intentional shooting at the car).

The court first ruled that the question of what consequences Burnette had intended by firing the gun was settled by her admission, and hence there was no need for a jury to construe what she had in mind when she pulled the trigger. It then concluded, based on Burnette's admission, that Lynn's claim sounded in negligence rather than battery and thus could proceed, apparently rejecting the idea of intent transferring from the tort of trespass to chattels to the tort of battery. Although the court's unwillingness to link trespass and battery in this way was probably sound, its handling of the case in other respects seems problematic, particularly its treatment of the defendant's admission as settling the question of her intent. Shouldn't the factfinder be asked to consider whether Burnette's description of her intent was self-serving? Could not a jury have reasonably concluded that, in shooting at the tire, Burnette acted for the purpose of scaring Lynn, or in the knowledge that she would scare him? If a jury could make that finding, would that change the outcome of the analysis as to whether Burnette committed battery or negligence?

On the problems of transferring intent from property torts to dignitary torts, consider the following hypothetical. *D* is invited to an ultra-chic party held on the ground floor of a department store after regular business hours. As he moves among the glamorous crowd, *D* aggressively fondles what he reasonably and sincerely believes to be a mannequin.

Much to his horror, he discovers that the "mannequin" is in fact *M*, a model who was hired by the party's organizers to imitate a mannequin. Is it plausible to assert that *D* has committed battery against *M*?

5. *Relational Wrongs and Transferred Intent.* In the *Palsgraf* decision discussed in Chapter 5, Judge Cardozo held that a negligence plaintiff cannot prevail merely by demonstrating wrongful conduct that happens to injure the plaintiff. In addition, she must prove that the conduct was a wrong *to her*. Does the application of transferred intent in a case such as *White* refute the idea that tort law — or at least dignitary tort law — contains a similar requirement? In their *Palsgraf* opinions, both Cardozo and Judge Andrews discuss transferred intent doctrine in articulating their respective positions on negligence law. Reconsider in light of what you now know whether either's treatment of the doctrine is convincing.

III. Defenses

It is sometimes open to parties sued for assault, battery, or false imprisonment to defeat liability notwithstanding the claimant's establishment of a prima facie case. This section focuses on four categories of defenses available to those sued for dignitary torts. Our coverage here is not exhaustive, but rather representative.

Defenses to dignitary torts typically assert that the alleged tortfeasor was *privileged* to act as she did, even though her conduct was prima facie tortious. Privileges recognized by dignitary tort law in turn tend to consist of *justifications*, as opposed to *excuses*. To claim a justification for one's conduct is to claim that one was entitled to engage in the conduct, notwithstanding its apparent wrongfulness. So, for example, a person sued for battery who asserts the privilege of self-defense is claiming that she was within her rights to cause intentionally a harmful touching of another because she actually and reasonably believed that doing so was necessary to protect herself from an imminent harmful or inappropriate touching. By contrast, when an actor asserts an excuse, she alleges that something about her condition or circumstances — for example, her diminished mental capacity — entitles her to an exemption from the rules of right conduct. As we have seen, tort law is generally reluctant to recognize excuses.

As is the case for claims of negligence (see Chapter 7), the burden of pleading and proving the defenses to dignitary torts usually rests on the alleged tortfeasor — if he fails to raise them by the appropriate procedures, or to prove them, they will be lost. However, some states' laws treat what we present as defenses as elements of the prima facie case. This is particularly so with the defense of *consent*, to which we turn first. Many states require *plaintiffs* to prove *absence of consent*, rather than leaving it to the defendant to prove that the victim consented. (Given that torts such as battery concern, at their core, the subjection of another to unwanted touchings, etc., it is perhaps not surprising that the issue of consent is sometimes singled out for this special treatment.)

Before considering consent and other defenses available to tortfeasors who have committed assault, battery, or false imprisonment, it will be helpful to highlight the *unavailability* of another potential defense — *comparative fault*. As explained briefly in Chapter 1, and more extensively in Chapter 7, it is open to a defendant being sued for *negligence* to argue in defense that the plaintiff's own fault contributed to her being injured. Thus, for example, car driver *D*, who carelessly runs over and injures pedestrian *P*, may attempt to establish that *P* was herself careless by stepping off the curb without checking for traffic. If *D* can establish that *P*'s carelessness, along with *D*'s, played a role in causing *P*'s injuries, then — depending on the rules of the particular jurisdiction and the factfinder's assignment of percentage fault to *D* and *P* — the effect of this showing will be to reduce *P*'s recovery or to bar her suit altogether.

For dignitary torts such as battery, the longstanding black-letter rule is that comparative fault doctrine has no place. For example, suppose *B* purposely induces *A* to ingest a drink containing poison. Under the majority rule, even if *B* can prove that had *A* exercised reasonable care he would have detected the poison (e.g., by taking notice of the poison's powerful bitter odor), *B* cannot invoke comparative fault to reduce *A*'s damages or bar his claim. However, some courts and legislatures have recognized, and some commentators have urged, that comparative fault be recognized as a distinct defense to dignitary tort claims. *See* Dan B. Dobbs, *The Law of Torts* § 206, at 517-522 (2000) (discussing the issue). Moreover, it may sometimes be the case that evidence of a victim's carelessness can be offered as relevant to the proof of a defense that is recognized in dignitary tort law. Thus, evidence that a victim acted with apparent disregard for his physical well-being might, in some circumstances, support an inference that he implicitly consented to being subject to defendant's wrongful conduct.

A.   *Consent*

The role played by consent in the law of dignitary torts is quite similar to the role played in negligence law by the doctrine of assumption of risk, discussed in Chapter 7. Whereas the latter doctrine excuses liability for harms caused by careless conduct on the ground that the plaintiff knowingly and voluntarily exposed herself to the risk of such carelessness, the doctrine of consent turns on the idea that the plaintiff cannot prevail because he has chosen to endure a bodily contact, or apprehension of contact, or confinement, that would otherwise be tortious. As with assumption of risk, consent can be communicated *expressly*, through a written or spoken statement, or it can be communicated *implicitly*, through conduct.

Koffman v. Garnett

574 S.E.2d 258 (Va. 2003)

Lacy, J.   In this case we consider whether the trial court properly dismissed the plaintiffs' second amended motion for judgment for failure to state causes of action for gross negligence, assault, and battery.

Because this case was decided on demurrer, we take as true all material facts properly pleaded in the motion for judgment and all inferences properly drawn from those facts.

In the fall of 2000, Andrew W. Koffman, a 13-year old middle school student at a public school in Botetourt County, began participating on the school's football team. It was Andy's first season playing organized football, and he was positioned as a third-string defensive player. James Garnett was employed by the Botetourt County School Board as an assistant coach for the football team and was responsible for the supervision, training, and instruction of the team's defensive players.

The team lost its first game of the season. Garnett was upset by the defensive players' inadequate tackling in that game and became further displeased by what he perceived as inadequate tackling during the first practice following the loss.

Garnett ordered Andy to hold a football and "stand upright and motionless" so that Garnett could explain the proper tackling technique to the defensive players. Then Garnett, without further warning, thrust his arms around Andy's body, lifted him "off his feet by two feet or more," and "slamm[ed]" him to the ground. Andy weighed 144 pounds, while Garnett weighed approximately 260 pounds. The force of the tackle broke the humerus bone in Andy's left arm. During prior practices, no coach had used physical force to instruct players on rules or techniques of playing football.

In his second amended motion for judgment, Andy, by his father and next friend, Richard Koffman, and Andy's parents, Richard and Rebecca Koffman, individually, (collectively "the Koffmans") alleged that Andy was injured as a result of Garnett's simple and gross negligence and intentional acts of assault and battery. . . . The trial court dismissed the action, finding that . . . the facts alleged were insufficient to state causes of action for gross negligence, assault, or battery because the instruction and playing of football are "inherently dangerous and always potentially violent."

In this appeal, the Koffmans . . . assert that they pled sufficient facts in their second amended motion for judgment to sustain their claims of gross negligence,* assault, and battery.

I.

In Ferguson v. Ferguson, 212 Va. 86, 92, 181 S.E.2d 648, 653 (1971), this Court defined gross negligence as "that degree of negligence which shows indifference to others as constitutes an utter disregard of prudence amounting to a complete neglect of the safety of [another]. It must be such a degree of negligence as would shock fair minded [people] although something less than willful recklessness." Whether . . . actions constitute gross negligence is generally a factual matter for resolution by the jury and becomes a question of law only when reasonable people cannot differ.

* [Virginia law immunizes public employees from liability for official acts involving ordinary negligence. Thus, the Koffmans were required to prove at least gross negligence on Garnett's part. — EDS.]

The disparity in size between Garnett and Andy was obvious to Garnett. Because of his authority as a coach, Garnett must have anticipated that Andy would comply with his instructions to stand in a non-defensive, upright, and motionless position. Under these circumstances, Garnett proceeded to aggressively tackle the much smaller, inexperienced student football player, by lifting him more than two feet from the ground and slamming him into the turf. According to the Koffmans' allegations, no coach had tackled any player previously so there was no reason for Andy to expect to be tackled by Garnett, nor was Andy warned of the impending tackle or of the force Garnett would use.

As the trial court observed, receiving an injury while participating in a tackling demonstration may be part of the sport. The facts alleged in this case, however, go beyond the circumstances of simply being tackled in the course of participating in organized football. Here Garnett's knowledge of his greater size and experience, his instruction implying that Andy was not to take any action to defend himself from the force of a tackle, the force he used during the tackle, and Garnett's previous practice of not personally using force to demonstrate or teach football technique could lead a reasonable person to conclude that, in this instance, Garnett's actions were imprudent and were taken in utter disregard for the safety of the player involved. Because reasonable persons could disagree on this issue, a jury issue was presented, and the trial court erred in holding that, as a matter of law, the second amended motion for judgment was inadequate to state a claim for gross negligence.

II.

The trial court held that the second amended motion for judgment was insufficient as a matter of law to establish causes of action for the torts of assault and battery. We begin by identifying the elements of these two independent torts. *See* Charles E. Friend, *Personal Injury Law in Virginia* § 6.2.1 (2d ed. 1998). The tort of assault consists of an act intended to cause either harmful or offensive contact with another person or apprehension of such contact, and that creates in that other person's mind a reasonable apprehension of an imminent battery. Restatement (Second) of Torts § 21 (1965); Friend § 6.3.1 at 226; Fowler V. Harper, et al., *The Law of Torts* § 3.5 at 3:18-:19 (3d ed. Cum. Supp. 2003).

The tort of battery is an unwanted touching which is neither consented to, excused, nor justified. *See* Washburn v. Klara, 263 Va. 586, 561 S.E.2d 682 (2002); Woodbury v. Courtney, 239 Va. 651, 391 S.E.2d 293 (1990). Although these two torts "go together like ham and eggs," the difference between them is "that between physical contact and the mere apprehension of it. One may exist without the other." W. Page Keeton, *Prosser and Keeton on Torts* § 10 at 46; *see also* Friend § 6.3.

The Koffmans' second amended motion for judgment does not include an allegation that Andy had any apprehension of an immediate battery. This allegation cannot be supplied by inference because any inference of Andy's apprehension is discredited by the affirmative allegations that Andy had no warning of an imminent forceful tackle by Garnett. The

Koffmans argue that a reasonable inference of apprehension can be found "in the very short period of time that it took the coach to lift Andy into the air and throw him violently to the ground." At this point, however, the battery alleged by the Koffmans was in progress. Accordingly, we find that the pleadings were insufficient as a matter of law to establish [an assault].

The second amended motion for judgment is sufficient, however, to establish a . . . battery. The Koffmans pled that Andy consented to physical contact with players "of like age and experience" and that neither Andy nor his parents expected or consented to his "participation in aggressive contact tackling by the adult coaches." Further, the Koffmans pled that, in the past, coaches had not tackled players as a method of instruction. Garnett asserts that, by consenting to play football, Andy consented to be tackled, by either other football players or by the coaches.

Whether Andy consented to be tackled by Garnett in the manner alleged was a matter of fact. Based on the allegations in the Koffmans' second amended motion for judgment, reasonable persons could disagree on whether Andy gave such consent. Thus, we find that the trial court erred in holding that the Koffmans' second amended motion for judgment was insufficient as a matter of law to establish a claim for battery. . . .*

Kinser, J. (concurring in part, dissenting in part). I agree with the majority opinion except with regard to the issue of consent as it pertains to the intentional tort of battery. In my view, the second amended motion for judgment filed by the plaintiffs, Andrew W. Koffman, by his father and next friend, and Richard Koffman and Rebecca Koffman, individually, was insufficient as a matter of law to state a claim for battery.

Absent fraud, consent is generally a defense to an alleged battery. In the context of this case, "[t]aking part in a game manifests a willingness to submit to such bodily contacts or restrictions of liberty as are permitted by its rules or usages." Restatement (Second) of Torts § 50, cmt. b (1965), quoted in Thompson v. McNeill, 53 Ohio St. 3d 102, 559 N.E.2d 705, 708 (1990). . . . However, participating in a particular sport "does not manifest consent to contacts which are prohibited by rules or usages of the game if such rules or usages are designed to protect the participants and not merely to secure the better playing of the game as a test of skill." Restatement (Second) of Torts § 50, cmt. b (1965) quoted in *Thompson*. . . .

The thrust of the plaintiffs' allegations is that they did not consent to "Andy's participation in aggressive contact tackling by the adult coaches" but that they consented only to Andy's engaging "in a contact sport with other children of like age and experience." They further alleged that the coaches had not previously tackled the players when instructing them about the rules and techniques of football.

It is notable, in my opinion, that the plaintiffs admitted in their pleading that Andy's coach was "responsible . . . for the supervision,

---

* Because we have concluded that a cause of action for an intentional tort was sufficiently pled, on remand, the Koffmans may pursue their claim for punitive damages.

training and instruction of the defensive players." It cannot be disputed that one responsibility of a football coach is to minimize the possibility that players will sustain "something more than slight injury" while playing the sport. Vendrell v. School District No. 26C, Malheur County, 233 Or. 1, 376 P.2d 406, 413 (1962). A football coach cannot be expected "to extract from the game the body clashes that cause bruises, jolts and hard falls." *Id.* Instead, a coach should ensure that players are able to "withstand the shocks, blows and other rough treatment with which they would meet in actual play" by making certain that players are in "sound physical condition," are issued proper protective equipment, and are "taught and shown how to handle [themselves] while in play." *Id.* The instruction on how to handle themselves during a game should include demonstrations of proper tackling techniques. *Id.* By voluntarily participating in football, Andy and his parents necessarily consented to instruction by the coach on such techniques. The alleged battery occurred during that instruction.

The plaintiffs alleged that they were not aware that Andy's coach would use physical force to instruct on the rules and techniques of football since neither he nor the other coaches had done so in the past. Surely, the plaintiffs are not claiming that the scope of their consent changed from day to day depending on the coaches' instruction methods during prior practices. Moreover, they did not allege that they were told that the coaches would not use physical demonstrations to instruct the players.

Additionally, the plaintiffs did not allege that the tackle itself violated any rule or usage of the sport of football. Nor did they plead that Andy could not have been tackled by a larger, physically stronger, and more experienced player either during a game or practice. Tackling and instruction on proper tackling techniques are aspects of the sport of football to which a player consents when making a decision to participate in the sport.

In sum, I conclude that the plaintiffs did not sufficiently plead a claim for battery. We must remember that acts that might give rise to a battery on a city street will not do so in the context of the sport of football. *See Thompson,* 559 N.E.2d at 707. We must also not blur the lines between gross negligence and battery because the latter is an intentional tort. I agree fully that the plaintiffs alleged sufficient facts to proceed with their claim for gross negligence. . . .

NOTES AND QUESTIONS

1. *Express Consent.* To the extent Koffman consented to harmful contact, he did so implicitly, by voluntarily participating on the football team. In many other instances, consent is expressly stated, either in a writing or by oral statement. For example, in a non-emergency room setting, surgical patients will typically be required to complete and sign a form indicating their consent to being subjected to a harmful contact (namely, the surgical procedure itself). These forms usually also require

the patient to attest that she has been informed of all relevant risks that attend the surgery. (Recall the discussion of informed consent claims in Chapter 3.) Here is an example of such a form:

CONSENT TO OPERATION, TREATMENT, OR OTHER PROCEDURE

1. (1) Date: _____ Time: _____ A.M. _____ P.M.
    (2) I authorize and consent to the performance upon

    _____ of the following operation, treatment,
    NAME OF PATIENT

    or procedure:

    _____

    _____

    _____

    to be performed by Dr. _____ and staff.

2. The nature, advisability, and purpose of the operation, treatment, or other procedure have been explained to me, together with the benefits hoped to result and the material risks. Alternatives to the operation, treatment, or other procedure, if any, and the risks of such alternatives have been explained to me. I understand the explanations that have been given me, and I understand that no guarantee is offered as to the results of the operation, treatment, or other procedure.

3. I authorize and consent to the operation, treatment, or other procedure by the physician and assistants to the physician performing the operation, treatment, or other procedure, by the nursing staff and by other employees of the ABC Medical Center.

4. I authorize and consent to the administration of anesthesia by the anesthesiology staff of ABC Medical Center.

5. I understand that during the course of the operation, treatment, or other procedure unforeseen conditions may be found that make an extension of the original operation, treatment, or other procedure advisable. I authorize and consent to such extension or other operation, treatment, or other procedure as is advisable in the professional judgment of my physician or physicians.

6. I authorize and consent to the disposal, use, retention, or donation by the ABC Medical Center at its discretion of all tissues,

materials, and substances that would normally be removed in the course of the operation, treatment, or other procedure.

7. I understand that my physician has determined that I require/may require transfusion of blood and/or blood products. I understand that the blood products may include risks of fever and chills (about 1 in 200), allergic reaction with itching, hives (about 1 in 200), and rare severe allergic reaction (about 1 in 25,000), resulting in death (less than 1 in 1,000,000). In rare instances there may be a chance of infectious blood borne diseases, including Hepatitis B (about 1 in 180,000), Hepatitis C (less than 1 in 1,600,000), HIV/AIDS (about 1 in 1,900,000), as well as other unforeseen risks. I understand that the Red Cross and other blood banks use precautions to minimize these risks by screening the blood/blood products and in blood typing.

8. I have been provided with information regarding transfusions and have had the opportunity to discuss the risks, benefits, alternatives, and risk of no transfusions with my physician. **I hereby authorize and consent to the administration of blood/blood products if deemed medically necessary by my physician(s).**

_____   _____   _____   AM PM
SIGNATURE (PATIENT / PATIENT'S   DATE   TIME
LEGALLY AUTHORIZED REPRESENTATIVE)

_____
WITNESS

* * * * * * * * * * * * * * * * *

I met with _____ and fully discussed the above-described procedure.

☐   Consent cannot be obtained due to an emergency of the following nature:

_____
_____
_____

_____   _____   _____   AM PM
PHYSICIAN SIGNATURE   DATE   TIME

2. *Implied Consent.* Voluntary participation in contact sports is a common example of implicit consent to harmful touchings. There are innumerable other settings in which a person can be deemed to have consented to touchings that might otherwise be tortious. For example, persons who enter crowded trains and buses will be deemed to have consented to at least some intentionally caused jostlings and other contacts, such as being pushed by another as he tries to cram his way onto the vehicle. In certain situations, a history of dealings between the parties might also be relevant. For example, if two persons have in the past playfully punched or shoved one another in certain situations, that fact may permit an inference of consent to similar contact in a subsequent similar situation. The defense of implied consent thus often requires judges and juries to make judgments turning on factors such as the age, gender, and sophistication of the parties, their relationship, if any, and various other circumstances associated with their interaction.

3. *Actual Consent versus Objective Indicia of Consent.* Suppose that *D* sincerely believes that *P* has consented to being harmfully touched, when in fact *D* is mistaken because he misunderstood something that *P* said, or because he misread certain nonverbal cues. If *D* causes a harmful touching of *P* and *P* sues for battery, may *D* avoid liability on the ground that he believed that *P* had consented? Or must consent actually have been given?

Courts have typically adopted a third route, which is to bar the imposition of liability on *D* only if he *actually* and *reasonably* believed that *P* has consented to the contact. O'Brien v. Cunard S.S. Co., 28 N.E. 266 (Mass. 1891) provides a famous illustration of this doctrine. O'Brien, a young immigrant, was vaccinated on board defendant's ship as it brought her to New York. After suffering an adverse reaction, she sued for battery, alleging that she never consented to the injection. The court concluded that the ship's doctor reasonably inferred that O'Brien consented by virtue of standing in a line of people receiving the vaccination, and by holding out her arm as did others in the line. Thus, even if a jury were to believe that O'Brien's actual intent was to refuse the vaccination, the ship's owner would be free from liability because its doctor actually and reasonably inferred consent under the circumstances.

What justifies a rule that would permit an injurer to escape liability on the ground that he reasonably but mistakenly perceived consent on the part of the victim? Why should the risk of error with regard to consent fall on the victim rather than the injurer?

4. *Fraud and Coercion.* A tortfeasor cannot benefit from the consent defense if he secures the victim's consent by misrepresentation or other forms of deceit. So, for example, if *D* induces *V* to imbibe a poisonous drink by representing that it is wine, *D* cannot invoke consent as a defense. As discussed in more detail in Module I, some smokers have attempted to argue that they suffered a battery (or, alternatively, a fraud resulting in physical injury) at the hands of cigarette manufacturers by being induced to inhale toxic chemicals on the basis of the manufacturers' misrepresentations, including the failure to disclose the presence of toxic additives such as ammonia. *See* Naegele v. R.J. Reynolds Tobacco Co., 50 P.3d 769 (Cal. 2002)

(reversing summary dismissal of claims by an ex-smoker for fraud). In certain instances, the injurer may owe the victim an affirmative duty to disclose information relevant to the victim's decision to consent, such that failure to disclose will constitute fraud. For an interesting and perhaps unusual application of this rule, *see* Neal v. Neal, 873 P.2d 871 (Idaho 1994) (in suit by a wife against an adulterous husband for battery, the jury may find that the husband fraudulently secured the wife's consent to sexual inter- course by failing to disclose to her that he was having an affair).

Consent secured through coercion by the tortfeasor — for example, through physical violence or threats of violence — also will not count as a defense to a suit for battery. Likewise, consent is not a defense if (1) the victim lacks the ability or judgment necessary to give meaningful consent, and (2) a reasonable person in the position of the tortfeasor would perceive this lack of capacity. Lack of capacity may result from youth, mental incom- petence, or some other condition or circumstance. *See, e.g.*, Elkington v. Foust, 618 P.2d 37 (Utah 1980) (stepfather not entitled to jury instruction on consent as a defense against a claim for sexual battery of a minor plaintiff).

5. *Subtler Forms of Coercion and Incapacity.* Apparent consent will sometimes be deemed ineffective if the defendant had reason to know that the consent was not freely given. Often in such cases a critical issue will be whether the alleged tortfeasor occupied a position of power or authority in relation to the victim. Thus, a patient who sues her therapist for battery based on a "consensual" sexual encounter between them can argue that the therapist should have known that the patient was not in a position to make a genuinely free choice about having sex with the therapist. For a fractured decision addressing several issues related to consent, *see* Reavis v. Slominski, 551 N.W.2d 528 (Neb. 1996). There, a dentist's receptionist sued her employer for battery after they had sex at an office party. A few years earlier, while also working as a receptionist for Slominski, Reavis had at times acceded to Slominski's persistent sexual advances. In the instance that took place at the party, Reavis initially resisted, but eventually acceded. Following the encounter, Reavis, guilt-ridden, informed her husband of it, and then attempted suicide.

In her suit for battery, Reavis claimed that she acquiesced to sex with Slominski out of fear of losing her job, and because sexual abuse she suffered as a child had habituated her into coping with sexual aggression by acquiescing. The plurality opinion in *Reavis* concluded that expert testi- mony as to the effects of the past abuse could be admitted on the issue of whether Reavis lacked the capacity genuinely to consent, and whether Slominski, based on their encounters a few years earlier, had reason to know of, and hence was exploiting, this vulnerability when he accosted her at the party. Concurring justices held that the evidence of abuse should not have been admitted, but that a jury could find that Reavis's consent was not voluntary because she reasonably feared that she would lose her job if she did not acquiesce. Several dissenters maintained that the evidence on past abuse was irrelevant, and that a threat of being fired is, as a matter of law, not sufficiently coercive to vitiate consent to sexual intercourse. (On this last point, note that even if threats to fire employees are not sufficient to vitiate consent in an action for battery, they often are sufficient to generate claims for sexual harassment under federal laws applicable to employers of a certain size. See Chapter 10.)

6. *Scope of Consent.* As *Koffman* indicates, even when a court determines that the victim has expressly or implicitly consented to some harmful or inappropriate contact, the question remains as to whether the contact in question was of the sort to which the plaintiff consented. In Mohr v. Williams, 104 N.W.12 (Minn. 1905), the plaintiff voluntarily underwent surgery to improve her hearing in one ear. During the operation, while the plaintiff was unconscious, the surgeon determined that the ear in question was not diseased, but that the plaintiff's other ear was in need of surgical repair, so he proceeded to operate on it. Despite the fact that procedure apparently went well, and occurred with the permission of Mohr's family physician, who was in the operating room at the time, Mohr sued the surgeon for battery and prevailed after the court determined that the surgeon had exceeded the scope of Mohr's consent by operating on a different part of the body than the part that she had consented to have touched. Notice how the consent form, *supra* Note 1, deals with this potential source of liability. Recall also Largey v. Rothman from Chapter 3, which primarily concerned the doctrine of informed consent, but also raised the issue of whether Ms. Largey, in consenting to a biopsy, had consented to the removal of lymph nodes.

7. *Consent to Illegal Activities.* As they sometimes do in connection with contractual assumptions of risk, see Chapter 7, courts will in certain situations deem otherwise valid consents void as against public policy. In his capacity as co-Reporter for the Second Restatement, Dean Wade disapprovingly noted in 1979 that most courts at that time deemed consent *ineffective* if the consented-to conduct amounted to a crime. Thus, if two persons chose to engage in a fist fight that constituted a criminal breach of the peace, either or both could sue the other for battery. *See* Restatement (Second) of Torts § 892C (1979) (Reporter's note). In place of this approach, the Restatement maintains that consent to conduct constituting a crime should suffice to establish a defense to a tort claim unless the conduct in question was rendered criminal by the legislature in part to protect the consenting person from his own choices. For example, if *A* and *B* were to participate in an unlicensed boxing match in which *A* severely injured *B*, a court applying Section 892(c) might hold that *B* can sue *A* for battery notwithstanding *B*'s consent to participate in the fight on the ground that the licensing scheme aimed to protect persons such as *B* by reducing the risk of gross mismatches, having competent referees to regulate the contest, etc. *See* Restatement, *supra*, § 892C, illus. 9.

B. Self-Defense and Defense of Others

When consent operates as an effective defense it does so out of respect for individual autonomy. At least under certain conditions, a competent and informed individual is accorded by tort law a right to choose to experience treatment at the hands of others that, absent the exercise of that choice, would be wrongful. The remaining defenses to be considered in this chapter do not derive from the law's respect for individuals' capacity to choose. Instead, they recognize that there are situations in which an actor is entitled to commit a tort such as battery against another.

Perhaps the most familiar of these entitlements consists of a privilege to use force against another to defend oneself—for example, the privilege to strike another to ward off the other's physical attack. Self-defense in one sense sits quite comfortably within tort doctrine. Essentially, the privilege permits a person to protect the very bodily integrity that is meant to be protected and vindicated by torts such as battery. Yet, in another sense, the fit is potentially awkward. One of the original and most basic functions of tort law is to provide legal redress for victims of wrongs as a substitute for private violence. To the extent tort recognizes a broad privilege of self-defense, it at least runs the risk of sanctioning resort to forcible "self-help." The difficulty of defining lines that will permit victims to protect themselves without sanctioning private violence is reflected in the various doctrines that determine the application of the self-defense privilege. The same difficulties are also apparent (perhaps to an even greater extent) when we encounter in Section III.C the related privilege to use force to protect one's property interests.

Haeussler v. De Loretto
240 P.2d 654 (Cal. App. 1952)

Vallée, J.　Appeal by plaintiff from a judgment for defendant in an action for damages for assault and battery. The cause was tried by the court without a jury.

The evidence, stated in the light most favorable to the prevailing litigant, discloses that on May 21, 1950, about 10:30 P.M., plaintiff went to the home of defendant, a neighbor, to inquire about his dog which was missing and which frequently had gone to defendant's home. The dog had been the subject of disagreement between the wives of the parties on several previous occasions. When defendant, in response to plaintiff's knock, opened the door, the dog ran out from inside the house. Defendant testified that plaintiff immediately started talking in a loud tone of voice, told him he did not want defendant or his wife to feed the dog or keep it at their house; that plaintiff kept "waving his hands, and while he talked, his face was pretty flushed and he was pretty excited, like he had been drinking, and he kept arguing with me and one word led to another, and I don't know the man, but I do know of him. I know he had trouble with the Teamster's Union and [that another man named] Frowiss and him beat up a couple of friends of mine, and I got a little afraid, and towards the end, after I had asked him to go three times, and he kept waving his hands, I thought he was going to strike me, and I struck him or pushed him, and I went in and closed the door." Plaintiff called the police but no arrest was made nor was any criminal action had.

The court found that plaintiff precipitated the argument; defendant ordered plaintiff to leave his premises; plaintiff advanced threateningly toward defendant; defendant struck him once; two of plaintiff's teeth were loosened, necessitating dental care; defendant used reasonable force in defense of himself and in removing plaintiff from his premises; plaintiff failed to prove by a preponderance of evidence that defendant used or attempted to use wilful and unlawful force upon the person of plaintiff.

The issue of self defense was pleaded by defendant and litigated. The determination of which of the two parties precipitated the fight, and whether defendant acted in self defense, and whether in so doing he used more force than was reasonably necessary under the circumstances, were questions for the trier of fact. One who is involved in an altercation with another has the right to use such force as is necessary to protect himself from bodily injury, and the question of the amount of force justifiable under the circumstances of a particular case is also one for the trier of fact. As the court found that defendant used reasonable force in defense of himself, it necessarily follows the force used was not wilful or unlawful and that plaintiff failed to sustain the burden of proof. Since the conflicts in the evidence were resolved in defendant's favor, and the foregoing narration of the evidence supports the findings, this court may not disturb the judgment.

NOTES AND QUESTIONS

1. *Self-Defense, Provocation, and Imminence.* Self-defense is available to a victim who actually and reasonably believes it is necessary to injure another to avoid *imminent* injuries to herself such as harmful contact or confinement. A longstanding and fierce debate in criminal law concerns whether a battered spouse, almost always a woman who has been subjugated and repeatedly abused by her husband, may claim self-defense as a justification for homicide even though the killing of the abusive spouse occurred at a moment when that spouse posed no imminent threat. *See* Dan B. Dobbs, *The Law of Torts* § 72, at 165-166 (2000) (discussing the debate).

The privilege of self-defense typically applies when the injury threatened consists of physical harm, inappropriate touching, or confinement. By contrast, it does not apply if the conduct in question threatens only to result in defamation of, or distress to, the victim. Relatedly, the law does not privilege the use of force to respond to nonthreatening provocations, such as tauntings or teasings. In many jurisdictions, a person who immediately precipitates the confrontation in which defensive force is used is barred from invoking the self-defense privilege unless, after precipitating it, the injurer disengages, or manifests an intent to disengage, such that his provocation ceases to provide the main impetus for the confrontation. Gortarez v. Smitty's Super Valu, Inc., 680 P.2d 807 (Ariz. 1984) (if defendant's security guard is found to have unjustifiably induced fight with patron in which patron was injured, the guard cannot claim self-defense).

In Landry v. Bellanger, 851 So. 2d 943 (La. 2003), the Louisiana Supreme Court considered the issues of provocation and self-defense in relation to one another. Two acquaintances were drinking in a bar. The victim became increasingly insulting and belligerent toward the defendant. Eventually, the defendant asked the plaintiff to step outside, apparently in an effort to avoid a further scene in the bar. When plaintiff continued to harangue the defendant and bumped him, the defendant punched the plaintiff in the face, which caused the plaintiff to fall, resulting in severe injuries. The state's high court first rejected earlier Louisiana decisions holding that a victim's initial provocation of a fight functions to bar him from suing the defendant for injuries caused by the fight. It next concluded that although Louisiana does not recognize comparative fault as a defense to a claim of battery, a jury would nonetheless be entitled to apportion responsibility between a batterer and a provoking victim on the ground that a victim's provocation of a fight is not a mere act of carelessness, but instead an "intentional" act. Finally, it held that this particular plaintiff's suit was barred because the defendant's punch was not merely a response to a provocation, but a reasonable effort to defend himself against plaintiff's physical aggression.

2. *Objectivity of the Threat.* As with the defense of consent, the injurer may invoke self-defense only if he actually and reasonably perceives an imminent risk of injury to himself. Suppose that D mistakenly but reasonably believes that the person walking purposefully and quickly toward him in the darkness is his psychotic and violent enemy E, when in fact it is innocent delivery person P, who resembles E. If D punches P, D can claim the privilege of self-defense as against a battery claim by P. Conversely, if D recognizes or should recognize P for who he actually is, yet punches him, D will have no defense, even if he harbored the sincere but unreasonable belief that delivery persons routinely attack people. As with the determination of reasonableness in negligence law, the reasonableness of D's perception of the threat to him is judged in light of the surrounding circumstances. Thus a jury can give D greater leeway to respond forcibly to perceived threats in an emergency situation than in a situation more conducive to the exercise of prudence.

3. *Proportionality and Deadly Force.* As *Haeussler* indicates, the injurer's response must be reasonable not only in being grounded in a reasonable perception of imminent harm, but also in consisting of an appropriate or proportional response to the perceived threat. The issue of proportionality arises most starkly when the alleged tortfeasor uses deadly force, that is, force intended or calculated to cause death. As a rule, the use of this degree of force is only justified when the injurer actually and reasonably perceives that the victim is threatening him with imminent death or serious bodily injury. For an impassioned opinion on behalf of the privilege to use deadly force, *see* Price v. Gray's Guard Serv., Inc., 298 So. 2d 461 (Fla. Ct. App.) (a security guard who was attacked from behind and being beaten with his own club was privileged to shoot his assailants), *cert. denied*, 305 So. 2d 208 (Fla. 1974). By contrast, a victim who reasonably perceives that he is about to be slapped, or subjected to a nonharmful yet offensive battery, or nonviolent confinement in the manager's office of a department store, will not be able to invoke self-defense to justify the use of *deadly* force.

4. *Conditional Threats, Dwellings, and Retreat.* Suppose *A* approaches *B* from behind as *B* is withdrawing cash from an ATM during daylight hours on a quiet, but not deserted, street. *A* says to *B*: "Give me your money, and you won't get hurt." May *A* use force against *B*? Deadly force? According to the Second Restatement, *A* is privileged as a matter of law to use *non*-deadly force, and is privileged to use deadly force unless the factfinder determines that *A* reasonably believed that he could secure his personal safety by handing the money to *B*. Restatement (Second) of Torts § 65(3), at 109 (1965).

Suppose *S*, sleeping upstairs alone in her home, awakens to hear someone coming up the stairs toward her room. Is *S* entitled to reach for the gun in her night table and fire it the moment the person enters her room? The Restatement suggests that a person may use deadly force whenever she is being "attacked" in her "dwelling." *Id.* § 65(2), at 108-09. Now suppose *A* hears a commotion near the entrance to a barn located on her property 100 feet from her dwelling. If *A* spies a person attempting to break into the barn, may she shoot at him? *See* Goldfuss v. Davidson, 679 N.E.2d 1099 (Ohio 1997) (defendant not entitled to a self-defense instruction on facts similar to these).

The propriety of using deadly force is sometimes bound up with the notion of "safe retreat" — the thought being that, if one actually believes that one can safely retreat from a confrontation that would otherwise justify the use of deadly force (say, by fleeing), one is not justified in using deadly force. Restatement, *supra*, § 65(3), at 109. The Restatement's rule of retreat does not apply, however, to the use of non-deadly force, or to the use of deadly force to ward off an intruder's attack in one's dwelling. *Id.* §§ 63(2), 65(2)(a).

5. *Defense of Others versus Defensive Use of Others.* The privilege to injure an attacker for the purpose of defending others operates more or less under the same rules that govern the privilege of self-defense. Thus, so long as *D* actually and reasonably believes that injuring *P* is necessary to avoid an imminent injury of the requisite type to one or more third parties, *D* is privileged to use proportionate force against *P* to prevent such injuries. By contrast, the necessity of sparing oneself from injury is generally held *insufficient* to excuse the injuring of an innocent third party. So, for example, if *X* were to grab innocent bystander *Y* to shield himself from *Z*'s physical attack, resulting in bodily injury to *Y*, *X* will be held liable to *Y* for battery. See the discussion of necessity in connection with trespass to property, *infra* Chapter 11.

C. Defense and Recapture of Property

Katko v. Briney
183 N.W.2d 657 (Iowa 1971)

Moore, C.J.   The primary issue presented here is whether an owner may protect personal property in an unoccupied boarded-up farm house against trespassers and thieves by a spring gun capable of inflicting death or serious injury.

We are not here concerned with a man's right to protect his home and members of his family. Defendants' home was several miles from the scene of the incident to which we refer infra.

Plaintiff's action is for damages resulting from serious injury caused by a shot from a 20-gauge spring shotgun set by defendants in a bedroom of an old farm house which had been uninhabited for several years. Plaintiff and his companion, Marvin McDonough, had broken and entered the house to find and steal old bottles and dated fruit jars which they considered antiques.

At defendants' request plaintiff's action was tried to a jury consisting of residents of the community where defendants' property was located. The jury returned a verdict for plaintiff and against defendants for $20,000 actual and $10,000 punitive damages.

After careful consideration of defendants' motions for judgment notwithstanding the verdict and for new trial, the experienced and capable trial judge overruled them and entered judgment on the verdict. Thus we have this appeal by defendants. . . .

Most of the facts are not disputed. In 1957 defendant Bertha L. Briney inherited her parents' farm land in Mahaska and Monroe Counties. Included was an 80-acre tract in southwest Mahaska County where her grandparents and parents had lived. No one occupied the house thereafter. Her husband, Edward, attempted to care for the land. He kept no farm machinery thereon. The outbuildings became dilapidated.

For about 10 years, 1957 to 1967, there occurred a series of trespassing and housebreaking events with loss of some household items, the breaking of windows and "messing up of the property in general." The latest occurred June 8, 1967, prior to the event on July 16, 1967 herein involved.

Defendants through the years boarded up the windows and doors in an attempt to stop the intrusions. They had posted "no trespass" signs on the land several years before 1967. The nearest one was 35 feet from the house. On June 11, 1967 defendants set "a shotgun trap" in the north bedroom. After Mr. Briney cleaned and oiled his 20-gauge shotgun, the power of which he was well aware, defendants took it to the old house where they secured it to an iron bed with the barrel pointed at the bedroom door. It was rigged with wire from the doorknob to the gun's trigger so it would fire when the door was opened. Briney first pointed the gun so an intruder would be hit in the stomach but at Mrs. Briney's suggestion it was lowered to hit the legs. He admitted he did so "because I was mad and tired of being tormented" but "he did not intend to injure anyone." He gave no explanation of why he used a loaded shell and set it to hit a person already in the house. Tin was nailed over the bedroom window. The spring gun could not be seen from the outside. No warning of its presence was posted.

Plaintiff lived with his wife and worked regularly as a gasoline station attendant in Eddyville, seven miles from the old house. He had observed it for several years while hunting in the area and considered it as being abandoned. He knew it had long been uninhabited. In 1967 the area around the house was covered with high weeds. Prior to July 16, 1967 plaintiff and McDonough had been to the premises and found several old bottles and fruit jars which they took and added to their collection of antiques. On the latter date about 9:30 P.M. they made a second trip to the Briney property. They entered the old house by removing a board from a porch window which was without glass. While McDonough was looking around the kitchen area plaintiff went to another part of the house. As he started to open the north bedroom door the shotgun went off striking him in the right leg above the ankle bone. Much of his leg, including part of the tibia, was blown away. Only by McDonough's assistance was plaintiff able to get out of the house and after crawling some distance was put in his vehicle and rushed to a doctor and then to a hospital. He remained in the hospital 40 days.

Plaintiff's doctor testified he seriously considered amputation but eventually the healing process was successful. Some weeks after his release from the hospital plaintiff returned to work on crutches. He was required to keep the injured leg in a cast for approximately a year and wear a special brace for another year. He continued to suffer pain during this period.

There was undenied medical testimony plaintiff had a permanent deformity, a loss of tissue, and a shortening of the leg.

The record discloses plaintiff to trial time had incurred $710 medical expense, $2056.85 for hospital service, $61.80 for orthopedic service and $750 as loss of earnings. In addition thereto the trial court submitted to the jury the question of damages for pain and suffering and for future disability.

Plaintiff testified he knew he had no right to break and enter the house with intent to steal bottles and fruit jars therefrom. He further testified he had entered a plea of guilty to larceny in the nighttime of property of less than $20 value from a private building. He stated he had been fined $50 and costs and paroled during good behavior from a 60-day jail sentence. Other than minor traffic charges this was plaintiff's first brush with the law. On this civil case appeal it is not our prerogative to review the disposition made of the criminal charge against him.

The main thrust of defendants' defense in the trial court and on this appeal is that "the law permits use of a spring gun in a dwelling or warehouse for the purpose of preventing the unlawful entry of a burglar or thief.". . .

In the statement of issues the trial court stated plaintiff and his companion committed a felony when they broke and entered defendants' house. [In its instructions to the jury, the court stated that property owners are not permitted to use excessive force, including force calculated to cause death or great bodily harm, to protect their property except to prevent the commission of felonies of violence and where human life is in danger. The instructions explained that breaking and entering is not a felony of violence.] . . .

The overwhelming weight of authority, both textbook and case law, supports the trial court's statement of the applicable principles of law. . . .

Restatement of Torts, section 85, page 180, states:

> The value of human life and limb, not only to the individual concerned but also to society, so outweighs the interest of a possessor of land in excluding from it those whom he is not willing to admit thereto that a possessor of land has, as is stated in § 79, no privilege to use force intended or likely to cause death or serious harm against another whom the possessor sees about to enter his premises or meddle with his chattel, unless the intrusion threatens death or serious bodily harm to the occupiers or users of the premises. . . . A possessor of land cannot do indirectly and by a mechanical device that which, were he present, he could not do immediately and in person. Therefore, he cannot gain a privilege to install, for the purpose of protecting his land from intrusions harmless to the lives and limbs of the occupiers or users of it, a mechanical device whose only purpose is to inflict death or serious harm upon such as may intrude, by giving notice of his intention to inflict, by mechanical means and indirectly, harm which he could not, even after request, inflict directly were he present.

In Volume 2, Harper and James, *The Law of Torts*, section 27.3, pages 1440, 1441, this is found: "The possessor of land may not arrange his premises intentionally so as to cause death or serious bodily harm to a trespasser. The possessor may of course take some steps to repel a trespass. If he is present he may use force to do so, but only that amount which is reasonably necessary to effect the repulse. Moreover if the trespass threatens harm to property only — even a theft of property — the possessor would not be privileged to use deadly force, he may not arrange his premises so that such force will be inflicted by mechanical means. If he does, he will be liable even to a thief who is injured by such device.". . .

[The court reviewed the holdings of similar cases from Iowa and other jurisdictions holding property owners liable for causing injury by means of excessive force.] In addition to civil liability many jurisdictions hold a land owner criminally liable for serious injuries or homicide caused by spring guns or other set devices.

In Wisconsin, Oregon and England the use of spring guns and similar devices is specifically made unlawful by statute.

The legal principles stated by the trial court in [its] instructions . . . are well established and supported by the authorities cited and quoted *supra*. There is no merit in defendants' objections and exceptions thereto. Defendants' various motions based on the same reasons stated in exceptions to instructions were properly overruled.

Plaintiff's claim and the jury's allowance of punitive damages, under the trial court's instructions relating thereto, were not at any time or in any manner challenged by defendants in the trial court as not allowable. We therefore are not presented with the problem of whether the $10,000 award should be allowed to stand. . . .

Larson, J. (dissenting). I respectfully dissent, first, because the majority wrongfully assumes that by installing a spring gun in the bedroom of their unoccupied house the defendants intended to shoot any intruder who attempted to enter the room. Under the record presented here, that was a fact question. Unless it is held that there property owners are liable for any injury to a intruder from such a device regardless of the intent with which it is installed, liability under these pleadings must rest upon two definite issues of fact, i.e., did the defendants intend to shoot the invader, and if so, did they employ unnecessary and unreasonable force against him? . . .

[Judge Larson's dissent first maintained that the jury should have been instructed that it could not impose liability unless it found that the defendants had intended to kill or seriously injure an intruder by setting up the spring gun. It further maintained that a reasonable jury could have found that such intent was lacking given Mr. Briney's testimony that the gun was set up to "scare" intruders, and that he (Briney) did not expect the buckshot to go through the bedroom door "quite that hard." The dissent then turned to the issue of punitive damages. — EDS.]

In the case at bar the plaintiff was guilty of serious criminal conduct, which event gave rise to his claim against defendants. Even so, he may be eligible for an award of compensatory damages which so far as the law is concerned redresses him and places him in the position he was prior to sustaining the injury. The windfall he would receive in the form of punitive damages is bothersome to the principle of damages, because it is a response to the conduct of the defendants rather than any reaction to the loss suffered by plaintiff or any measurement of his worthiness for the award.

When such a windfall comes to a criminal as a result of his indulgence in serious criminal conduct, the result is intolerable and indeed shocks the conscience. If we find the law upholds such a result, the criminal would be permitted by operation of law to profit from his own crime. . . .

We cannot in good conscience ignore the conduct of the plaintiff. He does not come into court with clean hands, and attempts to make a claim to punitive damages in part on his own criminal conduct. In such circumstances, to enrich him would be unjust, and compensatory damages in such a case itself would be a sufficient deterrent to the defendant or others who might intend to set such a device. . . .

The admonitory function of the tort law is adequately served where the compensatory damages claimed are high and the granted award itself may act as a severe punishment and a deterrence. In such a case as we have here there is no need to hold out the prospect of punitive damages as an incentive to sue and rectify a minor physical damage such as a redress for lost dignity. Certainly this is not a case where defendants might profit in excess of the amount of reparation they may have to pay. . . .

Jones v. Fisher
166 N.W.2d 175 (Wis. 1969)

This is an assault and battery action brought by the plaintiff-respondent, Aleta I. Jones, for compensatory and punitive damages against Jerome Paul Fisher and Clara Belle Fisher, his wife, defendants-appellants.

The defendants were the owners and operators of a nursing home in Middleton, Wisconsin. The plaintiff, age twenty-six, married but separated, started to work for the defendants as a nurse's aid in December of 1966. She cared for the home residents during the night hours, set up and gave medication, prepared and served breakfast and had some clean-up duties in the kitchen. Until the incident in question the relationship between the parties had been cordial and friendly. The defendants regarded her as a good employee and were personally fond of her.

In September, 1967, the plaintiff was told by her dentist that her teeth were in bad condition. She needed an upper plate but complained to Mrs. Fisher about the cost of her dental work. The Fishers volunteered and did loan her $200 to apply on her dental expenses. All but $10 of the proceeds of the loan was paid to the dentist.

Shortly after she obtained the upper plate she quit working for the Fishers. About a week or more after she quit, on November 6, 1967, at noon, she returned to the nursing home to get her check in the amount of $48 for her last week's work. Mrs. Fisher tried to convince the plaintiff to return to work at the nursing home. The plaintiff refused. Mr. Fisher entered the conversation and inquired when she was going to repay the $200. She told him he could take $20 out of the $48 check and that she would pay the balance at the rate of $20 per month. He told her that was not satisfactory and that she would have to pay the entire amount in three days or leave the upper plate for security. She refused to agree to these conditions. She was told to leave the teeth and an argument ensued. There is a dispute as to whether the Fishers used profane and indecent language toward her. She attempted to run out of the room. Mr. Fisher seized her arms and forced them in back of her. The evidence is unclear as to whether she was forced onto his lap or into a crouched position; if she kicked at Mr. Fisher; or if she threatened to kill him. In any event, Mrs. Fisher grabbed at her face and mouth and extracted the upper plate. Mr. Fisher released her and she immediately ran out of the house. The affray was less than fifteen minutes. At the trial she testified that her arms and her back hurt while she was being held and that her mouth, which was sore because the teeth did not fit properly, hurt when Mrs. Fisher took her plate out. She had no bruises nor scratches. She testified that she was in fear and was humiliated and embarrassed.

After she left the rest home she walked . . . to a drugstore where she called her subsequent employer and asked him to call his lawyer. She then walked . . . to the police station and reported the incident to two police officers. One of the officers went to the Fisher nursing home, obtained the teeth, returned to the station and gave Mrs. Jones her teeth. She testified she suffered humiliation, embarrassment and shame at the drugstore and at the police station and that she had these same emotions for about a week which made it difficult to sleep. She did not see a doctor or take any prescriptive medicine.

The jury found that both defendants had committed an assault and battery on her and awarded compensatory damages of $1,000 and punitive damages of $2,500 as to each defendant. . . .

Beilfuss, J. . . .

The defendants do not raise any issue as to the assault and battery finding. Their main thrust is that the damages, both compensatory and punitive, are excessive and ask this court to . . . fix a reasonable amount as an option to a new trial. . . .

The jury awarded the plaintiff $1,000 compensatory damages. Compensatory damages are to compensate the injured party for his actual damages and not as punishment of the defendant. If there is personal injury the award should include compensation for loss of earnings, pain and suffering, and permanent or future disability if such appears. The award can also include compensation for mental suffering such as humiliation, shame, embarrassment, and fear. Granted, mental suffering is many times difficult to evaluate in terms of monetary awards, nevertheless, it is compensable.

Considering the testimony and other proof in the record most favorable to the plaintiff, we find that plaintiff was subjected to a painful physical assault for a very few minutes at the most. She testified her arms and back hurt while she was held and that the soreness of her mouth was aggravated when the teeth were taken. There was no objective physical evidence of injury. She did not consult a physician, nor use prescriptive medicine. Her physical injury was nominal. She testified that she was nervous, humiliated and scared during the altercation at the nursing home, at the drugstore, the police station, and for about a week thereafter and still (at the time of trial) thinks about it. She was without her teeth for, at the most, an hour. Understandably she could suffer humiliation and shame during this period. Conceivably she could continue to suffer these emotions for some time thereafter, but her symptoms were all subjective and not supported by any medical testimony nor any other corroborating evidence. The lack of medical testimony or other corroborating evidence is not fatal to her claim for past suffering but it would have done much to add credence to her almost minimal testimony of her subjective emotions. . . .

The trial court was of the opinion the award for compensatory damages was high but not excessive. . . . In view of the limited, vague and uncorroborated testimony bearing . . . upon her mental distress, we are of the opinion the award for compensatory damages of $1,000 does . . . reflect an allowance for the effects of injury not sufficiently proved . . . and . . . a rate of compensation which is beyond reason . . . and, therefore, excessive. We are of the opinion that $500 is a reasonable award to Mrs. Jones for compensatory damages. . . . [Quotation marks omitted. — EDs.]

. . . In Kink v. Combs . . . we stated at page 79, 135 N.W.2d at page 797:

> . . . "Where the defendant's wrongdoing has been intentional and deliberate, and has the character of outrage frequently associated with crime, all but a few courts have permitted the jury to award in the tort action 'punitive' or 'exemplary' damages, or what is sometimes called 'smart money.'" Prosser, *Law of Torts* (2d Ed. 1955), p.9.
>
> "For the award of punitive damages it is sufficient that there be a showing of wanton, wilful, or reckless disregard of the plaintiff's rights. 6 C.I.S. Assault and Battery § 55b(3), p.904."

We are of the opinion that the jury could (they are not required to do so) award punitive damages based upon the facts before them. The conduct of Mr. and Mrs. Fisher was illegal, outrageous and grossly unreasonable. It may be as appellants contend that they erroneously thought they had a right to take the teeth as security for their loan. Even so, it was grossly unreasonable to use the tactics they did and subject the plaintiff to this outrage.

The principal problem that confronts us is whether the damages awarded are excessive. . . .

The evidence reveals that the defendants' own property was worth approximately $75,000, subject to a mortgage of $41,000, leaving an equity of about $34,000. Their net income for the years 1966 and 1967 was about $24,000 per year. It appears as though the nursing home operation was a joint venture between Mr. and Mrs. Fisher. In contrasting the punitive awards with the wealth of the defendants we must either assume the award was $5,000 or consider that each owned one-half of the wealth of the parties.

In viewing the wealth of the defendants, the character and extent of their acts, and the probable motivation, and then applying the standard of punishment and deterrence, the court is of the unanimous opinion that the assessment of $2,500 as punitive damages to each defendant was excessive. . . .

The majority of the court is of the opinion that an assessment of $1,000 as to each defendant is a reasonable amount for punitive damages. . . .

. . . [R]eversed and cause remanded to the trial court with the direction that the plaintiff have the option to elect to take judgment in the amounts fixed by the court in this opinion, plus taxable costs. . . .

Hansen, J. (dissenting) (joined by Hanley, J.). The majority opinion sustains the collecting of punitive damages in a case involving a one hour deprivation of dentures. Next may come the case approving such added damages for the near-identical deed of toupee-snatching. We do not minimize the unpleasantness of an hour spent without newly acquired dentures, nor of an hour spent without the adornment of a substitute headpiece. We agree that compensatory damages for the deprivation and humiliation involved are justified. We do not agree that the added penalty of punitive or vindictive damages is also warranted in such instance. . . .

. . . It has been said that . . . punitive awards are permitted in most jurisdictions ". . . as a punishment to the defendant and as a warning and example to deter him and others from committing like offenses in the future." [citation omitted] Can it seriously be contended that such underlying justification is present in the case before us? Would not the recollection of the compensatory damages paid render very unlikely a repetition by the husband and wife here involved of the offense of denture detention? Would not the $1,000 compensatory damage award, standing alone, be a sufficient deterrent to others who might be tempted to hold dentures as security for an unpaid loan? Are we dealing here with a propensity to grab, and hold upper plates that is marked either by a high rate of recidivism or contagion? Is there here present a situation that justifies the heavy-handed use of punishment to deter? We think not, particularly because we do not deal with a matter of plaintiff's rights, but the question of what the public interest requires and what the public policy should permit. . . .

Elsewhere it has been said that punitive damages "are imposed in view of the enormity of the offense." Under any of these tests, can it be fairly concluded that the unfortunate altercation between the parties here involved moves into that category of seriousness that warrants awarding of punishment damages?

Unless malice is equated with momentary loss of temper or is to be presumed from an act of poor judgment, there is no element of malevolence or vindictiveness present here. The bicuspid corpus delicti is present only because of an interest-free loan made by defendants to plaintiff. Granted that they expected her to remain in their employ and to pay them back from her earnings, goodwill, not illwill is evidenced by the transaction, the advancing of the $200 to pay the dentist.

Conceding that the taking of the upper plate which belonged to the plaintiff, even if paid for by the defendants, was an invasion of her rights, can it be termed "wanton or reckless"? It is evident that there was a mutually cordial, supportive and agreeable relationship between the old couple and the young lady who worked for them in their nursing home, almost up to the incident here involved. It was the lady's decision, loan unpaid, to go to work for someone else that precipitated a change in the relationship. Is this flareup of emotions, this shift in mood, this disappointment of expectations on the part of the employing couple a foundation for a finding of wanton and reckless disregard of the rights of another[?] If so, the most trivial of altercations and mildest of scuffles dons the garment of wantonness or recklessness.

Given the unfortunate escalation of unpleasantness in the argument of the parties, can its climax, the grabbing of the dentures, be found to have the "character of outrage frequently associated with crime"? If the police had been called to stop the argument, instead of being called to get the plate back, would they have made an arrest? If they had, would a district attorney have issued a state warrant for battery, or even for disorderly conduct, on the basis of what had taken place? If he had, would a misdemeanor court have considered the situation here to involve violation of a criminal statute or as a falling-out among friends to be settled by an apology and a handshake? Is this the type of situation that Prosser contemplated when he wrote of an "outrage frequently associated with crime"? We think it falls short of being that. Certainly, if punitive damages are to be imposed "in view of the enormity of the crime," this is no situation justifying their imposition. . . .

NOTES AND QUESTIONS

1. *Katko's Aftermath.* According to Professor Palmer, while their appeal to the Iowa Supreme Court was pending, the Brineys sold their farm to pay the judgment to Katko. The case apparently garnered considerable public attention, prompting the publication of strongly opinionated letters on both sides of the issue in Iowa newspapers. Sympathizers with the Brineys raised $7,000 in contributions. The state legislature took up legislation designed by its supporters to enhance the ability of property owners to use deadly force to protect their property, but the legislation was not enacted.

2. *Other Security Measures and Other Victims.* By what means were the Brineys entitled to protect their property? Prior to Katko's attempted robbery, they had boarded up the house and apparently had complained to police about the previous break-ins, but to no effect. Is the majority saying that they had no choice but to accept that they would lose their property to thieves? Suppose the Brineys kept in the farmhouse a large dog that was trained to attack intruders. Would they be subject to liability under the reasoning of *Katko?* In this regard, consider the various opinions issued in Mech v. Hearst, 496 A.2d 1099 (Md. Ct. App.), *cert. denied,* 501 A.2d 1323 (Md. 1985), in which the judges differed over whether use of a vicious guard dog to ward off trespassers is always reasonable as a matter of law, or whether, under certain circumstances, a jury might find that a guard dog serves as the equivalent of a spring gun.*

Suppose the person who was shot was not an intruder looking to steal the Brineys' property, but *B*, a 12-year-old boy who broke into the house because he thought it would make a "cool hideout." Or suppose *A*, an adult who was in the market to buy an old farmhouse, was told by a local realtor to "take a look at" a different farmhouse quite near the Brineys', and that *A* entered the Brineys' house in the mistaken belief that he was entitled to force his way in. Does either of these claimants present a stronger claim for recovery than Katko? If so, are we to conclude that the amount of force one may reasonably use to protect property varies according to the nature of the intruder and the reasons for his intrusion? Is one problem with a spring gun that it cannot discriminate between different sorts of intruders and intrusions?

3. *Unclean Hands and Punitive Damages.* In dissent, Judge Larsen invokes the doctrine of "unclean hands," an equitable doctrine that is applied by courts faced with requests for injunctive relief as opposed to damages. For example, suppose, *H*, the holder of a patent on a particular pain-relieving medicine, requests a court order to halt the production or sale of company *I*'s pain-relief product on the ground that it infringes on *H*'s patent. Now suppose there is evidence that *H* himself had engaged in fraud in the course of securing its patent by knowingly submitting false documentation to the Patent Office. In light of that evidence, the court might decline to exercise its equitable power to issue the requested injunction on the ground that those seeking equity must themselves have "clean hands." Does a similar rationale warrant a ruling that Katko — who was apparently looking to grab a few empty bottles from an unused dwelling — was not entitled to any punitive damages? If it applies to punitive damages, should it also bar him from collecting compensatory damages? Or is there something special about punitive damages that would warrant subjecting a claim for them to a special equitable principle?

---

* As indicated in Chapter 3, statutes in several jurisdictions impose strict liability on dog owners to persons who are attacked while on the owner's property by permission (or otherwise lawfully). The issue here pertains only to the right to use reasonable means to repel trespassers.

4. *Defense versus Recapture of Property.* As a rule, the privilege to use reasonable force to defend property applies only preventively. However, if the property has, in the owner's absence, momentarily been occupied by an intruder who has no right to be there, the owner may use reasonable force to remove him. Thus, if the Brineys had decided to visit the farmhouse just as Katko arrived, they could have undertaken reasonable efforts to remove him. By contrast, if an owner were forcibly to evict a person who is not entitled to occupy land, yet who enjoys "peaceable," nontransitory possession of it (e.g., a tenant whose lease has expired), the owner runs the risk of criminal penalty, and in some instances tort liability, to the wrongful possessor, even if the amount of force used by the owner is deemed reasonable. *See* Dan B. Dobbs, *The Law of Torts* § 80, at 181-186 (2000). Here, the aim of the law is to discourage self-help and encourage owners to apply to the courts for relief.

Even in situations of transitory occupation in which the owner is, in principle, permitted to take steps to eject the trespasser, the ejection must be reasonable given the circumstances. For example, absent an imminent threat of bodily harm or death, an owner may not respond to a trespass in a manner that risks imminent and serious bodily harm to the trespasser. In Whitten v. Cox, 799 So. 2d 1 (Miss. 2000), the plaintiffs were driving their pickup truck across defendant's land on their way to an adjacent property. The defendant fired his gun at the truck, forced the plaintiffs out of the truck at gunpoint, and handcuffed, physically abused, and threatened to kill them. The Mississippi Supreme Court upheld verdicts for the plaintiffs on claims of battery, assault, and false imprisonment, ruling that the jury was entitled to find that the defendant acted unreasonably in asserting his property rights as he did.

5. *Recapture of Chattels.* Roughly the same framework applies to efforts to recapture personal possessions (chattels). Thus, once "peaceable" possession of the chattel is enjoyed by another, the owner may not seek to retrieve it through the use of force without risking criminal or tort liability. However, a possessor may use reasonable force against another if the other has obtained only momentary possession of the chattel. Under the Uniform Commercial Code, a person or entity that has sold a good to another on credit, and who under the terms of the sale is entitled to repossess it for lack of timely payments, may repossess the good so long as the repossession does not involve a "breach of the peace." Thus, if car dealer *C* sells a car on credit to buyer *B*, and *B* fails to make required payments, such that *C* is entitled under the sales contract to repossess, *C* may proceed to tow the car away, even if it is parked in the publicly accessible driveway on *B*'s property. *C* may not repossess, however, if doing so involves the use of force against *B* or another, or breaking and entering onto *B*'s property.

While the owner or possessor of a chattel thus enjoys a qualified privilege to recapture it, the privilege does not protect the owner who *mistakenly* seizes property that is not actually hers. Suppose that *A* leaves her expensive and distinctively colored mountain bike in the doorway of a store while she buys a bottle of water. Suppose that moments later she comes out of the store, discovers that the bike is missing, and sees *B* riding nearby on a bike of the same appearance. *A* is privileged to use reasonable force to wrestle the bike away from *B* if it turns out that the bike actually is *A*'s. However, if *A* is mistaken, because *B* just happens to have an identical bike, *B* will be able to sue *A* for battery. This result follows even if *A* was entirely reasonable in believing that the bike on which *B* was riding was *A*'s. The limited privilege to recapture chattel is thus exercised at the possessor's peril.

Given this thumbnail description of the limited privilege to recapture chattel, one can readily conclude that the facts of *Jones* did not provide the Fishers with a basis for arguing that they were justified in grabbing Jones' dental plate. Even in closer cases, why should the law recognize any privilege to repossess? If a central point of tort law is to provide citizens with a legal avenue of redress *in lieu of self-help*, why recognize even a limited privilege?

6. Jones *and Damages*. Obviously the main concern in *Jones* is the jury's damage award, particularly its award of punitive damages on top of its compensatory award. As explained in detail in Chapter 8, and as noted above in the initial discussion of battery, compensatory awards are meant to provide the plaintiff with reasonable compensation for her injuries. In addition, juries are permitted (but not required) to award punitive damages, although only to victims of relatively egregious forms of mistreatment involving malice or wanton disregard. Among other things, such awards are intended to permit the victim an added measure of recourse against the tortfeasor, and deter the tortfeasor and others from behaving in a similar fashion in the future.

In *Jones*, the initial jury award of $6,000 in compensatory and punitive damages amounted to about three months' worth of income to the Fishers. To use rough equivalents, if the same events happened today, and the Fishers earned $72,000 per year, the jury's award to Jones would correspond to an $18,000 award — $3,000 in compensatory damages and $15,000 in punitives. Would a $3,000 compensatory award to a latter-day Jones shock the conscience? Would a $15,000 award strike you as so excessive relative to the defendants' wrong and its consequences as to warrant its reduction by half?

The dissenting opinion in *Jones* suggests that the Fishers are being punished for the equivalent of "toupee-snatching." It also observes, dryly, that the Fishers have not demonstrated the sort of "propensity to grab, and hold upper plates" that might indicate a need for a supplemental award to deter similar misconduct in the future. Is this use of sarcasm rhetorically effective? Does it reveal a particular understanding — possibly a misunderstanding — as to the wrong of battery and the point of punitive damages as a response to battery?

7. *Battery and Trespass,* Jones *and* Jacque. Jacque v. Steenberg Homes, Inc., 563 N.W.2d 154 (Wis. 1997), also decided by the Wisconsin Supreme Court, provides an interesting contrast to *Jones*. There, the Court was faced with a claim of trespass to land that resulted when employees of the defendant, Steenberg Homes, deliberately traversed plaintiffs' property with heavy equipment after the Jacques had pointedly denied them permission to do so. Because the Jacques' land was covered in snow, it

suffered no adverse effects from the trespass. The jury proceeded to award the plaintiffs nominal compensatory damages of $1, but also $100,000 in punitive damages. On appeal, the Court upheld the award, reasoning in part as follows:

> . . . This court has long recognized "[e]very person['s] constitutional right to the exclusive enjoyment of his own property for any purpose which does not invade the rights of another person." Diana Shooting Club v. Lamoreux, 114 Wis. 44, 59, 89 N.W. 880 (1902) (holding that the victim of an intentional trespass should have been allowed to take judgment for nominal damages and costs). . . .
>
> Yet a right is hollow if the legal system provides insufficient means to protect it. Felix Cohen offers the following analysis summarizing the relationship between the individual and the state regarding property rights:
>
> [T]hat is property to which the following label can be attached:
>
> To the world:
> Keep off X unless you have my permission, which I may grant or withhold.
> Signed: Private Citizen
> Endorsed: The state

Felix S. Cohen, *Dialogue on Private Property,* IX Rutgers Law Review 357, 374 (1954). Harvey and Lois Jacque have the right to tell Steenberg Homes and any other trespasser, "No, you cannot cross our land." But that right has no practical meaning unless protected by the State. . . . [A nominal] award does not constitute state protection.

The nature of the nominal damage award in an intentional trespass to land case further supports an exception to *Barnard.* Because a legal right is involved, the law recognizes that actual harm occurs in every trespass. . . . Thus, in the case of intentional trespass to land, the nominal damage award represents the recognition that, although immeasurable in mere dollars, actual harm has occurred. . . .

Society has an interest in punishing and deterring intentional trespassers beyond that of protecting the interests of the individual landowner. . . . Private landowners should feel confident that wrongdoers who trespass upon their land will be appropriately punished. When landowners have confidence in the legal system, they are less likely to resort to "self-help" remedies. . . . [O]ne can easily imagine a frustrated landowner taking the law into his or her own hands when faced with a brazen trespasser, like Steenberg, who refuses to heed no trespass warnings.

People expect wrongdoers to be appropriately punished. Punitive damages have the effect of bringing to punishment types of conduct that, though oppressive and hurtful to the individual, almost invariably go unpunished by the public prosecutor. . . . If punitive damages are not allowed in a situation like this, what punishment will prohibit the intentional trespass to land? Moreover, what is to stop Steenberg Homes from concluding, in the future, that delivering its mobile homes via an intentional trespass . . . is not more profitable than obeying the law? . . .

Id. at 160-161. Although *Steenberg* involved a claim seeking to vindicate a property right, does its reasoning shed any light on the situation in *Jones?* What do you make of the contrast between the *Steenberg* court's unanimous and unequivocal defense of property rights and the *Jones* majority's almost apologetic affirmance of a reduced punitive award? *Katko* turned in part on the idea that the right to bodily integrity is worthy of greater protection than the right to exclude others from one's land. Are the analyses of punitive damages in *Jones* and *Steenberg* consistent with that priority?

D.   Investigative Detention and Arrest

An arrest is a particular kind of detention, one in which a person is held for the purpose of securing his presence at a judicial proceeding, or to otherwise aid in the administration of the law. Restatement (Second) of Torts § 112, at 190 (1965). In various circumstances, an actor who arrests another will be privileged against tort liability that he might otherwise incur by virtue of having purposefully and forcibly detained another. The privilege arises not out of a right to defend oneself, others, or property, but instead to enable officials and private citizens to advance the cause of law enforcement and the operation of the legal system.

Grant v. Stop-N-Go Market of Texas, Inc.

994 S.W.2d 867 (Tex. Ct. App. 1999)

O'Connor, J.   Gerald Grant, the appellant, sued Stop-N-Go Market of Texas, Inc., the appellee, for false imprisonment and defamation. The trial court granted summary judgment in favor of Stop-N-Go. We reverse and remand. . . .

B.   FALSE IMPRISONMENT

. . . The elements of false imprisonment are (1) a willful detention, (2) without consent, and (3) without authority of law. [Randall's Food Mkts., Inc. v. Johnson, 891 S.W.2d 640, 644-645 (Tex. 1995).] Stop-N-Go argues it negated the first two elements of Grant's claim because it established Grant was not wilfully detained without his consent. Stop-N-Go argues Grant chose to remain in the store, and he could have left if he so desired. In the alternative, Stop-N-Go argues it negated the third element of a false imprisonment claim because its actions were authorized by law under Chapter 124 of the Civil Practice and Remedies Code.

1.   The Summary Judgment Evidence

As evidence to support its motion, Stop-N-Go presented the trial court with an affidavit from Gerald Calhoun, the store manager, and excerpts from Grant's deposition. Grant responded to Stop-N-Go's motion for summary judgment with excerpts from his deposition, Stop-N-Go's responses to interrogatories, the police report, and Stop-N-Go's response to a request for production. . . .

a.   Grant's Deposition Testimony

In his deposition, Grant said he went to the Stop-N-Go store with his girlfriend. His girlfriend stayed in the car, which was parked in front of the door to the store. Grant paid for a can of beer, and then decided he wanted to buy some potato chips. He left the bag with the can of beer on the counter, and picked out two bags of potato chips which were marked on sale, two for 99 cents. Grant returned to the clerk and laid both bags of potato chips on the counter along with a one dollar bill.

The store clerk rang up the chips at 69 cents each. Grant told the clerk that the chips were on sale. The store clerk said something to Grant, but Grant did not understand what was said because the clerk spoke with a heavy foreign accent. The store clerk and Grant went back to the chip display. The clerk told Grant that the chips he selected were not on sale, but that another brand was on sale. Although Grant thought the clerk was wrong, he decided to buy the brand that the clerk said was on sale because he was in a hurry.

As the clerk began to total the price for the two bags of chips, Grant noticed someone leaning through the window of his car and apparently talking to his girlfriend. The appellant became concerned for his girlfriend because he did not recognize the person. He went to the door to make sure she was alright. As Grant walked to the door, he picked up the one dollar bill which he had previously laid on the counter. Grant opened the door to the store with his right hand and held the dollar bill in his left hand. After determining that the person leaning on his car was an acquaintance, Grant returned to the counter, paid for the two bags of chips, and began to walk out of the store. As he walked away from the counter, Grant told the clerk that he (the clerk) needed to learn his job better, a reference to the verbal altercation concerning the price of the chips.

Just as Grant reached the door, the store manager, Calhoun, came from the back of the store, grabbed him by the arm, and said words to the effect, "he (the clerk) is doing his job well, let's talk about the cigarettes that you stole." Grant said he was pulled back when Calhoun grabbed his arm. When Calhoun made the accusation against Grant, his voice was loud enough that all the patrons in the store heard what he was saying. Calhoun said words to the effect, "everything was on a surveillance videotape and there is nothing to talk about."

Grant said Calhoun went behind the counter and asked the store clerk three times what it was that Grant had stolen. The clerk did not respond until Calhoun asked if a pack of cigarettes was on the counter, to which the clerk responded affirmatively. Calhoun repeated his accusation that Grant stole a pack of cigarettes and passed them through the door.

Grant tried to explain to Calhoun that he did not steal any cigarettes. Grant said Calhoun told him to shut up. Grant said he got real quiet after Calhoun told him to shut up because he was afraid. After Calhoun grabbed him and accused him of stealing, Grant felt he could not leave. He thought if he did leave, the police would come looking for him.

b.   Calhoun's Affidavit

In his affidavit, Calhoun said he was in the back room of the store where a monitor for the store's surveillance camera was located. On the monitor, he saw Grant pick up something from the counter which appeared to him to be a pack of cigarettes. Calhoun said Grant went to the door and stepped at least part way outside, while still holding the object in his hand. Calhoun said a car was parked directly in front of the door to the store. He then saw Grant return to the counter and complete his purchase. However, Calhoun did not see Grant return the item that he picked up from the counter.

Calhoun said he left the back room and approached Grant as he was leaving the store because, after watching the monitor, he believed Grant had passed a pack of cigarettes out the door. He put his hand on Grant's arm to get his attention, and then he asked Grant about the cigarettes he thought were stolen. Calhoun said his hand was only on Grant's arm for a few seconds because, as soon as Grant turned around, Calhoun quit touching his arm.

According to Calhoun's affidavit, Grant denied stealing any cigarettes. Calhoun thought Grant's attitude was hostile and somewhat threatening, and so he decided to call the police to investigate the matter. He said he feared a confrontation with Grant. Calhoun said that when he told Grant he was going to call the police, Grant responded by saying to go ahead and call the police.

The police arrived within 15 to 20 minutes. Calhoun said Grant and the officer viewed the surveillance video. He said Grant told the officer he had picked up a dollar before stepping out the door. Calhoun told the officer he thought the object Grant picked up looked like a pack of cigarettes. According to Calhoun, the officer said he would take Grant in, but Calhoun never asked or directed the officer to do so. Calhoun gave the officer the surveillance video, and then the officer left the store with Grant.

Calhoun said he had no physical contact with Grant other than the initial touching to get Grant's attention. Once he got his attention, Calhoun said he and Grant remained on opposite sides of the counter while they waited for the police. Calhoun said a woman, perhaps Grant's girlfriend, came into the store and waited with Grant. Calhoun said nobody threatened Grant, nobody told Grant he could not leave, nobody prevented Grant from leaving, and nobody told Grant he was under arrest. According to Calhoun, Grant had a clear path to the door, nothing prevented Grant from leaving the store, Grant was never directed to remain in the store, and Grant was not put in or asked to go to a back room.

c.   The Surveillance Videotape

Grant claims the surveillance videotape is the best evidence to determine the reasonableness of Calhoun's belief that he stole cigarettes and of Calhoun's actions. However, Stop-N-Go did not produce it. Grant presented the trial court with the police report and Stop-N-Go's responses to discovery requests, which all address the location of the videotape.

The police report and the discovery requests are all inconsistent. The police report states the videotape was returned to Stop-N-Go. In a response to interrogatories, Stop-N-Go said the videotape was at the corporate office of the Risk Management Department of National Convenience Stores. However, in a response to a request to produce the surveillance videotape, Stop-N-Go said, "none." During oral argument before this Court, Stop-N-Go said the tape was lost.[1]

d. The Police Report

In the police report, Officer Anderson said when he walked into the Stop-N-Go store, Calhoun and Grant were arguing. Calhoun told the officer Grant stole a pack of cigarettes, and that it would be on the surveillance video. Anderson said he took Grant to the station to view the videotape. After reviewing the tape with Sergeant Hartley, Anderson determined the allegations against Grant were unfounded and released him. Anderson said the videotape was returned to Stop-N-Go.

2. WILLFUL DETENTION WITHOUT CONSENT

Stop-N-Go relies on Morales v. Lee, 668 S.W.2d 867, 869 (Tex. App. — San Antonio 1984, no writ), to argue that Grant was not willfully detained without his consent as a matter of law.[2] It argues Grant was not detained because he was not restrained from moving from one place to another. . . .

. . . According to Grant, Calhoun told Grant he could not leave and that he (Calhoun) was calling the police. This contradicts Calhoun's affidavit, in which Calhoun said he did not tell Grant that he could not leave. This raises a genuine issue of material fact concerning whether Grant was detained, and whether he consented to stay in the store.

1. . . . Grant argues the trial court erred in granting summary judgment because it should have presumed the missing videotape was unfavorable to Stop-N-Go. Stop-N-Go argues Grant was not entitled to this presumption because he has not shown the videotape was intentionally destroyed. Although we need not decide this issue . . . , we note that Grant may be entitled to a jury instruction on this presumption.

2. In *Morales*, the plaintiff was an employee at a doctor's office. The doctor accused the plaintiff of stealing five dollars. When she denied it, he screamed, hollered, threatened her, and then fired her and told her to leave. The plaintiff won on her false imprisonment claim in a jury trial. The appellate court reversed because it found there was no evidence of false imprisonment.

Morales is distinguishable. It involved a full trial, where all the evidence was developed; here, it was a summary judgment proceeding. In *Morales*, the defendant only threatened to call the police, whereas here, Stop-N-Go actually did call the police.

Stop-N-Go also argues that threats of future actions, such as to call the police, are not sufficient to constitute false imprisonment. However, Calhoun did more than threaten to call the police; he actually called the police. Grant said he was afraid of what was going to happen; he had never been in trouble with the police before. He was afraid to try and leave the store because Calhoun had already grabbed him and told him not to leave. *Compare Johnson*, 891 S.W.2d at 645 (finding no detention of employee based on fear of what would happen because no one tried to stop her from leaving, no one guarded her, and she was not threatened). Grant was afraid that if he left, he would be labeled a fugitive from justice, causing even more damage to his reputation.

Under *Johnson*, when we assume these facts are true, we conclude Grant raised fact issues concerning whether he was willfully detained without his consent.

3. The Shopkeeper's Privilege

In its motion for summary judgment, Stop-N-Go claimed its actions were authorized by law under Civil Practice and Remedies Code section 124.001, the shopkeeper's privilege. If this is true, then Stop-N-Go would have negated the third element of Grant's false imprisonment claim. Grant argues he raised genuine issues of material fact regarding whether Stop-N-Go established this privilege as a matter of law.

Stop-N-Go's only summary judgment evidence was from an interested witness, Calhoun. Calhoun's affidavit explains what Calhoun saw on the surveillance monitor. The videotape is the best evidence of what happened. However, Stop-N-Go has refused to produce the videotape, and each time Stop-N-Go was asked for it, it gave a different reason why it could not be produced.

The shopkeeper's privilege provides that a person who reasonably believes another person has stolen, or is attempting to steal property, is privileged to detain that person in a reasonable manner and for a reasonable time to investigate ownership of the property. Tex. Civ. Prac. & Rem. Code § 124.001; Wal-Mart v. Resendez, 962 S.W.2d 539, 540 (Tex. 1998). Thus, there are three components to the shopkeeper's privilege: (1) a reasonable belief a person has stolen or is attempting to steal; (2) detention for a reasonable time; and (3) detention in a reasonable manner. *Id.* at 540.

Like the court in Wal-Mart Stores, Inc. v. Odem, 929 S.W.2d 513, 520 (Tex. App. — San Antonio 1996, writ denied), we are concerned with a false imprisonment arising out of a detention. *Odem* explained that the shopkeeper's privilege is limited in its application to false imprisonment claims arising from investigative detentions. The test of liability is not based on the store patron's guilt or innocence, but instead on the reasonableness of the store's action under the circumstances; the trier of fact usually determines whether reasonable belief is established. Whether Calhoun was reasonable in believing Grant had committed a theft, or reasonable in detaining Grant, is a question to be determined by the jury.

Stop-N-Go relies on *Resendez* to argue that a ten to 15 minute deten-tion is reasonable as a matter of law. This is a true statement of the law in *Resendez*. *See* 962 S.W.2d at 540. While *Resendez* held a ten to 15 minute detention was reasonable as a matter of law, it so held, "*without deciding the outer parameters* of a permissible period of time under section 124.001." *Id.* (emphasis added).

Resendez does not support Stop-N-Go's position, because Grant was detained for more than ten to 15 minutes. According to Calhoun, the police arrived 15 to 20 minutes after they were called. Once the police arrived, they viewed the tape at the store, and then they took Grant to the police station and viewed the tape again. Grant said he spent approxi-mately an hour in police custody. Thus, Grant's detention lasted for more than an hour and 20 minutes.

4.   CONCLUSION

Stop-N-Go did not negate any element of Grant's false imprisonment claim as a matter of law, and Grant raised genuine issues of material fact on each element. Therefore, summary judgment on this claim was improper.

[The court next denied summary judgment for the defendant on Grant's defamation claim. It concluded that a jury could find that Calhoun defamed Grant by stating in front of other customers that the store had videotaped Grant stealing cigarettes.]

Thurman v. City of Milwaukee
197 F. Supp. 2d 1141 (E.D. Wis. 2002)

Adelman, J.   Plaintiffs, the estate and survivors of Clarence Michael Thurman III, bring this action under 42 U.S.C. § 1983 against former Milwaukee police officer Keith Bernard Miller, who shot and killed Thurman subsequent to chasing and apprehending him, after Thurman stole a lawn mower from Miller's garage. Plaintiffs allege that Miller used excessive force in violation of the Fourth and Fourteenth Amendments. . . . Defendants now move for summary judgment.

I.   FACTS

In the afternoon of August 3, 1996, defendant Miller was off duty and at home. His son told him that there was a man in their garage. Miller went to the garage and saw Thurman walking out of the garage pulling Miller's lawn mower. Miller followed Thurman with his police revolver drawn, pointed the gun at Thurman and said something to the effect of "bring my lawn mower back."

A group of neighborhood boys observed the incident. None of the boys heard Miller identify himself as a police officer or saw him display a badge. Miller was wearing shorts and had no shoes on.

Thurman left the lawn mower and tried to flee. Miller apprehended him in an alley adjacent to his garage and grabbed him by the shirt collar. With his gun in one hand, he bent Thurman over and started punching him and kicking him in the stomach. One of the neighborhood boys, Calvin Green, testified that Miller pointed his gun at Thurman's head and threatened to kill him. Green said that Miller hit Thurman four to seven times with his gun.

At a certain point Miller's wife drove up. Thurman escaped Miller's grip by pulling out of his t-shirt and fled. Miller asked the boys if any of them knew the man who had run off and ascertained that one of them, Robert Spencer, knew where Thurman lived. Miller told Spencer to wait, and he went into his house and put his shoes on. He did not telephone the police or ask his wife to do so.

Miller's wife tried to dissuade her husband from chasing Thurman. Green said that Miller's wife told him "don't go blowing off your head," and Miller responded, "I'm just going to beat him down some more."

Miller got into his wife's van and told Spencer to show him where Thurman lived. Spencer got into the van with Miller and directed him to an alley in the vicinity of North 40th Street and Hampton Avenue where they saw some men in a garage. Spencer remained in the van while Miller got out and talked to the men.

Miller then got back into the van and drove off. Shortly after, Spencer observed Thurman several blocks away and pointed him out to Miller. Miller then drove his van at high speed, "about 65, 70" miles per hour in the alley toward Thurman. Spencer said that Miller's driving scared him, and that Miller almost hit several children. Miller then got out of the van and ran after Thurman. Spencer heard a shot a minute or two later.

Miller shot and killed Thurman. The only witness to the shooting was Michael Jones, who was then seven years old. Jones testified at deposition that when he saw Miller and Thurman they appeared to be boxing, and that Miller pulled a gun from his pocket and was trying to shoot it. He did not hear Miller identify himself as a police officer. He saw the gun fall to the ground, observed the two men struggle for the gun, heard a shot and saw Thurman fall down.

Miller testified at deposition that he had been on the police force for about a year and a half when the incident occurred. He further stated that he stopped working as a police officer in early 1997, was subsequently found to be disabled and was not presently employed. He testified that on August 3, 1996, when his son told him that a man was in the garage, he ran out with his gun in his hand, observed Thurman and identified himself as a police officer. He testified that Thurman tried to flee, and that he pursued and then caught him. He stated that he struck Thurman a number of times, but that Thurman ran away.

Miller testified at deposition that, prior to pursuing Thurman, he did not call for backup although "nine times out of ten, most likely I would call for backup." He stated that after he pursued Thurman in the van and caught him, the two of them struggled, and Miller's gun fell out of his pants onto the ground. Miller testified that he picked the gun off the ground and that Thurman came at him, and he shot him.

II. SUMMARY JUDGMENT

A. STANDARD

Summary judgment is required "if the pleadings, depositions, answers to interrogatories, and admissions on file, together with the affidavits, if any, show that there is no genuine issue as to any material fact and that the moving party is entitled to judgment as a matter of law." Fed. R. Civ. P. 56(c). . . .

In evaluating a motion for summary judgment, the court must draw all inferences in a light most favorable to the nonmoving party. However, it is "not required to draw every conceivable inference from the record — only those inferences that are reasonable." Bank Leumi Le-Israel, B.M. v. Lee, 928 F.2d 232, 236 (7th Cir. 1991).

In deadly force cases the threshold for refuting self-defense claims at the summary judgment stage is relatively low. Where the officer defendant is the only witness left alive to testify, the award of summary judgment to the defense may be made only with particular care. . . .

III. SECTION 1983 CLAIM

Title 42 U.S.C. § 1983 states that:

> Every person who, under color of any statute, ordinance, regulation, custom, or usage, of any State . . . subjects, or causes to be subjected, any citizen of the United States or other person within the jurisdiction thereof to the deprivation of any rights, privileges, or immunities secured by the Constitution and laws, shall be liable to the party injured in an action at law, suit in equity, or other proper proceeding for redress.

In order to prove a violation of § 1983, plaintiffs must show that defendants deprived Thurman of a federal constitutional right while acting under color of state law.

A. UNDER COLOR OF STATE LAW

In the present case defendants do not dispute that Miller was acting under color of state law. Moreover, the evidence indicates that, although off duty, Miller meets the "under color" requirement. He was acting pursuant to a Milwaukee Police Department rule providing that officers are "always subject to duty" even when they are "technically 'off-duty.'" *See* MPD Rule 4 § 2/02500. . . . Miller also shot Thurman with a department-issued weapon. . . .

Defendants, however, do dispute the issue of whether Miller deprived Thurman of a federal constitutional right. I now turn to that issue.

B. REASONABLENESS OF SEIZURE

The Fourth Amendment protects persons against unreasonable searches and seizures. All claims that law enforcement officers have used excessive force in the course of an arrest, investigatory stop or other "seizure" of a citizen who is not in custody are analyzed under the Fourth Amendment and its "reasonableness" standard. Graham v. Connor, 490 U.S. 386, 395, 109 S. Ct. 1865, 104 L. Ed. 2d 443 (1989). Thus, in analyzing plaintiffs' claims, the first question is whether a seizure occurred.

In Terry v. Ohio, 392 U.S. 1, 19 n.16, 88 S. Ct. 1868, 20 L. Ed. 2d 889 (1968), the Supreme Court held that a seizure occurs when a government actor "by means of physical force or show of authority, has in some way restrained the liberty of a citizen." *See also* Tennessee v. Garner, 471 U.S. 1, 7, 105 S. Ct. 1694, 85 L. Ed. 2d 1 (1985) ("Whenever an officer restrains the freedom of a person to walk away, he has seized that person."). When law enforcement officers are pursuing an individual a seizure can be a process or continuum, United States v. Bradley, 196 F.3d 762 (7th Cir. 1999). Nevertheless, a seizure "requires an intentional acquisition of physical control." Brower v. County of Inyo, 489 U.S. 593, 596, 109 S. Ct. 1378, 103 L. Ed. 2d 628 (1989).

The evidence in the present case indicates that two seizures occurred. The first seizure took place when Miller grabbed Thurman outside of his garage after observing him with the lawn mower. This seizure ended when Thurman slipped out of his shirt and ran away. The second seizure occurred when Miller caught Thurman after pursuing him in the van and on foot. Plaintiffs challenge the reasonableness of the second seizure.

In assessing reasonableness I consider the totality of the circumstances and balance the extent of the intrusion against the need for it. *Garner,* 471 U.S. at 5, 8-9, 105 S. Ct. 1694. In *Garner,* the Supreme Court addressed the issue of deadly force and held that "if the suspect threatens the officer with a weapon or there is probable cause to believe that he has committed a crime involving the infliction or threatened infliction of serious physical harm, deadly force may be used if necessary to prevent escape, and if, where feasible, some warning has been given." *Id.* at 11-12, 105 S. Ct. 1694. In applying this standard to the use of nondeadly force, the Court in *Graham,* articulated three factors that determine whether force was reasonable: (1) "the severity of the crime"; (2) "whether the suspect poses an immediate threat to the safety of the officer or others"; and (3) "whether he is actively resisting arrest or attempting to evade arrest by flight." *Graham,* 490 U.S. at 396, 109 S. Ct. 1865.

The reasonableness of a particular use of force must be judged from the perspective of a reasonable officer on the scene, rather than with the 20/20 vision of hindsight. The calculus of reasonableness must embody allowance for the fact that police officers are often forced to make split-second judgments — in circumstances that are tense, uncertain and rapidly evolving—about the amount of force necessary in a particular situation. Further, the reasonableness inquiry is an objective one: whether the officer's actions were "objectively reasonable" in light of the facts and circumstances confronting him, without regard to his underlying intent or motivation.

In the Seventh Circuit the test of whether a search and seizure challenged under the Fourth Amendment is unlawful is the same as the test of negligence at common law: unreasonableness in the circumstances. Villanova v. Abrams, 972 F.2d 792, 796 (7th Cir. 1992). In *Villanova,* Judge Posner expressed this test in terms of Learned Hand's famous formula for negligence, $B < PL$, where B is the burden of precautions, L is the loss if there is an accident that the precautions could have prevented, and P is the probability of an accident if the precautions are not taken. *Id.;* United States v. Carroll Towing Co., 159 F.2d 169, 173 (2d Cir. 1947); *Johnson,* 41 F. Supp. 2d at 925.

In assessing whether a police shooting is reasonable the totality of the circumstances is not "limited to the precise moment when [the officer] discharged his weapon." Deering v. Reich, 183 F.3d 645, 649 (7th Cir. 1999). Rather, I must assess "all of the events that occurred around the time of the shooting." *Id.* at 652. The actions of the police officer that led to the shooting are relevant. An officer who shoots a suspect in an effort to protect himself cannot escape liability if the danger he faced was created by his own unreasonable conduct. The reasonableness inquiry requires a court to "carve up the incident into segments and judge each on its own terms to see if the officer was reasonable at each stage." *Plakas,* 19 F.3d at 1150 (relying on Tom v. Voida, 963 F.2d 952 (7th Cir. 1992)).

Applying the foregoing principles and taking the evidence in the light most favorable to plaintiffs, I conclude that a reasonable jury could find that Miller's seizure of Thurman was unreasonable in the circumstances. A reasonable jury could conclude that Miller's conduct created a high probability of serious harm and was unjustified by any offsetting potential benefit to the public.

Thurman did not pose an immediate danger to the safety of anyone. The offense that he had committed, stealing a lawn mower from a garage, did not involve violence or the threat of violence. He did not possess a weapon, and he was not driving a car. Further, Miller had found out from Spencer where Thurman lived, thus it is unlikely that Thurman could have avoided apprehension for long. The fact that he had fled from Miller was of marginal significance because it did not make him more dangerous, because he may not have known Miller was a police officer, and because Miller knew where to find him. There was evidence in the record indicating that Miller did not identify himself as a police officer during either of his seizures of Thurman.

Moreover, Miller could have, but failed to, take precautions that would have decreased the probability of physical harm. Most importantly, before pursuing Thurman, he could have called 911 and requested backup or asked his wife to do so. Had Miller or his wife called for backup, a number of uniformed officers would have immediately appeared on the scene and could have pursued Thurman with or without

Miller's assistance. They would have been in a much better position to arrest Thurman safely than Miller was by himself.

Miller knew that he should have called for backup. He testified in his deposition that nine out of ten times he would have done so, but that he did not in the present case. There was no downside to calling for backup. On the contrary, it would have increased the likelihood that Thurman would have been promptly arrested and diminished the probability that someone would be harmed in the process. In the terminology of the Hand formula the burden of precautions, "B," was zero.

On the other hand, by pursuing Thurman on his own, Miller created a high probability that either he or Thurman would be injured or killed. Miller already knew from his struggle with Thurman outside his garage that it would be difficult to subdue him. He testified in his deposition that he was surprised by how strong Thurman was. Miller also knew that Thurman was disposed to flee from him if he could. Further, even assuming that Thurman could have been safely subdued, Miller possessed no handcuffs or other instrument to restrain him. Thus, the evidence suggests that Miller's attempt to arrest Thurman by himself was extremely imprudent.

The record contains other evidence suggesting that Miller was likely to injure or kill Thurman. In fact, the evidence indicates that Miller pursued Thurman with the conscious purpose of harming him. One of the witnesses testified that Miller told his wife that the reason that he was going after Thurman was "to beat him down some more."

Additionally, Miller's conduct suggests that he was in an emotional state that impaired his capacity to make reasoned judgments. A reasonable jury could infer from his decisions to have a boy accompany him while he pursued Thurman, and to drive sixty-five or seventy miles an hour in an alley where children were playing, that he was not behaving rationally. His judgment may have been impaired because the incident involved him personally. Miller acknowledged in his deposition that he was concerned by Thurman's presence proximate to his family. If Miller was as highly wrought as the evidence suggests, this too would have increased the likelihood of harm.

For the foregoing reasons, the probability that by not taking the precaution of requesting backup, Miller's conduct would lead to someone being physically harmed, the "P" in the Hand formula, was extremely high.

Finally, the "L" in the Hand formula, the loss that could have been prevented if precautions were taken, was significant. Miller was armed and headed for a confrontation that was likely to precipitate violence. It was entirely predictable that he would have to use his weapon to acquire physical control over Thurman. The loss that could have been prevented had he requested backup and behaved more deliberately, was death or serious injury.

Thus, application of the Hand formula, $B < PL$, leads to the conclusion that a reasonable jury could find that Miller's seizure of Thurman was unreasonable in the circumstances. The burden of precautions was nonexistent, and the probability that failure to take such precautions would lead to serious injury or the loss of life was high.

The City argues that Miller acted reasonably when he shot Thurman, because Thurman was resisting Miller's effort to subdue him. However, as previously indicated, the reasonableness inquiry is not "limited to the precise moment when [the officer] discharged his weapon." *Deering,* 183 F.3d at 649. The reasonableness inquiry requires scrutiny of the conduct leading up to the shooting. If the officer's own unreasonable conduct created the danger that required him to use deadly force the officer may be liable under § 1983. In the present case a reasonable jury could reach that conclusion.

C. QUALIFIED IMMUNITY

Defendants argue that summary judgment must be granted based on qualified immunity. Under the doctrine of qualified immunity "government officials performing discretionary functions, generally are shielded from liability for civil damages insofar as their conduct does not violate clearly established statutory or constitutional rights of which a reasonable person would have known." Harlow v. Fitzgerald, 457 U.S. 800, 818, 102 S. Ct. 2727, 73 L. Ed. 2d 396 (1982). . . .

. . . Taking the facts in the light most favorable to plaintiffs, Miller is not entitled to qualified immunity. As an objective matter, on August 3, 1996, a reasonable police officer would have known that it was unreasonable to precipitate a physical confrontation with a nonviolent and unarmed offender without calling for backup, without identifying himself as an officer, and with the intent to physically harm the offender. Qualified immunity is not designed to shield from civil liability the plainly incompetent. If Miller committed the acts alleged by plaintiffs his conduct may well fall into this category. Thus, summary judgment based on qualified immunity is inappropriate. . . .

NOTES AND QUESTIONS

1. *Arrests and Warrants.* Often when a person is detained by a governmental official such as a police officer, that detention is undertaken pursuant to an arrest warrant. An arrest warrant is a document issued by a judge, or some other official with the appropriate authority, that directs the recipient of the document to arrest an identifiable person (or persons). Restatement (Second) of Torts § 113, at 191 (1965). Typically, warrants are issued only upon the presentation of evidence to the judge (or other official issuing the warrant) that there is probable cause to believe that the person to be arrested has committed a crime. When a governmental official arrests a person pursuant to a warrant that is actually valid, or in good faith relies on a warrant that appears valid on its face, she is immune from liability for false imprisonment. However, this immunity only applies to actions undertaken within the scope of the warrant. Thus, if officer *O* arrests person *P* under a warrant that authorizes the arrest of different person *D*, *O* does not benefit from any immunity by

virtue of the warrant. Likewise, the arresting official may lose the protection provided by the warrant if she acts outside the authority it provides by using excessive force in arrest.

2. *Warrantless Arrests.* Although a warrant thus provides considerable protection from liability for false imprisonment, government officials and private citizens also enjoy a limited privilege to arrest even in the absence of a warrant. (The phrase "citizen's arrest" is a shorthand description of a situation in which such a privilege attaches.) There are two common scenarios in which one private citizen is privileged to arrest another. In the first, a serious criminal offense (usually a felony) has actually been committed. If that is the case, and if the actor who arrests the other acts with "probable cause" — objectively reasonable grounds — to believe that the other committed the offense in question, he is privileged to detain the other. However, even if these conditions are met, the privilege is lost if it turns out that the actor did not act out of a good-faith desire to aid in the administration of the law, but rather used the occasion to harass, extort, or intimidate the detainee.

In the second scenario, the detainee, in the presence of the defendant, is in the process of attempting a serious criminal offence, or commits (or is about to commit) a breach of the peace (e.g., by fighting in public). Under these circumstances, the privilege to arrest will attach, but only if it turns out that the actor was correct in his perceptions. Thus, if *D* detains *C* based on a reasonable but *false* belief that *C* is about to commit a serious crime, *D* cannot invoke the privilege. Restatement, *supra*, § 119(c)-(d) & cmt. o.

3. *Investigative Detentions and the Shopkeeper's Privilege.* The U.S. Supreme Court held in Terry v. Ohio, 392 U.S. 1 (1968), that the Fourth Amendment permits police officers briefly to detain persons for the purpose of investigating actual or possible criminal activity. Such investigative stops do not require probable cause to believe that the person has committed a crime, but instead the lower threshold of "reasonable suspicion." Merchants historically enjoyed a much more limited privilege to detain customers to investigate possible thefts. Specifically, they were privileged to detain actual shoplifters, but they exercised that privilege at their peril, because it would not apply if it turned out that they were mistaken, even if their mistake was a reasonable one. *See* Claggett v. State, 670 A.2d 1002 (Md. App.) (reviewing Maryland common law with respect to the privilege to detain a suspected thief, and noting that any such detention is at the shopkeeper's peril), *cert. denied*, 675 A.2d 992 (Md. 1996).

Through common law development and, more typically, legislation of the sort referenced in *Grant*, merchants have been granted the privilege to detain customers believed to have committed or attempted a theft of their property, even if it turns out that the suspect is innocent. These statutes require that store personnel have probable cause or reasonable grounds for believing that the customer has stolen or is about to steal store property. If they have such grounds, they may detain the suspect, but only for a reasonable period of time and in a reasonable manner. In a decision subsequent to *Grant*, another Texas appellate court held that detention of a suspected shoplifter for the period of an hour did not constitute an unreasonably long detention. Dillard Dept. Stores, Inc. v. Silva, 106 S.W.3d 789 (Tex. App. 2003). However, the court in the same case also ruled that a jury was entitled to find that the store had executed the detention in an unreasonable manner because, among other things, its security guard twice placed the suspect on the floor, handcuffed him before taking him to an office, ridiculed him while in custody, and never entertained the victim's request to go out to his car in the parking lot, in which receipts for the allegedly stolen property could be found.

Federal civil rights laws guarantee all persons the right to "make and enforce contracts." 42 U.S.C. § 1981. In certain circumstances, courts have interpreted Section 1981 to provide customers or prospective customers with a federal-law remedy against owners and operators of businesses who refuse to serve them, or otherwise discriminate against them, on the basis of race or national origin. Some of these suits have claimed that store detention policies are discriminatory in that they disproportionately target African-Americans and members of other minority groups for investigation and detention. *See, e.g.*, Hampton v. Dillard Dept. Stores, Inc., 247 F.3d 1091 (10th Cir. 2001), *cert. denied*, 534 U.S. 1131 (2002).

Because shoplifting apparently causes the average retail business substantial losses, storeowners have increasingly relied on technology, including hidden surveillance cameras, to guard against theft. These technologies can implicate other interests protected by the law of torts, including the interest in privacy. For example, the issue has arisen as to whether, or under what circumstances, a clothing store can be held liable for secretly videotaping or observing its customers in changing areas. *See generally Annotation: Retailer's Surveillance of Dressing or Fitting Rooms as Invasion of Privacy*, 38 A.L.R.4th 954 (1985).

4. *Excessive Force: Civil Rights and Battery*. As *Thurman* indicates, the privilege to arrest, even if otherwise properly invoked, is lost if the arrest is undertaken with excessive force. In *Thurman*, the complaint as to the use of excessive force is presented as a federal civil rights claim under 42 U.S.C. § 1983, although in principle it also or alternatively could have been brought as a battery claim. The gist of the section 1983 claim is that officer Miller's shooting of Thurman violated the right against being subjected to an unreasonable seizure guaranteed by the Fourth Amendment. See *supra* Section II.C (noting the overlap of certain federal civil rights claims and state common law claims for battery and false imprisonment). As explained in Note 3 following *Fotjik*, claims against private actors for use of excessive force in the course of an arrest may sometimes be brought as federal law civil rights claims. However, if the private actor is deemed not to have been acting "under color of law," the claim must sound in common law torts such as battery.

Whether it is brought as a federal civil rights claim or a common law battery action, the issue in a case such as *Thurman* will be the same:

whether the person invoking the privilege to arrest used excessive force in effecting the arrest. In Section 1983 actions, the burden is on the plaintiff to prove excessive force so as to establish that he was subjected to an "unreasonable" seizure in violation of the Constitution. Courts have split over whether, in a common law battery suit against a police officer claiming use of excessive force in arrest, the burden is on the plaintiff to prove excessiveness or on the defendant to prove reasonableness. Edson v. City of Anaheim, 74 Cal. Rptr. 2d 614 (Ct. App. 1998).

5. *Examples of Reasonable Force.* For a case upholding a store security guard's use of non-deadly force to apprehend a suspected shoplifter, see Watkins v. Sears Roebuck & Co., 735 N.Y.S.2d 75 (App. Div. 2001) (guard who broke suspect's leg in tackling him as he fled store with stereo used reasonable force as a matter of law). As to the justified use of deadly force, see *Edson, supra* Note 4, which upheld a jury's defense verdict on behalf of a police officer. The officer shot a suspect who had led police on a lengthy chase and who, at the end of the chase, had turned toward the officer and reached under his jacket and toward his waistband, leading the officer to believe that the suspect was reaching for a gun.

6. *Statutory Authorization of Deadly Force and Suspects' Constitutional Rights.* In Tennessee v. Garner, 471 U.S. 1 (1985), a police officer shot a teenager as he fled from a house that he had attempted to rob. At the time, the teenager was climbing a fence with his back to the officer, and the officer was "reasonably sure" that the teenager was unarmed. Tennessee statutory law permitted a police officer to use deadly force against a fleeing criminal suspect who had ignored a command to stop, even if the sole reason for using such force was to prevent the person from escaping. Reasoning that "[i]t is not better that all felony suspects die than that they escape," the Supreme Court struck down the statute on the ground that its authorization of the use of deadly force against a fleeing suspect who does not present an imminent physical danger to others violates the suspect's right to be free from unreasonable seizure.

7. *Qualified Immunity.* As noted in the last portion of *Thurman*, governmental actors stand to benefit from an additional defense against liability for arrests, namely the defense of qualified immunity. This defense shields officials from liability arising out of the exercise of "discretionary functions" unless they perform those functions in a manner that violates clearly established constitutional rights of which a reasonable official would have known. Although technically a separate defense, qualified immunity, as applied to allegations that a governmental actor applied excessive force to an arrestee, essentially duplicates the privilege to use reasonable force. Thus, if a jury is entitled to deem an actor's use of force excessive, it is likely that the immunity will not attach, because the right against being seized through unreasonable force is clearly established, and is one of which a reasonable official undertaking an arrest would know. Wilson v. Meeks, 52 F.3d 1547 (10th Cir. 1995).

REFERENCES/FURTHER READING

Intent and Substantial Certainty

John Finnis, *Intention in Tort Law*, in *Philosophical Foundations of Tort Law* 229 (David G. Owen, ed. 1995).

David J. Jung & David I. Levine, *Whence Knowledge Intent? Whither Knowledge Intent?*, 20 U.C. Davis L. Rev. 551 (1987).

Walter Probert, *A Case Study of Interpretation in Torts*: Garratt v. Dailey, 19 U. Tol. L. Rev. 73 (1987).

Ellen S. Pryor, *The Stories We Tell: Intentional Harms and the Quest for Insurance Funding*, 75 Tex. L. Rev. 1721 (1997).

Kenneth W. Simons, *Rethinking Mental States*, 72 B.U. L. Rev. 463 (1992).

Symposium on the Third Restatement of Torts, 54 Vand. L. Rev. 1133 *et seq.* (2001) (articles and commentary by Profs. Henderson & Twerski, Armour & Sebok).

Unintended Effects and Transferred Intent

William L. Prosser, *Transferred Intent*, 45 Tex. L. Rev. 650 (1967).

Osborne M. Reynolds, Jr., *Transferred Intent: Should Its "Curious Survival" Continue?*, 50 Okla. L. Rev. 529 (1997).

Osborne M. Reynolds, Jr., *Tortious Battery*, 37 Okla. L. Rev. 717 (1984).

Symposium on Vosburg v. Putney, 1992 Wis. L. Rev. 853 *et seq.* (articles and comments by Profs. Henderson, Rabin, Hurst, and Zile).

Apportionment of Responsibility

Ellen Bublick, *Citizen No-Duty Rules: Rape Victims and Comparative Fault*, 99 Colum. L. Rev. 1413 (1999).

Gail D. Hollister, *Using Comparative Fault to Replace the All-or-Nothing Lottery Imposed in Intentional Tort Suits in Which Both Plaintiff and Defendant Are at Fault*, 46 Vand. L. Rev. 121 (1993).

Consent

Heid M. Hurd, *The Moral Magic of Consent*, 2 Leg. Theory 121 (1996) & Larry Alexander, *The Moral Magic of Consent (II)*, 2 Leg. Theory 165 (1996).

Alan Wertheimer, *What Is Consent? And Is It Important?*, 3 Buff. Crim. L. Rev. 557 (2000).

Symposium, *Five Approaches to Legal Reasoning in the Classroom: Contrasting Perspectives on* O'Brien v. Cunard S.S. Co., 57 Mo. L. Rev. 346 (1992).

Self-Defense

Symposium, *Self-Defense and Relations of Domination: Moral and Legal Perspectives on Battered Women Who Kill*, 57 U. Pitt. L. Rev. 461 *et seq.* (1996) (articles and commentaries by Profs. Richards, Schneider, Armour, Young, Fletcher, Zipursky, Gauthier, Finklestein, Pendleton, Thompson, Ripstein, Sebok, Cohen, Chamallas, & Horowitz).

Defense of Property and Detention/Arrest

Geoffrey W. R. Palmer, *The Iowa Spring Gun Case: A Study in American Gothic*, 56 Iowa L. Rev. 1219 (1971).

Richard A. Posner, *Killing or Wounding to Protect a Property Interest*, 14 J.L. & Econ. 201 (1971).

Regina Austin, *Of False Teeth and Biting Critiques:* Jones v. Fisher *in Context*, 15 Touro L. Rev. 389 (1999).

Anne-Marie Harris, *Shopping While Black: Applying 42 U.S.C. § 1981 to Cases of Consumer Racial Profiling*, 23 Bos. Coll. Third World L.J. 1 (2003).

Domestic Violence and Intentional Torts

Jennifer Wiggins, *Domestic Violence Torts*, 75 S. Cal. L. Rev. 121 (2001).

CHAPTER 10

Infliction of Emotional Distress

Chapter 9 focused on wrongs that have been part of the common law of tort since the Middle Ages. In this chapter, we consider two torts that came to be recognized as causes of action only in the mid-twentieth century. The first of these falls squarely within the family of dignitary torts. It is called *intentional infliction of emotional distress* (IIED), although some courts refer to it as the tort of *outrage.* The latter name gives clear expression to the gist of the tort. It imposes liability on an actor who, by means of outrageous conduct, intentionally or recklessly causes severe emotional distress to another. In analyzing IIED, we also have occasion to consider related statutorily based claims for race, age, and gender discrimination.

The second tort covered in this chapter — *negligent infliction of emotional distress* (NIED) — returns us from dignitary torts to negligence. We have postponed consideration of this branch of negligence law until now because it is perhaps best understood in terms of its historical and analytic links to other torts you will have encountered, including assault and IIED.

I. INTENTIONAL INFLICTION OF EMOTIONAL DISTRESS

A. The Emergence of IIED

As was noted in the introduction to Chapter 9, the hallmark of actions for assault, battery, and false imprisonment is their concern to vindicate "dignitary" interests, such as the interest in controlling others' efforts to gain access to one's body. Given their ancient lineage, it is perhaps not surprising that these torts remain concerned with responding to basic forms of wrongdoing, such as intentional woundings and confinements. Conversely, they do not purport to address the full range of conduct in which one person subjects another to a serious indignity. Indeed, even the limited range of interests guarded by these torts benefits from only partial protection. For example, as we have seen, while assault permits victims to complain of threats of bodily harm, it only applies to threats of imminent harm.

Even when one takes into account the existence of other longstanding dignitary torts, such as actions for libel and slander, significant gaps remain. Consider the famous case of Wilkinson v. Downton, [1897] 2 Q.B. 57. There, a man appeared at plaintiff's home and, as a practical joke, falsely informed her that her husband had been "smashed up" in an accident, had suffered two broken legs, and had sent for the plaintiff to rescue him, all of which caused the plaintiff severe and lasting distress. Without specifying the cause of action on which the plaintiff could rely, the trial judge upheld the jury's verdict for the plaintiff. Because there was evidence that the victim had suffered nausea and other physical side effects from the experience, the defendant was held liable because he had "wilfully done an act calculated to cause physical harm to the plaintiff."

For an even more dramatic example, consider the facts of an American counterpart to *Wilkinson* — Nickerson v. Hodges, 84 So. 37 (La. 1920). Carrie Nickerson, a single woman in her early 40s, was privy to a family legend asserting that her relatives had buried a pot of gold on property owned by one John Smith. After visiting a fortune teller, who gave her what purported to be a map showing the pot's location on Smith's property, Nickerson, with the help of others, spent months digging on the property. (Smith consented to their activities, apparently in the slight hope that they might find something and share it with him.) At some point, Smith's daughter, Minnie, along with two others — William "Bud" Baker and H. R. Hayes — formulated a plan to "assist" the explorers in their quest.

> Accordingly they obtained an old copper kettle or bucket, filled it with rocks and wet dirt, and buried it [in the area where Nickerson was searching].... [A] note was written by Hayes ... directing whoever should find the pot not to open it for three days, and to notify all the heirs. This note was wrapped in tin, [and] placed [in between the pot's two lids].... [A]ccording to these three defendants, [their plan] was ... [for the discovery of the pot] to be an April fool; but ... the proper opportunity for the "find" did not present itself until April 14th. On that day Miss Nickerson and her associates were searching and digging near the point where the pot had been buried, when one Grady Hayes, a brother of H. R. Hayes, following directions from the latter, and apparently helping the explorers to hunt for the gold, dug up the pot and gave the alarm. All of those in the vicinity, of course, rushed to the spot, those who were "in" on the secret being apparently as much excited as the rest, and, after some discussion, it was decided to remove the [upper] lid. When this was done, the note was discovered, and H. R. Hayes advised Miss Nickerson that he thought it proper that its directions should be carried out, and that the bank at Cotton Valley, a few miles distant, was the best place to deposit the "gold" for safe-keeping, until the delays could run and the heirs be notified, as requested. Following this suggestion, the pot was placed in a gunny sack, tied up, and taken to the bank for deposit....
>
> As might have been supposed, it did not take long for the news to spread that Miss Nickerson and her associates in the search for fortune, had found a pot of gold, and the discussion and interest in the matter became so general that defendant A. J. Hodges, vice president of the bank, went over from his place of business in Cotton Valley to the bank, and he and [Gatling, the bank's cashier] ... decided to examine the pot, so that, in event it did contain gold, proper precautions to guard the bank might be taken.... These two undid the wire sufficiently to peep into the pot, and discovered that it apparently contained only dirt. They then replaced the lid and held their tongues until the reappearance of Miss Nickerson. However, the secret leaked out from other sources, that the whole matter was a joke, and this information too, became pretty well distributed.
>
> After depositing the pot in the bank, Miss Nickerson went to Minden, La., and induced Judge R. C. Drew to agree to accompany her to Cotton Valley

on the following Monday (the deposit at the bank having been made on Saturday) for the purpose of seeing that the ceremonies surrounding the opening of the treasure were properly conducted. . . . Some half a dozen other relatives of Burton and Lawson Deck were notified, and either accompanied or preceded Miss Nickerson to Cotton Valley.

With the stage thus set, the parties all appeared at the bank on Monday morning at about 11 o'clock, and among the number were H. R. Hayes, one of the defendants, who seems to have been one of the guiding spirits in the scheme, and one Bushong, the latter, we infer, from intimations thrown out by witnesses in the record, being at the time either an avowed or supposed suitor of Miss Nickerson's. Judge Drew, as the spokesman for the party, approached Gatling and informed him that it was desired that the pot be produced for the purpose of opening and examining the contents for the benefit of those thus assembled. The testimony of the witnesses varies a little as to just when the storm began; some say, as soon as the sack was brought out. Miss Nickerson discovered that the string was tied near the top, instead of down low around the pot, and immediately commenced to shout that she had been robbed; others insist that she was calm until the package was opened and the mocking earth and stones met her view. Be that as it may, she flew into a rage, threw the lid of the pot at Gatling, and for some reason, not clearly explained, turned the force of her wrath upon Hayes to such an extent that he appealed for protection, and Bushong, with another, held her arms to prevent further violence.

Miss Nickerson . . . some 20 years before had been an inmate of an insane asylum, to the knowledge of those who had thus deceived her. She was energetic and self-supporting in her chosen line of employment [as a salesperson] . . . until [this episode took place]. The conspirators, no doubt, merely intended what they did as a practical joke, and had no willful intention of doing the lady any injury. However, the results were quite serious indeed, and the mental suffering and humiliation must have been quite unbearable, to say nothing of the disappointment and conviction, which she carried to her grave some two years later, that she had been robbed.

Id., at 37-39.

Compare the wrong suffered by Nickerson at the hands of her tormentors with the wrong suffered by *V*, the hypothetical victim of the unwanted haircut described at the outset of Chapter 9. In important respects, their two cases are very different. For example, whereas Nickerson suffered severe embarrassment, disappointment, and humiliation, *V* experienced none of these. This and other differences notwithstanding, the two cases also share an important characteristic. In each, the crux of the complaint is that another (or others) acted toward the victim in a manner flouting well-entrenched norms of decent behavior. Still, whereas *V* could seek redress for the wrong done to him through the well-established cause of action for battery, no comparable doctrinal hook presented itself to Nickerson. The defendants' practical joke had evolved into an exercise in purposeful public humiliation perpetrated against a victim known to be unusually vulnerable. Yet nothing in the facts seemed to support a claim for battery, assault, false imprisonment, defamation, or any of the other denominated dignitary torts.

Undaunted, Nickerson did sue H. R. Hayes, William Baker, and Minnie Smith, among others, seeking compensation for expenses, lost wages, mental and physical suffering, and humiliation. (As noted by the court, she died prior to trial, leaving her legal heirs to proceed with the suit.) After the jury returned a defense verdict, the Louisiana Supreme Court reversed and ordered payment to Nickerson's survivors in the amount of $500. The court indicated that, had Nickerson still been alive, a substantially larger sum would have been appropriate to compensate her for the "wrong thus done." As was the case in *Wilkinson*, the court nowhere in its opinion purported to identify the cause of action that provided redress for this wrong.

In 1936, Professor Calvert Magruder published an influential article that attempted to fill the doctrinal void evidenced by decisions such as *Wilkinson* and *Nickerson*. Magruder began his analysis by noting the then-black-letter rule (discussed more extensively in Section II of this chapter) that the causation of emotional distress in another, *independent of any other harm or setback to that other*, did not count as an "injury" in the eyes of tort law, and hence was (almost) never *of itself* actionable. He then surveyed an array of cases in which plaintiffs had recovered substantial damage awards on claims of assault, battery, false imprisonment, and defamation even though the predicate injuries of which they complained were minimal. (For example, he identified cases in which battery plaintiffs had won damages for physically harmless but offensive contacts, and in which false imprisonment plaintiffs had similarly obtained damage awards for brief and not-unpleasant confinements.) Although each of these claims had been framed in terms of one of these other torts, Magruder argued that they in fact formed a class unto themselves—a class that was defined by two features.

First, in each case, the interest whose invasion nominally gave rise to the tort (e.g., the interest in bodily integrity or freedom from confinement) was *not* the interest primarily being vindicated by the jury's damage award. Instead, given the minimal nature of the predicate injury of which the plaintiffs had complained, these awards, on his view, had to be understood as mainly compensating the victim for his emotional distress. Second, Magruder argued that judges had been led in these cases to sidestep the black-letter rule against recovery for freestanding emotional distress because of the sheer outrageousness of the defendants' conduct.

In short, courts had, without knowing it, come to articulate a new tort cause of action. Under it, an actor could be held liable for conduct (a) that is *outrageous* (Magruder's phrase was "beyond all bounds of decency"); (b) that is undertaken for the *purpose* of causing the victim *emotional distress* so severe that it could be expected to affect adversely his physical health; and (c) that *causes* such distress (even if that distress does not actually generate the expected physical harm).

The cause of action outlined by Magruder has in one sense taken firm root in U.S. tort law. Indeed, the "outrage" or "IIED" tort is now recognized, under one name or another, in almost every U.S. jurisdiction. However, there is another sense in which the action still remains at the periphery of tort practice: Although they are today often pleaded, IIED claims appear *rarely to succeed*. The two cases excerpted below are in this respect unrepresentative: In each, the plaintiff prevails. Compare their facts to those of the cases discussed in the notes that follow them. Taken together, do the principal and note cases reveal a pattern as to who recovers and who does not? Do they give you a sense of why courts have been willing to recognize this new cause of action as a general matter, yet reluctant to permit particular plaintiffs to prevail on it?

B. Elements

Dickens v. Puryear
276 S.E.2d 325 (N.C. 1981)

Exum, J.   Plaintiff's complaint is cast as a claim for intentional infliction of mental distress. It was filed more than one year but less than three years after the incidents complained of occurred. . . . Defendants' motions for summary judgment were allowed on the ground that plaintiff's claim was for assault and battery; therefore it was barred by the one-year statute of limitations applicable to assault and battery.

. . . We hold that . . . plaintiff's claim is not altogether barred by the one-year statute because plaintiff's factual showing indicates plaintiff may be able to prove a claim for intentional infliction of mental distress, a claim which is governed by the three-year statute of limitations. . . .

. . . For a time preceding the incidents in question plaintiff Dickens, a thirty-one year old man, shared sex, alcohol and marijuana with defendants' daughter, a seventeen year old high school student. On 2 April 1975 defendants, husband and wife, lured plaintiff into rural Johnston County, North Carolina. Upon plaintiff's arrival defendant Earl Puryear, after identifying himself, called out to defendant Ann Puryear who emerged from beside a nearby building and, crying, stated that she "didn't want to see that SOB." Ann Puryear then left the scene. Thereafter Earl Puryear pointed a pistol between plaintiff's eyes and shouted "Ya'll come on out." Four men wearing ski masks and armed with nightsticks then approached from behind plaintiff and beat him into semi-consciousness. They handcuffed plaintiff to a piece of farm machinery and resumed striking him with nightsticks. Defendant Earl Puryear, while brandishing a knife and cutting plaintiff's hair, threatened plaintiff with castration. During four or five interruptions of the beatings defendant Earl Puryear and the others, within plaintiff's hearing, discussed and took votes on whether plaintiff should be killed or castrated. Finally, after some two hours and the conclusion of a final conference, the beatings ceased. Defendant Earl Puryear told plaintiff to go home, pull his telephone off the wall, pack his clothes, and leave the state of North Carolina; otherwise he would be killed. Plaintiff was then set free.[1]

---

1. [Earl Puryear was later convicted for the crime of conspiracy to commit simple assault. — EDS.]

Plaintiff filed his complaint on 31 March 1978. It alleges that defendants on the occasion just described intentionally inflicted mental distress upon him. He further alleges that as a result of defendants' acts plaintiff has suffered "severe and permanent mental and emotional distress, and physical injury to his nerves and nervous system." He alleges that he is unable to sleep, afraid to go out in the dark, afraid to meet strangers, afraid he may be killed, suffering from chronic diarrhea and a gum disorder, unable effectively to perform his job, and that he has lost $1000 per month income. . . .

II

. . . Defendants contend, and the Court of Appeals agreed, that this is an action grounded in assault and battery. Although plaintiff pleads the tort of intentional infliction of mental distress, the Court of Appeals concluded that the complaint's factual allegations and the factual showing at the hearing on summary judgment support only a claim for assault and battery. The claim was, therefore, barred by the one-year period of limitations applicable to assault and battery. Plaintiff, on the other hand, argues that the factual showing on the motion supports a claim for intentional infliction of mental distress[,] a claim which is governed by the three-year period of limitations.[8] At least, plaintiff argues, his factual showing is such that it cannot be said as a matter of law that he will be unable to prove such a claim at trial. . . .

A

. . . The interest protected by the action for battery is freedom from intentional and unpermitted contact with one's person; the interest protected by the action for assault is freedom from apprehension of a harmful or offensive contact with one's person. McCracken v. Sloan, 40 N.C. App. 214, 252 S.E.2d 250 (1979); *see also* Prosser, *Law of Torts* §§ 9, 10 (4th ed. 1971) (hereinafter "Prosser"). The apprehension created must be one of an immediate harmful or offensive contact, as distinguished from contact in the future. . . .

[A]s noted by Prosser, § 10, p.40, "(t)hreats for the future . . . are simply not present breaches of the peace, and so never have fallen within

---

8. Although defendants argue that even the tort of intentional infliction of mental distress is governed by the one-year statute of limitations, we are satisfied that it is not. The one-year statute, G.S. 1-54(3), applies to "libel, slander, assault, battery, or false imprisonment." As we go to some length in the opinion to demonstrate, the tort of intentional infliction of mental distress is none of these things. Thus the rule of statutory construction embodied in the maxim, *expressio unius est exclusio alterius*, meaning the expression of one thing is the exclusion of another, applies. No statute of limitations addresses the tort of intentional infliction of mental distress by name. It must, therefore, be governed by the more general three-year statute of limitations, G.S. 1-52(5), which applies to "any other injury to the person or rights of another, not arising on contract and not hereafter enumerated." . . .

the narrow boundaries of (assault)." Thus threats for the future are actionable, if at all, not as assaults but as intentional inflictions of mental distress.

The tort of intentional infliction of mental distress is recognized in North Carolina. Stanback v. Stanback, 297 N.C. 181, 254 S.E.2d 611 (1979). "[L]iability arises under this tort when a defendant's 'conduct exceeds all bounds usually tolerated by decent society' and the conduct 'causes mental distress of a very serious kind.'" *Id.* at 196, 254 S.E.2d at 622, quoting Prosser, § 12, p.56. In *Stanback* plaintiff alleged that defendant breached a separation agreement between the parties. She further alleged ... "that defendant's conduct in breaching the contract was 'wilful, malicious, calculated, deliberate and purposeful' ... (and) that 'she has suffered great mental anguish and anxiety ...' as a result of defendant's conduct in breaching the agreement ... (and) that defendant acted recklessly and irresponsibly and 'with full knowledge of the consequences which would result....'" *Id.* at 198, 254 S.E.2d at 622-23. We held ... that these allegations were "sufficient to state a claim for what has become essentially the tort of intentional infliction of serious emotional distress. Plaintiff has alleged that defendant intentionally inflicted mental distress." *Id.* at 196, 254 S.E.2d at 621-22.

The tort alluded to in *Stanback* is defined in the Restatement [(Second) of Torts Section] 46 [(1965)] as follows:

One who by extreme and outrageous conduct intentionally or recklessly causes severe emotional distress to another is subject to liability for such emotional distress, and if bodily harm to the other results from it, for such bodily harm.

The holding in *Stanback* was in accord with the Restatement definition of ... intentional infliction of mental distress. We now reaffirm this holding....

... This tort imports an act which is done with the intention of causing emotional distress or with reckless indifference to the likelihood that emotional distress may result. A defendant is liable for this tort when he "desires to inflict severe emotional distress ... (or) knows that such distress is certain, or substantially certain, to result from his conduct ... (or) where he acts recklessly ... in deliberate disregard of a high degree of probability that the emotional distress will follow" and the mental distress does in fact result. Restatement § 46, Comment i, p.77. "The authorities seem to agree that if the tort is wilful and not merely negligent, the wrongdoer is liable for such physical injuries as may proximately result, whether he could have foreseen them or not." Kimberly v. Howland, *supra*, 143 N.C. at 402, 55 S.E. at 780.

[The court reviewed earlier North Carolina cases, which suggested that except in cases of assault, the state's tort law does not permit recovery for fright alone, but does permit recovery for tortiously caused physical injury, such as a heart attack, resulting from fright. It distinguished those cases as concerned to define the necessary elements of a claim for *negligent* rather than intentional infliction of emotional distress. See *infra* Section II for a discussion of NIED and physical harm. — EDS.]

Stanback, in effect, was the first formal recognition by this Court of the relatively recent tort of intentional infliction of mental distress. This tort, under the authorities already cited, consists of: (1) extreme and outrageous conduct, (2) which is intended to cause and does cause (3) severe emotional distress to another. The tort may also exist where defendant's actions indicate a reckless indifference to the likelihood that they will cause severe emotional distress. Recovery may be had for the emotional distress so caused and for any other bodily harm which proximately results from the distress itself. . . .

C

The question [raised by the defendants' summary judgment motion] is . . . whether the evidentiary showing demonstrates as a matter of law that plaintiff's only claim, if any, is for assault and battery. If plaintiff, as a matter of law, has no claim for intentional infliction of mental distress but has a claim, if at all, only for assault and battery, then plaintiff cannot surmount the affirmative defense of the one-year statute of limitations and defendants are entitled to summary judgment. . . .

Although plaintiff labels his claim one for intentional infliction of mental distress, we agree with the Court of Appeals that "(t)he nature of the action is not determined by what either party calls it. . . ." Hayes v. Ricard, 244 N.C. 313, 320, 93 S.E.2d 540, 545-46 (1956). The nature of the action is determined "by the issues arising on the pleading and by the relief sought," *id.*, and by the facts which, at trial, are proved or which, on motion for summary judgment, are forecast by the evidentiary showing.

Here much of the factual showing at the hearing related to assaults and batteries committed by defendants against plaintiff. The physical beatings and the cutting of plaintiff's hair constituted batteries. The threats of castration and death, being threats which created apprehension of immediate harmful or offensive contact, were assaults. Plaintiff's recovery for injuries, mental or physical, caused by these actions would be barred by the one-year statute of limitations.

The evidentiary showing on the summary judgment motion does, however, indicate that defendant Earl Puryear threatened plaintiff with death in the future unless plaintiff went home, pulled his telephone off the wall, packed his clothes, and left the state. The Court of Appeals characterized this threat as being "an immediate threat of harmful and offensive contact. It was a present threat of harm to plaintiff. . . ." 45 N.C. App. at 700, 263 S.E.2d at 859. The Court of Appeals thus concluded that this threat was also an assault barred by the one-year statute of limitations.

We disagree with the Court of Appeals' characterization of this threat. The threat was not one of imminent, or immediate, harm. It was a threat for the future apparently intended to and which allegedly did inflict serious mental distress; therefore it is actionable, if at all, as an intentional infliction of mental distress.

The threat, of course, cannot be considered separately from the entire episode of which it was only a part. The assaults and batteries, construing the record in the light most favorable to the plaintiff, were apparently designed to give added impetus to the ultimate conditional threat of future harm. Although plaintiff's recovery for injury, mental or physical, directly caused by the assaults and batteries is barred by the statute of limitations, these assaults and batteries may be considered in determining the outrageous character of the ultimate threat and the extent of plaintiff's mental or emotional distress caused by it.[11]

Having concluded, therefore, that the factual showing on the motions for summary judgment was sufficient to indicate that plaintiff may be able to prove at trial a claim for intentional infliction of mental distress, we hold that summary judgment for defendants based upon the one-year statute of limitations was error and we remand the matter for further proceedings against defendant Earl Puryear. . . .

Littlefield v. McGuffey
954 F.2d 1337 (7th Cir. 1992)

Wood, J.   Susanne Littlefield sued Malcolm McGuffey, also known as Wally Mack among other persona, claiming he denied her rental housing because her boyfriend, the father of her daughter, was not of the same race as she. She sought relief under the Equal Opportunity in Housing provision of the Civil Rights Act of 1866 and the Fair Housing Act as amended by the Fair Housing Amendments Act of 1988: 42 U.S.C.A. §§ 1982, 3604, 3613, and 3617.* In addition she . . . raised a claim for intentional infliction of emotional distress under Illinois common law. The jury found Mr. McGuffey liable and awarded $50,000 in compensatory damages and $100,000 in punitive damages.

McGuffey thereupon moved for a judgment notwithstanding the verdict and, alternatively, for a new trial. Judge Williams denied both motions. She then entered judgment on the verdict [and] awarded attorney's fees. . . . Littlefield v. Mack, 750 F. Supp. 1395, 1404 (N.D. Ill. 1990). Defendant McGuffey appeals [these decisions]. For the reasons stated below we affirm.

---

11. We note in this regard plaintiff's statement in his deposition that "(i)t is not entirely (the future threat) which caused me all of my emotional upset and disturbance that I have complained about. It was the ordeal from beginning to end." If plaintiff is able to prove a claim for intentional infliction of mental distress it will then be the difficult, but necessary, task of the trier of fact to ascertain the damages flowing from the conditional threat of future harm. Although the assaults and batteries serve to color and give impetus to the future threat and its impact on plaintiff's emotional condition, plaintiff may not recover damages flowing directly from the assaults and batteries themselves.

* [42 U.S.C. § 1982 bans intentional discrimination by governmental or private actors against non-White citizens in connection with the ownership, purchase, sale, or lease of property. The Fair Housing Act also bans such acts, but in addition regulates a wider range of conduct pertaining to housing. — Eds.]

BACKGROUND

On September 14, 1988, Ms. Littlefield, who was then 23 years old, met Malcolm McGuffey at one of his apartment buildings. After viewing the advertised apartment she completed a rental application form and gave him a $280 check as a security deposit, leaving the name of the payee blank at McGuffey's request. Later, McGuffey filled in the name of the payee with the fictitious "Santa Maria Realty," claiming at trial to have chosen that name because it had been close to Columbus Day. He endorsed the check first as "Santa Maria Realty" then as "Osvaldo Kennardo," another persona of his. At their meeting McGuffey and Ms. Littlefield had agreed she, her younger sister Sandra, and her daughter Shaunte would occupy the two-bedroom apartment and that McGuffey would purchase and install a carpet with Ms. Littlefield paying the cost of installation. McGuffey gave Ms. Littlefield a key to the apartment, and between then and September 27 she, members of her family, and friends cleaned and painted the apartment and moved various belongings into it.

On September 27, 1988, Bruce Collins, accompanied by Shaunte, the two-year old daughter of Collins and Littlefield, took a check to McGuffey to pay for the carpet installation. When McGuffey realized Mr. Collins was not the same race as Ms. Littlefield but was the father of her daughter, he became quite agitated and exclaimed "the old man" had rented the apartment to someone else. At trial McGuffey admitted he sometimes referred to himself as "the old man."

After Collins left, McGuffey called Ms. Littlefield at work and told her she could not rent the apartment because "the boss" (another of McGuffey's persona) had rented it to someone else. He also told her he had changed the locks and had put her belongings out on the porch. This was but the first of many phone calls McGuffey made to Ms. Littlefield. That evening he called her at home, identified himself as Walley Luther, and, mimicking a stereotypical black manner of speaking, told her he wanted to move in with her and "six black guys, . . . quit work and take welfare . . . and drugs with [her] . . . and swap wives with Bruce." He called her at least two more times that night and several other times that week with similar, degrading messages.

Ms. Littlefield was not the only recipient of McGuffey's harassing, insulting and racist phone calls. Her sister, Kathleen Gutierrez, was called many times over the next week or so. McGuffey told her he was a member of the Ku Klux Klan and regularly asked how her sister, Susanne, "could have [gone] to bed with a nigger and how she could . . . have a nigger baby." On one occasion McGuffey attempted to lure Ms. Gutierrez outside on the pretext that she had to move her car because the church lot where it was parked was being caulked.

The phone calls did not suffice. In early November McGuffey tracked down Ms. Littlefield's new residence and left a note, written on a napkin taped to her door, threatening the life of Bruce Collins and repeating racist slurs. When she arrived home that evening, Ms. Littlefield found her sister, Sandra, hiding behind the door, clutching a broom.

Ms. Littlefield and her witnesses . . . testified to all these events and more. Additionally, Ms. Littlefield testified to numerous episodes of severe emotional distress. She became hysterical upon receiving McGuffey's call at work, went to the restroom, and cried; the rest of the day she suffered from stomach upset and diarrhea. She experienced numerous episodes of disquiet and fright, being particularly fretful because she feared for her daughter's safety. Ms. Littlefield also testified that when she came home at night with Shaunte, she would run from her car to her apartment, clutching her daughter in one arm, with her keys in one hand and a can of mace in the other.

McGuffey denied Ms. Littlefield's allegations, claiming he had not refused her rental housing on the basis of race and that he had not harassed her. He asserted, instead, he had learned from various businesses and prior landlords that she was a poor credit risk and had a history as an undesirable tenant. He presented no witnesses, however, that confirmed having given him the negative rental-history or credit information. On the other hand, Ms. Littlefield presented witnesses [who] generally testified [that] the credit information McGuffey claimed to have acquired would not be given out and that, anyway, Ms. Littlefield's credit history was respectable. The testimony of Brice Fawcett, Ms. Littlefield's former landlord, was notably damaging for the defendant. He contradicted everything McGuffey claimed to have been told by him; he stated Ms. Littlefield had been a good tenant; and he testified McGuffey did not interview him until October 1, four days after McGuffey evicted Ms. Littlefield. As the district court observed, "Mr. McGuffey's story therefore depended almost entirely on his own credibility, and he was, to put it mildly, a witness with credibility problems." *Littlefield*, 750 F. Supp. at 1398.

ANALYSIS

. . . Mr. McGuffey raises [various] issues, [including]: (1) whether the district court erred in admitting or refusing to admit certain items of evidence, . . . (4) whether there was sufficient evidence to support the damage awards, and (5) whether the award of attorney's fees was excessive. . . .

ADMISSION OF EVIDENCE

McGuffey claims the trial court made three errors regarding admission of evidence that singly and collectively denied him a fair trial. . . .

On the merits we review claims of reversible error in a trial court's decision to admit or exclude evidence only for abuse of discretion, giving the judge great deference. . . .

[The court rejected McGuffey's first claim of error. — Eds.]

McGuffey further asserts it was error for the district court to admit Ms. Littlefield's testimony about episodes of fear and anxiety not accompanied by medically significant, physical manifestations. This claim of error fails because in Illinois physical manifestation of emotional distress is not an element of the tort of intentional infliction of emotional distress.

Under Illinois common law the tort comprises three elements.

First, the conduct involved must be truly extreme and outrageous. Second, the actor must either intend that his conduct inflict severe emotional distress, or know that there is at least a high probability that his conduct will cause severe emotional distress. Third, the conduct must in fact cause severe emotional distress.

McGrath v. Fahey, 126 Ill. 2d 78, 127 Ill. Dec. 724, 533 N.E.2d 806, 809 (1988) (citing Public Finance Corp. v. Davis, 66 Ill. 2d 85, 4 Ill. Dec. 652, 360 N.E.2d 765 (1976)). These are the only elements enunciated by the court. Medically significant, physical manifestation of emotional distress is not among them....

[Discussion of McGuffey's third claim of error omitted. — EDS.]

JURY INSTRUCTIONS

... A court of review should "proceed cautiously when asked to set aside a jury's verdict and order a new trial, bound to consume substantial judicial resources, on the ground that the instructions contained erroneous or confusing passages." Needham v. White Laboratories, Inc., 847 F.2d 355, 360 (7th Cir. 1988)....

First, McGuffey finds fault with Plaintiff's Instruction No. 21 regarding her state-law claim of intentional infliction of emotional distress. He raises numerous allegations, the essence of which is that there was insufficient evidence of past, present, or future damages to justify giving the challenged instruction.

... There is sufficient evidence in the record to support giving the challenged instruction. A perusal of the facts recited above shows Ms. Littlefield presented evidence of her having suffered severe emotional distress. Additionally, there was some evidence of that distress continuing through the time of trial. Thus, the district court was not without justification for giving the instruction with respect to past, present, and future damages....

Next, McGuffey claims the court erred in giving, over his objection, an instruction that did not state the Fair Housing Act ("FHA") capped punitive-damage awards at $1,000. At the time McGuffey racially discriminated against Ms. Littlefield, as well as at the time she initiated her action against him, the Fair Housing Act contained [a $1,000 cap] on punitive-damage awards. 42 U.S.C.A. § 3612 (West 1977). In contrast, no similar statutory limitation existed (or now exists) on punitive damages awarded under 42 U.S.C. § 1982.[3] By the time the case went to trial, however, the Fair Housing Amendment Act of 1988, codified at 42 U.S.C. §§ 3601-3619, had gone into effect. It removed the cap on punitive-damage awards....

3. Under Illinois common law, punitive damages are not available in an action for intentional infliction of emotional distress because outrageous conduct is an element of the action. [Thus, an IIED plaintiff's compensatory award is deemed by Illinois law to be sufficiently punitive in itself. — EDS.] Knierim v. Izzo, 22 Ill. 2d 73, 174 N.E.2d 157, 165 (1961).

McGuffey's specific claim of error — the claim that the FHA's damage-limitation should have been stated in the jury instruction, although there was an accompanying § 1982 claim — fails. This is because the district court was correct when it instructed the jury on the law in effect at the time of decision rather than on the prior law.

It is a long-held, general principle "that a court is to apply the law in effect at the time it renders its decision, unless doing so would result in manifest injustice or there is statutory direction or legislative history to the contrary." Bradley v. Richmond School Board, 416 U.S. 696, 711, 94 S. Ct. 2006, 2016, 40 L. Ed. 2d 476 (1974) (Award of attorney's fees permitted for services rendered before effective date of statute where the statute became effective after trial court decision but before resolution of direct appeal.).

Applying the new § 3613 to McGuffey is not a manifest injustice and is not contrary to statutory direction or legislative history. . . . [N]o material injustice was worked on the defendant by the trial court's applying the law in effect at the time of decision. Moreover, McGuffey points to no statutory directive or legislative history that clearly demonstrates removal of the cap applies only to causes of action arising after the effective date of the amendments. We are not convinced by McGuffey's argument that the statute's general delay in its effective date until 180 days after enactment constitutes a statutory direction sufficient to overcome application of the principle enunciated in *Bradley.* The trial court properly refused McGuffey's proposed instruction. . . .

SUFFICIENT EVIDENCE

. . . McGuffey's next two claims of error are that there is insufficient evidence to support the jury's verdict awarding, on the one hand, $50,000 in compensatory damages and, on the other, $100,000 in punitive damages. A damage award will not be vacated "for excessiveness unless it is 'monstrously excessive' or there is 'no rational connection between the evidence on damages and the verdict.'" Matlock v. Barnes, 932 F.2d 658, 667 (7th Cir.), *cert. denied*, 502 U.S. 909, 112 S. Ct. 304, 116 L. Ed. 2d 247 (1991) (quoting Abernathy v. Superior Hardwoods, Inc., 704 F.2d 963, 972 (7th Cir. 1983)). . . .

McGuffey claims . . . [that] the amount of the award was the result of the jury's being carried away by passion and prejudice, due in large part to Ms. Littlefield's testimony about her emotional feelings.

But it is precisely the testimony about her emotional feelings and response to his terror tactics which supports the award for the claims of intentional infliction of emotional distress and racial discrimination. For example, Ms. Littlefield testified that after Mr. McGuffey called her at work to tell her she could not move into the apartment, she became scared, went to the washroom, cried for a half hour, and left work for the day without explaining to her boss why because she was too embarrassed. She also testified that in late October or early November 1988, after moving into an apartment with her daughter and sister, a terrifying note was discovered taped to her door. The note read: "By THE Time you read this

message Kiss your Niger [sic] friend goodbye Bitch → he's dead!!!"
Plaintiff's Exhibit A. Plaintiff's handwriting expert testified the note had
been written by McGuffey, but the defendant's expert was equivocal. All
death threats are heinous and would support a finding of intentional
infliction of emotional distress. This one all the more because it employs
the most venomous and loathsome of racist epithets.

In addition, Ms. Littlefield testified she purchased cleaning, repair,
and painting supplies, that she, members of her family, and friends cleaned
and painted the apartment she was never allowed to occupy, and that she
moved numerous personal items into it. This testimony belies McGuffey's
appellate argument that Ms. Littlefield suffered no out-of-pocket loss.

Lastly, the jury's award is not out of line with other, similar awards. In
Webb v. City of Chester, Ill., 813 F.2d 824 (7th Cir. 1987), we approved an
award that included $20,250 as compensation specifically for embarrass-
ment and humiliation where a police officer successfully asserted a claim
of sexually discriminatory discharge. In Webb we also noted awards had
passed appellate review where they "ranged from a low of $500 to a high
of over $50,000." Id. at 837. At least one Illinois appellate court has
approved a compensatory-damage award of $138,450 in an action that
included a claim for intentional infliction of emotional distress. . . .

We, therefore, affirm the jury's compensatory-damage award.

McGuffey's other complaint is about the amount of the punitive-
damage award. . . .

. . . [W]e, like the district court, conclude there is sufficient evidence
to support the jury's punitive-damage award. . . . Initially, McGuffey
rejected Ms. Littlefield as a tenant because of the race of her boyfriend and
their daughter. McGuffey's subsequent acts of harassment and intimidation were entirely gratuitous and did not begin until *after* his initial act of
racial discrimination. These later acts, as Judge Williams noted, included
the following: (a) he immediately removed her belongings from the apartment, exposing them to theft and vandalism and her to public ridicule and
humiliation; (b) he made numerous, blatantly racist, harassing phone calls
to Ms. Littlefield; (c) he made similar racist, harassing phone calls to
members of Ms. Littlefield's family who did not live with her; (d) he went
to her sister's home and physically intimidated her; and (e) there is, of
course, the death threat to Bruce Collins posted on Ms. Littlefield's door.
Not only is the evidence sufficient to support the award of punitive
damages, it also supports the award of compensatory damages for the
federal and state law claims. . . .

ATTORNEY'S FEES

In his final claim of error McGuffey asserts the fees awarded
Ms. Littlefield's attorneys should be reduced to reflect what he claims are
the reasonable hours spent on the litigation. . . . A district court's rulings
on attorney's fees will rarely be reversed on appeal, and then only for
abuse of discretion. . . .

McGuffey, nonetheless, asks us to reduce the fee awarded from
approximately $140,000 to nearly $50,000 by scrutinizing and excising

some 473 individual time-charges, the largest of which is for 9.5 hours and the smallest of which is for 0.1 hours. This we shall not do. . . .

McGuffey also argues the amount of the fees awarded is disproportionately large compared to the damages awarded: approximately $140,000 versus $150,000. The size of a damage award, however, is not the gauge of a plaintiff's victory. Rather, value is gauged more broadly . . . Ms. Littlefield prevailed on her federal law claims, receiving both compensatory and punitive damages. The latter certainly will punish McGuffey and, one hopes, deter him from further violations. The award is also likely to deter others. Therefore, we find the attorney's fees awarded are not unreasonable, and the award stands. . . .

NOTES AND QUESTIONS

1. *Section 46.* The ALI first endorsed the IIED cause of action in a 1948 "Supplement" to the First Restatement, which contained the following provision:

> § 46. One who, without a privilege to do so, intentionally causes severe emotional distress to another is liable (a) for such emotional distress, and (b) for bodily harm resulting from it.

The "without . . . privilege" clause tracked language that the reporter, Dean Prosser, had used in an article published shortly after Professor Magruder's that also purported to locate the new IIED tort within the interstices of existing case law. Prosser introduced this clause in part to block use of the tort against creditors who induced severe emotional distress in others simply by insisting on their legal right ("privilege") to foreclose on property securing defaulted loans. It was replaced in 1965 by the requirement of "extreme and outrageous conduct" when Section 46 was published as part of the Second Restatement. Apparently, the ALI thought that the change of language would more effectively limit the potential scope of the new tort.

2. *Assault and IIED: Conditional Threats Revisited.* As *Dickens* makes clear, IIED has been recognized by courts in part to deal with a special class of cases that closely resemble assault, yet do not meet the definition of that tort because the defendant intentionally induces in the plaintiff an apprehension of harmful contact that will take place in the indefinite future, rather than imminently.

One of the most prominent early American decisions adopting the new tort of IIED involved this sort of threat. In State Rubbish Collectors Assn. v. Siliznoff, 240 P.2d 282 (Cal. 1952), Siliznoff, an independent hauler, obtained a contract to haul garbage from a brewery. The brewery previously had used another hauler who belonged to the association. Two association officers prevailed on Siliznoff to join, and to abide by its rules, which would have required him to compensate the prior hauler for having taken over the brewery account. Siliznoff balked, inquiring what the consequences would be if he did not, whereupon the officials informed him that he would be beaten up and his truck destroyed. During the course of a two-hour nighttime meeting, the association's officers extracted a verbal promise from Siliznoff that he would join the association and abide by its rules. Siliznoff never signed the agreement, however, and, although association members did not carry out their threat, they did sue him for breach of his promise to join and pay compensation(!). Siliznoff successfully defended against this contract claim by pleading duress, and won a jury verdict of $8,750 in compensatory and punitive damages on a counterclaim for assault (although the trial court reduced the award to $4,750).

Writing for the California Supreme Court, Justice Roger Traynor upheld the award for the plaintiff. Agreeing with the defendants that their threats failed to constitute an assault because they were conditional, and because they referred to actions that would take place at some indefinite future time, the court nonetheless concluded that Siliznoff had established a valid tort claim. Following the formulation of the 1948 Restatement supplement, Traynor reasoned that it was sufficient for the plaintiff to establish that the defendants "intentionally subject[ed] [him] to the mental suffering incident to serious threats to his physical well-being. . . ." *Id.* at 284.

3. *Statutes of Limitations: Substitute or Supplement?* Suppose that Puryear had not issued the threat on which the *Dickens* court fastened in determining that the plaintiff had pleaded a valid claim of IIED. Could Dickens have still availed himself of the longer statute of limitations by arguing that the rest of Puryear's conduct, even though it amounted to an assault, battery, and false imprisonment, also amounted to IIED? Following Section 47 of the Second Restatement, some courts have answered that question with a "no." In these jurisdictions, when the defendant's conduct would be actionable as another tort such as battery, the statute of limitations for those other torts will control. *See* K.G. v. R.T.R., 918 S.W.2d 795, 799-800 (Mo. 1996) (IIED was intended to supplement, not supplant, existing torts; a claimant who is distressed as a result of acts constituting a battery must seek compensation for that distress within the time limits set for battery actions).

Some courts have not been as clear about the relation of IIED to torts such as battery. A notable example arose out of the suit brought by Paula Jones against President Bill Clinton. According to Jones's complaint, in 1991, then-Governor Clinton arranged for an Arkansas state trooper to bring Jones, a state employee, up to his hotel room. There, he allegedly pulled her next to him, rubbed her leg, and attempted to kiss her neck. Jones further alleged that when she extricated herself and sat on a sofa across the room, the Governor lowered his pants, exposed himself, and instructed her to kiss his penis. When Jones indicated that she wanted to leave, Governor Clinton relented, warning Jones that the matter should be kept between them.

In 1994, one day prior to the third anniversary of the date on which the alleged events took place, Jones filed suit. The suit raised various federal claims for civil rights violations and employment discrimination, but also state law claims, including one for IIED.* President Clinton's lawyers moved to dismiss on the ground that the conduct alleged by Jones in connection with her IIED claim in fact supported claims for battery and/or false imprisonment, which are subject to a one-year limitations period. The trial judge rejected this argument, concluding that the facts alleged by Jones made out a colorable claim of IIED. Jones v. Clinton, 974 F. Supp. 712 (E.D. Ark. 1997). The judge did not explain, however, whether she reached this conclusion because Jones had alleged conduct *apart* from the conduct that would have established a claim for battery or false imprisonment (e.g., the alleged solicitation of oral sex), or because Jones was authorized to sue for IIED even with respect to conduct that also constituted a battery or false imprisonment.

4. *Aggravated Torts?* Outside the statute of limitations context, courts sometimes permit plaintiffs to point to the same conduct to prove that they have been the victims of a more "traditional" tort and IIED. For example, in Miller v. National Broadcasting Co., 187 Cal. App. 3d 1463 (Ct. App. 1986), the defendant's television crew followed paramedics into the plaintiff's home without her permission and there filmed for broadcast the paramedics' unsuccessful attempt to resuscitate the plaintiff's husband, who had suffered a heart attack. The appellate court affirmed the trial court's denial of the defendant's summary judgment motion on claims for trespass, invasion of privacy, and IIED, even though the operative facts of the IIED claim seem to have been identical to those of the trespass and privacy claims.

Arguably, in cases such as *Miller*, the court's recognition of an IIED claim serves to indicate that the defendant has committed an "aggravated" (i.e., especially culpable) version of these other torts. Recognition of an IIED action in these contexts thus resembles a finding of malice or reckless indifference of the sort that justifies the imposition of punitive damages. See Chapter 8; *see also id.* (noting that defendant's conduct evidenced not just a trespass and an invasion of privacy, but also a callous disregard for plaintiff's rights). Consider in this regard Burgess v. Taylor, 44 S.W.3d 806 (Ky. Ct. App. 2001). Plaintiff was deeply attached to her two horses, but couldn't adequately maintain them on her property. Although she retained ownership, she arranged for them to live on defendants' farm after defendants professed to be fellow horse-lovers. Shortly thereafter, defendants sold the horses for slaughter, then attempted to cover up their actions. The intermediate appellate court upheld plaintiff's claim for IIED even though the action could and probably should have been framed as a claim for the tort of conversion — unlawful destruction of personal property. In effect, the outrageousness of the defendants' conduct marked this as an instance of particularly malicious or aggravated conversion.

---

* President Clinton's lawyers initially argued that the suit should be stayed during the term of his presidency. The Supreme Court, however, ruled that a sitting president enjoys no special privilege to delay litigation that does not concern actions connected with his office.

5. *Outrageous!: Law or Fact?* Comment d to Section 46 of the Restatement provides an oft-cited explication of the "extreme and outrageous conduct" requirement:

> d. ... It has not been enough that the defendant has ... intended to inflict emotional distress, or even that his conduct has been characterized by "malice," or a degree of aggravation which would entitle the plaintiff to punitive damages for another tort. Liability has been found only where the conduct has been so outrageous in character, and so extreme in degree, as to *go beyond all possible bounds of decency*, and to be regarded as *atrocious, and utterly intolerable* in a civilized community. Generally, the case is one in which the recitation of the facts to an average member of the community would arouse his resentment against the actor, and lead him to exclaim "*Outrageous!*" (emphasis added).

By contrast, comment d indicates that the tort is *not* available to remedy "mere *insults, indignities, threats, annoyances, petty oppressions, or other trivialities*" (emphasis added). Many courts, following comment h to Section 46, have held that the question of whether conduct is "extreme and outrageous" is a question of law for the court. Others, however, deem it for the jury. Compare Jalowy v. Friendly Home, Inc., 818 A.2d 698 (R.I. 2003) (outrageousness is a question of law for the court, although the court may need to rely on the jury to find certain facts in relation to this determination); Harris v. Jefferson Partners, L.P., 653 N.W.2d 496 (S.D. 2002) (outrageousness initially is a question for the trial court) *with* Miller v. National Broadcasting Co., 187 Cal. App. 3d 1463 (Ct. App. 1986) (the jury should be left to determine if defendant's conduct was outrageous).

6. *The High Bar of Outrageousness: Jones v. Clinton.* Regardless of whether it is cast as a question of law or a mixed question law and fact, the concept of "extreme and outrageous conduct" defies general description. Still, as a rough-and-ready rule, it is probably the case that judges are strongly *dis*inclined to deem conduct sufficiently abominable to meet the standard. Although it is in some respects unique because it took place in the midst of a storm of partisan politics, the trial judge's decision on the issue of outrageousness in Jones v. Clinton fairly conveys the height of this doctrinal hurdle.

As noted above, the claim in Jones v. Clinton was that then-Governor Clinton had arranged for a state trooper to bring Paula Jones, a state employee, to his hotel room, where he allegedly pulled her next to him, rubbed her leg, and attempted to kiss her, then exposed himself and solicited oral sex. After the lawsuit proceeded through discovery — which led to the now-infamous deposition in which President Clinton denied having had sex with White House intern Monica Lewinsky — the President's lawyers moved for summary judgment, in part on the ground that even if Jones's allegations were credited, they failed as a matter of law to establish outrageous conduct. The federal district judge agreed. Jones v. Clinton, 990 F. Supp. 657 (E.D. Ark. 1998). Specifically, the court reasoned that Jones had only alleged "a mere sexual proposition or encounter, albeit an odious one, that was relatively brief in duration, did not involve any coercion or threats of reprisal and was abandoned as soon as plaintiff made clear that the advance was not welcome." *Id.* at 677. (Jones's appeal of this and other rulings were dismissed when the parties settled.)

Do you suppose that an "average" citizen confronted with the conduct alleged by Jones would be inclined to exclaim "Outrageous!"?

7. *Other Examples of "Merely Offensive, Insulting, or Careless" Conduct.* Compare to *Jones* the following decisions in which other courts have ruled that the defendant's conduct was merely inappropriate, offensive, and/or careless, rather than extreme and outrageous:

- Defendant, a priest who became very friendly with plaintiff parishioner and his family, commenced an adulterous affair with plaintiff's wife. While "acknowledg[ing] what must be [the plaintiff's] acute sense of betrayal," the court held that the priest's conduct was insufficient as a matter of law to support a claim for IIED. The court's assessment was influenced by the state's abolition of tort actions for interference with marital relations. It also distinguished an earlier decision that had reached the opposite result on very similar facts. That decision, it reasoned, had turned on the fact that the priest had become romantically involved with the plaintiff's wife only after the plaintiff and his wife specifically sought out the priest for marriage counseling. Arlinghaus v. Gallenstein, 115 S.W.3d 351 (Ky. Ct. App. 2003) (distinguishing Osborne v. Payne, 31 S.W.3d 911 (Ky. 2000)).

- Plaintiff's home caught fire, causing property damage. Inspectors for the defendant, the plaintiff's insurer, quickly concluded, in part on the basis of racist assumptions, that the plaintiff had deliberately set the fire. In doing so, they ignored contrary evidence that would later lead a fire department investigator to conclude that the fire was caused accidentally. As a result, the insurer denied coverage for damage to the plaintiff's personal property. The court concluded that the conduct of the defendant's employees may have been negligent and offensive, but was not outrageous. Carrol v. Allstate Ins. Co., 815 A.2d 119 (Conn. 2003).

- Defendant, owner of an office building, was concerned that his tenant, a failing business, was attempting to sell its equipment to defeat his ability to collect on debts it owed to him. The defendant appeared at the building and launched a profanity-laced tirade at the plaintiff, the business's human resources director. The plaintiff hyperventilated and fainted, allegedly suffering a minor stroke. The appellate court affirmed summary judgment for the defendant on the ground that defendant's verbal abuse constituted neither an assault (as there was insufficient evidence that the plaintiff could reasonably apprehend that the defendant was about to cause her harmful or offensive contact), nor IIED (because the defendant's conduct was merely rude, not outrageous). Johnson v. Cantrell, 1999 WL 5083 (Tenn. Ct. App. 1999).

- Plaintiff, an African-American, entered the defendant's department store to pick up an item being held for her. A dispute arose with a store employee, who proceeded to call the plaintiff a "nigger." Although "by no means condon[ing] the derogatory and offensive language" used by the employee, the court held that, in and of itself, the utterance of an epithet during the course of a disagreement is not outrageous as a matter of law. Dawson v. Zayre Dept. Stores, 499 A.2d 648 (Pa. Super. Ct. 1985).

8. *Examples of Outrageous Conduct.* In addition to the main cases and to note cases such as *Siliznoff*, consider the following examples of conduct deemed by a judge or jury to be outrageous. Was the conduct in these cases obviously more egregious than some of the conduct found not to be outrageous in the decisions described in Notes 6 and 7?

- Defendant, the plaintiff's bitter ex-husband, copied photographs of the plaintiff, taken when they were married, that depicted the plaintiff naked and having sex. Included on the copies were the plaintiff's name, employer, and phone number. Defendant posted 60 of these documents in the neighborhood in which the plaintiff lived. Cheatam v. Pohle, 789 N.E.2d 467 (Ind. 2003) (noting and presuming the validity of the verdict in favor of the plaintiff).

- After jurors rendered a verdict against a doctor in a medical malpractice action, defendant, another doctor, placed a flyer in the mailbox of each physician who worked at a local hospital. The flyer identified by name and address each juror, and stated that each had found a doctor "guilty" of malpractice. Plaintiffs, the former jurors, alleged that the defendant's conduct was designed to prevent them from receiving adequate medical care at the only hospital in their locality. Burgess v. Busby, 544 S.E.2d 4 (N.C. Ct. App. 2001) (overturning the trial court's grant of the defendant's motion to dismiss the plaintiffs' IIED claims).

- In violation of several restraining orders, defendant, the plaintiff's former roommate, stalked the plaintiff by means of hundreds of phone calls to her and to her friends, at times issuing nonspecific threats of physical harm. Kloepfel v. Bokor, 66 P.3d 630 (Wash. 2003) (ruling that an IIED plaintiff need not demonstrate physical harm or physical symptoms in order to recover).

- Plaintiff, mother of two, filed a complaint alleging the following facts. Plaintiff was sexually assaulted by an intruder in her home in the middle of the night. After fighting with the assailant, the plaintiff managed to escape, but the assailant then locked her out of her apartment, leaving him alone with her two young children. Hearing the plaintiff's screams, the neighbors called the police. Defendant was the police officer in charge of the crime scene. Ignoring the plaintiff's hysterical pleas for assistance in rescuing her children, and notwithstanding that she had quite evidently fled her apartment under duress, the defendant interrogated the plaintiff rudely as to why she had left the children with a stranger, and why she had left the apartment without a key. He also refused to break down the door of the apartment, citing concern over being held liable for the property damage, even though a supervisor had ordered him to gain immediate entry into the apartment and the plaintiff had assured him that she would pay for any such damage. While the defendant delayed, the assailant raped the plaintiff's daughter. These allegations were deemed sufficient to survive a motion to dismiss for failure to state a claim for IIED. Doe v. Calumet City, 641 N.E.2d 498 (Ill. 1994), *overruled on other grounds,* In re Chicago Flood Litig., 680 N.E.2d 265 (Ill. 1997).

9. *Proof of Emotional Distress.* In addition to presenting evidence sufficient to establish intent (or recklessness) and extreme and outrageous conduct, an IIED plaintiff must also prove that the conduct has caused her *severe* emotional distress. Thus, in contrast to certain claims for NIED, discussed in Section II below, severity is incorporated as a component of the plaintiff's prima facie case. According to comment j to Restatement (Second) Section 46,

> some degree of transient and trivial emotional distress is a part of the price of living among people. The law intervenes only where the distress inflicted is *so severe that no reasonable man could be expected to endure it.* (Emphasis added).

The corresponding burden of proof placed on an IIED plaintiff can be illustrated by returning once again to Jones v. Clinton. As noted above, the trial court there granted a defense motion for summary judgment on the ground that the conduct alleged was not "outrageous." In addition, the court ruled that Jones had failed to produce evidence that would permit a reasonable jury to conclude that she had suffered the sort of severe distress described in comment j. In support of its conclusion, the trial judge noted that Jones (1) did not miss any work following the alleged incident, (2) continued to remain in her government job for 19 months without complaint even though it required her to go to the office of the governor on a daily basis, (3) never complained, formally or informally, to a supervisor, (4) never consulted a therapist or psychiatrist, (5) had two subsequent and admittedly "friendly" social encounters with Governor Clinton, and (6) did not suffer adverse effects in her marriage. "Plaintiff's actions and statements," the court concluded, "do not portray someone who experienced emotional distress so severe in nature that no reasonable person could be expected to endure it." 990 F. Supp. at 678. The court also refused to credit the declaration of Jones's expert "who, after a 3.5 hour meeting with the plaintiff and her husband a mere four days prior to the filing of President Clinton's motion for summary judgment, opine[d] that [the] alleged encounter . . . caused plaintiff to suffer severe emotional distress. . . ." *Id.*

10. *Dignitary or Harm-Based Tort?* By bringing order to what struck them and others as an ad hoc collection of cases, Magruder and Prosser performed the valuable service of providing an analytic structure that lawyers and judges could use to assess the merits of claims for wrongs of the sort seen in *Wilkinson*, *Nickerson*, *Dickens*, and *Littlefield*. Still, their insistence of proof of severe emotional distress as part of the plaintiff's prima facie case arguably points to a tension within their renditions of this cause of action.

As explained above, the common thread that Magruder and Prosser saw in the cases was that the defendant had acted in an outrageous manner for the purpose of causing severe emotional distress in the plaintiff. This description seems to emphasize two different features of the cases: the egregious way in which the defendant *mistreated* the plaintiff, but also the *emotional impact* that the plaintiff stood to suffer and did suffer from the mistreatment. The former emphasis arguably suggests that IIED belongs in the realm of dignitary torts along with actions such as assault and battery. On this view, the wrong done to Nickerson was the wrong of humiliating her. Likewise, the wrong done to Littlefield was that of discriminating against and harassing her because of her (and her boyfriend's) race. On a view that instead emphasizes the harm suffered by the victim, IIED more closely resembles actions such as negligence. In this rendition, the wrong done to both Nickerson and Littlefield was that of acting toward the plaintiffs in a manner calculated to cause them serious harm.

Admittedly, the difference between these two characterizations is subtle — they will end up covering a lot of the same ground simply because severe emotional distress is a common reaction to being badly mistreated. Nonetheless, it might be important. Conceived as a dignitary wrong, IIED in principle perhaps ought to permit victims such as Nickerson and Littlefield to recover *even if the defendant's conduct, for whatever reason, does not happen to cause the victim to suffer severe distress.* Conceived as a harm-based wrong, IIED will permit victims to recover only if their emotional reaction to their mistreatment is "extreme." As we have seen, victims of batteries and assaults are permitted to proceed with claims against intentional wrongdoers notwithstanding the absence of severe harm. Why should the rule be any different for IIED victims (many of whom will have been subjected to more egregious misconduct than victims of these other torts)? If the concern is to avoid "opening the floodgates," isn't it enough to maintain, as courts generally have done, a narrow definition of outrageousness?

11. *Punitive Damages: Common Law and Statute.* The rule of Illinois law cited in footnote 3 of *Littlefield* — which sets a per se bar on the award of punitive damages for IIED claims — appears to be unusual. Most states' courts will permit juries to award punitive damages based on proof of the elements of IIED. Can you make sense of the Illinois rule? If punitive damages are not warranted for IIED claims because those claims seek redress for being outrageously mistreated, wouldn't that same reasoning suggest the denial of recovery of such damages in cases of battery or false imprisonment?

As *Littlefield* notes, Congress amended the Fair Housing Act in 1988 by eliminating the $1,000 cap on punitive damage awards to successful FHA claimants. Because the 1998 amendments had not been enacted at the time of Littlefield's discriminatory acts, he argued that it was unfair to subject him to a penalty of which he had no notice. The *Littlefield* court obviously was unimpressed with this argument, in part because it regarded Littlefield's separate claim under 42 U.S.C. § 1982 as providing an independent ground for the jury's punitive award.

In 1994, the U.S. Supreme Court considered the retroactive effect of the punitive damages provisions of another piece of federal antidiscrimination legislation: the Civil Rights Act of 1991. That act for the first time allowed juries to award compensatory and punitive damages to victims of employment discrimination on the basis of race, gender, or religion. The Court concluded that these provisions could not be applied retroactively because it would unfairly saddle employers with substantial additional liability of which they had no notice. Landgraf v. USI Film Prods., 511 U.S. 244 (1994). Although *Landgraf* did not purport to interpret the FHA— which, unlike the laws amended by the Civil Rights Act, already provided for limited punitive damages prior to its amendment—its reluctance to apply new punitive damages provisions retroactively arguably runs counter to *Littlefield*'s analysis.

12. *Intent and Recklessness*. The extreme and outrageous conduct and emotional distress elements form the core of the IIED tort. However, they are not the only elements that a plaintiff must make out in order to recover. Most obviously, the plaintiff must offer proof sufficient to establish *intent*. Proof that the defendant acted for the purpose of causing the plaintiff severe emotional distress, or with knowledge that such distress was substantially certain to result, will suffice just as it does for claims of assault or battery. IIED differs from those torts, however, in that its standard formulations also permit liability to attach for *reckless* infliction of severe emotional distress through outrageous conduct. Consider how the recklessness standard is analyzed and applied in the following decision.

Doe 1 v. Roman Catholic Diocese of Nashville
2003 WL 22171558 (Tenn. Ct. App. 2003)

Cottrell, J.   ... John Doe 1, his mother, and John Doe 2 seek to hold the Roman Catholic Diocese of Nashville liable for injuries [to each of them] caused by the alleged outrageous conduct of the Diocese in its dealings with Edward McKeown, a former priest, who sexually molested John Doe 1 and John Doe 2 a number of years after his affiliation with the Diocese ended. The trial court granted the Diocese's summary judgment motion, finding the Does had failed as a matter of law to satisfy the threshold requirements for stating a claim for the tort of outrageous conduct....

Edward McKeown became a Catholic priest in 1970. In 1986, a parent reported to ... [the] Diocese ... that Mr. McKeown had molested her son when he was a minor attending a Diocesan school in 1972 or 1973.

Mr. McKeown admitted to the molestation when confronted by the [Diocese's] Bishop.[1] Mr. McKeown was evaluated and diagnosed with a sexual disorder.[2] He was sent to the Institute of Living in Hartford, Connecticut in October of 1986 for treatment.

Upon his release in March 1987, Mr. McKeown returned to Nashville where he continued counseling and underwent Depo-Provera injections, as recommended by the treatment facility. . . . In 1989, after learning about another . . . incident [of inappropriate conduct toward a young boy],[4] the Diocese . . . removed Mr. McKeown from the priesthood.[5] Charitable support for Mr. McKeown continued until 1994.[6]

Following his termination from the Diocese, Mr. McKeown moved off Diocesan property and into a mobile home community and began working for the Juvenile Court Clerk. He was transferred to the Metro Tax Assessor's Office in 1990, following receipt of information about Mr. McKeown's past. However, Mr. McKeown returned to work part-time in the Juvenile Court Clerk's office in 1994, while still at the Assessor's office. Sometime during this period of time, Mr. McKeown began to molest young boys again.

In 1991, Mr. McKeown met John Doe 2 and his mother at the mobile home community where they all lived. He befriended the family. In 1993, Mr. McKeown started taking John Doe 2 to school and to football games. In approximately 1994, John Doe 2 started spending the night at Mr. McKeown's trailer, and Mr. McKeown began molesting John Doe 2. During 1994, Mr. McKeown molested John Doe 2 on numerous occasions. . . .

[McKeown likewise repeatedly molested John Doe 1 from 1995 to 1999. In 1999 John Doe 1 told Jane Doe 1 of his abuse, and she reported McKeown to the police.] Mr. McKeown admitted to the abuse of John Doe 1 and other children from 1973 through 1999 and was criminally prosecuted. He is currently serving a twenty-five year prison term.

As this brief recitation of facts demonstrates, at the time John Doe 1 and John Doe 2 were sexually abused by Mr. McKeown, he had been removed from the priesthood for five years or more. He was not an employee of the Diocese, had no actual or apparent authority to represent the Diocese, and had no indicia of priesthood or other authority from the

---

1. There is some dispute regarding whether the Diocese, when it discovered the sexual abuse in 1986, reported the . . . abuse to state authorities. . . . Because the ruling of the trial court under review . . . did not require resolution of this factual dispute, the court found it did not prevent summary judgment.

2. Plaintiffs allege that during this evaluation Mr. McKeown admitted to molesting over thirty (30) boys over a fourteen (14) year period and that this information was included in reports sent to the Diocese.

4. Mr. McKeown gave an underage male a condom as a Christmas gift.

5. McKeown was ordered to halt performing any and all priestly functions, move off Diocesan property, and to not work for the Diocese in any capacity. . . . [T]he [trial] court specifically found that ". . . after 1989 Mr. McKeown had no active employment relationship with the Diocese and no responsibilities with the church."

6. . . . [T]he Diocese paid Mr. McKeown support of $1,500 per month. In addition, it continued health care benefits for Mr. McKeown, which included the cost of his treatment and therapy until 1990 or 1991. The total amount of support over the period amounted to over $50,000. . . .

church. John Doe 1 and John Doe 2 met Mr. McKeown as a neighbor, not through any church-related activities or functions. Neither child was Catholic or had any relationship with the Roman Catholic Church or the Nashville Diocese.

These facts shaped the kind of lawsuit available to the plaintiffs.... John Doe 1, Jane Doe 1 and John Doe 2 do not seek to impute liability to the Diocese for the conduct of Edward McKeown under the theories of respondeat superior or negligent hiring, supervision, and retention by the church. Instead, the Does fault the Diocese primarily for not properly investigating and reporting Mr. McKeown to the authorities so that he would have been prosecuted and imprisoned and, consequently, unable to molest them. Rather than seeking to hold the Diocese vicariously responsible for Mr. McKeown's conduct, they assert the Diocese is liable because of its own conduct.

Specifically, the Does argue that the Diocese "engaged in repeated acts designed to conceal wrongdoing by an employee out of fear of financial responsibility and embarrassment with knowledge that others are being or will be harmed by the active silence" which allowed Mr. McKeown to remain in the community and continue to prey on young boys such as the victims here.

... The cause of action against the Diocese was based solely on outrageous conduct....

Summary judgments enjoy no presumption of correctness on appeal. Accordingly, appellate courts must make a fresh determination that the [relevant legal] requirements ... have been satisfied. We must consider the evidence in the light most favorable to the non-moving party, and we must resolve all inferences in the non-moving party's favor....

"Outrageous conduct" and "intentional infliction of emotional distress" are simply different names for the same cause of action. Bain v. Wells, 936 S.W.2d 618, 622 n.3 (Tenn. 1997)....[13]

... The Restatement [Second of Torts] established the definition and elements of the tort that have been adopted by a majority of courts:

§ 46. OUTRAGEOUS CONDUCT CAUSING SEVERE EMOTIONAL DISTRESS

(1) One who by extreme and outrageous conduct intentionally or recklessly causes severe emotional distress to another is subject to liability for such emotional distress, and if bodily harm to the other results from it, for such bodily harm.

(2) Where such conduct is directed at a third person, the actor is subject to liability if he intentionally or recklessly causes severe emotional distress

(a) to a member of such person's immediate family who is present at the time, whether or not such distress results in bodily harm, or

(b) to any other person who is present at the time, if such distress results in bodily harm.

---

13. Plaintiffs have not sued the Diocese for negligent infliction of emotional distress, a separate tort based on theories of negligence including duty, breach of duty, cause in fact, proximate causation, and injury.

In Tennessee, the tort of outrageous conduct was first recognized by our Supreme Court in Medlin [v. Allied Inv. Co.], 217 Tenn. [469,] 398 S.W.2d [270] [(1966)]. . . . Later, in Miller v. Willbanks, 8 S.W.3d 607, 611-12 (Tenn. 1999), the Court described *Medlin* as holding that, in the context of *intentional* conduct, a plaintiff has a right to emotional tranquility that gives rise to a cause of action for its violation.

[*Medlin* incorporated into Tennessee law the "beyond all possible bounds of decency . . ." standard for outrageousness specified in comment d to Section 46 of the Second Restatement. It is reproduced in Note 5 following *Littlefield*. — EDS.] . . .

The[ ] [element of outrageousness], however, do[es] not define the scope of the tort. Regardless of how outrageous, unacceptable, or even despicable a defendant's conduct may be, not all such conduct results in liability to the particular plaintiff . . . in the absence of other required elements. . . .

First, the conduct complained of must be intentional or reckless. *Miller*, 8 S.W.3d at 612; *Bain*, 936 S.W.2d at 622. "A negligent or inadvertent act will not give rise to a claim of outrageous conduct." Johnson v. Woman's Hosp., 527 S.W.2d 133, 138 (Tenn. Ct. App. 1975). The intent requirement relates not just to the act, but also to its consequences. *See* W. Page Keeton, Prosser and Keeton on the Law of Torts, § 8 (5th ed. 1984) (intent includes the desire to bring about certain results as well as the knowledge those results are substantially certain to occur).

The Restatement groups this tort with other intentional torts, characterized as intentional invasions of interest in personality, including battery, assault, and false imprisonment. All involve acts that are tortious because they are intended to cause an invasion of a legally protected right. Restatement, *supra* § 6. . . . Section 46(1) itself relates the defendant's intent to the effect of his or her acts. Section 46 applies where the actor desires to inflict severe emotional distress and also where he knows that such distress is certain, or substantially certain, to result from his conduct. It also applies where the actor acts recklessly in deliberate disregard of a high degree of probability that the emotional distress will follow. Restatement, *supra* § 46 cmt. i. Additionally, the Restatement makes clear that the rule in § 46 "creates liability only where the actor intends to invade the interest in freedom from severe emotional distress." Restatement, *supra* § 47 cmt. a.

Accordingly, it has been held that a cause of action for intentional infliction of emotional distress must allege facts showing outrageous conduct which is "of a nature especially calculated to cause . . . mental distress of a very serious kind." Christensen v. Superior Court, 820 P.2d 181, 203-04 (Cal. 1992) (quoting Ochoa v. Superior Court, 703 P.2d 1, 4 n.5 (Cal. 1985)); *see also* Gibson v. Brewer, 952 S.W.2d 239, 249 (Mo. 1997) (holding that the conduct must be "intended only to cause extreme emotional distress to the victim."); Vallinoto v. DiSandro, 688 A.2d 830, 839 (R.I. 1997) (although plaintiff alleged the defendant's sexual misconduct was intentional, the tort also requires an intent to inflict emotional injuries). The intent or reckless disregard of the consequences must be specific to a particular person. Witherspoon v. Philip Morris Inc., 964 F.

Supp. 455, 463 (U.S. D.C. 1997) (holding that "[p]recedent demonstrates that the tort of intentional infliction of emotional distress requires a high standard of intent, that is, the intent must be to actually cause emotional harm and it must be specifically directed toward the person complaining of emotional harm")....

Tennessee courts have also related the intent requirement to the consequences or effect of defendant's acts. *Bain*, 936 S.W.2d at 622 (quoting the Restatement); *Women's Hosp.*, 527 S.W.2d at 138 ("which conduct intentionally or recklessly causes such severe emotional distress"). In *Women's Hospital*, the court found that the conduct complained of, displaying the body of a deceased prematurely born infant preserved in a jar of formaldehyde to the mother, was intentional, not inadvertent. "It is admitted in the proof that the display was exactly what was intended." *Id.* The court then concluded that "a jury could find that the conduct of displaying the infant in the manner and under circumstances described was outrageous conduct . . . and that such conduct recklessly caused severe emotional distress to [the mother]." *Id.* at 140....

Thus, the intent element requires that the defendant intend to cause emotional distress to the plaintiff or act in reckless disregard of that consequence to the plaintiff. In both situations, an identified individual (or group [of] individuals) is the object of the intent or reckless disregard.... The exception is where a bystander is emotionally distressed by conduct directed at another, and in that situation, the defendant's knowledge of the bystander's presence serves the purpose of establishing the substantial certainty or reckless disregard element. Keeton et al., *supra* § 12. This limitation is consistent with the remaining element of this intentional tort.

The final requirement for liability to attach is, as the trial court herein found, that the extreme or outrageous conduct must be directed at the plaintiff or occur in the presence of the plaintiff. This conclusion results from § 46 itself, which is divided into two subsections. The first subsection, § 46(1), concerns conduct directed at the plaintiff, and the second, § 46(2), concerns conduct directed at a third person. The requirements for recovery differ depending upon whether the plaintiff was the object of the conduct or was merely present when the conduct, directed at someone else, occurred. Johnson v. Caparelli, 625 A.2d 668, 671 (Pa. Super. 1993) (stating that § 46(1) applies to situations where a person suffers emotional distress as a result of outrageous conduct directed at that individual, while "by way of contrast," § 46(2) applies to persons who suffer emotional distress as a result of outrageous conduct directed at a third party)....

While § 46(1) does not expressly include the words, "directed at," it is clear from the structure of the entire section on "Outrageous Conduct Causing Severe Emotional Distress" that the requirement is understood. The second subsection begins by distinguishing itself from the first, stating it applies "where such conduct is directed at a third person." Restatement, *supra* § 46(2). Additionally, none of the fact situations used as examples in Section 46 involve a situation where the challenged conduct was not directed at a specific individual or individuals.

Comment l to the Restatement, § 46 provides clarification as to the second circumstance in which a defendant can be liable, sometimes called a bystander claim.

> l. Conduct directed at a third person. Where the extreme and outrageous conduct is directed at a third person, as where, for example, a husband is murdered in the presence of his wife, the actor may know that it is substantially certain, or at least highly probable, that it will cause severe emotional distress to the plaintiff. In such cases the rule of this Section applies. The cases thus far decided, however, have limited such liability to plaintiffs who were present at the time, as distinguished from those who discover later what has occurred. . . . The Caveat [to this section][18] is intended, however, to leave open the possibility of situations in which presence at the time may not be required. Furthermore, the decided cases in which recovery has been allowed have been those in which the plaintiffs have been near relatives, or at least close associates, of the person attacked. The language of the cases is not, however, limited to such plaintiffs. . . .

A number of courts have addressed the "directed at" requirement. "To support the cause of action, [i]t is not enough that the conduct be intentional and outrageous. It must be conduct directed at the plaintiff, or occur in the presence of a plaintiff of whom the defendant is aware." *Christensen*, 820 P.2d at 181. With regard to the first subsection of § 46, "Even malicious, wilful or wanton conduct will not warrant a recovery for the infliction of emotional distress if the conduct was not directed toward the plaintiff." Meagher v. Lamb Weston, Inc., 839 F. Supp. 1403, 1409 (D. Ore. 1993). . . .

The trial court herein held that the Does did not meet the requirement that the conduct of the Diocese, even if outrageous, must have been directed at a specific or particular person. The Does argue that the trial court engrafted a new element onto the tort. We respectfully disagree.

First, our review of authority convinces us that the trial court merely expressly stated what has been implicit in holdings by Tennessee's courts since the *Medlin* decision. In each of these cases, the conduct complained of was directed at the plaintiff. . . .

. . . As discussed above, the Restatement clearly includes a requirement that the outrageous conduct be directed at a particular individual, either the plaintiff or a third party in the plaintiff's presence. "Simply put, intentional conduct is 'directed' at a particular victim; inattention [or negligence] is not similarly 'directed at' a chosen victim." David Crump, *Evaluating Independent Torts Based Upon "Intentional" or "Negligent" Infliction of Emotional Distress: How Can We Keep the Baby from Dissolving in the Bath Water?*, 34 Ariz. L. Rev. 439, 464 (1992).

---

18. . . . [The Caveat to Section 46] recognizes certain situations may arise where presence of the plaintiff may not be required. The most often cited example occurred when a man committed suicide in the plaintiff's home, while she was in another room, with certain knowledge she would find his body. . . .

The trial court herein found:

> However one might judge the conduct of the Diocese, the plaintiffs' case is fatally flawed because there is simply not the appropriate link between the alleged conduct and the sexual assaults on the plaintiffs.

The court based this holding on the "directed at" element of the tort and its finding that even if the Diocese failed to report Mr. McKeown when it should have, that conduct was not directed at the plaintiffs or at anyone with whom the plaintiffs had a close personal relationship. . . .

The Does strenuously argue that the trial court misapplied and confused the concepts of intent, recklessness, foreseeability and causation in concluding there was not a sufficient link between the Diocese's conduct and the harm to the Does. Plaintiffs assert there was sufficient proof of intent on the part of the Diocese to avoid summary judgment on the basis that the actor need only intend the act, not the consequences of that act, relying on the "recklessly" language of § 46 . . . and on comment *i* to § 46 to the effect that § 46 applies not only where there is intent to inflict emotional distress . . . but also where the actor acts recklessly in deliberate disregard of a high degree of probability that emotional distress will follow. . . . [T]he plaintiffs argue that the intent element of intentional infliction of emotional distress can be satisfied by a showing that "any reasonable person knew or should have known that emotional distress may flow from the outrageous conduct."

While counsel for the plaintiffs has skillfully constructed this argument, we disagree that it sets forth the standard for this intentional tort. Intent, recklessness, and negligence connote different degrees of culpability and potential liability. Restatement, *supra* § 8A cmt. a. For conduct to be considered reckless, the probability that harm will result must be substantially greater than is required for ordinary negligence. Restatement, *supra* § 500 cmt. a. The difference in the degree of risk "is so marked as to amount substantially to a difference in kind." Restatement, *supra* § 500 cmt. g.

The plaintiffs' argument in this regard asks us to incorporate into this intentional tort concepts, such as foreseeability, that apply in negligence-based causes of action. We decline to do so because it would blur if not eradicate the distinction between intentional infliction of emotional distress and its negligence-based counterpart. They are separate torts addressed to substantially different types of conduct affording different types of damages. Additionally, the plaintiffs' arguments regarding intent do not dispense with the "directed at" requirement, and we have already determined that such a requirement exists, in spite of the plaintiffs' arguments to the contrary.

The tort of intentional infliction of emotional distress through outrageous conduct is limited in its scope and applicability. It was recognized solely to subject to liability a defendant who, beyond all bounds of decency "purposely causes a disturbance of another's mental and emotional tranquility." Calvert Magruder, *Mental and Emotional Disturbance in the Law of Torts*, 49 Harv. L. Rev. 1033, 1058 (1936).

Accordingly, it has been recognized by courts in only certain situations. "The requirements of the rule are rigorous, and difficult to satisfy." Keeton, et al., *supra* § 12, at 60-61.

The requirement of specific intent and the requirement that the outrageous conduct be directed at a particular person are related. They are consistent with similar requirements applicable to the other intentional torts with which they are grouped in the Restatement: battery, assault, and false imprisonment. All those torts, obviously, involve actions and intent toward a particular person. The requirements address concerns of expanding potential plaintiffs beyond those whose interest in emotional tranquility is directly affected by defendant's intentional conduct. They express the factor of proximity, whether temporal or physical, that ensures the distress suffered by the plaintiff is directly related to the defendant's conduct, and that the conduct itself is what provokes the outrage or distress. They also distinguish the intentional tort of outrageous conduct from the negligence based tort of negligent infliction of emotional distress. Adopting the foreseeability argument propounded by the plaintiffs here would eliminate that distinction.

. . . As the trial court found, unless the other elements necessary to proceed are present, it is not necessary to reach a decision on whether the conduct of the Diocese could be found by a jury to be outrageous under the applicable legal standard. Accordingly, we affirm the judgment of the trial court. . . .

NOTES AND QUESTIONS

1. *Recklessness and the "Directed At" Requirement.* Is the *Doe* court taking the position that the Diocese's alleged failure to report a known serial child molester to authorities was not reckless conduct? If not, what is missing from the plaintiffs' allegations such that, as a matter of law, the Diocese cannot be held liable? Assume that the plaintiffs have sufficiently alleged reckless and outrageous conduct by the Diocese causing severe emotional trauma. What does it mean for the court to say that this conduct was not "directed at" the plaintiffs? Where does that requirement come from?

Recall from Chapter 9 the doctrine of *transferred intent*, by which the intent to commit one dignitary tort against a victim can support a finding of liability for another dignitary tort against another victim. (Thus, if *D* shoots at *T*, intending to hit him, but succeeds only in causing *V* to apprehend that she is about to be shot, *D* can be held liable for assaulting *V*.) Because they tend to regard transferred intent as an anomalous holdover reflecting tort law's medieval (and criminal law) origins, courts and commentators generally insist that the doctrine has no place in the law of a "modern" cause of action such as IIED. *See, e.g.*, Dan B. Dobbs, *The Law of Torts* § 43, at 81 (2000). Thus, suppose that *D* intentionally but unsuccessfully shoots at *C*. Suppose further that *P*, *C*'s parent, later learns of *D*'s attempted shooting of *C* and suffers severe emotional distress as a result. *P* will not be permitted to combine *D*'s intent to batter

C with *D*'s having caused *P* severe emotional distress to generate a claim of IIED. Does the nonapplicability of transferred intent to IIED claims help support the *Doe* court's adoption of the "directed at" requirement?

2. *Recklessness and Known Vulnerabilities.* Just as an intentional touching that would not otherwise be offensive can be rendered offensive if the actor who causes the touching knows that it will offend the victim, so, too, conduct that might not otherwise be deemed extreme and outrageous may become so if it involves purposeful preying on — or even reckless disregard for — a plaintiff's known vulnerability. *See, e.g.,* Gordon v. Frost, 388 S.E.2d 362 (Ga. Ct. App. 1989) (upholding jury finding of outrageousness against a pharmacist who caused a patient to be arrested for fraud in reckless disregard for what he knew from repeated interactions to be her vulnerable emotional condition).

3. *Bystanders and Derivative Actions.* As noted in *Doe*, Section 46 of the Second Restatement of Torts contains two separate provisions. Section 46(1) is the basic provision that has been discussed throughout this chapter. Section 46(2) adds that:

> (2) Where . . . [extreme and outrageous] conduct is directed at a third person, the actor is subject to liability if he intentionally or recklessly causes severe emotional distress
> > (a) to a member of such person's immediate family who is present at the time . . . , or
> > (b) to any other person who is present at the time if such distress results in bodily harm.

As explained in commentary to Section 46(2), it is meant to account for instances in which, for example, assailant *A* intentionally and unjustifiably shoots spouse *S* in *the presence of* other spouse *O*.

Section 46(2)(a) tracks but also extends the principles that permit certain family members to sue for *loss of consortium* or for *wrongful death* when another family member is injured or killed. As explained in Chapter 6, in the preceding hypothetical, were *S* to survive *A*'s attack, *O* could bring a loss of consortium claim against *A* that would compensate *O* for any loss of economic or emotional support resulting from *S*'s having been injured. (Likewise, if *S* were to die as a result of *A*'s attack, *O* would likely be able to bring a wrongful death action.) Yet, while family members such as *O* stand to recover damages for lost economic and/or emotional support by means of these two "derivative" actions, state laws vary as to whether they are in addition entitled to recover compensation for the *emotional distress* suffered because of injury or death to their relative. To the extent they do *not* entitle a family member such as *O* to such compensation, Section 46(a)(2) provides a supplementary cause of action by rendering *A*'s act not only a wrong to *S* upon which *O* may sue derivatively, but also a wrong to *O* herself for which *O* may sue directly.

While Section 46(2)(a) is thus linked to statutorily based derivative actions that aim to compensate family members of a tort victim for their injuries, Section 46(2)(b) — which affords relief to complete strangers who witness the outrageous mistreatment of another — is not. Does this suggest that Section 46(2)(b) lacks a compelling justification? Should every intentional tort that occurs before witnesses give rise to satellite liability for emotional distress caused to them? If so, would a similar rationale apply to negligently caused injuries? Why or why not? See *infra* Section II.C (on bystander liability in negligence law).

4. *Defenses.* The various defenses canvassed in Chapter 9 in connection with the torts of assault, battery, and false imprisonment should in principle apply to claims for IIED. As a practical matter, however, the facts that might go toward establishing these defenses often are subsumed in the determination of whether a given actor's conduct was extreme and outrageous. For example, if a competent adult plaintiff knowingly and voluntarily consents to being subjected to conduct that otherwise might appear to be beyond all bounds of decency, his consent may render the conduct not outrageous as a matter of law. Still, one occasionally sees IIED suits in which affirmative defenses are discussed as such. *See, e.g.,* Smith v. Calvary Christian Church, 614 N.W.2d 590 (Mich. 2000) (church member whose behavior in consorting with prostitutes was revealed to his congregation pursuant to church practices may not sue for IIED; as an active member of the church he consented to such practices).

Because severe emotional distress is often induced by speech about, or depictions of, a person, IIED claims can sometimes run afoul of the First Amendment to the U.S. Constitution. In 1988, the Supreme Court ruled that the Rev. Jerry Falwell, leader of the "Moral Majority," could not recover on an IIED claim against Hustler Magazine for printing a mock advertisement in which Falwell was depicted as engaging in incest with his mother. According to the Court, individuals and entities enjoy a constitutional right to lampoon public figures such as Falwell, even if the lampooning is outrageous and done for the purpose of causing another to experience severe emotional distress. The Court explained:

> If it were possible by laying down a principled standard to separate [acceptable from unacceptable caricatures of public figures], public discourse would probably suffer little or no harm. But we doubt that there is any such standard, and we are quite sure that the pejorative description "outrageous" does not supply one. "Outrageousness" in the area of political and social discourse has an inherent subjectiveness about it which would allow a jury to impose liability on the basis of the jurors' tastes or views, or perhaps on the basis of their dislike of a particular expression. An "outrageousness" standard thus runs afoul of our longstanding refusal to allow damages to be awarded because the speech in question may have an adverse emotional impact on the audience.

Hustler Magazine v. Falwell, 485 U.S. 46, 55 (1988). In effect, *Falwell* adopts the rule that, as a matter of constitutional law, descriptions or depictions of public figures can never be deemed "outrageous." Is the adoption of this *per se* rule justified? If juries are (at least in some jurisdictions) entrusted to make judgments about outrageousness in other contexts, why should they not be permitted to do so in this one?

5. *Prima Facie Tort.* Recall from the introduction to this section that the IIED tort emerged in part out of an effort to unify a set of decisions involving wrongs that did not fit comfortably into then-recognized tort causes of action. In addition to employing IIED for this purpose, some states have recognized a separate cause of action designed to enable victims to pursue claims for intentional wrongs that continue to fall through doctrinal cracks. In states that recognize it, this miscellaneous action is referred to as the cause of action for *prima facie tort*.

Under New York law, for example, the formal elements of such a claim are (1) intentional infliction of harm; (2) resulting in special damages (i.e., discrete and measurable monetary losses); (3) without excuse or justification; (4) by an act or series of acts that would otherwise be lawful. Burns Jackson Miller Summit & Spitzer v. Lindner, 451 N.E.2d 459, 467 (N.Y. 1983). Under New York law, at least, the intent element for this tort is more narrowly drawn than in traditional dignitary tort law, requiring not only proof of intent to injure, but in addition proof that the actor formed this intent *solely* out of a "malevolent" desire to injure the plaintiff. *Id*. at 468. Thus, if *D* were intentionally to injure *P* for the purpose of advancing *D*'s economic self-interest, *D*'s conduct will *not* be actionable in prima facie tort because *D* has acted out of a desire to enrich himself, rather than exclusively out of malice toward the plaintiff. Although allegations of prima facie tort are common in tort suits brought within jurisdictions that recognize it, they appear to succeed even less frequently than IIED claims. Instead, the plaintiff will either prevail on some other cause of action, or will be denied relief altogether.

C. IIED Applied: Employment Discrimination

The workplace is in some respects a natural source of claims for IIED. Offices tend to be hierarchically organized. Because of this, they create power relations, and, with those, the potential for abuses of power. Workplaces also foster repetitive interactions among persons in close quarters, often under stressful conditions. Finally, modern law outside of tort law has increasingly attempted to regulate the workplace so as to constrain the ways in which employers can act toward employees, and employees can act toward one another. In particular, since the mid-1960s, federal statutes have rendered illegal and sanctionable various forms of employment discrimination, including discrimination based on age, gender, race, and disabilities. These and other factors have begun to give rise to employment-related IIED suits, the likes of which Magruder and Prosser probably never envisioned. Largely excluded from the ambit of negligence law through the adoption of workers' compensation schemes at the beginning of the twentieth century, the workplace is perhaps once again becoming a fertile source of tort claims.* Consider in the following cases how federal

---

* As indicated by the next two cases, courts entertaining employment discrimination suits expressly authorized by federal statutes are often asked to rule on "pendent" state law tort claims arising out of the same facts alleged in plaintiffs' federal law claims. In ruling on

laws that render certain forms of employment discrimination actionable interact with the IIED tort.

Wilson v. Monarch Paper Co.
939 F.2d 1138 (5th Cir. 1991)

Jolly, J.   In this employment discrimination case, Monarch Paper Company ... appeals a $3,400,000 jury verdict finding it liable for age discrimination ... under the Age Discrimination in Employment Act (ADEA), 29 U.S.C. § 621, and for intentional infliction of emotional distress under Texas state law.... Upon review of the entire record, we affirm.

I

Because Monarch is challenging the sufficiency of the evidence, the facts are recited in the light most favorable to the jury's verdict. In 1970, at age 48, Richard E. Wilson was hired by Monarch Paper Company. Monarch is an incorporated division of Unisource Corporation, and Unisource is an incorporated group of Alco Standard Corporation. Wilson served as manager of the Corpus Christi division until November 1, 1977, when he was moved to the corporate staff in Houston to serve as "Corporate Director of Physical Distribution." During that time, he routinely received merit raises and performance bonuses. In 1980, Wilson received the additional title of "Vice President." In 1981, Wilson was given the additional title of "Assistant to John Blankenship," Monarch's President at the time.

While he was Director of Physical Distribution, Wilson received most of his assignments from Blankenship. Blankenship always seemed pleased with Wilson's performance and Wilson was never reprimanded or counseled about his performance. Blankenship provided Wilson with objective performance criteria at the beginning of each year, and Wilson's bonuses at the end of the year were based on his good performance under that objective criteria. In 1981, Wilson was placed in charge of the completion of an office warehouse building in Dallas, the largest construction project Monarch had ever undertaken. Wilson successfully completed that project within budget.

---

these employment-related state law tort claims, a court must determine whether any or all such claims have been removed from the tort system by the relevant state's workers' compensation legislation. *Compare* Livitsanos v. Superior Court, 828 P.2d 1195 (Cal. 1992) (suit alleging IIED can be brought by employee against employer for employment-caused distress if the employer's conduct (1) contravenes fundamental public policy or (2) exceeds the inherent risks of employment) *with* Green v. Wyman-Gordon Co., 664 N.E.2d 808 (Mass. 1996) (IIED claim brought by employee against employer based on conduct arising out of, and in the course of, employment is barred by the exclusivity provisions of the Massachusetts Workers' Compensation laws: The plaintiff may only receive disability benefits as per those laws).

In 1981, Wilson saw a portion of Monarch's long-range plans that indicated that Monarch was presently advancing younger persons in all levels of Monarch management. Tom Davis, who was hired as Employee Relations Manager of Monarch in 1979, testified that from the time he started to work at Monarch, he heard repeated references by the division managers (including Larry Clark, who later became the Executive Vice President of Monarch) to the age of employees on the corporate staff, including Wilson.

In October 1981, Blankenship became Chairman of Monarch and Unisource brought in a new, 42-year-old president from outside the company, Hamilton Bisbee. An announcement was made that Larry Clark would be assuming expanded responsibilities in physical distribution. According to the defendants, one of Blankenship's final acts as President was to direct Clark (who was in his mid-forties at the time) to assume expanded responsibility for both the operational and physical distribution aspects of Monarch.

When Bisbee arrived at Monarch in November 1981, Wilson was still deeply involved in the Dallas construction project. Richard Gozon, who was 43 years old and the President of Unisource, outlined Blankenship's new responsibilities as Chairman of the company and requested that Blankenship, Bisbee, Wilson, and John Hartley of Unisource "continue to work very closely together on the completion of the Dallas project." Bisbee, however, refused to speak to Wilson or to "interface" with him. This "silent treatment" was apparently tactical; Bisbee later told another Monarch employee, Bill Shehan, "if I ever stop talking to you, you're dead." Shehan also testified that at a meeting in Philadelphia at about the time Bisbee became President of Monarch, Gozon told Bisbee, "I'm not telling you that you have to fire Dick Wilson. I'm telling you that he cannot make any more money."

As soon as the Dallas building project was completed, Bisbee and Gozon intensified an effort designed to get rid of Wilson. On March 8, 1982, Gozon asked for Bisbee's recommendations on how to remove Wilson from the Monarch organization. On March 9, 1982, Bisbee responded with his recommendation that Wilson be terminated, and that any salary continuance to Wilson be discontinued should Wilson elect to pursue an adversarial role toward Monarch. Gozon then asked the Unisource Employee Relations Manager, John Snelgrove, to meet with Wilson with the goal of attempting to convince Wilson to quit.

During the same time frame, . . . Bisbee and Clark began dismantling Wilson's job by removing his responsibilities and assigning them to other employees. Clark was also seen entering Wilson's office after hours and removing files.

Blankenship [died in June of 1982]. . . . Immediately [there]after . . . Bisbee and Snelgrove gave Wilson three options: (1) he could take a sales job in Corpus Christi at half his pay; (2) he could be terminated with three months' severance pay; or (3) he could accept a job as warehouse supervisor in the Houston warehouse at the same salary but with a reduction in benefits. The benefits included participation in the management bonus plan, and the loss of the use of a company car, a company club membership, and a company expense account.

Wilson accepted the warehouse position. Wilson believed that he was being offered the position of Warehouse Manager, the only vacant position in the Houston warehouse at the time. When Wilson reported for duty at the warehouse on August 16, 1982, however, he was placed instead in the position of an entry level supervisor, a position that required no more than one year's experience in the paper business. Wilson, with his thirty years of experience in the paper business and a college degree, was vastly overqualified and overpaid for that position.

Soon after he went to the warehouse, Wilson was subjected to harassment and verbal abuse by his supervisor, Operations Manager and Acting Warehouse Manager Paul Bradley (who had previously been subordinate to Wilson). Bradley referred to Wilson as "old man" and admitted posting a sign in the warehouse that said "Wilson is old." In Bradley's absence, Wilson was placed under the supervision of a man in his twenties. Finally, Wilson was further demeaned when he was placed in charge of housekeeping but was not given any employees to assist him in the housekeeping duties. Wilson, the former vice-president and assistant to the president, was thus reduced finally to sweeping the floors and cleaning up the employees' cafeteria, duties which occupied 75 percent of his working time.

In the late fall of 1982, Wilson began suffering from respiratory problems caused by the dusty conditions in the warehouse and stress from the unrelenting harassment by his employer. On January 6, 1983, Wilson left work to see a doctor about his respiratory problems. He was advised to stay out of a dusty environment and was later advised that he had a clinically significant allergy to dust. Shortly after January 6, 1983, Wilson consulted a psychiatrist who diagnosed him as suffering from reactive depression, possibly suicidal, because of on-the-job stress. The psychiatrist also advised that Wilson should stay away from work indefinitely.

Wilson filed an age discrimination charge with the [federal Equal Employment Opportunity Commission] in January 1983. Although he continued being treated by a psychiatrist, his condition deteriorated to the point that in March 1983, he was involuntarily hospitalized with a psychotic manic episode. Prior to the difficulties with his employer, Wilson had no history of emotional illness.

Wilson's emotional illness was severe and long-lasting. He was diagnosed with manic-depressive illness or bipolar disorder. After his first hospitalization for a manic episode, in which he was locked in a padded cell and heavily sedated, he fell into a deep depression. The depression was unremitting for over two years and necessitated an additional hospital stay in which he was given electroconvulsive therapy (shock treatments). It was not until 1987 that Wilson's illness began remission, thus allowing him to carry on a semblance of a normal life.

II

On February 27, 1984, Wilson filed suit against the defendants, alleging age discrimination and various state law tort and contract claims. The defendants filed a counterclaim, seeking damages in excess of $10,000 for libel and slander, but later dismissed it.[1] On November 30 and December 28, 1988, the case was tried before a jury on Wilson's remaining claims that the defendants (1) reassigned him because of his age; (2) intentionally inflicted emotional distress; and (3) terminated his long-term disability benefits in retaliation for filing charges of age discrimination under the ... (ADEA).

... The jury returned a ... verdict in favor of Wilson on his age discrimination claim, awarding him $156,000 in [lost wages and benefits], plus an equal amount in liquidated damages.* The jury also found in favor of Wilson on his claim for intentional infliction of emotional distress, awarding him past damages of $622,359.15, future damages of $225,000, and punitive damages of $2,250,000. The jury found in favor of the defendants on Wilson's retaliation claim. The district court entered judgment for $3,409,359.15 plus prejudgment interest....

III

Monarch ... argues that the district court erred in denying its motions for directed verdict, JNOV, and new trial on Wilson's claim for intentional infliction of emotional distress [and on Wilson's age discrimination claim].... [Also,] Monarch argues that the district court erred in denying its motions for directed verdict, JNOV, new trial, and remittitur with respect to the amount of back pay awarded on the age discrimination claim. With respect to the emotional distress claim, neither the quantum of actual damages or the award of punitive damages are appealed....

A

Wilson's claim for intentional infliction of emotional distress is a pendent state law claim.... The sole issue before us is whether Monarch's conduct was "extreme and outrageous."

---

1. ... [T]he trial court permitted] ... Wilson's attorney [to] argue[ ] to the jury that the filing of the counterclaim should be considered in determining whether the defendants engaged in outrageous conduct. The defendants argue that the district court's refusal to exclude such evidence was reversible error because "a defendant is never liable [for intentional infliction of emotional distress] where he has done no more than to insist upon his legal rights in a permissible way, even though he is well aware that such insistence is certain to cause emotional distress." Restatement (Second) of Torts § 46, comment g. ... Because the district court has broad discretion in evidentiary matters, we find no abuse in admitting the counterclaim into evidence because it is arguable whether the pleading was asserted in good faith.

* [A plaintiff who proves "willful" discrimination may be awarded double the amount of wages that are owed to him. The added portion is termed *liquidated* damages. — EDS.]

(1)

"Extreme and outrageous conduct" is an amorphous phrase that escapes precise definition. In Dean v. Ford Motor Credit Co., [885 F.2d 300, 306 (5th Cir. 1989),] however, we [noted that Texas law applies the "beyond all possible bounds of decency" standard specified in comment d to Section 46 of the Second Restatement.] . . .

The facts of a given claim of outrageous conduct must be analyzed in context, and ours is the employment setting. We are cognizant that "the work culture in some situations may contemplate a degree of teasing and taunting that in other circumstances might be considered cruel and outrageous." Keeton, et al., *Prosser & Keeton on Torts* (5th ed. 1984 & 1988 Supp.). We further recognize that properly to manage its business, every employer must on occasion review, criticize, demote, transfer, and discipline employees. *Id.* We also acknowledge that it is not unusual for an employer, instead of directly discharging an employee, to create unpleasant and onerous work conditions designed to force an employee to quit, i.e., "constructively" to discharge the employee. In short, although this sort of conduct often rises to the level of illegality, except in the *most* unusual cases it is not the sort of conduct, as deplorable as it may sometimes be, that constitutes "extreme and outrageous" conduct.

(2)

Our recent decision in *Dean* . . . *supra*, is instructive in determining what types of conduct in the employment setting will constitute sufficiently outrageous conduct so as to legally support a jury's verdict. In *Dean*, the plaintiff presented evidence that (1) when she expressed interest in transferring to a higher paying position in the collection department, she was told that "women don't usually go into that department"; (2) she was denied a transfer to the collection department, and a lesser qualified man was selected; (3) the defendant's attitude toward the plaintiff changed after she complained about alleged discriminatory treatment; (4) management began to transfer her from desk to desk within the administrative department; (5) a coworker testified she believed management was trying to "set . . . [the plaintiff] up"; (6) she was called upon to do more work than the other clerks "and subjected to unfair harassment"; and (7) management used "special" annual reviews (that only the plaintiff received) to downgrade her performance. 885 F.2d at 304-305, 306-307. Far more significant to the claim for intentional infliction of emotional distress, however, (8) the plaintiff proved that a supervisor, who had access to the employer's checks, intentionally placed checks in the plaintiff's purse in order to make it appear that she was a thief, or to put her in fear of criminal charges for theft. *Id.* We expressly held that the "check incidents" were "precisely what [took] this case beyond the realm of an ordinary employment dispute and into the realm of an outrageous one." *Id.* at 307. We concluded that without the "check incidents" the employer's conduct "would not have been outrageous." *Id.*

Wilson argues that Monarch's conduct is sufficiently outrageous to meet the *Dean* standard. . . . Monarch contends that Wilson's evidence of outrageous conduct, that is, his reassignment to a job he did not like, his strained relationship with the company president, and isolated references to his age, is the same evidence that he used to prove his age discrimination claim. According to Monarch, unless all federal court discrimination lawsuits are to be accompanied by pendent state law claims for emotional distress, this court must make it clear that ordinary employment disputes cannot support an emotional distress claim.[4] We agree with Monarch that more is required to prove intentional infliction of emotional distress than the usual ADEA claim.

(3)

In *Dean*, we found that the "check incidents" took the case beyond an ordinary discrimination case and supported the claim of infliction of emotional distress. Wilson contends that Monarch's conduct was equally outrageous as the "check incidents" in *Dean*. Generally, Wilson argues that an average member of the community would exclaim "Outrageous!" upon hearing that a 60-year-old man, with 30 years of experience in his industry, was subjected to a year-long campaign of harassment and abuse because his company wanted to force him out of his job as part of its expressed written goal of getting rid of older employees and moving younger people into management. More precisely, Wilson argues that substantial evidence of outrageous conduct supports the jury's verdict, including: (1) his duties in physical distribution were assigned to a younger person; (2) Bisbee deliberately refused to speak to him in the hallways of Monarch in order to harass him; (3) certain portions of Monarch's long-range plans expressed a desire to move younger persons into sales and management positions; (4) Bisbee wanted to replace Wilson with a younger person; (5) other managers within Monarch would not work with Wilson, and he did not receive his work directly from Bisbee; (6) he was not offered a fully guaranteed salary to transfer to Corpus Christi; (7) he was assigned to Monarch's Houston warehouse as a supervisor, which was "demeaning"; (8) Paul Bradley, the Warehouse Manager, and other Monarch managers,

---

4. Monarch presents a lengthy citation of cases from other jurisdictions that have, according to it, rejected similar conduct as being not outrageous. *See, e.g.*, Patterson v. McLean Credit Union, 491 U.S. 164, 109 S. Ct. 2363, 105 L. Ed. 2d 132 (1989) (racial harassment and increased work load falls far short of constituting outrageous conduct under North Carolina law); Mundy v. Southern Bell Tel. & Tel. Co., 676 F.2d 503 (11th Cir. 1982) (transfer to less desirable job, inaccurate and unsupported negative evaluations, and attempts to damage employee's credibility not outrageous under Florida law); Murphy v. American Home Prod. Corp., 58 N.Y.2d 293, 461 N.Y.S.2d 232, 448 N.E.2d 86 (Ct. App. 1983) (job transfer, discharge and forcible removal from employer's premises, and dumping employee's personal belongings in the street not sufficient egregious conduct under New York law to support finding of outrageous conduct).

All of the states that have adopted this tort have relied on the elements in § 46 of the Restatement (Second) of Torts, however, the minimum standard of proof required to establish extreme and outrageous conduct is significantly different from state to state. . . .

referred to Wilson as old; (9) Bradley prepared a sign stating "Wilson is old" and, subsequently, "Wilson is a Goldbrick"; and (10) Monarch filed a counterclaim against Wilson in this action. We are not in full agreement.

Most of Monarch's conduct is similar in degree to conduct in *Dean* that failed to reach the level of outrageousness. We hold that all of this conduct, except as explicated below, is within the "realm of an ordinary employment dispute," *Dean*, 885 F.2d at 307, and, in the context of the employment milieu, is not so extreme and outrageous as to be properly addressed outside of Wilson's ADEA claim.

(4)

Wilson argues, however, that what takes this case out of the realm of an ordinary employment dispute is the degrading and humiliating way that he was stripped of his duties and demoted from an executive manager to an entry level warehouse supervisor with menial and demeaning duties. We agree. Wilson, a college graduate with thirty years experience in the paper field, had been a long-time executive at Monarch. His title was Corporate Director of Physical Distribution, with the added title of Vice-President and Assistant to the President. He had been responsible for the largest project in the company's history, and had completed the project on time and under budget. Yet, when transferred to the warehouse, Wilson's primary duty became housekeeping chores around the warehouse's shipping and receiving area. Because Monarch did not give Wilson any employees to supervise or assist him, Wilson was frequently required to sweep the warehouse. In addition, Wilson also was reduced to cleaning up after the employees in the warehouse cafeteria after their lunch hour. Wilson spent 75 percent of his time performing these menial, janitorial duties.

Monarch argues that assigning an executive with a college education and thirty years experience to janitorial duties is not extreme and outrageous conduct. The jury did not agree and neither do we. We find it difficult to conceive a workplace scenario more painful and embarrassing than an executive, indeed a vice-president and the assistant to the president, being subjected before his fellow employees to the most menial janitorial services and duties of cleaning up after entry level employees: the steep downhill push to total humiliation was complete. The evidence, considered as a whole, will fully support the view, which the jury apparently held, that Monarch, unwilling to fire Wilson outright, *intentionally and systematically* set out to humiliate him in the hopes that he would quit.[5] A reasonable jury could have found that this employer conduct was intentional and mean spirited, so severe that it resulted in institutional confinement and treatment for someone with no history of mental problems.

---

5. Nevertheless, we are not unaware of the irony in this case: if Monarch had chosen only to fire Wilson outright, leaving him without a salary, a job, insurance, etc., it would not be liable for intentional infliction of emotional distress. There is some suggestion in the record, however, that Monarch was unwilling to fire Wilson outright because it had no grounds and perhaps feared a lawsuit. . . .

Finally, the evidence supports the conclusion that this conduct was, indeed, so outrageous that civilized society should not tolerate it. *Dean*, 885 F.2d at 307.[6] Accordingly, the judgment of the district court in denying Monarch's motions for directed verdict, JNOV and a new trial on this claim is affirmed.

[The court next upheld the verdict and award for Wilson's age discrimination claim.]

IV

In conclusion, we express real concern about the consequences of applying the cause of action of intentional infliction of emotional distress to the workplace. This concern is, however, primarily a concern for the State of Texas, its courts and its legislature. Although the award in this case is astonishingly high, neither the quantum of damages, nor the applicability of punitive damages has been appealed. . . .

Stockett v. Tolin
791 F. Supp. 1536 (S.D. Fla. 1992)

Marcus, J.   This action was brought by the Plaintiff, Michelle Ann Stockett, against her former employers, Frank Tolin ("Tolin") and three closely-held Florida corporations, Limelite Studios, Inc. ("Limelite Studios"), Directors Production Company ("DPC") and Limelite Video, Inc. ("Limelite Video"). . . . Plaintiff seeks relief under Title VII . . . for hostile work environment, *quid pro quo* sexual harassment . . . and several pendent common law torts. . . . The parties agreed to the trial of the common-law tort actions before the Court without a jury. . . .

I.   FINDINGS OF FACT . . .

3. Plaintiff is a 29 year-old woman, who was employed by the Defendants from December 30, 1985, through on or about April 22, 1987. . . .

4. Each of the corporate defendants, Limelite Studios, Limelite Video, and DPC is or was a closely-held Florida corporation with its principal place of business at 7355 N.W. 41st Street, Miami, Florida. Limelite Studios, which rents out stages, was incorporated in late 1982. Limelite Video, which is involved in the business of post-production work . . . , was incorporated on October 8, 1985. Both are active corporations. DPC . . . stopped doing business in the summer of 1986. . . .

5. Defendant Frank Tolin is a 71-year old man, who . . . owned most of the stock in the Defendant corporations and dominated the organization

---

6. We suppose that the threat of an emotional distress claim also provides the irony of "civilizing" discrimination; or stated differently, employers will have to behave like ladies and gentlemen when discriminating.

and operation of the Defendant companies. At all material times, he owned [the vast majority of stock issued by Video and Limelite Studios, and half of DPC's stock. He also served as a director of each entity, and held top managerial positions, along with others, included Wanda Rayle, his second-in-command, and Ron Fenster.]

6. Although Limelite Studios, Limelite Video and DPC were separate corporations, they were, as Fenster and Tolin referred to them, more like "departments" within one large company that also included [various other Limelite companies], all of which were engaged in businesses relating in some way to the production industry.... Tolin's headquarters were at the studios and he ran the Limelite companies, as well as Tolin Construction Company and his vast real estate holdings, from there.

7. Employees of the Tolin enterprises sometimes were paid by one company, sometimes by another. Supervisory personnel such as Wanda Rayle and Ron Fenster exercised authority over employees of all of the Tolin companies. One receptionist paid by Limelite Studios took in visitors for all the companies.... [I]ncome and monies from the companies were "pooled" and then disbursed as needed to the various corporations as intra-company loans or loans from Tolin.... Employees of Studio, Video, as well as other Tolin companies, were carried on the same group health insurance policy.... The companies shared one copy machine, a common phone system and a time clock.... Even Defendant's response to the EEOC's Notice and Charge of Discrimination is on letterhead [boasting that "Limelite" is the largest "Teleproduction Center Under One Roof" in the United States]. The letterhead shows one Broward phone number, one fax line and one toll-free number shared by all the companies....

9. Based on the "date hired" and "date term" shown on the 1986 and 1987 employee master lists, during 1986, Limelite Studios had 9 employees who worked twenty or more weeks, Video had 11 and DPC had 3; during 1987, Video had 19 employees who worked 20 or more weeks. During 1986, the Limelite companies (also including Limelite Mobile, Inc., Limelite Equipment Rental, Inc. and Limelite Motion Pictures, Inc.), had close to 50 employees altogether. At least 33 of these worked 20 or more weeks....

10. Stockett's involvement with ... Limelite began at a [party] ..., which she had attended with a girlfriend hoping to make some contacts that would help her either further a modeling career or break into the production industry. [There,] Plaintiff was introduced to Toby Ross, who was involved in an on-the-job internship training program sponsored by Florida State University, and to Ron Fenster and Tolin....

12. Soon thereafter, Stockett [obtained an internship and, through that, employment with Tolin's companies as described above]....

15. Tolin first approached Stockett in an offensive manner late in December 1985 while she was working as a receptionist.... The Defendant came up to her at the receptionist's desk, put his arms around her from behind, pressed his body up against her and said "I'd love to eat you all up." Stockett pushed him away and asked Tolin to stop. Stockett was confused by Tolin's conduct but not totally surprised; ... another employee had warned Stockett when she first started working at Limelite to stay away from Tolin because "he liked young girls."

16. On two occasions in 1986 within a month of each other, in the offices of Limelite Video, Tolin confined Stockett for a few seconds in her secretarial chair, where she was sitting and typing. Coming up behind her he pressed down on her shoulders so she couldn't get up, and then reached over and squeezed her breasts.

17. In January or February 1987, Stockett was changing clothes in the ladies room after work, getting ready to go to a circus. Tolin walked into the ladies bathroom and looked around a partition, smiled and said, "Hello." She screamed for him to leave. He stood there another few seconds and left. Tolin admits encountering Stockett in the ladies room, although he claims he just stuck his head in while turning off a light, saw she was there, apologized and left.

18. On another occasion, sometime in March or April 1987, after that bathroom incident, while Stockett worked at her desk, Tolin came up behind her, stuck his tongue in her ear and told her in the crudest terms that he wanted to perform oral sex on her. Stockett testified further that [, on another occasion,] the Defendant again approached her from behind, while she was working at her desk, stuck his tongue in her ear, and said with a four letter expletive that he wanted to have sexual intercourse with Plaintiff. On still other occasions, Stockett testified that while she was working, the Defendant would corner her, run his fingers up the front of her shirt, grab her breasts and pinch her nipples. During these assaults, he laughed and said, "You like that, don't you." Tolin also grabbed Plaintiff's buttocks whenever he could get close enough, as the Plaintiff walked down the hall. Stockett testified that incidents such as these occurred weekly throughout Stockett's employment. She further testified that Tolin's behavior was deeply offensive to her, altogether unsolicited, and that she regularly told the Defendant to leave her alone.

19. A few weeks before Stockett left Limelite in April 1987, Tolin's conduct became even more blatant. One night while Stockett was working late, about 6:30 or 7:00 P.M., she encountered Tolin. She thought no one else was in the building. Tolin pushed her up against the wall and began licking her neck. According to Plaintiff, Tolin said he "wanted to f—me." Tolin had his hands on Plaintiff's shoulders, his body was pressed against hers and he was "right in her face." Stockett testified that she was terrified; she couldn't think and she couldn't move. Stockett testified that . . . Marie Arnold, [an associate of Tolin's], walked by, noticed the look on Plaintiff's face and interrupted Defendant's embrace. . . . According to Arnold['s testimony], Stockett had tears in her eyes and from the look in Stockett's eyes and on her face, it was apparent that Stockett was afraid.

20. Finally, [during] . . . the week before Stockett left Limelite in April 1987, as Stockett was leaving her office, she encountered Tolin in a hallway. Tolin told Stockett he was going away and asked how long she had been working there. When she replied that she had worked there for about one and one-half years, Tolin said to her, "you've always got an excuse, I want to f—you." He added that he was tired of waiting. Stockett told Tolin that she worked hard at her job and asked him to leave her alone. Tolin responded with a torrent of sexually explicit comments that included, "Oh, you work hard. Do you f—hard?" Tolin bragged about his

sexual prowess, compared himself to a twenty year old, and, finally, demanded, "F—me or you're fired." Later that day, Stockett encountered Tolin again as he left for his trip. Tolin's parting words were, "I'll see you when I get back," a comment Plaintiff took as a direct threat. Stockett reported this incident to Marie Arnold, who, in turn, reported it to Wanda Rayle.

21. Stockett began thinking about leaving her job at the time of the incident Marie Arnold witnessed. It was not until Tolin directly threatened her and presented her with an ultimatum, however, that she decided she could no longer work at Limelite. The following Monday, on April 20, 1987, Stockett gave two weeks' notice . . . but stayed only a few extra days. Tolin was out of town and Stockett did not want to be there when he returned. . . .

22. The Court is satisfied from the full record that Plaintiff did not in any way encourage Tolin's verbal and physical advances. Repeatedly she pushed him away and told him to stop. She avoided Tolin by going in the opposite direction when she saw him. When she went into his office, she would tell another woman not to let the door be closed. She tried never to be alone with the Defendant.

23. Moreover, the evidence . . . strongly suggests that Stockett stayed as long as she did and put up with Tolin's conduct as long as she did because she needed the work and wanted to learn the business. The Plaintiff feared that she would be fired immediately and her opportunity in the industry would be destroyed, by a man whom she perceived as being rich and very powerful. . . .

25. Stockett's account of a pervasively hostile work environment marked by the Defendant's repeated and explicit sexual advances is corroborated by the testimony of many other female employees at the Defendant companies.

[The court recited corroborating testimony of witnesses who observed Tolin harass Stockett. It also reviewed testimony from numerous employees who stated that he had manhandled, chased, and/or crudely propositioned them, as well as actresses who were being filmed on sound stages on the premises. Others testified that Tolin's behavior was so widely known that female employees had developed a "buddy system" to ensure no one would be caught alone with him.] . . .

27. Stockett testified that she felt helpless and was disgusted by Tolin's advances. Although Tolin sometimes stopped bothering Stockett when she pushed him away, she couldn't stop him permanently. The advances affected Stockett's ability to do her job; she became very nervous and went out of her way to avoid Tolin. Stockett regularly cried at the office and during her drive home from work. Stockett testified that she no longer trusts men and is uneasy around them. Stockett has had several jobs since terminating her employment at Limelite, including as a cocktail waitress, as a receptionist with a production firm, some modelling jobs, and work as an "extra." Stockett now works as a manager of a cosmetic counter at Lord and Taylor. She testified that the reason she enjoys this job is that she doesn't have to work with any men. Additionally, Stockett's doctor told her that she was getting an ulcer, and for approximately one

year, Stockett has been taking Tagamet for stomach symptoms that include ... burning, and being sick to her stomach....

30. ... Wanda Rayle testified ... that ... complaints of sexual harassment ... were presented to Tolin regularly. Tolin would either deny the incident or tell Rayle that the business belonged to him.... Rayle testified that every female employee but two had complained about the Defendant's misconduct....

31. The Defendant Tolin himself admitted at trial to [some of these incidents, although he dismissed some as jokes or accidents, and others as momentary lapses.]

32. Stockett presented expert testimony by a clinical psychologist, Glenn R. Caddy, PH.D., regarding both the psychological effects of her experience at Limelite and why she tolerated Tolin's advances.... He testified that he spent 12 to 13 hours with Stockett and has administered formal tests including a "before and after" MMPI (Minnesota Multiphasic Personality Inventory)....

33. Caddy testified that sexual harassment is an example of a process known as victimization.... In [relatively] less violent, more chronic situations, such as those that he opined occurred in this case, a person slowly evolves a sense of helplessness in coping with the situation. This results in anxiety, depression, feelings of personal incompetence, loss of a sense of self confidence and worth, and the inability to develop strategies for handling the treatment.

34. Caddy testified, and the Court finds his testimony consistent with the evidence presented, that Stockett suffered severe emotional distress as a result of the harassment by Tolin....

a. ... Stockett suffered from sleep disturbances, depression and loss of energy, general anxiety, a sense of uncertainty, and anger....

b. ... Caddy ... characterized [Stockett's distress] as "extreme." According to Caddy, Stockett [faced a deteriorating situation]; the longer it went on, the more degraded and helpless she felt. Stockett felt she wasn't safe anywhere, even in the bathroom.

35. The evidence presented suggests that the Plaintiff is suffering continuing damage, particularly in her inability to trust men and in her overall sense of personal confidence. Dr. Caddy testified that the Plaintiff would require psychotherapy for six months to a year at a projected cost of $7,500....

37. Tolin's net worth is said to be at least $25 million.... The net worth figure offered by Tolin on a financial statement given a few days before the trial to a lending institution ... was $82 million.... Tolin spent approximately $20 million on equipment and conversion of the facilities where the Limelite businesses are housed, an investment concerning which he told the Miami Herald, "I'm still a very wealthy man. $20 million is a small fraction of my wealth."...

II.   CONCLUSIONS OF LAW ...

40. Title VII of the Civil Rights Act of 1964 ... provides in pertinent part:

(a) It shall be an unlawful employment practice for an employer—

(1) to fail or refuse to hire or to discharge any individual, or otherwise to discriminate against any individual with respect to his compensation, terms, conditions, or privileges of employment, because of such individual's race, color, religion, sex, or national origin. . . .

42 U.S.C. § 2000e-2. . . .

42. For sexual harassment to be actionable under Title VII, however, the harassing actor must be an "employer," as defined by 42 U.S.C. § 2000e(b), i.e., an individual or a firm that is "engaged in an industry affecting commerce who has fifteen or more employees for each working day in each of twenty or more calendar weeks in the current or preceding calendar year, and any agent of such a person. . . ." *Id.* Defendants here concede, as they must, that "Limelite Video is an 'employer' within the meaning of Title VII." Defendant corporations argue, however, that the jurisdictional requirements are not satisfied as to the remaining two corporate Defendants. We disagree, since we find that the Defendant corporations were sufficiently integrated so as to be considered one "employer" for purposes of Title VII.

43. A grouping of employers may be considered as one "employer" if they are highly integrated with respect to ownership and operations. . . .

44. In the instant case, there is strong evidence of interrelations of operations recognized by other courts as supporting the applicability of the integrated enterprise theory, including: sharing management services, such as check writing, sharing payroll and insurance programs, and the preparation of mutual policy manuals; sharing services of managers and personnel, using employees on the payroll of one entity to perform work for the benefit of another nominally separate entity; sharing use of office space, equipment and storage; and providing services principally for the benefit of another entity or operating the entities as a single unit.

Likewise, that the same persons—Tolin, Rayle and Fenster—essentially managed and supervised the different entities, and that the companies had common officers and boards of directors, is evidence of the kind of common management that supports the second prong of the interrelated test.

45. [The court noted that the Limelite entities maintained centralized control of labor relations though a single personnel department.]

46. The final factor to be considered in assessing applicability of the interrelated enterprise theory is the degree of common ownership or financial control over the entities. In this case, the evidence on that point strongly supports the theory's application. Frank Tolin controls all the companies and serves as an officer and director with each of them.

47. Defendants, then, taken together, are so integrated and interrelated as to constitute a single employer with 15 employees under Title VII. Therefore, they fall within the Court's jurisdiction. At all events, we observe again that Limelite Video alone had 19 employees who worked 20 or more weeks during 1987, which is sufficient to satisfy Title VII's jurisdictional requirements as to Video itself.

48. "Courts recognize two forms of sexual harassment: quid pro quo sexual harassment and hostile work environment sexual harassment." Steele v. Offshore Shipbuilding, Inc., 867 F.2d 1311, 1315 (11th Cir. 1989) (citing [Meritor Savings Bank v.] Vinson, 477 U.S. [57, 65-66, 106 S. Ct. 2399, 2404-2405 (1986)].... "Quid pro quo sexual harassment occurs when an employer alters an employee's job conditions as a result of the employee's refusal to submit to sexual demands." *Id.* (citing *Vinson*, 477 U.S. at 65, 106 S. Ct. at 2404 ...). Hostile environment sexual harassment occurs when an employer's conduct "has the purpose or effect of unreasonably interfering with an individual's work performance or creating an intimidating, hostile, or offensive environment." *Steele*, 867 F.2d at 1315 (citing *Vinson*, 477 U.S. at 67, 106 S. Ct. at 2405 (quoting 29 C.F.R. § 1604.11(a)(3) (1987)).... "[W]here sexual harassment is 'sufficiently pervasive so as to alter the conditions of employment and create an abusive working environment,' a Title VII claim is made out 'irrespective of whether the complainant suffers tangible job detriment.'" Phillips v. Smalley Maintenance Services, Inc., 711 F.2d 1524, 1529 (11th Cir. 1983) [authority quoted within quote omitted — EDS.].

49. In order to prove a hostile environment sexual harassment case, a plaintiff must demonstrate:

    a. that she belongs to a protected group, i.e., that she is a woman;
    b. that she was subject to unwelcome sexual harassment;
    c. that the harassment complained of was based upon sex, i.e., that the actor did not similarly harass male employees; and
    d. that the harassment involved affected a "term, condition or privilege" of employment.

Henson v. City of Dundee, 682 F.2d 897, 903-04 (11th Cir. 1982). Unwelcomeness means that an employee did not solicit or invite the alleged behavior. *Id.* at 903....

51. At the outset, "[f]or sexual harassment to be actionable, it must be sufficiently severe or pervasive 'to alter the conditions of [the victim's] employment and create an abusive working environment.'" *Meritor Savings Bank, supra* (citation omitted).... The requirement that the sexual harassment be pervasive both permits and may require the introduction of evidence of Tolin's similar harassment of other women....

52. Defendant Tolin, individually and as a managing agent for the corporate defendants, blatantly and repeatedly harassed Plaintiff and many other women who worked for him. His conduct included both constant sexually explicit, degrading, and vulgar language and repeated acts of physical abuse. His offensive sexual behavior was relentless, and can only be characterized as crossing all bounds of common decency. According to Plaintiff, she tolerated Tolin's advances because she wanted to keep her job. Finally, toward the end of Plaintiff's tenure, Tolin spelled out for her the quid pro quo terms of her continued employment: "F— me or you're fired!" On this record, then, Plaintiff has plainly established quid pro quo sexual harassment, [and] hostile environment sexual harassment....

53. Stockett is accordingly entitled to back pay from the date of termination of her employment with Defendant corporations (4/22/87) up to the date of trial (2/20/90) totalling 147 weeks. Therefore, at her rate of $16,380/year base pay, Stockett is entitled to back pay in the amount of $46,305, less $4,401 that she earned from other employment, for a total back pay award of $41,904.

54. Additionally, because of the working conditions detailed at the Tolin studios, reinstatement would be ineffective as a make-whole remedy, and Stockett is entitled to "front pay." Because of Stockett's testimony that she could not and would not return to the production industry in general, nor to the Tolin companies in particular, reinstatement would be a wholly ineffectual remedy. Front pay will therefore be awarded to make Plaintiff whole, but will be limited to one year, a reasonable time in which Plaintiff could have obtained comparable employment. . . .

55. Inasmuch as Tolin was managing agent and principal of each of the corporations, and since the evidence of a pervasively hostile work environment was well known to the principal officers, agents, and employees of the Defendant companies, each of the corporations . . . is responsible for . . . harassment by Tolin.

56. As an individual defendant, Tolin, as an agent for a corporate employer, is directly liable for his actions that violate Title VII. . . .

58. Plaintiff also asserts . . . claims for . . . battery, invasion of privacy, intentional infliction of emotional distress, and false imprisonment. . . . On the ample record presented, Plaintiff is entitled to prevail on her state-law claims.

59. [The court's description of the torts pleaded by Stockett is omitted. — EDS.] . . . Florida recognizes the tort of intentional infliction of emotional distress. . . .[4]

---

4. . . . [C]ourts . . . consistently have held that the allegations sufficient to state a claim for sexual harassment are sufficient to state a claim for emotional distress, and have generally found what one court called "a common thread — a continued course of sexual advances, followed by refusals and ultimately, retaliation." Shaffer v. National Can Corp., 565 F. Supp. 909, 915 (E.D. Pa. 1983). As phrased in Fawcett v. IDS Financial Services, 41 FEP Cases 589, 593, 1986 WL 9877 (W.D. Pa. 1986) . . . :

Other district courts have held that cases in which a supervisor has conducted a continued course of sexual advances and harassment, followed by refusals by the employee, and retaliation by the supervisor in the form of denying promotions or making the atmosphere of the work place oppressive, involved conduct that is sufficiently outrageous to state a cause of action for intentional infliction of emotional distress.

Also relevant to the determination is the persistence with which the Defendant, Tolin, conducted himself. As the court observed in Cummings v. Walsh Construction Co., 561 F. Supp. 872 (S.D. Ga. 1983), in denying a motion for summary judgment on an emotional-distress count:

While it is true that Professor Prosser states that a solicitation for sex to an unwilling woman has been held not to lead to liability, [Prosser], at 55, he states, at page 56, that prolonged or repeated invitation, when raised to the point of "hounding" the invitee, can lead to liability.

561 F. Supp. at 882.

61. We find that Stockett is entitled to recover for the tortious behavior of Tolin. Tolin's groping and kissing of Stockett constituted both an offensive and unwelcome touching (i.e., battery) and an invasion of her physical solitude (invasion of privacy). Tolin's battery of Plaintiff—the repeated and offensive touching of the most private parts of Plaintiff's body—constitutes an intrusion into her physical solitude. Similarly, the act of entering the ladies bathroom constitutes an invasion of her privacy. In addition, the act of pinning Plaintiff against the wall and refusing to allow her to escape, even though only done for a short period of time, was false imprisonment. Further, the evidence establishes repeated physical attacks, as well as repeated verbal licentiousness. Tolin's conduct toward Stockett can only be characterized as being wanton, willful, and in total disregard of her rights. An ordinary prudent person, viewing his cumulative behavior, would be compelled to find this to be outrageous. The sum total of Tolin's conduct therefore also constituted an intentional infliction of emotional distress.

62. Under Florida law, Plaintiff is entitled to a sum that will reasonably compensate her for ... pain, suffering and mental anguish [that she has already suffered or can reasonably be expected to suffer as a result of the defendant's conduct]. . . . We conclude that, as to the state torts of battery, invasion of privacy, false imprisonment, and intentional infliction of emotional distress, Plaintiff is entitled to compensatory damages in the aggregate amount of $250,000. . . .

Stockett suffered from severe emotional distress during the entire time she worked at Limelite because of the sexually hostile atmosphere and Tolin's advances toward her. She continues to suffer distress, a loss of self esteem, and other lingering effects of her experience, and she will continue to suffer such distress in the future. On this record, we are satisfied that these damages are not fanciful or fleeting in nature. . . . Stockett is entitled to compensation for past mental anguish and loss of capacity for enjoyment of life; for future psychological care; and for future mental anguish and loss of capacity for enjoyment of life. . . .

65. Plaintiff is ... entitled to recover punitive damages. . . . While a punitive damages award is a drastic and often disfavored remedy, under controlling Florida law the particularly extensive and egregious conduct evident here warrants [it]. . . .

71. Under controlling Florida law, we conclude that Tolin's relentless pursuit of Plaintiff and others warrants special remediation by this Court. The Court will impose punitive damages in this case. In doing so, this Court is guided by the following:

a. The "overwhelming" public policy of the State of Florida is against sexual harassment. [Cited authority omitted.]

b. Tolin evidenced extreme insensitivity to the inappropriateness of his behavior, its effect on his victims and, for that matter, on the reputation of his studio and industry. . . . The willfulness of his conduct was exemplified by his continuous assertions that "the business belonged to him" and that he "could do what he wanted."

c. There is potential for great harm to be caused by Tolin's behavior, and similar behavior by others. We are mindful that many of the women who are involved in the production and film industries are young and inexperienced. . . .

d. Tolin made oppressive and invasive demands on Plaintiff and blatantly attempted to extort sex from her as a condition of employment.

e. The cost to Stockett of performing the role of a "private attorney general" is real. It is worth repeating that a sexual harassment plaintiff, more so than perhaps any litigant besides a rape victim, is herself on trial. No corner of Ms. Stockett's life or psyche was beyond the attempted reach of the Defendants' inquiry. She pursued this action knowing that the most embarrassing and intimate details of her life likely would be discussed in a public courtroom. If sexual harassment is to be eradicated—particularly the degrading and pervasive conduct well-documented on this record—the sacrifice called for in terms of the victim's privacy and dignity must be recognized and her service rewarded for bringing the wrongdoer to account.

f. The great wealth of Tolin, and his observation that $20 million dollars is but a small fraction of his wealth must also be considered. This boast, which Defendant contends was meant only to impress his competitors, will be a yardstick against which others will measure any punitive damage award. He is known, indeed self-proclaimed, to be fabulously wealthy. Under Florida law, if a punitive damage award against Tolin is to have either a special or general deterrent effect, it will have to be sufficiently large to be punitive at all.

g. We also consider the pervasiveness of the sexually hostile atmosphere and the frequency with which Tolin accosted Plaintiff and so many other women on the premises, and the thoroughly egregious, wanton nature of Tolin's conduct. Video, Studios, and DPC each knowingly allowed Tolin to carry on his activities as he served as principal officer and agent of each of them. . . .

73. Furthermore, it is axiomatic that a corporation can act only through its agents. Thus, when the agent of a corporation who causes the harm is the managing agent or primary owner of the corporation, punitive damages may be assessed against the corporation for the acts of the managing agent.

Therefore, based on the evidence and arguments presented, it is

ORDERED AND ADJUDGED that Plaintiff, Michelle Ann Stockett, shall recover from the Defendants, Frank Tolin, Limelite Studios, Inc., Limelite Video, Inc. and Directors Production Company, jointly and severally, judgment for damages in the aggregate amount of $308,284 [$41,904 in back pay, $16,380 in front pay, and $250,000 in tort damages.]. . . . Additionally, it is

ORDERED AND ADJUDGED that Plaintiff shall have judgement for punitive damages in the amount of $1.00 against Directors Production Company, $5,000 against Limelite Studios, Inc., $50,000 against Limelite Video, Inc., and $1 million against Frank Tolin, for a total of $1,055,001 in punitive damages. . . . Finally, it is further

ORDERED AND ADJUDGED that Plaintiff, as a prevailing plaintiff in a Title VII action, is entitled to recover reasonable attorney's fees. . . .

NOTES AND QUESTIONS

1. *The ADEA and Title VII: Procedures.* The Age Discrimination in Employment Act (ADEA) and Title VII are but two of several important federal statutes regulating the terms and conditions of employment. Others include statutes that set the terms under which unions and management negotiate wages and working conditions, that bar discrimination on grounds of disability, and that mandate that employers of a certain size grant employees maternity and medical leaves.

As the foregoing cases attest, both Title VII and the ADEA expressly generate private rights of action for victims of certain forms of employment discrimination. However, they do so in a manner that involves an administrative law overlay. Title VII grants employees of businesses of the requisite size the right to sue, but they must first file charges with a federal agency, the Equal Employment Opportunity Commission (EEOC). The agency, in turn, must notify the employer of the charge of discrimination and investigate the matter within a specified period of time. In addition, the agency must decide whether it will commence its own lawsuit against the employer. Only after these steps have been taken may the plaintiff proceed to commence her claim. By this means, the statute is designed to promote prompt and relatively informal resolution of charges of employment discrimination.

With certain important variations, the ADEA likewise empowers individuals to sue after first filing notice with the EEOC. One such variation is that a Title VII plaintiff may proceed with her individual suit even if the EEOC decides to sue in its own right, whereas an ADEA plaintiff may not.

2. *Employment Discrimination: Dignitary or Economic Injury?* When Title VII was enacted in 1964, it described the redress available to litigants who commenced employment discrimination suits in terms of *equitable* rather than legal remedies. In particular, it stated that upon a finding by the court that the employer had engaged in *intentional* discrimination in violation of its substantive provisions, the court was authorized to (1) enjoin the conduct in question, and (2) order other equitable relief as it deemed appropriate.

The object of these remedies was often described by courts in terms familiar to tort students — that of making the plaintiff "whole." However, the goal here was *not* that of fully compensating the plaintiff for having been mistreated, but instead that of providing her with *the terms of employment she would have enjoyed* but for the defendant's discrimination. Thus, in the case of plaintiffs such as Stockett, who were effectively forced out of their jobs by discriminatory acts, the courts were to award *back pay* (wages and benefits the employee would have received between the time of termination and the time of trial). In addition, they could either order the employee's reinstatement (where feasible), or award *front pay* (wages and benefits that the employee would stand to earn going forward, until such time as she could reasonably be expected to find comparable work). As originally enacted, Title VII did not permit an award to the plaintiff of emotional distress or punitive damages. Hence the importance of Stockett's assertion of separate common law tort claims: They provided the basis for the award to Stockett of emotional distress and punitive damages.

In 1991, Congress amended Title VII in ways that have rendered private actions brought under the statute more akin to tort actions. Thus, employees can now recover compensatory and punitive damages directly under the statute, although these awards are subject to statutory caps that vary with the size of the employer. These amendments also for the first time directed that individual Title VII claims shall be tried before a jury, rather than the trial judge. As a result, Title VII plaintiffs are now, like typical dignitary tort plaintiffs, in a position to recover emotional distress and punitive damages as determined by juries, although those damages are subject to statutory caps.*

The ADEA, consistent with the original terms of Title VII, empowers courts to grant appropriate equitable relief to victims of age discrimination in employment. As evidenced by *Wilson*, the ADEA, unlike Title VII, has always permitted jury trials, as well as "liquidated" (i.e., double) damages for "willful violations" of the act. It does not authorize awards for emotional distress or punitive damages.

3. *Discrimination and IIED. Wilson* and *Stockett* hold that IIED (and other torts) can provide certain ADEA and Title VII plaintiffs with the ability to convert claims of discrimination into claims of "outrageous" discrimination that, depending on the contours of state law, may warrant large compensatory and punitive awards. Given the ADEA's refusal to permit recovery of such damages, and given that even the amended Title VII sets caps on emotional distress and punitive awards, is there anything problematic about the interaction in this context of state tort law and federal antidiscrimination law? Or do they work in a complementary fashion? Do you agree with the *Wilson* court's assessment that the particular discriminatory acts undertaken by Wilson's supervisors against him rise to the level of outrageous discrimination, as opposed to ordinary discrimination?

4. Harris: *Economic versus Dignitary Injury Revisited. Stockett* cites the Supreme Court's 1986 *Meritor Savings Bank* decision for the rule that a Title VII plaintiff complaining of gender discrimination may prevail by proving either *quid quo pro* harassment, or *hostile work environment* harassment. In Harris v. Forklift Systems, Inc., 510 U.S. 17 (1993), the Court elaborated on the requirements for proving the latter form of

---

* *Stockett* was issued after the enactment of the 1991 amendments. Apparently, however, the trial judge decided not to apply them "retroactively" to Tolin's discriminatory conduct, which took place before their enactment. (On the retroactivity of the amendments, see Note 9 following Littlefield v. McGuffey.) Given this decision, Stockett's Title VII claims had to be tried by the judge, without a jury. Moreover, as indicated in the text, Stockett could only hope to recover emotional distress and punitive damages by asserting parallel state law tort claims. The parties were entitled to try the latter claims before a jury, but opted to have the judge resolve Stockett's federal and state law claims by means of a single bench trial.

harassment. Harris, a manager at the company, alleged various wrongful acts by Hardy, the president of the company. They were described by the Court as follows:

... Hardy told Harris on several occasions, in the presence of other employees, "You're a woman, what do you know" and "We need a man as the rental manager"; at least once, he told her she was "a dumb ass woman." Again in front of others, he suggested that the two of them "go to the Holiday Inn to negotiate [Harris's] raise." Hardy occasionally asked Harris and other female employees to get coins from his front pants pocket. He threw objects on the ground in front of Harris and other women, and asked them to pick the objects up. He made sexual innuendos about Harris's and other women's clothing.

... Harris complained to Hardy about his conduct. Hardy said he was surprised that Harris was offended, claimed he was only joking, and apologized. He also promised he would stop, and based on this assurance Harris stayed on the job. But ... Hardy began anew: While Harris was arranging a deal with one of Forklift's customers, he asked her, again in front of other employees, "What did you do, promise the guy ... some [sex] Saturday night?" ...

Faced with these allegations, the lower courts dismissed Harris's claim on the ground that while Hardy's conduct was offensive, it was not "so severe as to be expected to seriously affect [Harris's] psychological well-being." The Supreme Court, however, reinstated her claim, reasoning as follows:

... Title VII comes into play before ... harassing conduct leads to a nervous breakdown. A discriminatorily abusive work environment, even one that does not seriously affect employees' psychological well-being, can and often will detract from employees' job performance, discourage employees from remaining on the job, or keep them from advancing in their careers. Moreover, even without regard to these tangible effects, the very fact that the discriminatory conduct was so severe or pervasive that it created a work environment abusive to employees because of their race, gender, religion, or national origin offends Title VII's broad rule of workplace equality....

... Certainly Title VII bars conduct that would seriously affect a reasonable person's psychological well-being, but the statute is not limited to such conduct. So long as the environment would reasonably be perceived, and is perceived, as hostile or abusive, there is no need for it also to be psychologically injurious.

This is not, and by its nature cannot be, a mathematically precise test.... But we can say that whether an environment is "hostile" or "abusive" can be determined only by looking at all the circumstances. These may include the frequency of the discriminatory conduct; its severity; whether it is physically threatening or humiliating, or a mere offensive utterance; and whether it unreasonably interferes with an employee's work performance. The effect on the employee's psychological well-being is, of course, relevant to determining whether the plaintiff actually found the environment abusive. But while psychological harm, like any other relevant factor, may be taken into account, no single factor is required.

Does this account of the wrong of workplace gender discrimination (in the form of maintaining a hostile work environment) help articulate the distinction between ordinary discrimination and outrageous discrimination? Is it fair to say, that on *Harris*'s description, claims seeking compensation for the maintenance of a hostile work environment remain, at their core, claims to vindicate an employee's *economic* interests, rather than the sort of dignitary interests protected by torts such as IIED?

5. *IIED and Employment: Other Applications.* Although wary of recognizing IIED causes of action arising out workplace interactions other than discrimination, courts do sometimes permit them. Often these involve gross abuses of the power that managers hold over their employees. *See, e.g.,* Agis v. Howard Johnson Co., 355 N.E.2d 315 (Mass. 1976) (employer who suspected employee theft began firing employees based on the alphabetical order of their names in order to force a confession; IIED liability upheld); Kaminski v. United Parcel Serv., 501 N.Y.S.2d 871 (App. Div. 1986) (affirming the trial court's refusal to dismiss employee's IIED claim; allegations that supervisors procured plaintiff's resignation by psychological and physical abuse deemed sufficient). As noted at the outset of this section, a predicate to recovery on any such claim is a finding that the plaintiff's injury does not give rise to a workers' compensation claim that would exclude recovery in tort.

II.   NEGLIGENT INFLICTION OF EMOTIONAL DISTRESS

The introduction to Part Three of this book, and to this chapter, indicated that we would *only now* be turning to consider the subject of negligence causing emotional distress. Of course, from the opening case of Walter v. Wal-Mart forward, we have seen numerous instances in which a plaintiff has recovered compensation for emotional distress caused by the negligence of another. Yet, for reasons we now explore, neither *Walter* nor any of these other cases involved claims for negligent infliction of emotional distress (NIED). Instead, each of these plaintiffs sought compensation for distress that flowed from a *physical harm* caused by the defendant's failure to take care not to cause that sort of harm.

Consider *Walter*. It is clear that the vast bulk of the jury's award to Ms. Walter was meant to compensate her for the immediate and lingering psychological effects of having been accidentally poisoned by Wal-Mart's careless pharmacist. Still, her claim was *not* that Wal-Mart breached a duty owed to her to take care against causing her to be upset or distressed. Rather, she claimed that Wal-Mart breached a duty to take care in dispensing medication so as not to poison her. In other words, the wrong of which Walter complained was not the wrong of *inattentiveness to her emotional well-being*, but inattentiveness to her physical well-being. Once Walter established that Wal-Mart committed the latter wrong, she became entitled to compensation for various losses that flowed from it, including the pain and suffering she experienced as a result of her illness. However, those losses were compensable only because they were *consequent to* (or *parasitic on*) the *predicate* injury of bodily harm. Walter's bodily harm — her illness — was the injury that rendered Wal-Mart's conduct actionable in the first place.*

By contrast to claims such as Walter's, a claim for NIED *does* assert that the defendant committed the particular wrong of failing to be sufficiently vigilant of the plaintiff's emotional well-being. For these sorts of claims, emotional distress is the injury that the defendant is supposed to have taken care not to cause. In such cases, the relationship between compensation for bodily harms and for emotional distress is inverted. (Thus, a true NIED claimant can recover compensation for having suffered a miscarriage or a heart attack if she can show that this sort of physical injury was consequent to the emotional distress that she suffered because the defendant failed to attend to a duty to be vigilant of her mental well-being.)

A.   *From No Injury to the Zone of Danger*

Wyman v. Leavitt
71 Me. 227 (1880)

[This suit involved two separate claims against a subcontractor alleging that the subcontractor acted carelessly by blasting rocks in an area adjacent to the land on which the Wymans lived, as a result of which rocks were thrown upon the property. One claim, brought by Mr. Wyman in his capacity as owner of the property, sought compensation for damage to the land. The second claim, brought on behalf of Mrs. Wyman, alleged that she suffered anxiety as a result of the blasting. At trial, Mrs. Wyman testified that she was in fear for her own safety, as well as that of their child. On that claim, the jury awarded $264 in damages. The defendant appealed. — EDS.]

Virgin, J.   ... As a general proposition, damages are recoverable when they are the natural and reasonable result of the defendant's unlawful act — that is when they are such a consequence as in the ordinary course of things, would flow from such an act. This is the broad rule, covering all the elements of damages, some of which do not enter into every case. The rule though correct as a general abstract statement has its limitations in particular cases.... Personal injury usually consists in pain inflicted both bodily and mental. When bodily pain is caused, mental follows as a necessary consequence, especially when the former is so severe as to create apprehension and anxiety. And not only the suffering experienced before the trial, but such as is reasonably certain to continue afterward, as the result of the injury, rightfully enters into the assessment of damages.

---

* As we saw in Chapter 9, courts confronted with certain dignitary torts will also allow recovery of compensation for "parasitic" emotional distress. A claimant who proves she has been the victim of an assault, battery, or false imprisonment at the hands of the defendant will thus be entitled to recover compensation for her distress over that mistreatment. Likewise, the common law has long permitted defamation plaintiffs to recover for distress associated with tortiously caused injury to reputation.

In [an action of] trespass for assault and battery, the jury may consider not only the mental suffering which accompanies and is a part of the bodily pain, but that other mental condition of the injured person which arises from the insult of the defendant's blows.... Or for an assault alone, when maliciously done, though no actual personal injury be inflicted.... So in various other torts to property alone when the tort-feasor is actuated by wantonness or malice, or a willful disregard of others' rights therein, injury to the feelings of the plaintiff, resulting from such conduct of the defendant, may properly be considered by the jury in fixing the amount of their verdict.

But we have been unable to find any decided case, which holds that mental suffering alone, unattended by any injury to the person, caused by simple actionable negligence, can sustain an action. And the fact that no such case exists, and that no elementary writer asserts such a doctrine, is a strong argument against it. On the contrary it has been held that a verdict, founded upon fright and mental suffering, caused by risk and peril, would in the absence of personal injury, be contrary to law. So it is said (in Lynch v. Knight, 9 Ho. L. 577, 598,) that, "mental pain and anxiety, the law cannot value, and does not pretend to redress when the unlawful act complained of causes that alone." Again, in Johnson v. Wells, 6 Nev. 224 (3 Am. R. 245), after a very elaborate examination, it was held that pain of mind aside and distinct from bodily suffering, cannot be considered in estimating damages in an action against a common carrier of passengers. If the law were otherwise, it would seem that not only every passenger on a train that was personally injured, but every one that was frightened by a collision or by the trains leaving the track, could maintain an action against the company. ... We are of the opinion, therefore, that Mrs. Wyman's testimony relating to her fears, as to her own personal safety, was erroneously admitted. Whether a fright of sufficient severity to cause a physical disease would support an action, we need not now inquire....

Robb v. Pennsylvania R.R. Co.
210 A.2d 709 (Del. 1965)

Herrmann, J.   The question before us for decision is this: May the plaintiff recover for the physical consequences of fright caused by the negligence of the defendant, the plaintiff being within the immediate zone of physical danger created by such negligence, although there was no contemporaneous bodily impact?

Considering the record in the light most favorable to the plaintiff, the facts may be thus summarized:

... On March 11, 1961, the plaintiff was driving an automobile up the lane toward her home when the vehicle stalled at [a] railroad grade crossing. A rut about a foot deep had been negligently permitted by the defendant to form at the crossing. The rear wheels of the automobile lodged in the rut and, although the plaintiff tried to move the vehicle for several minutes, she was unable to do so. While thus engaged in attempting to move the vehicle, the plaintiff saw the defendant's train bearing down upon her. With only seconds to spare, she jumped from the stalled vehicle and fled for her life. Immediately thereafter, the locomotive collided with the vehicle, hurled it into the air and demolished it. The plaintiff was standing within a few feet of the track when the collision occurred and her face was covered with train soot and dirt. However — and this is the nub of the problem — she was not touched by the train; there was no bodily impact; and she suffered no contemporaneous physical injury. Nevertheless, the plaintiff was greatly frightened and emotionally disturbed by the accident as the result of which she sustained shock to her nervous system. The fright and nervous shock resulted in physical injuries including cessation of lactation which interfered with the plaintiff's ability to nurse and otherwise care for her infant child. Her nervous and general physical condition resulting from the accident also obliged the plaintiff to abandon a horse breeding business and an article which she had been engaged to write for substantial compensation.

The defendant moved for summary judgment taking the position that . . . she may not recover because there was no "impact" and contemporaneous physical injury. The trial judge agreed and granted summary judgment in the defendant's favor, stating: "In spite of a modern trend to the contrary in other jurisdictions, I feel compelled to follow the 'impact theory' in this matter by reason of well established precedents in this State." The plaintiff appeals, asserting that there are no such governing precedents in Delaware. . . .

II.

. . . The two schools of thought in the matter at hand evolved from two lines of cases originating about the turn of the century. The impact rule was established in America by the leading cases of Ewing v. Pittsburgh, etc. R. Co., 147 Pa. 40, 23 A. 340, 14 L.R.A. 666 (1892); Mitchell v. Rochester R. Co., 151 N.Y. 107, 45 N.E. 354, 34 L.R.A. 781 (1896); and Spade v. Lynn & Boston R. Co., 168 Mass. 285, 47 N.E. 88, 38 L.R.A. 512 (1897). . . . The doctrine denying recovery was not accepted universally, however. In Purcell v. St. Paul, etc., Ry. Co., 48 Minn. 134, 50 N.W. 1034, 16 L.R.A. 203 (1892) and Mack v. South Bound R. Co., 52 S.C. 323, 29 S.E. 905, 40 L.R.A. 679 (1897) the contrary rule was adopted; and . . . the courts of an increasing number of jurisdictions have been adopting the rule allowing recovery for injury due to fright induced by negligence without impact; until today the latter is recognized as the majority rule.

The impact rule is based, generally speaking, upon three propositions . . . :

1)   It is stated that since fright alone does not give rise to a cause of action, the consequences of fright will not give rise to a cause of action. This is now generally recognized to be a non-sequitur, want of damage being recognized as the reason that negligence causing mere fright is not actionable. It is now generally agreed, even in jurisdictions which have adopted the impact rule, that

the gist of the action is the injury flowing from the negligence, whether operating through the medium of physical impact or nervous shock.

2) It is stated that the physical consequences of fright are too remote and that the requisite causal connection is unprovable... . The fallacies of this ground of the impact rule, viewed in the light of growing medical knowledge, were well stated by Chief Justice Maltbie in Orlo v. Connecticut Co., 128 Conn. 231, 21 A.2d 402 (1941). It was there pointed out that the early difficulty in tracing a resulting injury back through fright or nervous shock has been minimized by the advance of medical science; and that the line of cases permitting recovery for serious injuries resulting from fright, where there has been but a trivial impact in itself causing little or no injury, demonstrate that there is no insuperable difficulty in tracing causal connection between the wrongdoing and the injury via the fright.

3) It is stated that public policy and expediency demand that there be no recovery for the physical consequences of fright in the absence of a contemporaneous physical injury.... In recent years, this has become the principal reason for denying recovery on the basis of the impact rule. In support of this argument, it is said that fright is a subjective state of mind, difficult to evaluate, and of such nature that proof by the claimant is too easy and disproof by the party charged too difficult, thus making it unsafe as a practical matter for the law to deal with such claims. This school of thought concludes that to permit recovery in such cases would open a "Pandora's Box" of fictitious and fraudulent claims involving speculative and conjectural damages with which the law and medical science cannot justly cope.... The expediency ground was termed a matter of "administrative policy" for each jurisdiction in the Restatement of the Law of Torts, Sec. 436, Caveat to Subsection (2). It is noteworthy that this Caveat was removed by the 1948 Supplement to the Restatement (p.740) in recognition of the accelerating trend of the law away from the impact rule and of the proven reliability of medical testimony necessary to establish the causal connection between negligence and an ultimate injury....

III.

It is our opinion that the reasons for rejecting the impact rule far outweigh the reasons which have been advanced in its support.

The [first two grounds] for the rule have been discredited in the very jurisdictions which first gave them credence. As stated by Holmes, C.J., for the Supreme Judicial Court of Massachusetts, the *Spade* decision did not result from "a logical deduction from the general principles of liability in tort, but as a limitation of those principles upon purely practical grounds." Smith v. Postal Telegraph Cable Co., 174 Mass. 576, 55 N.E. 380, 47 L.R.A.

323 (1899). Or, as stated by the same eminent jurist on another occasion, [the liability] exemption from such damages [is] "an arbitrary exception, based upon a notion of what is practicable." Homans v. Boston Elevated R. Co., 180 Mass. 456, 62 N.E. 737, 57 L.R.A. 291 (1902)....

If more were needed to warrant a declination to follow the cause of action and the proximate cause arguments, reference to the fictional and mechanical ends to which the impact rule has been carried would suffice for the purpose. The most trivial bodily contact, itself causing little or no injury, has been considered sufficient to take a case out of the rule and permit recovery for serious physical injuries resulting from the accompanying fright. Token impact sufficient to satisfy the rule has been held to be a slight bump against the seat, Homans v. Boston Elevated R. Co., supra; dust in the eyes, Porter v. Del., L. & W.R.Co., 73 N.J.L. 405, 63 A. 860 (1906); [and] inhalation of smoke, Morton v. Stack, 122 Ohio St. 115, 170 N.E. 869 (1930)....

This leaves the public policy or expediency ground to support the impact rule. We think that ground untenable.

It is the duty of the courts to afford a remedy and redress for every substantial wrong. Part of our basic law is the mandate that "every man for an injury done him in his ... person ... shall have remedy by the due course of law...." Del. Const. Art. 1, Sec. 9, Del. C. Ann. Neither volume of cases, nor danger of fraudulent claims, nor difficulty of proof, will relieve the courts of their obligation in this regard. None of these problems are insuperable. Statistics fail to show that there has been a "flood" of such cases in those jurisdictions in which recovery is allowed ...; but if there be increased litigation, the courts must willingly cope with the task. As to the danger of illusory and fictional claims, this is not a new problem; our courts deal constantly with claims for pain and suffering based upon subjective symptoms only; and the courts and the medical profession have been found equal to the danger. Fraudulent claims may be feigned in a slight-impact case as well as in a no-impact case. Likewise, the problems of adequacy of proof, for the avoidance of speculative and conjectural damages, are common to personal injury cases generally and are surmountable, being satisfactorily solved by our courts in case after case.

We are unwilling to accept a rule, or an expediency argument in support thereof, which results in the denial of a logical legal right and remedy in all cases because in some a fictitious injury may be urged or a difficult problem of the proof or disproof of speculative damage may be presented. Justice is not best served, we think, when compensation is denied to one who has suffered injury through the negligence of another merely because of the possibility of encouraging fictitious claims or speculative damages in other cases. Public policy requires the courts, with the aid of the legal and medical professions, to find ways and means to solve satisfactorily the problems thus presented — not expedient ways to avoid them....

We hold, therefore, that where negligence proximately caused fright, in one within the immediate area of physical danger from that negligence, which in turn produced physical consequences such as would be elements of damage if a bodily injury had been suffered, the injured party is entitled to recover under an application of the prevailing principles of law as to negligence and proximate causation. Otherwise stated, where results, which are regarded as proper elements of recovery as a consequence of physical injury, are proximately caused by fright due to negligence, recovery by one in the immediate zone of physical risk should be permitted. . . .

We conclude, therefore, that the Superior Court erred in the instant case in holding that the plaintiff's right to recover is barred by the impact rule. The plaintiff claims physical injuries resulting from fright proximately caused by the negligence of the defendant. She should have the opportunity to prove such injuries and to recover therefor if she succeeds. The summary judgment granted in favor of the defendant must be reversed and the cause remanded for further proceedings.

Consolidated Rail Corp. v. Gottshall
512 U.S. 532 (1994)

Thomas, J.   These cases require us to determine the proper standard for evaluating claims for negligent infliction of emotional distress that are brought under the Federal Employers' Liability Act. . . .

I

Respondents James Gottshall and Alan Carlisle each brought suit under the Federal Employers' Liability Act (FELA), . . . 45 U.S.C. §§ 51-60, against their former employer, petitioner Consolidated Rail Corporation (Conrail). . . .

A

Gottshall was a member of a Conrail work crew assigned to replace a stretch of defective track on an extremely hot and humid day. The crew was under time pressure, and so the men were discouraged from taking scheduled breaks. They were, however, allowed to obtain water as needed. Two and one-half hours into the job, a worker named Richard Johns, a longtime friend of Gottshall, collapsed. Gottshall and several others rushed to help Johns, who was pale and sweating profusely. They were able to revive him by administering a cold compress. Michael Norvick, the crew supervisor, then ordered the men to stop assisting Johns and to return to work. Five minutes later, Gottshall again went to Johns' aid after seeing his friend stand up and collapse. Realizing that Johns was having a heart attack, Gottshall began cardiopulmonary resuscitation. He continued the process for 40 minutes.

Meanwhile, Norvick attempted to summon assistance, but found that his radio was inoperative; unbeknownst to him, Conrail had temporarily taken the nearest base station off the air for repairs. Norvick drove off to get help, but by the time he returned with paramedics, Johns had died.

The paramedics covered the body with a sheet, ordered that it remain undisturbed until the coroner could examine it, and directed the crew not to leave until the coroner had arrived. Norvick ordered the men back to work, within sight of Johns' covered body. The coroner, who arrived several hours later, reported that Johns had died from a heart attack brought on by the combined factors of heat, humidity, and heavy exertion.

The entire experience left Gottshall extremely agitated and distraught. Over the next several days, during which he continued to work in hot and humid weather conditions, Gottshall began to feel ill. He became preoccupied with the events surrounding Johns' death, and worried that he would die under similar circumstances. Shortly after Johns' funeral, Gottshall was admitted to a psychiatric institution, where he was diagnosed as suffering from major depression and post-traumatic stress disorder. During the three weeks he spent at the institution, Gottshall experienced nausea, insomnia, cold sweats, and repetitive nightmares concerning Johns' death. He lost a great deal of weight and suffered from suicidal preoccupations and anxiety. Gottshall has continued to receive psychological treatment since his discharge from the hospital.

Gottshall sued Conrail under FELA [alleging] . . . that Conrail's negligence had created the circumstances under which he had been forced to observe and participate in the events surrounding Johns' death. The District Court granted Conrail's motion for summary judgment. . . .

A divided panel of the United States Court of Appeals for the Third Circuit reversed. . . . Gottshall v. Consolidated Rail Corp., 988 F.2d 355 (1993). . . .

The panel majority concluded that there were genuine issues of material fact concerning whether Gottshall's injuries were foreseeable by Conrail, whether Conrail had acted unreasonably, and whether Conrail's conduct had caused cognizable injury to Gottshall. The court therefore remanded for trial. *Id.*, at 383. . . .

B

Respondent Carlisle began working as a train dispatcher for Conrail in 1976. In this position, he was responsible for ensuring the safe and timely movement of passengers and cargo. Aging railstock and outdated equipment made Carlisle's job difficult. Reductions in Conrail's work force required Carlisle to take on additional duties and to work long hours. Carlisle and his fellow dispatchers frequently complained about safety concerns, the high level of stress in their jobs, and poor working conditions. In 1988, Carlisle became trainmaster in the South Philadelphia yards. With this promotion came added responsibilities that forced him to work erratic hours. Carlisle began to experience insomnia, headaches, depression, and weight loss. After an extended period during which he was required to work 12- to 15-hour shifts for weeks at a time, Carlisle suffered a nervous breakdown.

Carlisle sued Conrail . . . for negligent infliction of emotional distress. He alleged that Conrail had breached its duty to provide him with a safe workplace by forcing him to work under unreasonably stressful conditions, and that this breach had resulted in foreseeable stress-related health problems. At trial, Carlisle called ... experts who testified that his breakdown and ensuing severe depression were caused at least in part by the strain of his job. The jury awarded Carlisle $386,500. . . .

The Third Circuit affirmed. . . . [It concluded] that "when it is reasonably foreseeable that extended exposure to dangerous and stressful working conditions will cause injury to the worker, the employer may be held to be liable under the FELA for the employee's resulting injuries." [Quoted authority omitted. — Eds.] The Third Circuit held that Carlisle had produced sufficient evidence that his injury had been foreseeable to Conrail. The court also found sufficient evidence that Conrail had breached its duty to provide Carlisle with a safe workplace by making his employment too demanding, and that this breach had caused Carlisle's injury. . . .

II

A

... Section 1 of FELA provides that "[e]very common carrier by railroad ... shall be liable in damages to any person suffering injury while he is employed by such carrier ... for such injury or death resulting in whole or in part from the negligence of any of the officers, agents, or employees of such carrier." 45 U.S.C. § 51. Our task today is determining under what circumstances emotional distress may constitute "injury" resulting from "negligence" for purposes of the statute. As we previously have recognized when considering § 51, when Congress enacted FELA in 1908, its "attention was focused primarily upon injuries and death resulting from accidents on interstate railroads." [Cited decision omitted.] Cognizant of the physical dangers of railroading that resulted in the death or maiming of thousands of workers every year, Congress crafted a federal remedy that shifted part of the " 'human overhead' " of doing business from employees to their employers. Tiller v. Atlantic Coast Line R. Co., 318 U.S. 54, 58, 63 S. Ct. 444, 446-447, 87 L. Ed. 610 (1943). *See also* Wilkerson v. McCarthy, 336 U.S. 53, 68, 69 S. Ct. 413, 420, 93 L. Ed. 497 (1949) (Douglas, J., concurring) (FELA "was designed to put on the railroad industry some of the cost for the legs, eyes, arms, and lives which it consumed in its operations"). In order to further FELA's humanitarian purposes, Congress did away with several common-law tort defenses that had effectively barred recovery by injured workers. . . .

We have liberally construed FELA to further Congress' remedial goal. [Citing cases.] . . .

That FELA is to be liberally construed, however, ... "does not make the employer the insurer of the safety of his employees while they are on duty. The basis of his liability is his negligence, not the fact that injuries occur." Ellis v. Union Pacific R. Co., 329 U.S. 649, 653, 67 S. Ct. 598, 600, 91 L. Ed. 572 (1947). And while "[w]hat constitutes negligence for the statute's purposes is a federal question," Urie [v. Thompson], 337 U.S.

[163], ... 174 [(1949]), 69 S. Ct., at 1027, we have made clear that this federal question generally turns on principles of common law: "[T]he Federal Employers' Liability Act is founded on common-law concepts of negligence and injury, subject to such qualifications as Congress has imported into those terms," *id.*, at 182, 69 S. Ct., at 1030-1031. Those qualifications, discussed above, are the modification or abrogation of several common-law defenses to liability, including contributory negligence and assumption of risk. Only to the extent of these explicit statutory alterations is FELA "an avowed departure from the rules of the common law." Sinkler v. Missouri Pacific R. Co., 356 U.S. 326, 329, 78 S. Ct. 758, 762, 2 L. Ed. 2d 799 (1958). Thus, although common-law principles are not necessarily dispositive of questions arising under FELA, unless they are expressly rejected in the text of the statute, they are entitled to great weight in our analysis. Because FELA is silent on the issue of negligent infliction of emotional distress, common-law principles must play a significant role in our decision.

B

We turn, therefore, to consider the right of recovery pursued by respondents in light of the common law. The term "negligent infliction of emotional distress" is largely self-explanatory, but a definitional point should be clarified at the outset. The injury we contemplate when considering negligent infliction of emotional distress is mental or emotional injury, *cf. id.*, at 568, 107 S. Ct., at 1417, apart from the tort law concepts of pain and suffering. Although pain and suffering technically are mental harms, these terms traditionally "have been used to describe sensations stemming directly from a physical injury or condition." Pearson, Liability to Bystanders for Negligently Inflicted Emotional Harm—A Comment on the Nature of Arbitrary Rules, 34 U. Fla. L. Rev. 477, 485, n.45 (1982). The injury we deal with here is mental or emotional harm (such as fright or anxiety) that is caused by the negligence of another and that is not directly brought about by a physical injury, but that may manifest itself in physical symptoms.

Nearly all of the States have recognized a right to recover for negligent infliction of emotional distress, as we have defined it. No jurisdiction, however, allows recovery for all emotional harms, no matter how intangible or trivial, that might be causally linked to the negligence of another. Indeed, significant limitations, taking the form of "tests" or "rules," are placed by the common law on the right to recover for negligently inflicted emotional distress....

Behind these limitations lie a variety of policy considerations, many of them based on the fundamental differences between emotional and physical injuries. "Because the etiology of emotional disturbance is usually not as readily apparent as that of a broken bone following an automobile accident, courts have been concerned ... that recognition of a cause of action for [emotional] injury when not related to any physical trauma may inundate judicial resources with a flood of relatively trivial claims, many of which may be imagined or falsified, and that liability may be imposed for highly remote consequences of a negligent act." Maloney v. Conroy, 208 Conn. 392, 397-398, 545 A.2d 1059, 1061 (1988). The last concern has been particularly significant. Emotional injuries may occur far removed in time and space from the negligent conduct that triggered them. Moreover, in contrast to the situation with physical injury, there are no necessary finite limits on the number of persons who might suffer emotional injury as a result of a given negligent act. The incidence and severity of emotional injuries are also more difficult to predict than those of typical physical injuries because they depend on psychological factors that ordinarily are not apparent to potential tortfeasors.

For all of these reasons, courts have ... placed substantial limitations on the class of plaintiffs that may recover for emotional injuries and on the injuries that may be compensable.... Some courts phrase the limitations in terms of proximate causation.... Other courts speak of the limitations in terms of duty; the defendant owes only a certain class of plaintiffs a duty to avoid inflicting emotional harm.... We shall refer to the common-law limitations as outlining the duty of defendants with regard to negligent infliction of emotional distress.

Three major limiting tests for evaluating claims alleging negligent infliction of emotional distress have developed in the common law. The first of these has come to be known as the "physical impact" test.... At the time Congress enacted FELA in 1908, most of the major industrial States had embraced this test. Under the physical impact test, a plaintiff seeking damages for emotional injury stemming from a negligent act must have contemporaneously sustained a physical impact (no matter how slight) or injury due to the defendant's conduct. Most jurisdictions have abandoned this test, but at least five States continue to adhere to it.

The second test has come to be referred to as the "zone of danger" test. It came into use at roughly the same time as the physical impact test, and had been adopted by several jurisdictions at the time FELA was enacted.... [T]he zone of danger test limits recovery for emotional injury to those plaintiffs who sustain a physical impact as a result of a defendant's negligent conduct, or who are placed in immediate risk of physical harm by that conduct.... The zone of danger test currently is followed in 14 jurisdictions....

[The third test permits recovery by relatives of a physical-injury victim who are traumatized by contemporaneously observing the victim being injured by the carelessness of the defendant. This test is discussed below in Section II.C. — EDS.]

III

A

Having laid out the relevant legal framework, we turn to the questions presented. As an initial matter, we agree with the Third Circuit that claims for damages for negligent infliction of emotional distress are cognizable under FELA.... We see no reason why emotional injury should not be held to be encompassed within that term, especially given that "severe emotional injuries can be just as debilitating as physical injuries." *Gottshall*, 988 F.2d, at 361. We therefore hold that, as part of its "duty to use reasonable care in furnishing its employees with a safe place to work," [Atchison, Topeka & Santa Fe Ry. v.] Buell, 480 U.S. [557,] 558 [(1987)], 107 S. Ct., at 1412, a railroad has a duty under FELA to avoid subjecting its workers to negligently inflicted emotional injury. This latter duty, however, is not self-defining. . . .

B

When setting out its view of the proper scope of recovery for negligently inflicted emotional distress under FELA, the Third Circuit explicitly refused to adopt any of the common-law tests described above; indeed, the court in *Gottshall* went so far as to state that "doctrinal common law distinctions are to be discarded when they bar recovery on meritorious FELA claims." 988 F.2d, at 369. . . . By the time . . . [it decided *Carlisle*, the court had] refined its test to two questions — whether there was convincing evidence of the genuineness of the emotional injury claim (with "genuine" meaning authentic and serious), and if there was, whether the injury was foreseeable. If these questions could be answered affirmatively by the court, there was "no bar to recovery under the FELA." 990 F.2d, at 98.

The Third Circuit's standard is fatally flawed in a number of respects. First, . . . [b]y treating the common-law tests as mere arbitrary restrictions to be disregarded if they stand in the way of recovery on "meritorious" FELA claims, the Third Circuit put the cart before the horse: The common law must inform the availability of a right to recover under FELA for negligently inflicted emotional distress, so the "merit" of a FELA claim of this type cannot be ascertained without reference to the common law.

Perhaps the court below believed that its focus on the perceived genuineness of the claimed emotional injury adequately addressed the concerns of the common-law courts in dealing with emotional injury claims. But the potential for fraudulent and trivial claims — the concern identified by the Third Circuit — is only one of the difficulties created by allowing actions for negligently inflicted emotional distress. A more significant problem is the prospect that allowing such suits can lead to unpredictable and nearly infinite liability for defendants. The common law consistently has sought to place limits on this potential liability by restricting the class of plaintiffs who may recover and the types of harm for which plaintiffs may recover. This concern underlying the common-law tests has nothing to do with the potential for fraudulent claims; on the contrary, it is based upon the recognized possibility of *genuine* claims from the essentially infinite number of persons, in an infinite variety of situations, who might suffer real emotional harm as a result of a single instance of negligent conduct.

Second, we question the viability of the genuineness test on its own terms. . . . [T]esting for the "genuineness" of an injury alone cannot appreciably diminish the possibility of infinite liability. Such a fact-specific test, moreover, would be bound to lead to haphazard results. Judges would be forced to make highly subjective determinations concerning the authenticity of claims for emotional injury, which are far less susceptible to objective medical proof than are their physical counterparts. To the extent the genuineness test could limit potential liability, it could do so only inconsistently....

Third, to the extent the Third Circuit relied on the concept of foreseeability as a meaningful limitation on liability, we believe that reliance to be misplaced. If one takes a broad enough view, *all* consequences of a negligent act, no matter how far removed in time or space, may be foreseen. Conditioning liability on foreseeability, therefore, is hardly a condition at all. "Every injury has ramifying consequences, like the ripplings of the waters, without end. The problem for the law is to limit the legal consequences of wrongs to a controllable degree." Tobin [v. Grossman], 24 N.Y.2d, at 619, 301 N.Y.S.2d, at 560, 249 N.E.2d, at 424....

This is true as a practical matter in the FELA context as well, even though the statute limits recovery to railroad workers. If emotional injury to Gottshall was foreseeable to Conrail, such injury to the other seven members of his work crew was also foreseeable. Because one need not witness an accident to suffer emotional injury therefrom, however, the potential liability would not necessarily have to end there; any Conrail employees who heard or read about the events surrounding Johns' death could also foreseeably have suffered emotional injury as a result. Of course, not all of these workers would have been as traumatized by the tragedy as was Gottshall, but many could have been. Under the Third Circuit's standard, Conrail thus could face the potential of unpredictable liability to a large number of employees far removed from the scene of the allegedly negligent conduct that led to Johns' death.[12]

Finally, the Third Circuit in *Carlisle* erred in upholding "a claim under the FELA for negligent infliction of emotional distress arising from work-related stress." 990 F.2d, at 97-98. We find no support in the common law for this unprecedented holding, which would impose a duty to avoid creating a stressful work environment, and thereby dramatically expand employers' FELA liability to cover the stresses and strains of everyday employment. Indeed, [this] . . . ruling would tend to make railroads the insurers of the emotional well-being and mental health of their employees. We have made clear, however, that FELA is not an insurance statute....

C

. . . We [conclude] . . . that the zone of danger test best reconciles the concerns of the common law with the principles underlying our FELA jurisprudence.

---

12. The Third Circuit did require that the emotional injury be "reasonably" foreseeable, but under the circumstances, that qualifier seems to add little. Suffice it to say that if Gottshall's emotional injury stemming from Johns' death was reasonably foreseeable to Conrail, nearly any injury could also be reasonably foreseeable.

As we did in Monessen [S. W. Ry. v. Morgan, 486 U.S. 330 (1988)], we begin with the state of the common law in 1908, when FELA was enacted. . . . [T]he right to recover for negligently inflicted emotional distress was well established in many jurisdictions in 1908. Although at that time, [most U.S. courts] favored the physical impact test . . . , the zone of danger test had been adopted by a significant number of jurisdictions. Moreover, because it was recognized as being a progressive rule of liability that was less restrictive than the physical impact test, the zone of danger test would have been more consistent than the physical impact test with FELA's broad remedial goals. Considering the question "in the appropriate historical context," *Monessen, supra,* 486 U.S., at 337, 108 S. Ct., at 1843, then, it is reasonable to conclude that Congress intended the scope of the duty to avoid inflicting emotional distress under FELA to be coextensive with that established under the zone of danger test. That is, an emotional injury constitutes "injury" resulting from the employer's "negligence" for purposes of FELA only if it would be compensable under the terms of the zone of danger test.

Current usage only confirms this historical pedigree. The zone of danger test . . . remains to this day a well-established "common-law concep[t] of negligence," [cited authority omitted], that is suitable to inform our determination of the federal question of what constitutes negligence for purposes of FELA.

The zone of danger test also is consistent with FELA's central focus on physical perils. . . . FELA was intended to provide compensation for the injuries and deaths caused by the physical dangers of railroad work by allowing employees or their estates to assert damages claims. By imposing liability, FELA presumably also was meant to encourage employers to improve safety measures in order to avoid those claims. . . . But while the statute may have been primarily focused on physical injury, it refers simply to "injury," which may encompass both physical and emotional injury. We believe that allowing recovery for negligently inflicted emotional injury as provided for under the zone of danger test best harmonizes these considerations. . . .

Respondents decry the zone of danger test as arbitrarily excluding valid claims for emotional injury. But "[c]haracterizing a rule limiting liability as 'unprincipled' or 'arbitrary' is often the result of overemphasizing the policy considerations favoring imposition of liability, while at the same time failing to acknowledge any countervailing policies and the necessary compromise between competing and inconsistent policies informing the rule." Cameron v. Pepin, 610 A.2d 279, 283 (Me. 1992). Our FELA cases require that we look to the common law when considering the right to recover asserted by respondents, and the common law restricts recovery for negligent infliction of emotional distress on several policy grounds: the potential for a flood of trivial suits, the possibility of fraudulent claims that are difficult for judges and juries to detect, and the specter of unlimited and unpredictable liability. Although some of these grounds have been criticized by commentators, they all continue to give caution to courts. We believe the concerns that underlie the common-law tests, and particularly the fear of unlimited liability, to be well-founded. . . .

IV

Because the Third Circuit applied an erroneous standard for evaluating claims for negligent infliction of emotional distress brought under FELA, we reverse the judgments below. In *Gottshall*, we remand for reconsideration under the zone of danger test announced today. Gottshall asserts before this Court that he would in fact meet the requirements of the zone of danger test, while Conrail disagrees. The question was not adequately briefed or argued before us, however, and we believe it best to allow the Third Circuit to consider the question in the first instance in light of relevant common-law precedent.

In *Carlisle*, however, we remand with instructions to enter judgment for Conrail. Carlisle's work-stress-related claim plainly does not fall within the common law's conception of the zone of danger, and Carlisle makes no argument that it does. Without any support in the common law for such a claim, we will not take the radical step of reading FELA as compensating for stress arising in the ordinary course of employment. In short, the core of Carlisle's complaint was that he "had been given too much — not too dangerous — work to do. That is not our idea of an FELA claim." *Lancaster, supra*, at 813.

The judgments of the Court of Appeals are reversed, and the cases are remanded for further proceedings consistent with this opinion.

[Concurrence of Justice Souter omitted. — EDs.]

Ginsburg, J., (dissenting) (joined by Blackmun and Stevens, JJ.) . . .

. . . In view of the broad language of [FELA], and this Court's repeated reminders that [it] is to be liberally construed, I cannot regard as faithful to the legislation and our case law under it the restrictive test announced in the Court's opinion. . . .

III

. . . The Court offers three justifications for its adoption of the "zone of danger" test. First, the Court suggests that the "zone" test is most firmly rooted in "the common law." The Court mentions that several jurisdictions had adopted the zone of danger test by 1908, *ante*, at 2406, and n.8 (citing cases from eight States), and that the test "currently is followed in 14 jurisdictions." *Ante*, at 2406. But that very exposition tells us that the "zone" test never held sway in a majority of States. . . .

The Court further maintains that the zone of danger test is preferable because it is "consistent with FELA's central focus on physical perils." *Ante*, at 2410. But, as already underscored, see *supra*, at 2413, the FELA's language "is as broad as could be framed. . . . On its face, every injury suffered [on the job] by any employee . . . by reason of the carrier's negligence was made compensable." *Urie*, 337 U.S., at 181, 69 S. Ct., at 1030. . . .

The Court's principal reason for restricting the FELA's coverage of emotional distress claims is its fear of "infinite liability" to an "infinite number of persons." The universe of potential FELA plaintiffs, however, is hardly "infinite." The statute does not govern the public at large. Only persons "suffering injury . . . while employed" by a railroad may recover . . . , and to do so, the complainant must show that the injury resulted from the railroad's negligence. 45 U.S.C. § 51. The Court expresses concern that the approach Gottshall and Carlisle advocate would require "[j]udges . . . to make highly subjective determinations concerning the authenticity of claims for emotional injury, which are far less susceptible to objective medical proof than are their physical counterparts." *Ante,* at 2409. One solution to this problem . . . would be to require such "objective medical proof" and to exclude, as too insubstantial to count as "injury," claims lacking this proof.

IV

. . . Instead of the restrictive "zone" test that leaves severely harmed workers remediless, however negligent their employers, the appropriate FELA claim threshold should be keyed to the genuineness and gravity of the worker's injury. . . .

NOTES AND QUESTIONS

1. *Predicate Injuries: Bodily Harm versus Property Damage.* Every U.S. court has long accepted *Wyman*'s observation that a jury may award compensation for (adequately proven) pain and suffering *parasitic* on a physical injury caused by the defendant's failure to take care not to cause bodily harm. This is why Antoinette Walter's recovery of compensation for her distress over her poisoning was routine.

Recall from Chapter 2 that the "general" duty to take reasonable care recognized by decisions such as Heaven v. Pender includes a duty to take care against damaging tangible property owned or possessed by another. Why, then, does the *Wyman* court seem unwilling to permit Mrs. Wyman to recover for her emotional distress as a loss consequent to the predicate injury of property damage? Here, she faced two problems. First, her husband appears to have been the sole owner of the land. Second, most courts are unwilling to treat negligent causation of tangible property damage as sufficient in itself to support a parasitic award of emotional distress damages to the property owner or possessor. For modern examples, see Erlich v. Menezes, 981 P.2d 978 (Cal. 1999); Stahli v. McGlynn, 366 N.Y.S.2d 209 (N.Y. App. Div. 1975). (Intentional causation of property damage, however, may sometimes permit such recovery. *See, e.g.,* Blache v. Jones, 521 So. 2d 530 (La. Ct. App. 1988).) However, the rule might be different if the property damaged by the defendant's carelessness has sentimental rather than just commercial value. For example, suppose Leavitt's careless blasting proximately caused the death of Mrs. Wyman's beloved pet dog, which she owned outright. Should she be able to recover emotional distress damages as parasitic on the injury to her "property"? Compare the majority and dissenting opinions in Rabideau v. City of Racine, 627 N.W.2d 795 (Wis. 2001); *see also* Tenn. Code Ann. § 44-17-403

(2001) (permitting up to $4,000 in damages for emotional distress resulting from the intentional or negligent killing of a pet).

2. *Injury Revisited*. Decisions such as *Wyman* are sometimes described as holding that a defendant owes *no duty* to others to take reasonable care not to cause them emotional distress. Although late-nineteenth-century courts may have at times expressed themselves in this way, such a description is misleading insofar as it suggests that the perceived problem with a claim such as Mrs. Wyman's resided in her inability to satisfy the duty element. In fact, courts at this time tended to deny liability on other grounds. Indeed, in quoting with approval the analysis of Lynch v. Knight, the *Wyman* court seems to concede, at least for purposes of analysis, that the defendant's conduct breached an obligation owed to Mrs. Wyman (i.e., was "unlawful") so as to cause her to suffer an adverse effect. The problem with her claim, instead, resided in the particular adverse effect of which she was complaining. According to *Wyman*, mental suffering alone, although undoubtedly a setback to Mrs. Wyman, did not count as the sort of setback that constitutes an *injury* required by the first element of the negligence cause of action. (To help grasp this point, you may wish to reconsider the analysis of the injury element provided at the outset of Chapter 2.) Without an injury of which to complain, Mrs. Wyman was in exactly the same position as a person who, although *at risk* of being hit by flying debris because of Leavitt's carelessness, was not struck by any debris, and was at all times completely oblivious to the danger. *Cf.* Canning v. Inhabitants of Williamstown, 55 Mass. 451 (1848) (neither peril nor fright constitutes an injury within the meaning of a statute permitting a person "injured" because of poor road conditions to recover damages from the person or party responsible for maintaining the road).

Suppose that the perceived absence of injury provides the basis for the *Wyman* court's holding. Is the court guilty of an inconsistency when it acknowledges that Mrs. Wyman *could prevail* if she could somehow prove that Leavitt conducted blasting *for the purpose* of causing her to apprehend that she was about to be struck by rocks? How is it that fear of being physically injured can at one and the same time constitute an injury that will support a claim of assault, yet not constitute an injury that will support a claim of negligence?

3. *The Issue of Gender Bias*. Some scholars, most prominently Professor Chamallas, have argued that the rule denying recovery for emotional distress owes its origins to the gender biases of nineteenth-century judges. It is no coincidence, they maintain, that the law developed special and restrictive rules for these claims, because such claims tended to be brought by female plaintiffs and sought relief for invasion of the sort of nonmaterial interest that male judges traditionally regarded as unmanly and unworthy of legal protection. *See* Spade v. Lynn & B.R. Co., 168 Mass. 285 (1897) (female trolley passenger suffered nervous shock as a result of a commotion caused by a conductors' negligence; rule against recovery for negligently inflicted nervous shock justified on the ground that actors cannot be held hostage to the "peculiar sensitiveness" of others). Professor Chamallas further notes that even as decisions such as *Robb* have whittled

away at the blanket no-duty rule, they have refused to go so far as to embrace a *Heaven*-like general duty to avoid causing emotional injury. This asymmetry, she claims, reveals a continuing bias in the law.

4. *NIED versus Ordinary Negligence: Impacts as Bodily Harms.* As noted in *Robb*, by the turn of the twentieth century, courts had begun to cabin the rule articulated in decisions such as *Wyman*. One common technique was to expand what would suffice to establish the requisite "predicate" physical injury. Under the *impact rule*, recovery for disturbance of emotional tranquility could be had if the defendant made even the most minimal physical contact with the plaintiff's person. By this means, courts moved certain "emotional distress" claims into the category of physical harm cases by, in effect, borrowing a page from battery law, under which any touching, no matter how slight, is sufficient. *See, e.g.*, Morton v. Stack, 170 N.E. 869 (Ohio 1930) (child trapped in burning building because of landlord's failure to provide a fire escape can recover for being traumatized; inhalation of smoke treated as sufficient to generate an impact).

While the impact rule was perhaps well intentioned as a corrective to the blanket rule denying claims for negligently inflicted emotional distress, the fix it provided was largely ad hoc. (Consider why the minimal touching requirements of battery law might be out of place in the context of negligence.) Perhaps the poster child for its unprincipled nature was the decision in Mitchell v. Rochester Ry. Co., 45 N.E. 354 (N.Y. 1896), which held that a pregnant woman who suffered a miscarriage as a result of being descended upon, but not touched, by a team of horses, could not recover. In light of decisions such as *Mitchell*, courts came to view the impact rule with considerable skepticism and have by and large replaced it with alternative rules permitting recovery. Courts have not always clearly stated whether these new rules are meant to supersede or supplement the impact rule (i.e., they have not explicitly stated that impact remains sufficient to permit recovery, even if not necessary). However, most hold or assume that trivial touchings are *not* sufficient to count as the sort of predicate injury that will support the award of emotional distress compensation as parasitic damages. *See, e.g.*, Metro-North Commuter R. Co. v. Buckley, 521 U.S. 424 (1997) (reproduced in Chapter 13) (declining to treat inhalation of asbestos particles as sufficient to constitute a predicate physical injury under the Federal Employers Liability Act).

5. *Extending Liability for Physical Harm.* While some courts were seizing on the impact rule as a means of mitigating the perceived harshness of the rule articulated in decisions such as *Wyman*, others pursued an alternative path. These courts focused not on *how the emotional distress came about* (i.e., whether it occurred contemporaneously with, or subsequent to, a bodily contact) but instead on *its consequences or effects* on the plaintiff. In particular, courts and commentators came to argue that a plaintiff who could establish that she had suffered a discrete bodily harm or diagnosable illness because of having been exposed to a sudden "shock" should be deemed to be suing not for emotional distress but for the consequent physical harm or illness. By this means, the plaintiff in

Mitchell, for example, could be understood to be suing for negligent driving that caused a miscarriage, a claim no different in kind from Antoinette Walter's claim to have been made physically ill by Wal-Mart's careless mishandling of her prescription.

Many commentators argued that a rule confining recovery to victims who could prove a physical harm flowing from their distress was superior to the impact rule on at least two counts. First, it is arguably consistent with decisions such as *Wyman* because it does *not* deem interference with the victim's interest in emotional tranquility as itself an injury. Second, by recognizing claims brought by those who suffered significant adverse physical effects as a result of distress, it seems likely to provide redress for persons who are among the most severely traumatized, whereas the impact rule worked in favor of the arbitrary class of persons who happen to have been touched. Still, before courts could proceed down this road, they had to overcome an important doctrinal barrier, one set not by the injury element, but by the requirement of proximate cause.

6. *The Problem of Remoteness.* The proximate cause problem arose because of a basic difference between a claim such as Antoinette Walter's, on the one hand, and a claim of the sort seen in *Mitchell*, on the other. In *Walter*, the distress experienced by the plaintiff followed as a consequence of her being poisoned — the distress played no significant role in her becoming ill in the first place. In *Mitchell*, by contrast, the defendant's careless driving brought about a miscarriage only via the medium of the plaintiff's emotional response to that carelessness. Many of the same courts that refused to recognize emotional distress as an injury unto itself treated this difference as providing a compelling reason not to impose liability even in cases such as *Mitchell*, in which carelessly caused distress produced physical harms. Claims such as Mitchell's were, in essence, claims for indirectly caused or "remote" harms, that is, harm not *proximately caused* by the carelessness of the defendant. In their view, it was the plaintiff's responsibility to control her reactions to the defendant's carelessness. To the extent she was "unable" or "unwilling" to do so, any consequent emotional distress was deemed to be her problem, rather than the defendant's doing.

For the foregoing reasons, proximate cause doctrine, at least as much as injury doctrine, blocked liability for physical harms arising out of carelessly caused emotional traumas. By the same token, as courts began to expand liability in this area, they did so *not* by recognizing that disturbance of emotional tranquility constitutes an injury, but instead by liberalizing proximate cause doctrine as it applied to claims of consequential physical harms. Specifically, they abandoned the idea that the causal connection between defendant's breach and plaintiff's injury was always too remote simply because the injury was linked to the breach through the plaintiff's emotional response to it.

With the abandonment of this *per se* rule of remoteness, potential liability for careless acts expanded *within* the domain of liability for carelessly caused *physical harms*. This explains why, when it came time for Dean Prosser to "restate" the law of negligence in 1965, he declined to treat decisions such as *Robb* as recognizing a cause of action for negligent infliction of emotional distress. Instead, he described them as claims for carelessness causing *physical harms* via an emotional traumatization of the plaintiff. *See* Restatement (Second) of Torts § 313(1) (1965) (noting that recoveries in cases such as *Robb* do not vindicate the victim's interest in emotional tranquility, but instead permit recovery for physical harms caused by emotional distress).

7. *From Remote to Proximate: The Special Salience of Shock. Robb* partakes of the expansionist strategy just described in Note 6. Yet it also emphasizes that it is not enough for the plaintiff to establish that she suffered consequential physical harm as a result of emotional distress caused by the defendant's carelessness. In addition, the court requires her distress to have come about in a particular way, or to be of a particular kind. Specifically, she must have experienced that distress as a result of *being imminently endangered* by the defendant's careless conduct. Thus, if we imagine that Mrs. Robb's car stalled 20 yards from the railroad crossing, she would apparently not be entitled to recover, even if she could prove that she was actually afraid for her life, and that she suffered the same illness as a result of that fear.

Given that *Robb*, like the Second Restatement, seems to treat claims such as Mrs. Robb's as claims for physical harms, what is the point of requiring her to have been (objectively) endangered? If she actually perceived a danger, and if she can prove that that trauma caused her to become physically ill, what is gained by denying her recovery simply because that fear proves to have been unfounded? For that matter, once we conceive of this class of negligence claims as falling within the class of claims for negligence causing physical harm, why should *fear of bodily injury* be privileged as a special form of distress that can (if it produces consequent physical harm) lay the basis for a claim in negligence? Why not other fears? Why not distress that has nothing to do with fear? Suppose, for example, Mrs. Robb was sitting in her car 30 yards from the grade crossing, but was severely traumatized because she witnessed the negligent killing of another driver whose car became stuck on the crossing. Why shouldn't she be entitled to recover for her illness notwithstanding that she was outside the "zone of danger"?

Again, history sheds some light here. It seems that the zone of danger requirement is in part an effort to express in more contemporary language the older idea of "nervous shock." As noted above, the effort to move past the impact rule crystallized around cases such as *Mitchell*, in which the plaintiff suffered an injury or illness after being exposed to a sudden threat of physical harm. These cases apparently struck many courts and commentators as presenting the most compelling grounds for rejecting the old proximate cause rule because this particular sort of shock was thought to be transmitted immediately and directly through the plaintiff's nervous system. In their view, a plaintiff who apprehends being killed or seriously harmed — particularly a female plaintiff — suffered an instant and literal fraying of the nerves. Thus, it could not be said of this sort of plaintiff that she had suffered harm that was *remotely* caused (because mediated by the plaintiff's mental response). Rather, the defendant had caused harm quite "directly," by physically damaging the plaintiff's nervous system.

Representative of this mindset is the decision in Lindley v. Knowlton, 179 Cal. 298 (1918). There, a mother whose children were attacked by her neighbor's pet chimpanzee was permitted to recover for lasting trauma associated with fending off the attack. Quoting an earlier California decision, Sloane v. Southern Cal. Ry. Co., 111 Cal. 668, 681 (1896), the Court explained:

> The nerves and the nerve centers of the body are a part of the physical system, and are not only susceptible of lesion from external causes, but are also liable to be weakened and destroyed from causes primarily acting on the mind. If these nerves or the entire nervous system is thus affected, there is a physical injury produced. . . .

Robb does not explicitly link its zone of danger requirement to a biological thesis of the sort propounded in *Lindley*. Still, it seems to share *Lindley*'s view that there is something particularly salient about having been distressed by virtue of having been imminently endangered.

8. *From Harm to Symptoms: The Emergence of True NIED Claims* Most jurisdictions have at least gone so far as to embrace *Robb*'s holding recognizing a negligence action for plaintiffs who suffer physical harms as a result of having been placed in imminent physical peril by another's carelessness. But this still leaves open the question of the doctrinal and theoretical basis on which they have done so. The choice of basis in turn has important implications for the scope of responsibility and liability in this area.

As noted, courts that sought to expand liability in this area originally required the plaintiff to have suffered a discrete physical harm such as a miscarriage or a heart attack. Many modern courts, however, have been willing to relax this requirement by accepting evidence that less obviously points to a discrete physical harm. (Might this be said of *Robb* itself?) Indeed, many courts, perhaps most, now permit recovery so long as the emotional trauma of being endangered generates in the plaintiff observable nontransient physical *symptoms*, such as nervous behavior or sleeplessness — what today might be deemed "post-traumatic stress disorder" (PTSD). *See, e.g.*, Dailey v. LaCroix, 384 Mich. 4 (1970); Tobin v. Grossman, 249 N.E.2d 419 (N.Y. 1969). A few courts have gone further and abandoned even the requirement of symptoms. *See* Corgan v. Meuhling, 574 N.E.2d 602 (Ill. 1991) (criticizing the physical manifestation test as an unnecessary restriction on recovery)).

By progressively watering down the physical harm requirement, modern courts have finally arrived at the position rejected by *Wyman*. In these cases, the complaint is no longer conceived as seeking recovery for *bodily harm* suffered by the plaintiff as a result of her emotional distress. Rather, the plaintiff is understood to be suing for, and is permitted to recover for, *emotional distress in and of itself*. The issue of proof of symptomology, in turn, does not arise because of a question as to whether the plaintiff has suffered a physical harm. Rather, the issue is whether the plaintiff has provided sufficient circumstantial evidence to permit the factfinder to conclude that she has actually suffered emotional distress.

9. *Scope of the Duty.* As *Gottshall* indicates, once emotional distress came to be recognized as an injury in its own right, the duty issue — that is, the issue of when one person can be said to be under an obligation to another to take reasonable care not to cause distress to another — moved to the forefront. Because of the peculiar historical path by which NIED claims emerged, they were, in effect, "born" with some built-in limitations that resemble "qualified" duty rules of the sort discussed in Chapter 2, Section III. For example, the requirement of "shock," which later manifested itself as the "zone of danger" requirement, has become a rule of qualified duty stating that all persons are under an obligation to take reasonable care not to conduct themselves in a manner *that physically endangers another so as to distress that other by placing her in fear of imminent bodily harm.*

Apart from historical considerations, can you think of reasons that might render the zone of danger limitation an intelligible qualified duty rule? Is there something about distress-through-endangerment that warrants its incorporation into a rule of duty? *Cf.* Wall v. Fairview Hosp. & Healthcare Servs., 584 N.W.2d 395 (Minn. 1998) (a claim for negligent infliction of emotional distress is essentially a claim for negligent causation of physical injury, except in these cases " '[f]ortune smiled and the imminent calamity did not occur.' ") (citation omitted).

10. *FELA and the Scope of the Zone of Danger Limitation.* The Federal Employers Liability Act (FELA) essentially creates a statutory negligence regime governing claims by railroad workers against their employers. Looking to common law as "persuasive" authority as to the meaning of the statute, the Supreme Court in *Gottshall* declined to extend NIED liability under FELA beyond the "zone of danger." Granted its decision, why is the Court willing to remand Gottshall's claim, especially given its dismissal of Carlisle's claim? Suppose that, on remand, Gottshall is prepared to testify that his distress consisted entirely of grief over his co-worker's death. Suppose further that an expert will testify that, by ordering Gottshall to continue to work under conditions of extreme physical and emotional distress, Conrail's foreman exposed Gottshall to the risk of imminent physical harm (e.g., a heart attack or heat stroke). Would a jury be permitted to enter a verdict for Gottshall on the basis of this testimony, or would some additional showing be required?

In two important subsequent decisions, the Supreme Court has reaffirmed *Gottshall*'s adherence to the zone of danger limitation on NIED liability under FELA, while also clarifying the circumstances under which exposure to toxic materials such as airborne asbestos can count as a predicate physical harm. See Chapter 13.

11. *Modern Recastings: Fraud and Floodgates.* At the same time that genuine NIED claims were first being recognized, and hence the duty issue was being brought to the fore, courts, particularly "progressive"

courts such as the California Supreme Court, were increasingly enchanted with the Prosserian idea that the "duty" issue in negligence cases does not actually concern the issue of whether the defendant was obligated to be vigilant of some interest of the plaintiff's, but instead provides a mere label for an inquiry into whether "policy" concerns warrant barring what would otherwise be a valid negligence claim. See Chapter 2. Because of this additional fortuity of timing, analysis of the limited scope of liability for NIED has been closely bound up with the identification of policy concerns that may or may not support those limitations. Thus, unlike the *Robb* court, most courts have — as *Gottshall* explains — maintained that macroconcerns of public policy are the only sorts of reasons that actually justify imposing special limits on NIED liability. In particular, they have emphasized two such concerns: (1) that, because distress is easy to feign, recognition of a broad duty would invite frivolous or fraudulent suits, and/or (2) that distress is so commonly the result of negligence as to threaten an overwhelming flood of litigation.

Does this pair of policy considerations make sense of the requirement of physical symptomology imposed by many courts on NIED plaintiffs? Is *Gottshall* correct to suppose that at least one of them also points toward reaffirmance of the zone of danger limitation on liability? Or might policy permit or warrant the expansion of NIED liability in at least some cases in which the plaintiff cannot point to physical symptoms of her distress, or cannot prove that she was in the zone of danger? These issues are further explored in Section II.C *infra*.

B.   Undertakings to Be Vigilant of Another's Emotional Well-Being

Even as late-nineteenth-century courts were busy asserting, with Lynch v. Knight, that "mental pain or anxiety the law cannot value, and does not pretend to redress," they were also recognizing exceptions to this rule. Thus, as was noted in the introduction to the materials on intentional infliction of emotional distress, courts would occasionally permit recovery for what appeared to be pure claims of distress against defendants who caused it through abominable misconduct. In addition, courts recognized a few pockets of liability even for carelessly caused emotional distress. In one common scenario, a telegraph company, *T*, would promise sender *S* to deliver promptly a telegram to recipient *R*. The telegram was meant to inform *R* that *R*'s close relative had passed away and that the relative's funeral was imminent. *T*, however, would carelessly fail to deliver the telegram, causing *R* to miss the funeral. Many courts permitted *R* to recover for the distress associated with missing the funeral. Of these, some treated *R*'s claims as sounding in contract. (These courts treated a plaintiff such as *R* as entitled to sue for damages from *T*'s breach as a "third-party beneficiary" to the contract between *S* and *T*.) Other courts treated such claims as tort actions in which the duty to attend to the recipient's emotional well-being was deemed to arise out of the implicit undertaking on the part of *T* to deliver an important and emotionally freighted message to *R* in a prompt fashion. *See, e.g.,* Mentzer v. Western Union Tel. Co., 62 N.W. 1 (Iowa 1895) (adopting both rationales).

In a related vein, courts have long recognized a duty to take reasonable care not to cause distress to family members when undertaking to dispose appropriately of the corpse of their decedent, regardless of whether those family members were the ones who contracted for funeral services. For a modern illustration, see Christensen v. Superior Court, 820 P.2d 181 (Cal. 1991) (recognizing a negligence cause of action for relatives of decedents distressed over defendants' mishandling of their decedents' corpses).

Finally, one other class of plaintiffs was frequently permitted to sue for negligence causing them emotional distress. These consisted of passengers — often young women — who sued common carriers for causing them, or even failing to protect them from, severe distress experienced in transit. *See, e.g.,* Wilson v. Northern Pac. R. Co., 32 P. 468 (Wash. 1893) (discussing and applying the rule of the common carrier cases in favor of a passenger who suffered distress after being erroneously caused to exit the train on which she was riding to pay an unnecessary additional fare). Similar claims were sometimes recognized by guests against inns and hotels.

Can one identify a set of principles that make sense of the courts' willingness to impose duties to be vigilant of others emotional well-being in these sorts of cases? Consider the following passage from Fitzsimmons v. Olinger Mortuary Ass'n, 17 P.2d 535, 536-537 (Colo. 1932), quoted in *Christensen, supra*:

> "One who prepares a human body for burial and conducts a funeral usually deals with the living in their most difficult and delicate moments. . . . The exhibition of callousness or indifference, the offer of insult and indignity, can, of course, inflict no injury on the dead, but they can visit agony akin to torture on the living. So true is this that the chief asset of a mortician and the most conspicuous element of his advertisement is his consideration for the afflicted. A decent respect for their feelings is implied in every contract for his services."

Christensen, 820 P.2d at 196. Do the other contracts or undertakings mentioned above carry with them a similar sort of obligation of "decent respect" for the feelings of certain others? If so, is this because of characteristics unique to the businesses of telegraph operators, morticians, and common carriers? Consider in this regard the following modern decision.

Beul v. ASSE Intl., Inc.
233 F.3d 441 (7th Cir. 2000)

Posner, J. In this . . . suit for negligence, governed (so far as the substantive issues are concerned) by Wisconsin law, the jury returned a verdict finding that plaintiff Kristin Beul's damages were $1,100,000 and that she was 41 percent responsible for them; in accordance with the verdict, judgment was entered against defendant ASSE International for $649,000 (59 percent of $1.1 million)....

The defendant is a nonprofit corporation that operates international student exchange programs. For a fee of $2,000 it placed Kristin, a 16-year-old German girl who wanted to spend a year in the United States, with the Bruce family of Fort Atkinson, Wisconsin. The family, which consisted of Richard Bruce, age 40, his wife, and their 13-year-old daughter, had been selected by Marianne Breber, the defendant's Area Representative in the part of the state that includes Fort Atkinson. Breber is described in the briefs as a "volunteer," not an employee; the only payment she receives from ASSE is reimbursement of her expenses. Nothing in the appeal, however, turns either on her "volunteer" status or on ASSE's nonprofit status. Charities are not immune from tort liability in Wisconsin, ... and ASSE does not deny that if Breber was negligent it is liable for her negligence under the doctrine of *respondeat superior*, even though she was not an employee of ASSE. The doctrine is nowadays usually described as making an employer liable for the torts of his employees committed within the scope of their employment, but strictly speaking the liability is that of a "master" for the torts of his "servant" and it extends to situations in which the servant is not an employee, provided that he is acting in a similar role, albeit as a volunteer....

There is also no argument that the contract between ASSE and Kristin's parents is the exclusive source of ASSE's legal duties to Kristin. Negligence in the performance of a contract that foreseeably results in personal injury, including as here emotional distress, is actionable under tort law.... As we pointed out in Rardin v. T & D Machine Handling, Inc., 890 F.2d 24, 29 (7th Cir. 1989), "tort law is a field largely shaped by the special considerations involved in personal-injury cases, as contract law is not. Tort doctrines are, therefore, prima facie more suitable for the governance of such cases than contract doctrines are" even when victim and injurer are linked by contract.

As the sponsor of a foreign exchange student, ASSE was subject to regulations of the United States Information Agency that require sponsors to train their agents, "monitor the progress and welfare of the exchange visit," and require a "regular schedule of personal contact with the student and host family." 22 C.F.R. §§ 514.10(e)(2), 514.25 (d)(1), (4) (now §§ 62.10(e)(2), 62.25(d)(1), (4)). These regulations are intended for the protection of the visitor, see "Exchange Visitor Program," 58 Fed. Reg. 15,180, 15,190 (1993) (statement of USIA accompanying promulgation of 26 C.F.R. § 514.25), and the jury was therefore properly instructed, under standard tort principles not challenged by ASSE, that it could consider the violation of them as evidence of negligence. There is no argument that the regulations create a private federal right of suit that would allow the plaintiffs to sue ASSE under the federal-question jurisdiction of the federal courts ..., or that Wisconsin is legally obligated to use the regulations to define the duty of care of a sponsor sued under state tort law.... But the district court was entitled to conclude that a state court would look to the regulations for evidence of the sponsor's duty of care. Courts in tort cases commonly take their cues from statutes or regulations intended to protect the safety of the class to which the tort plaintiff belongs.

ASSE is also a member of a private association of sponsors of foreign exchange students, the Council on Standards for International Educational Travel, which requires members to "maintain thorough, accurate, and continual communication with host families and school authorities." A jury could reasonably consider the Council's statement as additional evidence of the standard of care applicable to sponsors and it could also accept the plaintiff's argument that due care required Breber to try to develop rapport with Kristin so that Kristin would trust and confide in her and so that Breber could pick up any signals of something amiss that Kristin might be embarrassed to mention unless pressed.

Kristin Beul arrived in Wisconsin from Germany on September 7, 1995, and was met at the airport by Richard Bruce and his daughter. Marianne Breber did not go to the airport to meet Kristin. In fact, apart from a brief orientation meeting at a shopping mall in September with Kristin and one other foreign exchange student, at which Breber gave Kristin her phone number, she didn't meet with Kristin until January 21 of the following year — under unusual circumstances, as we'll see. She did call the Bruce home a few times during this period and spoke briefly with Kristin once or twice, but she made no effort to make sure that Kristin was alone when they spoke. She would ask in these calls how Kristin was doing and Kristin would reply that everything was fine. Breber did not talk to Mrs. Bruce, who would have told her that she was concerned that her husband seemed to be developing an inappropriate relationship with Kristin.

Kristin had led a sheltered life in Germany. She had had no sexual experiences at all and in fact had had only two dates in her lifetime. On November 17, 1995, Richard Bruce, who weighed almost 300 pounds and who was alone at home at the time except for Kristin, came into the loft area in which she slept and raped her.

This was the start of a protracted sexual relationship. In the months that followed, Bruce frequently would call the high school that Kristin was attending and report her ill. Then, with Mrs. Bruce off at work and the Bruce's daughter at school, Bruce would have sex with Kristin. By February 22, Kristin had been absent 27 days from school. Bruce brandished a gun and told Kristin that he would kill himself if she told anyone what they were doing together.

Curiously, in January Bruce and Kristin called Marianne Breber and told her that Mrs. Bruce appeared to be jealous of the time that her husband was spending with Kristin. Bruce invited Breber to dinner on January 21. Breber did not meet privately with either Kristin or Mrs. Bruce on that occasion, and she observed nothing untoward. In February, however, Mrs. Bruce told Breber that she and her husband were getting divorced, and Breber forthwith found another host family to take in Kristin. Kristin didn't want to leave the Bruce home, but on February 22 Breber arrived there with a sheriff's deputy to remove Kristin. The deputy asked Kristin in the presence of Richard Bruce and his daughter whether there was any inappropriate sexual activity between Richard and Kristin, and Kristin answered "no." The same day Breber, upon calling Kristin's school to tell them that Kristin would be out for a few days in connection with her change of residence, learned for the first time of Kristin's many absences.

Kristin lived with Breber for a few days between host families, but Breber didn't use the occasion to inquire about any possible sexual relationship between Kristin and Bruce. Breber told the new host family that Kristin was not to contact Bruce for a month, but she did not tell Bruce not to have any contact with Kristin. They continued to correspond and talk on the phone. Kristin had decided that she was in love with Bruce and considered herself engaged to him.

In April, Mrs. Bruce discovered some of Kristin's love letters and alerted the authorities. A sheriff's deputy interviewed Bruce. The next day Bruce, who had committed a misdemeanor by having sex with a 16 year old, Wis. Stat. § 948.09, killed himself, leaving a note expressing fear of jail. It is undisputed that the events culminating in Bruce's suicide inflicted serious psychological harm on Kristin; the jury's assessment of her damages is not claimed to be excessive.

The defendant argues that it was entitled to judgment as a matter of law, or alternatively to a new trial because of trial error. The first argument divides into three: there was insufficient proof of a causal relationship between the defendant's negligence in failing to keep closer tabs on Kristin Beul and her sexual involvement with Bruce culminating in his suicide; Bruce's criminal activity was the sole, or superseding, cause of her harm; and the harm was too "remote" in a legal sense from the defendant's failure of due care to support liability.

Since Kristin was determined to conceal her relationship with Bruce, the defendant argues, no amount of care by Breber would have warded off the harm that befell Kristin; she would have stonewalled, however pertinacious Breber had been in her questioning. This is conceivable, and if true would let ASSE off the hook; if there was no causal relation between the defendant's negligence and the plaintiff's harm, there was no tort.

But it is improbable, and the jury was certainly not required to buy the argument. Suppose Breber had inquired from the school how Kristin was doing — a natural question to ask about a foreigner plunged into an American high school. She would have learned of the numerous absences, would (if minimally alert) have inquired about them from Kristin, and would have learned that Kristin had been "ill" and that Richard Bruce had been home and taken care of her. At that point the secret would have started to unravel.

As for the argument that Bruce's misconduct was so egregious as to let ASSE off the hook, it is true that the doctrine of "superseding cause" can excuse a negligent defendant. Suicide by a sane person, unless clearly foreseeable by the tortfeasor, for example a psychiatrist treating a depressed person, is a traditional example of the operation of the doctrine.... So if Bruce's boss had refused him a raise and Bruce had responded by killing himself, the boss even if somehow negligent in failing to give him the raise would not be considered the legal cause of the death. Or if through the carelessness of the driver a truck spilled a toxic substance and a passerby scraped it up and poisoned his mother-in-law with it, the driver would not be liable to the mother-in-law's estate; the son-in-law's criminal act would be deemed a superseding cause.

Animating the doctrine is the idea that it is unreasonable to make a person liable for such improbable consequences of negligent activity as could hardly figure in his deciding how careful he should be. The doctrine is not applied, therefore, when the duty of care claimed to have been violated is precisely a duty to protect against ordinarily unforeseeable conduct, as in our earlier example of a psychiatrist treating depression. The existence of the duty presupposes a probable, therefore a foreseeable, consequence of its breach. (All that "foreseeable" means in tort law is probable ex ante, that is, before the injury that is the basis of the tort suit.) Thus a hospital that fails to maintain a careful watch over patients known to be suicidal is not excused by the doctrine of superseding cause from liability for a suicide, . . . any more than a zoo can escape liability for allowing a tiger to escape and maul people on the ground that the tiger is the superseding cause of the mauling.

So Kristin's high school would not have been liable for the consequences of Bruce's sexual activity with Kristin even if the school should have reported her frequent absences to Breber; the criminal activities with their bizarre suicide sequel were not foreseeable by the school. But part of ASSE's duty and Breber's function was to protect foreign girls and boys from sexual hanky-panky initiated by members of host families. Especially when a teenage girl is brought to live with strangers in a foreign country, the risk of inappropriate sexual activity is not so slight that the organization charged by the girl's parents with the safety of their daughter can be excused as a matter of law from making a responsible effort to minimize the risk. Sexual abuse by stepfathers is not uncommon, see, e.g., Diana E.H. Russell, *"The Prevalance and Seriousness of Incestuous Abuse: Stepfathers vs. Biological Fathers,"* 8 Child Abuse & Neglect 15 (1984), and the husband in a host family has an analogous relationship to a teenage visitor living with the family.

It is true (we turn now to the issue of remoteness) that when through the negligence of an alarm company, to which ASSE in its role as protector of foreign students from the sexual attentions of members of host families might perhaps be analogized, a fire or burglary is not averted or controlled in time, the company is generally not liable for the consequences; the consequences are deemed too remote. E.g., Edwards v. Honeywell, Inc., 50 F.3d 484, 491 (7th Cir. 1995). . . . There are two related considerations. One is that so many factors outside the alarm company's control determine the likelihood and consequences (whether in property loss or personal injury) of a failure of its alarm to summon prompt aid on a particular occasion that the company is bound to lack the information that it needs to determine what level of care to take to prevent a failure of its system. . . . A harm is not foreseeable in the contemplation of the law if the injurer lacked the information he needed to determine whether he must use special care to avert the harm. The second point is that the alarm company is not the primary accident avoider but merely a backup, and the principal responsibility for avoiding disaster lies with the victim. The points are related because both involve the difficulty a backup or secondary protector against disaster has in figuring out the consequence of a lapse on its part. Neither point supports ASSE, which was standing in the shoes of the parents of a young girl living in a stranger's home far from her homeland and could reasonably be expected to exercise the kind of care that the parents themselves would exercise if they could to protect their 16-year-old daughter from the sexual pitfalls that lie about a girl of that age in those circumstances. ASSE assumed a primary role in the protection of the girl. . . .

The defendant . . . complains about the following instruction to the jury: "You're instructed that the law of Wisconsin does not allow a child under the age of 18 to consent to an act of intercourse." This was a reference to the state's statutory rape law, but it was not elaborated further. The jury was instructed to consider the instructions as a whole and another instruction was that it was to consider Kristin's comparative fault. The jury assessed that fault at 41 percent, so obviously it did not think the age-of-consent instruction prevented it from considering Kristin's responsibility for the harm that befell her as a consequence of her sexual relationship with Bruce.

But should the jury have been told what the age of consent is in Wisconsin and, if so, was the information conveyed to the jury in the right way? The answer to the first question is yes. The age of consent fixed by a state represents a legislative judgment about the maturity of girls in matters of sex. Eighteen is a pretty high age of consent by today's standards and of course the law was not fixed by reference to German girls; but it is nonetheless a reminder that teenage children are not considered fully responsible in sexual matters, and this was something relevant to the jury's consideration of Kristin's share of responsibility for the disaster. The criminal law is frequently used to set a standard of care for civil tort cases . . . and that was essentially the use made of it here. It would have been error to instruct the jury that because Kristin was below the age of consent her comparative fault must be reckoned at zero. That would have given too much force to the criminal statute in this civil case, for the statute cannot be considered a legislative judgment that minors are utterly incapable of avoiding becoming ensnared in sexual relationships. A comparative-fault rule, moreover, requires gradations of victim responsibility that are alien to the normal criminal prohibition. Victim fault is not a defense, either partial or complete, to criminal liability. It is not a defense to a charge of rape that, for example, the victim was dressed provocatively, or drunk, or otherwise careless in the circumstances in which the rape occurred.

It would have been better, though, if the jury had been told how it should take the age of consent into account in their deliberations. It should have been told that in deciding how much responsibility to assign to Kristin for the events that gave rise to the harm for which she was suing, it could consider that the state had made a judgment that girls below the age of 18 should be protected by the criminal law from sexual activity even if they agree to it. As it was, the jury was left to tease out the relation between the age-of-consent instruction and the comparative-fault

instruction for itself. But we cannot think that it was other than a harmless error. Indeed, we are surprised that the jury assigned so large a
responsibility to this young foreign girl virtually abandoned by the agency
that was standing in for her parents. The jury verdict was rather favorable
to the defendant than otherwise.

Affirmed.

NOTES AND QUESTIONS

1. *Undertakings, Contracts, and Emotional Distress Damages.* In
Chapter 2, we learned from MacPherson v. Buick that a contractual relationship is not a prerequisite to the existence of a tort duty of care. *Beul*,
like some of its nineteenth-century predecessors, poses a different issue
bearing on the relation of tort and contract: If there is a contract between
defendant and plaintiff, and the plaintiff is injured by the defendant as a
result of the defendant inadequately performing — that is, breaching —
the contract, may the plaintiff sue in contract, tort, or both?

The short answer is the one given in *Beul*: A contractual relationship
between defendant and plaintiff *usually* does not of itself prevent the plaintiff from suing in tort, particularly if the suit alleges that the defendant's
performance or failure of performance caused *physical harm* to the plaintiff. For example, as discussed in Chapter 12, when a consumer contracts to
purchase a product from a company, the consumer usually is not thereby
barred from suing in tort for physical injuries caused by the product.
However, with respect to certain contracts and certain types of injuries,
particularly intangible economic injuries, courts are more willing to treat a
contractual relationship as strictly contractual, without any tort overlay.
These typically include business transactions (e.g., the sale and purchase of
goods or services between two firms), as well as sales of real property. In
these cases, even if one party negligently fails to attend to her end of the
contractual bargain so as to injure another, a tort action generally will not
lie and the aggrieved party's *only* remedy lies in a suit for breach of
contract.

The line between "merely" contractual relationships and contractual
relationships that can support tort duties of care has important implications for claimants seeking to recover for emotional distress injuries. When
contract law provides the exclusive source of the plaintiff's right to sue the
defendant, the plaintiff usually cannot recover emotional distress damages
that flow from the other party's breach of contract, even if that breach was
the product of carelessness and the distress was foreseeable to the defendant. *See, e.g.*, Erlich v. Menezes, 981 P.2d 978 (Cal. 1999) (a contractor
who negligently built a shoddy house for the plaintiffs in breach of their
contract is not liable for emotional distress caused to the plaintiffs by the
breach); Wehringer v. Standard Sec. Life Ins. Co., 440 N.E.2d 1331 (N.Y.
1982) (no right to recover for emotional distress resulting from breach of
a merely contractual duty). By contrast, as we learn from *Beul*, when a
contractual relationship is also deemed to support tort duties of care, a
plaintiff may be able to recover on a claim for pure emotional distress.

2. Beul *and NIED.* Judge Posner does not explicitly describe *Beul* as addressing a claim for negligent infliction of emotional distress. What exactly is the theory of Beul's negligence suit? Is the claim that ASSE owed it to her to take care to prevent her from suffering the physical or dignitary harms associated with Bruce's initial sexual assault? Or is the claim that ASSE breached a duty to prevent any inappropriate physical contact between Bruce and Kristin?

In its opinion denying ASSE's motion for J.N.O.V., the district court described Beul's suit as seeking compensation for the psychological harm associated with her emotionally tangled "relationship" with Bruce. Beul v. ASSE Intl., Inc., 65 F. Supp. 2d 963, 964 (E.D. Wis. 1999). In fact, the district court describes Bruce's initial assault less dramatically than does Judge Posner. We note this difference in characterization *not* to suggest that Bruce's act was less culpable than Posner's opinion suggests, but as indicative of the trial court's view that the crux of Beul's claim did not concern Bruce's assault *per se*, but rather his having coerced her into a disastrous relationship, and her complicated emotional response to its revelation and Bruce's subsequent suicide.*

Assume that the appropriate description of the gist of Beul's negligence claim is as a claim for NIED. On what basis is Judge Posner prepared to identify the requisite undertaking on the part of ASSE to look out for Kristin's emotional well-being? Notice his assertion that Kristin's school owed no such duty to her. Is it plausible to draw such a sharp distinction between ASSE and the school? Recall, in this regard, the description of a school's duties to high-school students in Rogers v. Retrum, *supra*, Chapter 3.

3. *Reviewing the Elements.* Judge Posner has argued in several academic works that leading jurists such as Holmes and Cardozo owe much of their influence to their superior prose. Obviously, he aims to emulate them in his own opinion-writing, and with considerable success. Leaving aside any disagreement you might have with the conclusions he and his colleagues reach in the decision, do you find that Judge Posner's "cradle-to-grave" analysis of Kristin Beul's negligence claim helps you to appreciate how to reason systematically and efficiently through a complex negligence case?

4. *Affirmative Duties and NIED.* To the extent *Beul* deems ASSE to have been obligated to take care with respect to Kristin Beul's emotional well-being, it seems to recognize not just a "negative" duty of taking care

---

* This interpretation of the nature of Beul's claim is also supported by the trial court's findings that a background check by ASSE would have revealed nothing untoward in the Bruces' past. Beul v. ASSE Intl., Inc., 55 F. Supp. 2d 942, 945, 949-950 (E.D. Wis. 1999). Admittedly, the trial judge did fault Breber for failing to advise Kristen on how she might attempt to handle the sexual advances of a host parent, which in turn might suggest a focus on the possible causal link between Breber's carelessness and the harm caused by Bruce's initial assault. However, that failure is listed as one of several that left Kristin to cope with the trauma of her ongoing interactions with Bruce and his subsequent suicide. 65 F. Supp. 2d at 965.

to avoid causing such distress, but an affirmative duty to protect her psychological well-being from risks of harm posed by others. Can you think of alternative scenarios in which a court should recognize an affirmative duty to take steps to rescue or protect persons from suffering emotional distress? *Compare* Rowell v. Holt, 850 So. 2d 474 (Fla. 2003) *with* Lauer v. City of New York, 733 N.E.2d 184 (N.Y. 2000). In *Powell*, the plaintiff was falsely arrested. At his arraignment, the plaintiff handed his lawyer documentary proof of his innocence. However, the lawyer carelessly delayed presenting the proof to a judge for ten days, during which time the plaintiff remained in prison. The Florida Supreme Court permitted the client to recover from his lawyer for the distress he experienced by virtue of being imprisoned.

In *Lauer*, a medical examiner (ME) employed by New York State conducted an autopsy on the plaintiff's infant son and concluded in his report that he died from blows to the head. The plaintiff thereby became the chief suspect in the police investigation of the boy's death. Several weeks after issuing the report, the ME conducted a follow-up autopsy and concluded that the son died of a birth defect. However, the ME did not issue an amended report or transmit his new findings to the police. Police continued to investigate the plaintiff for more than a year, as a result of which he suffered acute anguish and anxiety. Finally, a journalist uncovered the exonerating information in the ME's second report. On these facts, the New York Court of Appeals declined to recognize a duty of care owed by the ME to the plaintiff. Its stated concern was that recognition of such liability would interfere too greatly with the operation of the ME's office.

5. *Undertakings to Others*. As is apparent from the materials in this subsection, tort law treats certain relationships or interactions as generating a duty to be vigilant of others' emotional well-being. Is the converse true? That is, can certain actors plausibly argue that obligations already owed to persons other than the plaintiff ought to *preclude* the recognition of a duty to take care not to cause distress to the plaintiff? Suppose motorist *M* is involved in an accident with other driver *P*. Suppose further that an employee of *M*'s liability insurer *L* takes a "hard line" position in settlement negotiations with *P*, as a result of which the negotiations are heated and protracted, dragging on for two years before generating a settlement. May *P* sue *L* for NIED? *Cf.* Krupnick v. Hartford Accident & Indemnity Co., 28 Cal. App. 4th 185 (Ct. App. 1994) (motorist's insurer owes no duty to conduct settlement negotiations with reasonable care for the emotional well-being of plaintiffs injured by the insured driver).

The possibility that recognition of a claim for NIED will create a conflict among duties has figured prominently in suits against therapists who specialize in helping emotionally disturbed young women "recover" memories of early childhood abuse. Suppose therapist *T* is treating *Q*, the daughter of *F*. During therapy, *Q* becomes convinced that *F* sexually abused her, confronts him with these allegations, and severs all ties with him. *F*, distraught, sues *T*, claiming that this form of therapy is not medically sound and therefore negligent. Does *T* owe *F* a duty to conduct

Q's therapy with due care for *F*'s emotional well-being? In Doe v. McKay, 700 N.E.2d 1018 (Ill. 1998), the Illinois Supreme Court answered in the negative, noting that recognition of a duty to the parent might interfere with the therapist's duty to act in the best interests of her client. For its part, the Wisconsin Supreme Court was unimpressed with this argument. Sawyer v. Midelfort, 595 N.W.2d 423 (Wis. 1999).

6. *Employment and Undertakings.* Implicit in the Supreme Court's analysis in *Gottshall* is the assumption that the *employment relationship* does not carry with it an undertaking on the part of the employer to take reasonable care against causing severe emotional distress to its employees. (If there were such an undertaking, presumably Gottshall's and Carlisle's claim could proceed by analogy to the old undertaking cases and their modern counterparts, such as *Beul*.) Is this an obviously sound assumption? What, generally, might distinguish the employment relationship from the relationship of Kristin Beul to ASSE, or a train passenger to the train's operator? *Compare* Conaway v. Control Data Corp., 955 F.2d 358 (5th Cir.) (noting that Texas law does not recognize a duty owed by employers to employees to take care not to cause them distress by virtue of employment-related decisions; even a careless termination, for example, does not give rise to claim for NIED), *cert. denied*, 506 U.S. 864 (1992). Even granted the soundness of the Court's conclusion, can one argue that Gottshall's complaint alleges a viable cause of action other than NIED?

C.   *Beyond the Zone: Bystander Claims*

NIED liability is still subject to much more significant constraints than liability for negligence causing physical harms. Indeed, courts have generally been cautious about extending NIED theories outside of "zone of danger" and "undertaking" cases. By far the most prominent exception to this tendency involves the imposition of "bystander" liability — that is, liability to certain persons who witness another being injured or killed by the carelessness of the defendant. The next three cases all involve bystander claims. Consider carefully the differences among the approaches adopted by the three opinions.

Waube v. Warrington
258 N.W. 497 (Wis. 1935)*

Wickhem, J.   [Susie Waube was looking out the window of her house watching her daughter Dolores cross the road in front of it when she witnessed defendant Amber Warrington negligently run over and kill Dolores. According to the complaint, Susie was already frail at the time,

* [Overruled by Bowen v. Lumbermens Mut. Cas. Co., 517 N.W.2d 432, 442-443 (Wis. 1994) — EDS.]

and died two weeks later in part because of her anguish. Plaintiff, Susie's husband, brought a survival action against Amber Warrington, Amber's husband (the owner of the car), and the car's insurer. The survival action proceeded on the theory that, had Susie not died, she would have been able to recover compensation for her anguish via a cause of action for negligent infliction of emotional distress. — EDS.]

... [T]he question presented is whether the mother of a child who, although not put in peril or fear of physical impact, sustains the shock of witnessing the negligent killing of her child, may recover for physical injuries caused by such fright or shock.

The problem must be approached at the outset from the view-point of the duty of defendant and the right of plaintiff, and not from the view-point of proximate cause. The right of the mother to recover must be based, first, upon the establishment of a duty on the part of defendant so to conduct herself with respect to the child as not to subject the mother to an unreasonable risk of shock or fright, and, second, upon the recognition of a legally protected right or interest on the part of the mother to be free from shock or fright occasioned by the peril of her child. It is not enough to find a breach of duty to the child, follow the consequences of such breach as far as the law of proximate cause will permit them to go, and then sustain a recovery for the mother if a physical injury to her by reason of shock or fright is held not too remote.

Upon this point we adopt and follow the doctrine of Palsgraf v. Long Island R. R. Co., 248 N.Y. 339, 162 N.E. 99. ...

> Negligence is not actionable unless it involves the invasion of a legally protected interest, the violation of a right. ... The plaintiff sues in her own right for a wrong personal to her, and not as the vicarious beneficiary of a breach of duty to another. ... The passenger far away, if the victim of a wrong at all, has a cause of action, not derivative, but original and primary. His claim to be protected against invasion of his bodily security is neither greater nor less because the act resulting in the invasion is a wrong to another far removed.

... [Wisconsin case law holds that] ... in order to give rise to a right of action grounded on negligent conduct, the emotional distress or shock must be occasioned by fear of personal injury to the person sustaining the shock, and not fear of injury to his property or to the person of another.

Thus it may be said that the doctrine most favorable to plaintiff is not sufficiently broad to entitle him to recover. The question presented is whether there should be an extension of the rule to cases where defendant's conduct involves merely an unreasonable risk of causing harm to the child or spouse of the person sustaining injuries through fright or shock. ...

The only case squarely dealing with this problem is Hambrook v. Stokes Bros. [1925], 1 K.B. 141. [There, the defendant's employee parked the defendant's truck at the top of a hill without taking reasonable care to ensure that it would not roll away. When it did, it ran over the plaintiff's daughter as she walked to school. The plaintiff was nearby, but not herself endangered. She soon thereafter learned that a young girl had been run over by the truck, went to the hospital, and found her injured daughter there. According to the court, plaintiff "sustained a severe shock and consequent physical injuries from which she died." — EDS.] Viewing the matter from the standpoint of proximate cause rather than duty, the court held that ... defendant ought to have anticipated that if the unattended truck ran down this narrow street it might terrify some woman to such an extent, through fear of some immediate bodily injury to herself, that she would receive a mental shock with resultant physical injuries, and that defendant ought also to have anticipated that such a shock might result from the peril to the child of such a woman.

While the majority, mistakenly, as it seems to us, approach this problem from the standpoint of proximate cause, the dissenting opinion of Sargant, L.J., approaches it from the standpoint of duty. The dissenting opinion concedes that since it was defendant's duty to exercise due care in the management of his vehicle so as to avoid physical injury to those on or near the highway, this duty cannot be limited to physical injuries caused by actual physical impact. The dissenting opinion, however, states that ... "it would be a considerable and unwarranted extension of the duty of owners of vehicles towards others in or near the highway, if it were held to include an obligation not to do anything to render them liable to harm through nervous shock caused by the sight or apprehension of damage to third persons." The dissenting opinion concludes that there is no sound reason for erecting an exception in favor of the mother of a child, and points out that once the defendant's duty is held to extend to those outside the field of physical peril, a doctrine is stated to which no rational boundaries can be erected....

... Fundamentally, defendant's duty was to use ordinary care to avoid physical injury to those who would be put in physical peril, as that term is commonly understood, by conduct on his part falling short of that standard. It is one thing to say that as to those who are put in peril of physical impact, impact is immaterial if physical injury is caused by shock arising from the peril. It is the foundation of cases holding to this liberal ruling, that the person affrighted or sustaining shock was actually put in peril of physical impact, and under these conditions it was considered immaterial that the physical impact did not materialize. It is quite another thing to say that those who are out of the field of physical danger through impact shall have a legally protected right to be free from emotional distress occasioned by the peril of others, when that distress results in physical impairment. The answer to this question cannot be reached solely by logic, nor is it clear that it can be entirely disposed of by a consideration of what the defendant ought reasonably to have anticipated as a consequence of his wrong. The answer must be reached by balancing the social interests involved in order to ascertain how far defendant's duty and plaintiff's right may justly and expediently be extended. It is our conclusion that they can neither justly nor expediently be extended to any recovery for physical injuries sustained by one out of the range of ordinary physical peril as a result of the shock of witnessing another's danger. Such consequences are so unusual and extraordinary, viewed after the event, that a user of the highway may be said not to subject others to an unreasonable risk of them by the careless management of his vehicle. Furthermore, the liability imposed by such a doctrine is wholly out of proportion to the culpability of the negligent tort-feasor, would put an unreasonable burden upon users of the highway, open the way to fraudulent claims, and enter a field that has no sensible or just stopping point.

It was recognized by the court in the *Hambrook Case* that had the mother there merely been told of the injury to her child, instead of having been virtually a witness to the transaction, there would have been no liability. The court thus selected at least one arbitrary boundary for the extension.... [I]f the mother may recover, why not a child whose shock was occasioned by the peril of the mother? It is not necessary to multiply these illustrations. They can be made as numerous as the varying degrees of human relationship, and they shade into each other in such a way as to leave no definite or clear-cut stopping place for the suggested doctrine, short of a recovery for every person who has sustained physical injuries as a result of shock or emotional distress by reason of seeing or hearing of the peril or injury of another. No court has gone this far, and we think no court should go this far. It is our view that fairness and justice, as well as expediency, require the defendant's duty to be defined as heretofore stated.... Human wrong-doing is seldom limited in its injurious effects to the immediate actors in a particular event. More frequently than not, a chain of results is set up that visits evil consequences far and wide. While from the standpoint of good morals and good citizenship the wrong-doer may be said to violate a duty to those who suffer from the wrong, the law finds it necessary, for reasons heretofore considered, to attach practical and just limits to the legal consequences of the wrongful act....

Dillon v. Legg
441 P.2d 912 (Cal. 1968)

Tobriner, J. That the courts should allow recovery to a mother who suffers emotional trauma and physical injury from witnessing the infliction of death or injury to her child for which the tortfeasor is liable in negligence would appear to be a compelling proposition. As Prosser points out, "All ordinary human feelings are in favor of her [the mother's] action against the negligent defendant. If a duty to her requires that she herself be in some recognizable danger, then it has properly been said that when a child is endangered, it is not beyond contemplation that its mother will be somewhere in the vicinity, and will suffer serious shock." (Prosser, *Law of Torts* (3d ed. 1964) p.353.)

Nevertheless, past American decisions have barred the mother's recovery. Refusing the mother the right to take her case to the jury, these courts ground their position on an alleged absence of a required "duty" of due care of the tortfeasor to the mother....

We have concluded that [the grounds offered for these decisions are inadequate to justify] the frustration of the natural justice upon which the mother's claim rests....

... [P]laintiff's first cause of action alleged that ... defendant's negligent operation of his vehicle caused it to "collide with the deceased Erin Lee Dillon [as she lawfully crossed a street] resulting in injuries to decedent which proximately resulted in her death." (Complaint, p.3.) Plaintiff, as the mother of the decedent, brought an action for compensation for the loss.

Plaintiff's second cause of action alleged that she, Margery M. Dillon, "was in close proximity to the ... collision and personally witnessed said collision." She further alleged that "because of the negligence of defendants ... and as a proximate cause [*sic*] thereof plaintiff ... sustained great emotional disturbance and shock and injury to her nervous system" which caused her great physical and mental pain and suffering.

[Plaintiff's third cause of action asserted a claim for negligent infliction of emotional distress on behalf of Erin's sister Cheryl, who was alleged by plaintiff to have been standing near to Erin when Erin was struck down. — EDS.]

... [Defendant] moved for judgment on the pleadings, contending that "No cause of action is stated in that allegation that plaintiff sustained emotional distress, fright or shock induced by apprehension of negligently caused danger or injury or the witnessing of negligently caused injury to a third person. Amaya v. Home Ice, Fuel & Supply Co., 59 Cal. 2d 295 [29 Cal. Rptr. 33, 379 P.2d 513] (1963). Even where a child, sister or spouse is the object of the plaintiff's apprehension no cause of action is stated, *supra*, p.303, *unless the complaint alleges that the plaintiff suffered emotional distress, fright or shock as a result of fear for his own safety.* Reed v. Moore, 156 Cal. App. 2d 43 (1957) at page 45 [319 P.2d 80]." (Italics added.) The court granted a judgment on the pleadings against the mother's count, the second cause of action, and denied it as to the sister's count, the third cause of action. ...

The trial court apparently sustained the motion for judgment on the pleadings on the second cause ... because [Mrs. Dillon] was not within the zone of danger and denied that motion as to the third cause involving Cheryl because of the possibility that she was within such zone of danger or feared for her own safety. Thus we have before us a case that dramatically illustrates the difference in result flowing from the alleged requirement that a plaintiff cannot recover for emotional trauma in witnessing the death of a child or sister unless she also feared for her own safety because she was actually within the zone of physical impact.

... The case thus illustrates the fallacy of the rule that would deny recovery in the one situation and grant it in the other. ... [W]e can hardly justify relief to the sister for trauma which she suffered upon apprehension of the child's death and yet deny it to the mother merely because of a happenstance that the sister was some few yards closer to the accident. The instant case exposes the hopeless artificiality of the zone-of-danger rule. ...

We further note, at the outset, that defendant has interposed the defense that the contributory negligence of the mother, the sister, and the child contributed to the accident. If any such defense is sustained and defendant found not liable for the death of the child because of the contributory negligence of the mother, sister or child, we do not believe that the mother or sister should recover for the emotional trauma which they allegedly suffered. In the absence of the primary liability of the tort-feasor for the death of the child, we see no ground for an independent and secondary liability for claims for injuries by third parties. The basis for such claims must be the adjudicated liability and fault of defendant; that liability and fault must be the foundation for the tortfeasor's duty of due care to third parties who, as a consequence of such negligence, sustain emotional trauma.

We turn then to an analysis of the concept of duty, which, as we have stated, has furnished the ground for the rejection of such claims as the instant one. Normally the simple facts of plaintiff's complaint would establish a cause of action: the complaint alleges that defendant drove his car (1) negligently, as a (2) proximate result of which plaintiff suffered (3) physical injury. Proof of these facts to a jury leads to recovery in damages; indeed, such a showing represents a classic example of the type of accident with which the law of negligence has been designed to deal.

The assertion that liability must nevertheless be denied because defendant bears no "duty" to plaintiff "begs the essential question—whether the plaintiff's interests are entitled to legal protection against the defendant's conduct.... It [duty] is a shorthand statement of a conclusion, rather than an aid to analysis in itself.... But it should be recognized that 'duty' is not sacrosanct in itself, but only an expression of the sum total of those considerations of policy which lead the law to say that the particular plaintiff is entitled to protection." (Prosser, *Law of Torts, supra,* at pp.332-333.)

[The majority opinion reviews and adopts the arguments of Prosser and other scholars suggesting that the "duty" element of the negligence tort was not "originally" part of the tort, but was grafted on to it by late nineteenth-century judges anxious to limit jury discretion and the liability of nascent manufacturing and transportation industries. An element of such dubious origins, it suggests, ought to be regarded with great suspicion.—EDS.] ...

1. *This court in the past has rejected the argument that we must deny recovery upon a legitimate claim because other fraudulent ones may be urged.*

The denial of "duty" in the instant situation rests upon the prime hypothesis that allowance of such an action would lead to successful assertion of fraudulent claims. The rationale apparently assumes that juries, confronted by irreconcilable expert medical testimony, will be unable to distinguish the deceitful from the bona fide. The argument concludes that only a per se rule denying the entire class of claims that potentially raises this administrative problem can avoid this danger.

In the first instance, the argument proceeds from a doubtful factual assumption. Whatever the possibilities of fraudulent claims of physical injury by disinterested spectators of an accident, a question not in issue in this case, we certainly cannot doubt that a mother who sees her child killed will suffer physical injury from shock. "It seems sufficiently obvious that the shock of a mother at danger or harm to her child may be both a real and a serious injury." (Prosser, *Law of Torts, supra,* at p.353.) ...

In the second instance, and more fundamentally, the possibility that fraudulent assertions may prompt recovery in isolated cases does not justify a wholesale rejection of the entire class of claims in which that potentiality arises. The "contention that the rule permitting the maintenance of the action would be impractical to administer . . . is but an argument that the courts are incapable of performing their appointed tasks, a premise which has frequently been rejected." (Emden v. Vitz (1948) 88 Cal. App. 2d 313, 319 [198 P.2d 696].) . . .

Indeed, we doubt that the problem of the fraudulent claim is substantially more pronounced in the case of a mother claiming physical injury resulting from seeing her child killed than in other areas of tort law in which the right to recover damages is well established in California. For example, a plaintiff claiming that fear for his own safety resulted in physical injury makes out a well recognized case for recovery.[4] Moreover, damages are allowed for "mental suffering," a type of injury, on the whole, less amenable to objective proof than the physical injury involved here; the mental injury can be in aggravation of, or "parasitic to," an established tort. In fact, fear for another, even in the absence of resulting physical injury, can be part of these parasitic damages. The danger of plaintiffs' fraudulent collection of damages for nonexistent injury is at least as great in these examples as in the instant case.

In sum, the application of tort law can never be a matter of mathematical precision. In terms of characterizing conduct as tortious and matching a money award to the injury suffered as well as in fixing the extent of injury, the process cannot be perfect. Undoubtedly, ever since the ancient case of the tavernkeeper's wife who successfully avoided the hatchet cast by an irate customer (I de S et ux v. W de S, Y.B. 22 Edw. iii, f.99, pl.60 (1348)), defendants have argued that plaintiffs' claims of injury from emotional trauma might well be fraudulent. Yet we cannot let the difficulties of adjudication frustrate the principle that there be a remedy for every substantial wrong.

2. *The alleged inability to fix definitions for recovery on the different facts of future cases does not justify the denial of recovery on the specific facts of the instant case; in any event, proper guidelines can indicate the extent of liability for such future cases.*

In order to limit the otherwise potentially infinite liability which would follow every negligent act, the law of torts holds defendant amenable only for injuries to others which to defendant at the time were reasonably foreseeable.

4.   . . . [I]t is incongruous and somewhat revolting to sanction recovery for the mother if she suffers shock from fear for her own safety and to deny it for shock from the witnessed death of her own daughter. To the layman such a ruling must appear incomprehensible; for the courts to rely upon self-contradictory legalistic abstractions to justify it is indefensible. We concur with Judge Magruder's observation in 49 Harvard Law Review 1033, at page 1039: "Once accepting the view that a plaintiff threatened with an injurious impact may recover for bodily harm resulting from shock without impact, it is easy to agree with Atkin, L.J. ([Hambrook v. Stokes Bros., [1925] 1 K.B. 141, 158-159]), that to hinge recovery on the speculative issue whether the parent was shocked through fear for herself or for her children 'would be discreditable to any system of jurisprudence.'"

In the absence of "overriding policy considerations ... foreseeability of risk [is] of ... primary importance in establishing the element of duty." (Grafton v. Mollica (1965) 231 Cal. App. 2d 860, 865 [42 Cal. Rptr. 306]. ... As a classic opinion states: "The risk reasonably to be perceived defines the duty to be obeyed." (Palsgraf v. Long Island R.R. Co. (1928) 248 N.Y. 339, 344 [162 N.E. 99, 59 A.L.R. 253].) Defendant owes a duty, in the sense of a potential liability for damages, only with respect to those risks or hazards whose likelihood made the conduct unreasonably dangerous, and hence negligent, in the first instance. (*See* Keeton, *Legal Cause in the Law of Torts* (1963) 18-20; Seavey, *Mr. Justice Cardozo and the Law of Torts* (1939) 52 Harv. L. Rev. 372; Seavey, *Principles of Torts* (1942) 56 Harv. L. Rev. 72.) ...[5]

Since the chief element in determining whether defendant owes a duty or an obligation to plaintiff is the foreseeability of the risk, that factor will be of prime concern in every case. Because it is inherently intertwined with foreseeability such duty or obligation must necessarily be adjudicated only upon a case-by-case basis. We cannot now predetermine defendant's obligation in every situation by a fixed category; no immutable rule can establish the extent of that obligation for every circumstance of the future. We can, however, define guidelines which will aid in the resolution of such an issue as the instant one.

We note, first, that we deal here with a case in which plaintiff suffered a shock which resulted in physical injury and we confine our ruling to that case. In determining, in such a case, whether defendant should reasonably foresee the injury to plaintiff, or, in other terminology, whether defendant owes plaintiff a duty of due care, the courts will take into account such factors as the following: (1) Whether plaintiff was located near the scene of the accident as contrasted with one who was a distance away from it. (2) Whether the shock resulted from a direct emotional impact upon plaintiff from the sensory and contemporaneous observance of the accident, as contrasted with learning of the accident from others after its occurrence. (3) Whether plaintiff and the victim were closely related, as contrasted with an absence of any relationship or the presence of only a distant relationship.

The evaluation of these factors will indicate the *degree* of the defendant's foreseeability: obviously defendant is more likely to foresee that a mother who observes an accident affecting her child will suffer harm than to foretell that a stranger witness will do so. Similarly, the degree of foreseeability of the third person's injury is far greater in the case of his contemporaneous observance of the accident than that in which he

---

5. The concept of the zone of danger cannot properly be restricted to the area of those exposed to *physical* injury; it must encompass the area of those exposed to *emotional* injury. The courts, today, hold that no distinction can be drawn between physical injury and emotional injury flowing from the physical injury; indeed, in the light of modern medical knowledge, any such distinction would be indefensible. As a result, in awarding recovery for emotional shock upon witnessing another's injury or death, we cannot draw a line between the plaintiff who is in the zone of danger of physical impact and the plaintiff who is in the zone of danger of emotional impact. The recovery of the one, within the guidelines set forth *infra*, is as much compelled as that of the other.

subsequently learns of it. The defendant is more likely to foresee that shock to the nearby, witnessing mother will cause physical harm than to anticipate that someone distant from the accident will suffer more than a temporary emotional reaction. All these elements, of course, shade into each other; the fixing of obligation, intimately tied into the facts, depends upon each case.

In light of these factors the court will determine whether the accident and harm was *reasonably* foreseeable. Such reasonable foreseeability does not turn on whether the particular plaintiff as an individual would have in actuality foreseen the exact accident and loss; it contemplates that courts, on a case-to-case basis, analyzing all the circumstances, will decide what the ordinary man under such circumstances should reasonably have foreseen. The courts thus mark out the areas of liability, excluding the remote and unexpected.

In the instant case, the presence of all the above factors indicates that plaintiff has alleged a sufficient prima facie case. Surely the negligent driver who causes the death of a young child may reasonably expect that the mother will not be far distant and will upon witnessing the accident suffer emotional trauma. As Dean Prosser has stated: "when a child is endangered, it is not beyond contemplation that its mother will be somewhere in the vicinity, and will suffer serious shock." (Prosser, *The Law of Torts, supra*, at p.353. *See also* 2 Harper & James, *The Law of Torts, supra*, at p.1039.)

We are not now called upon to decide whether, in the absence or reduced weight of some of the above factors, we would conclude that the accident and injury were not reasonably foreseeable and that therefore defendant owed no duty of due care to plaintiff. In future cases the courts will draw lines of demarcation upon facts more subtle than the compelling ones alleged in the complaint before us. . . .

. . . [T]he argument that "there is no point at which such actions would stop" is no more plausible today than when it was advanced in Winterbottom v. Wright (1842) 10 M. & W. 109, 111. History has exposed the fallacy of the claim that abolition of privity . . . would lead to "the most absurd and outrageous consequences, to which I can see no limit" (p.114). In taking another giant step forward, in imposing product liability in tort, we were not halted by the spectre of an inability to pre-judge every future case. [Discussed in Chapter 11. — EDS.] The setting of boundaries upon that doctrine makes the problem of fixing lines of limitation here appear, by comparison, almost miniscule. The widening of the area of liability and the possibility of the encouragement of unfounded and undefinable claims in the products liability field was sweeping; here we deal with a comparatively isolated and unusual situation. We do not believe that the fear that we cannot successfully adjudicate future cases of this sort, pursuant to the suggested guidelines, should bar recovery in an otherwise meritorious cause. . . .

[T]he history of the cases [concerning negligent infliction of emotional distress] does not show the development of a logical rule but rather a series of changes and abandonments. Upon the argument in each situation that the courts draw a Maginot Line to withstand an onslaught of false claims, the cases have assumed a variety of postures. At first they insisted that there be no recovery for emotional trauma at all. Retreating from this position, they gave relief for such trauma only if physical impact occurred. They then abandoned the requirement for physical impact but insisted that the victim fear for her own safety, holding that a mother could recover for fear for her children's safety if she simultaneously entertained a personal fear for herself. The final anomaly would be the instant case in which the sister, who observed the accident, would be granted recovery because she was in the "zone of danger," but the *mother*, not far distant, would be barred from recovery.

The successive abandonment of these positions exposes the weakness of artificial abstractions which bar recovery contrary to the general rules. As the commentators have suggested, the problem should be solved by the application of the principles of tort, not by the creation of exceptions to them. Legal history shows that artificial islands of exceptions, created from the fear that the legal process will not work, usually do not withstand the waves of reality and, in time, descend into oblivion....

... [F]or some artificial reason [ordinary principles of negligence] liability [are] alleged to be unworkable in the most egregious case of them all: the mother's emotional trauma at the witnessed death of her child. If we stop at this point, however, we must necessarily question and reject not merely recovery here, but the viability of the judicial process for ascertaining liability or tortious conduct itself. To the extent that it is inconsistent with our ruling here, we therefore overrule Amaya v. Home Ice Fuel & Supply Co., *supra*, 59 Cal. 2d 295.

To deny recovery would be to chain this state to an outmoded rule of the 19th century which can claim no current credence. No good reason compels our captivity to an indefensible orthodoxy.

The judgment is reversed.

Traynor, C.J. (dissenting). I dissent for the reasons set forth in Amaya v. Home Ice, Fuel & Supply Co. (1963) 59 Cal. 2d 295, 297-315 [29 Cal. Rptr. 33, 379 P.2d 513]. In my opinion that case was correctly decided and should not be overruled.

Burke, J. (dissenting) (joined by McComb, J.) As recently as 1963 this court, in *Amaya*, thoroughly studied and expressly rejected the proposition (pp.298-299) that tort liability may be predicated on fright or nervous shock (with consequent bodily illness) induced solely by the plaintiff's apprehension of negligently caused danger or injury to a third person. As related in our *Amaya* opinion, plaintiff there was the mother of a 17-month-old boy who saw him struck by a truck; accordingly our ruling necessarily included all mothers of small children who observe them being injured. Yet today this court's *Amaya* decision is overruled by an opinion which disdains any discussion whatever of the history and policy of pertinent law painstakingly set forth in *Amaya*.

Every one of the arguments advanced in today's opinion was considered by this court and rejected, expressly or by fair implication, in *Amaya*. Further, as *Amaya* points out (p.304 of 59 Cal. 2d), in every jurisdiction in this country that had ruled on the point at issue the decisions up to that time (1963) were unanimous in upholding the rule of nonliability. . . .

. . . [T]he majority's "guidelines" (*ante*, pp.740-741) are simply a restatement of those suggested earlier by Professor Prosser (Prosser, *Torts* (2d ed., 1955) p.182) they have already been discussed and expressly rejected by this court in *Amaya* (pp.312-313). Upon analysis, their seeming certainty evaporates into arbitrariness, and inexplicable distinctions appear. As we asked in *Amaya*: What if the plaintiff was honestly *mistaken* in believing the third person to be in danger or to be seriously injured? What if the third person had assumed the risk involved? How "close" must the relationship be between the plaintiff and the third person? I.e., what if the third person was the plaintiff's beloved niece or nephew, grandparent, fiance, or lifelong friend, more dear to the plaintiff than her immediate family? Next, how "near" must the plaintiff have been to the scene of the accident, and how "soon" must shock have been felt? Indeed, what is the magic in the plaintiff's being actually present? Is the shock any less real if the mother does not know of the accident until her injured child is brought into her home? On the other hand, is it any less real if the mother is physically present at the scene but is nevertheless unaware of the danger or injury to her child until after the accident has occurred? No answers to these questions are to be found in today's majority opinion. Our trial courts, however, will not so easily escape the burden of distinguishing between litigants on the basis of such artificial and unpredictable distinctions.

Further, and again contrary to the assertions of the majority (*ante*, pp.732-733), no fallacy or incongruity appears in the rule permitting recovery to one within the physical zone of danger for trauma suffered from fear of impact, but denying it to a person outside that zone. The impact feared must be to oneself, and it must be an objective fear — not merely that of an excessively imaginative or timid plaintiff. . . .

As this court declared in *Amaya* (p.315 of 59 Cal. 2d), there is good sense in the conclusion of the court in Waube [v. Warrington] that "the liability imposed by such a doctrine is wholly out of proportion to the culpability of the negligent tort-feasor"; further, to permit recovery by every person who might adversely feel some lingering effect of the defendant's conduct would throw us into "the fantastic realm of infinite liability." Yet the majority opinion in the present case simply omits to either mention or discuss the injustice to California defendants flowing from such a disproportionate extension of their liability — an injustice which plainly constituted a "prime hypothesis" for rejection of the liability sought to be imposed by the plaintiffs in *Waube* and in *Amaya*.

Additionally, the majority fail to explain their bare assertion (*ante*, p.733) that contributory negligence of Erin will defeat any recovery by plaintiff mother and sister. The familiar and heretofore unquestioned principle is that the relationships of parent and child or of husband and wife *in themselves furnish no basis* for imputation of contributory negligence. Is this principle now abrogated in California? If so, it is a ruling extending far beyond the confines of the particular issue now before us, and reaches potentially every negligence action in which the plaintiffs are members of the same family. . . .

Thing v. La Chusa
771 P.2d 814 (Cal. 1989)

Eagleson, J.   The narrow issue presented by the parties in this case is whether the Court of Appeal correctly held that a mother who did not witness an accident in which an automobile struck and injured her child may recover damages from the negligent driver for the emotional distress she suffered when she arrived at the accident scene. The more important question this issue poses for the court, however, is whether the "guidelines" enunciated by this court in Dillon v. Legg . . . are adequate, or if they should be refined to create greater certainty in this area of the law.
. . .

. . . [We] conclude that the societal benefits of certainty in the law, as well as traditional concepts of tort law, dictate limitation of bystander recovery of damages for emotional distress. In the absence of physical injury or impact to the plaintiff himself, damages for emotional distress should be recoverable only if the plaintiff: (1) is closely related to the injury victim, (2) is present at the scene of the injury-producing event at the time it occurs and is then aware that it is causing injury to the victim and, (3) as a result suffers emotional distress beyond that which would be anticipated in a disinterested witness.

I. BACKGROUND

On December 8, 1980, John Thing, a minor, was injured when struck by an automobile operated by defendant James V. La Chusa. His mother, plaintiff Maria Thing, was nearby, but neither saw nor heard the accident. She became aware of the injury to her son when told by a daughter that John had been struck by a car. She rushed to the scene where she saw her bloody and unconscious child, who she believed was dead, lying in the roadway. Maria sued defendants, alleging that she suffered great emotional disturbance, shock, and injury to her nervous system as a result of these events, and that the injury to John and emotional distress she suffered were proximately caused by defendants' negligence.

The trial court granted defendants' motion for summary judgment, ruling that, as a matter of law, Maria could not establish a claim for negligent infliction of emotional distress because she did not contemporaneously and sensorily perceive the accident. Although prior decisions applying the guidelines suggested by this court in Dillon v. Legg, *supra*, 68 Cal. 2d 728, compelled the ruling of the trial court, the Court of Appeal reversed the judgment dismissing Maria's claim after considering the decision of this court in Ochoa v. Superior Court (1985) 39 Cal. 3d 159 [216 Cal. Rptr. 661, 703 P.2d 1]. The Court of Appeal reasoned that . . . contemporaneous awareness of a sudden occurrence causing injury to her child was not a prerequisite to recovery under *Dillon*.

We granted review to consider whether *Ochoa* supports the holding of the Court of Appeal. We here also further define and circumscribe the circumstances in which the right to such recovery exists. To do so it is once again necessary to return to basic principles of tort law. . . .

III.   LIMITATIONS IN NEGLIGENCE ACTIONS

[The court reviewed the progression in California law from *Amaya* to *Dillon*. — EDS.] . . .

The *Dillon* court anticipated and accepted uncertainty in the short term in application of its holding, but was confident that the boundaries of this NIED action could be drawn in future cases. . . . Underscoring the questionable validity of that assumption, however, was the obvious and unaddressed problem that the injured party, the negligent tortfeasor, their insurers, and their attorneys had no means short of suit by which to determine if a duty such as to impose liability for damages would be found in cases other than those that were "on all fours" with *Dillon*. Thus, the only thing that was foreseeable from the *Dillon* decision was the uncertainty that continues to this time as to the parameters of the third party NIED action.

IV.   POST-*DILLON* EXTENSION

The expectation of the *Dillon* majority that the parameters of the tort would be further defined in future cases has not been fulfilled. Instead, subsequent decisions of the Courts of Appeal and this court, have created more uncertainty. And, just as the "zone of danger" limitation was abandoned in *Dillon* as an arbitrary restriction on recovery, the *Dillon* guidelines have been relaxed on grounds that they, too, created arbitrary limitations on recovery. Little consideration has been given in post-*Dillon* decisions to the importance of avoiding the limitless exposure to liability that the pure foreseeability test of "duty" would create and towards which these decisions have moved. . . .

[The court reviewed post-*Dillon* decisions relaxing the requirement of "sensory and contemporaneous observance" by permitting bystanders to recover if they recognized that the victim was about to be injured, or if they came upon the victim almost immediately after she was injured. These decisions culminated in *Ochoa, supra*. The defendants operated a juvenile facility in which plaintiff's teenage son was incarcerated. Because they carelessly failed to provide appropriate medical treatment to the son, he contracted and died of pneumonia. For several days, Mrs. Ochoa visited her son at the facility, watched his condition deteriorate, and unsuccessfully pleaded with staff to let her family physician care for him. Shortly before his death, the defendants physically wrested Mrs. Ochoa away from her son even as he pleaded with her not to leave. Mrs. Ochoa's complaint clearly satisfied two of the *Dillon* guidelines — she was a close relative who was at the scene of the injury-producing careless conduct. Arguably, however, the remaining guideline was not met because the distress experienced by Mrs. Ochoa did not involve the shock of witnessing an accident causing instantaneous injury. The supreme court nonetheless permitted her to recover. It also clarified that a bystander NIED plaintiff need not be aware that the defendant's conduct was "tortious" at the time of its occurrence so long as she is aware of a causal connection between the conduct and the harm to her relative. — Eds.][6]

V. CLARIFICATION OF THE RIGHT TO RECOVER FOR NIED

Not surprisingly, this "case-to-case" or ad hoc approach to development of the law that misled the Court of Appeal in this case has not only produced inconsistent rulings in the lower courts, but has provoked considerable critical comment by scholars who attempt to reconcile the cases....

Proposals to eliminate the arbitrary results of the proliferating, inconsistent and often conflicting *Dillon* progeny include the suggestion that recovery be allowed in any case in which recovery for physical injury is permitted. (*See* Ochoa v. Superior Court, *supra*, 39 Cal. 3d 159, 178 [conc. opn. of Grodin, J.].) Another would limit recovery to the close-relatives class contemplated by *Dillon*, but allow recovery whenever mental distress to the plaintiff was foreseeable. (*Id.* at p. 196, conc. & dis. opn. of Bird, C.J.) At the other extreme, respondent here and amicus curiae Association for California Tort Reform argue, in essence, that the *Dillon* "guidelines" should be recognized as substantive limitations or elements of the tort....

We acknowledged and addressed one aspect of this problem in Elden v. Sheldon (1988) 46 Cal. 3d 267 [250 Cal. Rptr. 254, 758 P.2d 582], holding that cohabitation, without formal marriage, did not constitute the close relationship contemplated by the *Dillon* guidelines and that foreseeability of injury alone does not justify imposition of liability for negligently caused emotional distress. In so doing, we again recognized that policy considerations justify restrictions on recovery for emotional distress notwithstanding the sometimes arbitrary result, and that the court has an obligation to establish those restrictions. *Elden* confirmed that those policy considerations include both the burden on the courts in applying vaguely defined criteria and the importance of limiting the scope of liability for negligence. If the consequences of a negligent act are not limited an intolerable burden is placed on society. A "bright line in this area of the law is essential." (46 Cal. 3d 267, 277.)

The issue resolved in *Elden* was too narrow to create that "bright line" for all NIED actions. This case, however, presents a broader question and thus affords the court a better opportunity to meet its obligation to create a clear rule under which liability may be determined. In so doing we balance the impact of arbitrary lines which deny recovery to some victims whose injury is very real against that of imposing liability out of proportion to culpability for negligent acts. We also weigh in the balance the importance to the administration of justice of clear guidelines under

6. ... *Ochoa* upheld not only a cause of action by the mother of the deceased child, but also the father whose complaint alleged that he had visited the child only once and "was extremely distressed by what he saw." (39 Cal.3d 159, 165, fn.6.) His recovery was limited, however, to the distress suffered on the one occasion on which he witnessed the apparent neglect of his son by the defendants. He was not permitted to recover for distress suffered when he learned from his wife after her subsequent visits to the child of the continuing neglect of and suffering experienced by the child.

which litigants and trial courts may resolve disputes. Thus, as we did in *Elden, supra,* 46 Cal. 3d 267, we return to the concerns which prompted the *Amaya* court, *supra,* 59 Cal. 2d 295, to deny recovery for negligent infliction of emotional distress.

Among the concerns of the *Amaya* court was the social cost of imposing liability on a negligent tortfeasor for all foreseeable emotional distress suffered by relatives who witnessed the injury. The court again faced this problem in Borer v. American Airlines, Inc. (1977) 19 Cal. 3d 441 [138 Cal. Rptr. 302, 563 P.2d 858], in which the court was asked to recognize a child's right to recover for the loss of a parent's consortium, an action that, like NIED, seeks monetary damages for mental or emotional loss. Refusing to permit such "filial" consortium actions, the court concluded that the cause of action for loss of consortium must be narrowly circumscribed. "Loss of consortium is an intangible injury for which money damages do not afford an accurate measure or suitable recompense; recognition of a right to recover for such losses ... may substantially increase the number of claims asserted in ordinary accident cases, the expense of settling or resolving such claims, and the ultimate liability of the defendants." (*Id.* at p. 444.) The decision, we explained, was one of policy. We reasoned that we could not "ignore the social burden of providing damages ... merely because the money to pay such awards comes initially from the 'negligent' defendant or his insurer. Realistically the burden ... must be borne by the public generally in increased insurance premiums or, otherwise, in the enhanced danger that accrues from the greater number of people who may choose to go without any insurance. We must also take into account the cost of administration of a system to determine and pay [the] awards; ..." (*Id.* at p. 447.)

While we emphasized in *Borer, supra,* 19 Cal. 3d 441, that our refusal to extend the right to recover damages in consortium cases did not signal a refusal to allow damages for intangible losses in other contexts, the policy bases for the decision are relevant to defining the NIED cause of action. Crucial to the *Borer* decision were the intangible nature of the loss, the inadequacy of monetary damages to make whole the loss, the difficulty in measuring the damage, and the societal cost of attempting to compensate the plaintiff. Multiplication of the defendant's liability was an additional concern. The number of family members who might seek damages on the basis of a single incident could unreasonably enlarge the defendant's burden. We rejected a suggestion that principles enunciated in *Dillon* mandated recognition of the children's cause of action, noting what was then the *Dillon* limitation—that the *Dillon* plaintiff have suffered physical injury—which limited the class of potential plaintiffs. *(*19 Cal. 3d at p.450.)[8]

---

8. Similar concerns led the court to reject a parent's cause of action for loss of a child's consortium in a companion case. "Our opinion in Borer v. American Airlines, *supra,* [19 Cal. 3d] 441, explains the policy considerations which impelled us to conclude that a child should not have a cause of action for loss of parental consortium. Those reasons for the most part apply fully to the present issue of a parental claim for loss of filial consortium. The intangible character of the loss, which can never really be compensated by money damages; the difficulty of measuring damages; the dangers of double recovery or multiple claims and of extensive liability—all these considerations apply similarly to both cases." (Baxter v. Superior Court (1977) 19 Cal. 3d 461, 464 [138 Cal. Rptr. 315, 563 P.2d 871].)

... Ochoa v. Superior Court, *supra*, 39 Cal. 3d 159, *165*, footnote 6, offers additional guidance, justifying what we acknowledge must be arbitrary lines to similarly limit the class of potential plaintiffs if emotional injury absent physical harm is to continue to be a recoverable item of damages in a negligence action. The impact of personally observing the injury-producing event in most, although concededly not all, cases distinguishes the plaintiff's resultant emotional distress from the emotion felt when one learns of the injury or death of a loved one from another, or observes pain and suffering but not the traumatic cause of the injury. Greater certainty and a more reasonable limit on the exposure to liability for negligent conduct is possible by limiting the right to recover for negligently caused emotional distress to plaintiffs who personally and contemporaneously perceive the injury-producing event and its traumatic consequences.

Similar reasoning justifies limiting recovery to persons closely related by blood or marriage since, in common experience, it is more likely that they will suffer a greater degree of emotional distress than a disinterested witness to negligently caused pain and suffering or death. Such limitations are indisputably arbitrary since it is foreseeable that in some cases unrelated persons have a relationship to the victim or are so affected by the traumatic event that they suffer equivalent emotional distress. As we have observed, however, drawing arbitrary lines is unavoidable if we are to limit liability and establish meaningful rules for application by litigants and lower courts.

No policy supports extension of the right to recover for NIED to a larger class of plaintiffs. Emotional distress is an intangible condition experienced by most persons, even absent negligence, at some time during their lives. Close relatives suffer serious, even debilitating, emotional reactions to the injury, death, serious illness, and evident suffering of loved ones. These reactions occur regardless of the cause of the loved one's illness, injury, or death. That relatives will have severe emotional distress is an unavoidable aspect of the "human condition." The emotional distress for which monetary damages may be recovered, however, ought not to be that form of acute emotional distress or the transient emotional reaction to the occasional gruesome or horrible incident to which every person may potentially be exposed in an industrial and sometimes violent society. Regardless of the depth of feeling or the resultant physical or mental illness that results from witnessing violent events, persons unrelated to those injured or killed may not now recover for such emotional upheaval even if negligently caused. Close relatives who witness the accidental injury or death of a loved one and suffer emotional trauma may not recover when the loved one's conduct was the cause of that emotional trauma. The overwhelming majority of "emotional distress" which we endure, therefore, is not compensable.

... In identifying those persons and the circumstances in which the defendant will be held to redress the injury, it is appropriate to restrict recovery to those persons who will suffer an emotional impact beyond the impact that can be anticipated whenever one learns that a relative is injured, or dies, or the emotion felt by a "disinterested" witness. The class of potential plaintiffs should be limited to those who because of their relationship suffer the greatest emotional distress. When the right to recover is limited in this manner, the liability bears a reasonable relationship to the culpability of the negligent defendant....

We conclude, therefore, that a plaintiff may recover damages for emotional distress caused by observing the negligently inflicted injury of a third person if, but only if, said plaintiff: (1) is closely related to the injury victim;[10] (2) is present at the scene of the injury-producing event at the time it occurs and is then aware that it is causing injury to the victim; and (3) as a result suffers serious emotional distress — a reaction beyond that which would be anticipated in a disinterested witness and which is not an abnormal response to the circumstances.[12] These factors were present in *Ochoa* and each of this court's prior decisions upholding recovery for NIED.

... The merely negligent actor does not owe a duty the law will recognize to make monetary amends to all persons who may have suffered emotional distress on viewing or learning about the injurious consequences of his conduct.... Experience has shown that, contrary to the expectation of the *Dillon* majority, and with apology to Bernard Witkin, there are clear judicial days on which a court can foresee forever and thus determine liability but none on which that foresight alone provides a socially and judicially acceptable limit on recovery of damages for that injury.

VI

The undisputed facts establish that plaintiff was not present at the scene of the accident in which her son was injured. She did not observe defendant's conduct and was not aware that her son was being injured. She could not, therefore, establish a right to recover for the emotional distress she suffered when she subsequently learned of the accident and observed its consequences. The order granting summary judgment was proper.

The judgment of the Court of Appeal is reversed....

[**Kaufman, J.**, concurred in the result, arguing that the court should return to *Amaya*'s zone of danger rule.]

[**Mosk, J.**, dissented, arguing that the majority's decision marked an unwarranted departure from *Dillon* and subsequent precedents.]

Broussard, J., (dissenting)....

Under the majority's strict requirement, a mother who arrives moments after an accident caused by another's negligence will not be permitted recovery. No matter that the mother would see her six-year-old

---

10. ... Absent exceptional circumstances, recovery should be limited to relatives residing in the same household, or parents, siblings, children, and grandparents of the victim.

12. As explained by the Hawaii Supreme Court, "serious mental distress may be found where a reasonable [person] normally constituted, would be unable to adequately cope with the mental distress engendered by the circumstances of the case." (Rodrigues v. State (1970) 52 Hawaii 156, 173 [472 P.2d 509, 519-520].)

son immediately after he was electrocuted, lying in a puddle of water in a dying state, gagging and choking in his own vomit, as in Hathaway v. Superior Court (1980) 112 Cal. App. 3d 728 [169 Cal. Rptr. 435]. No matter that the mother would be following her daughters' car and would come upon the wreckage of the car "before the dust had settled" to find the mangled bodies of her daughters, who were dead or dying, as in Parsons v. Superior Court (1978) 81 Cal. App. 3d 506, 509 [146 Cal. Rptr. 495]....

II.

Of course I share the majority's policy concern that tortfeasors not face *unlimited* liability for their negligent acts. As stated above, the *Dillon* court recognized foreseeability as a general limit on tort liability....

To determine whether defendants owed plaintiff a duty of care in this case, I think it is fruitful to reexamine the second *Dillon* guideline in light of Rowland v. Christian (1968) 69 Cal. 2d 108 [70 Cal. Rptr. 97, 443 P.2d 561, 32 A.L.R.3d 496], our leading case defining a defendant's duty of care. In *Rowland*, decided just two months after *Dillon*, we held that in the absence of a statutory exception to the legislative mandate that all persons are liable for injuries caused by failure to exercise due care (Civ. Code, § 1714, subd. (a)), "no such exception should be made unless clearly supported by public policy. [Citations.] [para.] A departure from this fundamental principle involves the balancing of a number of considerations; the major ones are the foreseeability of harm to the plaintiff, the degree of certainty that the plaintiff suffered injury, the closeness of the connection between the defendant's conduct and the injury suffered, the moral blame attached to the defendant's conduct, the policy of preventing future harm, the extent of the burden to the defendant and consequences to the community of imposing a duty to exercise care with resulting liability for breach, and the availability, cost, and prevalence of insurance for the risk involved." (*Rowland, supra,* 69 Cal. 2d at pp.112-113....)

While our cases defining a bystander's cause of action for negligent infliction of emotional distress consistently emphasize the first of the *Rowland* factors—foreseeability of harm to plaintiff—discussion of the others has been limited. The second, fourth, and fifth factors may be disposed of quickly: certainty of injury is usually a jury question, particularly since we no longer require physical manifestations of mental distress (Hedlund v. Superior Court (1983) 34 Cal. 3d 695, 706, fn.8 [194 Cal. Rptr. 805, 669 P.2d 41, 41 A.L.R.4th 1063]); moral blame almost always militates in favor of recovery; and the policy of preventing future harm favors the plaintiff, but only slightly since, in most cases, any *Dillon* claim is simply added to the primary victim's complaint. The third, sixth and seventh factors, however, merit more discussion.

This court has emphasized the importance of the third *Rowland* factor —nexus between defendant's conduct and the risk of injury—in establishing limitations on recovery. In J'Aire Corp. v. Gregory (1979) 24 Cal. 3d 799, 808 [157 Cal. Rptr. 407, 598 P.2d 60], we stated that case law "[places] a limit on recovery by focusing judicial attention on the foreseeability of the injury and the nexus between the defendant's conduct and the plaintiff's injury." There, we limited recovery for the tort of negligent interference with economic advantage "to instances where the *risk of harm is* foreseeable and is *closely connected with the defendant's conduct*, where damages are not wholly speculative and the injury is not part of the plaintiff's ordinary business risk." (*Ibid.*, italics added.)

The sixth and seventh *Rowland* factors — the burden on the defendant and the community, and the cost and availability of insurance — also merit further evaluation. Amici curiae contend that recovery in this case would mark an unwarranted expansion of *Dillon*, resulting in a new category of plaintiffs, fewer settlements, higher administrative costs and premiums, delays in payment, increased litigation, and higher awards. Amici insist that *Dillon*'s second guideline should be applied strictly, as a prerequisite for recovery. . . .

The authorities upon which amici rely do not persuade me that *Dillon* has significantly contributed to any substantial increase in litigation and insurance premiums. Nor do I find any indication that other jurisdictions are retreating from *Dillon*. . . . As the *Dillon* court responded to the contention that otherwise meritorious claims should be barred out of fear of increases in the number of suits and of fraudulent claims: " ' "[We] should be sorry to adopt a rule which would bar all such claims on grounds of policy alone, and in order to prevent the possible success of unrighteous or groundless actions. Such a course involves the denial of redress in meritorious cases, and it necessarily implies a certain degree of distrust, which [we] do not share, in the capacity of legal tribunals to get at the truth in this class of claim." ' " (*Dillon, supra*, 68 Cal. 2d at p.744, quoting Hambrook v. Stokes Bros. (1925) 1 K.B. 141, quoting Dulieu v. White and Sons (1901) 2 K.B. 669, 681, opn. by Kennedy, J. . . .)

I also do not believe courts lack the means to prevent unmeritorious cases from going to trial. As the case at bar demonstrates, trial courts are well aware of their duty to determine before trial whether the defendant could have owed the plaintiff a duty of care under the facts. . . .

NOTES AND QUESTIONS

1. Waube *and* Palsgraf. Is *Waube* a fair application of *Palsgraf*? If the driver's conduct was careless, and if it caused genuine distress to Mrs. Waube, why shouldn't the law impose liability? What does it mean to say that the driver committed a wrong "from the standpoint of good morals and good citizenship" yet that Waube was not the victim of a tort committed by the driver? Suppose Erin Dillon was riding a bicycle at the time of the accident, and the negligent driver, in colliding with her, caused a part of the bike to fly off so as to strike and physically harm Mrs. Dillon. Would there be a duty problem with a claim seeking compensation for that injury? A proximate cause problem? If the answer to these questions is no, what is so different about these claims for emotional distress? Does the result in *Waube* — later abrogated by the Wisconsin Supreme Court — suggest that a "Cardozoan" approach to tort law is essentially "conserva-

tive" in terms of not permitting the expansion of negligence liability? Can you construct an argument that, without rejecting *Palsgraf*, produces a different result in *Waube*?

2. *Bystander Claims for Physical Harm versus NIED.* Like *Robb*, *Dillon* speaks in terms of permitting recovery for *physical harms* resulting to a plaintiff from distress caused by the defendant's careless conduct. Nonetheless, it has come to stand for the authorization of recovery even absent consequent physical injury (at least so long as there is sufficient proof of the sort of "severe" distress now required by *Thing*). Thus, like *Robb*, which was decided as a physical harm case, *Dillon* has been received by subsequent courts as a decision articulating the rules for NIED recovery.

3. *The California Revolution.* Dillon v. Legg was decided in 1968, which was also the year that the California Supreme Court abolished the status categories for premises liability claims in Rowland v. Christian, *supra*, Chapter 2 (Note 8 following *Salaman*). The two decisions not only substantially expanded tort liability, they brought to bear longstanding academic skepticism about the duty element in a manner that promised to revolutionize the law of negligence. Quoting Prosser, *Dillon* emphasizes that the invocation of a legal no-duty rule to resolve a case always "begs the essential question. . . ." What is the essential question? How does *Dillon* define the duty inquiry? What are the elements of negligence, according to *Dillon?* How does that formulation differ from the traditional formulation? Does the court's conception of negligence resemble Judge Andrews' conception of negligence as grounded in a "duty to the world"?

4. Dillon *and* Palsgraf. Suppose *Dillon* is rightly read as siding with Andrews in holding that a negligence plaintiff need not show a wrong to her, merely a wrong to someone resulting in injury to her. If so, is dissenting Justice Burke justified in being puzzled as to the effect the majority is prepared to give to a finding that Erin was contributorily negligent? Why should Erin's negligence defeat Mrs. Dillon's claim? Shouldn't it instead be treated as one of two careless acts by persons other than Mrs. Dillon, each of which functioned as a but-for cause of her emotional distress?

5. *Uses of History.* In an omitted portion of *Dillon*, the court relies on Prosser, who in turn relied on the British historian Percy Winfield, for the claim that the duty element was originally no part of the tort of negligence, but was tacked on by judges such as the Exchequer Barons of Winterbottom v. Wright (see Chapter 2), who were anxious to find a way to limit the imposition of tort liability on emerging industry. Suppose Winfield's historical claims are correct. In what ways should they inform the analysis of a contemporary negligence case? What does the *Dillon* court's invocation of this history tell us about how it conceives of the nature and purpose of negligence law?

6. *The Zone of Danger and Arbitrariness.* *Dillon* scores points by stressing the "hopeless artificiality" of rules that would permit Cheryl, who was in the zone of danger, to recover for her emotional distress, but would

bar recovery by Mrs. Dillon, standing a few feet further away. Is this line so arbitrary? Assuming that Cheryl were entitled to recover damages under the zone of danger rule, for what losses would she be compensated? Negligence law draws "arbitrary" lines in other contexts. Imagine two careless drivers, A and B. A strikes and injures pedestrian P. B narrowly misses pedestrian Q, who happens at the time to have his back turned and to be listening to a portable CD player, and thus is oblivious to the peril. If P sues A, A must pay P's damages. Q, however, has no cause of action against B. Is this an intolerably arbitrary result, in that A and B did the same bad thing, yet only A is made to pay? Would the *Dillon* court permit recovery by Q?

7. *Progressive or Paternalistic?* The *Dillon* court, along with Prosser and Magruder, decry the denial of redress to persons such as Mrs. Dillon. Such a rule, they suggest, offends "natural justice" and "discredit[s]" our legal system. What exactly are they so indignant about? On what grounds do they assert that cases such as *Dillon* present especially compelling claims for compensation?

8. *The* Dillon *Factors.* *Dillon* offers "guidelines" to help lower courts determine when bystanders may recover for negligence causing emotional distress. It says that these factors aid in the determination of whether the distress was reasonably foreseeable to the defendant. Do the factors set out by the court actually bear on foreseeability? Is distress to a close friend of a person killed by careless driving less foreseeable to the driver than distress to a relative? What about distress to a relative who learns about the death an hour after it occurs?

9. *Every Tort = Two Torts?* Assume that *Dillon*'s holding is grounded in the sense that negligence law would be callous insofar as it does not permit compensation for the "secondary" harms consisting of the grief caused to others when a victim is wrongfully killed (or injured). If that is the concern, should every instance of negligence causing serious injury warrant two lawsuits: one by the victim for his injuries, the second by those grieving over the fate or plight of the victim? If not, why not?

10. *From* Dillon *to* Thing. *Dillon* was handed down during the tumultous summer of 1968, which, in the eyes of some, marked the beginning of the end of the counterculture movement of the 1960s. By 1989, the nation was, generally speaking, in a more conservative mood, and the composition of the California Supreme Court reflected that transition. Equally or more saliently, the courts had begun to encounter phenomena such as liability insurance crises, and were now receiving *amicus* briefs from organizations such as the "Association for California Tort Reform" (founded in 1979). Note, in this regard, the *Thing* court's emphasis on the "social cost" of imposing liability. Does that sort of consideration figure at all in *Dillon*?

11. *Rules and Standards.* In many respects the argument between the majority and dissenters in *Thing* replicates the arguments seen in the *Testbank* decision, *supra* Chapter 2, over the relative desirability of clear rules — which promote consistency and predictability but exclude some

plausible claims — versus fuzzier standards — which promote the just resolution of individual cases, but generate uncertainty. The *Thing* majority, of
course, gives the nod to a rule-based approach. Having done so, does it
incur any obligation to explain why it picked the particular rules that it
did? Is it sufficient for a court to say, in effect: "We have to draw the line
somewhere, and this place is as good as any?"

12. *Proportionality and Social Cost. Dillon* asserted that its guidelines are designed to distinguish cases of "foreseeable" from unforeseeable emotional distress. We earlier questioned whether that assertion was
plausible. *Thing* converts those guidelines into rules, and justifies them as
necessary to avoid individually disproportionate and socially costly liability. Are these more convincing bases for drawing the lines so as to include
claims only by close relatives who witness the relevant accident? Do the
justices believe that a decision to allow claims by unmarried partners of
injury victims will tip the scales in terms of generating disproportionate
liability or excessive social costs? Even if they do, how can they justify
drawing the line on the basis of the mere presence or absence of a
marriage license?

13. *Wrongful Death and Loss of Consortium Revisited.* Recall from
Chapter 6 that statutes now provide actions for *wrongful death*, whereby
the surviving family members of a victim killed by a defendant's tortious
conduct may sue the defendant for (at least) the monetary value of lost
support and company. In addition, common law provides the *loss of
consortium* action, whereby spouse *S1* can recover from defendant *D* for
carelessly injuring spouse *S2* so as to deprive *S1* of *S2*'s companionship.

Under California law at the time of *Dillon* and *Thing*, the parents of a
child killed by a defendant's carelessness toward the child were entitled to
bring a wrongful death action and recover loss of consortium damages,
but not damages for their emotional distress over the death. *See* Duggett v.
Atchinson, T. & S. Fe Ry., 313 P.2d 557 (Cal. 1957). Meanwhile, in the
Baxter case, cited in a footnote by the *Thing* majority, the California
Supreme Court had held that a parent *cannot* bring a *loss of consortium
action* against a defendant for carelessly *injuring* her child so as to deprive
the parent of the child's companionship and support.

Does the law pertaining to wrongful death actions offer an alternative
(and perhaps stronger) justification for the limitation of bystander liability
to the victim's close relatives than either foreseeability (*Dillon*) or policy
(*Thing*)? Alternatively, could one argue that the rule barring recovery of
emotional distress damages in wrongful death actions, when coupled with
Baxter's bar on parental consortium actions, suggests that there should be
no recovery in cases such as *Dillon* and *Thing?* If parents are not permitted
to recover for the emotional distress associated with the loss of their child,
or with his having been injured, why should they recover for the emotional
distress they experience in *witnessing* their child being killed or injured?
Can one make sense of this distinct treatment? Recall the rationales that
originally led courts to adopt the zone of danger rule. Might some of these
support the imposition of liability in certain bystander cases? See Chapter
13 (discussing the *Buckley* decision).

14. *Bystander Liability Elsewhere*. Professor Dobbs reckons that a majority of the states now follow one or another version of *Dillon*. Dan B. Dobbs, *The Law of Torts* § 309, at 840 & n.11 (2000). In Wisconsin, for example, the rule of *Waube* has been overruled in favor of an approach similar to *Dillon*'s, under which a plaintiff may recover if she suffers severe emotional distress as a result of witnessing the careless injuring of a close relative under extraordinarily traumatic circumstances. Bowen v. Lumbermens Mut. Cas. Co., 517 N.W.2d 432 (Wis. 1994). However, a number of courts have rejected bystander NIED liability. Perhaps most notably, the year after *Dillon* was decided, the New York Court of Appeals rejected it, in part relying on the very same policy factors regarded by the California Supreme Court as favoring the imposition of liability. Tobin v. Grossman, 249 N.E.2d 419 (N.Y. 1969). Does the fact that *Dillon* and *Tobin* invoke the same duty factors to reach diametrically opposed results in nearly identical circumstances give rise to concern as to their relative malleability?

15. *All The Way to* Heaven? In deciding *Dillon*, the California Court declared that it was overruling *Amaya*'s zone of danger rule "to the extent inconsistent" with the authorization of Mrs. Dillon's cause of action. This declaration raises an obvious and important question: To what extent *is* the zone of danger rule inconsistent with *Dillon*? Courts that have embraced bystander liability sometimes appear to conclude that, by doing so, they have eliminated zone of danger as a limit on liability for *any and all* NIED claims, whether brought by a bystander or not. Given that the remaining limitations on the scope of bystander liability contained in decisions such as *Dillon* by their terms pertain only to bystanders, it might seem to follow that the net effect of such decisions is to remove all special limitations that courts had previously imposed on NIED claims. This in turn would suggest the embrace of a general Heaven v. Pender duty of reasonable care to avoid distressing others, one subject only to "policy" limitations applicable to special cases such as bystander claims. On this reasoning, all emotional distress claims ought to proceed on the same general principles that govern claims for negligent misfeasance causing physical harm.

Two states — Montana and Tennessee — have adopted this chain of reasoning and have explicitly purported to collapse completely the distinction between negligence causing physical harm and negligence causing emotional distress. The Tennessee case in which this change was announced, Camper v. Minor, 915 S.W.2d 437 (Tenn. 1996), is instructive as to what it might mean for a general, *Heaven*-like duty to attach with respect to others' emotional well-being. There, plaintiff, the driver of a cement truck, began to drive through an intersection after the traffic light turned green. Defendant, driving a small passenger car at a modest speed, ran a red light and crashed into the truck. The plaintiff testified in his deposition that, because of the relative size of the vehicles and their speed, he was not at all fearful for his physical safety. Instead, he became very upset when he exited his truck and viewed the deceased defendant in her car. Adopting the position that NIED claims should be analyzed no differently than claims for negligence causing physical harm, the court ruled that the truck driver's action could proceed on the theory that the defendant, by running a red light, carelessly risked foreseeable distress to others who might observe her injuring or killing herself.

If *Camper*'s purported collapsing of the line between physical harm and emotional distress cases is taken at face value, it would seem to follow that all persons subject to the decision now must exercise reasonable care not to conduct themselves in a way that might foreseeably cause serious distress to others. For example, a homeowner who carelessly lacerates his arm or falls off a ladder while doing yard work could presumably be sued by a stranger who happened to witness the aftermath of the accident. It may be, however, that the court did not mean the case to stand for such a broad proposition. In a subsequent case, for example, it seemed to circumscribe the *Camper* duty. Ramsey v. Beavers, 931 S.W.2d 527 (Tenn. 1996).

The oddity of the rule suggested by *Camper* may suggest a fallacy in the chain of inferences that led from *Dillon*'s "overruling" of *Amaya* to the adoption of a general duty to take care against causing emotional distress to others. Indeed, it hardly follows that by refusing to employ the zone of danger test to block the peculiarly salient claim of a close relative who observes her loved one being killed before her eyes, *Dillon* entails that emotional distress ought to be actionable whenever it is produced by careless conduct. Several courts, including the California Supreme Court, seem to have recognized this point, although they often have expressed it in confusing language. For example, in Burgess v. Superior Court, 831 P.2d 1197 (Cal. 1992), the court held that bystander cases form a limited exception to the general rules applicable to "direct" claims of NIED, that is, claims arising out of undertakings or physical endangerment.[*] A similar idea has been expressed in different language by the Texas Supreme Court, which has held that bystander claims operate under separate rules because they are the only "true" NIED claims, whereas other claims — including death telegram and undertaking claims that other states would treat as "direct" NIED claims — are permitted to proceed because they arise out of "independent" duties, that is, duties, other than the duty to take care against causing the plaintiff emotional distress. Boyles v. Kerr, 855 S.W.2d 593 (Tex. 1993).

REFERENCES/FURTHER READING

Francis H. Bohlen, *The Right to Recover for Injury Resulting from Negligence Without Impact*, 41 Am. L. Register 141 (1902), *reprinted in* Francis H. Bohlen, *Studies in the Law of Torts* 252-290 (1926).

---

[*] *Burgess* involved a malpractice claim by a mother against her obstetrician for carelessness in delivering her baby, which caused severe birth defects in the baby, and trauma to the plaintiff-mother. Because the mother was not herself endangered by the defendant's carelessness, and because she was unconscious during the delivery, the defendant argued that she was barred from recovering for NIED under *Thing*. The court held that *Thing* was inapplicable because this was an instance of "direct" infliction of emotional distress, rather than a bystander claim, and because an obstetrician is chargeable with a duty to look after the emotional well-being of the mother and baby, given that both are his patients in the period up to and including birth.

Martha Chamallas, *Removing Emotional Harm from the Core of Tort Law*,
    54 Vand. L. Rev. 751 (2001).
Martha Chamallas with Linda K. Kerber, *Women, Mothers, and the Law of
    Fright: A History*, 88 Mich. L. Rev. 814 (1990).
David Crump, *Evaluating Independent Torts Based upon "Intentional" or
    "Negligent" Infliction of Emotional Distress: How Can We Keep the
    Baby from Dissolving in the Bath Water?*, 34 Ariz. L. Rev. 439 (1992).
Julie A. Davies, *Direct Actions for Emotional Harm: Is Compromise
    Possible?*, 67 Wash. L. Rev. 1 (1992).
Richard Delgado, *Words That Wound: A Tort Action for Racial Insults,
    Epithets, and Name-Calling*, 17 Harv. C.R.-C.L. L. Rev. 133 (1982).
John L. Diamond, *Dillon v. Legg Revisited: Toward a Unified Theory of
    Compensating Bystanders and Relatives for Intangible Injuries*, 35
    Hastings L.J. 477 (1984).
Dennis P. Duffy, *Intentional Infliction of Emotional Distress and
    Employment at Will: The Case Against "Tortification" of Labor and
    Employment Law*, 74 B.U. L. Rev. 387 (1994).
Daniel Givelber, *The Right to Minimum Social Decency and the Limits of
    Evenhandedness: Intentional Infliction of Emotional Distress by
    Outrageous Conduct*, 82 Colum. L. Rev. 42 (1982).
John C. P. Goldberg & Benjamin C. Zipursky, *Unrealized Torts*, 88 Va. L.
    Rev. 1625 (2002).
Herbert F. Goodrich, *Emotional Disturbance as Legal Damage*, 20 Mich.
    L. Rev. 497 (1922).
Leon Green, *"Fright" Cases*, 27 Ill. L. Rev. 761 (1933).
Fowler V. Harper & Mary Coate McNeeley, *A Re-Examination of the Basis
    for Liability for Emotional Distress*, 1938 Wis. L. Rev. 426 (1938).
Charles Lawrence, *If He Hollers Let Him Go: Regulating Racist Speech on
    Campus*, 1990 Duke L.J. 431.
Calvert Magruder, *Mental and Emotional Disturbance in the Law of Torts*,
    49 Harv. L. Rev. 1033 (1936).
Virginia E. Nolan & Edmund Ursin, *Negligent Infliction of Emotional
    Distress: Coherence Emerging from Chaos*, 33 Hastings L.J. 583 (1982).
Richard N. Pearson, *Liability to Bystanders for Negligently Inflicted
    Emotional Harm — A Comment on the Nature of Arbitrary Rules*, 34 U.
    Fla. L. Rev. 477 (1982).
Robert C. Post, *The Constitutional Concept of Public Discourse:
    Outrageous Opinion, Democratic Deliberation, and* Hustler Magazine
    v. Falwell, 103 Harv. L. Rev. 601 (1990).
William L. Prosser, *Insult and Outrage*, 44 Cal. L. Rev. 40 (1956).
William L. Prosser, *Intentional Infliction of Mental Suffering: A New Tort*,
    37 Mich. L. Rev. 874 (1939).
Andrew J. Simons, *Psychic Injury and the Bystander: The
    Transcontinental Dispute Between California and New York*, 51 St.
    John's L. Rev. 1 (1976).
John W. Wade, *Tort Liability for Abusive or Insulting Language*, 4 Vand. L.
    Rev. 63 (1950).
Barbara Young Welke, *Recasting American Liberty: Gender, Race, Law and
    the Railroad Revolution, 1865-1920* (2001).

PART FOUR

LIABILITY WITHOUT FAULT AND PRODUCTS LIABILITY

CHAPTER 11

Property Torts and Ultrahazardous Activities

I. INTRODUCTION

The concept of *unreasonable* conduct has played the lead role in Anglo-American accident law over the past two centuries, and probably longer than that. This has meant that, for a wide array of accidentally caused injuries, the victim has been left to bear his or her losses unless able to show that another person caused them by failing to exercise reasonable care. As many of the cases in Chapters 9 and 10 indicate, some torts require wrongful conduct other than carelessness, such as intentional or reckless misconduct. But the bulk of the statutory and case law we have studied thus far has conditioned liability on the presence of conduct that is at least careless.

Even though fault has served as the predominant standard by which responsibility for accidentally caused injury has been assigned, it would be a mistake to say that the Anglo-American law of accidents just *is* negligence law. At a minimum, this sort of blanket statement is misleading because, as we have seen, negligence itself comes in many shades. What constitutes carelessness, or adequate proof of carelessness, varies significantly depending on, among other things, (a) the actor whose conduct is being assessed (is he a child? a professional?), (b) the capacity in which she was acting when undertaking the conduct (driver? landowner? rescuer?), (c) the nature of the conduct (misfeasance? nonfeasance?), and (d) the kind of injury suffered by the victim (physical? emotional? economic?). Second, and more directly to the point, tort law has long included case law that explicitly permits an injury victim to recover compensation from another without proof that he acted carelessly, let alone recklessly or with intent to injure. Some scholars have even gone so far as to suggest that prior to the nineteenth century, liability routinely attached without regard to fault. While this contention is probably exaggerated, there is no question that liability without fault has been, and remains, an important feature of U.S. tort law.

The most common label used by judges and lawyers to describe liability that attaches without proven or presumed carelessness, recklessness, or intentional wrongdoing is *strict liability*. Reliance on this phrase is in some ways unfortunate. First, it suggests that actors can be held responsible for injuries entirely without regard to what they do or don't do—as if an injury victim could randomly pick a name from the phone book and then instruct a court to order that person to pay for the victim's losses. In fact, when liability without fault does apply, it applies to actors who have chosen to undertake certain sorts of activities that they could have chosen to avoid. In this sense, at least, liability is not "strict."

Second, some tort causes of action today that are taken to fall within the category of strict liability turn out to share important features of negligence law, which has generated a good deal of terminological confusion. Products liability law, for example, has often been described as imposing strict liability, yet its standards for the imposition of liability frequently seem to contain notions of fault. Conversely, there are several forms of tort liability that have not traditionally been placed within the category of strict liability, but that are actionable without proof of fault, recklessness, or intent. These include torts vindicating certain property rights, such as trespass and conversion.

To avoid some of these confusions, we shall use the phrase "liability without fault" in place of strict liability. Within the ambit of the common law of tort,* such liability arguably applies in at least three different settings: (1) conduct that interferes with the possession, use, or enjoyment of land or personal possessions, (2) "ultrahazardous" activities, such as the use of explosives or the keeping of wild animals; and (3) the manufacture, design, and sale of defective products by manufacturers and certain other commercial actors. This chapter discusses cases falling within the first two categories. Chapter 12 turns to the important and politically contentious subject of products liability.

Before we undertake to examine these areas in detail, it is worth pausing to reflect on some of the considerations that underlie the choice between fault-based and no-fault liability regimes. We therefore begin this chapter with two older decisions addressing that issue. The first is a nineteenth-century decision that helped establish negligence as the dominant cause of action available in modern tort law to victims of accidentally caused injuries. The second is an early twentieth-century decision in which the U.S. Supreme Court considered and rejected constitutional challenges to the displacement of the common law of negligence by a statutory scheme of liability without fault.

Harvey v. Dunlop
[1843] Hill & Den. 193 (N.Y. Sup. Ct.)

TRESPASS tried at the Washington circuit in June, 1839, before Willard, C. Judge. The plaintiff declares against the defendant for throwing a stone at his daughter and putting out her eye.... [Defendant entered a general responsive plea of not guilty.] ... The case was this: The plaintiff's daughter (Clementine), who was about five, and the defendant, about six

---

* As we have seen, and will see further below, liability without fault has also been imposed by statutory and administrative schemes that have supplanted the common law of negligence as it applied to particular activities. Workers' compensation systems — which reimburse workers injured on the job for healthcare costs and lost wages without inquiring into the employer's fault — provide the most familiar examples of these sorts of schemes.

years of age, were associates and in the habit of playing together. In the fall of 1835 they went out to gather beech nuts, and, after being absent a few hours, returned to the plaintiff's house both of them crying. On being asked what the matter was, the defendant stated that he had thrown a stone and killed Clementine or put out her eye. Neither of them said whether the stone was thrown by accident or design, nor did it appear from any one having personal knowledge how this was on the trial, as the plaintiff's daughter was not sworn as a witness. The eye had become incurably blind. The plaintiff had repeatedly admitted that the defendant was not to blame though it was not shown that he could have had any knowledge on the subject save such as he obtained from the children themselves, and that the injury was accidental.

The judge charged the jury that in cases of this kind the plaintiff could not recover, unless he made out that the defendant had been guilty of a wrongful act. That if they were satisfied, from all the evidence in the cause, that the injury complained of was the result of unavoidable accident, or in other words, that it was one which ordinary care and foresight could not have prevented, their verdict should be for the defendant. The judge observed that there was no evidence, except the defendant's admissions, showing that he had committed the injury, and these gave no information whether it was done by accident or design. He then adverted to the omission of the plaintiff to produce his daughter as a witness, who alone could have explained how the injury happened; and concluded by instructing the jury that if they were satisfied the defendant had wrongfully thrown the stone, whether done willfully or through carelessness, they should find for the plaintiff. The jury rendered a verdict in favor of the defendant. The plaintiff made a case, and now moved for a new trial on the ground of misdirection of the judge.

Nelson, C.J. I am of opinion that the grounds upon which the learned judge placed the case before the jury were correct. No case or principle can be found, or if found can be maintained, subjecting an individual to liability for an act done without fault on his part; and this was substantially the doctrine of the charge. All the cases concede that an injury arising from inevitable accident, or, which in law or reason is the same thing, from an act that ordinary human care and foresight are unable to guard against, is but the misfortune of the sufferer, and lays no foundation for legal responsibility. Thus it is laid down that, "If one man has received a corporal injury from the voluntary act of another, an action of trespass lies, provided there was a neglect or want of due caution in the person who did the injury, although there was no design to injure." (Bac. Abr. tit. Trespass, D.) But if not imputable to the neglect of the party by whom it was done, or to his want of caution, an action of trespass does not lie, although the consequences of a voluntary act. (Weaver v. Ward, Hob., 134; Gibbons v. Pepper, 4 Mod., 405.) It was said by Dallas, C.J., in Wakeman v. Robinson (1 Bingh., 213), "if the accident happened entirely without default on the part of the defendant, or blame imputable to him, the action does not lie"; and the same principle is recognized in Bullock v. Babcock, (3 Wend., 391).

... [I]t was for the jury to determine upon the facts and circumstances before them, whether or not the defendant was in the wrong. In order to arrive at a decision upon this question the jury had a right to take into consideration the childhood of the parties, the friendly relations existing between them, the conduct of both on their return home, but more especially the repeated admissions of the plaintiff that the defendant was not to blame. The latter fact was very material, and must and should have produced a strong impression upon the minds of the jury in the absence of the testimony of Clementine, because the natural inference to be drawn from the declarations was that the plaintiff had received the information upon which they were based from his daughter's account of the transaction, and had frankly disclosed it though the admissions operated against his own interest. These admissions, taken in connection with the other facts and circumstances in the case, were undoubtedly decisive of the true character of the transaction, and they conduct us satisfactorily to the same conclusion arrived at by the jury, that the misfortune happened without fault on either side, and that it was one of those unhappy accidents to which children of the tender age of these parties are not unfrequently exposed in their little innocent plays and amusements — a result rather to be deplored than punished.

New trial denied.

N.Y. Central R.R. Co. v. White
243 U.S. 188 (1917)

Pitney, J.   A proceeding was commenced by [Mrs. White] before the Workmen's Compensation Commission of the State of New York, established by the Workmen's Compensation Law of that state, to recover compensation from the New York Central & Hudson River Railroad Company for the death of her husband, Jacob White, who lost his life September 2, 1914, through an accidental injury arising out of and in the course of his employment under that company. The Commission awarded compensation in accordance with the terms of the law; its award was affirmed, without opinion, by the appellate division of the supreme court for the third judicial department, whose order was affirmed by the court of appeals, without opinion. . . .

[The railroad contends] . . . that to award compensation to [Mrs. White] under the provisions of the Workmen's Compensation Law would deprive [the railroad] of its property without due process of law, and deny to it the equal protection of the laws, in contravention of the Fourteenth Amendment.* . . .

---

* [The railroad also argued that New York could not apply its workers' compensation law to railroads because that would interfere with the federal liability scheme established in 1908 with the enactment of the Federal Employers' Liability Act (FELA). (On FELA, see *Gottshall, supra,* Chapter 10.) The Court rejected the argument on the grounds that FELA only applies to injuries caused by trains operating in interstate commerce, and that White was injured by a train operating exclusively within the State of New York. — Eds.]

... The Workmen's Compensation Law of New York establishes forty-two groups of hazardous employments, defines "employee" as a person engaged in one of these employments upon the premises ...; defines ... "injury" and "personal injury" as meaning only *accidental injuries arising out of and in the course of employment* ...; and *requires every employer subject to its provisions to pay or provide compensation according to a prescribed schedule* for the disability or death of his employee resulting from an accidental personal injury arising out of and in the course of the employment, *without regard to fault as a cause* except where the injury is occasioned by the wilful intention of the injured employee to bring about the injury or death of himself or of another, or where it results solely from the intoxication of the injured employee while on duty, in which cases neither the injured employee nor any dependent shall receive compensation. [Emphasis added.— Eds.] By § 11 the prescribed liability is made exclusive [with an exception if an employer fails to meet its payment obligations under the statute]. Compensation under the act is not regulated by the measure of damages applied in negligence suits, but, in addition to providing surgical, or other like treatment, it is based solely on loss of earning power, being graduated according to the average weekly wages of the injured employee and the character and duration of the disability, whether partial or total, temporary or permanent; while in case the injury causes death, the compensation is known as a death benefit, and includes funeral expenses, not exceeding $100, payments to the surviving wife (or dependent husband) during widowhood (or dependent widowerhood) of a percentage of the average wages of the deceased, and if there be a surviving child or children under the age of eighteen years an additional percentage of such wages for each child until that age is reached.... Provision is made for the establishment of a Workmen's Compensation Commission with administrative and judicial functions, including authority to pass upon claims to compensation on notice to the parties interested. The award or decision of the Commission is made subject to an appeal, on questions of law only, to the ... [state's courts]. A fund is created, known as "the state insurance fund," for the purpose of insuring employers against liability under the law, and assuring to the persons entitled the compensation thereby provided. The fund is made up primarily of premiums received from employers, at rates fixed by the Commission in view of the hazards of the different classes of employment, and the premiums are to be based upon the total pay roll and number of employees in each class at the lowest rate consistent with the maintenance of a solvent state insurance fund and the creation of a reasonable surplus and reserve. Elaborate provisions are laid down for the administration of this fund. By § 50, each employer is required [to purchase insurance or otherwise maintain adequate funds to cover liabilities to its workers under the fund].

In a previous year, the legislature enacted a [similar scheme].... This was held by the Court of Appeals in Ives v. South Buffalo R. Co., 201 N.Y. 271 ... to be invalid because in conflict with due process of law provisions of the state Constitution and of the Fourteenth Amendment. Thereafter, and in the year 1913, a constitutional amendment was adopted, effective January 1, 1914, declaring [that no provision of the state constitution shall be construed to prevent the legislative implementation of a workers' compensation scheme.]

In December, 1913, the legislature enacted the law now under consideration, and in 1914 re-enacted it to take effect as to payment of compensation on July 1 in that year. The act was sustained by the court of appeals as not inconsistent with the 14th Amendment in Jensen v. Southern P. Co., 215 N.Y. 514, and that decision was followed in the case at bar.

The scheme of the act is so wide a departure from common-law standards respecting the responsibility of employer to employee that doubts naturally have been raised respecting its constitutional validity. The adverse considerations urged or suggested . . . are: (a) That the employer's property is taken without due process of law, because he is subjected to a liability for compensation without regard to any neglect or default on his part or on the part of any other person for whom he is responsible, and in spite of the fact that the injury may be solely attributable to the fault of the employee; (b) that the employee's rights are interfered with, in that he is prevented from having compensation for injuries arising from the employer's fault commensurate with the damages actually sustained, and is limited to the measure of compensation prescribed by the act; and (c) that both employer and employee are deprived of their liberty to acquire property by being prevented from making such agreement as they choose respecting the terms of the employment.

In support of the legislation, it is said that the whole common-law doctrine of employer's liability for negligence, with its defenses of contributory negligence, fellow servant's negligence, and assumption of risk, is based upon fictions, and is inapplicable to modern conditions of employment; that in the highly organized and hazardous industries of the present day the causes of accident are often so obscure and complex that in a material proportion of cases it is impossible by any method correctly to ascertain the facts necessary to form an accurate judgment, and in a still larger proportion the expense and delay required for such ascertainment amount in effect to a defeat of justice; that, under the present system, the injured workman is left to bear the greater part of industrial accident loss, which, because of his limited income, he is unable to sustain, so that he and those dependent upon him are overcome by poverty and frequently become a burden upon public or private charity; and that litigation is unduly costly and tedious, encouraging corrupt practices and arousing antagonisms between employers and employees. . . .

The close relation of the rules governing responsibility as between employer and employee to the fundamental rights of liberty and property is, of course, recognized. But those rules, as guides of conduct, are not beyond alteration by legislation in the public interest. No person has a vested interest in any rule of law, entitling him to insist that it shall remain unchanged for his benefit. The common law bases the employer's liability for injuries to the employee upon the ground of negligence; but negligence is merely the disregard of some duty imposed by law; and the nature and extent of the duty may be modified by legislation, with corresponding change in the test of negligence. Indeed, liability may be imposed for the consequences of a failure to comply with a statutory duty, irrespective of negligence in the ordinary sense; safety appliance acts being a familiar instance.*

The fault may be that of the employer himself, or — most frequently — that of another for whose conduct he is made responsible according to the maxim *respondeat superior*. In the latter case the employer may be entirely blameless, may have exercised the utmost human foresight to safeguard the employee; yet, if the alter ego, while acting within the scope of his duties, be negligent, — in disobedience, it may be, of the employer's positive and specific command, — the employer is answerable for the consequences. It cannot be that the rule embodied in the maxim is unalterable by legislation.

The immunity of the employer from responsibility to an employee for the negligence of a fellow employee is of comparatively recent origin, it being the product of the judicial conception that the probability of a fellow workman's negligence is one of the natural and ordinary risks of the occupation, assumed by the employee and presumably taken into account in the fixing of his wages. The doctrine has prevailed generally throughout the United States, but with material differences in different jurisdictions respecting who should be deemed a fellow servant and who a vice principal or alter ego of the master, turning sometimes upon refined distinctions as to grades and departments in the employment.... It needs no argument to show that such a rule is subject to modification or abrogation by a State upon proper occasion.

The same may be said with respect to the general doctrine of assumption of risk.... Plainly, these rules, as guides of conduct and tests of liability, are subject to change in the exercise of the sovereign authority of the State.

So, also, with respect to contributory negligence. Aside from injuries intentionally self-inflicted, for which the statute under consideration affords no compensation, it is plain that the rules of law upon the subject, in their bearing upon the employer's responsibility, are subject to legislative change; for contributory negligence, again, involves a default in some duty resting on the employee, and his duties are subject to modification.

It may be added, by way of reminder, that the entire matter of liability for death caused by wrongful act, both within and without the relation of employer and employee, is a modern statutory innovation, in which the States differ as to who may sue, for whose benefit, and the measure of damages....

... [I]t [is not] necessary, for the purposes of the present case, to say [whether] a State might ... [violate the Fourteenth Amendment's guarantee of] "due process of law" ... [by] suddenly set[ting] aside all common-law rules respecting liability as between employer and employee, without providing a reasonably just substitute.... [I]t perhaps may be doubted whether the State could abolish all rights of action, on the one hand, or all

---

* [On liability without fault under the safety appliance acts, see *Rigsby, supra*, Chapter 6. — EDS.]

defenses, on the other, without setting up something adequate in their stead. No such question is here presented, and we intimate no opinion upon it. The statute under consideration sets aside one body of rules only to establish another system in its place. If the employee is no longer able to recover as much as before in case of being injured through the employer's negligence, he is entitled to moderate compensation in all cases of injury, and has a certain and speedy remedy without the difficulty and expense of establishing negligence or proving the amount of the damages. Instead of assuming the entire consequences of all ordinary risks of the occupation, he assumes the consequences, in excess of the scheduled compensation, of risks ordinary and extraordinary. On the other hand, if the employer is left without defense respecting the question of fault, he at the same time is assured that the recovery is limited, and that it goes directly to the relief of the designated beneficiary. And just as the employee's assumption of ordinary risks at common law presumably was taken into account in fixing the rate of wages, so the fixed responsibility of the employer, and the modified assumption of risk by the employee under the new system, presumably will be reflected in the wage scale. The act evidently is intended as a just settlement of a difficult problem, affecting one of the most important of social relations, and it is to be judged in its entirety. We have said enough to demonstrate that, in such an adjustment, the particular rules of the common law affecting the subject matter are not placed by the Fourteenth Amendment beyond the reach of the lawmaking power of the State; and thus we are brought to the question whether the method of compensation that is established as a substitute transcends the limits of permissible state action....

Of course, we cannot ignore the question whether the new arrangement is arbitrary and unreasonable, from the standpoint of natural justice. Respecting this, it is important to be observed that the act applies only to disabling or fatal personal injuries received in the course of hazardous employment in gainful occupation. Reduced to its elements, the situation to be dealt with is this: Employer and employee, by mutual consent, engage in a common operation intended to be advantageous to both; the employee is to contribute his personal services, and for these is to receive wages, and, ordinarily, nothing more; the employer is to furnish plant, facilities, organization, capital, credit, is to control and manage the operation, paying the wages and other expenses, disposing of the product at such prices as he can obtain, taking all the profits, if any there be, and, of necessity, bearing the entire losses. In the nature of things, there is more or less of a probability that the employee may lose his life through some accidental injury arising out of the employment, leaving his widow or children deprived of their natural support; or that he may sustain an injury not mortal, but resulting in his total or partial disablement, temporary or permanent, with corresponding impairment of earning capacity. The physical suffering must be borne by the employee alone; the laws of nature prevent this from being evaded or shifted to another, and the statute makes no attempt to afford an equivalent in compensation. But, besides, there is the loss of earning power, — a loss of that which stands to the employee as his capital in trade. This is a loss arising out of the business, and, however it may be charged up, is an expense of the operation, as truly as the cost of repairing broken machinery or any other expense that ordinarily is paid by the employer. Who is to bear the charge? It is plain that, on grounds of natural justice, it is not unreasonable for the State, while relieving the employer from responsibility for damages measured by common-law standards and payable in cases where he or those for whose conduct he is answerable are found to be at fault, to require him to contribute a reasonable amount, and according to a reasonable and definite scale, by way of compensation for the loss of earning power incurred in the common enterprise, irrespective of the question of negligence, instead of leaving the entire loss to rest where it may chance to fall — that is, upon the injured employee or his dependents. Nor can it be deemed arbitrary and unreasonable, from the standpoint of the employee's interest, to supplant a system under which he assumed the entire risk of injury in ordinary cases, and in others had a right to recover an amount more or less speculative upon proving facts of negligence that often were difficult to prove, and substitute a system under which, in all ordinary cases of accidental injury, he is sure of a definite and easily ascertained compensation, not being obliged to assume the entire loss in any case, but in all cases assuming any loss beyond the prescribed scale.

Much emphasis is laid upon the criticism that the act creates liability without fault. This is sufficiently answered by what has been said, but we may add that liability without fault is not a novelty in the law. The common-law liability of the carrier, of the innkeeper, or him who employed fire or other dangerous agency or harbored a mischievous animal, was not dependent altogether upon questions of fault or negligence. Statutes imposing liability without fault have been sustained.

We have referred to the maxim, *respondeat superior*. In . . . Hall v. Smith, 2 Bing. 156, this maxim was said by Best, Ch. J., to be "bottomed on this principle, that he who expects to derive advantage from an act which is done by another for him, must answer for any injury which a third person may sustain from it." And this view has been adopted in New York. The provision for compulsory compensation, in the act under consideration cannot be deemed to be an arbitrary and unreasonable application of the principle, so as to amount to a deprivation of the employer's property without due process of law. The pecuniary loss resulting from the employee's death or disablement must fall somewhere. It results from something done in the course of an operation from which the employer expects to derive a profit. In excluding the question of fault as a cause of the injury, the act in effect disregards the proximate cause and looks to one more remote, — the primary cause, as it may be deemed, — and that is, the employment itself. For this, both parties are responsible, since they voluntarily engage in it as coadventurers, with personal injury to the employee as a probable and foreseen result. In ignoring any possible negligence of the employee producing or contributing to the injury, the lawmaker reasonably may have been influenced by the belief that, in modern industry, the utmost diligence in the employer's service is in some degree inconsistent with adequate care on the part of the employee for his own safety; that the more intently he devotes himself to the work, the less he can take precautions for his own security. And it is evident that the consequences of a disabling or fatal injury are precisely the same to the parties immediately affected, and to the community, whether the proximate cause be culpable or innocent. Viewing the entire matter, it cannot be pronounced arbitrary and unreasonable for the State to impose upon the employer the absolute duty of making a moderate and definite compensation in money to every disabled employee, or, in case of his death, to those who were entitled to look to him for support, in lieu of the common-law liability confined to cases of negligence.

This, of course, is not to say that any scale of compensation, however insignificant, on the one hand, or onerous, on the other, would be supportable. In this case, no criticism is made on the ground that the compensation prescribed by the statute in question is unreasonable in amount, either in general or in the particular case. Any question of that kind may be met when it arises.

But, it is said, the statute strikes at the fundamentals of constitutional freedom of contract....

... [W]e recognize that the legislation under review does measurably limit the freedom of employer and employee to agree respecting the terms of employment, and that it cannot be supported except on the ground that it is a reasonable exercise of the police power of the State. In our opinion it is fairly supportable upon that ground. And for this reason: The subject matter in respect of which freedom of contract is restricted is the matter of compensation for human life or limb lost or disability incurred in the course of hazardous employment, and the public has a direct interest in this as affecting the common welfare.... It cannot be doubted that the State may prohibit and punish self-maiming and attempts at suicide; it may prohibit a man from bartering away his life or his personal security ... and the authority to prohibit contracts made in derogation of a lawfully-established policy of the State respecting compensation for accidental death or disabling personal injury is equally clear.

We have not overlooked the criticism that the act imposes no rule of conduct upon the employer with respect to the conditions of labor in the various industries embraced within its terms, prescribes no duty with regard to where the workmen shall work, the character of the machinery, tools, or appliances, the rules or regulations to be established, or the safety devices to be maintained. This statute does not concern itself with measures of prevention, which presumably are embraced in other laws. But the interest of the public is not confined to these. One of the grounds of its concern with the continued life and earning power of the individual is its interest in the prevention of pauperism, with its concomitants of vice and crime. And, in our opinion, laws regulating the responsibility of employers for the injury or death of employees, arising out of the employment, bear so close a relation to the protection of the lives and safety of those concerned that they properly may be regarded as coming within the category of police regulations....

Judgment affirmed.

NOTES AND QUESTIONS

1. Harvey*'s Holding.* The opinion in *Harvey*, although short, is densely packed with statements supporting variations on the idea that at common law, fault or carelessness is required before tort liability will be imposed on an actor who accidentally injures another. Consider each of the following statements (emphases have been added to each). Are they equivalent to one another? If not, are some more plausible than others as generalizations about the common law of torts? Are some more persuasive than others as a matter of policy or principle?

   a. "No case or principle can be found, or if found can be maintained, subjecting an individual to liability for *an act done without fault on his part....*"
   b. "All the cases concede that an injury arising *from inevitable accident* ... is but the misfortune of the sufferer, and lays no foundation for legal responsibility."
   c. "[A]*n act that ordinary human care and foresight are unable to guard against*, is but the misfortune of the sufferer, and lays no foundation for legal responsibility."
   d. "But *if not imputable to the neglect of the party by whom it was done, or to his want of caution*, an action [under the writ] of trespass does not lie, although the consequences of a voluntary act."
   e. "[I]f the accident happened *entirely without default on the part of the defendant, or blame imputable to him*, the action does not lie ...."
   f. If a case presents a *"misfortune [that] happened without fault on either side*, and ... *was one of those unhappy accidents to which children* of the tender age of these parties *are not unfrequently exposed* in their little innocent plays and amusements" then it is best treated as a result "to be deplored [rather] than punished."

2. *Holmes on Fault.* Justice Nelson's contention that Anglo-American tort law has always required at least lack of prudence on the part of the defendant as a condition of imposing liability has proved highly contentious among legal historians.See Appendix B. Still, *Harvey*, along with Chief Justice Shaw's opinion for the Massachusetts Supreme Judicial Court in Brown v. Kendall, 60 Mass. 292 (1850), came to stand as leading early precedents in the emerging American law of negligence. Both decisions owe some of their influence to Justice Oliver Wendell Holmes. In his 1881 book *The Common Law*, which he wrote while still a practicing lawyer, Holmes praised *Harvey* and *Brown*, and offered several arguments in favor of *Harvey*'s claim that tort liability in modern Anglo-American law had never recognized — and ought not to recognize — strict liability, at least in the sense of liability that attaches simply by virtue of a causal connection between the defendant's act and the plaintiff's injury:

   The undertaking to redistribute losses [from the plaintiff to the defendant through the award of damages in a tort suit] simply on the ground that they resulted from the defendant's act would not only be open to [objections raised previously], but ... to the still graver one of offending the sense of justice. Unless my act is of a nature to threaten others, unless under the circumstances a prudent man would have foreseen the possibility of harm, it is no more justifiable to make me indemnify my neighbor against the consequences, than to make me do the same thing if I had fallen upon him in a fit, or to compel me to insure him against lightning.

Oliver W. Holmes, Jr., *The Common Law* 96 (1881). The chapters on tort law in *The Common Law* have long been interpreted as defending the universal application of a negligence standard of liability to accidentally caused injuries.* While it is difficult to interpret a textual passage in isolation, which of the various principles identified in Note 1, *supra*, does Holmes seem to be defending? On what grounds? What features of a system of liability without fault would render it offensive to "the sense of justice"?

3. *Common Law and the Constitution.* Law students are taught that U.S. law consists of a strict hierarchy comprised of common law, legislation, and constitutional law, in which legislation "trumps" common law, and constitutional law "trumps" legislation. The holding of *White* is mostly consistent with this picture, given its reaffirmation of state legislatures' authority to replace the common law of negligence with at least some versions of no-fault workers' compensation schemes.** Does *White* indicate that any and all manner of legislative reform of the common law is permissible? Suppose a state legislature were simply to abolish the common law of negligence, while putting nothing in its place. Or suppose it were to enact a statute that permits any innocent victim of a car accident to sue and obtain "full" compensation from any state resident who has been cited for a traffic violation in the past calendar year, regardless of whether that resident played any role in bringing about the victim's injuries. Would these modifications of the common law be constitutional? In recent years, several state high courts have invoked provisions in *state constitutions* to strike down state legislation restricting the reach of the common law of tort through devices such as damages caps. *See generally* 1 Jennifer Friesen, *State Constitutional Law: Litigating Individual Rights, Claims and Defenses* 6-1 to 6-67 (3d ed. 2000).

4. *Justice and the Constitution.* *Harvey* (and Holmes in the above excerpt) seems to suppose that liability without fault offends basic principles of justice by forcing *A* to pay for *B*'s loss even though *A* did nothing wrong. Is the gist of *White* that state legislatures are free to adopt *unjust* laws if they choose to? Does *White* concede that workers' compensation schemes entail an injustice as against employers? Employees? If not, what in the Court's view reconciles these departures from the idea of fault-based liability with notions of justice?

---

* In his recent book, *The Hidden Holmes*, Professor Rosenberg has argued that this reading is mistaken, and that Holmes was prepared to endorse the imposition of certain forms of liability "without fault."

** Discussions of some basic features of workers' compensation schemes are provided in notes in Chapter 4 (following *Aldridge*), Chapter 7 (following *Ranney*), and Chapter 8 (following *Kenton*).

5. *Justice Holmes and Fault.* By the time of decisions such as *White*, Holmes was a member of the U.S. Supreme Court. Notwithstanding his apparent embrace in *The Common Law* of fault as a liability threshold demanded by "the sense of justice," Justice Holmes signed on to a series of decisions upholding no-fault workers' compensation statutes against constitutional challenges. Indeed, in one such instance, he concurred in a decision upholding a scheme that entitled certain workers to no-fault recovery of *full* compensation (rather than scheduled damages):

> There is some argument made for the general proposition that immunity from liability when not in fault is a right inherent in free government.... But if it is thought to be public policy to put certain voluntary conduct at the peril of those pursuing it, whether in the interest of safety or upon economic or other grounds, I know of nothing to hinder. A man employs a servant at the peril of what that servant may do in the course of his employment and there is nothing in the Constitution to limit the principle to that instance.... Indeed the criterion which is thought to be free from constitutional objection, the criterion of fault, is the application of an external standard, the conduct of a prudent man in the known circumstances, that is, in doubtful cases, the opinion of the jury, which the defendant has to satisfy at his peril, and which he may miss after giving the matter his best thought.

Arizona Copper Co. v. Hammer, 250 U.S. 400, 431 (1919) (Holmes, J., concurring). Are you convinced by Holmes's argument that tort law's reliance on *respondeat superior* and the objective reasonable person standard indicate that it has, in these respects, adopted liability without consideration of fault?

6. *Ives and Substantive Due Process.* The New York Court of Appeals' decision in Ives v. South Buffalo Ry. Co., 94 N.E. 431 (N.Y. 1911), mentioned in *White*, struck down the predecessor to the statute upheld in *White*. *Ives* concluded that the earlier version of the act, which was substantially the same as the statute upheld in *White*, violated federal and state constitutional provisions protecting citizens against being deprived of liberty or property without due process of law, and barring government from taking private property without providing just compensation. In support of those conclusions, it reasoned in part as follows:

> ... One of the inalienable rights of every citizen is to hold and enjoy his property until it is taken from him by due process of law. When our Constitutions were adopted it was the law of the land that no man who was without fault or negligence could be held liable in damages for injuries sustained by another. That is still the law, except as to the employers enumerated in the new statute....
> It is conceded that this is a liability unknown to the common law and we think it plainly constitutes a deprivation of liberty and property under the Federal and State Constitutions, unless its imposition can be justified under the police power which is discussed [below]....
> ... In arriving at this conclusion we do not overlook the cogent economic and sociological arguments which are urged in support of the statute.... It is based upon the proposition that the inherent risks of an employment should in justice be placed upon the shoulders of the employer, who can

protect himself against loss by insurance and by such an addition to the price of his wares as to cast the burden ultimately upon the consumer; that indemnity to an injured employee should be as much a charge upon the business as the cost of replacing or repairing disabled or defective machinery, appliances or tools; that, under our present system, the loss falls immediately upon the employee who is almost invariably unable to bear it, and ultimately upon the community which is taxed for the support of the indigent; and that our present system is uncertain, unscientific and wasteful, and fosters a spirit of antagonism between employer and employee which it is to the interests of the state to remove....

. . . It would probably conduce to the welfare of all concerned if there could be a more equal distribution of wealth. Many persons have much more property than they can use to advantage and many more find it impossible to get the means for a comfortable existence. If the legislature can say to an employer, "you must compensate your employee for an injury not caused by you or by your fault," why can it not go further and say to the man of wealth, "you have more property than you need and your neighbor is so poor that he can barely subsist; in the interest of natural justice you must divide with your neighbor so that he and his dependents shall not become a charge upon the state?"...

In its final and simple analysis [the statute entails] taking the property of A and giving it to B, and that cannot be done under our Constitutions....

. . . In order to sustain legislation under the police power, the courts must be able to see that its operation tends in some degree to prevent some offense or evil, or to preserve public health, morals, safety, and welfare. If it discloses no such purpose, but is clearly calculated to invade the liberty and property of private citizens, it is plainly the duty of the courts to declare it invalid....

Concrete illustrations of what may and what may not be done under the police power are to be found in this very labor law of which the new statute is a part. As [New York's labor law] stood before [the enactment of the workers' compensation act, it] . . . regulated the hours of work in certain employments; it directed the payment of wages in cash at specified periods; it provided for the protection of employees engaged in the erection of buildings; it compelled the employer to guard dangerous and exposed machinery, to construct fire escapes and ventilating appliances, and to provide toilet facilities, pure drinking water, and sanitary arrangements; it prohibited the employment of women, and of children under certain ages, in specified occupations; it regulated the hours of labor of minors; . . . in short, it imposed upon the employer many restrictions and duties which were unknown to the common law. Broadly classified, all these and similar statutory provisions which are designed, in one way or another, to conserve the health, safety or morals of the employees, and to increase the duties and responsibilities of the employer, are rules of conduct which properly fall within the sphere of the police power. But the new addition to the labor law is of quite a different character. It does nothing to conserve the health, safety, or morals of the employees, and it imposes upon the employer no new or affirmative duties or responsibilities in the conduct of his business. Its sole purpose is to make him liable for injuries which may be sustained wholly without his fault, and solely through the fault of the employee, except where the latter fault is such as to constitute serious and willful misconduct. Under this law, the most thoughtful and careful employer, who has neglected no duty, and whose workshop is equipped with every possible appliance that may make for the safety, health, and morals of his employees, is liable in damages to any employee who happens to sustain injury through an accident which no human being can foresee or prevent, or which, if preventable at all, can only be prevented by the reasonable care of the employee himself. . . .

[There is,] we think, [a] vital distinction between legislation which imposes upon an employer a legal duty, for the failure to perform which he may be penalized or rendered liable in damages, and legislation which makes him liable notwithstanding he has faithfully observed every duty imposed upon him by law. . . .

94 N.E. at 439-440, 442-443. What does the Court of Appeals mean when it concludes that workers' compensation laws are unjustifiable because they fail to impose any new duties on employers? Is the imposition of liability without fault really comparable to officials simply taking the assets of *A* and giving them to *B*?

Ives supposed that employers have an initial right to engage in a lawful business, which right can only be abridged by legislation that serves a limited set of social objectives, such as the promotion of public health and morals. *White* clearly rejects *Ives*'s result. Does it also reject *Ives*'s analytic framework? Or does it conclude that the legislation achieves one of the objectives falling within the states' "police power"?

Within a few years of its issuance, *Ives* had not only been effectively overruled by decisions such as *White*, it had become a poster child for the evils of "substantive due process" — a slogan invoked to condemn judges' reliance on ambiguous constitutional provisions such as due process clauses to block legislation seeking to regulate markets, ameliorate harsh working conditions, and redistribute income. As you will learn in Constitutional Law, in the 1930s, the U.S. Supreme Court issued a series of decisions in which it backed away from the idea that the federal Constitution contains significant constraints on social and economic legislation, thus helping to clear the way for the New Deal and the modern administrative state.

II. PROPERTY TORTS

A. *Trespass to Land: Prima Facie Case*

Perhaps the oldest and least controversial instances of tort liability without intentional, reckless, or unreasonable conduct involve the tort of trespass to land. A trespass to land involves a certain kind of interference with rights conferred under the terms of property law onto possessors of land. Specifically, a trespass involves a *tangible invasion* by an actor of property possessed by another, whether by the actor herself, or by other persons, animals, mechanized devices, or natural or artificial substances for which the actor is responsible. Under the common law of trespass, it is immaterial to the issue of liability whether the actor who causes such an invasion took reasonable care to prevent it. All that matters, at least prima facie, is whether the actor set out to make contact with the property in question, and whether the actor did in fact make such contact. As the following case illustrates, liability in trespass thus may fall even on those who conduct themselves reasonably.

Burns Philp Food, Inc. v. Cavalea Contl. Freight, Inc.
135 F.3d 526 (7th Cir. 1998)

Easterbrook, J.   Nabisco broke up a tract of industrial real estate in Chicago. Cavalea Continental Freight bought several parcels and Burns Philp Food the remainder. In 1986 real estate records were changed to reflect these transactions, but something went awry. . . . [As a result, Burns Philp mistakenly paid property taxes on land owned by Cavalea. It notified Cavalea of the mistake in 1993.] Instead of resolving matters amicably, these neighbors have acted like the Hatfields and McCoys. Cavalea refused to pay a dime, leading Burns Philp to sue [in restitution to obtain reimbursement for the tax payments]. Cavalea filed a counterclaim accusing Burns Philp of building a fence that encroached onto its parcel. . . . The district judge held a bench trial . . . and entered a judgment from which, predictably, both sides have appealed.

[The court first held that Burns Philp could recover for taxes unwittingly paid on behalf of Cavalea for the five years immediately prior to the filing of the suit. — EDS.]

Now for Cavalea's counterclaim. Burns Philp constructed a fence on what it thought was the border between its property and Cavalea's. Whoever surveyed the land to fix the border for the fence did a lousy job. The border is 205 feet long. One end of the fence was located several feet inside Burns Philp's lot and the other was 20 feet into Cavalea's. Burns Philp thus occupied about 2,000 square feet of land that belonged to Cavalea. After . . . a survey [was conducted] in 1995, Cavalea learned that some of its land was on the other side of the fence. It did not notify Burns Philp of the problem until November 1995, when it filed the counterclaim seeking damages for trespass and an injunction requiring Burns Philp to remove the fence. Burns Philp responded by denying liability; it did not verify the accuracy of Cavalea's survey or move the fence back to the property line. In December 1996 Cavalea ripped out the fence and appurtenances without Burns Philp's leave and placed a large container right at the property line, interfering with the use of Burns Philp's loading dock. Burns Philp now concedes that Cavalea was entitled to do these things. But the district judge held that Cavalea is not entitled to damages, because it did not notify Burns Philp that the fence had been erected on its land. Trespass is a strict liability tort . . . ; Restatement (2d) of Torts § 158 (1982), and an obligation to notify the intruder is inconsistent with the idea of strict liability. Nonetheless, the district judge stated:

> [The notice requirement] may be difficult to rationalize in terms of the traditional law of trespass, but it's not difficult for me to rationalize in terms of elemental justice, and that's the way I come out.

In diversity litigation, however, state law prevails over notions of "elemental justice." The only question for decision is whether Illinois conditions damages on the landowner's notice to the trespasser. (Cavalea contends that the counterclaim filed in 1995 gave whatever notice state law requires, a possibility the district judge did not discuss, but we need not pursue that prospect.)

Burns Philp locates a notice-to-trespassers requirement in cases holding that a landowner who has consented to entry may not complain about trespass until the consent has been revoked. The proposition is unremarkable. Trespass is entry without consent; while the consent lasts there can be no trespass, and therefore no legal remedy. How can this assist Burns Philp? Cavalea did not consent to the construction of a fence on its land. Had it done so, a change of mind would not necessarily require demolition of the fence — the original consent may grant a license that can be revoked only with compensation. But Burns Philp did not seek anyone's consent to build the fence. It thought that the fence was on its land, and no one knew otherwise until 1995. Knowledge of a fence's existence is not equivalent to consent — not, at least, when the landowner does not suspect that the border has been crossed. Paths that cut diagonals across parcels with known borders and similarly obvious intrusions, where failure to protest might imply consent, pose different questions. Burns Philp built its fence under a claim of right; it did not seek an express license (or an easement) and did not obtain an implied one; it does not assert that principles of adverse possession entitle it to maintain the fence. Cavalea accordingly is entitled to damages — if it suffered monetary loss.

Cavalea offered evidence that it used the land along its border with Burns Philp to store trailers and freight containers, and that it could have stored 102 additional trailers or containers had the fence been located correctly. It charges shippers and truckers $25 per day to store loaded containers, 75 cents a day for empty truck trailers, and 55 cents a day for empty containers. Proposing that all 102 places would have been used all of the time, Cavalea demanded nearly $1 million in damages, which would make this the most valuable twentieth of an acre in Chicago. Burns Philp responds that its employees consistently noticed empty places at Cavalea's facility even before the fence was removed, and it argues that access to the extra land accordingly would not have added to Cavalea's receipts. Because it concluded that Cavalea could not maintain an action for trespass, the district judge did not resolve this dispute. It is not our place to play factfinder . . . , but we hope that it will prove possible for the new district judge (see Circuit Rule 36) to wrap things up after reviewing the existing record without taking additional evidence. . . .

The judgment is vacated and the case remanded for two purposes: to limit damages for unjust enrichment to the five-year period preceding suit, and to calculate and award the damages (if any) that Cavalea sustained from the trespass.

NOTES AND QUESTIONS

1. *Why Litigation?* Judge Easterbrook plainly expresses his annoyance that the parties sued one another "instead of resolving matters amicably." Is there something special about this case, as opposed to other disputes we have seen, that would suggest the parties acted inappropriately

in resorting to the courts? What steps might their attorneys have taken to encourage resolution of the matter without litigation?

2. *Elemental Justice.* What did the district judge mean when he suggested that "elemental justice" warranted the notice requirement advocated by Burns Philp? Judge Easterbrook rejected this idea, noting that, under the Supreme Court's 1938 *Erie* decision, a federal court exercising jurisdiction over a tort case on the basis of diversity of citizenship between the parties is obligated to follow state law, not to improvise a separate body of federal tort law. (See the discussion of *Erie* in Note 1 following the *Testbank* decision in Chapter 2.) Of course, Judge Easterbrook's analysis leaves open the possibility that a state court interpreting state tort law could invoke elemental justice in support of a notice requirement. Do you agree that notice of the sort at issue here is required by basic principles of fairness? Is it unjust to force Burns Philp to pay damages for erecting a fence on another's land, even though it had good reason to believe that the land was its own?

3. *Strict Liability and Intentionality.* The court cites the Second Restatement of Torts for the proposition that trespass is a strict liability tort. While that description is accurate in one respect, there is another respect in which trespass can also accurately be described as an *intentional* tort. As we have seen, trespass requires that one person act so as to cause a certain kind of interference with a property possessor's rights of exclusive possession and control. Implicit in this formulation is the idea that the defendant's interfering act must have been *intentionally undertaken.* These two aspects of the tort of trespass are not self-contradictory, even if they may at times appear to be. While the act itself must have been intentional, there need not be any intention to do harm to the plaintiff, or to invade property that the actor knows to be owned or possessed by someone else, just as there need not be any unreasonable conduct. Rather, it is enough if (a) the defendant intentionally "invades" a swath of land (by walking on it, driving across it, throwing things onto it, digging it up, flooding it, building on it, etc.), and (b) the plaintiff owns or possesses the swath in question. On the other hand, a defendant who undertakes no voluntary or intentional act with respect to a piece of land cannot have committed a trespass. Thus, for example, if *D* unintentionally loses control of his car and crashes it into a residence or commercial establishment, he has not committed a trespass—he had no intention to make contact with the property in question—even though he may have committed negligence. *Cf.* Restatement (Second) of Torts § 166, illust. 2 (1977) (driver overcome by paralytic stroke not liable in trespass to owner of lawn damaged by car); Hammontree v. Jenner, 97 Cal. Rptr. 739 (Ct. App. 1971) (declining to apply liability without fault to hold driver liable for property damages caused when a driver lost control of his car as a result of an unexpected seizure).

In Scribner v. Summers, 84 F.3d 554 (2d Cir. 1996), the plaintiff property owner could not sell his land because it had been contaminated by hazardous waste that had flowed onto the land from defendant's adjacent property. Defendant knew that by washing its furnaces, it was sending water contaminated with hazardous materials down a swale toward plaintiff's property. If the washing was intentional, the drainage was virtually certain, and the leakage from the swale highly foreseeable, may one conclude that the defendant trespassed onto plaintiff's land? See Chapter 9, Section II.A (discussing the relationship between knowledge and intentionality).

4. *Nature of the Interference*. Will *any* invasion onto another's property suffice to establish a trespass, no matter how minimal? Historically, the answer has been yes. The Case of the Thorns (Hulle v. Orynge), decided in 1466, presents a famous example of judicial concern for seemingly trivial claims of interference. The defendant in that case was held to have trespassed by trimming hedges on his property, which caused some thorns to fall onto his neighbor's land. According to the opinion of one of the judges: "Even though it was lawful for him to cut the thorns, it was not lawful to allow them to fall into another person's soil, for he was to cut them in such a way that they did not damage others."

Very minimal interferences continue be treated as actionable in modern trespass law. For example, a cable company or an internet service provider must obtain consent from those whose property has to be traversed with wires or other equipment in order to provide service to customers. If such consent is not obtained, the property owners will have trespass claims, even if the equipment takes up a miniscule amount of space. *Cf.* Loretto v. Teleprompter Manhattan CATV Corp., 458 U.S. 419 (1982) (regulations authorizing the attachment of small pieces of equipment to buildings without the consent of building owners constitutes a "taking" of property by government in violation of the Fifth Amendment; owners are entitled to just compensation from the government for the invasion).

What is the point of rendering such minimal interferences actionable? In related contexts, tort observes the maxim *de minimis non curat lex* — the law does not concern itself with trivialities. Why should trespass be different? Some scholars have argued that the explanation is purely historical. English property law, they maintain, tended to leave property boundaries very poorly defined. Thus, courts positively welcomed the commencement of even trivial trespass actions to give them occasion to undertake the important business of more clearly defining the parties' property lines.

5. *Invasions On, Below, and Above the Surface*. According to the Second Restatement, "a trespass may be committed on, beneath, or above the surface of the earth." Restatement (Second) of Torts § 159, at 281 (1965). Many contemporary cases are brought by a plaintiff whose land has been contaminated by underground leakage of gas or toxic waste. *See, e.g.*, JBG/Twinbrook Metro Ltd. Partnership v. Wheeler, 697 A.2d 898 (Md. 1997) (subsurface gas leakage supports claim for common law trespass). Under the maxim *cujus est solum ejus est usque ad coelum*, a property owner was deemed to own the space directly above his land all the way "up to the heavens." The arrival in the twentieth century of routine airplane travel rendered strict observance of this maxim untenable. In the 1920s, Congress

enacted legislation essentially annexing the skies for public use, subject to government regulation. United States v. Causby, 328 U.S. 256 (1946). However, a property owner can still complain of an above-surface trespass caused by particularly low-flying aircraft, or, for that matter, by rocks being hurled across his property even if they do not land on it.

6. *Failure to Leave or Remove.* A trespass can occur by means of inaction just as it can by action. Thus, one who is invited to enter one's land has consent to be there and is not a trespasser. However, the failure to leave when the consent has been withdrawn, or its duration has expired, can provide the basis for a trespass claim. Similarly, the failure to remove an object from another's land is a trespass, even if the initial placement of the object was not tortious. *See, e.g.*, Rogers v. Board of Road Commissioners, 30 N.W.2d 358 (Mich. 1948) (plaintiff/widow permitted to bring a trespass action for the death of her husband, which occurred when he collided with a snow fence erected by the defendant county on their property: The plaintiff's and decedent's consent to the fence remaining on the property had terminated at the end of the winter season).

7. *Who May Complain of a Trespass?* Property torts adhere to the "proper plaintiff" requirement that figured prominently in Judge Cardozo's articulation of the tort of negligence in Palsgraf v. Long Island R.R. See Chapter 5. Thus, a plaintiff cannot prevail on a claim of trespass to land unless the plaintiff herself owns or otherwise is lawfully in possession of the land trespassed upon. Lal v. CBS, Inc., 726 F.2d 97 (3d Cir. 1984). Courts have, however, stretched the idea of a possessory interest to include members of the property owners' household. Restatement (Second) of Torts § 162, at 291-292 (1965).

8. *Injury, Harm, and Damages.* The introductory materials to Chapter 9 pointed out that dignitary torts such as assault, battery, and false imprisonment are actionable without harm to the victim. In this respect, as in several others, these torts differ from the tort of negligence. The tort of trespass shares this feature — there is no requirement that the invasion in question cause harm to the property or loss of economic value. As in those cases, nonharmful trespasses will generate awards for nominal damages, but may also warrant punitive damages if the defendant can be proven to have acted willfully, with malice, or with reckless disregard for plaintiff's rights. See Chapter 6. A particularly striking case of a cause of action for trespass without actual damages is presented by Jacque v. Steenberg Homes, Inc., 563 N.W.2d 154 (Wis. 1997), discussed in the notes following Jones v. Fisher in Chapter 9. There, the court upheld an award that combined nominal compensatory damages with $100,000 in punitive damages where the defendant, in the face of the plaintiffs' express refusal to consent, crossed the plaintiffs' land with heavy equipment.

9. *Damages.* While physical damage to property is not required to support a claim for trespass, such harm, should it attend a trespass, is compensable in a trespass action. As the next case demonstrates, the tort of trespass to property might also be available to certain plaintiffs who suffer bodily harm in connection with invasions on land.

Kopka v. Bell Tel. Co.
91 A.2d 232 (Pa. 1952)

Stern, J.   ...

At the request of residents of a township in Indiana County for telephone service the Bell Telephone Company of Pennsylvania, defendant in this suit, had its engineers stake out a line along a road bordering the farm of the plaintiff, Walter V. Kopka. It then proceeded to obtain rights-of-way from property owners along the road upon which the line was to be constructed, but no such right was obtained from the plaintiff.

Under an arrangement between the Company and one Jud Sedwick, additional defendant, the latter proceeded to erect the necessary poles to carry the wires and for that purpose drilled holes, one of which was dug inside the road on plaintiff's property; in this hole there was to be placed an anchor rod supporting a guy wire for bracing one of the poles. The Company had indicated to Sedwick where the holes were to be dug and the poles and anchor rods erected. This particular hole, 6½ feet deep and 17 inches wide, was dug on December 19, 1947. Two days later, on the 21st, plaintiff was informed by a neighbor about it and went out to investigate, it having been dug without his permission or knowledge. It was in the latter half of the afternoon of a cloudy day and starting to get dark. While walking around to find the hole plaintiff's left leg slipped into it with the result that he allegedly sustained certain injuries. He testified, although there was strong evidence to the contrary, that there was no mound or ring of dirt thrown up around the hole and that the ground seemed level at that point. The hay field through which he passed he described as being "rough and rolling, grass growed up, kind of spongy and spots of snow around in the fields." Around where the hole was "it was all weeds and briars and whatever it was." Other testimony on behalf of the plaintiff was to the effect that that corner of the field "was left in weeds, briar and morning-glory vines."

Suit was instituted against the Telephone Company in the Court of Common Pleas of Allegheny County. The complaint alleged the defendant had, without plaintiff's permission, trespassed upon his farm and dug a hole there, and that property damage as well as personal injuries to plaintiff resulted from the negligence of defendant in thus trespassing and causing others to trespass on his farm, digging the hole there and leaving it unprotected and without barriers, thereby creating a dangerous trap. Defendant filed an answer denying that the acts complained of were done by its agents or employes, but that, on the contrary, the installation of the poles and anchor rods was made by Jud Sedwick, an independent contractor. Defendant brought Sedwick on the record as additional defendant, alleging that any damage done to plaintiff's property or injuries suffered by him were the result of additional defendant's negligence and not that of defendant. ...

The trial resulted in a verdict in favor of plaintiff and against defendant in the sum of $11,000, and a verdict in favor of the additional defendant. The court overruled defendant's motions for judgment n. o. v. and for a new trial, and ordered that judgment be entered on the verdict, from which judgment defendant now appeals.

It should be immediately obvious that, as far as plaintiff's cause of action was based upon alleged negligence in the failure to cover the hole and erect barriers, the verdict against defendant cannot be sustained. If, as plaintiff claims, Sedwick acted as defendant's agent, there would be a hopeless inconsistency between the verdict in his favor and the verdict against his employer, since, in that event, the latter could be liable only on the principle of respondeat superior. . . . On the other hand, if Sedwick was an independent contractor, it is of course axiomatic that his negligence, or that of his employes, in failing properly to perform the work entrusted to him, could not impose liability upon defendant. Only insofar, therefore, as the action is one for the unauthorized invasion of plaintiff's land — that is insofar as it is the common law action of *quare clausum fregit* — can plaintiff's recovery therein be justified. . . .

Before considering the question of the liability of a trespasser for personal injuries suffered by the possessor of land as an indirect result of the trespass, there are two relevant legal principles to be borne in mind. The first is that the fact that a trespass results from an innocent mistake and, in that sense, is not deliberate or wilful, does not relieve the trespasser of liability therefor or for any of the results thereof. Thus, in Restatement, Torts, § 163, comment (b), it is said: "If the actor intends to be upon the particular piece of land in question, it is not necessary that he intend to invade the actor's interest in the exclusive possession of his land. The intention which is required to make the actor liable . . . is an intention to enter upon the particular piece of land in question irrespective of whether the actor knows or should know that he is not entitled to enter thereon. It is, therefore, immaterial whether or not he honestly and reasonably believes that the land is his own, or that he has the consent of the possessor or of a third person having power to give consent on his behalf, or that he has a mistaken belief that he has some other privilege to enter." . . .

The second important principle to be noted is that one who authorizes or directs another to commit an act which constitutes a trespass to another's land is himself liable as a trespasser to the same extent as if the trespass were committed directly by himself, and this is true even though the authority or direction be given to one who is an independent contractor.

The liability of defendant Company for the trespass involved in the digging of the hole on plaintiff's land without his knowledge or consent being thus established, does such liability extend to the personal injuries sustained by him as the result of his falling into the hole? The authorities are clear to the effect that where the complaint is for trespass to land the trespasser becomes liable not only for personal injuries resulting directly and proximately from the trespass but also for those which are indirect and consequential. In Restatement, Torts, § 380, it is stated that "A trespasser on land is subject to liability for bodily harm caused to the possessor thereof . . . by any . . . condition created by the trespasser while upon the land *irrespective of whether the trespasser's conduct is such as would subject him to liability were he not a trespasser*." And in comment (c) to this section, it is said: "It is, therefore, not necessary to the liability of the trespasser that his conduct should be intentionally wrongful or recklessly or negligently disregardful of the interests of the possessor.... Thus, one who trespasses upon the land of another incurs the risk of becoming liable for any bodily harm which is caused to the possessor of the land ... by any conduct of the trespasser during the continuance of his trespass no matter how otherwise innocent such conduct may be."[4] And in comment (f) to § 163, it is said: "So too, he [a trespasser] is liable for any harm to the possessor ... if such harm is caused by the actor's presence on the land, irrespective of whether it was caused by conduct which, were the actor not a trespasser, would have subjected him to liability."

The authorities uniformly support the principle thus stated.

Of course, if the owner or possessor of the land, wilfully, voluntarily, or by negligence, himself brings about the injury to his person, such an injury cannot be said to be consequent upon the trespass to the land, and in that event the trespasser would not be liable therefor.... The question arises, therefore, in the present case whether plaintiff's accident was essentially due to an inexcusable failure on his own part to see the hole for which he was in fact searching. That question, however, was for the jury and cannot be determined as a matter of law. The hole was comparatively small in diameter and, according to his evidence, was in rough ground where there were grass, briars, weeds, vines and spots of snow, interfering, perhaps, with ordinary clearness of vision, especially on a late, cloudy afternoon in the latter part of December.

The verdict rendered in favor of plaintiff was undoubtedly excessive. It appears that he suffered a war injury to his side and left leg which resulted in a 50 per cent disability and for which he is receiving compensation from the Government. In the present accident he claims to have sustained injuries to his right foot and to his back. The foot injury was occasioned by a briar penetrating his shoe and causing a puncture in the sole of the foot; after treatment this injury cleared up entirely in a couple of months leaving but a small scar. The only professional testimony as to the back injury was that of a doctor who examined him five days before the trial, more than two years after the accident, for the purpose, not of treatment, but of testifying. This doctor stated that in his opinion plaintiff had a chronic inflammation of muscles and tissue in the lower part of the back, and an early osteoarthritis. The testimony as to the causal relation between the accident and the arthritic condition was extremely tenuous. Plaintiff received some diathermic treatment for his back, but his entire medical expenses amounted to $80. He was not hospitalized. His claims for losses occasioned by allegedly forced relinquishment of certain activities were open to serious question; ten months before the accident

---

4. The Restatement gives the following illustration of the principle enunciated in that section: "A is driving his car along the highway in a neighborhood with which he is unfamiliar. He asks B to direct him to a certain town. B tells him that he can take a short cut through a private road over which the public is not accustomed to travel which B asserts to be upon his own land but which, in fact, is on the land of C. While driving *carefully* along the road, he runs over D, C's three-year-old child, who *suddenly dashes out from the bushes* which border the road. A is liable to D and to C."

he had signed a statement to the Government that he was unable then to work because of the injury to his leg. On the whole, a verdict in the amount of $7,000 would seem generous compensation for the injuries he sustained, and the verdict should accordingly be reduced to that amount. . . .

As modified the judgment is affirmed.

Musmanno, J. (concurring and dissenting in part).   I concur with the majority opinion with regard to liability of the Bell Telephone Company for the injuries sustained by the plaintiff, but dissent from the decision to lop off $4,000 from the verdict returned by the jury. Expert testimony established that the plaintiff sustained a serious injury to his back and that the pathological condition resulting from that injury will become progressively worse. . . .

Bell, J. (concurring in part and dissenting in part) (joined by Stearne, J.). The majority concede that defendant Bell Telephone Company was not guilty of negligence, and that the plaintiff cannot recover on the theory of negligence which was the theory on which the case was actually and admittedly tried and passed upon in the Court below. Nevertheless, they sustain plaintiff's verdict on an entirely different theory, viz., a theory of absolute liability arising out of a non-negligent trespass to land. In order to reach this startling conclusion, the majority utterly ignore a principle which this Court has iterated over and over again: ". . . we will not review a case on a theory other than that upon which it was tried and passed upon in the court below. . . . An appellate court does not sit to review questions that were neither raised, tried nor considered in the trial court." . . .

[Judge Bell proceeded to emphasize that, in proceedings before the trial court and the supreme court, Kopka's attorney had stated that he was advancing a claim for negligence, and not a claim for trespass. Thus, according to Judge Bell, the majority were not entitled to salvage Kopka's claim by treating it as seeking compensation for personal injuries parasitic on a trespass to land.] . . .

There is still another reason why plaintiff's verdict cannot be sustained. . . .

Damages, nominal or otherwise, depending upon the circumstances, may be recovered in an action of trespass quare clausum fregit; but because liability imposes such a severe and heavy burden upon one who may be an innocent trespasser, the damages recoverable have heretofore been limited in Pennsylvania (a) to injury to the land; and (b) to direct, immediate and proximate injuries resulting from the trespass. I believe that this doctrine has been reaffirmed and restated by the majority opinion. But the majority go one step further and rule for the first time in Pennsylvania that the possessor of land may also recover in an action of trespass quare clausum fregit for all indirect and consequential injuries to the person which result from the trespass. With this new or extended doctrine I disagree. . . .

Absolute liability for damages to land resulting from a non-negligent trespass quare clausum fregit is an ancient and technical concept, which arose from the ancient Anglo-Saxon emphasis on property rights and the ancient theory that a man's home was his castle and inviolable. Absolute liability is contrary to the modern philosophy of civil responsibility and should be applied only where the principle of stare decisis requires it, or where there is an express statutory direction imposing absolute liability without negligence, as for example under the Workmen's Compensation Act. But the modern trend is undoubtedly and rapidly drifting away from these ancient conceptions which formed the basis for trespass quare clausum fregit. As this Court said in Summit Hotel Co. v. National Broadcasting Company, 336 Pa. 182 at pages 186-187, 8 A.2d 302, at page 304, 124 A.L.R. 968 *"In our State, the doctrine of absolute liability has been invoked, almost without exception, only in that small group of actions which redress injuries to land, and it is only as to these that it can be fairly said that the doctrine prevails.* This liability is a survival of the medieval law dictated by the landlord, in which the protection of the uninterrupted enjoyment of real property was a primary consideration."...

NOTES AND QUESTIONS

1. *Breaking the Close*. In medieval English common law, the term *trespass* was a synonym for *wrong*. Thus, the writ of trespass was used as the procedural vehicle to bring claims for a diverse array of wrongs, including trespasses to land, assaults, batteries, injuries caused "directly" by negligence, etc. See Appendix B. Writs of alleging interferences with property rights were distinguished from writs complaining of other wrongs by inclusion of the phrase *quare clausum fregit*, which asks the defendant to explain "why he broke the [plaintiff's] close." "Breaking the close" is another way of expressing the idea that the defendant acted so as to invade the borders of plaintiff's land. Of course, in *Kopka*, the breaking that really mattered concerned the plaintiff's body rather than the borders of his property. Would there have been any cause of action if the plaintiff had not been physically injured by falling into the hole?

2. *Trespass or Negligence?* Focus on the fifth paragraph of the majority opinion, beginning, "It should be immediately obvious that ...". The crux of this argument is that if the jury's verdict was not based on the contractor's negligence, it must have been based on strict liability for Bell Telephone's trespass. Is this analysis sound? Even granted that Bell was not liable for the careless acts of Sedwick, the independent contractor, might it still have been properly held liable for careless misfeasance or nonfeasance? How would you frame that allegation of negligence?

Note that, in certain ways, trespass doctrine extends liability beyond the law applicable in a negligence action. Thus, according to the majority, under the "authorization" doctrine, Bell Telephone can be held responsible for an independent contractor's invasion of plaintiff's property, even though Bell could not be held liable for his careless acts under a theory of *respondeat superior*. See Chapter 8.

3. *Parasitic Damages*. Bell Telephone's conduct is deemed tortious because it interfered with plaintiff's proprietary interests. Given that such an interference is the predicate injury, does it make sense to give damages sufficient to compensate plaintiff for bodily harm as parasitic on that injury? The dissent claims to agree with the majority's view that sometimes personal injuries are compensable in an action for trespass, but says that the majority "goes one step further" by allowing recovery for "all indirect and consequential injuries." In doing so, it seems to import from negligence law the language of proximate cause. See Chapter 5. Is there anything odd about trying to limit an action in trespass, which is based on liability *without carelessness*, by means of proximate cause, which, especially in its modern form, is premised on the idea that an actor should be held responsible for the realization of those *risks* that rendered his conduct *careless?* On the other hand, isn't the dissent right to insist that the personal injuries for which a trespasser is liable must be limited by some principle?

In Beavers v. West Penn Power Co., 436 F.2d 869 (3d Cir. 1971), the plaintiff, ten years old, was killed when he came into contact with the defendant's power lines. The plaintiff sued in trespass, and the federal district judge, applying Pennsylvania law, instructed the jury to find for the plaintiff if they found that the defendant's erection of power lines trespassed in the space above the plaintiff's home, regardless of whether the power lines had been negligently constructed or maintained. The Third Circuit upheld the instruction, noting that, as a trespasser, the defendant would be strictly liable for all personal injuries caused by the trespass, whether "proximate or indirect." Can this be right? Suppose in *Kopka* the plaintiff had gone out to observe the hole in his yard, returned safely to his kitchen, then seriously injured his finger with a kitchen knife because he was still fuming over the fact that the hole had been dug without his permission. Would liability in trespass attach?

4. *Injunctions and Self-Help*. Damages are the most typical remedy obtained by property owners who suffer trespasses. However, other forms of relief may be available to them. Depending on the equities of the situation, property owners may be able to obtain a court order enjoining *ongoing* trespassory activity. *See, e.g.*, Anntco v. Shrewsbury Bank & Trust Co., 230 N.E.2d 795 (Mass. 1967) (upholding the issuance of an injunction against the continuous discharge of water by defendant onto plaintiff's property); *see also* Restatement (Second) of Torts §§ 933-951 (1979) (discussing the factors to be considered in determining the propriety of granting injunctive relief in response to trespasses). In the case of buildings and other permanent structures that have been constructed wholly or partly on another's land, the issuance of an injunction ordering the removal of the structure may result in considerable hardship to the defendant. Different jurisdictions seemingly take different views on the relative significance of the hardship faced by the defendant in deciding whether to grant such an order. *Compare* Brink v. Summers, 227 N.E.2d 476 (Mass. 1967) (courts will order the removal of permanent trespassory structures notwithstanding the hardship such an order may impose, and even as

against innocent trespassers) *with* Hanson v. Estell, 997 P.2d 426 (Wash. App. Div. 2000) (affirming the trial court's refusal to order the relocation of a barn that encroached slightly on the claimants' property in light of the negligible harm caused by the encroachment and the considerable expense associated with moving the barn).

As we saw in connection with the *Katko* decision in Chapter 9, possessors of land may sometimes employ self-help to defend their property rights, but only insofar as such efforts are reasonable. Seizure, destruction, or damaging of trespassory objects or structures can, depending on the circumstances, be deemed reasonable if done for the purpose of preventing invasion. In such cases, the possessor enjoys a privilege that will defeat any tort claim brought by the owner of the object or structure complaining of its seizure or destruction. (For more on tort claims for damage to personal property, see the notes following the next case.) For example, landowners generally are permitted to remove limbs of neighbors' trees encroaching onto their property. Indeed, they may be required to do so to avoid forfeiting any claim to damages. Granberry v. Jones, 216 S.W.2d 721 (Tenn. 1949) (a homeowner who had long permitted the defendant's hedge to encroach onto his property is entitled to trim so much of the hedge as is on his property, but may not recover for damages allegedly caused to his house by the hedge). This limited right of reasonable self-help is presumably what entitled Cavalea to rip out the fence that Burns Philp had unwittingly constructed on Cavalea's property. Given the limited nature of the privilege, a landowner who engages in self-help runs the risk of being found to have acted unreasonably in destroying or seizing an object or structure that trespasses on its property. *See* Sears v. Summit, Inc., 616 P.2d 765 (Wyo. 1980) (landowner held not entitled to commandeer construction equipment located on his property for the purpose of forcing the trespassing construction crew to pay him compensation).

Vincent v. Lake Erie Transp. Co.
124 N.W. 221 (Minn. 1910)

O'Brien, J.   The Steamship Reynolds, owned by the defendant, was for the purpose of discharging her cargo on November 27, 1905, moored to plaintiff's dock in Duluth. While the unloading of the boat was taking place a storm from the northeast developed, which at about 10 o'clock P.M., when the unloading was completed, had so grown in violence that the wind was then moving at 50 miles per hour and continued to increase during the night. There is some evidence that one, and perhaps two, boats were able to enter the harbor that night, but it is plain that navigation was practically suspended from the hour mentioned until the morning of the 29th, when the storm abated, and during that time no master would have been justified in attempting to navigate his vessel, if he could avoid doing so. After the discharge of the cargo the Reynolds signaled for a tug to tow her from the dock, but none could be obtained because of the severity of the storm. If the lines holding the ship to the dock had been cast off, she would doubtless have drifted away; but, instead, the lines were kept fast, and as soon as one parted or chafed it was replaced, sometimes with a larger one. The vessel lay upon the outside of the dock, her bow to the east, the wind and waves striking her starboard quarter with such force that she was constantly being lifted and thrown against the dock, resulting in its damage, as found by the jury, to the amount of $500.

We are satisfied that the character of the storm was such that it would have been highly imprudent for the master of the Reynolds to have attempted to leave the dock or to have permitted his vessel to drift a way from it. One witness testified upon the trial that the vessel could have been warped into a slip, and that, if the attempt to bring the ship into the slip had failed, the worst that could have happened would be that the vessel would have been blown ashore upon a soft and muddy bank. The witness was not present in Duluth at the time of the storm, and, while he may have been right in his conclusions, those in charge of the dock and the vessel at the time of the storm were not required to use the highest human intelligence, nor were they required to resort to every possible experiment which could be suggested for the preservation of their property. Nothing more was demanded of them than ordinary prudence and care, and the record in this case fully sustains the contention of the appellant that, in holding the vessel fast to the dock, those in charge of her exercised good judgment and prudent seamanship. . . .

The appellant contends by ample assignments of error that, because its conduct during the storm was rendered necessary by prudence and good seamanship under conditions over which it had no control, it cannot be held liable for any injury resulting to the property of others, and claims that the jury should have been so instructed. An analysis of the charge given by the trial court is not necessary, as in our opinion the only question for the jury was the amount of damages which the plaintiffs were entitled to recover, and no complaint is made upon that score.

The* situation was one in which the ordinary rules regulating property rights were suspended by forces beyond human control, and if, without the direct intervention of some act by the one sought to be held liable, the property of another was injured, such injury must be attributed to the act of God, and not to the wrongful act of the person sought to be charged. If during the storm the Reynolds had entered the harbor, and while there had become disabled and been thrown against the plaintiffs' dock, the plaintiffs could not have recovered. Again, if while attempting to hold fast to the dock the lines had parted, without any negligence, and the vessel carried against some other boat or dock in the harbor, there would be no liability upon her owner. But here those in charge of the vessel deliberately and by their direct efforts held her in such a position that the

---

* [Our presentation of the court's opinion in *Vincent* reproduces, in relevant part, the text as it appears in the official Minnesota Reports (and West's Northwestern Reporter). For reasons explained in Note 2, *infra*, we are of the view that an error probably occurred during the original publication process, and that this sentence ought to begin with the words "If the" rather than the word "The." — EDS.]

damage to the dock resulted, and, having thus preserved the ship at the expense of the dock, it seems to us that her owners are responsible to the dock owners to the extent of the injury inflicted.

In Depue v. Flatau, 100 Minn. 299, 111 N.W. 1, 8 L.R.A. (N.S.) 485, this court held that where the plaintiff, while lawfully in the defendants' house, became so ill that he was incapable of traveling with safety, the defendants were responsible to him in damages for compelling him to leave the premises. If, however, the owner of the premises had furnished the traveler with proper accommodations and medical attendance, would he have been able to defeat an action brought against him for their reasonable worth?

In Ploof v. Putnam, 71 Atl. 188, 20 L.R.A. (N.S.) 152, the Supreme Court of Vermont held that where, under stress of weather, a vessel was without permission moored to a private dock at an island in Lake Champlain owned by the defendant, the plaintiff was not guilty of trespass, and that the defendant was responsible in damages because his representative upon the island unmoored the vessel, permitting it to drift upon the shore, with resultant injuries to it. If, in that case, the vessel had been permitted to remain, and the dock had suffered an injury, we believe the shipowner would have been held liable for the injury done.

Theologians hold that a starving man may, without moral guilt, take what is necessary to sustain life; but it could hardly be said that the obligation would not be upon such person to pay the value of the property so taken when he became able to do so. And so public necessity, in times of war or peace, may require the taking of private property for public purposes; but under our system of jurisprudence compensation must be made.

Let us imagine in this case that for the better mooring of the vessel those in charge of her had appropriated a valuable cable lying upon the dock. No matter how justifiable such appropriation might have been, it would not be claimed that, because of the overwhelming necessity of the situation, the owner of the cable could not recover its value.

This is not a case where life or property was menaced by any object or thing belonging to the plaintiff, the destruction of which became necessary to prevent the threatened disaster. Nor is it a case where, because of the act of God, or unavoidable accident, the infliction of the injury was beyond the control of the defendant, but is one where the defendant prudently and advisedly availed itself of the plaintiffs' property for the purpose of preserving its own more valuable property, and the plaintiffs are entitled to compensation for the injury done.

Order affirmed.

Lewis, J. (dissenting) (joined by Jaggard, J.). I dissent. It was assumed on the trial before the lower court that appellant's liability depended on whether the master of the ship might, in the exercise of reasonable care, have sought a place of safety before the storm made it impossible to leave the dock. The majority opinion assumes that the evidence is conclusive that appellant moored its boat at respondent's dock pursuant to contract, and that the vessel was lawfully in position at the time the additional cables were fastened to the dock, and the reasoning of the opinion is that, because appellant made use of the stronger cables to hold the boat in position, it became liable under the rule that it had voluntarily made use of the property of another for the purpose of saving its own.

In my judgment, if the boat was lawfully in position at the time the storm broke, and the master could not, in the exercise of due care, have left that position without subjecting his vessel to the hazards of the storm, then the damage to the dock, caused by the pounding of the boat, was the result of an inevitable accident. If the master was in the exercise of due care, he was not at fault. The reasoning of the opinion admits that if the ropes, or cables, first attached to the dock had not parted, or if, in the first instance, the master had used the stronger cables, there would be no liability. If the master could not, in the exercise of reasonable care, have anticipated the severity of the storm and sought a place of safety before it became impossible, why should he be required to anticipate the severity of the storm, and, in the first instance, use the stronger cables?

I am of the opinion that one who constructs a dock to the navigable line of waters, and enters into contractual relations with the owner of a vessel to moor at the same, takes the risk of damage to his dock by a boat caught there by a storm, which event could not have been avoided in the exercise of due care, and further, that the legal status of the parties in such a case is not changed by renewal of cables to keep the boat from being cast adrift at the mercy of the tempest.

NOTES AND QUESTIONS

1. *Property and Water.* The status of structures, such as docks, that extend from privately owned land into public waters is governed by complex rules of property and maritime law. It appears that, at the time *Vincent* was decided, Minnesota law deemed the lake bed on which Vincent's dock was built to be property held by the State of Minnesota in trust for the people of the state. Nonetheless, it also appears that Vincent, as the owner of lakefront property, retained a "riparian right" to construct a dock that extended out into the water in front of his property "to the point of navigability," and to exclusive use of the dock for private purposes (so long as the structure did not interfere with the public's use of the waterway, and subject to the state's authority to regulate use of the lake in the public interest). State v. Korrer, 148 N.W. 617 (Minn. 1914). In short, Vincent seems to have enjoyed a possessory interest in his dock equivalent to his interest in the land to which the dock was attached.

2. *Scrivener's Error?* The phrase "scrivener's error" refers to a typographical error in the text of official documents such as statutes and official court reports. If a court determines that such an error has occurred, it is entitled to correct the text after the fact. *See, e.g.*, United States Natl. Bank v. Independent Ins. Agents of America, Inc., 508 U.S. 439 (1993) (repunctuating a federal statute upon a finding that its existing punctuation resulted from a clerical error). As noted above in an asterisked footnote,

we conjecture that such an error can be found in the official text of *Vincent*. Moreover, we think the error is significant, in that its correction can shed light on the court's reasoning.

The apparent error, as noted above, is in the fourth paragraph of the excerpted opinion. Its first sentence, in our view, should start with the word "If" before the word "The." This conjecture is based on the remaining text of the paragraph, as well as the ultimate rationale adopted by the majority opinion. Notice, for example, that the second clause of the first sentence begins "*and* if." The use of the conjunction "and" to commence this clause seems to presuppose the presence of an initial "If." Notice also that the second and third sentences respectively begin with "If" and "Again if." Their wording suggests that the first three sentences were meant to form a parallel construction, in which the first sentence was to provide an abstract statement of the principle that would have applied *if* the events in *Vincent* were truly beyond human control, whereas the second and third would provide concrete illustrations of that principle. This inference is in turn reinforced by the "But here" phrase that commences the paragraph's fourth and final sentence. Use of that phrase suggests that the last sentence was meant to stand in opposition to each of the three preceding sentences, which it cannot do unless the first sentence is deemed to start with an "If."

With the missing text in place, the gist of the paragraph comes into much sharper relief. As written, the paragraph seems initially to suggest that the court regarded *Vincent* as a case in which property rights were suspended because natural forces had taken over the situation. Such a suggestion runs directly counter to the entire point of the paragraph, and the opinion as a whole, which concludes that Vincent's property rights were not suspended.

3. *Harvey v. Vincent*. Compare *Vincent* to Harvey v. Dunlop, the decision with which this chapter commenced. Are the two decisions consistent? Suppose Harvey's attorney had argued to the New York court as follows: "Dunlop's conduct in throwing a stone at my client's daughter cost Clementine her eye. The question of whether Dunlop was behaving unreasonably when he threw the stone should be irrelevant. Even if he was acting reasonably when he threw it, he is still the one who threw it and, in doing so, harmed my client's daughter. Thus, he is the one who should pay." Why might this sort of argument, which seems to prevail in *Vincent*, fail in *Harvey?*

4. *Tort or Contract?* At least for a time, the defendant's ship had permission to be moored at Vincent's dock. Indeed, that permission was presumably obtained through a contract by which the defendant paid for the privilege to use the dock for a specified period of time. Might *Vincent* best be understood, then, not as a tort case, but as a contract case in which the court is left to fill in a missing term as to the conditions under which Vincent's consent to entry expired? Suppose the court were to determine that the parties had implicitly agreed that the dockowner was entitled to revoke consent after the ship was unloaded regardless of the risks faced by

the ship after being cast off. What would be the appropriate measure of contractual damages?

5. *Tort or Restitution?* Although *Vincent* was treated by the court as a tort case, some scholars have argued that its outcome turns on principles drawn from another area of law, namely the law of *restitution* or *unjust enrichment*. The basic idea of restitution is that, at least in some circumstances, when one person voluntarily confers a benefit onto another, the beneficiary owes it to the other to pay for the benefit. Thus, in contrast to tort, the obligation to pay restitution can arise even if no wrong has been done that is in need of rectification. The *Vincent* majority's cable hypothetical example, in the penultimate paragraph, lends some credibility to this reading of *Vincent*. What benefit was voluntarily conferred by the plaintiff to the defendant? What is the value of that benefit?

6. *Private Necessity and Incomplete Privilege*. *Vincent* is most commonly analyzed today as standing for the proposition that *private necessity* supplies an *incomplete privilege* to commit trespass. *See, e.g.*, Dan B. Dobbs, *The Law of Torts* § 107, at 248-250 (2000). The "privilege" part of this phrase refers to the fact that the defendant is held to have been entitled to override the property owner's right to exclude — the owner lacks the authority he would otherwise possess to eject a trespasser. The privilege is "incomplete" because, as in *Vincent*, the defendant is still liable for compensatory damages that result from his exercise of the privilege.

The incomplete privilege of private necessity is to be contrasted with the complete privilege of *public necessity*, whereby a private citizen is entitled to use or destroy another's property in order to avert a greater harm to the public without suffering any sanction. However, the destruction or harming of private property in the name of public necessity typically will be effected by government officials. So, for example, a fire department official might order the burning of a private citizen's property to help divert a fire away from a heavily populated area. The clause of the Fifth Amendment to the U.S. Constitution that prohibits the government from "taking" private property without "just compensation" entails that in some, but by no means all of these instances, officials will be obligated to compensate the owner for her losses out of funds from the public fisc. Dobbs, *supra*, § 109, at 253-254.

7. Vincent *and* Ploof. The majority in *Vincent* relied in part on a Vermont decision, Ploof v. Putnam, 71 A. 188 (Vt. 1908). The facts and reasoning of that case were presented by the Vermont court as follows:

> It is alleged as the ground on recovery that on the 13th day of November 1904, the defendant was the owner of a certain island in Lake Champlain, and of a certain dock attached thereto, which island and dock were then in charge of the defendant's servant; that the plaintiff was then possessed of and sailing upon said lake a certain loaded sloop, on which were the plaintiff and his wife and two minor children; that there then arose a sudden and violent tempest, whereby the sloop and the property and persons therein were placed in great danger of destruction; that, to save these from

destruction or injury, the plaintiff was compelled to, and did, moor the sloop to defendant's dock; that the defendant, by his servant, unmoored the sloop, whereupon it was driven upon the shore by the tempest, without the plaintiff's fault; and that the sloop and its contents were thereby destroyed, and the plaintiff and his wife and children cast into the lake and upon the shore, receiving injuries. This claim is set forth in two counts — one in trespass, charging that the defendant by his servant with force and arms willfully and designedly unmoored the sloop; the other in case, alleging that it was the duty of the defendant by his servant to permit the plaintiff to moor his sloop to the dock, and to permit it to remain so moored during the continuance of the tempest, but that the defendant by his servant, in disregard of this duty, negligently, carelessly, and wrongfully unmoored the sloop. Both counts are demurred to generally.

There are many cases in the books which hold that necessity, and an inability to control movements inaugurated in the proper exercise of a strict right, will justify entries upon land and interferences with personal property that would otherwise have been trespasses. . . .

It is clear that an entry upon the land of another may be justified by necessity, and that the declaration before us discloses a necessity for mooring the sloop. . . .

Did the court in *Ploof* need to invoke the idea of necessity to salvage the plaintiff's cause of action against the dockowner? What role does necessity play in establishing liability in *Ploof*?

8. Ploof *and* Marrs. Compare *Ploof* to an earlier decision, Cincinnati, N.O. & T.P. Ry. Co. v. Marrs' Adm'x., 85 S.W. 188 (Ky. Ct. App. 1905). Marrs, heavily intoxicated, disembarked from the defendant's train late at night and proceeded to fall asleep in the defendant's trainyard between two tracks. The defendant's employees later roused Marrs and told him to leave. An hour later, while operating an engine in the yard, the employees ran over and killed Marrs, who had fallen asleep again, this time on a track. The jury awarded Marrs' widow $4,500, and the defendant appealed. In rejecting the appeal, the court reasoned in part as follows:

There was no relation of passenger and carrier between Marrs and appellant, and therefore his entrance into the private switchyard of the corporation made him a trespasser; and, if those in charge of the switch engine had run it over him when he was first found in the yard, then, undoubtedly, appellant would have been entitled to a peremptory instruction under the evidence as adduced on the trial, because, he being a trespasser, its employes owed him no duty, except to refrain, after his peril was discovered, from injuring him, if this could be done by the exercise of ordinary diligence. But having found him drunk and asleep in the yard, could they arouse him, and start him wandering in the dark through the network of switches and tracks, and then say, when they afterwards ran over him, that they owed him no lookout duty because he was a trespasser? We cannot sanction so cruel and inhuman a principle. [The defendant's employees had seen Marrs disembark from the train and recognized at the time that he was drunk.] . . . When they saw him in the switchyard, asleep, and aroused him, they recognized him as the man they had seen on the train. They knew he was still intoxicated, and the fact that within so short a time he was found by them asleep in the switchyard was all the evidence that reasonable men required to know that, owing to his condition, he was unable to take care of himself, and more than probably was dazed and lost. Under these circumstances, it was their duty either to see him safely out of the yard, or, in default of this, to exercise at least ordinary care to avoid injuring him in moving the switch engine about where, under the circumstances, it was reasonable to anticipate his presence.... [C]ommon humanity forbade them simply to arouse him from where they found him asleep, and start him on another walk, merely to sink into a torpor in the yard a second time. Indeed, the action of these men was a positive injury to the decedent, for, as he lay between tracks Nos. 3 and 4, he was then, at least, safe from being run over. When they aroused him from this position, and started him on his walk in the dark through the yards, they subjected him to the perilous chance, when again overcome by the liquor, of assuming a position of greater danger than he was occupying at first. This chance subsequently became a reality. When the unfortunate man was overcome a second time in the yard, he went to sleep on one of the tracks, instead of between them. Under the circumstances, the switching crew should have done either more or less than they did, so far as the safety of the decedent was concerned.

We fully concede that Marrs' being drunk did not make him any the less a trespasser, when he first went into the yard of the corporation, and his intoxication added no new duty from it to him then. But when its servants actually discovered him, trespasser though he was, they owed him the duty to refrain from injuring him, and this duty was as comprehensive as the helplessness of his condition demanded to insure his safety from injury by them....

. . . Under these circumstances, we think they, after having discovered his perilous condition, owed him the duty of refraining from injuring him by exercising the care for his safety which we have indicated.

Id. at 188-190.

Did the *Marrs* court assume that the plaintiff could only recover if the court was prepared to conclude that Marrs was *justified* in trespassing on the defendant's property? That is, did the court assume that there are certain apparent trespasses that are rendered nontrespassory because of the putative trespasser's urgent need to invade the land? Alternatively, if the court did *not* make that assumption, does *Marrs* suggest a way in which the *Ploof* court could have imposed liability on Putnam *without* invoking a "necessity" privilege? Instead of focusing on the *plaintiff's reason* for intentionally interfering with the defendant's property rights, could the *Ploof* court have focused on the *reasonableness of the defendant's response* to that interference? If so, how might that have helped clarify the issue faced by the court in *Vincent?*

9. *Incentivizing the Parties.* Given the *Vincent* court's assumption that both parties behaved reasonably, does it make sense even to inquire whether one party is responsible for having committed a tort? Would it be more productive to ask whether forward-looking policy considerations favor placing the loss on dockowners or boatowners? Is it socially productive to tell shipowners that if they remain safely tied to a dock in a storm, they will bear the costs of damage to that dock? Does the plaintiff have a sound response to these arguments? In light of the court's decision, how might shipowners and dockowners adjust their behavior?

B.   Consent (With Notes on Other Defenses)

Claims for trespass, like other tort claims, are subject to affirmative defenses. (Indeed, if *Vincent* is understood as a "necessity" case, it provides an example of such a defense, albeit a partial one.) In this section we focus on one particularly important defense, namely, consent to entry onto land. As with dignitary torts such as battery, the presence or absence of permission is centrally important to trespass law. Indeed, the gist of both battery and trespass is an *unpermitted* physical invasion of a physical space that the victim has the right to control. Thus, just as with battery law, it is sometimes the case that a state's trespass law will require plaintiffs to prove *absence of consent* as part of their prima facie cases. In most jurisdictions, however, the burden remains on the defendant to prove that the plaintiff permitted him to enter the property.

Copeland v. Hubbard Broadcasting, Inc.
526 N.W.2d 402 (Minn. Ct. App. 1995)

Lansing, J.   Homeowners appeal the district court's summary judgment against their trespass claim. . . . We . . . reverse the summary judgment on the trespass claim.

FACTS

In the spring of 1993, KSTP television [(owned and operated by Hubbard)] broadcast an investigative report on the practices of two metro-area veterinarians. One of the veterinarians, Dr. Sam Ulland, treated Greg and Betty Copeland's cat. Before an April 1993 visit to the Copeland home, Dr. Ulland received the Copelands' permission to bring along a student interested in a career in veterinary medicine. The student, Patty Johnson, did not tell the Copelands or Dr. Ulland that, in addition to being a part-time student at the University of Minnesota, she was also an employee of KSTP and was [secretly] videotaping Dr. Ulland's practice methods.

When the investigative report was broadcast, it included two brief video portions filmed inside the Copelands' house. The Copelands sued KSTP and Johnson (collectively KSTP) for trespass. . . . The district court . . . granted KSTP's summary judgment motion on the trespass claim.

ISSUES

I. Did the district court err in granting KSTP's motion for summary judgment on the homeowners' trespass claim? . . .

ANALYSIS

A trespass is committed when a person enters the land of another without consent. Consent may be implied from the conduct of the parties, but silence alone will not support an inference of consent. Consent may be geographically or temporally restricted.

The district court concluded that KSTP was entitled to summary judgment on the Copelands' trespass claim because Johnson did not exceed the geographic boundaries of the Copelands' consent and the Copelands did not expressly limit their consent to Johnson's educational or vocational goals. We read the case law differently. For reasons we will more fully discuss, we hold that KSTP is not entitled to summary judgment on either basis.

Minnesota case law establishes that an entrant may become a trespasser by moving beyond the possessor's invitation or permission. *See* State v. Brooks-Scanlon Lumber Co., 128 Minn. 300, 302, 150 N.W. 912, 913 (1915) (when consent given to cut mature trees, cutting of immature trees exceeded scope of consent and constituted trespass); Rieger v. Zackoski, 321 N.W.2d 16, 20 (Minn. 1982) (court correctly instructed jury that lawful entrant may become trespasser by moving beyond scope of possessor's invitation). Although trespass in *Brooks-Scanlon* related to tangible objects, the decision nonetheless demonstrates that the scope of consent can be exceeded even though the entrant remains within the geographic limits of the consent. . . .

In support of its motion for summary judgment, KSTP cites Baugh v. CBS, Inc., for the proposition that the scope of consent can be exceeded only when physical boundaries are crossed. *See* 828 F. Supp. 745, 756 (N.D. Cal. 1993). *Baugh* is, however, factually distinguishable. In *Baugh*, the homeowner granted the broadcaster permission to videotape events at her house so long as they were not shown on television. *Id.* at 752. The homeowner brought a trespass action when the videotape was subsequently broadcast. *Id.* at 756. The court held that the scope of consent was not exceeded because the plaintiff agreed to the initial videotaping and the homeowner's cause of action was not trespass. *Baugh* has limited applicability to this case because the Copelands did not consent to any videotaping.

Courts in other jurisdictions have recognized trespass as a remedy when broadcasters use secret cameras for newsgathering. Newsgathering does not create a license to trespass or to intrude by electronic means into the precincts of another's home or office. Dietemann v. Time, Inc., 449 F.2d 245, 249 (9th Cir. 1971).

Whether a possessor of land has given consent for entry is, when disputed, a factual issue. The district court determined that the Copelands did not present any evidence indicating that the scope of consent was limited to educational purposes. The record, however, indicates that consent was given only to allow a veterinary student to accompany Dr. Ulland. Viewing the evidence in the light most favorable to the Copelands[], there is sufficient evidence to withstand summary judgment. . . .

NOTES AND QUESTIONS

1. *The Various Aspects of Consent.* As with respect to dignitary torts, the issue of consent in trespass law has several dimensions. First, consent

comes in two basic forms: *express* and *implied*. Which form of consent did the defendant invoke in *Copeland*?

Second, assuming consent has been granted explicitly or implicitly, it immunizes only those trespasses that fall within the scope of consent, either spatially or temporally. For example, the consent of the dockowner in Vincent v. Lake Erie included a temporal limitation. Thus, once the consent expired, the shipowner's decision to remain at the dock arguably converted a permitted entry into a trespass.

Third, consent to enter can be limited by reference to the *purposes* for which entry has been authorized. Thus, a homeowner who consents to have a cable TV repairman on the premises to install or repair his cable connection does not thereby consent to have the repairman spend the afternoon sunning himself in the yard, or swimming in the homeowner's pool.

Fourth, the capacity of consent to operate as a defense will depend upon *the communicative context* in which the consent is signaled. For example, as we saw in Chapter 9, the issue will sometimes arise in suits for battery, assault, or false imprisonment whether the defendant was entitled from the circumstances reasonably to infer consent, even where none was actually given. As indicated by the court's opinion in *Burns Philp*, *supra*, reasonable mistake as to ownership generally will not suffice to excuse a trespass. The Second Restatement adopts a position with respect to mistake parallel to its treatment of consent. *See* Restatement (Second) of Torts §§ 164(b), 244(b) (1965) (reasonable but erroneous belief that possessor has consented to entry provides no defense to claim for trespass to land or chattel, or to claim for conversion).

Finally, even when consent is given, there will sometimes be an issue as to whether that consent has been given *knowingly and voluntarily*. Recall from Chapter 3 that, in the context of medical procedures, consent will only be deemed valid in some jurisdictions if obtained after disclosure of all material information. Is the court in *Copeland* suggesting that the plaintiffs' consent to entry was similarly invalid because the homeowners did not have enough information about the entry to which they were consenting? In this setting, is it plausible to believe that the lack of information about the presence of the video camera vitiated the plaintiffs' consent to entry? Or is there something else objectionable about the conduct here that is better captured by a different sort of tort claim? As it turns out, the Copelands unsuccessfully attempted to amend their complaint to include common law claims for invasion of privacy and a claim under federal and state statutes prohibiting surreptitious electronic surveillance of others. Would the consent issue be analyzed similarly in *Copeland* if the underlying claim were invasion of privacy rather than trespass?

2. *Media Trespass*. In the last 40 years, courts, led by the U.S. Supreme Court, have made it more difficult for claimants to sue for defamation (injury to reputation) or loss of privacy. The animating idea underlying these developments has been a sense among judges that a victim's interest in her reputation and/or her privacy must give way to the constitutionally protected rights of speakers and audiences to participate in the free exchange of information and ideas, even if that exchange

involves statements that might sully the reputations or invade the privacy of others. As defamation and privacy claims have become harder to win, some claimants who believe they have been injured by media attention have turned to the venerable tort of trespass. Here, the free speech concerns are not as pressing, because the plaintiff is not complaining, at least in the first instance, about the *dissemination of information* about her. Instead, she argues that the *methods of newsgathering* employed by the media are tortious, regardless of what happens to the information once gathered. The viability of these trespass actions, as well as the consent issues analyzed in Note 1 above, have been addressed by two important opinions issued by federal Courts of Appeals. *See* Desnick v. American Broadcasting Co., 44 F.3d 1345 (7th Cir. 1995) (Posner, C.J.) (rejecting a trespass action brought by a doctor who was subject to an exposé that included footage obtained by the use of a hidden camera worn by a producer pretending to be a patient); Food Lion, Inc. v. Capital Cities/ABC, Inc., 194 F.3d 505 (4th Cir. 1999) (upholding a trespass claim against reporters who obtained access to a supermarket's back-room meat-packing operation by submitting false resumes, but granting only nominal damages for the harm caused by the trespass itself, as opposed to the airing of information that was obtained in part through the trespass).

3. *Trespass to Chattel*. The tort of trespass to real property has a direct analogue when the interference affects not land but personal property, also known as chattel. The most notable difference between the two forms of trespass, under U.S. law, is the courts' reluctance to recognize a cause of action for trespass to chattels absent a showing of harm. *See* Restatement (Second) of Torts § 218, illus. 2 (1965) ("A, a child, climbs upon the back of B's large dog and pulls its ears. No harm is done to the dog, or to any other legally protected interest of B. A is not liable to B."). Examples of actionable trespasses to chattels would include the slashing of another's car tires, or a band player's unpermitted use, and subsequent damaging of, a fellow band member's instrument. Like trespass to land, it is the intentionality of the tortfeasor's act and whether it does in fact interfere with plaintiff's personal property that determines whether the tort has occurred. Therefore, liability can attach even if the defendant reasonably but erroneously believes that the plaintiff's property belongs to him, and thus had no intention to cause harm to *another's* property.

4. *Trespass in Cyberspace*. Until recently, the law of trespass to chattel formed an obscure corner of tort law. Thus judges, who were perhaps already surprised when the tort of trespass to land started to appear in modern litigation concerning investigative reporting, were no doubt more surprised to find claims for *trespass to chattel* popping up in legal disputes involving cyberspace. In these suits, the plaintiffs have generally been internet service providers, such as AOL, who have sued defendants for flooding their subscribers with "junk" e-mail. Invoking trespass to chattel, the providers have asserted that their computer equipment, used for storing and processing subscribers' e-mail, constitute chattels upon which the defendants have trespassed, and which have been damaged by being "clogged" through overuse. At least two courts have

recognized such claims. *See* America Online, Inc. v. LCGM, Inc., 46 F. Supp. 2d 444 (E.D. Va. 1998) (recognizing cause of action for damages and granting injunction); CompuServe, Inc. v. Cyber Promotions, Inc., 962 F. Supp. 1015 (S.D. Ohio 1997) (granting injunction). The California Supreme Court recently weighed in on the other side of this dispute, declining to recognize a cause of action trespass to chattels. Intel Corp. v. Hamidi, 71 P.3d 296 (Cal. 2003). *Hamidi*, did not, however, involve a claim by an internet service provider.

5. *Conversion.* When a defendant's use of another's personal property takes the form of an intentional exercise of "dominion or control over a chattel," the wrong complained of is no longer trespass to chattel, but instead the distinct tort of *conversion*. Restatement (Second) of Torts, § 222A, at 431 (1965). Conversions often take the form of criminal thefts, such as the intentional stealing of another's car or wallet, or the intentional killing of another's farm animal or pet. But conversions need not be criminal or even culpable. Thus, if *A* reasonably but mistakenly takes *B*'s umbrella, which looks almost exactly like his own, and never attempts to return it because he believes it to be his own, *A* has committed the tort of conversion. *Id.* at 433, illus. 2. Ranson v. Kitner, 31 Ill. App. 241 (1889), provides a famous example of liability for conversion without fault. There the defendant shot at an animal that he actually believed to be a wolf, but which turned out to be the plaintiff's dog. When the plaintiff sued for conversion, the defendant argued that he could not be found liable because he had no intent to injure anyone's property; rather he had intended the apparently lawful act of shooting a wild animal. The court rejected this argument, concluding that the defendant's mistake as to the un-owned condition of the animal, even if a reasonable mistake, was no excuse.

A gruesome contemporary case asserting a cause of action for conversion and trespass to chattel is Wint v. Alabama Eye & Tissue Bank, 675 So. 2d 383 (Ala. 1996), in which a widow sued an eye and tissue bank for removing the eyes from her deceased husband's corpse without family consent.

6. *Other Defenses.* Like the dignitary torts discussed in Chapter 9, property torts are subject to a wide range of affirmative defenses beyond consent. These usually are described as "privileges" to enter or take property. Well-recognized defenses to trespass to land include entry incidental to the use of a public highway or navigable stream; entry to reclaim goods; entry to abate a private nuisance; and entry in order to effect an arrest or otherwise prevent crimes. *See* Restatement (Second) of Torts §§ 176-213, at 306-407 (1965). A roughly parallel set of defenses exists for trespass to chattels and conversion. *See id.* §§ 259-273, at 489-507. Analysis of privileges requires careful attention to the scope of the privilege and conditions of its exercise, and to the possibility that it has been abused. *See, e.g.,* Yeager v. Hurt, 433 So. 2d 1176 (Ala. 1983) (government automobile theft investigator had the right to seize the plaintiff's motorcycle, but abused the right by failing to return it for two years, giving rise to a claim for trespass to chattel and conversion).

C. Nuisance

Certain tort causes of action are so frequently brought together that they have become linguistic couplets. "Assault and battery" is one example. "Trespass and nuisance" is another. As we saw in studying the former pair, these phrases, though familiar, can be misleading. While a single action or pattern of activity can often give rise to both causes of action, each has different elements and vindicates different (albeit related) interests. The same is true for trespass and nuisance. Trespass provides a potentially powerful means of protecting and vindicating one's rights to *exclude* persons, objects, and substances from one's property. Often, however, interferences with the *use and enjoyment* of property can occur even absent the sort of invasion that serves as the necessary predicate for a trespass suit. To the extent noninvasive interferences with property rights are tortious, they tend to be actionable as *nuisances*. As we now see, nuisance and trespass differ in various ways beyond the issue of invasiveness.

Sturges v. Bridgman
11 Ch. D. 852 (1879)

Thesiger, L.J.   The Defendant in this case is the occupier, for the purpose of his business as a confectioner, of a house in *Wigmore Street*. In the rear of the house is a kitchen, and in that kitchen there are now, and have been for over twenty years, two large mortars in which the meat and other materials of the confectionery are pounded. The Plaintiff, who is a physician, is the occupier of a house in *Wimpole Street*, which until recently had a garden at the rear, the wall of which garden was a party-wall between the Plaintiff's and the Defendant's premises, and formed the back wall of the Defendant's kitchen. The Plaintiff has, however, recently built upon the site of the garden a consulting-room, one of the side walls of which is the wall just described. It has been proved that in the case of the mortars, before and at the time of action brought, a noise was caused which seriously inconvenienced the Plaintiff in the use of his consulting-room, and which, unless the Defendant had acquired a right to impose the inconvenience, would constitute an actionable nuisance. The Defendant contends that he had acquired the right, either at common Law or under the *Prescription Act*, by uninterrupted user for more than twenty years.

In deciding this question one more fact is necessary to be stated. Prior to the erection of the consulting-room no material annoyance or inconvenience was caused to the Plaintiff or to any previous occupier of the Plaintiff's house by what the Defendant did. It is true that the Defendant in the 7th paragraph of his affidavit speaks of an invalid lady who occupied the house upon one occasion, about thirty years before, requested him if possible to discontinue the use of the mortars before eight o'clock in the morning; and it is true also that there is some evidence of the garden wall having been subjected to vibration, but this vibration, even if it existed at all, was so slight, and the complaint, if it could be called a complaint, of the invalid lady, and can be looked upon as evidence, was of so trifling a character, that, upon the maxim *de minimis non curat lex*,* we arrive at the conclusion that the Defendant's acts would not have given rise to any proceedings either at law or in equity. Here then arises the objection to the acquisition by the Defendant of any easement. . . . [Given that the operation of the kitchen had only a *de minimis* impact on the plaintiff's property prior to the construction of the consulting room, the plaintiff would have had no grounds during that period to seek an injunction against, or damages based on, the defendant's activities. Thus, the fact that the defendant has, until now, been at liberty to use the mortars cannot be regarded as evidence that the plaintiff had acquiesced in their use so as to forfeit his right to complain about them now. — EDS.]

It is said that if this principle is applied in cases like the present, and were carried out to its logical consequences, it would result in the most serious practical inconveniences, for a man might go — say into the midst of the tanneries of *Bermondsey*, or into any other locality devoted to a particular trade or manufacture of a noisy or unsavoury character, and, by building a private residence upon a vacant piece of land, put a stop to such trade or manufacture altogether. The case also is put of a blacksmith's forge built away from all habitations, but to which, in course of time, habitations approach. We do not think that either of these hypothetical cases presents any real difficulty. As regards the first, it may be answered that whether anything is a nuisance or not is a question to be determined, not merely by an abstract consideration of the thing itself, but in reference to its circumstances; what would be a nuisance in *Belgrave Square* would not necessarily be so in *Bermondsey*; and where a locality is devoted to a particular trade or manufacture carried on by the traders or manufacturers in a particular and established manner not constituting a public nuisance, Judges and juries would be justified in finding, and may be trusted to find, that the trade or manufacture so carried on in that locality is not a private or actionable wrong. As regards the blacksmith's forge, that is really an *idem per idem* case with the present. It would be on the one hand in a very high degree unreasonable and undesirable that there should be a right of action for acts which are not in the present condition of the adjoining land, and possibly never will be any annoyance or inconvenience to either its owner or occupier; and it would be on the other hand in an equally degree unjust, and, from a public point of view, inexpedient that the use and value of the adjoining land should, for all time and under all circumstances, be restricted and diminished by reason of the continuance of acts incapable of physical interruption, and which the law gives no power to prevent. The smith in the case supposed might protect himself by taking a sufficient curtilage to ensure what he does from being at any time an annoyance to his neighbour, but the neighbour himself would be powerless in the matter. Individual cases of hardship may occur in the strict carrying out of the principle upon which we found our judgment, but the negation of the principle would lead even more to individual hardship,

---

* ["The law does not concern itself with trivial matters." — EDS.]

and would at the same time produce a prejudicial effect upon the development of land for residential purposes. The Master of the Rolls in the Court below took substantially the same view of the matter as ourselves and granted the relief which the Plaintiff prayed for, and we are of opinion that his order is right and should be affirmed, and that this appeal should be dismissed with costs.

NOTES AND QUESTIONS

1. *Types of Nuisance*. Because the term *nuisance* is used colloquially to refer to various sorts of annoyance, it is worth emphasizing that in tort law, the term is restricted to ongoing interferences with another's right to use and enjoy *real property*. Suppose *D* crashes his boat into a public bridge, causing it to be shut down for repairs for six months, thereby forcing *P* to drive to and from work by an alternate and slower route. *P* might well regard the closing of the bridge as a "nuisance," but he will not have a nuisance action against *D* — no property rights of his have been affected. Many activities have been adjudged to cause sufficient interference with the use and enjoyment of property so as to amount to nuisances, at least under certain circumstances. These include a noisy racetrack, low-flying air traffic, an incessantly howling dog, the emission of pollutants, the operation of an animal farm in a nonrural setting, use of bright lights in a residential neighborhood, and the erection of structures that block another's access to air or light.

2. *Nuisance versus Trespass*. As mentioned above, there are both similarities and differences between trespass to land and nuisance as torts. The most salient similarities include the following: (a) both involve interferences with an interest in land; (b) both require as a condition of actionability that the plaintiff have a possessory interest in the relevant property; (c) both frequently involve requests for injunctive relief in addition to, or apart from, claims for damages; (d) neither requires proof of actual damages or harm; (e) neither requires proof that the defendant acted for the purpose of interfering with someone else's property rights; and (f) neither requires that defendant's conduct fall below the threshold of reasonableness.

As to differences, nuisance requires the defendant's conduct to have caused *unreasonable* interference with another's use and enjoyment of land, whereas trespass exists even for trivial interferences with the right of exclusive control and possession. In this respect, liability for trespass is more "strict" than liability in nuisance. Liability in trespass is also more one-sided, in that there is little, if any, consideration given to the value of trespassory activity in determining whether a trespass has occurred. In nuisance, by contrast, the defendant's interest in pursuing the putatively offending activity often enters into the analysis of whether a nuisance exists. Nuisance also requires a *continuing* interference, while trespass will be satisfied by a one-off event. On the other hand, trespass requires that the invasive act be an intentional using of the property in question, while nuisance does not.

3. *Private versus Public Nuisance.* A cause of action for nuisance can refer to two different sorts of action: a "private nuisance" and a "public nuisance." *Sturges*, and indeed the entire "nuisance" section of this chapter, focus on private nuisances. Prosser and Keeton succinctly distinguish the two as follows:

> A private nuisance is a civil wrong, based on a disturbance of rights in land. The remedy for it lies in the hands of the individual whose rights have been disturbed. A public or common nuisance, on the other hand, is a species of catch-all criminal offense, consists of an interference with the rights of the community at large, which may include anything from the obstruction of a highway to a public gaming-house or indecent exposure. As in the case of other crimes, the normal remedy is in the hands of the state.

W. Page Keeton, et al., *Prosser and Keeton on Torts* 618 (5th ed. 1984). This distinction notwithstanding, the two forms of nuisance sometimes overlap in practice. Thus, while it is normally government officials who have standing to bring a cause of action for public nuisance, the common law sometimes permits individuals to bring such a claim, although only if the individual has suffered an injury as a result of the nuisance of a sort that distinguishes her from the general population. *See, e.g.*, Blair v. Anderson, 570 N.E.2d 1337 (Ind. Ct. App. 1991) (where the operation of a landfill blocks the flow of water onto the plaintiffs' adjacent property, the plaintiffs have standing to bring a public nuisance action to enjoin its operation). Because of this special injury requirement, when a private plaintiff brings a public nuisance claim, it is almost always accompanied by a separate claim for private nuisance. In such a situation, the plaintiff in effect wears two hats. As private nuisance claimant, she seeks to enjoin and obtain redress for an interference with the use and enjoyment of *her* property. As public nuisance claimant, she seeks an injunction on behalf of the public health and welfare. In recognition of the fact that the public's interest is being advanced in public nuisance suits, public officials are often granted the right to make themselves parties to an otherwise private lawsuit if the suit includes a claim for public nuisance. *See, e.g.*, Hancock v. Terry Elkhorn Mining Co., 503 S.W.2d 710 (Ky. 1973) (state attorney general may intervene as of right in suit alleging public nuisance).

The tort of public nuisance has received increased attention recently as a number of U.S. cities have invoked this cause of action against gun manufacturers. The typical allegation in these suits is that the manufacturers' failure to protect against the sale of guns to criminals has created a public health hazard by significantly increasing the amount of gun violence and attendant physical carnage that takes place in these cities. *See, e.g.*, City of Chicago v. Beretta U.S.A. Corp., 785 N.E.2d 16 (Ill. App. 2002), *app. allowed*, 788 N.E.2d 727 (Ill. 2003).

4. *Nuisance versus Negligence.* Because the concept of *unreasonable* interference plays a central role in nuisance law, it is natural to ask whether nuisance is really just a branch of negligence law. The short answer is that nuisance is a separate tort, and that the unreasonableness

to which nuisance law refers does not necessarily characterize the defendant's *conduct*. Rather, it is the nature of the interference with the defendant's use and enjoyment of her property that must be "unreasonable" — that is, more onerous than a landowner should have to put up with. Dan B. Dobbs, *The Law of Torts* § 463, at 1321, n.5 (2000). The Restatement (Second) expresses a certain degree of skepticism about this distinction, suggesting that apart from intentionally caused interferences with the use and enjoyment of land, most other nuisances are in fact instances of faulty conduct on the part of the defendant. Restatement (Second) of Torts § 822 (1979). (Section 822(b) allows that some unintentionally caused nuisances may not be fault-based, but only if they arise out of ultrahazardous activities, discussed *infra*, Section III.) Professor Dobbs, however, suggests that, while there certainly are cases of nuisances caused by unreasonable conduct, the torts remain distinct in important ways. *See* Dobbs, *supra*, § 464, at 1324. Does *Sturges* suggest that the Restatement's division of nuisances essentially into two categories — intentional and unreasonable — is unsatisfactory? Was the interference there brought about intentionally? If not, would you describe the defendant's conduct as "unreasonable," as that term is typically used in negligence law?

5. *Zoning.* Cities and municipalities today enact elaborate zoning ordinances that set out to distribute systematically different forms of land use (industrial, retail, residential, etc.) in order to provide landowners with notice of what they may do and what they may expect others in their vicinity to do. Should the advent of zoning eliminate the need for a common law of nuisance? Trickett v. Ochs, 838 A.2d 66 (Vt. 2003) (evidence that the defendant's use of property conforms with applicable zoning laws is relevant to, but not dispositive of, the question of whether the use constitutes a nuisance).

6. *Coasean Analysis of Tort Law.* Nobel prize–winning economist Ronald Coase relied in part on *Sturges* to develop a set of claims that he articulated most famously in a famous 1960 article entitled *The Problem of Social Cost*. This note describes the basic features of Coasean analysis, using *Sturges* to help illustrate its key points.

a. *Reciprocal Causation and Entitlements.* Coase began with the observation that standard analyses of tort cases tend to have a unidirectional focus: They inquire whether there is some reason for making an injurer (D) pay compensation to a victim (P) for P's losses. Analyses of this sort invoking doctrinal reasoning might attempt to resolve this question by parsing precedents to determine whether P had a valid claim against D. Economic analyses might alternatively pose the question of whether it would promote the efficient use of resources to impose liability on D. Regardless of their differences, both forms of analysis assume that the liability flows in one direction: *from* the one whose activity interferes with another's use of his property (D) *to* the one whose use of his property is interfered with (P).

In Coase's view, standard analyses are in the foregoing respect fundamentally flawed. All torts, he maintained, are *reciprocal* — they consist of interactions between at least two actors whose activities interfere with each other. Recall the facts of *Sturges*. As framed by the court, the question was whether the confectioners' interference with the doctor's practice was sufficiently serious to constitute a nuisance. Yet, according to Coase, as an analytic matter, one might just as well ask whether the doctor's insistence on quiet was an interference with the business of the confectioner. To treat the confectioner as the party who has "interfered" with the doctor's activity, and hence as eligible for legal sanctioning, is unjustifiably to presume a baseline by which the doctor enjoys a prima facie *entitlement* to engage in the activity, whereas the confectioner does not. Yet the crux of the legal problem posed by a case such as *Sturges* is, presumably, to figure out *who should be* entitled to engage in what sort of activity. Thus, to *begin* the analysis by characterizing the defendant as a person who has interfered with the activities of the plaintiff is to beg the critical question. One must instead begin with the assumption that each person is at liberty to act in the manner that he wishes, then ask whether there is some reason for the law to assign a right to engage in the activity to one of the two.

b. *The Irrelevance of Entitlements in the Absence of Transaction Costs: The Coase Theorem.* The economic theory of legal rules that was conventionally accepted when Coase entered the field had two prongs. The first (often tacit) presumption was evaluative — economists presumed that the best outcome was one in which resources were allocated such that they realized their most efficient or wealth-enhancing use. The second seemed to follow swiftly from the first: Legal rules should be designed so as to confer the legal entitlement to a resource to those who are able to use the resource in the most efficient manner (i.e., to generate the most wealth for the least cost).

Accepting the first prong of economic analysis, Coase famously rejected the second by advancing what has become known as the "Coase Theorem." Specifically, he argued that in a world in which parties could enter private transactions *costlessly* — that is, instantly, effortlessly, with full information, etc. — resources would find their way to their most efficient use *regardless of to whom they are initially allocated by the law*. This surprising result follows from the supposition that it will always be to the advantage of a party who is unable to make maximally efficient use of a resource to sell that resource to a party who is able to make such use of it. In short, even when the law "misallocates" the entitlement to use a given resource by granting it to someone who can't make the best use of it, that entitlement will naturally "migrate" (by means of voluntary transactions) to the party who can make the most efficient use of the resource.

A variation on *Sturges* will illustrate the point. Suppose that the confectioner's use of mortars during the doctor's consulting hours earns the confectioner $100 in profits, yet costs the doctor $150 in lost profits. Now suppose that the doctor is granted a legal entitlement to use his property free of this interference. In this situation, the confectioner cannot make it worthwhile to the doctor to forgo consulting unless he can pay the doctor more than he stands to lose from not consulting. However, since the confectioner makes less than $150 from operating his machines, it would be economically irrational for him to make such a payment. So the property ends up being devoted to its more efficient use.

But now turn the example around. Suppose that the confectioner is deemed by the law to be the one with the property right, and yet the relative profits are the same as indicated above. In this situation, the doctor, if acting rationally, will pay the confectioner to cease using his mortars. After all, it costs the doctor $150 in profits that he would otherwise obtain, so he can pay the confectioner anything under $150 and still make a profit. Likewise, the confectioner will, if acting rationally, accept some amount over $100 to cease using his equipment. Thus, even if the legal rules are set up to give the confectioner the initial entitlement to the relevant resource (the right to use the space adjacent to the wall), a mutually acceptable transaction should be possible by which the resource is allocated to its highest-value use (consulting). Under these circumstances, the question of *to whom* to allocate the entitlement to act turns out to be uninteresting: Considerations of efficiency give us no reason to confer the entitlement on one or the other party.

  c. *The Irrelevance of Distribution: Kaldor-Hicks Efficiency.* To say that the choice of entitlement will, in the absence of transaction costs, have no differential effect on the attainment of the efficient result is *not* to say that it won't have *any* effects. In particular, alternative entitlement rules will have very different *distributional* effects. If the rule is adopted entitling the doctor to consult, the confectioner will lose out on $100 worth of business, while the doctor will retain the full value of the $150 he obtains from consulting. However, if the alternative rule is adopted, the doctor will have to pay the confectioner for the right to consult, which means that the confectioner will earn his $100 plus a bit more, while the doctor will retain only what is left of the $150 after he pays the confectioner.

  Still, while this distributional difference might matter to those interested in analyzing a problem such as the one posed in *Sturges* as a problem of *justice*, it does not matter (at least in the first instance) to efficiency analysis. In economic analysis, the concern is not *who* gets a bigger or smaller slice of the total pie of aggregate social wealth, but how to fashion rules to ensure that the pie is as big as it can be. Indeed, followers of Coase typically rely upon the so-called *Kaldor-Hicks* conception of efficiency, which quite deliberately defines efficiency without regard to distributional issues. Under Kaldor-Hicks, a reallocation of resources is efficient if it generates a *net* gain in societal wealth, such that the beneficiaries of the extra wealth *could* fully compensate all those who lose wealth as a result of the reallocation, *regardless* of whether such compensation is actually paid. Thus, on the assumptions given above, the Kaldor-Hicks efficient solution to the problem is to have the doctor consult because the profits generated by consulting are sufficiently great that the doctor *could* fully compensate the confectioner for the losses he suffers by not being permitted to use his machines. Whether the rule should be adopted that requires the doctor *actually* to pay that compensation is a different question. Indeed, as we saw above, on the assumption of no transaction costs, the Coasean analyst is completely *indifferent* as to whether such a rule is adopted, since either rule will result in the property being put to its highest use.

d. *The Payoff: Reintroducing Transaction Costs.* As explained above, Coase's chief theoretical insight is that legal rules will have no influence on the relative efficiency of resource allocations when parties can enter into transactions with one another effortlessly, when they have perfect information, and when there are no other impediments to agreement. But, as he understood, the world of no transaction costs is a fantasy world. Bargaining takes time and effort, and is often conducted under conditions of limited information by actors who are not fully "rational." Moreover, even if all these problems are put aside, there often remains a substantial impediment to agreement, namely, the distributional question of how to divide up the economic pie. For example, we posited above that absent a court-granted entitlement to the doctor to use the consulting room, the doctor will seek to purchase that entitlement from the confectioner. Yet we also noted that the amount the doctor will rationally pay, and that the confectioner will rationally accept, falls somewhere between $100 and $150. The parties might well find it hard to settle on a number, since the doctor wants to pay as little as possible over $100 and the confectioner wants to be paid as much as possible up to $150.

Why, then, is the Coase Theorem at all significant, given the omnipresence of transaction costs? Does their existence render Coasean analysis irrelevant? Quite the opposite. As Coase explained, once transaction costs are reintroduced, we finally arrive at an *economic* explanation as to why the choice of legal rules bearing on entitlements *does* matter after all. They matter precisely because parties cannot enter transactions with one another costlessly. And so the lesson of the Coase Theorem in the end turns out *not* to be that legal rules are unimportant to efficiency. Rather, it suggests that they are important to the efficient allocation of resources *because* transactions are costly. It follows, according to Coase, that legal rules should not (generally) be designed with the goal of directly steering resources to their most efficient uses. Rather, they should be designed to avoid or overcome situations in which parties face high transactions costs — significant impediments to bargaining. In short, law is most likely to promote efficient use of resources when it "greases the wheels" of consensual transactions, which in turn permits resources to migrate to their most efficient uses.

e. *Implications.* With this brief summary in mind, consider the implications of a Coasean approach for the analysis of tort law. Do Coase's insights advance the analysis of cases such as *Sturges?* What about Vincent v. Lake Erie? Is there something special about those cases that render his framework particularly useful and appropriate? Does the idea of reciprocal causation apply as comfortably to other tort claims, such as those for negligence or battery? For example, is it useful or appropriate to describe an instance of medical malpractice as an instance of reciprocal injuring? (What "injury" has the doctor suffered at the hands of his patient?) Recall from the end of Chapter 2 Judge Calabresi's concept of the "cheapest cost avoider," which he developed at the same time that Coase was writing his seminal articles. Can you see how the two approaches resemble one another?

Penland v. Redwood Sanitary Sewer Serv. Dist.
965 P.2d 433 (Or. Ct. App. 1998)

Haselton, J. ...

To "reset the scene," we reproduce the summary of undisputed facts ... :

[Defendant] District operates sewage-related facilities, including a sewage treatment plant, in rural Josephine County. As part of the sewage treatment process, the District reduces incoming raw sewage to sludge, or biosolids, a bacteria-laden condensed form of sewage, by draining the liquids from the solids. Before 1988, the District trucked the sludge to various sites for land application, which involved spreading the sludge over a large area for agricultural and disposal purposes.

In 1988, the District's manager, Weber, who was charged with day-to-day oversight of its operations, instituted a small-scale pilot composting operation at the treatment plant. In July 1990, the District instituted composting on a permanent basis.

In the initial stages of the composting process, sludge is solidified by being poured into an outdoor levee, or "drying ring," which is exposed to the open air. After about two weeks, the material loses enough moisture to be mixed with organic material for composting. The reduced sludge, or biosolids, is then mixed with organic materials, such as wood, animal bedding, including animal waste, and yard waste, provided by local residents and businesses. The bacteria in the sludge break down the mixture. In order for the bacteria to decompose the sludge, the mixture must be exposed to air. Thus, the mixture is placed in a large pile, approximately nine feet high, 20 feet wide, and 100 hundred feet long, and exposed to the open air. The composted material is first piled over a perforated pipe for aeration. After two to three weeks, the pile is removed from the pipe and is turned every two weeks for aeration. There are normally seven piles at one time, each in a different stage of the composting process. Defendant uses heavy equipment to move the piles as they decompose and to load the finished product.

After approximately 90 days, the material becomes finished compost, which defendant sells to the public as mulch or soil amendment. The product, called Jo-Gro, contains no nutrients for fertilizing but is valuable for retaining moisture in soils.

If the sludge mixture is not aerated, it becomes anaerobic and, as a result, generates hydrogen sulfide. Hydrogen sulfide can cause headaches, nausea, and throat problems, and its odor is akin to that of rotten eggs. Hydrogen sulfide is generally released whenever a compost pile or the sludge pool is disturbed, but some level of hydrogen sulfide is always present as a result of the composting operation.

Plaintiffs are landowners and homeowners who live in rural Josephine County near the plant and composting operation. Many lived in the neighborhood before the District instituted the permanent composting operation. The closest plaintiffs, the Penlands, live about 180 feet from the property where the composting activities take place. Plaintiffs and other neighbors began to notice odor, noise, and dust, which they associated with the composting operation, in October 1991. Beginning in February 1992, plaintiffs and others complained to the District that, because of the odor and noise they ascribed to the plant, they were unable to enjoy outdoor activities, such as gardening, sitting on their porches, and barbequing. In response to those complaints, the District undertook several measures, including placing sound deflection panels on the electric wood grinder. Plaintiffs apparently found those measures to be ineffective and their complaints continued....

[In the summer of 1994, after receiving the recommendation of an advisory committee, the District's board of directors voted] to continue the composting operation at the sewage plant while implementing 21 of the *ad hoc* committee's recommended mitigation measures. Those measures included using a quieter loader, constructing vegetation screens, adding sound mufflers to equipment, eliminating construction lumber demolition, applying a commercial deodorizer, mixing the sludge more rapidly and efficiently, using fly bait, and adding dust-reducing spray misters.

In August 1994, plaintiffs filed this action, seeking to enjoin the continuation of the composting operation. Plaintiffs alleged that that operation created a nuisance in that it created excessive odor, noise, and dust and interfered with the reasonable use of their properties.

146 Or. App. at 227-29, 934 P.2d 434 (footnote omitted).

[The issues before the court are whether the District's composting operation constitutes a nuisance and, if so, whether it should be enjoined.]

In determining whether the composting operation constitutes a nuisance — i.e., whether it substantially and unreasonably interferes with the use and enjoyment of plaintiffs' property — we must assess five factors: (1) the location of the claimed nuisance; (2) the character of the neighborhood; (3) the nature of the thing complained of; (4) the frequency of the intrusion; and (5) the effect upon the plaintiff's enjoyment of life, health and property. Whether a condition constitutes a nuisance depends on its effect on "an ordinarily reasonable [person], a normal person of ordinary habits and sensibilities."

The trial court, in oral remarks that comported with its ultimate written findings and conclusions, explained its application of those factors:

> I want to start out, first of all, before I go on to the issue of nuisance, I'd just like for the record — I know it's not really evidence, but I was taken on a view of the property and I think it's important that the record reflect, as everyone agrees, that this is a residential area. It fronts the Rogue River. The day we were out there, there were osprey flying over the river. There's fish. It's a beautiful, very much a residential, rural nature, despite the fact that it's been divided into small parcels....
>
> I do find that the nature of the defendant's use of its property has substantially changed since most of the plaintiffs purchased their property. It's changed from a use that would have been consistent with just the sewage treatment facility plant, with the rural residential nature of the surrounding properties, to a use that's more akin to, in the words of one of the defendant's witnesses, an industrial site. The changing nature, in this respect, of the defendant's use of the property, I do not believe could have been reasonably foreseen by the plaintiffs.
>
> I do find specifically that — I find the plaintiffs to be credible in their testimony. With respect to the noise regulations, the defendant's witnesses testified that they are to be enforced at the county level, not by DEQ; that DEQ lacks both the authority and the staff to pursue noise complaints, and that

the county has not done any testing as to the noise complaints on this property, nor pursued really any complaint in that respect. The acoustical expert hired by the county, by the sewage district, stated his opinion that the noise level at one point at least did result from the composting operations and that they exceeded established levels.

Odor is a very subjective type of issue. There is certainly testimony from many of the defendant's witnesses that there's no odor at all. I can't believe that. There is no dispute that hydrogen sulfide is produced by these operations. There's no dispute that hydrogen sulfide can cause the very symptoms that the plaintiffs testified they were experiencing. And in fact there has been no government agency that has tested for hydrogen sulfide levels at this site, so any finding that they're in compliance is not based on any study or any testing that has been done on the site.

I am completely convinced that the nature of the odor that's produced by the defendant's composting operations does cause some of the plaintiffs to gag, to be nauseated, to have headaches, to be unable to eat, and to be unable to sit in their yards or patios or otherwise utilize their yards. And by doing so, that the odor substantially and unreasonably interferes with the plaintiffs' use and enjoyment of their property. I also am convinced that the nature of the noise and the frequency of the noise at the site caused by the composting operations also substantially and unreasonably interferes with the plaintiffs' use and enjoyment of their property.

Without exhaustively detailing the evidence and our analysis, we agree with the trial court that the composting operation is a nuisance. The District's sewage treatment plant, including the composting operation, is located in an area zoned RR-1 (rural residential one-acre) on the Rogue River. Many, and perhaps all, of the plaintiffs live or own property within one-quarter mile of the facility.

Two dozen witnesses, sixteen of whom reside or own property near the treatment facility, testified that the composting operation frequently created an offensive odor. Those witnesses variously described the odor as: "Stench." "Real offensive." "Sickening, very sickening." "Between a rotten egg and a rotten skunk." "Like a cat litter box." "Never smelled anything like it in my life." "About 500 outhouses all at once." And "I was in World War II, and I smelled some dead bodies and it had a smell something like that." Plaintiffs' witnesses testified that the intensity and frequency of the odor varied but, in general, depending on the location, the odor could be unbearably nauseating as often as several times a week.

The District points to testimony by other witnesses, including scientists and experts in sewage treatment, that the composting operation did not generate an offensive odor — or at least not an odor that could be consistently detected as offensive at plaintiffs' property. In a related sense, the District argues that, given expert meteorological evidence based on evaluation of wind-direction data and the timing of certain plaintiffs' complaints, the source of the odor plaintiffs' witnesses described was a dairy across the river from the treatment plant.

Conversely, many of plaintiffs' witnesses testified that they could distinguish the dairy smell from the compost smell. . . .

Reduced to its essentials, the District's position is that plaintiffs' witnesses either collectively imagined, were mistaken, or lied about the odors emanating from the composting operation. The trial court, which observed the witnesses, expressly determined that plaintiffs' witnesses were credible. We give that assessment "great weight," . . . and, given the balance of the evidence, affirm the trial court's determination that the composting facility generated offensive odors that were consistently detectable on plaintiffs' property.

We further affirm the trial court's finding that the odor did, in fact, substantially and unreasonably interfere with plaintiffs' use and enjoyment of their property. Plaintiffs testified that the odor made them nauseated and prevented them from sitting on their decks or outside, or even from leaving their windows open at night for a summer breeze. For example, one plaintiff testified that she could not work in her garden when the odor was present and to get relief from the odor, "we have to go in the house or go to town or something." Another testified, "I can sit down and eat on the back porch with the dairy smell, but I can't with the Jo-Gro smell. I get sick." And a third testified, "we like to sleep with the windows open, and it is so offensive that I became sick at my stomach, and we had to close the windows to be able to sleep." Again, the trial court expressly found that testimony to be credible and, giving that assessment due deference, so do we.

The District argues, nevertheless, that, as a matter of law, there can be no nuisance because it has complied with all applicable regulations and permits in operating the composting facility. However, the District's purported regulatory compliance does not preclude a determination that its operation constitutes a nuisance. We categorically rejected an identical argument in Lunda v. Matthews, 46 Or. App. 701, 707, 613 P.2d 63 (1980). Thus, in affirming an injunction against a nuisance, we explained:

> "[D]efendants argue that the operation of their plant was reasonable as a matter of law because they had secured an air contaminant discharge permit from the Department of Environmental Quality and they had not been cited for violation of the fallout standards. Conformance with pollution standards does not preclude a suit in private nuisance." [Citation omitted.]

We proceed to the second, and final, issue: Do the equities warrant the issuance of an injunction abating the nuisance? Concerning that issue, the trial court observed:

> With respect to the balance of the equities in this case, and the remedy, I want to state first of all, I have no intention to join the Board of Directors of the sewage service district. I don't intend to micro-manage the affairs of the sewer service district. So for that reason I can't really get into a situation where I'm setting what needs to be done to remedy the situation. I considered the alternative of damages because of that difficulty, but quite frankly, I don't think I can ascertain the damages because I think what the damages might be today might be different two years from now once the capacity of the plant has doubled. And I don't think that damages, for that reason, are easily ascertained in this situation, nor do I think it would be a final solution. I think you would just be inviting further litigation down the line if I tried to go that route. . . .
>
> [T]he defendant, since they have been aware of the plaintiffs' complaint, have expanded their operations and further invested in the composting

operations on site, after becoming aware and having been notified of the complaints that were being made in this case. And I think that by doing that, quite frankly, it demonstrates some arrogance on the part of the defendant, as well as, doing so, they did it at their own risk. So I'm rejecting any consideration of the cost that has been expended since they've been aware of these complaints in balancing the equities. I don't think they're entitled to go out and make substantial expenditures when the case is in litigation and to try to use those as some way to avoid responsibility. . . .

[A]s I said, balancing the equities in this case is really the most difficult. . . . I don't deny that there are other people who are not in this courtroom — the other patrons of the district who are going to be affected by my decision — and that's been the hardest part probably of making this decision is those considerations. But having considered that and considered the lack of any other remedy that I feel like would fit in the premises, I am going to grant the request for an injunction.

In York v. Stallings, 217 Or. 13, 22, 341 P.2d 529 (1959), the Court enunciated the standard for issuance of injunctive relief. Once a nuisance is established,

> it does not follow that an injunction should issue as a matter of course. The court may refuse an injunction in certain cases *where the hardship caused to the defendant by the injunction would greatly outweigh the benefit resulting to the plaintiff.* The injunction does not issue as a matter of absolute or unqualified right but is subject to the sound discretion of the court.

Id. at 22, 341 P.2d 529 (emphasis added). *See also Jewett*, 281 Or. at 478, 575 P.2d 164 (reiterating the "greatly outweighs" standard).

Thus, we must compare the benefit to plaintiffs with the hardship to the District resulting from a permanent injunction. The benefit to plaintiffs is the ability to enjoy their property in a manner consistent with its rural character — to garden, and eat outside, and keep their windows open on summer evenings. For plaintiffs, an injunction would mean being able to use and enjoy their property as they did before the nuisance came to them — to live, and breathe, free from a pervasive, nauseating odor.

The concomitant detriment to the District is essentially, but not completely, economic. If use of the existing composting facility is enjoined, the District has, at least, two arguably feasible alternatives: (1) move the composting activities to another site; or (2) return to its prior practice of trucking the sludge and applying it to acceptable agricultural sites.[5] Either of those options, even if otherwise practicable, would involve substantial additional expense. In addition, a return to the District's prior practice of land application would result in loss of significant environmental benefits.

The District's plant manager, Robert Webber, and Steven Gilbert, an environmental engineer retained by the District, testified persuasively that

---

5. Although a third alternative would be for the District to buy out the plaintiffs, there is no evidence of the feasibility or expense of that option. A fourth alternative might be for the District to adopt additional and *effective* mitigation measures while maintaining the operation at its present site. There is, however, no evidence in this record concerning the practical availability and efficacy, much less the cost, of any such measures. . . .

composting was an environmentally superior alternative to land application of biosolids. Webber explained, in some detail, why returning to its
previous practice of land application was no longer a feasible alternative
for the District, notwithstanding the fact that many districts and nearby
municipalities in southern Oregon, including the City of Grants Pass,
continue that practice. The concerns that Webber identified include
groundwater contamination monitoring, site constraints, land use restrictions, sludge runoff, and grazing restrictions.

In contrast, the District's objections to relocating the composting
operation to an alternative, non-residential site appear to be purely
financial. That is, in contrast to land application, there is no evidence
that practical or legal impediments, including land use or environmental
restrictions, would somehow preclude such relocation. The capital cost
of relocating the existing composting operation (as distinct from any
expansion of that operation to accommodate projected population
growth and demands) would be approximately $1,000,000. The District
currently serves approximately 1,800 households. The additional capital
costs associated with relocating, amortized over a 20-year period, would
result in a $5.00 per month rate increase per household over that period.
In addition the District's annual operating costs would increase by
approximately $100,000, representing the expense of trucking the
present volume of bio-solids/sludge from the existing treatment plant to
the newly-relocated composting operation.

Assessing those alternatives, we conclude, as did the trial court, that
the hardship to the District from the issuance of an injunction does not
"greatly outweigh" the benefit to plaintiffs. There is no question that relocating the composting operation will, in fact, be expensive. Nevertheless,
two factors especially bear on our assessment of the equities.

First, although a precise apportionment is impossible, the District's
relocation expenses have been exacerbated by actions and additional
expenditures that the District undertook after becoming aware of the
Penlands' initial complaints in 1991 and of other plaintiffs' complaints by
late 1992. This was not merely a case of the nuisance coming to the homeowners, but of the District expanding its operations after plaintiffs
protested.

Second, although the additional cost to the District will be substantial, the impact will be ameliorated because it can be spread among the
District's rate-payers — over 1,800 households.[7] In that "cost-spreading"
respect, Thornburg v. Port of Portland, 233 Or. 178, 376 P.2d 100 (1962),
which involved an inverse condemnation claim by homeowners whose
property lay beneath jet flightpaths of the then-newly expanded Portland
Airport, is instructive. In reversing the trial court's limitation of the plaintiff property owners' claims, the court observed:

> [W]hen the government conducts an activity upon its own land which, after
> balancing the question of reasonableness, is sufficiently disturbing to the

7. Moreover, the number of the District's rate-payers is projected to double, and
perhaps even triple, over the 20-year amortization period.

use and enjoyment of neighboring lands to amount to a taking thereof, then the public, and not the subservient landowner, should bear the cost of such public benefit.... The real question was ... one of ... reasonableness based upon nuisance theories. In effect, the inquiry should have been whether the government had undertaken a course of conduct on its own land which, in simple fairness to its neighbors, required it to obtain more land so that the substantial burdens of the activity would fall upon public land, rather than upon that of involuntary contributors who happen to lie in the path of progress.

Thornburg, 233 Or. at 193-94, 376 P.2d 100 (footnote omitted).

So too here. If the District and those whom it serves are committed to the environmental values and benefits of composting, that may well be laudable. But the cost of that commitment should be commonly borne and not visited solely upon a handful of "involuntary contributors who happen to lie in the path of progress." *Id.* at 194, 376 P.2d 100. We emphasize that this is not a case of simple-minded "NIMBY"[8] parochialism — of narrow-minded refusal to assume burdens that are, reasonably and necessarily, part of living as a community. It is, rather, a clear and compelling case of living next to a public nuisance. The equities favor the issuance of an injunction.

Affirmed.

Boomer v. Atlantic Cement Co.
257 N.E.2d 870 (N.Y. 1970)

Bergan, J.   Defendant operates a large cement plant near Albany. These are actions for injunction and damages by neighboring land owners alleging injury to property from dirt, smoke and vibration emanating from the plant. A nuisance has been found after trial, temporary damages have been allowed; but an injunction has been denied.

The public concern with air pollution arising from many sources in industry and in transportation is currently accorded ever wider recognition accompanied by a growing sense of responsibility in State and Federal Governments to control it. Cement plants are obvious sources of air pollution in the neighborhoods where they operate.

But there is now before the court private litigation in which individual property owners have sought specific relief from a single plant operation. The threshold question raised by the division of view on this appeal is whether the court should resolve the litigation between the parties now before it as equitably as seems possible; or whether, seeking promotion of the general public welfare, it should channel private litigation into broad public objectives.

A court performs its essential function when it decides the rights of parties before it. Its decision of private controversies may sometimes greatly affect public issues. Large questions of law are often resolved by the manner in which private litigation is decided. But this is normally an

8. "Not in my backyard."

incident to the court's main function to settle controversy. It is a rare exercise of judicial power to use a decision in private litigation as a purposeful mechanism to achieve direct public objectives greatly beyond the rights and interests before the court.

Effective control of air pollution is a problem presently far from solution even with the full public and financial powers of government. In large measure adequate technical procedures are yet to be developed and some that appear possible may be economically impracticable.

It seems apparent that the amelioration of air pollution will depend on technical research in great depth; on a carefully balanced consideration of the economic impact of close regulation; and of the actual effect on public health. It is likely to require massive public expenditure and to demand more than any local community can accomplish and to depend on regional and interstate controls.

A court should not try to do this on its own as a by-product of private litigation and it seems manifest that the judicial establishment is neither equipped in the limited nature of any judgment it can pronounce nor prepared to lay down and implement an effective policy for the elimination of air pollution. This is an area beyond the circumference of one private lawsuit. It is a direct responsibility for government and should not thus be undertaken as an incident to solving a dispute between property owners and a single cement plant — one of many — in the Hudson River valley.

The cement making operations of defendant have been found by the court of Special Term to have damaged the nearby properties of plaintiffs in these two actions. That court, as it has been noted, accordingly found defendant maintained a nuisance and this has been affirmed at the Appellate Division. The total damage to plaintiffs' properties is, however, relatively small in comparison with the value of defendant's operation and with the consequences of the injunction which plaintiffs seek.

The ground for the denial of injunction, notwithstanding the finding both that there is a nuisance and that plaintiffs have been damaged substantially, is the large disparity in economic consequences of the nuisance and of the injunction. This theory cannot, however, be sustained without overruling a doctrine which has been consistently reaffirmed in several leading cases in this court and which has never been disavowed here, namely that where a nuisance has been found and where there has been any substantial damage shown by the party complaining an injunction will be granted.

The rule in New York has been that such a nuisance will be enjoined although marked disparity be shown in economic consequence between the effect of the injunction and the effect of the nuisance....

Although the court at Special Term and the Appellate Division held that injunction should be denied, it was found that plaintiffs had been damaged in various specific amounts up to the time of the trial and damages to the respective plaintiffs were awarded for those amounts. The effect of this was, injunction having been denied, plaintiffs could maintain successive actions at law for damages thereafter as further damage was incurred.

The court at Special Term also found the amount of permanent damage attributable to each plaintiff, for the guidance of the parties in the event both sides stipulated to the payment and acceptance of such perma-nent damage as a settlement of all the controversies among the parties. The total of permanent damages to all plaintiffs thus found was $185,000. This basis of adjustment has not resulted in any stipulation by the parties.

This result at Special Term and at the Appellate Division is a depar-ture from a rule that has become settled; but to follow the rule literally in these cases would be to close down the plant at once. This court is fully agreed to avoid that immediately drastic remedy; the difference in view is how best to avoid it.*

One alternative is to grant the injunction but postpone its effect to a specified future date to give opportunity for technical advances to permit defendant to eliminate the nuisance; another is to grant the injunction conditioned on the payment of permanent damages to plaintiffs which would compensate them for the total economic loss to their property present and future caused by defendant's operations. For reasons which will be developed the court chooses the latter alternative.

If the injunction were to be granted unless within a short period — e.g., 18 months — the nuisance be abated by improved methods, there would be no assurance that any significant technical improvement would occur.

The parties could settle this private litigation at any time if defendant paid enough money and the imminent threat of closing the plant would build up the pressure on defendant. If there were no improved techniques found, there would inevitably be applications to the court at Special Term for extensions of time to perform on showing of good faith efforts to find such techniques.

Moreover, techniques to eliminate dust and other annoying by-products of cement making are unlikely to be developed by any research the defendant can undertake within any short period, but will depend on the total resources of the cement industry nationwide and through-out the world. The problem is universal wherever cement is made.

For obvious reasons the rate of the research is beyond control of defendant. If at the end of 18 months the whole industry has not found a technical solution a court would be hard put to close down this one cement plant if due regard be given to equitable principles.

On the other hand, to grant the injunction unless defendant pays plaintiffs such permanent damages as may be fixed by the court seems to do justice between the contending parties. All of the attributions of economic loss to the properties on which plaintiffs' complaints are based will have been redressed.

The nuisance complained of by these plaintiffs may have other public or private consequences, but these particular parties are the only ones who have sought remedies and the judgment proposed will fully redress them. The limitation of relief granted is a limitation only within the four corners of these actions and does not foreclose public health or other public agencies from seeking proper relief in a proper court.

---

* Respondent's investment in the plant is in excess of $45,000,000. There are over 300 people employed there.

It seems reasonable to think that the risk of being required to pay permanent damages to injured property owners by cement plant owners would itself be a reasonable effective spur to research for improved techniques to minimize nuisance....

The orders should be reversed, without costs, and the cases remitted to ... grant an injunction which shall be vacated upon payment by defendant of such amounts of permanent damage to the ... plaintiffs as shall ... be determined by the court.

Jasen, J. (dissenting). I agree with the majority that a reversal is required here, but I do not subscribe to the newly enunciated doctrine of assessment of permament damages, in lieu of an injunction, where substantial property rights have been impaired by the creation of a nuisance....

The harmful nature and widespread occurrence of air pollution have been extensively documented. Congressional hearings have revealed that air pollution causes substantial property damage, as well as being a contributing factor to a rising incidence of lung cancer, emphysema, bronchitis and asthma.

The specific problem faced here is known as particulate contamination because of the fine dust particles emanating from defendant's cement plant. The particular type of nuisance is not new, having appeared in many cases for at least the past 60 years.... It is interesting to note that cement production has recently been identified as a significant source of particulate contamination in the Hudson Valley. This type of pollution, wherein very small particles escape and stay in the atmosphere, has been denominated as the type of air pollution which produces the greatest hazard to human health. We have thus a nuisance which not only is damaging to the plaintiffs,[5] but also is decidedly harmful to the general public.

I see grave dangers in overruling our long-established rule of granting an injunction where a nuisance results in substantial continuing damage. In permitting the injunction to become inoperative upon the payment of permanent damages, the majority is, in effect, licensing a continuing wrong. It is the same as saying to the cement company, you may continue to do harm to your neighbors so long as you pay a fee for it. Furthermore, once such permanent damages are assessed and paid, the incentive to alleviate the wrong would be eliminated, thereby continuing air pollution of an area without abatement.

It is true that some courts have sanctioned the remedy here proposed by the majority in a number of cases, but none of the authorities relied upon by the majority are analogous to the situation before us. In those cases, the courts, in denying an injunction and awarding money damages, grounded their decision on a showing that the use to which the property was intended to be put was primarily for the public benefit. Here, on the

---

5. There are seven plaintiffs here who have been substantially damaged by the maintenance of this nuisance. The trial court found their total permanent damages to equal $185,000.

other hand, it is clearly established that the cement company is creating a continuing air pollution nuisance primarily for its own private interest with no public benefit. . . .

I would enjoin the defendant cement company from continuing the discharge of dust particles upon its neighbors' properties unless, within 18 months, the cement company abated this nuisance.[7]

It is not my intention to cause the removal of the cement plant from the Albany area, but to recognize the urgency of the problem stemming from this stationary source of air pollution, and to allow the company a specified period of time to develop a means to alleviate this nuisance.

I am aware that the trial court found that the most modern dust control devices available have been installed in defendant's plant, but, I submit, this does not mean that better and more effective dust control devices could not be developed within the time allowed to abate the pollution.

Moreover, I believe it is incumbent upon the defendant to develop such devices, since the cement company, at the time the plant commenced production (1962), was well aware of the plaintiffs' presence in the area, as well as the probable consequences of its contemplated operation. Yet, it still chose to build and operate the plant at this site.

In a day when there is a growing concern for clean air, highly developed industry should not expect acquiescence by the courts, but should, instead, plan its operations to eliminate contamination of our air and damage to its neighbors.

Accordingly, the orders of the Appellate Division, insofar as they denied the injunction, should be reversed, and the actions remitted to Supreme Court, Albany County to grant an injunction to take effect 18 months hence, unless the nuisance is abated by improved techniques prior to said date.

NOTES AND QUESTIONS

1. *Unreasonable Interference.* The details provided in *Penland* certainly turn the stomach, but are they necessary in a judicial opinion? Even a quick sketch of the facts would make it obvious that the treatment plant generated foul odors. Is the court's desire to elaborate on *just how awful* the plaintiffs found the treatment plant related to the definition of a nuisance as a "substantial" and "unreasonable" interference with the plaintiffs' use and enjoyment of their property, as opposed to mere annoyance?

2. *Standards for Injunctive Relief.* Do the courts in *Penland* and *Boomer* use the same test to decide whether to issue an injunction? If they do, why do they reach contrary results? How can you account for the fact that the government entity is required to shut down in *Penland*, while only damages are required of the private entity in *Boomer?* Is that not backwards?

7. The issuance of an injunction to become effective in the future is not an entirely new concept. For instance, in Schwarzenbach v. Oneonta Light & Power Co., 207 N.Y. 671, 100 N.E. 1134, an injunction against the maintenance of a dam spilling water on plaintiff's property was issued to become effective one year hence.

3. *Dispute Resolution versus Policy-Making.* The majority in *Boomer* states, "A court performs its essential function when it decides the rights of parties before it." What conclusion did the court intend to be drawing from this statement about its role in *Boomer*? Was the majority focused exclusively on the task of resolving the dispute before it, or does it engage in broader public policy analysis?

4. *Environmental Statutes.* Since *Boomer* was decided in 1970, the federal and state governments have enacted far-reaching environmental statutes that have in turn generated complex regulatory schemes aimed at halting and ameliorating air, water, and soil pollution. Does the capacity of legislatures and regulators to enact comprehensive anti-pollution laws have any relevance to whether an injunction or damages was the right remedy in *Boomer*?

5. *New York Law Since* Boomer. Some New York cases subsequent to *Boomer* approved the issuance of injunctions for nuisances. *See, e.g.,* Little Joseph Realty, Inc. v. Babylon, 363 N.E.2d 1163 (N.Y. 1977) (defendant's violation of a zoning ordinance provides a further reason to enjoin nuisance, notwithstanding costs of doing so); Hoover v. Durkee, 622 N.Y.S.2d 348 (App. Div. 1995) (cost-balancing inquiry not needed to justify injunction against race track).

6. *Injunctive Relief versus Damages.* There is a robust academic literature addressing the question of the appropriate form of remedy for a nuisance — an injunction or damages. The most influential contribution to this literature was provided by Judge Calabresi and his co-author, A. Douglas Melamed, in an article entitled *Property Rules, Liability Rules, and Inalienability: One View of the Cathedral.* Employing economic analysis of the sort discussed above in connection with Professor Coase's analysis of nuisance cases, Calabresi and Melamed used cases such as *Boomer* to illustrate their claim that grants of injunctive relief — what they term the use of a *property rule* — are generally inadvisable when the class of potentially affected parties is large. Their basic point is that the issuance of injunctive relief in such circumstances can create significant impediments to negotiated settlements, which in turn can prevent property from reaching its highest-valued use.

Suppose, for example, the *Boomer* court were to decide that neighboring residents should enjoy the entitlement to use their properties free of dust and noise, *and* that they are entitled to an injunction to enforce that entitlement. Now suppose it turns out that Kaldor-Hicks efficiency is in fact achieved by permitting the factory to operate, because the profits generated by the factory more than outweigh the neighbors' losses. Because of the injunction, the efficient result can only be reached if the factory owner can convince each neighbor to accept a payment in return for waiving his right to complain of the nuisance. But negotiations with multiple parties are costly and often fruitless. For example, some of the residents might try to "hold out" for a larger share than their neighbors of the amount that the plant is willing to pay to keep operating. Thus, according to Calabresi and Melamed, it will likely be better for the court to refrain from enjoining the operation of the plant, and instead to order the payment of damages. By means of this *liability rule*, the residents' entitlement to the value of being free of the plant's pollution is still protected, albeit not with a veto power. Instead, the residents are guaranteed compensation for the value of their entitlement (assuming that damages are accurately assessed), but are in effect required to sell that entitlement at the demand of the plant owner.

Regardless of whether a property rule or liability rule appropriately resolves a nuisance case such as *Boomer*, Calabresi's and Melamed's broader point is that the structure of the rules and remedies for protecting entitlements is at least as important as the initial decision regarding how the entitlements are allocated.

III.   ULTRAHAZARDOUS ACTIVITIES

Rylands v. Fletcher
[1868] All E.R. 1

The Lord Chancellor (Lord Cairns): — The plaintiff in this case is the occupier of a mine and works under a close of land. The defendants are the owners of a mill in his neighbourhood, and they proposed to make a reservoir for the purpose of keeping and storing water to be used about their mill upon another close of land, which, for the purposes of this case, may be taken as being adjoining to the close of the plaintiff, although, in point of fact, some intervening land lay between the two.* Underneath the close of land of the defendants on which they proposed to construct their reservoir there were certain old and disused mining passages and works. There were five vertical shafts, and some horizontal shafts communicating with them. The vertical shafts had been filled up with soil and rubbish, and it does not appear that any person was aware of the existence either of the vertical shafts or of the horizontal works communicating with them. In the course of the working by the Plaintiff of his mine, he had gradually worked through the seams of coal underneath the close, and had come into contact with the old and disused works underneath the close of the defendants.

In that state of things the reservoir of the defendants was constructed. It was constructed by them through the agency and inspection of an engineer and contractor. Personally, the defendants appear to have taken no part in the works, or to have been aware of any want of security connected with them. As regards the engineer and the contractor, we must take it from the case that they did not exercise, as far as they were concerned, that reasonable care and caution which they might have exercised, taking notice, as they appear to have taken notice, of the vertical shafts filled up in the manner which I have mentioned. However, when the reservoir was

---

* [John Rylands owned the mill, along with Jehu Horrocks, who also managed it. They hired the engineers and contractors who selected the site for and built the reservoir. The reservoir was built on land owned by the Earl of Wilton under a license granted by the Earl to Rylands and Horrocks. — EDS.]

constructed, and filled, or partly filled, with water, the weight of the water bearing upon the disused and imperfectly filled-up vertical shafts, broke through those shafts. The water passed down them and into the horizontal workings, and from the horizontal workings under the close of the defendants it passed on into the workings under the close of the plaintiff, and flooded his mine, causing considerable damage, for which this action was brought. The Court of Exchequer, when the special case stating the facts to which I have referred, was argued, was of opinion that the plaintiff had established no cause of action. The Court of Exchequer Chamber,* before which an appeal from this judgment was argued, was of a contrary opinion, and the Judges there unanimously arrived at the conclusion that there was a cause of action, and that the plaintiff was entitled to damages.

The principles on which this case must be determined appear to me to be extremely simple. The defendants, treating them as the owners or occupiers of the close on which the reservoir was constructed, might lawfully have used that close for any purpose for which it might in the ordinary course of the enjoyment of land be used; and if, in what I may term the natural user [sic] of that land, there had been any accumulation of water, either on the surface or underground, and if, by the operation of the laws of nature, that accumulation of water had passed off into the close occupied by the plaintiff, the plaintiff could not have complained that that result had taken place. If he had desired to guard himself against it, it would have lain upon him to have done so, by leaving, or by interposing, some barrier between his close and the close of the defendants in order to have prevented that operation of the laws of nature.

... On the other hand if the defendants, not stopping at the natural use of their close, had desired to use it for any purpose which I may term a non-natural use, for the purpose of introducing into the close that which in its natural condition was not in or upon it, for the purpose of introducing water either above or below ground in quantities and in a manner not the result of any work or operation on or under the land, — and if in consequence of their doing so, or in consequence of any imperfection in the mode of their doing so, the water came to escape and to pass off into the close of the plaintiff, then it appears to me that that which the defendants were doing they were doing at their own peril; and, if in the course of their doing it, the evil arose to which I have referred, the evil, namely, of the escape of the water and its passing away to the close of the plaintiff and injuring the plaintiff, then for the consequence of that, in my opinion, the defendants would be liable....

These simple principles, if they are well founded, as it appears to me they are, really dispose of this case. The same result is arrived at on the principles referred to by BLACKBURN, J. in his judgment, in the Court of Exchequer Chamber, where he states the opinion of that Court as to the law in these words:

> We think that the true rule of law is, that the person who, for his own purposes, brings on his land and collects and keeps there anything likely to

---

* [Decisions of the Exchequer Court at this time could be appealed to an intermediate court designated (unhelpfully) as Exchequer Chamber. — EDS.]

do mischief if it escapes, must keep it in at his peril; and if he does not do so, is *prima facie* answerable for all the damage which is the natural consequence of its escape. He can excuse himself by shewing that the escape was owing to the Plaintiff's default; or, perhaps, that the escape was the consequence of *vis major*, or the act of God; but as nothing of this sort exists here, it is unnecessary to inquire what excuse would be sufficient. The general rule, as above stated, seems on principle just. The person whose grass or corn is eaten down by the escaping cattle of his neighbour, or whose mine is flooded by the water from his neighbour's reservoir, or whose cellar is invaded by the filth of his neighbour's privy, or whose habitation is made unhealthy by the fumes and noisome vapours of his neighbour's alkali works, is damnified without any fault of his own; and it seems but reasonable and just that the neighbour who has brought something on his own property (which was not naturally there), harmless to others so long as it is confined to his own property, but which he knows will be mischievous if it gets on his neighbour's, should be obliged to make good the damage which ensues if he does not succeed in confining it to his own property. But for his act in bringing it there no mischief could have accrued, and it seems but just that he should at his peril keep it there, so that no mischief may accrue, or answer for the natural and anticipated consequence. And upon authority this we think is established to be the law, whether the things so brought be beasts, or water, or filth, or stenches.

In that opinion, I must say I entirely concur. Therefore, I have to move your Lordships that the judgment of the Court of Exchequer Chamber be affirmed, and that the present appeal be dismissed with costs.

Lord Cranworth: — I concur with my noble and learned friend in thinking that the rule of law was correctly stated by BLACKBURN, J. in delivering the opinion of the Exchequer Chamber. If a person brings, or accumulates, on his land anything which, if it should escape, may cause damage to his neighbour, he does so at his peril. If it does escape, and cause damage, he is responsible, however careful he may have been, and whatever precautions he may have taken to prevent the damage. In considering whether a defendant is liable to a plaintiff for damage which the plaintiff may have sustained, the question in general is not whether the defendant has acted with due care and caution, but whether his acts have occasioned the damage.... The doctrine is founded on good sense, for when one person, in managing his own affairs, causes, however innocently, damage to another, it is obviously only just that he should be the party to suffer....

Klein v. Pyrodyne Corp.
810 P.2d 917 (Wash. 1991) (en banc)*

Guy, J.   The plaintiffs in this case are persons injured when an aerial shell at a public fireworks exhibition went astray and exploded near them. The defendant is the pyrotechnic company hired to set up and discharge

* [As amended by 817 P.2d 1359. — EDS.]

the fireworks. The issue before this court is whether pyrotechnicians are strictly liable for damages caused by fireworks displays. We hold that they are.

Defendant Pyrodyne Corporation (Pyrodyne) is a general contractor for aerial fireworks at public fireworks displays. Pyrodyne contracted to procure fireworks, to provide pyrotechnic operators, and to display the fireworks at the Western Washington State Fairgrounds in Puyallup, Washington on July 4, 1987. All operators of the fireworks display were Pyrodyne employees acting within the scope of their employment duties.

As required by Washington statute, Pyrodyne purchased a $1,000,000 insurance policy prior to the fireworks show. The policy provided $1,000,000 coverage for each occurrence of bodily injury or property damage liability. Plaintiffs allege that Pyrodyne failed to carry out a number of the other statutory and regulatory requirements in preparing for and setting off the fireworks. For example, they allege that Pyrodyne failed to properly bury the mortar tubes prior to detonation, failed to provide a diagram of the display and surrounding environment to the local government, failed to provide crowd control monitors, and failed to keep the invitees at the mandated safe distance.

During the fireworks display, one of the 5-inch mortars was knocked into a horizontal position. From this position an aerial shell inside was ignited and discharged. The shell flew 500 feet in a trajectory parallel to the earth and exploded near the crowd of onlookers. Plaintiffs Danny and Marion Klein were injured by the explosion. Mr. Klein's clothing was set on fire, and he suffered facial burns and serious injury to his eyes.

The parties provide conflicting explanations of the cause of the improper horizontal discharge of the shell. Pyrodyne argues that the accident was caused by a 5-inch shell detonating in its above-ground mortar tube without ever leaving the ground. Pyrodyne asserts that this detonation caused another mortar tube to be knocked over, ignited, and shot off horizontally. In contrast, the Kleins contend that the misdirected shell resulted because Pyrodyne's employees improperly set up the display. They further note that because all of the evidence exploded, there is no means of proving the cause of the misfire.

The Kleins brought suit against Pyrodyne under theories of products liability and strict liability. Pyrodyne filed a motion for summary judgment, which the trial court granted as to the products liability claim. The trial court denied Pyrodyne's summary judgment motion regarding the Kleins' strict liability claim, holding that Pyrodyne was strictly liable without fault and ordering summary judgment in favor of the Kleins on the issue of liability. Pyrodyne appealed the order of partial summary judgment to the Court of Appeals, which certified the case to this court. Pyrodyne is appealing solely as to the trial court's holding that strict liability is the appropriate standard of liability for pyrotechnicians. A strict liability claim against pyrotechnicians for damages caused by fireworks displays presents a case of first impression in Washington.

ANALYSIS

I. FIREWORKS DISPLAYS AS ABNORMALLY DANGEROUS ACTIVITIES

. . . The modern doctrine of strict liability for abnormally dangerous activities derives from Fletcher v. Rylands, 159 Eng. Rep. 737 (1865), *rev'd*, 1 L.R.-Ex. 265, [1866] All E.R. 1, 6, *aff'd sub nom.* Rylands v. Fletcher, 3 L.R.-H.L. 330, [1868] All E.R. 1, 12, in which the defendant's reservoir flooded mine shafts on the plaintiff's adjoining land. Rylands v. Fletcher has come to stand for the rule that "the defendant will be liable when he damages another by a thing or activity unduly dangerous and inappropriate to the place where it is maintained, in the light of the character of that place and its surroundings." W. Keeton, D. Dobbs, R. Keeton & D. Owen, *Prosser and Keeton on Torts* § 78, at 547-48 (5th ed. 1984).

The basic principle of Rylands v. Fletcher has been accepted by the Restatement (Second) of Torts (1977). *See generally Prosser and Keeton* § 78, at 551 (explaining that the relevant Restatement sections differ in some respects from the *Rylands* doctrine). Section 519 of the Restatement provides that any party carrying on an "abnormally dangerous activity" is strictly liable for ensuing damages. The test for what constitutes such an activity is stated in section 520 of the Restatement. Both Restatement sections have been adopted by this court, and determination of whether an activity is an "abnormally dangerous activity" is a question of law.

Section 520 of the Restatement lists six factors that are to be considered in determining whether an activity is "abnormally dangerous." The factors are as follows:

(a)   existence of a high degree of risk of some harm to the person, land or chattels of others;

(b)   likelihood that the harm that results from it will be great;

(c)   inability to eliminate the risk by the exercise of reasonable care;

(d)   extent to which the activity is not a matter of common usage;

(e)   inappropriateness of the activity to the place where it is carried on; and

(f)   extent to which its value to the community is outweighed by its dangerous attributes.

Restatement (Second) of Torts § 520 (1977). As we previously recognized in Langan v. Valicopters, Inc., *supra*, 88 Wash. 2d at 861-62, 567 P.2d 218 (citing Tent. Draft No. 10, 1964, of comment (f) to section 520), the comments to section 520 explain how these factors should be evaluated:

> Any one of them is not necessarily sufficient of itself in a particular case, and ordinarily several of them will be required for strict liability. On the other hand, it is not necessary that each of them be present, especially if others weigh heavily. Because of the interplay of these various factors, it is not possible to reduce abnormally dangerous activities to any definition. The essential question is whether the risk created is so unusual, either because

of its magnitude or because of the circumstances surrounding it, as to justify the imposition of strict liability for the harm that results from it, even though it is carried on with all reasonable care.

Restatement (Second) of Torts § 520, comment *f* (1977). Examination of these factors persuades us that fireworks displays are abnormally dangerous activities justifying the imposition of strict liability.

We find that the factors stated in clauses (a), (b), and (c) are all present in the case of fireworks displays. Any time a person ignites aerial shells or rockets with the intention of sending them aloft to explode in the presence of large crowds of people, a high risk of serious personal injury or property damage is created. That risk arises because of the possibility that a shell or rocket will malfunction or be misdirected. Furthermore, no matter how much care pyrotechnicians exercise, they cannot entirely eliminate the high risk inherent in setting off powerful explosives such as fireworks near crowds.

The dangerousness of fireworks displays is evidenced by the elaborate scheme of administrative regulations with which pyrotechnicians must comply. Pyrotechnicians must be licensed to conduct public displays of special fireworks. WAC 212-17-220. To obtain such a license, the pyrotechnician must take and pass a written examination administered by the director of fire protection, and must submit evidence of qualifications and experience, including "participation in the firing of at least six public displays as an assistant, at least one of which shall have been in the current or preceding year." WAC 212-17-225. The pyrotechnician's application for a license must be investigated by the director of fire protection, who must confirm that the applicant is competent and experienced. WAC 212-17-230. Licensed pyrotechnicians are charged with ensuring that the display is set up in accordance with all rules and regulations. WAC 212-17-235. Regulations also govern such matters as the way in which the fireworks at public displays are constructed, stored, installed, and fired. WAC 212-17-305, -310, - 315, and -335. The necessity for such regulations demonstrates the dangerousness of fireworks displays.

Pyrodyne argues that if the regulations are complied with, then the high degree of risk otherwise inherent in the displays can be eliminated. Although we recognize that the high risk can be reduced, we do not agree that it can be eliminated. Setting off powerful fireworks near large crowds remains a highly risky activity even when the safety precautions mandated by statutes and regulations are followed. The Legislature appears to agree, for it has declared that in order to obtain a license to conduct a public fireworks display, a pyrotechnician must first obtain a surety bond or a certificate of insurance, the amount of which must be at least $1,000,000 for each event.[3] RCW 70.77.285, .295.

---

3. The fact that the Legislature requires a liability policy for an activity does not in itself imply that the Legislature views the activity as being abnormally dangerous for purposes of imposing strict liability. The fact that the Legislature has mandated a $1,000,000 liability policy for pyrotechnicians, however, does suggest that the Legislature views public fireworks displays as involving a high risk even when the appropriate safety precautions are taken.

The factors stated in clauses (a), (b), and (c) together, and sometimes one of them alone, express what is commonly meant by saying an activity is ultrahazardous. Restatement (Second) of Torts § 520, comment *h* (1977). As the Restatement explains, however, "[l]iability for abnormally dangerous activities is not . . . a matter of these three factors alone, and those stated in Clauses (d), (e), and (f) must still be taken into account." Restatement (Second) of Torts § 520, comment *h* (1977). . . .

The factor expressed in clause (d) concerns the extent to which the activity is not a matter "of common usage." The Restatement explains that "[a]n activity is a matter of common usage if it is customarily carried on by the great mass of mankind or by many people in the community." Restatement (Second) of Torts § 520, comment *i* (1977). As examples of activities that are not matters of common usage, the Restatement comments offer driving a tank, blasting, the manufacture, storage, transportation, and use of high explosives, and drilling for oil. The deciding characteristic is that few persons engage in these activities. Likewise, relatively few persons conduct public fireworks displays. Therefore, presenting public fireworks displays is not a matter of common usage.

Pyrodyne argues that the factor stated in clause (d) is not met because fireworks are a common way to celebrate the 4th of July. We reject this argument. Although fireworks are frequently and regularly enjoyed by the public, few persons set off special fireworks displays. Indeed, the general public is prohibited by statute from making public fireworks displays insofar as anyone wishing to do so must first obtain a license. RCW 70.77.255.

The factor stated in clause (e) requires analysis of the appropriateness of the activity to the place where it was carried on. In this case, the fireworks display was conducted at the Puyallup Fairgrounds. Although some locations — such as over water — may be safer, the Puyallup Fairgrounds is an appropriate place for a fireworks show because the audience can be seated at a reasonable distance from the display. Therefore, the clause (e) factor is not present in this case.

The factor stated in clause (f) requires analysis of the extent to which the value of fireworks to the community outweighs its dangerous attributes. We do not find that this factor is present here. This country has a long-standing tradition of fireworks on the 4th of July. That tradition suggests that we as a society have decided that the value of fireworks on the day celebrating our national independence and unity outweighs the risks of injuries and damage.

In sum, we find that setting off public fireworks displays satisfies four of the six conditions under the Restatement test; that is, it is an activity that is not "of common usage" and that presents an ineliminably high risk of serious bodily injury or property damage. We therefore hold that conducting public fireworks displays is an abnormally dangerous activity justifying the imposition of strict liability.

This conclusion is consistent with the results reached in cases involving damages caused by detonating dynamite. This court has recognized that parties detonating dynamite are strictly liable for the damages caused by such blasting. . . . There are a number of similarities between fireworks and dynamite. Both activities involve licensed experts intentionally igniting for profit explosives that have great potential for causing damage. Moreover, after the explosion no evidence remains as to the original explosive. The notable difference between fireworks and dynamite is that with fireworks the public is invited to watch the display and with dynamite the public is generally prohibited from being near the blasting location. Because detonating dynamite is subject to strict liability, and because of the similarities between fireworks and dynamite, strict liability is also an appropriate standard for determining the standard of liability for pyrotechnicians for any damages caused by their fireworks displays.

II. PUBLIC POLICY AND STRICT LIABILITY FOR FIREWORKS DISPLAYS

Policy considerations also support imposing strict liability on pyrotechnicians for damages caused by their public fireworks displays, although such considerations are not alone sufficient to justify that conclusion. Most basic is the question as to who should bear the loss when an innocent person suffers injury through the nonculpable but abnormally dangerous activities of another. In the case of public fireworks displays, fairness weighs in favor of requiring the pyrotechnicians who present the displays to bear the loss rather than the unfortunate spectators who suffer the injuries. In addition,

> [t]he rule of strict liability rests not only upon the ultimate idea of rectifying a wrong and putting the burden where it should belong as a matter of abstract justice, that is, upon the one of the two innocent parties whose acts instigated or made the harm possible, but it also rests on problems of proof:
>
> > One of these common features is that the person harmed would encounter a difficult problem of proof if some other standard of liability were applied. For example, the disasters caused by those who engage in abnormally dangerous or extra-hazardous activities frequently destroy all evidence of what in fact occurred, other than that the activity was being carried on. Certainly this is true with explosions of dynamite, large quantities of gasoline, or other explosives.

Siegler v. Kuhlman, 81 Wash. 2d 448, 455, 502 P.2d 1181 (1972), *cert. denied*, 411 U.S. 983 ... (1973) (quoting Peck, *Negligence and Liability Without Fault in the Tort Law*, 46 Wash. L. Rev. 225, 240 (1971)). In the present case, all evidence was destroyed as to what caused the misfire of the shell that injured the Kleins. Therefore, the problem of proof this case presents for the plaintiffs also supports imposing strict liability on Pyrodyne.

III. STATUTORY STRICT LIABILITY FOR FIREWORKS

As well as holding Pyrodyne strictly liable on the basis that fireworks displays are abnormally dangerous activities, we also hold that RCW 70.77.285 imposes statutory strict liability.[4] The statute, which mandates

---

4. RCW 70.77.285 states: "Except as provided in RCW 70.77.355, the applicant for a permit under RCW 70.77.260(2) for a public display of fireworks shall include with the

insurance coverage to pay for *all* damages resulting from fireworks displays, establishes strict liability for any ensuing injuries.

An example of a statute which the appellate court has held to be a strict liability statute is RCW 16.08.040, which reads in part:

> The owner of any dog which shall bite any person . . . shall be liable for such damages as may be suffered by the person bitten, regardless of the former viciousness of such dog or the owner's knowledge of such viciousness.

See Beeler v. Hickman, 50 Wash. App. 746, 750-51, 750 P.2d 1282 (1988). The court in *Beeler* held that the language of the statute clearly established strict liability for the owner of the dog. Although RCW 70.77.285 does not establish strict liability in the same language as the dog bite statute, it nonetheless provides that pyrotechnicians shall pay for all damages to persons or property resulting from fireworks displays.

RCW 70.77.285 has been amended twice since it was enacted in 1961. Laws of 1961, ch. 228, § 34, p.2027; Laws of 1982, ch. 230, § 16, p.976; Laws of 1984, ch. 249, § 15, p.1253. Neither amendment changed the original disjunctive language mandating liability insurance coverage for "all damages to persons or property . . . *or* any negligence on the part of the applicant." The statutory language clearly indicates that the Legislature intended pyrotechnicians to carry insurance to cover any damages incurred as a result of the fireworks display. The rule of construction applied to the disjunctive "or" mandates that by use of "or," a failure to comply with any requirement in the statute imposes liability. Thus, by utilizing the disjunctive "or" the Legislature indicated that damages will be owed for all injuries caused by the fireworks display, regardless of whether they resulted from the pyrotechnician's negligence.[5]

Furthermore, no part of a statute should be deemed inoperative or superfluous unless it is the result of obvious mistake or error. This requires that every word, clause, and sentence of a statute be given effect, if possible. Pursuant to this requirement, both clauses of RCW 70.77.285 should be given effect. Therefore, it is necessary to interpret the statute as mandating coverage of all damages caused by fireworks displays,

---

application evidence of a bond issued by an authorized surety company. The bond shall be in the amount required by RCW 70.77.295 and shall be conditioned upon the applicant's payment of all damages to persons or property resulting from or caused by such public display of fireworks, or any negligence on the part of the applicant or its agents, servants, employees, or subcontractors in the presentation of the display. Instead of a bond, the applicant may include a certificate of insurance evidencing the carrying of appropriate public liability insurance in the amount required by RCW 70.77.295 for the benefit of the person named therein as assured, as evidence of ability to respond in damages. The local fire official receiving the application shall approve the bond or insurance if it meets the requirements of this section."

5. RCW 70.77.285 was enacted prior to the Washington adoption of the strict liability standard. The Restatement of Torts regarding abnormally dangerous activities was drafted in 1964. This court first applied the strict liability standard to abnormally dangerous activities in Siegler v. Kuhlman, 81 Wash. 2d 448, 502 P.2d 1181 (1972). That case stated, however, that strict liability was not a novel concept and that it was at least as old as Fletcher v. Rylands, *supra* at 453.

regardless of whether those damages were caused by negligence of the pyrotechnicians.

IV. POSSIBLE NEGLIGENT MANUFACTURE AS AN INTERVENING FORCE

Pyrodyne argues that even if there is strict liability for fireworks, its liability under the facts of this case is cut off by the manufacturer's negligence, the existence of which we assume for purposes of evaluating the propriety of the trial court's summary judgment. According to Pyrodyne, a shell detonated without leaving the mortar box because it was negligently manufactured. This detonation, Pyrodyne asserts, was what caused the misfire of the second shell, which in turn resulted in the Kleins' injuries. Pyrodyne reasons that the manufacturer's negligence acted as an intervening or outside force that cuts off Pyrodyne's liability. . . .

We note that the Restatement (Second) of Torts takes a position contrary to that advocated by Pyrodyne. Section 522 of the Restatement provides that:

> One carrying on an abnormally dangerous activity is subject to strict liability for the resulting harm although it is caused by the unexpectable
> (a) innocent, negligent or reckless conduct of a third person . . .

Restatement (Second) of Torts § 522 (1977). The comment to section 522 explains that "[i]f the risk [from an abnormally dangerous activity] ripens into injury, it is immaterial that the harm occurs through the unexpectable action of a human being." Restatement (Second) of Torts § 522, comment *a* (1977).

Thus, on the one hand, Pyrodyne urges us to adopt the view that any intervention by an outside force beyond the defendant's control is sufficient to relieve the defendant from strict liability for an abnormally dangerous activity. On the other hand, section 522 provides that no negligent intervention by a third person will relieve the defendant from strict liability for abnormally dangerous activities. We reject both positions. . . .

We hold that intervening acts of third persons serve to relieve the defendant from strict liability for abnormally dangerous activities only if those acts were unforeseeable in relation to the extraordinary risk created by the activity. The rationale for this rule is that it encourages those who conduct abnormally dangerous activities to anticipate and take precautions against the possible negligence of third persons. Where the third person's negligence is beyond the actor's control, this rule, unlike the *Siegler* dicta, nonetheless imposes strict liability if the third person negligence was reasonably foreseeable. Such a result allocates the economic burden of injuries arising from the foreseeable negligence of third persons to the party best able to plan for it and to bear it — the actor carrying on the abnormally dangerous activity.

In the present case, negligence on the part of the fireworks manufacturer is readily foreseeable in relation to the extraordinary risk created by conducting a public fireworks display. Therefore, even if such negligence may properly be regarded as an intervening cause, an issue we need not decide, it cannot function to relieve Pyrodyne from liability. This is not to say, however, that in a proper case a defendant in a strict liability action could not pursue a claim against a third party and enforce a right of contribution to an extent proportionate to that party's fault.

CONCLUSION

We hold that Pyrodyne Corporation is strictly liable for all damages suffered as a result of the July 1987 fireworks display. Detonating fireworks displays constitutes an abnormally dangerous activity warranting strict liability. Public policy also supports this conclusion. Furthermore, RCW 70.77.285 mandates the payment of all damages caused by fireworks displays, regardless of whether those damages were due to the pyrotechnicians' negligence. This establishes the standard of strict liability for pyrotechnicians. Therefore, we affirm the decision of the trial court.

Dolliver, J. (concurring) (joined by Smith & Callow, JJ.).   I concur fully with the result reached by the majority. In my opinion the statute, RCW 70.77.285, is decisive. While I harbor some belief the Legislature may not have intended the result reached by the majority, legislative intent is irrelevant when the language of the statute is plain on its face.

I am not in agreement, however, with the analysis reached by the majority relative to the application of Restatement (Second) of Torts § 520 (1977), which characterizes fireworks displays as "abnormally dangerous." . . .

I first note that *no other jurisdiction* has adopted a common law rule of strict liability for fireworks displays. While this state regularly does things differently from its companion jurisdictions and, indeed, its uniqueness is many times a source of justifiable pride, extreme care should be exercised before embarking on a new doctrine foreign to this state as well as to all others. . . .

[Judge Dolliver proceeded to list the six factors identified by section 520 of the Second Restatement as relevant to the determination whether an activity is ultrahazardous.]

The majority claims factors (a), (b), (c), and (d) are present while factors (e) and (f) are not present. I agree factors (e) and (f) do not apply for the reasons given by the majority. I also agree factors (a) and (b) are present. Where I disagree with the majority is in whether factors (c) and (d) are present. The majority says yes, I say no.

Fireworks, no less than motor vehicles, for example, are high risk instrumentalities. In reality, all instrumentalities inevitably involve some degree of risk. Nothing in human life is risk free. The real issue is whether the hazard can be reduced to acceptable limits. This analysis is particularly apt where, as here, the likelihood of injury to significant numbers of persons is great unless the risk is significantly reduced. Blasting at some remove from civilization is one thing; public, urban fireworks displays are another matter.

It is apparent the Legislature, recognizing the dangers of public fireworks displays, attempted to regulate comprehensively fireworks displays. RCW Ch. 70.77 (State Fireworks Law). There are strict and specific safety and licensing provisions. . . . The Legislature has made the determination, through the legislative process, that in fact the "high degree of risk" inherent in public fireworks displays can adequately be reduced by the "reasonable care" required by the statute. This being so, I do not believe this court should use a random case, as here, to tamper with this legislative judgment. Factor (c) has not been met.

In discussing factor (d), the majority states that since "few persons set off special fireworks displays" they are not a matter of common usage. I believe the majority misconstrues factor (d). The Restatement comment on clause (d) discusses activities carried on by only a few persons, e.g., blasting, the transportation of high explosives, the drilling of oil wells. What is significant is that each of the activities used for illustrative purposes is not only an activity which is not a matter of common usage, but it is also a solitary activity. In contrast to the large crowds which attend public fireworks displays, the examples listed in comment *d* are not for spectators and are done away from the public. Comment *d*, Restatement (Second) of Torts § 520, at 40 (1977). The viewing of a public fireworks display is in fact, in the words of the comment on clause (d), "customarily carried on by the great mass of mankind or by many people in the community." Comment *i*, at 39. None of the examples in the comment are in any way similar to public fireworks displays. While it is true the setting up and setting off of the fireworks in public displays are done by very few people, the more important "activity" is viewing the fireworks display. I would find factor (d) is not met.

I also disagree with the majority's treatment of the six factors as acting only in favor of strict liability. Properly construed, each of the factors may also mitigate against strict liability. In *New Meadows*, we expressly stated, "Factors (d), (e), and (f) clearly weigh against imposition of strict liability." *New Meadows*, 102 Wash. 2d at 502, 687 P.2d 212. The majority concedes "the value of fireworks to the community outweighs its dangerous attributes." Majority, at 921. Properly construed, therefore, factor (f) is not merely a nullity in the strict liability analysis, but should actually mitigate against the imposition of strict liability. . . .

Thus, while I agree with the result reached by the majority, I would confine the opinion to that which is contained in part II in its opinion.

NOTES AND QUESTIONS

1. *An Embarrassment of Torts?* One of the remarkable features of *Rylands* is that the fact pattern seems chock-full of well-established torts. If so, why did the House of Lords have occasion to articulate a special rule for "non-natural" uses of land? For example, couldn't it have found that the water flowing into plaintiff's mines constituted a subsurface trespass caused by the defendants? Why wasn't the setting up of a reservoir a nuisance? Why wasn't the creation of a significant hazard near to the plaintiff's land in and of itself negligent? Why wasn't the failure of the engineers hired by the mill owner to ascertain the existence of underground shafts negligence that could be attributed to the mill owner?

2. Rylands *versus* Vaughan. The House of Lords in *Rylands* imposes liability on the mill owner because his storage of water on his property created a very significant risk of property damage to his neighbor, which risk was in the end realized. But isn't this exactly what happened when Menlove formed a haystack in a manner that risked spontaneous combustion and hence the transmission of fire to his neighbor Vaughan's property? See Chapter 3. If so, why was the liability in Vaughan v. Menlove, decided 30 years prior to *Rylands*, governed by a fault standard, whereas *Rylands* was not? In attempting to square *Rylands* with his thesis that nineteenth-century English common law had generally moved away from strict liability, Holmes suggested that the decision be treated as imposing a form of burden shifting:

> . . . as there is a limit to the nicety of inquiry which is possible at trial, it may
> be considered that the safest way to secure care is to throw the risk upon the
> person who decides what precautions shall be taken.

Oliver W. Holmes, Jr., *The Common Law* 117 (1881). Is this a convincing reading or explanation of *Rylands?* Why wouldn't the same reasoning warrant the imposition of strict liability in *Vaughan?*

3. *Reservoirs and Dams*. Professor Simpson has argued that *Rylands* must be understood against the backdrop of two catastrophic and widely publicized English dam failures that had occurred, respectively, in 1852 and 1864, and which resulted in Parliamentary investigations and possibly an increasing disposition to hold responsible those who maintained large reservoirs of water.

4. *Wild Animals*. As noted by the *Rylands* Lords, a long line of English precedents imposed liability without fault on owners of wild animals for injuries caused by those animals. Strict liability for wild animals continues today. In Franken v. Sioux Center, 272 N.W.2d 422 (Iowa 1978), for example, the defendant city was held strictly liable for the injuries inflicted by a Bengal tiger that bit the plaintiff. As demonstrated by *Pingaro* in Chapter 3, a number of states by statute hold owners even of domesticated dogs strictly liable for dog-bite injuries. *See also* Cook v. Whitsell-Shermann, 796 N.E.2d 271 (Ind. 2003). For a careful analysis of strict liability, common law negligence, and statutory liability in connection with a dog-bite injury, see Borns v. Voss, 70 P. 3d 262 (Wyo. 2003).

5. *Natural versus Non-Natural Uses*. Lord Cairns' famous opinion turns on a distinction between "natural" and "non-natural" uses of the property. Thus, he supposes that if the water that flooded the plaintiff's mines had accumulated on defendants' property "naturally," plaintiff would have had no complaint. By contrast, if the defendants,

> not stopping at the natural use of their close, had desired to use it for any
> purpose which I may term a non-natural use, for the purpose of introducing
> into [their] close that which in its natural condition was not in or upon it . . .
> and if in consequence of their doing so . . . the water came to escape and to
> pass off into the close of the Plaintiff, then it appears to me that that which
> the Defendants were doing they were doing at their own peril. . . .

What *is* a non-natural use of land? And why does its "naturalness" matter? Is naturalness relative to particular locations? *See* Turner v. Big Lake Oil Co., 96 S.W.2d 221 (Tex. 1937) (the creation of reservoirs filled with salt water is a "natural" use of land, given that in certain parts of Texas one would naturally expect to find such reservoirs, since they are a necessary part of oil exploration).

A subsequent English decision qualified *Rylands* by allowing an "act of God" defense that exempted from liability defendants whose stored water escaped in part because of unprecedented rains. Nichols v. Marsland, (1876) 2 Ex. D. 1. Is *Nichols* consistent with *Rylands*'s focus on non-natural uses of land?

6. *The Restatement Formulations.* The drafters of the first torts Restatement synthesized a number of different pockets of strict liability, including Lord Cairns' concept of non-natural activities, into a new category dubbed *ultrahazardous activities*. This suggestive label was replaced in the Restatement (Second) with the related concept of *abnormally dangerous* activities. Do these formulations shed light on the sorts of activities that warrant liability without fault, either as interpretations of "non-natural," or on their own?

An influential answer to this question was provided by Professor Fletcher in his 1971 article, *Fairness and Utility in Tort Law*. Fletcher argued that, broadly speaking, risks come in two different categories. First, risks can be "reciprocal," in the sense that persons are exposing each other to roughly similar risks of injury. Such is the case, Fletcher supposed, as between drivers of cars — as they go about driving normally, they generate roughly comparable risks of injury to one another. According to Fletcher, fault ought to be the standard of liability for reciprocal risks, because each member of society tolerates (or assumes) a baseline of risk reciprocal to that which he generates. In turn, it is only exceptional risks — the risks associated, for example, with *careless* driving — that should generate tort liability in reciprocal risk situations.

Fletcher's second category consists of "non-reciprocal" risks. These are risks that are generated by unconventional activities, that is, risks of harm that are unilaterally imposed by one actor upon others. While fault is the fair liability standard for activities that, when undertaken in the usual manner, generate reciprocal risks, fairness requires the different rule of strict liability for non-reciprocal risks. Otherwise, Fletcher argued, the unilateral risk-creator will enjoy the right to impose risks on others even though those others enjoy no equivalent right.

Does Fletcher's distinction between reciprocal and non-reciprocal risks help make sense of *Rylands?* Have the negligence cases we have encountered typically involved careless conduct that, if undertaken with ordinary care, would generate risks reciprocal to those the victim was imposing on the actor engaged in the conduct?

7. *Fire and Explosives.* Older English common law appears to have imposed liability on those who deliberately lit fires in their homes or on their properties, but then failed to contain them, even if they used reasonable care to contain the fires. Injuries caused by blasting and explosives

have long been treated as a basis for liability without fault. *See, e.g.*, Laughon & Johnson, Inc. v. Burch, 278 S.E.2d 856 (Va. 1981). Some courts impose similar liability for injuries imposed by industries that transport or process hazardous materials. *Compare, e.g.*, T & E Indus., Inc. v. Safety Light Corp., 587 A.2d 1249 (N.J. 1991) (imposing strict liability on a company that processes radium) *with* Indiana Harbor Belt R.R. Co. v. American Cyanamid Co., 916 F.2d 1174 (7th Cir. 1990) (Posner, J.) (declining to apply liability without fault to a company transporting a hazardous chemical). Few courts other than the *Pyrodyne* court have addressed whether strict liability ought to apply to fireworks' promoters. Not all have answered positively. *See, e.g.*, Cadena v. Chicago Fireworks Mfg. Co., 697 N.E.2d 802 (Ill. Ct. App. 1998) (rejecting the imposition of liability without fault on a city for injuries arising out of its operation of a fireworks display).

   8. *Statutory Interpretation.* As an alternative basis for its holding, the *Pyrodyne* court relies on an insurance statute that, on its face at least, seems not to address the standard of liability to which Pyrodyne will be held. Yet the issue of the ability of an actor to absorb the costs of its hazardous activity figures prominently in many analyses of liability without fault, including Judge Robert Keeton's important article, *Conditional Fault in the Law of Torts*.

   Judge Keeton argued that the distinction between negligence liability and liability with fault can be better understood as involving a distinction between two "types" of fault. Fault of the first type — what we typically deem "negligent" conduct — involves activity that violates norms of behavior even granted that the actor who engages in the behavior has made provision for the payment of any damages his behavior causes. Thus, we tend to regard careless driving as exemplifying fault of the first type. A careless driver's conduct is condemned even if he has purchased insurance sufficient to provide reasonable compensation to those he injures. By contrast, liability "without fault" is in reality a second type of fault, dubbed by Keeton "conditional fault." Conditional fault describes risky conduct that we are nonetheless prepared to treat as permissible if the actor who undertakes it stands ready to provide reasonable compensation to those injured by such conduct. Thus, according to Keeton, we say of highly risky activities such as blasting that it is permissible, but only on the condition that those who engage in it are prepared to compensate those who are injured by it.

   Do you find Keeton's distinction between types of fault plausible? Does it help make sense of the majority's reading of the Washington insurance statute? How well does the category of conditional fault mesh with the multifactor test of Section 520 of the Second Restatement?

   9. *Causation, Proximate Cause, and Apportionment.* As indicated by the *Pyrodyne* court's analysis of the effect on the defendant's liability of possible "intervening" negligence on the part of the fireworks' manufacturer, even in situations in which the plaintiff is entitled to recover in tort on a no-fault basis, the courts engage in causation analysis of a sort more or less identical to the forms of analysis seen in Chapter 4. Thus, a plaintiff

suing for injuries allegedly flowing from the use of explosives must demonstrate that the blasting was an actual and proximate cause of her injuries. A famous example of a case in which blasting was held to be an actual cause, but not a proximate cause, of property damage, is Foster v. Preston Mill Co., 268 P.2d 645 (Wash. 1954). There, defendant's blasting operation frightened a mother mink that resided on a mink farm two miles from the blast sight, inducing her to kill her kittens, causing her owner substantial economic loss. The defendant was held not liable because of the fortuity of the causal link between his hazardous conduct and the injury suffered by the plaintiff. Finally, as indicated in Chapter 7, factfinders are at least sometimes required to "apportion" responsibility among multiple defendants, even when one of the defendants is being held liable without fault. In effect, the jury is asked to assign fault, even though fault is not required to impose liability on that party.

REFERENCES/FURTHER READING

Workers' Compensation and Strict Liability

Ernst Freund, *Constitutional Status of Workmen's Compensation*, 6 Ill. L. Rev. 432, 433, 435-436 (1912).
Gregory C. Keating, *The Theory of Enterprise Liability and Common Law Strict Liability*, 54 Vand. L. Rev. 1285 (2001).
David Rosenberg, *The Hidden Holmes: His Theory of Torts in History* (1995).
Eugene Wambaugh, *Workmen's Compensation Acts: Their Theory and Their Constitutionality*, 25 Harv. L. Rev. 129 (1912).

Trespass

Michael R. Siebecker, *Cookies and the Common Law: Are Internet Advertisers Trespassing on Our Computers?*, 76 S. Cal. L. Rev. 893 (2003).

Vincent v. Lake Erie and Necessity

Alan Brudner, *A Theory of Necessity*, 7 Oxford J. Leg. Stud. 339 (1987).
George C. Christie, *The Defense of Necessity Considered from the Legal and Moral Points of View*, 48 Duke L.J. 975 (1999).
Jules L. Coleman, *Risks and Wrongs* 371-372 (1992).
Richard Epstein, *A Theory of Strict Liability*, 2 J. Leg. Stud. 151 (1973).
Richard Epstein, *The Ubiquity of the Benefit Principle*, 67 S. Cal. L. Rev. 1369 (1994).
Stephen D. Sugarman, Vincent v. Lake Erie Transportation Co.: *Liability for Harm Caused by Necessity*, in Robert L. Rabin & Stephen D. Sugarman, *Tort Stories* 259 (2003).
Ernest J. Weinrib, *The Idea of Private Law* 196-203 (1995).

Nuisance

Guido Calabresi, *Some Thoughts on Risk Distribution and the Law of Torts*, 70 Yale L.J. 499 (1961).

Guido Calabresi & A. Douglas Melamed, *Property Rules, Liability Rules and Inalienability: One View of the Cathedral*, 85 Harv. L. Rev. 1089 (1972).

Ronald Coase, *The Problem of Social Cost*, 3 J. L. & Econ. 1 (1960).

Donald G. Gifford, *Public Nuisance as a Mass Products Liability Tort*, 71 U. Cin. L. Rev. 741 (2003).

Gideon Parchomovsky & Peter Siegelman, *Selling Mayberry: Communities and Individuals in Law and Economics*, 92 Cal. L. Rev. 75 (2004).

Symposium, *Property Rules, Liability Rules and Inalienability: A Twenty-Five Year Retrospective,* 106 Yale L.J. 2083 *et seq.* (1997).

Ultrahazardous Activities

David Abraham, *Liberty and Property: Lord Bramwell and the Political Economy of Liberal Jurisprudence,* 38 Amer. J. Leg. Hist. 288 (1994).

Kenneth S. Abraham, Rylands v. Fletcher: *Tort Law's Conscience*, in Robert L. Rabin & Stephen D. Sugarman, *Tort Stories* 207 (2003).

Francis H. Bohlen, *The Rule in* Rylands v. Fletcher, 59 U. Pa. L. Rev. 298 (1911).

Gerald W. Boston, *Strict Liability for Abnormally Dangerous Activity: The Negligence Barrier*, 36 San Diego L. Rev. 597 (1999).

George Fletcher, *Fairness and Utility in Tort Law*, 85 Harv. L. Rev. 537 (1972).

William K. Jones, *Strict Liability for Hazardous Enterprise*, 92 Colum. L. Rev. 1705 (1992).

Robert Keeton, *Conditional Fault in the Law of Torts*, 72 Harv. L. Rev. 401 (1959).

Gary T. Schwartz, Rylands v. Fletcher, *Negligence and Strict Liability*, in Peter Cane & Jane Stapleton, *The Law of Obligations: Essays in Celebration of John Fleming* 201 (1998).

Jed H. Shugerman, Note: *The Floodgates of Strict Liability: Bursting Reservoirs and the Adoption of* Fletcher v. Rylands *in the Gilded Age*, 110 Yale L.J. 333 (2000).

A.W.B. Simpson, *Legal Liability for Bursting Reservoirs: The Historical Context of* Rylands v. Fletcher, 13 J. Leg. Stud. 209 (1984).

Glanville Williams, *Liability for Animals* (1939).

CHAPTER 12

Products Liability

I. INTRODUCTION

Products liability stands at the center of modern tort law. When one encounters high-stakes, cutting-edge litigation in tort, it tends to involve claims for injuries caused by "defective" products. For this reason, products liability is also perhaps the most politically controversial branch of tort. This chapter introduces you to its basic features.

As we have seen, suits seeking redress for injuries caused by products are nothing new. Recall, for example, the New York Court of Appeals' decision in the 1852 case of Thomas v. Winchester, in which the plaintiff was poisoned by a mislabeled medicine and was permitted to sue the manufacturer. See Chapter 2. For most of the modern history of tort — roughly 1850 to 1970 — actions of this sort fell within one of two existing doctrinal categories. First, they might sound in negligence, as did Mrs. Thomas's claim, as well as the claim of Mr. MacPherson against the Buick Motor Co. Alternatively, some consumers injured by products sued not in tort but in *contract*, for breach of an express or implied *warranty*: a contractual promise that the product was safe for ordinary use. By contrast, suits today for product-related injuries are almost always grounded in a separate body of law called *strict products liability* or just *products liability*. The change in label signifies that claims for injuries caused by defective products are now governed by a body of law that generates its own principles of responsibility, distinct from those at work in the law of negligence and warranty.

If one were to pick a date for the emergence of products liability law as a distinct department, it would probably be 1963, the year in which the California Supreme Court decided Greenman v. Yuba Power Products, Inc., 377 P.2d 897 (Cal. 1963). In *Greenman*, a unanimous court led by Justice Roger Traynor permitted a man injured while using a defective power tool to recover from the manufacturer on a theory of liability that relied neither on proof of fault nor on warranty. Justice Traynor's opinion dubbed this action as one of "strict liability" in tort for defective products. Within two years, the American Law Institute issued Section 402A of the Second Restatement of Torts. Relying primarily on California doctrine, Section 402A did not so much "restate" an existing law of products liability as recommend its adoption. Lawyers and courts across the country quickly latched onto Section 402A as providing a superior approach to claims alleging injuries caused by product defects. Within a decade of *Greenman*, a majority of jurisdictions in the United States had adopted causes of action in strict products liability. Today all but a handful of states employ some version of products liability law.

To say that products liability has been widely adopted as a distinct theory of liability is *not* to say that it has proved uncontroversial. Quite the opposite — it has throughout its brief life generated intense debate. The main *theoretical* concern associated with the recognition of this separate department of tort law can be stated succinctly: If accidents have traditionally been handled by our tort law under the rubric of negligence, and if, as cases such as *Greenman* insist, products liability is really a form of liability without fault, what can explain why victims of this class of accidents are entitled to the benefit of not having to prove fault? Various thoughtful answers have been proposed to this question. For example, some have insisted that products liability is faithful to a historical baseline of strict liability for accidentally caused harms, and that negligence is the upstart in the field that is in need of justification. Others, by contrast, insist that negligence is the default rule for liability arising out of accidents, but that there is no difficulty reconciling products liability law with that default because the "strictness" of products liability is illusory — in reality it is a form of fault-based liability. Still others insist that products liability is strict, and that it is incompatible with the law's baseline commitment to fault as a threshold for liability, and therefore illegitimate.

In our view, it is mistake to privilege either "strict liability" or "negligence" as the core principle of our tort law, in part because it is a mistake to suppose that either of those concepts has a single or constant meaning. As explained in Chapter 11, notwithstanding the central importance of negligence-based concepts, there remain important areas in which one or another version of strict liability applies, including claims arising out of interferences with property rights, ultrahazardous activities, and workplace accidents. Likewise, we hope that Part Two established, among other things, that negligence liability itself is multifaceted, reflecting an array of duties that differ substantially in terms of what they demand of various actors. For these and other reasons, we are disinclined to suppose that tort law privileges any one theory of responsibility as paradigmatic. Thus, there is no reason to believe that products liability law — even assuming it differs substantially from other tort law — has come into the world with either a special claim of privilege or a special stigma attached to it.

More affirmatively, we are of the view that products liability is controversial in part because, as a later entrant into the world of torts, it has emerged as a doctrinal hybrid that contains cross-currents reflecting various aspects of tort law and policy with which you are now familiar. From negligence law, you will perceive an emphasis on manufacturers' duties of vigilance, and on the proper balance among precaution and harm. From property torts, you will see a concern for the consumer's legitimate expectations for her physical safety. From the law of ultrahazardous activities, you will encounter the idea that large-scale production sometimes poses unavoidable hazards. From workers' compensation, you will note the distinctively modernist sense of the propriety of risk spreading and the concern for an uneven playing field between the individual and the large commercial enterprise. And, as elsewhere in torts, you will see these concerns being given expression in doctrines bearing on everything from rules of evidence to standards of liability.

In explicating the law of products liability, this chapter focuses primarily on the law of California. It does so because the California courts have tended to pave the way in this area, because California law provides a representative cross-section of issues, and because it provides a contemporary opportunity to examine the development of doctrine within a precedent-based system. The goal of this chapter is primarily to lay out basic concepts, and to see how they apply in a variety of settings. But in doing so, we also explore the broader debates that this area has spawned on issues of practical, political, and theoretical importance.

A.   *Precursors*

Escola is a simple but memorable case. Like some other notable concurring opinions — including, for example, Justice Louis Brandeis's concurring opinion on the importance of free speech rights in Whitney v. California, 274 U.S. 357 (1927) — Justice Traynor's *Escola* opinion is far more famous and important than the majority's. Indeed, as *Greenman* will attest, it is Traynor's opinion that has rendered *Escola* a legal landmark. If *Greenman* is the case that made strict products liability the law, *Escola* is the case that best presents its rationales.

Escola v. Coca Cola Bottling Co.

150 P.2d 436 (Cal. 1944)

Gibson, C.J.   Plaintiff, a waitress in a restaurant, was injured when a bottle of Coca Cola broke in her hand. She alleged that defendant company, which had bottled and delivered the alleged defective bottle to her employer, was negligent in selling "bottles containing said beverage which on account of excessive pressure of gas or by reason of some defect in the bottle was dangerous . . . and likely to explode." This appeal is from a judgment upon a jury verdict in favor of plaintiff.

Defendant's driver delivered several cases of Coca Cola to the restaurant, placing them on the floor, one on top of the other, under and behind the counter, where they remained at least thirty-six hours. Immediately before the accident, plaintiff picked up the top case and set it upon a nearby ice cream cabinet in front of and about three feet from the refrigerator. She then proceeded to take the bottles from the case with her right hand, one at a time, and put them into the refrigerator. Plaintiff testified that after she had placed three bottles in the refrigerator and had moved the fourth bottle about 18 inches from the case "it exploded in my hand." The bottle broke into two jagged pieces and inflicted a deep five-inch cut, severing blood vessels, nerves and muscles of the thumb and palm of the hand. Plaintiff further testified that when the bottle exploded, "It made a sound similar to an electric light bulb that would have dropped. It made a loud pop." Plaintiff's employer testified, "I was about twenty feet from where it actually happened and I heard the explosion." A fellow employee, on the opposite side of the counter, testified that plaintiff "had the bottle, I should judge, waist high, and I know that it didn't bang either the case or the door or another bottle . . . when it popped. It sounded just like a fruit jar would blow up. . . ." The witness further testified that the contents of the bottle "flew all over herself and myself and the walls and one thing and another."

The top portion of the bottle, with the cap, remained in plaintiff's hand, and the lower portion fell to the floor but did not break. The broken bottle was not produced at the trial, the pieces having been thrown away by an employee of the restaurant shortly after the accident. Plaintiff, however, described the broken pieces, and a diagram of the bottle was made showing the location of the "fracture line" where the bottle broke in two.

One of defendant's drivers, called as a witness by plaintiff, testified that he had seen other bottles of Coca Cola in the past explode and had found broken bottles in the warehouse when he took the cases out, but that he did not know what made them blow up.

Plaintiff then rested her case, having announced to the court that being unable to show any specific acts of negligence she relied completely on the doctrine of res ipsa loquitur.

Defendant contends that the doctrine of res ipsa loquitur does not apply in this case, and that the evidence is insufficient to support the judgment.

Many jurisdictions have applied the doctrine in cases involving exploding bottles of carbonated beverages. Other courts for varying reasons have refused to apply the doctrine in such cases. . . .

Res ipsa loquitur does not apply unless (1) defendant had exclusive control of the thing causing the injury and (2) the accident is of such a nature that it ordinarily would not occur in the absence of negligence by the defendant.

Many authorities state that the happening of the accident does not speak for itself where it took place some time after defendant had relinquished control of the instrumentality causing the injury. Under the more logical view, however, the doctrine may be applied upon the theory that defendant had control at the time of the alleged negligent act, although not at the time of the accident, *provided* plaintiff first proves that the condition of the instrumentality had not been changed after it left the defendant's possession. As said in Dunn v. Hoffman Beverage Co., 126 N.J.L. 556, 20 A.2d 352, 354, "defendant is not charged with the duty of showing affirmatively that something happened to the bottle after it left its control or management; . . . to get to the jury the plaintiff must show that there was due care during that period." Plaintiff must also prove that she handled the bottle carefully. . . .

Upon an examination of the record, the evidence appears sufficient to support a reasonable inference that the bottle here involved was not damaged by any extraneous force after delivery to the restaurant by defendant. It follows, therefore, that the bottle was in some manner defective at the time defendant relinquished control, because sound and properly prepared bottles of carbonated liquids do not ordinarily explode when carefully handled.

The next question, then, is whether plaintiff may rely upon the doctrine of res ipsa loquitur to supply an inference that defendant's negligence was responsible for the defective condition of the bottle at the time it was delivered to the restaurant. Under the general rules pertaining to the doctrine, as set forth above, it must appear that bottles of carbonated liquid are not ordinarily defective without negligence by the bottling company. . . .

An explosion such as took place here might have been caused by an excessive internal pressure in a sound bottle, by a defect in the glass of a bottle containing a safe pressure, or by a combination of these two possible causes. The question is whether under the evidence there was a probability that defendant was negligent in any of these respects. If so, the doctrine of res ipsa loquitur applies. . . .

A chemical engineer for the Owens-Illinois Glass Company and its Pacific Coast subsidiary, maker of Coca Cola bottles, explained how glass is manufactured and the methods used in testing and inspecting bottles. He testified that his company is the largest manufacturer of glass containers in the United States, and that it uses the standard methods for testing bottles recommended by the glass containers association. A pressure test is made by taking a sample from each mold every three hours—approximately one out of every 600 bottles—and subjecting the sample to an internal pressure of 450 pounds per square inch, which is sustained for one minute. (The normal pressure in Coca Cola bottles is less than 50 pounds per square inch.) The sample bottles are also subjected to the standard thermal shock test. The witness stated that these tests are "pretty near" infallible.

It thus appears that there is available to the industry a commonly-used method of testing bottles for defects not apparent to the eye, which is almost infallible. Since Coca Cola bottles are subjected to these tests by the manufacturer, it is not likely that they contain defects when delivered to the bottler which are not discoverable by visual inspection. Both new and used bottles are filled and distributed by defendant. The used bottles are not again subjected to the tests referred to above, and it may be inferred that defects not discoverable by visual inspection do not develop in bottles after they are manufactured. Obviously, if such defects do occur in used bottles there is a duty upon the bottler to make appropriate tests before they are refilled, and if such tests are not commercially practicable the bottles should not be re-used. This would seem to be particularly true where a charged liquid is placed in the bottle. It follows that a defect which would make the bottle unsound could be discovered by reasonable and practicable tests.

Although it is not clear in this case whether the explosion was caused by an excessive charge or a defect in the glass there is a sufficient showing that neither cause would ordinarily have been present if due care had been used. Further, defendant had exclusive control over both the charging and inspection of the bottles. Accordingly, all the requirements necessary to entitle plaintiff to rely on the doctrine of res ipsa loquitur to supply an inference of negligence are present.

It is true that defendant presented evidence tending to show that it exercised considerable precaution by carefully regulating and checking the pressure in the bottles and by making visual inspections for defects in the glass at several stages during the bottling process. It is well settled, however, that when a defendant produces evidence to rebut the inference of negligence which arises upon application of the doctrine of res ipsa loquitur, it is ordinarily a question of fact for the jury to determine whether the inference has been dispelled.

The judgment is affirmed.

Traynor, J. (concurring). I concur in the judgment, but I believe the manufacturer's negligence should no longer be singled out as the basis of a plaintiff's right to recover in cases like the present one. In my opinion it should now be recognized that a manufacturer incurs an absolute liability when an article that he has placed on the market, knowing that it is to be used without inspection, proves to have a defect that causes injury to human beings. MacPherson v. Buick Motor Co., 217 N.Y. 382, 111 N.E. 1050 . . . established the principle, recognized by this court, that irrespective of privity of contract, the manufacturer is responsible for an injury caused by such an article to any person who comes in lawful contact with it. In these cases the source of the manufacturer's liability was his negligence in the manufacturing process or in the inspection of component parts supplied by others. Even if there is no negligence, however, public policy demands that responsibility be fixed wherever it will most effectively reduce the hazards to life and health inherent in defective products that reach the market. It is evident that the manufacturer can anticipate some hazards and guard against the recurrence of others, as the public cannot. Those who suffer injury from defective products are unprepared to meet its consequences. The cost of an injury and the loss of time or health may be an overwhelming misfortune to the person injured, and a needless one, for the risk of injury can be insured by the manufacturer and distributed among the public as a cost of doing business. It is to the public interest to discourage the marketing of products having defects that are a menace to the public. If such products nevertheless find their way into the market it is to the public interest to place the responsibility for whatever injury they may cause upon the manufacturer, who, even if he is not negligent in the manufacture of the product, is responsible for its reaching the market. However intermittently such injuries may occur and however haphazardly they may strike, the risk of their occurrence is a constant risk and a general one. Against such a risk there should be general and constant protection and the manufacturer is best situated to afford such protection.

The injury from a defective product does not become a matter of indifference because the defect arises from causes other than the negligence of the manufacturer, such as negligence of a submanufacturer of a component part whose defects could not be revealed by inspection, or unknown causes that even by the device of res ipsa loquitur cannot be classified as negligence of the manufacturer. The inference of negligence may be dispelled by an affirmative showing of proper care. If the evidence against the fact inferred is "clear, positive, uncontradicted, and of such a nature that it can not rationally be disbelieved, the court must instruct the jury that the nonexistence of the fact has been established as a matter of law." An injured person, however, is not ordinarily in a position to refute such evidence or identify the cause of the defect, for he can hardly be familiar with the manufacturing process as the manufacturer himself is. In leaving it to the jury to decide whether the inference has been dispelled, regardless of the evidence against it, the negligence rule approaches the rule of strict liability. It is needlessly circuitous to make negligence the basis of recovery and impose what is in reality liability without negligence. If public policy demands that a manufacturer of goods be responsible for their quality regardless of negligence there is no reason not to fix that responsibility openly.

In the case of foodstuffs, the public policy of the state is formulated in a criminal statute. [Indeed, various provisions of] the Health and Safety Code [impose penalties for the sale of "adulterated" food — food that is itself unwholesome or injurious to health, or that is delivered in a container so as to be injurious to health.] The criminal liability under the statute attaches without proof of fault, so that the manufacturer is under the duty of ascertaining whether an article manufactured by him is safe. . . . Statutes of this kind result in a strict liability of the manufacturer in tort to the member of the public injured.

The statute may well be applicable to a bottle whose defects cause it to explode. In any event it is significant that the statute imposes criminal liability without fault, reflecting the public policy of protecting the public from dangerous products placed on the market, irrespective of negligence in their manufacture. While the Legislature imposes criminal liability only with regard to food products and their containers, there are many other sources of danger. It is to the public interest to prevent injury to the public from any defective goods by the imposition of civil liability generally.

The retailer, even though not equipped to test a product, is under an absolute liability to his customer, for the implied warranties of fitness for proposed use and merchantable quality include a warranty of safety of the product. This warranty is not necessarily a contractual one. The courts recognize, however, that the retailer cannot bear the burden of this warranty, and allow him to recoup any losses by means of the warranty of safety attending the wholesaler's or manufacturer's sale to him. Such a procedure, however, is needlessly circuitous and engenders wasteful litigation. Much would be gained if the injured person could base his action directly on the manufacturer's warranty.

The liability of the manufacturer to an immediate buyer injured by a defective product follows without proof of negligence from the implied warranty of safety attending the sale. Ordinarily, however, the immediate buyer is a dealer who does not intend to use the product himself, and if the warranty of safety is to serve the purpose of protecting health and safety it must give rights to others than the dealer. . . . While the defendant's negligence in the *MacPherson* case made it unnecessary for the court to base liability on warranty, Judge Cardozo's reasoning recognized the injured person as the real party in interest and effectively disposed of the theory that the liability of the manufacturer incurred by his warranty should apply only to the immediate purchaser. It thus paves the way for a standard of liability that would make the manufacturer guarantee the safety of his product even when there is no negligence.

This court and many others have extended protection according to such a standard to consumers of food products, taking the view that the right of a consumer injured by unwholesome food does not depend "upon the intricacies of the law of sales" and that the warranty of the manufacturer to the consumer in absence of privity of contract rests on public policy. Dangers to life and health inhere in other consumers' goods that are defective and there is no reason to differentiate them from the dangers of defective food products.

In the food products cases the courts have resorted to various fictions to rationalize the extension of the manufacturer's warranty to the consumer: that a warranty runs with the chattel; that the cause of action of the dealer is assigned to the consumer; that the consumer is a third party beneficiary of the manufacturer's contract with the dealer. They have also held the manufacturer liable on a mere fiction of negligence: "Practically he must know it [the product] is fit, or take the consequences, if it proves destructive." Parks v. C. C. Yost Pie Co., 93 Kan. 334, 144 P. 202, 203. . . . Such fictions are not necessary to fix the manufacturer's liability under a warranty if the warranty is severed from the contract of sale between the dealer and the consumer and based on the law of torts (Decker & Sons v. Capps, *supra*; Prosser, *Torts*, p.689) as a strict liability. . . .

As handicrafts have been replaced by mass production with its great markets and transportation facilities, the close relationship between the producer and consumer of a product has been altered. Manufacturing processes, frequently valuable secrets, are ordinarily either inaccessible to or beyond the ken of the general public. The consumer no longer has means or skill enough to investigate for himself the soundness of a product, even when it is not contained in a sealed package, and his erstwhile vigilance has been lulled by the steady efforts of manufacturers to build up confidence by advertising and marketing devices such as trademarks. Consumers no longer approach products warily but accept them on faith, relying on the reputation of the manufacturer or the trade mark. Manufacturers have sought to justify that faith by increasingly high standards of inspection and a readiness to make good on defective products by way of replacements and refunds. The manufacturer's obligation to the consumer must keep pace with the changing relationship between them; it cannot be escaped because the marketing of a product has become so complicated as to require one or more intermediaries. Certainly there is greater reason to impose liability on the manufacturer than on the retailer who is but a conduit of a product that he is not himself able to test.

The manufacturer's liability should, of course, be defined in terms of the safety of the product in normal and proper use, and should not extend to injuries that cannot be traced to the product as it reached the market.

NOTES AND QUESTIONS

1. Res Ipsa *Revisited.* The jury and the trial court in *Escola* did not seem to balk at reaching a verdict for plaintiff under the rubric of a negligence cause of action and a sensitive application of *res ipsa*. The majority of the supreme court similarly seemed capable of affirming the judgment on a negligence theory. Is the majority's application of *res ipsa* plausible? (See Chapter 3.) Why did Justice Traynor think it was necessary to create a whole new cause of action if *res ipsa* would have sufficed?

2. *Are Products Different?* Assume that the defendant in *Escola* really did use reasonable care. How, then, would the situation here differ from that of Harvey v. Dunlop, *supra*, Chapter 11? In *Harvey*, the court refused to impose liability when one child partially blinded another with a stone, deeming it an unfortunate tragedy. Under the assumption that Coca Cola acted carefully, isn't Escola's injury likewise a tragic occurrence for which the defendant cannot be held responsible? Should it be enough that it was the company's bottle that caused the injury?

3. *Justifying Defect-Based Liability.* The first two paragraphs of Justice Traynor's concurrence set forth several mutually reinforcing justifications for a new conception of liability for injuries caused by defective products. These include (a) a suggestion that manufacturers owe to consumers a particularly demanding obligation to be vigilant of product safety (an obligation-based rationale); (b) an argument that manufacturers are best situated to take precautions, and therefore should be given strong incentives to take such precautions (a deterrence rationale); (c) an argument that manufacturers are best situated to spread the costs of accidental injuries caused by their products (a compensation-insurance rationale); (d) an observation that responsibility for injury stems from having marketed a product that caused injury, regardless of negligence (a causation-strict liability rationale); (e) an argument that victims' entitlement to compensation should not depend on the nature of the conduct that caused it (a compensation-equality rationale); (f) an analysis of disparities in power in litigation concerning evidence and procedure (a litigation-structure rationale); (g) an assertion that, if two ways of structuring the law lead to the same result, the more open and direct structure is preferable (a judicial-candor rationale).

It is worthwhile to identify the text in the opinion that corresponds to each of these rationales. Which of them is most persuasive? Which seem most important to Justice Traynor? Why does he put forward all of them, rather than simply the ones he views as most important? Are there any rationales that he should have mentioned that he did not? Do these rationales overlap with those put forward for liability without fault in the cases we examined in Chapter 11?

4. *Unprecedented?* Thanks in part to Justice Traynor's concurrence, Judge Cardozo's *MacPherson* opinion is today commonly heralded as setting modern tort law on a course that led naturally to the adoption of strict products liability. Yet *MacPherson* itself, as Traynor acknowledges,

was a negligence decision. Why does Traynor believe it provides any support whatsoever to the plaintiff in *Escola?* How can he cite *MacPherson* when his whole point is to urge liability *without negligence?*

Note 3 above identifies many of the policy arguments put forward by Justice Traynor. Yet, to say that reasons of policy or principle support a particular doctrine is not to address whether extant legal authorities justify its adoption. In fact, Justice Traynor cited a number of different sources in his scholarly and citation-filled opinion. These include negligence cases, criminal statutes, and warranty cases (the full opinion contains scores of citations). Which sources of authority seem most supportive of his efforts at doctrinal innovation? Does he interweave the different authorities effectively?

5. *Food Impurities versus Product Defects.* As Justice Traynor notes, numerous courts had, prior to *Escola*, recognized warranty-based causes of action for persons injured by ingesting "impure" or otherwise defective food products. A typical case, cited by Traynor, is Parks v. C. C. Yost Pie Co., 144 P. 202 (Kan. 1914), in which a widow recovered damages from a manufacturer whose ptomaine-poisoned pie killed her husband. Another of the many food liability cases cited by Justice Traynor was a well-known New York Court of Appeals decision authored by Judge Cardozo. Ryan v. Progressive Grocery Stores, 175 N.E. 105 (N.Y. 1931), permitted the plaintiff to recover on an implied warranty theory for injuries to his mouth caused by a pin contained in a loaf of bread sold by defendant. Is there any reason why foodstuffs — and in *Escola*, a soft drink bottle — should have been among the first sorts of products in which strict liability would apply? Did it aid Traynor's cause that he was able to write his opinion in a case in which the defective "product" was a bottled beverage?

6. Henningsen. The warranty roots of modern products liability law received their most important and influential treatment in a New Jersey Supreme Court decision. In Henningsen v. Bloomfield Motors, Inc., 161 A.2d 69 (N.J. 1960), Helen Henningsen was driving a ten-day-old Plymouth sedan when its steering wheel suddenly spun in her hands, causing the car to crash into a wall. Mrs. Henningsen and her husband Claus, who had purchased the car, sued the car dealer (Bloomfield Motors) and the car's manufacturer (Chrysler). The Henningsens brought causes of action in both negligence and warranty, but the trial court dismissed the negligence claim for lack of sufficient evidence of breach, and sent the case to trial on warranty claims alone. The jury returned verdicts for the plaintiffs against both defendants.

On appeal, Chrysler argued that a provision in the contract of sale that limited its liability to the cost of replacing any defective parts, and disclaimed any other liabilities, precluded recovery of tort compensation for Mrs. Henningsen's injuries on either an *express* or *implied* warranty theory. In addition, it argued that any warranties that accompanied the product were not for the benefit of non-privies, such as Mrs. Henningsen. The court declared the contract's disclaimer of liability for personal injuries void as against public policy. In support of this holding, it noted that the limitation was provided in fine print in a standard-form contract drafted and used by each of the "Big Three" U.S. auto makers, and hence that consumers were not likely to have any meaningful choice as to whether to accept it. The court also rejected the privity argument (161 A.2d at 80-81):

> There is no doubt that under early common-law concepts of contractual liability only those persons who were parties to the bargain could sue for a breach of it. In more recent times a noticeable disposition has appeared in a number of jurisdictions to break through the narrow barrier of privity when dealing with sales of goods in order to give realistic recognition to a universally accepted fact. The fact is that the dealer and the ordinary buyer do not, and are not expected to, buy goods, whether they be foodstuffs or automobiles, exclusively for their own consumption or use. Makers and manufacturers know this and advertise and market their products on that assumption; witness, the "family" car, the baby foods, etc. The limitations of privity in contracts for the sale of goods developed their place in the law when marketing conditions were simple, when maker and buyer frequently met face to face on an equal bargaining plane and when many of the products were relatively uncomplicated and conducive to inspection by a buyer competent to evaluate their quality. With the advent of mass marketing, the manufacturer became remote from the purchaser, sales were accomplished through intermediaries, and the demand for the product was created by advertising media. In such an economy it became obvious that the consumer was the person being cultivated. Manifestly, the connotation of "consumer" was broader than that of "buyer." He signified such a person who, in the reasonable contemplation of the parties to the sale, might be expected to use the product. Thus, where the commodities sold are such that if defectively manufactured they will be dangerous to life or limb, then society's interests can only be protected by eliminating the requirement of privity between the maker and his dealers and the reasonably expected ultimate consumer. In that way the burden of losses consequent upon use of defective articles is borne by those who are in a position to either control the danger or make an equitable distribution of the losses when they do occur.

The *Escola* majority avoided issues of privity by working within the domain of negligence law. *Henningsen*, by contrast, had to solve the privity problem within the law of warranty. It did so, first, by ruling that an implied warranty of fitness "runs with" a product, and thus passes through an intermediate seller to the ultimate consumer. Second, and equally important, it held that a manufacturer and consumer were barred by law from agreeing to waive this implied warranty. As between *Escola* and *Henningsen*, which sort of "stretch" seems more plausible to you? Which one is more likely to help accident victims in the long run? Is there something intuitive about grounding products liability claims in an implicit promise from the manufacturer that the product will perform more or less as expected?

7. *Modern Warranty Law*. Following *Henningsen*, a majority of jurisdictions abandoned the privity requirement in implied warranty actions. Today, under Article 2-314 of the Uniform Commercial Code (UCC), which has been adopted in one form or another by every state, all goods come with an implied warranty of *merchantability*, that is, a promise that the goods are safe and fit for ordinary use. Such warranties

can be waived, but only by conspicuous and specific language agreed to by the buyer at the time of sale. U.C.C. § 2-316(2). (Some states have adopted versions of Section 2-316 that void even conspicuous and specific waivers of implied warranties, at least with respect to personal injury claimants.) Breaches of this implied warranty that result in physical harms generate in the victim a claim for consequential damages for the losses associated with those harms. Contractual terms purporting to cap or otherwise limit such damages are generally deemed void as unconscionable. U.C.C. §§ 2-715, 2-719. The reach of the implied warranty of merchantability differs across jurisdictions. Some extend it only to the immediate family members of the purchaser of the product. Others go so far as to render the warranty enforceable by any foreseeable user of the product. *See* U.C.C. § 2-318 A-C (offering alternative provisions as to the class of persons protected by warranty).

In spite of sellers' (limited) ability to waive warranties, as well as limits in some jurisdictions on the class of persons who are entitled to complain of breaches of warranty, modern warranty law is capable of providing legal redress to many persons who suffer bodily harm because of a product not fit for ordinary use. In general, however, modern products liability law, in which issues of waiver and "standing" do not arise, has tended to push warranty theories of recovery to the side. There are some important exceptions to this tendency. For example, as we will see, there are some jurisdictions in which the UCC imposes warranty-based liability for product-related physical injuries even when the law of products liability does not. In these jurisdictions, at least, the question of whether to provide separate warranty and tort causes of action for injuries caused by products, or whether all such actions should be unified under a single heading, remains very much alive.

B.   The Emergence of Strict Products Liability

Greenman v. Yuba Power Prods., Inc.
377 P.2d 897 (Cal. 1963)

Traynor, J.   Plaintiff brought this action for damages against the retailer and the manufacturer of a Shopsmith, a combination power tool that could be used as a saw, drill, and wood lathe. He saw a Shopsmith demonstrated by the retailer and studied a brochure prepared by the manufacturer. He decided he wanted a Shopsmith for his home workshop, and his wife bought and gave him one for Christmas in 1955. In 1957 he bought the necessary attachments to use the Shopsmith as a lathe for turning a large piece of wood he wished to make into a chalice. After he had worked on the piece of wood several times without difficulty, it suddenly flew out of the machine and struck him on the forehead, inflicting serious injuries. About ten and a half months later, he gave the retailer and the manufacturer written notice of claimed breaches of warranties and filed a complaint against them alleging such breaches and negligence.

After a trial before a jury, the court ruled that there was no evidence that the retailer was negligent or had breached any express warranty and that the manufacturer was not liable for the breach of any implied warranty. Accordingly, it submitted to the jury only the cause of action alleging breach of implied warranties against the retailer and the causes of action alleging negligence and breach of express warranties against the manufacturer. The jury returned a verdict for the retailer against plaintiff and for plaintiff against the manufacturer in the amount of $65,000. The trial court denied the manufacturer's motion for a new trial and entered judgment on the verdict. The manufacturer and plaintiff appeal. . . .

Plaintiff introduced substantial evidence that his injuries were caused by defective design and construction of the Shopsmith. His expert witnesses testified that inadequate set screws were used to hold parts of the machine together so that normal vibration caused the tailstock of the lathe to move away from the piece of wood being turned permitting it to fly out of the lathe. They also testified that there were other more positive ways of fastening the parts of the machine together, the use of which would have prevented the accident. The jury could therefore reasonably have concluded that the manufacturer negligently constructed the Shopsmith. The jury could also reasonably have concluded that statements in the manufacturer's brochure were untrue, that they constituted express warranties,[1] and that plaintiff's injuries were caused by their breach.

The manufacturer contends, however, that plaintiff did not give it notice of breach of warranty within a reasonable time and that therefore his cause of action for breach of warranty is barred by section 1769 of the Civil Code. Since it cannot be determined whether the verdict against it was based on the negligence or warranty cause of action or both, the manufacturer concludes that the error in presenting the warranty cause of action to the jury was prejudicial.

Section 1769 of the Civil Code provides: "In the absence of express or implied agreement of the parties, acceptance of the goods by the buyer shall not discharge the seller from liability in damages or other legal remedy for breach of any promise or warranty in the contract to sell or the sale. But, if, after acceptance of the goods, the buyer fails to give notice to the seller of the breach of any promise or warranty within a reasonable time after the buyer knows, or ought to know of such breach, the seller shall not be liable therefor."

Like other provisions of the uniform sales act (Civ. Code, §§ 1721-1800), section 1769 deals with the rights of the parties to a contract of sale or a sale. It does not provide that notice must be given of the breach of a warranty that arises independently of a contract of sale between the parties. Such warranties are not imposed by the sales act, but are the

---

1. In this respect the trial court limited the jury to a consideration of two statements in the manufacturer's brochure. (1) "WHEN SHOPSMITH IS IN HORIZONTAL POSITION — Rugged construction of frame provides rigid support from end to end. Heavy centerless-ground steel tubing insures perfect alignment of components." (2) "SHOPSMITH maintains its accuracy because every component has positive locks that hold adjustments through rough or precision work."

product of common-law decisions that have recognized them in a variety of situations. It is true that in many of these situations the court has invoked the sales act definitions of warranties in defining the defendant's liability, but it has done so, not because the statutes so required, but because they provided appropriate standards for the court to adopt under the circumstances presented.

The notice requirement of section 1769, however, is not an appropriate one for the court to adopt in actions by injured consumers against manufacturers with whom they have not dealt. "As between the immediate parties to the sale (the notice requirement) is a sound commercial rule, designed to protect the seller against unduly delayed claims for damages. As applied to personal injuries, and notice to a remote seller, it becomes a booby-trap for the unwary. The injured consumer is seldom 'steeped in the business practice which justifies the rule,' (James, *Product Liability*, 34 Texas L. Rev. 44, 192, 197) and at least until he has had legal advice it will not occur to him to give notice to one with whom he has had no dealings." (Prosser, *Strict Liability to the Consumer*, 69 Yale L.J. 1099, 1130, footnotes omitted.) It is true that in [three of our prior decisions, this] court assumed that notice of breach of warranty must be given in an action by a consumer against a manufacturer. Since in those cases, however, the court did not consider the question whether a distinction exists between a warranty based on a contract between the parties and one imposed on a manufacturer not in privity with the consumer, the decisions are not [binding in this case]. We conclude, therefore, that even if plaintiff did not give timely notice of breach of warranty to the manufacturer, his cause of action based on the representations contained in the brochure was not barred.

Moreover, to impose strict liability on the manufacturer under the circumstances of this case, it was not necessary for plaintiff to establish an express warranty as defined in section 1732 of the Civil Code. A manufacturer is strictly liable in tort when an article he places on the market, knowing that it is to be used without inspection for defects, proves to have a defect that causes injury to a human being. Recognized first in the case of unwholesome food products, such liability has now been extended to a variety of other products that create as great or greater hazards if defective. [Citing state and federal cases involving products including a grinding wheel, bottle, vaccine, surgical pin, automobile, skirt, tire, home permanent, hair dye, and plane. — Eds.]

Although in these cases strict liability has usually been based on the theory of an express or implied warranty running from the manufacturer to the plaintiff, the abandonment of the requirement of a contract between them, the recognition that the liability is not assumed by agreement but imposed by law, and the refusal to permit the manufacturer to define the scope of its own responsibility for defective products (Henningsen v. Bloomfield Motors, Inc., 32 N.J. 358, 161 A.2d 69, 84-96 . . .) make clear that the liability is not one governed by the law of contract warranties but by the law of strict liability in tort. Accordingly, rules defining and governing warranties that were developed to meet the needs of commercial transactions cannot properly be invoked to govern the manufacturer's liability to those injured by their defective products unless those rules also serve the purposes for which such liability is imposed.

We need not recanvass the reasons for imposing strict liability on the manufacturer. They have been fully articulated in the cases cited above. (*See also* 2 Harper and James, *Torts*, §§ 28.15-28,16, pp.1569-1574; Prosser, *Strict Liability to the Consumer*, 69 Yale L.J. 1099; Escola v. Coca Cola Bottling Co., 24 Cal. 2d 453, 461, 150 P.2d 436, concurring opinion.) The purpose of such liability is to insure that the costs of injuries resulting from defective products are borne by the manufacturers that put such products on the market rather than by the injured persons who are power-less to protect themselves. Sales warranties serve this purpose fitfully at best. In the present case, for example, plaintiff was able to plead and prove an express warranty only because he read and relied on the representa-tions of the Shopsmith's ruggedness contained in the manufacturer's brochure. Implicit in the machine's presence on the market, however, was a representation that it would safely do the jobs for which it was built. Under these circumstances, it should not be controlling whether plaintiff selected the machine because of the statements in the brochure, or because of the machine's own appearance of excellence that belied the defect lurking beneath the surface, or because he merely assumed that it would safely do the jobs it was built to do. It should not be controlling whether the details of the sales from manufacturer to retailer and from retailer to plaintiff's wife were such that one or more of the implied warranties of the sales act arose. "The remedies of injured consumers ought not to be made to depend upon the intricacies of the law of sales." (Ketterer v. Armour & Co., D.C., 200 F. 322, 323; Klein v. Duchess Sandwich Co., 14 Cal. 2d 272, 282, 93 P.2d 799.) To establish the manufac-turer's liability it was sufficient that plaintiff proved that he was injured while using the Shopsmith in a way it was intended to be used as a result of a defect in design and manufacture of which plaintiff was not aware that made the Shopsmith unsafe for its intended use. . . .

The judgment is affirmed.

NOTES AND QUESTIONS

1. *Beyond Negligence and Warranty.* How does the holding of *Greenman* differ from the holdings in *Escola* and *Henningsen?* Would a *res ipsa* theory have succeeded in *Greenman?* Why not? Why was an implied warranty theory problematic in *Greenman?*

2. *From* Escola *to* Greenman. Compare the rationales provided in *Greenman* with those stated by Justice Traynor in his *Escola* concurrence. Which rationales, if any, are omitted in *Greenman?* Are any new ones added?

3. *Defect.* Justice Traynor uses the terms *defect*, *defectively designed or constructed*, *defective condition*, and numerous other cognates of "defect" in describing the gist of Greenman's complaint about the Shopsmith. Do these terms address the issue of carelessness? Or breach of

express or implied warranty? Do they concern all three? Is it possible for a product to contain a defect without the seller of the product having acted negligently in marketing it? Is it possible for the product to be defectively designed without a seller having acted negligently?

4. Vandermark. In Vandermark v. Ford Motor Co., 391 P.2d 168, 171-172 (Cal. 1964), the California Supreme Court extended *Greenman*, applying defect-based liability to the *retailer* of a product (Maywood Bell, a car dealer), not simply the manufacturer:

> Retailers like manufacturers are engaged in the business of distributing goods to the public. They are an integral part of the overall producing and marketing enterprise that should bear the cost of injuries resulting from defective products. In some cases the retailer may be the only member of that enterprise reasonably available to the injured plaintiff. In other cases the retailer himself may play a substantial part in insuring that the product is safe or may be in a position to exert pressure on the manufacturer to that end; the retailer's strict liability thus serves as an added incentive to safety. Strict liability on the manufacturer and retailer alike affords maximum protection to the injured plaintiff and works no injustice to the defendants, for they can adjust the costs of such protection between them in the course of their continuing business relationship. Accordingly, as a retailer engaged in the business of distributing goods to the public, Maywood Bell is strictly liable in tort for personal injuries caused by defects in cars sold by it.
>
> Since Maywood Bell is strictly liable in tort, the fact that it restricted its contractual liability to Vandermark is immaterial. Regardless of the obligations it assumed by contract, it is subject to strict liability in tort because it is in the business of selling automobiles, one of which proved to be defective and caused injury to human beings. . . .

As we explore in greater depth below, the modern rules of products liability law apply to *sellers* of the products at issue. Retailers and manufacturers both qualify as sellers, as do others in the chain of distribution. Reconsider the majority and concurring opinions in *Escola*. Would the *res ipsa* theory of the majority apply equally well to a car dealer such as Maywood Bell? Which of Justice Traynor's stated rationales in his *Escola* concurrence apply to a retailer? Which (if any) do not?

5. *Defect = Negligence?* As we will see, some scholars have suggested that products liability law is, in the end, just a variation on negligence law that provides the plaintiff with the advantage of being able to prove carelessness by identifying a fault in the defendant's product rather than in the defendant's production or distribution methods. Does *Vandermark* support this supposition?

6. *Risk Spreading: Manufacturers versus Retailers.* Maywood Bell was a smaller enterprise than Ford Motor Company. As such, it presumably possessed a lesser ability to spread the costs of product-related injuries. Is it obvious that a modestly sized retail operation can more readily secure liability insurance than an individual consumer can secure health insurance? As a rule, will retailers always be relatively less well suited to spread risk than manufacturers? Suppose Greenman had purchased his Yuba Shopsmith in

2004 at a Wal-Mart store. Wouldn't this reverse the size differential of *Vandermark?*

  7. *Users versus Bystanders.* When the New York Court of Appeals in MacPherson v. Buick eliminated the privity rule, it extended the duty of care owed by car manufacturers at least to a subset of foreseeable users of those cars, including the car's passengers. Recall, however, that the court declined to indicate whether the duty of care further extended to nonusers such as pedestrians and other bystanders. In Elmore v. American Motors Corp., 451 P.2d 84 (Cal. 1969), the California Supreme Court was faced with the same issue in the context of delineating the emerging cause of action for products liability. One of the plaintiffs was the driver (and owner) of an automobile with a defective drive shaft. The defect caused the owner's car to crash into a vehicle from the oncoming lane. The other plaintiff, whose action is discussed below, was the injured driver of the oncoming vehicle.

> In [*Greenman*], we pointed out that the purpose of strict liability upon the manufacturer in tort is to insure that "the costs of injuries resulting from defective products are borne by the manufacturers that put such products on the market rather than by the injured persons who are powerless to protect themselves." We further pointed out that the rejection of the view that such liability was governed by contract warranties rather than tort rules was shown by cases which had recognized that the liability is not assumed by agreement but imposed by law and which had refused to permit the manufacturer to define its own responsibility for defective products. Similarly, in Vandermark v. Ford Motor Co. . . . we held that, since the retailer is strictly liable in tort, the fact that it restricted its contractual liability was immaterial.
>
> These cases make it clear that the doctrine of strict liability may not be restricted on a theory of privity of contract. Since the doctrine applies even where the manufacturer has attempted to limit liability, they further make it clear that the doctrine may not be limited on the theory that no representation of safety is made to the bystander.
>
> The liability has been based upon the existence of a defective product which caused injury to a human being, and in both *Greenman* and *Vandermark* we did not limit the rules stated to consumers and users but instead used language applicable to human beings generally.
>
> It has been pointed out that an injury to a bystander "is often a perfectly foreseeable risk of the maker's enterprise, and the considerations for imposing such risks on the maker without regard to his fault do not stop with those who undertake to use the chattel. [A restriction on the recovery by bystanders] is only the distorted shadow of a vanishing privity which is itself a reflection of the habit of viewing the problem as a commercial one between traders, rather than as part of the accident problem." (2 Harper and James, *The Law of Torts* (1956) p.1572, fn.6.)
>
> If anything, bystanders should be entitled to greater protection than the consumer or user where injury to bystanders from the defect is reasonably foreseeable. Consumers and users, at least, have the opportunity to inspect for defects and to limit their purchases to articles manufactured by reputable manufacturers and sold by reputable retailers, where as the bystander ordinarily has no such opportunities. In short, the bystander is in greater need

of protection from defective products which are dangerous, and if any distinction should be made between bystanders and users, it should be made, contrary to the position of defendants, to extend greater liability in favor of the bystanders.

An automobile with a defectively connected drive shaft constitutes a substantial hazard on the highway not only to the driver and passenger of the car but also to pedestrians and other drivers. The public policy which protects the driver and passenger of the car should also protect the bystander, and where a driver or passenger of another car is injured due to defects in the manufacture of an automobile and without any fault of their own, they may recover from the manufacturer of the defective automobile.

Id. at 88-89. Can the idea of a negligence/warranty hybrid, pioneered in *Greenman* by Traynor (who signed on to *Elmore*) bear the weight put on it by *Elmore?* Once *Greenman* was decided, should defendants have presumed that the California court would not be inclined to distinguish users from bystanders? Is the *Elmore* court on solid ground when it states that, as compared to a product user, a bystander is likely to be more vulnerable and in greater need of the protection afforded by the deterrence effects of liability and by an available deep pocket? Is it important that a bystander, unlike a purchaser or user of the product, does not even benefit from the product, or from the lower cost that might be associated with a less safe product?

Those jurisdictions that have directly addressed the *Elmore* question overwhelmingly have permitted bystanders to recover on a products liability theory, for reasons similar to those articulated by the court. On this question, courts seem to maintain a sense — one that traces back to *MacPherson* — that any vestiges of the old privity doctrine must be eliminated.

C.   The Second and Third Restatements of Torts

In 1965, on the heels of *Greenman*, the American Law Institute added a new section to the Second Restatement of Torts that endorsed recognition of products liability as a separate heading of tort law. This provision — Section 402A — proved to be extraordinarily influential. During the 1960s and 1970s, state courts overwhelmingly adopted some form of Section 402A either judicially or legislatively. Indeed, it is fair to say that Section 402A has set the basic terms for analysis in product liability cases since its enactment. Its "black letter" reads as follows:

§ 402A   SPECIAL LIABILITY OF SELLER OF PRODUCT FOR PHYSICAL HARM TO USER OR CONSUMER

(1) One who sells any product in a defective condition unreasonably dangerous to the user or consumer or to his property is subject to liability for physical harm thereby caused to the ultimate user or consumer, or to his property, if

(a) the seller is engaged in the business of selling such a product, and

(b) it is expected to and does reach the user or consumer without substantial change in the condition in which it is sold.

(2) The rule stated in Subsection (1) applies although

(a) the seller has exercised all possible care in the preparation and sale of his product, and

(b) the user or consumer has not bought the product from or entered into any contractual relation with the seller.

As will become apparent in several decisions reproduced below, this text was accompanied by substantial commentary from the Reporter, Dean Prosser, that addressed an array of issues and that provided a fairly detailed legal framework for treatment of product liability actions.

Although Section 402A's adoption was aided by the fact that it was "ahead of the curve," the fact that it was drafted just at the time that products liability law was getting under way also meant that it could not help but fail to anticipate and provide guidance on important developments in the field. For this reason, the courts and legislatures that adopted Section 402A have also embellished and revised it.

Cronin v. J.B.E. Olson Corp.
501 P.2d 1153 (Cal. 1972) (In Bank)

Sullivan, J.   In this products liability case, the principal question which we face is whether the injured plaintiff seeking recovery upon the theory of strict liability in tort must establish, among other facts, not only that the product contained a defect which proximately caused his injuries but also that such defective condition made the product unreasonably dangerous to the user or consumer. We have concluded that he need not do so. Accordingly, we find no error in the trial court's refusal to so instruct the jury. . . .

On October 3, 1966, plaintiff, a route salesman for Gravem-Inglis Bakery Co. (Gravem) of Stockton, was driving a bread delivery truck along a rural road in San Joaquin County. While plaintiff was attempting to pass a pick-up truck ahead of him, its driver made a sudden left turn, causing the pick-up to collide with the plaintiff's truck and forcing the latter off the road and into a ditch. . . . The impact broke an aluminum safety hasp which was located just behind the driver's seat and designed to hold the bread trays in place. The loaded trays, driven forward by the abrupt stop and impact of the truck, struck plaintiff in the back and hurled him through the windshield. He sustained serious personal injuries.

The truck, a one-ton Chevrolet stepvan with built-in bread racks, was one of several trucks sold to Gravem in 1957 by defendant Chase Chevrolet Company (Chase), not a party to this appeal. Upon receipt of Gravem's order, Chase purchased the trucks from defendant J. B. E. Olson Corporation (Olson), which acted as sales agent for the assembled vehicle, the chassis, body, and racks of which were manufactured by three subcontractors. The body of the van contained three aisles along which there were welded runners extending from the front to the rear of the truck. Each rack held ten bread trays from top to bottom and five trays deep; the trays slid forward into the cab or back through the rear door to facilitate deliveries.

Plaintiff brought the present action against Chase, Olson and General Motors Corporation alleging that the truck was unsafe for its intended use because of defects in its manufacture, in that the metal hasp was exceedingly porous, contained holes, pits and voids, and lacked sufficient tensile strength to withstand the impact. . . .

At the trial, plaintiff's expert testified, in substance, that the metal hasp broke, releasing the bread trays, because it was extremely porous and had a significantly lower tolerance to force than a non-flawed aluminum hasp would have had. The jury returned a verdict in favor of plaintiff and against Olson in the sum of $45,000 but in favor of defendant Chase. . . . Judgment was entered accordingly. This appeal by Olson followed.

Defendant attacks the sufficiency of the evidence to support the verdict and the trial court's instruction on strict liability. The challenge to the evidence is multipronged, claiming in effect that plaintiff produced no evidence on several essential issues. We first turn to this challenge, considering defendant's arguments in the order presented.

1.   SUFFICIENCY OF THE EVIDENCE

. . . [Defendant argues] that plaintiff's evidence failed to show any condition of the hasp which could be considered defective. The gist of the argument on this point appears to be that "defectiveness" cannot be properly determined without proof of some standard set by knowledgeable individuals for the manufacture and use of the particular part under scrutiny and that plaintiff's expert applied "his own unilateral standard" in giving his opinion that the hasp was defective. In the absence of an appropriate standard, so it is argued, all proof must fail.

The argument lacks merit. Gravem purchased the van and its bread racks from Chase as a unit. Since there were no standard bread racks available, Chase in turn ordered them from Olson according to the latter's blueprint, and left to Olson the manufacture of a safe set of bread racks. Olson admitted through the testimony of its vice president that the purpose of the locking device on the bread rack (of which the hasp was a part) was to hold the trays in place and that it knew that the van was to be driven on public highways. In short, the evidence shows that the intended purpose of the locking device was to keep the bread trays from moving forward into the driver's compartment as a result of any foreseeable movements of the van in highway travel.

The record shows that the hasp, because it was defective, did not fulfill this purpose. Plaintiff's expert testified that the broken hasp was "extremely porous and extremely defective" as it was full of holes, voids and cracks. These flaws were in the metal itself and resulted in the hasp's lowered tolerance to force. He further stated that this condition could not be attributed to prolonged use. This conclusion was buttressed by the expert's testimony that the break in the hasp was a tensile fracture caused by sudden force rather than a fatigue fracture, which is by nature progressive. The hasp failed because "(i)t was just a very, very bad piece of metal. Simply would not stand any force—reasonable forces at all."

Olson's argument that the van was built only for "normal" driving is unavailing. We agree that strict liability should not be imposed upon a manufacturer when injury results from a use of its product that is not reasonably foreseeable. Although a collision may not be the "normal" or intended use of a motor vehicle, vehicle manufacturers must take accidents into consideration as reasonably foreseeable occurrences involving their products. The design and manufacture of products should not be carried out in an industrial vacuum but with recognition of the realities of their every day use. . . .

Defendant claims that the hasp was not intended to be used without inspection and repair. However, the expert testimony offered by plaintiff established that the hasp failed because of internal holes, cracks and voids not visible to the naked eye. In any event, the mere failure to discover defects in the product is not a defense in a strict liability case. . . .

2. THE INSTRUCTION ON STRICT LIABILITY

Defendant's remaining contention requires us to probe the essential elements of products liability. It is claimed that in instructing the jury as to the issues upon which plaintiff had the burden of proof[5] the trial court erred by submitting a definition of strict liability which failed to include, as defendant requested,[6] the element that the defect found in the product be "unreasonably dangerous." It is urged that without this element, for which Olson finds support in section 402A of the Restatement Second of Torts (1965) and in recent decisions of this court, a seller would incur absolute liability for any injury proximately caused by an intended use of a product, regardless of the insignificance of the risk posed by the defect or the fortuity of the resulting harm. . . .

---

5. That instruction reads in pertinent part as follows:

In this action, the plaintiff has the burden of proving by a preponderance of the evidence all of the facts necessary to prove the following issues as to each defendant seller:

1. That the seller placed the equipment on the market for use under circumstances where he knew that such equipment would be used without inspection for defects;
2. That there was a defect in the manufacture or design of the equipment involved;
3. That the user was not aware of the said defect;
4. That the equipment was being used for the purpose for which it was designed and intended to be used;
5. That the injuries and damages complained of were proximately caused by the said defect;
6. The nature and extent of the injuries and damages sustained by the plaintiff.

6. The court refused defendant's instruction which provided in pertinent part that, "Plaintiff has burden of proving: . . . (2) That the defective condition made it unreasonably dangerous to the user or consumer. . . ."

Until our decision in Greenman v. Yuba Power Products, Inc., *supra*, 59 Cal. 2d 57, 27 Cal. Rptr. 697, 377 P.2d 897, strict liability for defective products was, in effect, imposed *sub silentio* by extension of the warranty doctrine. . . .

Greenman [imposed liability based simply on the presence of a defect in the design and manufacture of a product].

During the following decade the *Greenman* Rule has been made applicable to retailers; bailors and lessors; wholesalers and distributors; and sellers of mass-produced homes. Its protection has been extended to bystanders. But throughout the development of the *Greenman* rule we have said very little to explain what we meant in that case by a "defect" which would give rise to liability if injury were proximately caused thereby.

The addition of section 402A [to the Restatement Second of Torts] upon its publication in 1965 quickly exerted a pervasive influence on the decisional law. . . .

We have not hesitated to reach conclusions contrary to those set forth in Restatement section 402A, but we and the Courts of Appeal have more frequently adopted than challenged its basic outlines. In numerous cases this court and the Courts of Appeal have referred to the Restatement and the *Greenman* standards in tandem, as if they were for all practical purposes identical. But in none of these cases did the decision turn, as it does in the instant case, on whether the jury must decide that the injuries were caused by a "defective" product or by a product in a "defective condition unreasonably dangerous." . . .

We begin with section 402A itself. According to the official comment to the section, a "defective condition" is one "not contemplated by the ultimate consumer, which will be unreasonably dangerous to him." (Rest. 2d Torts, § 402A, com. g.) Comment i, defining "unreasonably dangerous," states, "The article sold must be dangerous to an extent beyond that which would be contemplated by the ordinary consumer who purchases it, with the ordinary knowledge common to the community as to its characteristics." Examples given in comment i make it clear that such innocuous products as sugar and butter, unless contaminated, would not give rise to a strict liability claim merely because the former may be harmful to a diabetic or the latter may aggravate the blood cholesterol level of a person with heart disease. Presumably such dangers are squarely within the contemplation of the ordinary consumer. Prosser, the reporter for the Restatement, suggests that the "unreasonably dangerous" qualification was added to foreclose the possibility that the manufacturer of a product with inherent possibilities for harm (for example, butter, drugs, whiskey and automobiles) would become "automatically responsible for all the harm that such things do in the world." (Prosser, *Strict Liability to the Consumer in California* (1966) 18 Hastings L.J. 9, 23.)

The result of the limitation, however, has not been merely to prevent the seller from becoming an insurer of his products with respect to all harm generated by their use. Rather, it has burdened the injured plaintiff with proof of an element which rings of negligence. As a result, if, in the view of the trier of fact, the "ordinary consumer" would have expected the defective condition of a product, the seller is not strictly liable regardless of the expectations of the injured plaintiff. If, for example, the "ordinary consumer" would have contemplated that Shopsmiths posed a risk of loosening their grip and letting the wood strike the operator, another *Greenman* might be denied recovery. In fact, it has been observed that the Restatement formulation of strict liability in practice rarely leads to a different conclusion than would have been reached under laws of negligence.

Of particular concern is the susceptibility of Restatement section 402A to a literal reading which would require the finder of fact to conclude that the product is, first, defective and, second, unreasonably dangerous. A bifurcated standard is of necessity more difficult to prove than a unitary one. But merely proclaiming that the phrase "defective condition unreasonably dangerous" requires only a single finding would not purge that phrase of its negligence complexion. We think that a requirement that a plaintiff also prove that the defect made the product "unreasonably dangerous" places upon him a significantly increased burden and represents a step backward in the area pioneered by this court.

We recognize that the words "unreasonably dangerous" may also serve the beneficial purpose of preventing the seller from being treated as the insurer of its products. However, we think that such protective end is attained by the necessity of proving that there was a defect in the manufacture or design of the product and that such defect was a proximate cause of the injuries. Although the seller should not be responsible for all injuries involving the use of its products, it should be liable for all injuries proximately caused by any of its products which are adjudged "defective."

We can see no difficulty in applying the *Greenman* formulation to the full range of products liability situations, including those involving "design defects." A defect may emerge from the mind of the designer as well as from the hand of the workman.

The *Greenman* case itself indicated that "(t)o establish the manufacturer's liability it was sufficient that plaintiff proved that he was injured while using the Shopsmith in a way it was intended to be used as a result of a defect in design and manufacture. . .", thereby suggesting the difficulty inherent in distinguishing between types of defects. Although it is easier to see the 'defect' in a single imperfectly fashioned product than in an entire line badly conceived, a distinction between manufacture and design defects is not tenable.

The most obvious problem we perceive in creating any such distinction is that thereafter it would be advantageous to characterize a defect in one rather than the other category. It is difficult to prove that a product ultimately caused injury because a widget was poorly welded — a defect in manufacture — rather than because it was made of inexpensive metal difficult to weld, chosen by a designer concerned with economy — a defect in design. The proof problem would, of course, be magnified when the article in question was either old or unique, with no easily available basis for comparison. We wish to avoid providing such a battleground for clever counsel. Furthermore, we find no reason why a different standard, and one harder to meet, should apply to defects which plague entire product lines. We recognize that it is more damaging to a manufacturer to have an entire line condemned, so to speak, for a defect in design, than a single product for a defect in manufacture. But the potential economic loss to a manufacturer should not be reflected in a different standard of proof for an injured consumer.

In summary, we have concluded that to require an injured plaintiff to prove not only that the product contained a defect but also that such defect made the product unreasonably dangerous to the user or consumer would place a considerably greater burden upon him than that articulated in *Greenman*. We believe the *Greenman* formulation is consonant with the rationale and development of products liability law in California because it provides a clear and simple test for determining whether the injured plaintiff is entitled to recovery. We are not persuaded to the contrary by the formulation of section 402A which inserts the factor of an "unreasonably dangerous" condition into the equation of products liability.

We conclude that the trial court did not err by refusing to instruct the jury that plaintiff must establish that the defective condition of the product made it unreasonably dangerous to the user or consumer.

The judgment is affirmed.

NOTES AND QUESTIONS

1. *The Third Restatement.* In 1998, the ALI published a new set of provisions on products liability as a separate part of the Restatement, entitled the Restatement (Third) of Torts: Products Liability. Some states have adopted key provisions of the Third Restatement, while others have declined to. In some instances, this document elaborates or confirms the Section 402A approach; for other issues, it rejects or modifies Section 402A. Its most basic provision, however, at least nominally tracks the basic contours of Section 402A.

§ 1. LIABILITY OF COMMERCIAL SELLER OR DISTRIBUTOR FOR HARM CAUSED BY DEFECTIVE PRODUCTS

One engaged in the business of selling or otherwise distributing products who sells or distributes a defective product is subject to liability for harm to persons or property caused by the defect.

Restatement (Third) of Torts: Products Liability §1 (1998).

2. *Defect and Unreasonable Dangerousness in the Third Restatement.* The Reporters for the Third Restatement, Professors Henderson and Twerski, made several provocative decisions, many of which have received substantial attention from legal commentators and courts. (See *infra* Sections III through V). One decision that has received relatively little attention is their *deliberate and explicit reintroduction of a second filter, beyond "defect" itself*. Thus, according to Section 2(b) of the new Restatement, a defect in the *design* of a product, to be actionable, *must render the product "not reasonably safe."* The Reporters point out in notes to this provision that several courts have utilized the "not reasonably safe" formulation, and also that this formulation is slightly more neutral

than Section 402A's "unreasonably dangerous" requirement—the latter (unlike the former) may tend to lead juries to believe the defect must render the product extremely dangerous. At the end of the day, however, it is hard to resist the conclusion that the addition of "not reasonably safe"—beyond defect itself—flies in the face of decisions such as *Cronin*. Moreover, it is quite clear that most jurisdictions do not expressly include such a phrase in their formulations of the standard of liability in products cases. The Reporters' treatment of the standard for defectiveness is discussed in more detail in Section III, *infra*.

3. *Defect and Unreasonable Danger in* Cronin. What is the putative defect in *Cronin?* How does the court describe it? Assuming that the hasp was defective, would it be appropriate to describe the product as unreasonably dangerous in light of that defect? Alternatively, would it be fair to say that the defective hasp rendered the product "not reasonably safe"? Is the (assumed) defectiveness of the hasp, coupled with the plaintiff's injuries, a good enough reason to impose liability on the defendant? If so, would there be equal or nearly equal reason to impose liability even if the hasp itself had not been defective? Which of the *Escola* rationales warrant liability in *Cronin?* Is its holding more in the spirit of warranty or negligence? Does the answer to that question bear on whether there should be a separate "unreasonably dangerous" requirement?

4. *Comment i and Consumer Expectations.* Comment i to Section 402A, referred to in *Cronin*, is the origin of what has come to be called the *consumer expectations test* for product defects. The *Cronin* court contends that Prosser's purpose in writing comment i was to make it clear that Section 402A was not intended to create liability for products that were generally known to be dangerous or unhealthful, such as sugar and butter. Other examples referred to in comment i include "good" (i.e., ordinary, untainted) tobacco and properly functioning guns. What do you think the rationale might have been for excluding such products from the domain of Section 402A? Do you suppose a political decision was made to leave certain products untouched, so that strict liability could more easily achieve acceptance? Or do you think that the "consumer expectations" criterion seemed plausible for general reasons of policy and principle, and that items such as sugar, butter, tobacco, and guns were appropriately isolated for special treatment?

5. *Consumer Expectations and Negligence.* *Cronin* insinuates that comment i's reference to a product "more dangerous than reasonable consumers expect" had the unintended effect of introducing what appeared to be a negligence standard back into products liability law. Observing that a central aim of products liability law was to ease the demands that negligence law placed on victims of product-related injuries, the court thus concluded that comment i should not be read to require products liability plaintiffs routinely to prove that the product in question was more dangerous than the reasonable consumer would expect. Is this argument sound?

6. *Dangers and Obvious Defects*: Luque. In Luque v. McLean, 501 P.2d 1163 (Cal. 1972), decided the same day as *Cronin*, the California

Supreme Court rejected a lower court's holding that a plaintiff cannot recover in a design defect case unless he can prove that he was *unaware* that the product contained the defect at issue. In effect, *Luque* decided that it is possible for an obviously dangerous design attribute nevertheless to be a design defect. The plaintiff in that case recovered damages from the manufacturer of a lawnmower that lacked a guard and thereby permitted access to the mower's blades. Plaintiff, who was injured when he reached his fingers under the moving blades, was permitted to proceed with his claim.

II.   BASICS OF A PRODUCTS LIABILITY CLAIM

Neither the Second nor the Third Restatement expressly breaks down products liability claims by reference to the elements that constitute a prima facie case. Some jurisdictions offer such formulations, but these vary, at least superficially. We offer the following reconstruction of the elements of a products liability claim as an aid to analysis, not as an effort to mimic standard judicial usage:

Products Liability: Prima Facie Case

Actor *A* is subject to liability to person *P* in products liability if:
1. *P* has suffered an *injury;*
2. *A sold* a *product;*
3. *A* is a commercial *seller of such products;*
4. at the time it was sold by *A*, the product was in a *defective condition;* and
5. the defect functioned as an actual and proximate *cause* of *P*'s injury.

It may be instructive to compare this list of elements to the elements of a prima facie case of negligence. The injury and causation elements — 1 and 3, respectively — are plainly parallel to those of negligence. These concepts are examined later in the chapter. Nominally, at least, the duty and the breach elements are also plainly absent. In their place, we see three new elements: (2) the sale of a product; (3) by a seller; (4) in a defective condition.

A.   What Counts as an Injury?

Before turning to consider the doctrinally novel aspects of products liability causes of action, it is worth pausing to emphasize an obvious point that might nonetheless cause confusion if ignored. When complainants file products liability actions, they overwhelmingly do so to obtain redress for physical harm caused by product defects. This pattern is not entirely coincidental. As a rough-and-ready rule, product liability doctrine, like negligence law, is much more reticent in recognizing claims for other sorts of injuries allegedly flowing from product defects, such as intangible economic loss.

A particularly important question as to the injury element concerns whether the owner of a product can invoke products liability law to recover for a defect that causes damage to, or the destruction of, the *product itself*. The general rule, subject to exceptions that vary by jurisdiction, is that the owner cannot, and is instead left to the protections he was able to obtain in the contract of sale via express or implied warranties. This is sometimes dubbed the "economic loss" rule. *See, e.g.*, East River S.S. Corp. v. Transamerica Delaval, Inc., 476 U.S. 858 (1986) (shipowner complaining of damage to turbines caused by a defect in them must proceed in contract rather than admiralty/tort). By contrast, tangible property damage caused by a product defect to property *other than the product itself* is ordinarily actionable in products liability. If, for example, a defective water heater causes the plaintiff's house to burn down, the plaintiff can sue for the damage to her house in products liability.

Should products liability law be available on more or less the same terms as negligence law to support a limited set of claims for intangible economic loss (e.g., loss of future revenue) and "pure" emotional distress? As to the latter, suppose that in Dillon v. Legg, *supra*, Chapter 10, the driver was not careless, but instead ran over the plaintiff's daughter in the presence of the plaintiff because of a defect in the car he was driving. If California negligence law is prepared, in the right circumstances, to permit the plaintiff/parent to recover for "bystander" emotional distress from a careless driver, is there any reason it should not permit the plaintiff to recover against a manufacturer whose defective product causes emotional distress under roughly the same circumstances? *See* Shepard v. Superior Court, 142 Cal. Rptr. 612, 615 (Ct. App. 1977) (reinstating the products liability claims of the parents and brother of the decedent, who witnessed her fall to her death from a car in which they were driving, allegedly because of a defective door lock).

B.   What Is a "Product"?

Products liability, unsurprisingly, concerns injuries caused by *products*. As explained succinctly by the Third Restatement, "[s]ervices, even when provided commercially, are not products." Restatement (Third) of Torts: Products Liability § 19(b) (1998). Were the law otherwise, products liability could end up swallowing a great deal of tort law. For example, if healthcare services that involved the use of objects and materials were deemed to constitute the sale of a "product" to the patient, medical malpractice law would be dramatically altered.

Although it excludes the provision of services, the domain of products liability law remains vast, applying not only to foods and beverages, automobiles, and power tools, but also to large industrial machines, kitchen appliances, toys, recreational and sports equipment, pharmaceuticals, chemicals sold for commercial or residential use, certain medical devices, cosmetics and toiletries, airplanes, boats, motorcycles, protective gear, scientific equipment, packaging materials, farming equipment, pesticides,

chemical treatments, and so on. The following are offered as rough guidelines for identifying the boundary lines between products and non-prod-
ucts for purposes of determining the scope of products liability law. *Note
that the issue of whether something counts as a product may come out
differently if the question is being asked for some other purpose or in some
other area of the law.*

- As an item comes more closely to taking the form of *real property*, it is unlikely to qualify as a product. Thus, parcels of land
  and individual buildings and houses traditionally would not be
  deemed products. However, mass-produced or prefabricated
  homes are frequently considered products. *See, e.g.*, Oliver v.
  Superior Court, 259 Cal. Rptr. 160 (Ct. App. 1989) (distinguishing mass producers from isolated construction); *see generally*
  Restatement (Third), *supra*, § 19(a) & cmt. e.
- *Human body parts*, tissues, blood, blood products, and cells are
  usually not considered products. Restatement (Third), *supra*,
  § 19(c). As to blood and blood products, numerous jurisdictions
  have "blood shield laws," which eliminate strict liability for these
  products, and impose other liability limitations. As to other sorts of
  products involving human tissue, courts tend to exempt them from
  the reach of products liability law. *See, e.g.*, Cryolife, Inc. v. Superior
  Court, 2 Cal Rptr. 3d 396 (Ct. App. 2003) (tissue bank that provided
  tendon from cadaver exempted from products liability).
- Similarly, *live animals* sold as pets or livestock are frequently not
  considered products, though courts differ on this depending on
  the context in which the injury caused by the animal comes about.
  Compare Blaha v. Stuard, 640 N.W. 2d 85 (S.D. 2002) (dog that bit
  plaintiff not a "product") *with* Worrell v. Sachs, 563 A.2d 1387
  (Conn. Super. 1989) (dog that carried a disease when sold qualifies as "product").
- *Textual material* — such as encyclopedias, guides, or books —
  are generally not considered products, although maps and charts
  are sometimes held to fall within the ambit of products liability.
  See, e.g., Artiglio v. General Elec. Co., 71 Cal. Rptr. 2d 817 (Cal.
  App. 1998) (outlining the distinction and holding that an inaccu-
  rate map used by a pilot was a "product").
- *Intangibles*, such as electricity and x-rays, reside at the margin.
  They generally are not treated as products, but they occasionally
  qualify. *See* Restatement (Third), *supra*, § 19(a) & cmt (d).
- *Used products* are not normally subject to strict products liability,
  although detailed doctrine now exists that qualifies this rule. *See*
  Restatement (Third), *supra*, § 8 (Liability of Commercial Seller or
  Distributor of Defective Used Products).
- Finally, some jurisdictions deem a type of item to be a "product"
  but nevertheless have made a deliberate decision to *exempt* the
  product from the reach of product liability laws. Prescription
  drugs and vaccines are common examples of this category. See
  infra Section IV.

What is it about products—as opposed to services, real property, words, and activities—that has led our legal system (and those of dozens of other nations) to develop a special system of law leaning toward strict liability?

C.   Who or What Is a "Seller"?

From *Winterbottom* and *MacPherson* through *Henningsen* and *Escola* up to the present day, a critical question in litigation over injuries caused by products has been that of who can be sued. Cases such as *MacPherson*, *Escola*, and *Henningsen* direct our attention to the manufacturers of products. So does a great deal of high-profile litigation in recent years, such as litigation against companies that manufacture cigarettes or diet drugs, breast implants, or SUVs. But products liability law extends far beyond manufacturers, and always has. Indeed, as we saw from *Elmore*, retailers are liable under strict products liability. Thus, a consumer injured by a defective lawnmower purchased at a local hardware store can sue the local hardware store under a products liability theory because it sold the lawnmower. That consumer can also sue the manufacturer of the lawnmower, who likely sold the lawnmower either directly to the local hardware store, or through a distributor or distributors. If it was through distributors, the distributors are also "sellers" subject to products liability law. Indeed, while we normally think of the classic antecedents of products liability as eliminating privity, it is important to see that products liability law creates causes of action against various actors within a distributive chain. *See generally* Restatement (Third) of Torts: Products Liability § 20 ("Definition of 'One Who Sells or Otherwise Distributes'") (1998).

1. *Sellers and Strict Liability.* Because products liability applies to sellers, it often attaches liability to a person or entity that played no role in the design, manufacture, or inspection of the product. For this reason alone, many successful products liability actions really do impose a form of liability without fault. The Ford dealer who sells a new model of car with a flaw in the design of the transmission system will be held liable if the jury finds the car defective. Whether the dealer knew or could have known of the flaw, was entitled to rely on Ford's general reputation for quality, or had any ability to inspect or test the model for defects, is irrelevant. As we will see, liability for defectively designed products also attaches to manufacturers. But when it does, it is not as obviously a form of liability without fault, if it is that at all. Indeed, the issue of how "strict" liability is for design defects is the subject of intensive debate. Yet for large numbers of bread-and-butter cases in which sellers have little or no direct control over product quality, the phrase "strict liability" fits well. (Perhaps unsurprisingly, trade groups comprised of retailers have recently achieved some success obtaining legislative reforms that scale back their liability under such circumstances.)

2. *Sellers and the Law of Warranty.* Because of the fact that liability is placed on *sellers*, products liability law has an enduring—and often

legally important—relation to contract law and other forms of commercial law. Several states in fact locate their products liability law, in part, within their versions of the Uniform Commercial Code. Even those few jurisdictions that lack a tort of strict products liability have fairly close analogues within their contract law. *See, e.g.,* N.C.G.S. § 25-2-314 (implied warranty of merchantability attaches to products). In addition, many states have overlapping statutory law that provides what are essentially products liability actions under consumer protection laws or deceptive trade practices statutes. Such laws provided much of the impetus for state-government initiated tobacco products liability litigation that took place in the 1990s.

3. *Distribution Chains and Indemnification.* Distribution chains are often long, wide, and complicated by a variety of legal and commercial variables. For example, suppose a McDonald's franchise in a town in Illinois sells a "Happy Meal" to a family with a small child, and a component of the toy that comes with the Happy Meal injures the child. The distributional chain might include the franchise, McDonald's, the distributor that sold the toy to McDonald's, the manufacturer of the toy, and the manufacturer of the component of the toy that injured the child. There likely will be contracts among these companies that include indemnification clauses—provisions that permit one to sue another to recover costs expended in litigation and liability for injuries stemming from the products supplied. In fact, the capacity for members of such a distributive chain to insure themselves, and to negotiate with one another over indemnification, is among the reasons that our system does not consider strict liability for (not-at-fault) sellers to be inherently inequitable.

4. *Sellers, Not Buyers.* Early in Chapter 2 we saw that, thanks to decisions such as *MacPherson*, negligence law permits not just buyers of products, but also users of products, to sue sellers in negligence for product-related injuries. Products liability applies at least as broadly. Thus, despite its emphasis on "sellers," products liability law *does not* require the plaintiff to be a buyer of the product. Indeed, as Elmore v. American Motor Corp. indicated, the plaintiff need not even be a *user* of the product; a bystander hit by a defective car can sue sellers of the car. On this issue, jurisdictions tend to speak in the language of "easy duty" negligence cases, requiring only that the plaintiff be within a class of persons foreseeably put at risk by the defective product.

5. *In the Business Of.* A person or entity who sells a product does not automatically qualify as a "seller" of that product for purposes of products liability law. She must also be "in the business of selling (or marketing)" such products. Thus, a lawyer who contracts to purchase a new car, but then contracts to sell it to his neighbor before ever using it, would not qualify as a "seller" for products liability law. Similarly, the owner of pizza parlor that sells a brand new car that she never used would not count as a "seller" of the car (although, of course, she would count as a seller of pizzas and soft drinks).

6. *What Constitutes Selling.* It is enough to establish that an actor has "sold" a product if the actor took steps to place the product on the

market, or figured in the distributional chain through which the product is placed on the market. Thus, a sale can occur even if the actor did not transfer legal title to the product, and even if he did not enter a bargain in which ownership was transferred for consideration. So, for example, an automobile company or dealer cannot avoid products liability law by leasing the product, rather than selling it. Likewise, a distributor cannot avoid products liability law by organizing its transactions so that it never actually holds title to the products. Courts will look to the underlying reality of the transaction, and ask whether the defendant has placed the product in the stream of commerce. *See, e.g.,* Baker v. Promack Prods. West, Inc., 692 S.W.2d 844 (Tenn. 1985) (applying strict liability to lessors).

Similarly, an actual transfer or sale is not necessary to trigger products liability law, if the nature of the plaintiff's contact with the product is sufficiently close to the normal domain of the marketplace. Thus, just as a shopping mall owner would be liable to a visitor injured by an unsafe condition in the mall under an "invitee" theory even if the plaintiff did not actually come to the mall with the intention of purchasing anything, so a car manufacturer would be liable under a products liability theory for a plaintiff injured by a defect in a "demonstrator" car or a "loaner" — actual sale or transfer is not necessary.

7. *Sales versus Service.* In a number of contexts, a business or professional engaged in a service will utilize or sell a product to a consumer as part of the service. For example, a surgeon who inserts a plastic hip joint into a patient in a meaningful sense delivers the hip joint to the patient. Still, as noted above, if the courts deem the defendant to be engaged primarily in a service, rather than a sale, they will not treat the defendant as a seller of the product for products liability law. *See, e.g.,* Ayyash v. Henry Ford Health Sys., 533 N.W.2d 353 (Mich. App. 1995) (declining to apply strict products liability law to a hospital that implanted a defective jaw implant and relying upon the sales/service distinction), *app. denied,* 549 N.W.2d 561 (Mich. 1996).

8. *Component Parts.* If a component part — such as a bicycle tire — is defective, and because of the defect the larger product of which it is a part injures the plaintiff, the seller and manufacturer of the component part will be liable. However, there are numerous cases in which the component manufacturer is able to demonstrate that there was nothing intrinsically defective in *its* product; the problem was simply that the larger product did not function optimally with that particular component — for example, the bicycle manufacturer should have chosen a different wheel rim to match with the tire in question. The component part manufacturer or supplier in this setting frequently will avoid liability. *See, e.g.,* Artiglio v. General Elec. Co., 71 Cal. Rptr. 2d 817 (Cal. App. 1998) (manufacturer of silicone for silicone breast implants not subject to strict liability for defective breast implants); In re TMJ Implants Prods. Liab. Litig., 97 F.3d 1050 (8th Cir. 1996) (limiting liability of suppliers of Teflon to be used in jaw implants). However, when the plaintiff is able to argue that defendant had an ongoing relationship with the manufacturer of the larger part, and/or the defendant had adequate awareness of and involvement with the design or manufacture

of the product in which its part was being integrated, the question of whether the component manufacturer will face liability becomes much closer. *See* Restatement (Third), *supra*, § 5(b) (a seller or distributor of a component may be liable if it "substantially participates in the integration of the component into the design of the product" and "the integration of the component causes the product to be defective").

D. *The Key to Products Liability: Defect*

A cause of action for products liability exists only if the product in question is defective, and only if the defect that caused the injury was present in the product *when sold or* marketed by the defendant. While there are frequently important issues surrounding whether the product was defective when sold, the more significant issue is what counts as a "defect." Indeed, this is probably the single most important question in products liability law. Although the court in *Cronin, supra*, expressed skepticism about creating separate categories of defect, U.S. courts, including the California Supreme Court, have since adopted a *three-fold* classification that identifies three different kinds of defects: *manufacturing defects, design defects,* and *warning (or instructional) defects*. None of these labels perfectly captures the distinctive features of each category. For now, the following tentative description will suffice:

Manufacturing Defect. A particular product (e.g., Ms. Smith's 1999 Toyota Camry) has a manufacturing defect if it diverges from the manufacturer's own specifications for the product. *Escola*'s flawed soda bottle is a perfect example of a manufacturing defect: Coca Cola designed and filled its bottles in a manner designed to *prevent* them from exploding. Although the phrase "manufacturing defect" appropriately calls to mind an isolated "lemon" that comes off the assembly line in a substandard condition, it applies more broadly. Thus, an item need not be mass-produced to count as a product with a manufacturing defect. "Jean-Claude's Frozen Quiches" might be prepared lovingly and individually in Jean-Claude's small bakery, but if one of his pies contains a pin, it would still count as a product with a manufacturing defect. Second, the defect will be charged to the manufacturer so long as it emerges while the product is in its control or possession. If an automobile suffers a bent axle as it is being rolled off the manufacturer's car carrier and onto the dealer's lot, it will be deemed to have a manufacturing defect even though the problem developed after the product was assembled.

Design Defect. Design defects inhere in an entire line of products. The idea is that there is a flaw in the plan or specifications for the product. The flaw (or flaws) alleged may be small or technical, or may go to the essence of the product. Thus, for example, the allegation in *Greenman* that the set screws were too small to hold items in the Shopsmith was an allegation of a somewhat technical design defect. By contrast, one of the central allegations in recent litigation over surgical gloves made of latex is that the very idea of using latex as the primary material for such gloves is unacceptably risky given the severe allergic responses that some persons exposed to latex may suffer. This too is a design defect claim. There are many levels in between these two extremes. Plaintiffs commonly assert several design defects, or several reasons that together support the finding of design defect.

The issue of what criteria should be used by the factfinder to ascertain whether a design is defective is probably the most controversial and hotly debated question within products liability doctrine. Indeed, the next section is devoted almost entirely to this question. But several factors tend to play at least some role in most or all jurisdictions. These include: the significance of the risks of physical injury posed by the particular design; how ordinary consumers would expect the product to function; and whether there is a feasible, safer, and affordable alternative design. The task of fashioning these and other factors into an operative legal test has turned out to be a singularly important question in products liability law, with California and the American Law Institute playing leading roles in the debate. These issues are explored in Section III, *infra*.

Failure to Warn or Instruct.   The term *defect* and the phrase "defective condition" are well suited to the sort of flaw found in an exploding bottle or a power tool with screws that are too small to render it safe for normal use. The same cannot be said of the phrases "warning defects" or "failure to warn." Nonetheless, these phrases are used in the law to describe a distinct category of product defect. A product is defective for lack of adequate warnings when safety requires that the product be sold with a warning, but the product is sold without a warning (or without an adequate warning). A mislabeled product — paint thinner labeled as vodka, for example — would count as a product that is defective because of its misrepresentation as to the contents of the bottle. So, too, would a bottle of medication that is accompanied by dosage instructions incorrectly indicating that the user ingest an amount that is ten times larger than the proper dosage. Another classic failure to warn case might involve a microwave oven that fails to warn that heating metal objects inside it can cause an explosion or a fire. In all these cases, there is some language of warning or instruction that ought to have been included, and was not. The "defect" is the omission of the language.

Despite the fact that the word *defect* applies awkwardly to these cases, failure to warn claims are as firmly grounded in the law of products liability as are claims for manufacturing and design defects. As such, they generally require proof of the same basic elements as these other claims, are subject to the same defenses, and extend to the same sorts of actors. Moreover, as with manufacturing and design defects, one focuses on the product as sold or distributed, not on the conduct of the defendant. Failure to warn is examined in Section V of this chapter.

The tripartite division among kinds of defect has become a central feature of U.S. products liability law, and it is a goal of this chapter to clarify these divisions. Nevertheless, it is worth keeping in mind that the early products liability cases that you read in Section I of this chapter drew no such divisions, and that U.S. products liability law did not generally do so until the 1970s. Likewise, it is worth noting that products liability law in other nations does not necessarily utilize these categories. Thus, even though these categorizations will and should become part of your thinking about products liability law, it is worth remembering that they are no less a doctrinal construction than the various doctrines encountered in the law of negligence and battery, and that there are other ways to "slice the bologna."

In real-world products liability cases, it is common for a plaintiff to assert claims that fall within two or all three of the foregoing categories. Part of the skill involved in lawyering these cases involves selecting a plausible categorization, or refuting such a selection. The following case presents allegations and discussions of all three types of defect. The notes that follow provide greater detail on manufacturing defects (and other issues that arise in the case). Sections III-V of this chapter provide greater detail on design defects and failure to warn.

Gower v. Savage Arms, Inc.
166 F. Supp. 2d 240 (E.D. Pa. 2001)

McLaughlin, J.   The plaintiffs, John and Debra Gower, seek to hold Savage Arms, Inc. and Savage Sports Corporation liable . . . under a theory of "successor liability" for injuries John Gower sustained when his hunting rifle discharged inadvertently, shooting him in the foot. Gower alleges that the rifle was defective as follows. First, it was designed so that it could not be unloaded with the safety engaged (the "unloading defect"). Second, it was designed without a detent system, which would have made the safety mechanism more user-friendly ("the detent defect"). Third, it was manufactured with a metal ridge that impaired the functioning of the safety mechanism (the "manufacturing defect"). Fourth, it was not accompanied by adequate warnings. . . .

The Court grants the defendants' motion with respect to . . . the "unloading defect" [and] insufficient warnings, claims. The Court denies the defendants' motion for summary judgment with respect to successor liability. The Court further denies the defendants' motion for summary judgment with respect to the strict liability claims concerning the "detent defect" and the manufacturing defect . . . without prejudice to renew these arguments after the Court has reached a decision on the pending motion to exclude the testimony of plaintiffs' expert, James Mason.

I. FACTS IN THE LIGHT MOST FAVORABLE TO THE PLAINTIFFS

A. THE INCIDENT

The plaintiffs claim damages for injuries sustained in a hunting accident in 1997. On December 15, 1997, John Gower was hunting with his two brothers, Clark and Craig, and with his brother-in-law, Robert Swan, at Long Pond, Pennsylvania. They spent much of the day hunting for deer in the woods. At approximately 4:30 P.M., after a day of hunting, the plaintiff left the woods and headed toward the truck in which they had driven to Long Pond. As he emerged from the woods, he turned around for one more visual sweep of the woods and field. Gower was preparing to unload his gun when the gun discharged, shooting him in the foot.

Gower was wearing thick gloves, and his fingers were inside the trigger guard when the gun discharged. At the time of the discharge the plaintiff had not taken the gun off the "safe" position. The rifle was designed so as not to fire when in the "safe" position.

B.   The Rifle

The rifle at issue in this lawsuit is a Savage Model 99C lever action repeating center fire rifle, serial number E850706. It was manufactured in or around 1987 by Savage Industries, Inc. The plaintiff, John Gower, purchased the rifle in October, 1989 from the Quarry Sporting Goods Store. . . .

According to the uncontradicted testimony of Savage Industries' Inspections Supervisor Mark Kwiecien, who is now a Quality Assurance Coordinator for Savage Arms, all guns shipped out by Savage Industries in 1987 were shipped in boxes containing safety manuals. It is also uncontradicted that John Gower purchased the gun without its box and did not receive a safety manual with the gun. As confirmed by expert inspections after the incident and conceded by both parties at oral argument, the rifle was not working properly at the time of the accident. The safety mechanism could only be placed in the "safe" position with more than the usually required force.

C.   Corporate History

The rifle at issue in this law-suit was manufactured by Savage Industries, Inc. in 1987. In February 1988, Savage Industries filed for bankruptcy. Around this time, the owners of Savage Industries set up a company, named Savage Arms. In May, 1989 Savage Industries filed a motion in Bankruptcy Court to sell its remaining assets. In July of 1989, Savage Industries sold four of its eleven product lines, including the Model 99 product line, together with associated tooling, machinery, trademarks, trade-names, patents, trade secrets, and goodwill, to Savage Arms.

[Although successor companies are sometimes not obligated for torts committed by their predecessors, the court held that a jury could find, under a doctrine called the "product line" exception, that Savage Arms was liable for injuries caused by a defective rifle manufactured by Savage Industries, Inc. — Eds.] . . .

III.   DISCUSSION

C.   STRICT LIABILITY

The Pennsylvania Supreme Court has adopted Section 402A of the Restatement (Second) of Torts. . . . In order to succeed in a claim brought under 402A, the plaintiffs must show (1) that the product was defective, (2) that the defect existed at the time the product left the manufacturer's hands, and (3) that the defect caused the plaintiff's injury.

1.   *The Alleged Defects*

The plaintiffs allege the following four defects: (1) the gun was not accompanied by warnings; (2) the gun was defectively designed in that it cannot be unloaded while in the "safe" position (the "unloading defect"); (3) the gun was defectively designed in that it did not incorporate a detent system, which would have made the safety mechanism more "user-friendly" (the "detent defect"); and (4) the gun was defectively manufactured with a metal ridge that caused the gun's safety mechanism to fail over time (the "manufacturing defect").

a.   Insufficient Warnings

The Pennsylvania courts have recognized a cause of action under [Restatement (Second) §] 402A for insufficient warnings. For an insufficient warnings claim, the plaintiffs must establish the same three elements required under 402A for design defect claims, including causation.

The Court grants the defendant's motion for summary judgment with respect to the plaintiffs' insufficient warnings claim, because the plaintiffs have failed to present any evidence that the lack of instructions caused Gower's injury. In Sherk v. Daisy-Heddon, 498 Pa. 594, 450 A.2d 615 (1982), the Court held that the manufacturer of a BB gun was not liable for injuries sustained when the plaintiff fired the gun at a friend:

> Where, as here, the lethal propensity of a gun was known or should have been known to the user, liability cannot be imposed upon the manufacturer merely because the manufacturer allegedly has failed to warn of that propensity.

Id. at 618. The Court reasoned that insufficient warnings could not be the cause of the injury, because the plaintiff had independent knowledge of the gun's dangerous propensities.

John Gower had extensive training in the use and safety of firearms while in the United States military. In his deposition, John Gower testified that he was familiar with the Ten Commandments of Firearm Safety, one of which states: "Never point your gun at anything you don't want to shoot."

Gower also testified that he made a practice of complying with the No. 1 Commandment, which reads: "Don't rely on your gun's safety. Treat every gun as if it were loaded and ready to fire." The Court finds that Gower was aware of the dangers inherent in the use of a gun and that the holding of *Sherk* is applicable.

In addition, the plaintiffs have not provided any evidence that the gun was lacking instructions when it left the manufacturer's hands. Mark Kwiecien has testified that every rifle left the manufacturing plant with a manual. Gower has testified that he did not receive a manual when he purchased the gun from Quarry Sporting Goods off the rack (i.e. not in its original box). Gower has not produced any evidence, however, to contradict Kwiecien's statement that all guns were shipped with manuals. According to comment "n" to Section 388 of the Restatement (Second) of Torts, a supplier's duty to warn is discharged by providing information to third parties upon whom it can reasonably rely to communicate the information to the ultimate users of the product. . . .

b. The "Unloading Defect"

The plaintiffs allege that the Model 99 rifle is defectively designed in that the shooter must take the firearm off safety in order to unload the chamber. John Gower claims not to have been unloading the gun when it discharged, however. Therefore, the fact that the gun could not be unloaded while in the "safe" position is not causally related to Gower's injury. . . .

c. The "Detent Defect"

The plaintiffs' expert, James Mason, alleges that "lack of positive detents on the safety slide will leave an operator with the impression that the safety is 'on' when indeed the gun is ready to fire." According to James Mason's expert report, a safety mechanism with a detent system would make it easier for a user to tell whether the safety had been engaged, because the position of the safety would be more clearly visible and because the mechanism would make an audible clicking noise when placed into the "safe" position. A detent system would also prevent the safety from slipping into the "fire" position.

[The only evidence before the court on the issue of a defect in the design of the gun was the report of plaintiff's expert.] The Court notes that, in his report, James Mason described the "exemplar trigger system" as "adequate" and found only that the detent would make the rifle more "user friendly." On this basis, it seems unlikely that Mason's report would support a finding that the gun without the detent is [defective in design]. Nonetheless, the Court declines to rest its decision on this basis for two reasons.

First, the defendant, who bears the burden of proof for this threshold determination as to whether the product is [defective in design] has provided no evidence that would enable the Court to make this determination.

Second, the Court is unwilling to rely solely on Mason's report in making this determination without first deciding the defendants' pending *Daubert* motion regarding Mason. Mason's report does not clearly distinguish between the "detent defect" and the "manufacturing defect" or between the factual bases for his views on either one. Due to this lack of clarity in the writing of the report, the Court is unwilling to make a decision at this stage without holding a hearing in which Mason can more clearly explain the bases for and the meaning of his report. . . .

The Court, therefore, denies the defendant's summary judgment motion with respect to the "detent defect" claim without prejudice to the defendant to renew the motion after the Court's decision on the *Daubert* motion.

d.   The "Manufacturing Defect"

The plaintiffs allege that there was a manufacturing defect in the rifle in the form of a metal ridge that affected the functioning of the safety mechanism:

> The subject safety button has a shallow ridge on the bottom of its rear radius that contacts the rising radius of the slot. This contact limits (to about .133-inch) the free, unobstructed movement of the button to the rear when applying the safety. This defective condition was present at the time of manufacture.

For purposes of summary judgment, the question of whether the ridge rendered the gun defective is not difficult to answer. In Dambacher v. Mallis, 336 Pa. Super. 22, 485 A.2d 408 (1984), the court stated: "In a manufacturing defect case, the question whether the product is defective is relatively simple. Since the allegation is that something went awry in the manufacturing process, so that, for example, the product lacked a component it should have had, the finder of fact need only compare the product that caused the injury with other products that were manufactured according to specifications." *Id.* at 426. Mason undertook such a comparison and found that the subject rifle had the above-mentioned metal ridge, whereas an exemplar rifle of the same model did not.

. . . For the above reason, the Court denies the defendant's summary judgment motion with respect to the "manufacturing defect" claim without prejudice to the defendant to renew the motion after the Court's decision on the *Daubert* motion. . . .

NOTES AND QUESTIONS

1. Gower's *Subsequent History*. A subsequent unpublished opinion reveals later developments in *Gower*. As the court seems to have anticipated, the testimony of Mason, plaintiff's expert witness on the issue of design defect, was deemed inadmissible, and summary judgment was granted on the design defect claim. For this and other reasons the only issue left for trial was Gower's manufacturing defect claim.

2. *Proving Manufacturing Defect.* Fortunately for Gower, he appears to have faced a relatively straightforward task in proving that the gun contained a manufacturing defect. The dangerous feature of the rifle was visually identified by an expert, and the demonstration that it was a manufacturing defect was accomplished by comparing it to a prototype in which the defective feature did not exist. Proving a manufacturing defect is often not so easy, as the plaintiff in *Escola* learned. (Recall that she was unable to prove what went wrong with the bottle.) This helps explain why Escola's lawyer was drawn to *res ipsa loquitur*, as was the majority of the California Supreme Court. Does the advent of strict liability eliminate the need for a doctrine like *res ipsa?* The short answer is no. While the concept of manufacturing defect eliminates the need to identify unreasonable conduct on the part of the defendant, it substitutes its own question: What exactly was defective about the product? Particularly in cases in which the harmful product exploded or was destroyed or is missing, proof problems can be daunting. To this end, jurisdictions permit circumstantial evidence to prove manufacturing defect, as Section 3 of the Restatement (Third)'s provisions on products liability indicates:

§ 3. CIRCUMSTANTIAL EVIDENCE SUPPORTING INFERENCE OF PRODUCT DEFECT

It may be inferred that the harm sustained by the plaintiff was caused by a product defect existing at the time of sale or distribution, without proof of a specific defect, when the incident that harmed the plaintiff:

(a) was of a kind that ordinarily occurs as a result of a product defect; and

(b) was not, in the particular case, solely the result of causes other than product defect existing at the time of sale or distribution.

The Reporters note that Section 3 will most commonly apply to claims of manufacturing defect rather than design defect or failure to warn. *Compare* Speller v. Sears, Roebuck & Co., 790 N.E.2d 252 (N.Y. 2003) (permitting plaintiffs alleging that a wiring defect in a refrigerator manufactured by the defendant caused a fire that killed their decedent to prove both defect and causation by circumstantial evidence) *with* Myrlak v. Port Auth. of N.Y. & N.J., 723 A.2d 45 (N.J. 1999) (declining to apply Section 3 to a suit alleging injuries caused by defectively manufactured chair).

3. *Time of Sale.* A critical issue raised by Gower's manufacturing defect claim was whether the defect existed at the time of sale. The plaintiff, of course, alleged that the "ridge" that limited the movement of the safety button was present at that time, whereas the defendants argued that it was not. Normally, it is the plaintiff's burden to prove that the defect existed at the time of sale. However, this factual issue is so important and so often closely argued that several jurisdictions have passed legislation that set forth specific burdens of proof and production on this timing issue. Note that, as to the warning defect, the defendants were able

successfully to argue that the "defect" (assuming there was one) did not exist at the time of sale.

4. *Actual and Proximate Causation*. Cause-in-fact is as central to products liability claims as it is to negligence claims. In the main, actual causation issues in products liability cases are akin to those seen in standard negligence cases and tort cases more generally: They raise highly fact-intensive issues for the jury and are ordinarily governed by the but-for standard. (Note that the absence of proof as to but-for causation was the court's reason for rejecting Gower's "unloading defect" theory.) However, just as certain negligence cases such as Summers v. Tice have posed conceptually difficult issues pertaining to actual causation, certain "cutting-edge" causation doctrines have also developed primarily within products liability law. One such example is market share liability, discussed in Section IV, *infra*. And, as in negligence, the issue of proof of causation can in certain products liability cases be quite difficult. Indeed, as noted in Chapter 4, the field of "toxic torts" — which mainly involves products liability claims — has required lawyers to master complex bodies of evidence involving epidemiological studies and the use of statistics, and has pushed courts and scholars to refine tort principles and doctrines so as to arrive at satisfactory rules for proof of causation. The significance of these issues of proof of causation to modern negligence law, and by implication to modern products liability law, is attested to by the careful and elaborate attention devoted to them by the "Basic Principles" portion of the Third Restatement of Torts. *See* Restatement (Third) of Torts: Liability For Physical Harms (Basic Principles § 28 (Tentative Draft No. 2, Mar. 25, 2002). Discussion of the U.S. Supreme Court's decisions in the *Daubert* and *Metro North* cases — see Chapter 13 — provides occasion to examine these issues in greater depth.

Proximate cause principles comparable to those that apply in negligence are applied by courts to products liability claims. Thus, certain injuries caused only fortuitously by a product defect will not support a cause of action for lack of proximate cause. Indeed, the *Ventricelli* decision, which declined to impose liability for injuries caused to the driver of a rental car with a defective trunk lid on proximate cause grounds, discussed in the notes following *Metts* in Chapter 5, involved a products liability claim. The doctrine of superseding cause also is recognized in products liability cases. Thus, suppose *V* is injured because *T* purposely induced him to drive a new car with brakes that *T* knew to be defective. In a products liability suit by *V* against *M*, the manufacturer, *M* could argue the issue of superseding cause to the jury.

5. *Loss of Consortium*. An omitted portion of *Gower* addressed the issue of whether the plaintiff's wife could proceed with a loss of consortium claim derivative of Gower's underlying products liability claim. As a general rule, such claims stand on the same footing in products liability actions as they do in negligence actions. Similarly, if a defective product proximately causes a death, it will give rise to a survival action on behalf of the decedent and a wrongful death on behalf of statutory beneficiaries

such as immediate family members under the same terms as if the death had been caused by negligence. See Chapter 6.

6. *Successor Liability.* The specter of successor liability for "product lines" is obviously important for litigators representing plaintiffs or defendants in product liability actions. But it is also important for corporate lawyers contemplating the possible merger of two business entities, or the sale or purchase of a product line. Detailed doctrine exists both in and out of products liability law regarding when a successor corporation may be held liable for the predecessor corporation's torts. As *Gower* indicates, because of the "product line" doctrine, causes of action sounding in products liability enjoy a unique ability to prevail as against successor entities. Why should products liability law — which is generally less forgiving of defendants in its standards of liability — also have the capacity to stretch beyond sellers to product line owners? Is this a logical extension of products liability doctrine, or counterintuitive?

7. *Other Causes of Action.* The fact that a special cause of action called products liability exists for personal injury actions based on product dangers does not mean that it is the only cause of action a plaintiff can or will bring in such actions. Instead, the victim's lawyer is likely to file a complaint that might include causes of action for negligence, breach of implied warranty, breach of express warranty, and misrepresentation, as well as applicable state and federal statutory claims. Before learning what facts the defendant will allege and what defenses he will assert, the plaintiff will want to be in the best position possible to sustain her lawsuit by diversifying the causes of action on which she will rely, subject to the (minimal) requirement that each has a colorable basis given her attorney's diligent (if early) review of the facts.

8. *Relationship to Negligence.* Given the resemblance of a negligence complaint such as Mr. MacPherson's to a products liability claim of the sort raised by Gower, it is likely that many if not most complaints containing products liability claims will also include claims for negligence in the design and/or manufacture of the product, and for negligent failure to warn. It is natural to wonder whether these two sets of claims are essentially redundant, a problem felt particularly keenly with respect to design defect claims, in which the standard for defect sometimes closely resembles negligence law's reasonable person standard. As a matter of black-letter law, the rule is that these two bodies of law describe distinct causes of action. However, to the extent a plaintiff can recover in products liability for injuries caused by a defective product, he cannot recover again for the same injuries caused by the same product in negligence. Moreover, as was emphasized by Justice Traynor's *Escola* and *Greenman* opinions, products liability law in principle ought to free plaintiffs from relying on negligence by removing the burden of having to prove lack of reasonable care. The extent to which the shift to products liability has actually opened up a wider swath of liability than would have existed under a continuing regime of negligence law is very difficult to assess. Some lawyers and jurists have argued that, at least at times, plaintiffs may obtain strategic

advantages by framing a claim in negligence rather than in strict products liability. In particular, they suggest that by focusing the jury's attention on the issue of fault, the building of a negligence case is more likely to foster a sense among jurors that a genuine wrong has been done, and that compensation is therefore owed.

III.   Design Defect

Although many areas of products liability have been the subject of intensive debate, the issue of how to define a "design defect" has proved to be singularly controversial. In part, the debate is political. The issue here is how easy or difficult it should be for plaintiffs to recover on a claim that a manufacturer has designed and produced a line of products with features that pose risks of physical injury to product users. In equal part, it is theoretical, reflecting a significant gap left open by scholarship and judicial decisions written at the birth of products liability law. Here one must recall that the doctrine of strict products liability arose primarily in response to injuries caused by *manufacturing defects* — flaws in individual products, such as the overcharged and/or weakened bottle that injured Escola, the car that veered sharply as Mrs. Henningsen drove it, or a particular pie containing a toxin or foreign object. Plaintiffs who recovered in such cases did so because something went terribly wrong in the manufacture of one unit of a mass-produced product. The question, as Justice Traynor saw it, was whether to permit recovery for injuries caused by a flawed unit — that is, a product not up to its own specifications — in the absence of any evidence that the defendant failed to use reasonable care to guard against the creation of that flaw.

Whereas the concept of a flaw or defect is almost internally self-defining for manufacturing defects, it is not for design defects. In the former case, a reference to the manufacturer's own standards will provide the criteria for determining defectiveness: A product containing a danger that results from a departure from its intended design can be said to contain a manufacturing defect. There is no ready equivalent to this "internal" standard in the design defect context. Indeed, the very question posed by this type of case is: Should the product have been *designed* differently? For these cases, "defect" or "flaw" connotes deviation from some *external* standard(s). But which one(s)? To this question, courts have tended to fasten on two answers.

The first answer invokes a standard — mentioned above in Section I — that has come to be known as the *consumer expectations test*. It states, roughly, that a product is defective in design if aspects of its design render it more dangerous than an ordinary consumer would expect it to be. Part of the appeal of the consumer expectations test is that, notwithstanding the aforementioned differences between manufacturing and design defect claims, it seems to handle paradigm cases in both categories pretty well. Thus, one might naturally say of products containing manufacturing defects that they disappoint ordinary consumer expectations. In *Escola*, for example, the exploding bottle was more dangerous than an ordinary consumer would expect. Likewise, an automobile whose gas tank location causes it to burst into flames when rear-ended at a moderate speed would count as defectively designed under this test—an ordinary consumer would expect a new automobile to withstand such a collision, and certainly not to explode. The same conclusion might apply to a ski binding the design of which prevents it from releasing even under severe stress; a large roasting pan designed to hold a turkey that is built with small handles that make it difficult to hold the pan steady as it is removed from the oven; a shower door with glass that, when subjected to a moderate force, shatters into razor-sharp shards; and a throat lozenge prepared with ingredients that cause convulsions in a significant minority of the population. In all these cases, *the concept of a flaw or a defect can be given content by comparing the actual product to a prototype in the mind of the ordinary consumer*. In this regard, the consumer expectations test, although a feature of tort law, reveals its roots in the law of contract and warranty, which is primarily concerned to protect the expectations of the contracting parties (here the consumer).

The second answer to the question of what constitutes a design defect comes in the form of the *risk-utility test*. Predictably, it derives from the other parent of products liability law—negligence. According to this test, a product is defectively designed if the risks of its design outweigh its utility. For example, a food processor whose chopping blades continue to turn even though the lid has been removed—thus permitting someone to put his fingers in it while the blades are spinning—can be said to contain a design defect under the risk-utility test. Even if the danger posed by this feature is in some sense "expected," the product is still defective simply because the risks of someone losing a finger are outweighed by the minimal utility of being able to add food to the processor as its blades are spinning. Likewise, an automobile with a rear engine and little or no hood in front of the driver's compartment might be deemed defective under the risk-utility test. The question would be whether the utility of the design—better visibility, easier maneuverability, etc.—outweighs the heightened risk of bodily harm the design poses as compared to cars with more substantial front ends. As compared to the consumer expectations test, the risk-utility test is more overtly normative or evaluative. The question is no longer: What dangers do consumers tend to expect to encounter in a product such as this one? Instead, the question is: Should the product be designed differently given the relative risks and benefits posed by its current design?

As noted above, at least some of the controversy over the concept of design defect emerged from the (understandable) failure of early decisions such as *Greenman* and *Cronin*, and early authorities, such as Section 402A, to isolate and define design defects as distinct from manufacturing defects. However, by the mid-1980s, the consumer expectation test and the risk-utility had filled that void. Thus, today's controversies tend to take the form of debates about *which test ought to rule*. Naturally, this debate also provokes questions about what each of these tests really entails, and how litigants are to go about proving their cases under one or the other.

Within the context of this broad national debate, California case law again occupies a very special position. This is not simply because of California's leading role in the history of products liability law. It is also because the California Supreme Court has issued two leading opinions, reproduced below, in which it has expressly decided to incorporate *both* the consumer expectation test *and* the risk-utility test into California law, reasoning that the propriety of applying each will depend on the type of case before a given court. To reach this result, the court has had to strive mightily to isolate the differences between the two primary doctrinal tests for design defect.

A. *Applying the Risk-Utility Test for Design Defect*

While the richness of California case law in products liability provides an excellent focus for analyzing the central debates in design defect law, it also leaves something to be desired in terms of the thoroughness with which it has applied the risk-utility test for defect. To that end, we first take a brief detour into the law of New Jersey. Here we find a relatively clear exposition of a standard formulation of the risk-utility test.

Cepeda v. Cumberland Eng'g Co.*
386 A.2d 816 (N.J. 1978)

Conford, P.J.A.D.   We granted certification to review a decision of the Appellate Division reversing a judgment entered on a jury verdict for plaintiff. . . . The action, brought by a workman operating a "pelletizing" machine, was for . . . damages consequent upon the loss of four fingers of the left hand resulting from an accident in the course of such operation in 1968. Although the machine came from the manufacturer with a bolted guard which would have prevented the accident, the guard had apparently been removed before plaintiff came to work on the day of the accident.

The theory of plaintiff's action was that the machine was defectively designed from a safety standpoint, in that the guard was required to be removed frequently in the normal course of the operation of the machine; that it could have been expected that on some such occasion the guard would not be replaced before resumption of operations, whether inadvertently or otherwise; and that therefore the defendant manufacturer should have equipped it with an electronic "interlock" mechanism, readily available and capable of installation, which would have automatically prevented the operation of the machine when the guard was off. The defense was that the machine was not defectively designed as it met general standards of safety as of the date of its sale to plaintiff's employer,

* [For subsequent history of this decision, see footnotes 5 and 8 herein, and Note 10 following this excerpt. — EDS.]

1956, and as it was reasonably contemplated that the machine would not be operated with the guard off. It was further contended that plaintiff was guilty of contributory negligence in operating the machine with the guard off and that such negligence barred recovery, being a substantial factor in bringing about the accident.

[The jury concluded that the machine was defectively designed and that its defective features caused the plaintiff's injury. It further found that the plaintiff had been careless in using the machine without its guard, but that this carelessness was not a "proximate cause" of his injuries. It awarded the plaintiff $125,000.] . . .

II

The evidence in the case, taking the most favorable view of the proofs for the plaintiff which could have been entertained by a jury, is as follows.

Plaintiff was an 18 year old native of Santo Domingo who spoke and read no English, had had little schooling, and had worked for the employer, Rotuba Extruders, for eight months when this accident occurred on April 3, 1968. His foremen were Spanish-speaking, as was he. His duties included working on this machine, among other things. At the time, the plant was on a multi-shift operation, and plaintiff's shift was from midnight to 8:00 A.M.

The function of the machine was to draw multiple strands of plastic extruded by another machine into position for cutting into very small pellets, so that the product could be conveniently stored and shipped. When the guard was on the machine, the strands were introduced by the workman into the machine through a horizontal opening in the guard adjoining the table, too narrow to admit a man's hand. However, there was no functional bar to the effectuation of the process in the absence of the guard (plaintiff had worked the machine without the guard several hours on April 3, 1968 before the accident). The strands of plastic were then sucked up by the "nip-point" of two revolving rollers and carried to a rotating drum containing knives which cut the plastic into pellets. Thence the pellets were discharged into a chute. . . .

Plaintiff testified through an interpreter [that the] . . . guard was not on the machine when he came to work the night of the accident. He had not taken it off and did not know who had. The accident happened when the "ribbon" of plastic "caught" his hand and "pulled it inside" (the rollers). He said it "sucked (him) right in." When he was instructed in the use of the machine the guard was on, but he was never told of and did not realize its purpose until after the accident. He was never instructed that he was not to operate the machine if the guard was off. Asked whether the guard was ever off the machine before the night of the accident, he responded, "Why, sure." But he also said he had never operated the machine previously without the guard. He cleaned the machine with an air hose while the guard remained on.

One of plaintiff's supervising foremen testified . . . that he told him never to remove the guard from the machine because "the machine could take his hand and whole arm off." Plaintiff himself admitted on depositions that he knew "the rollers could take his hand."

Called as a witness for plaintiff, an officer and plant manager of the employer company testified that there were two types of situations wherein the guard had to be removed for thorough cleaning of the machine. One was when there was to be a drastic change in the color run of the plastic; the other, when the strands jammed the rollers. In either of these situations, "which happened from time to time," the guard had to be dismantled and the inside of the machine both blown out with air and cleaned of the clogging plastic with shears and other tools. There was evidence that it required only a few minutes to remove or install the guard. Operators of the machine were classified as unskilled. To the witness's knowledge, the machine was never operated without the guard.

A plant supervisor corroborated the foregoing testimony as to occasions for removal of the guard. There were times when changes in the color run would occur four times in one shift. Although no one was supposed to run the machine without the guard, the supervisor himself had once "caught his hand" in the machine. The circumstances of that event were not further developed. Only the foremen had the authority and tools to remove the guard.

Isaac Stewart, a consulting engineer for many years in "accident and material failure evaluation," testified for plaintiff to an opinion that when sold in 1956 the machine was "unsafely designed." This was for the reason that the necessity for removal of the guard for cleaning and unclogging the machine was of an "operational" nature rather than for maintenance purposes only. Operational removals mandated an interlock mechanism to prevent operability when the guard was off. An interlock could have been installed for $25 or $30. Such devices have been known since the turn of the century and were specified in many safety codes 50 years ago. An in-running nip roller is dangerous. As of 1956, machines of various types with "nip" rollers were guarded with interlocks. The witness mentioned examples of such use on machines in the printing, food, injection mold and plastic industries.

Defendant's vice-president, who was a design engineer of the company when this machine was manufactured, testified that the company manufactured many kinds of machines equipped with guards to protect workers, but none were equipped with interlock devices. In 1956 there were no industry safety standards for manufacturing pelletizers. It was not felt necessary to provide an interlock in view of the presence of a guard which was bolted and served an operational as well as a safety function. Interlocks were used only with hinged guards, not bolted ones requiring use of a wrench to remove them, such as that here involved. On cross-examination the witness conceded that interlocks had been known for a long time prior to 1956.

Seymour Bodner testified as a safety expert for defendant. His opinion that the machine met safety standards was premised on the factual assumption that the guards required removal only on "major cleanups" of the machine and that those were infrequent. He thought that "the operation of the machine without the guard (was) not to be anticipated."

General industry safety codes as of 1956 did not call for interlocks on guards. Interlocks can be rendered inoperative. On cross-examination, he conceded that if the guard had to be removed frequently there should have been an interlock.

III

. . . The heart of the approach we take toward resolution of the matter of defendant's affirmative liability in this case calls for a careful distinction between ordinary manufacturing defects and defects of design. . . . The present case is an example of the latter, where the product is made as intended, but is asserted to be dangerous in some way. . . . The distinction has been frequently drawn in the literature. However, there has not been uniformity in the views as to what, if anything, should be the difference in the criteria for strict liability in tort in the respective types of "defects" mentioned.

The black letter of Rest. 2d Sec. 402A does not draw the stated distinction, the requirement that the product be "in a defective condition unreasonably dangerous to the user or consumer" being facially applicable to both kinds of defects. However, Comment i of the section explains that the qualification "unreasonably dangerous" was meant to negate the notion that products normally useful, such as sugar, whiskey, tobacco, or butter, could be regarded as defective because, if used improperly, excessively or in an adulterated condition, they could also be harmful (*Id*. at p.352). The requisite of "unreasonably dangerous," however, also extends to other manufactured objects whose utility in ordinary use outweighs the potentiality of their harmfulness. As stated in Prosser, *Torts* (1971), p.659: "An ordinary pair of shoes does not become unreasonably unsafe merely because the soles become somewhat slippery when wet; nor is there unreasonable danger in a hammer merely because it can mash a thumb. Knives and axes would be quite useless if they did not cut."

In the case of a defect of a product in the sense of an abnormality unintended by the manufacturer, there would appear to be prima facie liability for physical harm proximately resulting from the defect to a user or consumer without any need for showing of unreasonable danger in any other sense. "(T)he product (would be) unreasonably dangerous as a matter of law and this would be true of virtually any fabrication or construction defect." P. Keeton, [*Product Liability and the Meaning of Defect*,] 5 St. Mary's L.J. [30,] 39 [(1973)]. *Cf.* J. Wade, [*On the Nature of Strict Tort Liability for Products*], 44 Miss. L.J. [825,] 837 [(1973)].[4] . . .

_____

4. In this article, Dean Wade comments critically on *Cronin v. J.B.E. Olson Corp.* . . . which holds a plaintiff need only prove a product is "defective," not that it is also "unreasonably dangerous." Among other things, the author says: ". . . the position of the California court in *Cronin*, in limiting the requirement to a defective product, would be much more sustainable if the strict liability for products which it applies were confined to the product which has its 'defect' developed unintentionally in the manufacturing process, thus leaving the design and warning cases to be handled under the negligence techniques." 44 Miss. L.J. at 837. . . .

Our present decisional concern, however, is with the design defect aspect of a manufacturer's strict liability in tort. The cases in this area of the law frequently confound considerations relating to contributory negligence, assumption of risk and misuse of the product by the plaintiff with other factors relevant to liability for design defect. We shall deal with the former aspects of the instant case hereinafter. At this point of the discussion, the point to be made is that in design defect liability analysis the Section 402A criterion of "unreasonably dangerous" is an appropriate one if understood to render the liability of the manufacturer substantially coordinate with liability on negligence principles. The only qualification is as to the requisite of foreseeability by the manufacturer of the dangerous propensity of the chattel manifested at the trial this being imputed to the manufacturer. "Since proper design is a matter of reasonable fitness, the strict liability adds little or nothing to negligence on the part of the manufacturer. . . ." Prosser, *Torts, supra,* p.659, n.72.

A most useful formulation of the foregoing principles, for purposes of practical judicial implementation in design defect cases, is contained in the . . . articles by Deans Wade and P. Keeton cited above. . . . In his most recent article Dean Wade has described the approach as follows:

> The time has now come to be forthright in using a tort way of thinking and tort terminology (in cases of strict liability in tort). There are several ways of doing it, and it is not difficult. The simplest and easiest way, it would seem, is to assume that the defendant knew of the dangerous condition of the product and ask whether he was then negligent in putting it on the market or supplying it to someone else. In other words, the scienter is supplied as a matter of law, and there is no need for the plaintiff to prove its existence as a matter of fact. Once given this notice of the dangerous condition of the chattel, the question then becomes whether the defendant was negligent to people who might be harmed by that condition if they came into contact with it or were in the vicinity of it. Another way of saying this is to ask whether the magnitude of the risk created by the dangerous condition of the product was outweighed by the social utility attained by putting it out in this fashion.

Wade, op. cit., *supra*, 44 Miss. L.J. at 834-835.

Dean Keeton put the matter thiswise:

> A product is defective if it is unreasonably dangerous as marketed. It is unreasonably dangerous if a reasonable person would conclude that the magnitude of the scientifically perceivable danger *as it is proved to be at the time of trial* outweighed the benefits of the way the product was so designed and marketed. Under the heading of benefits one would include anything that gives utility of some kind to the product; one would also include the infeasibility and additional cost of making a safer product. As the Court of Appeals for the Fifth Circuit has said, "(D)emanding that the defect render the product unreasonably dangerous reflects a realization that many products have both utility and danger." Ross v. Up-Right, Inc., 402 F.2d 943 (5th Cir. 1968) (emphasis in original).

P. Keeton, op. cit., *supra*, 5 St. Mary's L.J. at 37-38.

Our study of the decisions satisfies us that this risk/utility analysis rationalizes what the great majority of the courts actually do in deciding design defect cases where physical injury has proximately resulted from the defect. Several recent cases have expressly referred to and applied the stated analysis.

Dean Wade suggests that before determining whether the case for liability should be given to the jury the trial court should give consideration to whether a balanced consideration of the following factors did not preclude liability as a matter of law:

(1) The usefulness and desirability of the product — its utility to the user and to the public as a whole.

(2) The safety aspects of the product — the likelihood that it will cause injury, and the probable seriousness of the injury.

(3) The availability of a substitute product which would meet the same need and not be as unsafe.

(4) The manufacturer's ability to eliminate the unsafe character of the product without impairing its usefulness or making it too expensive to maintain its utility.

(5) The user's ability to avoid danger by the exercise of care in the use of the product.

(6) The user's anticipated awareness of the dangers inherent in the product and their avoidability, because of general public knowledge of the obvious condition of the product, or of the existence of suitable warnings or instructions.

(7) The feasibility, on the part of the manufacturer, of spreading the loss by setting the price of the product or carrying liability insurance.

Wade, op. cit., *supra*, 44 Miss. L.J. at 837-838.

If the case is sent to the jury, since it would not always be appropriate for the court to include in the instructions to the jury all seven of the factors mentioned above, Dean Wade suggests the following model instruction:

A (product) is not duly safe if it is so likely to be harmful to persons (or property) that a reasonable prudent manufacturer (supplier), who had actual knowledge of its harmful character would not place it on the market. It is not necessary to find that this defendant had knowledge of the harmful character of the (product) in order to determine that it was not duly safe.

Id., at 839-840.

Subject to substituting the Section 402A language, "defective condition unreasonably dangerous," for the Wade-preferred "not duly safe," we approve and adopt this instruction for incorporation into a charge in an action against a manufacturer for strict liability in tort based upon the design defect of a product.[5] Such a charge would be usefully amplified by

---

5. It must be recognized that since this formulation of liability is based upon whether a "reasonable prudent" manufacturer (with assumed knowledge of the dangerous proclivity of the article) would have marketed the article, Subsection (2)(a) of Rest. 2d Sec. 402A is not applicable in design defect cases. Subsection (2) states: "the rule stated in Subsection

the judge calling to the attention of the jury for their consideration any of the Wade factors mentioned above going into the risk-utility analysis for which there is specific proof in the case and especial significance (e.g., here, the manufacturer's ability to eliminate the unsafe character of the product without impairing its utility or incurring too much expense; the manufacturer's asserted expectation that the machine would be operated only with the guard). It should also here be noted, although the point will be repeated in another connection, *infra*, that while foreseeability by the defendant of the harmful character (dangerous proclivity) of the product is not a requisite to liability, foreseeability (objective) of the kind of use (or misuse) of the product which occurred is a relevant factor. . . .

Strict tort liability under Rest. 2d Sec. 402A for design defects is not appropriately circumscribed by the warranty test of whether the article is reasonably fit for its intended purpose or use, notwithstanding strict liability in tort began here and elsewhere by borrowing warranty concepts in order to avoid the need of establishing negligence. As pointed out by Dean Wade, in situations "involving design matters, the consumer would not know what to expect, because he would have no idea how safe the product could be made." Wade, op. cit., *supra*, 44 Miss. L.J. at 829. . . . The fact that the instant machine was commercially "reasonably fit for its intended purpose" of pelletizing plastic strands is obviously irrelevant to the postulate of strict tort liability to a workman injured by reason of the unsafety of the machine due to a design defect.

The general outline of a rationale for the affirmative case of strict liability for design defects in a manufactured product includes the condition that the product is not being misused or abnormally used except where such latter kinds of use are foreseeable, Rest. 2d Sec. 402A, Comment h. . . . Abnormal use or misuse has also been conceptualized as negating proximate cause—a view taken by the Appellate Division here. If it is the plaintiff who has misused the product, negation of liability is sometimes posited on contributory negligence. . . . However, abnormal use is not an affirmative defense; it is rather for the plaintiff, in undertaking to prove that the unreasonable dangerousness of the article caused the injury, to show there was no abnormal use.

It is, however, clear that many, if not most jurisdictions now acknowledge that in applying strict liability in tort for design defects manufacturers cannot escape liability on grounds of misuse or abnormal use if the actual use proximate to the injury was objectively foreseeable. Foreseeability in the foregoing application may be "reasonable foreseeability," (i.e., objective); it need not be actual.

In concluding this phase of the discussion of the law, we take notice of . . . Cronin v. J.B.E. Olson Corporation, *supra*, 104 Cal. Rptr. 433, 501

---

(1) applies although (a) the seller has exercised all possible care in the preparation and sale of his product." *See* Volkswagen of America, Inc. v. Young, *supra*, 321 A.2d at 747-748.

[In a subsequent opinion, the court reaffirmed its adoption of a risk-utility test for design defect, but reconsidered and rejected *Cepeda*'s introduction of the phrase "unreasonably dangerous" into its recommended jury instruction. *See* Suter v. San Angelo Foundry & Mach. Co., 406 A.2d 140 (N.J. 1979). — Eds.]

P.2d 1153. . . . [There,] the California Supreme Court . . . held that it would not follow the Sec. 402A requirement of "unreasonably dangerous" but look only to whether the product was "defective.". . . The court felt that retention of the test of "unreasonably dangerous" diluted the intent of the strict liability in tort doctrine to relieve plaintiffs of problems of proof of negligence.

Cronin has been widely criticized as providing no useful definition of an actionable defect, particularly in relation to a case of a product of unsafe design. As stated by Dean Keeton . . . ". . . the difficulty is that no content was given [by *Cronin*] to the concept of defect and this is vitally important when a plaintiff's theory is that a product, although fabricated and constructed as it was intended to be, subjected users or others to an inherent risk of harm that made the product defective." [Citation omitted.]

It should be apparent from our discussion above of the Wade-Keeton risk/utility analysis of strict liability for defective products that we approve the Rest. 2d Sec. 402A criterion of "unreasonably dangerous" if understood conformably therewith. It is probable, as intimated in the said discussion, that liability could be premised on the fact of defect alone, where that defect is the result of an unintended manufacturing error or mischance, and proximately related to the personal injury. In such case, the added Restatement requirement that the defect be unreasonably dangerous could either be discarded or held satisfied in such instance as a matter of law. We may leave definitive resolution of the matter to a case calling for it. It will suffice for purposes of the case at bar, which is clearly a situation of alleged design defect, that the Restatement criterion of "unreasonably dangerous" remains soundly applicable thereto. . . .

IV

In the light of the previous discussion of the facts and the law, the Appellate Division rationale for finding no affirmative basis for liability as a matter of law is plainly insupportable. . . . [T]he court gave insufficient consideration to the potential jury question arising from the evidence as to the foreseeability that the machine would sometimes be operated without the guard. . . . [T]he matter of potential misuse or abnormal use is inherent in the overall general issue of the alleged unreasonable dangerousness of the machine, and that issue was definitely submitted to the jury. And we are in disagreement with the Appellate Division's observation that there was no "evidence tending to suggest that the manufacturer should have foreseen such an occurrence."

As already indicated, there was credible evidence that the guard had to be removed frequently during operations. Human nature being what it is, we believe a jury might have inferred that a reasonable manufacturer, from that fact, could have objectively expected that on occasion production with the machine would be resumed without replacing a guard just removed in a clean-out operation. Even the defendant's safety expert conceded that if the facts as to frequency of need for removal of the guard were as testified to by plaintiff's witnesses, the machine would be unsafe without an interlock. In any event, balancing the degree of such objective foreseeability with the gravity of the risk to a workman operating the machine without the guard and the feasibility and inexpensiveness of installing an interlock in 1956, when the machine was sold, a jury could properly, on the evidence, have found the injury to have resulted from an unreasonably dangerous condition of the machine. That another jury could reasonably have found to the contrary, does not, of course, affect the validity of the stated conclusion. . . .

V

On defendant's appeal to the Appellate Division it raised the point that the jury's findings of contributory negligence of the plaintiff and of absence of proximate cause between such contributory negligence and the accident were inconsistent and that the latter finding was against the weight of the evidence. Alternative to a claim for reversal and exculpation of liability entirely, it sought a new trial on the grounds stated. The Appellate Division decision did not reach the issue. Before explaining why we think the defendant's demand for a new trial on such grounds is well-taken, we address the contention of plaintiff, endorsed by the dissent herein, that on these facts contributory negligence is not a defense at all, and that therefore any inconsistency in the special findings of the jury . . . is legally immaterial. . . .

The broad consensus of American decisional law and writing in the strict liability field, except to the extent that the concept of comparative fault is beginning to gain acceptance therein, is expressed by Comment n, Rest. 2d Sec. 402A, alluded to above. It reads:

> Contributory negligence of the plaintiff is not a defense when such negligence consists merely in a failure to discover the defect in the product, or to guard against the possibility of its existence. On the other hand the form of contributory negligence which consists in voluntarily and unreasonably proceeding to encounter a known danger, and commonly passes under the name of assumption of risk, is a defense under this Section as in other cases of strict liability. If the user or consumer discovers the defect and is aware of the danger, and nevertheless proceeds unreasonably to make use of the product and is injured by it, he is barred from recovery.

Thus, although a species of plaintiff's conduct frequently denominated as assumption of the risk is recognized as a defense to strict liability in tort, our New Jersey law subsumes conduct of that nature, for purposes of ordinary negligence actions under the general category of plaintiff's fault, or, as conventionally expressed, contributory negligence in its broad aspect.

However, it is implicit in Comment n and the generality of the cases that . . . mere carelessness or inadvertence . . . [cannot] be a defense to an action for strict liability in tort for injuries sustained as the result of a product defect, particularly if the defect is one of unsafe design. . . . [A]cceptance of "ordinary" contributory negligence as a defense in actions for strict liability in tort would be incompatible with the policy considerations which led to the adoption of strict tort liability in the first instance. The manufacturer's duty is imposed precisely to avert foreseeable inadvertent injury to a user of a product. Thus, in the case at bar, plaintiff's carelessness, if any, in getting his hand caught in the plastic strands is not a defense, and so much of the trial court charge on contributory negligence in the present case which could have been otherwise understood by the jury should not be repeated at the retrial.

We believe the law in this State and the vast majority of others accords with the foregoing hypothesis of a defense of contributory negligence to strict liability in tort based upon a voluntary and unreasonable encountering by the plaintiff of a known safety hazard of a machine where proximately contributive to the accident. . . .

It is our view that on the proofs a jury could find either way as to whether plaintiff unreasonably and voluntarily subjected himself to a known danger by operating the machine without the guard on it. . . .

. . . Until such time as consideration is given in this State to extending the principle of comparative negligence or fault to strict liability in tort,[8] the continuance of unreasonable voluntary exposure of oneself to a known danger as a defense to strict liability in tort seems a fair balance of justice and policy in this area.

As indicated at the head of this point, we are of the view that there is merit in defendant's contention, raised before the Appellate Division, that the jury's special findings both of contributory negligence and absence of proximate causal relation thereof with the accident, are so inconsistent as to require a new trial. If plaintiff was contributorily negligent within the parameters of the judge's charge, either in undertaking to work the machine without the presence of the guard or in any other aspect of his activity, there inevitably was a direct causal relation between such conduct and plaintiff's accident. . . .

. . . [A] just resolution of this controversy will require a new trial . . . on the issue of unreasonable voluntary exposure to a known risk by plaintiff. The jury will not be asked to make a determination of proximate cause as to the latter, if they find in the affirmative on that issue. Moreover, the issue of damages need not be retried. The verdict of damages returned at the trial will stand should plaintiff prevail on the merits at the retrial. . . .

The judgment of the Appellate Division is reversed, and the cause is remanded to the Law Division for a limited new trial, subject to the conditions stated hereinabove.

Schreiber, J. (joined by Hughes, C.J. and Pashman, J.) (concurring and dissenting). I concur in the majority's conclusion that the jury's adjudication of defendant's liability should be reinstated. However, I must respectfully dissent from its . . . [ruling recognizing a limited] defense of

8. The New Jersey Comparative Negligence Act became effective in 1973. L.1973, c. 146 (N.J.S.A. 2A:15-5.1 *et seq.*). As the cause of action here arose in 1968, the statute is not applicable thereto, even if otherwise considered pertinent. L.1973, c. 146, sec. 4.

[In a subsequent opinion, the court modified *Cepeda*'s analysis of contributory negligence in light of the changes wrought by the Act. See Note 10 following this case excerpt. — EDS.]

contributory negligence. . . . A manufacturer's duty to install a safety device should not be excused when the accident which occurred was the very same mishap which would have been prevented had the manufacturer fulfilled its duty to the plaintiff worker. . . .

NOTES AND QUESTIONS

1. *Judge and Jury.* Dean Wade was quite explicit in his influential article on the proper standard for assessing design defects that its seven-factor test was unworkably complex as a jury instruction, and thus should be used only to aid judicial review of the legal sufficiency of the plaintiff's case. (His proposed jury instruction is discussed below.) Numerous jurisdictions, like New Jersey, have heeded Wade's advice, and reserved the seven-factor test for such use. Could one devise an intelligible jury instruction that packs in the seven factors? If so, would that be a desirable instruction? Are some of the factors appropriately considered by a judge and not by a jury?

2. *The Hand Formula versus Wade-Keeton.* Do the factors of the Wade test essentially recapitulate the Hand Formula for determining reasonable care in negligence cases? If not, how does it differ? Is the test appropriately described as a "balancing" test? Is it really balancing "risks" and "utilities" associated with a product's design, or are other factors at work?

3. *Jury Instructions.* As noted in *Cepeda*, Dean Wade recommended an instruction on the issue of design defect under which the jury would ask whether the product "is so likely to be harmful to persons (or property) that a *reasonable prudent manufacturer (supplier)*, who had actual knowledge of its harmful character would not place it on the market." Although this instruction echoes negligence law's concept of breach, it diverges from that concept in one important respect. In determining whether a reasonable prudent manufacturer would have placed the product as designed on the market, the jury is asked to apply *hindsight* to determine the magnitude of the risks associated with the product's design. Thus, it must ask whether *a prudent manufacturer armed with actual knowledge of at least some of the harms that flow from the design of the product would still have marketed it with that design.* The critical difference between the legal standard for carelessness and Wade's conception of design defect is whether the reasonableness of the defendant's conduct is determined by reference to what one could be expected to know about the dangers associated with his conduct at the time of acting (a foresight-based conception of reasonableness) or by reference to what, after the fact, is actually known about the dangers associated with that conduct (a hindsight-based conception).

4. *The Role of Foreseeability.* Many courts that instruct juries on a risk-utility test today do so in a way that differs in two respects from Wade's recommended jury instructions. First, they focus more on the *product's*

risks and benefits, rather than on the decision facing the defendant at the time of design and manufacture. In short, they simply ask the jury to assess whether the risks of a given product design are outweighed by the utility of that design. However, most jurisdictions instruct the jury that, in assessing the risks associated with the product, they must count only *foreseeable* risks, again marking an adherence to basic norms of negligence law. A striking rejection of this precept is found in the Wisconsin Supreme Court's aggressive holding that a manufacturer could be held liable for injuries caused by allergic reactions to latex gloves notwithstanding the apparent unforeseeability of those reactions. *See* Green v. Smith & Nephew AHP, Inc., 629 N.W.2d 727 (Wis. 2001).

5. *The Significance of Available Alternative Designs.* Note that the third and fourth factors of the Wade test ask judges to consider the availability of substitute products, as well as the feasibility and reasonableness of adopting an alternative design. What is the difference, if any, between these two ideas? Why is it important to consider whether there exists a reasonable alternative design? Is a product's safety necessarily a relative issue? Does this requirement follow from the negligence roots of products liability? If there is no reasonable alternative design, does that mean the product cannot be defective? See Note 12 following *Soule, infra*.

One of the most controversial aspects of the Restatement (Third) of Products Liability is its assertion that, for the vast run of design defect cases, the availability of an alternative design does not (and should not) merely count as a factor in risk-utility analysis, but should constitute a necessary element of the plaintiff's prima facie case. Restatement (Third) of Torts: Products Liability § 2(b) (1998) (a product "is defective in design when the foreseeable risks of harm posed by the product could have been reduced or avoided by the adoption of a reasonable alternative design"); *id.* cmt. d (noting that subsection 2(b) sets a "requirement . . . that the plaintiff show a reasonable alternative design"). Both the descriptive and normative versions of this assertion have prompted voluminous critical commentary from trial lawyers, academics, and judges. See Note 7 following *Soule, infra*.

6. *Focus on the Consumer: Factors Five and Six.* The sixth factor of the Wade test addresses whether — either by virtue of common knowledge, or through warnings and instructions — the consumer can be made aware of the risk in question and its potential avoidability. Relatedly, the fifth factor considers whether the risk in question is the type of risk that can be diminished by user precaution. To see the interplay of these two factors, consider the example of automobile airbags. Although of considerable utility, airbags pose a risk of injury to children and smaller adults who sit in the front passenger seat, because the rapid inflation of the airbag into what would be the chest of an average adult can hit a shorter person in the head and break her neck. A risk-utility evaluation under factor six would recognize that the risk can be diminished by providing warnings to purchasers and users in the owner's manual and in the car itself. It might also require that users can to some degree protect against the realization of this risk by keeping children in the car's back seat(s). For these reasons,

factors five and six would counsel against a finding that cars with airbags are defective because of the risk posed to persons of small stature.

Factors five and six of the Wade test thus provide defense lawyers with an occasion to focus on the plaintiff's conduct as a basis for dismissing his case for failing to prove defect as a matter of law. The idea is that a putative design problem generating a substantial risk of physical harm should not qualify as a "defect" if there are means by which the risk could be avoided by the consumer, and the seller has ensured that consumers are aware of such a risk and how to act so as to minimize it. To return to the airbag example, the risk of an airbag breaking a passenger's neck may figure differently in the overall assessment of the car's design if it turns out that there are easy ways for consumers to avoid or reduce this risk, of which they are or can be made aware.

7. *The Plaintiff's Role: Element or Defense?* The preceding note, as well as *Cepeda* itself, highlight the difficult issues that courts confront in determining how a plaintiff's conduct ought to factor into his products liability claim. A basic ambiguity concerns the way in which a court ought to conceive the point of an argument such as the defendant's in *Cepeda*. On the one hand, by pointing to the plaintiff's "misuse" of its product, the defendant could be seeking to rebut the claim that the product was defective when it left the defendant's possession. (After all, at that time, it still had the guard on it.) On the other hand, it could aim to establish that the plaintiff is ineligible to complain about any defect in the product because his own carelessness was a but-for cause of his injuries. The former argument asserts that an element of the plaintiff's case — "defect" — is not satisfied. The latter, although occasionally phrased in terms of superseding cause, tends to be asserted in support of one or another affirmative defense. The next two notes consider each branch of this doctrinal fork in the road.

8. *Intended versus Foreseeable Use: Product "Misuse" and Defectiveness.* In the spirit of many of the policy reasons for which products liability was developed, plaintiffs commonly argue that part of making a product safe is designing it, or providing warnings for it, with the conduct of *ordinary consumers* very much in mind. For example, given that consumers (particularly children and young adults), occasionally shake soda bottles vigorously so that they spew foam once opened, one might well ask of Coca Cola that it use bottling techniques that minimize the risk of bottles exploding even when shaken. Thus, on this view, if a plaintiff is able to demonstrate a feasible design that would minimize injury generated in part by ordinary consumer behavior, the underlying policies of products liability law entail that the defendant should be held responsible to adopt that design. In opposition, defendants argue that to ignore a plaintiff's dangerous misuse of a product is to misplace responsibility. The defendant, on this view, has fulfilled its obligation to consumers by producing a product that is safe when used as *intended* by the seller. By contrast, products that injure only because of unintended usages, such as unsafe handling, are not properly described as defective.

Current doctrine in some sense splits the difference between these views. In general, sellers are obligated to make design (and warning) choices with all *foreseeable* uses of the product in mind. Thus, a plaintiff's careless use of a product will not of itself negate a claim of "defect" unless that carelessness is so gross and idiosyncratic as to count as unforeseeable to a reasonable seller at the time of manufacture or sale. *See, e.g.*, Baker v. International Harvester Co., 660 S.W.2d 21 (Mo. Ct. App. 1983) (dismissing the claim of the estate of a hunter who, without permission, jumped aboard a moving farm combine to shoot from it and then was killed when he fell off—that the combine posed a danger to those who would use it in such an unforeseeable manner does not render it defective). However, evidence as to the foreseeability of consumers' careless conduct is usually deemed *relevant* to the factfinder's determination as to whether the product was defectively designed.

9. *Which Affirmative Defense?* Even if the plaintiff's "misuse" of a product does not negate a claim of defectiveness, it may still form the basis of a plaintiff-conduct defense. The question then arises: Which defense? In principle, product misuse could be handled under the doctrines of contributory negligence, comparative responsibility, or assumption of risk. Alternatively, it could be identified as a special defense in its own right.

As *Cepeda* makes clear, products liability emerged at a time when the plaintiff's fault, if found to have contributed to his injuries, automatically barred his claims against others whose careless (or innocent) conduct also caused his injuries. Given this drastic effect, as well as the consumer-protection rationales relied upon by the likes of Justice Traynor, it is no surprise to find that early products liability decisions declined to recognize contributory negligence as a defense. Indeed, in a pre-*Cepeda* decision, the New Jersey Supreme Court had held that contributory negligence should *not* function as defense to a products liability claim. Bexiga v. Havir Mfg. Corp., 290 A.2d 281 (N.J. 1972). (In omitted portions of their opinions, the majority and dissenting justices in *Cepeda* dispute whether *Bexiga* thereby meant to exclude even the "implied assumption of risk" branch of New Jersey contributory negligence law.) Some courts that rejected the defense maintained that the problem was not only one of politics and policy, but was also conceptual. Because products liability is *not* premised on negligence but on defect, they reasoned, there was nothing against which to compare the plaintiff's fault—the jury would be faced with the task of comparing apples and oranges.

With the shift to regimes of comparative responsibility, courts have revisited and, by and large, rejected the foregoing reasons against recognition of plaintiff's fault as a partial (or even complete) bar to recovery. (Of course, as in negligence, the plaintiff's careless conduct must function as a but-for cause of the accident to count as a defense.) Thus, today, in most jurisdictions the jury will be asked to compare the "fault" attributable to the seller of the defective product with the "fault" of the plaintiff in misusing it. The lead California case recognizing comparative negligence as a defense to a products liability action is Daly v. General Motors Corp., 575 P. 2d 1162 (Cal. 1978); *see also* Restatement (Third), *supra*, § 17(b) (generally applicable rules of comparative fault apply in products liability). Under the rules of modified comparative responsibility regimes, a plaintiff whose fault passes a certain threshold relative to the defendant's will be barred from recovering.

As *Cepeda* demonstrates, and as we saw in connection with negligence law in Chapter 7, most courts have now folded *implied* assumption of risk into the comparative responsibility inquiry. Given that a major goal of decisions such as *Henningsen* and *Greenman* was to prevent sellers from inducing consumers to waive their rights to complain about product defects that cause personal injuries, one must assume that express assumption of risk has little role to play in this area.

Finally, in a minority of jurisdictions, "product misuse" remains a separate defense that serves as a bar to recovery. This practice is frowned upon by the Third Restatement. *See* Restatement (Third), *supra*, § 17, cmt. c ("Product misuse, alteration, and modification, whether by a third party or the plaintiff, are not discrete doctrines within products liability law.").

10. *From* Cepeda *to* Suter. Consider further the application of comparative responsibility principles to the facts of a case such as *Cepeda*, which, unfortunately, presents a fairly common form of products liability claim. (Note that such claims are in addition to, and avoid the damage limitations of, workers' compensation claims against employers.) At first blush, it may be tempting to assign a great deal of responsibility to the employee who operates a machine without a safety device that was put in place for his protection. Keep in mind, however, that the circumstances of, and the reasons for, the removal of such devices vary significantly. Sometimes the situation may be that of an employee needlessly endangering himself. Often, however, product alterations of this sort are made at the behest of, or with the approval of, management, perhaps because the safety device in question interferes with faster production, or because the defendant's prefabricated machine is modified once installed in the employer's plant in order to accommodate some special requirement of the employer's production process. Note also that just as manufacturers of consumer products sometimes are (or should be) well aware of patterns of consumer "misuse," so too manufacturers of industrial equipment are or should be aware that safety equipment is often removed.

In recognition of the special conditions of the industrial workplace, the New Jersey Supreme Court within a year revisited and modified *Cepeda*'s analysis of the role of plaintiff's fault. Suter v. San Angelo Foundry & Mach. Co., 406 A.2d 140 (N.J. 1979). In light of the enactment of the New Jersey Comparative Negligence Act, *Suter* first converted *Cepeda*'s complete contributory negligence defense into a partial comparative fault defense.* Second, and more to the present point, *Suter* declined to apply even the partial defense of comparative responsibility to one set

---

* Because the Act adopts a "modified" comparative fault scheme, the plaintiff's fault will still operate as a complete bar if the plaintiff is deemed more responsible for his injuries than the defendant.

of cases. These consist of instances, like *Cepeda* itself, in which an employee in an "industrial setting" is injured while using in a foreseeable manner an evidently dangerous product supplied by his employer. In the view of the *Suter* court, these sorts of dangerous encounters are sufficiently likely to be involuntary that it would be unjust to recognize even a partial comparative responsibility defense to a products liability action brought by the injured employee against a seller of the product.

B. The Changing Meaning of Design Defect in California Law

In *Cronin, supra,* the California Supreme Court declined to require products liability plaintiffs to prove that the product in question failed the consumer expectations test. Indeed, it went further, approving instructions that simply asked the jury to determine whether the product in question contained a defect, without elaborating on the definition of that concept. However, *Cronin* was decided in 1972, before commentators and courts had drawn the now-standard contrast between manufacturing and design defects. (Recall that, in fact, *Cronin* refused to draw that distinction.) Six years later, the court had occasion to revisit these issues. As you read the following opinion, ask yourself: To what extent is the court consciously changing California law? For whose benefit?

Barker v. Lull Eng'g Co.
573 P.2d 443 (Cal. 1978)

Tobriner, Acting C.J. In August 1970, plaintiff Ray Barker was injured at a construction site at the University of California at Santa Cruz while operating a high-lift loader manufactured by defendant Lull Engineering Co. and leased to plaintiff's employer by defendant George M. Philpott Co., Inc. Claiming that his injuries were proximately caused, inter alia, by the alleged defective design of the loader, Barker instituted the present tort action seeking to recover damages for his injuries. The jury returned a verdict in favor of defendants, and plaintiff appeals from the judgment entered upon that verdict, contending primarily that in view of this court's decision in Cronin v. J. B. E. Olson Corp. (1972) 8 Cal. 3d 121, 104 Cal. Rptr. 433, 501 P.2d 1153, the trial court erred in instructing the jury "that strict liability for a defect in design of a product is based on a finding that the product was unreasonably dangerous for its intended use. . . ." . . .

As we explain in more detail below, we have concluded from this review that a product is defective in design either (1) if the product has failed to perform as safely as an ordinary consumer would expect when used in an intended or reasonably foreseeable manner, or (2) if, in light of the relevant factors discussed below, the benefits of the challenged design [are outweighed by] the risk of danger inherent in such design. In addition, we explain how the burden of proof with respect to the latter "risk-benefit" standard should be allocated.

This dual standard for design defect assures an injured plaintiff protection from products that either fall below ordinary consumer expectations as to safety, or that, on balance, are not as safely designed as they should be. At the same time, the standard permits a manufacturer who has marketed a product which satisfies ordinary consumer expectations to demonstrate the relative complexity of design decisions and the trade-offs that are frequently required in the adoption of alternative designs. Finally, this test reflects our continued adherence to the principle that, in a product liability action, the trier of fact must focus on the product, not on the manufacturer's conduct, and that the plaintiff need not prove that the manufacturer acted unreasonably or negligently in order to prevail in such an action.

1. *The facts of the present case*

Plaintiff Barker sustained serious injuries as a result of an accident which occurred while he was operating a Lull High-Lift Loader at a construction site. The loader, manufactured in 1967, is a piece of heavy construction equipment designed to lift loads of up to 5,000 pounds to a maximum height of 32 feet. The loader is 23 feet long, 8 feet wide and weighs 17,050 pounds; it sits on four large rubber tires which are about the height of a person's chest, and is equipped with four-wheel drive, an automatic transmission with no park position and a hand brake. Loads are lift by forks similar to the forks of a forklift.

The loader is designed so that the load can be kept level even when the loader is being operated on sloping terrain. The leveling of the load is controlled by a lever located near the steering column, and positioned between the operator's legs. The lever is equipped with a manual lock that can be engaged to prevent accidental slipping of the load level during lifting.

The loader was not equipped with seat belts or a roll bar. A wire and pipe cage over the driver's seat afforded the driver some protection from falling objects. The cab of the loader was located at least nine feet behind the lifting forks.

On the day of the accident the regular operator of the loader, Bill Dalton, did not report for work, and plaintiff, who had received only limited instruction on the operation of the loader from Dalton and who had operated the loader on only a few occasions, was assigned to run the loader in Dalton's place. The accident occurred while plaintiff was attempting to lift a load of lumber to a height of approximately 18 to 20 feet and to place the load on the second story of a building under construction. The lift was a particularly difficult one because the terrain on which the loader rested sloped sharply in several directions.

Witnesses testified that plaintiff approached the structure with the loader, leveled the forks to compensate for the sloping ground and lifted the load to a height variously estimated between 10 and 18 feet. During the course of the lift plaintiff felt some vibration, and, when it appeared to several coworkers that the load was beginning to tip, the workers shouted to plaintiff to jump from the loader. Plaintiff heeded these warnings and leaped from the loader, but while scrambling away he was struck by a piece of falling lumber and suffered serious injury.

Although the above facts were generally not in dispute, the parties differed markedly in identifying the responsible causes for the accident. Plaintiff contended . . . that the accident was attributable to one or more design defects of the loader. Defendant, in turn, denied that the loader was defective in any respect, and claimed that the accident resulted either from plaintiff's lack of skill or from his misuse of its product. We briefly review the conflicting evidence.

[Plaintiff's principal expert witness testified that the loader's relatively narrow wheel base called for it to be equipped, as are cranes and certain other models of loaders, with "outriggers" — mechanical arms extending out from the sides of the machine that could stabilize it. The expert additionally testified that the loader should have been equipped with a roll bar or seat belts, which would have permitted the plaintiff to remain in the loader as it tipped over. Finally, several witnesses testified that the leveling lever was defective because it was too easy for the loader's operator to accidentally engage it. — EDS.]

. . . Defendants' experts testified that the loader was not unstable when utilized on the terrain for which it was intended, and that if the accident did occur because of the tipping of the loader it was only because plaintiff had misused the equipment by operating it on steep terrain for which the loader was unsuited.[2] [Defense experts further testified that outriggers were not necessary when the loader was used for its intended purpose and that no competitive loaders with similar lifting capacity were equipped with outriggers. They further testified that a roll bar was unnecessary because in view of the bulk of the loader it would not roll completely over. The witnesses also maintained that seat belts would have increased the danger of the loader by impairing the operator's ability to leave the vehicle quickly in case of an emergency. With respect to the claimed defects of the leveling device, the defense experts testified that the positioning of the lever was the safest and most convenient for the operator. — EDS.] . . .

After considering the sharply conflicting testimony reviewed above, the jury by a 10 to 2 vote returned a general verdict in favor of defendants. Plaintiff appeals from the judgment entered upon that verdict.

2. *The trial court erred in instructing the jurors that "strict liability for a defect in design . . . is based on a finding that the product was unreasonably dangerous for its intended use."*

Plaintiff principally contends that the trial court committed prejudicial error in instructing the jury "that strict liability for a defect in design of a

---

2. In support of this claim, defendants presented the testimony of Bill Dalton, the regular operator of the loader, who testified that he called in sick on the day of the accident because he knew that the loader was not designed to make the lifts scheduled for that day, and he was frightened to make lifts in the area where the accident occurred because of the danger involved. Dalton testified that he informed his supervisor that a crane, rather than a high-lift loader, was required for lifts on such sloping ground, but that the supervisor had not agreed to obtain a crane for such lifts.

product is based on a finding that the product was unreasonably dangerous for its intended use. . . ."[4] Plaintiff maintains that this instruction conflicts directly with this court's decision in *Cronin*, decided subsequently to the instant trial, and mandates a reversal of the judgment. Defendants argue, in response, that our *Cronin* decision should not be applied to product liability actions which involve "design defects" as distinguished from "manufacturing defects."

[The court proceeded to summarize the facts and holding of *Cronin*, *supra*.] . . .

Plaintiff contends that the clear import of . . . *Cronin* is that the "unreasonably dangerous" terminology of [Section 402A of the Second] Restatement should not be utilized in defining defect in product liability actions, and that the trial court consequently erred in submitting an instruction which defined a design defect by reference to the "unreasonably dangerous" standard.

In attempting to escape the apparent force of *Cronin*'s explicit language, defendants observe that the flawed hasp which rendered the truck defective in *Cronin* represented a manufacturing defect rather than a design defect, and they argue that *Cronin*'s disapproval of the Restatement's "unreasonably dangerous" standard should be limited to the manufacturing defect context. Defendants point out that one of the bases for our rejection of the "unreasonably dangerous" criterion in *Cronin* was our concern that such language, when used in conjunction with the "defective product" terminology, was susceptible to an interpretation which would place a dual burden on an injured plaintiff to prove, first, that a product was defective and, second, that it was additionally unreasonably dangerous. Defendants contend that the "dual burden" problem is present only in a manufacturing defect context and not in a design defect case.

In elaborating this contention, defendants explain that in a manufacturing defect case, a jury may find a product defective because it deviates from the manufacturer's intended result, but may still decline to impose liability under the Restatement test on the ground that such defect did not render the product unreasonably dangerous. In a design defect case, by contrast, defendants assert that a defect is defined by reference to the "unreasonably dangerous" standard and, since the two are equivalent, no danger of a dual burden exists. In essence, defendants argue that under the instruction which the trial court gave in the instant case, plaintiff was not required to prove both that the loader was defective and that such

---

4. The challenged instruction reads in full: "I instruct you that strict liability for the defect in design of a product is based on a finding that the product was unreasonably dangerous for its intended use, and in turn the unreasonableness of the danger must necessarily be derived from the state of the art at the time of the design. The manufacturer or lessor are not insurers of their products. However, an industry cannot set its own standards."

Plaintiff's challenge is limited to the portion of the instruction which provides that "strict liability for the defect in design of a product is based on a finding that the product was unreasonably dangerous for its intended use," and accordingly we express no opinion as to the propriety of the remaining portions of the instruction.

defect made the loader unreasonably dangerous, but only that the loader was defectively designed by virtue of its unreasonable dangerousness.

Although defendants may be correct, at least theoretically, in asserting that the so-called "dual burden" problem is averted when the "unreasonably dangerous" terminology is used in a design defect case simply as a definition of "defective condition" or "defect," defendants overlook the fact that our objection to the "unreasonably dangerous" terminology in *Cronin* went beyond the "dual burden" issue, and was based, more fundamentally, on a substantive determination that the Restatement's "unreasonably dangerous" formulation represented an undue restriction on the application of strict liability principles.

As we noted in *Cronin*, the Restatement draftsmen adopted the "unreasonably dangerous" language primarily as a means of confining the application of strict tort liability to an article which is "dangerous to an extent beyond that which would be contemplated by the ordinary consumer who purchases it, with the ordinary knowledge common to the community as to its characteristics." (Rest. 2d Torts, § 402A, com. i.) In *Cronin*, however, we flatly rejected the suggestion that recovery in a products liability action should be permitted only if a product is more dangerous than contemplated by the average consumer, refusing to permit the low esteem in which the public might hold a dangerous product to diminish the manufacturer's responsibility for injuries caused by that product. As we pointedly noted in *Cronin*, even if the "ordinary consumer" may have contemplated that Shopsmith lathes posed a risk of loosening their grip and letting a piece of wood strike the operator, "another Greenman" should not be denied recovery. (8 Cal. 3d at p.133, 104 Cal. Rptr. 433, 501 P.2d 1153.) Indeed, our decision in *Luque v. McLean* (1972) 8 Cal. 3d 136, 104 Cal. Rptr. 443, 501 P.2d 1163 decided the same day as *Cronin* aptly reflects our disagreement with the restrictive implications of the Restatement formulation, for in *Luque* we held that a power rotary lawn mower with an unguarded hole could properly be found defective, in spite of the fact that the defect in the product was patent and hence in all probability within the reasonable contemplation of the ordinary consumer.

Thus, our rejection of the use of the "unreasonably dangerous" terminology in *Cronin* rested in part on a concern that a jury might interpret such an instruction, as the Restatement draftsman had indeed intended, as shielding a defendant from liability so long as the product did not fall below the ordinary consumer's expectations as to the product's safety.[7] As *Luque* demonstrates, the dangers posed by such a misconception by the jury extend to cases involving design defects as well as to actions involving

---

7. This is not to say that the expectations of the ordinary consumer are irrelevant to the determination of whether a product is defective, for as we point out below we believe that ordinary consumer expectations are frequently of direct significance to the defectiveness issue. The flaw in the Restatement's analysis, in our view, is that it treats such consumer expectations as a "ceiling" on a manufacturer's responsibility under strict liability principles, rather than as a "floor." As we shall explain, past California decisions establish that at a minimum a product must meet ordinary consumer expectations as to safety to avoid being found defective.

manufacturing defects: indeed, the danger of confusion is perhaps more pronounced in design cases in which the manufacturer could frequently argue that its product satisfied ordinary consumer expectations since it was identical to other items of the same product line with which the consumer may well have been familiar.

Accordingly, contrary to defendants' contention, the reasoning of *Cronin* does not dictate that that decision be confined to the manufacturing defect context. . . . Consequently, we conclude that the design defect instruction given in the instant case was erroneous.

3. . . . *In . . . design defect cases, a court may . . . instruct a jury that a product is defective . . . if (1) the plaintiff proves that the product failed to perform as safely as an ordinary consumer would expect . . . , or (2) . . . the defendant fails to prove . . . that . . . the benefits of the challenged design outweigh the risk of danger inherent in the design.* . . .

As this court has recognized on numerous occasions, the term defect as utilized in the strict liability context is neither self-defining nor susceptible to a single definition applicable in all contexts. . . .

. . . [O]ur cases have employed two alternative criteria in ascertaining, in Justice Traynor's words, whether there is something "wrong, if not in the manufacturer's manner of production, at least in his product." (Traynor, *The Ways and Meanings of Defective Products and Strict Liability, supra*, 32 Tenn. L. Rev. 363, 366.)

First, our cases establish that a product may be found defective in design if the plaintiff demonstrates that the product failed to perform as safely as an ordinary consumer would expect when used in an intended or reasonably foreseeable manner. This initial standard, somewhat analogous to the Uniform Commercial Code's warranty of fitness and merchantability, reflects the warranty heritage upon which California product liability doctrine in part rests. As we noted in *Greenman*, "implicit in (a product's) presence on the market . . . (is) a representation that it (will) safely do the jobs for which it was built." (59 Cal. 2d at p.64, 27 Cal. Rptr. at p.701, 377 P.2d at p.901.) When a product fails to satisfy such ordinary consumer expectations as to safety in its intended or reasonably foreseeable operation, a manufacturer is strictly liable for resulting injuries. Under this standard, an injured plaintiff will frequently be able to demonstrate the defectiveness of a product by resort to circumstantial evidence, even when the accident itself precludes identification of the specific defect at fault.

As Professor Wade has pointed out, however, the expectations of the ordinary consumer cannot be viewed as the exclusive yardstick for evaluating design defectiveness because "(i)n many situations . . . the consumer would not know what to expect, because he would have no idea how safe the product could be made." (Wade, *On the Nature of Strict Tort Liability for Products, supra*, 44 Miss. L.J. 825, 829.) Numerous California decisions have implicitly recognized this fact and have made clear, through varying linguistic formulations, that a product may be found defective in design, even if it satisfies ordinary consumer expectations, if through hindsight the jury determines that the product's design embodies "excessive preventable danger," or, in other words, if the jury finds that the risk of danger inherent in the challenged design outweighs the benefits of such design.[10]

A review of past cases indicates that in evaluating the adequacy of a product's design pursuant to this latter standard, a jury may consider, among other relevant factors, the gravity of the danger posed by the challenged design, the likelihood that such danger would occur, the mechanical feasibility of a safer alternative design, the financial cost of an improved design, and the adverse consequences to the product and to the consumer that would result from an alternative design.

Although our cases have thus recognized a variety of considerations that may be relevant to the determination of the adequacy of a product's design, past authorities have generally not devoted much attention to the appropriate allocation of the burden of proof with respect to these matters. The allocation of such burden is particularly significant in this context inasmuch as this court's product liability decisions, from *Greenman* to *Cronin*, have repeatedly emphasized that one of the principal purposes behind the strict product liability doctrine is to relieve an injured plaintiff of many of the onerous evidentiary burdens inherent in a negligence cause of action. Because most of the evidentiary matters which may be relevant to the determination of the adequacy of a product's design under the "risk-benefit" standard, e.g., the feasibility and cost of alternative designs are similar to issues typically presented in a negligent design case and involve technical matters peculiarly within the knowledge of the manufacturer, we conclude that once the plaintiff makes a prima facie showing that the injury was proximately caused by the product's design, the burden should appropriately shift to the defendant to prove, in light of the relevant factors, that the product is not defective. Moreover, inasmuch as this conclusion flows from our determination that the fundamental public policies embraced in *Greenman* dictate that a manufacturer who seeks to escape liability for an injury proximately caused by its product's design on a risk-benefit theory should bear the burden of persuading the trier of fact that its product should not be judged defective, the defendant's burden is one affecting the burden of proof, rather than simply the burden of producing evidence.

Thus, to reiterate, a product may be found defective in design, so as to subject a manufacturer to strict liability for resulting injuries, under either of two alternative tests. First, a product may be found defective in design if the plaintiff establishes that the product failed to perform as safely as an ordinary consumer would expect when used in an intended or reasonably foreseeable manner. Second, a product may alternatively be found defective in design if the plaintiff demonstrates that the product's design proximately caused his injury and the defendant fails to establish,

---

10. In the instant case we have no occasion to determine whether a product which entails a substantial risk of harm may be found defective even if no safer alternative design is feasible. As we noted in Jiminez v. Sears, Roebuck & Co., *supra*, 4 Cal. 3d 379, 383, 93 Cal. Rptr. 769, 772, 482 P.2d 681, 684, Justice Traynor has "suggested that liability might be imposed as to products whose norm is danger." (Citing Traynor, *The Ways and Meaning of Defective Products and Strict Liability*, *supra*, 32 Tenn. L. Rev. 363, 367 *et seq.*)

in light of the relevant factors, that, on balance, the benefits of the challenged design outweigh the risk of danger inherent in such design.

. . . As we have indicated, we believe that the test for defective design set out above is appropriate in light of the rationale and limits of the strict liability doctrine, for it subjects a manufacturer to liability whenever there is something "wrong" with its product's design . . . while stopping short of making the manufacturer an insurer for all injuries which may result from the use of its product. This test, moreover, explicitly focuses the trier of fact's attention on the adequacy of the product itself, rather than on the manufacturer's conduct, and places the burden on the manufacturer, rather than the plaintiff, to establish that because of the complexity of, and trade-offs implicit in, the design process, an injury-producing product should nevertheless not be found defective.

Amicus . . . on behalf of the plaintiff . . . contends that any instruction which directs the jury to "weigh" or "balance" a number of factors, or which sets forth a list of completing considerations for the jury to evaluate in determining the existence of a design defect, introduces an element which "rings of negligence" into the determination of defect, and consequently is inconsistent with [*Cronin*]. . . .

. . . [P]ast design defect decisions demonstrate that, as a practical matter, in many instances it is simply impossible to eliminate the balancing or weighing of competing considerations in determining whether a product is defectively designed or not. In Self v. General Motors Corp., *supra*, 42 Cal. App. 3d 1, 116 Cal. Rptr. 575, for example, an automobile passenger, injured when the car in which she was riding exploded during an accident, brought suit against the manufacturer claiming that the car was defective in that the fuel tank had been placed in a particularly vulnerable position in the left rear bumper. One issue in the case, of course, was whether it was technically feasible to locate the fuel tank in a different position which would have averted the explosion in question. But, as the *Self* court recognized, feasibility was not the sole issue, for another relevant consideration was whether an alternative design of the car, while averting the particular accident, would have created a greater risk of injury in other, more common situations.

In similar fashion, weighing the extent of the risks and the advantages posed by alternative designs is inevitable in many design defect cases. As the *Self* court stated: "(W)e appreciate the need to balance one consideration against another in designing a complicated product so as to achieve reasonable and practical safety under a multitude of varying conditions." Inasmuch as the weighing of competing considerations is implicit in many design defect determinations, an instruction which appears to preclude such a weighing process under all circumstances may mislead the jury. . . .

Thus, the fact that the manufacturer took reasonable precautions in an attempt to design a safe product or otherwise acted as a reasonably prudent manufacturer would have under the circumstances, while perhaps absolving the manufacturer of liability under a negligence theory, will not preclude the imposition of liability under strict liability principles if, upon hindsight, the trier of fact concludes that the product's design is unsafe to consumers, users, or bystanders.

4. *Conclusion*

The technological revolution has created a society that contains dangers to the individual never before contemplated. The individual must face the threat to life and limb not only from the car on the street or highway but from a massive array of hazardous mechanisms and products. The radical change from a comparatively safe, largely agricultural, society to this industrial unsafe one has been reflected in the decisions that formerly tied liability to the fault of a tortfeasor but now are more concerned with the safety of the individual who suffers the loss. As Dean Keeton has written, "The change in the substantive law as regards the liability of makers of products and other sellers in the marketing chain has been from fault to defect. The plaintiff is no longer required to impugn the maker, but he is required to impugn the product." (Keeton, *Product Liability and the Meaning of Defect* (1973) 5 St. Mary's L.J. 30, 33.) . . .

We hold that a trial judge may properly instruct the jury that a product is defective in design (1) if the plaintiff demonstrates that the product failed to perform as safely as an ordinary consumer would expect when used in an intended or reasonably foreseeable manner, or (2) if the plaintiff proves that the product's design proximately caused his injury and the defendant fails to prove, in light of the relevant factors discussed above, that on balance the benefits of the challenged design outweigh the risk of danger inherent in such design.

Because the jury may have interpreted the erroneous instruction given in the instant case as requiring plaintiff to prove that the high-lift loader was ultrahazardous or more dangerous than the average consumer contemplated, . . . we cannot find that the error was harmless on the facts of this case. . . .

The judgment in favor of defendants is reversed.

NOTES AND QUESTIONS

1. *Whither* Cronin? Why might the trial judge in *Barker* have decided to include the "unreasonably dangerous" concept in his jury instructions, despite the fact that California's high court had clearly rejected that language in *Cronin?*

2. Barker's *First Prong: Consumer Expectations.* The first prong of the *Barker* test states that a product is defective in design if "the plaintiff demonstrates that the product failed to perform as safely as an ordinary consumer would expect when used in an intended or reasonably foreseeable manner." For a relatively straightforward application of this test, see West v. Johnson & Johnson Products, Inc., 220 Cal. Rptr. 437 (Ct. App. 1985). The plaintiff in that case suffered toxic shock syndrome, involving temperatures as high as 107 degrees, profound shock, extremely low blood pressure, skin rashes, and liver and kidney abnormalities. She alleged, and offered proof, that her use of an O.B.-brand tampon manufactured by the defendant had caused her to suffer these injuries, and that it was therefore defective in design. The judge sent the case to the jury on a

882 Chapter 12. Products Liability

consumer expectation test, and the jury found for the plaintiff. *West*, applying *Barker*, held that it was perfectly appropriate for the court to instruct on a consumer expectation test, and affirmed. Does the consumer expectation test capture why a product such as this is "defective"?

3. *Whose Expectations?* Could *Barker* have reached the result it did on the strength of the consumer expectations test alone? (Wasn't the problem on appeal simply the lower court's erroneous insertion of "unreasonably dangerous" into the jury instruction?) Why did the *Barker* court feel the need to add a second prong to its analysis? In thinking about these questions, does it help to ask who counts as the consumer in *Barker?* Is it the plaintiff, the purchaser, the company, or someone else? Did Mr. Barker actually have any expectations about the front end loader?

4. Barker's *Second Prong: Risk-Utility.* Who among the parties in *Barker* is advocating for the risk-utility test: plaintiff, defendant, or neither? Note that the second prong of *Barker* requires a *defendant* to *prove* that the benefits of the chosen design outweigh its risks. This unusually plaintiff-solicitous feature of the law is a direct application of Justice Traynor's longstanding desire to alleviate the plaintiff's burden of proof in product-injury cases. It also raises an interesting doctrinal question: *What, if anything, must a plaintiff prove, under the second prong, in order to impose upon defendant the burden of proving that the utility of the design outweighs its risks?* Is the second prong in effect a form of absolute liability, which provides an affirmative defense of risk-utility?

The answer appears to be no: The plaintiff must still make a prima facie case of defect before the burden shifts. But there is much greater ambiguity in the language of *Barker* than one might hope. The court appears to have intended that the plaintiff must first demonstrate that a design feature that presented a substantial risk actually caused the injury. That design feature, if shown to present a substantial risk that was in fact realized, is in effect considered prima facie evidence of a design defect. The defendant then bears the burden of proving that the utility of the design outweighs the risks it poses.

5. *From* Barker *to* Soule. *Barker* was decided in 1978. The following year witnessed the birth of the "Association for California Tort Reform," heralding the emergence of a powerful political and legal backlash against Justice Traynor's vision of products liability law as necessary to defend the interests of the consumer against the risks posed by modern products. Ever since, products liability has been at the center of disputes over the tort system. Consider the following decision in light of these developments. Is it faithful to the letter of *Barker?* To its spirit?

Soule v. General Motors Corp.
882 P.2d 298 (Cal. 1994)

Baxter, J.   Plaintiff's ankles were badly injured when her General Motors (GM) car collided with another vehicle. She sued GM, asserting that defects in her automobile allowed its left front wheel to break free, collapse rearward, and smash the floorboard into her feet. GM denied any defect and claimed that the force of the collision itself was the sole cause of the injuries. Expert witnesses debated the issues at length. Plaintiff prevailed at trial, and the Court of Appeal affirmed the judgment.

We granted review to resolve three questions. First, may a product's design be found defective on grounds that the product's performance fell below the safety expectations of the ordinary consumer (*see* Barker v. Lull Engineering Co. (1978) 20 Cal. 3d 413, 426-432, 143 Cal. Rptr. 225, 573 P.2d 443) if the question of how safely the product should have performed cannot be answered by the common experience of its users? [Second and third questions omitted. — EDS.]

We [conclude that] [t]he trial court erred by giving an "ordinary consumer expectations" instruction in this complex case. . . . However, . . . [the] error[] . . . [was] harmless on this record. We will therefore affirm the Court of Appeal's judgment.

FACTS

On the early afternoon of January 16, 1984, plaintiff was driving her 1982 Camaro in the southbound center lane of Bolsa Chica Road. . . . There was a slight drizzle, the roadway was damp, and apparently plaintiff was not wearing her seat belt. A 1972 Datsun, approaching northbound, suddenly skidded into the path of plaintiff's car. The Datsun's left rear quarter struck plaintiff's Camaro in an area near the left front wheel. Estimates of the vehicles' combined closing speeds on impact vary from 30 to 70 miles per hour.[1]

The collision bent the Camaro's frame adjacent to the wheel and tore loose the bracket that attached the wheel assembly (specifically, the lower control arm) to the frame. As a result, the wheel collapsed rearward and inward. The wheel hit the underside of the "toe pan" — the slanted floorboard area beneath the pedals — causing the toe pan to crumple, or "deform," upward into the passenger compartment.

Plaintiff received a fractured rib and relatively minor scalp and knee injuries. Her most severe injuries were fractures of both ankles, and the more serious of these was the compound compression fracture of her left ankle. This injury never healed properly. In order to relieve plaintiff's pain, an orthopedic surgeon fused the joint. As a permanent result, plaintiff cannot flex her left ankle. She walks with considerable difficulty, and her condition is expected to deteriorate.

After the accident, the Camaro was acquired by a salvage dealer, Noah Hipolito. Soon thereafter, plaintiff's son, Jeffrey Bishop, and her original attorney, Richard Hawkins, each inspected and photographed the car and

---

1. In its statement of facts, the Court of Appeal adopted testimony by an accident witness that at the moment of impact, the Datsun had slowed from 50 miles per hour to between 15 and 25 miles per hour, and the Camaro was traveling about 30 miles per hour. GM did not challenge this factual assumption in its petition for rehearing.

its damaged floorboard area. The failed bracket assembly was retrieved. However, Hipolito later discarded the damaged toe pan, repaired the Camaro, and resold it. Thus, except for the bracket assembly, no part of the vehicle was retained as evidence.

Plaintiff sued GM for her ankle injuries, asserting a theory of strict tort liability for a defective product. She claimed the severe trauma to her ankles was not a natural consequence of the accident, but occurred when the collapse of the Camaro's wheel caused the toe pan to crush violently upward against her feet. Plaintiff attributed the wheel collapse to a manufacturing defect, the substandard quality of the weld attaching the lower control arm bracket to the frame. She also claimed that the placement of the bracket, and the configuration of the frame, were defective designs because they did not limit the wheel's rearward travel in the event the bracket should fail.

The available physical and circumstantial evidence left room for debate about the exact angle and force of the impact and the extent to which the toe pan had actually deformed. The issues of defect and causation were addressed through numerous experts produced by both sides in such areas as biomechanics, metallurgy, orthopedics, design engineering, and crash-test simulation.

Plaintiff submitted the results of crash tests, and also asserted the similarity of another real-world collision involving a 1987 Camaro driven by Dana Carr. According to plaintiff's experts, these examples indicated that Camaro accidents of similar direction and force do not generally produce wheel bracket assembly failure, extensive toe pan deformation, or severe ankle injuries such as those plaintiff had experienced. These experts opined that without the deformation of the toe pan in plaintiff's car, her accident could not have produced enough force to fracture her ankles.

A metallurgist testifying on plaintiff's behalf examined the failed bracket from her car. He concluded that its weld was particularly weak because of excess "porosity" caused by improper welding techniques. Plaintiff's experts also emphasized the alternative frame and bracket design used by the Ford Mustang of comparable model years. They asserted that the Mustang's design, unlike the Camaro's, provided protection against unlimited rearward travel of the wheel should a bracket assembly give way.

GM's metallurgist disputed the claims of excessive weakness or porosity in the bracket weld. Expert witnesses for GM also countered the assertions of defective design. GM asserted that the Camaro's bracket was overdesigned to withstand forces in excess of all expected uses. According to expert testimony adduced by GM, the Mustang's alternative frame and bracket configuration did not fit the Camaro's overall design goals and was not distinctly safer for all collision stresses to which the vehicle might be subjected. Indeed, one witness noted, at least one more recent Ford product had adopted the Camaro's design.

A second major thrust of GM's defense was that the force of the collision, rather than any product defect, was the sole cause of plaintiff's ankle injuries. Using the results of accident reconstruction, computer simulations, and actual crash tests, GM sought to prove that the probable collision force concentrated on the left front wheel of plaintiff's Camaro exceeded the "yield strength" of any feasible weld or design. . . .

The court instructed the jury that a manufacturer is liable for "enhanced" injuries caused by a manufacturing or design defect in its product while the product is being used in a foreseeable way. Over GM's objection, the court gave the standard design defect instruction without modification. This instruction advised that a product is defective in design "if it fails to perform as safely as an ordinary consumer would expect when used in an intended or reasonably foreseeable manner *or* if there is a risk of danger inherent in the design which outweighs the benefit of the design." (Italics added.)

The jury was also told that in order to establish liability for a design defect under the "ordinary consumer expectations" standard, plaintiff must show (1) the manufacturer's product failed to perform as safely as an ordinary consumer would expect, (2) the defect existed when the product left the manufacturer's possession, (3) the defect was a "legal cause" of plaintiff's "enhanced injury," and (4) the product was used in a reasonably foreseeable manner. . . .

In a series of special findings, the jury determined that the Camaro contained a defect (of unspecified nature) which was a "legal cause" of plaintiff's "enhanced injury." The jury further concluded that although plaintiff was guilty of comparative fault, her conduct was not a legal cause of her enhanced injuries. Plaintiff received an award of $1.65 million.

GM appealed. Among other things, it argued that the trial court erred by instructing on ordinary consumer expectations in a complex design-defect case. . . .

Following one line of authority, the Court of Appeal concluded that a jury may rely on expert assistance to determine what level of safe performance an ordinary consumer would expect under particular circumstances. Hence, the Court of Appeal ruled, there was no error in use of the ordinary consumer expectations standard for design defect in this case. . . .

DISCUSSION

1. TEST FOR DESIGN DEFECT

A manufacturer, distributor, or retailer is liable in tort if a defect in the manufacture or design of its product causes injury while the product is being used in a reasonably foreseeable way. (Cronin v. J.B.E. Olson Corp. (1972) 8 Cal. 3d 121, 126-130, 104 Cal. Rptr. 433, 501 P.2d 1153 [*Cronin*]; Greenman v. Yuba Power Products, Inc. (1963) 59 Cal. 2d 57, 62, 27 Cal. Rptr. 697, 377 P.2d 897 [*Greenman*].) Because traffic accidents are foreseeable, vehicle manufacturers must consider collision safety when they design and build their products. Thus, whatever the cause of an accident, a vehicle's producer is liable for specific collision injuries that would not have occurred but for a manufacturing or design defect in the vehicle. . . .

. . . At a minimum, said *Barker*, a product *is* defective in design if it *does* fail to perform as safely as an ordinary consumer would expect. This principle, *Barker* asserted, acknowledges the relationship between strict tort liability for a defective product and the common law doctrine of warranty, which holds that a product's presence on the market includes an implied representation " 'that it [will] safely do the jobs for which it was built.' " . . . "Under this [minimum] standard," *Barker* observed, "an injured plaintiff will frequently be able to demonstrate the defectiveness of the product *by resort to circumstantial evidence, even when the accident itself precludes identification of the specific defect at fault.* [Citations.]"

However, *Barker* asserted, the Restatement had erred in proposing that a violation of ordinary consumer expectations was *necessary* for recovery on this ground. . . .

Thus, *Barker* concluded, "a product may be found defective in design, even if it satisfies ordinary consumer expectations, if through hindsight the jury determines that the product's design embodies 'excessive preventable danger,' or, in other words, if the jury finds that the risk of danger inherent in the challenged design outweighs the benefits of such design. [Citations.]" *Barker* held that under this latter standard, "a jury may consider, among other relevant factors, the gravity of the danger posed by the challenged design, the likelihood that such danger would occur, the mechanical feasibility of a safer alternative design, the financial cost of an improved design, and the adverse consequences to the product and to the consumer that would result from an alternative design. [Citations.]"

Barker also made clear that when the ultimate issue of design defect calls for a careful assessment of feasibility, practicality, risk, and benefit, the case should not be resolved simply on the basis of ordinary consumer expectations. As *Barker* observed, "past design defect decisions demonstrate that, as a practical matter, in many instances it is simply impossible to eliminate the balancing or weighing of competing considerations in determining whether a product is defectively designed or not. . . ."

An example, *Barker* noted, was the "crashworthiness" issue presented in Self v. General Motors Corp., *supra*, 42 Cal. App. 3d 1, 116 Cal. Rptr. 575. The debate there was whether the explosion of a vehicle's fuel tank in an accident was due to a defect in design. This, in turn, entailed concerns about whether placement of the tank in a position less vulnerable to rear end collisions, even if technically feasible, "would have created a greater risk of injury in other, more common situations." Because this complex weighing of risks, benefits, and practical alternatives is "implicit" in so many design-defect determinations, *Barker* concluded, "an instruction which appears to preclude such a weighing process under all circumstances may mislead the jury." . . .

[Although the foregoing analysis suggests that *Barker* contemplated that a consumer expectations instruction should *not* be given when the design defect issue raises a complex issue requiring the weighing of risks and benefits, subsequent decisions have suggested otherwise.] To [this] effect is West v. Johnson & Johnson Products, Inc. (1985) 174 Cal. App. 3d 831, 220 Cal.

Rptr. 437 (*West*). The plaintiff in *West* became seriously ill in February 1980, during her menstrual period. . . . [P]laintiff's physicians belatedly concluded that she had suffered TSS [toxic shock syndrome] caused by tampons which defendant had designed and produced. At trial, experts debated the nature of plaintiff's illness, and they also disputed whether the tampon design and materials used by defendant encouraged TSS. The trial court instructed only on the consumer expectations prong of *Barker*.

On appeal, defendant argued that the risk-benefit test alone was proper. However, *West* . . . [concluded that juries can be instructed on] the consumer expectations test in complex cases involving expert testimony. In a time before general awareness and warnings about TSS, the court reasoned, plaintiff "had every right to expect" that use of this seemingly innocuous product "would not lead to a serious (or perhaps fatal) illness. . . ." Hence, the consumer expectations instruction was appropriate. . . .[2]

In *Barker*, we offered two alternative ways to prove a design defect, each appropriate to its own circumstances. The purposes, behaviors, and dangers of certain products are commonly understood by those who ordinarily use them. By the same token, the ordinary users or consumers of a product may have reasonable, widely accepted minimum expectations about the circumstances under which it should perform safely. Consumers govern their own conduct by these expectations, and products on the market should conform to them.

In some cases, therefore, "ordinary knowledge . . . as to . . . [the product's] characteristics" (Rest. 2d Torts, *supra*, § 402A, com. i., p.352) may permit an inference that the product did not perform as safely as it should. *If* the facts permit such a conclusion, and *if* the failure resulted from the product's design, a finding of defect is warranted without any further proof. The manufacturer may not defend a claim that a product's design failed to perform as safely as its ordinary consumers would expect by presenting expert evidence of the design's relative risks and benefits.[3]

However, as we noted in *Barker*, a complex product, even when it is being used as intended, may often cause injury in a way that does not

---

2. Under the particular circumstances, use of the consumer expectations test alone was approved in Grimshaw v. Ford Motor Co. (1981) 119 Cal. App. 3d 757, 174 Cal. Rptr. 348. There, a 1972 Pinto was instantly engulfed in flames when another vehicle struck it from the rear at 28 to 37 miles per hour. There was evidence that Ford knew placement of the Pinto's fuel tank was unsafe. The theory of trial was consumer expectations. Two weeks before the case went to the jury, we decided *Barker*. Ford immediately requested a risk-benefit instruction, which the trial court refused. In a pre-*Campbell* appeal, the Court of Appeal affirmed. Noting both the timing and theory-of-trial problems, the court also observed that a risk-benefit instruction would actually have *prejudiced* Ford, because under *Barker*, it offered an *additional* means of recovery for design defect.

3. For example, the ordinary consumers of modern automobiles may and do expect that such vehicles will be designed so as not to explode while idling at stoplights, experience sudden steering or brake failure as they leave the dealership, or roll over and catch fire in two-mile-per-hour collisions. If the plaintiff in a product liability action proved that a vehicle's design produced such a result, the jury could find forthwith that the car failed to perform as safely as its ordinary consumers would expect, and was therefore defective.

engage its ordinary consumers' reasonable minimum assumptions about safe performance. For example, the ordinary consumer of an automobile simply has "no idea" how it should perform in all foreseeable situations, or how safe it should be made against all foreseeable hazards.

An injured person is not foreclosed from proving a defect in the product's design simply because he cannot show that the reasonable minimum safety expectations of its ordinary consumers were violated. Under *Barker*'s alternative test, a product is still defective if its design embodies "excessive preventable danger," that is, unless "the benefits of the . . . design outweigh the risk of danger inherent in such design." But this determination involves technical issues of feasibility, cost, practicality, risk, and benefit which are "impossible" to avoid. In such cases, the jury *must* consider the manufacturer's evidence of competing design considerations, and the issue of design defect cannot fairly be resolved by standardless reference to the "expectations" of an "ordinary consumer."

As we have seen, the consumer expectations test is reserved for cases in which the *everyday experience* of the product's users permits a conclusion that the product's design violated *minimum* safety assumptions, and is thus defective *regardless of expert opinion about the merits of the design.* It follows that where the minimum safety of a product is within the common knowledge of lay jurors, expert witnesses may not be used to demonstrate what an ordinary consumer would or should expect. Use of expert testimony for that purpose would invade the jury's function, and would invite circumvention of the rule that the risks and benefits of a challenged design must be carefully balanced whenever the issue of design defect goes beyond the common experience of the product's users.[4]

By the same token, the jury may not be left free to find a violation of ordinary consumer expectations whenever it chooses. Unless the facts actually permit an inference that the product's performance did not meet the minimum safety expectations of its ordinary users, the jury must engage in the balancing of risks and benefits required by the second prong of *Barker.*

---

4. Plaintiff insists that manufacturers should be forced to design their products to meet the "objective" safety demands of a "hypothetical" reasonable consumer who is fully informed about what he or she *should* expect. Hence, plaintiff reasons, the jury may receive expert advice on "reasonable" safety expectations for the product. However, this function is better served by the risk-benefit prong of *Barker.* There, juries receive expert advice, apply clear guidelines, and decide accordingly whether the product's design is an acceptable compromise of competing considerations.

On the other hand, appropriate use of the consumer expectations test is not necessarily foreclosed simply because the product at issue is only in specialized use, so that the general public may not be familiar with its safety characteristics. If the safe performance of the product fell below the reasonable, widely shared minimum expectations of those who *do* use it, perhaps the injured consumer should not be forced to rely solely on a technical comparison of risks and benefits. By the same token, if the expectations of the product's limited group of ordinary consumers are beyond the lay experience common to all jurors, expert testimony on the limited subject of what the product's actual consumers *do expect* may be proper. (*See, e.g.,* Lunghi v. Clark Equipment Co., *supra,* 153 Cal. App. 3d 485, 496, 200 Cal. Rptr. 387.)

Accordingly, as *Barker* indicated, instructions are misleading and incorrect if they allow a jury to avoid this risk-benefit analysis in a case where it is required. Instructions based on the ordinary consumer expectations prong of *Barker* are not appropriate where, as a matter of law, the evidence would not support a jury verdict on that theory. Whenever that is so, the jury must be instructed solely on the alternative risk-benefit theory of design defect announced in *Barker.*[5] . . .

GM argues at length that the consumer expectations test is an "unworkable, amorphic, fleeting standard" which should be entirely abolished as a basis for design defect. In GM's view, the test is deficient and unfair in several respects. First, it defies definition. Second, it focuses not on the objective condition of products, but on the subjective, unstable, and often unreasonable opinions of consumers. Third, it ignores the reality that ordinary consumers know little about how safe the complex products they use can or should be made. Fourth, it invites the jury to isolate the particular consumer, component, accident, and injury before it instead of considering whether the whole product fairly accommodates the competing expectations of all consumers in all situations. Fifth, it eliminates the careful balancing of risks and benefits which is essential to any design issue. . . .

We fully understand the dangers of improper use of the consumer expectations test. However, we cannot accept GM's insinuation that ordinary consumers lack any legitimate expectations about the minimum safety of the products they use. In particular circumstances, a product's design may perform so unsafely that the defect is apparent to the common reason, experience, and understanding of its ordinary consumers. In such cases, a lay jury is competent to make that determination. . . .

When use of the consumer expectations test is limited as *Barker* intended, the principal concerns raised by GM and the Council are met. Within these limits, the test remains a workable means of determining the existence of design defect. We therefore find no compelling reason to overrule the consumer expectations prong of *Barker* at this late date, and we decline to do so.

Applying our conclusions to the facts of this case, however, we agree that the instant jury should not have been instructed on ordinary consumer expectations. Plaintiff's theory of design defect was one of technical and mechanical detail. It sought to examine the precise behavior of several obscure components of her car under the complex circumstances of a particular accident. The collision's exact speed, angle, and point of impact were disputed. It seems settled, however, that plaintiff's Camaro received a substantial oblique blow near the left front wheel, and that the adjacent frame members and bracket assembly absorbed considerable inertial force.

5. Plaintiff urges that any limitation on use of the consumer expectations test contravenes *Greenman*'s purpose to aid hapless consumers. But we have consistently held that manufacturers are not insurers of their products; they are liable in tort only when "defects" in their products cause injury. *Barker* properly articulated that a product's design is "defective" only if it violates the "ordinary" consumer's safety expectations, *or* if the manufacturer cannot show the design's benefits outweigh its risks. . . .

An ordinary consumer of automobiles cannot reasonably expect that a car's frame, suspension, or interior will be designed to remain intact in any and all accidents. Nor would ordinary experience and understanding inform such a consumer how safely an automobile's design should perform under the esoteric circumstances of the collision at issue here. Indeed, both parties assumed that quite complicated design considerations were at issue, and that expert testimony was necessary to illuminate these matters. Therefore, injection of ordinary consumer expectations into the design defect equation was improper.

We are equally persuaded, however, that the error was harmless, because it is not reasonably probable defendant would have obtained a more favorable result in its absence. . . . As previously noted, the case was tried on the assumption that the alleged design defect was a matter of technical debate. Virtually all the evidence and argument on design defect focused on expert evaluation of the strengths, shortcomings, risks, and benefits of the challenged design, as compared with a competitor's approach. . . .

. . . We see no reasonable probability that the jury disregarded the voluminous evidence on the risks and benefits of the Camaro's design, and instead rested its verdict on its independent assessment of what an ordinary consumer would expect. Accordingly, we conclude, the error in presenting that theory to the jury provides no basis for disturbing the trial judgment.[8] . . .

[Concurring opinion of **Mosk, A.C.J.**, omitted. — EDS.]

Arabian, J. (concurring and dissenting). I concur in the majority's holding that the trial court committed instructional error in two respects, incorrectly charging the jury on the "consumer expectations" component of design defect liability, and improperly refusing defendant General Motors' requested instruction on legal causation. I cannot agree, however, with the conclusion that the latter error was harmless. . . .

NOTES AND QUESTIONS

1. *Crashworthiness and Increased Harm.* Notice that, in *Soule*, the claimed defect concerns the ability of a car to withstand a crash while protecting the occupants. Claims that cars and other vehicles are defective because of their lack of "crashworthiness" pose special difficulties, not just

8. In a separate argument, raised for the first time in GM's brief on the merits, . . . GM . . . urge[s] us to reconsider *Barker*'s holding — embodied in the standard instruction received by this jury — that under the *risk-benefit* test, the *manufacturer* has the burden of proving that the utility of the challenged design outweighs its dangers. . . .

. . . We are not persuaded. *Barker* allows the evaluation of competing designs, but it does not require proof that the challenged design is the safest possible alternative. The manufacturer need only show that given the inherent complexities of design, the benefits of its chosen design outweigh the dangers. Moreover, [while] modern discovery practice [sometimes enables plaintiffs to obtain engineering and other documents from defendants, it] neither redresses the inherent technical imbalance between manufacturer and consumer nor dictates that the injured consumer should bear the primary burden of evaluating a design developed and chosen by the manufacturer. . . .

on the issue of defect, but also as to actual causation. Thus, as in *Soule*, the factfinder is asked to determine whether a more passenger-protective design would have either prevented or lessened the severity of the injuries suffered by the plaintiffs. Does the latter sort of theory, in particular, ask too much of judges and juries? *See* Restatement (Third) of Torts: Products Liability § 16 (1998) (providing rules for allocating burdens of proof and for apportionment of liability in cases alleging injuries in the form of "increased harm").

2. *Who Wants Which Test?* The plaintiff in *Barker* advocated the use of the risk-utility test, but the plaintiff in *Soule* favored consumer expectations. Why this discrepancy? Meanwhile, General Motors (supported by amicus briefs submitted on behalf of an array of manufacturers) fervently supported an approach to design defect that would require all plaintiffs to proceed on a risk-utility theory. Why? Why do defendants in these situations believe that they will be better off if a products liability case revolves around a broad examination of risk-utility factors?

3. *Measuring Success.* Who "won" in *Soule?* Does the defendant have to pay the plaintiff? What should General Motors' lawyers tell the client about the result?

4. *Changing Course?* Recall from Chapter 10 the shift in the law of negligent infliction of emotional distress that occurred between 1968, when the California Supreme Court issued Dillon v. Legg, which opened new vistas of "NIED" liability, and 1987, at which time it issued Thing v. LaChusa in order to circumscribe that liability. Do you perceive a similar political progression (or regression) from *Escola* through *Soule?*

5. Soule *versus* Barker. In some respects, at least, *Soule* embraces *Barker*'s two-prong approach to design defect. Does it simply apply *Barker*, or does it alter or amend *Barker* in some way? Compare the following passages, the first from *Barker*, the second from *Soule*:

> Thus, to reiterate, *a product may be found defective in design*, so as to subject a manufacturer to strict liability for resulting injuries, *under either of two alternative tests*. First, a product may be found defective in design if the plaintiff establishes that the product failed to perform as safely as an ordinary consumer would expect when used in an intended or reasonably foreseeable manner. Second, a product may alternatively be found defective in design if the plaintiff demonstrates that the product's design proximately caused his injury and the defendant fails to establish, in light of the relevant factors, that, on balance, the benefits of the challenged design outweigh the risk of danger inherent in such design.

> [T]he consumer expectations test is reserved for cases in which the *everyday experience* of the product's users permits a conclusion that the product's design violated *minimum* safety assumptions, and is thus defective *regardless of expert opinion about the merits of the design.*" [Emphasis in original.] . . .
> [Except in such cases,] the jury *must be instructed solely* on the alternative risk-benefit theory of design defect announced in *Barker.*

On its face, the language of *Barker* is quite permissive about the two prongs: In any case *either* may be invoked. The implication is that a plaintiff may choose either prong as her theory of why the design was defective, and if she succeeds in providing evidence that can sustain that theory, and persuading the jury under her chosen theory, she will have proved design defect. *Soule* plainly rules out such a permissive framework. *The court must decide which prong is appropriate* and the criteria of selection for that decision are quite rigid. More particularly, the consumer expectations test is impermissible except when the *"everyday experience* of the product's users permits a conclusion that the product's design violated *minimum* safety assumptions, and is thus defective *regardless of expert opinion about the merits of the design."*

6. *The Realm of Everyday Experience.* Do you agree with the *Soule* court's application of its holding to the facts of the case? Does the everyday experience of jurors who are automobile users permit a conclusion that the Camaro violated minimum safety expectations? Why does the court conclude otherwise? Will all automobile crash cases need to proceed under the risk-utility test? Does the fact that jurors often have extensive experience with automobiles mean that they have no need for expert testimony to make a sound decision about whether there was a design defect?

7. *Risk-Utility and the Third Restatement.* *Soule* is very much in line with the views of the Reporters for the Third Restatement who have unabashedly advocated for a risk-utility test as the most defensible test for design defect from a doctrinal and policy perspective. Indeed, they go so far as to *define* design defect in terms of risk-utility analysis, expressed in terms of a burden on the plaintiff to prove the existence of a "reasonable alternative design."

§ 2.   CATEGORIES OF PRODUCT DEFECT

. . . A product . . .
   (b) is defective in design when the foreseeable risks of harm posed by the product could have been reduced or avoided by the adoption of a reasonable alternative design by the seller or other distributor, or a predecessor in the commercial chain of distribution, and the omission of the alternative design renders the product not reasonably safe. . . .

COMMENT: . . .

d. . . . Subsection (b) adopts a reasonableness ("risk-utility balancing") test. . . . [T]he test is whether a reasonable alternative design would, at a reasonable cost, have reduced the foreseeable risks of harm posed by the product and, if so, whether the omission of [that] design . . . rendered the product not reasonably safe. . . .

Notice that, in one respect, Section 2(b) is at least nominally more burdensome to plaintiffs than *Soule*. Whereas, in footnote 8, *Soule* declined to re-think *Barker*'s placement on the defendant of the burden of proving that the benefits of a product's design outweigh its costs, Section 2(b) places the burden of proving defectiveness (by means of proof of a reasonable alternative design) squarely on the plaintiff. This feature of the Third Restatement has been as controversial as its decision to treat risk-utility as the test for design defect in almost all cases. *See* Vautour v. Body Masters Sports Indus., Inc., 784 A.2d 1178 (N.H. 2001) (rejecting the proof of reasonable alternative design requirement); Dan B. Dobbs, *The Law of Torts* § 361, at 996-1002 (2000) (reviewing the debate).

Although risk-utility is accorded preeminent status by the Third Restatement, the Reporters do leave room the possibility that a design defect plaintiff will be relieved of the burden of proving the existence of a reasonable alternative design. *See* Restatement, *supra* § 2, cmt. b. Most important, Section 3 provides a "*res ipsa*" exception that, although prima-rily designed with claims of manufacturing defect in mind, may permit an inference of design defect from the mere causation of injury by a product, albeit only if the incident in which the plaintiff is harmed is "of a kind that ordinarily occurs as a result of a product defect." Restatement, *supra*, § 3(a).

Taking its design defect provisions together, the Restatement Third can be viewed as extending the changes that *Soule* wrought upon *Barker*. First, for any case in which some sort of sophisticated knowledge is required for an intelligent opinion about whether the product's design is defective, it requires risk-utility analysis. Second, the express rationale for its position is that, if the law is to repose confidence in the jury system in high-stakes personal injury cases, it must make sure that the jurors are adequately guided by experts and that their decisions are channeled by meaningful criteria. Third, it allows that there remains a handful of cases in which a product design's defectiveness is so plain that it would be inef-ficient and unfair to force the plaintiff to offer proof on the risk-utility factors.

The Reporters in their commentary tout risk-utility as superior from a normative point of view. They also vigorously assert that it accurately reflects the consensus position among courts at the time that Section 2 was adopted. Both their normative and their descriptive claims about the dominance of risk-utility analysis provoked a great deal of controversy in the American Law Institute, and a great deal of controversy remains, not only among lawyers and academics, but now in the courts. *See, e.g.*, Potter v. Chicago Pneumatic Tool Co., 694 A.2d 1319 (Conn. 1997) (discussing and criticizing Section 2(b) and adopting a consumer expectations test suitable to sophisticated products).

8. *Airbag Litigation.* California has continued its general drift away from consumer expectations and toward risk-utility. At least in form, however, the two-prong test remains the law, and serious debates continue on which prong to use for certain categories of cases. Indeed, a trio of reported cases on airbags illustrate the uncertainty that remains. *See* McCabe v. American Honda Motor Co., 123 Cal. Rptr. 2d 303 (Ct. App. 2002) (reversing summary judgment but leaving open for trial the question

whether the consumer expectations test or risk-utility test applies to allegations of a defectively designed airbag); Pruitt v. General Motors Corp., 86 Cal. Rptr. 2d 4 (Ct. App. 1999) (rejecting use of consumer expectations test in an airbag case); Bresnahan v. Chrysler Corp., 38 Cal. Rptr. 2d 446 (Ct. App. 1995) (permitting use of consumer expectations test in an airbag case).

9. *Latex Glove Litigation.* Despite occasional contrary indications from lower courts that consumer expectations still has a meaningful role to play, it is likely that in big ticket, products liability litigation, the risk-utility test will carry the day in California. Support for this hypothesis can be found in the California Court of Appeals' denial of a writ of mandate in Morson v. Superior Court, 109 Cal. Rptr. 2d 343 (Ct. App.), *rev. denied*, 2001 Cal. LEXIS 6949 (Cal. 2001). The plaintiffs in *Morson* were health-care workers. They filed numerous suits against a group of defendants whose members manufactured and distributed latex gloves. Plaintiffs asserted that the defendants knew by the early 1990s that 5 to 12 percent of health care workers who are commonly exposed to latex are sensitized to that substance to the point of developing allergic reactions ranging from skin discoloration, soreness, and rashes, to respiratory failure. (They also alleged that the latex gloves were defective because of the defendants' failure to warn that the gloves and their associated substances were extremely dangerous to those that may have an allergic or chemical reaction to them.)

In a coordinated proceeding designed to set common terms on which the trials of these claims would proceed in different courtrooms, the coordinating trial judge ruled that juries should not be instructed on the consumer expectations test. In response, the plaintiffs sought a writ of mandate: a special interlocutory appeal in which the appellant (usually styled the "petitioner") alleges that a lower court has committed such a gross error of law as to be acting outside the scope of its authority, and by which the petitioner seeks a "mandate" (a command) from the appellate court instructing the lower court to reverse its erroneous ruling. In their petition, plaintiffs argued that the trial judge in the coordinated proceeding committed a gross error by rejecting the contention that there was an ordinary consumer expectation among workers that they would not sustain injury simply by wearing — or being around those who were wearing — latex gloves for the purpose of protecting themselves from contact with infectious agents. According to the plaintiffs, the product was "a simple one that can give rise to simple consumer expectations of safety that have nothing to do with the chemical composition of the material from which the product is manufactured, or any other design characteristics for which specialized knowledge is required for understanding or taking appropriate precautions." *Id.* at 357.

The Court of Appeals confidently rejected this argument:

> [T]he protective or barrier function of the latex gloves, on which the Plaintiffs' safety argument is mainly premised, is not their only characteristic. These gloves are made of a particular material through a particular manufacturing process. The effect of this material and these processes may well be to

create in their users many degrees of allergic reactions. Understanding and assessing responsibility for such allergic reactions is a matter that is driven by the science of the manufacturing and preparation procedures, as well as the medical aspects of an individual's allergic reactions to various substances.

Plaintiffs' theory of design defect, therefore, is a complex one. When we re-formulate the Plaintiffs' underlying consumer expectations statements to comport with their actual arguments in these proceedings, we see that their simple formulation of an expectation that they would not be harmed by the use of this product is totally inaccurate. Rather, their arguments posit that exposure to the natural substance of latex may make their dormant, incipient, or developing allergies worse than they would otherwise have been. We find it an inevitable conclusion that before the issues of design defect can be adequately litigated and resolved, expert testimony will be essential to assist the finder of fact in understanding the pros and cons of Plaintiffs' arguments.

Id. Did the *Morson* court decide the issue correctly under *Soule?* Why were plaintiffs concerned enough to seek a writ of mandate? Because the issue was brought to the appellate court by means of this special procedure, rather than an ordinary post-trial appeal, the court could have denied the writ without reaching the merits simply by concluding that any error alleged by the petition was an ordinary legal error that should be pursued on appeal, rather than the sort of extraordinary error that warrants the issuance of a writ of mandate. Why, then, did the court go out of its way to deny the writ on the merits? Do you think that litigation under the risk-utility test will appropriately determine whether the latex gloves in question should be deemed to have contained a design defect? Do you think this form of analysis is a fair way to ascertain whether the manufacturers of the gloves should be held liable?

Morson is directly opposed to a contemporaneous decision of the Wisconsin Supreme Court. *See* Green v. Smith & Nephew AHP, Inc., 629 N.W.2d 727 (Wis. 2001). The trial court there had employed the consumer expectations test, and had declined to instruct the jury that the injuries alleged by the plaintiff must have been foreseeable. A majority of the Wisconsin Supreme Court affirmed the jury's verdict for the plaintiff, expressly declaring that Wisconsin law favors the consumer expectations test across the board, even for sophisticated products. In the process, the court expressly rejected the Third Restatement's embrace of risk-utility, its demand of foreseeability, and its requirement of proof of a reasonable alternative design.

10. *Whither Consumer Expectations?* Numerous jurisdictions retain a consumer expectations test as their sole test for design defect. Some seem to have retained the test as a matter of *stare decisis*. Others have adopted the test by statute. Still others — like Wisconsin and Connecticut — have considered and rejected the idea of shifting from consumer expectations to risk-utility. In contrast to *Soule* and the Third Restatement, *Potter* — the Connecticut case on point — maintains that courts are quite capable of articulating the consumer expectations test in a way that still permits expert testimony on technical and/or scientific matters, as well as on the

risks and benefits of alternative product designs. 694 A.2d 1319. Why did *Soule* conclude that expert testimony could not play a role in the application of the consumer expectations test? Was its reasoning sound?

11. *New York and the Return of Warranty.* As if the foregoing array of tests and standards were not enough, the New York Court of Appeals has indicated that even if its products liability law demands application of the risk-utility test and only that test, the consumer expectations test might still have a role to play through a separate cause of action for breach of implied warranty. *See* Denny v. Ford Motor Co., 662 N.E. 2d 730 (N.Y. 1995). In *Denny* — a case involving the roll-over of a passenger vehicle — the court held that many plaintiffs with product-related personal injury claims may proceed either in tort under the risk-utility test, or under an implied warranty theory governed by the consumer expectations test.

12. *Manifestly Unreasonable Designs.* Suppose a product contains a significant danger, but cannot be redesigned to avoid that danger. Is it ever open to a judge or jury to declare that the product is of so little utility that it cannot be sold without subjecting the seller to liability for injuries caused by its dangerous features?

Courts have occasionally rendered decisions suggesting as much. For example, the New Jersey Supreme Court rendered a famous decision in which it indicated that it was willing to declare all above-ground swimming pools ineliminably defective for posing an inherent and unavoidable risk of bodily harm to those who dive headfirst into them. O'Brien v. Muskin Corp., 463 A.2d 298 (N.J. 1983).* Other candidates for unavoidably unsafe products that have been mentioned by courts and commentators include asbestos, tobacco, handguns, and metal-tipped lawn darts for use by children. The Third Restatement grudgingly acknowledges that such products might exist. *See* Restatement, *supra* § 2, cmt. e (suggesting that a toy gun designed for use with hard rubber pellets to create a sense of "realism" might be deemed manifestly unreasonable even though no other design could more safely provide such realism).

13. *Design Defects and Punitive Damages.* In footnote 2 of *Soule*, the court mentions that Ford Motor Co. had in an earlier case — Grimshaw v. Ford Motor Co., 174 Cal. Rptr. 348 (Ct. App. 1981) — unsuccessfully requested that the jury be instructed to use the risk-utility test for design defect. *Grimshaw* is significant not only for that ruling, but for the verdict it subsequently produced.

Thirteen-year-old Richard Grimshaw died when the car he was riding in, a Ford Pinto, was involved in a collision and burst into flames. The plaintiff's allegation was that the Pinto was defectively designed because its gas tank was incorporated into the car's chassis in such a way as to make it susceptible to explode in response to relatively modest rear-end collisions. In support of this contention, the plaintiff introduced evidence that Ford

---

* *O'Brien* generated a prompt legislative response. *See* N.J.S. 2A:58C-3a(2) (1987) (blocking liability for products containing "inherent" dangers that are known or knowable to the ordinary consumer).

had performed an internal assessment of the reasonable alternative designs that could have protected the unshielded gas tank. The plaintiff maintained that Ford had chosen to forgo such designs because each would have added between $4 and $15 to the car's sticker price, as well as extra weight, and that Ford was determined to keep the Pinto at a weight of 2000 lbs. and a price of $2000. It further introduced into evidence testimony of a former Ford engineer who described the process by which Ford "had engaged in cost-benefit analyses" in deciding whether to change the Pinto's fuel tank design once it became aware of the risk that it could rupture at low-speed collisions. The jury found that the Pinto was defectively designed under California law and awarded Grimshaw $550,000 in compensatory damages. It also awarded $125 million in punitive damages, which the trial judge reduced to $3.5 million. Ford appealed the *Grimshaw* case, primarily to challenge the reduced punitive award. The Court of Appeal for the Fourth Appellate District upheld it.

Ford raised many issues on appeal. For example, it argued that the judge erred in permitting the plaintiff's attorney to refer to cost-benefit analysis in his closing argument to the jury. However, the main focus of Ford's argument concerned the question of whether it is ever appropriate to allow a jury to award punitive damages in a products liability suit, and if so, whether it is appropriate for a jury to use evidence of cost-benefit analyses as evidence of the sort of *malice* or *reckless indifference* that must be found before punitive damages may be awarded, especially if the evidence suggests that the cost-benefit calculations were performed in good faith (nonfraudulently). Recall from Chapter 8 that punitive damages are in principle *unavailable* to plaintiffs complaining of injuries resulting from ordinary negligence. Ford argued that, given this rule, it must follow that punitive damages are also unavailable for products liability claims, which, after all, were originally conceived as imposing a form of strict liability. Ford also argued that juries should not be permitted to infer malice from the fact that a design they deem to be defective resulted from a deliberate decision made in part on the basis of cost-benefit analysis. *Every* design choice, it argued, is the result of deliberation over costs and benefits, including safety. This in turn would entail that punitive damages ought to be available in any design defect suit, a proposition seemingly contradicted by the rule that punitive damages may only be awarded in unusual cases in which the defendant displays a particularly culpable (malicious or reckless) disposition.

The *Grimshaw* court rejected Ford's contention that a jury in a products liability case is not permitted to evaluate the reprehensibility of a manufacturer's design decisions. In so ruling, it noted that the plaintiff was not simply alleging that Ford had acted carelessly when it adopted the cheaper fuel tank design (it was not as if an engineer had made a mistake when solving an equation). Rather, the claim was that Ford had acted with "malice," which, under California law "may be inferred from . . . [a] showing that the defendants' conduct . . . was willful, intentional, and done in reckless disregard of its possible results." *Id.* at 386. The court concluded that, in some cases at least, the same evidence offered to prove that a product contains a design defect will also demonstrate that the designer acted with wanton or reckless disregard for consumers' safety. In such cases, the manufacturer is not being punished merely for engaging in cost-benefit analysis, but rather for engaging in such analysis on terms that suggest a wanton failure to take seriously the potential "costs" (in terms of injuries) associated with its product. Thus, for example, the evidence pertaining to the design process might show that the manufacturer was fully aware that the design chosen would create a significant risk of injury for x persons, and that another design, which was just as cheap and efficacious, would create a much smaller risk for a much smaller number of persons $(x-n)$. The court held that, in such circumstances, a jury could conclude that the decision to adopt the design demonstrates reckless disregard.

Ford made a number of arguments in addition to the argument that design choices found to be defective under the rules of products liability can never be viewed as reckless or wanton acts. These arguments concerned larger issues of policy, in particular the problems of "multiple punishment" and "overdeterrence." Both of these arguments turn on the fact that manufacturers of mass-produced products may sometimes face the prospect of a succession of suits, and a succession of jury verdicts imposing huge punitive damages awards.* The court rejected these arguments, and responded with a series of policy arguments of its own:

> ... [I]n commerce-related torts, the manufacturer may find it more profitable to treat compensatory damages as a part of the cost of doing business rather than to remedy the defect. Deterrence of such "objectionable corporate policies" serves one of the principal purposes of [California law]. Governmental safety standards and the criminal law have failed to provide adequate consumer protection against the manufacture and distribution of defective products. Punitive damages thus remain as the most effective remedy for consumer protection against defectively designed mass produced articles....

Id. at 382-383 (citations omitted). In a contemporaneous Wisconsin case involving its Mustang model, Ford made similar policy arguments with equally little success. *See* Wangen v. Ford Motor Co., 294 N.W.2d 437 (Wis. 1980).

Whether the allowance of punitive damages in products liability cases has in fact led to unpredictable and unbounded liability predicated on jurors' second-guessing of corporate cost-benefit analysis is very much a contested issue today. Despite the impression created by occasional awards of eye-popping magnitude (the vast bulk of which are reduced on appeal), punitive damages are rarely awarded, and when they are awarded,

---

* In general, there are no substantive or procedural rules that bar the same manufacturer from being subjected to multiple punitive damage awards for the same conduct (e.g., producing a defectively designed car model) in multiple proceedings in one or many jurisdictions. For example, the federal constitutional prohibition on "double jeopardy" does not apply to civil proceedings. Thus, the jury's award of punitive damages in *Grimshaw* would have no effect on the ability of a jury in another suit — whether brought in California or any other state — alleging injuries to another person caused by the Pinto's defective gas tank.

it is usually in cases involving allegations of fraud, battery, and other "intentional" torts, not products liability. Yet anecdotal evidence and some empirical research suggests that punitive damages are frequently requested in products liability complaints. This provides some evidence in support of the claim that the real danger of punitive damages in products liability litigation resides in their "shadow effect." That is, because of the unpredictability of when punitive damages will be awarded and in what amount, defendants will feel pressure to settle cases that they would have taken to trial or to settle for higher amounts than the compensatory damages demanded by the plaintiffs would have justified, out of fear of that their case may fall within the 3 to 4 percent of products liability cases in which punitive damages are awarded. Some of the issues associated with the award of punitive damages for injuries caused by conduct evincing "reckless disregard" are discussed in Chapters 8 and 13.

14. *Punitive Damages and Corporate Intentionality*. Consider Ford's argument that juries should not be entrusted with the task of distinguishing between the production of a defectively designed product and the *malicious* or *reckless* production of a defectively designed product. Design decisions in large manufacturing operations are rarely the result of a single person exercising broad discretion. Instead, like other corporate acts, they are collaborative among key personnel who work for the corporation. How should the factfinder determine the attitude of a corporation? One might look to the individual employees responsible for the conduct to which one attributes the attitude, but that may not capture the whole picture. (After all, it may be the case that no single actor within the production process possessed all the information that was possessed by the corporation as a whole.) If the plaintiff cannot point to any single actor's malicious or reckless attitude, should she be barred from obtaining punitive damages? Or is it appropriate to ascribe such attitudes to the corporation itself? In ordinary discourse, it is quite common to ascribe dispositions such as "greed" or "environmental irresponsibility" to a collective entity such as a corporation. Are there philosophical or policy-based objections to adopting similar usage in the language of products liability law?

IV. PRESCRIPTION DRUGS

We saw in Chapter 3 that, for a variety of reasons, courts have generally been inclined to give dispositive weight to professional custom in medical malpractice cases, even though they do not do the same for many other activities, including (as we saw in *MacPherson*) product design and manufacture. Likewise, these materials have at various points alluded to "tort reform" laws that have, for example, capped noneconomic damages, abolished the collateral source rule, and shortened statutes of limitations in suits for medical malpractice. Since the inception of products liability law, citizens, judges, and legislators have expressed a like concern about its application to drugs, vaccines, and medical devices. These instincts are reflected in the "blood shield" laws, and the laws exempting human tissues from the category of products, mentioned in Section II. More striking, perhaps, is that Congress has enacted legislation that essentially removes claims for injuries caused by vaccines from the tort system, instead providing relatively modest compensation to those who suffer (even grave) side effects from being inoculated.

Apart from the fact that interest groups such as doctors, pharmaceutical companies, and their insurers wield considerable political clout, there are several reasons for the consistent expression of concerns about tort law's interaction with the delivery of healthcare. One obvious concern is cost. Americans expend an increasing amount of their incomes on medical services, which have steadily increased in price. Moves to contain liability are thus partly grounded in the belief that doing so will help keep a lid on healthcare costs. A second concern is that lay jurors have limited expertise in these areas, and hence perhaps are not to be entrusted with difficult judgments about the complex design decisions pertaining to the manufacture of pharmaceuticals. Third, when medical products have defects, those defects are often likely to inflict significant damage on "sympathetic" plaintiffs. Here the worry is that juries will be moved to enter enormous and at times excessive verdicts. Finally, the provision of medical services, including the sale and use of medical products, is already subject to substantial legislative and administrative regulation, and often occurs through the medium of professionals such as physicians and pharmacists, suggesting a diminished need to rely on tort law in this area. (Whether these reasons, individually or together, provide a sound basis for restricting the application of products liability law to pharmaceuticals and other medical devices is, as you would expect, a hotly contested issue.)

Given that the foregoing considerations are very much on the minds of citizens, judges, and politicians, it will come as no surprise to discover that courts have frequently crafted liability-restrictive doctrines in the domain of prescription drugs. That is largely the "story" of this section. However, we begin with a case that points entirely in the opposite direction. Indeed, the following decision can fairly be described as implementing one of the most interesting and innovative plaintiff-oriented developments of twentieth-century tort law—a development known as *market share liability*. For reasons that will become apparent when you read the following cases, market share liability was adopted first in California, as a means of providing relief to plaintiffs pursuing claims against the manufacturers of a prescription drug.

A. *Product Identification and Apportionment*

One of the main motivations for modern products liability law was the desire among courts such as the California Supreme Court to relieve plaintiffs injured by products of potentially daunting problems of proof. Indeed, it was the difficulties that Ms. Escola faced in proving what went wrong in the manufacture of the exploding soda bottle that first prompted Justice Traynor to call for the adoption of strict products liability. There, and in many other cases, the difficulty faced by the plaintiff concerns lack of evidence bearing on the issue of defect.

Even a plaintiff who can establish that she has been injured by an arguably defective product may stand to lose her suit because of a more basic problem of proof—the inability to identify the relevant "seller(s)" of the product in question. For example, plaintiffs around the country have brought products liability suits against paint manufacturers, alleging injuries caused to children who have suffered lead poisoning after ingesting lead-based paint as it peels off window sills and walls. Apart from difficulties posed in proving design defect, this sort of plaintiff often confronts the graver problem of lacking any proof as to which among numerous manufacturers produced the paint that her child ingested. For example, imagine a tenant of an apartment that was painted years before she took occupancy by an independent contractor that had been hired by the landlord. In this situation, the likelihood of determining the brand of paint that was used may be quite small.

You may recall that we encountered a similar situation in Chapter 4, in the case of Summers v. Tice. There the California Supreme Court permitted a plaintiff to recover from each of two careless hunters because the plaintiff had no basis for proving which one of the two actually succeeded in shooting him. Might the court that decided both *Escola* and *Summers* be prepared to construct out of them an innovative doctrinal solution to problems of product identification?

Sindell v. Abbott Labs.
607 P.2d 924 (Cal. 1980)*

Mosk, J. This case involves a complex problem both timely and significant: may a plaintiff, injured as the result of a drug administered to her mother during pregnancy, who knows the type of drug involved but cannot identify the manufacturer of the precise product, hold liable for her injuries a maker of a drug produced from an identical formula?

Plaintiff Judith Sindell brought an action against eleven drug companies and Does 1 through 100, on behalf of herself and other women similarly situated. The complaint alleges as follows:

Between 1941 and 1971, defendants were engaged in the business of manufacturing, promoting, and marketing diethylstilbesterol (DES), a drug which is a synthetic compound of the female hormone estrogen. The drug was administered to plaintiff's mother and the mothers of the class she represents,[1] for the purpose of preventing miscarriage. In 1947, the Food and Drug Administration authorized the marketing of DES as a miscarriage preventative, but only on an experimental basis, with a requirement that the drug contain a warning label to that effect.

* [*cert. denied*, 449 U.S. 912 (1980).—Eds.]
1. The plaintiff class alleged consists of "girls and women who are residents of California and who have been exposed to DES before birth and who may or may not know that fact or the dangers" to which they were exposed. Defendants are also sued as representatives of a class of drug manufacturers which sold DES after 1941.

DES may cause cancerous vaginal and cervical growths in the daughters exposed to it before birth, because their mothers took the drug during pregnancy. The form of cancer from which these daughters suffer is known as adenocarcinoma, and it manifests itself after a minimum latent period of 10 or 12 years. It is a fast-spreading and deadly disease, and radical surgery is required to prevent it from spreading. DES also causes adenosis, precancerous vaginal and cervical growths which may spread to other areas of the body. The treatment for adenosis is cauterization, surgery, or cryosurgery. Women who suffer from this condition must be monitored by biopsy or colposcopic examination twice a year, a painful and expensive procedure. Thousands of women whose mothers received DES during pregnancy are unaware of the effects of the drug.

In 1971, the Food and Drug Administration ordered defendants to cease marketing and promoting DES for the purpose of preventing miscarriages, and to warn physicians and the public that the drug should not be used by pregnant women because of the danger to their unborn children.

During the period defendants marketed DES, they knew or should have known that it was a carcinogenic substance, that there was a grave danger after varying periods of latency it would cause cancerous and precancerous growths in the daughters of the mothers who took it, and that it was ineffective to prevent miscarriage. Nevertheless, defendants continued to advertise and market the drug as a miscarriage preventative. They failed to test DES for efficacy and safety; the tests performed by others, upon which they relied, indicated that it was not safe or effective. In violation of the authorization of the Food and Drug Administration, defendants marketed DES on an unlimited basis rather than as an experimental drug, and they failed to warn of its potential danger.[2]

Because of defendants' advertised assurances that DES was safe and effective to prevent miscarriage, plaintiff was exposed to the drug prior to her birth. She became aware of the danger from such exposure within one year of the time she filed her complaint. As a result of the DES ingested by her mother, plaintiff developed a malignant bladder tumor which was removed by surgery. She suffers from adenosis and must constantly be monitored by biopsy or colposcopy to insure early warning of further malignancy.

The first cause of action alleges that defendants were jointly and individually negligent in that they manufactured, marketed and promoted DES as a safe and efficacious drug to prevent miscarriage, without adequate testing or warning, and without monitoring or reporting its effects.

A separate cause of action alleges that defendants are jointly liable regardless of which particular brand of DES was ingested by plaintiff's mother because defendants collaborated in marketing, promoting and testing the drug, relied upon each other's tests, and adhered to an industry-wide safety standard. DES was produced from a common and mutually

---

2. It is alleged also that defendants failed to determine if there was any means to avoid or treat the effects of DES upon the daughters of women exposed to it during pregnancy, and failed to monitor the carcinogenic effects of the drug.

agreed upon formula as a fungible drug interchangeable with other brands of the same product; defendants knew or should have known that it was customary for doctors to prescribe the drug by its generic rather than its brand name and that pharmacists filled prescriptions from whatever brand of the drug happened to be in stock.

Other causes of action are based upon theories of strict liability, violation of express and implied warranties, false and fraudulent representations, misbranding of drugs in violation of federal law, conspiracy and "lack of consent."

Each cause of action alleges that defendants are jointly liable because they acted in concert, on the basis of express and implied agreements, and in reliance upon and ratification and exploitation of each other's testing and marketing methods.

Plaintiff seeks compensatory damages of $1 million and punitive damages of $10 million for herself. For the members of her class, she prays for equitable relief in the form of an order that defendants warn physicians and others of the danger of DES and the necessity of performing certain tests to determine the presence of disease caused by the drug, and that they establish free clinics in California to perform such tests.

Defendants demurred to the complaint. While the complaint did not expressly allege that plaintiff could not identify the manufacturer of the precise drug ingested by her mother, she stated in her points and authorities in opposition to the demurrers filed by some of the defendants that she was unable to make the identification, and the trial court sustained the demurrers of these defendants without leave to amend on the ground that plaintiff did not and stated she could not identify which defendant had manufactured the drug responsible for her injuries. Thereupon, the court dismissed the action. This appeal involves only five of ten defendants named in the complaint.[4] . . .

This case is but one of a number filed throughout the country seeking to hold drug manufacturers liable for injuries allegedly resulting from DES prescribed to the plaintiffs' mothers since 1947. According to a note in the Fordham Law Review, estimates of the number of women who took the drug during pregnancy range from 1½ million to 3 million. Hundreds, perhaps thousands, of the daughters of these women suffer from adenocarcinoma, and the incidence of vaginal adenosis among them is 30 to 90 percent. (Comment, *DES and a Proposed Theory of Enterprise Liability* (1978) 46 Fordham L. Rev. 963, 964-967 (hereafter Fordham Comment).) Most of the cases are still pending. With two exceptions, those that have been decided resulted in judgments in favor of the drug company defendants because of the failure of the plaintiffs to identify the manufacturer of the DES prescribed to their mothers. The same result was reached in a

---

4. Abbott Laboratories, Eli Lilly and Company, E.R. Squibb and Sons, The Upjohn Company, and Rexall Drug Company are respondents. The action was dismissed or the appeal abandoned on various grounds as to other defendants named in the complaint; e.g., one defendant demonstrated it had not manufactured DES during the period plaintiff's mother took the drug.

recent California case. The present action is another attempt to overcome this obstacle to recovery.

We begin with the proposition that, as a general rule, the imposition of liability depends upon a showing by the plaintiff that his or her injuries were caused by the act of the defendant or by an instrumentality under the defendant's control. . . .

There are, however, exceptions to this rule. Plaintiff's complaint suggests several bases upon which defendants may be held liable for her injuries even though she cannot demonstrate the name of the manufacturer which produced the DES actually taken by her mother. The first of these theories, classically illustrated by Summers v. Tice (1948) 33 Cal. 2d 80, 199 P.2d 1, places the burden of proof of causation upon tortious defendants in certain circumstances. The second basis of liability emerging from the complaint is that defendants acted in concert to cause injury to plaintiff. There is a third and novel approach to the problem, sometimes called the theory of "enterprise liability," but which we prefer to designate by the more accurate term of "industry-wide" liability, which might obviate the necessity for identifying the manufacturer of the injury-causing drug. We shall conclude that these doctrines, as previously interpreted, may not be applied to hold defendants liable under the allegations of this complaint. However, we shall propose and adopt a fourth basis for permitting the action to be tried, grounded upon an extension of the *Summers* doctrine.

I

Plaintiff places primary reliance upon cases which hold that if a party cannot identify which of two or more defendants caused an injury, the burden of proof may shift to the defendants to show that they were not responsible for the harm. This principle is sometimes referred to as the "alternative liability" theory.

The celebrated case of Summers v. Tice, *supra*, 33 Cal. 2d 80, 199 P.2d 1, a unanimous opinion of this court, best exemplifies the rule. In *Summers*, the plaintiff was injured when two hunters negligently shot in his direction. It could not be determined which of them had fired the shot which actually caused the injury to the plaintiff's eye, but both defendants were nevertheless held jointly and severally liable for the whole of the damages. We reasoned that both were wrongdoers, both were negligent toward the plaintiff, and that it would be unfair to require plaintiff to isolate the defendant responsible, because if the one pointed out were to escape liability, the other might also, and the plaintiff-victim would be shorn of any remedy. In these circumstances, we held, the burden of proof shifted to the defendants, "each to absolve himself if he can." We stated that under these or similar circumstances a defendant is ordinarily in a "far better position" to offer evidence to determine whether he or another defendant caused the injury.

In *Summers*, we relied upon Ybarra v. Spangard (1944) 25 Cal. 2d 486, 154 P.2d 687. There, the plaintiff was injured while he was unconscious during the course of surgery. He sought damages against several doctors and a nurse who attended him while he was unconscious. We held that it would be unreasonable to require him to identify the particular defendant who had performed the alleged negligent act because he was unconscious at the time of the injury and the defendants exercised control over the instrumentalities which caused the harm. Therefore, under the doctrine of res ipsa loquitur, an inference of negligence arose that defendants were required to meet by explaining their conduct. . . .

Defendants assert that these principles are inapplicable here. First, they insist that a predicate to shifting the burden of proof under *Summers-Ybarra* is that the defendants must have greater access to information regarding the cause of the injuries than the plaintiff, whereas in the present case the reverse appears. [We disagree.] . . .

. . . Because many years elapsed between the time the drug was taken and the manifestation of plaintiff's injuries she, and many other daughters of mothers who took DES, are unable to [identify the manufacturer of the particular DES that harmed her]. Certainly there can be no implication that plaintiff is at fault in failing to do so — the event occurred while plaintiff was in utero, a generation ago.

On the other hand, it cannot be said with assurance that defendants have the means to make the identification. . . . Nor . . . [is] the absence of evidence on this subject . . . due to the fault of defendants. . . . [T]he difficulty or impossibility of identification results primarily from the passage of time rather than from their allegedly negligent acts of failing to provide adequate warnings. Thus Haft v. Lone Palm Hotel (1970) 3 Cal. 3d 756, 91 Cal. Rptr. 745, 478 P.2d 465, upon which plaintiff relies, is distinguishable.[14]

It is important to observe, however, that while defendants do not have means superior to plaintiff to identify the maker of the precise drug taken by her mother, they may in some instances be able to prove that they did not manufacture the injury-causing substance. In the present case, for example, one of the original defendants was dismissed from the action upon proof that it did not manufacture DES until after plaintiff was born.

[The] . . . fact [that] defendants do not have greater access to information which might establish the identity of the manufacturer of the DES which injured plaintiff does not per se prevent application of the *Summers* rule.

Nevertheless, . . . [there] is an important difference between the situation involved in *Summers* and the present case. There, all the parties who were or could have been responsible for the harm to the plaintiff were

14. In *Haft*, a father and his young son drowned in defendants' swimming pool. There were no witnesses to the accident. Defendants were negligent in failing to provide a lifeguard, as required by law. We held that the absence of evidence of causation was a direct and foreseeable result of the defendants' negligence, and that, therefore, the burden of proof on the issue of causation was upon defendants. . . . There is no proper analogy to *Haft* here. While in *Haft* the presence of a lifeguard on the scene would have provided a witness to the accident and probably prevented it, plaintiff asks us to speculate that if the DES taken by her mother had been labelled as an experimental drug, she would have recalled or recorded the name of the manufacturer and passed this information on to her daughter. It cannot be said here that the absence of evidence of causation was a "direct and foreseeable result" of defendants' failure to provide a warning label.

joined as defendants. Here, by contrast, there are approximately 200 drug companies which made DES, any of which might have manufactured the injury-producing drug.

Defendants maintain that, while in *Summers* there was a 50 percent chance that one of the two defendants was responsible for the plaintiff's injuries, here since any one of 200 companies which manufactured DES might have made the product which harmed plaintiff, there is no rational basis upon which to infer that any defendant in this action caused plaintiff's injuries, nor even a reasonable possibility that they were responsible.

These arguments are persuasive if we measure the chance that any one of the defendants supplied the injury-causing drug by the number of possible tortfeasors. In such a context, the possibility that any of the five defendants supplied the DES to plaintiff's mother is so remote that it would be unfair to require each defendant to exonerate itself. There may be a substantial likelihood that none of the five defendants joined in the action made the DES which caused the injury, and that the offending producer not named would escape liability altogether. While we propose, *infra*, an adaptation of the rule in *Summers* which will substantially overcome these difficulties, defendants appear to be correct that the rule, as previously applied, cannot relieve plaintiff of the burden of proving the identity of the manufacturer which made the drug causing her injuries.

II

The second principle upon which plaintiff relies is the so-called "concert of action" theory. . . .

. . . The elements of this doctrine are prescribed in section 876 of the Restatement of Torts. The section provides, "For harm resulting to a third person from the tortious conduct of another, one is subject to liability if he (a) does a tortious act in concert with the other or pursuant to a common design with him, or (b) knows that the other's conduct constitutes a breach of duty and gives substantial assistance or encouragement to the other so to conduct himself, or (c) gives substantial assistance to the other in accomplishing a tortious result and his own conduct, separately considered, constitutes a breach of duty to the third person." With respect to this doctrine, Prosser states that "those who, in pursuance of a common plan or design to commit a tortious act, actively take part in it, or further it by cooperation or request, or who lend aid or encouragement to the wrongdoer, or ratify and adopt his acts done for their benefit, are equally liable with him. Express agreement is not necessary, and all that is required is that there be a tacit understanding. . . ." (Prosser, *Law of Torts* (4th ed. 1971), sec. 46, p.292.)

Plaintiff . . . alleges that defendants' wrongful conduct "is the result of planned and concerted action, express and implied agreements, collaboration in, reliance upon, acquiescence in and ratification, exploitation and adoption of each other's testing, marketing methods, lack of warnings . . . and other acts or omissions . . ." and that "acting individually and in concert, (defendants) promoted, approved, authorized, acquiesced in, and reaped profits from sales" of DES. These allegations, plaintiff claims, state a "tacit understanding" among defendants to commit a tortious act against her.

In our view, this litany of charges is insufficient to allege a cause of action under the rules stated above. The gravamen of the charge . . . is that defendants failed to adequately test the drug or to give sufficient warning of its dangers and that they relied upon the tests performed by one another and took advantage of each other's promotional and marketing techniques. These allegations do not amount to a charge that there was a tacit understanding or a common plan among defendants to fail to conduct adequate tests or give sufficient warnings, and that they substantially aided and encouraged one another in these omissions. . . .

III

A third theory upon which plaintiff relies is the concept of industry-wide liability, or according to the terminology of the parties, "enterprise liability." This theory was suggested in Hall v. E. I. Du Pont de Nemours & Co., Inc. (E.D.N.Y. 1972) 345 F. Supp. 353. In that case, plaintiffs were 13 children injured by the explosion of blasting caps in 12 separate incidents which occurred in 10 different states between 1955 and 1959. The defendants were six blasting cap manufacturers, comprising virtually the entire blasting cap industry in the United States, and their trade association. There were, however, a number of Canadian blasting cap manufacturers which could have supplied the caps. The gravamen of the complaint was that the practice of the industry of omitting a warning on individual blasting caps and of failing to take other safety measures created an unreasonable risk of harm, resulting in the plaintiffs' injuries. The complaint did not identify a particular manufacturer of a cap which caused a particular injury. . . .

We decline to apply this theory in the present case. At least 200 manufacturers produced DES; *Hall*, which involved 6 manufacturers representing the entire blasting cap industry in the United States, cautioned against application of the doctrine espoused therein to a large number of producers. Moreover, in *Hall*, the conclusion that the defendants jointly controlled the risk was based upon allegations that they had delegated some functions relating to safety to a trade association. There are no such allegations here, and we have concluded above that plaintiff has failed to allege liability on a concert of action theory.

Equally important, the drug industry is closely regulated by the Food and Drug Administration, which actively controls the testing and manufacture of drugs and the method by which they are marketed, including the contents of warning labels.[26] To a considerable degree, therefore, the standards followed by drug manufacturers are suggested or compelled by the

---

26. Federal regulations may specify the type of tests a manufacturer must perform for certain drugs (21 C.F.R. § 436.206 *et seq.*), the type of packaging used (§ 429.10), the warnings which appear on labels (§ 369.20), and the standards to be followed in the manufacture of a drug (§ 211.22 *et seq.*).

government. Adherence to those standards cannot, of course, absolve a manufacturer of liability to which it would otherwise be subject. But since the government plays such a pervasive role in formulating the criteria for the testing and marketing of drugs, it would be unfair to impose upon a manufacturer liability for injuries resulting from the use of a drug which it did not supply simply because it followed the standards of the industry.

IV

If we were confined to the theories of *Summers* and *Hall*, we would be constrained to hold that the judgment must be sustained. Should we require that plaintiff identify the manufacturer which supplied the DES used by her mother or that all DES manufacturers be joined in the action, she would effectively be precluded from any recovery. As defendants candidly admit, there is little likelihood that all the manufacturers who made DES at the time in question are still in business or that they are subject to the jurisdiction of the California courts. There are, however, forceful arguments in favor of holding that plaintiff has a cause of action.

In our contemporary complex industrialized society, advances in science and technology create fungible goods which may harm consumers and which cannot be traced to any specific producer. The response of the courts can be either to adhere rigidly to prior doctrine, denying recovery to those injured by such products, or to fashion remedies to meet these changing needs. Just as Justice Traynor in his landmark concurring opinion in Escola v. Coca Cola Bottling Company (1944) 24 Cal. 2d 453, 467-468, 150 P.2d 436, recognized that in an era of mass production and complex marketing methods the traditional standard of negligence was insufficient to govern the obligations of manufacturer to consumer, so should we acknowledge that some adaptation of the rules of causation and liability may be appropriate in these recurring circumstances. . . .

The most persuasive reason for finding plaintiff states a cause of action is that advanced in *Summers*: as between an innocent plaintiff and negligent defendants, the latter should bear the cost of the injury. Here, as in *Summers*, plaintiff is not at fault in failing to provide evidence of causation, and although the absence of such evidence is not attributable to the defendants either, their conduct in marketing a drug the effects of which are delayed for many years played a significant role in creating the unavailability of proof.

From a broader policy standpoint, defendants are better able to bear the cost of injury resulting from the manufacture of a defective product. . . . The manufacturer is in the best position to discover and guard against defects in its products and to warn of harmful effects; thus, holding it liable for defects and failure to warn of harmful effects will provide an incentive to product safety. These considerations are particularly significant where medication is involved, for the consumer is virtually helpless to protect himself from serious, sometimes permanent, sometimes fatal, injuries caused by deleterious drugs.

Where, as here, all defendants produced a drug from an identical formula and the manufacturer of the DES which caused plaintiff's injuries cannot be identified through no fault of plaintiff, a modification of the rule of *Summers* is warranted. As we have seen, an undiluted *Summers* rationale is inappropriate to shift the burden of proof of causation to defendants because if we measure the chance that any particular manufacturer supplied the injury-causing product by the number of producers of DES, there is a possibility that none of the five defendants in this case produced the offending substance and that the responsible manufacturer, not named in the action, will escape liability.

But we approach the issue of causation from a different perspective: we hold it to be reasonable in the present context to measure the likelihood that any of the defendants supplied the product which allegedly injured plaintiff by the percentage which the DES sold by each of them for the purpose of preventing miscarriage bears to the entire production of the drug sold by all for that purpose. Plaintiff asserts in her briefs that Eli Lilly and Company and 5 or 6 other companies produced 90 percent of the DES marketed. If at trial this is established to be the fact, then there is a corresponding likelihood that this comparative handful of producers manufactured the DES which caused plaintiff's injuries, and only a 10 percent likelihood that the offending producer would escape liability.

If plaintiff joins in the action the manufacturers of a substantial share of the DES which her mother might have taken, the injustice of shifting the burden of proof to defendants to demonstrate that they could not have made the substance which injured plaintiff is significantly diminished. While 75 to 80 percent of the market is suggested as the requirement by the Fordham Comment (at p.996), we hold only that a substantial percentage is required.

The presence in the action of a substantial share of the appropriate market also provides a ready means to apportion damages among the defendants. Each defendant will be held liable for the proportion of the judgment represented by its share of that market unless it demonstrates that it could not have made the product which caused plaintiff's injuries. In the present case, as we have seen, one DES manufacturer was dismissed from the action upon filing a declaration that it had not manufactured DES until after plaintiff was born. Once plaintiff has met her burden of joining the required defendants, they in turn may cross-complaint against other DES manufacturers, not joined in the action, which they can allege might have supplied the injury-causing product.

Under this approach, each manufacturer's liability would approximate its responsibility for the injuries caused by its own products. Some minor discrepancy in the correlation between market share and liability is inevitable; therefore, a defendant may be held liable for a somewhat different percentage of the damage than its share of the appropriate market would justify. It is probably impossible, with the passage of time, to determine market share with mathematical exactitude. But just as a jury cannot be expected to determine the precise relationship between fault and liability in applying the doctrine of comparative fault or partial indemnity, the difficulty of apportioning damages among the defendant producers in exact relation to their market share does not seriously militate against the rule we adopt. As we said in *Summers* with regard to the liability of independent tortfeasors, where a correct division of liability cannot be made "the trier of fact may make it the best it can." (33 Cal. 2d at p.88, 199 P.2d at p.5.)

We are not unmindful of the practical problems involved in defining the market and determining market share,[29] but these are largely matters of proof which properly cannot be determined at the pleading stage of these proceedings. Defendants urge that it would be both unfair and contrary to public policy to hold them liable for plaintiff's injuries in the absence of proof that one of them supplied the drug responsible for the damage. Most of their arguments, however, are based upon the assumption that one manufacturer would be held responsible for the products of another or for those of all other manufacturers if plaintiff ultimately prevails. But under the rule we adopt, each manufacturer's liability for an injury would be approximately equivalent to the damages caused by the DES it manufactured.

The judgments are reversed.

Richardson, J. (dissenting) (joined by Clark and Manuel, JJ.)

I respectfully dissent. In these consolidated cases the majority adopts a wholly new theory which contains these ingredients: The plaintiffs were not alive at the time of the commission of the tortious acts. They sue a generation later. They are permitted to receive substantial damages from multiple defendants without any proof that any defendant caused or even probably caused plaintiffs' injuries.

Although the majority purports to change only the required burden of proof by shifting it from plaintiffs to defendants, the effect of its holding is to guarantee that plaintiffs will prevail on the causation issue because defendants are no more capable of disproving factual causation than plaintiffs are of proving it. "Market share" liability thus represents a new high water mark in tort law. The ramifications seem almost limitless. . . . In my view, the majority's departure from traditional tort doctrine is unwise. . . .

The "market share" thesis may be paraphrased. Plaintiffs have been hurt by someone who made DES. Because of the lapse of time no one can prove who made it. Perhaps it was not the named defendants who made it, but they did make some. Although DES was apparently safe at the time it was used, it was subsequently proven unsafe as to some daughters of some users. Plaintiffs have suffered injury and defendants are wealthy. There should be a remedy. Strict products liability is unavailable because the element of causation is lacking. Strike that requirement and label what remains "alternative" liability, "industry-wide" liability, or "market share" liability, proving thereby that if you hit the square peg hard and often enough the round holes will really become square, although you may splinter the board in the process. . . .

---

29. Defendants assert that there are no figures available to determine market share, that DES was provided for a number of uses other than to prevent miscarriage and it would be difficult to ascertain what proportion of the drug was used as a miscarriage preventative, and that the establishment of a time frame and area for market share would pose problems.

NOTES AND QUESTIONS

1. *First Things First*. According to the *Sindell* court, what tort had been committed against the plaintiffs? Negligence? Products liability? In which variant?

2. Sindell *v.* Summers. Is *Sindell*'s purported rejection of the application of *Summers* merely verbal? What are the court's most significant reasons for concluding that "alternative" liability does not apply to the plaintiff's claims against DES manufacturers? What are the most important distinctions between market share liability and alternative liability?

3. *Outside of California*. Several state courts have adopted a version of market share liability in DES cases. *See, e.g.*, Conley v. Boyle Drug. Co., 570 So. 2d 275 (Fla. 1990); Hymowitz v. Eli Lilly & Co., 539 N.E.2d 1069 (N.Y. 1989); Collins v. Eli Lilly & Co., 342 N.W.2d 37 (Wis. 1984); Martin v. Abbott Labs., 689 P.2d 368 (Wash. 1984). Other courts have rejected it. *See* Sutowski v. Eli Lilly & Co., 696 N.E.2d 187 (Ohio 1998) (citing several other jurisdictions that have rejected it). Many have not addressed the question.

Among those states accepting market share liability in DES cases, there are several variations. The New York Court of Appeals' *Hymowitz* decision involved numerous cases consolidated for purposes of deciding several issues, including the the viability of a market share theory under New York law, as well as statute of limitations issues. As to the latter, the New York legislature had enacted a savings statute for DES plaintiffs that "revived" claims that would otherwise have been time-barred. The Court of Appeals upheld the constitutionality of the savings statute, and went on to endorse market share liability, in part relying on the statute as evidence of special legislative solicitude for DES claimants. Unlike *Sindell*, *Hymowitz* creates an *irrebuttable* presumption on causation under which each defendant is held liable to each DES plaintiff in proportion to its market share, *even if* a given defendant could show that its DES could not have caused a particular plaintiff's injury. *Hymowitz* also specifies that each manufacturer's market share is to be determined by its percentage of the national market for DES, rather than its share of the market in the state or locality in which the plaintiff's mother resided at the time of ingesting DES. (*Sindell* left this question open.) By contrast, in *Conley*, the Florida court held that market share should be calculated at a geographically narrow level, such as the state or preferably the county in which the plaintiff's mother purchased DES. Wisconsin's DES case — *Collins* — treats the defendant pharmaceutical companies as joint tortfeasors, although market share is deemed relevant to the jury's apportionment of responsibility among them.

4. *The Fordham Comment*. As may be apparent from the above excerpt, the California Supreme Court relied heavily on a law student note in the Fordham Law Review. Although it is rare for courts to attribute such significance to a student note (or a faculty article, for that matter), tort law has long been a fruitful area of academic scholarship by law students.

5. *Intergenerational Torts*. One of the most difficult aspects of DES litigation was the fact that the plaintiffs were one generation removed from

those who took the drug—their mothers. The intergenerational problem was only intensified in Enright v. Eli Lilly & Co., 570 N.E.2d 198 (N.Y. 1991), a case brought by *grandchildren* of the women who took DES. Should these plaintiffs have a cause of action in negligence for injuries traceable to their grandmothers' ingestion of DES? In products liability? The Court of Appeals held that the grandchildren could not bring a cause of action sounding in negligence because the manufacturers could not be charged with a duty to be vigilant of the effects of its product on third-generation victims.

6. *Beyond DES?* A wide array of products liability claimants face significant proof problems through no fault of their own. Consequently, theories of market share liability have been pleaded by plaintiffs seeking recovery for injuries allegedly caused by asbestos, tobacco, handguns, lead-based paint, latex gloves, blood clotting factors, and many other products. The effort to push market share liability beyond DES has been overwhelmingly rejected by courts. The few lower courts that have permitted the plaintiffs to proceed on a market share theory have consistently been reversed on appeal. There are, however, a handful of decisions in which a high court has permitted the extension of market share liability. Among the most notable is the Hawaii Supreme Court's decision in Smith v. Cutter Biological, Inc., 823 P.2d 717 (Haw. 1991), which extended market share liability to plaintiffs who alleged having contracted diseases from tainted blood products.

In declining to expand the domain of market share liability, courts have suggested that the DES cases featured an unusual set of conditions that are rarely seen in combination outside of that context. Among these were (1) the existence of systemic reasons, not bearing on the plaintiffs' diligence, for the absence of evidence on product identification; (2) the ability of the plaintiffs to bring before the court a group of defendants that were responsible for almost all sales of the product; (3) the fact that the product in question was entirely generic and fungible in terms of its design specifications, its manufacture, and its propensity to cause the same illness among differently situated victims; and (4) the availability of at least some reliable data on market shares. *See, e.g.*, Skipworth v. Lead Indus. Assn., Inc., 690 A.2d 169 (Pa. 1997) (rejecting the imposition of market share liability on manufacturers of lead-based paint because their paint products were not fungible and because the relevant temporal and geographical domains were so indefinite that appropriate data on market share would not be ascertainable).

7. *Causation and Apportionment.* Recall from Chapters 4 and 8 that, in suits against multiple alleged tortfeasors, the issue of *causation*—whether the wrongful acts of each of two or more defendants played a role in bringing about a plaintiff's injury—is distinct from the issue of *apportionment*—how liability should be divided among two or more actors found to have tortiously injured the plaintiff. *Sindell*'s adoption of market share liability seems in some respects to collapse that distinction. That is, the court appears to solve the evidentiary problem faced by the plaintiff on the issue of causation by implementing what it takes to be a fair scheme

of apportionment. Yet because it was focused on the issue of causation, the court in *Sindell* in fact left open a critical question of apportionment: Would the liability imposed on those DES defendants that failed to *dis*prove causation be *joint and several*, such that the plaintiff could recover from any one defendant the full amount owed to her by all defendants?* Eight years later, in Brown v. Superior Court, 751 P.2d 470 (Cal. 1988), the California court answered that question with a resounding no, concluding that market share liability would be several only. The court reasoned that *Sindell*, by imposing liability on each DES manufacturer in approximate proportion to the amount of harm actually caused by its DES, sought to strike an equitable balance between the plaintiff's interest in receiving redress and the defendant's interest in being assigned an appropriate amount of responsibility. Joint and several liability, it concluded, would upset this carefully struck balance. Almost all jurisdictions that relax the product identification requirement in DES cases follow *Brown* in rejecting joint and several liability.

B. Standards of Defectiveness for Prescription Drugs

The California Supreme Court's holding in Brown v. Superior Court on the issue of apportionment significantly refined *Sindell*'s concept of market share liability. As it turns out, *Brown* is equally if not more significant for another reason. This is because, before reaching the issue of apportionment, the *Brown* court addressed an issue of critical importance not only to DES litigation, but to many other claims alleging defects in pharmaceutical products.

The *Brown* plaintiffs, like Sindell, sought relief for DES-related injuries on several theories, including design defect and failure-to-warn claims. Noting that *Sindell* had merely presumed, rather than endorsed, the application of products liability theories to injuries caused by prescription drugs such as DES, the *Brown* court took the occasion to pass on the merit of these theories. In stark contrast to *Sindell*, *Brown* adopted a relatively plaintiff-unfriendly approach to liability, issuing the following rule (here paraphrased rather than quoted):

1. A plaintiff alleging injuries caused by use of a *prescription drug*
2. sold by the seller with adequate *warnings* of health risks
   a. that are posed by the drug's use, and
   b. of which the seller *knew or should have known* at the time of sale,

---

* Recall from the notes following Ravo v. Rogatnick in Chapter 8 that, by enabling the plaintiff to recover her full damages from one of two or more tortfeasors, joint and several liability puts the onus on the paying tortfeasor to collect contribution for its "overpayment" from the other tortfeasor(s). Thus, the main effect of joint and several liability is to shift from the victim to the paying tortfeasor the risk that one or more co-tortfeasors will be unavailable or insolvent.

3.   may *not* invoke *either* the consumer expectations test or the risk-utility test to impose liability on the seller.

Citing various sources, including, most importantly, comment k to Section 402A of the Second Restatement (discussed below), *Brown* concluded that the public interest would be best served by requiring personal injury claimants suing for injuries caused by prescription drugs to proceed exclusively on theories of manufacturing defect, negligence, warranty, or misrepresentation, or a failure-to-warn theory differing only subtly from negligence (but see Note 1, page 932, *supra*):

> If drug manufacturers were subject to strict liability, they might be reluctant to undertake research programs to develop some pharmaceuticals that would prove beneficial or to distribute others that are available to be marketed, because of the fear of large adverse monetary judgments. Further, the additional expense of insuring against such liability — assuming insurance would be available — and of research programs to reveal possible dangers not detectable by available scientific methods could place the cost of medication beyond the reach of those who need it most.

Dean Prosser summed up the justification for exempting prescription drugs from strict liability as follows:

> The argument that industries producing potentially dangerous products should make good the harm, distribute it by liability insurance, and add the cost to the price of the product, encounters reason for pause, when we consider that two of the greatest medical boons to the human race, penicillin and cortisone, both have their dangerous side effects, and that drug companies might well have been deterred from producing and selling them. . . .

(Prosser, *Torts* (4th ed. 1971) § 99, at p.661, fns. omitted.)

The possibility that the cost of insurance and of defending against lawsuits will diminish the availability and increase the price of pharmaceuticals is far from theoretical. . . .

For example, according to defendant E.R. Squibb & Sons, Inc., Benedictin [sic], the only antinauseant drug available for pregnant women, was withdrawn from sale in 1983 because the cost of insurance almost equalled the entire income from sale of the drug. Before it was withdrawn, the price of Benedictin increased by over 300 percent.

Drug manufacturers refused to supply a newly discovered vaccine for influenza on the ground that mass inoculation would subject them to enormous liability. The government therefore assumed the risk of lawsuits resulting from injuries caused by the vaccine. One producer of diphtheria-tetanus-pertussis vaccine withdrew from the market, giving as its reason "extreme liability exposure, cost of litigation and the difficulty of continuing to obtain adequate insurance." (Hearing Before Subcom. on Health and the Environment of House Com. on Energy and Commerce on Vaccine Injury Compensation, 98th Cong., 2d Sess. (Sept. 10, 1984) p.295.) There are only two manufacturers of the vaccine remaining in the market, and the cost of each dose rose a hundredfold from 11 cents in 1982 to $11.40 in 1986, $8 of which was for an insurance reserve. The price increase roughly paralleled an increase in the number of lawsuits from one in 1978 to 219 in 1985. Finally, a manufacturer was unable to market a new drug for the treatment of vision problems because it could not obtain adequate liability insurance at a reasonable cost. (N.Y. Times (Oct. 14, 1986) p.10.)

There is no doubt that, from the public's standpoint, these are unfortunate consequences. . . . It is not unreasonable to conclude in these circumstances that the imposition of [strict products] liability would not further the public interest in the development and availability of these important products.[10]

Brown, 751 P.2d at 479-480.

If *Sindell* was remarkable for its willingness to stretch the common law to permit recoveries by DES plaintiffs, *Brown* is equally notable for its tight-fisted approach. Indeed, relative to the rules employed by other states, *Brown*'s rejection of design defect liability for prescription drugs resides at the restrictive end of the liability spectrum. A recent Nebraska decision provides a rather different analysis of the issues posed by the application of design defect law to prescription drugs. It also demonstrates that, for better or worse, other states' courts are now willing to take on the pioneering mentality of the early California products liability decisions.

Freeman v. Hoffman-La Roche, Inc.

618 N.W.2d 827 (Neb. 2000)

Connolly, J.   . . . The appellant, Aimee Freeman, filed a petition alleging seven theories of recovery against the appellee pharmaceutical company, Hoffman-La Roche, Inc. (Hoffman). She seeks damages for injuries she sustained following her use of the prescription drug Accutane. Hoffman demurred on the basis that the petition failed to state a cause of action. Based on our decision in McDaniel v. McNeil Laboratories, Inc., 196 Neb. 190, 241 N.W.2d 822 (1976), the district court dismissed [the petition]. . . .

I.   BACKGROUND

Freeman's operative petition alleged the following facts: On or about September 23, 1995, Freeman presented herself to her physician for treatment of chronic acne. After examination, her physician prescribed 20 milligrams daily of Accutane. Hoffman is the designer, manufacturer, wholesaler, retailer, fabricator, and supplier of Accutane.

Freeman took the Accutane daily from September 27 through October 2, 1995, and from October 4 through November 20, 1995. Hoffman alleged that as a result of taking the Accutane, she developed multiple health problems. These problems included ulcerative colitis,

10. We express no opinion whether the products to which these examples relate were in fact beneficial to the public health. Our purpose is to demonstrate that there is a rational connection between the cost and availability of pharmaceuticals and the liability imposed on their manufacturers for injuries resulting from their use.

inflammatory polyarthritis, [and ocular inflammation with visual impairment]. As a result, Freeman alleged that she sustained various damages. . . .

Freeman alleged seven theories of recovery, the details of which are set out further in the analysis sections of this opinion: (1) strict liability on the bases that Hoffman distributed Accutane when it was not fit for its intended purpose and when the inherent risks outweighed the benefits of its use, and because it was unreasonably dangerous; (2) negligence on the bases that Hoffman performed negligent and careless research, testing, design, manufacture, and inspection of the product and failed to give adequate warnings of the risks of its use; (3) misrepresentation on the basis that Hoffman falsely represented to Freeman that Accutane was safe to use, thus inducing her to use the product; (4) failure to warn; (5) breach of implied warranty; (6) breach of express warranty; and (7) fear of future product failure on the basis that the actions of Hoffman caused Freeman to suffer mental distress and anxiety. . . .

IV.   ANALYSIS

1.   DESIGN DEFECT

Freeman alleges that Hoffman is strictly liable for her injuries on the bases that Accutane was not fit for its intended purpose, that the risks inherent in the design outweighed the benefits of its use, and that Accutane was more dangerous to Freeman than was anticipated due to undisclosed side effects. As facts supporting her allegations, Freeman alleges that Accutane is sold as an acne medication and that the side effects of Accutane present life-threatening conditions. Thus, Freeman's petition asserts that Hoffman is liable on the basis of a design defect. Hoffman, however, alleges that because Accutane was approved by the FDA, it is exempted from liability for a design defect pursuant to our decision in McDaniel v. McNeil Laboratories, Inc., 196 Neb. 190, 241 N.W.2d 822 (1976).

(a)   Second Restatement § 402 A

In dealing with products other than prescription drugs, this court has recognized a manufacturer's liability in tort for design defects. Liability arises when an article a manufacturer has placed in the market, knowing that it is to be used without inspection for defects, proves to have a defect which causes an injury to a human being rightfully using the product. We have also adopted and applied the test set out in the Second Restatement § 402 A. . . .

[Nebraska law thus ordinarily applies] the consumer expectations test for strict liability. See, e.g., Haag v. Bongers, 256 Neb. 170, 589 N.W.2d 318 (1999). . . . Prescription drugs, however, have been treated differently both by this court and by the Second Restatement.

(i)   Comment *k*. Exception for Unavoidably Unsafe Products

Under the Second Restatement, prescription drugs are treated specially under § 402A, comment *k*. Comment *k*. at 353-54 provides an exception from strict liability when a product is deemed to be "unavoidably unsafe" and states:

> There are some products which, in the present state of human knowledge, are quite incapable of being made safe for their intended and ordinary use. These are especially common in the field of drugs. An outstanding example is the vaccine for the Pasteur treatment of rabies, which not uncommonly leads to very serious and damaging consequences when it is injected. Since the disease itself invariably leads to a dreadful death, both the marketing and use of the vaccine are fully justified, notwithstanding the unavoidable high degree of risk which they involve. Such a product, properly prepared, and accompanied by proper directions and warning, is not defective, nor is it *unreasonably* dangerous. The same is true of many other drugs, vaccines, and the like, many of which for this very reason cannot legally be sold except to physicians, or under the prescription of a physician. It is also true in particular of many new or experimental drugs as to which, because of lack of time and opportunity for sufficient medical experience, there can be no assurance of safety, or perhaps even of purity of ingredients, but such experience as there is justifies the marketing and use of the drug notwithstanding a medically recognizable risk. The seller of such products, again with the qualification that they are properly prepared and marketed, and proper warning is given, where the situation calls for it, is not to be held to strict liability for unfortunate consequences attending their use, merely because he has undertaken to supply the public with an apparently useful and desirable product, attended with a known but apparently reasonable risk.

Application of comment *k*. has been justified under the law in some jurisdictions as a way to strike a balance between a manufacturer's responsibility and the encouragement of research and development of new products. Under certain instances, it is in the public interest to allow products to be marketed which are unsafe, because the benefits of the product justify its risks.

We applied § 402A, comment *k*. to a products liability action involving a prescription drug in McDaniel v. McNeil Laboratories, Inc. . . . In *McDaniel*, a woman was rendered permanently comatose after being given doses of a prescription drug, Innovar, during surgery. At the time of her surgery, Innovar and the warnings and information contained in the package inserts had been approved for use by the FDA. . . . On appeal, we placed emphasis on FDA approval of the drug, and citing to § 402 A, comment *k*., we held:

> An unavoidably unsafe drug which has been approved for marketing by the United States Food and Drug Administration, properly prepared, compounded, packaged, and distributed, and accompanied by proper approved directions and warnings, as a matter of law, is not defective nor unreasonably dangerous, in the absence of proof of inaccurate, incomplete,

misleading, or fraudulent information furnished by the manufacturer in connection with such federal approval or later revisions thereof.

McDaniel, 196 Neb. at 201, 241 N.W.2d at 828. Under the evidence presented, we determined that it was not error for the trial court to refuse to submit the issue of strict liability or warranty, either express or implied, to the jury.

(ii)   Interpretation of Comment *k.* in Other Jurisdictions

Comment *k.*, however, has been interpreted in a variety of ways in other jurisdictions, and there has been a wide range of disagreement regarding its application.

Only a few jurisdictions have interpreted comment *k.* in a manner that strictly excepts all prescription drugs from strict liability. Under the minority view, a drug that is properly manufactured and accompanied by an adequate warning of the risks known to the manufacturer at the time of sale is not defectively designed as a matter of law. Brown v. Superior Court (Abbott Laboratories), 44 Cal. 3d 1049, 245 Cal. Rptr. 412, 751 P.2d 470 (1988). . . . These jurisdictions are commonly described by legal commentators as providing manufacturers with a "blanket immunity" from strict liability for design defects in prescription drugs. Our decision in *McDaniel, supra*, generally falls under this category of interpretation of comment *k.*

(iii)   Cases Applying Risk-Utility Analysis Under Comment *k.*

[The categorical approach of *Brown* and *McDaniel* has been widely criticized.] . . . One court has stated:

> We believe that a more selective application [of comment *k.*] will encourage, rather than discourage, improvements in prescription products. Comment k was designed in part to protect new and experimental drugs. . . . "Comment k states: 'There are some products which, in the present state of human knowledge, are quite incapable of being made safe for their intended and ordinary use.' Obviously, for this to be true, the design must be as safe as the best available testing and research permits." . . . Thus, a product which is as safe as current testing and research permits should be protected. The reverse is also true; a product which is not as safe as current technology can make it should not be protected. (Citation omitted.)

Adams v. G.D. Searle & Co., Inc., 576 So. 2d 728, 732 (Fla. App. 1991).

The majority of jurisdictions that have adopted comment *k.* apply it on a case-by-case basis, believing that societal interests in ensuring the marketing and development of prescription drugs will be adequately served without the need to resort to a rule of blanket immunity. . . .

Although a variety of tests are employed among jurisdictions that apply comment *k.* on a case-by-case basis, the majority apply the comment as an affirmative defense, with the trend toward the use of a risk-utility test in order to determine whether the defense applies. When a risk-utility test is applied, the existence of a reasonable alternative design is generally the central factor. Because the application of comment *k.* is traditionally viewed as an exception and a defense to strict liability, courts generally place the initial burden of proving the various risk utility factors on the defendant. Thus, under these cases, the plaintiff's burden of proof for his or her prima facie case remains the same as it is in any products liability case in the given jurisdiction.

. . . [W]e conclude that the rule of law expressed in *McDaniel* has not held up over time. We now believe that societal interests in ensuring the marketing and development of prescription drugs can be served without resorting to a rule which in effect amounts to a blanket immunity from strict liability for manufacturers. Accordingly, we overrule *McDaniel* to the extent it applies comment *k.* to provide a blanket immunity from strict liability for prescription drugs. Accordingly, we must address how, or if, comment *k.* should be applied, or whether we should consider adopting provisions of the Third Restatement. We next address those provisions in considering what test should be applied.

(b) Third Restatement

The provisions of the Second Restatement regarding products liability were changed dramatically in the Third Restatement, published by the American Law Institute in 1997. As stated in the introduction to the Third Restatement, the institute was required to answer questions that were not part of the products liability landscape when the Second Restatement was completed. Thus, the Third Restatement is a complete overhaul of the Second Restatement in the area of products liability.

Section 6 of the Third Restatement pertains specifically to prescription drugs, with § 6(c) applying to design defects. Section 6 at 144-45 states in part:

> (a) A manufacturer of a prescription drug or medical device who sells or otherwise distributes a defective drug or medical device is subject to liability for harm to persons caused by the defect. A prescription drug or medical device is one that may be legally sold or otherwise distributed only pursuant to a health-care provider's prescription.
>
> (b) For purposes of liability under Subsection (a), a prescription drug or medical device is defective if at the time of sale or other distribution the drug or medical device:
>
> (1) contains a manufacturing defect as defined in § 2(a); or
>
> (2) is not reasonably safe due to defective design as defined in Subsection (c); or
>
> (3) is not reasonably safe due to inadequate instructions or warnings as defined in Subsection (d).
>
> (c) A prescription drug or medical device is not reasonably safe due to defective design if the foreseeable risks of harm posed by the drug or medical device are sufficiently great in relation to its foreseeable therapeutic benefits that reasonable health-care providers, knowing of such

foreseeable risks and therapeutic benefits, would not prescribe the drug
or medical device for any class of patients.

In addition, § 6, comment *b.* at 146-47, states in part:

> The traditional refusal by courts to impose tort liability for defective
> designs of prescription drugs and medical devices is based on the fact that a
> prescription drug or medical device entails a unique set of risks and bene-
> fits. What may be harmful to one patient may be beneficial to another. . . .
> Courts have also recognized that the regulatory system governing prescrip-
> tion drugs is a legitimate mechanism for setting the standards for drug
> design. In part, this deference reflects concerns over the possible negative
> effects of judicially imposed liability on the cost and availability of valuable
> medical technology. This deference also rests on two further assumptions:
> first, that prescribing health-care providers, when adequately informed by
> drug manufacturers, are able to assure that the right drugs and medical
> devices reach the right patients; and second, that governmental regulatory
> agencies adequately review new prescription drugs and devices, keeping
> unreasonably dangerous designs off the market.
>
> Nevertheless, unqualified deference to these regulatory mechanisms is
> considered by a growing number of courts to be unjustified. An approved
> prescription drug or medical device can present significant risks without corre-
> sponding advantages. At the same time, manufacturers must have ample
> discretion to develop useful drugs and devices without subjecting their design
> decisions to the ordinary test applicable to products generally under § 2(b).
> Accordingly, Subsection (c) imposes a more rigorous test for defect than does
> § 2(b), which does not apply to prescription drugs and medical devices. . . .
>
> . . . Subsections (c) and (d) recognize common-law causes of action for
> defective drug design and for failure to provide reasonable instructions or
> warnings, even though the manufacturer complied with governmental
> standards.

Section 6, comment *f.* at 149, states in part:

> A prescription drug or device manufacturer defeats a plaintiff's design
> claim by establishing one or more contexts in which its product would be
> prescribed by reasonable, informed health-care providers. That some indi-
> vidual providers do, in fact, prescribe defendant's product does not in itself
> suffice to defeat the plaintiff's claim. Evidence regarding the actual conduct
> of health-care providers, while relevant and admissible, is not necessarily
> controlling. The issue is whether, objectively viewed, reasonable providers,
> knowing of the foreseeable risks and benefits of the drug or medical device,
> would prescribe it for any class of patients. Given this very demanding objec-
> tive standard, liability is likely to be imposed only under unusual circum-
> stances. The court has the responsibility to determine when the plaintiff has
> introduced sufficient evidence so that reasonable persons could conclude
> that plaintiff has met this demanding standard.

As of this writing, no state court has faced the issue of whether to
adopt § 6(c). A few federal courts have discussed this section, but only to
the extent of either predicting whether the applicable state court would
adopt § 6(c) or declining to apply it in the absence of state precedent.

[Scholars have offered] several criticisms of § 6(c), which will be briefly summarized. First, [they argue,] it does not accurately restate the law. It has been repeatedly stated that there is no support in the case law for the application of a reasonable physician standard in which strict liability for a design defect will apply only when a product is not useful for any class of persons. Rather, as illustrated by the discussion of the treatment of comment *k.* under the Second Restatement in other jurisdictions, the majority of courts apply some form of risk-utility balancing that focuses on a variety of factors, including the existence of a reasonable alternative design. . . .

Second, the reasonable physician test is criticized as being artificial and difficult to apply. The test requires fact finders to presume that physicians have as much or more of an awareness about a prescription drug product as the manufacturer. The test also ignores concerns of commentators that physicians tend to prescribe drugs they are familiar with or for which they have received advertising material, even when studies indicate that better alternatives are available.

A third criticism of particular applicability to Freeman's case is that the test lacks flexibility and treats drugs of unequal utility equally. For example, a drug used for cosmetic purposes but which causes serious side effects has less utility than a drug which treats a deadly disease, yet also has serious side effects. In each case, the drugs would likely be useful to a class of patients under the reasonable physician standard for some class of persons. Consequently, each would be exempted from design defect liability. But under a standard that considers reasonable alternative design, the cosmetic drug could be subject to liability if a safer yet equally effective design was available. . . .

Fourth, the test allows a consumer's claim to be defeated simply by a statement from the defense's expert witness that the drug at issue had some benefit for any single class of people. Thus, it is argued that application of § 6(c) will likely shield pharmaceutical companies from a wide variety of suits that could have been brought under comment *k.* of the Second Restatement. . . . Thus, even though the rule is reformulated, any application of § 6(c) will essentially provide the same blanket immunity from liability for design defects in prescription drugs as did the application of comment *k.* in the few states that interpreted it as such.

We conclude that § 6(c) has no basis in the case law. We view § 6(c) as too strict of a rule, under which recovery would be nearly impossible. Accordingly, we do not adopt § 6(c) of the Third Restatement. . . .

We conclude that § 402 A, comment *k.*, of the Second Restatement should be applied on a case-by-case basis and as an affirmative defense in cases involving prescription drug products. Under this rule, an application of the comment does not provide a blanket immunity from strict liability for prescription drugs. Rather, the plaintiff is required to plead the consumer expectations test, as he or she would be required to do in any products liability case. The defendant may then raise comment *k.* as an affirmative defense. The comment will apply to except the prescription drug product from strict liability when it is shown that (1) the product is properly manufactured and contains adequate warnings, (2) its benefits justify its risks, and (3) the product was at the time of manufacture and distribution incapable of being made more safe.

In this case, because the application of comment *k.* is an affirmative defense, Freeman was only required to plead that the Accutane she took was unreasonably dangerous under a consumer expectations test. Freeman alleged that Accutane was unreasonably dangerous for use, that it was not fit for its intended purpose, that the risks inherent in the design outweighed the benefits of its use, and that Accutane was more dangerous to Freeman than was anticipated due to undisclosed side effects. As facts supporting her allegations, Freeman alleged that Accutane is sold as an acne medication and that the side effects of Accutane present life-threatening conditions. Thus, Freeman alleged facts that the Accutane was dangerous to an extent beyond that which would be contemplated by the ordinary consumer who purchases it, with the ordinary knowledge common to the community as to its characteristics. Accordingly, we conclude that Freeman has stated a theory of recovery based on a design defect. . . .

3.   FAILURE TO WARN

[The court considered Freeman's claim that Hoffman failed adequately to warn her, via her physician, of Accutane's dangers. The court's treatment of this claim is discussed in Part V of this chapter. — EDS.] . . .

4.   IMPLIED AND EXPRESS WARRANTY

Freeman also alleges in her petition theories of recovery for breach of implied warranty on the basis that Accutane was not fit for its intended purpose and for breach of express warranty on the basis that Hoffman expressly warranted that Accutane was of merchantable quality.

(a)   Implied Warranty

[The court concluded that implied-warranty claims for personal injuries caused by products are subsumed into product liability claims. — EDS.] . . .

(b)   Express Warranty

We treat Freeman's express warranty claim differently. Express warranty is grounded in terms of an express promise made as part of a pending purchase. Thus, unlike implied warranties, there is a clearer contractual difference between a theory of recovery based on express warranty and a tort theory of recovery based on a product defect. Thus, we are not convinced that we should endeavor to merge those theories of recovery. Accordingly, we address whether Freeman has stated a theory of recovery for breach of express warranty.

Neb. U.C.C. § 2-313 (Reissue 1992) requires that in order to create an express warranty, the seller must make an affirmation of fact or promise to the buyer which relates to the goods and becomes part of the basis of the bargain. The comments indicate that express warranties rest on "dickered" aspects of the individual bargain. See *id.*, comment 1.

The only allegation Freeman made regarding express warranty was that Hoffman expressly warranted to her that Accutane was of marketable condition and that she relied on this warranty. Freeman did not allege any factual basis for this assertion. Further, Hoffman did not allege that any such warranty was the basis of a bargain between herself and Hoffman. Thus, Freeman did not allege a theory of recovery for breach of express warranty.

5. MISREPRESENTATION

Freeman alleges a theory of recovery labeled simply "Misrepresentation" in her petition. In her general factual allegations, Freeman alleges that Hoffman knew of the danger of Accutane, but misled the medical community with incomplete and inaccurate information regarding the safety of the drug. In the section devoted to misrepresentation, Freeman alleges that Hoffman falsely represented to her that Accutane was safe to use as instructed and labeled, when in fact it was not safe. Freeman then alleges that she relied on the misrepresentation and that the misrepresentation induced her to use Accutane.

Section 9 of the Third Restatement pertains to liability of a commercial product seller or producer for harm caused by misrepresentation and provides: "One engaged in the business of selling or otherwise distributing products who, in connection with the sale of a product, makes a fraudulent, negligent, or innocent misrepresentation of material fact concerning the product is subject to liability for harm to persons or property caused by the misrepresentation."

Comment *b.* indicates that § 9 is derived from the Second Restatement § 402 B and that the provision regarding liability for innocent product misrepresentations is generally applied only to public misrepresentations, if applied at all. Comment *e.*, § 9, of the Third Restatement notes that separate causes of action available under the Uniform Commercial Code, such as breach of warranty, can be combined in the same case with a claim for misrepresentation. Comment *d.* notes that a plaintiff is not required to show that the product was defective at the time of sale or distribution within the meaning of other sections of the Third Restatement.

We have recognized fraudulent misrepresentation as a cause of action with the following elements:

(1) that a representation was made; (2) that the representation was false; (3) that when made, the representation was known to be false or made recklessly without knowledge of its truth and as a positive assertion; (4) that it

was made with the intention that the plaintiff should rely upon it; (5) that the plaintiff did so rely; and (6) that he or she suffered damage as a result.

Gibb v. Citicorp Mortgage, Inc., 246 Neb. 355, 360, 518 N.W.2d 910, 916 (1994). We decline to adopt § 9 of the Third Restatement, and we instead apply the principles stated in *Gibb*.

In Adams v. G.D. Searle & Co., Inc., 576 So. 2d 728 (Fla. App. 1991), the plaintiff alleged that she was injured by the use of a defective intrauterine device (IUD). The plaintiff then alleged that the pharmaceutical company had misrepresented and omitted specific material facts about the IUD to her and the prescribing physician with the intention to induce them to rely on the misrepresentations and omissions and that they did so to the plaintiff's detriment. The court concluded that such an allegation stated a cause of action for fraud.

Freeman's allegations are substantially the same as those in *Adams* and allege the elements set forth in *Gibb*. When the sections of Freeman's petition pertaining to general factual allegations and misrepresentation are read together, she has stated a cause of action for fraudulent misrepresentation. . . .

V. CONCLUSION

We overrule McDaniel v. McNeil Laboratories, Inc., 196 Neb. 190, 241 N.W.2d 822 (1976), to the extent it applies § 402A, comment *k.* of the Second Restatement to provide a blanket immunity from strict liability for prescription drugs. Instead, we require a plaintiff to plead that the drug was unreasonably dangerous under a consumer expectations test and apply comment *k.* as an affirmative defense on a case-by-case basis. . . . Further, in this case, we merge the theories of breach of implied warranty with the theories of design and manufacturing defects. We decline to adopt § 9 of the Third Restatement as the test for misrepresentation. . . .

Applying the allegations in Freeman's petition to the legal tests, we conclude that Freeman failed to state a theory of recovery for liability based on a manufacturing defect, express warranty, or negligence. Freeman did, however, state theories of recovery for liability based on a design defect, . . . and misrepresentation. Accordingly, the district court erred in sustaining Hoffman's demurrer. We reverse, and remand for further proceedings to allow Freeman to amend her petition.

NOTES AND QUESTIONS

1. **Brown *versus* Freeman.** Is the Nebraska Supreme Court correct in suggesting that a case-by-case application of comment k is superior to *Brown*'s blanket immunity? Why would it ever make sense to adopt a rule granting an immunity when more narrowly tailored approaches are possible? Particularly in cases in which the plaintiff has been seriously injured, isn't it appropriate to eschew worries about possible overinclusiveness, while retaining the comment k defense for those cases that truly merit it?

2. *Rejecting Section 6(c)*. The Nebraska court has much to say about what is wrong with Section 6(c) of the Third Restatement. Can you see what might have attracted the Reporters to the complex formulation of that section? Why did the Reporters evidently choose to preclude liability wherever there exists *any class of patients* for whom a reasonable healthcare provider would prescribe the medication? In light of this language, can one argue that Section 6(c) envisions that liability for prescription drugs will be narrower in products liability than under the law of negligence?

3. *EU Law*. The United States is hardly the only country to confront the issue of liability for injuries caused by prescription drugs. The European Union and its individual member countries have likewise struggled to develop fair and workable standards for liability for injuries caused by prescription drugs. Some member nations have adopted the "development risk" defense, which states that there shall be no liability for injuries from risks that a manufacturer neither knew of nor should have known of. Although such a defense is applied by some nations to products beyond pharmaceuticals, pharmaceuticals have clearly provided a central impetus for its adoption. As a compromise measure, EU law permits member states to choose whether or not to recognize the development risk defense. At this stage, most EU member nations do permit such a defense.

4. *Prescription versus Over-the-Counter Medications*. Debates over whether to apply special rules to claims for injuries caused by drugs concern only prescription medications, not those purchased directly by the consumer. Why are over-the-counter medications treated differently than prescription drugs?

5. *The Federal Vaccine Act*. In the interest of public health, federal law mandates and subsidizes childhood vaccination programs. Many of these vaccines, including the polio vaccine, involve the injection of small doses of "live" disease agents. The goal is to trigger a response from the recipient's immune system so as to render it subsequently capable of repelling the agent and preventing onset of the disease. However, in a tiny fraction of recipients, live vaccines cause the disease itself, as well as certain other devastating side effects. As indicated in the excerpt from Brown v. Superior Court at the start of this section, the prospect of substantial tort liability arising out of vaccine-related injuries appears to have adversely affected both the availability and cost of vaccines. In 1986, Congress responded by enacting the National Childhood Vaccine Injury Act, 42 U.S.C. §§ 300aa-1 *et seq*. Under the act, which is funded by a tax on the sale of vaccines, a victim alleging vaccine-related injuries must first seek compensation in a special federal court. In that court, there is no need to prove fault or defect. In addition, the claimant may, depending on the facts of the case, benefit from an irrebuttable presumption of causation. In exchange, the claimant is limited to recovering medical expenses and lost earnings, along with a maximum of $250,000 for pain and suffering. After the court has determined whether the claimant stands to recover, and, if so, in what amount, the claimant has the choice of accepting the

court's resolution or rejecting it and proceeding with an ordinary tort suit. However, the act contains several provisions that diminish the prospects for recovery in tort, including a liability standard that specifies that a vaccine may not be deemed defective if its production of side effects was "unavoidable." *See* Schafer v. American Cyanamid Co., 20 F.3d 1 (1st Cir. 1994) (Breyer, J.) (describing the act and holding that it does not prevent family members from proceeding with state-law loss-of-consortium claims arising out of vaccine-related injuries to their relative).

6. *Controversies Over the Third Restatement.* As indicated by *Freeman* and several note cases in this chapter, the Restatement (Third) of Products Liability has been criticized for displaying an overall tendency to disfavor plaintiffs in products liability actions. A thorough evaluation of the fairness of such criticism must include recognition of important sections of the Restatement that adopt provisions that may prove highly unpopular with defendants. One of these is Section 9, which appears to soften the usual *scienter* requirement in fraud. Thus, whereas a plaintiff alleging losses caused by reliance on a defendant's misrepresentation usually must establish that the defendant made the misrepresentation with *knowledge* of its falsity and an *intent* to deceive, Section 9 permits recovery for misrepresentations resulting from mere *carelessness* as to the falsity of the representation. Note that the Nebraska Supreme Court declines to adopt this provision in favor of the more defendant-friendly traditional approach.

V.   FAILURE TO WARN OR INSTRUCT

As noted in Section II, the third category of product defect identified by U.S. products liability law is quite different from the first two. Manufacturing and design defect claims allege that a danger lurks within physical features, aspects, or components of the product. Failure to warn claims, by contrast, assert that the product is defective not because of how it has been designed or made, but because it should have been delivered with more information for consumers about the dangers associated with it, and how to use it safely. As you read the following materials, consider whether these differences warrant the adoption by lawmakers of alternative accounts of key products liability concepts, including the core concept of "defect."

A.   Which Risks Require Warning?

Anderson v. Owens-Corning Fiberglas Corp.
810 P.2d 549 (Cal. 1991) (In Bank)

Panelli, J.   In this case we consider the issue "whether a defendant in a products liability action based upon an alleged failure to warn of a risk of harm may present evidence of the state of the art, i.e., evidence that the particular risk was neither known nor knowable by the application of scientific knowledge available at the time of manufacture and/or distribution." (Order on grant of review, May 3, 1990.) As will appear, resolution of this evidentiary issue requires an examination of the failure-to-warn theory as an alternate and independent basis for imposing strict liability and a determination of whether knowledge, actual or constructive, is a component of strict liability on the failure-to-warn theory. It is manifest that, if knowledge or knowability is a component, state-of-the-art evidence is relevant and, subject to the normal rules of evidence, admissible. . . .

. . . The California courts, either expressly or by implication, have to date required knowledge, actual or constructive, of potential risk or danger before imposing strict liability for a failure to warn. The state of the art may be relevant to the question of knowability and, for that reason, should be admissible in that context. Exclusion of state-of-the-art evidence, *when the basis of liability is a failure to warn*, would make a manufacturer the virtual insurer of its product's safe use, a result that is not consonant with established principles underlying strict liability.

BACKGROUND

Defendants[1] are or were manufacturers of products containing asbestos. Plaintiff Carl Anderson filed suit in 1984, alleging that he contracted asbestosis and other lung ailments through exposure to asbestos and asbestos products (i.e., preformed blocks, cloth and cloth tape, cement, and floor tiles) while working as an electrician at the Long Beach Naval Shipyard from 1941 to 1976. Plaintiff allegedly encountered asbestos while working in the vicinity of others who were removing and installing insulation products aboard ships. The complaint stated causes of action for negligence, breach of warranty, and strict liability and, inter alia, prayed for punitive damages. Pursuant to stipulation entered at the time of trial, plaintiff proceeded only on his cause of action for strict liability and did not seek punitive damages.

[At trial, the defendants sought to introduce evidence as to the state of scientific knowledge concerning the health risks of asbestos at the time it was manufactured and sold (so-called "state of the art" evidence). The trial court held that such evidence was not relevant to plaintiff's design defect claim, which was brought on a consumer-expectation theory. The defendants then argued that the plaintiff should not be permitted to assert a failure-to-warn claim, in part because it would be unfair to permit such a claim to proceed while excluding state of the art evidence. The court agreed and declined to permit the failure to warn claim to go to the jury. The jury returned a defense verdict on the plaintiff's design defect claim. — EDS.]

---

1. Owens-Corning Fiberglas Corporation, H.K. Porter Company, Inc., Fibreboard Corporation, Pittsburg-Corning Corporation, Owens-Illinois, Inc., Keene Corporation, AC and S, Inc., Armstrong World Industries, and GAF Corporation. As a result of bankruptcy petitions, proceedings have been stayed as to Raymark Industries, Inc., Celotex Corporation, and Eagle-Picher Industries, Inc., which were also named.

Plaintiff moved for a new trial, asserting that the court erred in precluding proof of liability on a failure-to-warn theory. . . . The court granted the motion. . . .

The Court of Appeal, in a two-to-one decision, upheld the order granting a new trial. . . .

DISCUSSION

FAILURE TO WARN THEORY OF STRICT LIABILITY

Though not without some history in this court, the theory of strict liability for failure to warn has been forged principally in the lower courts. [Discussion of lower court decisions omitted. — EDS.] . . .

These cases . . . did not discuss knowledge or knowability as a component of the failure to warn theory of strict liability. However, a knowledge or knowability component clearly was included as an implicit condition of strict liability. In that regard, California was in accord with authorities in a majority of other states.

Only when the danger to be warned against was "unknowable" did the knowledge component of the failure-to-warn theory come into focus. Such cases made it apparent that eliminating the knowledge component had the effect of turning strict liability into absolute liability. The first California case to discuss knowledge or knowability as a condition of strict liability in the failure to warn context was Oakes v. E.I. Du Pont de Nemours & Co., Inc., *supra*, 272 Cal. App. 2d 645, 77 Cal. Rptr. 709. Du Pont had distributed weed-killing spray products containing ingredients that proved dangerous to some human beings. Accepting the premise that knowledge or knowability was a factor in the obligation to warn under the Restatement Second of Torts (§ 402A, com. j.), the court stated:

> The rationale of the strict liability rule is that the injured person is helpless to protect himself from the *actually defective product*. It is only reasonable therefore that as between the injured user and the one who places the product on the market the latter should bear the loss. The same rationale would apply to the marketing of a product which contains an ingredient which the manufacturer knows or should know "by the application of reasonable developed human skill and foresight" is dangerous. But, in the view of this court, that is where the reason for the rule ceases and the rule of "strict" liability itself should stop. To exact an obligation to warn the user of unknown and unknowable allergies, sensitivities and idiosyncrasies would be for the courts to recast the manufacturer in the role of an insurer beyond any reasonable application of the rationale expressed above.

(272 Cal. App. 2d at pp.650-651, 77 Cal. Rptr. 709.) . . .

. . . [In deciding Brown v. Superior Court, (1988) 44 Cal. 3d 1049, 245 Cal. Rptr. 412, 751 P.2d 470, we concluded] that a manufacturer is not strictly liable for injuries caused by a prescription drug so long as it was properly prepared and accompanied by warnings of its dangerous propensities that were either known or reasonably scientifically knowable at the time of distribution. . . .

. . . [D]ecisions of the Courts of Appeal persuade us that California is well settled into the majority view that knowledge, actual or constructive, is a requisite for strict liability for failure to warn. . . . *Brown, supra*, 44 Cal. 3d 1049, 245 Cal. Rptr. 412, 751 P.2d 470, if not directly, at least by implication, reaffirms that position.

However, even if we are implying too much from the language in *Brown*, the fact remains that we are now squarely faced with the issue of knowledge and knowability in strict liability for failure to warn in other than the drug context. Whatever the ambiguity of *Brown*, we hereby adopt the requirement, as propounded by the Restatement Second of Torts and acknowledged by the lower courts of this state and the majority of jurisdictions, that knowledge or knowability is a component of strict liability for failure to warn.

One of the guiding principles of the strict liability doctrine was to relieve a plaintiff of the evidentiary burdens inherent in a negligence cause of action. . . . The proponents of the minority rule, including the Court of Appeal in this case, argue that the knowability requirement, and admission of state-of-the-art evidence, improperly infuse negligence concepts into strict liability cases by directing the trier of fact's attention to the conduct of the manufacturer or distributor rather than to the condition of the product. Similar claims have been made as to other aspects of strict liability, sometimes resulting in limitations on the doctrine and sometimes not. In *Cronin*, for example, we concluded that the "unreasonably dangerous" element, which the Restatement Second of Torts had introduced into the definition of a defective product, should not be incorporated into a plaintiff's burden of proof in a product liability action because it "rings of negligence." . . .

However, the claim that a particular component "rings of" or "sounds in" negligence has not precluded its acceptance in the context of strict liability. . . . [For example,] . . . in Daly v. General Motors Corp., *supra*, 20 Cal. 3d 725, 144 Cal. Rptr. 380, 575 P.2d 1162, that the principles of comparative negligence apply to actions founded on strict products liability. . . .

[Likewise,] . . . in Barker [v. Lull Engineering Co.], this court rejected the claim that the risk/benefit test was unacceptable because it introduced an element which "rings of negligence" into the determination of design defect. . . .

As these cases illustrate, the strict liability doctrine has incorporated some well-settled rules from the law of negligence and has survived judicial challenges asserting that such incorporation violates the fundamental principles of the doctrine. It may also be true that the "warning defect" theory is "rooted in negligence" to a greater extent than are the manufacturing- or design-defect theories. The "warning defect" relates to a failure extraneous to the product itself. Thus, while a manufacturing or design defect *can be* evaluated without reference to the conduct of the manufacturer, the giving of a warning cannot. The latter necessarily requires the communicating of something to someone. How can one warn of something that is unknowable? If every product that has no warning were defective per se and for that reason subject to strict liability, the mere fact of injury by an unlabelled product would automatically permit recovery. That is not, and has never been, the purpose and goal of the failure-to-warn theory of strict liability. Further, if a warning automatically precluded liability in every case, a manufacturer or distributor could easily escape liability with overly broad, and thus practically useless, warnings.

. . . Furthermore, despite its roots in negligence, failure to warn in strict liability differs markedly from failure to warn in the negligence context. Negligence law in a failure-to-warn case requires a plaintiff to prove that a manufacturer or distributor did not warn of a particular risk for reasons which fell below the acceptable standard of care, i.e., what a reasonably prudent manufacturer would have known and warned about. Strict liability is not concerned with the standard of due care or the reasonableness of a manufacturer's conduct. The rules of strict liability require a plaintiff to prove only that the defendant did not adequately warn of a particular risk that was known or knowable in light of the generally recognized and prevailing best scientific and medical knowledge available at the time of manufacture and distribution.[13] Thus, in strict liability, as opposed to negligence, the reasonableness of the defendant's failure to warn is immaterial.

Stated another way, a reasonably prudent manufacturer might reasonably decide that the risk of harm was such as not to require a warning as, for example, if the manufacturer's own testing showed a result contrary to that of others in the scientific community. Such a manufacturer might escape liability under negligence principles. In contrast, under strict liability principles the manufacturer has no such leeway; the manufacturer is liable if it failed to give warning of dangers that were known to the scientific community at the time it manufactured or distributed the product. Whatever may be reasonable from the point of view of the manufacturer, the user of the product must be given the option either to refrain from using the product at all or to use it in such a way as to minimize the degree of danger. . . . Thus, the fact that a manufacturer acted as a reasonably prudent manufacturer in deciding not to warn, while perhaps absolving the manufacturer of liability under the negligence theory, will not preclude liability under strict liability principles if the trier of fact concludes that, based on the information scientifically available to the manufacturer, the manufacturer's failure to warn rendered the product unsafe to its users.

---

13. The parties do not dispute the accepted definition of scienter in the failure to warn context, namely, actual or constructive knowledge. As noted in comment j of section 402A of the Restatement Second of Torts, constructive knowledge is knowledge which is obtainable "by the application of reasonable, developed human skill and foresight." As we have explained, however, the element of scienter is not necessarily determinative of the duty to warn or of the liability that flows from the failure to warn. Thus, a manufacturer with knowledge, actual or constructive, might have acted reasonably in failing to warn and might escape liability for negligence; the manufacturer's reasonable conduct, however, would not relieve the manufacturer of liability on a strict liability theory.

The foregoing examination of the failure-to-warn theory of strict liability in California compels the conclusion that knowability is relevant to imposition of liability under that theory. Our conclusion not only accords with precedent but also with the considerations of policy that underlie the doctrine of strict liability.

We recognize that an important goal of strict liability is to spread the risks and costs of injury to those most able to bear them.[14] However, it was never the intention of the drafters of the doctrine to make the manufacturer or distributor the insurer of the safety of their products. It was never their intention to impose *absolute* liability.

CONCLUSION

Therefore, in answer to the question raised in our order granting review, a defendant in a strict products liability action based upon an alleged failure to warn of a risk of harm may present evidence of the state of the art, i.e., evidence that the particular risk was neither known nor knowable by the application of scientific knowledge available at the time of manufacture and/or distribution. The judgment of the Court of Appeal is affirmed with directions that the matter be remanded to the trial court for proceedings in accord with our decision herein.

Broussard, J. (concurring).   I concur in the majority opinion, but write separately simply to emphasize the narrow scope of the opinion's holding. As the majority opinion properly recognizes, the issue presented by this case is whether so-called "state-of-the-art" evidence is admissible in a strict products liability action *when the plaintiff contends that a product is defective because it failed to contain an adequate warning of the risk that caused the injury.* I agree with the majority that when the plaintiff proceeds *on an absence-of-warning theory*, the defendant is entitled to present evidence that the risk in question was scientifically unknown at the time the product was manufactured and distributed. A warning, by its nature, presupposes that the risk to be warned against is capable of being known, and a rule which permits the trier of fact to find a product defective simply because it lacked a warning of a scientifically unknown risk would go a long way to making a manufacturer an insurer of any injuries caused by its product.

---

14. The suggestion that losses arising from unknowable risks and hazards should be spread among all users to the product, as are losses from predictable injuries or negligent conduct, is generally regarded as not feasible. Not the least of the problems is insurability. (*See* Henderson, *Coping with Time Dimension in Products Liability* (1981) 69 Cal. L. Rev. 919, 948-949; Wade, *On the Effect in Product Liability of Knowledge Unavailable Prior to Marketing* (1983) 58 N.Y.U. L. Rev. 734.) Dean Wade stated the dilemma, but provided no solution: "How does one spread the potential loss of an unknowable hazard? How can insurance premiums be figured for this purpose? Indeed, will insurance be available at all? Spreading the loss is essentially a compensation device rather than a tort concept. Providing compensation should not be the sole basis for imposing tort liability, and this seems more emphatically so in the situation where the defendant is no more able to insure against unknown risks than is the plaintiff." (58 N.Y.U. L. Rev. at p.755.)

The majority's holding in this case, however, does not mean that state-of-the-art evidence is admissible in all strict products liability cases. Although the majority finds no need to reach the issue here, in my view it is both prudent and appropriate to make it clear that state-of-the-art evidence would not necessarily be relevant when, for example, a plaintiff in a strict products liability action relies solely on the so-called "consumer expectation" prong of the design defect standard. . . .

Under the consumer expectation standard, when a product proves to be unexpectedly unsafe when used as intended by the manufacturer, an injured plaintiff is entitled to recover for the resulting injuries . . . without regard to whether the manufacturer knew or could have known at the time of manufacture or distribution of the specific safety problem that was inherent in its product. Thus, when the plaintiff in a strict products liability action relies solely on a consumer expectation theory, state-of-the-art evidence may not be relevant or admissible.

In this case, however, plaintiff sought to rely, inter alia, on the absence of a warning to prove that the product was defective. Under these circumstances, I agree with the majority that state-of-the-art evidence was admissible.

[Opinion of **Mosk, J.**, concurring and dissenting, omitted. — EDS.]

NOTES AND QUESTIONS

1. *Carlin v. Superior Court: Updating* Brown *after* Anderson. The California Supreme Court subsequently issued a decision reaffirming *Anderson*'s distinction between theories of strict liability and negligence liability for failure to warn. It also held that, *Brown* notwithstanding, the former theory applies even to prescription drugs. In Carlin v. Superior Court, 920 P.2d 1347 (Cal. 1996), the plaintiff alleged that she suffered severe side effects from the medication Halcion. She sued its manufacturer, the Upjohn Company, for failing to warn of these side effects. Upjohn argued that *Brown*'s refusal to permit a plaintiff to proceed with a design defect claim for injuries caused by prescription drugs entailed that only negligence-based liability ought to be recognized when the claim is for failure to warn. The majority of a sharply divided court disagreed, seeing "no reason to depart from our conclusion in *Anderson* that the manufacturer should bear the costs, in terms of preventable injury or death, of its own failure to provide adequate warnings of known or reasonably scientifically knowable risks." *Id*. at 1354. *Carlin* reiterated *Anderson*'s observation that "[w]hatever may be reasonable from the point of view of the manufacturer, the user of the product must be given the option either to refrain from using the product at all or to use it in such a way as to minimize the degree of danger." *Id*. at 1348 (quoting *Anderson*, 810 P.2d, at 559). *Carlin* also rejected Upjohn's argument that its compliance with Federal Food and Drug Administration (FDA) regulations should suffice to establish the adequacy of its warnings for purposes of California products liability law:

... The fact that the pharmaceutical drug industry is highly regulated does not distinguish it from numerous other industries. Moreover, as the dissenting opinion concedes, the FDA's approval of a particular warning is not determinative of liability. Nor have our courts adopted the approach of the narrow line of cases cited by the dissenting opinion which would insulate manufacturers for failure to warn if they merely gave FDA-approved warnings. . . .

Id. at 1353 n.4.

2. *How Thin a Line?* Rhetoric aside, is there really a meaningful line to be drawn between strict liability and negligence in the failure to warn context? In attempting to draw that line, *Anderson* states:

> Negligence law in a failure-to-warn case requires a plaintiff to prove that a manufacturer or distributor did not warn of a particular risk for reasons which fell below the acceptable standard of care, i.e., what a reasonably prudent manufacturer would have known and warned about. Strict liability is not concerned with the standard of due care or the reasonableness of a manufacturer's conduct. *The rules of strict liability require a plaintiff to prove only that the defendant did not adequately warn of a particular risk that was known or knowable in light of the generally recognized and prevailing best scientific and medical knowledge available at the time of manufacture and distribution.* Thus, in strict liability, as opposed to negligence, the reasonableness of the defendant's failure to warn is immaterial." [Emphasis added.]

Unfortunately, the italicized sentence is either false, or at best elliptical, as the court in effect concedes a few sentences later:

> Thus, the fact that a manufacturer acted as a reasonably prudent manufacturer in deciding not to warn, while perhaps absolving the manufacturer of liability under the negligence theory, will not preclude liability under strict liability principles if the trier of fact concludes that, based on the information scientifically available to the manufacturer, *the manufacturer's failure to warn rendered the product unsafe to its users.* [Emphasis added.]

In other words, strict liability for failure to warn requires proof that the defendant failed adequately to warn of a risk not just when the risk was known or knowable, but also when the failure to warn of that risk *renders the product unsafe* to its users. Thus, in evaluating the width of the line between negligence and strict liability in the failure to warn context, one must ask: Are there known or knowable dangers such that the failure to warn of them would render a product unsafe to its users, yet of which a reasonably prudent manufacturer would not warn? Even if this category is small, why else might it matter to make a strict products liability action for failure to warn available to plaintiffs?

3. *Obvious Dangers versus Patent Defects.* Black-letter failure to warn law states that the failure to warn of *obvious* dangers is not actionable. (Compare *Salaman, supra,* Chapter 2, stating the rule of negligence law that landowners need not alert licensees of dangerous conditions on

the property when such conditions are readily observable.) In Maneely v. General Motors Corp., 108 F.3d 1176 (9th Cir. 1997), the plaintiffs were sleeping in the back of a pickup truck as it drove down a highway. After the driver fell asleep, the pickup crashed, causing the plaintiffs to be thrown against the walls of the pickup truck's bed, resulting in paralyzing injuries. Although the obviousness of a risk is generally a question of fact, the court affirmed a grant of summary judgment for GM, reasoning that, as matter of California law, GM had no obligation to warn of the "obvious" risks of forcible impact associated with riding in the bed of a pickup truck.

The so-called patent defect rule once served as a direct analog in design defect law to the obvious defect rule of failure to warn law. Under the patent defect rule, an obvious danger could not render a product defectively designed. Although most jurisdictions have now rejected this rule, as has the Restatement (Third) of Products Liability, the obvious danger rule has remained a feature of failure to warn law. What, if anything, might explain this discrepancy?

4. *Failure to Warn and Design Defect.* Comment j to Section 402A states in part: "Where warning is given, the seller may reasonably assume that it will be read and heeded; and a product bearing such a warning, which is safe for use if it is followed, is not in defective condition, nor is it unreasonably dangerous." Read literally, comment j thus appears to immunize sellers from liability for any design defect, no matter how dangerous, so long as they have warned and/or instructed users on how to use the product safely. The Third Restatement follows several commentators and courts in rejecting this idea:

> In general, when a safer design can reasonably be implemented and risks can reasonably be designed out of a product, adoption of the safer design is required over a warning that leaves a significant residuum of such risks. . . . Warnings are not . . . a substitute for the provision of a reasonably safe design.

Restatement (Third) of Torts: Products Liability § 2, cmt. l (1998); *see also* Glover v. Bic Corp., 6 F.3d 1318 (9th Cir. 1993) (applying Oregon law).

5. *Which Dangers Require a Warning?* A seller need not warn of every known or knowable danger that is not obvious. Whether a warning is required, as Note 2, *supra*, indicates, involves whether "the omission of the instructions or warnings renders the product not reasonably safe." Restatement (Third), *supra*, § 2(c). Whether a product is not reasonably safe because of the absence of adequate warnings or instructions is normally for the jury to decide. Given this standard, how should manufacturers go about identifying those dangers of which they should warn? How should lawyers advise client-sellers as to which warnings and instructions are necessary?

A particularly thorny contemporary issue in this area involves whether warnings are required about possible allergic reactions to a product or some ingredient or constituent element of a product. In Livingston v. Marie Callender's, Inc., 85 Cal. Rptr. 2d 528 (Ct. App. 1999), the plaintiff suffered an allergic reaction to monosodium glutamate (MSG) in the defendant's soup. The defendant argued that there was no duty to warn of possible allergic reaction to MSG. Invoking the Second and Third Restatements, the court ruled that the issue was for the jury:

> Restatement Second of Torts, section 402A, comment j states: "Directions or warning. In order to prevent the product from being unreasonably danger-ous, the seller may be required to give directions or warning, on the container, as to its use. The seller may reasonably assume that those with common allergies, as for example to eggs or strawberries, will be aware of them, and he is not required to warn against them. *Where, however, the product contains an ingredient to which a substantial number of the popu-lation are allergic, and the ingredient is one whose danger is not generally known, or if known is one which the consumer would reasonably not expect to find in the product, the seller is required to give warning against it, if he has knowledge, or by the application of reasonable, developed human skill and foresight should have knowledge, of the presence of the ingredient and the danger.* Likewise in the case of poisonous drugs, or those unduly dangerous for other reasons, warning as to use may be required." (Italics added.) The recently adopted Restatement Third of Torts: Products Liability, section 2, comment k, similarly states: "Cases of adverse allergic or idiosyncratic reactions involve a special subset of products that may be defective because of inadequate warnings. . . . [¶] The general rule in cases involving allergic reactions is that a warning is required when the harm-causing ingredient is one to which a substantial number of persons are aller-gic." Further, . . . comment k notes: "The ingredient that causes the allergic reaction must be one whose danger or whose presence in the product is not generally known to consumers. . . . When the presence of the allergenic ingredient would not be anticipated by a reasonable user or consumer, warnings concerning its presence are required."

Id. at 532-533.

6. *Proliferation = Dilution?* Professors Henderson and Twerski, the Reporters for the Third Restatement's provisions on products liability, have argued that the ease with which many jurisdictions permit plaintiffs to recover for failure to warn is having the perverse effect of reducing the efficacy of warnings. Because the issuance of further warnings is relatively cheap, manufacturers, they suppose, are inclined to attempt to ward off liability by warning of virtually any conceivable danger that might be asso-ciated with their product, no matter how remote. This proliferation of warnings in turn creates a culture in which consumers become dismissive of warnings because of their overuse. Thus, by too easily permitting failure to warn claims in the name of consumer safety, the law ends up diminish-ing safety.

7. *Adequacy of Warning.* A manufacturer's inclusion of a warning with the product, and its inclusion of instructions as to certain precau-tions, will not necessarily relieve the manufacturer of liability for ensuing injuries *even under a failure to warn theory*. This is because warnings and instructions must be *adequate* to notify the consumer of the existence and nature of the hazard at issue. The issue of adequacy is normally for the

jury. Although there are cases in which warnings are clearly inadequate—imagine a manufacturer that purports to alert consumers of a severe, nonobvious risk of a product in a small-font footnote buried in the product's owners' manual—adequacy is ordinarily highly context-specific, requiring a judgment that cannot be reduced to hard and fast rules. *See* Restatement (Third), *supra*, § 2, comment ("No easy guideline exists for courts to adopt in assessing the adequacy of product warnings and instructions. In making their assessments, courts must focus on many factors, such as content and comprehensibility, intensity of expression, and the characteristics of expected user groups."). Thus, for purposes of litigation as well as client counseling, consideration will have to be given to the placement and prominence of the warning on the product itself and/or in accompanying packaging or instructional materials; the nature of the risk(s) posed by the product; the extent to which the risk and its consequences, if realized, are defined and communicated by the warning; the precautions that can or should be taken in light of the warning; whether the warning is given in conjunction with other information that might cause confusion or a downplaying of the danger; and what the seller knows or should know about likely reactions to the warnings.

Some of the nuances of the "adequacy" issue are illustrated by Schwoerer v. Union Oil Co., 17 Cal. Rptr. 2d 227 (Ct. App. 1993). The plaintiff sued the manufacturers and distributors of a solvent that he had inhaled and touched while working with it. As a result, he alleged that he suffered multiple physical ailments, including permanent liver damage. The trial court granted summary judgment for the defendants, but the Court of Appeals reversed, finding that the adequacy of the warnings issued by the defendants was an issue of fact on which reasonable factfinders could disagree. It was undisputed that the defendants provided "material safety data sheets" (MSDS) to the plaintiff's employer, and that these contained warnings stating, among other things, that persons using the solvent should wear impermeable gloves, boots, aprons, and should also wear a gas mask or other breathing apparatus in situations in which significant inhalation might occur. The sheets further indicated that contact with the solvent could produce skin irritation, rashes, and dermatitis; that inhalation could cause respiratory tract irritation, dizziness, fatigue, nausea, and asphyxiation; and that chronic over-exposure to the solvent might have effects of an unspecified nature on the central nervous system.

For purposes of summary judgment, it was assumed that the plaintiff did not receive this information from his employer and was not equipped with protective clothing or goggles. On appeal, the central issue was whether the warnings were adequate as a matter of law, such that the issue should be taken away from the factfinder. The Court of Appeals concluded that they were not, reasoning as follows:

> It cannot be disputed that liver damage is far more apt to have a devastating effect on one so afflicted than is dermatitis, as to which the MSDS do warn.

Since, for our purposes, defendants are assumed to have known of this devastating potential yet failed to warn against it, defendants have not shown the warnings provided in the MSDS are adequate as a matter of law.

Id. at 232. Assume that the plaintiff did receive the information described above. Was *Schwoerer* rightly decided? Was it enough, on this assumption, that the plaintiff was put on notice that he was dealing with materials that were clearly not benign? That there was a possible connection between inhalation and unspecified dangers to the central nervous system?

B.   Proving Actual Causation in a Failure to Warn Case

When suit is brought for injuries caused by an ordinary consumer product that is alleged to lack proper warnings, the premise of the suit is that the warning would have been read by the consumer and heeded by him, thus avoiding the injury. Yet, even when an adequate warning is provided, there is no guarantee that a consumer will read it, nor, if he reads it, that he will adjust his conduct in light of it. In short, failure to warn claims pose issues of causation comparable to those encountered in connection with "informed consent" medical malpractice claims. See Chapter 3. Thus, courts have been required to consider what sort of showing a plaintiff must make to permit the factfinder to conclude that an adequate warning that was not in fact given would have been noticed and heeded had it been given. Before turning to an exploration of that issue, however, we must first discuss a related and prior question: *To whom* should warnings be given?

1. *The Learned Intermediary Doctrine.* In many cases, the obvious answer to the "to whom" question will be the correct answer. Thus, if the product in question is an ordinary consumer product such as a lawnmower or a toaster, any required warnings must be conveyed directly to the consumer through labels on the product, and/or in accompanying packaging or instructional materials. For some products, however, the question of who needs to be warned is not so obvious. Indeed, as the next case demonstrates, when the product that is alleged to be defective for lack of adequate warnings is a prescription drug, tort law generally obliges sellers to provide warnings and instructions only to the prescribing physician, not the consumer. The rule of tort law that specifies this result is known as the *learned intermediary doctrine*. Freeman v. Hoffman-La Roche, Inc., the case from Section IV in which the plaintiff sued the manufacturer of a prescription acne medication on various theories, including failure to warn, describes this doctrine succinctly:

Pharmaceutical products have historically been treated differently in regard to a duty to warn. Although in ordinary product cases, a manufacturer's duty to warn runs directly to the consumer of the product, in cases involving prescription drugs, it is widely held that the duty to warn extends only to members of the medical profession and not to the consumer. Annot., 57 A.L.R.5th 1 (1998) (collecting cases). This concept, known as the learned intermediary doctrine,

> is based upon the premise that, as a medical expert, a patient's prescribing or treating physician is in the best position to evaluate the often complex information provided by the manufacturer concerning the risks and benefits of its drug or product and to make an individualized medical judgment, based on the patient's particular needs and susceptibilities, as to whether the patient should use the product.

57 A.L.R.5th at 26.

The learned intermediary doctrine is provided for in § 6(d) of the Third Restatement. Section 6(d) at 145 states:

> A prescription drug or medical device is not reasonably safe due to inadequate instructions or warnings if reasonable instructions or warnings regarding foreseeable risks of harm are not provided to:
>
> (1) prescribing and other health-care providers who are in a position to reduce the risks of harm in accordance with the instructions or warnings; or
>
> (2) the patient when the manufacturer knows or has reason to know that health-care providers will not be in a position to reduce the risks of harm in accordance with the instructions or warnings. . . .

618 N.W.2d 827, 841-842 (Neb. 2000). The *Freeman* court proceeded to incorporate the learned intermediary doctrine into Nebraska law, and to permit Freeman to press her failure to warn claim on the ground that Hoffman had, according to her allegations, failed to provide adequate warnings of the risks of Accutane to physicians.

2. *Exceptions.* Plaintiffs suing for certain prescription medicines have sometimes succeeded in arguing that warnings ought to have been given directly to consumers. *See, e.g.,* MacDonald v. Ortho Pharmaceutical Corp., 475 N.E.2d 65 (Mass. 1985) (manufacturer owes a duty to warn the consumer directly of health risks associated with use of contraceptive). With the rise of direct-to-consumer advertising for prescription drugs ranging from antacids to antidepressants, the argument is now being made that many of the original rationales for the learned intermediary doctrine have faded away. The most striking evidence of this nascent trend is the decision of the New Jersey Supreme Court in Perez v. Wyeth Labs., Inc., 734 A.2d 1245 (N.J. 1999) (when a drug manufacturer advertises directly to patients, it can incur liability for failing to include adequate warnings of health risks in the advertising itself).

With this sketch of the learned intermediary doctrine in mind, consider now the issues mentioned at the outset of this section as to the burden plaintiffs do or should face in proving causation within a failure to warn claim.

Motus v. Pfizer Inc.

196 F. Supp. 2d 984 (C.D. Cal. 2001)*

Matz, J.

I. INTRODUCTION

Six days after Dr. Gerald Trostler prescribed Zoloft to Victor Motus, Mr. Motus took his life. His widow, Flora Motus, sued Zoloft's manufacturer, Pfizer Inc., for failing to adequately warn that Zoloft can cause those who ingest it to commit suicide. She alleges five claims: (1) "wrongful death/negligence"; (2) strict liability; (3) "survival action"; (4) fraud; and (5) breach of warranty. Each of Ms. Motus's claims is premised on the allegation that Pfizer's "package insert and marketing materials do not warn . . . that [Zoloft] can cause some people to think and act in violent or suicidal ways." First Amended Complaint ("FAC") ¶ 20. She alleges that Pfizer's failure to warn of this risk caused her husband to commit suicide.

Pfizer now moves for summary judgment on the ground that Ms. Motus cannot prove that its alleged failure to warn or inadequate warning caused her injury. Pfizer argues that Ms. Motus has no evidence that Dr. Trostler would have acted differently had adequate warnings been provided. The Court agrees with Pfizer, and accordingly grants it summary judgment on all claims.

II. FACTUAL BACKGROUND

A. DR. TROSTLER PRESCRIBES ZOLOFT TO VICTOR MOTUS

Mr. Motus first saw Dr. Trostler on July 16, 1998 because he was having trouble controlling his diabetes and cholesterol. Mr. Motus did not mention any symptoms of anxiety or depression during his first visit, nor during his next three visits to Dr. Trostler on July 27, August 25, and October 13. Mr. Motus visited Dr. Trostler for the last time on November 6, 1998. During that visit, Mr. Motus appeared "unhappy," "depressed," and "frustrated," and he "had a lot on his mind that he wanted to share" with Dr. Trostler. Mr. Motus told Dr. Trostler that his savings of $150,000 were gone, that he was losing $5,000 to $10,000 per week on a bad investment, that he could not sleep, that he was the president of a school district, that he had a political problem and that he had some numbness in his hands. Mr. Motus also told Dr. Trostler that he was contemplating bankruptcy.

As a result of these revelations, Dr. Trostler concluded that Mr. Motus was moderately depressed. Dr. Trostler did not think that Mr. Motus was suicidal or sufficiently depressed to warrant sending Mr. Motus to a mental health professional. Dr. Trostler prescribed Mr. Motus 25 milligrams of Zoloft for seven days, followed by 50 milligrams of Zoloft for fourteen days.

* [aff'd, 2004 U.S. App. LEXIS 1944 (9th Cir.).—EDS.]

To fill this prescription, Dr. Trostler gave Mr. Motus a sample packet of Zoloft, which he had received from a Pfizer representative. The sample packet did not have any warning printed on it. Dr. Trostler opined that the box containing the sample packets probably did contain a package insert (i.e., an insert that contains information about the drug, including warnings), or that each sample packet originally came with the package insert attached, but he could not recall removing the package insert from the packets or whether one package insert came in the box of samples.

Dr. Trostler did not provide Mr. Motus with a package insert or any other written information concerning Zoloft, and he could not recall whether he had any promotional materials for Zoloft in his office at the time he prescribed Zoloft for Mr. Motus. Dr. Trostler did not warn Mr. Motus that taking Zoloft could cause him to have suicidal thoughts or experience akathisia[, a condition that may entail muscle twitches, agitation, and restlessness]. He did not discuss with Mr. Motus any contraindications of taking Zoloft, and was not aware of any contraindications that would have suggested Mr. Motus was not a good candidate for Zoloft. During Dr. Trostler's deposition, Plaintiff's lawyer asked: "If you had been told that Zoloft can cause an increased risk in suicide during the first few weeks of drug treatment, is that the kind of information you would pass on to your patients?" Dr. Trostler responded, "Yes."

Dr. Trostler told Mr. Motus to call him if his condition worsened or if he experienced any side effects, and he also had Mr. Motus schedule a follow-up appointment for November 26 (i.e., twenty days later). Before Mr. Motus took his life, Dr. Trostler did not speak to Mr. Motus or any member of Mr. Motus's family and he did not know whether Mr. Motus experienced adverse reactions to Zoloft, such as confusion, akathisia, or suicidal thoughts. Six days later, on November 12, 1998, Mr. Motus committed suicide by shooting himself.

B.   HOW DID DR. TROSTLER LEARN ABOUT ZOLOFT?

Dr. Trostler could not recall reviewing any information from Pfizer before deciding to prescribe Zoloft to Mr. Motus, although he "may have" relied on some unspecified written information from an "article or seminar." He stated that his familiarity with Zoloft was "probably multi-source," and included "reading articles" and attending "drug company meetings." By "drug company meetings," Dr. Trostler meant physician meetings such as seminars, lectures or conferences, where information was delivered by various people, including drug company representatives. Dr. Trostler stated that the articles he read were "occasional articles that appear[ed] in journals to which I subscribe," such as the New England Journal of Medicine and the Annals of Internal Medicine. Dr. Trostler stated that he also received "hundreds of journals that come to the office unsolicited."

Plaintiff argues that Dr. Trostler obtained information from sources other than the package insert, such as "PDR's" (Physician's Desk Reference), "Dear Doctor" letters and promotional activities of sales people. There is no evidence that he obtained information about Zoloft from the first two sources. As to sales representatives, Dr. Trostler stated that before the death of Mr. Motus, he "probably did have conversations about Zoloft with Pfizer representatives, but I don't specifically recall." When asked whether he recalled any particular meeting where Zoloft was discussed, Dr. Trostler responded "No," and he could not remember the substance of any conversations he may have had with a Pfizer representative concerning Zoloft. Dr. Trostler also could not recall whether Pfizer representatives brought him scientific articles or patient information brochures in 1998. Nor could Dr. Trostler recall whether he discussed Zoloft with his colleagues.

Even though Dr. Trostler stated that he could not recall any particular meeting in which he discussed Zoloft with a Pfizer representative, certain parts of his deposition indicate that he did, in fact, recall the substance of at least some meetings. For example, when asked: "In talking to Zoloft representatives . . . did they recommend different medical conditions to prescribe Zoloft to treat?," Dr. Trostler replied "Yes," and indicated that depression and panic attacks were two of those conditions. Dr. Trostler also stated that in discussing Zoloft with Pfizer's representatives, they never told him that Zoloft could: (1) cause akathisia; (2) worsen a patient's situation; (3) cause a patient to have suicidal thoughts; (4) cause a patient to experience a feeling so acute that death is a welcome result; or (5) increase the risk that a patient would commit suicide. Dr. Trostler could not recall whether the drug representatives told him that once he prescribed Zoloft, he needed to closely supervise his patient.

C. WHY DID DR. TROSTLER DECIDE TO PRESCRIBE ZOLOFT FOR VICTOR MOTUS?

Dr. Trostler stated that he relied solely on his "training and experience" in making his clinical evaluation that Mr. Motus was depressed. He admitted that he prescribed drugs without having previously reviewed the package insert, and that he first reviewed the package insert for Zoloft after Mr. Motus committed suicide.[2] Dr. Trostler stated that his "clinical experience" was the "ultimate determinant" for whether he would prescribe a drug, and that he would not prescribe a drug based on what a drug representative told him if he had concerns about a drug's safety or effectiveness.

---

2. The package insert made the following references to suicide. First, the "Adverse Reactions" section listed "suicide ideation and attempt" as events that had occurred in clinical trials and the frequency with which they had occurred. Second, the "Adverse Reactions" section stated "It is important to emphasize that although the events reported occurred during treatment with Zoloft, they were not necessarily caused by it." Third, the "Precautions" section stated, "The possibility of a suicide attempt is inherent in depression and may persist until significant remission occurs. Close supervision of high-risk patients should accompany initial drug therapy. Prescriptions for Zoloft should be written for the smallest quantity of tablets consistent with good patient management in order to reduce the risk of overdose." It is not disputed that the Food and Drug Administration ("FDA") approved this labeling.

When asked: "In deciding to prescribe Mr. Motus Zoloft, did you rely specifically on any statements made to you by Pfizer representatives?," Dr. Trostler replied, "No." When asked: "Did you rely on any materials provided to you by Pfizer sales representatives in making your decision to prescribe Zoloft to Mr. Motus?," Dr. Trostler replied, "No." When asked: "Did any written material provided to you by a Pfizer representative regarding Zoloft cause you to prescribe Zoloft to Mr. Motus?," Dr. Trostler replied, "No."

D.   DR. TROSTLER'S AWARENESS OF A POSSIBLE RELATIONSHIP BETWEEN ZOLOFT AND SUICIDE BEFORE HE PRESCRIBED ZOLOFT TO MR. MOTUS

Dr. Trostler stated that he was aware, before he prescribed Zoloft to Mr. Motus, that there were some claims that [the class of antidepressants known as selective seritonin reuptake inhibitors (SSRIs), which includes Zoloft] . . . [is] linked to increased suicide and violence, but that he discounted these claims based on his personal experience. Indeed, even as late as his deposition, Dr. Trostler stated, "My personal belief is that SSRIs do not cause people to commit suicide." He stated in particular that he "was aware that there had been some publicity about individuals taking SSRI's and committing suicide or violent behavior." When asked, however, whether he was "aware that serotonin is associated with suicide and violence," Dr. Trostler responded "No," and also indicated that he had never seen any articles discussing the subject. Dr. Trostler could not recall reading any articles about Zoloft and suicide or suicidal ideation.

What is *absent* from Dr. Trostler's deposition may be as significant for purposes of this motion as what he did say. Plaintiff never asked Dr. Trostler whether he would have changed his decision to prescribe Zoloft to Mr. Motus if Pfizer had provided a specified warning about the risk of suicide associated with ingestion of the drug. Plaintiff also never asked Dr. Trostler whether the warning she thinks was required would have affected what Dr. Trostler said to Mr. Motus at the time he prescribed him Zoloft.

III.   DISCUSSION

Pfizer moves for summary judgment on the ground that even if the warnings on the Zoloft package inserts or elsewhere were inadequate, Ms. Motus cannot prove that the inadequacy caused her injury — i.e., led to Mr. Motus's death — because, in deciding to prescribe Zoloft for Mr. Motus, Dr. Trostler did not rely on any information from Pfizer. The absence of an adequate warning that Zoloft can cause suicide or akathisia is immaterial, Pfizer argues, because even if such a warning had been provided it would not have changed either Dr. Trostler's decision to prescribe Zoloft or the information he relayed to Mr. Motus about Zoloft. Pfizer also argues that Ms. Motus cannot prove that the absence of an adequate warning . . . caused her injury, because Dr. Trostler already was aware of claims that

SSRIs like Zoloft could increase suicidality and violence when he prescribed Zoloft to Mr. Motus. Therefore, Pfizer argues, because Dr. Trostler was already aware of the "risk" at issue, the failure to warn him of the risk could not have been the cause of Mr. Motus's death. . . .

B.   CALIFORNIA LAW GOVERNING FAILURE-TO-WARN CASES

California law applies in this diversity action. It is well-settled that a manufacturer of prescription drugs owes to the medical profession the duty of providing adequate warnings if it knows, or has reason to know, of any dangerous side effects of its drugs. Carlin v. The Superior Court of Sutter County, 13 Cal. 4th 1104, 1112-13, 56 Cal. Rptr. 2d 162, 920 P.2d 1347 (1996). California follows the learned intermediary doctrine, which states that in the case of prescription drugs, the duty to warn "runs to the physician, not to the patient." *Id.* at 1116, 56 Cal. Rptr. 2d 162, 920 P.2d 1347 (citations omitted). Thus, a manufacturer discharges its duty to warn if it provides adequate warnings to the physician about any known or reasonably knowable dangerous side effects, regardless of whether the warning reaches the patient.

A plaintiff asserting causes of action based on a failure to warn must prove not only that no warning was provided or the warning was inadequate, but also that the inadequacy or absence of the warning caused the plaintiff's injury.

Pfizer tacitly concedes for purposes of this summary judgment motion that its warning about the risk of suicide was inadequate. It moves for summary judgment on the ground that Ms. Motus cannot demonstrate that the inadequate warning was the proximate cause of her injury, because she has failed to demonstrate that the inclusion of an adequate warning would have altered Dr. Trostler's decision to prescribe Zoloft to Mr. Motus. If it is not genuinely disputable that Dr. Trostler would have prescribed Zoloft to Mr. Motus even if Pfizer had provided an adequate warning about the risk of suicide, then Ms. Motus cannot prove proximate cause, and Pfizer is entitled to summary judgment.

C.   THE BURDEN OF PROOF AND THE REBUTTABLE PRESUMPTION

Both sides agree that under California law [on actual causation] Plaintiff must prove that Pfizer's alleged failure to warn or inadequate warning was a "substantial factor" in bringing about Mr. Motus's death. . . . The threshold issue here is whether she can do so by invoking the rebuttable presumption, adopted by some states, that had there been an adequate warning, the doctor would have heeded it. Courts have premised the adoption of this presumption on the following language in comment j of section 402A of the Restatement (Second) of Torts:

> Where warning is given, the seller may reasonably assume that it will be read and heeded; and a product bearing such a warning, which is safe for use if followed, is not in defective condition, nor is it unreasonably dangerous.

Under the rebuttable presumption, once the plaintiff establishes that the manufacturer provided inadequate warnings, the burden shifts to the defendant to show that an adequate warning would not have affected the doctor's conduct in prescribing the drug. If the defendant fails to make that showing, "the presumption satisfies the plaintiff's burden of demonstrating that the inadequate warning was the proximate cause of the ingestion of the drug." [Quoted authority omitted. — EDS.] The rebuttable presumption is simply a burden-shifting device that makes it easier for a plaintiff to prove causation.

By contrast, in states that have not adopted the rebuttable presumption, the plaintiff in a prescription drug case bears the full burden of proving through affirmative evidence that the inadequate warning was the proximate cause of the injury, or, in other words, that an adequate warning to the prescribing physician would have altered the physician's conduct. . . .

In this case, if the presumption applies, Pfizer must come forward with evidence affirmatively demonstrating that an adequate warning would not have affected Dr. Trostler's decision to prescribe Zoloft to Mr. Motus. If the rebuttable presumption does not apply, Pfizer may prevail by showing that Plaintiff lacks evidence establishing that an adequate warning would have affected Dr. Trostler's decision to prescribe Zoloft. Pfizer need not produce its own evidence; pointing to an absence of evidence on Plaintiff's part is sufficient.

D.   DOES CALIFORNIA APPLY THE REBUTTABLE PRESUMPTION?

"A federal court sitting in diversity must follow the law directed by the Supreme Court of the state whose law is found to be applicable, and if there is no direct decision by the highest court of that state, the federal court should determine what it believes that state's highest court would find if the issue were before it." Plummer v. Lederle Laboratories, 819 F.2d 349, 355 (2d Cir. 1987) (citation omitted).

Plaintiff asserts that California has adopted the presumption, and that it applies to this case. . . .

As Defendant argues in its supplemental brief, California appellate courts — citing comment j to section 402A of the Restatement (Second) of Torts — have reasoned that when an adequate warning is provided to the plaintiff, the defendant *manufacturer* "may assume that it will be read and heeded." Plaintiff has cited no California case using comment j to shift either the burden of proof as to causation or the burden of going forward to a defendant in a failure-to-warn case.

Moreover, even if California *had* adopted the rebuttable presumption in failure-to-warn cases generally, California courts would not necessarily apply that presumption in the prescription drug context, which raises distinct policy concerns. . . . [In] *Brown v. Superior Court of City and County of San Francisco*, 751 P.2d 470 (1988) . . . the California Supreme Court . . . noted:

[There is] an important distinction between prescription drugs and other products such as construction machinery . . . , a lawnmower . . . , or perfume . . . , the producers of which were held strictly liable. In the latter cases, the product is used to make work easier or to provide pleasure, while in the former it may be necessary to alleviate pain or to sustain life. Moreover, unlike other important medical products (wheelchairs, for example), harm to some users from prescription drugs is unavoidable. Because of these distinctions, the broader public interest in the availability of drugs must be considered in deciding the appropriate standard of liability for injuries resulting from their use.

Id. at 1063, 245 Cal. Rptr. 412, 751 P.2d 470. . . .

[*Brown*'s admonition notwithstanding,] [t]he Court recognizes the difficulty in predicting how the California Supreme Court would rule on the issue whether prescription drug manufacturers should be subject to the application of the rebuttable presumption. In *Carlin*, for example, the California Supreme Court held that manufacturers of prescription drugs can be held strictly liable for failing to warn of risks that are scientifically knowable, but which were not actually known to the drug manufacturer at the time it manufactured the drug. In reaching this conclusion, the *Carlin* Court minimized the differences between strict liability rules in the prescription drug context and in the non-prescription drug context. . . . If in fact California had adopted the rebuttable presumption in a failure-to-warn case involving a product other than a prescription drug, this language in *Carlin* might be some indication that the California Supreme Court would also adopt the rebuttable presumption in the prescription drug failure-to-warn context.

But in fact, no California court *has* adopted or applied that presumption, and several California courts have decided whether proximate cause has been or can be established in prescription drug and medical device failure-to-warn cases without mentioning the rebuttable presumption. For example, in Plenger v. Alza Corp., 11 Cal. App. 4th 349, 13 Cal. Rptr. 2d 811 (1992), the plaintiffs sued an IUD manufacturer after their wife and mother died as a result of an infection caused by her use of an IUD. The plaintiffs alleged that the warnings the manufacturer gave the decedent's doctor were inadequate. . . . The court granted summary judgment to the defendant on the ground that the risk of infection and death was so well known in the medical profession that the failure to warn the physician of that risk could not be the legal cause of the decedent's death. If the rebuttable presumption had been applied in *Plenger*, the court would have assumed that the doctor would have heeded an adequate warning about the risk of infection and death from the implantation of IUDs, and so the defendant would have had the burden to demonstrate with affirmative evidence that the doctor still would have implanted the IUD even if an adequate warning had been provided. . . .

Perhaps the most persuasive California case on this point is Ramirez v. Plough, Inc., 6 Cal. 4th 539, 25 Cal. Rptr. 2d 97, 863 P.2d 167 (1993), a failure-to-warn case involving a non-prescription drug. In *Ramirez*, an infant sued a drug manufacturer, alleging that he contracted Reyes Syndrome as a result of ingesting non-prescription aspirin. The product label, which was entirely in English, contained a warning that aspirin has been associated with Reyes Syndrome and stated that the dosage for a child under two should be "as directed by doctor." *Id.* at 543-44, 25 Cal. Rptr. 2d 97, 863 P.2d 167. The plaintiff's mother, who was literate only in Spanish, did not consult a doctor before giving him aspirin. The mother did not ask anyone to translate the label or package insert into Spanish, even though other members of her household could have done so.

The primary question in *Ramirez* was whether the drug manufacturer had a duty to provide warnings in Spanish. The Court concluded it did not. After losing on this ground, the plaintiff asserted an alternative ground of liability: that, lack of Spanish warnings aside, the English label provided defective warnings. The Court rejected this argument because the plaintiff's mother "neither read nor obtained translation of the product labeling. Thus, there is no conceivable causal connection between the representations or omissions that accompanied the product and plaintiff's injury." The Court did not apply or even mention any rebuttable presumption that the plaintiff's mother would have read and heeded an adequate warning. *Ramirez* is strong evidence that the Court would not apply the rebuttable presumption in this case, involving a prescription drug.

Given that other no other court applying California law in this context has adopted the presumption, and several courts have failed to do so when the presumption could have been critical, this Court will not apply it here.

E.   THERE IS NO EVIDENCE THAT ADEQUATE WARNINGS WOULD HAVE CHANGED DR. TROSTLER'S CONDUCT

Given the Court's conclusion that the "rebuttable presumption" is not applicable, Pfizer may prevail in its motion for summary judgment if Ms. Motus has failed to adduce evidence that Dr. Trostler would have acted differently had Pfizer provided an adequate warning about the risk of suicide associated with the ingestion of Zoloft. Ms. Motus has introduced no such evidence.

Mr. Motus did not disclose any contraindications to Dr. Trostler suggesting that he was not a good candidate for Zoloft. . . .

Mr. Motus did not exhibit symptoms that became progressively worse over a period of time. *Cf.* McEwen v. Ortho Pharmaceutical Corp., 270 Or. 375, 528 P.2d 522, 539 (1974) (substantial evidence supported finding that adequate warnings would have changed doctor's decision to permit plaintiff to continue using birth control pills because plaintiff had cumulative symptoms that developed over a period of time). . . . Under *McEwen* . . ., Motus may have been able to create a genuine issue if, for example, Dr. Trostler became aware that Mr. Motus experienced adverse reactions to Zoloft such as confusion, akathisia, or suicidal thoughts. But Mr. Motus ingested Zoloft for, at most, only six days and Dr. Trostler testified in his deposition that he did not speak to Mr. Motus or any member of his family after he prescribed Zoloft to Mr. Motus.

Nor has Ms. Motus produced evidence that the risk of suicide associated with Zoloft is so high that it would have affected Dr. Trostler's (or any reasonable physician's) decision to prescribe Zoloft to a moderately depressed patient. "The burden [is] on the plaintiff to demonstrate that the additional non-disclosed risk was sufficiently high that it would have changed the treating physician's decision to prescribe the product for the plaintiff." Thomas [v. Hoffman-LaRoche, Inc.], 949 F.2d [806,] 815 ([5th Cir.] 1992) (plaintiff who suffered seizures after taking Accutane failed to prove that an inadequate warning caused her injuries because the risk of seizures from Accutane is so low that it could not have affected the doctor's decision to prescribe the medication); *see also* Willett v. Baxter Int'l, Inc., 929 F.2d 1094, 1099 (5th Cir. 1991) (unlikely that doctor would have changed his mind to implant artificial heart valves where the risk undisclosed by the warnings — a .03 percent per annum rate of failure due to soot pockets — was minimal and "plaintiff failed to present any specific evidence that this . . . risk would have changed [the doctor's] decision"). . . .

Next, Plaintiff has presented no evidence that Dr. Trostler relied on statements from Pfizer in making his decision to prescribe Zoloft to Mr. Motus. Dr. Trostler's recollection of how he learned about Zoloft is vague. But he did state unequivocally that in making that decision, he did not rely either on any statements Pfizer representatives made to him nor any written materials they may have provided to him. Indeed, Dr. Trostler stated that he did not read the package insert or PDR entry for Zoloft until after Mr. Motus committed suicide. It follows that the inclusion of adequate warnings in that information would not have affected his decision. . . .

Ms. Motus argues that Dr. Trostler's credibility is a jury question. Plaintiff is correct that some courts permit a plaintiff to get past the summary judgment phase even when a prescribing doctor makes unequivocal statements demonstrating that adequate warnings would not have changed his or her decision to prescribe a drug. . . .

The Court [rejects this argument]. If Dr. Trostler's testimony on this point were "equivocal or uncertain," or if there was evidence placing his credibility in question, the Court might agree that it should "reserve the issue of credibility for the jury's determination." [Quoted authority omitted.] Here, there is no such equivocal evidence in the record, nor evidence undermining Dr. Trostler's veracity. Indeed, Plaintiff never asked Dr. Trostler what could have been (depending on the answer) the following dispositive question: "Dr. Trostler, if even without reading the package insert you had become aware that Pfizer itself had disclosed that [whatever is the precise warning regarding suicide that plaintiff considers necessary], would you have prescribed Zoloft to Mr. Motus?"

Plaintiff's lawyer did ask Dr. Trostler: "If you had been told that Zoloft can cause an increased risk in suicide during the first few weeks of drug treatment, is that the kind of information you would pass on to your patients?" Dr. Trostler responded, "Yes." Plaintiff argues that this response creates a genuine issue as to whether Dr. Trostler would have changed his behavior had Pfizer provided adequate warnings. The Court does not agree. Given that this case is about the sufficiency of the warnings accompanying Zoloft, the appropriate question would have been: "If Zoloft's package insert had contained a warning that Zoloft can cause an increased risk in suicide during the first few weeks of drug treatment, would you have prescribed Zoloft to Mr. Motus?" But Plaintiff's lawyer did not ask this question, and at the hearing, in response to the Court's inquiry why not, he displayed commendable candor in acknowledging that he, and probably defense counsel as well, were afraid of how Dr. Trostler might respond. The testimony Dr. Trostler did give does not establish that if that warning had been provided, he would not have prescribed Zoloft or would have told Mr. Motus something other than what he did say.

On this record Plaintiff has failed to create a question of fact for the jury, especially given that it would appear to be against Dr. Trostler's professional interest to testify as he did. (It is hardly a testament to his diligence that he did not read the package insert before prescribing Zoloft to Mr. Motus.) . . .

G.   OVERPROMOTION

In her complaint, Plaintiff alleges that Pfizer overpromoted Zoloft: "Pfizer aggressively distributed and marketed Zoloft, encouraging all types of physicians (including those who have no specialized training or expertise in the mental health field such as Dr. Trostler) to dispense and prescribe Zoloft, not only for depression, but also for other maladies." Plaintiff alleges that this alleged overpromotion "has nullified what warnings Pfizer has given regarding this drug." On the basis of these allegations, Plaintiff argues that Pfizer's "overpromotion" caused Dr. Trostler to prescribe Zoloft despite his awareness of the alleged risk that Zoloft can cause patients to commit suicide.

An overpromotion theory is one way that a plaintiff in a failure-to-warn case can overcome the manufacturer's argument either (1) that it provided adequate warnings or (2) that the doctor's decision to prescribe a drug despite his awareness of its dangers was an intervening cause sufficient to vitiate the manufacturer's liability. *See* Stevens v. Parke, Davis & Co., 9 Cal. 3d 51, 65, 107 Cal. Rptr. 45, 507 P.2d 653 (1973) ("[A]n adequate warning to the [medical] profession may be eroded or even nullified by overpromotion of the drug through a vigorous sales program which may have the effect of persuading the prescribing doctor to disregard the warnings given.") . . .

The logic of an overpromotion theory is that the manufacturer's aggressive marketing caused a physician to discount a known risk when prescribing a drug to a patient. Because this Court's ruling is based only on the ground that Plaintiff failed to prove that Dr. Trostler would not have prescribed Zoloft if an adequate warning had been provided, not on his awareness of claims that SSRI drugs were linked to increased suicide, there is no need to address whether Pfizer's alleged overpromotion contaminated Dr. Trotsler's decision. [In any event,] . . . it would appear that Plaintiff could not demonstrate that Pfizer's alleged overpromotion caused Dr. Trostler to prescribe Zoloft to Mr. Motus.

IV.   CONCLUSION

Ms. Motus points to no evidence establishing that Dr. Trostler would have acted differently had Pfizer provided an adequate warning about the alleged risk that Zoloft causes those who ingest it to commit suicide. She is therefore unable to create a genuine issue as to whether Pfizer's alleged failure to provide an adequate warning caused her injuries. All of Plaintiff's claims are premised to some extent on the allegation that Pfizer's failure to warn caused her injuries. Accordingly, Defendant is entitled to summary judgment.

NOTES AND QUESTIONS

1. *Actual Causation*. Like manufacturing defect and design defect claims, failure to warn actions require the plaintiff to prove that the defect (the absence of an adequate warning) actually caused the plaintiff's injury. Unlike the other two sorts of defect cases, however, the application of cause-in-fact to failure to warn cases necessarily raises the speculative question of whether someone would have selected a different course of conduct if different, or greater, information or warnings had been provided. As noted above, failure to warn cases in this respect involve an issue similar to the causation issue in informed consent cases, see Chapter 3, as well as fraud.

Previous sections of this chapter have indicated that, at its inception, products liability law was expressly designed to ease a plaintiff's burden in suing a product seller for a product-related injury. It is therefore not surprising that courts developed doctrinal devices — such as the heeding presumption mentioned (but not applied) in *Motus* — that, in effect, put a thumb on the plaintiff's side of the scale in failure to warn cases. However, we have also seen a number of courts displaying hostility to the proliferation of products liability claims, which might suggest diminished receptiveness to devices aiding plaintiffs, particularly when it relates to an issue as central as causation. Do you find the federal district judge's application of California law evenhanded? Which parts of the opinion do you believe would be most vulnerable on appeal?

2. *The Heeding Presumption*. As *Motus* indicates, numerous jurisdictions have adopted what is termed the *heeding presumption* in failure to warn cases. A striking application of the heeding presumption is found in House v. Armour of America, Inc., 929 P.2d 340 (Utah 1996). The plaintiff in *House* was the widow of a police officer who was shot and killed while on a SWAT mission. The defendant was the manufacturer of the body armor vest worn by the deceased officer, which vest was penetrated by a bullet shot from a rifle. The plaintiff argued that the manufacturer should have warned of the limitations of their vest — that is, that it would not necessarily protect against rifle fire. While contesting the duty to warn of such limitations, the defendant also argued that it would not have made any difference because Officer House would have undertaken the same

path of risky conduct in any case. Relying on the heeding presumption, the court said that there was at least an issue for the jury as to whether House might have behaved differently by, for example, taking other precautions against being shot.

Comment j to Section 402A of the Second Restatement, quoted in *Motus*, is often cited as an authority for adoption of the heeding presumption. Reexamine the text of the comment. Does it clearly speak to the issue of causation?

3. *Predicting the Development of California Law.* Do you agree with the district court's prediction in *Motus* that the California Supreme Court would not, in an appropriate case, adopt the heeding presumption? Was the federal court nonetheless on strong ground given that the case before it concerned warnings as to the effects of a prescription drug? Would a contrary ruling have offered much of a benefit to the plaintiff given that the heeding presumption is rebuttable, and that the defendant was prepared to offer evidence to rebut it?

4. *The Antidepressant Controversy.* As *Motus* indicates, Zoloft is one among several antidepressant medications called SSRIs (of which the best known is Prozac). Several other pharmaceutical companies have been sued in similar actions around the country, based on the suicide of family members who had been prescribed SSRIs. In these cases, the causation question is complicated—both in medicine and in law—by the fact that as a group, the set of patients who are prescribed this medication are much likelier than average to attempt or commit suicide. There is, however, some controversy over whether, for one or more of the SSRIs, there exist subsets of patients who are at increased risk of suicide as they begin to take their medication. The controversy has fluctuated over the past 15 years, both in North America and in Europe. Does it make sense to foreclose these medical causation questions as a matter of law? Or should juries have broad discretion to rule on them on a case-by-case basis? The FDA is trusted to make these decisions for the broader purpose of drug regulation and public health; should its decisions on drug safety be given deference on issues of tort liability? How much deference?

5. *Sophisticated Users.* In *House, supra* Note 2, the defendant argued at trial that the amount of information a manufacturer must provide with its product depends upon the sophistication and background knowledge of the relevant pool of consumers. In this view, the manufacturer's duty to a "sophisticated user" will be narrower, because certain risks that will not be obvious to the layperson may be obvious (or at least reasonably discoverable) to the sophisticated user. The Utah Supreme Court's opinion held that a jury can take into account the sophistication of a user such as House in determining whether he could be expected to be aware of the vulnerability of the vest to rifle-fire. The sophisticated user principle is accepted in various forms in a large number of jurisdictions.

6. *Failure to Warn, Causation, and Cost Spreading.* Some products liability suits involve allegations and proof of egregious wrongdoing, for example, the realization of a risk of injury recklessly imposed. At the other

end, one sometimes sees cases that approach "pure" cost spreading—those in which the defendant has done nothing obviously wrong, but nonetheless is well positioned to bear and spread the cost of a hapless victim's injuries. Courts and commentators routinely purport to reject loss spreading as itself sufficient to justify the imposition of liability: hence the oft-repeated mantras that products liability is not "absolute" liability, and that sellers are not "insurers" of consumers. Still, failure to warn doctrine, like other forms of products liability, continues to provide occasional cases that, at least viewed in hindsight, approach this end of the spectrum.

Ayers v. Johnson & Johnson Baby Prods. Co., 818 P.2d 1337 (Wash. 1991), is one such example. A 15-month-old baby boy opened his sister's handbag and pulled out an unmarked vial that contained baby oil that his sister was taking to school. The boy's mother noticed him putting the vial to his mouth and she yelled at him in response. Upon hearing his mother, the startled infant aspirated the baby oil (inhaled it into his lungs) rather than swallowing it. Tragically, the baby oil, by coating the boy's lungs, caused serious oxygen deprivation, which in turn left the boy permanently paralyzed and mentally retarded. The family sued Johnson & Johnson for failing to warn that the baby oil was dangerous if aspirated. In defense, Johnson & Johnson pointed out that it has sold hundreds of millions of bottles of baby oil and that, so far as it or the court could tell, this was the only episode of its kind. It also noted that aspiration of any number of commonly available, nontoxic fluids might have produced the same result. Nevertheless, the jury returned a multimillion-dollar verdict, which verdict was upheld by the Washington Supreme Court in a decision that relied on, among other plaintiff-friendly rulings, a markedly relaxed review of what counts as sufficient proof of actual causation.

East Penn Mfg. Co. v. Pineda, 578 A.2d 1113 (D.C. Ct. App. 1990), similarly displays "heroic" efforts by a trial judge and an appellate court to keep alive a jury verdict in a failure to warn suit arising out of tragic facts. The plaintiff was an experienced mechanic with little education who suffered an acid burn from an exploding battery manufactured by defendant. The acid burned his face and virtually blinded him in the right eye. The explosion occurred while he was recharging the battery, during which procedure he failed to use various safety precautions that would have prevented the explosion. The plaintiff's lawyers argued at trial that the battery-maker ought to have warned of all the dangers of recharging, and ought to have instructed users on proper precautions. (The battery itself did have a warning, but the warning was not detailed and was in any case covered in dust.) Although D.C. law incorporates a heeding presumption, East Penn rebutted the heeding presumption by presenting Pineda's admission, in his deposition, that he did not read the label on the battery. One might have supposed that his admission would spell defeat for his claim, but it did not. Upholding a jury verdict for plaintiff, the court concluded that the jury was entitled to find that if a better set of warnings had been provided, some of Pineda's co-workers might have read them and conveyed the information to Pineda, which might have caused him to use different precautions.

Most likely, jurors and judges involved in these cases understandably sympathized with the plaintiffs and their families. Is there anything wrong with decisions such as *Ayers* or *Pineda?* Are they the sort of decision contemplated by Justice Traynor's *Escola* concurrence?

REFERENCES/FURTHER READING

History

Mark Geistfeld, Escola v. Coca Cola Bottling Co., *Strict Products Liability Unbound*, in Robert L. Rabin & Stephen D. Sugarman, *Tort Stories* 259 (2003).

Oscar S. Gray, *Reflections on the Historical Context of Section 402A*, 10 Touro L. Rev. 75 (1993).

James R. Hackney, Jr., *The Intellectual Origins of American Strict Products Liability: A Case Study in American Pragmatic Instrumentalism*, 39 Am. J. Leg. Hist. 443 (1995).

James A. Henderson, Jr. & Theodore Eisenberg, *The Quiet Revolution in Products Liability: An Empirical Study of Legal Change*, 37 UCLA L. Rev. 479 (1990).

James A. Henderson, Jr. & Aaron D. Twerski, *Closing the American Products Liability Frontier: The Rejection of Liability Without Defect*, 66 N.Y.U. L. Rev. 1263 (1991).

Gregory C. Keating, *The Theory of Enterprise Liability and Common Law Strict Liability*, 54 Vand. L. Rev. 1285 (2001).

David G. Owen, *The Graying of Products Liability Law: Paths Taken and Untaken in the New Restatement*, 61 Tenn. L. Rev. 1241 (1994).

George L. Priest, *The Invention of Enterprise Liability: A Critical History of the Intellectual Foundations of Modern Tort Law*, 14 J. Leg. Stud. 461 (1985).

George L. Priest, *Strict Products Liability: The Original Intent*, 10 Cardozo L. Rev. 2301 (1989).

William L. Prosser, *The Fall of the Citadel (Strict Liability to the Consumer)*, 50 Minn. L. Rev. 791 (1966).

William L. Prosser, *The Assault upon the Citadel (Strict Liability to the Consumer)*, 69 Yale L.J. 1099 (1960).

William L. Prosser, *The Implied Warranty of Merchantable Quality*, 27 Minn. L. Rev. 117 (1943).

Marshall S. Shapo, *Products Liability: The Next Act*, 26 Hofstra L. Rev. 761 (1998).

G. Edward White, *Tort Law: An Intellectual History* (Exp. ed. 2003).

Underpinnings

John B. Attanasio, *The Principle of Aggregate Autonomy and the Calabresian Approach to Products Liability*, 74 Va. L. Rev. 677 (1988).

Leslie Bender, *Feminist (Re)Torts: Thoughts on the Liability Crisis, Mass Torts, Power, and Responsibilities*, 1990 Duke L.J. 848 (1990).

Anita Bernstein, *Product Dynamism in the Law*, in Floyd Rudmin & Marsha Richins (eds.), *Meaning, Measure and Morality of Materialism* (1992).

Carl Bogus, *War on the Common Law: The Struggle at the Center of Products Liability*, 60 Mo. L. Rev. 1 (1995).

Guido Calabresi & Jon T. Hirschoff, *Toward a Test for Strict Liability in Torts*, 81 Yale L.J. 1055 (1972).

Alan Calnan, *A Consumer-Use Approach to Products Liability*, 33 U. Mem. L. Rev. 755 (2003).

Steven P. Croley & Jon D. Hanson, *Rescuing the Revolution: The Revised Case for Enterprise Liability*, 91 Mich. L. Rev. 683 (1993).

Richard A. Epstein, *Products Liability: The Search for the Middle Ground*, 56 N.C. L. Rev. 643 (1978).

Mark Geistfeld, *The Political Economy of Neo-Contractual Proposals for Products Liability Reform*, 72 Tex. L. Rev. 803 (1994).

Mark Geistfeld, *Implementing Enterprise Liability: A Comment on Henderson and Twerski*, 67 N.Y.U. L. Rev. 1157 (1992).

Peter Huber, *Safety and the Second Best: The Hazards of Public Risk Management in the Courts*, 85 Colum. L. Rev. 277 (1985).

Fleming James, Jr., *Products Liability* (Pts. I & II), 34 Tex. L. Rev. 44, 192 (1955).

Gregory C. Keating, *The Idea of Fairness in the Law of Enterprise Liability*, 95 Mich. L. Rev. 1266 (1997).

William M. Landes & Richard A. Posner, *A Positive Economic Analysis of Products Liability*, 14 J. Leg. Stud. 535 (1985).

David G. Owen, *Rethinking the Policies of Strict Products Liability*, 33 Vand. L. Rev. 681 (1980).

Alan Schwartz, *The Case Against Strict Liability*, 60 Fordham L. Rev. 819 (1992).

Gary T. Schwartz, *Foreword: Understanding Products Liability*, 67 Cal. L. Rev. 435 (1979).

Marshall S. Shapo, *A Representational Theory of Consumer Protection: Doctrine, Function and Legal Liability for Product Disappointment*, 60 Va. L. Rev. 1109 (1974).

Roger Traynor, *The Ways and Meanings of Defective Products and Strict Liability*, 32 Tenn. L. Rev. 363 (1965).

Design Defect

Sheila L. Birnbaum, *Unmasking the Test for Design Defect: From Negligence [to Warranty] to Strict Liability to Negligence*, 33 Vand. L. Rev. 593 (1980).

Richard L. Cupp, Jr., *The Continuing Search for Proper Perspective: Whose Reasonableness Should Be at Issue in a Product Design Defect Analysis?*, 30 Seton Hall L. Rev. 233 (1999).

Richard L. Cupp, Jr. & Danielle Polage, *The Rhetoric of Strict Liability versus Negligence: An Empirical Analysis*, 77 N.Y.U. L. Rev. 874 (2002).

Mary J. Davis, *Design Defect Liability: In Search of a Standard of Responsibility*, 39 Wayne L. Rev. 1217 (1993).

Richard A. Epstein, *The Risks of Risk/Utility*, 48 Ohio St. L.J. 469 (1987).

James A. Henderson, Jr., *Coping with the Time Dimension in Products Liability*, 69 Cal. L. Rev. 919 (1981).

James A. Henderson, Jr., *Judicial Review of Manufacturers' Conscious Design Choices: The Limits of Adjudication*, 73 Colum. L. Rev. 1531 (1973).

James A. Henderson, Jr. & Aaron D. Twerski, *The Products Liability Restatement in the Courts; An Initial Assessment*, 27 Wm. Mitchell L. Rev. 7 (2000).

James A. Henderson, Jr. & Aaron D. Twerski, *Achieving Consensus on Defective Product Design*, 83 Cornell L. Rev. 867 (1998).

W. Page Keeton, *The Meaning of Defect in Products Liability Law — A Review of Basic Principles*, 45 Mo. L. Rev. 579 (1988).

W. Page Keeton, *Product Liability and the Meaning of Defect*, 5 St. Mary's L.J. 30 (1973).

Douglas A. Kysar, *The Expectations of Consumers*, 103 Colum. L. Rev. 1700 (2003).

David G. Owen, *Toward a Proper Test for Design Defectiveness: "Micro-Balancing" Costs and Benefits*, 75 Tex. L. Rev. 1661 (1997).

Jerry J. Phillips, *The Unreasonably Unsafe Product and Strict Liability*, 72 Chi.-Kent L. Rev. 129 (1996).

William C. Powers, Jr., *The Persistence of Fault in Products Liability*, 61 Tex. L. Rev. 777 (1983).

Victor E. Schwartz, *Unavoidably Unsafe Products: Clarifying the Meaning and Policy Behind Comment K*, 42 Wash. & Lee L. Rev. 1139 (1985).

John W. Wade, *On the Nature of Strict Tort Liability for Products*, 44 Miss. L.J. 825 (1973).

Ellen Wertheimer, *Ockham's Scalpel: A Return to a Reasonableness Standard*, 43 Vill. L. Rev. 321 (1998).

Ellen Wertheimer, *The Smoke Gets in Their Eyes: Product Category Liability and Alternative Feasible Designs in the Third Restatement*, 61 Tenn. L. Rev. 1429 (1994).

Prescription Drugs

Anita Bernstein, Hymowitz v. Eli Lilly and Co., *Markets of Mothers*, in Robert L. Rabin & Stephen D. Sugarman, *Tort Stories* 151 (2003).

George W. Conk, *Is There a Design Defect in the Restatement (Third) of Torts: Products Liability?* 109 Yale L.J. 1087 (2000).

Richard L. Cupp, Jr., *Rethinking Conscious Design Liability for Prescription Drugs: The Restatement (Third) Standard Versus a Negligence Approach*, 63 Geo. Wash. L. Rev. 76 (1994).

James A. Henderson, Jr. & Aaron D. Twerski, *Drug Designs Are Different*, 111 Yale L.J. 151 (2001).

M. Stuart Madden, *The Enduring Paradox of Products Liability Law Relating to Prescription Pharmaceuticals*, 21 Pace L. Rev. 313 (2001).

Robert M. McKenna, *The Impact of Product Liability Law on the Development of a Vaccine against the AIDS Virus*, 55 U. Chi. L. Rev. 943 (1988).

Arthur Ripstein & Benjamin C. Zipursky, *Corrective Justice in an Age of Mass Torts*, in Gerald J. Postema, *Philosophy and The Law of Torts* 214 (2001).

Naomi Scheiner, *Comment: DES and a Proposed Theory of Enterprise Liability*, 46 Fordham L. Rev. 963 (1978).

Teresa Moran Schwartz, *Prescription Products and the Proposed Restatement (Third)*, 61 Tenn. L. Rev. 1357 (1994).

Victor E. Schwartz & Liberty Mahshigian, *National Childhood Vaccine Injury Act of 1986: An Ad Hoc Remedy or Window for the Future?*, 48 Ohio St. L.J. 387 (1987).

Michael J. Wagner & Laura L. Peterson, *The New Restatement (Third) of Torts — Shelter from the Product Liability Storm for Pharmaceutical Companies and Medical Device Manufacturers?*, 53 Food & Drug L.J. 225 (1998).

Failure to Warn

Mark Geistfeld, *Inadequate Product Warnings and Causation*, 30 U. Mich. J.L. Ref. 309 (1997).

James A. Henderson, Jr. & Aaron D. Twerski, *Doctrinal Collapse in Products Liability: The Empty Shell of Failure to Warn*, 65 N.Y.U. L. Rev. 265 (1990).

Howard Latin, *"Good" Warnings, Bad Products, and Cognitive Limitations*, 41 UCLA L. Rev. 1193 (1994).

M. Stuart Madden, *The Duty to Warn in Products Liability: Contours and Criticism*, 89 W. Va. L. Rev. 221 (1987).

Aaron Twerski, *et al.*, *The Use and Abuse of Warnings in Products Liability —Design Defect Litigation Comes of Age*, 61 Cornell L. Rev. 495 (1976).

Causation, Damages, and Defenses

David Fischer, *Products Liability—Proximate Cause, Intervening Cause, and Duty*, 52 Mo. L. Rev. 547 (1987).

David G. Owen, *Problems in Assessing Punitive Damages Against Manufacturers of Defective Products*, 49 U. Chi. L. Rev. 1 (1982).

Michael Rustad, *In Defense of Punitive Damages in Products Liability: Testing Tort Anecdotes with Empirical Data*, 78 Iowa L. Rev. 1 (1992).

Aaron D. Twerski, *The Many Faces of Misuse*, 29 Mercer L. Rev. 403 (1978).

PART FIVE

TORTS AT THE SUPREME COURT

CHAPTER 13

Torts at the Supreme Court

I. INTRODUCTION

We have emphasized from the first pages of this book that the common law of tort is primarily state law. Even when federal courts hear tort claims by virtue of "diversity" or "supplemental" jurisdiction, they have been required — since the U.S. Supreme Court's 1938 decision of Erie v. Tompkins — to apply state law to resolve the substantive issues raised by those claims. Thus, it is hardly surprising that, while a class in civil procedure or constitutional law will likely feature many Supreme Court opinions, classes in torts — except insofar as they touch on special areas, such as defamation and privacy, in which free speech rights come into play — usually do not.

As recently as a decade ago, the assumption that the nation's most powerful court was nothing but a bit player in tort would have been roughly accurate. The major tort developments of the second half of the twentieth century, including the expansion (and contraction) of negligence liability, and the birth of products liability, were engineered by state courts (and legislatures). By contrast, the Supreme Court's docket was during this time most notable for cases that raised issues of racial justice, reproductive rights, free speech, the boundaries of law enforcement, and the role of the regulatory state in areas such as labor relations, healthcare, and the environment.

Today things are different. To be sure, Erie is still the law, and hence the federal courts, including the Supreme Court, formally remain out of the business of formulating substantive rules of tort law. Nonetheless, the current Court is, indirectly, very much in that business, and lawyers addressing issues of tort law in the new century must be alert to this reality. This chapter points out some of the most important ways in which the Court — and the lower federal courts — are playing and will play a significant role in the development of tort or tort-related doctrines.

Before engaging in that task, however, we should emphasize two points. First, it is important to recall that there are some longstanding pockets of federal tort law, several of which we have already encountered. These include areas of statutory tort law such as the old Safety Appliance Acts (see *Rigsby*, *supra*, Chapter 6), the Federal Tort Claims Act (see *Downs*, *supra*, Chapter 7), and FELA (see *Gottshall*, *supra*, Chapter 10). They also include areas governed by federal common law, such as admiralty (see *Testbank*, *supra*, Chapter 2, *Carroll Towing*, *supra*, Chapter 3, and *Reliable Transfer*, *supra*, Chapter 7). By these means, as well as through cases brought under the federal courts' diversity jurisdiction, titans of the federal bench, such as Holmes (in his years on the Supreme

Court) and Hand, Calabresi and Posner, have played a role in crafting important if isolated pieces of federal and, to a lesser extent, state, tort law.

Second, we have gone out of our way to point out another respect in which "federal" tort law can be said to exist. If tort law is understood as the means by which private individuals who are wrongfully injured by others seek rectification for those wrongs, then private rights of action afforded by federal statutes outlawing sexual harassment, employment discrimination, civil rights violations, securities fraud, and electronic invasions of privacy are in an extended sense "torts." To the degree that the U.S. Supreme Court has made available causes of action to aggrieved individuals in cases such as *Borak*, *Bivens*, and *Harris*, it can be said to have played an important role in the world of torts, writ large.

Still, it is primarily in the last decade that the Supreme Court has set out to shape doctrine affecting core areas of tort law. Thus, in two short and seemingly technical opinions on the law of evidence — Daubert v. Merrell Dow Pharmaceuticals, Inc., 509 U.S. 579 (1993), and Kumho Tire Co. v. Carmichael, 526 U.S. 137 (1999) — the Court has changed the ground rules for litigating toxic tort claims and products liability suits more generally. In a series of decisions including BMW of North America, Inc. v. Gore, 517 U.S. 559 (1996), the Justices have fashioned an increasingly elaborate and intrusive set of federal constitutional limits on punitive damage awards. In Metro-North Commuter R.R. Co. v. Buckley, 521 U.S. 424 (1997), the Court revisited the scope of liability for emotional distress under FELA, and, in the process, offered what will likely turn out to be an influential answer to the question of what counts as an "injury" sufficient to support a tort claim. Notably, it asked and answered this question in a suit arising out of a worker's prolonged exposure to asbestos, a known toxin that has produced by far the largest amount of litigation and liability in the history of American tort law. Asbestos was equally at the center of Amchem Prods., Inc. v. Windsor, 521 U.S. 591 (1997), and Ortiz v. Fibreboard Corp., 527 U.S. 815 (1999), in which the Court rejected innovative attempts to achieve aggregate settlements of masses of asbestos claims on the ground that the settlements violated rights accorded by the Federal Rules of Civil Procedure to individual litigants to have their claims tried separately. Finally, in a wobbly course of decisions culminating in Geier v. American Honda Motor Co., 529 U.S. 861 (2000), the Court has displayed an increasing willingness to find that federal safety legislation and regulations have "preempted" state tort law — that is, rendered it void because it conflicts with directives issued by Congress and federal regulators. In this manner, a Court that is often accused of undermining congressional power in the name of states' rights has demonstrated considerable willingness to permit federal law to displace states' decisions about the content of the obligations citizens owe one another.

Why has the Supreme Court suddenly become important to torts? There is no simple answer. Clearly, tort law's expansion and front-page visibility in the later years of the twentieth century have played a role. Equally clearly, cries over "junk" science, "obscene" punitive damage verdicts, "extortionate" settlements, and "drummed-up" litigation have registered, at least to some degree, with some of the Justices. Still, epithets like "judicial activism" don't seem to offer much by way of explanatory value. (For example, *Daubert*, *Amchem*, and *Geier* can all be understood as displaying fidelity and deference to the work of the federal legislative and/or executive branches.) Nor can one point to a solid block of "conservative" Justices caught in the thrall of modern tort reform movements. As you will see, the decisions excerpted below have instead been issued by shifting coalitions of Justices of varying political leanings. By setting forth several of the Court's leading "tort" decisions from the past decade, we hope to permit you to begin to formulate your own answers to these important questions.

II. TORTS AND EVIDENCE: GUIDELINES FOR EXPERT TESTIMONY IN PERSONAL INJURY CASES

As was noted in Chapter 12, the 1960s and 1970s saw a rapid development in certain aspects of tort law, most noticeably a trend toward more expansive forms of products liability. Equally important, however, were related changes in procedural and evidentiary law. By the middle of the twentieth century, an array of legal scholars and judges had critiqued traditional rules preventing the admission of various forms of evidence at trial as setting arbitrary and unnecessarily restrictive limitations on the ability of litigants to prove and defend lawsuits. Confident that judges and juries, aided by the process of adversarial litigation, are capable of separating fact from fiction, these jurists advocated for a more permissive set of evidence rules. Eventually, in 1975, Congress responded by enacting the Federal Rules of Evidence, which effected a broad liberalization of the rules applicable to suits brought in federal court. Many state courts and legislatures followed suit, often using the Federal Rules as their model.

In the following decision — *Daubert* — the Supreme Court considered the effect of Congress's enactment of a particular rule of evidence — Rule 702 — which authorizes parties to enlist expert witnesses to testify on their clients' behalf. Specifically, the question was whether Rule 702 had incorporated "the *Frye* test," a doctrine which, prior to the adoption of the rules, had been employed by federal courts to determine whether to admit expert testimony on matters of *scientific knowledge*. The *Frye* test derived its name from a lower federal court decision, Frye v. United States, 293 F. 1013, 1014 (D.C. Ct. App. 1923), in which the court barred an expert from testifying to the results of a primitive and scientifically controversial lie-detector test that he had conducted in connection with a criminal prosecution. In support of this result, *Frye* reasoned that an expert should not be permitted to present jurors with a scientific hypothesis or theory relevant to the resolution of a lawsuit unless the methodology on which the expert relies is "generally accepted" in the scientific community. From the time *Frye* was decided, defendants consistently advocated its use as necessary to prevent jurors from being swayed by putative experts who indulge in speculative "junk" science.

Prior to *Daubert*, the lower federal courts had split on the issue of whether *Frye* had survived the adoption of the Federal Rules. Some held that it had. Others held that it had not, in part because the rule does not mention *Frye*, and in part because the rules as a whole were intended to liberalize the admission of evidence. As you will see, the Supreme Court in *Daubert* accepted the latter position, and held that the *Frye* test has no place within the Federal Rules. Indeed, Justice Blackmun, who wrote the opinion for the Court, quite clearly thought that he was giving force to the "liberal" spirit of the Federal Rules. By rejecting *Frye*, he seemed to believe, the Court was embracing a system that would let jurors decide difficult scientific issues on which experts disagreed. Still, notwithstanding its general tenor, Justice Blackmun's opinion concludes on a note of caution, suggesting that even though district courts should not employ the *Frye* test, they should continue to play *some* role in determining whether a purported scientific expert really can claim to be bringing scientific expertise to bear on a particular issue. It then offered some guidelines, distinct from the *Frye* test, to help trial judges perform this "gatekeeping" role.

In one of those unpredictable twists characteristic of our precedent-based system, *Daubert* has since come to stand for a position quite opposed to the one that Justice Blackmun's opinion appears to have intended. Indeed, *Daubert* and its progeny — including subsequent federal court decisions, congressional modifications of Rule 702, and comparable changes in many states' evidence law — have bolstered the idea that trial judges must play an *aggressive* role in barring testimony from plaintiffs' experts who offer novel or speculative theories on issues such as actual causation or reasonable alternative design. As a result, the allocation of authority between judge and jury to resolve factual disputes in tort cases has shifted markedly toward judges. Moreover, the general tenor of tort litigation has shifted from the pro-plaintiff orientation of the 1960s and 70s to one more favorable to defendants. Indeed, tort plaintiffs today find themselves increasingly having to go to the trouble and (often considerable) expense of establishing the bona fides of experts who will be called to testify on issues such as design defect and cause-in-fact.

Daubert v. Merrell Dow Pharmaceuticals, Inc.

509 U.S. 579 (1993)

Blackmun, J.   In this case we are called upon to determine the standard for admitting expert scientific testimony in a federal trial.

I

Petitioners Jason Daubert and Eric Schuller are minor children born with serious birth defects. They and their parents sued respondent in California state court, alleging that the birth defects had been caused by the mothers' ingestion of Bendectin, a prescription antinausea drug marketed by respondent. Respondent removed the suits to federal court on diversity grounds.

After extensive discovery, respondent moved for summary judgment, contending that Bendectin does not cause birth defects in humans and that petitioners would be unable to come forward with any admissible evidence that it does. In support of its motion, respondent submitted an affidavit of Steven H. Lamm, physician and epidemiologist, who is a well-credentialed expert on the risks from exposure to various chemical substances. Doctor Lamm stated that he had reviewed all the literature on Bendectin and human birth defects — more than 30 published studies involving over 130,000 patients. No study had found Bendectin to be a human teratogen (i.e., a substance capable of causing malformations in fetuses). On the basis of this review, Doctor Lamm concluded that maternal use of Bendectin during the first trimester of pregnancy has not been shown to be a risk factor for human birth defects.

Petitioners did not (and do not) contest this characterization of the published record regarding Bendectin. Instead, they responded to respondent's motion with the testimony of eight experts of their own, each of whom also possessed impressive credentials. These experts had concluded that Bendectin can cause birth defects. Their conclusions were based upon "in vitro" (test tube) and "in vivo" (live) animal studies that found a link between Bendectin and malformations; pharmacological studies of the chemical structure of Bendectin that purported to show similarities between the structure of the drug and that of other substances known to cause birth defects; and the "reanalysis" of previously published epidemiological (human statistical) studies.

The District Court granted respondent's motion for summary judgment. The court stated that scientific evidence is admissible only if the principle upon which it is based is " 'sufficiently established to have general acceptance in the field to which it belongs.'" 727 F. Supp. 570, 572 (S.D. Cal. 1989), quoting United States v. Kilgus, 571 F.2d 508, 510 (CA9 1978). The court concluded that petitioners' evidence did not meet this standard. Given the vast body of epidemiological data concerning Bendectin, the court held, expert opinion which is not based on epidemiological evidence is not admissible to establish causation. Thus, the animal-cell studies, live-animal studies, and chemical-structure analyses on which petitioners had relied could not raise by themselves a reasonably disputable jury issue regarding causation. Petitioners' epidemiological analyses, based as they were on recalculations of data in previously published studies that had found no causal link between the drug and birth defects, were ruled to be inadmissible because they had not been published or subjected to peer review.

The United States Court of Appeals for the Ninth Circuit affirmed. 951 F.2d 1128 (1991). Citing Frye v. United States, 54 App. D.C. 46, 47, 293 F. 1013, 1014 (1923), the court stated that expert opinion based on a scientific technique is inadmissible unless the technique is "generally accepted" as reliable in the relevant scientific community. The court declared that expert opinion based on a methodology that diverges "significantly from the procedures accepted by recognized authorities in the field ... cannot be shown to be 'generally accepted as a reliable technique.'" Id., at 1130, quoting United States v. Solomon, 753 F.2d 1522, 1526 (CA9 1985).

... Contending that reanalysis is generally accepted by the scientific community only when it is subjected to verification and scrutiny by others in the field, the Court of Appeals rejected petitioners' reanalyses as "unpublished, not subjected to the normal peer review process and generated solely for use in litigation.". . . .

We granted certiorari, in light of sharp divisions among the courts regarding the proper standard for the admission of expert testimony.

II

A. . . .

The *Frye* test has its origin in a short and citation-free 1923 decision concerning the admissibility of evidence derived from a systolic blood pressure deception test, a crude precursor to the polygraph machine. In what has become a famous (perhaps infamous) passage, the then Court of Appeals for the District of Columbia described the device and its operation and declared:

> "Just when a scientific principle or discovery crosses the line between the experimental and demonstrable stages is difficult to define. Somewhere in this twilight zone the evidential force of the principle must be recognized, and while courts will go a long way in admitting expert testimony deduced from a well-recognized scientific principle or discovery, *the thing from which the deduction is made must be sufficiently established to have gained general acceptance in the particular field in which it belongs.*" 54 App. D.C., at 47, 293 F., at 1014 (emphasis added).

Because the deception test had "not yet gained such standing and scientific recognition among physiological and psychological authorities as would justify the courts in admitting expert testimony deduced from the discovery, development, and experiments thus far made," evidence of its results was ruled inadmissible. *Ibid.*

The merits of the *Frye* test have been much debated, and scholarship on its proper scope and application is legion. Petitioners' primary attack, however, is not on the content but on the continuing authority of the rule. They contend that the *Frye* test was superseded by the adoption of the Federal Rules of Evidence. We agree.

We interpret the legislatively enacted Federal Rules of Evidence as we would any statute. Rule 402 provides the baseline:

> All relevant evidence is admissible, except as otherwise provided by the Constitution of the United States, by Act of Congress, by these rules, or by other rules prescribed by the Supreme Court pursuant to statutory authority. Evidence which is not relevant is not admissible.

"Relevant evidence" is defined as that which has "any tendency to make the existence of any fact that is of consequence to the determination of the action more probable or less probable than it would be without the evidence." Rule 401. The Rule's basic standard of relevance thus is a liberal one.

Frye, of course, predated the Rules by half a century. . . .

Here there is a specific Rule that speaks to the contested issue. Rule 702, governing expert testimony, provides:

> If scientific, technical, or other specialized knowledge will assist the trier of fact to understand the evidence or to determine a fact in issue, a witness qualified as an expert by knowledge, skill, experience, training, or education, may testify thereto in the form of an opinion or otherwise.

Nothing in the text of this Rule establishes "general acceptance" as an absolute prerequisite to admissibility. Nor does respondent present any clear indication that Rule 702 or the Rules as a whole were intended to incorporate a "general acceptance" standard. The drafting history makes no mention of *Frye*, and a rigid "general acceptance" requirement would be at odds with the "liberal thrust" of the Federal Rules and their "general approach of relaxing the traditional barriers to 'opinion' testimony." [Quoted authority omitted.] Given the Rules' permissive backdrop and their inclusion of a specific rule on expert testimony that does not mention "general acceptance," the assertion that the Rules somehow assimilated *Frye* is unconvincing. *Frye* made "general acceptance" the exclusive test for admitting expert scientific testimony. That austere standard, absent from, and incompatible with, the Federal Rules of Evidence, should not be applied in federal trials.

B

That the *Frye* test was displaced by the Rules of Evidence does not mean, however, that the Rules themselves place no limits on the admissibility of purportedly scientific evidence. Nor is the trial judge disabled from screening such evidence. To the contrary, under the Rules the trial judge must ensure that any and all scientific testimony or evidence admitted is not only relevant, but reliable.

The primary locus of this obligation is Rule 702, which clearly contemplates some degree of regulation of the subjects and theories about which an expert may testify. "*If scientific,* technical, or other specialized *knowledge will assist the trier of fact* to understand the evidence or to determine a fact in issue" an expert "may testify *thereto.*" (Emphasis added.) The subject of an expert's testimony must be "scientific . . . knowledge."[8] The adjective "scientific" implies a grounding in the methods and procedures of science. Similarly, the word "knowledge" connotes more than subjective belief or unsupported speculation. The term "applies to any body of known facts or to any body of ideas inferred from such facts or accepted as truths on good grounds." Webster's Third New International Dictionary 1252 (1986). Of course, it would be unreasonable to conclude that the subject of scientific testimony must be "known" to a certainty; arguably, there are no certainties in science. *See, e.g.,* Brief for Nicolaas

---

8. Rule 702 also applies to "technical, or other specialized knowledge." Our discussion is limited to the scientific context because that is the nature of the expertise offered here.

Bloembergen et al. as *Amici Curiae* 9 ("Indeed, scientists do not assert that they know what is immutably 'true' — they are committed to searching for new, temporary, theories to explain, as best they can, phenomena"); Brief for American Association for the Advancement of Science et al. as *Amici Curiae* 7-8 ("Science is not an encyclopedic body of knowledge about the universe. Instead, it represents a *process* for proposing and refining theoretical explanations about the world that are subject to further testing and refinement" (emphasis in original)). But, in order to qualify as "scientific knowledge," an inference or assertion must be derived by the scientific method. Proposed testimony must be supported by appropriate validation — i.e., "good grounds," based on what is known. In short, the requirement that an expert's testimony pertain to "scientific knowledge" establishes a standard of evidentiary reliability.

Rule 702 further requires that the evidence or testimony "assist the trier of fact to understand the evidence or to determine a fact in issue." This condition goes primarily to relevance. "Expert testimony which does not relate to any issue in the case is not relevant and, ergo, non-helpful." [Quoted authority omitted.] . . . [S]cientific validity for one purpose is not necessarily scientific validity for other, unrelated purposes. The study of the phases of the moon, for example, may provide valid scientific "knowledge" about whether a certain night was dark, and if darkness is a fact in issue, the knowledge will assist the trier of fact. However (absent creditable grounds supporting such a link), evidence that the moon was full on a certain night will not assist the trier of fact in determining whether an individual was unusually likely to have behaved irrationally on that night. Rule 702's "helpfulness" standard requires a valid scientific connection to the pertinent inquiry as a precondition to admissibility.

That these requirements are embodied in Rule 702 is not surprising. Unlike an ordinary witness, *see* Rule 701, an expert is permitted wide latitude to offer opinions, including those that are not based on firsthand knowledge or observation. *See* Rules 702 and 703. Presumably, this relaxation of the usual requirement of firsthand knowledge — a rule which represents "a 'most pervasive manifestation' of the common law insistence upon 'the most reliable sources of information,' " Advisory Committee's Notes on Fed. Rule Evid. 602, 28 U.S.C. App., p.755 (citation omitted) — is premised on an assumption that the expert's opinion will have a reliable basis in the knowledge and experience of his discipline.

C

Faced with a proffer of expert scientific testimony, then, the trial judge must determine at the outset, pursuant to Rule 104(a),[10] whether

---

10. Rule 104(a) provides:

"Preliminary questions concerning the qualification of a person to be a witness, the existence of a privilege, or the admissibility of evidence shall be determined by the court, subject to the provisions of subdivision (b) [pertaining to conditional admissions]. In making its determination it is not bound by the rules of evidence except those with respect to privileges." These matters should be established by a preponderance of proof.

the expert is proposing to testify to (1) scientific knowledge that (2) will assist the trier of fact to understand or determine a fact in issue. This entails a preliminary assessment of whether the reasoning or methodology underlying the testimony is scientifically valid and of whether that reasoning or methodology properly can be applied to the facts in issue. We are confident that federal judges possess the capacity to undertake this review. Many factors will bear on the inquiry, and we do not presume to set out a definitive checklist or test. But some general observations are appropriate.

Ordinarily, a key question to be answered in determining whether a theory or technique is scientific knowledge that will assist the trier of fact will be whether it can be (and has been) tested. "Scientific methodology today is based on generating hypotheses and testing them to see if they can be falsified; indeed, this methodology is what distinguishes science from other fields of human inquiry." [Quoted authority omitted.]

Another pertinent consideration is whether the theory or technique has been subjected to peer review and publication. Publication (which is but one element of peer review) is not a *sine qua non* of admissibility; it does not necessarily correlate with reliability.... The fact of publication (or lack thereof) in a peer reviewed journal thus will be a relevant, though not dispositive, consideration in assessing the scientific validity of a particular technique or methodology on which an opinion is premised.

Additionally, in the case of a particular scientific technique, the court ordinarily should consider the known or potential rate of error....

Finally, "general acceptance" can yet have a bearing on the inquiry. A "reliability assessment does not require, although it does permit, explicit identification of a relevant scientific community and an express determination of a particular degree of acceptance within that community." [Quoted authority omitted.] Widespread acceptance can be an important factor in ruling particular evidence admissible, and "a known technique which has been able to attract only minimal support within the community," *Downing*, 753 F.2d, at 1238, may properly be viewed with skepticism.

The inquiry envisioned by Rule 702 is, we emphasize, a flexible one. Its overarching subject is the scientific validity and thus the evidentiary relevance and reliability — of the principles that underlie a proposed submission. The focus, of course, must be solely on principles and methodology, not on the conclusions that they generate.

Throughout, a judge assessing a proffer of expert scientific testimony under Rule 702 should also be mindful of other applicable rules. Rule 703 provides that expert opinions based on otherwise inadmissible hearsay are to be admitted only if the facts or data are "of a type reasonably relied upon by experts in the particular field in forming opinions or inferences upon the subject." Rule 706 allows the court at its discretion to procure the assistance of an expert of its own choosing. Finally, Rule 403 permits the exclusion of relevant evidence "if its probative value is substantially outweighed by the danger of unfair prejudice, confusion of the issues, or misleading the jury...." Judge Weinstein has explained: "Expert evidence can be both powerful and quite misleading because of the difficulty in evaluating it. Because of this risk, the judge in weighing possible prejudice against probative force under Rule 403 of the present rules exercises more control over experts than over lay witnesses." Weinstein, 138 F.R.D., at 632.

III

. . . Petitioners and, to a greater extent, their *amici* exhibit a different concern. They suggest that recognition of a screening role for the judge that allows for the exclusion of "invalid" evidence will sanction a stifling and repressive scientific orthodoxy and will be inimical to the search for truth. It is true that open debate is an essential part of both legal and scientific analyses. Yet there are important differences between the quest for truth in the courtroom and the quest for truth in the laboratory. Scientific conclusions are subject to perpetual revision. Law, on the other hand, must resolve disputes finally and quickly. The scientific project is advanced by broad and wide-ranging consideration of a multitude of hypotheses, for those that are incorrect will eventually be shown to be so, and that in itself is an advance. Conjectures that are probably wrong are of little use, however, in the project of reaching a quick, final, and binding legal judgment — often of great consequence — about a particular set of events in the past. We recognize that, in practice, a gatekeeping role for the judge, no matter how flexible, inevitably on occasion will prevent the jury from learning of authentic insights and innovations. That, nevertheless, is the balance that is struck by Rules of Evidence designed not for the exhaustive search for cosmic understanding but for the particularized resolution of legal disputes. . . .

To summarize: "General acceptance" is not a necessary precondition to the admissibility of scientific evidence under the Federal Rules of Evidence, but the Rules of Evidence — especially Rule 702 — do assign to the trial judge the task of ensuring that an expert's testimony both rests on a reliable foundation and is relevant to the task at hand. Pertinent evidence based on scientifically valid principles will satisfy those demands.

The inquiries of the District Court and the Court of Appeals focused almost exclusively on "general acceptance," as gauged by publication and the decisions of other courts. Accordingly, the judgment of the Court of Appeals is vacated, and the case is remanded for further proceedings consistent with this opinion.

Rehnquist, C.J. (concurring in part and dissenting in part) (joined by Stevens, J.). The petition for certiorari in this case presents two questions: first, whether the rule of Frye v. United States, 54 App. D.C. 46, 293 F. 1013 (1923), remains good law after the enactment of the Federal Rules of Evidence; and second, if *Frye* remains valid, whether it requires expert scientific testimony to have been subjected to a peer review process in order to be admissible. The Court concludes, correctly in my view, that the *Frye* rule did not survive the enactment of the Federal Rules of Evidence, and I therefore join Parts I and II-A of its opinion. The second question presented in the petition for certiorari necessarily is mooted by this holding, but the Court nonetheless proceeds to construe Rules 702 and 703 very much in the abstract, and then offers some "general observations." . . .

I defer to no one in my confidence in federal judges; but I am at a loss to know what is meant when it is said that the scientific status of a theory depends on its "falsifiability," and I suspect some of them will be, too.

I do not doubt that Rule 702 confides to the judge some gatekeeping responsibility in deciding questions of the admissibility of proffered expert testimony. But I do not think it imposes on them either the obligation or the authority to become amateur scientists in order to perform that role. I think the Court would be far better advised in this case to decide only the questions presented, and to leave the further development of this important area of the law to future cases.

NOTES AND QUESTIONS

1. *Who Won?* *Daubert* at first blush seems like a victory for the plaintiffs' bar. Indeed, initial commentary on *Daubert* expressed this point of view. Yet *Daubert* has become a powerful defense weapon in both federal court and in state courts that have chosen to follow the Court's lead in interpreting and applying state-law rules of evidence. By emphasizing the need for trial judges to play a gatekeeping role in evidentiary matters, *Daubert* helped give birth to an increasingly widespread practice of conducting pre-trial hearings on whether a given expert, usually one hired by the plaintiff, will be permitted to testify at trial. While *Daubert* hearings are certainly not the rule in tort cases, they have become an important aspect of tort litigation, particularly in toxic torts and other cases in which proof of actual causation is difficult. Can you see how the Court's deployment of its (relatively broad) conception of valid scientific method might alter the playing field of tort litigation in favor of defendants?

2. *Law versus Science.* The Bendectin litigation that came before the Supreme Court in *Daubert* graphically demonstrates an extraordinarily difficult problem of proof that has been the subject of endless debates among courts, legislators, and academics. As the Court ultimately indicated in *Daubert*, when the Bendectin litigation got under way, the plaintiffs were able to back their allegations of a possible causal link between Bendectin and birth defects with the testimony of "qualified" experts. Granted the admissibility of their testimony, the plaintiffs seemed to have presented enough of a case to get to the jury on the issue of causation. Given the vast potential liability in these cases, it would thus seem that the corporate defendants ought to have been prepared to settle for substantial amounts, lest they expose their shareholders to (cumulatively) bankrupting jury verdicts. And yet since the time these cases were first filed, a strong consensus has developed within the medical and scientific community, based on enormous quantities of epidemiological data, that there is no demonstrable causal connection between Bendectin and the sort of birth defects alleged by the defendants. The upshot, it is argued, is that, because tort litigation often proceeds in advance of adequate science, it threatens to impose massive liability on the basis of allegations that can turn out to

be utterly unfounded. Indeed, critics of the tort system have contended that this is exactly what has happened in suits by Vietnam War veterans alleging links between exposure to chemical defoliants such as Agent Orange and cancer and birth defects, as well as in litigation linking silicone breast implants to autoimmune diseases.

3. *Post*-Daubert *Rulings.* In General Electric Co. v. Joiner, 522 U.S. 136 (1997), the Supreme Court held that courts of appeals should apply an "abuse of discretion" standard to district courts' reliability determinations for experts under *Daubert.* Perhaps more significant was the Court's ruling in Kumho Tire Co. v. Carmichael, 526 U.S. 137 (1999). In comparison to *Daubert*, the facts of *Kumho* were humdrum. It involved a single plaintiff alleging a standard products liability claim — that his car crashed and injured him because of a defect in a tire manufactured by the defendant. The issue was whether the trial judge was required to subject to *Daubert* scrutiny the plaintiff's "tire expert," who was prepared to identify the defect in the tire and explain how it contributed to the crash. The plaintiff argued that *Daubert* pertained only to "scientific" expertise, not to testimony involving relatively straightforward issues of physics and mechanical engineering. The Court rejected plaintiff's proposed distinction, and held that trial courts are required to assess the methodologies and qualifications of any and all proposed expert witnesses.

Numerous state courts and legislatures have extended their versions of *Daubert* along the lines of *Kumho Tire*. Likewise, an amended version of Federal Rule of Evidence 702, which incorporates *Daubert* and *Kumho*, became effective in December 2000. As amended, Rule 702 now reads:

> If scientific, technical, or other specialized knowledge will assist the trier of fact to understand the evidence or to determine a fact in issue, a witness qualified as an expert by knowledge, skill, experience, training, or education, may testify thereto in the form of an opinion or otherwise, if (1) the testimony is based upon sufficient facts or data, (2) the testimony is the product of reliable principles and methods, and (3) the witness has applied the principles and methods reliably to the facts of the case.

III.   TORTS AND PUNISHMENT (AND DETERRENCE): CONSTITUTIONAL LIMITS ON PUNITIVE DAMAGES

As noted in Chapter 8, state tort law has long recognized that, for certain forms of egregious wrongdoing, plaintiffs are entitled to seek not only compensatory damages, but also punitive damages. Although there were lively jurisprudential debates in the nineteenth century about the propriety of awarding tort damages that "punish," it is only since about 1980 that punitive damages have become a political hot potato. In part, this change has resulted from the perception that judges and juries have displayed an increasing willingness to conclude that corporations and other businesses have displayed "reckless disregard" for consumer safety by mass-marketing products knowing (statistically, at least) that features of those products would cause injuries. This in turn has raised the prospect — and in some cases the reality — of large-scale and multiple punitive damage awards. See Chapter 12, Section III (on design defect and punitive damages).

By the late 1980s, members of the defense bar began mounting arguments that some punitive damage awards can be so arbitrary and excessive, relative to the nature of a given defendant's misconduct and the harm it caused, as to violate the defendant's federal constitutional rights. When that argument first made its way to the Supreme Court, the Justices seemed unimpressed. Thus, in Browning-Ferris Industries of Vt., Inc. v. Kelco, 492 U.S. 257 (1989), a majority rejected the argument that punitive damages are "fines" subject to the Eighth Amendment's ban on "excessive fines." Still, several Justices wondered aloud whether the award of such damages might sometimes violate a defendant's Fourteenth Amendment right not to be deprived of its property "without due process of law."

Two years later, in Pacific Mut. Life Ins. Co. v. Haslip, 499 U.S. 1 (1991), the Court took a further step, with seven of eight participating Justices endorsing the proposition that the Due Process Clause entails that states must afford defendants adequate *procedural* protections if they are going to permit the imposition of punitive damages. A majority of five, however, upheld the award under review in that case after determining that Alabama law provided adequate protections. Alabama law at the time required the jury to be instructed that it was free not to award punitive damages, and that, in the event it chose to do so, it could only set its award at an amount necessary to punish and deter the defendant's misconduct. It further required trial judges to review any punitive award and to state on the record its reasons for upholding or interfering with that award. Finally, it provided for appellate review under a multi-factor standard that, in substance, is more exacting than the "shocks the conscience" standard used for judicial review of compensatory damages.

In Honda Motor Co. v. Oberg, 512 U.S. 415 (1994), the Court invoked *Haslip* to strike down a 1910 amendment to the Oregon state constitution that denied trial or appellate courts any power to review jury awards for excessiveness. (The amendment did not affect courts' power to set aside verdicts altogether. Rather, it barred them from applying "shock the conscience" review to the size of the award.) The Court held that Due Process requires that state law mandate meaningful judicial review of punitive damage awards for excessiveness.

Haslip, Oberg, and an intervening decision, TXO Production Corp. v. Alliance Resources Corp., 509 U.S. 443 (1993), revealed that several members of the Court believed not only that the Due Process Clause mandates certain procedural protections, but also that it sets a substantive limit on the size of punitive damage awards. Nevertheless, no majority of Justices had yet held that a particular award violated this substantive limit, nor had the Court spelled out in any detail by what standards "excessiveness" would be measured. The sale of a partially repainted BMW would provide them with the occasion to fill these lacunae. Notably, the sale occurred under the law of Alabama, whose procedures for post-trial review of punitive damage awards have already been determined in *Haslip* to satisfy the procedural component of due process.

BMW of North America, Inc. v. Gore
517 U.S. 559 (1996)

Stevens, J.   The Due Process Clause of the Fourteenth Amendment prohibits a State from imposing a "'grossly excessive'" punishment on a tortfeasor. TXO Production Corp. v. Alliance Resources Corp., 509 U.S. 443, 454 (1993) (and cases cited). The wrongdoing involved in this case was the decision by a national distributor of automobiles not to advise its dealers, and hence their customers, of predelivery damage to new cars when the cost of repair amounted to less than 3 percent of the car's suggested retail price. The question presented is whether a $2 million punitive damages award to the purchaser of one of these cars exceeds the constitutional limit.

I

In January 1990, Dr. Ira Gore, Jr. (respondent), purchased a black BMW sports sedan for $40,750.88 from an authorized BMW dealer in Birmingham, Alabama. After driving the car for approximately nine months, and without noticing any flaws in its appearance, Dr. Gore took the car to "Slick Finish," an independent detailer, to make it look "'snazzier than it normally would appear.'" Mr. Slick, the proprietor, detected evidence that the car had been repainted.[1] Convinced that he had been cheated, Dr. Gore brought suit against petitioner BMW of North America (BMW), the American distributor of BMW automobiles. Dr. Gore alleged, *inter alia*, that the failure to disclose that the car had been repainted constituted suppression of a material fact....

At trial, BMW acknowledged that it had adopted a nationwide policy in 1983 concerning cars that were damaged in the course of manufacture or transportation. If the cost of repairing the damage exceeded 3 percent of the car's suggested retail price, the car was placed in company service for a period of time and then sold as used. If the repair cost did not exceed 3 percent of the suggested retail price, however, the car was sold as new without advising the dealer that any repairs had been made. Because the $601.37 cost of repainting Dr. Gore's car was only about 1.5 percent of its suggested retail price, BMW did not disclose the damage or repair to the Birmingham dealer.

Dr. Gore asserted that his repainted car was worth less than a car that had not been refinished. To prove his actual damages of $4,000, he relied on the testimony of a former BMW dealer, who estimated that the value of a repainted BMW was approximately 10 percent less than the value of a new car that had not been damaged and repaired.[4] To support his claim

---

1. The top, hood, trunk, and quarter panels of Dr. Gore's car were repainted at BMW's vehicle preparation center in Brunswick, Georgia. The parties presumed that the damage was caused by exposure to acid rain during transit between the manufacturing plant in Germany and the preparation center.

4. The dealer who testified to the reduction in value is the former owner of the Birmingham dealership sued in this action. He sold the dealership approximately one year before the trial.

for punitive damages, Dr. Gore introduced evidence that since 1983 BMW had sold 983 refinished cars as new, including 14 in Alabama, without disclosing that the cars had been repainted before sale.... Using the actual damage estimate of $4,000 per vehicle, Dr. Gore argued that a punitive award of $4 million would provide an appropriate penalty for selling approximately 1,000 cars for more than they were worth....

The jury returned a verdict finding BMW liable for compensatory damages of $4,000. In addition, the jury assessed $4 million in punitive damages, based on a determination that the nondisclosure policy constituted "gross, oppressive or malicious" fraud.[6]

BMW filed a post-trial motion to set aside the punitive damages award. The company introduced evidence to establish that its nondisclosure policy was consistent with the laws of roughly 25 States defining the disclosure obligations of automobile manufacturers, distributors, and dealers. The most stringent of these statutes required disclosure of repairs costing more than 3 percent of the suggested retail price; none mandated disclosure of less costly repairs. Relying on these statutes, BMW contended that its conduct was lawful in these States and therefore could not provide the basis for an award of punitive damages....

The trial judge denied BMW's post-trial motion, holding, *inter alia*, that the award was not excessive. On appeal, the Alabama Supreme Court also rejected BMW's claim that the award exceeded the constitutionally permissible amount. 646 So. 2d 619 (1994). The court's excessiveness inquiry applied the factors articulated in Green Oil Co. v. Hornsby, 539 So. 2d 218, 223-224 (Ala. 1989), and approved in Pacific Mut. Life Ins. Co. v. Haslip, 499 U.S. 1, 21-22, 113 L. Ed. 2d 1, 111 S. Ct. 1032 (1991). Based on its analysis, the court concluded that BMW's conduct was "reprehensible"; the nondisclosure was profitable for the company; the judgment "would not have a substantial impact upon [BMW's] financial position"; the litigation had been expensive; no criminal sanctions had been imposed on BMW for the same conduct; ... and the punitive award bore a "reasonable relationship" to "the harm that was likely to occur from [BMW's] conduct as well as ... the harm that actually occurred." 646 So. 2d at 625-627.

The Alabama Supreme Court did, however, rule in BMW's favor on one critical point: The court found that the jury improperly computed the amount of punitive damages by multiplying Dr. Gore's compensatory damages by the number of similar sales in other jurisdictions. Having found the verdict tainted, the court held that "a constitutionally reasonable punitive damages award in this case is $2,000,000" and therefore ordered a remittitur in that amount. The court's discussion of the amount of its remitted award expressly disclaimed any reliance on "acts that occurred in other jurisdictions"; instead, the court explained that it had used a "comparative analysis" that considered Alabama cases, "along with cases from other jurisdictions, involving the sale of an automobile where

---

6. The jury also found the Birmingham dealership liable for Dr. Gore's compensatory damages and the German manufacturer liable for both the compensatory and punitive damages. The dealership did not appeal the judgment against it. The Alabama Supreme Court held that the trial court did not have jurisdiction over the German manufacturer and therefore reversed the judgment against that defendant.

the seller misrepresented the condition of the vehicle and the jury awarded punitive damages to the purchaser."[11] *Id.*, at 628....

II

Punitive damages may properly be imposed to further a State's legitimate interests in punishing unlawful conduct and deterring its repetition. In our federal system, States necessarily have considerable flexibility in determining the level of punitive damages that they will allow in different classes of cases and in any particular case. Most States that authorize exemplary damages afford the jury similar latitude, requiring only that the damages awarded be reasonably necessary to vindicate the State's legitimate interests in punishment and deterrence. Only when an award can fairly be categorized as "grossly excessive" in relation to these interests does it enter the zone of arbitrariness that violates the Due Process Clause of the Fourteenth Amendment. For that reason, the federal excessiveness inquiry appropriately begins with an identification of the state interests that a punitive award is designed to serve. We therefore focus our attention first on the scope of Alabama's legitimate interests in punishing BMW and deterring it from future misconduct.

No one doubts that a State may protect its citizens by prohibiting deceptive trade practices and by requiring automobile distributors to disclose presale repairs that affect the value of a new car. But the States need not, and in fact do not, provide such protection in a uniform manner....

Th[is] diversity [of regulatory approaches] demonstrates that reasonable people may disagree about the value of a full disclosure requirement. Some legislatures may conclude that affirmative disclosure requirements are unnecessary because the self-interest of those involved in the automobile trade in developing and maintaining the goodwill of their customers will motivate them to make voluntary disclosures or to refrain from selling cars that do not comply with self-imposed standards. Those legislatures that do adopt affirmative disclosure obligations may take into account the cost of government regulation, choosing to draw a line exempting minor repairs from such a requirement. In formulating a disclosure standard, States may also consider other goals, such as providing a "safe harbor" for automobile manufacturers, distributors, and dealers against lawsuits over minor repairs.

... [W]e do not doubt that [while] Congress has ample authority to enact ... a [disclosure] policy for the entire Nation, it is clear that no single State could do so, or even impose its own policy choice on neighboring States....

---

11. ... In light of the Alabama Supreme Court's conclusion that (1) the jury had computed its award by multiplying $4,000 by the number of refinished vehicles sold in the United States and (2) that the award should have been based on Alabama conduct, respect for the error-free portion of the jury verdict would seem to produce an award of $56,000 ($4,000 multiplied by 14, the number of repainted vehicles sold in Alabama).

We think it follows from these principles of state sovereignty and comity that a State may not impose economic sanctions on violators of its laws with the intent of changing the tortfeasors' lawful conduct in other States.[17] Before this Court Dr. Gore argued that the large punitive damages award was necessary to induce BMW to change the nationwide policy that it adopted in 1983. But by attempting to alter BMW's nationwide policy, Alabama would be infringing on the policy choices of other States....

... The Alabama Supreme Court therefore properly eschewed reliance on BMW's out-of-state conduct and based its remitted award solely on conduct that occurred within Alabama. The award must be analyzed in the light of the same conduct, with consideration given only to the interests of Alabama consumers, rather than those of the entire Nation. When the scope of the interest in punishment and deterrence that an Alabama court may appropriately consider is properly limited, it is apparent — for reasons that we shall now address — that this award is grossly excessive.

III

Elementary notions of fairness enshrined in our constitutional jurisprudence dictate that a person receive fair notice not only of the conduct that will subject him to punishment, but also of the severity of the penalty that a State may impose. Three guideposts, each of which indicates that BMW did not receive adequate notice of the magnitude of the sanction that Alabama might impose for adhering to the nondisclosure policy adopted in 1983, lead us to the conclusion that the $2 million award against BMW is grossly excessive: the degree of reprehensibility of the nondisclosure; the disparity between the harm or potential harm suffered by Dr. Gore and his punitive damages award; and the difference between this remedy and the civil penalties authorized or imposed in comparable cases. We discuss these considerations in turn.

Degree of Reprehensibility

Perhaps the most important indicium of the reasonableness of a punitive damages award is the degree of reprehensibility of the defendant's conduct. As the Court stated nearly 150 years ago, exemplary damages imposed on a defendant should reflect "the enormity of his offense." Day v. Woodworth, 54 U.S. 363, 13 HOW 363, 371, 14 L. Ed. 181 (1852). This principle reflects the accepted view that some wrongs are more blameworthy

---

17. State power may be exercised as much by a jury's application of a state rule of law in a civil lawsuit as by a statute. See New York Times Co. v. Sullivan, 376 U.S. 254, 265, 11 L. Ed. 2d 686, 84 S. Ct. 710 (1964) ("The test is not the form in which state power has been applied but, whatever the form, whether such power has in fact been exercised"); San Diego Building Trades Council v. Garmon, 359 U.S. 236, 247, 3 L. Ed. 2d 775, 79 S. Ct. 773 (1959) ("Regulation can be as effectively exerted through an award of damages as through some form of preventive relief").

than others. Thus, we have said that "nonviolent crimes are less serious than crimes marked by violence or the threat of violence." Solem v. Helm, 463 U.S. 277, 292-293, 77 L. Ed. 2d 637, 103 S. Ct. 3001 (1983). Similarly, "trickery and deceit," *TXO,* 509 U.S. at 462, are more reprehensible than negligence. In *TXO,* both the West Virginia Supreme Court and the Justices of this Court placed special emphasis on the principle that punitive damages may not be "grossly out of proportion to the severity of the offense." *Id.,* at 453, 462. . . .

In this case, none of the aggravating factors associated with particularly reprehensible conduct is present. The harm BMW inflicted on Dr. Gore was purely economic in nature. The presale refinishing of the car had no effect on its performance or safety features, or even its appearance for at least nine months after his purchase. BMW's conduct evinced no indifference to or reckless disregard for the health and safety of others. To be sure, infliction of economic injury, especially when done intentionally through affirmative acts of misconduct, or when the target is financially vulnerable, can warrant a substantial penalty. But this observation does not convert all acts that cause economic harm into torts that are sufficiently reprehensible to justify a significant sanction in addition to compensatory damages.

[Gore's lawyers pointed out that BMW had repeatedly failed to disclose minor damage and repairs to buyers notwithstanding that several states have legislation requiring disclosure to buyers, and that the common law in every state renders fraudulent misrepresentation tortious. The Court rejected an inference of extreme reprehensibility from these facts, noting that the statutes reasonably could have been interpreted by BMW not to apply to minor repairs, and likewise that common law fraud only applies to "material" misrepresentations. Thus, BMW's conduct, even if a wrong under Alabama law, was not part of a pattern of deliberate wrongdoing. — EDS.] . . .

That conduct is sufficiently reprehensible to give rise to tort liability, and even a modest award of exemplary damages does not establish the high degree of culpability that warrants a substantial punitive damages award. Because this case exhibits none of the circumstances ordinarily associated with egregiously improper conduct, we are persuaded that BMW's conduct was not sufficiently reprehensible to warrant imposition of a $2 million exemplary damages award.

Ratio

The second and perhaps most commonly cited indicium of an unreasonable or excessive punitive damages award is its ratio to the actual harm inflicted on the plaintiff. The principle that exemplary damages must bear a "reasonable relationship" to compensatory damages has a long pedigree. Scholars have identified a number of early English statutes authorizing the award of multiple damages for particular wrongs. Some 65 different enactments during the period between 1275 and 1753 provided for double, treble, or quadruple damages. Our decisions in both *Haslip* and *TXO* endorsed the proposition that a comparison between the compensatory award and the punitive award is significant.

In *Haslip* we concluded that even though a punitive damages award of "more than 4 times the amount of compensatory damages" might be "close to the line," it did not "cross the line into the area of constitutional impropriety." 499 U.S. at 23-24. *TXO*, following dicta in *Haslip*, refined this analysis by confirming that the proper inquiry is "'whether there is a reasonable relationship between the punitive damages award and *the harm likely to result* from the defendant's conduct as well as the harm that actually has occurred.'" *TXO*, 509 U.S. at 460 (emphasis in original), quoting *Haslip*, 499 U.S. at 21. Thus, in upholding the $10 million award in *TXO*, we relied on the difference between that figure and the harm to the victim that would have ensued if the tortious plan had succeeded. That difference suggested that the relevant ratio was not more than 10 to 1.

The $2 million in punitive damages awarded to Dr. Gore by the Alabama Supreme Court is 500 times the amount of his actual harm as determined by the jury. Moreover, there is no suggestion that Dr. Gore or any other BMW purchaser was threatened with any additional potential harm by BMW's nondisclosure policy. The disparity in this case is thus dramatically greater than those considered in *Haslip* and *TXO*.

Of course, we have consistently rejected the notion that the constitutional line is marked by a simple mathematical formula, even one that compares actual *and potential* damages to the punitive award. Indeed, low awards of compensatory damages may properly support a higher ratio than high compensatory awards, if, for example, a particularly egregious act has resulted in only a small amount of economic damages. A higher ratio may also be justified in cases in which the injury is hard to detect or the monetary value of noneconomic harm might have been difficult to determine. It is appropriate, therefore, to reiterate our rejection of a categorical approach. Once again, "we return to what we said . . . in *Haslip:* 'We need not, and indeed we cannot, draw a mathematical bright line between the constitutionally acceptable and the constitutionally unacceptable that would fit every case. We can say, however, that [a] general concer[n] of reasonableness . . . properly enter[s] into the constitutional calculus.'" *Id.*, at 458 (quoting *Haslip*, 499 U.S. at 18). In most cases, the ratio will be within a constitutionally acceptable range, and remittitur will not be justified on this basis. When the ratio is a breathtaking 500 to 1, however, the award must surely "raise a suspicious judicial eyebrow." *TXO*, 509 U.S. at 481 (O'Connor, J., dissenting).

Sanctions for Comparable Misconduct

Comparing the punitive damages award and the civil or criminal penalties that could be imposed for comparable misconduct provides a third indicium of excessiveness. As Justice O'Connor has correctly observed, a reviewing court engaged in determining whether an award of punitive damages is excessive should "accord 'substantial deference' to legislative judgments concerning appropriate sanctions for the conduct at issue." Browning-Ferris Industries of Vt., Inc. v. Kelco Disposal, Inc., 492 U.S. at 301 (opinion concurring in part and dissenting in part).... In this case the $2 million economic sanction imposed on BMW is substantially greater than the statutory fines available in Alabama and elsewhere for similar malfeasance.

The maximum civil penalty authorized by the Alabama Legislature for a violation of its Deceptive Trade Practices Act is $2,000; other States authorize more severe sanctions, with the maxima ranging from $5,000 to $10,000. Significantly, some statutes draw a distinction between first offenders and recidivists; thus, in New York the penalty is $50 for a first offense and $250 for subsequent offenses. None of these statutes would provide an out-of-state distributor with fair notice that the first violation — or, indeed the first 14 violations — of its provisions might subject an offender to a multimillion dollar penalty....

The judgment is reversed, and the case is remanded for further proceedings not inconsistent with this opinion.

Breyer, J. (concurring) (joined by O'Connor and Souter, JJ.)....

[In *Haslip*, this Court emphasized] the constitutional importance of legal standards that provide "reasonable constraints" within which "discretion is exercised," that assure "meaningful and adequate review by the trial court whenever a jury has fixed the punitive damages," and permit "appellate review [that] makes certain that the punitive damages are reasonable in their amount and rational in light of their purpose to punish what has occurred and to deter its repetition."

This constitutional concern ... arises out of the basic unfairness of depriving citizens of life, liberty, or property, through the application, not of law and legal processes, but of arbitrary coercion. Requiring the application of law, rather than a decisionmaker's caprice, does more than simply provide citizens notice of what actions may subject them to punishment; it also helps to assure the uniform general treatment of similarly situated persons that is the essence of law itself.

... The standards the Alabama courts applied here ... provided no significant constraints or protection against arbitrary results.

First, the Alabama statute that permits punitive damages does not itself contain a standard that readily distinguishes between conduct warranting very small, and conduct warranting very large, punitive damages awards. That statute permits punitive damages in cases of "oppression, fraud, wantonness, or malice." Ala. Code § 6-11-20(a) (1993). But the statute goes on to define those terms broadly, to encompass far more than the egregious conduct that those terms, at first reading, might seem to imply.... The statute ... authorizes punitive damages for the most serious kinds of misrepresentations, say, tricking the elderly out of their life savings, for much less serious conduct, such as the failure to disclose repainting a car, at issue here, and for a vast range of conduct in between.

Second, the Alabama courts, in this case, have applied the "factors" intended to constrain punitive damages awards in a way that belies that purpose. Green Oil Co. v. Hornsby, 539 So. 2d 218 (Ala. 1989), sets forth seven factors that appellate courts use to determine whether or not a jury award was "grossly excessive" and which, in principle, might make up for the lack of significant constraint in the statute. But, as the Alabama courts have authoritatively interpreted them, and as their application in this case illustrates, they impose little actual constraint.

[Justice Breyer reviewed the other *Green Oil* factors and concluded that, as interpreted by the Alabama Supreme Court, they failed to provide adequate standards by which to review punitive damage awards. — EDS.]

The upshot is that the rules that purport to channel discretion in this kind of case, here did not do so in fact. That means that the award in this case was both (a) the product of a system of standards that did not significantly constrain a court's, and hence a jury's, discretion in making that award; and (b) grossly excessive in light of the State's legitimate punitive damages objectives.

. . . [O]ne cannot expect to direct jurors like legislators through the ballot box; nor can one expect those jurors to interpret law like judges, who work within a discipline and hierarchical organization that normally promotes roughly uniform interpretation and application of the law. Yet here Alabama expects jurors to act, at least a little, like legislators or judges, for it permits them, to a certain extent, to create public policy and to apply that policy, not to compensate a victim, but to achieve a policy-related objective outside the confines of the particular case. . . .

. . . I recognize that it is often difficult to determine just when a punitive award exceeds an amount reasonably related to a State's legitimate interests, or when that excess is so great as to amount to a matter of constitutional concern. Yet whatever the difficulties of drawing a precise line, once we examine the award in this case, it is not difficult to say that this award lies on the line's far side. The severe lack of proportionality between the size of the award and the underlying punitive damages objectives shows that the award falls into the category of "gross excessiveness" set forth in this Court's prior cases.

These two reasons *taken together* overcome what would otherwise amount to a "strong presumption of validity." *TXO*, 509 U.S. at 457. And, for those two reasons, I conclude that the award in this unusual case violates the basic guarantee of nonarbitrary governmental behavior that the Due Process Clause provides. . . .

Scalia, J. (dissenting) (joined by Thomas, J.).   Today we see the latest manifestation of this Court's recent and increasingly insistent "concern about punitive damages that 'run wild.'" Pacific Mut. Life Ins. Co. v. Haslip, 499 U.S. 1, 18, 113 L. Ed. 2d 1, 111 S. Ct. 1032 (1991). Since the Constitution does not make that concern any of our business, the Court's activities in this area are an unjustified incursion into the province of state governments.

. . . [A] state trial procedure that commits the decision whether to impose punitive damages, and the amount, to the discretion of the jury, subject to some judicial review for "reasonableness," furnishes a defendant with all the process that is "due." I do not regard the Fourteenth Amendment's Due Process Clause as a secret repository of substantive guarantees against "unfairness" — neither the unfairness of an excessive civil compensatory award, nor the unfairness of an "unreasonable" punitive award. What the Fourteenth Amendment's procedural guarantee assures is an opportunity to contest the reasonableness of a damages judgment in state court; but there is no federal guarantee a damages award actually *be* reasonable....

II

One might understand the Court's eagerness to enter this field, rather than leave it with the state legislatures, if it had something useful to say. In fact, however, its opinion provides virtually no guidance to legislatures, and to state and federal courts, as to what a "constitutionally proper" level of punitive damages might be....

... "Alabama does not have the power," the Court says, "to punish BMW for conduct that was lawful where it occurred and that had no impact on Alabama or its residents." That may be true, though only in the narrow sense that a person cannot be *held liable to be punished* on the basis of a lawful act. But if a person has been held subject to punishment because he committed an *un*lawful act, the *degree* of his punishment assuredly *can* be increased on the basis of any other conduct of his that displays his wickedness, unlawful or not. Criminal sentences can be computed, we have said, on the basis of "information concerning every aspect of a defendant's life," Williams v. New York, 337 U.S. 241, 250-252, 93 L. Ed. 1337, 69 S. Ct. 1079 (1949).... Why could the Supreme Court of Alabama not consider lawful (but disreputable) conduct, both inside and outside Alabama, for the purpose of assessing just how bad an actor BMW was?...

III

... [T]he Court identifies "[t]hree guideposts" that lead it to the conclusion that the award in this case is excessive....

... In truth, the "guideposts" mark a road to nowhere; they provide no real guidance at all. As to "degree of reprehensibility" ... we learn that "'nonviolent crimes are less serious than crimes marked by violence or the threat of violence,'" and that "'trickery and deceit'" are "more reprehensible than negligence" ... As to the ratio of punitive to compensatory damages, we are told that a "'general concer[n] of reasonableness ... enter[s] into the constitutional calculus,'" though even "a breathtaking 500 to 1" will not necessarily do anything more than "'raise a suspicious judicial eyebrow[.]'" And as to legislative sanctions provided for comparable misconduct, they should be accorded "'substantial deference.'" One expects the Court to conclude: "To thine own self be true."....

Ginsburg, J. (dissenting) (joined by Rehnquist, C.J.).

The Court ... unnecessarily and unwisely ventures into territory traditionally within the States' domain, and does so in the face of reform measures recently adopted or currently under consideration in legislative arenas. The Alabama Supreme Court, in this case, endeavored to follow this Court's prior instructions; and, more recently, Alabama's highest court has installed further controls on awards of punitive damages. I would therefore leave the state court's judgment undisturbed, and resist unnecessary intrusion into an area dominantly of state concern. . . .

II

A

Alabama's Supreme Court reports that it "thoroughly and painstakingly" reviewed the jury's award, *ibid*, according to principles set out in its own pathmarking decisions and in this Court's opinions in *TXO* and Pacific Mut. Life Ins. Co. v. Haslip, 499 U.S. 1, 21, 113 L. Ed. 2d 1, 111 S. Ct. 1032 (1991). 646 So. 2d at 621. The Alabama court said it gave weight to several factors, including BMW's deliberate ("reprehensible") presentation of refinished cars as new and undamaged, without disclosing that the value of those cars had been reduced by an estimated 10%, the financial position of the defendant, and the costs of litigation. *Id.*, at 625-626. These standards, we previously held, "impos[e] a sufficiently definite and meaningful constraint on the discretion of Alabama factfinders in awarding punitive damages." *Haslip*, 499 U.S. at 22. Alabama's highest court could have displayed its labor pains more visibly, but its judgment is nonetheless entitled to a presumption of legitimacy. . . .

B

The Court finds Alabama's $2 million award not simply excessive, but grossly so, and therefore unconstitutional. The decision leads us further into territory traditionally within the States' domain, and commits the Court, now and again, to correct "misapplication of a properly stated rule of law." The Court is not well equipped for this mission. Tellingly, the Court repeats that it brings to the task no "mathematical formula," no "categorical approach," no "bright line." It has only a vague concept of substantive due process, a "raised eyebrow" test . . . as its ultimate guide.[5] . . .

For the reasons stated, I dissent from this Court's disturbance of the judgment the Alabama Supreme Court has made. . . .

NOTES AND QUESTIONS

1. *On Remand.* When the *Gore* case returned to the Alabama Supreme Court, it ordered a new trial unless Dr. Gore would accept a remittitur of all but $50,000 of the jury's award of punitive damages. 701

5. . . . What is the Court's measure of too big? Not a cap of the kind a legislature could order, or a mathematical test this Court can divine and impose. Too big is, in the end, the amount at which five Members of the Court bridle.

So. 2d, at 515. The plaintiff accepted that amount. How did the Alabama Court determine that $50,000 set the maximum permissible award under the Constitution?

2. Leatherman *and* State Farm. In two subsequent decisions, the Court has continued to emphasize the need for trial and appellate judges to exercise substantial control over punitive damage awards. First, it held that federal appellate courts are obligated to undertake *de novo* review of the jury's punitive award (i.e., should not defer to the trial court's ruling as to whether a particular award was constitutionally excessive). Cooper Indus., Inc. v. Leatherman Tool Group, Inc., 532 U.S. 424 (2001). Note the contrast with *Gasperini* (mentioned in Chapter 8 in the notes following *Kenton*), in which the Court held that federal appellate courts may *not* engage in hard-look review of compensatory damage awards.

The second decision, State Farm Mut. Auto Ins. Co. v. Campbell, 538 U.S. 408 (2003), involved a suit by a car owner (and his spouse) against his liability insurer for willfully mishandling the defense of a negligence suit that resulted in a large judgment against the owner. (For a brief discussion of the insurer's role in defending tort suits, see Chapter 8, Section IV.) The jury awarded the owner $1 million in compensatory damages. At the punitive phase of the trial, the owner's attorneys introduced evidence that the insurer's conduct toward the owner was part of a nationwide scheme for denying policyholders the coverage that was owed to them under a variety of different types of insurance policies. On the basis of that evidence, the jury issued a $145 million punitive award, which was upheld on appeal by Utah's high court. Relying on *Gore*, the Supreme Court struck the award on the ground that due process bars plaintiffs from relying on evidence of egregious misconduct that does not pertain directly to the mistreatment of the plaintiff himself.

Writing for a six-Justice majority, Justice Kennedy also offered refinements (arguably in the form of dicta) to the "ratio" prong of the *Gore* test. Pulling together statements from *Haslip* and *Gore*, his opinion asserted that: (1) "few awards exceeding a single-digit ratio between punitive and compensatory damages, to a significant degree, will satisfy due process"; (2) a "4-to-1 ratio" often will be "close to the line of constitutional impropriety"; (3) higher ratios may be appropriate when " 'a particularly egregious act has resulted in only a small amount of economic damages,' " where " 'the injury is hard to detect,' " or where " 'the monetary value of noneconomic harm might have been difficult to determine' "; and (4) lower ratios, perhaps as low as 1-to-1, may "reach the outermost limit of the due process guarantee" when "compensatory damages are substantial." Having said all this, *State Farm* also reiterated that it was not prepared to draw "bright line" rules, and that the "precise award in any case ... must be based upon the facts and circumstances of the defendant's conduct and the harm to the plaintiff."

3. *Federal versus State Constraints*. Justice Ginsburg noted in an appendix to her *Gore* dissent that state legislatures had already taken various steps to control jury awards of punitive damages. A few have gone so far as to abolish punitive damages as a matter of common law, permitting them

only when specifically authorized by statute. N.H. Rev. Stat. Ann. § 507:16. Others set dollar caps on punitive awards (or caps in the form of a maximum ratio to compensatory damages), or require a substantial portion of any punitive award to be paid to the state. Still others set heightened standards of proof. With this degree of legislative activity, Justice Ginsburg argued, the Court was venturing into an area where its efforts were not needed. Is that a convincing rationale for declining to recognize a right against having to pay excessive punitive damages?

4. Mathias *Revisited*. Recall the *Mathias* case from Chapter 8, in which the Seventh Circuit upheld a $186,000 punitive award on top of a $5,000 compensatory award against the corporate owner of a motel that rented rooms in the knowledge that they were infested with bedbugs. Mathias v. Accor Economy Lodging, Inc., 347 F.3d 672 (7th Cir. 2003). *Mathias* was decided after *Gore* and *State Farm*, yet concluded that the award did not violate their guidelines on constitutional excessiveness. Writing for the Circuit Court, Judge Posner contrasted the punitive award against the motel owner, which was 37.5 times the compensatory award, with the awards in cases such as *State Farm* and the suit arising from the *Exxon Valdez* oil spill, in which "huge" compensatory damages were provided. In those cases, he reasoned, the Supreme Court has forbidden punitive damages with multiples higher than single digits. *Mathias*, however, presented a different type of case because the actual injury to the plaintiffs was very small, and was as much an indignity as it was an economic or physical loss:

> . . . [O]ne function of punitive-damages awards is to relieve the pressures on an overloaded system of criminal justice by providing a civil alternative to criminal prosecution of minor crimes. An example is deliberately spitting in a person's face, a criminal assault but because minor readily deterrable by the levying of what amounts to a civil fine through a suit for damages for the tort of battery. Compensatory damages would not do the trick in such a case, and this for three reasons: because they are difficult to determine in the case of acts that inflict largely dignatory harms; because in the spitting case they would be too slight to give the victim an incentive to sue, and he might decide instead to respond with violence . . . and because to limit the plaintiff to compensatory damages would enable the defendant to commit the offensive act with impunity provided that he was willing to pay.

347 F.3d, at 676-677.

Is Judge Posner correct to place the wrong committed by the motel managers in *Mathias* in the same category as intentionally spitting in someone's face? Surely some wrong was committed, and the decision to expose the plaintiffs to bedbugs produced great anger, distress, and probably embarrassment on their part. But was the attitude of the managers such that one could infer that they wished to offend the dignity of their customers? Does it help clarify analysis to describe the injury arising from the tort as "dignitary"? Judge Posner also reasoned that a punitive award that is large in relation to a compensatory award may be necessary to create adequate incentives to sue (and thus to make sure that the wrongdoer does not profit from his wrongdoing) particularly when the losses caused by the defendant's misconduct come in the form of small increments of harm experienced by many victims. As Judge Posner noted, the $191,000 awarded by the *Mathias* jury had a certain arithmetic logic to it — it equalled $1000 times the total number of rooms in the hotel.

Recall that, in the end, the Alabama Supreme Court implemented *Gore* by ordering the punitive damages in the case reduced to $50,000, and that there were 14 Alabama residents who had been defrauded by BMW, including Dr. Gore. Would this 12.5-to-1 ratio have been accepted by the *State Farm* court? Can Judge Posner claim that he has faithfully followed *Gore* and *State Farm*?

5. Romo. In *Romo v. Ford Motor Co.*, 113 Cal. App. 4th 738 (Cal. Ct. App. 2003), the Romo family's 1978 Ford Bronco swerved to avoid another driver, then tipped over, killing three and injuring three others. The Romos argued that the deaths and injuries were caused by the lack of a rollbar or a metal roof in the rear of the Bronco's cab. The jury found that Ford had "willfully and consciously ignored the dangers to human life" inherent in its design of the Bronco. It then awarded the Romos $5 million in compensatory damages and $290 million in punitive damages. Although the jury award had been issued before *State Farm* was decided, the California Supreme Court ordered the Fifth Appellate District Court to review the award in light of the Supreme Court's decision. Reasoning that *State Farm* explicitly forbids juries from using punitive damages to punish the defendant for wrongs it inflicted on anyone other than the plaintiff, and noting *State Farm*'s emphasis on single-digit ratios, the court determined that a roughly 5:1 ratio was appropriate given the "extreme reprehensibility" of Ford's conduct. It thus reduced the jury's award to $23.7 million. In doing so, it held that *State Farm* had, in effect, overruled the "deterrence" rationale for punitive damages that California had adopted in the *Grimshaw* case (discussed in the concluding notes to Section III of Chapter 12).

Can *Mathias*, which involved a small injury, and *Romo*, which involved a huge injury, be reconciled? Does it make sense to say that the Due Process Clause allows a 37.5 multiple in a case involving bedbugs and yet mandates a multiple of 5 in a case involving an apparently egregious and deadly design defect? In his dissent to *Gore*, Justice Scalia predicted that, "in truth, [the *Gore*] 'guideposts' mark a road to nowhere; they provide no real guidance at all." Has this prediction come true?

IV. TORTS WITHOUT INJURIES?: UNRIPENED PHYSICAL HARM AND MEDICAL MONITORING CLAIMS

In Chapter 10, we encountered the *Gottshall* decision, in which the Supreme Court held that a railroad worker who cannot prove that he has suffered bodily harm as a result of his employer's carelessness can still recover under the Federal Employers' Liability Act (FELA) for negligently caused emotional distress, but only if that distress arises because the employer carelessly placed him in immediate danger of such harm. Left open was the question of what, exactly, counts as bodily harm. Broken bones and diagnosed diseases clearly do. What about less dramatic invasions of bodily integrity? In particular, the question soon arose as to whether inhalation of large quantities of a known toxin can count as a bodily harm in and of itself, thus permitting recovery by a FELA plaintiff who was not immediately endangered by that exposure. A second and related issue concerned whether such a plaintiff might recover for a very different form of injury, namely, the intangible economic losses suffered because sound medical practices warrant a regime of medical monitoring to gauge the effects of such an exposure on the plaintiff's long-term health.

As it turns out, the Supreme Court, in the *Buckley* decision excerpted below, confronted these questions in a very special context—that of litigation arising out a worker's on-the-job exposure to airborne asbestos fibers. Asbestos, a natural fiber that functions as an effective heat insulator, had for decades been used in the construction of buildings, industrial boilers, ship engines, and vehicle braking systems. In the construction process, *millions* of workers were exposed over extended periods to high concentrations of asbestos fibers. Inhalation of these fibers can cause asbestosis, a nonmalignant condition causing minor-to-severe breathing impairments. It can also cause lung cancer and mesothelioma, a devastating form of cancer in the lining of the lung. At least some of these dangers were known at a relatively early date by prominent manufacturers such as Johns Manville. As we see in the next section, the physical devastation wrought by asbestos has generated a genuine litigation crisis—tens of thousands of product liability suits have been launched by injured plaintiffs seeking compensation in amounts that, in the aggregate, exceed the available assets of manufacturers and distributors of asbestos. In these circumstances, it is impossible to suppose that the Justices' analyses of the "injury" issue in *Buckley* were not influenced by the larger context of modern asbestos litigation. Indeed, the majority opinion, written by Justice Breyer, explicitly refers to that context in support of its conclusions.

Yet, while the questions about injury addressed in *Buckley* were of a piece with these more general problems of asbestos litigation, they also arose in a context that was, in another respect, quite isolated. As we saw in Chapters 4 and 8, when it comes to claims *against their employers*, employees suffering from work-related illnesses are usually entitled to receive only the modest, scheduled amounts authorized under workers' compensation statutes. However, in enacting FELA, Congress long ago ordained that the members of a single industry—railroads—would remain subject to negligence liability *in their capacity as employers*. Thus, *Buckley* provides the unusual sight of an employer, rather than a manufacturer or distributor, being sued in tort for carelessly injuring a plaintiff by exposing him to asbestos.

In sum, *Buckley* is a fascinating opinion because, on the one hand, it raises a set of theoretical, almost esoteric, questions in an odd pocket of (federal) negligence law. On the other hand, it raises those questions against the backdrop of a cluster of pressing practical and political problems generated by the most massive and unruly body of tort litigation ever encountered by U.S. courts.

Metro-North Commuter R.R. Co. v. Buckley
521 U.S. 424 (1997)

Breyer, J.   The basic question in this case is whether a railroad worker negligently exposed to a carcinogen (here, asbestos) but without symptoms of any disease can recover under the Federal Employers' Liability Act (FELA), 35 Stat. 65, as amended, 45 U.S.C. § 51 *et seq.*, for negligently inflicted emotional distress. We conclude that the worker before us here cannot recover unless, and until, he manifests symptoms of a disease....

I

Respondent, Michael Buckley, works as a pipefitter for Metro-North, a railroad. For three years (1985-1988) his job exposed him to asbestos for about one hour per working day. During that time Buckley would remove insulation from pipes, often covering himself with insulation dust that contained asbestos. Since 1987, when he attended an "asbestos awareness" class, Buckley has feared that he would develop cancer — and with some cause, for his two expert witnesses testified that, even after taking account of his now-discarded 15-year habit of smoking up to a pack of cigarettes per day, the exposure created an *added* risk of death due to cancer, or to other asbestos-related diseases of either 1% to 5% (in the view of one of plaintiff's experts), or 1% to 3% (in the view of another). Since 1989, Buckley has received periodic medical check-ups for cancer and asbestosis. So far, those check-ups have not revealed any evidence of cancer or any other asbestos-related disease.

Buckley sued Metro-North under the FELA, a statute that permits a railroad worker to recover for an "injury ... resulting ... from" his employer's "negligence." 45 U.S.C. § 51. He sought damages for his emotional distress and to cover the cost of future medical check-ups. His employer conceded negligence, but it did not concede that Buckley had actually suffered emotional distress, and it argued that the FELA did not permit a worker like Buckley, who had suffered no physical harm, to recover for injuries of either sort. After hearing Buckley's case, the District Court dismissed the action. The court found that Buckley did not "offer sufficient evidence to allow a jury to find that he suffered a real emotional injury." App. 623. And, in any event, Buckley suffered no "physical impact"; hence any emotional injury fell outside the limited set of circumstances in which, according to this Court, the FELA permits recovery. *Id.*, at 620; *see* Consolidated Rail Corporation v. Gottshall, 512 U.S. 532, 114 S. Ct. 2396, 129 L. Ed. 2d 427 (1994). The District Court did not discuss Buckley's further claim for the costs of medical monitoring.

Buckley appealed, and the Second Circuit reversed. 79 F.3d 1337 (1996). Buckley's evidence, it said, showed that his contact with the insulation dust (containing asbestos) was "massive, lengthy, and tangible," *id.*, at 1345, and that the contact "would cause fear in a reasonable person," *id.*, at 1344. Under these circumstances, the court held, the contact was what this Court in *Gottshall* had called a "physical impact" — a "physical impact" that, when present, permits a FELA plaintiff to recover for accompanying emotional distress. The Second Circuit also found in certain of Buckley's workplace statements sufficient expression of worry to permit sending his emotional distress claim to a jury. Finally, the court held that Buckley could recover for the costs of medical check-ups because the FELA permits recovery of all reasonably incurred extra medical monitoring costs whenever a "reasonable physician would prescribe . . . a monitoring regime different than the one that would have been prescribed in the absence of" a particular negligently caused exposure to a toxic substance. *Id.*, at 1347 (internal quotation marks omitted).

We granted certiorari to review the Second Circuit's holdings in light of *Gottshall.*

II

The critical question before us in respect to Buckley's "emotional distress" claim is whether the physical contact with insulation dust that accompanied his emotional distress amounts to a "physical impact" as this Court used that term in *Gottshall.* [Justice Breyer proceeded to review *Gottshall*'s analysis, including its holding that FELA permits recovery on a claim of NIED for]

> "those plaintiffs who *sustain a physical impact* as a result of a defendant's negligent conduct, or who are placed in immediate risk of physical harm by that conduct." *Id.*, at 547-548 (emphasis added).

The case before us, as we have said, focuses on the italicized words "physical impact." The Second Circuit interpreted those words as including a simple physical contact with a substance that might cause a disease at a future time, so long as the contact was of a kind that would "cause fear in a reasonable person." 79 F.3d at 1344. In our view, however, the "physical impact" to which *Gottshall* referred does not include a simple physical contact with a substance that might cause a disease at a substantially later time — where that substance, or related circumstance, threatens no harm other than that disease-related risk.

First, *Gottshall* cited many state cases in support of its adoption of the "zone of danger" test quoted above. And in each case where recovery for emotional distress was permitted, the case involved a threatened physical contact that caused, or might have caused, immediate traumatic harm.

Second, *Gottshall*'s language, read in light of this precedent, seems similarly limited. *Gottshall*, 512 U.S. 532 at 555 ("zone of danger test . . . is consistent with FELA's central focus on physical perils"); *id.*, at 556 (quoting Lancaster v. Norfolk & Western R. Co., 773 F.2d 807, 813 (CA7 1985), *cert. denied*, 480 U.S. 945, 94 L. Ed. 2d 788, 107 S. Ct. 1602 (1987)) (FELA seeks to protect workers " 'from physical invasions or menaces' ").

Taken together, language and cited precedent indicate that the words "physical impact" do not encompass every form of "physical contact." And, in particular, they do not include a contact that amounts to no more than an exposure — an exposure, such as that before us, to a substance that poses some future risk of disease and which contact causes emotional distress only because the worker learns that he may become ill after a substantial period of time.

Third, common-law precedent does not favor the plaintiff. Common law courts do permit a plaintiff who suffers from a disease to recover for related negligently caused emotional distress, and some courts permit a plaintiff who exhibits a physical symptom of exposure to recover. But with only a few exceptions, common law courts have denied recovery to those who, like Buckley, are disease and symptom free.

Fourth, the general policy reasons to which *Gottshall* referred — in its explanation of why common law courts have restricted recovery for emotional harm to cases falling within rather narrowly defined categories — militate against an expansive definition of "physical impact" here. Those reasons include: (a) special "difficulty for judges and juries" in separating valid, important claims from those that are invalid or "trivial," *Gottshall*, 512 U.S. at 557; (b) a threat of "unlimited and unpredictable liability," *ibid.*; and (c) the "potential for a flood" of comparatively unimportant, or "trivial," claims, *ibid.*

To separate meritorious and important claims from invalid or trivial claims does not seem easier here than in other cases in which a plaintiff might seek recovery for typical negligently caused emotional distress. The facts before us illustrate the problem. The District Court, when concluding that Buckley had failed to present "sufficient evidence to allow a jury to find . . . a real emotional injury," pointed out that, apart from Buckley's own testimony, there was virtually no evidence of distress. App. 623-625. Indeed, Buckley continued to work with insulating material "even though . . . he could have transferred" elsewhere, he "continued to smoke cigarettes" despite doctors' warnings, and his doctor did not refer him "either to a psychologist or to a social worker." *Id.*, at 624. The Court of Appeals reversed because it found certain objective corroborating evidence, namely "workers' complaints to supervisors and investigative bodies." 79 F.3d at 1346. Both kinds of "objective" evidence — the confirming and disconfirming evidence — seem only indirectly related to the question at issue, the existence and seriousness of Buckley's claimed emotional distress. Yet, given the difficulty of separating valid from invalid emotional injury claims, the evidence before us may typify the kind of evidence to which parties and the courts would have to look. . . .

More important, the physical contact at issue here — a simple (though extensive) contact with a carcinogenic substance — does not seem to offer much help in separating valid from invalid emotional distress claims. That is because contacts, even extensive contacts, with serious carcinogens are common. *See, e.g.*, Nicholson, Perkel & Selikoff, *Occupational Exposure to Asbestos: Population at Risk and Projected Mortality — 1980-2030*, 3 Am. J. Indust. Med. 259 (1982) (estimating that 21 million Americans have been exposed to work-related asbestos); U.S. Dept. of Health and Human Services, 1 Seventh Annual Report on Carcinogens 71 (1994) (3 million workers exposed to benzene, a majority of Americans exposed outside the workplace); Pirkle, et al., *Exposure of the U.S. Population to Environmental Tobacco Smoke*, 275 JAMA 1233,

1237 (1996) (reporting that 43% of American children lived in a home with at least one smoker, and 37% of adult nonsmokers lived in a home with at least one smoker or reported environmental tobacco smoke at work). They may occur without causing serious emotional distress, but sometimes they do cause distress, and reasonably so, for cancer is both an unusually threatening and unusually frightening disease. *See* Statistical Abstract of United States 94 (1996) (23.5 percent of Americans who died in 1994 died of cancer); American Cancer Society, Cancer Facts & Figures — 1997, p.1 (half of all men and one third of all women will develop cancer). The relevant problem, however, remains one of evaluating a claimed emotional reaction to an *increased* risk of dying. An external circumstance — exposure — makes some emotional distress more likely. But how can one determine from the external circumstance of exposure whether, or when, a claimed strong emotional reaction to an *increased* mortality risk (say from 23% to 28%) is reasonable and genuine, rather than overstated — particularly when the relevant statistics themselves are controversial and uncertain (as is usually the case), and particularly since neither those exposed nor judges or juries are experts in statistics? The evaluation problem seems a serious one.

The large number of those exposed and the uncertainties that may surround recovery also suggest what *Gottshall* called the problem of "unlimited and unpredictable liability." Does such liability mean, for example, that the costs associated with a rule of liability would become so great that, given the nature of the harm, it would seem unreasonable to require the public to pay the higher prices that may result? The same characteristics further suggest what *Gottshall* called the problem of a "flood" of cases that, if not "trivial," are comparatively less important. In a world of limited resources, would a rule permitting immediate large-scale recoveries for widespread emotional distress caused by fear of future disease diminish the likelihood of recovery by those who later suffer from the disease?

We do not raise these questions to answer them (for we do not have the answers), but rather to show that general policy concerns of a kind that have led common law courts to deny recovery for certain classes of negligently caused harms are present in this case as well. That being so, we cannot find in *Gottshall*'s underlying rationale any basis for departing from *Gottshall*'s language and precedent or from the current common-law consensus. That is to say, we cannot find in *Gottshall*'s language, cited precedent, other common law-precedent, or related concerns of policy, a legal basis for adopting the emotional-distress recovery rule adopted by the Court of Appeals.

Buckley raises several important arguments in reply. He points out, for example, that common law courts do permit recovery for emotional distress where a plaintiff has physical symptoms; and he argues that his evidence of exposure and enhanced mortality risk is as strong a proof as an accompanying physical symptom that his emotional distress is genuine.

This argument, however, while important, overlooks the fact that the common law in this area does not examine the genuineness of emotional harm case by case. Rather, it has developed recovery-permitting categories the contours of which more distantly reflect this, and other, abstract general policy concerns. . . . The relevant question here concerns the validity of a rule that seeks to redefine such a category. It would not be easy to redefine "physical impact" in terms of a rule that turned on, say, the "massive, lengthy, [or] tangible" nature of a contact that amounted to an exposure, whether to contaminated water, or to germ-laden air, or to carcinogen-containing substances, such as insulation dust containing asbestos. . . .

Finally, Buckley argues that the "humanitarian" nature of the FELA warrants a holding in his favor. We do not doubt that the FELA's purpose militates in favor of recovery for a serious and negligently caused emotional harm. *Cf. Gottshall*, 512 U.S. at 550. But just as courts must interpret that law to take proper account of the harms suffered by a sympathetic individual plaintiff, so they must consider the general impact, on workers as well as employers, of the general liability rules they would thereby create. Here the relevant question concerns not simply recovery in an individual case, but the consequences and effects of *a rule of law that would permit that recovery*. And if the common law concludes that a legal rule permitting recovery here, from a tort law perspective, and despite benefits in *some* individual cases, would on balance cause more harm than good, and if we find that judgment reasonable, we cannot find that conclusion inconsistent with the FELA's humanitarian purpose.

III

Buckley also sought recovery for a different kind of "injury," namely the economic cost of the extra medical check-ups that he expects to incur as a result of his exposure to asbestos-laden insulation dust. The District Court, when it dismissed the action, did not discuss this aspect of Buckley's case. But the Second Circuit, when reversing the District Court, held that "a reasonable jury could award" Buckley the "costs" of "medical monitoring" in this case. 79 F.3d at 1347. We agreed to decide whether the court correctly found that the FELA permitted a plaintiff without symptoms or disease to recover this economic loss.

The parties do not dispute — and we assume — that an exposed plaintiff can recover related reasonable medical monitoring costs if and when he develops symptoms. As the Second Circuit pointed out, a plaintiff injured through negligence can recover related reasonable medical expenses as an element of damages. No one has argued that any different principle would apply in the case of a plaintiff whose "injury" consists of a disease, a symptom, or those sorts of emotional distress that fall within the FELA's definition of "injury." . . .

Other portions of the Second Circuit's opinion, however, indicate that it may have rested this portion of its decision upon a broader ground, namely that medical monitoring costs themselves represent a separate negligently caused economic "injury," 45 U.S.C. § 51, for which a negligently exposed FELA plaintiff (including a plaintiff without disease or symptoms) may recover to the extent that the medical monitoring costs that a reasonable physician would prescribe for the plaintiff exceed the medical monitoring costs that "would have been prescribed in the absence of [the] exposure." 79 F.3d at 1347 (citation omitted). This portion of the opinion ... suggests the existence of an ordinary, but separate, tort law cause of action permitting (as tort law ordinarily permits) the recovery of medical cost damages in the form of a lump sum [damages award].... As so characterized, the Second Circuit's holding, in our view, went beyond the bounds of currently "evolving common law." *Gottshall*, at 558 (Souter, J., concurring).

Guided by the parties' briefs, we have canvassed the state-law cases that have considered whether the negligent causation of this kind of harm (i.e., causing a plaintiff, through negligent exposure to a toxic substance, to incur medical monitoring costs) by itself constitutes a sufficient basis for a tort recovery.... [S]everal important State Supreme Court cases have permitted recovery. Ayers v. Jackson, 106 N.J. 557, 525 A.2d 287 (1987); Hansen v. Mountain Fuel Supply Co., 858 P.2d 970 (Utah 1993); Potter v. Firestone Tire & Rubber Co., 6 Cal. 4th 965, 863 P.2d 795 (1993); *see also* Burns v. Jaquays Mining Corp., 156 Ariz. 375, 752 P.2d 28 (Ct. App. 1987).

We find it sufficient to note, for present purposes, that the cases authorizing recovery for medical monitoring in the absence of physical injury do not endorse a full-blown, traditional tort law cause of action for lump-sum damages — of the sort that the Court of Appeals seems to have endorsed here. Rather, those courts, while recognizing that medical monitoring costs can amount to a harm that justifies a tort remedy, have suggested, or imposed, special limitations on that remedy. *Compare Ayers, supra,* at 608, 525 A.2d at 314 (recommending in future cases creation of "a court-supervised fund to administer medical-surveillance payments"); *Hansen, supra*, at 982 (suggesting insurance mechanism or court-supervised fund as proper remedy); *Potter, supra*, 1010, n.28, 863 P.2d at 825, n.28 (suggesting that a lump-sum damages award would be inappropriate); *Burns, supra*, 381, 752 P.2d at 34 (holding that lump-sum damages are not appropriate) *with*, e.g., Honeycutt v. Walden, 294 Ark. 440, 743 S.W.2d 809 (1988) (damages award for future medical expenses made necessary by physical injury are awarded as lump-sum payment); Rice v. Hill, 315 Pa. 166, 172 A. 289 (1934) (same); and Restatement (Second) of Torts § 920A(2) (1977) (ordinarily fact that plaintiff is insured is irrelevant to amount of tort recovery). We believe that the note of caution, the limitations, and the expressed uneasiness with a traditional lump-sum damages remedy are important, for they suggest a judicial recognition of some of the policy concerns that have been pointed out to us here — concerns of a sort that *Gottshall* identified.

Since, for example, the particular, say cancer-related, costs at issue are the *extra* monitoring costs, over and above those otherwise recommended, their identification will sometimes pose special "difficulties for judges and juries." *Gottshall*, 512 U.S. at 557. Those difficulties in part can reflect uncertainty among medical professionals about just which tests are most usefully administered and when. And in part those difficulties can reflect the fact that scientists will not always see a medical need to provide systematic *scientific* answers to the relevant *legal* question, namely whether an exposure calls for *extra* monitoring. Buckley's sole expert . . . was equivocal about the need for *extra* monitoring, and the defense had not yet put on its case.

Moreover, tens of millions of individuals may have suffered exposure to substances that might justify some form of substance-exposure-related medical monitoring. . . . And that fact, along with uncertainty as to the amount of liability, could threaten both a "flood" of less important cases (potentially absorbing resources better left available to those more seriously harmed) and the systemic harms that can accompany "unlimited and unpredictable liability" (say, for example, vast testing liability adversely affecting the allocation of scarce medical resources). The dissent assumes that medical monitoring is not a "costly" remedy. But Buckley here sought damages worth $950 annually for 36 years; by comparison, of all claims settled by the Center for Claims Resolution, a group representing asbestos manufacturers, from 1988 until 1993, the average settlement for plaintiffs *injured* by asbestos was about $12,500, and the settlement for non-malignant plaintiffs among this group averaged $8,810. . . .

We do not deny important competing considerations—of a kind that may have led some courts to provide a form of liability. Buckley argues, for example, that it is inequitable to place the economic burden of such care on the negligently exposed plaintiff rather than on the negligent defendant. He points out that providing preventive care to individuals who would otherwise go without can help to mitigate potentially serious future health effects of diseases by detecting them in early stages; again, whether or not this is such a situation, we may assume that such situations occur. And he adds that, despite scientific uncertainties, the difficulty of separating justified from unjustified claims may be less serious than where emotional distress is the harm at issue.

We do not deny that Justice Ginsburg paints a sympathetic picture of Buckley and his co-workers; this picture has force because Buckley *is* sympathetic and he *has* suffered wrong at the hands of a negligent employer. But we are more troubled than is the dissent by the potential systemic effects of creating a new, full-blown, tort law cause of action—for example, the effects upon interests of other potential plaintiffs who are not before the court and who depend on a tort system that can distinguish between reliable and serious claims on the one hand, and unreliable and relatively trivial claims on the other. The reality is that competing interests are at stake—and those interests sometimes can be reconciled in ways other than simply through the creation of a full-blown, traditional, tort law cause of action.

We have not tried to balance these, or other, competing considerations here. We point them out to help explain why we consider the limitations and cautions to be important—and integral—parts of the state-court decisions that permit asymptomatic plaintiffs a separate tort claim for medical monitoring costs. That being so, we do not find sufficient support in the common law for the unqualified rule of lump-sum damages recovery that is, at least arguably, before us here. And given the mix of competing general policy considerations, plaintiff's policy-based arguments do not convince us that the FELA contains a tort liability rule of that *unqualified* kind.

This limited conclusion disposes of the matter before us. We need not, and do not, express any view here about the extent to which the FELA might, or might not, accommodate medical cost recovery rules more finely tailored than the rule we have considered.

IV

For the reasons stated, we reverse the determination of the Second Circuit, and we remand the case for further proceedings consistent with this opinion.

Ginsburg, J. (concurring and dissenting) (joined by Stevens, J.). . . .

Buckley's extensive contact with asbestos particles in Grand Central's tunnels, as I comprehend his situation, constituted "physical impact" as that term was used in *Gottshall*. Nevertheless, I concur in the Court's judgment with respect to Buckley's emotional distress claim. In my view, that claim fails because Buckley did not present objective evidence of severe emotional distress. Buckley testified at trial that he was angry at Metro-North and fearful of developing an asbestos-related disease. However, he sought no professional help to ease his distress, and presented no medical testimony concerning his mental health. Under these circumstances, Buckley's emotional distress claim fails as a matter of law. *Cf. Gottshall*, 512 U.S. at 563-564, 566-567 (Ginsburg, J., dissenting) (describing as "unquestionably genuine and severe" emotional distress suffered by one respondent who had a nervous breakdown, and another who was hospitalized, lost weight, and had, *inter alia*, suicidal preoccupations, anxiety, insomnia, cold sweats, and nausea). . . .

II

. . . It is not apparent why (or even whether) the Court reverses the Second Circuit's determination on Buckley's second claim. The Court of Appeals held that a medical monitoring claim is solidly grounded, and this Court does not hold otherwise. Hypothesizing that Buckley demands lump-sum damages and nothing else, the Court ruminates on the appropriate remedy without answering the anterior question: Does the plaintiff have a claim for relief? Buckley has shown that Metro-North negligently exposed him to "extremely high levels of asbestos," 79 F.3d at 1341, and that this exposure warrants "medical monitoring in order to detect and treat [asbestos-related] diseases as they may arise." *Id.*, at 1346. Buckley's expert medical witness estimated the annual costs of proper monitoring at $950. We do not know from the Court's opinion what more a plaintiff must show to qualify for relief.

A

In my view, the Second Circuit rightly held that a railworker negligently exposed to asbestos states a claim for relief under the FELA; recovery in such cases, again as the Court of Appeals held, should reflect the difference in cost between the medical tests a reasonable physician would prescribe for unexposed persons and the monitoring regime a reasonable physician would advise for persons exposed in the way Michael Buckley and his co-workers were.

Recognizing such a claim would align the FELA with the "evolving common law." *Gottshall*, 512 U.S. at 558 (Souter, J., concurring). "[A medical monitoring] action has been increasingly recognized by state courts as necessary given the latent nature of many diseases caused by exposure to hazardous materials and the traditional common law tort doctrine requirement that an injury be manifest." Daigle v. Shell Oil Co., 972 F.2d 1527, 1533 (CA10 1992). . . . As the Court understates, several state high courts have upheld medical monitoring cost recovery. In a path-marking opinion, the United States Court of Appeals for the Third Circuit, interpreting Pennsylvania law, recognized a right to compensation for monitoring "necessary in order to diagnose properly the warning signs of disease." *See Paoli I*, 916 F.2d at 851; *see also Paoli II*, 35 F.3d at 785-788. Similarly, a number of Federal District Courts interpreting state law, and several state courts of first and second instance, have sustained medical monitoring claims. This Court, responsible for developing FELA law, finds little value in these decisions.

These courts have answered the question this Court passes by: What are the elements of a compensable medical monitoring claim? The Third Circuit, for example, has enumerated: A plaintiff can recover the costs of medical monitoring if (1) he establishes that he was significantly exposed to a proven hazardous substance through the negligent actions of the defendant; (2) as a proximate result of the exposure, the plaintiff suffers a significantly increased risk of contracting a serious latent disease; (3) by reason of the exposure a reasonable physician would prescribe a monitoring regime different from the one that would have been prescribed in the absence of the exposure; and (4) monitoring and testing procedures exist that make the early detection and treatment of the disease possible and beneficial. *See Paoli I*, 916 F.2d at 852; *Paoli II*, 35 F.3d at 788. Each factor must be shown by competent expert testimony.

A claim so defined comports with the terms of the FELA. Under the FELA, a railroad "shall be liable in damages to any person suffering injury while he is employed by such carrier . . . for such injury . . . resulting in whole or in part from the negligence of any of the officers, agents, or employees of such carrier." 45 U.S.C. § 51. The "injury" sustained by an asbestos-exposed worker seeking to recover medical monitoring costs is the invasion of that employee's interest in being free from the economic burden of extraordinary medical surveillance. *See* Restatement (Second) of Torts § 7 (1964) (defining injury as "the invasion of any legally protected interest of another"); *see* Friends for All Children, Inc. v. Lockheed Aircraft Corp., 241 U.S. App. D.C. 83, 746 F.2d 816, 826 (CADC

1984) ("It is difficult to dispute that an individual has an interest in avoiding expensive diagnostic examinations just as he or she has an interest in avoiding physical injury."); Ayers v. Jackson, 106 N.J. 557, 591, 525 A.2d 287, 304 (1987).

Traditional tort principles upon which the FELA rests warrant recognition of medical monitoring claims of the kind Buckley has asserted. As the Third Circuit explained, the policy reasons for recognizing this tort are obvious[:]

> "Medical monitoring claims acknowledge that, in a toxic age, significant harm can be done to an individual by a tortfeasor, notwithstanding latent manifestation of that harm. Moreover, ... recognizing this tort does not require courts to speculate about the probability of future injury. It merely requires courts to ascertain the probability that the far less costly remedy of medical supervision is appropriate. Allowing plaintiffs to recover the cost of this care deters irresponsible discharge of toxic chemicals by defendants and encourages plaintiffs to detect and treat their injuries as soon as possible. These are conventional goals of the tort system...." *Paoli I*, 916 F.2d at 852....

On all counts — exposure, increased risk of devastating disease, and the necessity of monitoring — Michael Buckley's complaint presents a textbook case. Through its stipulations, Metro-North has acknowledged that it failed "to use [the] reasonable care [the FELA requires] in furnishing its employees with a safe place to work." *Buell*, 480 U.S. at 558. At trial, "competent expert testimony ... established both that Buckley suffered a substantial impact from asbestos that ... significantly increased his risk of contracting an asbestos-related disease and that Buckley should receive medical monitoring in order to ensure early detection and cure of any asbestos-related disease he develops." 79 F.3d at 1347. Thus, Metro-North, "through [its] negligence, caused the plaintiff, in the opinion of medical experts, to need specific medical services — a cost that is neither inconsequential nor of a kind the community generally accepts as part of the wear and tear of daily life. Under [the] principles of tort law, the [tortfeasor] should pay." *Friends for All Children*, 746 F.2d at 825.

B

The Court, as I read its opinion, leaves open the question whether Buckley may state a claim for relief under the FELA. The Court does not question the medical need for monitoring. It recognizes that cancer, one of the diseases Buckley faces an increased risk of suffering, is "unusually threatening and unusually frightening," and that detection of disease in early stages "can help to mitigate potentially serious future health effects," *ante*, at 18. On the other hand, the Court notes there may be "uncertainty among medical professionals about just which tests are most usefully administered and when."

It is not uncommon, of course, that doctors will agree that medical attention is needed, yet disagree on what monitoring or treatment course is best. But uncertainty as to which tests are best or when they should be administered is not cause to deny a claim for relief. Fact triers in tort cases routinely face questions lacking indubitably clear answers. . . .

Occupational Safety and Health Administration (OSHA) regulations governing permissible levels of asbestos exposure in the workplace make it plain that medical monitoring is no "trivial" matter, *see ante*, at 19; the regulations are instructive on appropriate standards for necessary monitoring, *see* 29 CFR § 1910.1001 (1996); *see also* 29 U.S.C. § 655(b)(7) (authorizing Secretary of Labor to require employers to provide medical monitoring to employees exposed to hazardous substances). OSHA's regulations direct employers to provide medical monitoring for employees exposed to certain levels of asbestos, and they describe in detail the monitoring employers must make available. *See* 29 CFR § 1910.1001(l), App. D, App. E (1996). These regulations apply to all industries covered by the Occupational Safety and Health Act of 1970 (Act). Although the Act does not apply to state public employers such as Metro-North, *see* 29 U.S.C. § 652(5), New York State has adopted OSHA standards for its public employers, *see* N.Y. Lab. Law §§ 27-a(3)(c), (4)(a) (McKinney 1986 and Supp. 1997). Had Metro-North assiduously attended to those standards, Buckley might have been spared the costs he now seeks to recover.

Finally, the Court's anticipation of a "'flood' of less important cases" and "'unlimited and unpredictable liability'" is overblown. The employee's "injury" in the claim at stake is the economic burden additional medical surveillance entails; if an employer provides all that a reasonable physician would recommend for the exposed employee, the employee would incur no costs and hence have no claim for compensation. Nor does the FELA claim Buckley states pave the way for "tens of millions of individuals" with similar claims. It is doubtful that many legions in the universe of individuals ever exposed to toxic material could demonstrate that their employers negligently exposed them to a known hazardous substance, and thereby substantially increased the risk that they would suffer debilitating or deadly disease. Withholding relief, moreover, is dangerous, for lives will be lost when grave disease is diagnosed too late.

C

The Court emphasizes most heavily that several courts, while authorizing recovery for medical monitoring, have imposed or suggested special limitations on the tort remedy. *See ante*, at 15-16. In lieu of lump-sum damages, the Court indicates, a court-supervised fund might be the better remedy.

It is scarcely surprising that the Second Circuit did not consider relief through a court-supervised fund. So far as the record before us shows, no party argued in the District Court, the Second Circuit, or even this Court, that medical monitoring expenses may be recoverable, but not through a lump sum, only through a court fund. The question aired below was the prime one the Court obscures: Does Buckley's medical monitoring claim warrant any relief? . . .

The Court today reverses the Second Circuit's determination that Buckley has stated a claim for relief, but remands the case for further proceedings. If I comprehend the Court's enigmatic decision correctly, Buckley may replead a claim for relief and recover for medical monitoring, but he must receive that relief in a form other than a lump sum. Unaccountably, the Court resists the straightforward statement that would enlighten courts in this and similar cases: A claim for medical monitoring is cognizable under the FELA; it is a claim entirely in step with " 'evolving common law.' " I therefore dissent from the Court's judgment to the extent it relates to medical monitoring.

NOTES AND QUESTIONS

1. Ayers. The Court in *Buckley* makes clear that, so far as FELA liability is concerned, a *de minimis* physical impact will not count as the sort of predicate injury that will support an award of compensatory damages for emotional distress associated with that impact. At what point, one may fairly ask, does an impact become an injury? The Court confronted this question in yet another recent FELA case, Norfolk & West. Ry. Co. v. Ayers, 538 U.S. 135 (2003). In *Ayers*, the claimants sought to recover for emotional distress, including for fear of cancer. However, unlike Buckley, these claimants alleged that they suffered from *asbestosis*, a disease involving the scarring of lung tissue by asbestos fibers. Asbestosis is almost never fatal, and apparently is not causally related to the development of other asbestosis-related diseases, such as lung cancers. Instead, it produces symptoms ranging from mild to severe shortness of breath, coughing, and fatigue.

Justice Ginsburg, writing for a 5 to 4 majority, concluded that asbestosis constitutes a predicate injury that supports recovery for emotional distress damages "related" to the disease, including damages for plaintiff's fear of contracting cancer in the future. The dissenters agreed that asbestosis constitutes a predicate physical injury, but argued that fear-of-cancer damages could not be awarded parasitically on that injury, because the plaintiff's distress *was not over asbestosis itself*, but over the prospect that the same exposure to asbestos that caused the plaintiff to develop asbestosis might someday cause him to develop cancer.

2. *Zone of Danger Revisited.* The *Buckley* majority obviously concluded that Buckley could not establish that he was endangered, otherwise he could have proceeded under the holding of *Gottshall*. This observation provides an occasion to reconsider the zone of danger rule discussed in Chapter 10. What is so significant about the risk of imminent bodily harm, as opposed to long-term health risks? As noted in Chapter 10, courts at the turn of the twentieth century may have been under the impression that "near misses" have a physical effect on the nervous system that distress over less immediate harms does not. Is there an alternative explanation, more normative and less biologically dependent, that can explain why Buckley should not get to recover for his fear of future injury?

Two of us have argued that the "zone of danger" test is best understood as one important instantiation of a more general requirement that NIED claimants prove that the defendant's carelessness placed them in a situation that generated the sort of extreme stress that a reasonable person should not be required to endure. These are situations, we suggest, "in which a reasonable person cannot be expected to keep a stiff upper lip; she cannot be expected to avoid responding by tumbling into severe emotional distress, that is, situations in which the mountain is a mountain, not a molehill." Instances of being exposed to imminent bodily harm provide important examples of such situations, but are not the only ones. For example, suppose a defendant were carelessly to expose his neighbor to radioactive materials, thereby rendering the neighbor and each member of his family 20 times more likely than the general population to develop a very rare form of cancer by the age of 60. In this view, liability ought to attach for the distress associated with having been exposed to the sort of threat that would cast a pall over the life of even a person of ordinary resilience. Could the same be said for Buckley? While most of us would undoubtedly regard any increase in the percentage likelihood of contracting lung cancer to be highly undesirable, can one say of a small marginal increase in the risk of cancer (Justice Breyer posits a shift from 23 to 28 percent) that it is itself sufficient to generate the sort of pall that would entitle a person of ordinary fortitude to experience severe distress?

3. *Medical Monitoring and Right versus Remedy.* In her separate opinion, Justice Ginsburg expresses puzzlement over the majority's treatment of Buckley's claim to be entitled to compensation by virtue of the fact that Metro North's carelessness caused him to incur reasonable expenses for medical tests that he would not otherwise have had to incur. Her puzzlement stems from the fact that the majority seems to acknowledge the validity of this sort of claim, yet links its validity to the form of the remedy sought by Buckley. Thus, it seems to reason that insofar as Buckley sought lump-sum damages, he failed to state a cause of action for reimbursement. However, if he sought a court order enjoining Metro North to pay for his medical monitoring, he might well have a cognizable claim. Justice Ginsburg is surely right to puzzle over this apparent conflation of right and remedy. Can you think of an explanation as to why the majority might have linked the two? Is Buckley's medical monitoring claim a claim for negligence causing pure economic loss? (See *Testbank*, Chapter 2.) Might there be another way to characterize what Metro North did to Buckley, and how its conduct might translate into an obligation to make reasonable efforts to assist him in detecting the onset of cancer in the future?

V.   TORTS, FAIRNESS, AND EFFICIENCY: MASS TORTS AND CLASS ACTIONS

One of the most innovative features of the Federal Rules of Civil Procedure is Rule 23, which permits a special type of lawsuit known as the *class action*. The hallmark of a class action is that a single named plaintiff, or a small group of named plaintiffs, litigate the suit not just on behalf of themselves, but for a large group of similarly situated persons. Suppose evidence emerges that Company *C* violated federal securities laws by defrauding 1,000 investors of $500 each. Given that federal securities laws sometimes generate private rights of action (see *Borak*, Chapter 6), each individual investor has a potentially valid federal-law claim against the company. Rule 23 in turn provides a procedural mechanism by which one such investor may be entitled to sue *as representative of the class of all the defrauded investors*. In principle, if a class action such as this goes forward and is resolved through settlement or verdict, all members of the class are bound by that resolution, whether favorable or unfavorable. If the representative plaintiff prevails, for example, each class member receives some part of the award, even though none participated in the actual litigation.

Rule 23 was designed in part with cases like the foregoing example in mind, in which each member of a large group suffers a relatively modest injury. The benefits it provides for such cases are perhaps apparent. First, it saves time and money by avoiding repetitive litigation in courtrooms around the country of substantially the same facts. Second, it promotes fairness by ensuring that persons who suffer identical or nearly identical injuries from the same wrong receive comparable treatment. Third, it gives clients and lawyers an incentive to commence the litigation in the first place. Few if any clients or attorneys will expend money to litigate a single $500 claim. But if one thousand $500 claims are pooled together, the representative plaintiff — and more important, her lawyer — may well have a sufficient incentive to endure the expense and bother of litigation. By the same token, class actions ensure that the deterrent effects of tort liability are not dissipated in cases of conduct that threatens to cause modest harms to a large number of victims.

By departing from the traditional form of civil litigation, in which an individual plaintiff represented by his own attorney pursues a claim, class actions thus promise to deliver a number of benefits. For the same reasons, however, they pose certain risks. Two such risks are particularly noteworthy. First, they only stand to promote the efficient resolution of claims if class members actually possess nearly identical claims against a given defendant (or defendants): only then does it make sense to try these claims in a single proceeding brought by a *representative* plaintiff. By way of contrast — to take a deliberately overstated example — suppose our imagined securities-fraud plaintiff sought to sue not only as the representative of the defrauded investors, but also as the representative of "anyone who has suffered a legally actionable wrong at the hands of Company *C* in the past three years." As thus defined, the class would inevitably include persons with dramatically different claims, including, for example, an employee of *C* who claims to have been wrongfully discharged, or a public utility claiming that *C* hasn't paid its electric bill. Simply put, there is little to be gained in terms of efficiency or fairness by trying in one lawsuit a welter of claims grounded on completely different factual allegations and legal theories.

Even granted a basic commonality among class members' claims, there is a second concern raised by class actions. A class action creates something like a principal-agent relationship between the class members and the litigant who purports to sue on their behalf. In any principal-agent relationship, there is always the risk that the agent will not fully or faithfully pursue the interests of the principal. In this context, one worry is that the representative plaintiff and/or his attorney will agree to "sell out" the members of the class in exchange for a "sweetheart" deal for him or themselves. So, for example, one might be concerned that our representative securities-fraud litigant will accept from Company *C* a substantial payment in exchange for agreeing to a binding settlement in which *C* pays each other class member only $50 of the $500 owed.

The drafters of Rule 23 were well aware of these and other risks associated with class actions, and they accordingly created a variety of mechanisms for protecting against their realization. Some of these mechanisms confer rights on potential class members that are designed to permit them to protect their own interests. For example, a litigant purporting to represent a class must give effective *notice* of the class action to class members so that they are likely to be informed that someone else is litigating on their behalf. More substantively, members are usually given the right to *opt out* of a class action if they conclude, for whatever reason, that they do not want their legal rights determined by a representative proceeding.

Most important for our immediate purposes, Rule 23 imposes on federal district judges various oversight responsibilities not present in ordinary A v. B litigation. First and foremost, the district judge is charged with the task of "certifying the class," that is, deciding, through the application of certain standards set out in Rule 23, whether efficiency and fairness will likely be served by letting the litigation proceed as a class action and, if so, who should be included in the class. Absent certification, a plaintiff has no right or ability to sue in a representative capacity: A suit purporting to be a class action does not actually become a class action until the class is certified. In addition, the district court must approve the means through which the named plaintiff aims to notify class members of the litigation. Finally, if the parties in the case reach a settlement, the district judge is required by Rule 23 to scrutinize the agreement to ensure that is not merely a windfall to the named plaintiff, but a fair result for class members.

In the period immediately after Rule 23's 1966 enactment, the Rule was not frequently invoked in tort cases, for several reasons. First, personal injury cases typically involved a large enough potential verdict, and individualized enough facts, that there was neither the need nor the incentive to proceed by means of a class action. Second, and of equal importance, the Advisory Committee notes to Rule 23 explicitly stated that its drafters did not design it to handle personal injury litigation. Third, torts affecting a modest number of victims could be litigated together using "joinder" and other procedural devices less ambitious than the class action device. Fourth, tort actions — as opposed to civil rights or securities-fraud actions — generally are governed by state law, which can raise difficult "choice-of-law" issues if different states' laws apply to claims brought by different members of a single class.

By the 1980s, however, courts began to see and authorize tort class actions. Industrial disasters, hotel fires, and airplane crashes with large numbers of victims all provided plausible occasions for the use of Rule 23. More significantly, the emergence of design defect litigation, in which the central allegation was that a mass-produced product, such as a particular drug or car model, had been defectively designed, raised the possibility that hundreds or thousands of plaintiffs might bring suit in courts around the country against a single manufacturer for the same alleged wrong. In a period in which judicial dockets were becoming increasingly clogged, and in which key changes in the composition and operation of the plaintiffs' bar (including the use of advertising) enabled lawyers to amass large groups of clients, the class action suddenly emerged as a promising device for handling these sorts of tort claims. The rise in the number of federal class actions was paralleled by an increase in state class actions as well, since many states had created "mini" versions of Rule 23, which allowed state courts to certify classes if criteria similar to those developed under the federal rule were satisfied. Through these and other developments, the modern phenomenon of high-profile, multimillon dollar "mass torts" emerged. (This even though federal appellate courts continued to wonder aloud whether Rule 23 really permitted tort class actions, with neither Congress nor the Supreme Court answering the question.)

By the late 1980s, the manufacture, sale, and use of one particular product — asbestos — provided the basis for by far the most sprawling, complex, and momentous instances of mass tort litigation. As noted in the introduction to the *Buckley* case in Section IV, manufacturers and distributors of asbestos were confronted with tens of thousands of product liability claims brought by workers and others claiming to have been injured by exposure to asbestos. In response, scores of companies that produced or used asbestos threatened or entered bankruptcy. The apparent lack of adequate funds to pay tort claimants in turn raised the prospect of an unseemly "race to the courthouse," in which plaintiffs recovered not on the basis of the strength of their claims, but simply because they happened to get their claims in first. Meanwhile, the court system, already swamped with growing criminal dockets, was in danger of being overwhelmed with asbestos-related suits.

Faced with these prospects, lawyers and federal district judges began efforts to craft class actions that would resolve, on an aggregate level, a wide variety of claims against a large number of defendants. Yet, although the deployment of Rule 23 promised to bring some order and fairness to the chaos of asbestos litigation, it also raises a number of red flags. Victims' suits have sought compensation for a wide array of physical injuries ranging from the trivial to the fatal, as well as emotional and economic harms of the sort discussed in *Buckley*. Their exposure to asbestos occurred at various times, in a vast array of circumstances, and involved inhalation of substantially varying amounts of asbestos. In addition, a victim's own conduct — in particular, her smoking habits — complicates the inquiry into the causal significance of her asbestos exposure. Finally, for different plaintiffs, determinations of issues such as injury, causation, and comparative fault may have to be adjudicated under different states' laws, depending in part on the place of manufacture and exposure.

In short, the courts have found themselves confronted with litigation that simultaneously cries out for, yet warns against, the use of the class action device, by which a massive inventory of individual personal injury claims would be adjudicated through a modest number of representative litigations. In turn, a premium has been placed on the adoption of innovative techniques for obtaining the benefits of the class action without unduly risking inefficiencies and unfairness. Consider, in this light, the ingenious efforts of the litigants that led to the Supreme Court's *Amchem* decision, excerpted below. Essentially, the lawyers on both sides concluded that the best way to proceed was, first, to negotiate an elaborate global settlement that purported to resolve the claims of tens of thousands of asbestos victims, including thousands who were not "at the table" to negotiate the terms of the settlement. Needless to say, a settlement agreement cannot bind someone who is not a party to it, so the next and crucial step for the lawyers was to file a class action. In doing so, the plaintiffs' lawyers had no intention of litigating the merits of their clients' claims. Instead, the class action was filed for the sole purpose of getting a federal court to certify the class, and approve the settlement, *which would then render the settlement agreement binding on persons who had not agreed to it* (just as a class action binds class members who do not themselves participate in the actual litigation of the underlying suit). The question put to the Court was whether Rule 23 grants district courts the authority to entertain and resolve this sort of "settlement class action," and, if so, under what circumstances and standards. Beyond this already important question, *Amchem* presented the Court with an important opportunity to shed light on the larger question of the viability of mass tort class actions under Rule 23.

Amchem Prods., Inc. v. Windsor
521 U.S. 591 (1997)

Ginsburg, J.   This case concerns the legitimacy under Rule 23 of the Federal Rules of Civil Procedure of a class-action certification sought to achieve global settlement of current and future asbestos-related claims. The class proposed for certification potentially encompasses hundreds of thousands, perhaps millions, of individuals tied together by this commonality: Each was, or some day may be, adversely affected by past exposure to asbestos products manufactured by one or more of 20 companies. Those companies, defendants in the lower courts, are petitioners here.

The United States District Court for the Eastern District of Pennsylvania certified the class for settlement only, finding that the proposed settlement was fair and that representation and notice had been adequate. That court enjoined class members from separately pursuing asbestos-related personal-injury suits in any court, federal or state, pending the issuance of a final order. The Court of Appeals for the Third Circuit vacated the District Court's orders, holding that the class certification failed to satisfy Rule 23's requirements in several critical respects. We affirm the Court of Appeals' judgment.

I

A

The settlement-class certification we confront evolved in response to an asbestos-litigation crisis. *See* Georgine v. Amchem Products, Inc., 83 F.3d 610, 618, and n.2 (C.A.3 1996) (citing commentary). A United States Judicial Conference Ad Hoc Committee on Asbestos Litigation ... described facets of the problem in a 1991 report:

"[This] is a tale of danger known in the 1930s, exposure inflicted upon millions of Americans in the 1940s and 1950s, injuries that began to take their toll in the 1960s, and a flood of lawsuits beginning in the 1970s. On the basis of past and current filing data, and because of a latency period that may last as long as 40 years for some asbestos related diseases, a continuing stream of claims can be expected. The final toll of asbestos related injuries is unknown. Predictions have been made of 200,000 asbestos disease deaths before the year 2000 and as many as 265,000 by the year 2015.

The most objectionable aspects of asbestos litigation can be briefly summarized: dockets in both federal and state courts continue to grow; long delays are routine; trials are too long; the same issues are litigated over and over; transaction costs exceed the victims' recovery by nearly two to one; exhaustion of assets threatens and distorts the process; and future claimants may lose altogether." Report of The Judicial Conference Ad Hoc Committee on Asbestos Litigation 2-3 (Mar. 1991).

Real reform, the report concluded, required federal legislation creating a national asbestos dispute-resolution scheme. *See id.*, at 3, 27-35. ... To this date, no congressional response has emerged.

In the face of legislative inaction, the federal courts—lacking authority to replace state tort systems with a national toxic tort compensation regime—endeavored to work with the procedural tools available to improve management of federal asbestos litigation. ... [T]he Judicial Panel on Multidistrict Litigation (MDL Panel) ... transferred all asbestos cases then filed, but not yet on trial in federal courts to a single district, the United States District Court for the Eastern District of Pennsylvania. ... The [transfer] order aggregated pending cases only; no authority resides in the MDL Panel to license for consolidated proceedings claims not yet filed.

B

After the consolidation, attorneys for plaintiffs and defendants formed separate steering committees and began settlement negotiations. Ronald L. Motley and Gene Locks—later appointed, along with Motley's law partner Joseph F. Rice, to represent the plaintiff class in this action—cochaired the Plaintiffs' Steering Committee. Counsel for the Center for Claims Resolution (CCR), the consortium of 20 former asbestos manufacturers now before us as petitioners, participated in the Defendants' Steering Committee. Although the MDL Panel order collected, transferred, and consolidated only cases already commenced in federal courts, settlement negotiations included efforts to find a "means of resolving . . . future cases." Record, Doc. 3, p.2 (Memorandum in Support of Joint Motion for Conditional Class Certification). . . .

In November 1991, the Defendants' Steering Committee made an offer designed to settle all pending and future asbestos cases by providing a fund for distribution by plaintiffs' counsel among asbestos-exposed individuals. The Plaintiffs' Steering Committee rejected this offer, and negotiations fell apart. CCR, however, continued to pursue "a workable administrative system for the handling of future claims."

To that end, CCR counsel approached the lawyers who had headed the Plaintiffs' Steering Committee in the unsuccessful negotiations, and a new round of negotiations began; that round yielded the mass settlement agreement now in controversy. At the time, the former heads of the Plaintiffs' Steering Committee represented thousands of plaintiffs with then-pending asbestos-related claims—claimants the parties to this suit call "inventory" plaintiffs. CCR indicated in these discussions that it would resist settlement of inventory cases absent "some kind of protection for the future."

Settlement talks thus concentrated on devising an administrative scheme for disposition of asbestos claims not yet in litigation. In these negotiations, counsel for masses of inventory plaintiffs endeavored to represent the interests of the anticipated future claimants, although those lawyers then had no attorney-client relationship with such claimants.

Once negotiations seemed likely to produce an agreement purporting to bind potential plaintiffs, CCR agreed to settle, through separate agreements [outside the parameters of the present class action], the claims of plaintiffs who had already filed asbestos-related lawsuits. In one such agreement, CCR defendants promised to pay more than $200 million to gain release of the claims of numerous inventory plaintiffs. After settling the inventory claims, CCR, together with the plaintiffs' lawyers CCR had approached, launched this case, exclusively involving persons outside the MDL Panel's province—plaintiffs without already pending lawsuits.[3]

C

The class action thus instituted was not intended to be litigated. Rather, within the space of a single day, January 15, 1993, the settling parties—CCR defendants and the representatives of the plaintiff class described below—presented to the District Court a complaint, an answer, a proposed settlement agreement, and a joint motion for conditional class certification.

_____
3. It is basic to comprehension of this proceeding to notice that no transferred case is included in the settlement at issue, and no case covered by the settlement existed as a civil action at the time of the MDL Panel transfer.

The complaint identified nine lead plaintiffs, designating them and members of their families as representatives of a class comprising all persons who had not filed an asbestos-related lawsuit against a CCR defendant as of the date the class action commenced, but who (1) had been exposed — occupationally or through the occupational exposure of a spouse or household member — to asbestos or products containing asbestos attributable to a CCR defendant [in the United States], or (2) whose spouse or family member had been so exposed. Untold numbers of individuals may fall within this description. All named plaintiffs alleged that they or a member of their family had been exposed to asbestos-containing products of CCR defendants. More than half of the named plaintiffs alleged that they or their family members had already suffered various physical injuries as a result of the exposure. The others alleged that they had not yet manifested any asbestos-related condition. The complaint delineated no subclasses; all named plaintiffs were designated as representatives of the class as a whole.

The complaint invoked the District Court's diversity jurisdiction and asserted various state-law claims for relief, including (1) negligent failure to warn, (2) strict liability, (3) breach of express and implied warranty, (4) negligent infliction of emotional distress, (5) enhanced risk of disease, (6) medical monitoring, and (7) civil conspiracy. Each plaintiff requested unspecified damages in excess of $100,000. CCR defendants' answer denied the principal allegations of the complaint and asserted 11 affirmative defenses.

A stipulation of settlement accompanied the pleadings; it proposed to settle, and to preclude nearly all class members from litigating against CCR companies, all claims not filed before January 15, 1993, involving compensation for present and future asbestos-related personal injury or death. An exhaustive document exceeding 100 pages, the stipulation presents in detail an administrative mechanism and a schedule of payments to compensate class members who meet defined asbestos-exposure and medical requirements. The stipulation describes four categories of compensable disease: mesothelioma; lung cancer; certain "other cancers" (colon-rectal, laryngeal, esophageal, and stomach cancer); and "non-malignant conditions" (asbestosis and bilateral pleural thickening). Persons with "exceptional" medical claims — claims that do not fall within the four described diagnostic categories — may in some instances qualify for compensation, but the settlement caps the number of "exceptional" claims CCR must cover.

For each qualifying disease category, the stipulation specifies the range of damages CCR will pay to qualifying claimants. Payments under the settlement are not adjustable for inflation. Mesothelioma claimants — the most highly compensated category — are scheduled to receive between $20,000 and $200,000. The stipulation provides that CCR is to propose the level of compensation within the prescribed ranges; it also establishes procedures to resolve disputes over medical diagnoses and levels of compensation.

Compensation above the fixed ranges may be obtained for "extraordinary" claims. But the settlement places both numerical caps and dollar limits on such claims.[6] The settlement also imposes "case flow maximums," which cap the number of claims payable for each disease in a given year.

Class members are to receive no compensation for certain kinds of claims, even if otherwise applicable state law recognizes such claims. Claims that garner no compensation under the settlement include claims by family members of asbestos-exposed individuals for loss of consortium, and claims by so-called "exposure-only" plaintiffs for increased risk of cancer, fear of future asbestos-related injury, and medical monitoring. "Pleural" claims, which might be asserted by persons with asbestos-related plaques on their lungs but no accompanying physical impairment, are also excluded. Although not entitled to present compensation, exposure-only claimants and pleural claimants may qualify for benefits when and if they develop a compensable disease and meet the relevant exposure and medical criteria. Defendants forgo defenses to liability, including statute of limitations pleas.

Class members, in the main, are bound by the settlement in perpetuity, while CCR defendants may choose to withdraw from the settlement after ten years. A small number of class members — only a few per year — may reject the settlement and pursue their claims in court. Those permitted to exercise this option, however, may not assert any punitive damages claim or any claim for increased risk of cancer. Aspects of the administration of the settlement are to be monitored by the AFL-CIO and class counsel. Class counsel are to receive attorneys' fees in an amount to be approved by the District Court.

D

. . . Objectors raised numerous challenges to the settlement. They urged that the settlement unfairly disadvantaged those without currently compensable conditions in that it failed to adjust for inflation or to account for changes, over time, in medical understanding. They maintained that compensation levels were intolerably low in comparison to awards available in tort litigation or payments received by the inventory plaintiffs. And they objected to the absence of any compensation for certain claims, for example, medical monitoring, compensable under the tort law of several States. Rejecting these and all other objections, Judge Reed concluded that the settlement terms were fair and had been negotiated without collusion. He also found that adequate notice had been given to class members and that final class certification under Rule 23(b)(3) was appropriate. . . .

---

6. Only three percent of the qualified mesothelioma, lung cancer, and "other cancer" claims, and only one percent of the total number of qualified "non-malignant condition" claims can be designated "extraordinary." Average expenditures are specified for claims found "extraordinary"; mesothelioma victims with compensable extraordinary claims, for example, receive, on average, $300,000.

The objectors appealed. The United States Court of Appeals for the Third Circuit vacated the certification, holding that the requirements of Rule 23 had not been satisfied. *See* 83 F.3d 610 (1996)....

III

... Rule 23(a) states four threshold requirements applicable to all class actions: (1) numerosity (a "class [so large] that joinder of all members is impracticable"); (2) commonality ("questions of law or fact common to the class"); (3) typicality (named parties' claims or defenses "are typical ... of the class"); and (4) adequacy of representation (representatives "will fairly and adequately protect the interests of the class").

In addition to satisfying Rule 23(a)'s prerequisites, parties seeking class certification must show that the action is maintainable under Rule 23(b)(1), (2), or (3)....

In the 1966 class-action amendments, Rule 23(b)(3), the category at issue here, was "the most adventuresome" innovation....

Framed for situations in which "class-action treatment is not as clearly called for" as it is in Rule 23(b)(1) and (b)(2) situations, Rule 23(b)(3) permits certification where class suit "may nevertheless be convenient and desirable." Adv. Comm. Notes, 28 U.S.C. App., p.697. To qualify for certification under Rule 23(b)(3), a class must meet two requirements beyond the Rule 23(a) prerequisites: Common questions must "predominate over any questions affecting only individual members"; and class resolution must be "superior to other available methods for the fair and efficient adjudication of the controversy." In adding "predominance" and "superiority" to the qualification-for-certification list, the Advisory Committee sought to cover cases "in which a class action would achieve economies of time, effort, and expense, and promote ... uniformity of decision as to persons similarly situated, without sacrificing procedural fairness or bringing about other undesirable results." *Ibid*....

Rule 23(b)(3) includes a nonexhaustive list of factors pertinent to a court's "close look" at the predominance and superiority criteria:

> (A) the interest of members of the class in individually controlling the prosecution or defense of separate actions; (B) the extent and nature of any litigation concerning the controversy already commenced by or against members of the class; (C) the desirability or undesirability of concentrating the litigation of the claims in the particular forum; (D) the difficulties likely to be encountered in the management of a class action.

In setting out these factors, the Advisory Committee for the 1966 reform anticipated that in each case, courts would "consider the interests of individual members of the class in controlling their own litigations and carrying them on as they see fit." Adv. Comm. Notes, 28 U.S.C. App., p.698. They elaborated:

> "The interests of individuals in conducting separate lawsuits may be so strong as to call for denial of a class action. On the other hand, these interests may be theoretic rather than practical; the class may have a high degree

of cohesion and prosecution of the action through representatives would be quite unobjectionable, or the amounts at stake for individuals may be so small that separate suits would be impracticable." *Ibid.*

As the Third Circuit observed in the instant case: "Each plaintiff [in an action involving claims for personal injury and death] has a significant interest in individually controlling the prosecution of [his case]"; each "ha[s] a substantial stake in making individual decisions on whether and when to settle." 83 F.3d, at 633.

While the text of Rule 23(b)(3) does not exclude from certification cases in which individual damages run high, the Advisory Committee had dominantly in mind vindication of "the rights of groups of people who individually would be without effective strength to bring their opponents into court at all." Kaplan, Prefatory Note 497. As concisely recalled in a recent Seventh Circuit opinion:

> "The policy at the very core of the class action mechanism is to overcome the problem that small recoveries do not provide the incentive for any individual to bring a solo action prosecuting his or her rights. A class action solves this problem by aggregating the relatively paltry potential recoveries into something worth someone's (usually an attorney's) labor." Mace v. Van Ru Credit Corp., 109 F.3d 338, 344 (1997).

To alert class members to their right to "opt out" of a (b)(3) class, Rule 23 instructs the court to "direct to the members of the class the best notice practicable under the circumstances, including individual notice to all members who can be identified through reasonable effort." Fed. Rule Civ. Proc. 23(c)(2).

No class action may be "dismissed or compromised without [court] approval," preceded by notice to class members. Fed. Rule Civ. Proc. 23(e). The Advisory Committee's sole comment on this terse final provision of Rule 23 restates the Rule's instruction without elaboration: "Subdivision (e) requires approval of the court, after notice, for the dismissal or compromise of any class action." Adv. Comm. Notes, 28 U.S.C. App., p.699.

In the decades since the 1966 revision of Rule 23, class-action practice has become ever more "adventuresome" as a means of coping with claims too numerous to secure their "just, speedy, and inexpensive determination" one by one. . . .

Among current applications of Rule 23(b)(3), the "settlement only" class has become a stock device. Although all Federal Circuits recognize the utility of Rule 23(b)(3) settlement classes, courts have divided on the extent to which a proffered settlement affects court surveillance under Rule 23's certification criteria. . . .

IV

We granted review to decide the role settlement may play, under existing Rule 23, in determining the propriety of class certification. The Third Circuit's opinion stated that each of the requirements of Rule 23(a)

and (b)(3) "must be satisfied without taking into account the settlement."
83 F.3d, at 626 (quoting *GM Trucks*, 55 F.3d, at 799). That statement, petitioners urge, is incorrect.

We agree with petitioners to this limited extent: Settlement is relevant to a class certification. The Third Circuit's opinion bears modification
in that respect. But, as we earlier observed, the Court of Appeals in fact
did not ignore the settlement; instead, that court homed in on settlement
terms in explaining why it found the absentees' interests inadequately
represented. The Third Circuit's close inspection of the settlement in that
regard was altogether proper.

Confronted with a request for settlement-only class certification, a
district court need not inquire whether the case, if tried, would present
intractable management problems, *see* Fed. Rule Civ. Proc. 23(b)(3)(D),
for the proposal is that there be no trial. But other specifications of the
Rule — those designed to protect absentees by blocking unwarranted or
overbroad class definitions — demand undiluted, even heightened, attention in the settlement context. Such attention is of vital importance, for a
court asked to certify a settlement class will lack the opportunity, present
when a case is litigated, to adjust the class, informed by the proceedings as
they unfold. *See* Rule 23(c), (d).[16]

And, of overriding importance, courts must be mindful that the Rule
as now composed sets the requirements they are bound to enforce. . . .
Courts are not free to amend a rule outside the process Congress ordered,
a process properly tuned to the instruction that rules of procedure "shall
not abridge . . . any substantive right." [28 U.S.C. § 2072(b).]

Rule 23(e), on settlement of class actions, reads in its entirety: "A class
action shall not be dismissed or compromised without the approval of the
court, and notice of the proposed dismissal or compromise shall be given
to all members of the class in such manner as the court directs." This
prescription was designed to function as an additional requirement, not a
superseding direction, for the "class action" to which Rule 23(e) refers is
one qualified for certification under Rule 23(a) and (b). *Cf. Eisen*, 417 U.S.,
at 176-177, 94 S. Ct., at 2151-2152 (adequate representation does not
eliminate additional requirement to provide notice). Subdivisions (a) and
(b) focus court attention on whether a proposed class has sufficient unity
so that absent members can fairly be bound by decisions of class representatives. That dominant concern persists when settlement, rather than trial,
is proposed.

The safeguards provided by the Rule 23(a) and (b) class-qualifying
criteria, we emphasize, are not impractical impediments — checks shorn
of utility — in the settlement-class context. First, the standards set for the
protection of absent class members serve to inhibit appraisals of the

---

16. Portions of the opinion dissenting in part appear to assume that settlement
counts only one way — in favor of certification. To the extent that is the dissent's meaning,
we disagree. Settlement, though a relevant factor, does not inevitably signal that class-
action certification should be granted more readily than it would be were the case to be
litigated. For reasons the Third Circuit aired, proposed settlement classes sometimes
warrant more, not less, caution on the question of certification.

chancellor's foot kind — class certifications dependent upon the court's gestalt judgment or overarching impression of the settlement's fairness.

Second, if a fairness inquiry under Rule 23(e) controlled certification, eclipsing Rule 23(a) and (b), and permitting class designation despite the impossibility of litigation, both class counsel and court would be disarmed. Class counsel confined to settlement negotiations could not use the threat of litigation to press for a better offer, *see* Coffee, *Class Wars: The Dilemma of the Mass Tort Class Action*, 95 Colum. L. Rev. 1343, 1379-1380 (1995), and the court would face a bargain proffered for its approval without benefit of adversarial investigation, *see*, e.g., Kamilewicz v. Bank of Boston Corp., 100 F.3d 1348, 1352 (C.A.7 1996) (Easterbrook, J., dissenting from denial of rehearing en banc) (parties "may even put one over on the court, in a staged performance"), *cert. denied*, 520 U.S. 1204, 117 S. Ct. 1569, 137 L. Ed. 2d 714 (1997).

Federal courts, in any case, lack authority to substitute for Rule 23's certification criteria a standard never adopted — that if a settlement is "fair," then certification is proper. Applying to this case criteria the rule-makers set, we conclude that the Third Circuit's appraisal is essentially correct. Although that court should have acknowledged that settlement is a factor in the calculus, a remand is not warranted on that account. The Court of Appeals' opinion amply demonstrates why — with or without a settlement on the table — the sprawling class the District Court certified does not satisfy Rule 23's requirements.[17]

A

We address first the requirement of Rule 23(b)(3) that "[common] questions of law or fact . . . predominate over any questions affecting only individual members." The District Court concluded that predominance was satisfied based on two factors: class members' shared experience of asbestos exposure and their common "interest in receiving prompt and fair compensation for their claims, while minimizing the risks and transaction costs inherent in the asbestos litigation process as it occurs presently in the tort system." 157 F.R.D., at 316. The settling parties also contend that the settlement's fairness is a common question, predominating over disparate legal issues that might be pivotal in litigation but become irrelevant under the settlement.

The predominance requirement stated in Rule 23(b)(3), we hold, is not met by the factors on which the District Court relied. The benefits asbestos-exposed persons might gain from the establishment of a grand-scale compensation scheme is a matter fit for legislative consideration, but it is not pertinent to the predominance inquiry. That inquiry trains on the

---

17. We do not inspect and set aside for insufficient evidence District Court findings of fact. Rather, we focus on the requirements of Rule 23, and endeavor to explain why those requirements cannot be met for a class so enormously diverse and problematic as the one the District Court certified.

legal or factual questions that qualify each class member's case as a genuine controversy, questions that preexist any settlement.[18]

The Rule 23(b)(3) predominance inquiry tests whether proposed classes are sufficiently cohesive to warrant adjudication by representation.... If a common interest in a fair compromise could satisfy the predominance requirement of Rule 23(b)(3), that vital prescription would be stripped of any meaning in the settlement context.

The District Court also relied upon this commonality: "The members of the class have all been exposed to asbestos products supplied by the defendants...." 157 F.R.D., at 316. Even if Rule 23(a)'s commonality requirement may be satisfied by that shared experience, the predominance criterion is far more demanding. Given the greater number of questions peculiar to the several categories of class members, and to individuals within each category, and the significance of those uncommon questions, any overarching dispute about the health consequences of asbestos exposure cannot satisfy the Rule 23(b)(3) predominance standard.

The Third Circuit highlighted the disparate questions undermining class cohesion in this case:

> "Class members were exposed to different asbestos-containing products, for different amounts of time, in different ways, and over different periods. Some class members suffer no physical injury or have only asymptomatic pleural changes, while others suffer from lung cancer, disabling asbestosis, or from mesothelioma.... Each has a different history of cigarette smoking, a factor that complicates the causation inquiry.
>
> The [exposure-only] plaintiffs especially share little in common, either with each other or with the presently injured class members. It is unclear whether they will contract asbestos-related disease and, if so, what disease each will suffer. They will also incur different medical expenses because their monitoring and treatment will depend on singular circumstances and individual medical histories." [Citation omitted.]

Differences in state law, the Court of Appeals observed, compound these disparities.

No settlement class called to our attention is as sprawling as this one. Even mass tort cases arising from a common cause or disaster may, depending upon the circumstances, satisfy the predominance requirement. The Advisory Committee for the 1966 revision of Rule 23, it is true, noted that "mass accident" cases are likely to present "significant questions, not only of damages but of liability and defenses of liability, ... affecting the individuals in different ways." Adv. Comm. Notes, 28 U.S.C. App.,

---

18. In this respect, the predominance requirement of Rule 23(b)(3) is similar to the requirement of Rule 23(a)(3) that "claims or defenses" of the named representatives must be "typical of the claims or defenses of the class." The words "claims or defenses" in this context — just as in the context of Rule 24(b)(2) governing permissive intervention — "manifestly refer to the kinds of claims or defenses that can be raised in courts of law as part of an actual or impending law suit." Diamond v. Charles, 476 U.S. 54, 76-77, 106 S. Ct. 1697, 1711, 90 L. Ed. 2d 48 (1986) (O'Connor, J., concurring in part and concurring in judgment).

p.697. And the Committee advised that such cases are "ordinarily not appropriate" for class treatment. *Ibid.* But the text of the Rule does not categorically exclude mass tort cases from class certification, and District Courts, since the late 1970's, have been certifying such cases in increasing number. *See* Resnik, *From "Cases" to "Litigation,"* 54 Law & Contemp. Prob. 5, 17-19 (Summer 1991) (describing trend). The Committee's warning, however, continues to call for caution when individual stakes are high and disparities among class members great. As the Third Circuit's opinion makes plain, the certification in this case does not follow the counsel of caution. That certification cannot be upheld, for it rests on a conception of Rule 23(b)(3)'s predominance requirement irreconcilable with the Rule's design.

B

Nor can the class approved by the District Court satisfy Rule 23(a)(4)'s requirement that the named parties "will fairly and adequately protect the interests of the class." The adequacy inquiry under Rule 23(a)(4) serves to uncover conflicts of interest between named parties and the class they seek to represent. . . . "[A] class representative must be part of the class and 'possess the same interest and suffer the same injury' as the class members."

As the Third Circuit pointed out, named parties with diverse medical conditions sought to act on behalf of a single giant class rather than on behalf of discrete subclasses. In significant respects, the interests of those within the single class are not aligned. Most saliently, for the currently injured, the critical goal is generous immediate payments. That goal tugs against the interest of exposure-only plaintiffs in ensuring an ample, inflation-protected fund for the future.

The disparity between the currently injured and exposure-only categories of plaintiffs, and the diversity within each category are not made insignificant by the District Court's finding that petitioners' assets suffice to pay claims under the settlement. Although this is not a "limited fund" case certified under Rule 23(b)(1)(B), the terms of the settlement reflect essential allocation decisions designed to confine compensation and to limit defendants' liability. For example, as earlier described, the settlement includes no adjustment for inflation; only a few claimants per year can opt out at the back end; and loss-of-consortium claims are extinguished with no compensation.

The settling parties, in sum, achieved a global compromise with no structural assurance of fair and adequate representation for the diverse groups and individuals affected. Although the named parties alleged a range of complaints, each served generally as representative for the whole, not for a separate constituency. In another asbestos class action, the Second Circuit spoke precisely to this point:

"[W]here differences among members of a class are such that subclasses must be established, we know of no authority that permits a court to approve a settlement without creating subclasses on the basis of consents by members of a unitary class, some of whom happen to be members of the distinct subgroups. The class representatives may well have thought that the Settlement serves the aggregate interests of the entire class. But the adversity among subgroups requires that the members of each subgroup cannot be bound to a settlement except by consents given by those who understand that their role is to represent solely the members of their respective subgroups." In re Joint Eastern and Southern Dist. Asbestos Litigation, 982 F.2d 721, 742-743 (1992), *modified on reb'g sub nom.* In re Findley, 993 F.2d 7 (1993).

The Third Circuit found no assurance here — either in the terms of the settlement or in the structure of the negotiations — that the named plaintiffs operated under a proper understanding of their representational responsibilities. *See* 83 F.3d, at 630-631. That assessment, we conclude, is on the mark.

C

Impediments to the provision of adequate notice, the Third Circuit emphasized, rendered highly problematic any endeavor to tie to a settlement class persons with no perceptible asbestos-related disease at the time of the settlement. Any persons in the exposure-only category, the Court of Appeals stressed, may not even know of their exposure, or realize the extent of the harm they may incur. Even if they fully appreciate the significance of class notice, those without current afflictions may not have the information or foresight needed to decide, intelligently, whether to stay in or opt out.

Family members of asbestos-exposed individuals may themselves fall prey to disease or may ultimately have ripe claims for loss of consortium. Yet large numbers of people in this category — future spouses and children of asbestos victims — could not be alerted to their class membership. And current spouses and children of the occupationally exposed may know nothing of that exposure. . . .

V

The argument is sensibly made that a nationwide administrative claims processing regime would provide the most secure, fair, and efficient means of compensating victims of asbestos exposure. Congress, however, has not adopted such a solution. And Rule 23, which must be interpreted with fidelity to the Rules Enabling Act and applied with the interests of absent class members in close view, cannot carry the large load CCR, class counsel, and the District Court heaped upon it. . . .

For the reasons stated, the judgment of the Court of Appeals for the Third Circuit is *Affirmed.**

* [Justice O'Connor recused herself from participating in *Amchem.* — EDS.]

Breyer, J. (concurring in part and dissenting in part) (joined by Stevens, J.)

Although I agree with the Court's basic holding that "[s]ettlement is relevant to a class certification," I find several problems in its approach that lead me to a different conclusion. First, I believe that the need for settlement in this mass tort case, with hundreds of thousands of lawsuits, is greater than the Court's opinion suggests. Second, I would give more weight than would the majority to settlement-related issues for purposes of determining whether common issues predominate. Third, I am uncertain about the Court's determination of adequacy of representation, and do not believe it appropriate for this Court to second-guess the District Court on the matter without first having the Court of Appeals consider it. Fourth, I am uncertain about the tenor of an opinion that seems to suggest the settlement is unfair. And fifth, in the absence of further review by the Court of Appeals, I cannot accept the majority's suggestions that "notice" is inadequate.

These difficulties flow from the majority's review of what are highly fact-based, complex, and difficult matters, matters that are inappropriate for initial review before this Court. The law gives broad leeway to district courts in making class certification decisions, and their judgments are to be reviewed by the court of appeals only for abuse of discretion. . . . Indeed, the District Court's certification decision rests upon more than 300 findings of fact reached after five weeks of comprehensive hearings. Accordingly, I do not believe that we should in effect set aside the findings of the District Court. That court is far more familiar with the issues and litigants than is a court of appeals or are we, and therefore has "broad power and discretion . . . with respect to matters involving the certification" of class actions.

I do not believe that we can rely upon the Court of Appeals' review of the District Court record, for that review, and its ultimate conclusions, are infected by a legal error. . . . There is no evidence that the Court of Appeals at any point considered the settlement as something that would help the class meet Rule 23. I find, moreover, the fact-related issues presented here sufficiently close to warrant further detailed appellate court review under the correct legal standard. And I shall briefly explain why this is so.

I

First, I believe the majority understates the importance of settlement in this case. Between 13 and 21 million workers have been exposed to asbestos in the workplace — over the past 40 or 50 years — but the most severe instances of such exposure probably occurred three or four decades ago. This exposure has led to several hundred thousand lawsuits, about 15% of which involved claims for cancer and about 30% for asbestosis. About half of the suits have involved claims for pleural thickening and plaques — the harmfulness of which is apparently controversial. (One expert below testified that they "don't transform into cancer" and are not "predictor[s] of future disease," App. 781.) Some of those who suffer from the most serious injuries, however, have received little or no compensation. These lawsuits have taken up more than 6% of all federal civil filings in one recent year, and are subject to a delay that is twice that of other civil suits.

Delays, high costs, and a random pattern of noncompensation led the Judicial Conference Ad Hoc Committee on Asbestos Litigation to transfer all federal asbestos personal-injury cases to the Eastern District of Pennsylvania in an effort to bring about a fair and comprehensive settlement. It is worth considering a few of the Committee's comments. *See* Judicial Conference Report 2 (" 'Decisions concerning thousands of deaths, millions of injuries, and billions of dollars are entangled in a litigation system whose strengths have increasingly been overshadowed by its weaknesses.' The ensuing five years have seen the picture worsen: increased filings, larger backlogs, higher costs, more bankruptcies and poorer prospects that judgments — if ever obtained — can be collected" (quoting Rand Corporation Institute for Civil Justice)); *id.,* at 13 ("The transaction costs associated with asbestos litigation are an unconscionable burden on the victims of asbestos disease." "[O]f each asbestos litigation dollar, 61 cents is consumed in transaction costs.... Only 39 cents were paid to the asbestos victims" (citing Rand finding)); *id.,* at 12 ("Delays also can increase transaction costs, especially the attorneys' fees paid by defendants at hourly rates. These costs reduce either the insurance fund or the company's assets, thereby reducing the funds available to pay pending and future claimants. By the end of the trial phase in [one case], at least seven defendants had declared bankruptcy (as a result of asbestos claims generally")); see also J. Weinstein, Individual Justice in Mass Tort Litigation 155 (1995)....

Although the transfer of the federal asbestos cases did not produce a general settlement, it was intertwined with and led to a lengthy year-long negotiation between the cochairs of the Plaintiff's Multi-District Litigation Steering Committee (elected by the Plaintiff's Committee Members and approved by the District Court) and the 20 asbestos defendants who are before us here. Georgine v. Amchem Products, Inc., 157 F.R.D. 246, 266-267 (E.D. Pa. 1994); App. 660-662. These "protracted and vigorous" negotiations led to the present partial settlement, which will pay an estimated $1.3 billion and compensate perhaps 100,000 class members in the first 10 years. 157 F.R.D., at 268, 287. "The negotiations included a substantial exchange of information" between class counsel and the 20 defendant companies, including "confidential data" showing the defendants' historical settlement averages, numbers of claims filed and settled, and insurance resources. *Id.,* at 267. "Virtually no provision" of the settlement "was not the subject of significant negotiation," and the settlement terms "changed substantially" during the negotiations. *Ibid.* In the end, the negotiations produced a settlement that, the District Court determined based on its detailed review of the process, was "the result of arms-length adversarial negotiations by extraordinarily competent and experienced attorneys." *Id.,* at 335.

The District Court, when approving the settlement, concluded that it improved the plaintiffs' chances of compensation and reduced total legal fees and other transaction costs by a significant amount. Under the previous system, according to the court, "[t]he sickest of victims often go uncompensated for years while valuable funds go to others who remain unimpaired by their mild asbestos disease." *Ibid.* The court believed the settlement would create a compensation system that would make more money available for plaintiffs who later develop serious illnesses.

I mention this matter because it suggests that the settlement before us is unusual in terms of its importance, both to many potential plaintiffs and to defendants, and with respect to the time, effort, and expenditure that it reflects. All of which leads me to be reluctant to set aside the District Court's findings without more assurance than I have that they are wrong. I cannot obtain that assurance through comprehensive review of the record because that is properly the job of the Court of Appeals and that court, understandably, but as we now hold, mistakenly, believed that settlement was not a relevant (and, as I would say, important) consideration.

Second, the majority, in reviewing the District Court's determination that common "issues of fact and law predominate," says that the predominance "inquiry trains on the legal or factual questions that qualify each class member's case as a genuine controversy, questions that preexist any settlement." I find it difficult to interpret this sentence in a way that could lead me to the majority's conclusion. If the majority means that these pre-settlement questions are what matters, then how does it reconcile its statement with its basic conclusion that "settlement is relevant" to class certification, or with the numerous lower court authority that says that settlement is not only relevant, but important?

Nor do I understand how one could decide whether common questions "predominate" in the abstract — without looking at what is likely to be at issue in the proceedings that will ensue, namely, the settlement. . . .

The majority may mean that the District Court gave too much weight to the settlement. But I am not certain how it can reach that conclusion. It cannot rely upon the Court of Appeals, for that court gave no positive weight at all to the settlement. Nor can it say that the District Court relied solely on "a common interest in a fair compromise," for the District Court did not do so. Rather, it found the settlement relevant because it explained the importance of the class plaintiffs' common features and common interests. The court found predominance in part because:

> "The members of the class have all been exposed to asbestos products supplied by the defendants and all share an interest in receiving prompt and fair compensation for their claims, while minimizing the risks and transaction costs inherent in the asbestos litigation process as it occurs presently in the tort system." 157 F.R.D., at 316.

The settlement is relevant because it means that these common features and interests are likely to be important in the proceeding that would ensue — a proceeding that would focus primarily upon whether or not the proposed settlement fairly and properly satisfied the interests class members had in common. That is to say, the settlement underscored the importance of (a) the common fact of exposure, (b) the common interest in receiving *some* compensation for certain rather than running a strong risk of *no* compensation, and (c) the common interest in avoiding large legal fees, other transaction costs, and delays.

Of course, as the majority points out, there are also important differences among class members. Different plaintiffs were exposed to different products for different times; each has a distinct medical history and a different history of smoking; and many cases arise under the laws of different States. The relevant question, however, is *how much* these differences matter in respect to the legal proceedings that lie ahead. Many, if not all, toxic tort class actions involve plaintiffs with such differences. . . .

Third, the majority concludes that the "representative parties" will not "fairly and adequately protect the interests of the class." Rule 23(a)(4). It finds a serious conflict between plaintiffs who are now injured and those who may be injured in the future because "for the currently injured, the critical goal is generous immediate payments," a goal that "tugs against the interest of exposure-only plaintiffs in ensuring an ample, inflation-protected fund for the future."

I agree that there is a serious problem, but it is a problem that often exists in toxic tort cases. And it is a problem that potentially exists whenever a single defendant injures several plaintiffs, for a settling plaintiff leaves fewer assets available for the others. With class actions, at least, plaintiffs have the consolation that a district court, thoroughly familiar with the facts, is charged with the responsibility of ensuring that the interests of no class members are sacrificed.

But this Court cannot easily safeguard such interests through review of a cold record. . . .

Further, certain details of the settlement that are not discussed in the majority opinion suggest that the settlement may be of greater benefit to future plaintiffs than the majority suggests. The District Court concluded that future plaintiffs receive a "significant value" from the settlement due to a variety of its items that benefit future plaintiffs, such as: (1) tolling the statute of limitations so that class members "will no longer be forced to file premature lawsuits or risk their claims being time-barred"; (2) waiver of defenses to liability; (3) payment of claims, if and when members become sick, pursuant to the settlement's compensation standards, which avoids "the uncertainties, long delays and high transaction costs [including attorney's fees] of the tort system"; (4) "some assurance that there will be funds available if and when they get sick," based on the finding that each defendant "has shown an ability to fund the payment of all qualifying claims" under the settlement; and (5) the right to additional compensation if cancer develops (many settlements for plaintiffs with noncancerous conditions bar such additional claims). 157 F.R.D., at 292. For these reasons, and others, the District Court found that the distinction between present and future plaintiffs was "illusory." *Id.,* at 317-318.

I do not know whether or not the benefits are more or less valuable than an inflation adjustment. But I can certainly recognize an argument that they are. (To choose one more brief illustration, the majority chastises the settlement for extinguishing loss-of-consortium claims, *ante,* at 2251, 2252, but does not note that, as the District Court found, the "defendants' historical [settlement] averages, upon which the compensation values are based, include payments for loss of consortium claims, and, accordingly, the Compensation Schedule is not unfair for this ascribed reason," 157

F.R.D., at 278.) The difficulties inherent in both knowing and understanding the vast number of relevant individual fact-based determinations here counsel heavily in favor of deference to district court decisionmaking in Rule 23 decisions. Or, at the least, making certain that appellate court review has taken place with the correct standard in mind.

Fourth, I am more agnostic than is the majority about the basic fairness of the settlement. The District Court's conclusions rested upon complicated factual findings that are not easily cast aside. It is helpful to consider some of them, such as its determination that the settlement provided "fair compensation . . . while reducing the delays and transaction costs endemic to the asbestos litigation process" and that "the proposed class action settlement is superior to other available methods for the fair and efficient resolution of the asbestos-related personal injury claims of class members." 157 F.R.D., at 316 (citation omitted); *see also id.*, at 335. . . . I do not intend to pass judgment upon the settlement's fairness, but I do believe that these matters would have to be explored in far greater depth before I could reach a conclusion about fairness. And that task, as I have said, is one for the Court of Appeals.

Finally, I believe it is up to the District Court, rather than this Court, to review the legal sufficiency of notice to members of the class. The District Court found that the plan to provide notice was implemented at a cost of millions of dollars and included hundreds of thousands of individual notices, a wide-ranging television and print campaign, and significant additional efforts by 35 international and national unions to notify their members. Every notice emphasized that an individual did not currently have to be sick to be a class member. And in the end, the District Court was "confident" that Rule 23 and due process requirements were satisfied because, as a result of this "extensive and expensive notice procedure," "over six million" individuals "received actual notice materials," and "millions more" were reached by the media campaign. *Id.*, at 312, 333, 336. Although the majority, in principle, is reviewing a Court of Appeals' conclusion, it seems to me that its opinion might call into question the fact-related determinations of the District Court. To the extent that it does so, I disagree, for such findings cannot be so quickly disregarded. And I do not think that our precedents permit this Court to do so.

II

The issues in this case are complicated and difficult. The District Court might have been correct. Or not. Subclasses might be appropriate. Or not. I cannot tell. And I do not believe that this Court should be in the business of trying to make these fact-based determinations. That is a job suited to the district courts in the first instance, and the courts of appeals on review. But there is no reason in this case to believe that the Court of Appeals conducted its prior review with an understanding that the settlement could have constituted a reasonably strong factor in favor of class certification. For this reason, I would provide the courts below with an opportunity to analyze the factual questions involved in certification by vacating the judgment, and remanding the case for further proceedings.

NOTES AND QUESTIONS

1. *Ortiz*. The Supreme Court revisited the propriety of a settlement-only class action in the asbestos area in *Ortiz v. Fibreboard Corp.*, 527 U.S. 815 (1999). Unlike *Amchem*, *Ortiz* came to the Supreme Court from a Court of Appeals (the Fifth Circuit) that had affirmed the District Court's certification. More important, the settling parties in *Ortiz* did not seek the same type of class action certification as those in *Amchem*. Rather, they invoked Federal Rule of Civil Procedure 23(b)(1)(B), which, by incorporating the historic practices of equity courts, permits federal courts to create a mandatory class action in certain *limited fund* cases. The theory was that members of the class were all seeking to recover from one large limited settlement fund. Following *Amchem*, however, the Court reversed, in a 7 to 2 decision (with Justices Breyer and Stevens dissenting). For the majority, Justice Souter wrote that 23(b)(1)(B)'s concept of a limited fund did not encompass a fund whose limitations were created by the settling parties themselves. Echoing Justice Ginsburg in *Amchem*, he also faulted the class for failing to provide adequate structural protections for different subclasses of potential plaintiffs.

2. *The Aftermath of Amchem*. The years after the Court's decision in *Amchem* have seen a substantial new wave of asbestos-related bankruptcies, an expansion of asbestos litigation to reach additional companies not conventionally regarded as part of the asbestos industry (e.g., corporations that owned workplace premises on which asbestos-containing products were used), and continued delays in the provision of compensation to plaintiffs. Efforts to design and enforce private administrative-type compensation systems for asbestos claims, moreover, have not abated. Instead, they largely have gravitated from the vehicle of "settlement class actions" to that of corporate reorganization plans under a special provision of the federal Bankruptcy Code for the handling of asbestos-related claims. *See* 11 U.S.C. § 524(g).

Justice Ginsburg and Chief Justice Rehnquist have each made clear their view that the asbestos problem "cries out" for a legislative solution. Congress has certainly tried — numerous times. The most recent effort was the Asbestos Victims Fairness Compensation Act, S. 1125, which proposed the creation of a $114 billion trust fund for asbestos claimants, and the simultaneous termination of asbestos litigation by injured persons. The bill stalled in the Senate in the fall of 2003, with some interest groups reportedly claiming that no fund with less than $153 billion would be acceptable. It remains to be seen whether the negotiating process can be re-energized.

VI. TORT LAW AND THE ADMINISTRATIVE STATE: PREEMPTION

The Supremacy Clause of Article VI of the United States Constitution provides that "the Laws of the United States . . . shall be the Supreme Law of the Land; and the Judges in every state shall be bound thereby, any Thing in the Constitution or Laws of any State to the Contrary notwithstanding." By virtue of this clause, federal statutes, as well as agency regulations validly issued under them, *preempt* conflicting state laws (i.e., so long as the federal laws themselves fall within Congress's constitutional powers, and do not violate individuals' rights). For example, a federal statute imposing specific limits on the emission of air pollutants by automobiles would preempt — render null and void — any state statute that purports to impose less stringent limits.

Federal preemption of state law extends not just to state statutes and regulations, but also to tort law. Thus, insofar as federal law *relieves* certain actors of obligations to take care not to injure others, state tort law that would impose liability for a breach of those obligations is preempted. Suppose that Congress, in an effort to reduce transportation costs, authorizes all trains to drive at speeds of up to 45 mph regardless of weather and track conditions, time of day, etc. With such a federal law in place, a negligence suit brought by a person whose car was struck by a train could not be predicated on the theory that the train's operator failed to act reasonably *because he was driving at 45 mph*. To be clear, the imagined statute would *not* free train owners and operators from *all* obligations under state tort law. It would, however, preempt claims predicated on duties that are inconsistent with the rights granted to them by the statute. (Train owners and operators would continue, for example, to be under obligation to use reasonable care to ensure that their equipment is in good working order. Likewise, they would remain subject to liability for injuries caused by other forms of driver carelessness, such as falling asleep at the controls and thereby failing to heed a stop signal.)

Until the mid-twentieth century, the potential for conflict between federal law and state tort law was relatively modest, simply because the federal government played a much smaller regulatory role in the first 150 years of the country's existence. With the post-New Deal emergence of the modern administrative state, the situation has changed dramatically. Congress, as well as an array of federal agencies, now regulate vast fields of activity, including the emission of industrial pollutants, the manufacture and marketing of goods, the use of highways, railways, and airports, etc. As a result, the occasions for federal-state conflict, and hence for instances of federal preemption of state tort law, are today much more plentiful. Moreover, because a finding of preemption essentially grants immunity from tort liability for any claim deemed preempted, it is not surprising to find defendants increasingly turning to the federal courts, including the Supreme Court, to achieve a form of nationwide "tort reform" through the application of preemption doctrine. And so, in the last 25 years, the Court has found itself considering, among other questions, whether federal water pollution control schemes preempt individuals from bringing nuisance and trespass actions against polluters, International Paper Co. v. Ouellette, 479 U.S. 481 (1987); whether federally mandated warnings on cigarette packages preempt failure-to-warn, breach-of-warranty, and fraud suits brought by smokers against tobacco companies, Cipollone v. Liggett Group, Inc., 505 U.S. 504 (1992);

whether regulations as to the design of railroad grade crossings preempt negligence actions against railroads for failure to render such crossings reasonably safe, CSX Transp., Inc. v. Easterwood, 507 U.S. 658 (1993); and whether laws requiring FDA approval of certain medical devices preempt product liability actions alleging defects in those products, Medtronic, Inc. v. Lohr, 518 U.S. 470 (1996). Lower federal courts have faced an even larger array of preemption claims.

Preemption comes in two basic forms: *express* and *implied*. Express preemption occurs when Congress includes within a regulatory statute a provision that specifically declares that the statute is intended to preempt the operation of conflicting state law. Implied preemption occurs when a federal statute regulates an activity that is also regulated by state law, yet is silent as to its effect on that law. Here the courts are left to determine whether, because of an *actual conflict* between the provisions of federal and state law, the latter must give way, not because Congress explicitly said it must, but because the conflict is so direct and significant that one may presume that Congress intended that the conflicting state law be suspended.

Consider the interplay of express and implied preemption in the following decision concerning federal automobile safety regulations. Do the majority and dissent have the same understanding of the relation between the express and implied versions of the doctrine?

Geier v. American Honda Motor Co.
529 U.S. 861 (2000).

Breyer, J.   This case focuses on the 1984 version of a Federal Motor Vehicle Safety Standard promulgated by the Department of Transportation under the authority of the National Traffic and Motor Vehicle Safety Act of 1966, 80 Stat. 718, 15 U.S.C. § 1381 *et seq.* (1988 ed.). The standard, FMVSS 208, required auto manufacturers to equip some but not all of their 1987 vehicles with passive restraints. We ask whether the Act pre-empts a state common-law tort action in which the plaintiff claims that the defendant auto manufacturer, who was in compliance with the standard, should nonetheless have equipped a 1987 automobile with airbags. We conclude that the Act, taken together with FMVSS 208, pre-empts the lawsuit.

I

In 1992, petitioner Alexis Geier, driving a 1987 Honda Accord, collided with a tree and was seriously injured. The car was equipped with manual shoulder and lap belts which Geier had buckled up at the time. The car was not equipped with airbags or other passive restraint devices.

Geier and her parents, also petitioners, sued the car's manufacturer, American Honda Motor Company, Inc., and its affiliates (hereinafter American Honda), under District of Columbia tort law. They claimed, among other things, that American Honda had designed its car negligently and defectively because it lacked a driver's side airbag. The District Court dismissed the lawsuit. The court noted that FMVSS 208 gave car manufacturers a choice as to whether to install airbags. And the court concluded that petitioners' lawsuit, because it sought to establish a different safety standard — i.e., an airbag requirement — was expressly pre-empted by a provision of the Act which pre-empts "any safety standard" that is not identical to a federal safety standard applicable to the same aspect of performance, 15 U.S.C. § 1392(d) (1988 ed.)....

The Court of Appeals agreed with the District Court's conclusion but on somewhat different reasoning....

Several state courts have held to the contrary, namely, that neither the Act's express pre-emption nor FMVSS 208 pre-empts a "no airbag" tort suit. All of the Federal Circuit Courts that have considered the question, however, have found pre-emption.... We now hold that this kind of "no airbag" lawsuit conflicts with the objectives of FMVSS 208, a standard authorized by the Act, and is therefore pre-empted by the Act.

In reaching our conclusion, we consider three subsidiary questions. First, does the Act's express pre-emption provision pre-empt this lawsuit? We think not. Second, do ordinary pre-emption principles nonetheless apply? We hold that they do. Third, does this lawsuit actually conflict with FMVSS 208, hence with the Act itself? We hold that it does.

II

We first ask whether the Safety Act's express pre-emption provision pre-empts this tort action. The provision reads as follows:

> "Whenever a Federal motor vehicle safety standard established under this subchapter is in effect, no State or political subdivision of a State shall have any authority either to establish, or to continue in effect, with respect to any motor vehicle or item of motor vehicle equipment[,] any safety standard applicable to the same aspect of performance of such vehicle or item of equipment which is not identical to the Federal standard." 15 U.S.C. § 1392(d) (1988 ed.).

American Honda points out that a majority of this Court has said that a somewhat similar statutory provision in a different federal statute — a provision that uses the word "requirements" — may well expressly pre-empt similar tort actions.... Petitioners reply that this statute speaks of pre-empting a state-law "safety *standard*," not a "requirement," and that a tort action does not involve a safety *standard*. Hence, they conclude, the express pre-emption provision does not apply.

We need not determine the precise significance of the use of the word "standard," rather than "requirement," however, for the Act contains another provision, which resolves the disagreement. That provision, a "saving" clause, says that "[c]ompliance with" a federal safety standard "does not exempt any person from any liability under common law." 15 U.S.C. § 1397(k) (1988 ed.). The saving clause assumes that there are some significant number of common-law liability cases to save. And a reading of the express pre-emption provision that excludes common-law tort actions gives actual meaning to the saving clause's literal language, while leaving adequate room for state tort law to operate — for example, where federal law creates only a floor, i.e., a minimum safety standard. *See, e.g.,* Brief for United States as *Amicus Curiae* 21 (explaining that common-law claim that a vehicle is defectively designed because it lacks antilock brakes would not be pre-empted by 49 C.F.R. § 571.105 (1999), a safety standard establishing minimum requirements for brake performance).... We have found no convincing indication that Congress wanted to pre-empt, not only state statutes and regulations, but also common-law tort actions, in such circumstances. Hence [a] broad reading [of the pre-emption provision] cannot be correct. The language of the ... provision permits a narrow reading that excludes common-law actions. Given the presence of the saving clause, we conclude that the pre-emption clause must be so read.

III

We have just said that the saving clause *at least* removes tort actions from the scope of the express pre-emption clause. Does it do more? In particular, does it foreclose or limit the operation of ordinary pre-emption principles insofar as those principles instruct us to read statutes as pre-empting state laws (including common-law rules) that "actually conflict" with the statute or federal standards promulgated thereunder? Petitioners concede, as they must in light of Freightliner Corp. v. Myrick, 514 U.S. 280, 115 S. Ct. 1483, 131 L. Ed. 2d 385 (1995), that the pre-emption provision, by itself, does not foreclose (through negative implication) "any possibility of implied [conflict] pre-emption," *id.,* at 288, 115 S. Ct. 1483 (discussing Cipollone v. Liggett Group, Inc., 505 U.S. 504, 517-518, 112 S. Ct. 2608, 120 L. Ed. 2d 407 (1992)). But they argue that the saving clause has that very effect.

... We now conclude that the saving clause (like the express pre-emption provision) does *not* bar the ordinary working of conflict pre-emption principles.

Nothing in the language of the saving clause suggests an intent to save state-law tort actions that conflict with federal regulations. The words "[c]ompliance" and "does not exempt," 15 U.S.C. § 1397(k) (1988 ed.), sound as if they simply bar a special kind of defense, namely, a defense that compliance with a federal standard automatically exempts a defendant from state law, whether the Federal Government meant that standard to be an absolute requirement or only a minimum one. *See* Restatement (Third) of Torts: Products Liability § 4(b), Comment *e* (1997) (distinguishing between state-law compliance defense and a federal claim of pre-emption). It is difficult to understand why Congress would have insisted on a compliance-with-federal-regulation precondition to the provision's applicability had it wished the Act to "save" all state-law tort actions, regardless of their potential threat to the objectives of federal safety standards promulgated under that Act. Nor does our interpretation conflict with the purpose of the saving provision, say, by rendering it ineffectual. As we have previously explained, the saving provision still makes clear that the express pre-emption provision does not of its own force pre-empt common-law tort actions. And it thereby preserves those actions that seek to establish greater safety than the minimum safety achieved by a federal regulation intended to provide a floor.

.... [W]e conclude that the saving clause foresees—it does not fore-close—the possibility that a federal safety standard will pre-empt a state common-law tort action with which it conflicts. . . .

IV

The basic question, then, is whether a common-law "no airbag" action like the one before us actually conflicts with FMVSS 208. We hold that it does.

In petitioners' and the dissent's view, FMVSS 208 sets a minimum airbag standard. As far as FMVSS 208 is concerned, the more airbags, and the sooner, the better. But that was not the Secretary's view. The Department of Transportation's (DOT's) comments, which accompanied the promulgation of FMVSS 208, make clear that the standard deliberately provided the manufacturer with a range of choices among different passive restraint devices. Those choices would bring about a mix of different devices introduced gradually over time; and FMVSS 208 would thereby lower costs, overcome technical safety problems, encourage technological development, and win widespread consumer acceptance—all of which would promote FMVSS 208's safety objectives.

A

The history of FMVSS 208 helps explain why and how DOT sought these objectives. *See generally* Motor Vehicle Mfrs. Assn. of United States, Inc. v. State Farm Mut. Automobile Ins. Co., 463 U.S. 29, 34-38, 103 S. Ct. 2856, 77 L. Ed. 2d 443 (1983). In 1967, DOT, understanding that seatbelts would save many lives, required manufacturers to install manual seatbelts in all automobiles. It became apparent, however, that most occupants simply would not buckle up their belts. DOT then began to investigate the feasibility of requiring "passive restraints," such as airbags and automatic seatbelts. In 1970, it amended FMVSS 208 to include some passive protection requirements, while making clear that airbags were one of several "equally acceptable" devices and that it neither " 'favored' [n]or expected the introduction of airbag systems." [Cited authority omitted.] In 1971, it added an express provision permitting compliance through the use of nondetachable passive belts, and in 1972, it mandated full passive protection for all front seat occupants for vehicles manufactured after August 15, 1975. Although the agency's focus was originally on airbags, at no point did FMVSS 208 formally require the use of airbags. From the start, as in 1984, it permitted passive restraint options.

DOT gave manufacturers a further choice for new vehicles manufactured between 1972 and August 1975. Manufacturers could either install a passive restraint device such as automatic seatbelts or airbags or retain manual belts and add an "ignition interlock" device that in effect forced occupants to buckle up by preventing the ignition otherwise from turning on. The interlock soon became popular with manufacturers. And in 1974, when the agency approved the use of detachable automatic seatbelts, it conditioned that approval by providing that such systems must include an interlock system *and* a continuous warning buzzer to encourage reattachment of the belt. But the interlock and buzzer devices were most unpopular with the public. And Congress, responding to public pressure, passed a law that forbade DOT from requiring, or permitting compliance by means of, such devices. Motor Vehicle and School Bus Safety Amendments of 1974, § 109, 88 Stat. 1482 (previously codified at 15 U.S.C. § 1410b(b) (1988 ed.)).

That experience influenced DOT's subsequent passive restraint initiatives. In 1976, DOT Secretary William T. Coleman, Jr., fearing continued public resistance, suspended the passive restraint requirements. He sought to win public acceptance for a variety of passive restraint devices through a demonstration project that would involve about half a million new automobiles. But his successor, Brock Adams, canceled the project, instead amending FMVSS 208 to require passive restraints, principally either airbags or passive seatbelts.

Andrew Lewis, a new DOT Secretary in a new administration, rescinded the Adams requirements, primarily because DOT learned that the industry planned to satisfy those requirements almost exclusively through the installation of detachable automatic seatbelts. This Court held the rescission unlawful. *State Farm, supra,* at 34, 46, 103 S. Ct. 2856. And the stage was set for then-DOT Secretary, Elizabeth Dole, to amend FMVSS 208 once again, promulgating the version that is now before us.

B

Read in light of this history, DOT's own contemporaneous explanation ... makes clear that the 1984 version of FMVSS 208 reflected the following significant considerations. First, buckled up seatbelts are a vital ingredient of automobile safety. Second, despite the enormous and unnecessary risks that a passenger runs by not buckling up manual lap and shoulder belts, more than 80% of front seat passengers would leave their manual seatbelts unbuckled. 49 Fed. Reg. 28983 (1984) (estimating that only 12.5% of front seat passengers buckled up manual belts). Third, airbags could make up for the dangers caused by unbuckled manual belts, but they could not make up for them entirely. *Id.,* at 28986 (concluding that, although an airbag plus a lap and shoulder belt was the most "effective" system, airbags alone were *less* effective than buckled up manual lap and shoulder belts).

Fourth, passive restraint systems had their own disadvantages, for example, the dangers associated with, intrusiveness of, and corresponding public dislike for, nondetachable automatic belts. Fifth, airbags brought with them their own special risks to safety, such as the risk of danger to out-of-position occupants (usually children) in small cars. *Id.,* at 28992,

29001; *see also* 65 Fed. Reg. 30680, 30681-30682 (2000) (finding 158 confirmed airbag-induced fatalities as of April 2000, and amending rule to add new requirements, test procedures, and injury criteria to ensure that "future air bags be designed to create less risk of serious airbag-induced injuries than current air bags, particularly for small women and young children"); U.S. Dept. of Transportation, National Highway Traffic Safety Administration, National Accident Sampling System Crashworthiness Data System 1991-1993, p.viii (Aug. 1995) (finding that airbags caused approximately 54,000 injuries between 1991 and 1993).

Sixth, airbags were expected to be significantly more expensive than other passive restraint devices, raising the average cost of a vehicle price $320 for full frontal airbags over the cost of a car with manual lap and shoulder seatbelts (and potentially much more if production volumes were low). 49 Fed. Reg. 28990 (1984). And the agency worried that the high replacement cost—estimated to be $800—could lead car owners to refuse to replace them after deployment. *Id.,* at 28990, 29000-29001; *see also id.,* at 28990 (estimating total investment costs for mandatory airbag requirement at $1.3 billion compared to $500 million for automatic seat-belts). Seventh, the public, for reasons of cost, fear, or physical intrusive-ness, might resist installation or use of any of the then-available passive restraint devices, *id.,* at 28987-28989—a particular concern with respect to airbags, *id.,* at 29001 (noting that "[a]irbags engendered the largest quantity of, and most vociferously worded, comments").

FMVSS 208 reflected these considerations in several ways. Most importantly, that standard deliberately sought variety—a mix of several different passive restraint systems. It did so by setting a performance requirement for passive restraint devices and allowing manufacturers to choose among different passive restraint mechanisms, such as airbags, automatic belts, or other passive restraint technologies to satisfy that requirement. And DOT explained why FMVSS 208 sought the mix of devices that it expected its performance standard to produce. DOT wrote that it had *rejected* a proposed FMVSS 208 "all airbag" standard because of safety concerns (perceived or real) associated with airbags, which concerns threatened a "backlash" more easily overcome "if airbags" were "not the only way of complying." *Id.,* at 29001. It added that a mix of devices would help develop data on comparative effectiveness, would allow the industry time to overcome the safety problems and the high production costs associated with airbags, and would facilitate the develop-ment of alternative, cheaper, and safer passive restraint systems. And it would thereby build public confidence necessary to avoid another inter-lock-type fiasco.

The 1984 FMVSS 208 standard also deliberately sought a *gradual* phase-in of passive restraints. *Id.,* at 28999-29000. It required the manufacturers to equip only 10% of their car fleet manufactured after September 1, 1986, with passive restraints. *Id.,* at 28999. It then increased the percentage in three annual stages, up to 100% of the new car fleet for cars manufactured after September 1, 1989. And it explained that the phased-in requirement would allow more time for manufacturers to develop airbags or other, better, safer passive restraint systems. It would help develop information about the comparative effectiveness of different systems, would lead to a mix in which airbags and other nonseatbelt passive restraint systems played a more prominent role than would otherwise result, and would promote public acceptance.

Of course, as the dissent points out, FMVSS 208 did not guarantee the mix by setting a ceiling for each different passive restraint device. In fact, it provided a form of extra credit for airbag installation (and other nonbelt passive restraint devices) under which each airbag-installed vehicle counted as 1.5 vehicles for purposes of meeting FMVSS 208's passive restraint requirement. 49 C.F.R. § 571.208, S4.1.3.4(a)(1) (1999); 49 Fed. Reg. 29000 (1984). But why should DOT have bothered to impose an airbag ceiling when the practical threat to the mix it desired arose from the likelihood that manufacturers would install, not too many airbags too quickly, but too few or none at all? After all, only a few years earlier, Secretary Dole's predecessor had discovered that manufacturers intended to meet the then-current passive restraint requirement almost entirely (more than 99%) through the installation of more affordable automatic belt systems. The extra credit, as DOT explained, was designed to "encourage manufacturers to equip *at least some* of their cars with airbags." 49 Fed. Reg. 29001 (1984) (emphasis added) (responding to comment that failure to mandate airbags might mean the "end of . . . airbag technology"). . . . The credit provision *reinforces* the point that FMVSS 208 sought a gradually developing mix of passive restraint devices; it does not show the contrary.

Finally, FMVSS 208's passive restraint requirement was conditional. DOT believed that ordinary manual lap and shoulder belts would produce about the same amount of safety as passive restraints, and at significantly lower costs — *if only auto occupants would buckle up.* Thus, FMVSS 208 provided for rescission of its passive restraint requirement if, by September 1, 1989, two-thirds of the States had laws in place that, like those of many other nations, required auto occupants to buckle up (and which met other requirements specified in the standard). The Secretary wrote that "coverage of a large percentage of the American people by seatbelt laws that are enforced would largely negate the incremental increase in safety to be expected from an automatic protection requirement." [Cited authority omitted.] In the end, two-thirds of the States did not enact mandatory buckle-up laws, and the passive restraint requirement remained in effect.

In sum, as DOT now tells us through the Solicitor General, the 1984 version of FMVSS 208 "embodies the Secretary's policy judgment that safety would best be promoted if manufacturers installed *alternative* protection systems in their fleets rather than one particular system in every car." Brief for United States as *Amicus Curiae* 25. . . . Petitioners' tort suit claims that the manufacturers of the 1987 Honda Accord "had a duty to design, manufacture, distribute and sell a motor vehicle with an effective and safe passive restraint system, including, but not limited to, airbags." App. 3 (Complaint, ¶ 11).

In effect, petitioners' tort action depends upon its claim that manufacturers had a duty to install an airbag when they manufactured the 1987

Honda Accord. Such a state law—i.e., a rule of state tort law imposing such a duty—by its terms would have required manufacturers of all similar cars to install airbags rather than other passive restraint systems, such as automatic belts or passive interiors. It thereby would have presented an obstacle to the variety and mix of devices that the federal regulation sought. It would have required all manufacturers to have installed airbags in respect to the entire District-of-Columbia-related portion of their 1987 new car fleet, even though FMVSS 208 at that time required only that 10% of a manufacturer's nationwide fleet be equipped with any passive restraint device at all. It thereby also would have stood as an obstacle to the gradual passive restraint phase-in that the federal regulation deliberately imposed. In addition, it could have made less likely the adoption of a state mandatory buckle-up law. Because the rule of law for which petitioners contend would have stood "as an obstacle to the accomplishment and execution of" the important means-related federal objectives that we have just discussed, it is pre-empted....

... FMVSS 208 sought a gradually developing mix of alternative passive restraint devices for safety-related reasons. The rule of state tort law for which petitioners argue would stand as an "obstacle" to the accomplishment of that objective. And the statute foresees the application of ordinary principles of pre-emption in cases of actual conflict. Hence, the tort action is pre-empted.

The judgment of the Court of Appeals is affirmed.

Stevens, J. (dissenting) (joined by Souter, Thomas, and Ginsburg, JJ.).

Airbag technology has been available to automobile manufacturers for over 30 years. There is now general agreement on the proposition "that, to be safe, a car must have an airbag." Indeed, current federal law imposes that requirement on all automobile manufacturers. The question raised by petitioners' common-law tort action is whether that proposition was sufficiently obvious when Honda's 1987 Accord was manufactured to make the failure to install such a safety feature actionable under theories of negligence or defective design. The Court holds that an interim regulation motivated by the Secretary of Transportation's desire to foster gradual development of a variety of passive restraint devices deprives state courts of jurisdiction to answer that question. I respectfully dissent from that holding, and especially from the Court's unprecedented extension of the doctrine of pre-emption....

I

The question presented is whether either the National Traffic and Motor Vehicle Safety Act of 1966 (Safety Act or Act), 80 Stat. 718, 15 U.S.C. § 1381 *et seq.* (1988 ed.), or the version of Standard 208 promulgated by the Secretary of Transportation in 1984, 49 C.F.R. § 571.208, S4.1.3-S4.1.4 (1998), pre-empts common-law tort claims that an automobile manufactured in 1987 was negligently and defectively designed because it lacked "an effective and safe passive restraint system, including, but not limited to, airbags." App. 3. In Motor Vehicle Mfrs. Assn. of

United States, Inc. v. State Farm Mut. Automobile Ins. Co., 463 U.S. 29, 34-38, 103 S. Ct. 2856, 77 L. Ed. 2d 443 (1983), we reviewed the first chapters of the "complex and convoluted history" of Standard 208. It was the "unacceptably high" rate of deaths and injuries caused by automobile accidents that led to the enactment of the Safety Act in 1966. *Id.*, at 33, 103 S. Ct. 2856. The purpose of the Act, as stated by Congress, was "to reduce traffic accidents and deaths and injuries to persons resulting from traffic accidents." 15 U.S.C. § 1381. The Act directed the Secretary of Transportation or his delegate to issue motor vehicle safety standards that "shall be practicable, shall meet the need for motor vehicle safety, and shall be stated in objective terms." § 1392(a). The Act defines the term "safety standard" as a "minimum standard for motor vehicle performance, or motor vehicle equipment performance." § 1391(2).

Standard 208 covers "[o]ccupant crash protection." Its purpose "is to reduce the number of deaths of vehicle occupants, and the severity of injuries, by specifying vehicle crashworthiness requirements . . . [and] equipment requirements for active and passive restraint systems." 49 C.F.R. § 571.208, S2 (1998). The first version of that standard, issued in 1967, simply required the installation of manual seatbelts in all automobiles. Two years later the Secretary formally proposed a revision that would require the installation of "passive occupant restraint systems," that is to say, devices that do not depend for their effectiveness on any action by the vehicle occupant. The airbag is one such system.[2] The Secretary's proposal led to a series of amendments to Standard 208 that imposed various passive restraint requirements, culminating in a 1977 regulation that mandated such restraints in all cars by the model year 1984. The two commercially available restraints that could satisfy this mandate were airbags and automatic seatbelts; the regulation allowed each vehicle manufacturer to choose which restraint to install. In 1981, however, following a change of administration, the new Secretary first extended the deadline for compliance and then rescinded the passive restraint requirement altogether. In *Motor Vehicle Mfrs. Assn.*, we affirmed a decision by the Court of Appeals holding that this rescission was arbitrary. On remand, Secretary Elizabeth Dole promulgated the version of Standard 208 that is at issue in this case.

The 1984 standard provided for a phase-in of passive restraint requirements beginning with the 1987 model year. In that year, vehicle manufacturers were required to equip a minimum of 10% of their new passenger cars with such restraints. While the 1987 Honda Accord driven by Ms. Geier was not so equipped, it is undisputed that Honda complied with the 10% minimum by installing passive restraints in certain other 1987 models. This minimum passive restraint requirement increased to

---

2. . . . The lifesaving potential of these devices was immediately recognized, and in 1977, after substantial on-the-road experience with both devices, it was estimated by [the National Highway Traffic Safety Administration (NHTSA)] that passive restraints could prevent approximately 12,000 deaths and over 100,000 serious injuries annually. 42 Fed. Reg. 34298." Motor Vehicle Mfrs. Assn. of United States, Inc. v. State Farm Mut. Automobile Ins. Co., 463 U.S. 29, 35, 103 S. Ct. 2856, 77 L. Ed. 2d 443 (1983).

25% of 1988 models and 40% of 1989 models; the standard also mandated that "after September 1, 1989, all new cars must have automatic occupant crash protection." 49 Fed. Reg. 28999 (1984). . . . In response to a 1991 amendment to the Safety Act, the Secretary amended the standard to require that, beginning in the 1998 model year, all new cars have an airbag at both the driver's and right front passenger's positions.

Given that Secretary Dole promulgated the 1984 standard in response to our opinion invalidating her predecessor's rescission of the 1977 passive restraint requirement, she provided a full explanation for her decision not to require airbags in all cars and to phase in the new requirements. The initial 3-year delay was designed to give vehicle manufacturers adequate time for compliance. The decision to give manufacturers a choice between airbags and a different form of passive restraint, such as an automatic seatbelt, was motivated in part by safety concerns and in part by a desire not to retard the development of more effective systems. An important safety concern was the fear of a "public backlash" to an airbag mandate that consumers might not fully understand. The Secretary believed, however, that the use of airbags would avoid possible public objections to automatic seatbelts and that many of the public concerns regarding airbags were unfounded.

Although the standard did not require airbags in all cars, it is clear that the Secretary did intend to encourage wider use of airbags. One of her basic conclusions was that "[a]utomatic occupant protection systems that do not totally rely upon belts, such as airbags . . . , offer significant additional potential for preventing fatalities and injuries, at least in part because the American public is likely to find them less intrusive; their development and availability should be encouraged through appropriate incentives." [Quoted authority omitted.] The Secretary therefore included a phase-in period in order to encourage manufacturers to comply with the standard by installing airbags and other (perhaps more effective) nonbelt technologies that they might develop, rather than by installing less expensive automatic seatbelts.[4] As a further incentive for the use of such technologies, the standard provided that a vehicle equipped with an airbag or other nonbelt system would count as 1.5 vehicles for the purpose of determining compliance with the required 10, 25, or 40% minimum passive restraint requirement during the phase-in period. 49 C.F.R. § 571.208, S4.1.3.4(a)(1) (1998). . . . [T]here is no mention, either in the text of the final standard or in the accompanying comments, of the possibility that the risk of potential tort liability would provide an incentive for manufacturers to install airbags. Nor is there any other specific evidence of an intent to preclude common-law tort actions.

---

4. "If the Department had required full compliance by September 1, 1987, it is very likely all of the manufacturers would have had to comply through the use of automatic belts. Thus, by phasing-in the requirement, the Department makes it easier for manufacturers to use other, perhaps better, systems such as airbags and passive interiors." 49 Fed. Reg. 29000 (1984).

II

Before discussing the pre-emption issue, it is appropriate to note that there is a vast difference between a rejection of Honda's threshold arguments in favor of federal pre-emption and a conclusion that petitioners ultimately would prevail on their common-law tort claims. I express no opinion on the possible merit, or lack of merit, of those claims. I do observe, however, that even though good-faith compliance with the minimum requirements of Standard 208 would not provide Honda with a complete defense on the merits,[6] I assume that such compliance would be admissible evidence tending to negate charges of negligent and defective design.[7] In addition, if Honda were ultimately found liable, such compliance would presumably weigh against an award of punitive damages. Silkwood v. Kerr-McGee Corp., 485 F. Supp. 566, 583-584 (W.D. Okla. 1979) (concluding that substantial compliance with regulatory scheme did not bar award of punitive damages, but noting that "[g]ood faith belief in, and efforts to comply with, all government regulations would be evidence of conduct inconsistent with the mental state requisite for punitive damages" under state law). . . .

III

When a state statute, administrative rule, or common-law cause of action conflicts with a federal statute, it is axiomatic that the state law is without effect. On the other hand, it is equally clear that the Supremacy Clause does not give unelected federal judges *carte blanche* to use federal law as a means of imposing their own ideas of tort reform on the States. Because of the role of States as separate sovereigns in our federal system, we have long presumed that state laws — particularly those, such as the provision of tort remedies to compensate for personal injuries, that are within the scope of the States' historic police powers — are not to be pre-empted by a federal statute unless it is the clear and manifest purpose of Congress to do so.

[Justice Stevens's opinion here reviews and, like the majority's opinion, rejects Honda's contention that the Safety Act's preemption provision expressly preempts state tort cause of action. — EDS.] . . .

6. Wood v. General Motors Corp., 865 F.2d 395, 417 (C.A.1 1988) (collecting cases). The result would be different, of course, if petitioners had brought common-law tort claims challenging Honda's compliance with a mandatory minimum federal standard — e.g., claims that a 1999 Honda was negligently and defectively designed *because* it was equipped with airbags as required by the current version of Standard 208. Restatement (Third) of Torts: General Principles § 14(b), and Comment g (Discussion Draft, Apr. 5, 1999) ("If the actor's adoption [or rejection] of a precaution would require the actor to violate a statute, the actor cannot be found negligent for failing to adopt [or reject] that precaution"). . . .

7. Restatement (Third) of Torts: Products Liability § 4(b), and Comment e (1997); Contini v. Hyundai Motor Co., 840 F. Supp. 22, 23-24 (S.D.N.Y. 1993). *See also* Restatement (Second) of Torts § 288C, and Comment a (1964) (negligence); McNeil Pharmaceutical v. Hawkins, 686 A.2d 567, 577-579 (D.C. 1996) (strict liability).

IV

Even though the Safety Act does not expressly pre-empt common-law claims, Honda contends that Standard 208—of its own force—implicitly pre-empts the claims in this case.

> We have recognized that a federal statute implicitly overrides state law either when the scope of a statute indicates that Congress intended federal law to occupy a field exclusively, English v. General Elec. Co., 496 U.S. 72, 78-79, 110 S. Ct. 2270, 110 L. Ed. 2d 65 (1990), or when state law is in actual conflict with federal law. We have found implied conflict pre-emption where it is "impossible for a private party to comply with both state and federal requirements," id., at 79, 110 S. Ct. 2270, or where state law "stands as an obstacle to the accomplishment and execution of the full purposes and objectives of Congress." Hines v. Davidowitz, 312 U.S. 52, 67, 61 S. Ct. 399, 85 L. Ed. 581 (1941).

Freightliner Corp. v. Myrick, 514 U.S. 280, 287, 115 S. Ct. 1483, 131 L. Ed. 2d 385 (1995). In addition, we have concluded that regulations "intended to pre-empt state law" that are promulgated by an agency acting nonarbitrarily and within its congressionally delegated authority may also have pre-emptive force. In this case, Honda relies on the last of the implied pre-emption principles stated in *Freightliner*, arguing that the imposition of common-law liability for failure to install an airbag would frustrate the purposes and objectives of Standard 208.

Both the text of the statute and the text of the standard provide persuasive reasons for rejecting this argument. The saving clause of the Safety Act arguably denies the Secretary the authority to promulgate standards that would pre-empt common-law remedies.[16] Moreover, the text of Standard 208 says nothing about pre-emption, and I am not persuaded that Honda has overcome our traditional presumption that it lacks any implicit pre-emptive effect.

Honda argues, and the Court now agrees, that the risk of liability presented by common-law claims that vehicles without airbags are negligently and defectively designed would frustrate the policy decision that the Secretary made in promulgating Standard 208. This decision, in their view, was that safety—including a desire to encourage "public acceptance of the airbag technology and experimentation with better passive restraint systems"—would best be promoted through gradual implementation of a passive restraint requirement making airbags only one of a variety of

---

16. The Court contends, in essence, that a saving clause cannot foreclose *implied* conflict pre-emption. The cases it cites to support that point, however, ... do not establish ... that a saving clause in a given statute cannot deprive a *regulation* issued pursuant to that statute of any implicit pre-emptive effect. As stated in the text, I believe the language of this particular saving clause unquestionably limits, and possibly forecloses entirely, the preemptive effect that safety standards promulgated by the Secretary have on common-law remedies. Under that interpretation, there is by definition no frustration of federal purposes—that is, no "tolerat[ion of] actual conflict"—when tort suits are allowed to go forward. ...

systems that a manufacturer could install in order to comply, rather than through a requirement mandating the use of one particular system in every vehicle. . . .

There are at least three flaws in this argument that provide sufficient grounds for rejecting it. First, the entire argument is based on an unrealistic factual predicate. Whatever the risk of liability on a no-airbag claim may have been prior to the promulgation of the 1984 version of Standard 208, that risk did not lead any manufacturer to install airbags in even a substantial portion of its cars. If there had been a realistic likelihood that the risk of tort liability would have that consequence, there would have been no need for Standard 208. The promulgation of that standard certainly did not *increase* the pre-existing risk of liability. Even if the standard did not create a previously unavailable pre-emption defense, it likely *reduced* the manufacturers' risk of liability by enabling them to point to the regulation and their compliance therewith as evidence tending to negate charges of negligent and defective design. Given that the pre-1984 risk of liability did not lead to widespread airbag installation, this reduced risk of liability was hardly likely to compel manufacturers to install airbags in all cars — or even to compel them to comply with Standard 208 during the phase-in period by installing airbags exclusively.

Second, even if the manufacturers' assessment of their risk of liability ultimately proved to be wrong, the purposes of Standard 208 would not be frustrated. In light of the inevitable time interval between the eventual filing of a tort action alleging that the failure to install an airbag is a design defect and the possible resolution of such a claim against a manufacturer, as well as the additional interval between such a resolution (if any) and manufacturers' "compliance with the state-law duty in question," by modifying their designs to avoid such liability in the future, it is obvious that the phase-in period would have ended long before its purposes could have been frustrated by the specter of tort liability. Thus, even without pre-emption, the public would have been given the time that the Secretary deemed necessary to gradually adjust to the increasing use of airbag technology and allay their unfounded concerns about it. Moreover, even if any no-airbag suits were ultimately resolved against manufacturers, the resulting incentive to modify their designs would have been quite different from a decision by the Secretary to mandate the use of airbags in every vehicle. For example, if the extra credit provided for the use of nonbelt passive restraint technologies during the phase-in period had (as the Secretary hoped) ultimately encouraged manufacturers to develop a nonbelt system more effective than the airbag, manufacturers held liable for failing to install passive restraints would have been free to respond by modifying their designs to include such a system *instead of* an airbag.[18] It seems

18. The Court's failure to "understand [this point] correctly," is directly attributable to its fundamental misconception of the nature of duties imposed by tort law. A general verdict of liability in a case seeking damages for negligent and defective design of a vehicle that (like Ms. Geier's) lacked any passive restraints does not amount to an immutable, mandatory "rule of state tort law imposing . . . a duty [to install an airbag]." Rather, that verdict merely reflects the jury's judgment that the manufacturer of a vehicle without any passive restraint system breached its duty of due care by designing a product that was not

clear, therefore, that any potential tort liability would not frustrate the Secretary's desire to encourage both experimentation with better passive restraint systems and public acceptance of airbags.

Third, despite its acknowledgment that the saving clause "preserves those actions that seek to establish greater safety than the minimum safety achieved by a federal regulation intended to provide a floor," the Court completely ignores the important fact that by definition all of the standards established under the Safety Act—like the British regulations that governed the number and capacity of lifeboats aboard the *Titanic*—impose minimum, rather than fixed or maximum, requirements. The phase-in program authorized by Standard 208 thus set minimum percentage requirements for the installation of passive restraints, increasing in annual stages of 10, 25, 40, and 100%. Those requirements were not ceilings, and it is obvious that the Secretary favored a more rapid increase. The possibility that exposure to potential tort liability might accelerate the rate of increase would actually further the only goal explicitly mentioned in the standard itself: reducing the number of deaths and severity of injuries of vehicle occupants. Had gradualism been independently important as a method of achieving the Secretary's safety goals, presumably the Secretary would have put a ceiling as well as a floor on each annual increase in the required percentage of new passive restraint installations. For similar reasons, it is evident that variety was not a matter of independent importance to the Secretary. Although the standard allowed manufacturers to comply with the minimum percentage requirements by installing passive restraint systems other than airbags (such as automatic seatbelts), it encouraged them to install airbags and other nonbelt systems that might be developed in the future. The Secretary did not act to ensure the use of a variety of passive restraints by placing ceilings on the number of airbags that could be used in complying with the minimum requirements....

V

For these reasons, it is evident that Honda has not crossed the high threshold established by our decisions regarding pre-emption of state laws that allegedly frustrate federal purposes: it has not demonstrated that allowing a common-law no-airbag claim to go forward would impose an obligation on manufacturers that directly and irreconcilably contradicts any primary objective that the Secretary set forth with clarity in Standard 208.... Given our repeated emphasis on the importance of the presumption against

---

reasonably safe because a reasonable alternative design—"including, but not limited to, airbags," App. 3—could have reduced the foreseeable risks of harm posed by the product. *See* Restatement (Third) of Torts: Products Liability § 2(b), and Comment *d* (1997); *id.,* § 1, Comment *a* (noting that § 2(b) is rooted in concepts of both negligence and strict liability). Such a verdict obviously does not foreclose the possibility that more than one alternative design exists the use of which would render the vehicle reasonably safe and satisfy the manufacturer's duty of due care. Thus, the Court is quite wrong to suggest that, as a consequence of such a verdict, only the installation of airbags would enable manufacturers to avoid liability in the future.

pre-emption, see, e.g., CSX Transp., Inc. v. Easterwood, 507 U.S., at 663-664, 113 S. Ct. 1732; Rice v. Santa Fe Elevator Corp., 331 U.S. 218, 230, 67 S. Ct. 1146, 91 L. Ed. 1447 (1947), this silence lends additional support to the conclusion that the continuation of whatever common-law liability may exist in a case like this poses no danger of frustrating any of the Secretary's primary purposes in promulgating Standard 208....

Our presumption against pre-emption is rooted in the concept of federalism. It recognizes that when Congress legislates "in a field which the States have traditionally occupied ... [,] we start with the assumption that the historic police powers of the States were not to be superseded by the Federal Act unless that was the clear and manifest purpose of Congress." Rice v. Santa Fe Elevator Corp., 331 U.S., at 230, 67 S. Ct. 1146.... The signal virtues of this presumption are its placement of the power of pre-emption squarely in the hands of Congress, which is far more suited than the Judiciary to strike the appropriate state/federal balance (particularly in areas of traditional state regulation), and its requirement that Congress speak clearly when exercising that power. In this way, the structural safeguards inherent in the normal operation of the legislative process operate to defend state interests from undue infringement. In addition, the presumption serves as a limiting principle that prevents federal judges from running amok with our potentially boundless (and perhaps inadequately considered) doctrine of implied conflict pre-emption based on frustration of purposes — i.e., that state law is pre-empted if it "stands as an obstacle to the accomplishment and execution of the full purposes and objectives of Congress." Hines v. Davidowitz, 312 U.S. 52, 67, 61 S. Ct. 399, 85 L. Ed. 581 (1941).

While the presumption is important in assessing the pre-emptive reach of federal statutes, it becomes crucial when the pre-emptive effect of an administrative regulation is at issue. Unlike Congress, administrative agencies are clearly not designed to represent the interests of States, yet with relative ease they can promulgate comprehensive and detailed regulations that have broad pre-emption ramifications for state law. We have addressed the heightened federalism and nondelegation concerns that agency pre-emption raises by using the presumption to build a procedural bridge across the political accountability gap between States and administrative agencies. Thus, even in cases where implied regulatory pre-emption is at issue, we generally "expect an administrative regulation to declare any intention to pre-empt state law with some specificity." California Coastal Comm'n v. Granite Rock Co., 480 U.S. 572, 583, 107 S. Ct. 1419, 94 L. Ed. 2d 577 (1987).... This expectation ... serves to ensure that States will be able to have a dialog with agencies regarding pre-emption decisions *ex ante* through the normal notice-and-comment procedures of the Administrative Procedure Act (APA), 5 U.S.C. § 553....

Because neither the text of the statute nor the text of the regulation contains any indication of an intent to pre-empt petitioners' cause of action, and because I cannot agree with the Court's unprecedented use of inferences from regulatory history and commentary as a basis for implied pre-emption, I am convinced that Honda has not overcome the presumption against pre-emption in this case. I therefore respectfully dissent.

NOTES AND QUESTIONS

1. *Preemption versus Regulatory Compliance.* As both *Geier* opinions point out, even when a federal statute or regulation does not preempt state tort law, it can still factor into the resolution of a tort suit. For example, an auto manufacturer's compliance with applicable federal design regulations can be presented as evidence that the design it chose was not "defective," or to bar the award of punitive damages as a matter of law.

2. Buckman *and* Sprietsma. In Buckman Co. v. Plaintiffs' Legal Committee, 531 U.S 341 (2001), a class of patients sued the manufacturer of allegedly defective screws used in surgery. Pursuant to federal law pertaining to medical devices, the manufacturer had sought and received approval for the screws from the Food and Drug Administration (FDA). However, the plaintiffs alleged that the manufacturer had obtained approval by submitting false documentation to the agency. A majority of seven held that the plaintiffs' "fraud-on-the-FDA" claims were implicitly preempted because their recognition would upset the carefully constructed administrative apparatus established by Congress for regulating the design and use of medical devices.

In omitted portions of their opinions, Justices Breyer and Stevens disagreed about whether the Court owed deference to the Department of Transportation's own views, expressed in briefs submitted to the Court, as to the preemptive effect of Standard 208. In a unanimous 2002 decision, the Court held that neither the Federal Boat Safety Act of 1971, nor the Coast Guard's considered decision to *not* exercise its authority under the Act to issue a regulation requiring propeller guards on outboard motors, preempted a suit alleging that a particular motor was defectively designed because it lacked a guard. Sprietsma v. Mercury Marine, 537 U.S. 51 (2002). In so holding, the Court paid deference to the Coast Guard's statements that it did not regard its refusal to issue a regulation on propeller guards as having preemptive effect.

3. *ERISA Preemption.* The Employment Retirement Income Security Act (ERISA) sets federal standards for how companies must set up and fund retirement and benefit plans for their employees. It purports to "supersede[ ]" state laws that "relate to any employment benefit plan" governed by the statute. 29 U.S.C. § 1144. Health care is increasingly provided by means of contracts between employers and managed care organizations (MCOs), through which employees are enrolled in a health care plan that is administered by the MCO and paid for by contributions from employer and employees. Because of these sorts of arrangements, the issue of ERISA's preemptive effect has been heavily litigated in recent years. For example, some plaintiffs have sought recovery in tort for deaths or serious illnesses on allegations that an MCO negligently refused to approve or pay for a necessary medical procedure that was covered under the relevant plan. The issue is whether such a claim amounts to a state law that "relate[s] to an[ ] employment benefit plan." The Supreme Court has thus far declined to address this question, although it has addressed related issues of ERISA preemption. *See, e.g.,* Pegram v. Herdrich, 530 U.S. 211 (2000).

REFERENCES/FURTHER READING

Daubert *and Science in the Courts*

Marcia Angell, *Science on Trial: The Clash of Medical Evidence and the Law in the Breast Implant Case* (1996).

Erica Beecher-Monas, *The Heuristics of Intellectual Due Process: A Primer for Triers of Science*, 75 N.Y.U. L. Rev. 1563 (2000).

David E. Bernstein, Frye, Frye *Again: The Past, Present, and Future of the General Acceptance Test*, 41 Jurimetrics J. 385 (2001).

David S. Caudill, *Give Me a Line In a U.S. Supreme Court Opinion Or In Official Commentary To the Rules of Evidence For Admissibility Of Experts In Court, and I Will Move the [Legal] World*, 39 Hous. L. Rev. 437 (2002).

Michael D. Green, *Bendectin and Birth Defects: The Challenges of Mass Toxic Substances Litigation* (1996).

Edward J. Imwinkelried, *Should The Courts Incorporate A Best Evidence Ruling Into The Standard Determining The Admissibility Of Scientific Testimony?: Enough Is Enough Even When It Is Not The Best*, 50 Case W. Res. L. Rev. 19 (1999).

Sheila Jasanoff, *Science at the Bar* (1995).

Gore *and the Constitutional Scrutiny of Punitive Damages**

Theodore Eisenberg & Martin T. Wells, *The Predictability of Punitive Damages Awards in Published Opinions, The Impact of* BMW v. Gore *on Punitive Damages Awards, and Forecasting Which Punitive Awards Will Be Reduced*, 7 S. Ct. Econ. Rev. 59 (1999).

John C. Jeffries, Jr., *A Comment on the Constitutionality of Punitive Damages*, 72 Va. L. Rev. 139 (1986).

Lisa Litwiller, *Has the Supreme Court Sounded the Death Knell for Jury-Assessed Punitive Damages? A Critical Re-Examination of the American Jury*, 36 U.S.F.L. Rev. 411 (2002).

Richard W. Murphy, *Punitive Damages, Explanatory Verdicts, and the Hard Look*, 76 Wash. L. Rev. 995 (2001).

Colleen P. Murphy, *Judgment as a Matter of Law on Punitive Damages*, 75 Tul. L. Rev. 459 (2000).

Victor E. Schwartz, Mark A. Behrens, Rochelle M. Tedesco, *Selective Due Process: The United States Supreme Court Has Said That Punitive Damages Awards Must Be Reviewed for Excessiveness, but Many Courts Are Failing to Follow the Letter and Spirit of the Law*, 82 Or. L. Rev. 33 (2003).

---

* For additional analyses of *Gore* and punitive damages, see also the References/Further Reading section at the end of Chapter 8.

Buckley *and Fear of Disease*

Kenneth Abraham, *Liability for Medical Monitoring and the Problem of Limits*, 88 Va. L. Rev. 1975 (2002).

Mark Geistfeld, *The Analytics of Duty: Medical Monitoring and Related Forms of Economic Loss*, 88 Va. L. Rev. 1921 (2002).

John C. P. Goldberg & Benjamin C. Zipursky, *Unrealized Torts*, 88 Va. L. Rev. 1625 (2002).

James A. Henderson, Jr. & Aaron D. Twerski, *Asbestos Litigation Gone Mad: Exposure-Based Recovery for Increased Risk, Mental Distress, and Medical Monitoring*, 53 S.C. L. Rev. 815 (2002).

Andrew R. Klein, *Fear of Disease and the Puzzle of Future Cases in Tort*, 35 U.C. Davis L. Rev. 965 (2002).

Amchem *and Mass Torts*

John C. Coffee, Jr., *Class Wars: The Dilemma of the Mass Tort Class Action*, 95 Colum. L. Rev. 1343 (1995).

Samuel Issacharoff, *Governance and Legitimacy in the Law of Class Actions*, 1999 S. Ct. Rev. 337.

Richard A. Nagareda, *Autonomy, Peace, and Put Options in the Mass Tort Class Action*, 115 Harv. L. Rev. 747 (2002).

George L. Priest, *Procedural versus Substantive Controls of Mass Tort Class Actions*, 26 J. Legal Stud. 521 (1997).

David Rosenberg, *The Regulatory Advantage of Class Action*, in *Regulation Through Litigation* (W. Kip Viscusi, ed. 2002).

Peter H. Schuck, *Agent Orange on Trial: Mass Toxic Disasters in the Courts* (1986).

Geier *and Preemption*

Mary J. Davis, *Unmasking the Presumption in Favor of Preemption*, 53 S.C. L. Rev. 967 (2002).

Steven Gardbaum, *The Nature of Preemption*, 79 Cornell L. Rev. 767 (1994).

Roderick M. Hills, Jr., *Against Preemption: How Federalism Can Improve the National Legislative Process*, http://papers.ssrn.com/sol3/papers.cfm?abstract_id = 412000 (2003).

Keith N. Hylton, *Preemption and Products Liability: A Positive Theory*, http://papers.ssrn.com/sol3/papers.cfm?abstract_id = 433661 (2003).

Russell Korobkin, *The Failed Jurisprudence of Managed Care and How to Fix It: Reinterpreting ERISA Preemption*, 51 UCLA L. Rev. 457 (2003).

Caleb Nelson, *Preemption*, 86 Va. L. Rev. 225 (2000).

APPENDIX A

MATERIALS CONCERNING WALTER v. WAL-MART STORES, INC.

Sections I-VI of this appendix reproduce documents referenced in the discussion of Walter v. Wal-Mart in Chapter 1. Section VII provides further information about the litigation and discusses additional procedural, substantive, and tactical issues it posed. The authors gratefully acknowledge the assistance of Steven Silin, Esq. and Mark Franco, Esq. in assembling these materials.

I. Plaintiff's Complaint

STATE OF MAINE   SUPERIOR COURT
KNOX, SS.   CIVIL ACTION
                                                       DOCKET NO.

ANTOINETTE WALTER,   *
                                            *
        Plaintiff,   *
                                            *
vs.   *
                                            *   **COMPLAINT AND DEMAND**
                                            *   **FOR JURY TRIAL**
WAL-MART STORES, INC., #1797,   *
an Arkansas Corporation with a place of   *
business located in Rockland, Maine,   *
                                            *
        Defendant,   *

1.   At all times pertinent hereto the Plaintiff was a resident of Rockland, County of Knox and
      State of Maine.

2.   That at all times relevant hereto the Defendant was an Arkansas corporation doing business
      in Rockland, County of Knox and State of Maine and did operate a pharmacy at that location.

3.   That on or about May 7, 1997, Plaintiff's physician, Dr. Stephen Ross, wrote Plaintiff a
      prescription for Chlorambucil (2 mg.).

4.   That on or about that date the Defendant by or through one of its employees or agents, did
      undertake to fill that prescription and did fill that prescription in a negligent, careless and
      reckless manner, specifically included but not limited to substituting a different drug,
      Melthalan, for the drug prescribed by Dr. Ross.

5.   That as a result of the Defendant's actions as aforesaid the Plaintiff did suffer severe, painful
      and permanent, physical and emotional injuries, including an extended hospitalization
      because of the adverse reaction that the inappropriately filled medication caused.

6.   Because of the Defendant's actions as aforesaid the Plaintiff did incur and will continue to
      incur great expenses in an effort to heal the said injuries.

7.   The Plaintiff does hereby make a demand for trial by jury.

        WHEREFORE, Plaintiff demands judgment against this Defendant in an amount which will fairly and reasonably compensate her together with interest and costs.

        DATED at Lewiston, Maine this 12th day of May, 1998.

                                        _____
                                        Steven D. Silin, Esquire -- Bar Roll #2686
                                        Attorney for Plaintiff

II.   Defendant's Answer

STATE OF MAINE	SUPERIOR COURT
KNOX, SS.	CIVIL ACTION
	DOCKET NO.: CV-98-035

ANTOINETTE WALTER

    Plaintiff

    v.

WAL-MART STORES, INC.

    Defendant

ANSWER TO PLAINTIFF'S
COMPLAINT AND DEMAND
FOR JURY TRIAL

NOW COMES Defendant Wal-Mart Stores, Inc. (hereinafter referred to as "Wal-Mart") and answers Plaintiff's Complaint and Demand for Jury Trial as follows:

1.   Defendant Wal-Mart admits the allegations contained in Paragraph 1 of Plaintiff's Complaint.

2.   Defendant Wal-Mart admits the allegations contained in Paragraph 2 of Plaintiff's Complaint.

3.   Defendant Wal-Mart has insufficient information with which to form a belief as to the truth of the allegations contained in Paragraph 3 of Plaintiff's Complaint and therefore, denies same.

4.   Defendant Wal-Mart denies the allegations contained in Paragraph 4 of Plaintiff's Complaint.

5.   Defendant Wal-Mart denies the allegations contained in Paragraph 5 of Plaintiff's Complaint.

6.   Defendant Wal-Mart denies the allegations contained in Paragraph 6 of Plaintiff's Complaint.

7.   Defendant Wal-Mart admits the allegations contained in Paragraph 7 of Plaintiff's Complaint.

STATE OF MAINE   SUPERIOR COURT
KNOX, SS.   CIVIL ACTION
                                        DOCKET NO: CV-98-035

ANTOINETTE WALTER   )
)
        Plaintiff   )
)
)   ANSWER TO PLAINTIFF'S
vs.   )   COMPLAINT AND DEMAND
)   FOR JURY TRIAL
WAL-MART STORES, INC.   )
)
        Defendant   )

        NOW COMES Defendant Wal-Mart Stores, Inc. (hereinafter referred to as "Wal-Mart") and answers Plaintiff's Complaint and Demand for Jury Trial as follows:

        1.   Defendant Wal-Mart admits the allegations contained in Paragraph 1 of Plaintiff's Complaint.

        2.   Defendant Wal-Mart admits the allegations contained in Paragraph 2 of Plaintiff's Complaint.

        3.   Defendant Wal-Mart has insufficient information with which to form a belief as to the truth of the allegations contained in Paragraph 3 of Plaintiff's Complaint and, therefore, denies same.

        4.   Defendant Wal-Mart denies the allegations contained in Paragraph 4 of Plaintiff's Complaint.

        5.   Defendant Wal-Mart denies the allegations contained in Paragraph 5 of Plaintiff's Complaint.

        6.   Defendant Wal-Mart denies the allegations contained in Paragraph 6 of Plaintiff's Complaint.

        7.   Defendant Wal-Mart admits the allegations contained in Paragraph 7 of Plaintiff's Complaint.

WHEREFORE, Defendant Wal-Mart respectfully requests that Plaintiff's Complaint be dismissed and for its costs and for such other relief the Court deems just and appropriate.

AFFIRMATIVE DEFENSES

1.   The Plaintiff's Complaint fails to state a claim upon which relief may be granted.

2.   The negligence of the Plaintiff was equal to or greater than the alleged negligence of the Defendant.

3.   The Plaintiff's claim is barred by the doctrine of mitigation of damages.

Dated at Portland, Maine, this 28th day of May, 1998.

Mark V. Franco, Esq.
Attorney for Defendant Wal-Mart Stores, Inc.

THOMPSON & BOWIE
Three Canal Plaza
P. O. Box 4630
Portland, ME 04112
(207) 774-2500

III. Requests for Documents and Interrogatories

STATE OF MAINE
KNOX, SS.

SUPERIOR COURT
CIVIL ACTION
DOCKET NO: CV-98-035

ANTOINETTE WALTER   )
)
   Plaintiff   )
)
)   REQUEST FOR PRODUCTION
vs.   )   OF DOCUMENTS PROPOUNDED
)   TO PLAINTIFF
WAL-MART STORES, INC.)
)
   Defendant   )

    NOW COMES Defendant, Wal-Mart Stores, Inc., and requests, pursuant to Rule 34 of the Maine Rules of Civil Procedure, that Plaintiff, Antoinette Walter, produce for inspection and copying by the Defendant at the offices of Thompson & Bowie, Three Canal Plaza, Portland, Maine, within thirty (30) days, the following documents:

    1.   A certified, legible copy of any memoranda, notes, correspondence, reports including pharmacology reports, or other documents of any kind, of any hospital, laboratory, clinic or other medical or health facility, by or at which the Plaintiff has been examined. treated, or tested within the last ten years;

    2.   Legible copies of any and all reports, correspondence, memoranda, notes including office notes or other documents of any kind whatsoever reflecting the examination, testing, or treatment provided by any physician, technician, physical therapist, or other practitioner of the healing arts, or psychologist, psychiatrist, marriage and/or sex counselor, or other treating individual, relative to the Plaintiff within ten years prior to this request;

    3.   Legible copies of any report, list, memoranda, graph, correspondence or other documents of any kind, reflecting in any way test or treatment or examination performed on or with the Plaintiff, within the ten years prior to the date of this request;

    4.   Each and every statement, bill, check or other document of any kind reflecting any medical expenses on the part of the Plaintiff, related to the occurrence of which the Plaintiff's complained in this action;

5.   Each and every document of any kind which relates in any way to the damages which are not of a medical nature which the Plaintiff claims to have suffered or incurred in relation to the subject matter of this action;

6.   Any and all notes, memoranda, correspondence, reports, or other documents of any kind, reflecting treatment, examination, testing, or consultation for each and every psychologist, psychiatrist, psychotherapist, or similar health professional, relating to injuries allegedly sustained by the Plaintiff relative to the occurrence which forms the subject matter of this suit;

7.   Each and every document in the nature of a report or otherwise reflecting any of the Plaintiff's expert's opinions concerning the subject matter of this action,

Dated at Portland, Maine, this 26th day of June, 1998.

_____
Mark V. Franco, Esq.
Attorney for Defendant Wal-Mart Stores, Inc.
Bar Roll No: 2967

THOMPSON & BOWIE
Three Canal Plaza
P. O. Box 4630
Portland, ME 04112
(207) 774-2500

STATE OF MAINE   SUPERIOR COURT
KNOX, SS.   CIVIL ACTION
                                        DOCKET NO: CV-98-035

ANTOINETTE WALTER   )
)
        Plaintiff   )
)
)   INTERROGATORIES
vs.   )   PROPOUNDED BY DEFENDANT
)   TO PLAINTIFF
WAL-MART STORES, INC.   )
)
        Defendant   )

NOW COMES the Defendant, Wal-Mart Stores, Inc., in the above-entitled action and requests the Plaintiff, Antoinette Walter, answer under oath the Interrogatories below within thirty (30) days of service in accordance with Rule 33 of the Maine Rules of Civil Procedure. The Plaintiff is further requested to provide supplemental information to Defendant as it becomes available so that the answers may remain true and accurate until this matter is finally adjudicated.

DEFINITIONS

A.   "Person" shall include the plural, as well as the singular, and shall include, in addition to natural persons, any firm, corporation, association, partnership or other form of entity.

B.   To "identify" a person shall mean to state with respect thereto·

    a.   His full name;
    b.   His present of last known business and/or home address;
    c.   His employer and employment position, both now and during that time period which is the subject of the particular inquiry.

C.   "Document" shall include but not be limited to any written, recorded, filmed or graphic material, whether produced or reproduced or on paper, cards, tapes, film, electric facsimile, computer storing device or any other media, including but not limited to papers, books, letters, photographs, objects, tangible things, correspondence, telegrams, cables, telex messages, memoranda, notes, notations, records, work papers, transcripts, minutes, reports and recordings of telephone or other conversations, or of interviews or of conferences, or of other meetings, affidavits, statements, charts, graphs, specifications, drawings, blueprints, summaries, opinions, proposals, reports, studies, analyses, audits, evaluations, contracts, agreements, journals, statistical records, ledgers, books of account, bookkeeping entries, financial statements, tax returns, vouchers, checks, check stubs, invoices, receipts, desk calendars, appointment books, diaries, lists, tabulations, summaries, sound recordings, computer printouts, data processing reports and output, microfilms, all records kept by electronic photographic or mechanical means, and things similar to any of the foregoing however denominated.

D.   To "identify" a document shall mean to state with respect thereto:

a.   The type of document;

b.   Its date, and if it bears no date its approximate date;

c.   The name of the person who prepared it and/or sent or delivered it;

d.   The name of each person to whom it was addressed and/or delivered;

e.   Its nature and substance, with sufficient particulars to enable it to be identified;

f.   Its physical location, and the name and address of its present custodian;

g.   The person or persons in possession or control of the original writing, including their full names and current addresses.

E.   To "identify" an oral communication shall mean to state with respect thereto:

a.   The date and place where the communication occurred;

b.   The name and current address of each person who participated in the communication, and the name and current address of each person who was present at the time it was made;

c.   By whom each such person was employed, and whom each person represented or purported to represent in making the communication;

d.   A complete and accurate statement of what each person said;

e.   A complete identification of each document regarding or relating to the communication.

F.   The term "the incident" as used in these Interrogatories shall mean the incident which occurred on or about the date, which allegedly caused the damage, as set forth in your Complaint.

G.   When referring to non-natural persons, to "identify" means to state the full name, form (e.g., corporation, partnership, Professional Association, etc.), state the origin and principal place of business.

H.   When referring to objects or things (other than documents), to identify means to describe the object or thing by stating its approximate size (dimensions) and weight, color, function, purpose, the materials of which it is (or was) composed, and any and all serial numbers or other identifying numbers, letters, or marks. When the request to identify objects or things refers to a group or class, the identifying marks, letters or numbers of a series, so long as all items in the series are substantially identical.

INTERROGATORIES

1.   Please identify yourself by stating your full name, present address, present employment position, if any, date of birth, the full name and present address of your spouse, if you are married, your height and weight as of the time of the incident referred to in the Complaint, color of hair, color of eyes, Social Security number, and the names, ages and addresses of your children, if any.

2.   Please state each of the addresses at which you have lived during the past ten (10) years, together with the inclusive dates for each such residence address.

3.   Please state the full names, current addresses, employment positions and employers of each and every person who, to your knowledge or to that of your agents, attorneys or employees have knowledge of any of the facts concerning the incident referred to in the Complaint. Identify all documents which relate to each of these persons and the incident.

4.   State the full name, current address and employment position of each person who investigated on your behalf the matters which are the subject of this suit. Identify each and every document which relates in any way to this Interrogatory answer.

5.   Set forth in full the substance of any admission by a party or by an alleged agent of a party, and include within your answer the name of the person making each such admission, the date and time of the admission, and the name and address of all

persons present at the time of the admission. Identify each and every document which relates in any way to each such admission.

6.   Please itemize in complete and exhaustive detail each and every element of damage which you claim or contend is associated with the incident. Identify all documents presently in your possession, or of which you, your agents, servants, employees or attorneys are aware, which in any way substantiates these damages.

7.   Do you claim or contend that you incurred any other damages as a result of the incident? If so, please itemize in complete and exhaustive detail each and every element of damage, other than that referred to in the previous Interrogatory, which you claim or contend resulted from the incident. Identify all documents presently in your possession, or of which you, your agents, servants, employees or attorneys are aware, which in any way substantiates these damages.

8.   If you, or anyone on your behalf, has obtained any statements concerning the accident which is the subject matter of this lawsuit, describe separately each such statement by setting forth the name and address of the person who gave it, the name, address and employment position of the person who took it, the date it was taken, whether it was written or recorded, whether it was reduced to writing, whether it was signed and the present location of all notes, recordings, transcripts or other writings of any kind pertaining to each statement.

9.   If you have made an insurance claim or have been reimbursed by any insurer for any of the losses or damages claimed in this suit, state with respect to each such claim or reimbursement the name and address of the insurer, the policy number under which the claim or reimbursement was made, the nature of insurance coverage provided, the amount claimed, and the amount of each reimbursement made. Identify all documents which relate in any way to the claim or reimbursement.

10.   Please identify and itemize by source, date and amount all expenses, including medical expenses, which you claim in this lawsuit as having resulted from the incident.

11.   Please identify each and every physician, technician, physical therapist, hospital, laboratory, clinic or other medical person or facility by whom or at which you have been examined, tested or treated during the ten (10) year period immediately preceding the date of the incident. Include within your answer the inclusive dates during which each such exam, test or treatment occurred, together with the name, type and/or description of each such examination, test or treatment and the reason therefore.

12.   Please identify each and every physician, technician, physical therapist, hospital, laboratory, clinic or other medical person or facility by whom or at which you have been examined, tested or treated from the date of the incident up to and including the present date; and include within your answer the dates of each exam, test or treatment, and the name, type and/or description of each such examination, test or treatment, and the reason therefore.

13.   If you have had physical complaints of any kind since the incident, set forth in complete and exhaustive detail the nature of each such complaint, including the dates and times of each complaint; and describe the frequency, intensity and duration of each complaint.

14.   Please describe in detail each and every diagnosis you have received from each and every doctor you have consulted to date concerning injuries you may have suffered as a result of the incident.

15.   If you were at any time confined as a result of injuries sustained in this accident, please describe in detail:

    a.   The period of time you were confined in any hospital;

    b.   The period of time you were confined to bed; and,

    c.   The period of time you were confined to your home.

16.   Please describe in complete and exhaustive detail your symptoms at the present time, including the sites and intensities of any pain.

17.   Please describe in complete and exhaustive detail any and all injuries, painful symptoms, and/or congenital defects you had suffered before the incident, and further indicate how recently before the incident you had been treated for such difficulties, by date.

18.   Please describe in detail each and every occupational activity which you were able to perform before the incident that you were unable to perform to any extent as a consequence of the incident.

19.   Please describe in detail each and every activity, other than activities referred to in the preceding Interrogatory, which you were able to perform before the incident which you claim you cannot perform now as a result of the incident.

20.   Do you claim or contend that you are entitled to damages for pain and suffering?

21.   If so, please list in precise detail each and every occurrence, symptom or other factor which in any way supports this claim or contention.

22.   State how the occurrence which is the subject of this suit took place setting forth, in detail, the events in the order in which they occurred.

23.   Identify each expert witness you will call by stating his name, address, employment position and a summary of his qualifications as an expert; state the subject matter of which he is expected to testify, the substance of all facts and opinions to which he is expected to testify, and a summary of the grounds for each opinion he will give.

Dated at Portland, Maine, this 26th day of June, 1998.

(signature)

Mark V. Franco, Esq.
Attorney for Defendant Wal-Mart Stores, Inc.
Bar Roll No: 2967

THOMPSON & BOWIE
Three Canal Plaza
P. O. Box 4630
Portland, ME 04112
(207) 774-2500

STATE OF MAINE   SUPERIOR COURT
KNOX, SS.   CIVIL ACTION
                                                  DOCKET NO: 98-035

ANTOINETTE WALTER,   *
                                       *
                                       *
                                       *   **PLAINTIFF'S REQUEST FOR**
                                       *   **PRODUCTION OF DOCUMENTS**
             Plaintiff   *   **PROPOUNDED TO DEFENDANT**
                                       *
WAL-MART STORES, INC. #1797   *
                                       *
                                       *
             Defendant   *

In accordance with the provisions of Rule 34, M.R.Civ.P., the Plaintiff requests the
Defendant, to produce for inspection and copying in the offices of Plaintiff's Attorney, 129 Lisbon
Street, Lewiston, Maine on or before August 14, 1998 the following:

1.   All documents relating in any way to the filling of the prescription for the Plaintiff on
      or about May 7, 1997, that is the prescription which underlies this complaint,
      specifically included but not limited to all prescription slips, invoices, incident
      reports, subsequent directives pertaining to any policies with respect to filling of
      prescriptions or substituting of prescriptions, or any other documents of any kind
      relating in any way to the filling of the prescription which is the basis of the
      complaint in this case.

2.   Any and all guidelines, manuals, policies or regulations or any other related
      documents which relate generally to the filling of prescriptions or substituting of
      prescriptions used, referred to, made available to, or relied upon by pharmacy
      employees of the Defendant with respect to the filling or substituting of prescriptions
      as of May 7, 1997 or at any point subsequent.

3.   Any and all documents supporting, or anything relied upon by any employee of the
      Defendant with respect to, the appropriateness of substituting Chlorambucil
      (Leukeran) with Melphalan (Alkeran).

4.   All literature within the Defendant's possession, custody or control pertaining to Chlorambucil (Leukeran) and Melphalan (Alkeran), derived from medical texts or other medical literature, manuals, guidelines, manufacturer's literature or from any other source, specifically including but not limited to information on dosage and administration, clinical pharmacology, indications and usage, precautions, adverse reactions, contraindications, warnings, substitution with other drugs, or possible anticipated adverse reactions.

DATED: July 14, 1998

Steven D. Silin, Esquire -- Bar Roll #2686
ATTORNEY FOR PLAINTIFF

STATE OF MAINE   SUPERIOR COURT
KNOX, SS.   CIVIL ACTION
                                            DOCKET NO. 98-035

ANTOINETTE WALTER,   *
                                            *
        Plaintiff,   *
                                            *
                                            *
vs.   *   **PLAINTIFF'S INTERROGATORIES**
                                            *   **PROPOUNDED TO DEFENDANT**
                                            *
WAL-MART STORES, INC., #1797,   *
                                            *
        Defendant,   *

Plaintiff, by and though counsel, requests that the Plaintiff answer, under oath, the following Interrogatories and Request for Production of Documents within thirty days of service upon them in accordance with Rules 33 and 34 of the Maine Rules of Civil Procedure. The Defendant is further requested to provide supplemental information to Plaintiff as it becomes available to them so that the answers may remain true and accurate until this matter is finally adjudicated.

1.   Please state the name, address, age, social security number, telephone number, height, weight, name and address of present employer and present occupation or position of each and every person answering these Interrogatories.

2.   Have any statements been taken from you or anyone else, by you or anyone acting on your behalf relating to the occurrence which is the subject matter of this lawsuit? If so, for each statement, please state the following:

      a.   The name of the person who gave the statement;
      b.   The substance of said statement;
      c.   The date upon which said statement was taken;
      d.   The name of the person who took the statement;
      e.   Whether or not the statement was reduced to writing;
      f.   The present location of the statement and the name and address of the person who is now in possession of it; and
      g.   If you will do so without a formal Notice to Produce, please attach a copy of all statements described in your answer to this Interrogatory if they are in your or your attorney's possession.

3.   Please describe in detail the substance of any admission by a party or agent of a party with respect to the facts which give rise to this action, including within your answer the names and addresses of the person or persons making each admission, the substance of each admission, date and time of each admission and the names and addresses of any person present at the time of each admission.

4.   State the full name and last known address of each and every person known to you, your agents, servants, employees or attorneys who has or may have information with regard to the subject matter of this lawsuit and summarize what you understand this information to be.

5.   Please state the full name and complete address of each and every person you intend to call upon on your behalf as an expert witness in this matter. and, as to each such person, please state:

    a.   In what field this witness is an expert, and a resume of his/her education and experience and qualifications in such field;

    b.   The date, place and form of each occasion when he/ she has been offered as an expert witness and, with respect to each such occasion, the subject matter upon which he/she was called to testify, whether he/she did in fact qualify as an expert, and a detailed description of the technical area, if any, in which he/she is qualified as an expert;

    c.   The name of each organization with which he/she is affiliated and with respect to his/her testimony, the full name and complete address of each person, firm or corporation with whom he/she has consulted concerning his/her testimony;

    d.   The date of publication, publisher, or any text, textbook, article or other published material which was authored by said expert;

    e.   The subject matter in which the expert is expected to testify;

    f.   The substance of all facts and opinions to which the expert is expected to testify and a summary of the grounds for each such opinion; and

    g.   A description of any reports, memoranda, correspondence, notes or writings of any kind in any way related to his/her anticipated testimony and the date, author, addressee and substance of each.

6.   Please state the name and current address of each and every person who you intend to call as a witness and who will testify to the facts.

7.   The name of the pharmacist and/or pharmacy technician or assistant involved in the filling or execution of the prescription for Plaintiff Antoinette Walter at the Rockland Wal-Mart Store on or about May 7, 1997 for Chlorambucil -- as prescribed by Dr. Stephen Ross, and the following information:

    a.   Current address;
    b.   Current employment status;
    c.   Position as of May 7, 1997 and as of this date;
    d.   License status as of May 7, 1997 and as of this date;
    3.   Educational training and employment background prior to May 7, 1997.

8.   With respect to any pharmacist or pharmacy technicians, not included in the previous interrogatory answer, that were on duty at the Rockland Wal-Mart Store on May 7, 1997 please provide the following information:

    a.   Name;
    b.   Current address;
    c.   Current employment status;
    d.   Employment position as of May 7, 1997;
    e.   License status as of May 7, 1997 and as of this date;
    f.   Educational training and employment background prior to May 7, 1997.

9.   The name and current employment position of any and all Wal-Mart personnel or any other individuals who investigated or made inquiry into the specific prescription practices which underlies the Complaint in this case, including but not limited to any state or other governmental regulatory or oversight board or personnel. With respect to any such individuals please provide their address and position.

DATED: July 14, 1998

                                    Steven D. Silin, Esquire — Bar Roll #2686
                                    ATTORNEY FOR PLAINTIFF

C:\FILES\CLIENTS\WALTER\WALINTE3.DIS

IV. Notice of Deposition of Antoinette Walter

STATE OF MAINE   SUPERIOR COURT
KNOX, SS.   CIVIL ACTION
                                        DOCKET NO: CV-98-035

ANTOINETTE WALTER   )
)
     Plaintiff   )
)
)   NOTICE TO TAKE ORAL
vs.   )   DEPOSITION OF PLAINTIFF
)   ANTOINETTE WALTER
WAL-MART STORES, INC.   )
)
     Defendant   )

NOTICE TO TAKE ORAL DEPOSITION OF PLAINTIFF
ANTOINETTE WALTER

TO: Steven D. Silin, Esq.
      Berman & Simmons, P.A.
      129 Lisbon Street, P.O. Box 961
      Lewiston, ME 04243-0961

Please take notice that on Thursday, November 19, 1998 at the offices of
Edward B. Miller, 32 School Street, Rockland, Maine, Defendant Hoyt's Cinemas
Corporation in the above action will take the deposition of Plaintiff Antoinette beginning
at 1:30 p.m. on said day, upon oral examination, pursuant to the Maine Rules of Civil
Procedure, before Bickford & Melton, a Notary Public, or before some other officer
authorized by law to administer oaths. The deposition will continue from day to day until
completed.

Ms. Walter is requested to bring with her copies of all medical and hospital reports
concerning the examination, treatment, diagnosis and prognosis of the injuries allegedly
sustained in this accident, and proof of any alleged loss of earnings and loss of earning
capacity, which may not have been previously supplied.

Ms. Walter is requested to produce at her deposition, copies of all notes,
memoranda, letters, contracts, photographs and any other documents of any kind which
have not previously been supplied.

Dated at Portland, Maine, this 26th day of October, 1998.

[signature]

Mark Y. Franco, Esq.
Attorney for Defendant Hoyt's Cinemas Corp.
Bar No. 2967

THOMPSON & BOWIE
Three Canal Plaza
P. O. Box 4630
Portland, ME 04112
(207) 774-2500

V. Jury Verdict Form

V. Jury Verdict Form

STATE OF MAINE
KNOX, SS.

SUPERIOR COURT
CIVIL ACTION
DOCKET NO. 98-035

ANTOINETTE WALTER,   *
                                      *
        Plaintiff,   *
                                      *
                                      *   JURY VERDICT FORM
vs.   *
                                      *
                                      *
WAL-MART STORES, INC., #1797,   *
                                      *
        Defendant,   *

1.   What are Antoinette Walter's total damages?

      $ _550,000ρ00_

Number of Jurors concurring in verdict   _8_

Number of Jurors not concurring in verdict   _0_

DATED: _2-23-99_   _Robert La. Bradstreet_
                                         FOREPERSON

VI. Consent Agreement: *In re: Henry Lovin, III*

STATE OF MAINE
BOARD OF PHARMACY

In re:)   CONSENT
Henry Lovin, III, R.Ph.   )   AGREEMENT
Complaint No. PHR–148   )

PARTIES

This document is a Consent Agreement regarding disciplinary action against
Henry Lovin, III's license to practice pharmacy in the State of Maine. The parties to
this Consent Agreement are: Henry Lovin, III, R.Ph. ("Mr. Lovin"), the State of
Maine Board of Pharmacy ("the Board") and the Maine Department of the Attorney
General ("the Attorney General"). This Consent Agreement is entered into
pursuant to 32 M.R.S.A. § 13741(2) and 10 M.R.S.A. § 8003(5).

FACTS

1. Mr. Lovin is a licensee of the Board.

2. On or about February 13, 1998, the Board received a complaint from State
Pharmacy Inspector Tonya Dickey, a copy of which is annexed hereto and made a
part hereof as Exhibit A and which the Board docketed as Complaint No. PHR–148.

3. On June 9, 1998, the Board voted to offer Mr. Lovin this Consent
Agreement, in order to resolve Complaint No. PHR–148.

COVENANTS

4. Mr. Lovin admits violations alleged in Complaint No. PHR–148.

5. As discipline for conduct admitted in ¶ 4 above, Mr. Lovin shall, no later

- 2 -

than thirty (30) days after the date of the last signature hereto, pay the Board a
monetary penalty of Five Hundred Dollars ($500.00), which payment is to be made
to "Treasurer, State of Maine" and remitted to Kelly B. Webster, Complaints &
Investigations Clerk, Maine Department of Professional and Financial Regulation,
35 State House Station, Augusta, Maine 04333. Further, effective April 1, 1999, Mr.
Lovin's license shall be SUSPENDED for fourteen (14) consecutive days.

6. In his regular application for license renewal, Mr. Lovin shall submit to
the Board proof of fifteen (15) extra hours of continuing professional education on a
topic relevant to Complaint No. PHR–148.

7. This Consent Agreement is not appealable and is effective until modified
or rescinded by the parties hereto.

8. The Board and the Department of the Attorney General may communicate
and cooperate regarding any matter related to this Consent Agreement.

9. This Consent Agreement is a public record within the meaning of
1 M.R.S.A. § 402 and will be available for inspection and copying by the public
pursuant to 1 M.R.S.A. § 408.

10. Nothing in this Consent Agreement shall be construed to affect any right
or interest of any person not a party hereto.

11. Mr. Lovin acknowledges by his signature hereto that he has read this
Consent Agreement, that he has had an opportunity to consult with an attorney
before executing this Consent Agreement, that he executed this Consent Agreement

- 3 -

of his own free will and that he agrees to abide by all terms and conditions set forth

herein.

DATED: 3/6/99   _____ RPh
                                   HENRY LOVIN, III, R.Ph.

DATED: 3/9/99   _____ RPh.
                                   President
                                   Maine Board of Pharmacy

DATED: 3/9/99   _____
                                   JAMES M. BOWIE
                                   Assistant Attorney General

STATE OF MAINE
DEPARTMENT OF PROFESSIONAL
AND FINANCIAL REGULATION
OFFICE OF LICENSING AND REGISTRATION
BOARD OF COMMISSIONERS OF THE PROFESSION OF PHARMACY
35 STATE HOUSE STATION
AUGUSTA, MAINE
04333-0035

ANGUS S. KING, JR.
GOVERNOR

S. CATHERINE LONGLEY
COMMISSIONER

ANNE L. HEAD
DIRECTOR

February 5, 1998

To: Kelly Webster

Please file a complaint against the following license: Henry Lovin III RPh
                                                        25 Wadsworth St.
                                                        Thomaston, ME 04861
                                                        License No. 2960

The statutes and regulation being cited for violation are:

Title 32:   Section 13784 (1) Patient Information Regulation
            Section 13794 Labeling of Prescriptions
Board Rules, Chapter 16 (1)(B) Patient Counseling Requirements

   The above violations are being cited for the error in dispensing caused by Henry Lovin III RPh on a prescription for Antoinette Walter dated 5/7/97.

Sincerely,

Tonya Dickey RPh
Pharmacy Inspector

PHONE: (207)624-8603 (Voice)

INSPECTOR VOICE MAIL: (207)624-8604

Printed on recycled paper
(207) 624-8563 (TDD)

FAX: (207)624-8637

VII. Supplemental Notes and Questions

Section II of Chapter 1 discussed some of the basic procedural and substantive issues associated with Antoinette Walter's negligence action against Wal-Mart. The notes that follow provide additional information about the suit and pose additional questions raised by it.

1. *What Went Wrong?* Recall that the trial judge, Judge Marsano, entered judgment as a matter of law for the plaintiff, in effect ruling that a reasonable jury would have to find that Wal-Mart breached the duty of reasonable care it owed to Walter so as to cause her injury. The evidence presented at trial pertaining to Wal-Mart's breach of duty — i.e., its carelessness — was minimal: it consisted entirely of brief testimony from Henry Lovin, the pharmacist employed by Wal-Mart. That testimony came under direct examination from Mr. Silin, the plaintiff's attorney:

MR. SILIN:	. . . As I understand it, what you did when you saw [Walter's] prescription receipt, in your mind you thought Alkeran is the brand . . . name for Chlorambucil. Is that what you did?
MR. LOVIN:	Yes, unfortunately. . . .
MR. SILIN:	You went ahead and filled the prescription with the Alkeran drug instead of the Chlorambucil or the Leukeran drug prescribed by Dr. Ross?
MR. LOVIN:	Yes.
MR. SILIN:	You would agree with me, would you not, that that was a serious error?
MR. LOVIN:	Definitely.
MR. SILIN:	That was not the kind of substitution [that] . . . you intentionally or purposely or knowingly [would] make if you were even remotely trying to satisfy the proper standard of care for a pharmacist?
MR. LOVIN:	No. . . .
MR. SILIN:	This wasn't a purposeful substitution you made because you thought it would be appropriate for the prescription that was written?
MR. LOVIN:	No.
MR. SILIN:	This simply was an error that you made, a mistake, a serious mistake that resulted in the wrong drug being given to Antoinette Walter?
MR. LOVIN:	Yes.
MR. SILIN:	As I understand it, at the time this prescription was filled there were various protocols in place at Wal-Mart, and I assume at every other pharmacy on the face of this planet, certainly in this part of the country to help prevent this very

	thing from ever occurring . . . [and] in the literature [from Wal-Mart] it talks about a four-point step process to double check, triple check that under no circumstances is a wrong drug prescribed for a patient; is that correct?
MR. LOVIN:	Right. . . .
MR. SILIN:	[To follow this protocol,] . . . what you need to do is to check the stock bottle against the doctor's prescription to make sure . . . [they match]?
MR. LOVIN:	True.
MR. SILIN:	So would you agree with me that would have been the second error that you did in this case. The first being mixing up the brand names. . . . Then the second mistake was failing to check the stock bottle against the written prescription provided by the doctor?
MR. LOVIN:	Yes.
MR. SILIN:	That's something that is incumbent upon you as a pharmacist practicing safe pharmacy, complying with the standard of pharmacy care to check the stock bottle against the prescription?
MR. LOVIN:	That's correct.
MR. SILIN:	If you had, you would have, don't you agree, discovered the mistake that you had made?
MR. LOVIN:	Yes. . . .
MR. SILIN:	An additional check in your process . . . is for you to . . . counsel the patient, showing her the drug that is prescribed, discussing what it's used for and discussing that in the context of the doctor's specific prescription?
MR. LOVIN:	Yes.
MR. SILIN:	Would you agree with me that . . . if you had done that, that yet once again your error would have been detected?
MR. LOVIN:	It very definitely could have been. . . .
MR. SILIN:	There were three chances to find out about [the mistake] and correct it. All three of those checkpoints were missed by you; would you agree with that?
MR. LOVIN:	Yes.

On cross-examination conducted by the defense attorney, Mr. Franco, the jury learned that Henry Lovin's father had been a pharmacist, and that Lovin, age 51 at the time of trial, had worked in, and eventually taken over, his father's store before moving to Maine and joining Wal-Mart. Lovin further testified that he had wanted to be a pharmacist since he was a teenager. He professed horror at what had happened to Ms. Walter: "Obviously I [have] been in this career all my life. I went into it to help people, not to cause anybody harm."

The trial transcript does not shed any more light on the explanation for Lovin's error. For example, no evidence was introduced concerning Lovin's general practices as a pharmacist, his record for safety prior to this incident, or the performance evaluations that he had received from his superiors at Wal-Mart. One may perhaps infer from the absence of such evidence that Lovin's mistake was a one-off lapse that came about through an unfortunate sequence of errors. Assuming that this was the case, does it affect your assessment of Lovin's conduct? Is it plausible to argue that a jury was at least permitted to conclude that, although Lovin made a mistake, it was *not* a careless mistake?

2. *A Reasonable Mistake?* In fact, attorney Franco made exactly this argument in opposition to plaintiff's motion for judgment as a matter of law (obviously without success):

MR. FRANCO: With respect to the plaintiff's . . . motion [for judgment as a matter of law], the defendant objects. [It would] be unusual for a trial court to take the issue of negligence away from the jury in a case such as this. . . .

The uncontroverted facts of the case are Mr. Lovin dispensed the wrong medication to Ms. Walter. The law is clear that the fact that somebody makes a mistake in the exercise of their duties, whatever it may be, it doesn't have to be just a pharmacist, it could be in the exercise of driving an automobile, it could be in the exercise of maintaining . . . premises. . . .

There are human factors involved in the law that have to be recognized. Mistakes are made everyday. That doesn't mean that a mistake translates into negligence as a matter of law. If that were the case . . . we might as well just rid the system of the law of negligence. A mistake equals negligence basically means strict liability.

We are not here to talk about strict liability. Whether or not this was an acceptable mistake, whether or not this is a mistake that falls within what a jury would consider to be . . . a reasonable mistake under the circumstances, is up for them to decide, not for this Court to decide as a matter of law. . . .

Franco's observation that mistakes are made every day is surely correct. But how does it support his contention that the jury was entitled to conclude that Lovin acted with reasonable care for Ms. Walter's well-being? What does he have in mind when he says that the jury could have found that Lovin made an "acceptable" or "reasonable" mistake?* What does the trial and appellate courts' rejection of this argument tell you about negligence law's conception of what it means to be act with reasonable care?

3. *How Do We Know How Pharmacists and Pharmacies Should Conduct Themselves?* As indicated in Section II of Chapter 1, attorney Franco also argued that Judge Marsano should grant judgment as a matter of law in favor of Wal-Mart. Among other things, Franco argued that the plaintiff had failed to produce an expert to establish a standard or benchmark against which to assess the reasonableness of Lovin's conduct. Here

---

* For a decision endorsing the idea that the commission of a mistake does not necessarily entail a finding of carelessness, see Myers v. Beem, 712 P.2d 1092 (Colo. 1985). There, the defendant attorney admitted that he "screwed up" in representing his client, yet the state Supreme Court held that the client was not entitled to a directed verdict on a subsequent claim against the attorney for legal malpractice because a reasonable jury could find that the lawyer's mistake was not a careless mistake. To note the ruling in *Myers* is not to suggest that the Maine Supreme Court erred in reaching the opposite conclusion in *Walter*. As indicated in Chapter 1, even superficially similar precedents are often distinguishable. Certainly *Walter* does not suggest that *all* instances of error constitute instances of carelessness. Rather it holds only that the evidence pertaining to Lovin's errors conclusively established that he was careless.

is part of that argument, which was made to the judge without the jury present:

MR. FRANCO: Your Honor, at this point the defendant would also move for [judgment as a matter of law]. This is what is called a professional tort or an allegation of professional tort. A professional tort . . . requires testimony of an expert witness as to the appropriate standard of care attributable to the defendant.

The [Maine Supreme] Court has made it clear in every case in which they have spoken on this subject that expert testimony is necessary as a matter of law to prove malpractice. What we are talking about is malpractice. We can dance around various terms all we want.. But we are talking about [a] professional dispensing a medication. . . .

In the case of a . . . medical professional or a quasi-medical professional, it's the burden of the plaintiff to prove negligence, that is the failure of reasonable care. Reasonable care is that degree of care which a reasonably careful pharmacist would use under similar or like circumstances.

In order to prove the elements . . . of negligence, the plaintiff is required at the outset to establish what the standard of practice is applicable to pharmacists and the pharmacy profession. The record contains no evidence of the standard applicable to Mr. Lovin in this case. The only evidence in this case that was discussed in the context of the standard of practice is the standard of practice that is exercised by Wal-Mart. That is their own practice — their own prescription drug check . . . the four-point check.

There has been an acknowledgement on the part of Mr. Lovin that he made a mistake. There is no question about that. There has never been a question that a mistake was made in the four-point check, in adhering or failing to adhere to the Wal-Mart standard of practice. That Wal-Mart standard of practice doesn't necessarily mean that that's the standard of practice in the pharmacy industry. In fact, there has been no evidence of that. . . .

. . . Mr. Lovin . . . was not here as an expert witness.

Does Franco have a point in noting the absence of any evidence indicating whether other national or local pharmacies follow a protocol like Wal-Mart's? Suppose most of them don't have such a protocol. Would this fact affect your judgment about Wal-Mart's responsibility for Walter's injury?

Obviously, the Maine Supreme Court agreed with Judge Marsano that Franco's objections were off-base, and that the plaintiff was not required to produce an expert to testify whether other pharmacies have in place protocols such as Wal-Mart's, or whether other pharmacists routinely follow those protocols. Its ground for doing so was that certain instances of professional malpractice are so straightforward as to be identifiable by judges and juries without the help of expert testimony as to how prudent members of the profession ordinarily conduct themselves. (It is perhaps also worth noting that, as stated in the Consent Agreement reached between Lovin and the Maine Board of Pharmacy, Lovin's conduct violated Maine regulations as to the proper methods for dispensing prescription medication. The role of regulations in setting standards of care for tort law is discussed in Chapter 6.)

4. *Respondeat Superior Revisited*. Recall the brief discussion of the doctrine of *respondeat superior* in Section II of Chapter 1, under which even employers with reasonable policies and procedures are held responsible for injuries to customers and others caused by an employee's careless performance of his job. Is it fair to say that Franco's arguments in favor of judgment as a matter of law for Wal-Mart, and against entry of judgment for Walter, are really arguments against the application of that well-established doctrine? Do they collapse the issue of whether Lovin behaved reasonably in this instance with the issue of whether Wal-Mart had adopted reasonable policies for the dispensation of prescription medications?

5. *Accepting Responsibility?* Recall from footnote 1 of the Maine Supreme Court's opinion that attorney Franco opened by telling the jury that "Wal-Mart has never denied responsibility for this incident," and that the major issue it would need to decide is how much compensation was owed to Walter. How could he take that position and then proceed to argue that Wal-Mart was entitled to judgment as a matter of law on the issue of breach, and to contest the entry of judgment as a matter of law for Walter? In a concurring opinion, omitted from the excerpt of Walter v. Wal-Mart in Chapter 1, three Justices of the Maine Supreme Court indicated displeasure with the defense's approach:

> **Wathen, C.J.** (concurring) (joined by Rudman and Dana, JJ.).
> [¶ 40] I concur in the result, but I reach that result on different grounds. . . . In my judgment, defense counsel in this case admitted liability in his opening statement when he told the jury that Wal-Mart had never denied liability and that the only issue concerned the amount of fair and just compensation. Having made that statement, he then sought to try the issue of liability behind the jurors' backs. To countenance such a strategy would be to ignore the requirement of the Maine Bar Rules that trial counsel employ "such means only as are consistent with truth, and shall not seek to mislead the . . . jury . . . by any artifice or false statement of fact or law." M. Bar R. 3.7(e)(1)(i). . . .

6. *Trial Tactics: Stipulating and Blaming*. Judge Marsano ruled that a reasonable jury not only *could* conclude that Lovin breached the legal standard of reasonable care, but that it *would have to* reach that conclusion. Yet attorney Silin could hardly have been certain at the outset that the judge would issue such a ruling, or that the Supreme Court would uphold any such ruling. Nonetheless, prior to trial, Silin never retained the services of an expert who could testify that Lovin failed to act as would an average qualified pharmacist. Indeed, Silin never even deposed Lovin. What might explain these tactical decisions? Was Silin being cavalier? Was he attempting to minimize the costs of preparing for trial? Or was he justifiably

confident that, even if he could not obtain a directed verdict, he could convince a jury that Lovin's error was negligence?

The answer seems to reside in the fact that Silin had obtained through discovery a copy of a letter that Lovin had written in response to an inquiry from the Maine Board of Pharmacy.[*] In that letter, Lovin apparently expressly acknowledged his mistakes and expressed great remorse over them. In light of this "smoking gun," and conversations between himself and Franco, Silin expected until just before trial that Wal-Mart would *stipulate to liability*, i.e., formally concede at the outset of trial that Lovin had acted unreasonably so as to cause injury to Walter. Even if no stipulation was reached, however, he believed that the letter provided more than enough information to establish that Lovin had acted unreasonably so as to breach a duty owed to Walter.

Consider the following portion of the trial transcript, which reflects a conversation that was held outside of the jury's hearing at the commencement of the trial. Ask yourself whether the issue of stipulating to Lovin's negligence was something the two lawyers had adequately discussed with one another before the trial.

> **MR. SILIN:** I've . . . thought until probably . . . last week . . . that we were going to stipulate to liability. I still don't know how liability is an issue. They want it both ways, to admit to liability but to still have the jury somehow give them an out. I now realize because they are not stipulating to anything that I have to [sic]. I didn't intend until I thought about [it] last week . . . to call Mr. Lovin to establish the elements of negligence in this case. I have no reason to think he's not going to admit everything in there. I have the [letter] to keep him honest. . . .
>
> **MR. FRANCO:** Your Honor, at this point I'm not prepared to stipulate to liability simply because it's my understanding from speaking to Steve [Silin] that if I had done that, he would fight me tooth and nail over Mr. Lovin testifying at all. I think it's an important part of my case for Mr. Lovin to testify.
>
> **THE COURT:** I understand that quite often logic yield[s] to tactics; that's where we are at.

Franco's stated reason for refusing to stipulate to liability — to guarantee that Lovin would be able to testify at trial — was in one respect well-taken. Rules of evidence bar the introduction of superfluous or irrelevant testimony. Thus, if the only issues left after stipulation as to liability were the issues of the extent of Walter's damages and whether she failed to mitigate them, the judge might well have ruled that Lovin could not testify because Lovin had nothing to say about those issues. Still, why do you suppose that Franco was so anxious to ensure that Lovin would testify at trial? (Here it may be helpful to recall from Note 1 the nature of the testimony from Lovin elicited by Franco.)

---

[*] The Board's inquiry ultimately led to the Consent Agreement reproduced in Part VI of this appendix (pages 1070-1072).

Is there any other explanation for the failure of Silin and Franco to stipulate to liability? Keep in mind that lawyers are ultimately answerable to their clients, and that decisions about litigation strategy, although usually made by trial counsel in consultation with their clients, are sometimes insisted upon by the client, particularly when the client is a sophisticated business with in-house lawyers of its own. Thus, it is quite possible that Wal-Mart instructed Franco not to stipulate to liability. In hindsight, would Franco and/or Wal-Mart have been well-advised to stipulate that Wal-Mart was liable to Walter for at least some damages? Suppose the jury had never heard Lovin testify to his mistakes, and suppose Silin was not able to harp on Wal-Mart's refusal to "accept responsibility" in his opening and closing statements. Would the jury have returned a damage award of the same magnitude?

7. *Settlement.* Stipulation is a method by which the parties can agree to set aside uncontested issues so as to limit the issues submitted to the jury at trial. Settlement agreements, by contrast, provide a method for resolving all the issues in a case, including damages, and for doing so prior to trial, if possible.

Today, most tort suits are resolved by settlements reached at some point after the filing of the complaint and prior to trial. Such agreements offer various advantages to the parties, including, most importantly, the promise of a prompt disposition of the dispute, and the avoidance of often substantial litigation expenses. The latter is of particular value to defendants, but also provides incentives to settle for plaintiffs. A plaintiff's attorney operating under a contingent fee agreement will often stand to recover a fixed percentage of the plaintiff's recovery, regardless of whether it is received as a settlement payment or a jury award. Still, as the litigation progresses, the plaintiff's lawyer will be required to invest additional hours of work in the litigation. Thus, unless there is reason to believe that the jury will render an award substantially larger than a figure at which the defendant might settle, the plaintiff's attorney's rate of compensation (per hour devoted to the case) will decrease over time.

The typical tort settlement agreement consists of a document, signed by both parties, in which the defendant disavows responsibility or liability for the plaintiff's injury, but nonetheless agrees to pay a certain amount to the plaintiff in order to avoid the trouble and expense of fully litigating the dispute. Often such agreements include confidentiality provisions that forbid either side from disclosing the nature of the lawsuit or the terms of the settlement. This practice is controversial, with critics arguing that such provisions withhold from the public important information about dangers facing the general populace. (For example, imagine that a driver is injured when his car rolls over as he swerves to avoid an obstacle. Now suppose that he sues the car's manufacturer, claiming that it was negligent in producing a car that was prone to roll over under normal driving conditions. If that suit is resolved by a confidential settlement, it cannot serve as a warning to thousands of other drivers who might be at risk of injury through roll-overs.) Some courts have recently promulgated so-called "sunshine" rules that mandate that settlement agreements be publicly available.

Given that tort suits often result in settlement, it is worth pondering why no settlement was reached in *Walter*. Indeed, the failure of the lawyers to come to terms prior to trial is in some respects quite surprising. The issues in the case were not complex by the standards of ordinary tort litigation. Thus, while attorney Silin could not be certain that a jury would find for his client, nor could he predict exactly what they would award her, he had plenty of reason for optimism. Likewise, the defendant's lawyer, Franco, certainly had grounds to worry that the jury would find for Walter and that they would award her a substantial sum. So why couldn't they resolve the matter with a negotiated settlement? Silin's first offer of settlement sought an amount in the neighborhood of $250,000. However, Franco apparently was authorized to offer only about $100,000. Despite further conversations during the course of litigation, the two attorneys could not get any closer to settlement. Does the following excerpt offer insight into the settlement dynamics of the case?

Wal-Mart Shifting Litigation Strategy
The Retailer Settles Cases, Prompting Lawyers To Ask, "What's Happening?"

Catherine Aman & Gary Young
The National Law Journal
September 30, 2002

In late July, Wal-Mart Stores Inc. settled a suit brought by Robert McClung, whose wife was abducted from the parking lot at a Memphis, Tenn., store in 1990 and murdered.

For any other company, resolving a horrific case like this would be routine, but Wal-Mart has a long history of refusing to negotiate with plaintiffs. Indeed, for more than a decade the retailing colossus fought tooth-and-nail against McClung and his lawyer, Bruce Kramer of Borod & Kramer in Memphis. When Wal-Mart first proposed mediation this past May, Kramer said he was "more than skeptical."...

The shift in litigation strategy is just one of several significant changes in the company's law department during the past year....

With 4,300 stores worldwide and 100 million shoppers a week, Wal-Mart has more exposure than a Playboy centerfold. According to spokesman William Wertz, the company is sued roughly 5,000 times a year, and, typically, has about 10,000 pending cases. Until recently, Wal-Mart routinely reacted to these challenges by playing judicial hardball.

"They absolutely would not consider settling anything," said Mary Jo O'Neill, acting regional attorney for the Equal Employment Opportunity Commission in Phoenix. Her agency has brought dozens of employment suits against the company in the past decade. "It was part of the corporate culture."

Several factors probably forced Wal-Mart to rethink its legal strategy. Among these are a string of embarrassing and expensive court losses in the late 1990s; widespread negative publicity for its hard-nosed litigation style; a threatened $18 million sanction for discovery abuse in 1999; and the 2000 appointment of a new chief executive officer, H. Lee Scott, who appears to back the changes in the law department.

"Wal-Mart has probably recognized that, based on the litigation strategy they chose in the past, they've created a horrible reputation for themselves among judges and lawyers," said Gilbert Adams III, an associate in the Beaumont, Texas, practice of his father, Gilbert T. Adams. The younger Adams, who has brought several suits against the company, added, "That horrible reputation is causing them difficulty litigating cases." . . .

Wal-Mart has also dropped a long-standing policy of retaining only those outside counsel who would work for a flat, per-case fee. Wertz said that the change was prompted by a desire to hire the most qualified attorneys, many of whom insist on hourly compensation. But the change may also reflect a reconsideration of the company's hardball tactics. Critics have long charged that flat-fee arrangements added to Wal-Mart's intransigence, since the company did not have to pay the price for stalling, rejecting settlement offers and insisting on trial. Wertz would not comment on whether Wal-Mart was now settling more cases than in the past. . . .

8. *Summing Up.* What is your impression of tort law in light of the foregoing account of Walter v. Wal-Mart? What were the procedural and substantive aspects of the tort system able or unable to accomplish in this instance? Perhaps it will be helpful to break these questions down into other, slightly more manageable questions.

First, and most obviously, one can ask about the desirability of the result: a verdict of $550,000 for the plaintiff, upheld by the trial judge and the Maine Supreme Court. Attorney Silin argued to the jury that Ms. Walter — already 80 at the time — incurred about $70,000 in medical expenses.* Thus, so far as the jury was concerned, the vast bulk of the award — $480,000 — compensated her for the distress, suffering, and lost quality of life associated with illness she was caused to suffer by Wal-Mart's carelessness. Does this figure seem appropriate, excessive, or inadequate? As measured against what criteria or scales? What does this sum represent or accomplish?

Second, one might ask what was accomplished in terms of process. Clearly, both sides were given the ability to discover and present a lot of

---

* Fixing the amount of Walter's medical expenses at $70,000 turns out to involve something more than simple arithmetic. Silin based that figure on the total amount billed by medical providers for the services rendered to Walter during and after her hospitalization. As explained in Chapter 1, Section III.A.3, Walter herself did not actually pay the full amount of these bills: at least 80% of the charges were probably covered by Medicare — federally-funded health insurance for senior citizens. However, the jury was not told of this fact because of the *collateral source rule*, a doctrine that specifies that jurors are not allowed to consider other sources of compensation to a tort victim in determining damages. The collateral source rule thus dictated that the jury was to be presented with a figure representing Walter's "expenses" even though she didn't pay most of them. Even so, there remained a question as to what that figure should be. This is because the amount of reimbursement paid by the government to providers of medical services to Medicare patients is *not* determined by the amount the providers charge, but rather by schedules set by the government that are invariably lower than those charges. Indeed, in this case, the government's schedules dictated payment to Walter's providers of about $34,000 — roughly half the amount nominally charged by Walter's healthcare providers. Franco argued to the trial judge that the jury should thus have been instructed that Walter's medical "expenses" were $34,000 (what was actually paid) not $70,000 (what the providers billed). Obviously, the judge was unpersuaded.

information to the jury, even though, as it turned out, the jury was permitted to decide only a small portion of the case. Thus, the trial judge and the jury heard from Lovin himself about how the error was caused. They also heard from Walter and a friend of hers about what she did and didn't do after the error occurred, and how it adversely affected her life. And they heard from two doctors—Walter's doctor and an expert hired by Wal-Mart—about the medical effects of the error. In this respect, the procedures of tort law seemed to permit a relatively complete investigation into what went wrong as a predicate to the judge's and the jury's assignation of responsibility. Could similarly complete information have been obtained by other means? Is there any potential downside to a system that is geared to permit litigants to explore in great depth all the different facets of a dispute?

Another aspect of tort law revealed by *Walter* is that tort suits tend to place the alleged victim and injurer in a starkly adversarial posture, one that can easily block potentially sensible resolutions of disputes even if the key actors — the attorneys and the trial judge — are proceeding in good faith. Moreover, it may at times induce some of these actors to behave in a manner that might strike you as less than ideal. These observations in turn suggest that the proper functioning of tort law cannot help but depend in part on the exercise of good judgment by the professionals who make up the tort bar and bench.

TABLE OF CASES

Principal cases are in italics.

INDEX